The Law of
Torts

The Law of
Torts

Tenth Edition

Margaret Brazier LLB, Barrister

Professor in Law
at the University of Manchester

John Murphy LLB, LLM

Lecturer in Law
at the University of Manchester

Butterworths
London Edinburgh Dublin
1999

United Kingdom	Butterworths, a Division of Reed Elsevier (UK) Ltd, Halsbury House, 35 Chancery Lane, LONDON WC2A 1EL and 4 Hill Street, EDINBURGH EH2 3JZ
Australia	Butterworths, a Division of Reed International Books Australia Pty Ltd, CHATSWOOD, New South Wales
Canada	Butterworths Canada Ltd, MARKHAM, Ontario
Hong Kong	Butterworths Asia (Hong Kong), HONG KONG
India	Butterworths India, NEW DELHI
Ireland	Butterworth (Ireland) Ltd, DUBLIN
Malaysia	Malayan Law Journal Sdn Bhd, KUALA LUMPUR
New Zealand	Butterworths of New Zealand Ltd, WELLINGTON
Singapore	Butterworths Asia, SINGAPORE
South Africa	Butterworths Publishers (Pty) Ltd, DURBAN
USA	Lexis Law Publishing, CHARLOTTESVILLE, Virginia

A CIP Catalogue record for this book is available from the British Library.

ISBN 0 406 89103 6

Printed and bound in Great Britain by The Bath Press, Bath

Visit us at our website: http://www.butterworths.co.uk

Preface

The original author of this work, Professor Harry Street, died tragically early 15 years ago. *Street on Torts* remains his creation and the Faculty of Law at the University of Manchester continues to miss him. He set for all of us, whether we were lucky enough to know him personally or not, an impossibly high standard of scholarship which we strive to live up to.

Keeping abreast of the law of torts becomes ever more difficult. The past six years have seen a flood of cases across the whole range of torts. The trend to restrict the development of negligence, especially in relation to liability for pure economic loss, appears tentatively to be reversing itself in the decisions of the House of Lords in *White v Jones* and *Spring v Guardian Assurance plc*. Their Lordships acknowledge in those key cases a strong impulse to do justice to hard-done by plaintiffs. Concern to keep the potential liability of public authorities within bounds, however, continues to manifest itself in *X v Bedfordshire County Council* and *Stovin v Wise*. The insoluble problems of setting limits to claims for psychiatric harm recur again in *White v Chief Constable of South Yorkshire Police*. Developments have by no means been confined to the tort of negligence. *Hunter v Canary Wharf* reviews the tort of private nuisance. *Martin v Watson* breathed new life into malicious prosecution. The Human Rights Act 1998 will, in the lifetime of this edition, pose profound challenges for all students of torts.

It continues to be our objective to present an account of the law of torts as a whole. Negligence is not the only tort! Nonetheless we are well aware that in choosing to cover a whole range of torts constraints of space mean that there are topics which we do not deal with as fully as we would wish. Economic loss on its own has generated enough case law in the last 10 years to occupy several hundred pages. We have had to be selective and, particularly in the part on negligence, have focused largely on the leading cases. We do not claim to have achieved fully comprehensive coverage of every case. Our hope is that we can offer the reader an understanding of the broad framework of the law of torts and the opportunity to develop his or her own critical appraisal of the law.

We thank our colleagues in the Faculty who have given us advice and support in the preparation of this edition, in particular Andrew Grifiths, Hazel Carty and Margaret Halliwell. We thank our fellow teachers on the tort course, Caroline Bridge and Anthony Ogus, whose ideas and criticisms offer us such stimulus. Helen Mulholland and Chris Suddeth gave valuable assistance in researching key chapters of the text and have our grateful thanks for all their work. We must also thank Shirley Tiffany who patiently typed up nearly half the manuscript and offered us both constant, cheerful support. Last, but not least, we thank all our students who serve as guinea pigs for any new ideas of ours.

We have sought to incorporate developments in the law up to 1 November 1998. Where possible later developments, notably *White v Chief Constable of South Yorkshire Police,* have been added in at proof stage.

Margaret Brazier
John Murphy
March 1999

Contents

Preface   v
Abbreviations   xxvii
Table of statutes   xxix
Table of cases   xxxv

Part I

Introduction

Chapter I

The law of torts   3

SECTION 1.   WHAT IS A TORT?   3
SECTION 2.   HUMAN RIGHTS AND PROTECTED INTERESTS   4
  (A)   The Human Rights Act 1998   4
  (B)   Rights and wrongs   7
  (C)   Interests protected by the law of torts   7
    (1)   Intentional invasion of personal and proprietary interests   7
    (2)   Interests in economic relations, business and trading interests   7
    (3)   Interests in intellectual property   8
    (4)   Negligent interference with personal, proprietary and economic interests   8
    (5)   Further protection of personal and proprietary interests   8
    (6)   Reputation   9
    (7)   Due process   9
    (8)   Miscellaneous interests: 'convention rights'   9
    (9)   'Eurotorts'   9
SECTION 3.   ISSUES COMMON TO ALL TORTS   10
  (A)   A law of tort or a law of torts?   11
  (B)   Malice or motive   11

(C)   'Ghosts from the past': forms of action   11
SECTION 4.   GENERAL ISSUES AND THE LAW OF TORTS   12
   (A)   Conflict between certainty and justice   12
   (B)   Judicial caution in respect of non-material harms   13
   (C)   The judges and laissez-faire   13
   (D)   Limits of the effectiveness of the law of torts   13
   (E)   Loss distribution   13
   (F)   Deterrence   14
   (G)   Economics and law   15
SECTION 5.   TORT AND OTHER BRANCHES OF LAW   15

Part II

Intentional invasions of interests in person and property

Chapter 2

Intentional torts today   23

SECTION 1.   TRESPASS AND NEGLIGENCE   23
SECTION 2.   INTENTION AND TRESPASS   26
SECTION 3.   RELEVANCE OF TRESPASS TODAY   27

Chapter 3

Intentional torts to the person   30

SECTION 1.   INTRODUCTION   30
SECTION 2.   BATTERY   30
   (A)   State of mind of the defendant   31
   (B)   No consent by the plaintiff   32
   (C)   The character of the act of the defendant   33
   (D)   Damages   34
SECTION 3.   ASSAULT   34
   (A)   The character of the defendant's conduct   35
SECTION 4.   INTENTIONAL PHYSICAL HARM OTHER THAN TRESPASS
              TO PERSON   36
SECTION 5.   FALSE IMPRISONMENT   38
   (A)   State of mind   38
   (B)   Character of the act   38
   (C)   Knowledge of the plaintiff   41
   (D)   Who is liable for a false imprisonment?   41
   (E)   Damages   42
SECTION 6.   OTHER FORMS OF COMPENSATION   43

Chapter 4

Goods 44

SECTION 1.   INTRODUCTION 44
SECTION 2.   CONVERSION 46
  (A)   Interest of the plaintiff 47
      (1)   Bailment 47
      (2)   Lien and pledge 48
      (3)   Sale 49
      (4)   Licensee 49
      (5)   Finder 50
      (6)   Jus tertii (third party rights) 51
  (B)   The subject matter 52
  (C)   Human body products 52
  (D)   State of mind of the defendant 53
  (E)   Acts of conversion 54
      (1)   Taking goods or dispossessing 54
      (2)   Destroying or altering 55
      (3)   Using 55
      (4)   Receiving 56
      (5)   Disposition without delivery 57
      (6)   Disposition and delivery 57
      (7)   Misdelivery by carrier 58
      (8)   Refusal to surrender on demand 59
      (9)   Goods lost or destroyed 59
      (10) Residual acts amounting to a conversion 60
  (F)   Conversion as between co-owners 60
  (G)   Remedies: damages 61
  (H)   Remedies: other forms of relief 66
  (I)   Limitation of actions 67
SECTION 3.   TRESPASS TO GOODS 67
  (A)   Forms of trespass 68
  (B)   Character of the act of the defendant 68
  (C)   State of mind of the defendant 69
  (D)   The interest of the plaintiff 69
  (E)   Damages 71
      (1)   Measure 71
      (2)   Trespass ab initio 71
SECTION 4.   RESIDUAL TORTS 72

Chapter 5

Land 73

SECTION 1.   TRESPASS 73
  (A)   Types of acts 73
  (B)   Subject matter 76

(C)   State of mind of the defendant   77
(D)   The interest of the plaintiff in the land   77
(E)   Damages   80
SECTION 2.   ACTIONS BY REVERSIONERS   81

Chapter 6

Defences to intentional torts to the person and property   82

SECTION 1.   MISTAKE AND INEVITABLE ACCIDENT   82
(A)   Mistake as such is no defence   82
(B)   Inevitable accident   83
SECTION 2.   CONSENT   83
(A)   General   83
(B)   Consent to medical treatment   85
SECTION 3.   CONTRIBUTORY NEGLIGENCE   88
SECTION 4.   SELF-DEFENCE   88
SECTION 5.   DEFENCE OF THE PERSON OF ANOTHER   89
SECTION 6.   DEFENCE OF ONE'S PROPERTY   90
SECTION 7.   DEFENCE OF THE PROPERTY OF ANOTHER   92
SECTION 8.   PREVENTING CRIME   92
SECTION 9.   NECESSITY   92
(A)   Distinguished from defence of property   92
(B)   Scope   93
      (1)   Private necessity   93
      (2)   Public necessity   94
SECTION 10.   THE MENTAL HEALTH ACTS   95
SECTION 11.   DISCIPLINE   95
(A)   Children   95
      (1)   By parents   95
      (2)   By schoolteachers and others responsible for their children for their
            training and education   96
(B)   Passengers in public transport   97
SECTION 12.   ARREST, SEARCH AND SEIZURE   97
(A)   Arrest   97
      (1)   By a policeman with a warrant   97
      (2)   Arrest without warrant   98
(B)   Reasonable cause   99
(C)   Manner of arrest   100
(D)   Entry, search and seizure   101
SECTION 13.   JUDICIAL ACTS   102
SECTION 14.   STATUTORY AUTHORITY   103
SECTION 15.   ACTS CONNECTED WITH PARLIAMENTARY PROCEEDINGS   104
SECTION 16.   EXECUTIVE ACTS   104
(A)   Act of state   104
(B)   Prerogative   105

SECTION 17.   AN ACT WHICH IS ALSO A CRIME   105
  (A)   Assault and battery   105
SECTION 18.   PLAINTIFF A WRONGDOER   105
SECTION 19.   SELF-HELP REMEDIES   108

Part III

Intentional interference with economic interests

Chapter 7

Interference with economic interests   113

SECTION 1.   'RIGHTS' AND ECONOMIC INTERESTS   113
SECTION 2.   FREE COMPETITION; UNFAIR COMPETITION   115
SECTION 3.   ECONOMIC LOSS AND NEGLIGENCE   116
SECTION 4.   ECONOMIC TORTS AND ECONOMIC REGULATION   117

Chapter 8

False representations   118

SECTION 1.   DECEIT   118
  (A)   False representation   119
  (B)   Knowledge of falsity   120
  (C)   Intention to deceive   120
  (D)   Reliance of the plaintiff   121
  (E)   Loss   122
  (F)   Agency   123
  (G)   Statute of Frauds Amendment Act 1828   124
  (H)   Misrepresentation Act 1967   125
SECTION 2.   PASSING OFF - UNFAIR TRADING   126
  (A)   The misrepresentation   127
    (1)   Marketing a product as that of the plaintiff   127
    (2)   Using the plaintiff's name   127
    (3)   Using the plaintiff's trade name   128
    (4)   Using the plaintiff's trade mark   129
    (5)   Imitating appearance of the plaintiff's goods   129
    (6)   Selling inferior goods to those of the plaintiff, thereby misleading the purchaser   130
    (7)   False advertising   130
    (8)   Misrepresentations designed to cash in on another's goodwill   131
    (9)   Character merchandising   132
  (B)   In the course of a trade   132

(C) A representation to customers or ultimate customers   132
(D) Calculated to injure goodwill   133
(E) Proof of damage   134
(F) Defences   134
(G) Remedies   135
      (1) Injunction   135
      (2) Damages   135
(H) Unfair trading and passing off   135
SECTION 3.   INJURIOUS FALSEHOOD   136
(A) Interests protected   136
(B) Disparagement   138
(C) False statement   138
(D) Publication   139
(E) Malice   139
(F) Damage   140
(G) Defences   141
(H) Injurious falsehood and defamation   141

Chapter 9

Unlawful interference with trade   143

SECTION 1.   CONSPIRACY   144
(A) Combination   144
(B) The purpose of the defendants   145
(C) Justification   147
SECTION 2.   INDUCING BREACH OF CONTRACT   148
(A) Kinds of contract   149
(B) Breach of other obligations   149
(C) Breach of contract   149
(D) Knowledge of the contract   151
(E) 'Inducement' and 'interference'   151
      (1) Direct persuasion or procurement   152
      (2) Direct intervention   152
      (3) Indirect procurement   153
      (4) Inconsistent dealings   154
(F) State of mind of the defendant   154
(G) Damage   155
(H) Justification   155
(I) Remedies   157
      (1) Damages   157
      (2) Injunction   157
SECTION 3.   UNLAWFUL INTERFERENCE WITH TRADE   158
(A) Intimidation: unlawful threats   158
(B) Unlawful conduct   159
SECTION 4.   ECONOMIC TORTS AND TRADE UNIONS   162

Chapter 10

Intellectual property interests   163

SECTION 1.   COPYRIGHT, PATENTS AND SIMILAR INTERESTS   163
SECTION 2.   BREACH OF CONFIDENCE   164
  (A)   The obligation of confidentiality   164
  (B)   Public interest   166
  (C)   Remedies   167

Part IV

Negligent invasions of interests in person and property and economic interests

Chapter 11

Duty of care I:
the neighbour principle   171

SECTION 1.   INTRODUCTION   171
SECTION 2.   PROXIMITY AND POLICY   172
  (A)   Duty-situations   172
  (B)   The rise and fall of Anns   174
  (C)   Limiting the categories of negligence   179
  (D)   The unforeseeable plaintiff   180
SECTION 3.   OMISSIONS   182
SECTION 4.   THE LIABILITY OF PUBLIC AUTHORITIES   182
  (A)   General   182
  (B)   Exercise of a discretionary power   183
  (C)   Failure to exercise a statutory power   188
  (D)   Public service immunities?   190
SECTION 5.   DUTY AND THIRD PARTIES   193
SECTION 6.   DUTIES IN TORT AND CONTRACT   196

Chapter 12

Duty of care II:
recognised harm   199

SECTION 1.   INTRODUCTION   199
SECTION 2.   HARM TO PERSONS   200

(A)   Duty to the unborn   200
(B)   Duty to rescuers   202
(C)   Liability for psychiatric harm   203
SECTION 3.   POLICY AND PUBLIC INTEREST   210
SECTION 4.   PHYSICAL DAMAGE TO PROPERTY   212
SECTION 5.   'PURE' ECONOMIC LOSS   215
(A)   Statements and 'special relationships'   215
(B)   The extended *Hedley Byrne* principle   220
(C)   Beyond *Hedley Byrne*?   224
SECTION 6.   HUMAN RIGHTS AND THE DUTY OF CARE   228

Chapter 13

Breach of duty   231

SECTION 1.   THE STANDARD OF CARE   231
(A)   Law, not fact   231
(B)   The guiding principles of law   233
   (1)   The likelihood of harm   233
   (2)   The seriousness of the risk and the risk of serious injury   233
   (3)   The utility of the act of the defendant   233
   (4)   The cost of avoiding the harm   234
(C)   The relation between standard of care and duty   235
SECTION 2.   THE REASONABLE 'MAN'   237
(A)   Children   237
(B)   Adults affected by disability or infirmity   238
(C)   Intelligence and knowledge   239
(D)   Skill   240
(E)   The circumstances of the plaintiff   242
(F)   The 'hurly burly of life'   243
(G)   Reasonable anticipation   243
(H)   Foreseeable acts of third parties   244
(I)   General practice of the community   245
SECTION 3.   PROFESSIONAL NEGLIGENCE   246
(A)   The background   246
(B)   Duty and breach   246
(C)   The reasonable 'professional'   248
(D)   Patients and doctors   249
SECTION 4.   EMPLOYERS' LIABILITY TO THEIR EMPLOYEES   250
(A)   A personal, non-delegable duty   251
(B)   The provision of competent staff   253
(C)   Adequate premises and plant   254
(D)   A proper system of working   254
SECTION 5.   PROVING NEGLIGENCE   256
(A)   Law and fact   256
(B)   Onus of proof   257

(C)   Res ipsa loquitur   258
       (1)   'The doctrine is dependent on the absence of explanation'   259
       (2)   The harm must be of such a kind that it does not ordinarily happen if
              proper care is being taken   259
       (3)   The instrumentality causing the accident must be within the
              exclusive control of the defendant   260
              (a)   The meaning of 'control'   260
              (b)   Where one of two or more persons is in control   261
(D)   THE EFFECT OF RES IPSA LOQUITUR   262

Chapter 14

Causation   264

SECTION 1.   CAUSE AND EFFECT   264
SECTION 2.   EVIDENCE OF CAUSATION   265
SECTION 3.   MULTIPLE CAUSES   269
    (A)   Novus actus interveniens   269
    (B)   Concurrent causes   273
    (C)   Consecutive causes   273
SECTION 4.   REMOTENESS OF DAMAGE   274
    (A)   *Re Polemis* and the *Wagon Mound*   274
    (B)   Foreseeable type of harm   275
    (C)   The means by which the harm was caused   276
    (D)   Extent of the damage   278
    (E)   The 'thin skull' rule   279

Chapter 15

Defences to negligence   281

SECTION 1.   CONTRIBUTORY NEGLIGENCE   281
    (A)   Risk   282
    (B)   That the plaintiff's negligence was a contributory factor   282
    (C)   The negligence of the plaintiff   286
    (D)   The scope of the Law Reform (Contributory Negligence) Act 1945   289
    (E)   Apportionment of damages   291
SECTION 2.   VOLUNTARY ASSUMPTION OF RISK   292
    (A)   Is assumption of risk properly regarded as a defence?   292
    (B)   Illustrations of when the plaintiff is deemed to have assumed the risk   294
        (1)   Suits by employees against employers   294
        (2)   Drunken drivers/drunken pilots   296
        (3)   Dangerous activities   298
    (C)   Voluntary act   298
SECTION 3.   EXCLUDING LIABILITY   300

Chapter 16

Liability for defective premises and structures   303

SECTION 1.   OCCUPIERS' LIABILITY   303
  (A)   Liability to visitors: the Occupiers' Liability Act 1957   304
      (1)   Who is an occupier?   304
      (2)   Scope of the Act   305
          (a)   Visitors   305
          (b)   Against what risks does the Act afford protection?   308
      (3)   The common duty of care   309
          (a)   General principles   309
          (b)   Warning   312
          (c)   Assumption of risk   312
          (d)   Contributory negligence   313
          (e)   Liability for independent contractors   313
      (4)   Some special cases within the Act   314
          (a)   Fixed or movable structures   314
          (b)   Damage to property   315
          (c)   Liability in contract   316
      (5)   Exclusion of liability   317
  (B)   Liability to non-visitors: the Occupiers' Liability Act 1984   320
  (C)   Common law liability and activities on land   322
  (D)   Liability to those outside the premises   323
  (E)   Liability to those on adjoining premises   324
SECTION 2.   LIABILITY OF NON-OCCUPIERS   325
  (A)   The Defective Premises Act 1972   326
  (B)   Builders and contractors: physical damage   327
  (C)   Builders and contractors: other loss   329
  (D)   Professional advisers   331
  (E)   Local authorities   331
  (F)   Landlords   332

Part V

Invasions of interests in person and property where intentional or negligent conduct need not always be proved

Chapter 17

Product liability   337

SECTION 1.   INTRODUCTION   337

SECTION 2.   CONSUMER PROTECTION AND THE CHANGING
             COMMON LAW   338
  (A)   The limitations of contract   338
  (B)   The action for negligence   340
        (1)   The narrow rule in *Donoghue v Stevenson* – defective products   341
        (2)   Range of defendants   341
        (3)   Products   342
        (4)   Ultimate consumer   342
        (5)   Sale   343
        (6)   Intermediate examination   343
        (7)   Preparation or putting up   344
        (8)   Continuing duty of care   344
        (9)   Economic loss   344
        (10) Proving negligence   345
        (10) Proving causation   347
  (C)   Action for breach of statutory duty   347
SECTION 3.   THE STRICT LIABILITY REGIME   348
  (A)   The European Directive and the Consumer Protection
        Act 1987   348
  (B)   Who can sue under the Act?   349
  (C)   On whom is strict liability imposed?   350
  (D)   Products   351
  (E)   Defining 'defect'   351
  (F)   General defences   353
  (G)   The 'development risks' defence   354
  (H)   Causation   355
  (I)   Limitation   356

Chapter 18

Nuisance   357

SECTION 1.   NUISANCE AS A SEPARATE TORT   357
  (A)   Scope of the law of nuisance   357
  (B)   Nuisance and environmental law   359
  (C)   Nuisance and other torts   360
SECTION 2.   THE BASIS OF NUISANCE LIABILITY   362
  (A)   Substantial interference   362
        (1)   Interference with the use or enjoyment of land   363
              (a)   The sensitivity of the plaintiff   364
              (b)   Location of the plaintiff's premises   365
        (2)   Material damage to land   366
        (3)   Interference with servitudes   368
  (B)   Unreasonableness   368
        (1)   The seriousness of the interference   369
              (a)   The duration of the harm   369
              (b)   The extent of the harm   370

(c)   The character of the harm   370
(d)   Social value of the use interfered with   371
(2)   Reasonable user of the defendant's land   371
(a)   The defendant's motive   372
(b)   Location of the defendant's enterprise   373
(c)   Fault   374
(d)   The kind of user   375
(e)   Impracticability of preventing or avoiding the interference   375

SECTION 3.   WHO CAN SUE?   376
(A)   Owners and resident occupiers   376
(B)   Reversioners   377
(C)   Plaintiffs suffering personal injuries, damage to chattels or economic loss   377

SECTION 4.   WHO CAN BE SUED?   378
(A)   Creators   378
(B)   Occupiers   380
(1)   Acts of a trespasser   380
(2)   Acts of nature   381
(3)   Nuisances created by independent contractors   382
(4)   Acts of a previous occupier   382
(C)   Landlords   382

SECTION 5.   MUST THE INTERFERENCE EMANATE FROM THE DEFENDANT'S LAND?   383

SECTION 6.   DEFENCES   384
(A)   Statutory authority   384
(B)   Prescription   385
(C)   The plaintiff's conduct   385
(D)   Other defences   386

SECTION 7.   REMEDIES   387
(A)   Damages   387
(B)   Injunction   388

SECTION 8.   PUBLIC NUISANCE   389
(A)   Nature of public nuisance   389
(1)   The relator action   389
(2)   Civil actions for 'special damage'   390
(B)   The relationship between public nuisance and private nuisance   392
(C)   Remedies in public nuisance   393
(1)   Injunction   393
(2)   Damages   394

Chapter 19

Rylands v Fletcher   395

SECTION 1.   INTRODUCTION   395
SECTION 2.   'THINGS' WITHIN THE RULE   397

SECTION 3.   PARTIES   398
(A)   Who may be sued?   398
(B)   Who may sue?   401
SECTION 4.   THE NON-NATURAL USE OF LAND   402
SECTION 5.   ESCAPE   404
SECTION 6.   FORESEEABILITY OF HARM   405
SECTION 7.   DEFENCES   406
(A)   Statutory authority   406
(B)   Consent of the plaintiff   407
(C)   Contributory negligence   407
(D)   Act of third parties: *Rylands v Fletcher* or negligence?   408
(E)   Act of God   409
(F)   Necessity   410
SECTION 8.   NUISANCE AND *RYLANDS v FLETCHER*   410

Chapter 20

Animals   413

SECTION 1.   NEGLIGENCE AND STRICT LIABILITY   413
SECTION 2.   DAMAGE DONE BY DANGEROUS ANIMALS   413
(A)   Dangerous species   413
(B)   Non-dangerous species   414
(C)   Liability for either kind of dangerous animal   415
SECTION 3.   LIABILITY FOR STRAYING LIVESTOCK   416
SECTION 4.   LIABILITY FOR INJURY DONE BY DOGS TO LIVESTOCK   416

Chapter 21

Breach of statutory duty   417

SECTION 1.   INTRODUCTION   417
SECTION 2.   ELUSIVE PARLIAMENTARY INTENT   419
SECTION 3.   THE NATURE OF THE ACTION   423
SECTION 4.   WHAT THE PLAINTIFF MUST PROVE   423
(A)   An obligation on the defendant   423
(B)   The statute must impose the burden on the defendant   424
(C)   The statute protects the plaintiff's interest by way of a cause of action
in tort   425
(1)   The state of the pre-existing common law   425
(2)   Alternative remedies provided by statute   426
(3)   Public and private rights   427
(D)   The harm suffered by him is within the scope of the general class of risks at
which the statute is directed   428
(E)   The plaintiff was one of the persons protected by
the statute   429
(F)   When damage must be proved   429

(G)   The conduct of the defendant was of such a character as to violate the statute   429

(H)   A breach of the duty   430

(I)   Causation   430

SECTION 5.   DEFENCES   430

(A)   The relation between criminal and tortious liability   430

(B)   Assumption of risk   430

(C)   Contributory negligence   431

(D)   Act of third party   432

SECTION 6.   PROPOSALS FOR REFORM   432

Part VI

Interests in reputation – defamation

Chapter 22

Defamation   435

SECTION 1.   INTRODUCTION   435

(A)   Background issues   435

SECTION 2.   ELEMENTS OF DEFAMATION   439

(A)   The meaning of defamatory   439

(1)   Injury to reputation   439

(a)   Words of abuse   440

(b)   Words of opinion   441

(c)   Other examples of injured reputation   441

(2)   Who may be defamed   442

(3)   The interpretation of defamatory statements   443

(a)   Innuendo   443

(b)   The roles of judge and jury in construing what is defamatory   445

(4)   Immateriality of the defendant's knowledge   446

(B)   Reference to the plaintiff   447

(1)   Class libels   447

(2)   Unintentional references to the plaintiff   448

(C)   'Malicious' publication   448

SECTION 3.   DISTINGUISHING LIBEL AND SLANDER   451

(A)   Criteria for distinguishing libel from slander   451

(C)   Juridical differences between libel and slander   452

(D)   Exceptional cases where slander is actionable per se   452

(1)   Imputation of crime   452

(2)   Imputation of certain types of disease   453

(3)   Slander in respect of office, profession, calling, trade or business   454

(4)   Imputation of the unchastity of a woman   454
(E)   Special damage and remoteness of damage   455

Chapter 23

Defences and remedies   457

SECTION 1.   CONSENT AND ASSUMPTION OF RISK   457
SECTION 2.   JUSTIFICATION   458
SECTION 3.   INNOCENT DISSEMINATORS   461
(A)   Innocent publication: the common law   461
(B)   Defamation Act 1996, s 1   462
(C)   Offer of amends: Defamation Act 1996, ss 2-4   463
SECTION 4.   ABSOLUTE PRIVILEGE   464
(A)   Parliamentary proceedings   464
(B)   Executive matters   464
(C)   Judicial proceedings   466
(D)   Solicitor-client communications   467
(E)   Reports of judicial proceedings   468
SECTION 5.   QUALIFIED PRIVILEGE   468
(A)   Malice   469
    (1)   Establishing malice   469
        (a)   The defendant does not believe in the truth of
            his statement   469
        (b)   Abuse of the purpose of the privilege   470
        (c)   The inclusion of extraneous matter   471
        (d)   Unreasonable publication to persons outside the scope of
            the privilege   471
    (2)   Judge and jury and the burden of proof in respect of malice   471
    (3)   Excess of privilege and malice   472
    (4)   Joint publishers and malice   472
(B)   Instances of qualified privilege   473
    (1)   General principle   473
    (2)   Privileged reports   474
    (3)   Statements to protect an interest   476
        (a)   The public interest   476
        (b)   The interest of the publisher   476
        (c)   Instances of common interest   477
    (4)   Statements in pursuance of a legal, social or moral duty   477
SECTION 6.   FAIR COMMENT   479
(A)   Matters of public interest   479
(B)   Comment on true facts   480
(C)   Comment must be honest and not actuated by malice   482
(D)   Burden of proof and the functions of judge and jury   483
SECTION 7.   APOLOGY   484

SECTION 8.   REMEDIES   485
  (A)   Damages   485
  (B)   Injunction   487

Part VII

Misuse of process

Chapter 24

Misuse of process   491

SECTION 1.   MALICIOUS PROSECUTION AND RELATED CLAIMS   491
  (A)   Institution of proceedings   492
  (B)   Nature of proceedings   493
  (C)   Termination in favour of plaintiff   494
  (D)   Absence of reasonable and probable cause   494
  (E)   Malice: improper purpose   496
  (F)   The Crown Prosecution Service   497
  (G)   Defences   497
SECTION 2.   ABUSE OF PROCESS   498
SECTION 3.   WITNESS IMMUNITY   498
SECTION 4.   MISFEASANCE IN PUBLIC OFFICE   499

Part VIII

Remedies and parties

Chapter 25

Vicarious liability   503

SECTION 1.   IMPORTANCE OF THE DISTINCTION BETWEEN EMPLOYEES AND
              INDEPENDENT CONTRACTORS   503
SECTION 2.   CRITERIA FOR DISTINGUISHING EMPLOYEES AND
              INDEPENDENT CONTRACTORS4   504
  (A)   Control   504
  (B)   Some particular cases examined   505
       (1)   Hospital staff   506
       (2)   Borrowed employees   506
SECTION 3.   IS THERE A SEPARATE CATEGORY OF AGENTS?   507

SECTION 4.   LIABILITY IN RESPECT OF AN INDEPENDENT
              CONTRACTOR   509
  (A)   Authorising him to commit a tort   509
  (B)   Torts where intentional or negligent conduct need not always be
        proved   510
  (C)   Negligence   510
        (1)   Personal negligence on the part of the employer   510
        (2)   Non-delegable duties – those duty-situations where the duty
              extends to a responsibility for the negligent acts of an
              independent contractor   510
SECTION 5.   WHERE THE EMPLOYER IS NOT LIABLE FOR THE ACTS OF AN
              INDEPENDENT CONTRACTOR   513
  (A)   No breach by employer of any duty imposed on him by the law
        of torts   513
  (B)   Collateral negligence   514
SECTION 6.   LIABILITY IN RESPECT OF EMPLOYEES   515
  (A)   The commission of a tort by the employee   515
  (B)   The course of employment   516
  (C)   Relevant factors in determining whether the act was committed in the
        course of employment   516
        (1)   Mode of doing the work that an employee is employed to do   516
        (2)   Authorised limits of time and space   517
        (3)   Express prohibition   518
        (4)   Connection with employer's work   520
        (5)   Deliberate criminal conduct   521
                 Fraud   522
  (D)   Statutory duty and vicarious liability   523

Chapter 26

Remedies   525

SECTION 1.   EXTRA-JUDICIAL   525
SECTION 2.   JUDICIAL   525
  (A)   Damages   525
        (1)   Nominal   525
        (2)   Contemptuous   526
        (3)   General and special damages distinguished   526
        (4)   Personal injuries   526
        (5)   Damages and tax   526
        (6)   'Parasitic' damages   527
        (7)   Aggravated and exemplary damages   527
        (8)   Mitigation of damage   530
        (9)   Successive actions on the same facts   531
              (a)   Violation of two rights separately protected   531

(b)   Consequential damage where two torts protect the
same interest   532

(c)   Successive acts   532

(d)   One tortious act causing damage on different occasions   533

(B)   Tort and contract   533

(C)   Tort and restitution   534

(1)   Election of remedies   534

(2)   Advantages of proceedings in tort or restitution   535

(D)   Account   535

(E)   Injunctions   535

(1)   As a remedy per se, or as an addition to damages   535

(2)   Injunction and declaratory judgment as a remedy where an action in
tort does not lie   537

Chapter 27

Compensation for personal injuries   539

SECTION 1.   INTRODUCTORY   539

SECTION 2.   AWARDS OF DAMAGES TO LIVING PLAINTIFFS   540

(A)   Pecuniary losses   542

(1)   Loss of earnings   542

(2)   Medical, nursing and hospital expenses   545

(3)   Additional pecuniary losses and expenses   546

(4)   Deduction for benefits received   548

(B)   Non-pecuniary losses   549

(1)   Pain and suffering   549

(2)   Loss of amenities   550

(3)   Assessing the quantum   550

(4)   Provisional awards   551

(5)   Interest   552

(C)   Damage or destruction of goods   552

SECTION 3.   DEATH   553

(A)   Survival of causes of action   553

(B)   Death as a cause of action   554

(1)   Historical introduction   554

(2)   Who may sue?   555

(3)   Nature of the act complained of   555

(4)   The nature of the interests protected   556

(5)   Period of limitation   557

(6)   Assessment of damages   557

SECTION 4.   ALTERNATIVE COMPENSATION SYSTEMS   561

(A)   Responsibility and the welfare state   561

(B)   Other compensation systems   562

(1)   Criminal Injuries Compensation Scheme   562

(2)   Occupational sick pay   563

(3)   Occupational pensions   563

(4)   Industrial Injuries Scheme   563
(5)   Trade unions   563
(6)   Insurance   563
(C)   The Pearson Report   563

Chapter 28

Extinction of remedies   566

SECTION 1.   WAIVER   566
SECTION 2.   SATISFACTION   567
SECTION 3.   JUDGMENT   567
SECTION 4.   RELEASE   568
SECTION 5.   ACCORD AND SATISFACTION   568
SECTION 6.   LIMITATION   569
(A)   Period of limitation   569
(B)   When does a cause of action accrue?   571
(C)   Special rules for personal injuries   572
(D)   Latent damage other than personal injuries   574
(E)   Continuing wrongs   576
(F)   Effect of disability of the plaintiff   576
(G)   Postponement of limitation period in case of fraud or concealment   577
SECTION 7.   DEATH   578

Chapter 29

Parties   579

SECTION 1.   THE CROWN   579
(A)   Vicarious liability   579
(B)   Non-vicarious liability   579
(C)   Exceptions   580
(1)   Judicial errors   580
(2)   Armed forces   580
(3)   Certain statutes imposing liability in tort   581
SECTION 2.   FOREIGN STATES   581
SECTION 3.   AMBASSADORS   581
SECTION 4.   POSTAL AUTHORITIES   582
SECTION 5.   HIGHWAY AUTHORITIES   582
SECTION 6.   CORPORATIONS   584
(A)   Liability   584
(B)   Power to sue   585
SECTION 7.   TRADE UNIONS AND OTHER UNINCORPORATED BODIES   585
(A)   Trade unions   585
(B)   Other unincorporated bodies   586

(1)   Liability as defendants   586
    (a)   Substantive   586
    (b)   Procedural   586
(2)   Capacity as plaintiffs   587
SECTION 8.   PARTNERS   588
SECTION 9.   HUSBAND AND WIFE   588
SECTION 10.   MENTALLY DISORDERED PERSONS   589
SECTION 11.   MINORS   590
(A)   Liability   590
    (1)   Where the act of the minor is also a breach of contract   590
    (2)   Liability of the parent   591
(B)   Capacity to sue   591
SECTION 12.   BANKRUPTS   591
(A)   Liability   591
(B)   Capacity to sue   592
SECTION 13.   ASSIGNEES   593
SECTION 14.   CONVICTED PERSONS   593
SECTION 15.   JOINT TORTS   594
(A)   Categories   594
    (1)   Joint tortfeasors   594
    (2)   Several concurrent tortfeasors   595
    (3)   Several tortfeasors causing different damage   596
(B)   The importance of the distinction between joint tortfeasors, several concurrent tortfeasors and other tortfeasors   596
(C)   The distinction between joint tortfeasors and several concurrent tortfeasors   597
(D)   Contribution   598
    (1)   Scope   598
    (2)   Who may claim contribution   598
    (3)   Those from whom contribution may be claimed   599
    (4)   Amount of contribution recoverable   599

Appendix 1

Convention rights   603

Appendix 2

Defamation Act 1996   609

Index   613

Abbreviations

American Restatement	Restatement of the Law of Torts (American Law Institute)
Aus LJ	Australian Law Journal
Blackstone	Commentaries on the Laws of England, by Sir William Blackstone (1796)
Camb LJ	Cambridge Law Journal
Can BR	Canadian Bar Review
Clerk and Lindsell	Law of Torts by JF Clark and WHB Lindsell (16th edn, 1989)
Comyns	Comyns' Digest of the Laws of England (5th edn, 1822)
Fleming	Law of Torts by JG Fleming (7th edn, 1987)
Gatley	Law and Practice of Libel and Slander by JC Gatley (8th edn, 1981)
Green	Judge and Jury, by Leon Green (Kansas, 1990)
Halsbury	The Laws of England (4th edn, 1973-83)
Harper and James	Law of Torts by FV Harper and F James (1956)
Harv LR	Harvard Law Review
HFI	History of English Law, by Sir William Holdsworth (1922-38)
LQR	Law Quarterly Review
MLR	Modern Law Review
Munkman	Employer's Liability at Common Law by J Munkman (11th edn, 1991)
Pollock	The Law of Torts by Sir F Pollock (15th edn, 1952, by PA Landon)
Porter Report	Report of the Committee on the Law of Defamation (Cmnd 7636, 1948)
Prosser	Handbook of the Law of Torts by WL Prosser (3rd edn, 1964)
Report	Third Report of the Law Reform Committee (Occupiers, Liability to Invitees, Licensees and Trespassers) (Cmnd 9305, 1954)
Russell	On Crime (12th edn, 1964, by JWC Turner)
Salmond & Heuston	Law of Torts by Sir John Salmond (20th edn, 1991, by RFV Heuston)
UTLJ	University of Toronto Law Journal
Williams *Animals*	Liability for Animals by Glanville L Williams (1939)

Williams *Bankruptcy*	Law and Practice in Bankruptcy by Sir Ronald Williams (19th edn, 1979, by Muir Hunter)
Williams *Joint Torts*	Joint Torts and Contributory Negligence by Glanville L Williams (1950)
Winfield & Jolowicz	Law of Torts by Sir Percy Winfield (4th edn, 1948)
Winfield *Present Law*	Present Law of Abuse of Legal Procedures, by PH Winfield
Winfield *Province*	Province of the Law of Trusts by PH Winfield (1931)

Table of statutes

PAGE

Administration of Justice Act 1982: 552, 554
s 1(1)(b) 550
   (3)(a) 555
2 527
4(1), (2) 553
Animals Act 1971
s 2(1) 413
   (2) 414, 415
3 416
4(1)(b) 416
5(1) 415, 416
   (2) 415
   (3) 91, 415
   (4)-(6) 416
6(2) 414
   (3), (5) 415
7 416
   (1) 108
9 91
10 .... 415, 416
11 .... 414, 416

Banking Act 1979
s 47 88
Bills of Exchange Act 1882
s 80 58

Carriage by Air Act 1961 555
Carriage of Passengers by Road Act 1974: 555
Cheques Act 1957
s 1 58
Children Act 1989
s 8(1) 86
10 86
Children and Young Persons Act 1933
s 1(7) 95
Chronically Sick and Disabled Persons Act
   1970 561
Civil Aviation Act 1982
s 49(3) 76
76(1) 76
   (2) 77
   (3) 600

PAGE

Civil Liability (Contribution) Act
   1978 .... 289, 356, 581
s 1(1)-(4) 597, 598, 599
2(1), (2) 599
   (3) 600
3, 4 598
Clean Air Act 1993 360
Coal Mines Act 1911 430
Common Law Procedure Act 1852 11
Companies Act 1985
s 35, 35A, 35B 585
Congenital Disabilities (Civil Liability) Act
   1976 .... 202, 581
s 1(1) 201
   (7) 289
2 201
4(5) 201
Consumer Credit Act 1974
Pt VII(ss 87-104) 48
Pt IX(ss 127-144) 48
Consumer Protection Act 1961
s 3 .... 337, 348
Consumer Protection Act 1987 ... 290, 341
s 1(2) 351
   (a)-(c) 350
   (3) 351
2(1) 349, 355
   (2)(a)-(c) 350
   (3) 350, 356
3(1) 350
   (2)(a), (b) 352
   (c) 352, 353
4 348
   (1)(a)–(d) 353
   (e) 338, 354, 355
   (f) 354
5(2), (3) 349
   (5) 570
6 353
   (3) 349
   (4) 354
10 348
39 348

PAGE

Consumer Protection Act 1987—contd
s 41 .... 337, 348, 419
Sch 1 570
Consumer Safety Act 1978
s 6 337
Copyright, Designs and Patents Act 1988
Pt III(ss 213-264) 163
s 253 138
Courts and Legal Services Act 1990
s 8 .... 437, 486
23 465
108 .... 102, 103
Criminal Injuries Compensation Act
1995 .... 43, 562
Criminal Justice Act 1948
s 70 593
Criminal Justice and Public Order Act
1994 98
Criminal Law Act 1967
s 3 .... 90, 92, 98
Criminal Law Act 1977
s 60 43
Crown Proceedings Act 1947 535
s 1 579
2 534
(1) 580
(b), (c) 579
(2), (3) 524, 580
(5) 580
(6) 579
3 579
9 582
10 580
28 464
Crown Proceedings (Armed Forces) Act
1987 .... 192, 580

Damages Act 1996
s 2 .... 541, 542
3 .... 544, 554
5 541
Defamation Act 1952 .... 460, 581
s 2 454
3 140
4 463
5 .... 436, 437, 459, 485
6 481
7 .... 437, 445, 475
8 436
(2) 437
(3) 437
9 436
(1)(c) 437
10 436
Defamation Act 1996 581
s 1(1), (2) 462
(3)(a)-(e) 462
(5) 462
2 484
(3), (4) 463
3 484
(2) 463
4 484

PAGE

Defamation Act 1996—contd
s 4(2)-(5) 463
5 569
9(1) 474
13 438
(4), (5) 464
14(2) 468
(3) 468, 474
15(1), (2) 475
(3) 474
(4)(a) 475
Sch 1 474
para 14 475
Sch 2 463
Defective Premises Act 1972 ..... 326, 351
s 1 331
(3) 327
2 327
3 .... 327, 328
4 327
(3) 333
(4) 332
Diplomatic Privileges Act 1964
Sch 1 581
Disposal of Uncollected Goods Act
1952 46
Distress for Rent Act 1737
s 19 71
Dramatic and Musical Performers'
Protection Act 1958 161
s 2 421

Employers' Liability (Compulsory Insurance)
Act 1969 .... 421, 512
Employer's Liability (Defective Equipment)
Act 1969 512
Employment Act 1990 162
Environmental Protection Act 1990 ... 360
European Communities Act 1972
s 2(1) 349

Factories Act 1937 429
Factors Act 1889
s 1(1) 56
2(1) 56
Family Law Act 1996
s 62 555
Family Law Reform Act 1969
s 1(1) 590
8(3) 86
Fatal Accidents Act 1976 .... 227, 597
s 1(1) 554
(2)-(5) 555
(6) 557
1A 203, 553
(1) 556
(2)(a), (b) 556
(4) 557
2(2), (4) 555
3(1) 557
(3)-(5) 559
4 .... 559, 560
5 555

PAGE

Fatal Accidents Act 1976—*contd*
s 12(1) 572
33 572
Fires Prevention (Metropolis) Act
1774 .... 386, 412
Food Act 1984 389

Guard Dogs Act 1975 415

Health and Safety at Work etc Act 1974
s 2-9 420
15 420
17(1) 250
47(1)(a) 420
(2) 419, 420
Highways Act 1980 389
s 58(1) 582
Human Fertilisation and Embryology Act
1990
s 44 201
Human Rights Act 1998 .... 4, 200
s 1, 3 5
6(3)(a) 5
(b) 6, 460
7, 8, 11 5

Insolvency Act 1986
s 382 591
International Transport Conventions Act
1983 555

Justices of the Peace Act 1979
s 44 102
45 103

Latent Damage Act 1986 .... 197, 290,
327, 569, 575
s 3 576
Law of Libel Amendment Act 1888
s 3 .... 468, 475
Law of Property Act 1925
s 40 79
Law Reform (Contributory Negligence)
Act 1945 ...... 285, 291, 292, 300,
313, 354, 408, 415, 416,
431, 531, 555, 581,
601
s 1 283
(1) 289
4 290
Law Reform (Husband and Wife) Act 1962
s 1(1) 588
Law Reform (Married Women and Joint
Tortfeasors) Act 1935
s 3 588
6 601
(1) 597
Law Reform (Miscellaneous Provisions)
Act 1934
s 1 572
(1) 438, 553
(2)(a) 553

PAGE

Law Reform (Miscellaneous Provisions)
Act 1934—*contd*
s 1(2)(c) 554
3(5) 554
14(1), (2) 572
Law Reform (Personal Injuries) Act 1948
s 2(4) 561
Legal Aid Act 1974
s 7 437
Sch 1 437
Libel Act 1843
s 2 484
Limitation Act 1980 .... 67, 581
s 2 570
4A 569
10(3)-(5) 599
11 .... 570, 572, 574
(1) 556, 569
(5)-(7) 553
12(1) 556
(2) 557
14 575
14A 569, 575
14B 575
30(1) 570
33 .... 557, 575
38(1) 570
Local Government Act 1974
s 32 465

Magistrates' Courts Act 1980
s 2 98
24(4)-(6) 98
26 98
27(7) 98
30(1), (10) 101
125(2) 97
Maritime Conventions Act 1911
s 1 283
Married Women's Property Act 1882
s 17 588
Medicines Act 1968 353
Mental Health Act 1983 .... 95, 187
Pt IV(ss 56-64) 87
Mental Health (Patients in the Community)
Act 1995 95
Merchant Shipping Act 1995 555
Metropolitan Fire Brigade Act 1865
s 12 94
Minors' Contracts Act 1987 590
Misrepresentation Act 1967
s 2(1) 125
(2) 126

Occupiers Liability Act 1957 . 12, 303, 305,
306, 307, 321, 583
s 1(1) 315
(2) 304, 308, 309
(3) 314
(a) 315
2(1) 312, 316
(2) 309, 313

PAGE

Occupiers Liability Act 1957—*contd*
s 2(3) 310, 312, 313
  (b) 311
  (4)(a) 312
   (b) 313, 314, 318
  (5) 312
  (6) 308, 310
3(1) 318
 (2) 317
 (3) 317, 318
5(1) 316, 317
6 580
Occupiers' Liability Act 1984 ..... 91, 304,
                306, 308, 309,
                311, 319, 323
s 1(3) 320
  (a), (b) 321
  (4), (5) 321
  (6) 322
  (7) 320
  (8) 322
Offences Against the Person Act 1861
s 31 91
 45 105

Parliamentary Commissioner Act 1967
s 10(5) 464
Parliamentary Papers Act 1840
s 1 464
 2 474
Partnership Act 1890
s 10, 12 588
Patents Act 1977 163
s 70 138
Police and Criminal Evidence Act
    1984 .... 28, 97, 101
s 1(9) 102
 8, 18 102
 19 60
 24 98
  (6) 83
 25 .... 98, 100
 28 100
 32(4) 102
 54(7) 102
 55 102
 117 98
Post Office Act 1969 570
s 29(1)-(3) 582
Powers of Criminal Courts Act 1973
s 35-38 43
Prison Act 1952 .... 40, 95
Prosecution of Offences Act 1985 497
Protection from Harassment Act
    1997 .... 165, 439
s 2 .... 37, 38
 3 .... 419, 438
  (2) 159

Registered Design Act 1949 163
s 26 138
Rehabilitation of Offenders Act 1974 .. 460

PAGE

Road Traffic Act 1972
s 35(5) 245
Road Traffic Act 1988
s 300 300

Sale and Supply of Goods Act 1994: 337, 339
Sale of Goods (Amendment) Act
    1994 .... 56, 60
Sale of Goods Act 1893 .... 337, 338
Sale of Goods Act 1979
s 10B 60
 11(2) 56
 14(2)(b) 339
  (3) 339
 20A 60
 21 56
Sex Discrimination Act 1975 521
Slander of Women Act 1891 454
Social Security Act 1989
s 22 548
Sch 4 548
Social Security (Recovery of Benefits) Act
    1997 561
State Immunity Act 1978
s 3, 5, 6 581
Statute of Frauds Amendment Act 1828
s 6 124
Supply of Goods and Services Act 1982 . 16
s 4 339
 13 .... 246, 339
Supreme Court Act 1981
s 32A 554
 34A 552
 35A 559
 37(1) 536
 50 .... 388, 538

Theatres Act 1968
s 4, 7 452
Torts (Interference with Goods) Act
    1977 .... 44, 72
s 1 46
  (b) 71
 2(1) 64
  (2) 45, 46, 53, 59, 67
  (3) 67
 3 64
  (1) 66, 67
  (2)(a)-(c) 66, 67
  (4)(a), (b) 66
  (5) 67
 6(1) 64, 67
  (2) 64, 67
  (3) 64
 7(2) 61
 8 61
  (1) 51, 71
  (2) 51
 10(1) 71
  (a) 60, 61
  (b) 61
  (3) 61

PAGE

Torts (Interference with Goods) Act
1977—*contd*
s 11 290
(1) 71, 88
(2) 61
(3) 60
12, 13 46
14(1) 52
32 67
40 67
Sch 1 46
Trade Marks Act 1994
s 2(2) 129
56(2) 163
Trade Union and Labour Relations Act 1974
s 13(1) 162
Trade Union and Labour Relations
(Consolidation) Act 1992 162
s 10 .... 442, 586
11, 12 442
15 505
20, 23 586

PAGE

Trade Union and Labour Relations
(Consolidation) Act 1992—*contd*
s 226, 244 586
Trade Union Reform and Employment Rights
Act 1993
s 17-21 162

Unfair Contract Terms Act 1977 .. 322, 337
s 1 300
(1)(c) 318
(3)(b) 319
2(1) 300, 318
(2) 318
(3) 301, 318
6 339
11(1) 318
(3) 301, 318
13(1) 301
14 .... 318, 319

Vaccine Damage Payments Act 1979 .. 562

War Damage Act 1965
s 1(1) 105

List of cases

PAGE

A

AB v South West Water Services Ltd (1993), CA 123, 394, 527, 528, 529
AMF International Ltd v Magnet Bowling Ltd (1968) 304, 313, 314, 315, 316
AVX Ltd v EGM Solders Ltd (1982) 59
Abbassy v Metropolitan Police Comr (1990), CA 100
Abbott v Refuge Assurance Co Ltd (1962), CA 496
Abrath v North Eastern Rly Co (1883), CA; on appeal (1886), HL 496
Ackerley v Parkinson (1815) 103
Acrow (Automation) Ltd v Rex Chainbelt Inc (1971), CA 160
Acton Corpn v Morris (1953), CA 73, 75
Adam v Ward (1917), HL 445, 469, 470, 471, 472, 473
Adams v Kelly (1824) 449
Adams v Ursell (1913) 366
Adamson v Jarvis (1827) 600
Addie (Robert) & Sons (Collieries) Ltd v Dumbreck (1929), HL 305, 308
Addis v Crocker (1961), CA 466
Admiralty Comrs v SS Amerika (1917), HL 554
Admiralty Comrs v SS Volute (Owners) (1922), HL 283
Affutu-Nartoy v Clarke (1984) 83
Air Canada v Secretary of State for Trade (1983), CA; affd sub nom Air Canada v Secretary
    of State for Trade (No 2) (1983), HL 466
Airedale National Health Service Trust v Bland (1993), HL 29
Aitken v Bedwell (1827) 41
Aitken v Gardiner and Watson (1956) 63
Ajello v Worsley (1898) 140
Al-Adsani v Kuwait (1994), CA 581
Al-Fayed v The Observer Ltd (1986) 487
Al-Kandari v JR Brown & Co (1988), CA 221
Al-Nakib Investments (Jersey) Ltd v Longcroft (1990) 218
Al Saudi Banque v Clark Pixley (a firm) (1990) 218, 220
Albert v Lavin (1982), CA; affd (1982), HL 89, 99
Albion, The. See Stone (Thomas) (Shipping) Ltd v Admiralty, The Albion
Alcock v Chief Constable of South Yorkshire Police (1991), CA; affd (1992),
    HL 191, 203, 204, 205, 206, 207, 230
Alcock v Wraith (1991), CA 510, 511
Alcott v Millar's Karri and Jarrah Forests Ltd (1904), CA 140
Aldred v Nacanco (1987), CA 517
Aldworth v Stewart (1866) 97
Alexander v Jenkins (1892), CA 441, 454
Alexander v North Eastern Rly Co (1865) 459
Alexander v Southey (1821) 45, 59
Alexandrou v Oxford (1993), CA 190
Alford v National Coal Board (1952), HL 431, 520

PAGE

Ali (Saif) v Sydney Mitchell & Co (a firm) (1980), HL 220, 498
Aliakmon, The. See Leigh and Sillivan Ltd v Aliakmon Shipping Co Ltd, The Aliakmon
Allason v Campbell (1996) 140
Allbutt v General Council of Medical Education and Registration (1889), CA 474
Allen v Bloomsbury Health Authority (1993) 547
Allen v Flood (1898), HL 113, 143, 148, 491
Allen v Gulf Oil Refining Ltd (1981), HL 182, 384
Allen v Metropolitan Police Comr (1980) 28
Allen v Wright (1838) 99
Allen (W H) & Co v Brown Watson (1965) 128
Alliance and Leicester Building Society v Edgestop Ltd (1994); affd on other grounds (1995),
    CA 290
Allied Maples Group Ltd v Simmons & Simmons (a firm) (1995), CA 266, 267
Allsop v Allsop (1860) 455
Allsop v Church of England Newspaper Ltd (1972), CA 444, 445
Almeroth v Chivers & Sons Ltd (1948), CA 386
Amann v Damm (1860) 478
American Cyanamid Co v Ethicon Ltd (1975), HL 158, 537
American Express Co v British Airways Board (1983) 582
Ancell v McDermott (1993), CA 190
Anchor Brewhouse Developments Ltd v Berkley House (Docklands Developments) Ltd
    (1987) 76
Anderson v Gorrie (1895), CA 102
Anderson v Oppenheimer (1880), CA 407
André & Cie SA v Ets Michel Blanc & Fils (1977); affd (1979), CA 125
Andreae v Selfridge & Co Ltd (1938), CA 363, 375, 387
Andrews v Freeborough (1967), CA 553
Andrews v Hopkinson (1957) 342
Andrews v Mockford (1896), CA 121
Andrews v Schooling (1991), CA 327
Anglo-Newfoundland Development Co Ltd v Pacific Steam Navigation Co (1924), HL ... 245
Anglo-Scottish Beet Sugar Corpn Ltd v Spalding UDC (1937) 123
Anheuser-Busch Inc v Budejovicky Budvar Narodni Podnik, Budweiser Case (1984), CA ... 127
Annabel's (Berkeley Square) v Schock (1972), CA 133
Anns v Merton London Borough Council (1978),
    HL 174, 183, 184, 213, 326, 329, 332, 342, 385, 569
Ansell v Thomas (1974), CA 41
Antec International Ltd v South Western Chicks (Warren) Ltd (1998) 129
Anthony v Haney (1832) 93, 108
Apley Estates Co Ltd v De Bernales (1946); affd (1947), CA 568, 597
Apollinaris Co Ltd v Norrish (1875) 128
Appleton v Garrett (1996) 85, 528
Arab Monetary Fund v Hashim (No 8) (1993); on appeal (1993), CA 598
Arbuthnot Latham Bank Ltd v Trafalgar Holding Ltd (1998), CA 569
Archer v Brown (1985) 123
Arenson v Casson Beckman Rutley & Co (1977), HL 103
Argy Trading Development Co Ltd v Lapid Developments Ltd (1977) 220
Argyll (Duchess of) v Duke of Argyll (1967) 164
Armagas Ltd v Mundogas SA, The Ocean Frost (1986), CA; affd (1986), HL 124, 508,
                                                                              522, 523
Armory v Delamirie (1722) 50
Armstrong v Strain (1952), CA 123
Arneil v Paterson (1931), HL 597
Arnison v Smith (1889), CA 121
Arpad, The (1934), CA 58, 65
Arthur v Anker (1997), CA 84, 109
Ash v Hutchinson & Co (Publishers) Ltd (1936), CA 532, 594
Ash v Lady Ash (1696) 95, 591
Ashby v Tolhurst (1937), CA 53
Ashby v White (1703) 426, 429, 525
Ashcroft v Mersey Regional Health Authority (1983); affd (1985), CA 257
Ashdown v Samuel Williams & Sons Ltd (1957), CA 317, 319
Ashton v Turner (1981) 107, 175

PAGE

Aspro Travel Ltd v Owners Abroad Group plc (1995), CA 445, 446, 447, 458, 476
Associated British Ports v Transport and General Workers' Union (1989), CA; revsd (1989), HL
    149, 150, 158, 160, 161
Associated Newspapers Ltd v Dingle. See Dingle v Associated Newspapers Ltd
Associated Newspapers plc v Insert Media Ltd (1991), CA 126, 131
Astaire v Campling (1965), CA 440
Aswan Engineering Establishment Co v Lupdine Ltd (Thurgar Bolle, third party) (1987),
    CA 344, 345
Athletes Foot Marketing Associates Inc v Cobra Sports Ltd (1980) 132
Atkinson v Fitzwalter (1987), CA 460, 485
Atkinson v Newcastle and Gateshead Waterworks Co (1877), CA 417, 425, 427
Attersoll v Stevens (1808) 70, 78
Attia v British Gas plc (1988), CA 175, 204, 210
A-G v Copeland (1902), CA 385
A-G v Corke (1933) 398
A-G v Cory Bros & Co Ltd (1918); on appeal (1919), CA; revsd (1921), HL 400
A-G v Doughty (1752) 365
A-G v Gastonia Coaches Ltd (1977) 392
A-G v Guardian Newspapers Ltd (1987), HL 166
A-G v Hastings Corpn (1950), CA 373
A-G v Jonathan Cape Ltd (1976) 166
A-G v News Group Newspapers Ltd (1987), CA 487
A-G v Nissan (1970), HL 105
A-G v Tomline (1880), CA 81
A-G and General Council of Medical Education of United Kingdom Registration v Barrett
    Proprietaries Ltd (1932) 134
A-G for New South Wales v Perpetual Trustee Co Ltd (1951), HC of A 158
A-G (on the relation of Glamorgan County Council and Pontardawe RDC) v PYA Quarries
    Ltd (1957), CA 390, 392
A-G's Reference (No 2 of 1983) (1984), CA 89, 91
Attwood v Chapman (1914) 466
Atwood v Ernest (1853) 61
Austin v Dowling (1870) 42
Australian Newspaper Co v Bennett (1894), PC 446
Auty v National Coal Board (1985), CA 540, 543

B

B (a minor), Re (1981), CA 86
B (a minor), Re (1987), HL 86
B v Croydon Health Authority (1994), CA 87
BBMB Finance (Hong Kong) Ltd v Eda Holdings Ltd (1991), PC 62
Badkin v Powell (1776) 70
Bagot v Stevens, Scanlan & Co Ltd (1966) 196
Baird v Williamson (1863) 399
Baker v Barclays Bank Ltd (1955) 61
Baker v Bolton (1808) 554
Baker v Carrick (1894), CA 473, 479
Baker v E Longhurst & Sons Ltd (1933), CA 236
Baker v James (1921) 252
Baker v Market Harborough Industrial Co-operative Society Ltd (1953), CA 261
Baker v T E Hopkins & Son Ltd (1959), CA 202, 270, 294, 297, 299
Baker v Willoughby (1970), HL 273
Balden v Shorter (1933) 137, 139
Baldwin v Cole (1704) 59
Balfour v Barty-King (Hyder & Sons (Builders) Ltd, third parties) (1956); affd (1957),
    CA 398, 404, 412, 511
Ball v Consolidated Rutile (1991) 390
Ball v Ray (1873) 373
Ballard v North British Rly Co (1923) 252, 259, 262, 263
Ballett v Mingay (1943), CA 590
Balme v Hutton (1833), Ex Ch 70
Balmer v Hayes (1950) 426

PAGE

Bamford v Turnley (1862), Ex Ch 358, 372
Banbury v Bank of Montreal (1918), HL 125
Bank View Mills Ltd v Nelson Corpn (1942); revsd (1943), CA 596
Bank voor Handel en Scheepvaart NV v Slatford (1953), CA; revsd sub nom Bank voor Handel
    en Scheepvaart NV v Administrator of Hungarian Property (1954), HL 505, 579
Banque Bruxelles Lambert SA v Eagle Star Insurance Co Ltd (1997), HL 123, 274
Banque Financière de la Cité SA (formerly Banque Keyser Ullmann SA) v Westgate Insurance
    Co Ltd (formerly Hodge General and Mercantile Co Ltd) (1991), HL 119, 220, 275
Barclays Bank plc v Fairclough Building Ltd (1995), CA 291, 600, 601
Barfoot v Reynolds (1734) 89
Barker v Braham and Norwood (1773) 509
Barker v Furlong (1891) 57, 71
Barker v Herbert (1911), CA 391
Barkway v South Wales Transport Co Ltd (1948), CA; revsd (1950), HL 259, 262
Barnes (an infant) v Hampshire County Council (1969), HL 174
Barnes v Irwell Valley Water Board (1939), CA 341
Barnes v Nayer (1986), CA 84, 290
Barnes v Ward (1850) 391
Barnett v Chelsea and Kensington Hospital Management Committee (1969) 265, 512
Barnett v Cohen (1921) 556
Barnett v Earl of Guildford (1855) 79
Barnett v H and J Packer & Co Ltd (1940) 342
Barrett v Associated Newspapers Ltd (1907), CA 140
Barrett v Enfield London Borough Council (1997), CA 187
Barrett v Ministry of Defence (1995), CA 195, 282
Barrette v Franki Compressed Pile Co of Canada Ltd (1955) 411
Barretts & Baird (Wholesale) Ltd v Institution of Professional Civil Servants (1987) 159
Barrow v Arnaud (1846), Ex Ch 66
Barrow v Bankside Members Agency Ltd and Bankside Underwriting Management Ltd (1995);
    affd sub nom Barrow v Bankside Agency Ltd (1995), CA 531
Bartlett v Tottenham (1932) 398
Bartonshill Coal Co v McGuire (1858), HL 503
Barwick v English Joint Stock Bank (1867) 521
Basébé v Matthews (1867) 494
Basely v Clarkson (1681) 77
Batcheller v Tunbridge Wells Gas Co (1901) 398
Bates v Parker (1953), CA 311
Bates v Stone Parish Council (1954), CA 308
Batts Combe Quarry Ltd v Ford (1943), CA 154
Batty v Metropolitan Property Realisations Ltd (1978), CA 196, 213, 326, 329, 342
Baume & Co Ltd v A H Moore Ltd (1958), CA 133
Bavins Junior and Sims v London and South Western Bank Ltd (1900), CA 52
Baxter v Taylor (1832) 81
Baxter v Woolcombers Ltd (1963), CA 287
Bayley v Manchester, Sheffield and Lincolnshire Rly Co (1873), Ex Ch 24, 516
Bayoumi v Protim Services Ltd (1996), CA 327
Beach v Freeson (1972) 476
Beaman v ARTS Ltd (1949), CA 67, 577
Beard v London General Omnibus Co (1900), CA 517
Beatson v Skene (1860) 466
Beaudesert Shire Council v Smith (1966), HC of A 379
Beaumont v Humberts (1990), CA 220
Beckham v Drake (1849) 592
Beckwith v Shordike (1767) 74
Behrens v Bertram Mills Circus Ltd (1957) 288, 413, 557
Belgische Radio en Televisie and Société Belge des Auteurs, Compositeurs et Éditeurs
    (BRT) v SV SABAM and NV Fonior: 127/73 (1974), ECJ 9
Bell v Secretary of State for Defence (1986), CA 581
Bell v Stone (1798) 441
Belmont Finance Corpn Ltd v Williams Furniture Ltd (1979), CA 144
Belsize Motor Supply Co v Cox (1914) 48, 61
Benjamin v Storr (1874) 390, 394, 418, 428
Benmax v Austin Motor Co Ltd (1955), HL 257

PAGE

Bennett v Chemical Construction (GB) Ltd (1971), CA 258
Bennett v Metropolitan Police Comr (1995) 155, 499
Bennett v Tugwell (1971) 298
Benning v Wong (1969) 401, 407
Benson v Biggs Wall & Co Ltd (1982) 558
Bents Brewery Co Ltd v Hogan (1945) 152, 155
Berkoff v Burchill (1996), CA 439
Bermingham v Sher Bros (1980) 311
Bernina, The. See Mills v Armstrong, The Bernina
Bernstein of Leigh (Baron) v Skyviews and General Ltd (1978) 76, 165
Berrill v Road Haulage Executive (1952) 288
Berry v British Transport Commission (1962), CA 493
Berry v Humm & Co (1915) 557
Best v Samuel Fox & Co Ltd (1952), HL 455
Best v Wellcome Foundation Ltd (1994) 347
Bhoomidas v Port of Singapore Authority (1978), PC 506
Biba Group Ltd v Biba Boutique (1980) 128
Bidwell v Briant (1956) 279
Billings (AC) & Sons Ltd v Riden (1958), HL 327, 342
Birch v Mills (1995) 413
Bird v Holbrook (1828) 36, 91
Bird v Jones (1845) 38, 39
Bird v O'Neal (1960), PC 147
Bird v Pearce (Somerset County Council, third party) (1979), CA 215, 583
Bird v Randall (1762) 157
Bird v Tower Hamlets London Borough Council (1969) 583
Birkett v Hayes (1982), CA 551, 552
Birkett v James (1978), HL 574
Birse Construction Ltd v Haiste Ltd (1996), CA 596, 597
Bishop v Consolidated London Properties Ltd (1933) 324
Bishop v Cunard White Star Co Ltd, The Queen Mary (1950) 558
Bisney v Swanston (1972), CA 80
Black v Christchurch Finance Co (1894), PC 408, 511
Blackham v Pugh (1846) 476
Blackshaw v Lord (1984), CA 476, 478
Blades v Higgs (1861) 108
Blades v Higgs (1865) 108
Blake v Barnard (1840) 35
Blake v Lanyon (1795) 150
Blamires v Lancashire and Yorkshire Rly Co (1873) 245
Blankley v Godley (1952) 76
Blenheim Borough and Wairau River Board v British Pavements (Canterbury) Ltd (1940) .. 64
Blennerhasset v Novelty Sales Services Ltd (1933) 439
Bliss v Hall (1838) 385
Bloodworth v Gray (1844) 453, 454
Bloxam v Sanders (1825) 49
Blue Circle Industries plc v Ministry of Defence (1996); varied (1998), CA 428
Blundy, Clark & Co Ltd v London and North Eastern Rly Co (1931), CA 390
Blyth v Birmingham Waterworks Co (1856) 237
Boakes v Postmaster-General (1962), CA 582
Boaler v Holder (1887) 494
Bodley v Reynolds (1846) 64
Bognor Regis UDC v Campion (1972) 442
Bolam v Friern Hospital Management Committee (1957) 87, 240, 248
Bolitho v City and Hackney Health Authority (1998), HL 248, 249, 269
Bollinger v Costa Brava Wine Co Ltd (1960) 131
Bollinger v Costa Brava Wine Co (No 4) (1961) 131
Bolton v Stone. See Stone v Bolton
Bone v Seale (1975), CA 367
Bonnard v Perryman (1891), CA 487
Bonnington Castings Ltd v Wardlaw (1956) 268, 430
Bookbinder v Tebbit (1989), CA 443, 459
Booth v Arnold (1895), CA 454

PAGE

Booth & Co (International) Ltd v National Enterprise Board (1978) 426
Boothman v British Northrop (1972), CA 291
Boswell-Wilkie Circus (Pty) Ltd v Brian Boswell Circus (Pty) Ltd (1985); affd (1986) 127
Botterill v Whytehead (1879) 469
Bottomley v Bannister (1932), CA 181
Bottomley v FW Woolworth & Co Ltd (1932), CA 461
Bourgoin SA v Ministry of Agriculture, Fisheries and Food (1986), CA 424, 499
Bowater v Rowley Regis Corpn (1944), CA 295, 298
Bowen v Anderson (1894) 382
Bowen v Hall (1881), CA 148
Bower v Peate (1876) 382, 510
Bowmakers Ltd v Barnet Instruments Ltd (1945), CA 106
Box v Jubb (1879) 408
Boxes Ltd v British Waterways Board (1971), CA 400
Boxsius v Goblet Frères (1894), CA 450, 472
Boy Andrew (Owners) v St Rognvald (Owners) (1948), HL 284, 285
Boyce v Douglas (1807) 595
Boyle v Kodak Ltd (1969), HL 431, 432
Brand v Hammersmith and City Rly Co (1867), Ex Ch; revsd sub nom Hammersmith and
    City Rly Co v Brand (1869) 103, 360
Brandeis Goldschmidt & Co Ltd v Western Transport Ltd (1981), CA 63, 66
Brandon v Osborne Garrett & Co (1924) 288
Bracebridge Engineering Ltd v Darby (1990), EAT 521
Bradburn v Great Western Rly Co (1874) 548
Bradburn v Lindsay (1983) 324
Braddock v Bevins (1948), CA 441, 477
Bradford v Robinson Rentals Ltd (1967) 276
Bradford Corpn v Pickles (1895), HL 4, 368, 372, 491
Bradford Third Equitable Benefit Building Society v Borders (1941), HL 119, 120
Bradlaugh v Gossett (1884), DC 104
Bradley v Copley (1845) 49
Bradshaw v Waterlow & Sons Ltd (1915), CA 496
Braham v J Lyons & Co Ltd (1962), CA 425
Braithwaite v South Durham Steel Co Ltd (1958) 306
Bray v Palmer (1953), CA 261
Brekkes Ltd v Cattel (1972) 152
Brent Walker Group plc v Time Out Ltd (1991), CA 480
Brew Bros Ltd v Snax (Ross) Ltd (1970), CA 383
Brewer v Dew (1843) 68, 592
Brewer and Gregory v Sparrow (1827) 568
Brice v Brown (1984) 209, 276, 279
Bridges v Hawkesworth (1851) 51
Bridgman v Stockdale (1953) 477
Bridgmont v Associated Newspapers Ltd (1951), CA 448
Bridlington Relay Ltd v Yorkshire Electricity Board (1965) 364
Brierly v Kendall (1852) 71
Briess v Woolley (1954), HL 119, 515
Brimelow v Casson (1924) 156
Brinsmead v Harrison (1872), Ex Ch 597
Brinsmead (John) & Sons Ltd v Brinsmead and Waddington & Sons Ltd (1913); on appeal
    (1913), CA 128
Bristol and West of England Bank v Midland Rly Co (1891), CA 59
Bristol Conservatories Ltd v Conservatories Custom Built Ltd (1989), CA 132, 136
Bristow v Cormican (1878), HL 79
British Cast Plate Manufacturers (Governor & Co) v Meredith (1792) 94
British Celanese Ltd v AH Hunt (Capacitors) Ltd (1969) .. 225, 369, 378, 393, 401, 404, 412
British Columbia Electric Rly Co Ltd v Loach (1916), PC 283
British Data Management plc v Boxer Commercial Removals plc (1996), CA 487
British Economical Lamp Co Ltd v Empire, Mile End, Ltd (1913) 60
British Homophone Ltd v Kunz and Crystallate Gramophone Record Manufacturing Co Ltd
    (1935) 151
British Industrial Plastics Ltd v Ferguson (1940), HL 151, 154
British Motor Trade Association v Gray (1951) 149

PAGE

British Motor Trade Association v Salvadori (1949) 154, 157
British Railway Traffic and Electric Co Ltd v CRC Co Ltd and LCC (1922) 139
British Railways Board v Herrington (1972), HL 320
British Road Services Ltd v Arthur V Crutchley & Co Ltd (Factory Guards Ltd, Third Parties)
  (1967); on appeal (1968), CA 521
British Russian Gazette and Trade Outlook Ltd v Associated Newspapers Ltd (1933), CA .. 568
British Transport Commission v Gourley (1956), HL 526, 542
British Vacuum Cleaner Co Ltd v New Vacuum Cleaner Co Ltd (1907) 128
Broadley v Guy Clapham & Co (1994), CA 572
Broadway Approvals Ltd v Odhams Press Ltd (1965), CA 482
Brock v Richards (1951), CA 413
Broder v Saillard (1876) 367, 399
Bromley v Mercer (1922), CA 333, 391
Brooke v Bool (1928), DC 594
Brooks v J and P Coates (UK) Ltd (1984) 569, 572, 573
Brooks v London and North Western Rly Co (1884), DC 240
Broom v Morgan (1953), CA 515
Broome v Agar (1928), CA 446
Brown v Brash and Ambrose (1948), CA 78
Brown v Chapman (1848) 42
Brown v Hawkes (1891); affd (1891), CA 496
Brown v Raphael (1958), CA 121
Brown v Rolls Royce Ltd (1960) 245
Brown v Smith (1853) 486
Brown v Thompson (1968), CA 600
Brown, Jenkinson & Co Ltd v Percy Dalton (London) Ltd (1957), CA 121
Browne v DC Thomson & Co (1912) 447
Browne v Dawson (1840) 79
Browne v Dunn (1893), HL 468
Browning v War Office (1963), CA 548
Brownlie v Campbell (1880), HL 119
Bruce v Odhams Press Ltd (1936), CA 448
Brunner v Williams (1975), DC 75
Brunsden v Humphrey (1884), CA 531
Brunswick (Duke) v Harmer (1849) 571
Bryan v Maloney (1994), HC of A 330
Bryanston Finance Ltd v de Vries (1975), CA 472, 477, 597
Bryanston Leasings Ltd v Principality Finance Ltd (1977) 60, 66
Bryant v Wardell (1848) 48
Bryce v Rusden (1886) 485
Buck v English Electric Co Ltd (1978) 572
Buckland v Guildford Gas Light and Coke Co (1949) 174
Buckland v Johnson (1854) 568
Buckley and Toronto Transportation Commission v Smith Transport Ltd (1946) 590
Budden v BP Oil Ltd (1980), CA 232, 245
Building and Civil Engineering Holidays Scheme Management Ltd v Post Office (1966), CA: 582
Bull v Bull (1955), CA 78, 79
Bull v Devon Area Health Authority (1993), CA 504, 512
Bulmer (H P) Ltd and Showerings Ltd v J Bollinger SA and Champagne Lanson Père et Fils
  (1978), CA 134
Bunker v Charles Brand & Son Ltd (1969) 313, 315
Bunyan v Jordon (1936) 37
Burgess v Burgess (1853) 128
Burgess v Florence Nightingale Hospital For Gentlewomen (1955) 557, 558
Burmah Oil Co (Burma Trading) Ltd v Lord Advocate (1965), HL 94, 105
Burmah Trading Corpn v Mirza Mahomed Allay Sherazee and Burmah Co Ltd (1878) 64
Burn v Morris (1834) 567
Burnard v Haggis (1863) 590
Burnett v British Waterways Board (1973), CA 299
Burnett v George (1993), CA 537
Burnie Port Authority v General Jones Pty Ltd (1994) 409
Burns v Edman (1970) 107, 557
Burnside v Emerson (1968), CA 583

PAGE
Buron v Denman (1848) 105
Burris v Azadani (1995), CA 37
Burroughes v Bayne (1860) 69
Burton v Davies (1953) 39
Burton v Hughes (1824) 54
Burton v Islington Health Authority (1993), CA 200
Bush v Smith (1953), CA 73, 592
Bushel v Miller (1718) 45, 55
Butler (or Black) v Fife Coal Co Ltd (1912), HL 253, 420
Butler v Standard Telephones and Cables Ltd (1940) 379
Butterfield v Forrester (1809) 281
Bux v Slough Metals Ltd (1974), CA 245
Byrne v Boadle (1863) 259
Byrne v Deane (1937), CA 440, 450
Byron (Lord) v Johnston (1816) 127, 132
Bywell Castle, The (1879), CA 288

C

C (adult: refusal of treatment), Re (1994) 94
C (a minor) v Hackney London Borough Council (1996), CA 568
C v Mirror Group Newspapers (1996), CA; revsd (1997), HL 577
CHC Software Care Ltd v Hopkins & Wood (1993) 136
Cadbury-Schweppes Pty Ltd v Pub Squash Co Pty Ltd (1981), PC 130, 134
Cakebread v Hopping Bros (Whetstone) Ltd (1947), CA 431
Caledonian Rly Co v Walker's Trustees (1882), HL 390
Callis v Gunn (1964), DC 33
Caltex Oil (Australia) Pty Ltd v Dredge Willemstad (1976), HC of A 221
Calvet v Tomkies (1963), CA 141
Cambridge Nutrition Ltd v BBC (1990), CA 166
Cambridge University Press v University Tutorial Press (1928) 136
Cambridge Water Co Ltd v Eastern Counties Leather plc (1994), HL 358, 359, 360, 361,
                                                        371, 372, 374, 375, 396, 397,
                                                        403, 405, 406, 409, 411, 412
Camden Nominees Ltd v Forcey (or Slack) (1940) 156
Camdex International Ltd v Bank of Zambia (1998), CA 593
Camellia Tanker Ltd SA v International Transport Workers' Federation (1976), CA 152
Caminer v Northern and London Investment Trust Ltd (1951), HL 236, 239, 324
Campbell v Northern Ireland Housing Executive (1996) 305, 307
Campbell v Paddington Corpn (1911) 527, 585
Campbell v Spottiswoode (1863) 482
Campbell and Cosans v United Kingdom (1982) 96
Camporese v Parton (1983) 478
Canadian Pacific Rly Co v Lockhart (1942), PC 519
Canadian Shredded Wheat Co Ltd v Kellogg Co of Canada Ltd (1938), PC 128
Candler v Crane Christmas & Co (1951), CA 174, 216
Candlewood Navigation Corpn Ltd v Mitsui OSK Lines Ltd, The Mineral Transporter, The
        Ibaraki Maru (1986), PC 179, 213, 215
Canterbury v Spence (1972); on appeal (1972) 232
Canterbury City Council v Howletts & Port Lympne Estates Ltd (1997) 415
Caparo Industries plc v Dickman (1989), CA; on appeal (1990), HL . 117, 177, 217, 247, 390
Capital and Counties Bank Ltd v George Henty & Sons (1882), HL 439, 443
Capital and Counties plc v Hampshire County Council (1997), CA 180, 189, 191, 418
Capps v Miller (1989), CA 287, 289, 291, 292
Carlgarth, The (1927), CA 310
Carmarthenshire County Council v Lewis (1955), HL 194, 243
Carmen v Fox Film Corpn (1923) 157
Carmichael v National Power plc (1998), CA 506
Carr-Glynn v Frearsons (a firm) (1998) 223
Carslogie Steamship Co Ltd v Royal Norwegian Government (1952), HL 270
Carstairs v Taylor (1871) 407, 408
Cartledge v E Jopling & Sons Ltd (1963), HL 569, 572, 574
Case of Gloucester Grammar School (1410) 115

PAGE

Case of Thorns (1466) 77
Casey v Automatic Renault Canada Ltd (1966) 492
Cassell & Co Ltd v Broome (1972), HL 460, 485, 526, 528, 529
Cassidy v Daily Mirror Newspapers Ltd (1929), CA 444, 445, 446, 447
Cassidy v Ministry of Health (1951), CA 260, 261, 323, 504, 506, 512, 514, 515
Castle v St Augustine's Links Ltd (1922) 391
Caswell v Powell Duffryn Associated Collieries Ltd (1940), HL 282, 431
Catnic Components Ltd v Hill & Smith Ltd (1983) 164, 529
Cattle v Stockton Waterworks Co (1875) 155, 225, 401, 402
Cavalier v Pope (1906), HL 333
Cavanagh v London Transport Executive (1956) 600
Cavanagh v Ulster Weaving Co Ltd (1960), HL 245
Cavendish, The. See Oceangas (Gibraltar) Ltd v Port of London Authority, The Cavendish
Cawdor (Lord) v Lewis (1835) 81
Caxton Publishing Co Ltd v Sutherland Publishing Co (1939), HL 54, 63, 567
Cayzer Irvine & Co v Carron Co (1884), HL 245
Cellactite and British Uralite Ltd v HH Robertson Co Inc (1957), CA 139
Cellular Clothing Co v Maxton and Murray (1899), HL 128
Century Insurance Co Ltd v Northern Ireland Road Tranport Board (1942), HL 516
Chadwick v British Transport Commission (or British Railways Board) (1967) 202, 203
Chant v Read (1939) 532
Chapman v Honig (1963), CA 160
Chapman v Lord Ellesmere (1932), CA 457, 474, 475, 477
Chapman v Pickersgill (1762) 493
Charing Cross West End and City Electric Supply Co v Hydraulic Power Co (1914), CA ... 405
Charleston v News Group Newspapers Ltd (1995), HL 443
Charlton v Forrest Printing Ink Co Ltd (1980), CA 255
Charrington v Simons & Co Ltd (1971) 537
Chatterton v Gerson (1981) 85, 250
Chatterton v Secretary of State for India in Council (1895), CA 464
Chaudhry v Prabhakar (1988), CA 217, 239, 241
Cheater v Cater (1918), CA 325
Cherneskey v Armadale Publishers Ltd (1979) 483
Cheticamp Fisheries Co-operative Ltd v Canada (1995) 158, 160
Chettle v Denton (1951), CA 322
Chinery v Viall (1860) 49, 62
Chinn v Morris (1826) 39
Chomley v Watson (1907) 447
Christie v Davey (1893) 372, 411
Christie v Leachinsky (1947), HL 100
Christmas v General Cleaning Contractors Ltd and Caledonian Club Trust Ltd (1952), CA;
    affd sub nom General Cleaning Contractors Ltd v Christmas (1953), HL 253, 256,
                                                                           299, 311
Christopherson v Bare (1848) 32
Chubb Cash Ltd v John Crilley & Son (1983), CA 54, 62
Church of Scientology of California v Johnson-Smith (1972) 464
Church of Scientology of California v Miller (1987), CA 164, 166
Citizens' Life Assurance Co v Brown (1904), PC 473
City Motors (1933) Pty Ltd v Southern Aerial Super Service Pty Ltd (1961) 47
City of Lincoln, The (1889), CA 269
Clark v Molyneux (1877), CA 469
Clark v Oxfordshire Health Authority (1998), CA 506
Clarke v Army and Navy Co-operative Society (1903), CA 340
Clarke v Bruce Lance & Co (a firm) (1988), CA 223, 248
Clarke v Dickson (1858) 566
Clarke v Dickson (1859) 566
Clarke v Holmes (1862), Ex Ch 239
Clarke v Taylor (1836) 459
Clarke and Wife v Brims (1947) 425
Clarkson v Lawson (1830) 460
Clay v A J Crump & Sons Ltd (1964), CA 331, 343
Clay v Pooler (1982) 542, 558
Clayards v Dethick and Davis (1848) 288, 299

PAGE

Clayton v Woodman & Son (Builders) Ltd (1961); revsd (1962), CA 215
Cleary v Booth (1893), DC 96
Clegg v Dearden (1848) 75
Cleghorn v Oldham (1927) 298
Clissold v Cratchley (1910), CA 498
Close v Steel Co of Wales Ltd (1962), HL 428
Clowes v National Coal Board (1987) 266
Clunis v Camden and Islington Health Authority (1998), CA 107, 211, 547
Clutterbuck v Chaffers (1816) 450
Clydesdale Bank Ltd v Paton (1896), HL 125
Cobbett v Grey (1849) 39
Cockcroft v Smith (1705) 89
Coco v AN Clark (Engineers) Ltd (1969) 164
Codd v Cabe (1876), DC 89
Cohen v Daily Telegraph Ltd (1968), CA 480
Cohen v Morgan (1825) 492
Cole v De Trafford (No 2) (1918), CA 262
Cole v Turner (1704) 33
Colfar v Coggins and Griffiths (Liverpool) Ltd (1945), HL 254
Colledge v Bass Mitchells & Butlers Ltd (1988), CA 549
Colley v Hart (1890) 138
Collingwood v Home and Colonial Stores Ltd (1936), CA 401, 404
Collins v Hertfordshire County Council (1947) 323, 506, 511, 512
Collins v Renison (1754) 91
Collins v Wilcock (1984) 13, 28, 31
Colls v Home and Colonial Stores Ltd (1904), HL 363
Colonial Mutual Life Assurance Society Ltd v Producers and Citizens Assurance Co of
    Australia Ltd (1931) 508
Columbia Picture Industries Inc v Robinson (1987) 536
Colvilles Ltd v Devine (1969), HL 263
Colwill v Reeves (1811) 70
Compania Colombiana de Seguros v Pacific Steam Navigation Co (1965) 593
Compton v McClure (1975) 517
Condon v Basi (1985), CA 83, 241
Condon v Condon (1978) 292
Conley v Strain (1988) 271
Conn v David Spencer Ltd (1930) 39
Consejo Regulador de las Denominaciones Jerez-Xere-Sherry y Manzanilla de Sanlucar de
    Barrameda v Matthew Clark & Sons (1992) 131
Consolidated Co v Curtis & Son (1892) 54, 57
Consorzio del Prosciutto di Parma v Marks & Spencer plc (1991), CA 127
Constantine v Imperial Hotels Ltd (1944) 525
Control Risks Ltd v New English Library (1989), CA 481
Conway v George Wimpey & Co Ltd (1951), CA 323
Conway v Rimmer (1968), HL 466
Cook v Alexander (1974), CA 474
Cook v Beal (1697) 89
Cook v Broderip (1968) 253, 314
Cook v Cox (1814) 451
Cook v JL Kier & Co Ltd (1970), CA 550
Cook v Lewis (1951) 261, 597
Cook v Square D Ltd (1992), CA 252, 256, 513
Cook v Ward (1830) 457
Cooke v Forbes (1867) 388
Cooke v Midland Great Western Rly of Ireland (1909), HL 308, 311
Cookson v Harewood (1932), CA 457
Cookson v Knowles (1979), HL 543, 544, 559
Cooney v Edeveain (1897), CA 480
Cooper v Crabtree (1882), CA 77
Cooper v Lawson (1838) 459
Cooper v Railway Executive (Southern Region) (1953) 432
Cooper v Willomatt (1845) 47
Coote v Stone (1971), CA 426

PAGE

Cope v Sharpe (No 2) (1912), CA 93
Corbett v Barking, Havering and Brentwood Health Authority (1991), CA 559, 560
Corbett v Burge, Warren and Ridgley Ltd (1932) 498
Cornman v Eastern Counties Rly Co (1859) 244
Cornwell v Myskow (1987), CA 441, 480, 482, 487
Cotton v Derbyshire Dales District Council (1994), CA 313
Couch v Steel (1854) 417
County Hotel and Wine Co v London and North Western Rly Co (1918); on appeal (1919), CA;
    affd (1921), HL 533
Coupey v Henley (1797) 90
Coupland v Eagle Bros Ltd (1969) 313
Covell v Laming (1808) 33, 68, 74
Coward v Baddeley (1859) 31
Coward v Wellington (1836) 455
Cox v Glue (1848) 76
Coxhead v Richards (1846) 479
Craig v Frost (1936) 96
Creed v John McGeoch & Sons Ltd (1955) 391
Cresswell v Eaton (1991) 560
Cresswell v Sirl (1948), CA 92
Crest Homes Ltd v Ascott (1980), CA 487
Croft v Day (1843) 127
Crofter Hand Woven Harris Tweed Co Ltd v Veitch (1942), HL 145, 147
Croke (a minor) v Wiseman (1981), CA 545, 546
Cropper v Chief Constable of the South Yorkshire Police (1990), CA 491
Crossley v Rawlinson (1981) 278
Crowhurst v Amersham Burial Board (1878) 398, 399
Crown River Cruises Ltd v Kimbolton Fireworks Ltd and London Fire & Civil Defence
    Authority (1996) 368, 369, 396, 400, 405
Cruise v Terrell (1922), CA 78
Crump v Lambert (1867); affd (1867) 363
Cummings v Granger (1977), CA 414, 415
Cummings (or McWilliams) v Sir William Arrol & Co Ltd (1962), HL 273, 430
Cunard v Antifyre Ltd (1933) 324, 369, 376, 378
Cunard Steamship Co v Stacey (1955), CA 151
Cunningham v Harrison (1973), CA 545, 548
Cunningham v Reading Football Club Ltd (1992) 310
Cunningham-Howie v FW Dimbleby & Sons Ltd (1951), CA 481
Curtis v Betts (1990), CA 414, 415
Cushing v Peter Walker & Son (Warrington and Burton) Ltd (1941) 383
Cutler v McPhail (1962) 597
Cutler v United Dairies (London) Ltd (1933), CA 299
Cutler v Vauxhall Motors Ltd (1971), CA 549
Cutler v Wandsworth Stadium Ltd (1949), HL 422, 425, 427
Cynat Products Ltd v Landbuild (Investment and Property) Ltd (1984) 513

D

D (a minor) (wardship: sterilisation), Re (1976) 86
D (a minor) v Department of the Environment (NI) (1992) 311
D v Meah (1986) 34
D & F Estates Ltd v Church Comrs for England (1989), HL 214, 226, 326, 329
D and L Caterers Ltd and Jackson v D'Ajou (1945), CA 442, 453
DDSA Pharmaceuticals Ltd v Times Newspapers Ltd (1973), CA 445
Daborn v Bath Tramways Motor Co Ltd and Smithey (1946), CA 234
Daily Mirror Newspapers Ltd v Gardner (1968), CA 149, 152
Dakhyl v Labouchere (1908), HL 446
Dale v Wood (1822) 89
Dallison v Caffery (1965), CA 101
Dalton v Angus (1881), HL 510, 513
Daly v Chief Constable of Merseyside Police unreported 190
Daly v General Steam Navigation Co Ltd, The Dragon (1980), CA 323, 544, 547
Daly v Liverpool Corpn (1939) 238

PAGE

Danby v Beardsley (1880) 492
Daniels v Griffiths (1998), CA 467
Daniels v Jones (1961), CA 559
Daniels and Daniels v R White & Sons Ltd and Tarbard (1938) 346, 351
Danish Mercantile Co Ltd v Beaumont (1950) 137
Dann v Hamilton (1939) 294, 296
Daressa, The (1971) 278
Darley Main Colliery Co v Mitchell (1886), HL 368, 369, 533
Darling Island Stevedoring and Lighterage Co Ltd v Long (1956) 523
Davey v Harrow Corpn (1958), CA 381, 399
David v Abdul Cader (1963), PC 499
Davidson v Chief Constable of North Wales (1994), CA 42, 98, 492
Davie v New Merton Board Mills Ltd (1959), HL 253, 512
Davies (or Davis) v Mann (1842) 283
Davies v Powell Duffryn Associated Collieries Ltd. See Yelland v Powell Duffryn Associated
   Collieries Ltd (No 2)
Davies v Solomon (1871) 455, 527
Davies v Swan Motor Co (Swansea) Ltd (1949), CA 284, 285, 291
Davies v Taylor (1974), HL 556
Davis v Billing (1891), CA 460
Davis v Bromley Corpn (1908), CA 499
Davis v Bunn (1936) 262
Davis v Foots (1940), CA 333
Davis v Oswell (1837) 64
Davison v Leggett (1969), CA 261
Dawkins v Lord Paulet (1869) 465
Dawkins v Lord Rokeby (1873), Ex Ch; affd (1875) 465, 466
Dawrant v Nutt (1960) 288
Dawson v Great Northern and City Rly Co (1905), CA 593
Day v Bream (1837) 462
Dean v Hogg (1834) 90
Deane v Clayton (1817) 36, 91
De Beers Abrasive Products Ltd v International General Electric Co of New York Ltd
   (1975) 138
De Buse v McCarthy (1942), CA 472
Deerness v John R Keeble & Son (Brantham) Ltd (1983), HL 574
De Francesco v Barnum (1890) 154
De Franco v Metropolitan Police Comr (1987), CA 51
De Freville v Dill (1927) 40, 215
Defries v Milne (1913), CA 593
De Jetley Marks v Lord Greenwood (1936) 149
Delaney v TP Smith Ltd (1946), CA 79
De Martell v Merton and Sutton Health Authority (1992), CA 200
De Meza and Stuart v Apple, Van Straten, Shena and Stone (1975), CA 290
Denaby and Cadeby Main Collieries Ltd v Yorkshire Miners' Association (1906), HL 150
Dennis v Charnwood Borough Council (1983), CA 574
Department of Social Security v Butler (1995), CA 537
Department of Transport v North West Water Authority (1984), HL 384
Department of the Environment v Thomas Bates & Son Ltd (1991), HL . 213, 226, 326, 329
Derbyshire County Council v Times Newspapers Ltd (1993), HL 436, 442
Derrick v Williams (1939), CA 532
Derry v Peek (1889), HL 120, 216
Deshane v Deere & Co (1993), Ont CA 352
Devereux v Barclay (1819) 58
Devonshire v Jenkins (1979) 81
Dewar v City and Suburban Racecourse Co (1899) 373
Dewey v White (1827) 94
Deyong v Shenburn (1946), CA 199
Dhaliwal v Personal Representatives of Hunt (1995), CA 544
Dibble (HE) Ltd (trading as Mill Lane Nurseries) v Moore (West, third party) (1970), CA .. 60
Dibdin v Swan (1793) 480
Dickinson v Burrell (1866) 593
Dicks v Brooks (1880), CA 137
Dietz v Lennig Chemicals Ltd (1969), HL 558

PAGE

Dimbleby & Sons Ltd v National Union of Journalists (1984), CA; affd (1984), HL . 150, 158
Dingle v Associated Newspapers Ltd (1961), CA; affd sub nom Associated Newspapers Ltd
    v Dingle (1964), HL 485, 487, 596
DPP v Junes (1999) 77
Dixon v Bell (1816) 340
Dixon v Dixon (1904) 159
Dixon v Smith (1860) 486
Dobbie v Medway Health Authority (1994), CA 572
Dobell v Stevens (1825) 122
Dobson v North Tyneside Health Authority (1996), CA 53
Docker v Chief Constable of West Midland Police (1998), CA 499
Dodd Properties (Kent) v Canterbury City Council (1980), CA 278, 357, 530, 552
Dodds v Dodds (1978) 556, 558
Dodwell v Burford (1669) 33
Doe d Rochester (Bishop) v Bridges (1831) 418
Dolbey v Goodwin (1955), CA 558
Dolby v Newnes (1887) 439, 441
Doltis (J) Ltd v Isaac Braithwaite & Sons (Engineers) Ltd (1957) 404
Dominion Mosaics and Tile Co Ltd v Trafalgar Trucking Co Ltd (1990), CA 80
Dominion Natural Gas Co Ltd v Collins and Perkins (1909), PC 342
Domsalla v Barr (t/a AB Construction) (1969), CA 526
Donaghey v Boulton and Paul Ltd (1968), HL 275, 428
Donald v Suckling (1866) 49, 56
Donaldson v McNiven (1952); affd (1952), CA 232, 244, 591
Donnelly v Jackman (1970) 33
Donnelly v Joyce (1974), CA 546
Donoghue v Stevenson. See M'Alister (or Donoghue) v Stevenson
Donovan v Union Cartage Co Ltd (1933) 242
Doodeward v Spence (1908) 53
Dooley v Cammell Laird & Co Ltd (1951) 210, 600
Dougal v McCarthy (1893), CA 75
Doughty v Turner Manufacturing Co Ltd (1964), CA 275, 277
Douglas Valley Finance Co Ltd v S Hughes (Hirers) Ltd (1969) 54
Dove v Banhams Patent Locks Ltd (1983) 571, 574
Dow Corning Corpn v Hollis (1995) 344
Dowling v Time Inc (1954), CA 482
Downs v Chappell (1996), CA 121
Doyle v Olby (Ironmongers) Ltd (1969), CA 123
Dragon, The. See Daly v General Steam Navigation Co Ltd, The Dragon
Drane v Evangelou (1978), CA 73, 81, 529, 530
Dransfield v British Insulated Cables Ltd (1937) 343
Draper v Hodder (1972), CA 277, 413
Draper v Trist (1939), CA 133, 134
Drinkwater v Kimber (1951); affd (1952), CA 289, 595
Driver v William Willett (Contractors) Ltd (1969) 331
Drummond v British Building Cleaners Ltd (1954), CA 253, 256
Drummond-Jackson v British Medical Association (1970), CA 441
Duck v Mayeu (1892), CA 597
Duckworth v Johnson (1859) 556
Duffy v Thanet District Council (1984) 516
Dulieu v White & Sons (1901) 203
Dumbell v Roberts (1944), CA 33
Dunford and Elliott Ltd v Johnson and Firth Brown Ltd (1978), CA 164
Dunlop v Woollahra Municipal Council (1982), PC 499
Dunlop Pneumatic Tyre Co Ltd v Maison Talbot, Earl of Shrewsbury and Talbot and Weigel
    (1904), CA 141
Dunlop Rubber Co Ltd v Dunlop (1921), HL 439
Dunn v Birmingham Canal Navigation Co (1872); affd (1872), Ex Ch 408
Dunn v Large (1783) 80
Dunne v North Western Gas Board (1964), CA 400
Dunster v Abbott (1953), CA 323
Dunton v Dover District Council (1977) 393, 537
Dunwich Corpn v Sterry (1831) 71
D'Urso v Sanson (1939) 270, 299

PAGE

Dutton v Bognor Regis UDC (1972), CA 328
Dyer v Munday (1895), CA 105
Dymond v Pearce (1972), CA 392, 394

E

EC Commission v United Kingdom: C-300/95 (1996), ECJ 349, 355
EMI Records Ltd v Riley (1981) 588
Eason v Newman (1596) 59
Easson v London and North Eastern Rly Co (1944), CA 236, 260, 262
East v Chapman (1827) 485
East v Maurer (1991), CA 123
East Suffolk Rivers Catchment Board v Kent (1941), HL 189
Eastern and South African Telegraph Co Ltd v Cape Town Tramways Companies Ltd
    (1902), PC 365, 408
Eastman v South West Thames Regional Health Authority (1991), CA 242
Easycare Inc v Bryan Lawrence & Co (1995) 141
Eddis v Chichester Constable (1969), CA 67, 577
Edelsten v Edelsten (1863) 135
Edge (William) & Sons Ltd v William Niccolls & Sons Ltd (1911), HL 130, 134
Edgington v Fitzmaurice (1885), CA 121, 122
Edmondson v Birch & Co Ltd and Horner (1907), CA 472
Edmondson v Nuttall (1864) 62
Edwards v Bell (1824) 459
Edwards v Railway Executive (1952), HL 307
Edwards v Times Newspapers Ltd (1997) 443
Egerton v Home Office (1978) 580
Egger v Viscount Chelmsford (or Davies) (1965), CA 473, 483
Eglantine Inn Ltd v Isaiah Smith (1948) 450
El Ajou v Dollar Land Holdings plc (1994), CA 144
Elborow v Allen (1622) 140
Electrical, Electronic Telecommunication and Plumbing Union v Times Newspapers Ltd
    (1980) 442, 586
Electrochrome Ltd v Welsh Plastics Ltd (1968) 225
Elguzouli-Daf v Metropolitan Police Comr (1995), CA 497, 499
Elleanor v Cavendish Woodhouse Ltd and Comerford (1972), CA 517
Ellen v Great Northern Rly Co (1901), CA 568
Elliot's Case (1629) 104
Elliotson v Feetham (1835) 386
Elliott v Boynton (1924), CA 79
Elliott v London Borough of Islington (1991), CA 388
Ellis v John Stenning & Son (1932) 65
Ellis v Sheffield Gas Consumers Co (1853) 509
Ellison v Ministry of Defence (1996) 371, 397, 403, 406, 410, 412
Ellor v Selfridge & Co Ltd (1930) 259
Elvin and Powell Ltd v Plummer Roddis Ltd (1933) 58
Elwes v Brigg Gas Co (1886) 50
Emanuel (H & N) Ltd v Greater London Council (1971), CA 412
Embrey v Owen (1851) 525
Emeh v Kensington and Chelsea and Westminster Area Health Authority (1985),
    CA 211, 271, 530, 547
Emerald Construction Co v Lowthian (1966), CA 151, 154, 155
Emerson v Grimsby Times and Telegraph Co Ltd (1926), CA 439, 441
Emmens v Pottle (1885), CA 461
Empresa Exportadora de Azucar v Industria Azucarera Nacional SA, The Playa Larga and
    The Marble Islands (1983), CA 49, 55, 62
England v Cowley (1873) 60
England v National Coal Board (1953), CA; on appeal sub nom National Coal Board v
    England (1954), HL 245, 420, 523
English v Wilsons and Clyde Coal Co Ltd (1936); on appeal sub nom Wilsons and Clyde
    Coal Co Ltd v English (1938), HL 251, 254
Entick v Carrington (1765) 29
Ephraim v London Borough of Newham (1992), CA 332

PAGE

Esso Petroleum Co Ltd v Kingswood Motors (Addlestone) Ltd (1974) 157
Esso Petroleum Co Ltd v Mardon (1976), CA 196, 217
Esso Petroleum Co Ltd v Southport Corpn. See Southport Corpn v Esso Petroleum Co Ltd
Euro-Diam Ltd v Bathurst (1990), CA 106
Eurymedon, The (1938), CA 283
Evans v Harlow (1844) 138, 441
Evans v London Hospital Medical College (1981) 492, 498
Evans (C) & Sons Ltd v Spritebrand Ltd (1985), CA 584
Everett v Griffiths (1920), CA; affd (1921), HL 103, 187
Everett v Ribbands (1952), CA 494
Excelsior Wire Rope Co Ltd v Callan (1930), HL 323
Exchange Telegraph Co Ltd v Gregory & Co (1896), CA 154, 155
Eyre v Measday (1986), CA 247

F

F v West Berkshire Health Authority (1990), HL 28, 31, 33, 69, 85, 87, 88, 93
F v Wirral Metropolitan Borough Council (1991), CA 149
Faccini Dori v Recreb Srl: C-91/92 (1994), ECJ 349
Fagan v Metropolitan Police Comr (1969) 33
Fairhurst v St Helens and Knowsley Health Authority (1995) 546
Fairline Shipping Corpn v Adamson (1975) 521, 584
Falconer v ASLEF and NUR (1986) 153, 161
Fardon v Harcourt-Rivington (1932), HL 413
Farmer v Hyde (1937), CA 468
Farmer Giles Ltd v Wessex Water Authority (1990), CA 80
Farrant v — (1822) 56
Farrer v Nelson (1885) 381
Farrington v Leigh (1987), CA 447
Fawcett v Smethurst (1914) 590
Fay v Prentice (1845) 375
Fayed v Al-Tajir (1988), CA 465
Fennings v Lord Grenville (1808) 61
Ferguson v Earl of Kinnoul (1842), HL 429
Ferguson v Welsh (1987), HL 306, 309, 313, 314
Fielding v Variety Inc (1967), CA 141
Filliter v Phippard (1847) 386
Films Rover International Ltd v Cannon Film Sales Ltd (1986) 537
Findlay v Blaylock (1937) 149
Fine Art Society Ltd v Union Bank of London Ltd (1886), CA 56
Firman v Ellis (1978), CA 574
First National Commercial Bank plc v Humberts (a firm) (1995), CA 571
Firth v Bowling Iron Co (1878) 398
Fish v Kapur (1948) 260
Fisher v CHT Ltd (No 2) (1966), CA 304
Fisher v Harrods Ltd (1966) 342
Fisher v Prince (1762) 65
Fisons v Norton Healthcare Ltd (1994) 129
Fitter v Veal (1701) 531
Fitzgerald v Ford (1996), CA 546, 551
Fitzgerald v Lane (1987), CA; affd (1989), HL 273, 287, 292, 595, 600
Fitzgerald v Northcote (1865) 96
Fleming v Dollar (1889), DC 460
Fletcher v Rylands and Horrocks (1866); affd sub nom Rylands v Fletcher (1868) ... 361, 362,
                                                                          375, 378, 395, 398,
                                                                          400, 401, 403, 407, 510
Flying Fish, The (1865) 530
Fogg v McKnight (1968) 24
Fookes v Slaytor (1979), CA 281
Forbes v Kemsley Newspapers Ltd (1951) 128
Forbes v Wandsworth Health Authority (1997), CA 573
Ford v Foster (1872) 129, 134
Forde v Skinner (1830) 33

PAGE

Forrester v Tyrrell (1893), CA 452
Forsdick v Collins (1816) 55
Forsdike v Stone (1868) 485
Forsikringsaktieselskapet Vesta v Butcher, Bain Dawles Ltd and Aquacultural Insurance
    Services Ltd (1989), CA; affd (1989), HL 197, 291, 533
Forster v Outred & Co (a firm) (1982), CA 571
Fosbroke-Hobbes v Airwork Ltd and British-American Air Services Ltd (1937) 259
Foskett v Mistry (1984), CA 237
Foster v Warblington UDC (1906), CA 376
Fouldes v Willoughby (1841) 45, 55, 68
Fowler v Hollins (1872), Ex Ch; affd sub nom Hollins v Fowler (1875) 54, 55, 56, 57, 58
Fowler v Lanning (1959) 24, 25, 83
Fowles v Bedfordshire County Council (1996) 303
Foxcroft v Lacy (1613) 447
France v Gaudet (1871) 65
France v Parkinson (1954), CA 261, 288
Francis v Cockrell (1870) 316
Francis, Day and Hunter Ltd v Twentieth Century Fox Corpn Ltd (1939), PC 127
Francovich and Bonifaci v Italy: C-6, 9/90 (1991), ECJ 9
Fraser v Berkeley (1836) 88
Fraser v Evans (1969), CA 165
Fraser v Mirza (1993), HL 469, 470, 471, 476
Fray v Blackburn (1863) 102
Freeman v Home Office (No 2) (1984); affd (1984), CA 32, 83
Freeman v Rosher (1849) 509
Friends' Provident Life Office v Hillier Parker May & Rowden (a firm) (Estates and General
    plc, third parties)) (1997), CA 596, 598
Fritz v Hobson (1880) 387, 394
Froom v Butcher (1976), CA 232, 287, 289, 292, 531
Frost v Chief Constable of South Yorkshire Police (1998), CA; revsd sub nom White v Chief
    Constable of South Yorkshire Police (1999), HL 13, 191, 192, 200, 203,
                                           204, 208, 209, 215
Fullam v Newcastle Chronicle and Journal Ltd (1977), CA 443
Furniss v Cambridge Daily News Ltd (1907), CA 474

G

GWK Ltd v Dunlop Rubber Co Ltd (1926); on appeal (1926), CA 152, 157
Galashiels Gas Co Ltd v O'Donnell (or Millar) (1949), HL 429
Gallagher v Humphrey (1862) 322
Gallagher v N McDowell Ltd (1961) 328
Gammell v Wilson (1982), CA; affd (1982), HL 554
Gandy v Jubber (1864); revsd (1865), Ex Ch 382
Garden Cottage Foods Ltd v Milk Marketing Board (1982); revsd (1984), HL 9, 424, 537
Gardiner v Moore (1969) 595, 597
Garner v Morrall (1935) 260
Garnham, Harris and Elton Ltd v Alfred W Ellis (Transport) Ltd (1967) 58
Gaunt v Fynney (1872) 363, 367, 371
Gayler and Pope Ltd v B Davies & Son Ltd (1924) 27
Geddis v Bann Reservoir (Proprietors) (1878), HL 104
Gee v Metropolitan Rly Co (1873) 260
Gee v Pritchard (1818) 538
General Cleaning Contractors Ltd v Christmas. See Christmas v General Cleaning Contractors
    Ltd and Caledonian Club Trust Ltd
General Electric Co Ltd v Pryce's Stores (1933) 130
Generale Bank Nederland NV v Export Credit Guarantee Department (1998), CA; affd
    (1999), HL 523
George v Pinnock (1973), CA 542, 545
Gerard v Dickenson (1590) 136
Germanic, The (1904) 237
Gerrard v Crowe (1920), PC 93
Gerrard v Staffordshire Potteries Ltd (1995), CA 428
Gibbings v O'Dea & Co Ltd (1948-9) 440

PAGE

Gibbons v Duffell (1932), HC of A 465
Gibbons v Pepper (1695) 33
Gibbs v Cruikshank (1873) 532
Gibbs v Pike and Wells (1842) 498
Gibbs v Rea (1998), PC 493, 495
Giblan v National Amalgamated Labourers' Union of Great Britain and Ireland (1903), CA: 147
Gilding v Eyre (1861) 494
Giles v Walker (1890), DC 399
Gillard v Britton (1841) 62
Gillette Safety Razor Co and Gillette Safety Razor Ltd v Franks (1924) 130
Gillette UK Ltd v Edenwest Ltd (1994) 133
Gillick v BBC (1995), CA 443
Gillick v West Norfolk and Wisbech Area Health Authority (1986), HL 86
Gillingham Borough Council v Medway (Chatham) Dock Co Ltd (1993) 360, 366, 384,
                                                                             389, 390
Gillmore v LCC (1938) 298, 316
Gilson v Kerrier RDC (1976), CA 407
Ginty v Belmont Building Supplies Ltd (1959) 431
Gizzonio v Chief Constable of Derbyshire Constabulary (1998), CA 494, 496, 500
Glamorgan Coal Co Ltd v South Wales Miners' Federation (1903), CA; affd sub nom South
         Wales Miners' Federation v Glamorgan Coal Co Ltd (1905), HL 154, 155
Glasgow Corpn v Muir (1943), HL 231, 233, 237, 244, 277, 308
Glasgow Corpn v Taylor (1922), HL 242, 307, 311
Gleaves v Deakin (1980), HL 452
Gledhill (G H) & Sons Ltd v British Perforated Toilet Paper Co (1911); on appeal (1911),
         CA 129
Glegg v Bromley (1912), CA 593
Glenwood Lumber Co Ltd v Phillips (1904) 52
Glinski v McIver (1962), HL 495
Glover v London and South Western Rly Co (1867) 34
Glyn, Mills Currie & Co v East and West India Dock Co (1880); affd (1881), HL 57
Godwin v Uzoigwe (1993), CA 159
Goffin v Donnelly (1881) 466
Goh Choon Seng v Lee Kim Soo (1925), PC 516
Gold v Essex County Council (1942), CA 506, 511
Gold v Haringey Health Authority (1986); revsd (1988), CA 212, 250
Goldman v Hargrave (1967), PC 235, 324, 359, 360, 379, 381, 386
Goldrei, Foucard & Son v Sinclair and Russian Chamber of Commerce in London (1918),
         CA 122
Goldsmith v Bhoyrul (1997) 436
Goldsmith v Sperrings Ltd (1977), CA 449, 461
Goldsoll v Goldman (1914); affd (1915), CA 155
Goodburne v Bowman (1833) 460
Goodwill v British Pregnancy Advisory Service (1996), CA 181, 212, 219
Gordon v Harper (1796) 47, 70
Gorris v Scott (1874) 428
Gosden v Elphick and Bennet (1849) 42
Goslin v Corry (1844) 485
Gough v National Coal Board (1954), CA 308, 311
Gough v Thorne (1966), CA 237, 287
Grand Hotel Co of Caledonia Springs v Wilson (1904), PC 133
Graham v Dodds (1983), HL 558
Graham v Peat (1801) 79
Graham v Rechem International (1996) 412
Graham v Saville (1945), CA 84, 122
Grainger v Hill (1838) 39, 55, 498
Gran Gelato Ltd v Richcliff (Group) Ltd (1992) 125, 291
Granada Group Ltd v Ford Motor Co Ltd (1973) 133
Granby (Marquis) v Bakewell UDC (1923) 387
Grant v Australian Knitting Mills Ltd (1936), PC 172, 342, 343, 346, 515
Grant v National Coal Board (1956), HL 428
Grant v Sun Shipping Co Ltd (1948), HL 244, 287
Grappelli v Derek Block (Holdings) Ltd (1981), CA 443, 448

PAGE

Gray v Jones (1939) 453
Great Lakes Steamship Co v Maple Leaf Milling Co Ltd (1924), PC 279
Greater Nottingham Co-operative Society Ltd v Cementation Piling and Foundations Ltd
    (1989), CA 226
Grech v Odhams Press Ltd (1958); affd (1958), CA 480
Green v All Motors Ltd (1917), CA 57
Green v Bartram (1830) 90
Green v Button (1835) 136, 156
Green v Chelsea Waterworks Co (1894), CA 406
Green v De Havilland (1968) 496
Green v Goddard (1702) 91
Greene v Chelsea Borough Council (1954), CA 305
Greenhalgh v British Railways Board (1969), CA 306, 310
Greening v Wilkinson (1825) 63
Greenock Corpn v Caledonian Rly Co (1917), HL 409, 410
Greenway v Fisher (1824) 57
Greenwood v Bennett (1973), CA 16, 63
Greer v Faulkner (1908) 64
Greers Ltd v Pearman and Corder Ltd (1922), CA 137, 139
Gregory v Duke of Brunswick (1844); on appeal (1846), Ex Ch; on appeal (1849), HL ... 145
Gregory v Kelly (1978) 287, 292
Gregory v Piper (1829) 74
Gregory v Portsmouth City Council (1997), CA 493
Greig v Insole (1978) 151, 152, 154
Grein v Imperial Airways Ltd (1937), CA 555
Greyvensteyn v Hattingh (1911), PC 93
Grice v Stourport Tennis Hockey and Squash Club (1997), CA 587
Griffith v Jenkins (1992), HL 554
Griffiths v Liverpool Corpn (1967), CA 583
Griffiths v Williams (1995), CA 550, 551
Grinham v Willey (1859) 42
Groom v Crocker (1939), CA 441, 469
Gros v Crook (1969) 483, 508
Gross v Lewis Hillman Ltd (1970), CA 119
Grosvenor Hotel Co v Hamilton (1894), CA 367, 387
Grote v Chester and Holyhead Rly Co (1848) 511
Groves v Lord Wimborne (1898), CA 417, 427
Grovit v Doctor (1997), HL 569
Guay v Sun Publishing Co Ltd (1952); affd (1953) 140
Guest v Warren (1854) 532
Guinness (Arthur), Son & Co (Dublin) Ltd v The Freshfield (Owners), The Lady Gwendolen
    (1965), CA 584
Gunter v Astor (1819) 157
Guppy's (Bridport) Ltd v Brookling (1983), CA 529

H

H v Norfolk County Council (1997), CA 192
HL Motor Works (Willesden) Ltd v Alwahbi (1977), CA 552
Hadmor Productions Ltd v Hamilton (1983), HL 158
Hague v Deputy Governor of Parkhurst Prison. See R v Deputy Governor of Parkhurst Prison,
    ex p Hague
Hale v Hants and Dorset Motor Services Ltd (1947), CA 273
Hale v Jennings Bros (1938), CA 398, 401, 404, 408, 412
Haley v London Electricity Board (1965), HL 242
Halford v Brookes (1992), CA 574
Hall v Beckenham Corpn (1949) 378
Hall v Brooklands Auto-Racing Club (1933), CA 244
Hall v Wilson (1939) 559
Hall & Co Ltd v Pearlberg (1956) 526
Hall (J and E) Ltd v Barclay (1937), CA 62
Halley, The. See Liverpool, Brazil and River Plate Steam Navigation Co Ltd v Benham, The
    Halley

PAGE

Halliday v Holgate (1868) 49
Halsey v Brotherhood (1881), CA 139
Halsey v Esso Petroleum Co Ltd (1961) 359, 366, 367, 372, 378, 391, 398
Hambrook v Stokes Bros (1925), CA 204
Hamilton v Anderson (1858), HL 467
Hamlyn v John Houston & Co (1903), CA 588
Hammersmith and City Rly Co v Brand. See Brand v Hammersmith and City Rly Co
Hammerton v Earl of Dysart (1916), HL 525
Hamps v Darby (1948), CA 68, 91
Handcock v Baker (1800) 90
Hannah v Peel (1945) 51
Hannam v Mann (1984), CA 291
Hanson v Wearmouth Coal Co Ltd and Sunderland Gas Co (1939), CA 408
Harakas v Baltic Mercantile and Shipping Exchange Ltd (1982), CA 487
Hardaker v Idle District Council (1896), CA 511, 514
Hardy v Central London Rly Co (1920), CA 307, 323
Hardy v Ryle (1829) 576
Hargreaves v Bretherton (1959) 160, 498
Harnett v Bond (1925), HL 39
Harper v Charlesworth (1825) 78
Harper v GN Haden & Sons (1933), CA 390, 391, 392
Harper v Godsell (1870) 61
Harrington (Earl) v Derby Corpn (1905) 576
Harris v Birkenhead Corpn (1976), CA 305
Harris v De Pinna (1886), CA 363
Harris v Empress Motors Ltd (1983), CA 544
Harris v Lubbock (1971), CA 482
Harris v Warren and Phillips (1918) 130
Harrison v British Railways Board (1981) 289
Harrison v Bush (1856) 476
Harrison v Duke of Rutland (1893), CA 77
Harrison v Michelin Tyre Co Ltd (1985) 516
Harrison v National Coal Board (1951), HL 245, 424, 523
Harrison v Southwark and Vauxhall Water Co (1891) 372
Harrods Ltd v R Harrod Ltd (1923), CA 133
Harrold v Watney (1898), CA 391
Harrow London Borough Council v Donohue (1993), CA 74
Hart v Chief Constable of Kent (1983) 100
Hartley v Birmingham City District Council (1992), CA 574
Hartley v Moxham (1842) 68
Hartwell v Grayson Rollo and Clover Docks Ltd (1947), CA 305
Harvey v RG O'Dell Ltd (1958) 600, 601
Harvey v Road Haulage Executive (1952), CA 285
Haseldine v CA Daw & Son Ltd (1941), CA 173, 240, 314, 341, 342, 343
Hasselblad (GB) Ltd v Orbinson (1985), CA 465, 466
Havana Cigar and Tobacco Factories Ltd v Oddenino (1924), CA 129
Hawkins v Coulsdon and Purley UDC (1954), CA 305, 343
Hawkins v McGee (1929) 198
Hay v Hughes (1975), CA 560
Hay (or Bourhill) v Young (1943), HL 172, 181, 204, 242
Hayden v Hayden (1992), CA 560
Haydon v Kent County Council (1978), CA 583
Haynes v Harwood (1935), CA 202, 239, 270, 299, 401
Hayward v Thompson (1982), CA 447, 448, 485
Headford v Bristol and District Health Authority (1995), CA 577
Healing (Sales) Pty Ltd v Inglis Electrix Pty Ltd (1968) 62
Heap v Ind Coope and Allsopp Ltd (1940), CA 383
Heath v Keys (1984) 80
Heatons Transport (St Helens) Ltd v Transport and General Workers' Union (1973), HL . 507
Heaven v Pender (1883), CA 171, 172, 173, 237, 340
Hebditch v MacIlwaine (1894), CA 476
Hedley Byrne & Co Ltd v Heller & Partners Ltd (1964), HL 15, 173, 199, 215, 216, 302
Hegarty v EE Caledonia Ltd (1996); on appeal (1997), CA 208

PAGE

Hegarty v Shine (1878); affd (1878), CA 84, 108
Hellwig v Mitchell (1910) 453
Helman v Horsham and Worthing Assessment Committee (1949), CA 78
Helstan Securities Ltd v Hertfordshire County Council (1978) 48
Henderson v Henry E Jenkins & Sons and Evans (1970), HL 259
Henderson v Merrett Syndicates (1995), HL 15, 197, 215, 218, 220, 247, 290, 533, 576
Henderson & Co v Williams (1895), CA 59
Henley v Cameron (1949), CA 285
Henwood v Harrison (1872) 479
Heranger, SS (Owners) v SS Diamond (Owners) (1939), HL 236, 287
Herbage v Pressdram Ltd (1984), CA 461
Herd v Weardale Steel Coal and Coke Co Ltd (1913), CA; affd (1915), HL 39, 40
Herniman v Smith (1938), HL 494, 495
Herring v Boyle (1834) 41
Herschtal (or Herschthal) v Stewart and Ardern Ltd (1940) 341
Heslop v Chapman (1853) 497
Heugh v London and North Western Rly Co (1870) 58
Hevican v Ruane (1991) 207
Hewett v Alf Brown's Transport Ltd (1992), CA 256
Hewitt v Bonvin (1940), CA 508
Heydon v Smith (1610) 68
Hickman v Maisey (1900), CA 77
Hicks v British Transport Commission (1958), CA 287
Hicks v Faulkner (1881); affd (1882), CA 494
Hilbery v Hatton (1864) 509
Hilder v Associated Portland Cement Manufacturers Ltd (1961) 324
Hill v Chief Constable of West Yorkshire (1988), CA; affd (1989), HL 176, 190,
                                                                          194, 229, 272
Hill v Lovett (1992) 308, 413
Hill v Perrott (1810) 534
Hill v Tupper (1863) 76, 78
Hillesden Securities Ltd v Ryjak Ltd (1983) 64, 65, 66
Hillier v Air Ministry (1962) 405
Hills v Potter (1983) 85
Hindustan Steam Shipping Co Ltd v Siemens Bros & Co Ltd (1955) 344
Hines v Winnick (1947) 128, 132
Hiort v Bott (1874) 58
Hiort v London and North Western Rly Co (1879), CA 46
Hivac Ltd v Park Royal Scientific Instruments Ltd (1946), CA 150, 164
Hoare & Co v McAlpine (1923) 408, 411
Hobbs v CT Tinling & Co Ltd (1929), CA 486, 487
Hobbs (E) (Farms) Ltd v Baxenden Chemical Co Ltd (1992) 344, 404
Hodge & Sons v Anglo-American Oil Co (1922), CA 343
Hodgson v Sidney (1866) 592
Hodgson v Trapp (1989), HL 544, 549
Hoffman-La Roche v DDSA Pharmaceuticals (1969), CA 134
Holden v Chief Constable of Lancashire (1987), CA 529
Holden v White (1982), CA 304
Holdsworth Ltd v Associated Newspapers Ltd (1937), CA 442
Hole v Sittingbourne and Sheerness Rly Co (1861) 425, 510, 514
Holgate-Mohammed v Duke (1984), HL 99, 101
Holliday v National Telephone Co (1899), CA 511
Holling v Yorkshire Traction Co Ltd (1948) 324
Hollins v Fowler. See Fowler v Hollins
Hollywood Silver Fox Farm Ltd v Emmett (1936) 359, 372
Holman v Johnson (1775) 106
Holmes v Bagge (1853) 90
Holmes v Mather (1875) 27, 33
Holmes v Norfolk County Council (1981) 304
Holmes v Wilson (1839) 75
Holt v Payne Skillington (1996), CA 197, 290
Holtham v Metropolitan Police Comr (1987), CA 99
Home v Bentinck (1820), Ex Ch 466

PAGE

Home Brewery Co Ltd v William Davis & Co (Leicester) Ltd (1987) 74, 361
Home Office v Dorset Yacht Co Ltd (1970), HL 174, 183, 194, 272
Honeywill and Stein Ltd v Larkin Bros (London's Commercial Photographers) Ltd (1934),
    CA 504, 511
Hook v Cunard SS Co Ltd (1953) 42, 96, 97
Hopper v Reeve (1817) 34
Hornal v Neuberger Products Ltd (1957), CA 120, 458
Horrocks v Lowe (1975), HL 469, 470, 472
Horsfall v Thomas (1862) 122
Horsfield v Brown (1932) 97
Hosking v De Havilland Aircraft Co Ltd (1949) 425, 510
Hotson v East Berkshire Area Health Authority (1987), HL 266
Hough v London Express Newspaper Ltd (1940), CA 444
Houghland v R R Low (Luxury Coaches) Ltd (1962), CA 59
Houldsworth v City of Glasgow Bank and Liquidators (1880), HL 508
Hounslow London Borough Council v Twickenham Garden Developments Ltd (1971) 79
Housecroft v Burnett (1986), CA 540, 542, 545, 551
Howard v Furness Houlder Argentine Lines Ltd and A and R Brown Ltd (1936) 404
Howard v Harris (1884) 59
Howard v Shirlstar Container Transport Ltd (1990), CA 106
Howard Marine and Dredging Co Ltd v A Ogden & Sons (Excavations) Ltd (1978), CA ... 125
Hubbard v Pitt (1976), CA 76, 384
Hubbuck & Sons v Wilkinson, Heywood and Clark (1899), CA 138
Hucks v Cole (1993), CA 248
Hudson v Ridge Manufacturing Co Ltd (1957) 253, 516
Hughes v Lord Advocate (1963), HL 275, 276
Hughes v McKeown (1985) 547
Hughes v National Union of Mineworkers (1991) 190, 192
Hughes v Percival (1883), HL 324, 510, 511
Hulley v Silversprings Bleaching Co (1922) 385
Hulton (E) & Co v Jones (1910), HL 446, 448
Humphreys v Dreamland (Margate) Ltd (1930), HL 305
Humphries (or Humphreys) v Cousins (1877) 398, 400, 407
Hunt v Dowman (1618) 81
Hunt v Great Northern Rly Co (1891), CA 477
Hunt v Severs (1994), HL 546
Hunter v British Coal Corpn (1998), CA 209
Hunter v Butler (1996), CA 557
Hunter v Canary Wharf Ltd (1995), CA; revsd (1997), HL 5, 37, 357, 359, 360,
                                                              364, 365, 371, 373, 376,
                                                              377, 378, 401, 402, 412
Huntley v Thornton (1957) 147
Hurdman v North Eastern Rly Co (1878), CA 367, 399
Hurley v Dyke (1979), HL 343
Hurlstone v London Electric Rly Co (1914), CA 509
Hurrell v Ellis (1845) 72
Hussain v Lancaster City Council (1998), CA 379
Hussain v New Taplow Paper Mills Ltd (1987), CA; affd (1988), HL 548, 549
Hussien v Chong Fook Kam (1970), PC 99
Hutchins v Maughan (1947) 68
Hutchinson v Davidson (1945) 80
Huth v Huth (1915), CA 449, 450
Huxford v Stoy Hayward & Co (1989) 218
Hyams v Peterson (1991) 444
Hyde v Tameside Area Health Authority (1981), CA 108
Hyde Corpn v Oldham Ashton and Hyde Electric Tramway Ltd (1900), CA 76

I

IBL Ltd v Coussens (1991), CA 63, 65, 66
ICI Ltd v Shatwell (1965), HL 294, 296, 297, 431, 523
Ibaraki Maru, The. See Candlewood Navigation Corpn Ltd v Mitsui OSK Lines Ltd,
    The Mineral Transporter, The Ibaraki Maru

PAGE

Ichard v Frangoulis (1977) 550
Ilford UDC v Beal (1925) 379
Ilkiw v Samuels (1963), CA 517, 542
Illustrated Newspapers Ltd v Publicity Services (London) Ltd (1938) 132
Incledon v Watson (1862) 119
Independent Broadcasting Authority v EMI Electronics Ltd and BICC Construction Ltd
     (1980), HL 347
India (Republic) and Government of the Republic of India (Ministry of Defence) v India
     Steamship Co Ltd, The Indian Grace (1992), CA; revsd sub nom India (Republic) v
     India Steamship Co Ltd, The Indian Endurance, The Indian Grace (1993), HL 532
Initial Services Ltd v Putterill (1968), CA 165
IRC v Rossminster Ltd (1980), HL 103
Innes v Wylie (1844) 33
Insurance Comr v Joyce (1948) 293, 297
Invercargill City Council v Hamlin (1994), NZCA; affd (1996), PC 214, 330, 571
Inverugie Investments Ltd v Hackett (1995), PC 64, 80
Iqbal v London Transport Executive (1973), CA 517, 519
Irene's Success, The. See Schiffahrt und Kohlen GmbH v Chelsea Maritime Ltd,
     The Irene's Success
Iron Trades Mutual Insurance Co Ltd v JK Buckenham Ltd (1990) 197, 290, 534, 575
Isaack (or Isack) v Clark (or Clarke) (1615) 59
Isaacs (M) & Sons Ltd v Cook (1925) 465, 468
Island Records Ltd, ex p (1978), CA 161, 417, 538
Island Records Ltd v Tring International plc (1995) 567
Issa v Hackney London Borough Council (1997), CA 419, 422, 425

J

JEB Fasteners Ltd v Marks, Bloom & Co (a firm) (1981); on appeal (1983), CA 220, 290
Jackson v Adams (1835) 453
Jacobs v LCC (1950), HL 391
Jacobs v Morton and Partners (1994) 331, 345
Jacobs v Seward (1872), HL 61, 79
Jaggard v Sawyer (1995), CA 388
James v Boston (1845) 477
Jameson v Central Electricity Generating Board (Babcock Energy, third party) (1998),
     CA; revsd (1998), HL 597, 599
Jamieson & Co v Jamieson (1898), CA 130
Janvier v Sweeney (1919), CA 36
Jasperson v Dominion Tobacco Co (1923), PC 152
Jauffir v Akhbar (1984) 323
Jaundrill v Gillett (1996) 414, 415
Jay's Ltd v Jacobi (1933) 127
Jefferies v Duncombe (1809) 451
Jefford v Gee (1970), CA 552
Jegon v Vivian (1871) 80
Jennings v Rundall (1799) 590
Jerred v Roddam Dent & Son Ltd (1948) 600
Jobling v Associated Dairies Ltd (1982), HL 274
Joel v Morison (1834) 518
John v MGN Ltd (1997), CA 437, 486, 528, 529
John Lewis & Co Ltd v Tims. See Tims v John Lewis & Co Ltd
Johnson v Coventry Churchill International Ltd (1992) 505
Johnson v Diprose (1893), CA 70
Johnson v Emerson and Sparrow (1871) 493
Johnson v Rea Ltd (1962), CA 182
Johnson (Assignee of Cumming) v Stear (1863) 61
Johnson Electric Industrial Manufacturing Ltd v Mabuchi-Motor KK (1986) 138
Johnston & Co v Orr Ewing & Co (1882), HL 134
Johnstone v Bloomsbury Health Authority (1992), CA 197, 242, 255, 290, 301, 533
Johnstone v Pedlar (1921), HL 105
Johnstone v Sutton (1786), Ex Ch; affd (1787), HL 494
Jolley v London Borough of Sutton (1998), CA 310
Jolliffe v Willmett & Co (1971) 83

PAGE

Jones v Boyce (1816) 241, 287
Jones v Carter (1846) 566
Jones v Chapman (1849) 79
Jones v Dumbrell (1981) 119
Jones v Festiniog Rly Co (1868) 396, 398, 401
Jones v Jones (1916), HL 454
Jones v Livox Quarries Ltd (1952), CA 282, 286
Jones v Llanrwst UDC (1911) 377
Jones v Manchester Corpn (1952), CA 512, 601
Jones v Pollard (1997), CA 437
Jones v Skelton (1963), PC 445
Jones v Stroud District Council (1988), CA 574
Jones v Swansea City Council (1990), HL 499, 500
Jones v Tower Boot Co Ltd (1997), CA 521
Jones Bros (Hunstanton) Ltd v Stevens (1955), CA 150, 155
Jordin v Crump (1841) 91
Joseph (D) Ltd v Ralph Wood & Co Ltd (1951) 65
Joyce v Motor Surveys Ltd (1948) 137, 140
Joyce v Sengupta (1993), CA 138, 140, 141, 437
Junior Books Ltd v Veitchi Co Ltd (1983), HL 175, 225, 227, 345

K

K v JMP Co Ltd (1976), CA 559
K v P (J, third party) (1993) 599
Kahler v Midland Bank Ltd (1950), HL 47
Kaliningrad, The and The Nadezhda Krupskaya (1997) 154, 155, 156
Kandalla v British Airways Board (1981) 556
Kapetan Georgis, The. See Virgo Steamship Co SA v Skaarup Shipping Corpn,
    The Kapetan Georgis
Kapfunde v Abbey National plc (1999) 224
Karflex Ltd v Poole (1933) 48
Kark (Norman) Publications v Odhams Press Ltd (1962) 129
Kars v Kars (1996) 546
Kavanagh, Re, ex p Bankrupt v Jackson (Trustee) (1950), CA 592
Kay v Ayrshire and Arran Health Board (1987), HL 266, 267
Kay v ITW Ltd (1968), CA 517
Kaye v Robertson (1991), CA 137, 140
Kealey v Heard (1983) 259, 261, 311
Kean v McGivan (1982), CA 132
Kearney v London and Brighton Rly Co (1870); affd (1871) 259
Keating v Elvan Reinforced Concrete Co Ltd (1967); affd (1968), CA 544
Keeble v Hickeringill (1706) 113
Kelly v Bastible (1996), CA 574
Kelly v O'Malley (1889) 474, 475
Kelly v Partington (1833) 479
Kelly v Tinling (1865) 479
Kelsen v Imperial Tobacco Co (of Great Britain and Ireland) Ltd (1957) 76, 361
Kemsley v Foot (1952), HL 480, 481
Kenfield Motors v Hayles and Rees (1998) 288
Kennard v Cory Bros & Co Ltd (1921), HL 398, 405, 407
Kennaway v Thompson (1981), CA 362, 389, 537
Kent v British Railways Board (1995), CA 542
Keppel Bus Co Ltd v Sa'ad bin Ahmad (1974), PC 520
Kerby v Redbridge Health Authority (1994) 550
Kerr v Kennedy (1942) 454
Ketteman v Hansel Properties Ltd (1987), HL 575
Khashoggi v IPC Magazines Ltd (1986), CA 458, 460
Khashoggi v Smith (1980), CA 165
Khorasandjian v Bush (1993), CA 37, 376, 384, 402
Kiam v Neil (1995), CA 437
Kiddle v City Business Properties Ltd (or City Business Premises Ltd) (1942) 386, 407
Kimberley-Cark Ltd v Fort Sterling Ltd (1997) 126
King v Liverpool City Council (1986), CA 272

PAGE

King v Phillips (1953), CA 237
King v Smith (1995), CA 252
King v Victoria Insurance Co Ltd (1896), PC 593
King's Prerogative in Saltpetre (1606) 94
Kingshott v Associated Kent Newspapers Ltd (1991), CA 475
Kirk v Gregory (1876) 68, 69, 93
Kirkham v Boughey (1958) 531
Kirkham v Chief Constable of the Greater Manchester Police (1990), CA .   106, 108, 191, 270
Kirklees Metropolitan Borough Council v Wickes Building Supplies Ltd (1993), HL 424
Kitchen v Royal Air Forces Association (1958), CA 578
Kite, The (1933) 263
Knapp v Railway Executive (1949), CA 429
Knight v Fellick (1977), CA 261
Knight v Home Office (1990) 235
Knight v Wilson (1949) 56
Knightley v Johns (1982), CA 191, 271, 272
Knupffer v London Express Newspaper Ltd (1944), HL 447, 448
Kondis v State Transport Authority (1984), HC of A 252
Konskier v B Goodman Ltd (1928), CA 75
Kooragang Investments Pty Ltd v Richardson and Wrench Ltd (1982), PC 124, 508, 522
Koursk, The (1924), CA 273, 594, 595
Kralj v McGrath (1986) 290, 527, 549
Kroeker v Jansen (1995) 546
Kubach v Hollands (1937) 341, 344
Kuchenmeister v Home Office (1958) 39
Kwei Tek Chao (t/a Zung Fu Co) v British Traders and Shippers Ltd (1954) 124
Kynaston v DPP (1987) 102

L

Lady Gwendolen, The. See Guinness (Arthur), Son & Co (Dublin) Ltd v The Freshfield
    (Owners), The Lady Gwendolen
Lake v King (1670) 464
Lamb v Camden London Borough Council (1981), CA 272
Lamine v Dorrell (1705) 534
Lampert v Eastern National Omnibus Co Ltd (1954) 288, 455, 527
Lampitt v Poole Borough Council (Taylor, third parties) (1991), CA 598
Lancashire and Yorkshire Rly Co, London and North Western Rly Co and Graeser Ltd
    v MacNicoll (1918), DC 55, 60
Lancashire County Council v Municipal Mutual Insurance Ltd (1997) 528
Lancashire Waggon Co v Fitzhugh (1861) 57
Lane v Dixon (1847) 78
Lane v Holloway (1968), CA 88, 107
Lane v Shire Roofing Co (Oxford) Ltd (1995), CA 504, 505
Langbrook Properties Ltd v Surrey County Council (1969) 174, 324
Langham v Wellingborough School Governors and Fryer (1932), CA 262
Langridge v Levy (1837); affd sub nom Levy v Langridge (1838), Ex Ch 120, 122, 340
LaPlante v LaPlante (1995) 195
Laskey, Jaggard and Brown v United Kingdom (1997), ECtHR 84
Latham v R Johnson and Nephew Ltd (1913), CA 307, 308
Latimer v AEC Ltd (1952); affd (1953), HL 234, 235, 252
Latter v Braddell (1881), CA 84
Laughton v Bishop of Sodor and Man (1872) 476, 477
Laurie v Raglan Building Co Ltd (1942), CA 259
Lavender v Betts (1942) 74
Lavender v Diamints Ltd (1948); revsd (1949), CA 429, 431
Law v Llewellyn (1906), CA 467
Law Debenture Trust Corpn plc v Ural Caspian Oil Corpn Ltd (1995), CA 149
Lawless v Anglo-Egyptian Cotton and Oil Co (1869) 472
Lawrence v Chester Chronicle (1986), CA 458
Laws v Florinplace Ltd (1981) 363
Lazenby v White (1871) 129
Leach v Money (1765) 104

PAGE

League Against Cruel Sports Ltd v Scott (1986) 74, 77
Leakey v National Trust for Places of Historic Interest or Natural Beauty (1980),
    CA 361, 376, 381, 399, 412
Leame v Bray (1803) 33
Leanse v Lord Egerton (1943) 391
Lee v Atkinson and Brooks (1609) 56
Lee v Haley (1869) 134
Lee v Lancashire and Yorkshire Rly Co (1871) 568
Lee v Sheard (1956), CA 542
Lee v Thompson (1989), CA 197, 290, 533
Lee (Joe) Ltd v Lord Dalmery (1927) 149
Lee Kar Choo v Lee Lian Choon (1967), PC 134
Lee Ting Sang v Chung Chi-Keung (1990), PC 505
Leeds Industrial Co-operative Society Ltd v Slack (1924), HL 74
Leeman v Montagu (1936) 375
Le Fanu v Malcomson (1848) 448
Legal and General Mortgage Services Ltd v HPC Professional Services (1997) 287
Leigh and Sillivan Ltd v Aliakmon Shipping Co Ltd, The Aliakmon (1985), CA; affd
    (1986), HL 174, 179, 213, 227
Leitch (William) & Co Ltd v Leydon (1931), HL 68, 83
Le Lievre v Gould (1893), CA 172
Lemmon v Webb (1894), CA; affd (1895), HL 73, 108
Lemon v Simmons (1888) 453
Lemos v Kennedy Leigh Development Co Ltd (1961), CA 536
Lemprière v Lange (1879) 122
Lennard's Carrying Co Ltd v Asiatic Petroleum Co Ltd (1915), HL 584
Leslie (R) Ltd v Sheill (or Shiell) (1914), CA 591
Letang v Cooper (1965), CA 23, 25, 31, 77, 570
Letang v Ottawa Electric Rly Co (1926), PC 293
Lever v Goodwin (1887), CA 135
Levy v Langridge. See Langridge v Levy
Leward v Basely (1695) 89
Lewis v Chief Constable of the South Wales Constabulary (1991), CA 97
Lewis's Trusts, Re (1953) 78
Lewisham Borough Council v Maloney (1948), CA 78
Ley v Hamilton (1935), HL 485
Liddle v North Riding of Yorkshire County Council (1934), CA 77
Liebig's Extract of Meat Co Ltd v Hanbury (1867) 129
Liesbosch, Dredger (Owners) v SS Edison (Owners) (1933), HL 278, 530, 552
Liff v Peasley (1980), CA 574
Lilley v Roney (1892), DC 467
Lim Poh Choo v Camden and Islington Area Health Authority (1980), HL: 544, 545, 547, 550
Limbrick v French (1993) 286
Limpus v London General Omnibus Co Ltd (1862), Ex Ch 519
Lincoln v Daniels (1962), CA 466, 467
Lindsey County Council v Marshall (1937), HL 511
Lineker v Raleigh Industries Ltd (1980), CA 430
Linotype Co Ltd v British Empire Type-Setting Machine Co Ltd (1899), HL 441
Lion Laboratories Ltd v Evans (1985), CA 164, 166
Lister v Perryman (1870), HL 99, 495
Lister v Romford Ice and Cold Storage Co Ltd (1957), HL 600, 601
Liverpool, Brazil and River Plate Steam Navigation Co Ltd v Benham, The Halley (1868): 505
Liverpool Corpn v H Coghill & Son Ltd (1918) 385
Livingstone v Ministry of Defence (1984), CA 32
Livingstone v Rawyards Coal Co (1880), HL 80
Lloyd v David Syme & Co Ltd (1986), PC 445
Lloyd v Grace, Smith & Co (1912), HL 124, 508, 521
Lloyde v West Midlands Gas Board (1971), CA 258, 260
Lloyds Bank Ltd v Chartered Bank of India, Australia and China (1929), CA ... 52, 56
Locabail International Finance Ltd v Agroexport, The Sea Hawk (1986), CA 537
Lochgelly Iron and Coal Co v M'Mullan (1934), HL 171, 424
Lock v Ashton (1848) 42
Lockett v A and M Charles Ltd (1938) 339

PAGE

Lockhart v Barr (1943), HL 346
Lockhart v Harrison (1928), HL 446
Lodge Holes Colliery Co Ltd v Wednesbury Corpn (1908), HL 387
Logan v Uttlesford District Council and Hammond (1986), CA 599
London Artists Ltd v Littler (1969), CA 480
London Association for Protection of Trade v Greenlands Ltd (1916), HL 476, 479, 586
London Computer Operators Training Ltd v BBC (1973), CA 445
London Corpn v Appleyard (1963) 51
LCC v Cattermoles (Garages) Ltd (1953), CA 516, 519
London County Freehold and Leasehold Properties Ltd v Berkeley Property and Investment
    Co Ltd (1936), CA 123
London Ferro-Concrete Co Ltd v Justicz (1951), CA 140
London Graving Dock Co Ltd v Horton (1951), HL 312
London Passenger Transport Board v Upson. See Upson v London Passenger Transport Board
Long v Hepworth (1968) 570
Long v Smithson (1918), DC 151
Longden v British Coal Corpn (1995), CA 548
Longdon-Griffiths v Smith (1951) 473, 477, 586
Longhurst v Metropolitan Water Board (1948), HL 324
Longmeid v Holliday (1851) 340
Lonrho Ltd v Shell Petroleum Co Ltd (No 2) (1982), HL 144, 145, 146, 153, 159,
                                                          160, 418, 424, 427, 538
Lonrho plc v Fayed (1990), CA; on appeal (1992), HL 114, 115, 116, 144, 146, 160
Lonrho plc v Fayed (No 2) (1991) 149
Lord v Price (1874) 48
Losinjska Plovidba v Transco Overseas Ltd, The Orjula (1995) 345
Lotan v Cross (1810) 70
Lotus Cars Ltd v Jaguar Cars Ltd (1982) 157
Loudon v Ryder (1953), CA 34, 78
Loudon v Ryder (No 2) (1953) 73, 139, 537
Love v Port of London Authority (1959) 279
Loveday v Renton (1990) 347
Lowery v Walker (1911), HL 308
Lows v Telford (1876), HL 79
Lucas-Box v Associated Newspapers Group plc (1986), CA 458
Lucas-Box v News Group Newspapers Ltd (1986), CA 446
Ludgate v Lovett (1969), CA 262
Lumley v Gye (1853) 148, 151, 157
Lumley v Wagner (1852) 157
Luxmoore-May v Messenger May Baverstock (a firm) (1990), CA 249
Lyde v Barnard (1836) 125
Lynch v Knight (1861) 452, 455, 456
Lyne v Nicholls (1906) 138, 140
Lyon and Lyon v Daily Telegraph Ltd (1943), CA 483
Lyons (J) & Sons v Wilkins (1899), CA 384
Lyons, Sons & Co v Gulliver (1914), CA 390

M

M v Calderdale Health Authority (1998) 512
MB (an adult: medical treatment), Re (1997), CA 28, 85, 93, 94
MTM Construction Ltd v William Reid Engineering Ltd (1998), OH 510
Maberley v Henry W Peabody & Co of London Ltd, Rowland Smith Motors Ltd and
    Rowland Smith (1946) 387, 533
M'Alister (or Donoghue) v Stevenson (1932) 173, 174, 198, 337, 340, 345
McAuley v Bristol City Council (1992), CA 332
McC (a minor), Re (1985), HL 103
McCafferty v Metropolitan Police District Receiver (1977), CA 572
McCain Foods Ltd v Grand Falls Industries Ltd (1991) 344
McCall v Abelesz (1976), CA 74
McCamley v Cammell Laird Shipbuilders Ltd (1990), CA 549, 551
McCombe v Read (1955) 379
M'Combie v Davies (1805) 56
McConkey v Amec plc (1990), CA 507

PAGE

McCulloch v Lewis A May (Produce Distributors) Ltd (1947) 133, 134
McDermid v Nash Dredging and Reclamation Co Ltd (1987), HL 251, 252, 255, 256, 512
MacDonald v Glasgow Western Hospitals Board of Management (1954) 512
McDonald's Corpn v Steel (1997) 437
McDonald's Hamburgers Ltd v Burgerking (UK) Ltd (1986); revsd (1987), CA 139
Macdougall v Knight (1890), CA 532
McFarlane v EE Caledonia Ltd (1994), CA 208
McGeown v Northern Ireland Housing Executive (1995), HL 304, 306
McGhee v National Coal Board (1972), HL 252, 266, 430
McGowan v Stott (1923), CA 259, 260, 262
M'Gregor v Gregory (1843) 441
McHale v Watson (1964); on appeal (1966), HC of A 238
Macievich v Anderson (1952), CA 389
McIlkenny v Chief Constable of West Midlands (1980), CA; affd sub nom Hunter v Chief
    Constable of West Midlands Police (1981), HL 105
Mackay v Borthwick (1982) 287
McKay v Essex Area Health Authority (1982), CA 175, 201, 211
Mackay v Ford (1860) 467
McKean v McIvor (1870) 58
McKerman v Fraser (1931) 147
McKew v Holland and Hannen and Cubitts (Scotland) Ltd (1969) 270
McKinnon Industries Ltd v Walker (1951), PC 365, 388
McLaren v Bradstreet (1969) 278
M'Laughlin v Pryor (1842) 509
MacLeay v Tait (1906), HL 121
M'Leod v M'Ghie (1841) 52
McLoughlin v O'Brian (1983), HL 175, 203, 205
McManus v Bowes (1938), CA 150
McMeechan v Secretary of State for Employment (1997), CA 506
McMillan v Lord Advocate (1991) 313
MacMillan Magazines Ltd v RCN Publishing Co Ltd (1998) 138
McNaughton (James) Papers Group Ltd v Hicks Anderson & Co (1991), CA 218
McNichol v Grandy (1932) 449
McPhail v Persons (names unknown) (1973), CA 74
M'Pherson v Daniels (1829) 449, 458
McQuire v Western Morning News Co (1903), CA 483
McWhirter v Manning (1954) 449
Mafo v Adams (1970), CA 123
Mahesan S/O Thambiah v Malaysia Government Officers' Co-operative Housing Society Ltd
    (1979), PC 124, 534
Mahon v Osborne (1939), CA 259, 261
Mahon v Rahn (1997), CA 467
Mair v Wood (1948) 588
Maira, The. See National Bank of Greece SA v Pinios Shipping Co, The Maira Maitland v
    Raisbeck and RT and J Hewitt Ltd (1944), CA 393
Makanjuola v Metropolitan Police Comr (1992), CA 521
Malachy v Soper (1836) 136, 137, 139, 140
Malcolm v Broadhurst (1970) 276, 278, 279
Malette v Shulman (1991) 85
Malfroot v Noxal Ltd (1935) 341
Mallett v Dunn (1949) 288
Maloco v Littlewoods Ltd (1987), HL 272
Malone v Laskey (1907), CA 376
Malone v Metropolitan Police Comr (1979) 165
Malone v Rowan (1984) 559
Malyon v Plummer (1964), CA 557
Malz v Rosen (1966) 492, 496
Manchester Airport plc v Dutton (1999) 79
Manchester Corpn v Farnworth (1930), HL 104, 367, 384
Manchester Corpn v Markland (1936), HL 244
Manchester Ship Canal Co v Manchester Racecourse Co (1901), CA 158
Manders v Williams (1849) 47
Mangena v Edward Lloyd Ltd (1908); on appeal (1909), CA 474
Mangena v Wright (1909) 480

PAGE

Mansfield v Weetabix Ltd (1998), CA 238
Manton v Brocklebank (1923), CA 27, 68, 69
Manus, Akt v R J Fullwood and Bland Ltd (1954) 135
Mapp v News Group Newspapers Ltd (1998), CA 445
Marcroft Wagons Ltd v Smith (1951), CA 78
Marengo v Daily Sketch and Sunday Graphic Ltd (1948), HL 135
Mareva Cia Naviera SA v International Bulkcarriers SA, The Mareva (1975), CA 536
Margarine Union GmbH v Cambay Prince Steamship Co Ltd (1969) 179
Marintrans AB v Comet Shipping Co Ltd, The Shinjitsu Maru (No 5) (1985) 291
Mariola Marine Corpn v Lloyd's Register of Shipping, The Morning Watch (1990) 219
Markt & Co Ltd v Knight Steamship Co Ltd (1910), CA 588
Marriage v East Norfolk Rivers Catchment Board (1950), CA 104
Marrinan v Vibart (1963), CA 144, 467, 498
Marshall v Osmond (1983), CA 234, 241
Marston v British Railways Board (1976) 573
Martin v LCC (1899), CA 391
Martin v Porter (1839) 80
Martin v Temperley (1843) 505
Martin v Watson (1994), CA; revsd (1996), HL 492, 494, 496
Mason v Clarke (1955), HL 76, 78, 79
Mason v Levy Auto Parts of England Ltd (1967) 404, 412
Mason v Williams and Williams Ltd and Thomas Turton & Sons Ltd (1955) 342, 346
Masper v Brown (1876) 105
Massam v Thorley's Cattle Food Co (1880), CA 129
Masson Seeley & Co Ltd v Embosotype Manufacturing Co (1924) 131
Masters v Brent London Borough Council (1978) 367
Matania v National Provincial Bank Ltd and Elevenist Syndicate Ltd (1936), CA: 369, 382, 510
Matthews v Wicks (1987), CA 416
Maxey Drainage Board v Great Northern Rly Co (1912), DC 93
Maxim's Ltd v Dye (1978) 132
Maynard v West Midlands Regional Health Authority (1984), HL 248
Maynegrain Pty Ltd v Compafina Bank (1984), PC 49
Mayo v Seaton UDC (1903) 367
Meade v London Borough of Haringey (1979), CA 149
Meah v McCreamer (1985) 27
Meah v McCreamer (No 2) (1986) 27, 547
Mears v London and South Western Rly Co (1862) 72
Mediana (Owners) v Comet (Owners, Master and Crew of the Lightship), The Mediana
    (1900), HL 71, 525, 552
Meekins v Henson (1964) 473, 588
Meering v Grahame-White Aviation Co Ltd (1919), CA 41
Meggs v Liverpool Corpn (1968), CA 583
Mehmet v Perry (1977) 560
Melhuish v Clifford (1998) 587
Mentmore Manufacturing Co Ltd v Fomento (Sterling Area) Ltd (1955), CA 138, 140
Mercantile Marine Service Association v Toms (1916), CA 587
Mercer v South Eastern and Chatham Rly Co's Managing Committee (1922) 182
Meridian Global Funds Management Asia Ltd v Securities Commission (1995), PC 144
Merivale v Carson (1887), CA 480, 482, 483
Merkur Island Shipping Corpn v Laughton (1983), CA; affd (1983), HL .. 114, 143, 153, 158
Merlin v British Nuclear Fuels plc (1990) 428
Merricks v Nott-Bower (1965), CA 465
Merrington v Ironbridge Metal Works Ltd (1952) 299
Mersey Docks and Harbour Board v Coggins and Griffiths (Liverpool) Ltd (1947), HL: 251, 506
Mersey Docks and Harbour Board Trustees v Gibbs (1866) 182, 239
Metall und Rohstoff AG v ACLI Metals (London) Ltd (1984), CA 123
Metall und Rohstoff AG v Donaldson Lufkin & Jenrette Inc (1990), CA 146, 498
Metropolitan Asylum District Managers v Hill (1881), HL 104, 384
Metropolitan Properties Ltd v Jones (1939) 376
Meux's Brewery Co v City of London Electric Lighting Co (1895), CA 377
Meye v Electric Transmission Ltd (1942) 75
Michael v Spiers and Pond Ltd (1909) 453, 455
Middlebrook Mushrooms Ltd v Transport and General Workers' Union (1993), CA 151

PAGE

Midland Bank plc v Bardgrove Property Services Ltd (1991); affd (1992), CA 174
Midland Bank Trust Co Ltd v Green (No 3) (1982), CA 144, 588
Midland Bank Trust Co Ltd v Hett, Stubbs and Kemp (a firm) (1979) 196, 290
Midwood & Co v Manchester Corpn (1905), CA 369, 378, 379, 401, 404, 412
Miles v Forest Rock Granite Co (Leicestershire) Ltd (1918), CA 399
Millar v Bassey (1993), CA 155
Millard v Serck Tubes Ltd (1969), CA 428
Miller v Jackson (1977), CA 362, 383, 385, 537
Miller v London Electrical Manufacturing Co Ltd (1976), CA 572
Miller v South of Scotland Electricity Board (1958) 327
Millington v Fox (1838) 129
Mills v Armstrong, The Bernina (1888), HL 288
Mills v Brooker (1919) 54
Mills v Hassall (1983) 549
Mineral Transporter, The. See Candlewood Navigation Corpn Ltd v Mitsui OSK Lines Ltd,
    The Mineral Transporter, The Ibaraki Maru
Minister of Health v Bellotti (1944), CA 75
Ministry of Housing and Local Government v Sharp (1970), CA 220
Mint v Good (1951), CA 324, 332, 383, 391
Minter v Priest (1930), HL 468
Miraflores (Owners) v George Livanos (Owners) (1967), HL 600
Mirage Studios v Counter Feat Clothing Co Ltd (1991) 126, 132
Mitchell v Faber and Faber Ltd (1998) 443
Mitchell v Hirst, Kidd and Rennie Ltd (1936) 468
Mitchell v Mulholland (No 2) (1972), CA 543
Moeliker v A Reyrolle & Co Ltd (1977), CA 550
Mogul Steamship Co v McGregor Gow & Co (1892), HL 145, 160
Mohamed Amin v Jogendra Kumar Bannerjee (1947), PC 492
Molinari v Ministry of Defence (1994) 552
Mollo v BBC (1963) 440
Mond v Hyde (1998), CA 467
Monk v Warbey (1935), CA 421, 427
Monks v Dykes (1839) 78
Monson v Tussauds Ltd (1894), CA 451, 487
Montgomery v Thompson (1891), HL 128
Montreal v Montreal Locomotive Works Ltd (1947) 505
Moore v Canadian Pacific Steamship Co (1945) 479
Moore v DER Ltd (1971), CA 552
Moore v News of the World Ltd (1972), CA 459
Moore v Oastler (1836) 485, 530
Moore v R Fox & Sons (1956), CA 262, 263
Moore v Regents of the University of California (1990) 53
Moorgate Mercantile Co Ltd v Finch and Read (1962), CA 54
Morahan v Archer (1957) 526
Morales v Eccleston (1991), CA 237, 287
More v Weaver (1928), CA 468
Morgan v Lingen (1863) 440
Morgan v Marquis (1853) 61
Morgan v Odhams Press Ltd (1971), HL 447
Morgan v Powell (1842) 80
Morgan Crucible Co plc v Hill Samuel & Co Ltd (1991), CA 218
Morgans v Launchbury (1973), HL 508
Moriarty v Brooks (1834), Ex Ch 90, 91
Moriarty v McCarthy (1978) 546
Morison v London County and Westminster Bank Ltd (1914), CA 56
Morning Watch, The. See Mariola Marine Corpn v Lloyd's Register of Shipping,
    The Morning Watch
Morrell v International Thomson Publishing Ltd (1989), CA 446, 458
Morris v Baron & Co (1918), HL 568
Morris v Blaenau Gwent District Council (1982), CA 416
Morris v Breaveglen Ltd (t/a Anzac Construction Co) (1993), CA 507
Morris v CW Martin & Sons Ltd (1966), CA 521
Morris v Ford Motor Co Ltd (1973), CA 600

PAGE

Morris v Luton Corpn (1946), CA 236
Morris v Murray (1991), CA 293, 294, 297, 298, 300, 322
Morris v West Hartlepool Steam Navigation Co Ltd (1956), HL 257
Morris v Winsbury-White (1937) 261
Morris Motors Ltd v Lilley (t/a G and L Motors) (1959) 130
Morriss v Marsden (1952) 27, 535, 589
Morton-Norwich Products Inc v Intercen Ltd (No 2) (1981) 164, 529
Moss v Christchurch RDC (1925) 387
Mott v Shoolbred (1875) 393
Mouse's Case (1608) 94
Moy v Stoop (1909) 359, 373, 376
Muirhead v Industrial Tank Specialities Ltd (1986), CA 226, 228, 345
Mulcahy v Ministry of Defence (1996), CA 172, 192, 581
Mulgrave v Ogden (1591) 55
Mulholland and Tedd Ltd v Baker (1939) 412
Mullard v Ben Line Steamers Ltd (1971), CA 431
Mullett v Mason (1866) 122
Mullin v Richards (1998), CA 237, 287
Mulliner v Florence (1878), CA 48
Mullis v United States Lines Co (1969) 313
Munro v Willmott (1949) 64
Munster v Lamb (1883), CA 467
Murdoch v Glacier Metal Co Ltd (1998), CA 365
Murphy v Brentwood District Council (1991), HL 8, 14, 117, 177, 178, 180, 183,
                                    213, 226, 227, 324, 326, 328, 329,
                                    330, 332, 345, 422, 569, 575
Murphy v Culhane (1977), CA 84, 88, 290, 321, 555
Murray v East India Co (1821) 571
Murray v Harringay Arena Ltd (1951), CA 289, 293
Murray v Minister of Defence (1985) 35
Murray v Ministry of Defence (1988), HL 41
Murray v Shuter (1976), CA 553
Musgrove v Pandelis (1919), CA 398, 401, 412
Musurus Bey v Gadban (1894), CA 571, 582
Mutual Life and Citizens' Assurance Co Ltd v Evatt (1971), PC 217
Myroft v Sleight (1921) 440

N

NWL Ltd v Woods, The Nawala (1979), HL 158
Nahhas v Pier House (Cheyne Walk) Management Ltd (1984) 522
Nance v British Columbia Electric Rly Co Ltd (1951), PC 286
Nash v Eli Lilly & Co (1993), CA 572, 573, 574
Nash v Sheen (1953) 33
National Bank of Greece SA v Pinios Shipping Co, The Maira (1989), CA; on appeal sub nom
    National Bank of Greece SA v Pinios Shipping Co (1990), HL 290, 533
National Coal Board v England. See England v National Coal Board
National Coal Board v J E Evans & Co (Cardiff) Ltd (1951), CA 24, 27, 69
National Mercantile Bank v Rymill (1881), CA 57
National Provincial Bank Ltd v Ainsworth (1965), HL 78
National Telephone Co v Baker (1893) 398
Nationwide Building Society v Lewis (1998), CA 588
Nawala, The. See NWL Ltd v Woods, The Nawala
Nea Tyhi, The (1982) 179
Neate v Harding (1851) 534
Nelmes v Chief Constable of Avon and Somerset Constabulary (1993), CA 416
Nelson v Raphael (1979) 508
Nettleship v Weston (1971), CA 240, 293, 296, 297
Netz v Ede (1946) 105
Neutrogena Corpn v Golden Ltd (1995), CA 134
Neville v London Express Newspapers Ltd (1919), HL 525
New York Times v Sullivan (1964) 438
Newport Association Football Club Ltd v Football Association of Wales Ltd (1995) 160

PAGE

News Group Newspapers Ltd v Society of Graphical and Allied Trades '82 (No 2)
(1987) 153, 392
Newstead v London Express Newspaper Ltd (1940), CA 448
Newsweek Inc v BBC (1979), CA 134
Newton v Edgerley (1959) 591
Ng Chun Pui v Lee Chuen Tat (1988), PC 241, 258, 263
Nicholas H, The. See Rich (Marc) & Co AG v Bishop Rock Marine Co Ltd, The Nicholas H
Nicholls v Ely Beet Sugar Factory Ltd (1936), CA 393, 525
Nichols v Marsland (1876), CA 270, 409
Nicolls v Bastard (1835) 47
Nield v London and North Western Rly Co (1874) 93
Nitrigin Eireann Teoranta v Inco Alloys Ltd (1992) 214, 331, 343
Noble v Harrison (1926), DC 403, 411
North Central (or General) Wagon and Finance Co Ltd v Graham (1950), CA 48
Northam v Bowden (1855) 49
Northern Sandblasting Pty Ltd v Harris (1997), HC of A 332
Northern Territory v Mengel (1995) 155
Northwestern Utilities Ltd v London Guarantee and Accident Co Ltd (1936), PC: 233, 404, 407
Nor-Video Services Ltd v Ontario Hydro (1978) 364
Norwood v Navan (1981), CA 508
Nottingham v Aldridge (1971) 508
Nunan v Southern Rly Co (1924), CA 556
Nyberg (or Nyburg) v Handelaar (1892), CA 61
Nykredit Mortgage Bank plc v Edward Erdman Group Ltd (No 2) (1997) 571

O

Oakley v Lyster (1931), CA 60
Oakley v Walker (1977) 550
Ocean Frost, The. See Armagas Ltd v Mundogas SA, The Ocean Frost
Oceangas (Gibraltar) Ltd v Port of London Authority, The Cavendish (1993) 505
O'Connell v Jackson (1972), CA 287, 289, 292
O'Connor v Waldron (1935), PC 466
Oddy v Lord Paulet (1865) 471
Oertli (T) AG v E J Bowman (London) Ltd, William Page & Co (Turmix Sales) Ltd,
Farnsworth, Parness and Marlow (1956); on appeal (1957), CA; affd (1959), HL .. 594
Office Cleaning Services Ltd v Westminster Office Cleaning Association (1944), CA; affd
(1946), HL 133
Ogwo v Taylor (1988), HL 202, 203, 207, 269, 299, 309
O'Hara v Chief Constable of Royal Ulster Constabulary (1997), HL 99
Oliver v Ashman (1962), CA 544
Oliver v Birmingham and Midland Motor Omnibus Co Ltd (1933) 289
Olley v Marlborough Court Ltd (1949), CA 515
Olotu v Home Office (1997), CA 5, 30, 40, 422
Ontario Ltd (384238) v The Queen in Right of Canada (1983) 55
O'Reilly v Imperial Chemical Industries Ltd (1955) 251
O'Reilly v Mackman (1983), HL 184
Orjula, The. See Losinjska Plovidba v Transco Overseas Ltd, The Orjula
Ormiston v Great Western Rly Co (1917) 453
Oropesa, The (1943), CA 531, 532
O'Rourke v Camden London Borough Council (1988) 422, 426
Osborn v Thomas Boulter & Son (1930), CA 451, 452
Osborn v Veitch (1858) 35
Osborne v London and North Western Rly Co (1888), DC 293
Osman v Ferguson (1993), CA 190, 194, 229
Osman v United Kingdom (1999), ECtHR 6, 191, 229
O'Sullivan v Williams (1992), CA 47, 61, 70, 531
Oughton v Seppings (1830) 534
Overseas Tankship (UK) Ltd v Miller Steamship Co Pty, The Wagon Mound (No 2)
(1967), PC 233, 235, 239, 275, 361,
374, 387, 393, 394, 527
Overseas Tankship (UK) Ltd v Morts Dock and Engineering Co Ltd, The Wagon Mound (1961),
PC 25, 275, 406

PAGE
Owen v Lewyn (1672) 58
Owen v Northampton Borough Council (1992), CA 587
Owen v O'Connor (1964) 527
Owens v Brimmell (1977) 286, 287, 292, 296, 297

P

PLG Research Ltd v Ardon International Ltd (1993) 594
Pacific Colcotronis, The. See UBAF Ltd v European American Banking Corpn, The Pacific
    Colcotronis
Padbury v Holliday and Greenwood Ltd (1912), CA 514
Padmore v Lawrence (1840) 476
Page v Read (1984) 305
Page v Smith (1996), HL 204
Page v Smith (No 2) (1996), CA 266
Page Motors Ltd v Epsom and Ewell Borough Council (1981), CA 381
Paine & Co Ltd v St Neots Gas and Coke Co (1939), CA 76
Palfrey v Greater London Council (1985) 549
Palmer v Durnford Ford (a firm) (1992) 498
Palsgraf v Long Island Railroad Co (1928) 181, 233
Pamplin v Express Newspapers Ltd (No 2) (1988), CA 485
Pape v Cumbria County Council (1992) 242
Paris v Levy (1860) 480
Paris v Stepney Borough Council (1950), CA; revsd (1951), HL: 231, 233, 242, 244, 255, 296
Parker v British Airways Board (1982), CA 50
Parker v Godin (1728) 57
Parker-Knoll Ltd v Knoll International Ltd (1962), HL 128
Parkes v Prescott (1869), Ex Ch 449
Parkinson v Liverpool Corpn (1950), CA 241
Parmiter v Coupland (1840) 439
Parry v Cleaver (1970), HL 548
Parsons v Surgey (1864) 477
Parsons (H) (Livestock) Ltd v Uttley Ingham & Co Ltd (1978), CA 279
Pasley v Freeman (1789) 118
Pasmore v Oswaldtwistle UDC (1898), HL 425
Patel v Patel (1988), CA 37
Patel v WH Smith (Eziot) Ltd (1987), CA 74
Paterson Zochonis & Co Ltd v Merfarken Packaging Ltd (1986), CA 195
Patrick v Colerick (1838) 108
Payne v Rogers (1794) 383
Peabody Donation Fund (Governors) v Sir Lindsay Parkinson & Co Ltd (1985),
    HL 176, 326, 571
Peachey v Wing (1826) 70
Pearce v Secretary of State for Defence (1988), HL 581
Pearson v Rose and Young Ltd (1951), CA 56
Peck (Polly) (Holdings) plc v Trelford (1986), CA 446, 460, 482
Peek v Gurney (1873) 119, 120
Penfolds Wines Pty Ltd v Elliott (1946) 56, 70
Pennington v Norris (1956) 292
Penny v Wimbledon UDC and Iles (1899), CA 391, 511, 514
Penton v Caldwell (1945) 477
Pepper (Inspector of Taxes) v Hart (1993), HL 570
Perera v Peiris (1949), PC 473
Perera v Vandiyar (1953), CA 74
Performing Right Society Ltd v Mitchell and Booker (Palais de Danse) Ltd (1924) 504
Perkowski v Wellington Corpn (1959) 308
Perl (P) (Exporters) Ltd v Camden London Borough Council (1984), CA 193, 195, 196,
                                                                          325, 381
Perry v Kendricks Transport Ltd (1956), CA 398, 401, 409, 412
Perry v Sidney Phillips & Son (a firm) (1982), CA 80, 530
Perry (Howard E) & Co Ltd v British Railways Board (1980) 45, 59, 60, 66
Peruvian Guano Co Ltd v Dreyfus Bros & Co (1892), HL 530
Peters v Bradlaugh (1888) 458
Peters v Prince of Wales Theatre (Birmingham) Ltd (1943), CA 407

PAGE

Petre (Lord) v Heneage (1701) 55
Philips v Naylor (1859) 496
Philips v William Whiteley Ltd (1938) 241
Phillips v Britannia Hygienic Laundry Co (1923); on appeal (1923), CA .. 245, 425, 427, 513
Phillips v Clagett (1843) 568
Phillips v Homfray (1883), CA; on appeal sub nom Phillips v Fothergill (1886), HL 534
Phillips v Perry (1997) 311
Philpott v Kelley (1835) 55
Phipps v Rochester Corpn (1955) 308, 311
Pickard v Smith (1861) 511
Pickering v Liverpool Daily Post and Echo Newspapers plc (1991), HL 4, 419, 429
Pickering v Rudd (1815) 74
Pickett v British Rail Engineering Ltd (1980), HL 544, 556
Pickford v Imperial Chemical Industries plc (1998), HL 268
Pickles v National Coal Board (intended action) (1968), CA 572
Pigney v Pointers Transport Services Ltd (1957) 270, 555
Pike v Waldrum and Peninsular and Oriental Steam Navigation Co (1952) 42
Piller (Anton) KG v Manufacturing Processes Ltd (1976), CA 536
Pilmore v Hood (1838) 120
Pirelli General Cable Works Ltd v Oscar Faber & Partners (1983), HL 569, 571, 574
Pitt v Donovan (1813) 469
Pitts v Hunt (1991), CA 105, 292, 297, 300
Plange v Chief Constable of South Humberside Police (1992), CA 99
Plasycoed Collieries Co Ltd v Partridge, Jones & Co Ltd (1912), DC 48
Platform Home Loans Ltd v Oyston Shipways Ltd (1998), CA; revsd (1999), HL 287
Plato Films Ltd v Speidel (1961), HL 460, 487
Playa Larga and The Marble Islands, The. See Empresa Exportadora de Azucar v Industria
    Azucarera Nacional SA, The Playa Larga and The Marble Islands
Playa Larga, The (Owners of Cargo lately laden on board) v I Congreso del Partido (Owners),
    Marble Islands, The (Owners of Cargo lately laden on board) v I Congreso del Partido
    (Owners), I Congreso del Partido (1983), HL 581
Plomien Fuel Economiser Co Ltd v National School of Salesmanship Ltd (1943), CA 134
Plumb v Cobden Flour Mills Co Ltd (1914), HL 518
Plummer v Charman (1962), CA 477
Plymouth Mutual Co-operative and Industrial Society Ltd v Traders' Publishing Association
    Ltd (1906), CA 482
Poland v John Parr & Sons (1927), CA 520
Polemis and Furness Withy & Co, Re (1921), CA 274
Polhill v Walter (1832) 120
Polkinhorn v Wright (1845) 91
Pontardawe RDC v Moore-Gwyn (1929) 399
Pontiac Marina Pte Ltd v CDL Hotels International Ltd (1997) 132
Ponting v Noakes (1894) 404
Port Swettenham Authority v TW Wu & Co (M) Sdn Bhd (1979), PC 521, 522
Porter v Barking and Dagenham London Borough Council (1990) 243
Portland Managements Ltd v Harte (1977), CA 79
Possfund Custodian Trustee Ltd v Diamond (McGrigor Donald (a firm), third party) (1996): 121
Poulton v London and South Western Rly Co (1867) 584
Pounder v London Underground Ltd (1995) 555
Powell v Birmingham Vinegar Brewery Co Ltd (1896), CA; revsd sub nom Birmingham
    Vinegar Brewery Co Ltd v Powell (1897), HL 128
Powell v Fall (1880), CA 396
Powell v Gelston (1916) 449
Powell v Phillips (1972), CA 245
Powell v Rees (1837) 534
Powell v Streatham Manor Nursing Home (1935), HL 257
Practice Direction (1984) 542
Practice Direction (1992) 542
Practice Direction (Mareva and Anton Piller orders: forms) (1997) 536
Practice Note (1993) 86
Praed v Graham (1889), CA 485
Pratt v Swaine (1828) 571
Prebble v Television New Zealand Ltd (1995), PC 438, 464
Preist v Last (1903), CA 339

PAGE

Preston v Mercer (1656) 362
Pride of Derby and Derbyshire Angling Association Ltd v British Celanese Ltd (1953),
  CA 404, 537, 596
Pridham v Hemel Hempstead Corpn (1970), CA 583
Printers and Finishers Ltd v Holloway (1964) 158, 165
Prior v Wilson (1856) 458
Pritchard v Briggs (1980), CA 156, 158
Pritchard v JH Cobden Ltd (1988), CA 543, 544, 547
Pritchard v Post Office (1950), CA 242
Procea Products Ltd v Evans & Sons Ltd (1951) 134
Prole v Allen (1950) 587
Prosser v Edmonds (1835) 593
Prosser (A) & Son Ltd v Levy (1955), CA 407
Protheroe v Railway Executive (1951) 317
Proudman v Allen (1954) 93
Prudential Assurance Co Ltd v Lorenz (1971) 149
Prudential Assurance Co Ltd v Newman Industries Ltd (1981) 587
Pullman v Walter Hill & Co (1891), CA 449, 450
Purcell v Sowler (1877), CA 479
Purdew and Purdew v Seress-Smith (1993) 466
Purefoy Engineering Co Ltd v Sykes Boxall & Co Ltd, Sykes and Boxall (1955), CA 131
Pursell v Horn (1838) 34
Pwllbach Colliery Co Ltd v Woodman (1915), HL 386
Pym v Great Northern Rly Co (1863), Ex Ch 557

Q

Qualcast (Wolverhampton) Ltd v Haynes (1959), HL 236
Quarman v Burnett (1840) 504
Quartz Hill Consolidated Gold Mining Co v Eyre (1883), CA 493
Queen Mary, The. See Bishop v Cunard White Star Co Ltd, The Queen Mary
Quinn v Leathem (1901), HL 144, 145, 154
Quinn v Scott (1965) 234, 239
Quintas v National Smelting Co Ltd (1961), CA 292

R

R (a minor), Re (1992), CA 86
R v Barnard (1837) 119
R v Billinghurst (1978) 83
R v Bird (1985), CA 89
R v Bottrill, ex p Kuechenmeister (1947), CA 105
R v Bournewood Community and Mental Health NHS Trust, ex p L (1998) 95
R v Brown (1994), HL 32, 84
R v Chief Constable of North Wales Police, ex p AB (1998), CA 5
R v Clarence (1888), CCR 84
R v Cotesworth (1704) 33
R v Day (1845) 34
R v Deputy Governor of Parkhurst Prison, ex p Hague (1991), HL: 40, 419, 422, 425, 426, 593
R v Graham-Campbell, ex p Herbert (1935) 104
R v Howell (1982), CA 99
R v Hughes (1994), CA 102
R v Ireland (1998), HL 35
R v Kelly (1998), CA 53
R v Latimer (1886), CCR 31
R v Meade and Belt (1823) 35
R v Newport (Salop) Justices, ex p Wright (1929), DC 96
R v Roberts (1953) 101
R v Rule (1937), CCA 476
R v Russell (1827) 392
R v St George (1840) 35
R v St George's Union (1871) 78
R v Secretary of State for Social Services, ex p Hincks (1979); affd (1980), CA 422
R v Secretary of State for the Home Department, ex p Fire Brigades Union (1995), HL ... 562

PAGE

R v Self (1992), CA 98
R v Shorrock (1994), CA 390, 393
R v Telfer (1976) 100
R v Ward (1836) 392
RB Policies at Lloyd's v Butler (1950) 67, 571
RCA Corpn v Pollard (1983), CA 161, 418, 538
Racz v Home Office (1994), HL 500, 521, 529
Radley v London and North Western Rly Co (1876), HL 283
Radstock Co-operative and Industrial Society v Norton-Radstock UDC (1968), CA 379
Raggett v Findlater (1873) 128
Railways Comr v McDermott (1967), PC 322
Railways Comr v Quinlan (1964), PC 327
Rainham Chemical Works Ltd v Belvedere Fish Guano Co (1921), HL 397, 398, 399,
                                                                400, 403, 594
Ramsey v Hartley (1977), CA 592, 593
Rand v Craig (1919), CA 519
Rantzen v Mirror Group Newspapers (1986) Ltd (1994), CA 5, 436, 437, 486
Rapier v London Tramways Co (1893), CA 358, 359
Ratcliffe v Evans (1892), CA 136, 140, 441
Ravenga v Mackintosh (1824) 496
Ravenscroft v Rederiaktiebolaget Transatlantic (1991); revsd (1992), CA 207
Rayner v Mitchell (1877) 518
Razzel v Snowball (1954), CA 512
Read v Coker (1853) 35
Read v Croydon Corpn (1938) 341
Read v Friendly Society of Operative Stonemasons of England, Ireland and Wales (1902);
     varied (1902), CA 150, 156
Read v Harries (1995) 544
Read v J Lyons & Co Ltd (1945), CA; affd (1947), HL 336, 342, 359, 376, 396, 397,
                                                        400, 401, 402, 403, 404, 405
Reckitt & Colman Products Ltd v Borden Inc (1990), HL 127, 129, 134, 136
Reddaway v Bentham Hemp-Spinning Co (1892), CA 135
Reddaway (Frank) & Co Ltd v George Banham & Co Ltd (1896), HL 128
Redland Bricks Ltd v Morris (1970), HL 537
Redpath v Belfast and County Down Rly (1947) 548
Reeves v Metropolitan Police Comr (1998), CA 106, 108, 270, 299
Reffell v Surrey County Council (1964) 426
Regan v Williamson (1976) 560
Reid v Fairbanks (1853) 63
Reid v Rush & Tompkins Group plc (1989), CA 255
Reliance Car Facilities Ltd v Roding Motors (1952), CA 48
Rely-a-Bell Burglar and Fire Alarm Co Ltd v Eisler (1926) 157
Resolute Maritime Inc v Nippon Kaiji Kyokai, The Skopas (1983) 125, 126
Reuter (RJ) Co Ltd v Mulhens (1954), CA 139
Revill v Newbery (1996), CA 88, 89, 91, 106, 303, 309, 320
Revis v Smith (1856) 467
Rey v Lecouturier (1908), CA; affd sub nom Lecouturier v Rey (1910), HL 128
Reynolds v Clark (1725) 73
Reynolds v Kennedy (1748) 494
Reynolds v Metropolitan Police Comr (1985), CA 493
Reynolds v Shipping Federation Ltd (1924) 145
Reynolds v Times Newspapers Ltd (1998), CA 436, 477
Rhodes v Moules (1895), CA 63
Rice v Reed (1900), CA 567
Rich v Basterfield (1847) 379
Rich v LCC (1953), CA 323, 591
Rich (Marc) & Co AG v Bishop Rock Marine Co Ltd, The Nicholas H (1996), HL .. 178, 180,
                                                                        212
Richards v Davies (1921) 76
Richards v Naum (1967), CA 465
Richardson v Atkinson (1723) 55
Richardson v Pitt-Stanley (1995), CA 419, 421, 425, 427
Richardson v Silvester (1873), DC 120
Richardson v Stephenson Clarke Ltd (1969) 252

PAGE

Riches v DPP (1973), CA 496
Riches v News Group Newspapers Ltd (1986), CA 485, 528
Richley v Faull (1965) 259
Rickards v Lothian (1913) 397, 403, 408
Ricket v Directors etc of the Metropolitan Rly Co (1867) 390, 391
Ricketts v Erith Borough Council (1943) 591
Ricketts v Thos Tilling Ltd (1915), CA 517
Rickless v United Artists Corpn (1988), CA 421
Riddick v Thames Board Mills Ltd (1977), CA 450, 473
Riding v Smith (1876) 137
Rigby v Chief Constable of Northamptonshire (1985) 94, 191, 234, 396, 398,
                                                              400, 405, 409, 410
Rima Electric Ltd v Rolls Razor Ltd (1965) 136
Rimmer v Liverpool City Council (1985), CA 327, 328, 331
Rivers v Cutting (1982), CA 513
Rivlin v Bilainkin (1953) 464
Rivtow Marine Ltd v Washington Ironworks (1974) 344
Roberts v Johnstone (1989), CA 545
Roberts v Ramsbottom (1980) 238
Roberts v Read (1812) 24
Roberts v Roberts (1657) 95
Roberts v Tayler (1845) 90
Roberts v Wyatt (1810) 47
Robertson v Ridley (1989), CA 587
Robinson v Balmain New Ferry Co Ltd (1910), PC 40
Robinson v Beaconsfield RDC (1911), CA 510, 514
Robinson v Chambers (No 2) (1946) 452
Robinson v Kilvert (1889), CA 364
Robinson v Post Office (1974), CA 273, 279
Robinson v Ward (1958) 454
Robson v Hallett (1967) 75, 308
Rodgers v Maw (1846) 534
Roe v Minister of Health (1954), CA 172, 181, 240, 261, 506, 515
Rogers v Austin (1997) 531
Rogers v Macnamara (1853) 72
Rogers v Night Riders (a firm) (1983), CA 513
Rogers v Rajendro Dutt (1860), PC 4
Rogers v Spence (1844), Ex Ch; affd (1846) 592
Rogers v Whitaker (1993) 232
Roles v Nathan (1963), CA 311, 312
Roncarelli v Duplessis (1959) 499
Rondel v Worsley (1969), HL 190, 220
Ronex Properties Ltd v John Laing Construction Ltd (1983), CA 598
Rookes v Barnard (1964), HL 123, 150, 159, 527
Rooth v Wilson (1817) 70
Rose v Buckett (1901), CA 592
Rose v Ford (1937), HL 553
Rose v Miles (1815) 391
Rose v Plenty (1976), CA 323, 519, 520
Ross v Associated Portland Cement Manufacturers Ltd (1964), HL 431
Ross v Caunters (1980) 175, 221, 248, 290
Ross v Fedden (1872) 407
Ross v Rugge-Price (1876) 421
Rost v Edwards (1990) 464, 466
Rouse v Gravelworks Ltd (1940), CA 404
Rouse v Squires (1973), CA 273, 285
Rowling v Takaro Properties Ltd (1988), PC 176, 385
Roy v Prior (1971), HL 493, 498
Royal Aquarium and Summer and Winter Garden Society v Parkinson (1892), CA: 466, 469, 470
Royal Baking Powder Co v Wright, Crossley & Co (1900), HL 137, 138
Royscot Trust Ltd v Rogerson (1991), CA 125
Rubber Improvement Ltd v Daily Telegraph Ltd (1964), HL 439, 444, 445, 458, 526
Ruddiman & Co v Smith (1889), DC 517

PAGE

Rushmer v Polsue and Alfieri Ltd (1906), CA; affd sub nom Polsue and Alfieri Ltd v Rushmer (1907), HL 366
Russell v Duke of Norfolk (1949), CA 457
Russell v Notcutt (1896), CA 444
Ruxley Electronics and Construction Ltd v Forsyth (1995), HL 371
Ryan v Fildes (1938) 96
Ryeford Homes Ltd and Mewburn Property Co Ltd v Sevenoaks District Council (1989) 378, 393, 402, 404
Rylands v Fletcher. See Fletcher v Rylands and Horrocks

S

S v Newham London Borough Council (1998), CA 478
S v W (child abuse: damages) (1995), CA 570
S and K Holdings Ltd v Throgmorton Publications Ltd (1972), CA 460
S-C (mental patient: habeas corpus), Re (1996), CA 95
SCM (UK) Ltd v WJ Whittall & Son Ltd (1971), CA 225
SOS Kinderdorf International v Bittaye (1996), PC 156
Sachs v Miklos (1948), CA 63
Sack v Jones (1925) 366
Sadgrove v Hole (1901), CA 450
Sadler v Great Western Rly Co (1896), HL 595
Sadler v South Staffordshire and Birmingham District Steam Tramways Co (1889), CA 33
Said v Butt (1920) 149
St Albans City and District Council v International Computers Ltd (1996), CA 342
St Anne's Well Brewery Co v Roberts (1928), CA 382, 383, 400, 404
St George's Healthcare NHS Trust v S (1998), CA 85, 93
St Helen's Smelting Co v Tipping (1865) 367, 370
Sales Affiliates Ltd v Le Jean Ltd (1947) 136
Salsbury v Woodland (1970), CA 511, 514
Sampson v Hodson-Pressinger (1981), CA 368, 412
Samuel (No 2), Re (1945), CA 57
Samuel and Escombe v Rowe (1892) 63
Sanders-Clark v Grosvenor Mansions Co Ltd and D'Allessandri (1900) 372
Sanderson v Marsden and Jones (1922), CA 55
Saunders v Edwards (1987), CA 106, 123
Saunders v Leeds Western Health Authority (1993) 260
Savile v Roberts (1698) 493
Savoy Hotel plc v BBC (1982) 538
Sayers v Harlow UDC (1958), CA 41
Scala Ballroom (Wolverhampton) Ltd v Ratcliffe (1958), CA 146
Scarsbrook v Mason (1961) 594
Schiffahrt und Kohlen GmbH v Chelsea Maritime Ltd, The Irene's Success (1982) 179
Schloendorff v Society of New York Hospital (1914) 85
Schneider v Eisovitch (1960) 278
Schneider v Heath (1813) 119
Schneider v Leigh (1955), CA 465
Scott v London and St Katherine Docks Co (1865), Ex Ch 258
Scott v Matthew Brown & Co Ltd (1884) 90
Scott v Sampson (1882), DC 486, 487
Scott v Shepherd (1773) 31, 33, 269
Scott v Stansfield (1868) 467
Scuriaga v Powell (1979); affd (1980), CA 212
Sea Hawk, The. See Locabail International Finance Ltd v Agroexport, The Sea Hawk
Seager v Copydex Ltd (1967), CA 165
Seaman v Cuppledick (1615) 89
Seaman v Netherclift (1876), CA 467
Secretary of State for Defence v Guardian Newspapers Ltd (1985), HL 66
Secretary of State for the Environment v Essex, Goodman & Suggitt (1986) 571
Secretary of State for the Home Department v Robb (1995) 93
Sedleigh-Denfield v O'Callaghan (1940), HL 359, 362, 363, 367, 378, 380, 384, 393, 412
Sefton v Tophams Ltd (1965), CA; revsd sub nom Tophams Ltd v Earl of Sefton (1967), HL 158

PAGE

Selby Bridge (Proprietors) v Sunday Telegraph Ltd (1966) 442
Seligman v Docker (1949) 381, 399
Sellars v Best (1954) 533
Selvanayagam v University of the West Indies (1983), PC 271, 530
Series 5 Software Ltd v Clarke (1995) 536
Seton Laing & Co v Lafone (1887), CA 59
Sewai Jaipur v Arjun Lal (1937), PC 76
Sewell v National Telephone Co Ltd (1907), CA 42
Seymour v Butterworth (1862) 479
Seymour v Greenwood (1861), Ex Ch 24
Shanson v Howard (1997) 444
Shapiro v La Morta (1923), CA 37, 137, 139, 140
Sharman v Merritt and Hatcher Ltd (1916) 475
Sharp v Avery and Kerwood (1938), CA 215
Sharpe v E T Sweeting & Son Ltd (1963) 328
Sharrod v London and North Western Rly Co (1849) 24
Shearman v Folland (1950), CA 545
Shears v Mendeloff (1914) 149
Sheldon v RHM Outhwaite (Underwriting Agencies) Ltd (1996), HL 577
Shelfer v City of London Electric Lighting Co (1895), CA 388, 537
Shelley v Paddock (1980), CA 123
Shepheard v Whitaker (1875) 441
Shepherd v Post Office (1995), CA 555
Shepherd (or Shepard or Sheppard or Sheperd) v Wakeman (1662) 137
Sheppard v Glossop Corpn (1921), CA 189
Sheridan v New Quay Co (1858) 56, 57
Shiels v Cruikshank (1953) 558
Shiffman v Grand Priory in British Realm of Venerable Order of the Hospital of St John of
    Jerusalem (1936) 398, 408
Shinjitsu Maru (No 5), The. See Marintrans AB v Comet Shipping Co Ltd, The Shinjitsu Maru
    (No 5)
Shipley v Todhunter (1836) 443
Shipping Co Uniform Inc v International Transport Workers' Federation, The Uniform Star
    (1985) 150
Shirvell v Hackwood Estates Co Ltd (1938), CA 325
Shorland v Govett (1826) 72
Short v J & W Henderson Ltd (1946), HL 504
Shrewsbury's (Countess) Case (1600) 78
Shrosbery v Osmaston (1877) 497
Sidaway v Board of Governors of the Bethlem Royal Hospital and the Maudsley Hospital
    (1985), HL 85, 232, 250
Sigurdson v British Columbia Electric Rly Co Ltd (1953), PC 285
Silcott v Metropolitan Police Comr (1996), CA 496, 499, 500
Sim v Stretch (1936), HL 439, 440
Simaan General Contracting Co v Pilkington Glass Ltd (No 2) (1988), CA: 213, 226, 344, 345
Sime v Sutcliffe Catering Scotland Ltd (1990) 507
Simkiss v Rhondda Borough Council (1982), CA 311
Simmonds v Newport Abercarn Black Vein Steam Coal Co (1921), CA 429
Simmons v Lillystone (1853) 55
Simmons v Mitchell (1880), PC 453
Simms, Re, ex p Trustee (1934), CA 65
Simon v Islington Borough Council (1943), CA 426, 582
Simpson v Norwest Holst Southern Ltd (1980), CA 573
Simpson v Savage (1856) 377
Simpson v Weber (1925), DC 74
Sindell v Abbott Laboratories (1980) 356
Singer Machine Manufacturers v Wilson (1877), HL 129
Singer Manufacturing Co v Loog (1882), HL 134
Sirros v Moore (1975), CA 103
Siveyer v Allison (1935) 108
Skopas, The. See Resolute Maritime Inc v Nippon Kaiji Kyokai, The Skopas
Skuse v Granada Television Ltd (1996), CA 439, 443
Slade v Battersea and Putney Group Hospital Management Committee (1955) 309, 323

PAGE

Slater v Clay Cross Co Ltd (1956), CA 296, 323
Slazengers Ltd v C Gibbs & Co (1916) 441
Slim v Daily Telegraph Ltd (1968), CA 445
Slipper v BBC (1991), CA 449, 450, 456
Smeaton v Ilford Corpn (1954) 400, 404, 406
Smith v Ainger (1990), CA 414
Smith v Austin Lifts Ltd (1959), HL 256
Smith v Baker & Sons (1891), HL 252, 295, 300
Smith v Chadwick (1884), HL 119, 121
Smith v Drumm (1996) 331
Smith v East Elloe RDC (1956), HL 498
Smith v Enright (1893) 527
Smith v Eric S Bush (1990), HL 117, 217, 219, 247, 301, 331
Smith v Giddy (1904) 361, 371
Smith v Leech Brain & Co Ltd (1962) 279
Smith v Leurs (1945) 193
Smith v Littlewoods Organisation Ltd (1987), HL ... 182, 194, 195, 230, 325, 380, 401, 409
Smith v London and South Western Rly Co (1870), Ex Ch 181
Smith v Manchester City Council (or Manchester Corpn) (1974), CA 544
Smith v Scott (1847) 485
Smith v Scott (1973) 379, 398
Smith v Stages (1989), HL 517
Smith v Stone (1647) 74
Smith v Tunbridge Wells Health Authority (1994) 250
Smithies v National Association of Operative Plasterers (1909), CA 150, 156
Smoker v London Fire and Civil Defence Authority (1991), HL 549
Smolden v Whitworth (1997) 294
Snook v Mannion (1982) 308
Soane v Knight (1827) 480
Sochacki v Sas (1947) 259, 404
Société Anonyme de Remorquage à Hélice v Bennetts (1911) 155
Société Commerciale de Réassurance v ERAS (International) Ltd, Re ERAS EIL appeals
    (1992), CA 575
Society of Incorporated Accountants v Vincent (1954) 132
Sole v W J Hallt Ltd (1973) 316
Solloway v McLaughlin (1938), PC 63, 65
Solomon v Frinigan (1866) 105
Somerville v Hawkins (1851) 476
Sorrell v Smith (1925), HL 145, 147, 148
South Australia Asset Management Corpn v York Montague Ltd (1996), HL 274
South Hetton Coal Co v North-Eastern News Association (1894), CA 442, 483
South Staffordshire Water Co v Sharman (1896) 50
South Wales Miners' Federation v Glamorgan Coal Co Ltd. See Glamorgan Coal Co Ltd v
    South Wales Miners' Federation
Southport Corpn v Esso Petroleum Co Ltd (1953); on appeal (1954), CA; affd sub nom
    Esso Petroleum Co Ltd v Southport Corpn (1956), HL 24, 74, 94, 379
Southwark London Borough Council v Williams (1971), CA 93
Spalding (A G) & Bros v A W Gamage Ltd (1918), CA 135
Spalding (A G) & Bros v A W Gamage Ltd and Benetfink & Co Ltd (1915), HL: 126, 130, 133
Sparham-Souter v Town and Country Developments (Essex) Ltd (1976), CA 574
Spartan Steel and Alloys Ltd v Martin & Co (Contractors) Ltd (1973), CA 180, 225, 527
Speed v Thomas Swift & Co Ltd (1943), CA 254
Speed Seal Products Ltd v Paddington (1986), CA 498
Spencer v London and Birmingham Rly Co (1836) 394
Spencer-Ward v Humberts (1995), CA 575
Spicer v Smee (1946) 369, 382, 383, 386
Spill v Maule (1869) 471, 477
Spittle v Bunney (1988), CA 560
Spring v Guardian Assurance plc (1995), HL 139, 177, 223, 267, 469, 478
Springhead Spinning Co v Riley (1868) 161, 537
Square v Model Farm Dairies (Bournemouth) Ltd (1939), CA 425
Stacy v Sherrin (1913) 94
Stafford v Conti Commodity Services Ltd (1981) 220

PAGE

Stanbury v Exeter Corpn (1905) 523, 524
Stanley v Powell (1891) 27
Stanley v Saddique (1992), CA 560
Stansbie v Troman (1948), CA 271
Stanton v Ewart F Youlden Ltd (1960) 554
Staples v West Dorset District Council (1995), CA 313
Stapley v Annetts (1969), CA 494
Stapley v Gypsum Mines Ltd (1953), HL 283, 284, 291
Statnigros v Storhaug & Partners (1953) 153
Staveley Iron and Chemical Co Ltd v Jones (1956), HL 286, 431, 515
Stein v Blake (1995), HL 593
Stennett v Hancock and Peters (1939) 343, 513
Stephen (Harold) & Co Ltd v Post Office (1978), CA 582
Stephens v Anglian Water Authority (1987), CA 180
Stephens v Avery (1988) 164, 166
Stephens v Myers (1830) 35
Stephenson v Donaldson & Sons (1981) 441
Sterman v EW & WJ Moore (a firm) (1970), CA 23
Stern v Piper (1997), CA 474
Stevens v Kitchener (1887) 476
Stevens v Midland Counties Rly Co (1854) 496
Stevenson (or Stephenson) Jordan and Harrison Ltd v MacDonald and Evans (1952), CA .. 505
Steward v Young (1870) 139
Stewart v West African Terminals Ltd (1964), CA 275
Stimpson v Wood & Son (1888), DC 556
Stockdale v Hansard (1839) 464
Stoke-on-Trent City Council v W & J Wass Ltd (1988), CA 361
Stokes v Guest, Keen and Nettlefold (Bolts and Nuts) Ltd (1968) 245
Stone v Bolton (1950), CA; on appeal sub nom Bolton v Stone (1951), HL ... 231, 324, 361,
369, 391, 406, 411
Stone (Thomas) (Shipping) Ltd v Admiralty, The Albion (1952) 581
Stone v Taffe (1974), CA 306
Storey v Ashton (1869) 518
Storey v Challands (1837) 455
Stovin v Wise (Norfolk County Council, third party) (1996), HL 15, 172, 176, 180, 182,
183, 185, 188, 189, 193,
195, 196
Strand Electric and Engineering Co Ltd v Brisford Entertainments Ltd (1952), CA 64, 65
Stratford (J T) & Son Ltd v Lindley (1965), HL 151, 153, 158
Street v Mountford (1985), HL 78
Stroud v Bradbury (1952) 91
Stuart v Bell (1891), CA 479
Stubbings v Webb (1993), HL 25, 570, 574, 577, 591
Sturges v Bridgman (1879), CA 358, 363, 365, 370, 373, 385, 386
Sturtevant Engineering Co Ltd v Sturtevant Mill Co of USA Ltd (1936) 128
Sumner v William Henderson & Sons Ltd (1963), CA 253
Sun Life Assurance Co of Canada v WH Smith & Son Ltd (1933), CA 461
Surtees v Kingston-upon-Thames Borough Council (1991), CA 243, 591
Sutcliffe v Chief Constable of West Yorkshire (1996), CA 60
Sutcliffe v Pressdram Ltd (1991), CA 456, 486
Sutcliffe v Sayer (1987), CA 331
Sutcliffe v Thackrah (1974), HL 103
Sutherland Shire Council v Heyman (1985), HC of A 177
Sutton v Population Services Family Planning Programme Ltd (1981) 549
Swadling v Cooper (1930), CA; revsd (1931), HL 284
Swain v Puri (1996), CA 321
Swan v Salisbury Construction Co Ltd (1966), PC 259
Swift v Jewsbury (1874), Ex Ch 125
Swinney v Chief Constable of Northumbria Police (1997), CA 190
Swiss Bank Corpn v Lloyds Bank Ltd (1979); revsd (1982), CA; affd (1982), HL 155
Syeds v Hay (1791) 57
Sykes v North Eastern Rly Co (1875) 557
Sykes v Sykes (1824) 127

PAGE

Sylvester v Chapman Ltd (1935) 299
Szalatnay-Stacho v Fink (1946); affd (1947), CA 465

T

T (adult: refusal of treatment), Re (1993), CA 28, 85, 93
T (a minor) (wardship: medical treatment), Re (1997), CA 86, 94
T v North Yorkshire County Council (1998), CA 522
T v T (1988) 88
Tadd v Eastwood (1985), CA 466
Taff Vale Rly Co v Jenkins (1913), HL 556
Tai Hing Cotton Mill Ltd v Liu Chong Hing Bank Ltd (1986), PC 196, 290, 533
Taittinger v Allbev Ltd (1993), CA 131, 134
Tameside and Glossop Acute Services Trust v CH (1995) 87
Tamlin v Hannaford (1950), CA 579
Tang Man Sit (personal representatives) v Capacious Investments Ltd (1996) 567
Tappenden (t/a English and American Autos) v Artus (1964), CA 57
Tarasoff v Regents of the University of California (1976) 166
Targett v Torfaen Borough Council (1992), CA 331, 333, 342
Tarrant v Rowlands (1979) 583
Tate and Lyle Industries Ltd v Greater London Council (1983), HL 104, 213, 376,
                                                                          384, 390, 391
Taylor v Chester (1869) 106
Taylor v Hall (1742) 454
Taylor v Liverpool Corpn (1939) 325
Taylor v O'Connor (1971), HL 543, 558
Taylor v Perkins (1607) 453
Taylor v Plumer (1815) 52
Taylor v Rover Co Ltd (1966) 513
Taylor v Rowan (1835) 70
Taylor v Serious Fraud Office (1997), CA; affd (1998), HL 467
Taylor v Smyth (1991) 144
Taylor (CR) (Wholesale) Ltd v Hepworths Ltd (1977) 387
Telnikoff v Matusevitch (1991), CA; on appeal (1992), HL 479, 481, 482
Temperton v Russell (1893), CA 148, 156
Tempest v Snowden (1952), CA 495
Tennent v Earl of Glasgow (1864), HL 387, 409
Tetley v Chitty (1986) 368, 379
Thaarup v Hulton Press Ltd (1943), CA 441
Thacker v Crown Prosecution Service (1997), CA 497
Thake v Maurice (1986); revsd (1986), CA 198, 212, 247
Tharpe v Stallwood (1843) 71
Thatcher v Great Western Rly Co (1893), CA 323
Thatcher v Littlejohn (1978), CA 552
Theaker v Richardson (1962), CA 444, 449
Thomas v Bath District Health Authority (1995), CA 530
Thomas v Bradbury, Agnew & Co Ltd (1906), CA 480, 483
Thomas v British Railways Board (1976), CA 306, 322
Thomas v Gulf Oil Refining Ltd (1979) 174
Thomas v National Union of Mineworkers (South Wales Area) (1986) 35, 384
Thomas v Quartermaine (1887), CA 172, 295
Thomas v Thomas (1835) 385
Thomas v Whip (1715) 534
Thomas v Wignall (1987), CA 544
Thomas and Evans Ltd v Mid-Rhondda Co-operative Society Ltd (1941), CA 404
Thompson v Anglo-Saxon Petroleum Co Ltd (1955) 514
Thompson v Bankstown Municipal Council (1953), HC of A 309, 323
Thompson v Bernard (1807) 453
Thompson v Brown Construction (Ebbw Vale) Ltd (1981), HL 573
Thompson v Clive Alexander and Partners (1992) 327
Thompson v Earthy (1951) 75
Thompson v Gibson (1841) 379
Thompson v LCC (1899), CA 595

PAGE

Thompson v Metropolitan Police Comr (1998), CA 28, 42, 528, 529
Thompson v Price (1973) 559
Thompson v Smith's Shiprepairers (North Shields) Ltd (1984) 245, 252, 569
Thompson v Ward (1953), CA 78
Thompson-Schwab v Costaki (1956), CA 363, 365, 366
Thomson (D C) & Co Ltd v Deakin (1952), CA 148, 149, 151, 152, 153
Thorley v Lord Kerry (1812) 440
Thornton v Kirklees Metropolitan Borough Council (1979), CA 422, 426
Thorpe v Brumfitt (1873) 387
Three Rivers District Council v Bank of England (No 3) (1996) 500
Three Rivers District Council v Bank of England (No 4) (1998) 499, 500
Thurston v Charles (1905) 527, 532
Tickell v Read (1773) 89
Tidy v Battman (1934), CA 236
Tilley v Stevenson (1939), CA 244, 403
Timothy v Simpson (1835) 98
Tims v John Lewis & Co Ltd (1951), CA; revsd sub nom John Lewis & Co Ltd v Tims
    (1952), HL 100, 101, 493
Tinkler v Poole (1770) 54
Tinsley v Dudley (1951), CA 316
Tinsley v Milligan (1994), HL 106
Titchener v British Railways Board (1983), HL 322
Todd v Flight (1860) 382
Todd v Hawkins (1837) 477, 479
Toff v McDowell (1993) 368, 383, 412
Tolhausen v Davies (1888); affd (1888), CA 322
Tolley v JS Fry & Sons Ltd (1931), HL 440, 444
Tolley v Morris (1979), HL 576, 577
Tolstoy Miloslavsky v United Kingdom (1995), ECtHR 436
Toogood v Spyring (1834) 472, 473, 476
Topp v London Country Bus (South West) Ltd (1993), CA 401, 409
Toronto Power Co Ltd v Paskwan (1915), PC 254
Torquay Hotel Co Ltd v Cousins (1969), CA 148, 149, 152, 158
Tournier v National Provincial and Union Bank of England (1924), CA 439, 446
Townsend v Stone Toms & Partners (1981), CA 597
Townsend v Wathen (1808) 36, 72
Trapp v Mackie (1979), HL 466
Treasure Cot Co Ltd v Hamley Bros Ltd (1950) 135
Tremain v Pike (1969) 275, 276
Tremayne v Hill (1987), CA 287
Trenberth (John) Ltd v National Westminster Bank Ltd (1979) 537
Trendtex Trading Corpn v Crédit Suisse (1982), HL 593
Trevett v Lee (1955), CA 386, 392, 393
Trollope & Sons v London Building Trades Federation (1895), CA 147
Trotman v British Railways Board (1975) 245
Trotter v Maclean (1879) 80
Truth (NZ) Ltd v Avery (1959) 482
Tsikata v Newspaper Publishing plc (1997), CA 475, 478
Tuberville v Savage (1669) 33, 36
Tucker v Newman (1839) 377
Tullay v Reed (1823) 91
Tunbridge Wells Corpn v Baird (1896), HL 76
Turner v Ambler (1847) 496
Turner v Mansfield Corpn (1975), CA 258, 262
Turner (otherwise Robertson) v Metro-Goldwyn-Mayer Pictures Ltd (1950),
    HL 89, 443, 470, 480, 482, 484
Turner v Ministry of Defence (1969), CA 548
Tuson v Evans (1840) 472
Tussaud v Tussaud (1890) 127, 128
Tuttle v Buck (1909) 114
Tutton v AD Walter Ltd (1986) 320
Twine v Bean's Express Ltd (1946); affd (1946), CA 323, 519

PAGE

U

UBAF Ltd v European American Banking Corpn, The Pacific Colcotronis (1984), CA: 125, 571
UCB Bank plc v David J Pinder plc (1998) 287
Udale v Bloomsbury Area Health Authority (1983) 211
Ultramares Corpn v Touche (1931) 117, 200
Underwood (A L) Ltd v Bank of Liverpool and Martins (1924), CA 56
Uniform Star, The. See Shipping Co Uniform Inc v International Transport Workers'
    Federation, The Uniform Star
Union Bank of Canada v Rideau Lumber Co (1902) 64
Union Credit Bank Ltd v Mersey Docks and Harbour Board (1899) 58
Union Transport Finance Ltd v British Car Auctions Ltd (1978), CA 48, 54
United Australia Ltd v Barclays Bank Ltd (1941), HL 535, 566, 567, 568
United Biscuits (UK) Ltd v Asda Stores Ltd (1997) 130
United Merthyr Collieries Co, Re (1872) 80, 81
United States of America and Republic of France v Dollfus Mieg et Cie SA and Bank of
    England (1952), HL 66, 70
Universe Tankships Inc of Monrovia v International Transport Workers Federation, The
    Universe Sentinel (1983), HL 535
Upson v London Passenger Transport Board (1947), CA; affd sub nom London Passenger
    Transport Board v Upson (1949), HL 244, 423, 427
Usill v Hales (1878) 474
Uxbridge Permanent Benefit Building Society v Pickard (1939), CA 507

V

Vacwell Engineering Co Ltd v BDH Chemicals Ltd (1971); revsd (1971), CA 277, 343
Valpy v Sanders (or Saunders) (1848) 567
Van Oppen & Co Ltd v Tredegars Ltd (1921) 60
Vancouver General Hospital v McDaniel (1934), PC 245
Vandyke v Fender (Sun Insurance Office Ltd, third party) (1970), CA 517, 600
Vasey v Surrey Free Inns (1996), CA 521
Vaughan v Ellis (1608) 137
Vaughan v Menlove (1837) 171, 237, 239
Vaughan v Roper & Co Ltd (1947), CA 254
Veal v Heard (1930) 467
Verney v Wilkins (1962) 426
Vernon v Bosley (1997), CA 204, 205
Verschures Creameries Ltd v Hull and Netherlands Steamship Co Ltd (1921), CA 566
Vicars v Wilcocks (1806) 456
Victoria Park Racing and Recreation Grounds Co Ltd v Taylor (1937), HC of A 365
Victorian Railways Comrs v Coultas (1888), PC 203
Videan v British Transport Commission (1963), CA 202, 309
Vincent v Lake Erie Transportation Co (1910) 93
Vine Products Ltd v Mackenzie & Co Ltd (1969) 131
Virgo Steamship Co SA v Skaarup Shipping Corpn, The Kapetan Georgis (1988) 225
Vizetelly v Mudie's Select Library Ltd (1900), CA 461
Vodafone Group plc v Orange Personal Communications Services Ltd (1997) 138
Vokes (C G) Ltd v Evans & Marble Arch Motor Supplies Ltd (1931), CA 127

W

W (a minor) (medical treatment), Re (1992), CA 86
W v Egdell (1990), CA 165, 166
W v Essex County Council (1998), CA 187
W v Meah (1986) 27, 34
W v Metropolitan Police Comr (1997), CA 190
Wagner v International Rly Co (1921) 202
Wagon Mound, The. See Overseas Tankship (UK) Ltd v Morts Dock and Engineering Co
    Ltd, The Wagon Mound
Wagon Mound (No 2), The. See Overseas Tankship (UK) Ltd v Miller SS Co Pty,
    The Wagon Mound (No 2)

PAGE

Wah Tat Bank Ltd v Chan Cheng Kum (1975), PC 597
Wakley v Cooke (1849) 458
Walker v Baird (1892), PC 105
Walker v Clyde and Wren (1861) 60
Walker v Northumberland County Council (1995) 209, 235, 255
Walker (John) & Sons Ltd v Henry Ost & Co Ltd (1970) 131
Walker (Peter) & Son Ltd v Hodgson (1909), CA 482
Walkley v Precision Forgings Ltd (1979), HL 574
Wallace v Newton (1982) 414
Walley v Holt (1876) 590
Wallis v Hands (1893) 77
Walsh v Ervin (1952) 390
Walsh v Holst & Co Ltd (1958), CA 261, 511
Walter v Ashton (1902) 133
Walter v Selfe (1851); affd (1852) 358, 364, 369
Walton v British Leyland (1978) 344
Waple v Surrey County Council (1998), CA 467
Ward v Chief Constable of West Midlands Police (1997), CA 495
Ward v Hertfordshire County Council (1970), CA 309
Ward v Macauley (1791) 70
Ward v Ritz Hotel (London) (1992), CA 310
Ward v Tesco Stores Ltd (1976), CA 260
Ward v Weeks (1830) 456
Ward Lock & Co Ltd v Operative Printers' Assistants' Society (1906), CA 384
Ware v Garston Haulage Co Ltd (1944), CA 393
Ware and De Freville Ltd v Motor Trade Association (1921), CA 115, 159, 441
Warner v Riddiford (1858) 39, 84, 101
Warnink (Erven) BV v J Townend & Sons (Hull) Ltd (1979), HL 117, 126, 131, 132, 135
Warren v Henlys Ltd (1948) 520
Warren v Warren (1834) 450
Warren v Warren (1996), CA 103
Wason, ex p (1869) 464
Wason v Walter (1868) 474
Wasson v Chief Constable of the Royal Ulster Constabulary (1987) 290
Watkin v Hall (1868) 458
Watkins v Birmingham City Council (1975), CA 507
Watkins v Lee (1839) 494
Watson v Buckley Osborne Garrett & Co Ltd and Wyrovoys Products Ltd (1940) 342
Watson v MacLean (1858), Ex Ch 52
Watson v Murray & Co (1955) 75, 80
Watson v M'Ewan (1905), HL 467
Watson (administrators of) v Willmott (1991) 555, 561
Watt v Hertfordshire County Council (1954), CA 234, 293
Watt v Jamieson (1954) 371
Watt v Kesteven County Council (1955), CA 422
Watt v Longsdon (1930), CA 479
Watt (or Thomas) v Thomas (1947), HL 257
Watts v Aldington (1993), CA 597
Watts v Enfield Rolling Mills (Aluminium) Ltd (1952), CA 429
Watts v Spence (1976) 125
Watts v Times Newspapers Ltd (Schilling & Lom (a firm), third party) (1997), CA 478
Waverley Borough Council v Fletcher (1996), CA 50
Wearing v Pirelli Ltd (1977), HL 428
Weaver v Commercial Process Co Ltd (1947) 600
Weaver v Ward (1616) 26, 33, 589
Webb v Beavan (1883) 452
Webb v Times Publishing Co Ltd (1960) 473, 474
Weddell v JA Pearce & Major (1988) 592
Weld-Blundell v Stephens (1920), HL 193, 456
Weldon v Times Book Co Ltd (1911), CA 461
Wellaway v Courtier (1918), DC 76
Weller & Co v Foot and Mouth Disease Research Institute (1966) 115, 225, 402
Wells v Cooper (1958), CA 241

PAGE

Wells v Smith (1914) 122
Wells v Wells (1998), HL 543, 544
Welsh v Chief Constable of the Merseyside Police (1993) 497, 580
Wenlock v Moloney (1967), CA 592
Wenman v Ash (1853) 450, 476
Wennhak v Morgan (1888), DC 70, 450
Wentworth v Wiltshire County Council (1993), CA 304, 421, 428, 584
Wershof v Metropolitan Police Comr (1978) 98, 496
West v Bristol Tramways Co (1908), CA 396, 398, 411
West v Smallwood (1838) 42
West v West (1911), CA 466
West (H) & Son Ltd v Shephard (1964), HL 549
West London Commercial Bank Ltd v Kitson (1884), CA 122
Western Counties Manure Co v Lawes Chemical Manure Co (1874) 136
Western Engraving Co v Film Laboratories Ltd (1936), CA 398, 404
Westhoughton Coal and Cannel Co Ltd v Wigan Coal Corpn Ltd (1939), CA ... 400
Westripp v Baldock (1938); affd (1939), CA 74
Westwood v Post Office (1974), HL 431
Whalley v Lancashire and Yorkshire Rly Co (1884), CA 93, 399
Whatman v Pearson (1868) 518
Wheat v E Lacon & Co Ltd (1966), HL 304
Wheatley v Lodge (1971), DC 100
Wheeler v Copas (1981) 315
Wheeler v J J Saunders Ltd (1995), CA 366, 384, 389, 413
Wheeler v Morris (1915), CA 324
Wheeler v New Merton Board Mills Ltd (1933), CA 430
Wheta v Scandlyn (1952) 81
White v Batey & Co Ltd (1892) 477
White v Blackmore (1972), CA 312, 317, 319
White v Chief Constable of South Yorkshire Police. See Frost v Chief Constable of South
    Yorkshire Police
White v Holbrook Precision Castings (1985), CA 253
White v J and F Stone (Lighting and Radio) Ltd (1939), CA 449, 472
White v Jones (1995), HL 13, 117, 198, 200, 221, 222, 248, 290
White v Mellin (1895), HL 130, 138, 139, 141
White v Morris (1852) 70
White v Riley (1921), CA 145, 155
White v St Albans City and District Council (1990), CA 320, 321
White v White (1950), CA 590
Whiteford v Hunter (1950), HL 245
Whitehouse v Jordan (1981), HL 249, 257
Whiteley Ltd v Hilt (1918), CA 48
Whiting v Hillingdon London Borough Council (1970) 304
Whitmores (Edenbridge) Ltd v Stanford (1909) 400
Whitwham v Westminster Brymbo Coal & Coke Co (1896); affd (1896), CA ... 80
Wickham Holdings Ltd v Brooke House Motors Ltd (1967); CA 48, 62
Wicks v Fentham (1791) 494
Wieland v Cyril Lord Carpets Ltd (1969) 270, 275, 277
Wilchick v Marks and Silverstone (1934) 382, 383
Wilde v Waters (1855) 60
Wilkes v Hungerford Market Co (1835) 390
Wilkins v Leighton (1932) 382
Wilkins (Fred) & Bros Ltd v Weaver (1915) 150
Wilkinson v Ancliff (BLT) Ltd (1986), CA 572
Wilkinson v Downton (1897) 36, 121, 140
Wilks (formerly infant) v Cheltenham Home Guard Motor Cycle and Light Car Club (1971),
    CA 294
Williams v Archer (1847), Ex Ch 66
Williams v Banks (1859) 497
Williams v Birmingham Battery and Metal Co (1899), CA 252
Williams v Cardiff Corpn (1950), CA 311
Williams v Humphrey (1975) 25, 31, 590
Williams v Hursey (1959), HC of A 152

PAGE

Williams v Natural Life Health Foods Ltd (1998), HL 198, 215, 219, 220, 223, 224
Williams v Peel River Land and Mineral Co Ltd (1886), CA 66
Williams (J B) Co v H Bronnley & Co Ltd (1909), CA 129
Williamson v Freer (1874) 472
Williamson v John I Thornycroft & Co Ltd (1940), CA 559
Wills v Wells (1818) 52
Willis (RH) & Son (a firm) v British Car Auctions Ltd (1978), CA 54, 58
Willson v Ministry of Defence (1991) 552
Wilsher v Essex Area Health Authority (1987), CA; revsd (1988), HL 240, 248, 262,
                                                                          268, 278, 512
Wilson, Re, ex p Vine (1878), CA 592
Wilson v Barker (1833) 70
Wilson v Hodgson's Kingston Brewery Co (1915), DC 514
Wilson v Housing Corpn (1997) 149
Wilson v Lombank Ltd (1963) 61, 62, 70
Wilson v National Coal Board (1981), HL 549
Wilson v Newberry (1871) 398
Wilson v Pringle (1987), CA 27, 31, 590
Wilson v Tyneside Window Cleaning Co (1958), CA 254
Wilson v United Counties Bank Ltd (1920), HL 592
Wilson v Waddell (1876), HL 399
Wilsons and Clyde Coal Co Ltd v English. See English v Wilsons and Clyde Coal Co Ltd
Wilts United Dairies Ltd v Thomas Robinson, Sons & Co Ltd (1957); affd (1958),
    CA 130, 140
Wing v London General Omnibus Co (1909), CA 260
Winkfield, The (1902), CA 47, 52, 70
Winnipeg Condominium Corpn No 36 v Bird Construction Co Ltd (1995), Can SC 330
Winstanley v Bampton (1943) 470, 476
Winter v Bancks (1901), DC 58
Winter v Cardiff RDC (1950), HL 255
Winterbottom v Wright (1842) 171, 340
Winterbourne v Morgan (1809) 75
Wise v Kaye (1962), CA 550
Withers v Perry Chain Co Ltd (1961), CA 233, 296
Wolverhampton New Waterworks Co v Hawkesford (1859) 426
Wombles Ltd v Wombles Skips Ltd (1977) 133
Wong (Edward) Finance Co Ltd v Johnson, Stokes and Master (1984), PC 248
Wood v Bell (1856) 49
Wood v Conway Corpn (1914), CA 388
Wood v Lane and Cleaton (1834) 39
Wood v Morewood (1841) 64, 80
Woodrup v Nicol (1993), CA 545
Woodward's Trade Mark, Re, Woodward Ltd v Boulton Macro Ltd (1915) 128
Wooldridge v Sumner (1963), CA 239, 241, 294, 297
Woollerton and Wilson Ltd v Richard Costain Ltd (1970) 537
Worlsey (E) & Co Ltd v Cooper (1939) 140
Worsfold v Howe (1980), CA 237
Wotherspoon v Currie (1872), HL 128
Woyka & Co v London and Northern Trading Co (1922), CA 123
Wren v Weild (1869) 137, 139
Wright v British Railways Board (1983), HL 540, 552
Wright v Cedzich (1930) 455
Wright v Cheshire County Council (1952), CA 245
Wright v Dunlop Rubber Co (1972), CA 344, 354
Wright v Lodge (1993), CA 265, 271
Wright v Wilson (1699) 38
Wright v Woodgate (1835) 470
Wright, Layman and Umney Ltd v Wright (1949), CA 127
Wringe v Cohen (1940), CA 366, 383
Wyatt v Hillingdon London Borough Council (1978), CA 426

PAGE

X

X v Bedfordshire County Council (1995), HL 177, 182, 183, 185, 190, 192,
228, 418, 422, 423, 426, 427
X v Y (1988) 165, 166

Y

Y (mental incapacity: bone marrow transplant) Re, (1997) 29, 88
Yachuk v Oliver Blais Co Ltd (1949), PC 237
Yarmouth v France (1887) 295
Yelland v Powell Duffryn Associated Collieries Ltd (No 2) (1941), CA; on appeal sub nom
Davies v Powell Duffryn Associated Collieries Ltd (1942), HL 553, 558
Yepremian v Scarborough General Hospital (1980) 512
Yianni v Edwin Evans & Sons (1982) 287
Youl v Harbottle (1791) 58
Young v Box & Co (1951) 519
Young v Edward Box & Co Ltd (1951), CA 323
Young v Macrae (1862) 138
Young v Percival (1974), CA 558
Young v Rankin (1934) 95, 591
Young (Edward) & Co Ltd v Holt (1947) 135
Youssoupoff v Metro-Goldwyn-Mayer Pictures Ltd (1934), CA 440, 441, 451
Yuen Kun-yeu v A-G of Hong Kong (1988), PC 176

Part I

Introduction

CONTENTS

CHAPTER   PAGE

1 The law of torts   3

Chapter 1

The law of torts

✓

SECTION I. WHAT IS A TORT?

The very word *tort* may pose a conundrum for the novice law student. Crime and contract will be terms with which he or she is already familiar, but what does tort mean? What is the law of torts about? Much ink has been spilt in attempts to define a tort with very little success. Winfield's classic definition declared:[1]

> Tortious liability arises from the breach of a duty primarily fixed by law; such duty is towards persons generally and its breach is redressable by an action for unliquidated damages.

Yet this definition does little more than purport to assist us to distinguish tort from other branches of law. Historically, in contract, for example, the duties undertaken by the parties were generally fixed by agreement. By contrast, duties in tort were imposed on all citizens. And while in crime redress was by means of punishment by the state, in tort the redress was primarily by way of an award of compensation. Today, as we shall see at the end of this chapter, even those distinctions between tort and other branches of law are sometimes blurred. Partly for this reason, what tort is about remains somewhat mysterious. Perhaps the best explanation we can offer is this. Tort is that branch of the civil law relating to obligations imposed by operation of law on all natural and artificial persons. It concerns the basic duties one person owes to another whether he likes it or not. No further, or better, attempt at defining tort will be made here, since, as Pollock rightly said:[2]

> there is ... rather too much talk about definitions. A definition, strictly speaking, is nothing but an abbreviation in which the user of the term defined may please himself ...

It is the function and purpose of the law of torts that are of greater import, and these are matters which can be explained in comparatively simple terms. What does the law of torts do?

What the law of torts does is to define the obligations imposed on one member of society to his or her fellows and to provide for compensation for harms caused by

1 Winfield *Province of the Law of Tort* (1931), p 92; and see *Clerk and Lindsell* 1-01.
2 Book review (1931) 47 LQR 588.

breach of such obligations.[3] Tort is often described as centrally concerned with loss-adjustment and judged by its success or otherwise as a compensation system. Of course many tort actions have as their objective the pursuit of monetary compensation for a loss inflicted on the plaintiff by the defendant. At the heart of the dispute is often the question of who should bear the relevant loss. Should it lie where it falls on the unfortunate plaintiff? Or is the conduct of the defendant such that the law should shift the loss to him? In the tort of negligence, and many of the torts discussed in Parts IV and V, loss adjustment is a core issue and tort's 'success' must be judged at least in part by its efficacy as a compensation system.

The law of torts protects fundamental human interests. It concerns those situations where one person's conduct causes or threatens to cause harm to the interests of others. 'Interests' may be defined as the kinds of claims, wants or desires that people seek to satisfy in life, which a civilised society ought to recognise. Not every human desire can qualify as a legally protected interest. Society must determine which of the many human interests are so fundamental that the law should recognise those interests and compensate those whose interests are violated by others. In the first edition of this work, Street's emphasis on the plaintiff's interests as opposed to the defendant's wrongdoing was perceived as radical, even bizarre.

We retain and endorse his emphasis on interests. No claim in tort can succeed, however morally reprehensible the defendant's conduct, unless the court first recognises that the harm suffered by the plaintiff involves violation of an interest sufficient to confer on the plaintiff a legal right to protection of that interest.[4] The starting point of any analysis of the law of torts must be a consideration of those rights that tort protects. It is apparent that one of the functions of the law of torts is the protection of what are popularly known as human rights. To date, tort has developed this role in piecemeal fashion. Succeeding chapters will show how case law developed civil liberties in England. The Human Rights Act 1998 will ultimately have a profound impact on the law of torts. The Act reinforces the role of torts in protecting human interests, but will also enable the courts to break free of some of the restrictions on developing protection of interests deriving from the historical origins of the common law.

SECTION 2.   HUMAN RIGHTS AND PROTECTED INTERESTS

We attempt now to identify those interests which common law has traditionally protected, to consider how a human rights analysis could alter the definition or scope of such interests and to evaluate whether interests hitherto unknown to the common law may emerge. First, a brief explanation of just what the Human Rights Act 1998 does, and does not, provide is called for.

(A)   THE HUMAN RIGHTS ACT 1998

2/10/00

The Human Rights Act 1998 is not expected to come into force until some time in 2000. Its impact must be to a large extent a matter of speculation. All that can be said with

---

3   For a very different analysis of the role of tort, Markesinis and Deakin *Tort Law* (3rd ed) contend (in Chapter 11) that tort is centrally concerned with 'accidents'.

4   See, for example, *Rogers v Rajendro Dutt* (1860) 25 JP 3; *Bradford Corpn v Pickles* [1895] AC 587, HL; *Pickering v Liverpool Daily Post and Echo Newspapers plc* [1991] 2 AC 370, HL. For an elegant analysis of the fundamental basis of the law of torts, see Cane *Anatomy of Tort Law* (1997).

certainty is that the Act will radically alter the law of torts. What follows is not a comprehensive account of the Act, but an attempt to predict how the Act may affect the law of torts in the course of the life of the current edition of this work.

Contrary to what is often said in the popular press, the Human Rights Act does not incorporate the European Convention on Human Rights into English law. The Act provides (1) that, wherever possible, primary and subordinate legislation must be interpreted in a way which is compatible with 'Convention rights'[5] and (2) that it is unlawful for any public authority to act in a way which is incompatible with a 'Convention right'.[6] 'Convention rights' mean[7] the fundamental rights and freedoms set out in Articles 2 to 12 and 14 of the Convention, Articles 1 to 3 of the First Protocol (concerning rights to property, education and free elections) and Articles 1 and 2 of the sixth Protocol (abolishing the death penalty). Reference to relevant Articles and Protocols will be made from time to time throughout this work and all the relevant Articles and Protocols are set out in full in Appendix A. Section 11 of the Act makes it crystal clear that 'Convention rights' are in addition to, not in substitution for, rights and freedoms already endorsed at common law. It may, at first glance, seem odd that no express provision of the Act appears to require that the judges develop the common law in a manner consistent with 'Convention rights'. Two factors explain that apparent omission. First, for some years now English judges have, wherever possible, sought to ensure that the common law is consistent with such rights.[8] Second, section 6 of the Act, which makes it unlawful for any public authority to act in a way incompatible with 'Convention rights' provides that courts are classified as public authorities.[9] Thus, a judge adjudicating on a claim in tort must, by virtue of section 6, consider compatibility with 'Convention rights' and ensure consistency between common law and 'Convention rights'.[10]

For the tort lawyer, the most crucial element of the Act is the provision that 'Convention rights' are directly enforceable against public authorities, and that an individual who considers that his rights have been violated can sue for damages.[11] Where an individual considers that a public authority has acted in breach of 'Convention rights', a number of rather different outcomes must be considered. First, in many cases, the self-same rights conferred by the Convention are already recognised by the law of torts. For example, Article 5 provides for a right to liberty and security and protects the citizen against arbitrary detention. The ancient tort of false imprisonment protects that same fundamental interest. A person alleging unlawful arrest by the police will not need to resort to claiming a breach of Article 5. He can perfectly well sue in false imprisonment. In determining whether that arrest was lawful, the court will be mindful of the provisions of Article 5 and the jurisprudence of the European Court of Human Rights.[12]

What if a 'Convention right' is not so well established in domestic law. Arguably privacy is not.[13] The plaintiff might then elect to bring his claim under the Act alleging

5   See s 3. For an introductory account of the Act, see Ewing 'The Human Rights Act and Parliamentary Democracy' (1999) 62 MLR 79.
6   See ss 6-8.
7   See s 1.
8   See, for example, *Rantzen v Mirror Group Newspapers* [1993] 4 All ER 975, CA; *Olotu v Home Office* [1997] 1 WLR 329, CA; *R v Chief Constable of North Wales Police, ex p AB* [1998] 3 WLR 7, CA.
9   See s 6(3)(a).
10   Otherwise the court itself acts unlawfully.
11   See ss 7-8.
12   As is already the case, well illustrated in the judgments of the Court of Appeal in *Olotu v Home Office* [1997] 1 WLR 328, CA.
13   Something very close to a tort of invasion of privacy seemed to be developing in this country, but see now *Hunter v Canary Wharf Ltd* [1997] AC 655, HL discussed post, ch 18.

breach of Article 8 which requires respect for private and family life. If he elects for a Convention remedy alone, however, he can sue under the Act only if the defendant is a *public authority*. Were we to discover that the Home Office is bugging our office, suing a government department as a public authority should be straightforward. But, what if a tabloid newspaper invades our homes splashing our private business all over its front page? It is arguable that the newspaper, too, may be classified as a public authority, for section 6(3)(b) classifies as a public authority '*any person certain of whose functions are functions of a public nature*'. State schools and universities thus clearly qualify as public bodies. So may the press, churches,[14] and charities such as the RSPCA and NSPCC.

What if the wrongdoer is an entirely private individual – let's say, a colleague who invades our privacy by persistently peering through our window and monitoring our private correspondence? In practical terms, very often, some common law remedy may be found within which to frame a cause of action which will be reinforced by reference to 'Convention rights'. The 'snooper' who peers through windows and opens mail could be liable for harassment[15] and trespass to goods.[16] If no common law remedy at all can be identified so the defendant appears to be immune from liability, Article 6 of the Convention comes into play. Article 6 grants a right that, in determination of his civil rights and obligations, everyone is entitled to a fair trial. It grants a right of access to justice. If no remedy for violation of Article 8 (right to privacy) appears to exist, the court must in effect develop a remedy, or the court acts unlawfully in failing to implement Article 8. And the UK government is in breach of the Convention in failing to provide a legal remedy, violating the citizen's right to access to justice.

Article 6 will affect the development of the law of torts in two ways. Relatively rarely, Article 6 will come into play because the common law offers no remedy for violation of a 'Convention right'. More commonly, the Article will be pleaded in order to overcome some restriction on the plaintiff's common law right. The common law recognises a right to life and freedom from bodily harm.[17] However, consider the following case. It is a well-established principle of common law that there is no duty to be a 'Good Samaritan'. An adult who stands by and does nothing to help a drowning child commits no tort as long as the child is a stranger to her. For as we shall see, pure omissions are not actionable at common law.[18] Could the child's parents argue that the absence of any obligation to rescue the child violated his right to life (under Article 2)? Will long established principles of common law have to be revisited and revised?

Finally we must note that in relation to primary legislation the courts' role remains limited by doctrines of Parliamentary sovereignty. Section 3 of the Act requires only that judges try to interpret statutes consistently with 'Convention rights'. The Act grants no power to strike down legislation. The judiciary are limited to issuing a declaration of incompatibility requiring ministers to take essentially political action to remedy the inconsistency between the domestic legislation and the European Convention.

---

14 The churches were concerned that they could be liable for breach of 'Convention rights' in upholding doctrine, for example by refusing to conduct marriage ceremonies between homosexuals. Section 13 of the Act seeks to reinforce the importance of freedom of religion.

15 See post at p 37.

16 See post at ch 4.

17 As by the provision of blanket immunity for the police; see *Osman v United Kingdom* [1999] 1 FLR 193, ECHR.

18 See post at p 182.

(B)   RIGHTS AND WRONGS

Before reviewing the kinds of interests (including 'Convention rights') protected by the common law, the relationship within the law of torts of rights and wrongs must be very briefly addressed. It is not enough to identify the kinds of interest torts protect. The kinds of wrongdoing considered sufficient to violate those interests must also be identified. Deliberate, intentional, invasion of an interest can easily be classified as demanding that the law intervene to require the defendant to compensate for the harm he has caused the plaintiff. Certain interests, however, may be so crucial to the plaintiff, and so vulnerable to accidental harm, that negligence on the part of the defendant engages his liability in tort. Exceptionally, the relationship of plaintiff and defendant or the nature of the defendant's conduct gives rise to strict liability. In such instances, the law requires the defendant to bear an absolute responsibility for protecting the plaintiff's interests. This intricate relationship between rights and wrongs is further elaborated in the next section.

(C)   INTERESTS PROTECTED BY THE LAW OF TORTS

One key issue must be flagged up here. It is not uncommon for the central question in a claim in tort to be how the law reconciles competing interests. For example, every citizen can assert a right to liberty as well as a right to freedom from deliberately inflicted physical harm. Protecting A's compelling interest in the latter may necessarily involve restriction of B's right to the former. Hence defences justifying what might otherwise constitute tortious conduct are of crucial importance. And it will be noted that nearly all 'Convention rights' are qualified and/or on occasion must be prioritised.

We look now at the kinds of interests which the law of torts protects, broadly in the order in which the relevant torts are dealt with in the body of this work.

(1)   INTENTIONAL INVASION OF PERSONAL AND PROPRIETARY INTERESTS

The protection of the person from deliberately inflicted physical harm and restriction on freedom of movement, and the protection of interests in tangible property, especially the right to non-interference with land and goods, were originally the most important concerns of the law of torts. Their importance will be recognised by dealing first with the invasion of these interests by intentional conduct: the relevant torts include interference with goods and trespass in its various forms. It is these torts which provide the foundation of the protection of 'Convention rights' to life (Article 2), to freedom from torture or degrading treatment (Article 3), to freedom from slavery (Article 4), to liberty (Article 6) and to peaceful possession of property (First Protocol).

(2)   INTERESTS IN ECONOMIC RELATIONS, BUSINESS AND TRADING INTERESTS[19]

The extensive protection afforded to individuals' interests in freedom from physical harm and in their property is not mirrored by similar protection of interests in economic and business activities. The so-called 'economic torts' remain unclear in their scope and bedevilled by their relationship with ever-changing legislation on trade union immunities. Furthermore, very real difficulties exist in reconciling protection of one individual's economic interests with the concept of free competition in a market economy. Torts in this area include deceit, passing off, interference with contractual

---

19   See P Cane *Tort Law and Economic Interests* (1996, 2nd ed).

relations, conspiracy and intimidation. 'Convention rights' would not appear to play any immediate role in these economic torts.

(3)   INTERESTS IN INTELLECTUAL PROPERTY

Interests in tangible property, land and goods are, as we shall see, well protected by the common law. Intellectual property in confidential information, copyright, and patents, poses greater problems. Much of the law in this field is statutory and interests in intellectual property generally overlap with interests in economic relations. But this is not invariably so. For example, breach of confidence, as yet an embryonic and even disputed tort, protects a patient's right to confidentiality from his doctor as much as a multinational company's right to protection of their trade secrets.

(4)   NEGLIGENT INTERFERENCE WITH PERSONAL, PROPRIETARY AND ECONOMIC INTERESTS

Protection of persons and property limited to deliberately inflicted harm would be manifestly inadequate in our complex and overcrowded world. Nor would such limited protection meet the requirements of the Human Rights Convention to safeguard life and bodily security. Since the landmark decision in *Donoghue v Stevenson* in 1932 the courts have, albeit with occasional trepidation, developed the tort of negligence as it safeguards interests in physical safety. Indeed there are those who now argue that personal injuries law has become '... a separate and self-contained area of the law'.[20] For the present though, principles analogous to those defining the duty to avoid inflicting personal injury apply to actual material damage to property.[1] Defining the boundary between such material damage and 'pure' economic loss has proved problematic.[2] Just as protection of economic interests from deliberate harm has proved problematic, so have the judges adopted a cautious and unpredictable approach to protecting economic interests from negligently inflicted harm.

(5)   FURTHER PROTECTION OF PERSONAL AND PROPRIETARY INTERESTS

Personal and proprietary interests rank so highly in the order of priority of interests protected by the law of torts, and within the hierarchy of 'Convention rights' that further torts have emerged offering protection for those interests against conduct which is not necessarily, or cannot be proved to be, either intentional or negligent. There are torts of ancient origin such as nuisance and, later, the rule in *Rylands v Fletcher*. These highlight the importance vested by the common law in the landowner's interest in his enjoyment of his property, a right the common law perhaps prioritised over rights to freedom from injury. The action for breach of statutory duty represents the common law's response to parliamentary intervention usually to improve standards of public health and personal safety. More importantly and recently strict liability for injuries caused by defective and dangerous goods has been introduced into English law at the behest of the European Community.

---

20   Ibid at p 9.
1   Ibid ch 2 questions the assumption on which damage to property is regarded as other than economic loss. But note the potential impact of the First Protocol (right to peaceful enjoyment of property).
2   See *Murphy v Brentwood District Council* [1990] 2 All ER 908, HL.

(6) REPUTATION

The law of torts has long protected an individual's interest in his reputation via the torts of libel and slander. To some extent the developing tort of breach of confidence also fulfils this function. Pressure for a tort of invasion of privacy also arises in part from the perceived defects in the torts of libel and slander. Protection of reputation and privacy, however, provoke a classic case of how to reconcile competing interests. Freedom of speech is equally asserted as a fundamental interest. Your interest in protecting your reputation and/or privacy may on occasion inhibit our freedom of speech.

(7) DUE PROCESS

A right to protection from malicious abuse of the judicial process is recognised in the tort of malicious prosecution and its ancillary tort of abuse of process. Now it seems that a tort to prevent abuse of the administrative process is in its early infancy.

(8) MISCELLANEOUS INTERESTS: 'CONVENTION RIGHTS'

The antiquity and somewhat piecemeal development of torts means that there are a number of residual torts which defy classification. More importantly, the question arises of whether the principles developed by the common law offer adequate coverage of 'Convention rights'. Does the Convention recognise interests unknown to the common law? The most obvious example of a possible lacuna in the law of tort has already been noted: the protection of privacy guaranteed in the Convention by Article 8. However privacy is also an excellent example of how dangerous it may be to look at any alleged human right in isolation. Article 10 establishes a right to freedom of expression, to hold opinions and disseminate information. The media and others fear that a right to privacy, if developed without proper safeguards, could undermine that latter right. Unscrupulous individuals whose conduct adversely affects others' interests would seek to use Article 8 to prevent public knowledge of their own activities.

Article 8 may be the most obvious example of a 'Convention right' set to take root in the common law in the next century when the Human Rights Act comes into force. Other 'Convention rights', too, have no directly analogous common law protection. Article 12 protects the right to marry and found a family. Article 9 protects freedom of thought and religion. Article 11 protects freedom of assembly. Just how such rights will find the requisite protection and just how appropriate remedies will develop will be crucial to the development of the law of torts in the coming decade.

(9) 'EUROTORTS'

In addition to seeking to come to terms with the impact of the European Convention on Human Rights on the law of torts, the influence of European Community Law on the development of this branch of the law must be noted. The European Court of Justice has held that certain breaches of Community law create rights which national courts must protect and that they must devise remedies for violation of these rights.[3] Where a provision of Community law has direct effect, breach of such a rule has been classified by the English courts as a breach of statutory duty.[4] However in *Francovich v Italian Republic*[5] the European Court of Justice held that failure by a member state to implement

---

3   Case 127/73: *Belgische Radio en Televisie v SV SABAM* [1974] ECR 51.
4   *Garden Cottage Foods Ltd v Milk Marketing Board* [1984] AC 130, HL; discussed post at 424.
5   Case C-6 and 9-90: [1993] 2 CMLR 66. See Craig (1997) 113 LQR 67.

a directive from the Community designed to protect the interests of particular individuals gave rise to a claim in damages. The form of the remedy was for national courts to define. How such a 'Eurotort' fits into the classification of torts within the common law remains to be fully worked out.[6] What is clear beyond doubt, however, is that students of torts cannot ignore European law, nor keep the common law and European law in separate pigeon holes.

SECTION 3. ISSUES COMMON TO ALL TORTS

Emphasis on the new, especially the impact of the Human Rights Act, must not obscure the fact that law of torts has an ancient history within the common law. In most branches of English law the effect of historical accidents and procedural requirements has often been to obstruct orderly and scientific exposition; this is especially true of torts where the sources, until very recent times, are to be found mainly in common law and not in statute. The difficulties in tort are magnified by the fact that the situations where clashes of interests occur have been continually increasing and taking on new forms, with the result that the development and expansion of the law has been called for.

In the nineteenth century railways, and in the twentieth motor vehicles, have had a great impact on the law relating to accidents. Broadcasting and television have necessitated changes in the law of defamation, and in the future satellite broadcasting, cable television, and pre-eminently the internet, will no doubt occasion more. Pirating of tapes, both sound and video, is now posing new issues in economic torts. The complexities of modern industrial organisation, trade unions, company conglomerates, induce reactions in tort law from judges and Parliament alike. More involved methods of manufacture and marketing of goods have been factors influencing the introduction of strict liability for defective goods; relationships are infinitely more diverse than when the maker of goods customarily used to sell them directly to the person who used them.

In the light of these considerations it would not be surprising, therefore, if the law of torts has in some instances aims other than protecting the interests of, and compensating for (or even preventing the recurrence of), harms sustained by private individuals. Occasionally, the effect of the law of torts is to aid the administration of the criminal law (as with the former rule that prosecutions for felony had to precede an action in tort on the same facts) or to punish a wrongdoer (eg by the award of exemplary damages[7]). These deviations are, however, justifiable, or at least explicable on historical or other grounds. Thus they need not prevent our accepting that the primary aim of the law of torts is to compensate those who have suffered harm through the invasion of certain of their interests occasioned by the conduct of others.[8]

Three issues are common, then, to all cases in tort.

1   What interests does the law of torts protect?
2   Against what general types of conduct, malicious, intentional, negligent, or accidental, are these several interests protected?
3   When will conduct of a defendant, which would normally be a tort in accordance with points 1 and 2 above, not subject him to liability because there is some special circumstance which requires an exception to the general rule? Thus, to arrest another is ordinarily a tort, but a police officer, or even a private person, may in certain circumstances be authorised to make an arrest, whereupon he will have a defence

---

6   See further *Clerk & Lindsell* 1-03 to 1-04.
7   See p 527ff, post.
8   For another view, see Williams 'The Aims of the Law of Tort' (1951) CLP 137.

to an action in tort. Many defences are common to most and perhaps all torts; these are often styled general defences. Examples of these general defences are consent, statutory authority and judicial act. For convenience, these defences will be discussed in the part of the book dealing with intentional interference with persons and property, but it must be firmly grasped that they are capable of being defences to torts other than those examined in that part.

(A)   A LAW OF TORT OR A LAW OF TORTS?

A discussion of the question whether there is a law of tort or a law of torts is thus rendered superfluous. It is inconsistent with the authorities to contend that the infliction of unjustifiable harm is always a tort. On the other hand, there is no fixed catalogue of circumstances which alone and for all time mark the limit of what are torts. There is no problem peculiar to the law of torts here. Certain situations have been held to be torts and will continue to be so in the absence of statutory repeal (similarly, others have been held not to be torts, and courts upon which those decisions are binding will follow them). These fundamental points are also often camouflaged behind the Latin maxims *damnum sine injuria* and *injuria sine damno*, which (not because of their aid to understanding, but because the student may meet them elsewhere) must be shortly explained. *Damnum sine injuria* merely means that one may have suffered damage and yet have no action in tort; in short, the damage is not to an interest protected by the law of tort. *Injuria sine damno* is a shorthand version of the rule that some interests are so important that their violation is an actionable tort without proof of damage.

(B)   MALICE OR MOTIVE

Likewise it is unprofitable to dwell here on the importance of motive or malice. It follows from what has been said that an act, even though it is malicious, will not be a tort unless the interest which it violates is protected by some tort. On the other hand, if the interest interfered with is rated so low in the hierarchy of tort-protected interests that only malicious invasions are forbidden, that will be a case where malice will be essential to liability: which these are the reader will discover as he or she progresses through the book.

The catalogue of torts is very much more extensive than it was, say, 200 years ago. This expansion has been mainly the work of the judges, in whose handling of the precedents one may detect the same characteristics as are found in other branches of the law: logic and the use of analogy; appropriate, though imprecise, reflection of contemporary social and economic attitudes; recognition of the guiding (and sometimes cramping) effects of history and the like.

(C)   'GHOSTS FROM THE PAST': FORMS OF ACTION

Until the passing of the Common Law Procedure Act 1852 and the Judicature Act 1875 a plaintiff could only sue in tort if he brought his cause of action within a recognised form of action – ie one for which some particular writ of summons was available. Although the forms of action are now abolished, many old cases cannot be understood without some knowledge of forms of action.[9] Moreover, classifications of torts derive from the various writs, so that rules worked out under them have necessarily been the jumping-off place for any growth in the law of torts which has taken place since. Many seemingly arbitrary divisions between one tort and another today are explained only by reference to the forms of action. Thus, the writ of trespass lay only for direct injuries; the form of action known as action on the case developed separately for indirect injuries: it will be seen that even now trespass is not committed where the injury is indirect.[10]

A plaintiff does not have to *plead* a tort of negligence, trespass or whatever. In his pleading he merely sets out the relevant facts. Torts 'overlap' when on those facts he might have succeeded by contending at trial that they satisfied the requirements of either tort. To state, for example, that the plaintiff might have succeeded had he relied on nuisance rather than on negligence means that if the plaintiff had argued that the facts proved satisfied all the requirements of the tort of nuisance he would have succeeded even though those facts did not contain all the elements of the tort of negligence. The plaintiff's error will be one of oral argument, not of pleading, except when he fails to plead an allegation of fact which, although not material in negligence, would have been requisite for nuisance. Strictly speaking, a judge could find for the plaintiff merely by holding that, on the facts proved, there was a tort. But, given the splitting up into compartments of the law of torts, he will ordinarily decide that the plaintiff wins because the defendant has committed some specific tort. The law does not say that intentionally and carelessly inflicted harm will be tortious in certain circumstances. Instead, it defines the limits of each tort, many of which overlap – for example, the same facts could be negligence, nuisance and *Rylands v Fletcher* – and says to the plaintiff: 'You win if you establish facts which satisfy the definitions of any one of those torts'. With regard to any particular decided case, the student is then concerned to know, not only that the plaintiff has succeeded on certain facts, but also which tort has been committed, for he or she then learns the elements of that tort. Normally a court cannot be expected to find for a litigant on the basis of arguments which he has not advanced in court. If the facts pleaded constitute nuisance but not negligence he can hardly complain at losing when he fails to argue before the court that the tort of nuisance has been committed.

SECTION 4.   GENERAL ISSUES AND THE LAW OF TORTS

(A)   CONFLICT BETWEEN CERTAINTY AND JUSTICE

The conflict between the demands of certainty and justice is a recurrent theme in case law. The claims of certainty are less pressing in the case of the law of torts than in some other branches – for example, the law of property. The purchaser of land must be assured that the law on the faith of which he acquires a good title is not liable to change; it is less important that the law should settle precisely and for all time, say, the limits of liability of health authorities for harm caused to their patients. Yet, the development of some torts has been seriously affected by the judicial urge for that certainty which is believed by many to result from making rigid categories. The courts, for example, once thought fit to divide entrants on to land into three rigid categories – invitees, licensees and trespassers – in order to determine the duty of occupiers to them in respect of their personal safety, with the result that in 1957 the Occupiers' Liability Act had to be passed

9   Williams and Hepple *Foundations of the Law of Tort* ch 2.
10   See ch 5 post.

in order to clear up the confusion that this method had brought about.[11] As we shall see, too, the judicial will to introduce predictable rules defining liability for economic loss has to some extent been undermined by a judicial desire to allow for 'hard cases'.[12]

(B)   JUDICIAL CAUTION IN RESPECT OF NON-MATERIAL HARMS

Damages in many torts cannot be fixed with mathematical precision: the problem, say, of calculating damages in the tort of false imprisonment is different entirely from that of measuring damages in an action for breach of contract based on failure to perform a contract for the sale of goods. The courts have properly been on their guard to restrain gold-digging actions. Sometimes, they have perhaps been excessively wary, and later courts have had to overrule earlier decisions; for example, the courts at first refused to recognise nervous shock as a head of damage, and even today seek to place limits on recovery for such psychiatric harm, fearful of imposing open-ended liability on the tortfeasor.[13]

(C)   THE JUDGES AND *LAISSEZ-FAIRE*

Much of the law relating to economic transactions is only understood if the implied judicial acceptance of laissez-faire is considered. This is merely one facet of the individualism of the law of torts, especially in the nineteenth century, and is an influence which still persists, although less pervasively, in the face of the modern tendency towards collectivism.[14]

(D)   LIMITS OF THE EFFECTIVENESS OF THE LAW OF TORTS

The law of torts is essentially practical. Judges have little patience with trivial claims; for example, they may deny a remedy by way of trespass to the person for mere touching.[15] They recognise the limits of the wrongs which the law is capable of redressing, however morally reprehensible they may be; avarice, brutal words, ingratitude, for instance, are not dealt with by the law of torts. Along with this is a judicial dread of a flood of actions. For this reason the courts have so far been reluctant to allow claims for negligently inflicted foreseeable economic loss where the range of claimants as a result of one incident might be large.[16]

(E)   LOSS DISTRIBUTION

The traditional approach of the law of torts has been merely to ask whether a loss which B has suffered should be shifted to A. If A were at fault, the answer would usually be to shift that loss from innocent B to wrongdoer A. Many judges – for instance Viscount Simonds 20 years ago, and Lord Diplock more recently – say that this is indeed the

---

11 See ch 15 post.
12 See for example *White v Jones* [1995] 1 All ER 691, HL discussed post at p 222ff. See also Murphy 'Expectation Losses, Negligent Omissions and the Tortious Duty of Care' [1996] CLJ 43.
13 As in *White v Chief Constable of South Yorkshire Police* [1999] 1 All ER 1, HL.
14 See generally Cane *Tort Law and Economic Interests* (1996, 2nd edn).
15 See *Collins v Wilcock* [1984] 1 WLR 1172 discussed post.
16 See ch 12 post.

only judicial function in the law of torts. There is, however, another view: by spreading the loss from an individual victim to many who benefit from an activity that has caused it, the loss is more easily borne. The employer whose workman is injured can spread the loss through raising the price of his product. The same argument applies where his product injures a consumer. This principle of loss distribution is seen in the firm acceptance of vicarious liability: that an employer is answerable for the torts committed by those who work for him. It is the reason why courts have rejected the argument that if a manufacturer has a contractual liability to X he cannot have a tortious liability to Y; the manufacturer is today answerable to the eventual user of his carelessly made defective goods.

This notion of loss distribution is reinforced by insurance.[17] The employer or manufacturer or vehicle owner can readily insure (and indeed is often compelled to do so) against the risk of his negligently inflicting harm on third parties. He pays the premium which can be reflected in the price mechanism or result in all those who are in the same class of insured persons paying premiums reflecting the damages which insurers have to meet. Some judges overtly acknowledge that judges are the readier to find negligence, or to make high compensatory awards, when they know that the damages will be paid by an insurance company.[18] It must be said that other judges take notice of insurance in order to refuse an extension of tort boundaries. For example, the Law Lords have refused to make car owners vicariously liable whenever members of their family have negligently caused accidents, and other judges have refused to allow claims for widespread economic losses on the ground that insurance companies have fixed their premiums on the assumption that such liabilities did not exist and would therefore not be covered by their insurance policies.

(F)   DETERRENCE

The imposition of tort liability operates not simply to transfer the relevant loss from victim to tortfeasor but also to deter the tortious conduct in question. Put at its simplest the more tort claims that are brought against a careless driver the higher his insurance premiums will rise. Imposing strict liability for breaches of statutory duties on employers and for the manufacture of defective products on producers encourages maintenance of the highest standards to avoid the economic cost of liability. But the operation of deterrence in torts has its problems. In many instances the tortfeasor's conduct is in no sense 'calculated negligence'. For deterrence to be effective the courts must ensure 'tort does not pay'. Extension of the availability of exemplary damages is one means to ensure that end but the price for that may be to confuse the functions of tort and criminal law.[19] Moreover, judges are on occasion cautious about invoking principles of deterrence, fearful they will lead to over-cautious, defensive conduct. This concern is particularly evident in medical litigation despite the fact that hard evidence of defensive medicine is scanty.

17   See *Cane* ch 9; Stapleton 'Tort, Insurance and Ideology' (1995) 58 MLR 520.
18   See *Murphy v Brentwood District Council* [1990] 2 All ER 908 at 923 (per Lord Keith), HL.
19   See further Law Commission Consultation Paper No 132 *Aggravated, Exemplary and Restitutionary Damages* (1993).

(G) ECONOMICS AND LAW

Much academic interest has been engendered by economic analysis of law.[20] The law is criticised and evaluated on the basis of criteria of economic efficiency. So in the context of torts the crucial issue becomes whether the operation of the particular tort is cost effective.[1] The principal objectives should not be to eliminate all damage but to deter conduct resulting in damage where the cost of accident prevention is less than the cost of the accident occurring. On such criteria any change from negligence-based liability to strict liability would have to depend on proof that the total additional costs to the potential defendants, additional precautions, insurance and so on did not exceed the total cost to individuals of the risk created by the enterprise. Concepts of fairness and justice can be relevant only if susceptible to being assigned economic value.

Economic analysis is a useful tool to attain an understanding of the operation of certain torts, in particular negligence and product liability. It offers a measure by which our often confused system of compensation law may be judged and found wanting. Economic analysis can never be an all-embracing explanation of the objective of the law of torts, nor have English judges expressly relied on academic exposition of economic analysis when making law.[2] Economic efficiency is simply one of the several and sometimes contradictory objectives of tort. Tort law does not reflect the market-place and efficiency must always be subordinated to justice to individuals.

SECTION 5. TORT AND OTHER BRANCHES OF LAW

For some writers the juridical divisions between torts and other areas of the common law – principally the law of contract and the law of restitution – have become so blurred that they prefer not to talk of three separate branches of the common law but, instead, of a general law of obligations.[3] Historically, contract law alone was concerned with the obligation to fulfil undertakings voluntarily made (so long as good consideration had been provided). By contrast, as we have seen, the obligation underlying torts is one to refrain from violating another's legally recognised rights and interests. Finally, with its roots in Roman Law, restitution concerns the obligation to reverse unjust enrichment. While obligations lawyers recognise that it is possible to distinguish these three areas of law in this way, they contend that it is only possible to do so in broad terms. They believe that there are too many areas of overlap (in terms of the bases of damages awarded and the sources of the obligations) for this distinction to be worthwhile. For example, the burgeoning tort law associated with voluntary assumptions of responsibility stemming from the decision in *Hedley Byrne & Co v Heller & Partners Ltd*,[4] is seen by some to undermine the cardinal principles that only contractual obligations are created by the parties themselves and that tortious obligations are imposed by rules of law.

---

20 For a general introduction to economic analysis see P Burrows and C G Veljanowski *Readings in the Economic of Law and Regulation* (1984).
1 Calabresi *The Cost of Accidents* (1970); Posner *The Economic Analysis of Law* (3rd edn, 1987); Posner *Tort Law-Cases and Economic Analysis* (1982) illustrates the application of economic analysis in case law in the USA.
2 Although they do take economic efficiency into account in determining the limits of liability for negligence; see in particular *Stovin v Wise* [1996] AC 923, HL. See post on the limits of liability for economic loss.
3 See Cane *The Anatomy of Tort Law* (1997) pp 182-196; Cooke and Oughton *The Common Law of Obligations* (1992).
4 [1964] AC 465, HL. See also *White v Jones*, supra; *Henderson v Merrett Syndicate* [1994] 3 All ER 506, HL.

There are also other areas of overlap that persuade such writers that it is better to talk in terms of a general law of obligations. For instance, both contract and tort concern awards of damages for harm done (whether broken promises or broken legs),[5] while contract and restitution seek to compensate for benefits conferred.[6] At the same time, both tort and restitution can operate purely by virtue of rules of law.[7] In consequence of these juridical connections, the argument in favour of reconceptualising the common law in terms of a law of obligations is not without considerable force. Nonetheless, we believe that the clearest grasp of the principles, aims and objectives of tort law, together with an appreciation of its distinctiveness in terms of the range of interests it protects, may best be derived from its exposition in isolation from the law of contract and the law of restitution.

Finally, it should be noted that certain types of conduct simultaneously constitute both a crime and a tort; thus the thief who steals your watch commits both the crime of theft and the tort of conversion. The function of criminal law is to protect the interest of the public at large (or of the state), whereas the primary aim of the law of torts is to protect the interests of individuals rather than to punish certain categories of wrongdoer.

5   Furthermore, while the measure of damages in contract was once distinctively that of 'expectation loss', this has begun to feature also in the law of tort: see *White v Jones*, supra. Sea also Murphy 'Expectation Losses, Negligent Omissions and the Tortious Duty of Care' (1996) 55 CLJ 43.
6   In contract, if A builds B a fence for which B fails to pay, B is in breach of contract. If the benefit is conferred extra contractually, however, the action will lie in restitution (eg, *Greenwood v Bennett* [1973] QB 195, CA: A, believing the car he bought from a thief to be his own, effected several improvements upon it; B, the true owner, to whom the car had to be returned was liable to A in respect of his unjust enrichment in the form of those car improvements).
7   Occasionally, contractual obligations are imposed by rules of law – eg, the duty to perform a service with reasonable care imposed by s 13 of the Supply of Goods and Services Act 1982. But these obligations are imposed only within the pre-existing framework of reciprocal, voluntary obligations.

Part II

Intentional invasions of interests in person and property

CONTENTS

CHAPTERS		PAGE
2	Intentional torts today	23
3	Intentional torts to the person	30
4	Goods	44
5	Land	73
6	Defences to intentional torts to the person and property	82

Chapter 2

Intentional torts today

The examination of the rules of the various torts will begin with a discussion of those torts which effect an intentional interference with interests in the person and in property. Most of the torts examined in this Part are forms of trespass: the separate tort of negligence will be examined in Part IV. Before proceeding to a detailed consideration of these various torts, we may usefully consider three matters of general importance: the relationship of trespass to negligence; the sense in which, in trespass, an intentional act on the part of the defendant is required, and, most importantly, the context in which intentional torts, in particular trespass, remain relevant today.

SECTION I. TRESPASS AND NEGLIGENCE[1]

Compensation for injuries to the person and to property was first given by the courts from at least the thirteenth century onwards. By this time writs of trespass were in common use. A suit in trespass could succeed only where the interference was 'direct'; the action on the case was developed for injuries not 'directly' inflicted. The Court of Appeal has held that it is still not enough to set out in the writ the facts and the relief or remedy sought – the writ must also state the cause of action.[2] An allegation of trespass will still fail if the act of the defendant is not direct,[3] although, of course, some other right of action in tort may lie.

Until the judgment of Lord Denning MR in *Letang v Cooper*[4] (in 1965) one could say that trespass and negligence overlapped in that both might be available where direct injuries were sustained as a result of non-accidental conduct. Nevertheless, trespass is properly addressed under the heading of 'intentional invasions' because, in practice, the separate tort of negligence is almost always relied on if the conduct of the defendant is negligent, not intentional, for the following reasons.

1   Whatever its history, trespass in its modern context whether to the person, goods or land, has come to be the means by which the common law protects the citizen from deliberate violation of his fundamental rights to security of his person and property.

---

1   See Trindade (1971) 20 ICLQ 706.
2   *Sterman v E W & W J Moore Ltd* [1970] 1 QB 596, [1970] 1 All ER 581, CA.
3   For the meaning of 'direct' in the various forms of trespass, see pp 33, 73, post.
4   [1965] 1 QB 232, CA.

2   A claim based on negligence is not affected by any doubt there may be whether the injury is direct.

3   The writ of trespass did not lie against an employer for the torts of his employees.[5]

However, there may still be particular cases where a plaintiff perceives some advantage to be gained from styling his claim trespass rather than negligence, even though the essence of the claim is that another's carelessness caused him injury. Relying on the historical precedents that injury resulting from *direct* applications of force fall within the ambit of trespass to the person, the plaintiff may seek to avoid some obstacle fatal to a claim in the modern tort of negligence. It may be that substantively in trespass a plaintiff does not need to prove that the defendant owed him a duty of care,[6] merely that he was careless as to the risk of direct injury to someone. It is impossible to determine the issue with any certainty because in claims for 'negligent trespass' the courts have not clarified whether 'negligent' means simply careless, or such conduct as would give rise to an action in negligence. In practice, examples of careless conduct causing direct injury which would not give rise to a duty of care are hard to find today. Consider the following examples. (1) A party is out in a country park, shooting game. The defendant's eyesight is poor and she shoots wildly, injuring a fellow 'sportsman' some yards ahead of her. Proving a duty to avoid injury to her fellow will not be problematic. (2) Aware of her fallibility, the defendant removes herself from the crowd, again shooting wildly, she injures an abandoned child who has fallen asleep hidden in the undergrowth. There may be no duty to the child in such circumstances, but, however inept her shooting, is the defendant in the latter case in any sense careless? Trespass requires proof of either intention or negligence on any analysis. A claim does not lie (at any rate in modern times) on simple proof of direct injury.[7]

A second possible substantive advantage to be gained from suing for negligent trespass, rather than in the tort of negligence, relates to the principles governing remoteness of damage in negligence.[8] Even where carelessness is proved, in the tort of negligence the defendant is only responsible for injuries or harm of a kind reasonably foreseeable by him. If the defendant ought only to have foreseen a risk of damage to

---

5   *Sharrod v London and North Western Rly Co* (1849) 4 Exch 580. Nevertheless, under the old writ system an action on the case would have lain against the master even for the intentional wrongdoing of a servant: *Seymour v Greenwood* (1861) 7 H & N 355; *Bayley v Manchester, Sheffield and Lincolnshire Rly Co* (1873) LR 8 CP 148, Ex Ch. Although then, Lord Tucker accurately states in *Esso Petroleum Co Ltd v Southport Corpn* [1956] AC 218 at 244,[1955] 3 All ER 864 at 873, HL that trespass does not lie against the servant's master, this does not mean that the master can only be sued if the servant's conduct constitutes negligence, an action derived from the old action on the case will lie against the master where an act committed by his servant in the course of his employment, although it does not constitute negligence, does constitute an intentional trespass. This distinction between trespass and negligence is therefore of little importance since the abolition of the forms of action eg *National Coal Board v J E Evans & Co (Cardiff) Ltd and Maberley Parker Ltd* [1951] 2 KB 861, [1951] 2 All ER 310, CA, and see p 26, post. This same difference may give trespass an advantage over negligence. Suppose that a trespass is committed in circumstances which humiliate or insult the plaintiff but he suffers no other damage. No action in negligence would lie but under the rules about aggravated damages in trespass (p 527, post) that damage would be recoverable in trespass; see *Fogg v McKnight* [1968] NZLR 330.

There is at least another minor difference. Trespass is actionable per se; in negligence damage must be proved. If, therefore, there is an interval between the wrongful act and the occurrence of damage, an action in trespass may be time-barred before one of negligence; cf *Roberts v Read* (1812) 16 East 215.

6   As to the definition of 'duty of care' see post at p 171 et seq.

7   *Fowler v Lanning* [1959] 1 QB 426.

8   See post at p 275 et seq.

the plaintiff's goods by impact, he is not liable if in the event his carelessness results in damage by fire.[9] Trespass is actionable per se and generally all the damage actually ensuing from the defendant's unlawful act are recoverable.[10]

Nonetheless fascinating though academic debate may be on the substantive advantages of negligent trespass, where trespass is preferred to negligence the reason will generally be to gain some procedural advantage. In *Fowler v Lanning*[11] the plaintiff in his statement of claim alleged simply that the defendant shot the plaintiff seeking to avoid having to give particulars (details) of either intention or negligence on the part of the defendant and arguing that in trespass the burden of disproving intention or carelessness in causing direct injury fell on the defendant. Diplock J proffered an elegant analysis of the development of the torts of trespass and negligence concluding that the onus of proving negligence lies with the plaintiff regardless of whether he calls his claim trespass or negligence.

Diplock J overtly sought to ensure that the plaintiff could not gain an unfair advantage by resurrecting the heritage of distinctions based on the old forms of action. Any judge's instinct will be that if a plaintiff is the victim of carelessness he should succeed in the tort of negligence or fail. He will strive to deny the continuance of different rules in trespass when the effect would be to give a remedy in trespass for careless conduct in circumstances where an action in negligence would fail. What remains uncertain is how far a judge will feel free to attain his objective when to do so entails ignoring the historical origins and basis of trespass.

In *Letang v Cooper* the facts were as follows.[12]

> The defendant negligently drove his Jaguar on an hotel's grass car park over the legs of the plaintiff who was sunbathing. More than three years later, the plaintiff sued the defendant. Rules on limitation of actions[13] provide that actions for 'negligence, nuisance or breach of duty' are barred after three years and other tort actions are barred after six years. The plaintiff relied on trespass in an effort to prevent her action from being time-barred.

Naturally the Court of Appeal did not wish to reach the absurd conclusion that trespass would still lie, although negligence would not. Lord Denning MR and Danckwerts LJ held that the distinction between trespass and case is obsolete; that there is no overlap of trespass and negligence; if the act is intentional it is trespass and not negligence; if the act is negligent, it is negligence and not trespass. Diplock LJ accepted that trespass could still be committed negligently, but expressly refrained from considering whether there were any substantive differences between negligent trespass and negligence. He argued that it did not matter *how* the plaintiff described his cause of action. If the essence of the complaint was breach of a duty of care the rules relating to negligence applied. Lord Denning gave another ground for ruling that the action was statute barred. He maintained that the phrase 'breach of duty' in the Limitation Act embraced intentional trespass as well as negligence. That argument has been decisively rejected by the House of Lords in *Stubbings v Webb*.[14] Nonetheless *Letang v Cooper* illustrates the judicial policy to avoid overlap of trespass and negligence. Yet even today we cannot

---

9   *The Wagon Mound* [1961] AC 388, [1961] 1 All ER 404, PC.
10 Consider the facts of *Williams v Humphrey* (1975) Times, 20 February. The plaintiff recovered in trespass when he suffered a serious ankle injury after the defendant pushed him into a swimming pool. In negligence would he have had to have shown that that kind of injury was foreseeable?
11 [1959] 1 QB 426.
12 [1965] 1 QB 232, [1964] 2 All ER 929, CA.
13 See post ch 30.
14 [1993] AC 449, [1993] 1 All ER 322, see post at p 570. The Law Commission has issued proposals to resolve some of the more ludicrous aspects of the rules of limitation: See Law Commission Consultation Paper No 151, *Limitation of Actions*.

conclusively assert that trespass has no relevance when negligent conduct is relied on.

SECTION 2.   INTENTION AND TRESPASS

The mental state of the doer of an act is often important in tort. It is essential to distinguish motive, intention, negligence, accident, and involuntariness. A voluntary act may be regarded as a muscular contraction or relaxation that is not effected under compulsion. In order, however, to determine whether a tort has been committed intentionally, one must ask: what constitutes for the purpose of the particular tort an invasion of the interest of the plaintiff, and then whether the defendant, in doing this act, desired that invasion as a consequence. There is, however, one refinement of this which causes difficulties. If in the circumstances he had knowledge that his conduct was substantially certain to result in that act (not merely that he might have foreseen the result) his act would still be deemed to be intentional. Consequences ulterior to those consequences which constitute the tortious invasion of the interest of the plaintiff may be desired by the defendant. For example, a defendant may disable the plaintiff in order to prevent him from competing against him in a race; when, as in battery, the tort itself is concerned with the intentional striking, those desired consequences more remote than the striking itself may be called 'motive'. 'Motive' is also properly used to describe the emotion which prompts the defendant to commit the act, for example, rage, hatred or jealousy. An act is negligent when a reasonable person would have foreseen that it would lead to the particular invasion of the plaintiff's interest which constitutes that tort. There are some torts where there may be a liability for acts that are neither intentional nor negligent, for accidental acts. Yet, in such cases, although the doer neither intended nor ought to have foreseen the consequences he must have done the act: there must be a muscular reaction which is something more than a reflexive one, one which is not effected under compulsion.

If a man throws a stone at a woman, his trespass to her person is intentional; that he threw it because she had jilted him would be immaterial in determining his liability in trespass – that would be his motive. If he did not throw the stone for the purpose of hitting her but ought to have foreseen that it was likely that the stone would hit her, his act would be unintentional but nevertheless negligent. If the stone hit her solely because it rebounded off a tree at which he had thrown it his conduct would be voluntary, the hit would be accidental. But if, while he was holding the stone in his hand, a third party seized his arm and by twisting it compelled him to release his hold on it, whereupon it fell on the woman, his conduct would be involuntary and could never give rise to liability on his part.

That trespass (and the rules are the same whether it be trespass to person, land, or goods) may be committed either intentionally or negligently, and that it cannot be committed involuntarily[15] is plain – but what about the non-negligent and unintentional act. The early common lawyers were not interested so much in the mental state of the defendant but were satisfied to ask whether the defendant by his act inflicted on the plaintiff the harm complained of.[16] With the development of the modern tort of negligence in the nineteenth century, the problem of accidental trespass became

15 *Fowler v Lanning*, supra; *Weaver v Ward* (1616) Hob 134.
16 HEL vol viii 456–8.

important and was examined in a series of important cases.[17] The effect of these cases (however challengeable their interpretation of older cases may be[18]) is that a suit alleging trespass based on an unintentional act will not now succeed.

SECTION 3.   RELEVANCE OF TRESPASS TODAY

A glance at indices to the law reports will reveal several judgments in negligence and perhaps a handful of judgments in trespass to the person, goods or land. Does this evidence indicate either that these intentional torts are failing in their purpose, or that trespass should be regarded as of only historic interest? Certainly not. First the boundaries set by the trespass torts on intentional, deliberate interference with another's person or property are well understood in society generally. All sorts of grey areas exist in negligence, for example the extent to which the law protects individuals against emotional distress,[19] or businesses against loss of profits.[20] Fewer such grey areas afflict trespass. That the civil law complements the criminal law in prohibiting one person from beating another, or seizing his goods, or invading his land, is clear beyond debate. As it is often grey areas of the law which generate contested litigation, a proliferation of trespass claims is not to be expected. The obligations imposed on each member of society to his or her fellows are in general defined with precision by the trespass torts.[1]

Secondly, good practical reasons can be seen to explain why even if many individuals did, or do, breach those obligations imposed on them by the trespass torts, few victims would go to court to sue for compensation. The tort of trespass to the person overlaps to a considerable extent with crimes of assault. The rate of reported criminal assaults far exceeds that of writs issued for trespass to the person. This is because, of course, the perpetrator of the criminal assault is rarely worth suing. He has no funds from which compensation may be claimed. If the criminal has funds then he can and may well be pursued in the civil courts. In 1986 the press made a great hullabaloo over the award of just over £17,000 in damages to two women who had been viciously and sexually assaulted. They hailed it as a novel case of compensation for rape victims.[2] In law the women's claim was far from novel. There can scarcely be a clearer example of trespass to the person than rape. What was exceptional was that the rapist had earlier been awarded £45,000 compensation for injuries which he had suffered in a road accident. These injuries included brain damage resulting in a change of personality responsible for the aggressive and perverted sexual impulses motivating his attacks on the women.[3] In recent years there has been a small but steady stream of cases brought in battery by victims of criminal attacks. On occasion a victim has succeeded in tort after a failed

17   *Holmes v Mather* (1875) LR 10 Exch 261; *Stanley v Powell* [1891] 1 QB 86; *Gayler and Pope Ltd v B Davies & Son Ltd* [1924] 2 KB 75; *Manton v Brocklebank* [1923] 2 KB 212, CA; *National Coal Board v JE Evans & Co (Cardiff) Ltd* [1951] 2 KB 861, CA; *Fowler v Lanning, supra;* cf *Morriss v Marsden* [1952] 1 All ER 925.

18   See *Pollock 128* (Editor's Excursus B).

19   See later at pp 203–210.

20   See later in ch 12.

1   But see *Wilson v Pringle* [1987] QB 237 post at p 31.

2   *W v Meah* [1986] 1 All ER 935. The main interest of the case is that the women were awarded only £17,000. Was this sufficient compensation for their injuries and trauma?

3   *Meah v McCreamer* [1985] 1 All ER 367; and see Meah's unsuccessful attempt to recover the £17,000 which he was ordered to pay his victims from insurers of the defendant in the road accident claim *Meah v McCreamer (No 2)* [1986] 1 All ER 943. Consider generally the circumstances in which victims of criminal assault can use the trespass torts. Parents of two of the young women murdered by Peter Sutcliffe, the 'Yorkshire Ripper', recovered for their loss occasioned by the battery that led to their daughters' deaths after criminal bankruptcy proceedings against Sutcliffe resulted in funds being available for them to claim against.

criminal prosecution. This is because in a civil claim it only need be proven on the balance of probabilities that the attack occurred and that the defendant was responsible, whereas in a criminal case guilt must be proven beyond all reasonable doubt.

Finally, estimating the importance of litigation in the trespass torts from judgments cited in an index under the headings of assault and battery or trespass is misleading. There are several important judgments on police powers the essence of which are the limits the trespass torts place on the police in the execution of their duties. In the last few years the trespass torts have been the means by which the law has sought to define patients' rights to accept or reject medical treatment. The intentional torts offer a ready means by which to vindicate the fundamental human rights guaranteed by the European Convention on Human Rights, and about to be brought into domestic law by the Human Rights Act.

First, the Police and Criminal Evidence Act 1984 authorises police officers to do a variety of acts which, were they not justifiable as the exercise of statutory powers to arrest persons, or seize goods, or enter property, would constitute trespass. Where an officer exceeds those powers he commits a trespass and a civil action will lie against him and his chief constable. For example, an arresting officer may use reasonable force. For several officers to thrust an elderly man to the floor of a police van and sit on him exceeds any reasonable degree of force required.[4] In cases such as this we shall see that the issue as it reaches law reports is not, has there been a trespass; it is, rather, was the behaviour of the police such an abuse of power that they ought to have to pay additional exemplary damages.[5]

Additionally, a series of cases explore the limits of police powers to take informal action to pursue their inquiries at the stage where officers are not yet ready to arrest or formally search a person. What steps may a policeman take to attract a citizen's attention, to encourage him to answer his questions? A tap on the shoulder to attract the man's attention is permissible. Grabbing and holding his elbow is not.[6] The policeman may not exceed the generally acceptable contacts we all impliedly agree to in our crowded society. His conduct may be judged in the light of the task which he has in hand. But he has no powers additional to those of the ordinary citizen save those expressly conferred on him by statute. Judgments on these vital issues of civil liberties arise generally not by means of the individual aggrieved suing the police but in a criminal prosecution for assaulting a police officer in the execution of his duty. The man touched by the police officer pushes him off. The question of whether he has criminally assaulted the officer depends on whether the prior act of the officer exceeded his lawful powers so making that act a trespass against the accused to which he could respond with reasonable force.

Second, in the medical context, any physical contact with a patient constitutes a battery, unless authorised by the patient or a guardian competent to act on her behalf. Battery has been the vehicle by which the courts have addressed key questions of human rights, including rights to life itself. Such questions have included whether severely mentally handicapped women can be sterilised,[7] whether blood transfusions may be administered to an unconscious patient who had earlier refused to sanction a procedure,[8] whether a woman in labour could be subjected to surgery to save her baby but against her will,[9] whether a mentally handicapped woman could be used as a bone

---

4   *Allen v Metropolitan Police Comr* [1980] Crim LR 441.
5   *Thompson v Metropolitan Police Comr* [1998] QB 498, CA.
6   See *Collins v Wilcock* [1984] 3 All ER 374, [1984] 1 WLR 1172; and see generally *Clerk and Lindsell* ch 16.
7   *F v Berkshire Health Authority* [1989] 2 All ER 545, HL.
8   *Re T (Adult: Refusal of Medical Treatment)* [1993] Fam 95, [1992] 4 All ER 649, CA.
9   *Re MB* (1997) 8 Med LR 217, CA.

marrow donor to save her sister's life[10] and even in what circumstances the common law sanctioned passive euthanasia.[11]

Third, the intentional torts, and trespass in particular, have never been at death's door. Trespass torts have, and still do, define the limits of acceptable conduct between citizen and citizen, and between the individual and the state. They play a crucial role in support of rights to individual security, autonomy and freedom. The common law built the foundations of civil liberties in England within the framework of trespass.[12] The Human Rights Act will be unlikely to consign the intentional torts to history. True, the citizen deprived of his liberty by the state, degraded by police brutality or unlawfully spied on by the security services may have an additional or alternative 'Convention remedy'. But the established torts of trespass to the person, goods and land and pre-eminently false imprisonment already vindicate the citizen's rights. What the Human Rights Act may do is allow the common law judges to develop yet further the scope of the intentional torts, to lay to rest some of their historical baggage. An interest in privacy may at last be recognised overtly. Nor, in excitement surrounding the impact of the Human Rights Act on the protection of the citizen against the state, must the importance of the enforcement of rights between citizens be forgotten. The state is not the only the powerful actor who may descend to misuse of power.

---

10 *Re Y* [1997] Fam 110, [1997] 2 WLR 556.
11 *Airedale NHS Trust v Bland* [1993] AC 789, [1993] 1 All ER 821, HL.
12 And not just trespass to the person, for example, in *Entick v Carrington* (1765) 2 Wils 275 trespass to land and goods provided the context for the guarantee of the citizen's right to freedom from unlawful searches and seizures by the Crown.

Chapter 3

Intentional torts to the person

SECTION 1. INTRODUCTION

The torts of battery, assault and false imprisonment discussed in this chapter are among the most ancient of their kind. Analysis of these torts will demonstrate that in the protection offered to both bodily integrity and liberty, the scope of tort may be limited by its historical antecedents. The language is on occasion archaic. Yet the intentional torts to the person continue to provide safeguards of the most basic human rights and the judges have shown a willingness to innovate to ensure that tort keeps pace with modern society. Even prior to the enactment of the Human Rights Act, common law judges have sought to test how far the conditions of a particular tort match the relevant provisions of the European Convention on Human Rights.[1] Articles 2 and 3 guarantee the right to life and freedom from torture and degrading treatment. Article 5 asserts the right to liberty and security of person, and complemented by Article 6, seeks to ensure that the state cannot detain persons without substantial grounds justifying that deprivation of liberty, and procedures which comply with natural justice. Article 8 establishes a right to respect for private and family life. The very same fundamental interests protected, as will be seen, only partially by the existing common law are articulated in a more comprehensive, if less developed, form by the Convention.

Once the Act is in force (some time in 2000) certain claims for battery and false imprisonment against public authorities, notably the police, may be litigated at least in part as a claim under the Act. And in all future development of these torts which are the key to civil liberties, the Convention must be addressed and may provide fresh impetus to the continued development of these torts, which are now considered in detail.

SECTION 2. BATTERY

The form of trespass to the person known as battery is any act of the defendant which directly and either intentionally or negligently causes some physical contact with the person of the plaintiff without the plaintiff's consent.

---

1   See, for example, *Olotu v Home Office* [1997] 1 All ER 385, [1997] 1 WLR 328, CA.

(A) STATE OF MIND OF THE DEFENDANT

Today, whatever the historical definition of battery may be, most suits for battery are likely to be based on an intentional act of the defendant.[2] What is crucial, then, is to define what state of mind is required of the defendant to render him liable in battery. He must have intended a contact with the plaintiff. But is proof of a deliberate voluntary touching of the plaintiff sufficient? He need not have intended the plaintiff any harm. Battery is actionable per se without proof of any injury or damage to the plaintiff. He must have understood that his conduct was beyond the bounds of physical contact '… generally acceptable in the ordinary conduct of everyday life.'[3] The Court of Appeal said in *Wilson v Pringle*[4] that the plaintiff must show that the defendant's touching of the plaintiff was a 'hostile' touching. Hostility is not to be equated with ill-will or malevolence. It means an understanding by the defendant that he is doing something that the plaintiff may object to, that the plaintiff may regard as an unlawful intrusion on his rights to physical privacy and personal autonomy. Thus bare allegations that one 13-year-old boy jumped on another in the course of horseplay were insufficient of themselves to establish a battery. Further evidence of intent to injure or distress the plaintiff was called for. Had a grown man engaged in similar conduct the result might well have been different. Off the sports field, mature adults do not generally regard it as acceptable conduct for their colleagues to leap at them and wrestle them to the ground.

Lord Goff in *F v West Berkshire Health Authority*[5] doubted that the use of the word 'hostile', however defined, was appropriate to describe the necessary state of mind in battery. A surgeon operating on a patient to preserve her life and health may be motivated by his judgment as to her best interests, not hostility towards her. Yet if she is competent to do so, and has refused to consent to a particular course of treatment, he commits a battery. Lord Goff preferred to define battery thus. Any deliberate touching of another's body, beyond the bounds of acceptable everyday conduct, is, in the absence of lawful excuse, capable of constituting a battery. Where a person by reason of some permanent or temporary mental incapacity cannot consent himself to medical or other necessary procedures that lawful excuse may have to be found in a principle of necessity.[6]

Battery is both a tort and a crime and in many cases it is accordingly important to know to what extent criminal cases are relevant in tort. Perhaps the position is accurately stated in *Scott v Shepherd*:[7] 'And though criminal cases are no rule for civil ones, yet in trespass I think there is an analogy.' If A intends to hit B with a stone thrown by him in circumstances that would have amounted to the crime of battery were he to hit B, but A hits C instead, although with regard to C the conduct of A is neither intentional nor negligent, A commits a crime.[8] The point is undecided in tort; it is difficult to forecast whether the English courts would, like the American ones, follow the criminal analogy

---

2   *Letang v Cooper* [1965] 1 QB 232, [1964] 2 All ER 929, CA; see above at pp 25.
3   *Collins v Wilcock* [1984] 3 All ER 374 at 378, [1984] 1 WLR 1172 at 1178.
4   [1987] QB 237, [1986] 2 All ER 440, contrast the facts and decision of this case with *Williams v Humphrey* (1975) Times, 20 February (15-year-old schoolboy liable for prank of pushing another boy into swimming pool).
5   [1989] 2 All ER 545 at 564.
6   See post at p 93.
7   (1773) 2 Wm Bl 892 at 899 (per De Grey CJ); cf *Coward v Baddeley* (1859) 4 H & N 478 at 480 (per Pollock CB).
8   *R v Latimer* (1886) 17 QBD 359 (unlawful wounding).

by having recourse to a fiction of 'transferred' intent.[9] It is arguable that such conduct should be branded as morally wrong, and thus deserving of criminal punishment, and yet that, unless the defendant could have foreseen harm to the plaintiff, there is an insufficient relationship towards him to entitle him to a remedy in tort. Both motive and malice are irrelevant in determining liability for battery, though either may affect the amount of damages.

(B)   NO CONSENT BY THE PLAINTIFF

The absence of consent is so inherent in the notion of a tortious invasion of interests in the person that the absence of consent must be established by the plaintiff. So, it has been held that 'an assault must be an act against the will of the party assaulted: and therefore it cannot be said that a party has been assaulted by his own permission'.[10]

Any lingering doubt that the onus of proving absence of consent lies on the plaintiff was laid to rest in *Freeman v Home Office (No 2)*.[11] A prisoner alleged that he had been injected with powerful mood-changing drugs against his will. The judge held that the essence of battery is a specific and unpermitted intrusion on the plaintiff's body. Unless the plaintiff can establish that the intrusion was unpermitted no battery is proved. A contrary result would potentially have posed severe problems for all doctors, not just prison medical officers. Any contact with the patient, from surgery, through vaccinations to examining sore throats with a spatula would be prima facie a battery. The doctor would have to prove consent. Where minor procedures were in issue and no written consent had been obtained, or if records were lost, or the doctor had died,[12] this would pose acute difficulties for the defendant. On the other hand in the context of actions by suspects against the police, or prisoners against prison authorities, casting the burden of proving lack of consent on them, their word against those in power, against 'respectable' members of society, may make the action for battery a less effective weapon to enforce civil liberties for all.

What constitutes a valid consent is often a fundamental issue, especially in cases of 'medical trespass'. It may be a question of exactly what the patient consented to, or indeed whether he was competent to give consent. Logically, as it is for the plaintiff to prove absence of consent, such matters might be expected to be dealt with here. In practice once the plaintiff has raised sufficient evidence to cast doubt on the reality of a purported consent, consent is still treated as a 'defence' and so reality of consent is discussed later in this text in chapter 6, section 2.

---

9   *American Restatement, Torts* (2d) & 32. Winfield, in a note at (1935) 83 U of Pennsylvania LR 416, n 15 accepted this doctrine of transferred intent in the English law of torts. Is an intention to cause an apprehension of harm enough? Eg A swings a golf club near B in order to alarm him; without negligence on his part, the head flies off and hits B. Can B sue A? In *Livingstone v Ministry of Defence* [1984] NI 356, NI CA it was held that where the defendant fired a baton round injuring the plaintiff it mattered not whether he fired at P or another person; the defendant was guilty of battery unless he could prove lawful justification for his act.

10   *Christopherson v Bare* (1848) 11 QB 473 at 477 (per Patteson J). Though note that in criminal law consent is *not* an absolute defence to assault: *R v Brown* [1994] AC 212, HL.

11   [1983] 3 All ER 589 at 594–5; affd by the Court of Appeal, [1984] QB 524, [1984] 1 All ER 1036.

12   As had the prison doctor in *Freeman v Home Office (No 2)*.

(C) THE CHARACTER OF THE ACT OF THE DEFENDANT

There is no battery unless there is an act by the defendant. Merely to obstruct entrance to a room by standing still is not of itself enough.[13] No battery is committed if there is an incident over which the defendant has no control.[14]

There can be no battery unless there is contact with the plaintiff. Is any contact, however slight, enough? It would be rational to say that this tort protects not merely the interest in freedom from bodily harm, but also that in freedom from insult. Lord Goff has suggested that battery protects a person '...not only against physical injury but against any form of physical molestation'.[15] Such a formulation explains why spitting in the face is battery but touching another in a crowd is not. Further, the views of Holt CJ, 'that the least touching of another in anger is battery' but that 'if two or more meet in a narrow passage, and without any violence or design of harm, the one touches the other gently, it is no battery'[16] may be reconciled as follows. The courts cannot, and should not be expected to, give protection against these unavoidable incidents of everyday life, and thus his second statement[17] can be classed as an example of a permitted contact, and for the reasons already given, not tortious. Battery, then, protects a person against all unpermitted contacts, irrespective of whether there is physical harm. So, taking fingerprints,[18] spitting in one's face,[19] cutting one's hair against one's will[20] are all batteries.

As for all trespasses to the person, the act must be a 'direct' one; it is not enough that the act 'causes' the contact. Contact must immediately follow from the act of the defendant;[1] it must be a continuation of his act.[2] For a ship to ram another may be a trespass despite the effect of the current,[3] but where A struck B's horse which ran off and threw B, who was trampled on by the horse of a third party, B could not recover damages from A in trespass.[4] The contact must be with the person of the plaintiff. But, is it trespass to the person to throw over a carriage or chair in which the plaintiff is

---

13 *Innes v Wylie* (1844) 1 Car & Kir 257 at 263 (per Lord Denman CJ). A motorist who accidentally drives his car on to a police constable's foot while parking his car commits no battery but does he if he then ignores the constable's plea to 'Get off my foot'?; *Fagan v Metropolitan Police Comr* [1969] 1 QB 439, [1968] 3 All ER 442.

14 The defendant was not liable when a frightened horse ran away with him and collided with the plaintiff; *Gibbons v Pepper* (1695) 2 Salk 637; *Weaver v Ward* (1616) Hob 134; *Holmes v Mather* (1875) LR 10 Exch 261.

15 See *F v West Berkshire Health Authority* [1989] 2 All ER 545 at 563 HL.

16 *Cole v Turner* (1704) 6 Mod Rep 149.

17 This explains, too, the dictum in *Tuberville v Savage* (1669) 1 Mod Rep 3, that striking another on the breast in discourse is not actionable. What if a police constable who knows that a passing pedestrian does not wish to answer his questions continues to tap him on the shoulder so that he will stop to be interrogated? See *Donnelly v Jackman* [1970] 1 All ER 987.

18 *Dumbell v Roberts* [1944] 1 All ER 326 at 330, CA (per Scott LJ); *Callis v Gunn* [1964] 1 QB 495, [1963] 3 All ER 677.

19 *R v Cotesworth* (1704) 6 Mod Rep 172.

20 *Forde v Skinner* (1830) 4 C & P 239; cf *Nash v Sheen* (1953) Times, 13 March (application to the plaintiff's hair of a 'tone-rinse', the dye in which caused a rash by the defendant hairdresser, to whom the plaintiff went for a permanent wave, held to be actionable trespass).

1 *Leame v Bray* (1803) 3 East 593 at 603 (per Le Blanc J).

2 *Scott v Shepherd* (1773) 2 Wm Bl 892 at 899 (per De Grey CJ).

3 *Covell v Laming* (1808) 1 Camp 497.

4 *Dodwell v Burford* (1669) 1 Mod Rep 24. Is it battery if A pulls away B's chair as he is about to sit on it, whereupon B falls to the floor? If X cuts a rope to which Y is holding, or if X waggles it? Presumably to daub a towel with the intention that another should wipe his face on it, which he does, is too indirect for trespass. It is important to notice that there may be a claim for intentional infliction of harm even though trespass is not proved. Cf *Sadler v South Staffs etc Tramways Co* (1889) 23 QBD 17, CA.

sitting?[5] If battery protected against insult generally and not merely against bodily harm, then contact with anything so closely attached to or associated with the person that it could be regarded as part thereof would be treated as a battery. The matter was investigated in *Pursell v Horn*[6] where it was decided that throwing water on to the clothes being worn by the plaintiff was not necessarily battery. This case suggests that contact with things attached to the person may be battery only if there is a transmission of force to the body of the plaintiff.[7] The protection from insult or indignity afforded by the tort of battery is limited to insult or indignity inflicted by touching another person, however trivial the touching may be.[8]

(D) DAMAGES

Battery, like all suits in trespass, is actionable per se, ie without proof of damage. It seems also that, once the tort is proved, consequential loss in respect of goods, as well as the personal damage sustained, can be recovered.[9] Despite the doubt whether there is a battery when the contact injures merely feelings without causing physical contact, the courts can award additional damages on account of insult or injury to feelings for a battery which has also caused harm.[10]

SECTION 3. ASSAULT

That type of trespass to the person known as assault is any act of the defendant which directly and either intentionally or negligently[11] causes the plaintiff immediately to apprehend a contact with his person.

It may seem surprising that historically the law of tort should protect an interest in freedom from one particular form of mental anxiety. The explanation may be that since assaults were likely to result in breaches of the peace, trespass was invoked in order to enforce the criminal law. This association with criminal law, and the fact that the search for a rational basis for compensation in the form of the plaintiff's apprehension[12] is comparatively recent, explain the emphasis in the old cases on the intention of the defendant rather than on the effect produced on the plaintiff. There is therefore difficulty in reconciling some old and new cases.

---

5   *Hopper v Reeve* (1817) 7 Taunt 698.
6   (1838) 8 Ad & El 602.
7   Lord Denman CJ, at 604: 'It must imply personal violence'. Parke B held in *R v Day* (1845) 4 LTOS 493 that it was the crime of battery to slit with a knife the clothes which a man was wearing, and although the man's hand was cut this did not seem material because it was cut in reaching for the knife.
8   Street asked is kissing a sleeping lady in the presence of her friends battery and suggested that it was. Today presumably, a lady reversing roles is equally liable?
9   *Glover v London and South Western Rly Co* (1867) LR 3 QB 25.
10   *London v Ryder* [1953] 2 QB 202, [1953] 1 All ER 741, CA. There is little in the way of authority on quantum of damages for battery; in *W v Meah, D v Meah* [1986] 1 All ER 935 Woolf J awarded Miss W £6,750 for a horrifying and degrading sexual assault and Mrs D £10,250 for a brutal rape.
11   It is in accordance with principle to include foreseeable though unintended harm, but decisions are lacking. Eg if a defendant unintentionally brandishes a stick close to a lady, but without intending to hit or alarm her, it is submitted that his conduct is tortious if he could reasonably foresee that his act would have one of those effects.
12   Cf Comyns, II, 275.

(A) THE CHARACTER OF THE DEFENDANT'S CONDUCT

The law of assault is substantially the same as that of battery except that apprehension of contact, not the contact itself, has to be established. Usually when there is a battery, there will also be an assault, but not, for instance, when a person is hit from behind. To point a loaded gun at the plaintiff, or to shake a fist under his nose, or to curse him in a threatening manner, or to aim a blow at him which is intercepted, or to surround him with a display of force,[13] is to assault him. Clearly, if the defendant by his act intends to commit a battery and the plaintiff apprehends it, it is an assault. Within the tort[14] of assault what must be apprehended, however, is actual physical contact. Photographing a person against his will is an intrusion on his privacy but not an actionable assault.[15]

The effect of the origin of this tort on the present law is seen when one asks whether to brandish an unloaded pistol is an assault. In 1840 it was still being said that this was not assault because the defendant could not have intended a battery.[16] Tindal CJ had said 10 years previously that 'it is not every threat, when there is no actual physical violence, that constitutes an assault, there must, in all cases, be the means of carrying the threat into effect'.[17] These cases have not been overruled, but it is the ratio of one criminal case that to point an unloaded gun at the plaintiff is an assault.[18] An act which causes a reasonable person to apprehend a battery constitutes assault. The test for what constitutes reasonable apprehension of an imminent battery is *objective* not subjective. If, with no prior knowledge of the plaintiff's mental frailty, the defendant innocuously waves his hand in the air to emphasise a point he is making in conversation, there is no assault even though the plaintiff's paranoia causes him to believe that the defendant is about to strike him.

Where the intervention of the police, or other protective measures, ensure that threats of violence and abuse cannot be carried out by the defendants, there is no assault committed.So where working miners were bussed into their collieries with police guards, the threats yelled at them by strikers were not assaults.[19] The plaintiffs knew, as reasonable men, that those threats could not be carried out there and then. The distress and emotional strain caused to them by the abuse was not the result of apprehension of an immediate battery. The tort of assault as a means of protecting freedom from mental anxiety can thus be seen as limited in scope.

It was once suggested that mere words could not constitute an assault.[20] The House of Lords in the criminal case of *R v Ireland*[1] have finally squashed that particular fallacy. Words which instil a reasonable fear of a battery do amount to assault for '...means by which persons of evil disposition may intentionally or carelessly cause another to fear

13 *Read v Coker* (1835) 13 CB 850.
14 Note developments in the criminal law bringing conduct designed to cause psychiatric injury within the ambit of the criminal law: *R v Ireland* [1998] AC 147, HL; it is thought that developments in relation to the tort of intentional infliction of harm will make any similar expansion of the tort of assault unlikely.
15 *Murray v Minister of Defence* [1985] 12 NIJB 12.
16 *Blake v Barnard* (1840) 9 C & P 626; Winfield, regarded this as the ratio, but it seems that the ratio of Lord Abinger was that since the plaintiff in his declaration averred that a 'loaded' gun was pointed at him, and then sought a verdict at the trial on the basis that it was unloaded, there was no evidence to go to the jury on the facts set out in the declaration.
17 *Stephens v Myers* (1830) 4 C & P 349 at 349–50. In *Osborn v Veitch* (1858) 1 F & F 317 it was held that to point a loaded gun at half-cock at the plaintiff was an assault but this was because there was ''a present ability' of doing the act threatened'.
18 *R v St George* (1840) 9 C & P 483.
19 *Thomas v NUM* [1985] 2 All ER 1 at 24.
20 The case usually relied on is *R v Meade and Belt* (1823) 1 Lew CC 184, where it is said obiter (at 185 per Holroyd J) that 'no words or singing are equivalent to an assault'.
1 [1998] AC 147, [1997] 4 All ER 225.

immediate and unlawful violence vary according to circumstances'.[2] On the other hand, words accompanying an act may explain what might otherwise be an assault, as when the defendant with hand on sword said: 'If it were not assize-time, I would not take such language from you'.[3]

SECTION 4.   INTENTIONAL PHYSICAL HARM OTHER THAN TRESPASS TO PERSON

A wilful act (or statement) of the defendant, calculated to cause physical harm to the plaintiff and in fact causing physical harm to him, is a tort.

This was established by Wright J, in *Wilkinson v Downton*:[4]

> The plaintiff was told by the defendant, who knew it to be untrue, that her husband had been seriously injured in an accident. Believing this, she suffered nervous shock resulting in serious physical illness, and was held to have a cause of action.

The Court of Appeal upheld *Wilkinson v Downton* in *Janvier v Sweeney*:[5]

> The defendants, private detectives, told the plaintiff that unless she procured certain letters belonging to her mistress for them, they would disclose to the authorities that her fiancé, an internee, was a traitor; they knew that they had no such evidence. She recovered damages for the physical illness brought on by nervous shock occasioned by the defendants' conduct.

Nor is this tort limited to 'nervous shock' cases. Because of the rule that intentional acts which indirectly cause harm are not trespasses, there are many situations where, but for the judgment in *Wilkinson v Downton*, there might be no action. Putting poison in another's tea, digging a pit into which it is intended that another shall fall, perhaps passing on an infectious disease – these are not trespasses, but should properly be regarded as intentional physical harms within the principle of *Wilkinson v Downton*. The old cases declaring that it is a tortious act deliberately to set spring guns or other mechanical devices with the intention of injuring trespassers seem to belong to this category – the acts are in each instance consequential and thus not trespasses.[6] It seems confusing to speak of negligence when the defendant has deliberately inflicted the harm.

It has been suggested that it is wrong to state that in this tort one must prove that the defendant intended to cause the harm, and that the cases decide that one need only prove an intention to do the act.[7] But Wright J said:[8] 'One question is whether the defendant's act was so plainly calculated to produce some effect of the kind which was produced that an intention to produce it ought to be imputed to the defendant'. Remembering that intention covers the case where a person must be presumed to have intended the natural consequences of his conduct, it seems clear that the defendant must be proved to have intended to violate the interest of the plaintiff in his freedom

2   [1997] 3 WLR 534 at 550 per Lord Hoffmann.
3   *Tuberville v Savage* (1669) 1 Mod Rep 3.
4   [1897] 2 QB 57, 66 LJQB 493 (the fuller report).
5   [1919] 2 KB 316, CA.
6   *Deane v Clayton* (1817) 7 Taunt 489 (court equally divided whether it was actionable on the case to set iron spikes for dogs); *Bird v Holbrook* (1828) 4 Bing 628 (setter of spring gun liable in case to pursuer of stray fowl); cf *Townsend v Wathen* (1808) 9 East 277 and p 91, post.
7   Goodhart, Book Review (1994) 7 MLR 88.
8   [1897] 2 QB 57 at 59.

from physical harm – an intention to do an act the non-remote consequence of which is physical harm is not enough.[9] That a joke is the motive, as in *Wilkinson v Downton*, is irrelevant.

For nearly a century the tort defined in *Wilkinson v Downton*, while theoretically filling gaps in the trespass torts, appeared to fall into disuse. Recent case law has developed the principles on which *Wilkinson v Downton* is founded to provide a substantial degree of protection from harassment, at least where the defendant's conduct threatens injury to the plaintiff's physical or mental health. In *Khorasandjian v Bush*[10] the plaintiff's former boyfriend refused to accept that their friendship was over and persistently pursued her and her family with visits and abusive telephone calls. In *Burris v Azadani*[11] the defendant rejected the plaintiff's refusal to enter into a relationship with him. He made pestering telephone calls and issued constant threats to harm himself and her. The Court of Appeal held in both cases that the defendant's conduct was tortious and granted the plaintiff an injunction to protect her from further harassment. It was suggested that given earlier dicta[12] harassment per se did not constitute a tort; only where harassment threatened actual injury to health was any tort committed.[13] A modern tort of harassment may be wider in scope. In *Khorasandjian v Bush* the majority in the Court of Appeal held that harassing telephone calls constitute the tort of private nuisance and that the plaintiff could sue in nuisance even though she had no proprietary interest in her parents' home where she was living at the time. The House of Lords in *Hunter v Canary Wharf Ltd*[14] overruled that part of the judgment in *Khorasandjian* which sought to extend the ambit of the tort of nuisance but nonetheless considered that the defendant's persecution of his ex-girlfriend was tortious, Lord Hoffman put it thus:

'I do not therefore say that *Khorasandjian v Bush* was wrongly decided. But it must be seen as a case of intentional harassment not nuisance'.[15]

Moreover his Lordship also appeared to suggest that injury to health is not a pre-requisite of any emergent tort of harassment. Mere distress, inconvenience or discomfort may suffice.

Such has been public concern and media debate about harassment, popularly described as 'stalking', that Parliament enacted the Protection from Harassment Act 1997. Section 1 provides that conduct amounting to harassment of another becomes a criminal offence unless justifiable for the purpose of detecting or preventing crime, or authorised by law, or, in the particular circumstances, that conduct was reasonable. The victim of such harassment, be it actual or apprehended, is granted a right to sue in tort for breach of statutory duty by section 2 of the Act. Lord Hoffmann has suggested[16] that the creation of a statutory tort of harassment will obviate the need for any further

---

9   This interpretation of the case is supported by Lush J, in *Shapiro v La Morta* (1923) 130 LT 622 at 625. Cf *Bunyan v Jordon* (1937) 57 CLR 1 (H Ct Australia): D fired revolver into the air, thereby inflicting nervous shock resulting in physical illness; because D intended merely to frighten – a mere transient shock, not a nervous breakdown or other physical harm – held not liable. This tort is not committed unless there is actual illness with ascertainable objective physical consequences; anguish or fright is not enough.
10   [1993] QB 727, [1993] 3 All ER 669, CA.
11   [1995] 1 WLR 1372; and see *Burnett v George* [1992] 1 FLR 525.
12   See *Patel v Patel* [1988] 2 FLR 179, C.A.
13   Fricker [1992] Fam Law 158.
14   [1997] AC 655, HL.
15   [1997] 2 WLR 684 at 709; and see *Burris v Azadani* [1995] 1 WLR 1372 at 1378 per Sir Thomas Bingham MR.
16   [1997] 2 WLR 684 at 709.

development of the common law. We are not so certain. The 1997 Act provides no concrete definition of harassment. Conduct constitutes harassment if the defendant ought to know that his activities amount to harassment or a reasonable person would consider such conduct amounted to harassment. What degree of distress or harm is required to render unsocial behaviour harassment remains to be determined. Where a line is properly drawn between undesirable conduct and *criminal* conduct will be crucial to the fate of the Act.[17] Analogous questions affect the possible development of the common law. It is clear now that persecution making another's life a nightmare and disturbing his mental welfare is tortious. Tort protects the victim of a rejected lover. How far does or should tort go to protect people from other kinds of distress? Can the politician relentlessly pilloried by the press sue at common law or under the Act?[18] Will the development of torts of harassment go at least some way to protect an interest in privacy, even without reference to Article 8 of the European Convention?

SECTION 5. FALSE IMPRISONMENT

The trespass rather inadequately known as false imprisonment[19] may be defined as *an act of the defendant which directly and intentionally or negligently causes the confinement of the plaintiff within an area delimited by the defendant.*

Usually when there is a false imprisonment there will also be an assault or battery, but not, for example, where A voluntarily enters a room and B then locks the door. This tort protects the interest in freedom from confinement, from loss of liberty.

(A) STATE OF MIND

Normally this tort must be intentional in the sense that the defendant must intend to do an act which is at least substantially certain to effect the confinement. Malice is irrelevant. On principle negligence ought to be enough. Accordingly, if a person locks a door, being negligently unaware of the presence of somebody in the room, this should be false imprisonment.

(B) CHARACTER OF THE ACT

Like other trespasses, this tort is actionable per se but the courts have not thought that so great a protection ought to be afforded against any restraint of the person; so there must be a total restraint.[20] To prevent a man from crossing a bridge except by making a detour around part of the area of the bridge which has been closed off is not false imprisonment. Nor, so it was held in an old case,[1] was it false imprisonment if A were able to escape from his confinement by a nominal trespass on the land of a third party.[2]

---

17 For under the Act liability in tort is dependent on proof of the crime of harassment.
18 What will constitute 'reasonable conduct' on the part of an investigating journalist?
19 'False' in the sense of 'false' step; the confinement need not be in 'prison'.
20 Partial restraint may be the subject of an action on the case, on proof of damage; *Wright v Wilson* (1699) 1 Ld Raym 739; *Bird v Jones* (1845) 7 QB 742 at 752 (per Patteson J).
1 *Bird v Jones* supra.
2 *Wright v Wilson* supra; the court thought that a special action on the case would lie.

Every confinement of the person is an imprisonment, whether it be in a common prison or in a private house, or in the stocks, or even by forcibly detaining one in the public streets.[3]

One may be confined in a house,[4] in a prison,[5] in a mine,[6] or in a vehicle.[7] How large the area of confinement can be obviously depends on the circumstances of each particular case – it could be tortious to restrict a man to a large country estate, or perhaps even to restrain him from leaving, say, the Isle of Man, yet if A prevented B from landing in England from the Continent that act could not be a false imprisonment.[8] The boundaries of the area of confinement must be fixed by the defendant. As Coleridge J said in *Bird v Jones*:[9]

Some confusion seems...to arise from confounding imprisonment of the body with mere loss of freedom:...imprisonment...includes the notion of restraint within some limits defined by a will or power exterior to our own.

Lord Denman, in his dissenting judgment in the same case, said:[10]

As long as I am prevented from doing what I have a right to do, of what importance is it that I am permitted to do something else?...If I am locked in a room, am I not imprisoned because I might effect my escape through a window, or because I might find an exit dangerous or inconvenient to myself, as by wading through water...?

Although this contention was rejected so far as the adequacy of a partial restraint is concerned, it is thought that, if someone can only escape at the risk of personal injury or if it is otherwise unreasonable[11] for him to escape, it constitutes the tort of false imprisonment. The barriers need not be physical; when a Commissioner in Lunacy wrongfully used his authority to dissuade the plaintiff from leaving his office, he was liable in false imprisonment.[12] Restraint on movement in the street even by a mere threat of force which intimidates a person into compliance without laying hands on him is false imprisonment.[13] A restraint effected by an assertion of authority is enough – so those who seek compensation because they have been wrongfully arrested by policemen claim for false imprisonment, and need not establish that the policeman touched them.[14] The plaintiff need not risk violence by resisting his arrester.

Once a person is lawfully detained, changes in the conditions of his detention will not render that detention unlawful. In a series of cases prisoners sought to assert that

3 Blackstone, III, 127.
4 *Warner v Riddiford* (1858) 4 CBNS 180.
5 *Cobbett v Grey* (1849) 4 Exch 729.
6 *Herd v Weardale Steel, Coal and Coke Co Ltd* [1915] AC 67, HL.
7 *Burton v Davies* [1953] QSR 26 (Queensland), driving a car at such a speed as to prevent a passenger from alighting is false imprisonment.
8 But in *Kuchenmeister v Home Office* [1958] 1 QB 496, [1958] 1 All ER 485, it was held to be imprisonment for imigration officers to prevent an alien from proceeding from an airport to an aircraft and from embarking on it, even though the Aliens Order, 1953, authorised them to prescribe limits within which he must remain.
9 (1845) 7 QB 742 at 744.
10 (1845) 7 QB 742 at 754–5.
11 If A removes B's bathing costume in a swimming pool and B does not leave the pool until he has found someone to lend him another costume, is he falsely imprisoned?
12 *Harnett v Bond* [1925] AC 669, HL.
13 Can you imprison by telephone? Is a threat of force to a member of one's family sufficient?
14 *Warner v Riddiford* (1858) 4 CBNS 180, especially at 204 (per Willes J); *Chinn v Morris* (1826) 2 C & P 361; *Grainger v Hill* (1838) 4 Bing NC 212; *Wood v Lane* (1834) 6 C & P 774. What if a plaintiff is accused of shoplifting, but in order to avoid the embarrassment of a converation in a crowded store he accompanies the store detective to the office; cf *Conn v David Spencer Ltd* [1930] 1 DLR 805?

solitary confinement ultra vires the Prison Rules or detention in intolerable conditions, such as the notorious 'control units', or insanitary police cells, constituted false imprisonment. The House of Lords[15] finally rejected such claims. Once a prisoner is lawfully imprisoned by virtue of the Prison Act 1952 he no longer enjoys any 'residual liberty', and the prison authorities are entitled to restrain and define his movements. That does not mean that a prisoner subjected to intolerable hardship is remediless. In appropriate circumstances he may have an action for assault and battery, and, if the conditions of confinement affect his health, he may be able to sue for negligence. It is thought that a similar analysis applies to detention by police officers. For, if a remedy in false imprisonment lay, once an arrested person could establish that the conditions of his detention render his further detention unlawful, the logical consequence would be that from that moment on he could go free, using reasonable force if necessary to effect his escape.

Nor can a person held on remand for a period beyond the 112-day limit set by the Prosecution of Offences (Custody Time Limits) Regulations 1987 sue the prison authorities for false imprisonment.[16] The plaintiff was lawfully in the custody of the prison governor and only an order of the Crown Court could secure her release. The failure of the Crown Prosecution Service to act to bring her to trial or arrange her release on bail, and her own surprising failure to apply for bail, did not affect the validity of her detention. The governor lacked any independent authority to free the plaintiff. The plaintiff's right was not to be released from gaol per se, but to an order of the court releasing her on bail.

False imprisonment must result from a direct act of the defendant, depriving the plaintiff of his liberty by that act. So, it is not false imprisonment to cause a person to be temporarily detained in an asylum by making false statements to the authorities about his behaviour,[17] or to dig a pit into which the plaintiff falls.[18] However short the period of detention, an action for false imprisonment will lie, provided that the other requirements of the tort are satisfied.

A person who is held liable in false imprisonment will normally have performed some positive act. *Herd v Weardale Steel, Coal and Coke Co*[19] posed the problem of whether there might be liability in respect of a mere omission:[20]

> The plaintiff, a miner employed by the defendants, descended their mine in pursuance of his contract of employment. During his shift the plaintiff requested the defendants to carry him to the surface in their cage. In refusing this request the defendants committed no breach of contract: their contractual obligation was to transport him to the surface at the end of his shift. The action in false imprisonment failed.[1]

---

15 *Hague v Deputy Governor of Parkhurst Prison* [1992] 1 AC 58, [1991] 3 All ER 733.

16 *Olotu v Home Office* [1997] 1 WLR 328 CA. (The Court of Appeal expressly addressed for how far their findings were compatible with Article 5 of the Human Rights Convention).

17 But an action on the case lay against a medical practitioner, who negligently certified that the plaintiff was insane, whereupon she was detained in a mental hospital: *De Freville v Dill* (1927) 96 LJKB 1056.

18 It may be the tort of intentionally causing physical harm; ch 3, section 3, ante. Is it false imprisonment to deflate the tyres of the invalid chair in which a cripple is travelling, or to take away the ladder of a tiler who is on the roof?

19 [1913] 3 KB 771, CA; affd [1915] AC 67, HL.

20 Because both are acts of commission, not of omission, consider the example of a student forbidden to leave the lecture room until the end of the lecture, and a conductor who will not allow one who has boarded the wrong bus to alight without paying his fare.

1   Cf *Robinson v Balmain New Ferry Co Ltd* [1910] AC 295 at 299, PC: 'There is no law requiring the defendants to make the exit from their premises gratuitous to people who come there upon a definite contract which involves their leaving the wharf by another way;'

This case is authority for the proposition that failure to provide a means of egress from premises is not a tort where there is no duty to provide it: thus, if A falls down the mine of B while trespassing it is not false imprisonment should B refuse to bring him to the surface in his lift.[2] What it does not decide is whether the failure to carry out a duty, whether contractual or otherwise, may constitute a false imprisonment even though there is no positive act on the part of the defendant. The House of Lords did not consider this point, but the two judges who constituted the majority in the Court of Appeal held that the omission to perform a contractual duty was not a false imprisonment.[3] Of course, the unhappy victim in such circumstances would retain a remedy in contract. Nonetheless, it would seem right that a person whose confinement is continued in breach of either a contractual or non-contractual duty to release him should additionally enjoy a remedy in false imprisonment.[4]

(C) KNOWLEDGE OF THE PLAINTIFF

Surprisingly, perhaps, there is no requirement that the plaintiff alleging false imprisonment was aware of the relevant restraint on his freedom at the time of his confinement. Prior to 1988 the authorities on this issue were in conflict. In *Herring v Boyle*[5] an action brought on behalf of a schoolboy detained at school by his headmaster during the holidays because his parents had not paid the fees failed. The judge found that the boy was unaware of his detention. But in *Meering v Grahame-White Aviation Co*[6] a man persuaded by works police to remain in an office, but unaware that had he tried to leave he would have been prevented from doing so, successfully recovered damages for his imprisonment. The House of Lords in *Murray v Minister of Defence*[7] endorsed that latter judgment. Actual knowledge of detention is not a necessary element of the tort of false imprisonment. Proof of a total restraint of liberty is sufficient. Lord Griffiths declared:[8]

> The law attaches supreme importance to the liberty of the individual and if he suffers a wrongful interference with that liberty it should remain actionable even without proof of special damage.

(D) WHO IS LIABLE FOR A FALSE IMPRISONMENT?

The usual question to be asked when deciding who can be sued for false imprisonment is: who was 'active in promoting and causing' the confinement?[9] It is often necessary to determine who can be sued when a person is detained and charged for an offence

2   And if B's refusal caused A to die of starvation?
3   Per Buckley and Hamilton LJJ [1913] 3 KB 771, CA.
4   Eg a prisoner not released on completion of his sentence. Consider too the case of someone accidentally confined but then not freed by another with a duty to do so. What about the classic case of the 'lady locked in the lavatory': *Sayers v Harlow UDC* [1958] 2 All ER 342, [1958] 1 WLR 623, CA.
5   (1834) 1 Cr M & R 377.
6   (1919) 122 LT 44.
7   [1988] 2 All ER 521, [1988] 1 WLR 692.
8   [1988] 1 WLR 692 at 704.
9   *Aitken v Bedwell* (1827) Mood & M 68. In *Ansell v Thomas* [1974] Crim LR 31, CA, a managing director left his factory early only because two policemen summoned by his co-directors threatened to eject him forcibly if he did not leave; the co-directors were held liable in trespass. A person may be liable in false imprisonment either because he himself effected the arrest or, in line with the general principle that he who instigates another to commit a tort is a joint tortfeasor because he actively promoted the arrest of another.

where the arrest is unjustified by law.[10] (The separate question of when lawful arrest is a defence will be examined later.)

Giving information to the police, on the basis of which a police officer exercises his own judgment and arrests the plaintiff does not impose on the informer responsibility for that arrest, however likely it is that arrest will ensue from the information proffered. Thus a store detective was not liable when the plaintiff was arrested on the basis of information which she gave to police officers, even though her information proved to be erroneous.[11] Even signing the charge sheet at the police station will not necessarily render the private citizen liable for the detention of the plaintiff.[12] It must be shown that the plaintiff's detention was truly the act of the defendant rather than of the police officers concerned. So where a police officer refused to take the plaintiff into custody unless the defendant charged him and signed the charge sheet, the defendant not the police officer was held responsible for that detention.[13]

If the defendant wrongfully gives the plaintiff into custody and then the magistrate remands the plaintiff the defendant is answerable in false imprisonment for damages only up to the time of the judicial remand. Once a judicial act interposes, liability for false imprisonment ceases.[14] It is important to distinguish false imprisonment from malicious prosecution, a tort concerned with the abuse of the judicial process, and which, unlike false imprisonment, calls for proof of malice and of absence of reasonable cause.[15] Therefore, if A wrongfully prefers a complaint against B before a magistrate who then issues a warrant or tries him forthwith or remands him, A has not committed the tort of false imprisonment,[16] even if the magistrate has no jurisdiction.[17]

(E) DAMAGES

False imprisonment is actionable without proof of damage. In addition to damages for loss of liberty the court may compensate for injury to feelings and loss of reputation.[18]

In claims for false imprisonment, awards of damages are currently made by juries. The amounts of such awards against the police escalated in recent years with an award of £200,000 in exemplary damages[19] being made in one such action brought by Mr Hsu. In *Thompson v Metropolitan Police Comr*,[20] where the police appealed against the award to Mr Hsu, the Court of Appeal issued guidelines on the criteria which should now determine awards of compensation for false imprisonment and malicious prosecution. Judges directing the jury on the issue of damages must address the following matters. Save in exceptional cases, damages are to be awarded only to compensate the plaintiff for the injury suffered, not to punish the defendant. Basic damages to compensate the plaintiff for loss of liberty would generally start at about

---

10 See *Pike v Waldrum and P & O Navigation Co* [1952] 1 Lloyd's Rep 431 on the liability of naval authorities and a ship's captain for the arrest of a seaman.

11 *Davidson v Chief Constable of North Wales* [1994] 2 All ER 597; and see *Gosden v Elphick* (1849) 4 Exch 445.

12 *Sewell v National Telephone Co* [1907] 1 KB 557, CA; *Grinham v Willey* (1859) 4 H & N 496.

13 *Austin v Dowling* (1870) LR 5 CP 534.

14 *Lock v Ashton* (1848) 12 QB 871.

15 See ch 26, post.

16 *Brown v Chapman* (1848) 6 CB 365.

17 *West v Smallwood* (1838) 3 M & W 418.

18 *Hook v Cunard Steamship Co Ltd* [1953] 1 All ER 1021, [1953] 1 WLR 682.

19 As to exemplary damages generally see pp 5–27 et seq post and note the proposals to reform the law relating to aggravated and exemplary damages Law Commission Report No 247, *Aggravated, Exemplary and Restitutionary Damages*.

20 [1998] QB 498, [1997] 2 All ER 762, CA.

£500 for the first hour of detention, but thereafter be calculated on a reducing scale to allow around £3,000 for 24 hours unlawful imprisonment and a 'progressively reducing scale' for subsequent days. Aggravated damages should be awarded only on evidence of humiliating circumstances surrounding the detention, or especially malicious or oppressive behaviour by police officers. Aggravated damages would rarely be less than £1000 but would not generally approach double the figure for basic damages. Exemplary damages must be exceptional, based on a judgment that the sum of basic and aggravated damages is inadequate to punish the defendant for oppressive and arbitrary behaviour, for abuse of power. Juries must note that an award of exemplary damages constitutes a windfall for the plaintiff and that where damages come out of police funds, the burden of payment falls on the police budget affecting perhaps the operational efficiency of the service. The amount of exemplary damages must be no more than what is sufficient to mark the jury's disapproval of police behaviour. A particularly disgraceful instance of misbehaviour might merit an award of £25,000 and £50,000 should be regarded as an absolute maximum. The award of £200,000 to Mr Hsu was reduced to a mere £15,000.

Given the facts in both Mr Hsu's case, and the second case with which the police's appeal against his award was joined, which show ample evidence of gross brutality, it might be asked why the appeal court was so anxious to reduce levels of damages for false imprisonment. Was it solely to protect police funds? Another crucial factor, however, is this. Awards for pain and suffering in personal injury claims remain relatively low.[1] A plaintiff suffering two broken legs, enduring weeks of hospitalisation and some continuing incapacity might be awarded only about £50,000. How should compensation for loss of liberty and transient humiliation compare to compensation for injury?

SECTION 6.   OTHER FORMS OF COMPENSATION

Many of the torts discussed in this chapter will also be crimes. A court which has convicted a person of an offence (other than a road traffic offence) may require him to compensate the victim for any personal injury, loss or damage resulting.[2]

The Criminal Injuries Compensation Scheme[3] further provides for awards of compensation to victims of crime who have sustained personal injuries. Awards are subject to a statutory tariff and will generally be of lesser amounts than would be awarded to a successful plaintiff in a tort claim.

1   See per Lord Woolf at 413.
2   Sections 35 to 38 of the Powers of Criminal Courts Act 1973, as amended by s 60 of the Criminal Law Act 1977. The maximum award by a magistrates' court is £5,000.
3   See now the Criminal Injuries Compensation Act 1995.

Chapter 4

Goods

SECTION 1. INTRODUCTION

The law might be expected to protect persons whose title to, or possession of, goods is interfered with, or whose goods are damaged by intentional conduct. Broadly speaking, English law does this but not in any systematic way. As Sir John Salmond said:[1]

> ...we are still called upon to observe distinctions and subtleties that have no substance or justification in them, but are nothing more than an evil inheritance from the days when forms of action and of pleading held the legal system in their clutches. In no branch of the law is this more obvious than in that which relates to the different classes of wrongs which may be committed with respect to goods. In particular the law of trover and conversion is a region still darkened with the mists of legal formalism, through which no man will find his way by the light of nature or with any other guide save the old learning of writs and forms of action and the mysteries of pleading.

Unfortunately, Salmond's criticism of the law of torts as it protects interests in goods is as pertinent today as it was in 1903. This is so despite a systematic review by the Law Reform Committee[2] of the several and ancient torts concerning goods which are often collectively referred to as the chattel torts. Their proposal that all those torts relating to intentional interference with goods should be replaced by a single tort of 'wrongful interference with chattels' was, as we shall see, only implemented to a very limited extent by Parliament in the Torts (Interference with Goods) Act 1977.[3] Hence students must still attempt to understand the historical development of the various chattel torts.

The action for *trespass to goods*, trespass *de bonis asportatis*, affords a remedy where there has been a direct interference with goods in the plaintiff's possession at the time of the trespass, whether that be by taking the goods from him or damaging the goods without removing them. It is of no help where the relevant interference with the goods is indirect, nor, generally, is trespass available where the goods are not in the

1 (1903) 21 LQR 43.
2 See the 18th Report of the Law Reform Committee (Conversion and Detinue) (1971) Cmnd 4774.
3 See Palmer 'The Application of the Torts (Interference with Goods) Act 1977 to Actions in Bailment' (1978) 41 MLR 629 and 'The Abolition of Detinue' [1981] Conv 62, and see Thorneley [1977] CLJ 248.

possession of the plaintiff. Thus if student A lends his book overnight to student B, who gives it or sells it to C, trespass may not lie against C.

The oldest of the chattel torts, the writ of *detinue*, developed to provide a remedy for wrongful detention of goods. A person with a right to immediate possession of goods could, by way of an action in detinue, recover the goods themselves or payment of their value and consequential damages for their detention upon evidence that the defendant had wrongfully refused to deliver up the goods on demand. The loss or destruction of the goods where the defendant owed the plaintiff a duty to take care of those goods (as a bailee)[4] was no justification for failing to redeliver the goods. In many instances the facts which gave rise to a remedy in detinue simultaneously created a cause of action in conversion, the latest of the major chattel torts to evolve. Detinue is abolished by the Torts (Interference with Goods) Act 1977. The one clear instance of detinue (loss or destruction of goods in breach of duty by a bailee) which did not constitute conversion at common law is 'converted' into a statutory conversion by section 2(2) of that Act.[5]

The action for *conversion* (originally called *trover*) developed upon a legal fiction.[6] The original form of the pleadings alleged that the defendant had found the plaintiff's chattels (hence the name 'trover') and had wrongfully converted them to his own use. The allegation of finding (trover) could not be contested and the essence of the tort became the wrongful conversion of the goods to the use of the defendant. Once refusal to deliver up the goods was treated as evidence of conversion,[7] conversion and detinue became largely concurrent torts. As seizing goods and carrying them away is quite clearly a wrongful conversion of goods, conversion is also often available concurrently with trespass. But merely moving or damaging goods without converting them to the defendant's own use remains remediable in trespass alone.[8] The action for conversion lies not only where the plaintiff has actual possession of the relevant goods but also where he has a right to immediate possession of the goods. Consider again the earlier example of the aggrieved student A. Should B refuse to return the book to him he commits conversion. Should B have sold the book to C who also refuses to deliver the book back to its true owner A, both B and C may be sued for conversion.

The major extant chattel torts of trespass and conversion predominantly protect interests in possession. *Residual torts* derived from the action on the case protect the rights of owners not in possession in certain cases. Trespass and conversion deal with intentional interference with goods. Where goods are lost or damaged as a result of the defendant's breach of a duty of care, an action may lie in *negligence*.

The archaic nature of the chattel torts adds to the intrinsic difficulty of the subject of interference with goods. That intrinsic difficulty is unavoidable in that, as the essence of trespass or conversion is very often whether the defendant wrongfully and unlawfully dealt with the plaintiff's goods, the basic question of law in issue may be one of contract

4   When goods are entrusted by one person (the bailor) to another (the bailee) a bailment is created which imposes on the bailee duties towards the bailor in respect of those goods. The nature of the bailment whether it is gratuitous or for reward, voluntary or involuntary, will determine the scope of the duty owed by the bailee. Bailments may be for a fixed term (hire of a car for one week) or at will. This will be relevant to determine the relevant rights to sue in conversion of bailor and bailee. See N E Palmer *Bailment* (2nd edn).

5   See *Palmer* (supra) who argues that there are other instances of detinue in relation to breach of bailment not now actionable as conversion. The issue is discussed but not decided in *Howard E Perry & Co Ltd v British Railways Board* [1980] 2 All ER 579, [1980] 1 WLR 1375.

6   For details of the history of detinue and conversion and the interplay between the historic chattel torts, see Milsom 'Not Doing is No Trespass' [1954] CLJ 105; Simpson 'The Introduction of the Action on the Case for Conversion' (1959) 75 LQR 364.

7   See *Alexander v Southey* (1821) 5 B & Ald 247.

8   *Bushel v Miller* (1718) 1 Stra 128; *Fouldes v Willoughby* (1841) 8 M & W 540.

or personal property,[9] or even abstruse questions of mercantile law.[10] For example, A enters into a conditional sale agreement with B to purchase a car. Before A has completed all the payments on the car he sells it to C. When B seeks to recover the car or its value from C via an action for conversion the court will have to consider the authority (if any) of A to sell the car to B. That will depend on:

1   the terms of the contract between A and B; and
2   the relevant rules of the law of personal property on title to goods.

What the Law Reform Committee had hoped to do was at least to simplify the tortious remedies available to plaintiffs. One statutory tort of 'wrongful interference with chattels' was recommended which would lie wherever goods were intentionally interfered with without lawful justification. Negligent interference would remain actionable, if at all, only under the existing law of negligence.

The Torts (Interference with Goods) Act 1977 introduces a collective description 'wrongful interference with goods'[11] to cover conversion, trespass to goods, negligence resulting in damage to goods or to an interest in goods and any other tort insofar as it results in damages to goods or an interest in goods. This is done to facilitate common treatment of all chattel torts in respect to remedies and procedure. The Act neither redefines nor replaces the existing substantive rules on trespass, conversion, or the residual chattel torts. The substantive impact of the Act is extremely limited. Detinue is abolished[12] and the one clear instance of detinue which did not constitute conversion at common law (wrongful loss or destruction of goods by a bailee) is declared to be conversion by section 2(2). New provision is made for bailees to dispose of uncollected goods.[13]

The main impact of the 1977 Act is, as we shall see, to simplify and rationalise the remedies and procedures relating to chattel torts. The intricacies of conversion and its relationship to trespass must still be explored. As conversion is in practical terms the pre-eminent chattel tort it is dealt with first.

SECTION 2.   CONVERSION

Conversion may be defined as an intentional[14] dealing with goods which is seriously inconsistent with the possession or right to immediate possession of another person.

This tort protects the plaintiff's interest in the dominion and control of his goods; it does not protect his interest in its physical condition. This is why the tort is much concerned with problems of title to personal property, and so often involves complex rules of commercial law.[15]

---

9   See A P Bell *Modern Law of Personal Property* (1989).
10   See *The Future Express* [1993] 2 Lloyd's Rep. 542, CA.
11   Torts (Interference with Goods) Act 1977, s 1.
12   Torts (Interference with Goods) Act 1977, s 2.
13   Without statutory authority to do so bailees (eg drycleaners) disposing of uncollected goods would be liable for conversion for so doing. Sections 12,13 and Sch 1 repeal and replace the earlier and unsatisfactory Disposal of Uncollected Goods Act 1952.
14   At common law an act of conversion had to be a voluntary act; hence once detinue was abolished, the need to make the wrongful loss or destruction of goods by a bailee in breach of duty a statutory conversion; see post at p 59.
15   As in *The Future Express* supra. The tort appears to be actionable without proof of special damage: *Hiort v London and North Western Rly Co* (1879) 4 Ex D 188.

(A) INTEREST OF THE PLAINTIFF

The plaintiff must have either possession or the right to immediate possession.[16] English law in this respect favours possession at the expense of ownership. For example if a landlord has rented out furnished accommodation for a fixed term and a third party commits an act of conversion in respect of some of the furniture, the landlord has no right to sue in conversion, although the tenant may.[17]

(I) BAILMENT

Where goods have been entrusted to another so as to create a bailment, the bailee can sue third parties in conversion.[18] If the bailment is at will then the bailor may also sue because he is then deemed to have an immediate right to possession.[19]

A bailment which originally gave to the bailor no immediate right to possess may become a bailment at will. *Manders v Williams*[20] is illustrative:

> The plaintiff brewer supplied porter (stout) in casks to a publican on condition that he was to return empty casks within six months; it was held that the plaintiff could sue a sheriff who seized (within six months of their being supplied) some empty casks in execution for a debt of the publican, because, once the casks were empty, the effect of the contract was to make the publican a bailee at will, whereupon the plaintiff was entitled to immediate possession.

However, where bailor and bailee enjoy concurrent rights to sue in conversion they cannot both exercise those rights and so effect double recovery against the defendant. Either bailor or bailee may sue but whichever first obtains damages that concludes the case.[1] The successful claimant must then account to the other for the proportion of the damages representing his interest in the property. So where the owner of a car had lent the vehicle to his girlfriend, and the car was damaged while in her possession, his successful claim for damages based on his right to recover the car at will, precluded a second action by the girlfriend albeit she had possession of the car at the time the damage was done.[2] In very many cases however the crucial issue for the bailor, the owner of the goods, is whether he does enjoy a right to immediate possession of the goods – is the bailment, or has it become, a bailment at will or has some wrongful act of the bailee ended the bailment; for if a bailee does a wrongful act which may be deemed to terminate the bailment, the bailor may sue. Sale of the goods by the bailee will ordinarily terminate the bailment and the bailor can then sue either the bailee or the third party.[3]

16 *The Future Express* supra; *Gordon v Harper* (1796) 7 Term Rep 9. As to equitable rights to possess see *Clerk & Lindsell* para 13-80.
17 *Gordon v Harper* supra; and see *Roberts v Wyatt* (1810) 2 Taunt 268; *City Motors (1933) Pty Ltd v Southern Super Aerial Service Pty Ltd* (1961) 106 CLR 477, H Ct Australia.
18 The bailment gives him the right to possession of the goods for the period of the bailment. In *The Winkfield* [1902] P 42, CA, the Postmaster-General, as bailee, could recover the full value of mail lost through the wrongdoing of the defendant.
19 As the bailment can be terminated at will, the owner retains the right to demand the goods back instantly, the right to immediate possession. *Nicolls v Bastard* (1835) 2 Cr M & R 659; *Kahler v Midland Bank Ltd* [1950] AC 24 at 56 (per Lord Radcliffe), [1949] 2 All ER 621 at 641.
20 (1849) 4 Exch 339.
1   *Nicolls v Bastard* [1835–42] All ER Rep 429 at 430.
2   *O'Sullivan v Williams* [1992] 3 All ER 385, CA.
3   *Cooper v Willomatt* (1845) 1 CB 672: of course, at the conclusion of the purported act of sale the bailee's interest is forfeited and the bailor is entitled to immediate possession, but if the sale is one which passes a goods title to the third party, at what moment of time can the bailor be said to have and immediate right to possess and thus a right to sue the bailee in conversion?

Destruction of the goods[4] or dealing with them in a manner wholly inconsistent with the terms of the bailment,[5] will have the same result. It will be a difficult matter of interpretation of contract to decide whether a particular act of the bailee determines the bailment, or, at least, makes it determinable at will. This is especially true and important in the case of hire-purchase agreements.[6] These normally prohibit the hirer from selling or otherwise disposing of the goods,[7] and empower the owner to terminate the agreement if the prohibition is disregarded; if the agreement dispenses with notice to the hirer of termination, the owner can sue a party who purchases from the hirer in unwitting contravention of such a prohibition.[8] In *Whiteley Ltd v Hilt*:[9]

> The hire-purchase agreement empowered the hirer to purchase a piano after payment of the final instalment. It did not prohibit her from transferring the piano during the hiring period. It was held that the owners had no cause of action against the transferee who had paid all the instalments remaining owing.

With this may be compared *Belsize Motor Supply Co v Cox*:[10]

> The owners were authorised to determine the agreement if the hirers parted with possession of the hired goods. It was held that the owners could recover from a pledgee of the hirer only the instalments which were still owing and that the agreement continued in force despite the transfer of the goods.

In effect, the courts treat hire-purchase agreements as sui generis in that they are regarded as creating a proprietary interest separate from the contractual interest under the bailment agreement.[11]

(2)   Lien and pledge

In certain limited cases where goods are entrusted to another to carry out certain services (eg repairs), the person in possession of those goods acquires a lien over the goods, that is to say a right to retain the goods until he is paid for his services.[12] The holder of a lien, too, may sue in conversion,[13] but if he wrongfully parts with the possession of the goods he loses his lien, and his act is a conversion which ends the bailment and entitles the owner to sue him.[14] A pledge (deposit of goods as security for a debt),

---

4   *Bryant v Wardell* (1848) 2 Exch 479 at 482.
5   *Plasycoed Collieries Co Ltd v Partridge, Jones & Co Ltd* [1912] 2 KB 345 at 351 (per Hamilton J); but not presumably a mere excess of permitted user.
6   And see now Consumer Credit Act 1974, Parts VII and IX.
7   It is standard practice in hire-purchase agreements, by express terms, to make the benefits of the hirer's option to purchase unassignable: *Helstan Securities Ltd v Hertfordshire County Council* [1978] 3 All ER 262.
8   *North Central Wagon and Finance Co Ltd v Graham* [1950] 2 KB 7, [1950] 1 All ER 780, CA (sale by bailee made hiring determinable at will of bailor: as explained in *Reliance Car Facilities Ltd v Roding Motors* [1952] 2 QB 844, [1952] 1 All ER 1355), CA; *Union Transport Finance Ltd v British Car Auctions Ltd* [1978] 2 All ER 385, CA (damages recovered from auctioneer who sold car on instructions of a hire-purchaser).
9   [1918] 2 KB 808, CA.
10   [1914] 1 KB 244; *Wickham Holdings Ltd v Brooke House Motors Ltd* [1967] 1 All ER 117.
11   Cf *Karflex Ltd v Poole* [1933] 2 KB 251 at 263–4, [1933] All ER Rep 46 at 50–51 (per Goddard J).
12   See *Bell* ch 6.
13   In *Lord v Price* (1874) LR 9 Exch 54, the buyer of goods in possession of the seller, who had a lien for the price, could not sue a third party. Is it desirable to prevent the owner from suing a third party if a carrier has a lien?
14   *Mulliner v Florence* (1878) 3 QBD 484, CA.

however, confers something more than the personal right of retention given by a lien – for there is, in addition, a power to sell in default of payment on the agreed date. So, in *Donald v Suckling*[15] it was held that a repledge by the pledgee did not end the pledge and the original pledgor could not sue the second pledgee without tendering the sum owing. Similarly, the assignee of a pledgor cannot sue the pledgee who sells the goods because, until the sum owing is tendered, there is no immediate right to possession.[16]

(3) Sale

It is often difficult to discover which of the parties to a contract for the sale of goods has an interest sufficient to support an action in conversion. The crucial question is whether at the date of the alleged conversion the buyer has a sufficient right to immediate possession of the goods. In *Empresa Exportadora de Azucar v IANSA*,[17] the plaintiffs had contracted to buy, and had paid for, two cargoes of sugar to be shipped to them in Chile by the defendants from Cuba. On the orders of the Cuban government, after a military take-over in Chile, the ship discharging the first cargo sailed away with the cargo only partially unloaded and the second ship was diverted back to Cuba part way through its voyage. The buyers were held to have an immediate right to possession of both the partially unloaded cargo and the diverted cargo and succeeded in their action for conversion against the sellers. Sales on credit terms pose rather more difficulties. In *Bloxam v Sanders*[18] it was held that, where goods were sold on credit, the buyer could ordinarily sue the seller in conversion if he wrongfully sold them to a third party, but that, if the seller exercised his right of stoppage in transitu upon the buyer becoming insolvent, the buyer could no longer sue. In the absence of credit terms, the court further declared, the buyer, although he may have the property in the goods, has no right to immediate possession until he tenders or pays the price. In *Chinery v Viall*[19] the seller of goods on credit terms had resold them to a third party. Stating that their decision did not turn on the fact that the original contract was a sale on credit, the court held that 'where there has been no default by the buyer' the buyer may sue the seller. It is thought that *Bloxam v Sanders* is to be preferred, and that a buyer to whom property has passed, but who has not been given credit terms, has no immediate right to possess until he tenders the price. All too often problems of conversion turn on such questions of personal property law.[20]

(4) Licensee

Sometimes a licensee may be able to sue in conversion. In *Northam v Bowden*[1] the plaintiff had a licence to prospect certain land for tin, and the defendant, without permission, carted away some of the soil on this land. It was held that 'if the plaintiff

---

15 (1866) LR 1 QB 585. A mere equitable pledge may be sufficient: *Maynegrain Pty Ltd v Compafina Bank* [1984] 1 NSWLR 258.
16 *Halliday v Holgate* (1868) LR 3 Exch 299. Cf *Bradley v Copley* (1845) 1 CB 685. The assignee of a bill of sale which authorises the borrower to remain in possession of the goods cannot sue in conversion for a wrongful seizure of the goods by a sheriff, because, until the assignee has demanded payment and been refused, or the borrower has otherwise defaulted in payment, he has no immediate right to possession.
17 [1983] 2 Lloyd's Rep 171, CA (a defence of 'act of state' was rejected).
18 (1825) 4 B & C 941.
19 (1860) 5 H & N 288.
20 See, for example *Wood v Bell* (1856) 5 E & B 772 (punching of name on keel of ship evinced intention to pass property from the ship to the plaintiff who had commissioned it).
1   (1855) 11 Exch 70.

had a right to the gravel and soil for the purpose of getting any mineral that could be found in it, he had such a possession of the whole as entitled him to maintain an action for its conversion against a wrongdoer'.[2] Apart from such cases of profits à prendre, licensees of goods are bailees and call for no separate treatment.

(5)   FINDER

The popular maxim 'finders-keepers' has some considerable substance to it. The rule that possession is sufficient to ground a claim in conversion means that in certain circumstances someone who finds a chattel can keep it and protect his right to do so against third parties. The rules regarding finding were authoritatively settled in *Parker v British Airways Board*[3] although their application to particular facts is often difficult:

> The finder of a chattel acquires rights over it if the true owner is unknown and the chattel appears to have been abandoned or lost and he takes it into his care and control. He acquires a right to keep it against all but the true owner or one who can assert a prior right to keep the chattel which was subsisting at the time when the finder took the chattel into his care and control.

In the classic case of *Armory v Delamirie*:[4]

> A chimney sweeper's boy found a jewel and handed it to an apprentice of a goldsmith to be valued. He removed the jewel from its setting and handed back the setting to the boy and offered him 1½d for the jewel. The boy refused the offer for the jewel whereupon the goldsmith declined to return the jewel to him. The court found for the boy against the goldsmith in trover.

Any employee or agent who finds goods in the course of his employment does so on behalf of his employer who acquires a finder's rights. Anyone with finder's rights has an obligation to take reasonable steps to trace the true owner.

However, an occupier of land or a building has rights superior to those of a finder over goods in, under, or attached to that land or building. Thus, a medieval gold brooch buried eight inches under the soil in a public park found by the use of a metal detector,[5] and a prehistoric boat embedded in the soil six feet below the surface,[6] belong to the landowner. Similar rules apply to ships, vehicles and aircraft. An occupier of premises has rights superior to those of a finder over goods upon or in, but not attached to, the premises only if, before the finding, he has manifested an intention to exercise control over the building and the things which may be upon it or in it.

This last rule is difficult to apply, as the cases show. In *Parker v British Airways Board*:[7]

> The plaintiff was in the defendants' first class lounge at Heathrow Airport awaiting his flight. He found a gold bracelet on the floor and handed it to the defendants' employee with his name and address and a request that it be returned to him if unclaimed. Nobody claimed it and

---

2   (1855) 11 Exch 70 at 73 (per Martin B).
3   [1982] QB 1004, [1982] 1 All ER 834, CA. See especially the judgment of Donaldson LJ.
4   (1722) 1 Stra 505.
5   *Waverley Borough Council v Fletcher* [1996] QB 334, CA; and see *South Staffordshire Water Co v Sharman* [1896] 2 QB 44.
6   *Elwes v Brigg Gas Co* (1886) 33 Ch D 562.
7   [1982] QB 1004, [1982] 1 All ER 834, CA; and see *Waverley Borough Council v Fletcher* supra at 781–786.

the defendants failed to return it and sold it. The Court of Appeal held that the proceeds belonged to the plaintiff.

The defendants had shown no intention beforehand to exercise such control over the lounge as to displace the plaintiff's rights as a finder.

In *Bridges v Hawkesworth*[8] the finder of a packet of bank notes lying on the floor in the public part of a shop was held to be entitled to them as against the owner of the shop. A soldier billeted in a house who found a brooch loose in a crevice on top of a window frame there was held entitled as against the non-occupying owner to the brooch.[9] By contrast, owners of premises were entitled, as against demolition workmen-finders, to bank notes found by the latter in a box in the wall safe of an old cellar.[10] An occupier with a superior claim to a finder must also take reasonable steps to trace the true owner.

(6) JUS TERTII (THIRD PARTY RIGHTS)

Under the unamended common law a plaintiff often succeeded in conversion even though the defendant could show that a third party had a better title than the plaintiff. As it was said, the defendant could not plead jus tertii. A most significant procedural reform implemented by the 1977 Act, a reform of procedure which in effect also amends substantive law, is the abolition of the common law rules on jus tertii.[11]

The defendant in an action of conversion or other wrongful interference is now entitled to prove that a third party has a better right than the plaintiff with respect to all or any part of the interest claimed by the plaintiff. The aims of this reform were to avoid multiplicity of actions by allowing interested third parties to apply to be joined in actions, to protect defendants against the risk of being liable to two different claimants in respect of the same interference, and to limit the plaintiff's damages to his actual loss.

The Act authorised the making of rules of court to implement this change.[12] Under those rules, the plaintiff in an action for conversion is required to give particulars of his title and to identify any person who, to his knowledge, has or claims an interest in the goods.[13] The defendant is authorised to apply for directions as to whether any person should be joined with a view to establishing whether he has a better right than the plaintiff, or has a claim as a result of which the defendant might be doubly liable.[14] The relevant date for ascertaining the interest of the third party is the date of the alleged conversion.[15] Where a party fails to appear at the hearing or to comply with a direction, the court may by order deprive him of any right of action against the defendant for the wrong, either unconditionally or subject to such terms and conditions as might be specified.[16]

These rules abolish the former principle that a possessor of goods could recover for the full amount of their value although he was not the owner, and even though he

8 (1851) 21 LJQB 75.
9 *Hannah v Peel* [1945] KB 509, [1945] 2 All ER 288.
10 *London Corpn v Appleyard* [1963] 2 All ER 834, but was this because the goods were 'attached' to the premises perhaps?
11 Torts (Interference with Goods) Act 1977, s 8(1).
12 Torts (Interference with Goods) Act 1977, s 8(2).
13 RSC Ord 15, r 10A(1). Would it be sufficient for P to plead that D stole the car from X (unknown) and therefore X has the better title?
14 RSC Ord 15, r 10A(4).
15 *De Franco v Metropolitan Police Comr* (1987) Times, 8 May, CA.
16 RSC Ord 15, r 10A(4).

was not personally liable to the owner to that extent.[17] The same rules abolish the principle that a bailee was estopped from denying his bailor's title: the bailee when sued by his bailor can now have a named third party joined in.

(B)   THE SUBJECT MATTER

Any goods can be the subject matter of conversion. Although cheques are of value only as choses in action, the courts have satisfied the demands of commercial convenience by allowing the full value represented by them to be recovered in actions for conversion. So, where a banker has not handled actual cash or notes but has merely made the appropriate entries by way of credit or debit balances, the courts will treat the conversion as being of the goods, that is of the piece of paper, the cheque, under which the money was transferred, and the value of the goods converted as being the sum represented by the cheque.[18] This doctrine, which is certainly applicable to all negotiable instruments, makes substantial inroads on any possible rule, traceable to the former fiction of losing and finding, that conversion does not lie in respect of rights in intangible property. But this is not the limit of the doctrine; in *Bavins Junr and Sims v London and South Western Bank*[19] all the judges in the Court of Appeal thought that the full value of a non-negotiable document evidencing a debt could be recovered in an action for conversion. It would seem that whenever a particular intangible right is represented in the ordinary course of business by a special written instrument, even though not negotiable, the value of the right is recoverable in an action for conversion of the instrument. So, a life insurance policy[20] or a guarantee[1] may be converted.

These rules are unaffected by the 1977 Act which provides that unless the context otherwise requires 'goods' includes all goods personal other than things in action and money.[2] The Act thus retains the common-law rule that money as currency (though not as coins[3]) does not fall within the ambit of conversion. The rule that a document evidencing a thing in action, although not the thing in action itself, can be converted, is also unaffected.

(C)   HUMAN BODY PRODUCTS

Advances in medical science pose some fascinating conundrums concerning property rights in human body products. If a husband about to undergo chemotherapy stores sperm to enable his wife to conceive via artificial insemination at some later date, will the sperm bank be liable for conversion if they take that sperm and use it, without the donor's consent, to inseminate a patient other than his wife? Blood is taken from a patient who is HIV positive and then used without his consent or knowledge to develop

---

17 Eg *Glenwood Lumber Co v Phillips* [1904] AC 405. Decisions like *The Winkfield* [1902] P 42, CA are affected. There the Postmaster-General, as bailee, was able to recover the full value of mail lost through the defendant's wrongdoing even though he was not accountable to the bailors for the loss. Now the Post Office would have to identify the bailors, whereupon the defendant could join them in the proceedings and the damages would be apportioned as between bailors and bailee.

18 *Lloyds Bank v Chartered Bank of India, Australia and China* [1929] 1 KB 40, CA, at 55–6 (per Scrutton LJ).

19 [1900] 1 QB 270.

20 *Wills v Wells* (1818) 2 Moore CP 247; *Watson v MacLean* (1858) EB & E 75.

1   *M'Leod v M'Ghie* (1841) 2 Man & G 326.

2   Torts (Interference with Goods) Act 1977, s 14(1).

3   Eg money in a bag: *Taylor v Plumer* (1815) 3 M & S 562.

an AIDS vaccine from which doctors make their fortune. Such scenarios raise three questions pertinent to the tort of conversion. (1) Do human body products constitute goods? (2) Does the 'donor' continue to enjoy any possessory rights over those 'goods'? (3) Are there policy grounds for discouraging such actions in conversion? Only a partial answer can be offered to any of these questions. It is well established that there is no property in a dead body. In *Dobson v North Tyneside Health Authority*,[4] the plaintiff's daughter collapsed at work. She was admitted to the first defendant's hospital, but discharged five days later with a provisional diagnosis of epilepsy. Two months later she was re-admitted to hospital and two brain tumours were diagnosed. She died before a planned operation could be performed. An autopsy was carried out and her brain removed and preserved. Her body was then returned to her family for burial, minus the brain. The brain was stored at the second defendant's hospital but subsequently disposed of. The plaintiffs sued in conversion alleging that the defendants' failure to keep and preserve the brain deprived them of the opportunity to discover whether the deceased's tumours were benign or malignant and thus deprived them of evidence crucial in a claim for medical negligence against the first defendant.

The Court of Appeal dismissed the claim for conversion re-affirming the principle that *generally* there is no property right in a corpse, or its parts. Only where some significant process has been undertaken to alter that body, or preserve it for scientific or exhibition purposes, can any title to the body be claimed. So a museum possessing a valuable Egyptian mummy can assert a claim to that mummy, and, apparently, doctors who deliberately preserved a two-headed foetus could maintain a similar claim.[5]

Dobson expressly addresses property in tissues and organs taken from the dead. Dicta in the judgment suggest a similar analysis may apply to products taken from living human bodies. Unless and until, some special process alters the very nature of the body product in England, as in the US,[6] a claim in conversion for misuse of such products looks likely to fail.[7]

(D)   STATE OF MIND OF THE DEFENDANT

Save for the statutory conversion created by section 2(2) of the 1977 Act there can only be a conversion if there is intentional conduct resulting in an interference with the goods of the plaintiff.

In *Ashby v Tolhurst*:[8]

A third party had driven away the plaintiff's car which he had left in the car park of the defendants. At the trial the plaintiff gave evidence that the attendant told him that he had 'given' the car to the third party. His case in conversion rested on the assertion that this word 'imports that the attendant took some active step to place this thief in possession of the motor car' but it was found 'impossible to collect that meaning out of the words'. There was therefore no conversion, quite apart from the fact that the conditions on the ticket were also deemed to exclude liability.

If the defendant intends that dealing with the goods which, in fact, interferes with the control of the plaintiff, that act will be conversion:

---

4   [1996] 4 All ER 474, [1997] 1 WLR 596, CA.
5   *Doodeward v Spence* (1908) 6 CLR 406. And see now *R v Kelly* [1998] 3 All ER 741, CA.
6   See the famous case of *Moore v Regents of the University of California* 793 P 2d 479 (Cal 1990) where the plaintiff failed to assert property rights in a cell-line developed from his excised spleen.
7   See generally Matthews 'Whose Body? People as Property' [1983] CLP 193.
8   [1937] 2 KB 242, [1937] 2 All ER 837, CA.

though the doer may not know of or intend to challenge the property or possession of the true owner.[9]

Mistake and good faith are irrelevant:

the liability…is founded upon what has been regarded as a salutary rule for the protection of property, namely that persons deal with the property in chattels or exercise acts of ownership over them at their peril.[10]

So, as against the true owner, it is no defence for an auctioneer, after selling goods on behalf of a client, honestly delivering them to the buyer, and paying the proceeds of sale to his client, to say that he was unaware that his client did not own the goods.[11] And bailiffs seizing and selling a cash register at auction were liable to the plaintiff who had sold the cash register under an HP agreement whereby he retained property in the register until all payments were made, albeit the bailiffs had no reason to believe possession of the goods vested in any person other than the company against whom the seizure order was made and in whom physical possession of the register vested.[12]

(E) ACTS OF CONVERSION

In some of the acts of conversion now to be enumerated, especially those involving a sale of the goods, it is unchallengeably clear that the act is sufficiently inconsistent with the rights of the true owner to be a conversion. In many of the other ways of committing conversion, the courts have a discretion whether they will treat the act as sufficiently inconsistent with the right of the true owner to be a conversion – this is especially true in the case of physical damage to the goods and breach of bailment.

The courts have not fully spelt out the factors which go to the exercise of their discretion: the most important probably are the extent and duration of the control or dominion exercised over the goods, the intention and motive of the defendant, the amount of harm caused to the goods, and the expense and inconvenience suffered by the owner.

(1) TAKING GOODS OR DISPOSSESSING

To take goods out of the possession of another may be to convert them. To steal, or to seize under legal process without justification,[13] is a conversion. If, after lopping off the branches of his neighbour's apple tree when they overhang his land, a householder appropriates the fruit, he commits conversion.[14] Merely to remove goods from one

---

9   *Caxton Publishing Co Ltd v Sutherland Publishing Co* [1939] AC 178 at 202, [1938] 4 All ER 389 at 404 (per Lord Porter); *Douglas Valley Finance Co Ltd v S Hughes (Hirers) Ltd* [1969] 1 QB 738, [1966] 3 All ER 214.

10   *Fowler v Hollins* (1872) LR 7 QB 616 at 639 (per Cleasby B); affd sub nom *Hollins v Fowler* (1875) LR 7 HL 757; followed in *Union Transport Finance Ltd v British Car Auctions Ltd* [1978] 2 All ER 385, CA and *R H Willis & Son v British Car Auctions Ltd* [1978] 2 All ER 392, CA.

11   *Consolidated Co v Curtis & Son* [1892] 1 QB 495. In *Moorgate Mercantile Co Ltd v Finch and Read* [1962] 1 QB 701, [1962] 2 All ER 467, CA, the borrower of a car had it confiscated upon conviction for carrying in it uncustomed watches. This was rightly held to be a conversion, for the confiscation was the result of his intentional act of carrying the watches in the car.

12   *Chubb Cash Ltd v John Crilley & Son* [1983] 2 All ER 294, [1983] 1 WLR 599, CA.

13   *Tinkler v Poole* (1770) 5 Burr 2657; *Burton v Hughes* (1824) 2 Bing 173; *Chubb Cash Ltd v John Crilley (a firm)* (supra).

14   *Mills v Brooker* [1919] 1 KB 555.

place to another is not conversion;[15] where a porter moved goods of another in order to reach his own, and negligently failed to replace them, he was not liable in conversion for their subsequent loss.[16] It may be, however, that if they are moved to an unreasonable place with a consequent risk of loss, this is conversion; in *Forsdick v Collins*,[17] for instance, the defendant came into possession of land on which the plaintiff had a block of Portland stone and the removal of the Portland stone by the defendant 'to a distance' was held to be a conversion. A deprivation of the goods which is more than a mere moving of the goods, but in reality deprives the plaintiffs of the use of the goods for however short a time, will generally constitute conversion.[18] To make the plaintiff hand over goods under duress is conversion.[19]

(2) DESTROYING OR ALTERING

To destroy goods is to convert them, if done intentionally.[20] The quantum of harm constituting a destruction for this purpose is clearly a question of degree, but damage as such is not a conversion.[1] A change of identity not amounting to destruction is enough; for example, to draw out part of a vessel of liquor and fill it up with water is conversion,[2] but perhaps merely to cut a log in two is not.[3] If goods are applied for a purpose which eliminates their utility as goods in their original form, for instance the making of wine from grapes, or of clothing from cloth, this is conversion;[4] but it is not to bottle another's wine in order to preserve it.[5]

(3) USING

'If a man takes my horse and rides it and then redelivers it to me nevertheless I may have an action against him, for this is a conversion...'[6] To use goods as your own is ordinarily to convert them; it was thus conversion for a person, to whom carbolic acid drums were delivered by mistake, to deal with them as his own by pouring the contents into his tank.[7] 'The wearing of a pearl is a conversion.'[8] In *Mulgrave v Ogden*[9] it was said:

> No law compelleth him that finds a thing to keep it safely; as if a man finds a garment, and suffers it to be moth-eaten; or if one find a horse, and giveth it no sustenance: but if a man find a thing and useth it, he is answerable, for it is conversion: so if he of purpose misuseth it; as if one finds paper, and puts it into the water, etc, but for negligent keeping no law punisheth him.

15 *Fouldes v Willoughby* (1841) 8 M & W 540, where the defendant removed the plaintiff's horses from a ferry boat on to the shore because he did not wish the plaintiff to travel in the boat.
16 *Bushel v Miller* (1718) 1 Stra 128.
17 (1816) 1 Stark 173; cf *Sanderson v Marsden and Jones* (1922) 10 Ll L Rep 467, CA (defendant removing timber from quay to his premises not a conversion).
18 *Empresa Exportadora de Azucar v IANSA* [1983] 2 Lloyd's Rep 171, CA; but see to the contrary *384238 Ontario Ltd v The Queen in Right of Canada* (1983) 8 DLR (4th) 676.
19 *Grainger v Hill* (1838) 4 Bing NC 212.
20 Accidental destruction is not conversion: *Simmons v Lillystone* (1853) 8 Exch 431.
1   *Fouldes v Willoughby*, supra, at 549 (per Alderson B).
2   *Richardson v Atkinson* (1723) 1 Stra 576.
3   Dictum of Parke B, in *Simmons v Lillystone* supra at 442.
4   Cf *Hollins v Fowler* (1875) LR 7 HL 757 at 764, 768 (dictum of Blackburn J, that a miller innocently grinding another's corn commits conversion).
5   *Philpott v Kelly* (1835) 3 Ad & El 106.
6   Rolle *Abridgement*, tit Action sur Case, 5.
7   *Lancashire and Yorkshire Rly Co v MacNicoll* (1918) 88 LJKB 601.
8   *Petre (Lord) v Heneage* (1701) 12 Mod Rep 519 at 520 (per Holt CJ).
9   (1591) Cro Eliz 219.

The claim of the plaintiff 'would not be defeated by the fact that the defendant whom he sues for the misuse of his temporary dominion of the property claims to be an agent for someone else'.[10] In a Scottish case a vendor who, without negligence, used a boat sold by him has been held liable in conversion to the buyer to whom property had passed.[11]

A mere misuse by a bailee, unaccompanied by any denial of title, is not a conversion although it might be some other tort.[12]

(4) RECEIVING

Voluntarily[13] to receive goods in consummation of a transaction which is intended by the parties to give to the recipient some proprietary rights in the goods may be a conversion actionable by the owner.[14] It has been held a conversion for a purchaser so to receive goods,[15] or for a banker to receive a cheque from a person who has no title to it and to credit the proceeds to his account.[16] If the defendant in good faith receives the goods for the purposes of storage or transport[17] he does not commit conversion. There is no act asserting a proprietary interest in the goods, because it is not the main purpose of such transactions to pass interests in the goods. Receipt of goods by way of pledge is conversion if the delivery of the goods is conversion.[18]

It needs to be noted, however, that there are many instances where the demands of commercial convenience have been thought to outweigh the need to protect owners of goods: indeed, Parliament and the courts have in certain circumstances gone so far as to hold that receivers of goods from persons with no title commit no conversion, and sometimes that they even acquire a good title to them,[19]

For example, the true owner of goods may be precluded by his conduct from denying the seller's authority to sell, whereupon the buyer will acquire a good title.[20] Where an agent having authority in the ordinary course of his business to dispose of goods is in possession of such goods with the consent of the owner, any disposition of them made by him in the course of the business of a mercantile agent to a bona fide purchaser for value is as valid as if he had the authority of the owner.[1]

---

10 *Morison v London County and Westminster Bank Ltd* [1914] 3 KB 356, at 386, CA (per Phillimore LJ, obiter).
11 *Knight v Wilson* 1949 SLT 26.
12 *Lee v Atkinson and Brooks* (1609) Yelv 172 (when hirer of horse deviates, action on case lies) approved in *Donald v Suckling* (1866) LR 1 QB 585 at 615, by Blackburn J, who said that if the act is repugnant to the bailment, it is conversion, but 'where the act, though unauthorised, is not repugnant to the contract as to show a disclaimer' it is not the case. *Penfolds Wines Pty Ltd v Elliott* (1946) 74 CLR 204; Palmer *Bailment* (1979) 754.
13 Receipt by an involuntary bailee is not conversion.
14 Cf *M'Combie v Davies* (1805) 6 East 538 at 540 (per Lord Ellenborough CJ): 'Certainly a man is guilty of a conversion who takes my property by assignment from another who has no authority to dispose of it; for what is that but assisting that other in carrying his wrongful act into effect?'
15 *Farrant v* — (1822) 3 Stark 130.
16 *Fine Arts Society v Union Bank of London* (1886) 17 QBD 705, CA; *AL Underwood Ltd v Bank of Liverpool* [1924] 1 KB 775, CA; *Lloyds Bank Ltd v Chartered Bank of India, Australia and China* [1929] 1 KB 40, CA.
17 Per Blackburn J, in *Hollins v Fowler* (1875) LR 7 HL 757 at 767; cf *Sheridan v New Quay Co* (1858) 4 CBNS 618 (carrier).
18 Sale of Goods Act 1979, s 11(2).
19 The ancient doctrine of market overt was abolished by the Sale of Goods (Amendment) Act 1994.
20 Sale of Goods Act 1979, s 21.
1 Factors Act 1889, ss 1(1), 2(1). For the limits of this doctrine see *Pearson v Rose & Young Ltd* [1951] 1 KB 275 CA.

(5) DISPOSITION WITHOUT DELIVERY

A person who agrees to sell goods to which he has no title and who does not transfer possession of them does not thereby ordinarily commit conversion, for the bargain and sale is void if the seller has no rights in the goods.[2]

(6) DISPOSITION AND DELIVERY

Ordinarily a person who without lawful authority disposes of goods with the intention of transferring the title or some other right in the goods, and who delivers the goods, thereby commits a conversion. A sale and a pledge[3] may each constitute such a disposition. In *Syeds v Hay*[4] the rule applied to a sea-captain who delivered goods to a wharfinger in the wrongful belief that the wharfinger had a lien on them.

The main difficulty arises where the defendant is an innocent transferor. Innocence of itself is no defence; so the auctioneer who sells in good faith goods which do not belong to his client commits conversion by handing them over to the buyer.[5] Yet it is felt that this need to support the validity of commercial dealings must, in the interests of innocent defendants, have some limits.

In *Hollins v Fowler*[6] Lord Blackburn said:

> one who deals with goods at the request of the person who has the actual custody of them, in the bona fide belief that the custodier is the true owner, or has the authority of the true owner, should be excused for what he does if the act is of such a nature as would be excused if done by the authority of the person in possession, if he was a finder of the goods or intrusted with their custody.

This did not exclude from liability the defendants in the instant case, who were acting as cotton brokers, buying, not as agents on account of a certain customer as principal, but in expectation of finding a customer. The principle seems to be this: if the defendant has himself negotiated the transaction and then disposes of the goods in pursuance of it, he is liable; if, on the other hand, someone else has effected the transaction, and the defendant acting on his behalf merely delivers in consummation of that transaction, it is not conversion by the defendant. Therefore, a packer shipping goods on the order of his principal does not commit conversion;[7] nor in similar circumstances do mere carriers[8] or warehousemen.[9] *National Mercantile Bank v Rymill*[10] marks the furthest limit of this exception and is distinguishable from *Consolidated Co v Curtis* only in that the auctioneer did not negotiate the sale. Goods were deposited with the defendant auctioneer to sell; the seller eventually sold them himself, and, on his instructions, the

2 *Lancashire Waggon Co v Fitzhugh* (1861) 6 H & N 502; he may, however, be liable for injurious falsehood; see ch 8, post.
3 *Parker v Godin* (1728) 2 Stra 813.
4 (1791) 4 Term Rep 260. But if someone entrusts another with a chattel to be used by him, the bailor impliedly authorises the bailee to allow a lien for the cost of necessary repairs to be created over it: *Green v All Motors Ltd* [1917] 1 KB 625, CA; *Tappenden v Artus* [1964] 2 QB 185, [1963] 3 All ER 213, CA.
5 *Consolidated Co v Curtis & Son* [1892] 1 QB 495; *Barker v Furlong* [1891] 2 Ch 172 at 181.
6 (1875) LR 7 HL 757 at 766–7; in *Re Samuel (No 2)* [1945] Ch 408, [1945] 2 All ER 437n, a solicitor who received jewellery from the agent of his bankrupt client and handed it to another agent on his client's instruction knowing of the intention to sell it, was held to be acting ministerially and not liable in conversion.
7 *Greenway v Fisher* (1824) 1 C & P 190.
8 *Sheridan v New Quay Co* (1858) 4 CBNS 618.
9 *Glyn Mills Currie & Co v East and West India Dock Co* (1880) 6 QBD 475 at 491 (per Bramwell B); affd (1881) 7 App Cas 591, HL.
10 (1881) 44 LT 767, CA.

defendant handed them to the buyer and in so doing was held not liable in conversion to the true owner.

In *R H Willis & Son v British Car Auctions Ltd* Lord Denning treated the *Rymill* case as a departure from *Hollins v Fowler* by a court anxious to protect the auctioneer, and decided that an auctioneer is liable in conversion to the true owner where goods are sold by his intervention, under the hammer or as the result of a provisional bid.[11]

If an involuntary bailee, acting reasonably, delivers goods to one who is not entitled to them he does not commit conversion. Thus, where, upon goods being refused at the consignee's late place of business, the carrier took them back to his store and notified the consignee, and then handed them to a former employee of the consignee (being unaware that this man had left the consignee's employment), this was no conversion.[12] If the defendant is not placed in the dilemma of the involuntary bailee and none the less makes himself a party to an unauthorised transfer he commits conversion. In *Hiort v Bott*,[13] for example,

> an invoice and delivery order were mistakenly sent by the plaintiffs to the defendant. Thinking that he was thereby correcting the error, on his own initiative the defendant indorsed the delivery order over to the plaintiff's agent, who thereby obtained the goods for himself. This was conversion.[14]

In the case of cheques and some other negotiable instruments there is a limited statutory exemption from liability. A banker paying a cheque (even though not indorsed or irregularly indorsed) in good faith and in the ordinary course of business to the collecting banker is in the same position as if he had paid it to the true owner.[15]

(7)   MISDELIVERY BY CARRIER

A carrier[16] or warehouseman[17] who by mistake delivers goods to the wrong person, commits a conversion whether or not his mistake was innocent.[18] But failure to deliver because the goods have been lost or destroyed by accident or carelessness is not conversion.[19] Nor is it conversion for a bailee[20] or pledgee[1] without notice of the claim of the true owner to return goods to the person from whom he received them.

11 [1978] 2 All ER 392, CA where the police seized a gig from A, and, when he was later found not guilty of stealing it, after demand by the true owner for possession, handed it back to A: this was a conversion by the police actionable by the true owner; *Winter v Bancks* (1901) 84 LT 504.

12 *Heugh v London and North Western Rly Co* (1870) LR 5 Exch 51; cf *Elvin and Powell Ltd v Plummer Roddis Ltd* (1933) 50 TLR 158, where plaintiff's counsel conceded that the defendant did not intend to deny the title of the plaintiff.

13 (1874) LR 9 Exch 86.

14 Contra, if as in *Elvin and Powell v Plummer Roddis*, supra, the goods themselves had been delivered to the defendant and handed by him to the third party.

15 Bills of Exchange Act 1882, s 80, as amended by s 1 of the Cheques Act 1957.

16 *Youl v Harbottle* (1791) Peake 68, NP.

17 *Devereux v Barclay* (1819) 2 B & Ald 702.

18 If the carrier delivers in accordance with the seller's instructions (or even as a carrier would interpret his instructions according to the usual course of business although he in fact delivered them to a person to whom the seller did not intend delivery to be made) this is not a misdelivery: *McKean v McIvor*(1870) LR 6 Exch 36. It is conversion by a carrier to deliver goods to another carrier by whom they are misappropriated, unless the defendant carrier is authorised to make a sub-contract; *Garnham, Harris and Elton Ltd v Alfred W Ellis (Transport) Ltd* [1967] 2 All ER 940.

19 *Owen v Lewyn* (1672) 1 Vent 223; *The Arpad* [1934] P 189 at 232, CA (per Maugham LJ).

20 *Hollins v Fowler* (1875) LR 7 HL 757 at 767 (per Blackburn J). Otherwise the bailee would be in an impossible position, for if he retained he could not plead a title paramount of which he was unaware.

1   *Union Credit Bank Ltd v Mersey Docks and Harbour Board* [1899] 2 QB 205.

(8) REFUSAL TO SURRENDER ON DEMAND

A refusal to surrender goods upon lawful and reasonable demand is a conversion.[2] In particular, this covers the situation where the possession of the defendant was originally lawful; it may be invoked, for example, where the receiving is not itself actionable.

Many of the cases on wrongful detention were actions of detinue. With the abolition of detinue, conversion will now apparently lie in every case in which detinue would formerly have lain. The most important case since the 1977 Act is *Howard E Perry & Co Ltd v British Railways Board*.[3]

> The defendants admitted that the plaintiffs owned and were entitled to immediate possession of steel held by them as carriers in their depots. There was a national steelworkers' strike, and their union had sought the support of railway unions. The defendants feared sympathetic industrial action by their employees if they allowed the plaintiffs to collect the steel. Their refusal to allow the plaintiffs to enter the depots and collect the steel was held wrongful.

There is a large amount of case law on this topic, but the principles are quite simple. Even if the defendant no longer has possession at the time of the demand and refusal it is no defence for him to prove that, prior to the accrual of the plaintiff's title, he wrongfully parted with them.[4] If the defendant refuses to surrender in circumstances where it would be unreasonable for him to do so immediately on demand, this is not conversion. The defendant may postpone surrender until after he has had a reasonable time in which to confirm the title of the claimant, or, if he is an employee, to consult his employer.[5] This reasonableness is a question of fact; many factors may be relevant – the time of the demand, the expense and inconvenience of immediate compliance, the knowledge on the part of the defendant of the claimant's title, and of his identity, and whether the defendant has adequately conveyed to the plaintiff the grounds for his temporary refusal. The doctrine of estoppel may sometimes operate to prevent the defendant from setting up facts which would otherwise have justified a refusal.[6]

(9) GOODS LOST OR DESTROYED

At common law there could be no conversion where there was no voluntary act. Section 2 of the Torts (Interference with Goods) Act 1977, which abolishes detinue, therefore further provides in section 2(2):

> An action lies in conversion for loss or destruction of goods which a bailee has allowed to happen in breach of his duty to his bailor (that is to say it lies in a case which is not otherwise conversion, but would have been detinue before detinue was abolished).

Bailees are required to take reasonable care of goods in their keeping and will be liable for the loss or destruction of such goods unless they can disprove fault,[7] but they are

2   *Eason v Newman* (1596) Cro Eliz 495; *Isaack v Clark* (1615) 2 Bulst 306 at 310 (per Dodderidge J); *Baldwin v Cole* (1704) 6 Mod Rep 212.
3   [1980] 2 All ER 579, [1980] 1 WLR 1375.
4   *Bristol and West of England Bank v Midland Rly Co* [1891] 2 QB 653, CA.
5   *Alexander v Southey* (1821) 5 B & Ald 247.
6   *Seton, Laing & Co v Lafone* (1887) 19 QBD 68, CA; *Henderson & Co v Williams* [1895] 1 QB 521, CA.
7   A bailee will ordinarily be liable unless he disproves fault; *Houghland v R R Low (Luxury Coaches) Ltd* [1962] 1 QB 694, [1962] 2 All ER 159, CA. An involuntary bailee is not liable for failure to return merely because he has lost it; *Howard v Harris* (1884) 1 Cab & El 253, but he is liable if he destroys or damages the goods. If the bailee is unaware that the goods on his premises are not his property, ie an 'unconscious bailee', he is under a duty to exercise reasonable care to ascertain that they were his own before he destroys them; *AVX Ltd v EGM Solders Ltd* (1982) Times, 7 July.

not insurers of the goods. In *Sutcliffe v Chief Constable of West Yorkshire*[8] the police seized the plaintiff's vehicle under powers conferred by section 19 of the Police and Criminal Evidence Act 1984. The car was kept in the police station yard which was well lit and adjacent to the police station. The yard could not be locked as police cars required constant access to the yard. An arson attack destroyed the plaintiff's car. The Court of Appeal dismissed the plaintiff's claim for conversion. The attack was unprecedented. In the circumstances of their custody of the plaintiff's property the defendant had done all that was reasonable to take care of the vehicle.

Denial of title is not of itself conversion.[9] There may, however, be conversion of goods although the defendant has not physically dealt with them,[10] or been in physical possession of them,[11] if his acts deprive the plaintiff of his right to possession or amount to a substantial interference with that right.[12] But a mere threat to prevent an owner in possession from removing his goods will not of itself amount to conversion.[13]

Where goods are left on land, and the occupier refuses to allow the owner of the goods to enter the land and retrieve them, the refusal is not necessarily conversion.[14] It may become conversion, however, if the occupier sets up in himself any right in respect of the goods,[15] or denies the plaintiff most of the rights of ownership, including the right to possession, for a period which is plainly indefinite.[16]

(10) RESIDUAL ACTS AMOUNTING TO A CONVERSION

It must be emphasised again that the above are not exhaustive categories of acts of conversion. There are other acts which are not capable of being readily classified and which may yet fall within the definition of conversion. In these residual cases the judicial discretion whether to treat the act as sufficiently inconsistent with the true owner's rights for a conversion is especially important.

(F) CONVERSION AS BETWEEN CO-OWNERS[17]

Co-ownership does not afford a defence to certain proceedings in conversion. Section 10(1)(a) of the 1977 Act provides that co-ownership is no defence to an action founded on conversion where the defendant, without the authority of the other co-owner, destroys the goods, or disposes of them in a way giving a good title to the entire property in the goods, or otherwise does anything equivalent to the destruction of the other

---

8   [1996] RTR 86, CA.
9   Torts (Interference with Goods) Act 1977, s 11(3). Cf *Oakley v Lyster* [1931] 1 KB 148, CA.
10 *Van Oppen & Co Ltd v Tredegars Ltd* (1921) 37 TLR 504.
11 Eg *Oakley v Lyster* [1931] 1 KB 148, CA (conversion of hardcore on another's land by taking possession of part thereof and total denial and repudiation of owner's right to remainder); and see *Halsbury's Laws* (4th edn) para 1427.
12 *Oakley v Lyster* [1931] 1 KB 148, CA; *Lancashire and Yorkshire Rly Co, London and North Western Rly Co and Graeser Ltd v MacNicoll* (1918) 88 LJKB 601.
13 *England v Cowley* (1873) LR 8 Exch 126 (landlord wishing to distrain stated that he would not permit holder of bill of sale to remove goods unless rent was paid).
14 *Wilde v Waters* (1855) 24 LJCP 193 at 195, Maule J; *British Economical Lamp Co Ltd v Empire Mile End Lane Ltd* (1913) 29 TLR 386.
15 *Walker v Clyde* (1861) 10 CBNS 381; *H E Dibble Ltd v Moore* [1970] 2 QB 181, [19169] 3 All ER 1465, CA.
16 *Howard E Perry & Co Ltd v British Railways Board* [1980] 2 All ER 579 at 583, per Sir Robert Megarry VC; *Bryanston Leasings Ltd v Principality Finance Ltd* [1977] RTR 45.
17 Note ss 20A and 10b of the Sale of Goods Act 1979 (inserted by the Sale of Goods (Amendment) Act 1995) whereby a buyer of a quantity of goods forming part of a larger bulk becomes a proportionate *co-owner* of those goods.

interest in the goods. This principle was well established at common law, and section 10(1)(a) is declared to be by way of restatement of existing law.[18] Thus a partner who paid cheques into a third person's bank account was, by excluding his co-owner's right to enjoy the proceeds, liable for conversion.[19] A co-owner cannot, however, be sued for conversion if he merely makes use of the common property in a reasonable way.[20] Nor was there necessarily a conversion where the co-owner took and kept the goods.[1] The law required (and still does) a destruction of the goods or something equivalent to it.[2]

The 1977 Act, however, does alter the common law by further providing in section 10(1)(b) that it is also no defence to an action founded on conversion where the defendant, without the authority of the other co-owner, purports to dispose of the goods in such a way as would give a good title to the entire property in the goods if he were acting with the authority of all co-owners of the goods. At common law, a sale and delivery by a co-owner which did not pass title was not a conversion because it was not akin to destruction of the plaintiff's property.

The foregoing rules do not affect the law concerning execution or enforcement of judgments, or concerning any form of distress.[3]

(G) REMEDIES: DAMAGES

The major effect of the 1977 Act is to rationalise the remedies available to plaintiffs suing in conversion both in relation to the damages which may be awarded and in making provision for specific return of the goods by way of orders for delivery.

(1) At common law a plaintiff with a limited interest in the goods could normally recover their full value from a third party. Under section 8 of the 1977 Act and rules of court the plaintiff now has to identify any other person whom he knows to have an interest in the goods and any such interested party may be joined, whereupon the damages may be apportioned amongst the interested parties in proportion to their respective interests.[4] Where the other interested party is not traced, as in cases of finding, or a missing bailor, the plaintiff in possession can recover the full value of the goods, but is liable to account to the true owner.[5]

Where the defendant has an interest in the goods, then the plaintiff's damages in respect of the interference with his interest are limited to the value of that interest.[6] An unpaid seller who sold to a third party has been held liable to the original buyer, to

---

18 Torts (Interference with Goods) Act 1977, s 10(3).
19 *Baker v Barclays Bank Ltd* [1955] 2 All ER 571, [1955] 1 WLR 822.
20 As, for instance, by cutting grass and making hay in the common field (*Jacobs v Seward* (1872) LR 5 HL 464) or extracting the oil and the other valuable parts of a dead whale which is owned in common (*Fennings v Lord Grenville* (1808) 1 Taunt 241).
1   The bailee of common property from one co-owner is not guilty of conversion if he refuses to deliver the property on the demand of another co-owner (*Atwood v Ernest* (1853) 13 CB 881; *Harper v Godsell* (1870) LR 5 QB 422) unless the latter has a special property in the entire chattel (*Nyberg v Handelaar* [1892] 2 QB 202, CA).
2   *Morgan v Marquis* (1853) 9 Exch 145; *Baker v Barclays Bank Ltd* [1955] 2 All ER 571.
3   Torts (Interference with Goods) Act 1977, s 11(2).The rules apply equally to intentional trespass to goods as they apply to conversion.
4   Torts (Interference with Goods) Act 1977, s 7(2) and p 51, ante.
5   *Wilson v Lombank Ltd* [1963] 1 All ER 740; *O'Sullivan v Williams* [1992] 3 All ER 385 at 387, CA.
6   *Johnson v Stear* (1863) 15 CBNS 330, CA (owner suing pledgee); *Belsize Motor Supply Co v Cox* [1914] 1 KB 244 (owner suing assignee of hirer).

whom he had not delivered the goods,[7] who was not in default, only for the value of the goods less the contract price owing to him; the policy behind this is lucidly explained by Bramwell B:[8]

> a man cannot by merely changing the form of action[9] entitle himself to recover damages greater than the amount to which he is in law entitled, according to the true facts of the case and the real nature of the transaction.

(2)   The plaintiff in conversion is entitled to be compensated to the extent of the value to him of the goods of which he has been deprived. This will often appropriately be the market value of the goods. Where goods are of a kind which can be readily bought in the market the actual market value will be the appropriate measure; otherwise the replacement value in a comparable state[10] or the original cost minus depreciation will be the standard. Where the actual value of the plaintiff's interest in the goods is less than the market value he may be awarded the value of that interest and not the higher market value.[11] In *Wickham Holdings Ltd v Brooke House Motors*[12] the hirer of a car sold the car in breach of his hire purchase agreement. The finance company, who owned the car, were held able to recover from the ultimate purchaser of the vehicle only the value of the outstanding hire purchase instalments due, and not the higher value of the car itself. In *Chubb Cash Ltd v John Crilley & Son (a firm)*[13] the plaintiff sold a cash register on hire purchase terms. He then assigned the instalments due under the agreement to a credit company in return for a loan agreeing to pay all instalments due should the purchaser of the register default on the hire purchase company. In his action for conversion against bailiffs who had seized the cash register the plaintiff was awarded only the market value of the goods and not the higher amount due under his agreement with the credit company. That consequential loss was held to be irrecoverable.

Where a negotiable instrument or other document ordinarily representing a chose in action is converted, the value which the document represents, and not merely its value as a piece of paper, is the basis of the quantum of damages.

(3)   'The general rule is that a plaintiff whose property is irreversibly converted has vested in him a right to damages for conversion measured by the value of the property at the date of conversion.'[14] Once a claim for conversion has accrued to the plaintiff it is not open to him to delay the issue of his writ and thereby base his action on a subsequent demand and refusal – the duty to mitigate damages operates.[15]

A rule basing damages on value at the date of conversion can be seen to work to the plaintiff's benefit in certain circumstances. If the goods decrease in value between

---

7   If an unpaid seller takes goods out of the buyer's possession he is liable in conversion for the full value of the goods without deduction for the unpaid price: *Healing (Sales) Pty Ltd v Inglis Electrix Pty Ltd* (1968) 42 ALJR 280, H Ct Australia, following *Gillard v Britton* (1841) 8 M & W 575.

8   *Chinery v Viall* (1860) 5 H & N 288.

9   Ie from breach of contract to conversion.

10   *J & E Hall Ltd v Barclay* [1937] 3 All ER 620, CA.

11   But see *Edmondson v Nuttall* (1864) 17 CBNS 280; and *Wilson v Lombank Ltd* [1963] 1 All ER 740 (a case in trespass).

12   [1967] 1 All ER 117, [1967] 1 WLR 295, CA.

13   [1983] 2 All ER 294, [1983] 1 WLR 599, CA.

14   *BBMB Finance (Hong Kong) Ltd v Eda Holdings Ltd* [1991] 2 All ER 129, PC.

15   *Empresa Exportadora de Azucar v IANSA* [1983] 2 Lloyd's Rep 171, CA.

the date of the conversion and the date of judgment the plaintiff may still recover the value at the date of conversion.[16] In *Solloway v McLaughlin*[17]

> The defendant broker fraudulently and contrary to his instructions sold shares of the plaintiff deposited with him. By the time of the trial the defendants had bought in replacement an equivalent number of the shares at a greatly reduced market value. Although the net result was to put the plaintiff in a better position than if his instructions had been obeyed, he was held entitled to recover the difference between the value of the shares at the time of the conversion and the value of the shares since bought in replacement.

However, the general rule is not immutable. In conversion, as in other torts, the fundamental purpose of an award of damages is to compensate the plaintiff for the loss he actually sustains.[18] Thus, the market value (even where ascertainable) at conversion will not necessarily mark the top limit of damages recoverable in conversion in the following instances:

(i) Evidence comes in later to show what was the value at conversion.[19]

(ii) The market value of the goods rises between the date of the cause of action and trial. If the act of conversion relied on by the plaintiff is a sale, and by the time when the plaintiff knows or ought to know of the sale the value has increased, the plaintiff can recover that higher value.[20] There is some authority also for the view that the plaintiff may recover from a broker who has sold his stock its increased value within a reasonable time for buying replacement stock,[1] that is the court estimates the value of the chance of a profit.[2] In *Greening v Wilkinson*:[3]

> The defendant refused to hand over to the plaintiff the plaintiff's warrants for cotton and relying on this demand and refusal the warrants were worth 6d per lb and at trial 10$\frac{1}{2}$d. The jury awarded damages on the basis of 10$\frac{1}{2}$d per lb in accordance with Abbott CJ's ruling that they 'may give the value at the time of the conversion, or at any subsequent time, at their discretion, because the plaintiff might have had a good opportunity of selling the goods if they had not been detained'.[4]

(iii) If the defendant converts the plaintiff's goods and he then increases their value the plaintiff cannot ordinarily recover that increased value.[5] Thus where the defendant converted a partially built ship which he then completed at his own expense the court's view was that the plaintiff was entitled to recover the market value of the completed ship less the expense incurred by the defendant in completing it.[6] Where the act of conversion relied on takes place after the

---

16 *Rhodes v Moules* [1895] 1 Ch 236; the defendants converted the plaintiff's bearer shares, the market price of which dropped after the conversion, and the Court of Appeal refused to allow the defendant to satisfy the judgment against him by purchasing the same number of shares for the plaintiff.

17 [1938] AC 247, [1937] 4 All ER 328, PC; *BBMB Finance v Edna Holdings Ltd* supra.

18 *Brandeis Goldschmidt & Co v Western Transport Ltd* [1981] QB 864, CA; *IBL Ltd v Coussens* [1991] 2 All ER 133 at 1390, CA.

19 *Caxton Publishing Co Ltd v Sutherland Publishing Co* [1939] AC 178 at 203, HL (per Lord Porter).

20 *Sachs v Miklos* [1948] 2 KB 23, [1948] 1 All ER 67, CA.

1 *Samuel and Escombe v Rowe* (1892) 8 TLR 488.

2 *Aitken v Gardiner* (1956) 4 DLR (2d) 119 (Ontario HC).

3 (1825) 1 C & P 625.

4 Lord Porter left open the soundness of this judgment in *Caxton Publishing Co Ltd v Sutherland Publishing Co* [1939] AC 178 at 203, HL.

5 *Caxton Publishing Co Ltd v Sutherland Publishing Co* supra; *Greenwood v Bennett* [1973] QB 195, [1972] 3 All ER 586, CA.

6 *Reid v Fairbanks* (1853) 13 CB 692 (the parties settled the size of the damages awarded).

improvement made to the goods, section 6(1) of the Act is applicable now. If the defendant has improved the goods in the mistaken but honest belief that he had a good title to them an allowance is made for the extent to which at the time at which the goods fall to be valued in assessing damages, the value of the goods is attributable to the improvement. If, for example, the improver is sued for later selling the goods, the statutory allowance applies.[7] A similar allowance is enjoyed by purported purchasers of goods improved by another, provided again that the purchaser acted in good faith.[8] Subsequent purchasers enjoy the same protection.[9] Thus an eventual buyer in good faith of a stolen car when sued by the true owner will have the damages reduced to reflect any improvements made on it since the theft. The Act leaves it uncertain whether the common law rule that an improver who did not act in good faith was entitled to a deduction still survives, or whether the statutory requirement of good faith must be taken to supersede the common law. At common law special rules applied to goods severed from the land such as coal and other minerals,[10] and timber:[11] if, for instance, the defendant innocently severed the plaintiff's coal he was liable only for the value of the coal in the seam, but if his act was wilful, he was liable for its value immediately after severance.[12] These rules may be unaffected by the Act.[13]

(iv) If the plaintiff incurs pecuniary loss as a direct consequence of the conversion he may recover this as special damage in addition to the market value of the goods. A workman deprived of his tools recovered loss of wages;[14] the owner of a converted pony could claim the cost of hiring another.[15] In *Strand Electric and Engineering Co Ltd v Brisford Entertainments Ltd*[16] (an action in detinue):

> In the course of their business the plaintiffs hired to the defendants some switchboards. The plaintiffs claimed the return of the goods and damages for their detention. Besides ordering the return of the goods the court awarded damages on the basis of a reasonable hiring charge for the entire period of detention until judgment. Nor were the damages to be limited to the loss of profit of the plaintiff; the fact that for some of the period during which the defendant detained the equipment the plaintiff would not have been able to find another hirer was irrelevant.

(v) Although detinue is abolished by section 2(1) of the 1977 Act, section 3 of the Act, in effect, preserves the remedies for what would previously have constituted

---

7   And see *Munro v Willmott* [1949] 1 KB 295, [1948] 2 All ER 983 at common law (where plaintiff relied on a demand and refusal rather than an earlier conversion, the plaintiff could not recover the value as increased by the defendant's improvement).

8   Torts (Interference with Goods) Act 1977, s 6(2).

9   Torts (Interference with Goods) Act 1977, s 6(3).

10   The English cases have concerned coal; the rule was applied to shale in *Blenheim Borough and Wairau River Board v British Pavements (Canterbury) Ltd* [1940] NZLR 564.

11   *Burmah Trading Corpn v Mirza Mahomed Allay Sherazee and Burmah Co Ltd* (1878) LR 5 Ind App 130; *Union Bank of Canada v Rideau Lumber Co* (1902) 4 OLR 721; *Greer v Faulkner* (1908) 40 SCR 399 (Canada).

12   *Wood v Morewood* (1841) 3 QB 440n.

13   The Act applies only where the defendant improves goods; it seems doubtful whether severing minerals to make them saleable is to 'improve' them.

14   *Bodley v Reynolds* (1846) 8 QB 779.

15   *Davis v Oswell* (1827) 7 C & P 804.

16   [1952] 2 QB 246, [1952] 1 All ER 796, CA; confirmed in *Inverugie Investments v Hackett* [1995] 3 All ER 841, 845, PC. Where a defendant converted a Rolls Royce on hire from the plaintiffs and then put it out of his power to return it, he remained liable for the hiring charges, namely over £13,000, until it was returned, although its value when converted was only £7,500, *Hillesden Securities Ltd v Ryjak Ltd* [1983] 2 All ER 184, [1983] 1 WLR 959.

detinue by making such remedies available in conversion.[17] Where the defendant has possession of the goods at the time that proceedings are begun, he cannot, by disposing of the goods, reduce his liability for loss occasioned by detention of a profit earning chattel to the market value thereof. However, where the remedy lies in damages while the general rule in conversion is that the value of the converted goods is ascertained at the date of conversion, in detinue authority suggested that the relevant date should be the date of judgment. In *IBL Ltd v Coussens*[18] the defendant converted two cars by wrongful refusal to return them to the plaintiff. The plaintiff asserted that he was entitled to the damages based on the value of the cars at the date of judgment. The Court of Appeal held that in such cases of temporary deprivation of property, where no irreversible act of conversion is committed, evidence must be adduced as to the true loss suffered by the owner of the goods. The measure of damages was not to be fixed arbitrarily at *either* the date of conversion or the date of judgment. Their Lordships remitted the case back to the master for evidence of (a) the value of the cars, and (b) what the plaintiffs would have done with the cars had they been returned when requested. If, for example, the plaintiffs would have sold the cars between the dates of conversion and judgment, the value of the cars at that time, plus interest, would represent a proper measure of damages.

(vi) The effect as between the parties to a satisfied judgment for damages in conversion is to transfer the title to the defendant.[19] It follows that the court will not award damages for loss of use as well as the value of the goods where the effect would be doubly to compensate the plaintiff: the capacity for profitable use is part of the value of the goods. Thus where the defendant converted certain manufacturing plant of the plaintiff, he was liable for the value of the plant when converted but not for loss of use between that date and trial.[20] On the other hand, if the defendant wrongfully detained goods and later sold them it seems that the plaintiff could recover in addition to their value the loss of use from the date of the unlawful detention until sale,[1] and indeed until the plaintiff had a reasonable opportunity to buy a replacement after learning of that sale,[2] but not for loss of use until trial.

(vii) It is doubtful in what circumstances a buyer who does not recover his goods can claim a loss of re-sale profit.[3] Where the action of conversion based on non-delivery is an alternative to an action in contract and the seller is unaware of the re-sale contract, this loss of profit is not recoverable as such in conversion, although where there is no market in the goods the re-sale price may be evidence of value.[4]

The courts will, if the defendant returns the goods before trial, reduce the damages in conversion by the amount of its value at that time:[5] in short, the court will not enforce a sale on the defendant, and 'subject to the payment of costs and special damages (if there are any) an action for damages for conversion can always be stayed if the

---

17 *Hillesden Securities Ltd v Ryjak Ltd* [1983] 2 All ER 184, [1983] 1 WLR 959.
18 [1991] 2 All ER 133, CA.
19 *Ellis v John Stenning & Son* [1932] 2 Ch 81, [1932] All ER Rep 597.
20 *Re Simms, ex p Trustee* [1934] Ch 1, [1933] All ER Rep 302, CA.
1 *Strand Electric and Engineering Co Ltd v Brisford Entertainments Ltd* [1952] 2 QB 246, [1952] 1 All ER 796, CA, at 255 and 801 respectively (per Denning LJ).
2 *Re Simms, ex p Trustee* [1934] Ch 1 at 30 (per Romer LJ).
3 This loss was recovered in *France v Gaudet* (1871) LR 6 QB 199.
4 *The Arpad* [1934] P 189, CA. Conversely, a buyer still recovered the market value from a seller not delivering to him, although the loss of the buyer on his contract of re-sale is less than this sum; *D Joseph Ltd v Ralph Wood & Co Ltd* [1951] WN 224.
5 *Fisher v Prince* (1762) 3 Burr 1363; *Solloway v McLaughlin* [1938] AC 247 at 258–9, [1937] 4 All ER 328 at 332, 333, PC.

defendant offers to hand over the property in dispute'.[6] The value of the goods when returned is set off against the damages calculated as set out in the preceding paragraphs. Where goods acquired by the plaintiff for use in a manufacturing process have been wrongfully detained and later returned to him, the plaintiff must show that a loss of profit or other pecuniary loss has resulted from the detention.[7] If he fails to prove that he would have used the goods at any time before their return, he cannot recover the fall in their market value over the period of their detention and may receive only nominal damages.[8] It will be otherwise where he has purchased the goods for re-sale during the period of detention.[9]

(H) REMEDIES: OTHER FORMS OF RELIEF

The 1977 Act introduces common remedies for all forms of 'wrongful interferences with goods'. Section 3 provides that in proceedings for conversion, or for any other chattel tort, against a person in possession or control of goods,[10] the following relief may be given, as far as is appropriate:[11] an order for delivery and for payment of any consequential damages;[12] an order for delivery of the goods, but giving the defendant the alternative of paying damages by reference to the value of the goods, together in either alternative with payment of any consequential damages;[13] or damages.[14]

If it is shown to the court's satisfaction that an order for delivery and payment of any consequential damages has not been complied with, the court may revoke the order (or the relevant part of it)[15] and make an order for payment of damages by reference to the value of the goods.[16]

Where an order is made for delivery but giving the defendant the alternative of paying damages,[17] the defendant may satisfy the order by returning the goods at any time

6   *USA and Republic of France v Dollfus Mieg et Compagnie SA and Bank of England* [1952] AC 582 at 619, [1952] 1 All ER 572 at 590, HL (per Lord Radcliffe).
7   *Brandeis Goldschmidt & Co Ltd v Western Transport Ltd* [1981] QB 864 at 870, [1982] 1 All ER 28 at 31, CA per Brandon LJ; *Williams v The Peel River Land and Mineral Co Ltd* (1886) 55 LT 689 at 692–693, CA per Bowen LJ. See also *Williams v Archer* (1847) 5 CB 318; *Barrow v Arnaud* (1846) 8 QB 595, 604, Ex Ch.
8   *Williams v Peel Land and Minerals Co Ltd* (1886) 55 LT 689 at 692–693, CA per Bowen LJ; *Bryanston Leasings Ltd v Principality Finance Ltd* [1977] RTR 45; *Brandeis Goldschmidt & Co Ltd v Western Transport Ltd* [1981] QB 864 at 871, [1982] 1 All ER 28 at 32, CA per Brandon LJ.
9   *Brandeis Goldschmidt & Co Ltd v Western Transport Ltd* [1981] QB 864 at 873, [1982] 1 All ER 28 at 34, CA per Brandon LJ.
10 Even though the defendant is no longer in possession at the date of judgment, the liability in damages for what was formerly detinue remains under s 3: *Hillesden Securities Ltd v Ryjack Ltd* [1983] 2 All ER 184.
11 Torts (Interference with Goods) Act 1977, s 3(1). See *Secretary of State for Defence v Guardian Newspapers Ltd* [1985] AC 339, [1984] 3 All ER 601, HL (the plaintuiff sought delivery up of a photostatic copy of a secret ministerial memorandum).
12 Torts (Interference with Goods) Act 1977, s 3(2)(a). Cf *Howard E Perry & Co Ltd v British Railways Board* [1980] 2 All ER 579, [1980] 1 WLR 1375.
13 Torts (Interference with Goods) Act 1977, s 3(2)(b). For principles governing the application of s 3(2)(b) orders see *IBL Ltd v Coussens* [1991] 2 All ER 133, CA. Cf *Howard E Perry & Co Ltd v British Railways Board* supra.
14 Torts (Interference with Goods) Act 1977, s 3(2)(c).
15 Torts (Interference with Goods) Act 1977, s 3(4)(a).
16 Torts (Interference with Goods) Act 1977, s 3(4)(b).
17 Ie under Torts (Interference with Goods) Act 1977, s 3(2)(b). An order for delivery of the goods under s 3(2)(a) or 3(2)(b) of the Act may impose such conditions as may be determined by the court, or pursuant to rules of court and, in particular, where damages by reference to the value of the goods would not be the whole of the value of the goods, may require an allowance

before execution of judgment, but without prejudice to liability to pay any consequential damages.[18] Where goods are not detained (as where they are lost or destroyed) the normal form of judgment is for damages.

(I)   LIMITATION OF ACTIONS

The Limitation Act 1980 provides that once the period of limitation has expired, the plaintiff's title to the goods is extinguished.[19] The Act further provides that where there are successive conversions in respect of the same goods, whether by the same person or not, the cause of action is extinguished after six years from the first conversion.[20] If the action is based on fraud, or if the right of action is concealed by fraud, the period of limitation (normally six years under the Act) does not begin to run until the plaintiff discovers or ought to have discovered the fraud.[1] The first part of this has no application to conversion which is not an action based on fraud, but if the circumstances of the commission of a conversion are such that a plaintiff could not reasonably be expected to know that the conversion was taking place, this is a concealment of the right of action within the Act.[2] The Limitation Act 1980 also has complex provisions designed to enable owners from whom goods are stolen to sue the thief without limit of time.[3]

SECTION 3.   TRESPASS TO GOODS

An intentional or negligent interference with goods in the possession of the plaintiff is a trespass provided that the interference is direct.

This tort protects several interests. First, it protects the plaintiff's interest in the retention of possession of his goods (though the tort of conversion also protects this interest and is more often relied on for this purpose than is trespass). Secondly, trespass protects his interest in the physical condition of his goods and, thirdly, his interest in the inviolability of his goods, ie protection against intermeddling.

---

to be made by the claimant to reflect the difference: s 3(2)(b). For example, a bailor's action against the bailee may be one in which the measure of damages is not the full value of the goods. Then, the court may order delivery of the goods, but require the bailor to pay the bailee a sum reflecting the difference: Torts (Interference with Goods) Act 1977. Where an allowance is to be made under s 6(1) or 6(2) of the Act in respect of an improvement of the goods and an order is made under s 3(2)(a) or 3(2)(b) of the Act, the court may assess the allowance to be made in respect of the improvement and by the order require, as a condition for delivery of the goods, that allowance to be made by the claimant.

18 Torts (Interference with Goods) Act 1977, s 3(5).
19 Torts (Interference with Goods) Act 1977, s 2(3)(2). *R B Policies at Lloyd's v Butler* [1950] 1 KB 76, [1949] 2 All ER 226.
20 Torts (Interference with Goods) Act 1977, s 3(1).
1   Torts (Interference with Goods) Act 1977, s 32. The section adds that a subsequent bona fide purchaser is not prejudiced by these provisions should the owner seek to recover the property from him; and see *Eddis v Chichester Constable* [1969] 2 Ch 345, [1969] 2 All ER 912, CA.
2   *Beaman v ARTS Ltd* [1949] 1 KB 550, [1949] 1 All ER 465, CA.
3   Torts (Interference with Goods) Act 1977, s 40.

(A)   FORMS OF TRESPASS

It follows that trespass to goods assumes various forms. Taking goods out of the possession of another,[4] moving them from one place to another,[5] or even bringing one's person into contact with them,[6] or directing a missile at them[7] have all been held to be trespasses.

(B)   CHARACTER OF THE ACT OF THE DEFENDANT

There cannot be a trespass if the interference is indirect.[8] Thus, to lock the room in which the plaintiff has his goods is not a trespass to them.[9] Although he who mixes a drug with the feed of a racehorse commits a trespass *quoad* the feed, his act does not become a trespass to the racehorse when the stable boy later gives this feed to it.[10] Nor is it clear whether it is trespass to cause the goods of a plaintiff to come into harmful contact with some other object; for example, to drive sheep over the edge of a cliff into the sea below.[11]

It is trespass to goods to cut and take away trees,[12] to beat a dog[13] or to shoot racing pigeons[14] (whether or not the goods were capable of being stolen is irrelevant[15]).

In order to decide whether a mere touching of goods is a trespass one must ask whether trespass to goods is actionable per se. A dictum of Lord Blanesburgh in *Willian Leitch & Co Ltd v Leydon*[16] is often cited[17] to support the view that it is always actionable per se. There in fact it was left undecided whether the proprietor of a soda fountain committed a trespass by filling with soda water, for his customers, bottles which he knew to belong to the plaintiffs, mineral water manufacturers. The dictum of Lord Blanesburgh is only a summary of the argument of counsel for the appellant which the noble lord expressly stated must not be taken to be his own view. Some, on the other hand, state that there is clear authority for the proposition that trespass is actionable per se, but only where there is a dispossession of the plaintiff.[18] Yet in *Kirk v Gregory*[19] a woman, who moved rings belonging to a man who had just died from one room in his house to another was held liable in nominal damages for this asportation, ie for this carrying away of the goods from one place to another. This case has been treated as consistent with this latter view by saying of it that 'there was a complete asportation while the intermeddling lasted'.[20] But an asportation or moving of the goods

---

4   *Brewer v Dew* (1843) 11 M & W 625.
5   *Kirk v Gregory* (1876) 1 Ex D 55; *Fouldes v Willoughby* (1841) 8 M & W 540 at 544–5 (per Lord Abinger).
6   *Fouldes v Willoughby* (1841) 8 M & W 540 at 549 (per Alderson B obiter): 'Scratching the panel of a carriage would be a trespass.'
7   *Hamps v Darby* [1948] 2 KB 311 [1948] 2 All ER 474, CA.
8   *Covell v Laming* (1808) 1 Camp 497.
9   *Hartley v Moxham* (1842) 3 QB 701.
10 Unless the poison goes from the hand of the defendant directly into the mouth of the animal. *Hutchins v Maughan* [1947] VLR 131 (Victoria Sup Ct) carries the point in the text.
11 It is not trespass merely because one's animal inflicts direct injury on goods, *Manton v Brocklebank* [1923] 2 KB 212, CA, especially per Atkin LJ at 229.
12 *Heydon v Smith* (1610) 2 Brownl 328.
13 *Wright v Ramscot* (1667) 1 Saund 84.
14 *Hamps v Darby* [1948] 2 KB 311, [1948] 2 All ER 474, CA.
15 [1948] 2 KB 311 at 322, 478, respectively (per Evershed LJ).
16 [1931] AC 90 at 106, HL.
17 Eg *Salmond* 89.
18 Eg *Pollock* 264.
19 (1876) 1 Ex D 55.
20 *Pollock* 265n36.

is not necessarily a dispossession:[1] if in gently reversing my car I touch the bumper of another car, the brake of which has not been applied, and, without damaging it, cause it to move a few inches, I have not dispossessed the owner, though I have asported it. There are good reasons for making trespass to goods always actionable per se, and it is thought that it is both consistent with the authorities and in accordance with the general principle of trespass so to hold. Otherwise, people could touch museum exhibits with impunity; the law would leave remediless the perhaps not oversensitive person who declined to wear her Armani blouse again after her flatmate had 'borrowed' it to wear to a party. Perhaps the correct question is not whether trespass to goods is actionable per se. It should be in conformity with the general principles applying to all trespass torts. The question should rather be, was the relevant touching beyond what is acceptable in everyday life.[2] Picking up and admiring a friend's Armani blouse (worth £300) may not be an act one would expect her to object to; is wearing it without her permission?

(C)   STATE OF MIND OF THE DEFENDANT

The problem of whether there is liability for trespasses which are neither intentional nor negligent has been examined already. In *National Coal Board v J E Evans & Co Cardiff Ltd*[3] the Court of Appeal held that a contractor whose servant, while excavating, damaged the cable of the plaintiff and whose act was neither intentional nor negligent,[4] was not liable in trespass to goods. There is, then, no liability for an accidental trespass to goods.[5] But, if the defendant intended to interfere, his trespass is intentional even though he did not know that his act amounted to a trespass;[6] if, for example, he believed that the goods interfered with were his own.

(D)   THE INTEREST OF THE PLAINTIFF

The plaintiff must be in possession of the goods at the time of the interference. Possession connotes both the power (*factum*) of exercising physical control and the intention (*animus*) to exercise such control on his own behalf. Whether the plaintiff is the owner is immaterial. So if A intends to catch a butterfly, which is in his garden, and before he can do so it flies on to the highway where B catches it, A has no possession

1   Cf Channell B, in *Burroughes v Bayne* (1860) 5 H & N 296 at 305–6.
2   On analogy with trespass to the person; see *F v West Berkshire Health Authority* [1989] 2 All ER 545 discussed supra at p28.
3   [1951] 2 KB 861, [1951] 2 All ER 310. Although the ratio is probably that the injury was caused by the conduct of the plaintiff (see especially Cohen LJ at 875) all three judges gave considered judgments to the effect that there was no liability for accidental trespass to goods.
4   He willed the operation of the machine which was excavating the earth, but he neither desired nor ought to have foreseen that damage to the cable which constituted the tortious invasion of the plaintiff's interest. His act, therefore, was neither intentional nor negligent.
5   In *Manton v Brocklebank* [1923] 2 KB 212 at 229, CA, Atkin LJ held that 'whether a horse directly injures goods, or a dog accomplishes an 'asportavit' of a golf ball, he does not involve his owner in liability for trespass to goods, at any rate unless the owner has intentionally caused the act complained of'. Why negligence should not be enough for trespass here is not clear, and it is relevant that a finding of no negligence was made.
6   HEL vol viii, 466, seems confused on this. He thinks that because of cases such as *Kirk v Gregory* (1876) 1 Ex D 55, the rule for trespass to goods is more strict than for trespass to persons. This is not so; for instance, if a father hits a child through mistakenly identifying her as his daughter in circumstances that would have afforded him a defence but for his error, he would be liable for battery.

– there is *animus* but not *factum*. On the other hand, he has possession of the butterfly specimens in his natural history collection. Lord Esher has said:

> The plaintiff in an action of trespass must at the time of the trespass have the present possession of the goods, either actual or constructive, or a legal right to the immediate possession.[7]

Thus, a cyclist who parks his cycle outside a shop remains in possession of it, but if a thief rides away on it, the thief then has the possession although he obtained it wrongfully.

Therefore, if A took B's gun and handed it to C, B could not sue C in trespass (unless he showed that C authorised or ratified A's act), because B would have had no possession at the time when C received possession from A.[8] If a lodger holds goods on sale or return from a shopkeeper, and those goods are seized in pursuance of a lawful execution on the landlord's goods, this has been held to be a trespass to the lodger.[9] If X and Y both claim the right to goods which neither has previously possessed, and in a scuffle for them X snatches them from Y's hand Y has not possession to found a suit in trespass.[10] A bailee, even a gratuitous one,[11] can sue in trespass. The Crown could therefore sue in respect of the loss of Post Office mails.[12] Where a landlord demised land to the plaintiff for 21 years, with liberty to dig a half acre of brick-earth annually, and to dig in excess of that at an agreed price, the plaintiff could sue a third party who took away brick-earth from the land.[13] A bailor does not have possession and therefore cannot ordinarily sue in trespass for an act done to the goods bailed.[14] If, however, the bailor has an immediate right to possession as in the case of a bailment at will, for example where a young man had lent his car to his girlfriend while he was on holiday,[15] he may then sue.[16]

Want of possession precluded success in the following cases: against a police commissioner who, while in possession of the certificate of character of the plaintiff, wrote across it: 'Dismissed the police service';[17] by the assignees of a bankrupt against a sheriff who seized goods when unaware of a secret act of bankruptcy by the bankrupt.[18] For the same reason a telephone subscriber would have no action in trespass if the police tapped his telephone line. There are three apparent exceptions to the rule that possession is essential:

1   In *White v Morris*[19] it was held that, where goods were assigned as security for a loan upon trust to permit the assignor to remain in possession until default in

7   *Johnson v Diprose* [1893] 1 QB 512 at 515, CA.
8   *Wilson v Barker* (1833) 4 B & Ad 614; cf *Badkin v Powell* (1776) 2 Cowp 476. And see *Wilson v Lombank Ltd* [1963] 1 All ER 740.
9   *Colwill v Reeves* (1811) 2 Camp 575; contra 'If a man puts corn into my bag...because it is impossible to distinguish what was mine from what was his' (per Lord Ellenborough obiter at 576).
10 *Peachey v Wing* (1826) 5 LJOSKB 55.
11 *Rooth v Wilson* (1817) 1 B & Ald 59.
12 *The Winkfield* [1902] P 42, CA.
13 *Attersoll v Stevens* (1808) 1 Taunt 183.
14 *Gordon v Harper* (1796) 7 Term Rep 9; *Ward v Macauley* (1791) 4 Term Rep 489 but see Lord Porter in *United States of America and Republic of France v Dollfus Mieg et Cie SA* [1952] AC 582 at 611, [1952] 1 All ER 572, HL.
15 *O'Sullivan v Williams* [1992] 3 All ER 385, CA.
16 *Lotan v Cross* (1810) 2 Camp 464; *Penfolds Wines Pty Ltd v Elliott* (1946) 74 CLR 204 at 226–8 (per Dixon J).
17 *Taylor v Rowan* (1835) 7 C & P 70; cf *Wennhak v Morgan* (1888) 20 QBD 635.
18 *Balme v Hutton* (1833) 9 Bing 471.
19 (1852) 11 CB 1015.

repayment, the assignee could sue in trespass while the goods were still in the assignor's possession. It may be assumed, despite lack of authority for such a general proposition, that all trustees may sue for trespass to goods in the hands of the beneficiary on the basis that they share possession with him.[20]

2   The title of executors or administrators relates back to the death of the deceased, and this entitles them to sue for a trespass committed between the date of the death and that of the grant.[1]

3   The owner of a franchise in wrecks has been deemed to have constructive possession of a wreck so as to enable him to sue in trespass a person who seized a cask of whisky before he could do so.[2]

'Trespass to goods' is expressly included within the definition of a 'wrongful interference with goods' in the Torts (Interference with Goods) Act 1977.[3] Therefore the defence of jus tertii is no longer available,[4] and the statutory rules regarding co-ownership also apply, as in an appropriate case are all forms of relief provided for by that Act.[5]

(E)   DAMAGES

(1)   MEASURE

Where the plaintiff has been deprived of the goods, he is entitled to their value by way of damages. This rule applies to suits by bailees against third parties, but when the assignee under a bill of sale wrongfully seized from the assignor goods comprised in the bill, the damages awarded to the assignor were limited to the value of his interest in them.[6] A plaintiff may recover general damages for loss of use of goods (as distinct from special damages for loss of profits from the goods) although he would not have been using them during the period within which he has been deprived of their use.[7] The provisions of the Torts (Interference with Goods) Act 1977 relating to damages apply to actions for trespass to goods.[8]

(2)   TRESPASS AB INITIO[9]

Where any person having by authority of law[10] entered on land or seized goods, or arrested a person, subsequently commits a trespass his original act will in certain circumstances be deemed itself to be a trespass.[11]

---

20   See *Barker v Furlong* [1891] 2 Ch 172 (conversion).
1   *Tharpe v Stallwood* (1843) 5 Man & G 760.
2   *Dunwich Corpn v Sterry* (1831) 1 B & Ad 831.
3   Torts (Interference with Goods) Act 1977, s 1(b).
4   Torts (Interference with Goods) Act 1977, s 8(1). Section 11(1) excludes contributory negligence as a defence in proceedings based on intentional trespass.
5   Torts (Interference with Goods) Act 1977, s 10(1).
6   *Brierly v Kendall* (1852) 17 QB 937.
7   *The Mediana* [1900] AC 113 at 117–8 (per Earl of Halsbury LC).
8   See ante.
9   See *Clerk and Lindsell* at 23–29 and the seventh edition of this work at p 56.
10   Authority of law, as distinct from permission of another – for example, it covers one who enters an inn, but not the buyer of a ticket for a seat at a theatre.
11   The Distress for Rent Act 1737, s 19, abolished this rule in the case of distress for rent.

The doctrine has little practical relevance today. Its importance is mainly limited[12] to the fact that, presumably, damages may be assessed on the basis that the entire conduct of the defendant and not merely his subsequent wrongful act is tortious.[13]

SECTION 4.   RESIDUAL TORTS

There are many circumstances where the violation of interests in goods is not protected by trespass, conversion or even the tort of negligence. The action analogous to the old action on the case has proved very fruitful in filling these gaps; and what now follows is to be treated as illustrative of this wider right of action and not as exhaustively defining the circumstances in which it may be held available in the future. These torts are forms of 'wrongful interference with goods' so that, where relevant, the provisions of the Act of 1977 apply.

Trespass and conversion are especially restrictive in that they are not available to a plaintiff who neither possesses nor has an immediate right to possess the goods. The leading case of *Mears v London and South Western Rly Co*[14] has firmly established that if goods are destroyed or damaged, the owner may sue without having possession or an immediate right to possess. The rule benefits, for example, a bailor, a purchaser where the vendor has a lien for unpaid purchase money, and a mortgagee. He must prove damage to his interest – taking the goods from the possessor without affecting title is insufficient. Presumably, the act complained of must be wrongful in the sense that it is one which, had the plaintiff had possession or the immediate right to it, would have grounded a suit in trespass, or conversion. So, where the employer of the plaintiff, a conductor of a public transport vehicle, endorsed on the plaintiff's licence (which was in the employer's possession) 'discharged for being 1s 4d short' he was liable in case for defacing it.[15]

Credit agreements present interesting problems in this respect. If a car which is the subject of a credit agreement is seriously damaged, can the owner sue in case? If the hirer exercises his option to buy, what does the owner lose? And, yet, if (as is likely in such an event), the hirer does not exercise it, the owner is left without effective remedy other than in case. It seems that, until the hirer opts, the owner is to be regarded as the reversioner and can sue.

It will be recalled, too, that a bailee disregarding the terms of his bailment may sometimes be liable in case, though not in conversion[16] and that to deny the plaintiff access to his goods or to interfere with his freedom of using them is also actionable on the case.[17] Further, to place baited traps on one's land near the highway so as to attract dogs into the traps, and in consequence of which dogs are so trapped, is a tort of this category.[18]

---

12   It may also matter where the entrant sues the occupier of the land. If the entrant becomes a trespasser ab initio the occupier will be able to use reasonable force to eject him, whereas the mere commission of a misfeasance after lawful entry would not justify forcible ejection from the land. It might also affect the duty owed to him by an occupier in respect of the state of the premises and acts done therein; ch 16, post.
13   *Shorland v Govett* (1826) 5 B & C 485, obiter.
14   (1862) 11 CBNS 850.
15   *Rogers v Macnamara* (1853) 14 CB 27; cf *Hurrell v Ellis* (1845) 2 CB 295 (recovered damages for loss of employment where libel did not lie).
16   See ante.
17   See ante.
18   *Townsend v Wathen* (1808) 9 East 277.

Chapter 5

Land

SECTION I. TRESPASS

Intentionally or negligently entering or remaining on, or directly causing any physical matter to come into contact with, land in the possession of another is a trespass (trespass quare clausum fregit).

This tort protects the interest of the plaintiff in having his land free from physical intrusion. Because of this emphasis on physical interference with possession, it follows that it is not the function of the tort to protect ownership as such. Nonetheless, because the owner is often in possession, the purpose of many a suit in trespass is not the recovery of damages but the settlement of disputed rights over land, and a judgment may be backed by the sanction of an injunction if the action succeeds. The use of this action in tort as a means of resolving disputes on title has been facilitated by the rule that trespass is actionable per se.[1]

(A) TYPES OF ACTS

As with all forms of trespass, the immediate act must constitute the trespass complained of; it is not trespass if the invasion of the plaintiff's land is merely consequential upon the act of the defendant. So, a plaintiff landowner who complains that the defendant has erected a spout to drain away water from the eaves of the house of the defendant, as a result of which water has dripped on to the plaintiff's adjoining land, can sue only in nuisance, not in trespass.[2] How difficult it is to draw the line between 'direct' and

---

1   *Bush v Smith* (1953) 162 Estates Gazette 430, CA. The growing awareness of the scope of the declaratory judgment could lead to a declining use of trespass for this purpose; cf *Loudon v Ryder (No 2)* [1953] Ch 423, [1953] 1 All ER 1005; *Acton Corpn v Morris* [1953] 2 All ER 932, CA. (The defendant locked the door of his house, thereby denying the plaintiff access to his upper flat. Though the court doubted whether this was trespass, it held that the plaintiff could have a declaration of his right of access.) The action for recovery of land is also important in this connection, p 81, post. A plaintiff who does not mention trespass to land in his pleadings is not restricted to his alternative claim for breach of contract, and so can claim exemplary damages for the trespass: *Drane v Evangelou* [1978] 2 All ER 437, CA.

2   *Reynolds v Clarke* (1725) 2 Ld Raym 1399, cf *Lemmon v Webb* [1894] 3 Ch 1, at 24, CA (per Kay LJ), (and [1895] AC 1, HL) that the encroachment of boughs and roots of trees is not trespass.

'consequential' is shown by *Gregory v Piper*,[3] which held that it was trespass where rubbish, which was placed near the plaintiff's land, on drying, rolled on to it, because this was the result of natural forces. To enter another's land is a trespass.[4] Of course, such an entry may be an assertion of title, and then the action in trespass will, in effect, determine who has title.[5] To cause some foreign matter[6] to enter or come into physical contact with the land of the plaintiff is a trespass. Firing a gun into the soil,[7] placing a ladder against,[8] or driving nails into,[9] the wall of the plaintiff, encouraging a dog to run to his land,[10] removing the doors and windows,[11] and throwing a person on to another's land,[12] are all trespasses. But in all cases the intrusion on the plaintiff's land must result from some act or omission on the part of the defendant, or persons for whom he is responsible. The intrusion on the plaintiff's deer sanctuary by a pack of hounds does not of itself impose liability for trespass on the master of hounds.[13] Liability for trespass to land is not absolute.

To remain on land after a trespassory entry thereon is in itself also a trespass, a 'continuing trespass' as it is commonly styled. So, if A places goods on B's land and is successfully sued by B in trespass for this act, he is liable, if he fails thereafter to remove them, to further actions in trespass for the continued presence of the goods on the land.[14] If, on the other hand, he merely commits an act such as digging a hole, or removing goods, ie he does not wrongfully allow anything to remain on the land, the

---

3   (1829) 9 B & C 591. This, it seems, cannot be reconciled with the decision of Denning LJ in *Southport Corpn v Esso Petroleum Co Ltd* [1954] 2 QB 182 at 195–6, [1954] 2 All ER 561 at 570, CA supported by Lords Radcliffe and Tucker [1956] AC at 242, 244, HL, respectively (discharge of oil from ship, which, when carried by tide on to plaintiff's foreshore, held not to constitute a trespass, because that was consequential, not direct). See also *Covell v Laming* (1808) 1 Camp 497 (defendant at the helm guided his ship in a certain direction. The wind and waves were only instrumental in carrying along the ship in the direction in which he guided it. Upon the ship's colliding with the plaintiff's ship, held to be a trespass). And see *Home Brewery Co Ltd v William Davis & Co (Leicester) Ltd* [1987] QB 339, [1987] 1 All ER 637 (water squeezed out from osier bed filled in by defendant flooding the plaintiff's higher land *quaere* trespass or nuisance).
4   A squatter, ie 'one who, without any colour of right, enters on an unoccupied house or land, intending to stay there as long as he can', is a trespasser: per Lord Denning at 456 in *McPhail v Persons, Names Unknown* [1973] Ch 447, [1983] 3 All ER 393, CA.
5   If the defendant has not entered, it will normally be impossible, then, to use an action in trespass as a means of settling a dispute in title.
6   Perhaps anything having size or mass, including gases, flames, beams from searchlights and mirrors, but not vibrations.
7   *Pickering v Rudd* (1815) 4 Camp 219 at 220 (per Lord Ellenborough).
8   *Westripp v Baldock* [1938] 2 All ER 779; affd [1939] 1 All ER 279, CA.
9   *Simpson v Weber* (1925) 133 LT 46.
10 *Beckwith v Shordike* (1767) 4 Burr 2092.
11 *Lavender v Betts* [1942] 2 All ER 72. But not the defendant's turning off the gas and electricity at the meter in his cellar, for the purpose of evicting the tenant of rooms on an upper floor, because the consequence is indirect: *Perera v Vandiyar* [1953] 1 All ER 1109, [1953] 1 WLR 672. This is now a criminal offence under s 1 of the Protection from Eviction Act 1977, but no action for breach of statutory duty lies: *McCall v Abelesz* [1976] QB 585, [1976] 1 All ER 727, CA.
12 *Smith v Stone* (1647) Sty 65.
13 *League Against Cruel Sports Ltd v Scott* [1986] QB 240, [1985] 2 All ER 489.
14 If the plaintiff seeks an injunction, the court has a discretion to award damages in lieu of such injunction which also take into account the likely future damage. This, in effect, settles the price which the defendant must pay for the right to commit the trespass in the future, and no subsequent action will lie in respect thereof: *Leeds Industrial Co-operative Society v Slack* [1924] AC 851, HL. Nevertheless prima facie the landowner is entitled to his injunction even where the acts complained of cause no harm, *Patel v WH Smith (Eziot) Ltd* [1987] 1 WLR 853, CA; *Harrow London Borough Council v Donohue* [1993] NPC 49, CA.

fact that the harm thus occasioned continues is not enough to make it a continuing trespass; damage can be recovered once only for such a trespass.[15] There is a continuing trespass only when that which continued after the first action is itself a trespass; hence, for a person to remain or leave goods[16] there is such a trespass. A person who is on land with the permission of the possessor has been held a trespasser if he remains there for an unreasonable time after the termination of the permission.[17] 'When a householder lives in a dwelling-house to which there is a garden in front and does not lock the gate of the garden, it gives an implied licence to any member of the public who has lawful reason for doing so to proceed from the gate to the front door or back door, and to inquire whether he may be admitted and to conduct his lawful business.'[18] If the licence is withdrawn he is also not a trespasser during the reasonable time which he takes to leave the premises.[19] In *Konskier v B Goodman Ltd*[20] the facts were as follows:

> The defendant builder had permission from the possessor of a building to leave rubbish there while demolishing part of it. During the currency of this licence, the plaintiff became tenant of the building and was held entitled to recover in trespass from the builder when the latter did not remove the rubbish after the expiry of the licence.

If a tenant, with the consent of the landlord, stays on at the expiration of his term, so that he thereby becomes a tenant, either from year to year or at his will, his remaining is not an act of trespass so long as the tenancy has not been properly determined.[1] If however, he is a mere tenant at sufferance (thus remaining without permission of the landlord) the landlord may enter and demand possession and sue in trespass.[2] *Watson v Murray & Co* provides an illustration (if not an extension[3]) of the types of acts which may constitute trespass to land.[4]

> The defendants, who were sheriff's officers, seized goods in the plaintiff's shop under writs of execution. It was held that each of the following acts amounted to trespass: locking the plaintiff's premises so as to exclude her therefrom when they had lotted the goods for the purpose of a sale; opening her premises for a public viewing of the goods; affixing posters on her premises.

---

15   *Clegg v Dearden* (1848) 12 QB 576 at 601.
16   *Holmes v Wilson* (1839) 10 Ad & El 503.
17   *Minister of Health v Bellotti* [1944] KB 298, [1944] 1 All ER 238, CA cf the conflicting obiter dicta of Lord Ellenborough and Bayley J in *Winterbourne v Morgan* (1809) 11 East 395 at 402, 405 respectively.
18   *Robson v Hallett* [1967] 2 QB 939 at 953–4, per Diplock LJ, [1967] 2 All ER 407, CA. In *Brunner v Williams* (1975) 73 LGR 266, a weights and measures inspector was held to have no implied licence to enter a plaintiff's garden to see whether a coal dealer was infringing the Weights and Measures Act 1963; all he may do is go to the plaintiff's door and ask permission;
19   *Robson v Hallett* [1967] 2 QB 939 at 953–4, per Diplock LJ, [1967] 2 All ER 407.
20   [1928] 1 KB 421, CA. Presumably, the defendant's successor in title to the chattels would also be liable in trespass for knowingly allowing them to remain on the plaintiff's land.
1   *Dougal v McCarthy* [1893] 1 QB 736 at 739–40 (per Lord Esher); *Meye v Electric Transmission Ltd* [1942] Ch 290.
2   If the deceased tenant's widow remains there after his death she, too, can be sued in trespass: *Thompson v Earthy* [1951] 2 KB 596, [1951] 2 All ER 235.
3   Were all the acts here held to be trespasses sufficiently direct? See *Acton Corpn v Morris* [1953] 2 All ER 932, CA, not cited in the present case.
4   [1955] 2 QB 1, [1955] 1 All ER 350.

(B) SUBJECT MATTER

The tort is trespass to land; obviously, then, to walk on the surface of the plaintiff's land is enough to constitute the tort of trespass. Anything attached to the soil, and capable of being separately possessed, may be the subject matter of trespass *quaere clausum fregit*: damage to grass[5] or turnips,[6] or a profit à prendre such as a fishery.[7]

Possession of land may be separated, as it were, horizontally so that, for instance, A may possess the pasturage, B the surface and subsoil, and C the minerals below; each of them may sue if the subject matter of his possession is invaded. Highway authorities, for example, often have the surface of streets vested in them by statute: and so they (not the owners of the adjoining land[8]) may sue for surface trespasses, such as breaking up the street,[9] or erecting structures on the highway.[10] It may be trespass to tunnel beneath the surface of land, to mine there, to use a cave beneath it or to drive building foundations through the soil; in the absence of specific provision to the contrary, the owner of the surface is presumed to own that which is underground.

It is trespass to invade that portion of the airspace which is requisite for the ordinary use of the land and the structures upon it.[11] An aircraft does not infringe any of the plaintiff's rights to airspace by being flown over his land for the purpose of photographing it.[12]

Apart from the position at common law, the Civil Aviation Act 1982[13] provides that, with the exception of aircraft belonging to or exclusively employed in the service of Her Majesty,[14] no action shall lie in respect of trespass or nuisance by reason only of the flight of an aircraft over any property at a height above the ground, which, having regard to weather and other circumstances of the case, is reasonable.[15] Subject to the same exception, the owner of an aircraft is liable for all material loss or damage to persons or property caused by that aircraft, whether in flight, taking off[16] or landing, or by a

---

5   *Richards v Davies* [1921] 1 Ch 90 at 94–5 (per per Lawrence J).

6   *Wellaway v Courtier* [1918] 1 KB 200.

7   Cf *Hill v Tupper* (1863) 2 H & C 121 at 127 (per Pollock CB): *Mason v Clarke* [1955] AC 778, HL (right to take rabbits). But not an easement: *Paine & Co v St Neots Gas and Coke Co* [1939] 3 All ER 812, CA.

8   In *Hubbard v Pitt* [1976] QB 142, [1975] 3 All ER 1, CA Lord Denning held that where the surface of a pavement was vested in the local highway authority the adjoining owner could not sue for trespass to the pavement. In *Randall v Tarrant* [1955] 1 All ER 600, CA, a motorist who parked his car on the highway and then trespassed on the adjoining field was held not to be a trespasser on the highway.

9   *Hyde Corpn v Oldham Ashton and Hyde Electric Tramway Ltd* (1900) 64 JP 596, CA.

10 *Sewai Jaipur v Arjun Lal* [1937] 4 All ER 5, PC; they are not thereby authorised to build lavatories underneath; *Tunbridge Wells Corpn v Baird* [1896] AC 434, HL. See also *Cox v Glue* (1848) 5 CB 533.

11 *Kelsen v Imperial Tobacco Co of Great Britain and Ireland Ltd* [1957] 2 QB 334, [1956] 2 All ER 343 (defendant's advertising sign projecting into airspace above plaintiff's shop held a trespass); *Anchor Brewhouse Developments v Berkley House Docklands Developments Ltd* (1987) 284 Estates Gazette 625 (crane passing over land without permission).

12 *Baron Bernstein of Leigh v Skyviews and General Ltd* [1978] QB 479, [1977] 2 All ER 902.

13 Section 76.

14 Civil Aviation Act 1982, ss 49(3), 76(1).

15 Civil Aviation Act 1982, s 76(1). The section applies to all flights which are at a reasonable height and comply with statutory requirements, but the ordinary liabilities in trespass or nuisance would arise for any other wrongful activity carried on by or from the aircraft, such as deliberate emission of vast quantities of smoke that polluted the plaintiff's land; *Baron Bernstein of Leigh v Skyviews and General Ltd* [1978] QB 479 at 489, [1977] 2 All ER 902 at 906 (per Griffiths J).

16 The ordinary common law applies to accidents caused by the aircraft, while taxiing to the take-off point; *Blankley v Godley* [1952] 1 All ER 436n.

person in it or articles falling from it, without proof of negligence or intention or other cause of actionc.[17]

A highway is land in the possession and ownership of a person (who, except for any rights in respect of the surface enjoyed by a highway authority is presumed to be the owner of the adjoining land) subject to a public right of way. If a person uses a highway for purposes other than those 'reasonably incident to its user'[18] as a highway (which may include a peaceful demonstration[18a]) his act is a trespass. The purpose need not be unlawful in itself; interrupting a shoot[19] obtaining information on the speed and performance of racehorses on the adjoining land of the owner of the highway soil,[20] have been held trespasses.

(C) STATE OF MIND OF THE DEFENDANT

The rules here seem to be essentially similar to those for other forms of trespass. If the defendant intended to enter the land on which he in fact is, then he trespassed, whether or not he intended to invade the plaintiff's interest in his own exclusive possession. Mistake, as such, is no defence in trespass; it will not avail the defendant that he thought that he was on his own land.[1] As with all torts, there is no liability if there is no voluntary act on the part of the defendant; a person thrown on to the land by a third party is not liable in trespass.[2] *Letang v Cooper* notwithstanding, it must be assumed for the time being that a negligent unintentional act of trespass is enough; for example, if A intentionally throws a stone on to C's land and, as he should have foreseen, it ricochets on to B's land, this is trespass to B's land as well as C's. On the other hand, it is thought that an unintentional non-negligent act is not trespass.[3]

In *League Against Cruel Sports Ltd v Scott*[4] the plaintiffs owned land which they maintained as a deer sanctuary and on which hunting was prohibited. Hounds from a local hunt intruded on the sanctuary and disturbed the deer. Park J held that the master of the hounds could not be liable in trespass unless it could be proved that he (or some person for whom he was responsible) either deliberately encouraged the dogs to enter the plaintiffs' land, or by negligence failed to prevent them intruding on the sanctuary.

(D) THE INTEREST OF THE PLAINTIFF IN THE LAND

If the plaintiff has a legal estate and exclusive possession then he may sue in trespass. The tenant (not the landlord) can sue if a third party trespasses on the land demised.[5]

17 Civil Aviation Act 1982, s 76(2).
18 *Liddle v Yorkshire (North Riding) County Council* [1934] 2 KB 101 at 127.
18a *DPP v Jones* (1999) Times, 5 March.
19 *Harrison v Duke of Rutland* [1893] 1 QB 142, CA.
20 *Hickman v Maisey* [1900] 1 QB 752, CA.
1 *Basely v Clarkson* (1681) 3 Lev 37.
2 [1965] 1 QB 232, [1964] 2 All ER 929, CA.
3 Contra dicta (perhaps not ratio) of the *Case of Thorns* (1466) YB 6 Edw 4 fo 7 pl 18.
4 [1986] QB 240, [1985] 2 All ER 489.
5 *Cooper v Crabtree* (1882) 20 Ch D 589, CA. A plaintiff with an *Interesse termini* could not sue if he never took possession; *Wallis v Hands* [1893] 2 Ch 75.

So, too, the owner of an equitable interest with possession can sue.[6] A statutory possession will found an action of trespass.[7]

The Court of Appeal has held that 'a person may have such a right of exclusive possession of property as will entitle him to bring an action for trespass against the owner of that property but which confers no interest whatever in the land'.[8] Those whose interests fall short of those of a lessee may nonetheless be able to sue in trespass if in fact they have exclusive occupation. Whether a lodger can sue in trespass would rest on whether on the facts he had exclusive occupation – it would be relevant whether he had an outdoor key and whether he could bar access to the rooms.[9]

In *National Provincial Bank Ltd v Ainsworth*[10] the House of Lords unanimously held that a deserted wife at that time had no proprietary interest in the matrimonial home, but only a personal right. Nonetheless Lord Upjohn stated that she had exclusive occupation and could therefore bring proceedings against trespassers. In *Hill v Tupper*:[11]

X Co leased certain land, which adjoined their canal, to the plaintiff. He was also given 'the sole and exclusive rights' to let out on hire pleasure boats for use on the canal. Subsequently, the defendant set up a rival concern, whereupon he was sued in trespass by the plaintiff. The latter conceded that X Co could sue the defendant in trespass but at the same time he argued that he himself could do so.

Since the plaintiff's concession was tantamount to an admission that he did not have exclusive occupation, it is not surprising that the court dismissed the action. It did, however, add that only if he could prove that his interest was a new species of property could he succeed,[12] and that it was the policy of the law not to allow the creation of

6   *Mason v Clarke* [1955] AC 778, HL. Another example is *London v Ryder* [1953] 2 QB 202, [1953] 1 All ER 741, CA, where the plaintiff was entitled to the premises under a declaration of trust merely (and see *Re Lewis's Trusts* (1953) Times, 26 March) and yet recovered damages for trespass to the land. A beneficiary under a trust for sale may also sue: *Bull v Bull* [1955] 1 All ER 253 at 255 (per Denning LJ, obiter).

7   *Cruise v Terrell* [1922] 1 KB 664, CA; *Lewisham Borough Council v Maloney* [1948] 1 KB 50, [1947] 2 All ER 36, CA. Whether a landlord of a tenant at will can sue third parties in trespass is undecided: *Attersoll v Stevens* (1808), 1 Taunt 183: *Shrewsbury's (Countess) Case* (1600) 5 Co Rep 13b.

8   *Marcroft Wagons Ltd v Smith* [1951] 2 KB 496 at 501, [1951] 2 All ER 271 at 274, CA (per Evershed MR). *Brown v Brash and Ambrose* [1948] 2 KB 247, [1948] 1 All ER 922, CA and *Thompson v Ward* [1953] 2 QB 153, [1953] 1 All ER 1169, CA, show that a statutory tenant who leaves his premises even for a period of five to ten years with the intention of eventually returning there and who'clothes his inward intention with some formal, outward and visible sign of it' (per Asquith LJ), at 254, in *Brown v Brash and Ambrose*) by installing someone as licensee or maybe by leaving furniture there, has the right to sue in trespass anyone who occupies the premises, eg the landlord.

9   *Lane v Dixon* (1847) 3 CB 776; *Monks v Dykes* (1839) 4 M & W 567; *Helman v Horsham and Worthing Assessment Committee* [1949] 2 KB 335, [1949] 1 All ER 776 (per Evershed LJ), at 347, 783 respectively; *R v St George's Union* (1871) LR 7 QB 90. Similarly, a plaintiff who could not rely on possession under his lease from the Crown because it was void for non-compliance with a statute was held to have 'actual possession...sufficient to entitle the party possessing it to maintain trespass against persons who have no title at all, and are mere wrongdoers': *Harper v Charlesworth* (1825) 4 B & C 574 at 591 (per Bayley J). The House of Lords in *Street v Mountford* [1985] AC 809, [1985] 2 All ER 289 held that where the intention evidenced by the agreement between the parties was to grant exclusive possession for a period of time and at a rent there will normally be found to be a tenancy in any case.

10   [1965] AC 1175, [1965] 2 All ER 472, HL.

11   (1863) 2 H & C 121.

12   It will be recalled that interference with a profit à prendre may be trespass; p 76, ante.

new rights in land. However, note that in *Manchester Airport plc v Dutton*[13] a licensee who had not yet entered into occupation was entitled to eject trespassers who had set up a protest camp

It is no defence to a wrongdoer that the possession of the plaintiff is unlawful. The fact of possession is enough.[14] But as against the true owner, the rule is different; in *Delaney v TP Smith Ltd*[15] the plaintiff entered property held under a lease which was unenforceable because it did not comply with requirements of section 40 of the Law of Property Act 1925 relating to a memorandum in writing, and it was held that he was unable to sue his landlord in trespass for ejecting him. Two other dicta are important here:

> A mere trespasser cannot, by the very act of trespass, immediately and without acquiescence, give himself what the law understands by possession against the person whom he ejects, and drive him to produce his title, if he can, without delay, reinstate himself in his former possession.[16]

> If there are two persons in a field, each asserting that the field is his, and each doing some act in the assertion of the right of possession, and if the question is, which of those two is in actual possession, I answer, the person who has the title is in actual possession, and the other is a trespasser.[17]

If a plaintiff has a right to immediate possession of the land, he can, once he has entered upon it, sue for trespasses committed by third parties between the date of accrual of his right and his entry;[18] this is often called trespass by relation.[19] The ratio decidendi of the House of Lords in *Jacobs v Seward* was:[20]

> …unless there be an actual ouster of one tenant in common by another, trespass will not lie by the one against the other so far as the land is concerned.

13 (1999) Times, 5 March, CA. 'In recent years it has been established that a person who has no more than a licence may yet have possession of the land.' per Megarry J in *Hounslow London Borough Council v Twickenham Garden Developments Ltd* [1971] Ch 233 at 257, [1970] 3 All ER 326. But see *Street v Mountford* (supra) on the distinction between tenancies and occupational licences.

14 *Graham v Peat* (1801) 1 East 244. In *Mason v Clarke* [1955] AC 778, [1955] 1 All ER 914, HL, Viscount Simonds and Lord Oaksey (contra, Lord Keith) held that the bare possession of a profit à prendre was enough to found an action in trespass. This was obiter because the successful plaintiff had in fact an equitable title to the profit. Cf *Bristow v Cormican* (1878) 3 App Cas 641, HL.

15 [1946] KB 393, CA.

16 *Browne v Dawson* (1840) 12 Ad & El 624 at 629. In *Portland Managements Ltd v Harte* [1977] QB 306, [1976] 1 All ER 225, CA, it was held that if the plaintiff proves ownership and his intention to resume possession the onus is on the defendant to prove that he is not a trespasser.

17 *Jones v Chapman* (1849) 2 Exch 803 at 821 (Maule J), approved *Lows v Telford* (1876) 1 App Cas 414 at 426, HL (per Lord Selborne).

18 *Barnett v Guildford (Earl)* (1855) 11 Exch 19.

19 Suppose that the effect of a proviso for forfeiture in a lease is that the lease subsists until proceedings for forfeiture are brought; this doctrine of trespass by relation would not then allow a lessor, who is entitled by the terms of the lease to forfeit it, to claim damages for the period between the act giving ground for forfeiture and the issue of the writ: *Elliott v Boynton* [1924] 1 Ch 236, CA.

20 (1872) LR 5 HL 464 at 472; and holding that it was not an ouster for a tenant in common to put a lock on the gate to a field and make hay there, cf *Bull v Bull* [1955] 1 QB 234, [1955] 1 All ER 253, CA.

(E) DAMAGES

The plaintiff is entitled to full restitution for his loss. Generally, the depreciation in selling value will be an adequate measure for destruction of, or damage to, land and buildings, though sometimes the plaintiff can also recover special damages, for example business profits,[1] or perhaps the cost of replacement premises.[2] However, where the cost of reinstatement or repair exceeds the diminution in value of the property, those costs may be awarded as damages provided expenditure on such reinstatement and repair is reasonable.[3] And the cost of repair will always be important evidence of the plaintiff's loss, especially where there is no market in which the value of the property may be ascertained or the plaintiff can prove that it was reasonable to have the property restored.[4] All tests such as market value or replacement cost are subordinate to the over-riding principle of restoring the plaintiff to the same position as before the tort was committed.[5]

The measure of damages for wrongful occupancy of land is the reasonable rental value of the land during the time of the defendant's occupancy. So in *Inverugie Investments Ltd v Hackett*,[6] the plaintiffs were awarded the equivalent of the letting value of the whole of the holiday apartment block wrongfully occupied by the defendant trespassers, even though in practice only about 35–40% of the apartments were actually rented out by the defendants, or could have been by the plaintiffs. The plaintiffs were entitled to compensation for the wrongful use of their property, regardless of whether they had suffered any actual loss from being deprived of the use of that property or whether the defendants had in fact benefited from their wrongdoing.

Where goods such as coal or other minerals or trees are severed from the land, the measure of damages depends upon whether the act is wilful or innocent.[7] If his severance is innocent the defendant can deduct his cost of severance from the value of the goods.[8] If the act is wilful the defendant cannot deduct his expenses of severing, although he can deduct subsequent expenses such as hauling coal to the surface.[9] Whether in either case the defendant can also deduct an additional sum by way of

---

1   *Watson v Murray & Co* [1955] 2 QB 1, [1955] 1 All ER 350; cf *Dunn v Large* (1783) 3 Doug KB 335 (when defendant ejected plaintiff from inn, closed it down and sent custom elsewhere, plaintiff refused loss of sale value, but only because he did not specially plead it).
2   *Dominion Mosaics and Tile Co v Trafalgar Trucking Co* [1990] 2 All ER 246, CA.
3   *Heath v Keys* [1984] CLY 3568; measure of damages based on the cost of repair is only available when the plaintiff does in fact intend to carry out repairs: *Perry v Sidney Phillips & Son* [1982] 3 All ER 705, [1982] 1 WLR 1297, CA.
4   For a lucid statement, see *Hutchinson v Davidson* 1945 SC 395.
5   *Farmer Giles Ltd v Wessex Water Authority* [1990] 18 EG 102, CA. In *Bisney v Swanston* (1972) 225 Estates Gazette 2299, CA, D put a trailer on P's transport cafe ground so as to interfere with P's business as much as possible. As well as damages for loss of business, £250 aggravated damages were awarded against D for intending to interfere with malice and spite.
6   [1995] 1 WLR 713, PC; and see *Whitwham v Westminster Brymbo Coal and Coke Co* [1896] 1 Ch 894; affd [1896] 2 Ch 538, CA.
7   'Wilful' includes 'fraudulent'; whether it includes 'negligent' is doubtful: *Wood v Morewood* (1841) 3 QB 440n; *Re United Merthyr Collieries Co* (1872) LR 15 Eq 46; Fry J said obiter in *Trotter v Maclean* (1879) 13 Ch D 574 at 587 that the burden of proving wilfulness is on the plaintiff.
8   *Jegon v Vivian* (1871) 6 Ch App 742.
9   *Martin v Porter* (1839) 5 M & W 351; *Morgan v Powell* (1842) 3 QB 278. If the plaintiff could not himself reach the seam in order to extract the mineral, his damages are based on what a third party would pay him by way of royalty for permission to extract: *Livingstone v Rawyards Coal Co* (1880) 5 App Cas 25, HL.

profit for his work, or whether the plaintiff is entitled to the value of the severed goods less only the defendant's actual expenses, is not settled.[10]

A tenant who is unlawfully evicted by his landlord may recover exemplary damages in trespass – to teach the landlord that tort does not pay.[11]

SECTION 2.   ACTIONS BY REVERSIONERS

Although trespass is not available to those without possession whose interests in land are violated, they are not remediless. A landlord will ordinarily have contractual rights against tenants who damage his interest, for example by allowing premises to fall into disrepair, and that branch of the law of property known as waste will also afford a remedy of a tortious nature to a landlord who establishes that his tenant has damaged the reversionary interest.[12]

If a non-possessory interest in land is violated by a third party, an action derived from the old action on the case may lie. The plaintiff must prove 'such permanent injury as would be necessarily prejudicial to the reversioner';[13] it was not enough to prove that the defendant's cart wheels had made an impression on the surface of the land.[14]

10 *Jegon v Vivian*, supra and *A-G v Tomline* (1880) 14 Ch D 58 would allow the innocent defendant his profit; contra *Re United Merthyr Collieries Co* (1872) LR 15 Eq 46. *Tai Te Wheta v Scandlyn* [1952] NZLR 30, held that even an innocent trespasser could not set off the value of improvements done by him to the land; see also *Lord Cawdor v Lewis* (1835) 1 Y & C Ex 427.
11 *Drane v Evangelou* [1978] 2 All ER 437. Suprisingly, however, *Devonshire v Jenkins* (1979) 129 NLJ 849 held that exemplary damages were not recoverable if in fact the evicting landlord did not obtain that profit which he sought by his attempted unlawful eviction.
12 Landlord-tenant relationships of this kind are customarily, and appropriately, treated in textbooks of real property, and not in those on torts.
13 *Baxter v Taylor* (1832) 5 B & Ad 72 at 75 (per Taunton J).
14 Ibid. For a lessee to deny access to a reversioner entitled to enter and view is also actionable on the case: *Hunt v Dowman* (1618) Cro Jac 478.

Chapter 6

Defences to intentional torts to the person and property

In this chapter will be discussed all the important defences which may be available in respect of the torts so far described. It must not be thought that these defences apply only to these torts. Many of them, for example, consent, statutory authority, *ex turpi causa*, are general defences, and are capable of being defences to almost any tort. However defences have a particular importance in the context of the intentional torts for this reason. The key question in claims for trespass and the like is often likely to be not was a prima facie trespass committed, but was there in the actual circumstances of the case any lawful excuse or justification for that trespass? The tort of false imprisonment developed to protect the self-same right to liberty as that articulated in Article 5 of the Human Rights Convention. The heart of most common law claims for false imprisonment is whether the detention of an alleged criminal is justifiable. Articles 5 and 6 of the Convention assert the right to liberty and security of the person in ten brief words, and then devote over a page to possible justifications for deprivation of such a right. Defences to intentional torts are crucial in defining the scope of individual rights.

SECTION I.   MISTAKE AND INEVITABLE ACCIDENT

(A)   MISTAKE AS SUCH IS NO DEFENCE

It has been shown[1] that mistake is no defence to intentional torts. If the defendant intended to drive his tractor on to the plaintiff's land, then his reasonable mistake that the land was his own will be no defence.[2] Mistake must, however, be distinguished from inevitable accident. If the defendant shows that the tractor went on to that land solely because of a defect in the steering which no amount of care could have prevented, he will not be liable; for in such a case he neither intended to do that which he has done (ie enter the land which in fact belongs to the plaintiff), nor could he have avoided doing so by taking every care.

Although mistake is no defence in tort, it may be relevant, in deciding if some other defence is open to the defendant, to know whether he was mistaken as to some fact. If

---

1   See p 77, ante.
2   Similarly, where there is liability for negligent acts, if, though his act is not intentional, he foresees the consequences, mistake about the surrounding circumstances will not afford him a defence.

a policeman arrests without warrant someone who in fact has not committed an arrestable offence, and whom he had no grounds for believing to have committed one, this is false imprisonment; if, on the other hand, he mistakenly believed on reasonable grounds that the plaintiff had committed an arrestable offence the defence of lawful arrest is open to him.[3]

(B)   INEVITABLE ACCIDENT

It may perhaps once have been the case that the defendant was liable in trespass unless he could establish that his violation of the plaintiff's interest was a result of 'inevitable accident'. Whatever the historical niceties of the writ of trespass such a doctrine no longer prevails. In *Fowler v Lanning*[4] the plaintiff's pleadings in a claim for trespass asserted baldly 'the defendant shot the plaintiff'. Diplock J held that the pleadings disclosed no valid cause of action. For trespass to lie, the plaintiff must aver and prove that the defendant acted either intentionally or negligently. The onus of establishing evidence of tortious conduct rests on the plaintiff. Thus there is no call for a *defence* of 'inevitable accident' for if the facts of the case rest on such an event no cause of action will exist.

SECTION 2.   CONSENT

(A)   GENERAL

The common law will not permit someone who has freely assented to conduct by another to sue that other for damages resulting from that conduct: volenti non fit injuria. Consent may take two forms, either where the plaintiff expressly consents to an invasion of his interest which would otherwise be a tort (this form is conveniently called consent), or a willingness on the part of the plaintiff to run the risk of injury from a particular source of danger (often called assumption of risk).

It is convenient to treat consent as a defence although it will be recalled that it is now clear that in trespass to the person, but not in trespass to land, the burden of proving want of consent is on the plaintiff.[5] Consent may be given expressly by words or be inferred from conduct. A boxer cannot complain if his opponent hits him with a straight left to the nose. A footballer consents to those tackles which the rules permit, and, it is thought, to those tackles contravening the rules where the rule infringed is framed to maintain the skill of the game; but it is otherwise if his opponent gouges out an eye or perhaps even tackles against the rules and dangerously. Such conduct is entirely beyond what the player agreed to risk when embarking on the game.[6]

Establishing just what can reasonably be inferred from conduct can be problematic. If a plaintiff has habitually allowed children to play on his field, consent may constitute

---

3   Police and Criminal Evidence Act 1984, s 24(6)
4   [1959] 1 QB 426, [1959] 1 All ER 290.
5   *Freeman v Home Office (No 2)* [1984] QB 524, [1983] 3 All ER 589 at 594–5; affd [1984] 1 All ER 1036, CA. On one interpretation, Lord Blanesburgh in *William Leitch & Co Ltd v Leydon* [1931] AC 90 at 109, [1930] All ER Rep 754 at 762, HL, could be applying the rule relating to assault to trespass to goods. In *Jolliffe v Willmett & Co* [1971] 1 All ER 478, a wife living apart from her husband authorised an inquiry agent to enter her husband's flat; the inquiry agent's defence of leave and licence failed when the husband sued him for trespass to land.
6   See *R v Billinghurst* [1978] Crim LR 553; *Affutu-Nartoy v Clarke* (1984) Times, 9 February. As to duty of care owed by one competitor to another see *Condon v Basi* [1985] 2 All ER 453, [1985] 1 WLR 866, CA.

a defence to a claim against a frolicking child, but not, perhaps, against a party of adults using the field for a firework display? *Arthur v Anker*[7] explored the boundaries of consent in a very relevant modern context. It was held that where a person unlawfully parked his car on another's land, knowing full well that the owners asserted a right to wheelclamp trespassing vehicles and charge for their release, he impliedly consented not only to the otherwise unlawful detention of his car, so that there was no trespass to goods, but also to being required to pay a reasonable fee to ensure the declamping of the vehicle. A sensible person would reasonably appreciate that by electing to defy the wheelclamping warnings, he took on himself the risk of the detention of his vehicle.

Consent must be to the act complained of. The tenant may have consented to her landlord's entering the land to examine repairs but not to his assaulting her. Fraud may invalidate an apparent consent but only, it has been held, if the fraud is as to the very nature of the act consented to. Thus nineteenth century judgments held that a woman's consent to sexual intercourse was not vitiated by her ignorance that her lover was infected with syphilis.[8] Any fraud was purely collateral to the essence of the act.[9] Consent obtained by duress is no consent.[10] An important question is the effect of consent obtained by a show of authority – for example, the policeman, who, without formally arresting or charging a suspect, asks him to accompany him to the police station, has no defence if the plaintiff goes because of an assertion of authority by him: consent obtained by show of authority is no consent.[11] Equally, if the plaintiff is drunk or otherwise incapable of giving consent, then there is no defence.[12]

The overriding interest of the state in maintaining order and punishing wrongdoers is such that has been held on the highest authority that it is not necessarily a defence in criminal law that the victim has consented to the criminal act.[13] No considerations of policy prevent the courts from holding that consent to a crime is a valid defence in tort, and it may be assumed that the courts will hold that consent may be a defence in tort in such circumstances.[14]

---

7   [1997] QB 564, [1996] 3 All ER 783, CA.
8   *R v Clarence* (1888) 22 QBD 23, 44; *Hegarty v Shine* (1878) 14 Cox CC 124. Do you think that *Hegarty v Shine* would be decided the same way today in a different moral climate? Would consent to intercourse defeat a claim in trespass where the plaintiff had been infected with AIDS?
9   What if the defendant impersonates the plaintiff's husband, or a bigamist 'marries' the innocent plaintiff and has intercourse (held actionable in *Graham v Saville* [1945] 2 DLR 489, Ontario CA), or the singing teacher convinces his pupil that intercourse will improve her voice? To what does the plaintiff consent? Is it intercourse, marital intercourse, intercourse free from venereal disease, any penetration? Should the test be whether the mistake induced relates to that which is harmful or offensive in the act?
10   Yet in *Latter v Braddell* (1881) 50 LJQB 448, a servant who complied, reluctantly, crying and under protest, with an order of her mistress that she be medically examined to check whether she was pregnant, was held to have consented.
11   *Warner v Riddiford* (1858) 4 CBNS 180. Submissions in *Freeman v Home Office* (supra) that the relationship between prisoner and prison doctor was such that the former could never freely consent to treatment by the latter failed. But the judge at first instance made it clear that in looking at the reality of a prisoner's consent to medical treatment the doctor's power to affect the prisoner's situation must be borne in mind.
12   Must the plaintiff's consent be manifested to the defendant? Is it enough if the defendant reasonably believes that the plaintiff has consented?
13   *R v Brown* [1994] 1 AC 212, HL; the European Court of Human Rights subsequently ruled that the decision in *Brown* did not constitute a violation of Article 8 of the Convention: *Laskey, Jaggard and Brown v United Kingdom* (1997) 24 EHRR 39.
14   *Barnes v Nayer* (1986) Times, 19 December, CA; *Murphy v Culhane* [1977] QB 94, [1976] 3 All ER 533 where the Court of Appeal held that the defence of consent might be available in respect of a crime, and at the same time also held that a plea of ex turpi causa might also be open to the defendant, (See p 105, post.)

(B)   CONSENT TO MEDICAL TREATMENT

Any physical contact with a patient without his consent to that contact is prima facie a battery.[15] Consent need not be written and in practice will often be implied from conduct, for example holding out your arm to receive an injection. Where surgery or more serious invasive treatment is contemplated patients will usually be asked to sign a standard consent form agreeing to the operation or other treatment 'the effect and nature of which have been explained to me'. Such a consent is ineffective unless an adequate explanation of the broad nature of what is to be done to the patient is given to him.[16] But a failure to warn the patient of the risks or side-effects of the treatment proposed will not vitiate the patient's consent.[17] It may be a breach of the doctor's duty to give the patient proper and skilled advice, but as such it will be actionable only in negligence[18] and not in battery. Only when the defendant actively misleads the patient will a claim in battery normally be appropriate.[19]

Where the patient is adult, conscious and competent, the law's requirement for consent to treatment recognises and enforces the right to self-determination, to autonomy. In *F v West Berkshire Health Authority*[20] Lord Goff endorsed the famous principle enunciated by an American judge Cardozo J in *Schloendorff v Society of New York Hospital*:[1]

Every human being of adult years and sound mind has a right to determine what shall be done with his own body...

It is no defence to an action in battery for a doctor to assert that he acted in what he believed to be the patient's interests, or even to preserve her life. Thus, if a Jehovah's Witness has unequivocally refused to authorise a blood transfusion, a doctor administering blood against her will commits a battery.[2] But in cases of doubt where it is unclear whether the patient did freely, and with full understanding of what was at stake, reject life-saving treatment, the Court of Appeal has said that doctors act lawfully in erring on the side of preserving life.[3] Slight authority suggesting that a pregnant woman might be required to submit to a Caesarian section to protect the interests of the viable foetus was ultimately overruled by the Court of Appeal.[4] Their Lordships asserted that the foetus lacked any legal personality to justify violation of its mother's autonomy, providing that the mother remained mentally competent.

15   *F v West Berkshire Health Authority* [1989] 2 All ER 545, HL; see also Brazier *Medicine Patients and the Law* (2nd edn, 1992) ch 4.
16   *Chatterton v Gerson* [1981] QB 432 at 443 (per Bristow J).
17   *Chatterton v Gerson* (supra) at 444; *Freeman v Home Office (No 2)* (supra); *Hills v Potter* [1983] 3 All ER 716. The bringing of actions in battery where the essence of the claim is inadequate advice was deplored by their Lordships in *Sidaway v Governors of Bethlem Royal Hospital and the Maudsley Hospital* [1985] 2 WLR 480 at 489.
18   See *Sidaway v Governors of Bethlem Royal Hospital* (supra) discussed post at p 250.
19   See *Appleton v Garrett* [1996] PIQR P 1.
20   Supra at 564.
1   211 NY 125 (1914) at 12.
2   *Malette v Shulman* [1991] 2 Med LR 162.
3   *Re T (adult: refusal of medical treatment)* [1992] 4 All ER 649, CA. (T had signed a form refusing blood transfusion and later lapsed into unconsciousness. She was not herself a Jehovah's Witness and signed the form after some time alone in her mother's company. Her mother was a devout Witness. The Court of Appeal found that she had not been properly advised of the consequences of refusing a transfusion and might have been unduly influenced by her mother.)
4   *Re MB* [1997] 8 Med LR 217; but note their wide definition of 'temporary mental incapacity'; *St George's Healthcare NHS Trust v S* [1998] 3 All ER 673, CA.

The Family Law Reform Act 1969, section 8, provides that a minor over 16 may effectively consent to surgical, medical or dental treatment. In the case of children under 16, that Act preserves the common law that providing the individual child is mature enough to make his or her own decision on the treatment proposed, the child herself can give an effective consent to treatment.[5] Thus Mrs Gillick's attempt to ensure that no girl under 16 could lawfully be prescribed the Pill without parental agreement failed. By a majority the House of Lords held that a doctor faced with a request by a young girl for contraceptive treatment (or an abortion) should always try to persuade his patient to consult her family. But should she refuse to do, so he might lawfully treat her provided that he was satisfied that she had a sufficient understanding of what was involved in the treatment and its implications for her. Children under 16 thus acquired the capacity to authorise treatment for themselves once competent to do so. But it seems that though a *Gillick competent* child can consent to treatment, there is no similar capacity to refuse treatment. The Court of Appeal[6] has held that the parental power to consent on the minor's behalf continues even after the minor acquires an independent capacity to consent for himself. It does not matter whether this capacity derives from achieving the necessary maturity to be *Gillick competent*, or reaching the age of 16 and acquiring a statutory capacity under the Family Law Reform Act. In either case the right to consent does not import an unqualified right to refuse treatment. The position is this. Consent by *either* the minor *or* any person with parental responsibility for him authorises treatment and ensures that any necessary physical contacts entailed in treatment are not batteries. Lord Donaldson MR[7] cautioned doctors to give serious consideration to any objections to treatment by a minor, but such objections do not constitute an absolute bar on treatment.

In the case of younger children parental consent to treatment will be effective to authorise treatment beneficial to the child.[8] No battery is committed by a doctor who with parental consent vaccinates a protesting four-year-old against measles. Where treatment proposed is not clearly and unequivocally beneficial to the child, parental consent alone may be insufficient to authorise that treatment. Several cases have been heard relating to the sterilisation of mentally handicapped girls. Where the surgery is proposed not to deal with some immediate physical problem, such as a hysterectomy to remove a cancerous uterus, the authorisation of the court must be sought before such serious and generally irreversible surgery is performed or the surgeon may risk liability for battery and prosecution for criminal assault.[9] When the patient is under 18, authorisation can be sought by means of a specific issue order under the Children Act 1989[10] or, preferably, by invoking the inherent jurisdiction of the High Court.[11]

Where a patient is over 18 but incapable of consenting to medical treatment on his own behalf English law found itself in a state of some confusion. Once a person reaches the age of majority, the law currently makes no provision for anyone else to be endowed with authority to act for him in matters relating to his personal welfare and health. Others may be appointed to administer his property and look after his finances, but not to

5   Section 8(3); *Gillick v West Norfolk and Wisbech Area Health Authority* [1986] AC 112, [1985] 3 All ER 402.
6   *Re W (a minor) (medical treatment)* [1993] Fam 64, [1992] 4 All ER 627, CA and see *Re R (a Minor) (Wardship: Medical Treatment)* [1991] Fam 11, [1991] 4 All ER 177, CA.
7   *Re W* [1992] 4 All ER 627 at 639–640.
8   *Re D* [1976] Fam 185, [1976] 1 All ER 326 and see *Re B* [1981] 1 WLR 1421. Note that in *Re T* [1997] 1 WLR 242 the Court of Appeal, endorsing parental refusal of a liver transplant for their infant son, appeared to regard parental objections to treatment as crucial in defining the child's interests.
9   *Re B (a minor) (wardship: sterilisation)* [1987] 2 All ER 206 at 214, HL.
10   See s 8(1), s 10.
11   *Practice Note (Sterilisation: minors and mental health patients)* [1993] 3 All ER 222.

authorise medical treatment or any other procedures relating to the incapable individual's person.[12] There, when a patient needing immediate surgery is rushed into a casualty unit after a road accident, and when a person suffering from such profound mental handicap as to be unable to consent to treatment himself needs medical care, hospital staff face a real dilemma. Not to treat such patients would appear to be a breach of their professional duty of care. To treat them without consent might lead to liability in battery.

In the case of the patient suffering some temporary incapacity, after an accident or because he is under anaesthesia, it has long been accepted that doctors act lawfully in doing whatever is necessary to preserve the patient's life and prevent any permanent damage to health. Two rather different arguments were advanced to support that contention. (1) In the absence of evidence to the contrary, hospital staff were entitled to assume that the patient as a reasonable person implicitly consented to whatever measures were immediately required to save his life and restore him to consciousness. (2) A defence of emergency or necessity rendered the relevant treatments lawful. In *F v West Berkshire Health Authority*[13] the House of Lords preferred to endorse a defence of necessity rather than to rely on rather artificial assumptions of tacit consent. In the case of the temporarily unconscious patient such an approach accords with common sense. And remember it is not only the doctor and nurse in the hospital who need legal justification to intervene and make contact with the accident victim. The 'Good Samaritan' who comes to his aid as he lies bleeding in the road, the ambulance workers and hospital porters all must touch the patient in a manner which in the absence of legal excuse will constitute a battery.

Even so, the House of Lords in *F* also elected to extend the defence of necessity to patients suffering some permanent mental incapacity. Where a patient will never be able to authorise treatment on his own behalf, Part IV of the Mental Health Act 1983 makes provision to dispense with the requirement for consent to psychiatric treatment in the case of patients detained under the Act. Elaborate safeguards are built into the statute to protect such patients and the provisions to dispense with consent extend beyond patients whose mental handicap prevents them making any judgment at all to those whose mental disorder distorts any judgment they may make. But the provision for dispensing with consent is extremely limited in scope. (1) It applies only to patients formally detained in a mental hospital, and very few are. (2) The section speaks of treatment for psychiatric disorder only and not treatment for physical ills.[14] Faced with this legal limbo, the House of Lords ruled that treatment of a patient incapable of consenting to treatment was lawful on grounds of necessity providing that what was to be done was in the best interests of the patient and would be endorsed by a reasonable body of medical opinion.[15] This 'best interests' necessity principle applies to all forms of treatment from routine dental treatment and daily nursing care to radical and irreversible measures such as abortion and sterilisation. Their Lordships advised that in the case of radical or potentially irreversible surgery doctors ought to apply to the court for a declaration that what was proposed was lawful, but in the case of adults application for judicial permission is not mandatory.[16]

---

12 See *Brazier*, ch 5.
13 [1989] 2 All ER 545, at 565–6 HL.
14 Though note that feeding an anorexic patient has been held to constitute treatment for psychiatric disorder: *B v Croydon Health Authority* [1996] Fam 133; as has Caesarian surgery: *Tameside and Glossop Acute Services Trust v CH* [1996] 1 FLR 762.
15 See *Bolam v Friern Hospital Management Committee* [1957] 1 WLR 582; post at p 248.
16 Though Lord Griffiths dissented on this issue and argued that the courts did have jurisdiction to require doctors to seek a declaration before proceeding to carry out radical or irreversible surgery in such cases.

In *F v West Berkshire Health Authority*, F was a 36-year-old woman cared for as a voluntary patient in a mental hospital. She was said to have a mental age of five to six. She was thought by staff to have started a full sexual relationship with a male patient and it was proposed that she be sterilised. The Law Lords unanimously endorsed surgery. But could such action genuinely be categorised as 'necessary' or are the bounds of necessity being overstretched in such cases?[17] On the other hand would it be right simply to leave F to become pregnant and then debate whether abortion was 'necessary'?[18] The potential elasticity of the concept of medical necessity remains troublesome. Consider the case of *Re Y (Mental Patient: Bone Marrow Donation)*.[19] A judge issued a declaration that bone marrow could lawfully be harvested from the defendant, a young woman suffering from profound mental disability and living in residential care, to be 'donated' to her elder sister who was suffering from cancer. The procedure was deemed 'necessary' because of the potential impact on the defendant of her sister's premature death. She would be distressed herself and the effect on the women's elderly mother would be such that the mother's health might deteriorate. Moreover, the mother relied largely on the sister to visit her disabled daughter. The loss of sister and the weakening of the bond with the mother would damage Y's interests thus rendering the bone marrow 'donation' necessary.

Cases like *Re Y* illustrate the crucial social and ethical decisions prompted by society's duty to care for those unable to make their own decisions. The judges have done their best to mould the ancient torts to meet modern needs. The Law Commission conducted a thorough review of the law on treatment of patients with mental incapacity.[20] Now it looks as though government intends to implement their proposals to modernise and clarify the relevant legal principles.[1]

SECTION 3.   CONTRIBUTORY NEGLIGENCE

This defence is fully examined in what is obviously its most appropriate place, in negligence.[2] Contributory negligence is no defence to proceedings founded on conversion or intentional trespass to goods.[3] The defence is available in battery.[4]

SECTION 4.   SELF-DEFENCE

An act which might otherwise constitute trespass to the person may be justified if the defendant is able to establish that he acted in self-defence.[5] He was merely repelling

---

17 See MA Jones 'Justifying Medical Treatment without Consent' (1989) 5 PN 178.
18 Consider the worst-case scenario in *T v T* [1988] Fam 52, [1988] 1 All ER 613 (19-year-old girl with a mental age of 2½, doubly incontinent and incapable of communicating with others had become pregnant).
19 [1997] Fam 110, [1997] 2 WLR 556.
20 Law Commission Report No 231 *Mental Incapacity*.
1   *Who Decides?* (Consultation Paper Issued by the Lord Chancellor's Department) Cm 3803 (1997).
2   See pp 281 et seq, post.
3   Torts (Interference with Goods) Act 1977, s 11(1), except that the defence is open to a collecting banker sued for conversion of a cheque; Banking Act 1979, s 47.
4   *Murphy v Culhane* [1977] QB 94, [1976] 3 All ER 533, CA; *Barnes v Nayer* (supra); *Revill v Newbery* [1996] QB 567, [1996] 1 All ER 291, CA.
5   Even though the provocation by the plaintiff may not on the facts justify the battery, it may be a ground for reducing damages: *Fraser v Berkeley* (1836) 7 C & P 621 at 624 (per Lord Abinger); *Lane v Holloway* [1968] 1 QB 379, [1967] 3 All ER 129, CA.

an attack, or threatened attack, on the part of the plaintiff. The defendant must prove that in the circumstances it was reasonable that he should defend himself and that the force used by him was reasonable. So, in *Cockcroft v Smith*:[6]

> The clerk of a court sued an attorney for biting off his forefinger in a scuffle in court. Holt CJ held that in itself it was no defence that the plaintiff had first run his fingers towards the defendant's eyes, for a man must not 'in case of a small assault, give a violent or an unreasonable return'.

The right to use reasonable force to protect oneself against injury or threat of injury applies equally to resisting unlawful arrest.[7]

What is reasonable force is a question of fact in each case.[8] It will be material to consider whether the plaintiff could have escaped, whether he resisted with the most reasonable means available, whether the act of the defendant went beyond the limits of defence to mere revenge, whether the defendant continued to use violence after the danger had passed, and whether the plaintiff's attack was, or was reasonably expected to be, violent.[9] It has been said that, even though the force used is no greater than is requisite for protection, it is still no defence unless the defendant also proves that the force used was not disproportionate to the nature of the evil sought to be avoided; but the cases do not establish such a legal rule.[10] The relation between the harm threatened by the plaintiff and the means of defence used is one element of fact to be considered in deciding the general question of reasonableness.[11] Suppose that A pins B against a wall and repeatedly kisses her against her will, and the only means whereby she can compel A to desist is by lacerating his wrists with scissors, having failed to push him away because of his superior size and strength. Does her defence fail because the evil of wounding is contended to outweigh the 'evil' of unwanted kisses?

SECTION 5.   DEFENCE OF THE PERSON OF ANOTHER

The cases clearly establish that an employee may justify a battery in defence of his employer and an employer[12] may lawfully strike someone in defence of his employee.[13] A wife may defend her husband and a man may defend any member of his household.[14]

---

6   (1705) 2 Salk 642. In fact the plaintiff failed on a finding that his act did endanger the defendant's eye.
7   *Codd v Cabe* (1876) 1 Ex D 352.
8   Cf Holmes J, in Holmes-Laski *Letters*, v.1, 335, on the supposed duty in law to retreat to the wall before killing assailant; 'I think it an instance of an early statement ossifying by repetition into an absolute principle when rationally it is only one of the circumstances to be considered with the rest in deciding whether the defendant exceeds the reasonable limits'. The notion of any duty to retreat was expressly condemned by the Court of Appeal in *R v Bird* [1985] 2 All ER 513, [1985] 1 WLR 816. As to force exerted where the danger is miscalculated but the intervention based on a reasonable mistake, see *Albert v Lavin* [1982] AC 546, CA. The point was not considered in affirming the decision in the House of Lords [1982] AC at 546.
9   See *Revill v Newbery* [1996] QB 567, [1996] 1 All ER 291, CA.
10   *Cook v Beal* (1697) 1 Ld Raym 176; *Cockroft v Smith*, supra; *Dale v Wood* (1822) 7 Moore CP 33. In each case the force used was unnecessary for self-defence.
11   Cf *Turner v Metro-Goldwyn-Meyer Pictures Ltd* [1950] 1 All ER 449 at 471, HL (per Lord Oaksey obiter): 'If you are attacked by a prize-fighter you are not bound to adhere to the Queensbury rules in your defence.'
12   *Barfoot v Reynolds* (1734) 2 Stra 953.
13   *Seaman v Cuppledick* (1615) Owen 150, *Tickell v Read* (1773) Lofft 215; contra *Leward v Basely* (1695) 1 Ld Raym 62.
14   *A-G's Reference (No 2 of 1983)* [1984] QB 456, [1984] 1 All ER 988, CA; *Leward v Basely*, supra. In more egalitarian times may it be assumed a woman too may defend her family?

It may be that the defence extends to the protection of other persons, although authority is lacking; for instance, that a guard could defend railway passengers. It is submitted that the question ought always to be: 'Was it reasonable for the defendant to protect the other person in this way?'

As with self-defence, the conduct of the defendant must be reasonable in all the circumstances, and it is conceivable that one relevant factor may be the relationship between the defendant and the person whom he defended, ie that one may use greater force in defence of a close relative than of a stranger; at least, the facts must probably[15] be such as to have justified the third person in defending himself. If the defendant acted in order to prevent the plaintiff from perpetrating a felony jeopardising the life of a third party, that was on the authority of *Handcock v Baker*, in itself a defence[16] a dictum there suggested that 'it is lawful for a private person to do anything to prevent the perpetration of a felony'.[17] Felonies were abolished by the Criminal Law Act 1967 and it is suggested that any general right to intervene to prevent a criminal attack on another is now provided for solely by section 3 of that 1967 Act. If the defendant goes beyond merely protecting another and chastises the attacker, then, unless he has the defence of discipline, he is liable for that act of chastisement.

SECTION 6. DEFENCE OF ONE'S PROPERTY

One may use reasonable force to defend land or chattels in one's possession against any person threatening to commit or committing a trespass to the property. The defendant must have such possession as would enable him to sue the plaintiff in trespass. Thus the captain of a cricket club who removed the plaintiff from the field could not plead that he had ejected a trespasser, because the captain did not have possession of the field.[18] Similarly, in *Scott v Matthew Brown & Co Ltd*:[19]

> The defendant was on the land merely as a result of ejecting the plaintiff by an act of trespass whereupon the plaintiff, the true owner, at once re-entered. The defendant forcibly removed him, and was held not to have sufficient possession to sue in trespass, and therefore to have no defence against the action of battery by the plaintiff.

If the defendant has a mere right to possess, but not actual possession, he may have some other defence, re-entry in the case of land, or recaption in the case of chattels, but he cannot successfully plead that he was defending his property.[20]

To remain on land after permission has expired is trespass: therefore the defence is available to a defendant who ejects such a person.[1] A threatened intrusion is also sufficient: if the plaintiff has taken the key of the defendant's car and is about to enter the car, the defendant may resist this potential trespass to his chattel.

As with defence of the person, if the defendant has a reasonable belief that force is essential to end the trespass, he may use it although he is mistaken in thinking it to be necessary, but if he mistakenly believes that the plaintiff is a trespasser, he has no

---

15 There is one doubtful case when the defendant reasonably but mistakenly believes that the third party had, in the circumstances, the privilege to defend himself.
16 A bystander may also use force to arrest another committing a breach of the peace in his presence, p 99, post.
17 (1800) 2 Bos & P 260 at 265 (per Chambre J). See also *Coupey v Henley* (1797) 2 Esp 539.
18 *Holmes v Bagge* (1853) 1 E & B 782; *Dean v Hogg* (1834) 10 Bing 345.
19 (1884) 51 LT 746.
20 *Roberts v Tayler* (1845) 1 CB 117 at 126–7 (per Tindal CJ).
1 *Green v Bartram* (1830) 4 C & P 308; *Moriarty v Brooks* (1834) 6 C & P 684, Ex Ch.

defence. What is reasonable force depends here also on the facts, though guidance may be sought from decided cases:[2]

> If a person enters another's house with force and violence, the owner of the house may justify turning him out (using no more force than is necessary), without a previous request to depart; but if the person enters quietly, the other party cannot justify turning him out, without a previous request to depart.

As the law does not value interests in property so highly as those in the person, the use of force in defence of the former is, then, harder to justify than in the case of self-defence. Firing a shotgun at a burglar who had broken into a garden shed, but shown no overt intention of violence to the person was held in *Revill v Newbery*[3] to be disproportionate force in defence of property, albeit the plaintiff's damages were reduced by two thirds in the light of his contributory fault. Consider two key issues. Would firing the shotgun have been reasonable had the defendant shouted a warning yet the plaintiff still failed to desist in his criminal enterprise? Had the burglar entered via the plaintiff's bedroom window late at night, would the degree of force be justifiable? May it be that unless the plaintiff resists his expulsion so as to bring the rules of self-defence into play, force likely to cause death or serious bodily harm will not be justifiable in defence of property?[4]

The courts have often had to consider the extent to which a defendant could use mechanical devices or other methods to protect his property. No principle is set out explicitly in the series of cases, but the test here is also one of reasonableness. To deter trespassers by barbed wire or spiked railings on the confines of one's land is reasonable, and there is no liability if another is injured by them;[5] but deliberately and without notice to set spring guns or any device calculated to kill or cause grievous bodily harm is not reasonable.[6]

Where dogs (or theoretically other animals) are used to protect property, under the Animals Act 1971 a person is not liable under that Act to impose strict liability[7] 'for any damage caused by an animal kept on any premises or structure to a person trespassing there, if it is proved either (a) that the animal was not kept there for the protection of persons or property; or (b) (if the animal was kept there for the protection of persons or property) that keeping it there for that purpose was not unreasonable.'[8] Section 9 of the Animals Act creates a special statutory defence for the killing of or injury to dogs worrying livestock. The defence is available only if (or the defendant reasonably believed it to be so) the dog is worrying or is about to worry the livestock and there are no reasonable means of ending or preventing the worrying; or the dog

---

2 *Tullay v Reed* (1823) 1 C & P 6 (per Park J); cf *Green v Goddard* (1702) 2 Salk 641; *Polkinhorn v Wright* (1845) 8 QB 197.

3 [1996] QB 567 CA; and see *Collins v Renison* (1754) Say 138; *Moriarty v Brooks* (1834) 6 C & P 684 Ex Ch; cf *Stroud v Bradbury* [1952] 2 All ER 76.

4 As to when killing intruding animals may be justified, see *Hamps v Darby* [1948] 2 KB 311, [1948] 2 All ER 474, CA.

5 See *Deane v Clayton* (1817) 7 Taunt 489.

6 *Bird v Holbrook* (1828) 4 Bing 628, distinguished in *Jordin v Crump* (1841) 8 M & W 782 (setting, with notice, dog spears for the purpose of protecting game against dogs held lawful); see now Offences against the Person Act 1861, s 31. In *A-G Reference (No 2 of 1983)* [1984] QB 456, [1984] 1 All ER 988, CA, the accused had armed himself with petrol bombs to repel rioters who had earlier smashed into his shop. The Court of Appeal held he was entitled to acquittal if his object was to protect his family or his property from imminent attack and the force employed was reasonable. As to an occupier's duty of care to a trespasser see now the Occupiers' Liability Act 1984 discussed post at p 320.

7 Chapter 20, post.

8 Section 5(3).

has been worrying livestock, has not left the vicinity and is not under the control of any person and there are no practicable means of ascertaining to whom it belongs. The defendant must further notify the police within 48 hours of the killing or injury.[9]

SECTION 7.   DEFENCE OF THE PROPERTY OF ANOTHER

Blackstone states that it is a defence to protect the property of other members of one's household,[10] and although one might expect the courts to confine this defence within narrow limits, by analogy with defence of the person of another it may be assumed to exist.

SECTION 8.   PREVENTING CRIME

The above discussion relates to the right given to individuals at common law to defend themselves, their property and other closely related persons. Section 3 of the Criminal Law Act 1967 confers a public right to use 'such force as is reasonable in the prevention of crime'. Very often, where someone uses force to defend herself or her child from attack it matters not whether her defence is categorised as self-defence at common law or invokes the authority to use force to prevent crime bestowed on every citizen by section 3. The private and the public rights to use force defensively must be distinguished in at least two instances. It is unclear whether at common law any private right justifies the use of force to repel an attack on a stranger. Section 3 clearly does where that attack is criminal. But in a second instance the right to use force conferred by section 3 is clearly inferior to the private right of self-defence conferred at common law. Should your attacker be insane, or a child under 10, no crime may be committed. Can section 3 be invoked to authorise force against what is reasonably believed to be, but in fact is not, and could not be, a criminal offence?

SECTION 9.   NECESSITY

(A)   DISTINGUISHED FROM DEFENCE OF PROPERTY

As a justification for a trespass, defence of property is sometimes difficult to distinguish from necessity. Confusion is all the more likely because, in deciding whether defence of property is available, one may have to consider whether the act of the defendant was reasonably necessary for that defence. The difference is that self-defence or defence of property presupposes that the plaintiff is prima facie a wrongdoer: the defence of necessity contemplates the infliction of harm on an innocent plaintiff. When, for instance, the defendant barricades his land against flood-water and, in consequence, the plaintiff's land is flooded, the defence of necessity may lie against the plaintiff who is not responsible for creating the threat of danger. Obviously, then, the law may be expected to attach a greater importance to the plaintiff's interest, and, accordingly, to restrict the scope of the defence.

---

9   Either livestock or land must belong to the defendant, *or* he must have authority to act on the owner's behalf. There was a substantially similar defence at common law, eg *Cresswell v Sirl* [1948] 1 KB 241, [1947] 2 All ER 730, CA, except that the police need not be notified. Section 9 does not repeal the common-law defence expressly – perhaps it is still available although the police were not notified.

10   Book III, 3; no modern cases have been traced.

(B) SCOPE

(1) PRIVATE NECESSITY

One may lawfully[11] protect one's person and property[12] (and that of another[13]) against the threat of harm even though the consequence is that an innocent person suffers a loss.

How far does a defence of private necessity extend? Where lies the boundary between the needs of one and the rights of others? It has been held that the removal of the goods of a lately deceased person is justified only if necessary for their safety.[14] One may do what is necessary to protect one's own property against a threatened flood,[15] even though flooding of one's neighbour's land ensues, and it has been held to be justifiable to divert locusts from one's land although the result is that they damage the crops of one's neighbour instead.[16] But homeless persons who enter empty houses of a local authority which are awaiting development to provide housing do not have the defence of necessity for their trespass; the Court of Appeal restricted the application of the defence to an urgent situation of imminent peril.[17]

As we have seen earlier, modern case law on the scope of necessity has focused on its application in the context of medical treatment. A doctor is justified by the defence of necessity in operating to save the life of an unconscious patient and in giving what she judges to be appropriate care to mentally incapacitated patients.[18] But can necessity be invoked even to save a patient's life if the doctor knows that the patient objects to what he wishes to do? The answer today is resoundingly no. Where the patient is mentally competent, and freely, with full understanding of the seriousness of a decision to refuse treatment, so refuses life-saving treatment, no defence of necessity can now be invoked to justify imposing treatment against that person's will.[19] Even where in the latter stages of pregnancy the interests of a viable foetus are at stake, the maternal right to bodily integrity now prevails.[20] Nor may prisoners on hunger strike lawfully be forcibly fed.[1] Necessity in terms of a third party's or society's interest in saving life

11 There is no English authority (contra *Vincent v Lake Erie Transportation Co* 109 Minn 456 (1910) USA) that the privilege is incomplete in the sense that he must compensate the plaintiff for the actual loss sustained by him; an obiter dictum of Tindal CJ in *Anthony v Haney* (1832) 8 Bing 186 at 193 sometimes cited as such authority is solely on recaption.

12 *Cope v Sharpe (No 2)* [1912] 1 KB 496, CA (defendant justified in burning heather on plaintiff's land in order to prevent fire on plaintiff's land spreading to land on which defendant's master had shooting rights).

13 *Proudman v Allen* [1954] SASR 336 (defendant, believing that plaintiff's unoccupied car was about to run into another vehicle, jumped into the driving seat with the result that the car ran into the sea and sank – held no trespass).

14 *Kirk v Gregory* (1876) 1 Ex D 55.

15 *Nield v London and North Western Rly Co* (1874) LR 10 Exch 4 at 7 (per Bramwell B); *Maxey Drainage Board v Great Northern Rly Co* (1912) 106 LT 429 at 430 (per Lush J) Div Ct; *Gerrard v Crowe* [1921] 1 AC 395, PC. If the defendant's land is already flooded he may not divert that flood water on to the plaintiff's land: *Whalley v Lancashire and Yorkshire Rly Co* (1884) 13 QBD 131.

16 *Greyvensteyn v Hattingh* [1911] AC 355, PC (the defendant entered land of a third party while diverting them).

17 *Southwark London Borough Council v Williams* [1971] Ch 734, [1971] 2 All ER 175, CA.

18 *F v West Berkshire Health Authority* [1989] 2 All ER 545, HL.

19 *Re T (adult: refusal of medical treatment)* [1993] Fam 95, [1992] 4 All ER 649, CA.

20 *Re MB* [1997] 8 Med LR 217; *St George's Healthcare NHS Trust v S* [1998] 3 All ER 673, CA.

1 *Secretary of State for the Home Department v Robb* [1995] Fam 127, overruling *Leigh v Gladstone* [1909] 26 TLR 139.

cannot override individual autonomy so long as the individual at risk is mentally competent.[2]

(2) PUBLIC NECESSITY

There are ancient judgments that provide that a citizen might lawfully enter another's land to erect fortifications for the defence of the realm[3] or to fight fires.[4] Public necessity was also relied on to justify throwing cargo overboard in order to save the lives of the ship's passengers.[5] Whether compensation is payable to the victims of acts committed because of public necessity is obscure.[6] Lord Donaldson MR in justifying medical intervention in cases where real doubt existed as to whether the patient had freely refused life-saving treatment invoked the public, societal, interest in preserving life.[7]

In order to raise the defence of either public or private necessity there must be both an actual (or what to a reasonable man seems to be) danger, and the steps taken must in the light of the facts be reasonable.[8] If the plaintiff relies on an allegedly negligent act the defence of necessity need not be considered, for the same standard is then applied to determine the issues of both necessity and negligence, viz, the reasonable man.[9]

Thus in *Rigby v Chief Constable of Northampton*[10] the police were held liable for firing a CS gas canister into the plaintiff's shop to flush out a dangerous psychopath without having adequate fire-fighting equipment available. The shop was burned out. The judge held that necessity was a good defence to trespass in such an emergency, but that the police were liable in negligence for their failure to ensure that they had sufficient fire-fighting back-up when the canister was released onto the plaintiff's property.

2   As to what constitutes mental competence, see *Re C* [1994] 1 WLR 290; *Re MB* [1997] 8 Med LR 217. Difficult practical issues will continue to arise. A woman sees a youth who looks about 14 swaying at the edge of a high roof. She believes him to be helplessly drunk and drags him away. In fact he is 21, terminally ill and had deliberately opted for suicide. Is she, should she be, protected by a defence of necessity?

3   YB 8 Ed 4 f 23 Mich pl. 41 (per counsel); YB 21 H 7, 27 (dictum of Kingsmill J – the point was taken on demurrer but no judgment given on it); *The Case of the King's Prerogative in Saltpetre* (1606) 12 Co Rep 12 (obiter dictum in resolution of judges).

4   *Deway v White* (1827) Mood & M 56 (defendant justified in throwing down plaintiff's chimney because of fire risk that it would otherwise fall on highway below); per Kingsmill J, supra, and *Case of Saltpetre*, supra (justified in destroying buildings); fire brigades now have statutory authority dating from Metropolitan Fire Brigade Act 1865, s 12 to commit such trespass – Viner, Abr Trespass K a pl 3 (justified in taking to safety goods in burning house).

5   *Mouse's case* (1608) 12 Co Rep 63; cf *Southport Corpn v Esso Petroleum Co Ltd* [1954] 2 QB 182, [1954] 2 All ER 561; revsd [1956] AC 218, [1955] 3 All ER 864, HL; cf also the restricted common law right to deviate from a foundrous highway at least where it is public, and the land entered belongs to a person responsible for the highway's foundrous state (*Stacy v Sherrin* (1913) 29 TLR 555).

6   No: Bohlen 39 HLR 370; Glanville Williams *Current Legal Problems* vol 6, 216. Yes: Scott and Hildesley *Case of Requisition* p 136 et passim; Buller J (obiter) in *British Cast Plate Manufacturers (Governor & Co) v Meredith* (1792) 4 Term Rep 794 at 797; Ambiguous: dicta in *Case of Saltpetre*, supra. Inconclusive: obiter dicta in *Burmah Oil Co Ltd v Lord Advocate* [1965] AC 75, [1964] 2 All ER 348, HL.

7   *Re T (adult: refusal of medical treatment)* [1997] 1 WLR 242, CA.

8   *Cope v Sharp (No 2)* p 93 ante, illustrates both these requirements.

9   *Southport Corpn v Esso Petroleum Co Ltd* supra.

10   [1985] 2 All ER 985, [1985] 1 WLR 1242.

SECTION 10.   THE MENTAL HEALTH ACTS

Persons who suffer from such a degree of mental disorder that they pose a risk of harm to themselves or to others may be subject both to detention and compulsory treatment against their will. Provisions of both the Mental Health Act 1983 and the Mental Health (Patients in the Community Act) 1995 may justify conduct otherwise constituting false imprisonment and battery. The detailed principles underlying mental health law cannot be elaborated here, but it must be noted that the courts are vigilant to ensure compliance with the Acts and protect the rights of the mentally ill citizen as much as his healthy colleague.[11] The Master of the Rolls has declared:[12]

> [N]o adult citizen of the United Kingdom is liable to be confined to any institution against his will.

SECTION 11.   DISCIPLINE

Where force is used neither in self-defence nor in the prevention of crime, but rather to punish the offender, the trespass against him, be it a battery or a false imprisonment, must now generally be justified by statutory authority, for example the Prison Act 1952 or the Mental Health Act 1983. The sanction given by the common law to those in authority disciplining those subject to their authority is virtually a matter of legal history alone now. It is nearly a century ago that it was finally determined that a husband has no right to discipline his wife whether by beating her or imprisoning her. Exercise of disciplinary powers remains a defence to an action in tort only in relation to children and in the bizarre case of passengers on ships and aircraft.

(A)   CHILDREN

(1)   BY PARENTS

Save in the case of injuries inflicted before birth where children are expressly excluded from suing their mothers, children are not prevented from suing their parents even while they remain minors.[13] Section 1(7) of the Children and Young Persons Act 1933 presumes, however, that parents can justify an assault and battery by way of chastisement provided reasonable force by way of correction is used. And similarly parents may be able to justify detention of their children by way of punishment as a defence to an action of false imprisonment. It is suggested, however, that there is only a right to detain where it is reasonable in the circumstances; and that whereas a parent, who locked up her 12-year-old son at night to prevent him from going out joy-riding, might have a defence to an action of false imprisonment, a parent, who detained a 17-year-old daughter whereby she was prevented from sitting her A levels or even going out with her boyfriend, would have no defence. Change in social *mores* and in the status of children have diminished parental rights of discipline. A growing body of opinion supports outlawing any right of physical punishment. Article 3 of the Human

---

11 But note the difficult case of *R v Bournewood Community Health Service Trust, ex p L* [1998] 3 All ER 289.
12 *Re S-C (Mental patient: habeas corpus)* [1996] 1 All ER 532, 534 CA.
13 In *Ash v Lady Ash* (1696) Comb 357 a daughter was able to sue her mother in trespass to the person; in *Roberts v Roberts* (1657) Hard 96, an infant obtained an injunction against her father to prevent waste and in the Scottish case of *Young v Rankin* 1934 SC 499, a child passenger in a car driven by his father was held to be able to sue his father for injuries received consequent upon his father's negligent driving.

Rights Convention bans inhuman or degrading treatment and may thereby outlaw all physical chastisement be the recipient child or adult, and a recent (as yet unreported) decision of the European Court of Human Rights has held that beating a child with a cane violates Article 3.

(2) BY SCHOOLTEACHERS AND OTHERS RESPONSIBLE FOR THEIR CHILDREN FOR THEIR TRAINING AND EDUCATION

At common law, head and assistant teachers, both at boarding and day schools, and in the maintained and the independent sectors, had the right to use reasonable force to correct the children under their tutelage.[14] Following a decision of the European Court of Human Rights,[15] section 47 of the Education (No 2) Act 1987 prohibits corporal punishment in maintained schools and for state-funded pupils in independent schools. Use of force to punish a child as opposed to limited force needed to protect a child from harming himself or others will be no defence to an action for assault and battery. The defence of exercise of disciplinary powers will remain available to teachers in independent schools against fee paying pupils, and the defence of disciplinary powers will remain available to all teachers in respect of acts not involving beating the child where available at common law, for example to justify detention after school or confiscating the child's property. A pretty serious breach of discipline would have to be shown to justify detaining or, in particular, locking up a child.[16] Disciplinary powers may afford a defence to trespass to goods as where a teacher removed from a boy a pocket book which, he thought, would identify the ringleaders in a school conspiracy to disturb order.

In independent schools where corporal punishment is not yet prohibited correction may be administered (even at a day school) for acts done outside school affecting school discipline.[17] The force used must be reasonable in the circumstances – presumably the offence, the age and physique of the child, his past behaviour, the punishment, the injury inflicted, are all material. It may be that, consistent with the change of public opinion on the matter, the lawful limits of this disciplinary power are growing even narrower – a moderate box on the ear of an unruly 10-year-old causing deafness was held unjustifiable as long ago as 1938.[18] Probably, not only must the teacher use force which is objectively reasonable, but he also himself must have thought it reasonably necessary in the circumstances.[19]

The basis of the defence is the need to maintain order in the particular organisation responsible for the training of the child, and school rules and parental instructions are factors to be taken into consideration when deciding what is reasonable, but are not in themselves conclusive.[20] Again the Human Rights Convention looks set to end at last all corporal punishment.

14 *Fitzgerald v Northcote* (1865) 4 F & F 656 (headmaster, boarding school); *Ryan v Fildes* [1938] 3 All ER 517 (assistant mistress, day school).
15 *Campbell and Cosans v UK* (1982) 4 EHRR 293 (corporal punishment contrary to the parents' wishes violated Article 8 of the Convention).
16 *Fitzgerald v Northcote* supra.
17 *Cleary v Booth* [1893] 1 QB 465 (fighting on the way to school); *R v Newport (Salop) Justices, ex p Wright* [1929] 2 KB 416, Div Ct (smoking in street after school).
18 *Ryan v Fildes* [1938] 3 All ER 517; there is a significant reference to Tucker J: 'In these days', at 520.
19 See *Hook v Cunard SS Co Ltd* [1953] 1 All ER 1021, on the somewhat analogous case of powers of a ship's captain to place a seaman under arrest in the interest of ship's discipline.
20 And see *Craig v Frost* (1936) 30 QJP 140 (Queensland): defendant teacher ordered child not to gallop horse to and from school, whereas father permitted galloping. Held since the order was reasonable in the interests of the child's safety, teacher's disciplinary powers overrode parental instructions.

(B) PASSENGERS IN PUBLIC TRANSPORT

The captain of a ship may use reasonable force against anyone on his ship who commits 'some act calculated in the apprehension of a reasonable man to interfere with the safety of the ship or the due prosecution of the voyage',[1] provided also, it seems, that he believes it necessary for the purpose.[2] A captain was not therefore justified in detaining a passenger in his cabin for a week because the passenger put his hand to his nose to the captain and did not apologise.[3] The cases traced have only been concerned with ships, but the same defence may be available to captains of aircraft, and, though perhaps in a restricted class of events, to those in charge of rail and road transport.

SECTION 12.   ARREST, SEARCH AND SEIZURE

The powers of arrest, search and seizure conferred on police officers, and to a limited extent on private citizens, by the Police and Criminal Evidence Act 1984 are in practice the most important of all the defences discussed in this chapter. Lawful arrest, search or seizure may constitute a defence to false imprisonment, battery or interference with goods. Unlawful arrest may justify action which would otherwise be a battery by the person resisting arrest. The 1984 Act to some degree codifies earlier case law and legislation on police powers as well as conferring new powers and duties on the police. Nevertheless a fair amount of pre-1984 Act case law remains relevant to the definition of police powers.[4] The Human Rights Act will require that provision for lawful arrest meets the principles set out in Article 5 of the Convention, as in general they would appear to do.

(A)   ARREST

(1)   By a policeman with a warrant

A policeman who arrests a person under a warrant acts lawfully and commits no trespass. Even if there is a 'defect of jurisdiction' in the magistrate who issued the warrant, a constable is statutorily exempt from liability if he acts in obedience to the warrant.[5] Thus it has been held that this section protects a constable obeying an 'invalid or unlawful warrant'.[6] But even if the warrant is good the constable is protected only if he acts in obedience to it: he is liable if he arrests the wrong person, or acts outside his jurisdiction.[7] And he must produce the warrant on demand and will be liable if he fails to do so. The arrested person having sight of the warrant may then be able to sue the magistrate if the warrant itself is defective.

---

1   *Aldworth v Stewart* (1866) 4 F & F 957 at 961 (per Channell B).
2   *Hook v Cunard SS Co Ltd* [1953] 1 All ER 1021.
3   *Aldworth v Stewart* supra.
4   *Lewis v Chief Constable of South Wales Constabulary* [1991] 1 All ER 206 at 208 CA (per Balcombe LJ).
5   Constables Protection Act 1750, s 6; see generally *Clerk and Lindsell* paras 27-118–27-120.
6   *Horsfield v Brown* [1932] 1 KB 355 at 369; quaere whether a constable is protected if the warrant is irregular in form eg it is not signed by a qualified magistrate or does not specify the cause of arrest.
7   As to constables' jurisdiction see now the Magistrates' Courts Act 1980, s 125(2).

(2)   ARREST WITHOUT WARRANT

Section 24 of the Police and Criminal Evidence Act 1984 provides for a category of 'arrestable offences'. These are criminal offences (1) for which the sentence is fixed by law, (2) for which a statute authorises imprisonment for five years, (3) a list of specific offences in subsections, and (4) inciting, conspiring or attempting to commit any of the above offences. Any person, constable or private citizen, may arrest without warrant anyone who is or whom, with reasonable cause, he suspects to be, in the act of committing an arrestable offence.[8] Any person may further arrest anyone whom he has reasonable cause to believe has committed an arrestable offence provided that that arrestable offence has in fact been committed.[9] Private citizens act at their peril. If despite appearances no crime has been committed at all they may be liable for false imprisonment consequent on the unlawful arrest.[10] Constables enjoy greater powers. Even though no arrestable offence has been committed, a constable may, if he reasonably suspects that such an offence has been committed, arrest any person, whom he, with reasonable cause, suspects to be guilty of that offence.[11] And he may arrest any person who is, or whom he, with reasonable cause, suspects to be about to commit an arrestable offence.[12] Section 117 of the 1984 Act expressly authorises constables to use reasonable force in the exercise of any of their powers under the Act including effecting an arrest. Private citizens arresting a person under the 1984 Act must rely on section 3 of the Criminal Law Act 1967 which authorises the use of reasonable force by anyone in the prevention of crime.

Section 25 of the Police and Criminal Evidence Act 1984 provides a significant extension to police powers of arrest, a power of general arrest, not limited to arrestable (ie relatively grave offences). Constables who have reasonable cause to believe that any offence is being or has been committed may arrest any person reasonably suspected of that offence if it appears to the constable that the service of a summons is impracticable or inappropriate because any of the general arrest conditions is satisfied. The general arrest conditions are wide in scope. They include inter alia that the constable believes that the suspected person has given a false name, or refuses to give a satisfactory address for service of a summons, or that he may, unless arrested, injure himself or another, or cause damage to property, or commit an offence against public decency. And, it must not be overlooked that in addition to police powers of arrest in respect of arrestable offences and the novel general arrest power under the 1984 Act, that statute expressly preserves a number of specific arrest powers under earlier Acts,[13] and almost every year new legislation confers further arrest powers on the police.[14] Finally common law powers to intervene to prevent breaches of the peace are unaffected by the 1984 Act. Constables and private citizens may arrest without warrant a person committing a breach of the peace, or who, having committed such a breach, is reasonably believed to be about to renew it,[15] or where an imminent breach is reasonably

8   Magistrates' Courts Act 1980, s 24(4).
9   Magistrates' Courts Act 1980, s 24(5).
10   R v Self [1992] 3 All ER 476, CA (a store detective arrested a customer whom she saw putting a bar of chocolate in his pocket; he was acquitted of theft and the arrest was found to be unlawful).
11   Magistrates' Courts Act 1980, s 24(6). Hence it may be crucial to ascertain whether responsibility for an arrest lies with a constable, or the person who informed him of the possible crime and sought to have a suspect detained: see Davidson v Chief Constable of North Wales [1994] 2 All ER 597, CA.
12   Magistrates' Courts Act 1980, s 27(7).
13   Magistrates' Courts Act 1980, ss 26 and 2. Various other statutes confer a variety of powers on private citizens too.
14   For example, the Criminal Justice and Public Order Act 1994.
15   Timothy v Simpson (1835) 1 Cr M & R 757. Police are not entitled to arrest for obstruction of an officer in the execution of his duty unless the disturbance caused or was likely to cause a breach of the peace: Wershof v Metropolitan Police Comr [1978] 3 All ER 540, CA.

apprehended.[16] Exceptionally a person may be detained without a formal arrest in order to prevent, or stop, a breach of the peace.[17]

(B)   REASONABLE CAUSE

Powers of arrest, and the police's complementary crime prevention powers of search and seizure, are generally dependent on reasonable cause for relevant suspicion.[18] The adjustment of the conflict between the citizen's interest in personal freedom and the public interest in efficient enforcement of the criminal law is a delicate one. Traditionally the common law has dictated that the courts show no tendency to attach excessive weight to the second, to the detriment of the first factor. So the burden of proving reasonable cause, of justifying the arrest, lies on the defendant,[19] albeit that in malicious prosecution it is on the plaintiff. Jury trial is still available in actions for false imprisonment. The jury must find the facts on which the matter depends, but what amounts to reasonable cause is a question of law for the judge.[20] Mere suspicion, a policeman's hunch, is insufficient, but suspicion is a lesser state of mind than knowledge of guilt.[1] To have reasonable cause for suspicion, a constable must himself have subjective grounds for forming such an opinion, and be able to justify those grounds objectively, to show that there is reasonable evidence to support his suspicion. A constable who arrested a person simply because he was ordered to do so by a superior officer would act unlawfully because he himself would have had no basis on which to form reasonable grounds for suspicion. But where a briefing from senior officers gave information about the plaintiff's suspected involvement in a terrorist murder, that briefing was found sufficient to establish that the arresting constable who identified the plaintiff from the briefing had reasonable cause to suspect him of the crime.[2] Once reasonable cause for suspicion is established, the constable need not generally prove that arrest was necessary. Constables are endowed with a discretion to arrest; they are rarely under a duty to do so. The House of Lords in *Holgate-Mohammed v Duke*[3] held that the constable's discretion to arrest could be challenged only if he could be proved to have acted on some immaterial or irrelevant consideration. Arrest of a woman in the belief that once in police custody she would more readily confess was held to be not unreasonable. An arrest for the purpose of using the period in custody to dispel or confirm suspicion by questioning the suspect or seeking further evidence was well within the discretion of a constable. Taking advantage of suspicion of crime to arrest your wife's lover and incarcerate him for a few hours would be clearly unlawful! And the Court of Appeal has held that a constable carrying out an arrest when he well knows there is no possibility of a charge being made acts unlawfully.[4]

---

16   *R v Howell* [1982] QB 416, [1981] 3 All ER 383, CA.
17   *Albert v Lavin* [1982] AC 546, [1981] 3 All ER 878, HL.
18   As is the related provision of Article 5(1)(c) of The Human Rights Convention.
19   *Holtham v Metropolitan Police Comr* (1987) Times, 28 November; *Allen v Wright* (1838) 8 C & P 522.
20   *Lister v Perryman* (1870) LR 4 HL 521.
1   *Shaaban Bin Hussien v Chong Fook Kam* [1970] AC 942, [1969] 3 All ER 1626, PC.
2   *O'Hara v Chief Constable of the Royal Ulster Constabulary* [1997] AC 286, HL; *Hussien v Chong Fook Kam*, [1970] AC 942, [1969] 3 All ER 1626, PC.
3   [1984] AC 437, [1984] 1 All ER 1054.
4   *Plange v Chief Constable of South Humberside Police* (1992) Times, 23 March, CA.

(C)   MANNER OF ARREST

Section 28 of the Police and Criminal Evidence Act 1984 sets out the basic rules governing the manner of a lawful arrest.[5] An arrested person must be told as soon as is practicable both:

(1)   that he is under lawful arrest; and

(2)   what are the grounds for the arrest.

That information must be volunteered by the arrestor regardless of whether the fact of, or the ground for, the arrest, appears obvious.[6] Only escape before the arrestor can practicably explain the arrest and its grounds can now excuse a failure to impart the relevant information.[7] But the dual requirement of section 28 is very basic and earlier case law elaborating the criteria for valid arrest remain relevant. For example, an arrested person must be told why he is being detained in plain simple English and given enough details to enable him to understand fully why he is being arrested.[8] It is not enough to tell him that he has been arrested 'for burglary'.[9] He has to be told in general terms when and where he is suspected of having committed burglary. The practical difficulties confronted by police officers making an arrest should not be overlooked and precise legal language need not be used. So where a constable told the arrested person she was arresting him for unlawful possession of a car, the Court of Appeal held that that was sufficient to make clear to him that he was being detained on reasonable suspicion of either theft or unlawful handling of the vehicle.[10] Should an arrested person be deaf or unable to understand English, if the arrestor should have been aware of the problem he must take reasonable steps to try to communicate with his suspect. But the arrest will not be invalid because the arrestor cannot immediately summon an interpreter to his side.[11] And arrest by words alone will generally not be sufficient unless the arrested person submits to arrest. Some physical contact is required to bring the arrested person, nominally at least, under the arrestor's control.[12]

One novel problem concerning the manner of arrest arises from the introduction of the general arrest power in section 25 of the 1984 Act. Will it be sufficient for a constable to inform a suspect of the offence constituting the ground of the arrest? Or must he further explain why he is invoking the general arrest power? On principle the latter should be the correct approach. Rules governing the manner of arrest are designed to enable arrested persons to become aware that their liberty has been lawfully curtailed: that they cannot lawfully resist detention.[13] The general arrest power, which theoretically permits arrest for any offence, even a parking offence, must require that the constable tell the arrested person what exceptional circumstance justifies arrest.

Private citizens effecting an arrest must, as soon as is reasonable, hand the arrested person over to the police. They cannot imprison suspects on their own premises, or launch their own investigations. But that does not always mean the police must be

---

5   Section 28 largely enacts the common law rules derived from the classic decision in *Christie v Leachinsky* [1947] AC 573, [1947] 1 All ER 567, HL. Compare the judgment of Viscount Simon at 587 with the provision now made by s 28.

6   Magistrates' Courts Act 1980, s 28(2), (4). And see Article 5(2) of the Human Rights Convention.

7   Magistrates' Courts Act 1980, s 28(5).

8   *Christie v Leachinsky* (supra) per Viscount Simon at 587.

9   *R v Telfer* [1976] Crim LR 562.

10 *Abbassy v Metropolitan Police Comr* [1990] 1 All ER 193 (note too that in judging the sufficiency of information given to the arrested person by a constable, earlier conversations between the two may be taken into account).

11 *John Lewis & Co Ltd v Tims* [1952] AC 676 at 681, HL; *Wheatley v Lodge* [1971] 1 WLR 29 at 34.

12 *Hart v Chief Constable of Kent* [1983] RTR 484, DC.

13 See *Christie v Leachinsky* supra per Viscount Simon at 587.

summoned instantly. In *John Lewis & Co v Tims*[14] the plaintiff was arrested by the defendants' store detectives. She was held for some 20 to 60 minutes while the manager decided whether to call the police. The House of Lords found that in the circumstances the delay and its purpose was reasonable.

Police officers have rather wider powers after an arrest. Generally a constable arresting a person must take him as soon as is practicable to a police station.[15] However, he may delay taking him there immediately where '...the presence of that person elsewhere is necessary in order to carry out such investigations as it is reasonable to carry out immediately.'[16] So he may, where appropriate, take the arrested person to his home or place of employment to, for example, check out an alibi claim, or establish evidence of identity or to look for stolen property.[17] The 1984 Act further provides detailed rules that are intended to ensure that, normally, arrested persons are taken only to designated police stations properly equipped to receive and hold arrested persons.

Occasionally suspects may be taken by police to the police station without arrest in order 'to help the police with their inquiries'. The police can then decide after questioning the suspect whether to charge him. There is no power to hold suspects without arrest for 'questioning'.[18] In a case where a deaf mute had been detained without arrest for three nights in a police station before being charged, Devlin J told the jury[19] 'You may sometimes read in novels and detective stories, perhaps written by people not familiar with police procedure, that persons are sometimes taken into custody for questioning. There is no such power in this country. A man cannot be detained unless he is arrested.'

Only if the evidence establishes that the plaintiff freely agreed to go to and remain in the police station can liability for false imprisonment in such a case be rebutted.[20] The unlawful practice of detention without arrest must be distinguished from another more common practice. A person is arrested on a minor charge while further inquiries about a more serious matter are pursued. Providing lawful grounds exist for the first arrest the decision to exercise the discretion to arrest the person on that charge can be challenged only if it can be proved to have been effected in bad faith or for some irrelevant or improper purpose.[1]

(D) ENTRY, SEARCH AND SEIZURE

The Police and Criminal Evidence Act 1984 confers on constables powers to enter premises, search persons and property and to seize evidence which are far greater in extent than the uncertain and ill-defined powers enjoyed by the police at common law. Exercise of powers of entry, search and seizure will in an appropriate case provide a good defence to actions for trespass whether to land, person, or goods, and to actions for conversion.

14   [1952] AC 676, [1952] 1 All ER 1203.
15   Magistrates' Courts Act 1980, s 30(1).
16   Magistrates' Courts Act 1980, s 30(10).
17   See *Dallison v Caffery* [1965] 1 QB 348, [1964] 2 All ER 610, CA.
18   Save by virtue of the exceptional provision made by the Prevention of Terrorism (Temporary Provisions) Act 1989.
19   *R v Roberts* (1953) Manchester Guardian, 25 March.
20   See *Warner v Riddiford* (1858) 4 CBNS 180 (show of authority may negate apparent consent: on whom would the burden of proving absence of consent fall?).
1   See *Holgate-Mohammed v Duke* [1984] AC 437, [1984] 1 All ER 1054, HL.

Detailed exposition of the powers provided for by the 1984 Act is beyond the scope of a work on torts.[2] Police powers include power to stop and search persons in public places for stolen or prohibited articles.[3] Powers of entry to effect an arrest for an arrestable offence are conferred by section 17 as is a surprisingly new power,[4] to enter premises to save life or lives or prevent serious damage to property. Arrested persons may be personally searched for items with which they may injure themselves or others, or effect an escape, or which may constitute evidence relating to an offence.[5] But the extent of a body search in such circumstances is strictly limited[6] and detailed conditions are laid down for the conduct and authorisation of an intimate search,[7] though a simple visual examination of the plaintiff's open mouth has been held not to constitute an intimate search.[8] Premises may be entered and searched where the occupier has been arrested for an arrestable offence for evidence concerning that or any related offence.[9] Any premises on which a person is arrested for any offence may be searched.[10] All these powers are additional to the power to seek a search warrant from magistrates.[11] This list is by no means conclusive. Three major questions relating to the ambit of police powers of search and seizure as defences to intentional torts still await a conclusive answer:

1   The protection for the citizen against unjust infringement of his liberty under the Act lies in the immensely detailed rules laid down in the Act for the execution of such powers, including rules as to making comprehensive records of searches undertaken. Will the courts enforce these rules to the letter holding any infringement, however minor, fatal to a defence based on the Act?

2   Will earlier case law requiring that police explain the grounds for any search of a person as they would be required to explain an arrest still hold good?

3   And most importantly, what is the exact scope of section 19 of the Act? For section 19 appears to provide that whenever police are lawfully on premises they may seize anything reasonably believed to be evidence of or the fruits of any crime, thus evading other provisions of the Act, such as section 18, which limit police powers of entry to seizure of evidence relating to the crime for which the arrested person has been arrested or a related offence.

SECTION 13.   JUDICIAL ACTS

No action in tort lies against a judge[12] or a magistrate[13] for any act done within his jurisdiction even though there may be evidence that he acted in bad faith. The risk of frivolous and vexatious actions discrediting the judicial process as a whole is perceived as outweighing the risk of harm occasioned by a corrupt or malicious judge.[14] Where a judge or a magistrate acts outside his jurisdiction the position is more complex. Judges

2   See *Clerk & Lindsell* ch 16.
3   Police and Criminal Evidence Act 1984, s 1.
4   No such power existed at common law. And see *Kynaston v DPP* (1987) 87 Cr App Rep 200, DC.
5   Police and Criminal Evidence Act 1984, s 32.
6   See Police and Criminal Evidence Act 1984, ss 1(9), 32(4), 54(7).
7   Police and Criminal Evidence Act 1984, s 55.
8   *R v Hughes* [1994] 1 WLR 876.
9   Police and Criminal Evidence Act 1984, s 18.
10   Police and Criminal Evidence Act 1984, s 18.
11   Police and Criminal Evidence Act 1984, s 8.
12   *Fray v Blackburn* (1863) 3 B & S 576; *Anderson v Gorrie* [1895] 1 QB 668, CA.
13   Section 44 of the Justices of the Peace Act 1979 as amended by s 108 of the Courts and Legal Services Act 1990.
14   See M Brazier 'Judicial Immunity and the Independence of the Judiciary' [1976] PL 397.

of the Supreme Court are the sole arbiters of their own jurisdiction and therefore cannot be proved to have acted beyond that jurisdiction save in the most blatant case where no sort of authority for a purported judicial act could be invoked.[15] Judges of inferior courts operate within a limited jurisdiction defined and enforced by the superior courts. A judgment made by a district judge or a magistrate can be quashed (rendered a nullity) by the High Court. Will the individual judge then be liable for any tort, for example, false imprisonment, resulting from that invalid judgment? Lord Denning in *Sirros v Moore*[16] contended that such liability only arose if the plaintiff could prove that the judge acted in bad faith. The House of Lords in *Re McC* held that in so far as he sought to apply such a doctrine to magistrates he was wrong[17] and reached no conclusive opinion as far as judges of other inferior courts were concerned. Parliament in response to *Re McC* legislated to clarify the liability of magistrates. A magistrate cannot now be liable for an act beyond his jurisdiction unless he acted in bad faith.[18] So judges of the High Court and above can only be liable for an act flagrantly beyond their authority (and so, very obviously, in bad faith), magistrates are liable only for a deliberate excess of jurisdiction, but judges of county and Crown courts remain in a sort of judicial limbo. But is it justifiable to grant any judge immunity from the consequences of his mistakes' an immunity not shared by other professionals? Albeit that in some cases other persons, for example members of tribunals,[19] may share in the limited immunity of judges[20] of inferior courts and in their related immunity from proceedings for libel and slander.[1]

It should be noted that it may also be a defence to false imprisonment, trespass or conversion that the act was done in execution of the judicial process.[2]

SECTION 14. STATUTORY AUTHORITY

Public bodies and officials may only do acts which would be unlawful in others if they are authorised to do them by statute. Of course, as government has become increasingly regulatory and far-reaching in its effects, more and more such powers have been given. The question before the courts in tort cases of this type is whether the Act in question authorised the official to commit the tort complained of.[3]

Certain guiding principles have been worked out by the courts in order to answer this question. Either a duty or a power to do the act will afford a defence.[4] The defendant must prove that the tort would be an inevitable result of performing the act authorised: if, for instance, a local authority built an efficient electricity generating station, the fumes from which damaged crops of the plaintiff, they would only have a defence if they proved

---

15 *Re McC* [1985] AC 528, [1984] 3 All ER 908, HL.
16 [1975] QB 118, [1974] 3 All ER 776, CA.
17 Supra at 541–2 (per Lord Bridge). And note *Warren v Warren* [1996] 3 WLR 1129, 1137, CA.
18 Section 45 of the Justices of the Peace Act 1979 as amended by s 108 of the Courts and Legal Services Act 1990.
19 See M Brazier 'Judicial Immunity and the Independence of the Judiciary' [1976] PL 397.
20 Some judicial or quasi-judicial function must be conferred on the individual by statute. Simply because a professional duty includes acting fairly will not confer any immunity from suit *Sutcliffe v Thackrah* [1974] AC 727, [1974] 1 All ER 859, HL (no immunity for architect certifying amount of building work done). *Arenson v Casson, Beckman, Rutley & Co* [1977] AC 405, [1975] 3 All ER 901 (defence possibly available to arbitrators but not valuers; and dicta in that decision even doubt the availability of immunity to arbitrators in all cases).
1 *Ackerley v Parkinson* (1815) 3 M & S 411; *Everett v Griffiths* [1921] 1 AC 631.
2 See *Clerk & Lindsell* ch 16.
3 *IRC v Rossminster Ltd* [1980] AC 952 [1980] 1 All ER 80, HL is a recent example of the difficult problems of statutory construction which may arise.
4 *Hammersmith and City Rly Co v Brand* (1869) LR 4 HL 171.

not merely that an efficient station had been built, but also that they had used all reasonable care[5] in the light of current technical and scientific skill to prevent the commission of a tort; however, they have an absolute defence, regardless of proving these precautions, if they can discharge the very heavy burden of proving that the Act authorised them to disregard these matters.[6]

In determining whether Parliament intended to deprive the plaintiff of a right to sue, the presence of some alternative special provision in the Act for compensating those injured by the statutory activity may be material, and sometimes even decisive. It is also important to look at the nature of the power. Powers to execute some particular work or carry on some particular undertaking, such as building a reservoir or a gasworks, 'are, in the absence of clear provision to the contrary in the Act, limited to the doing of the particular things authorised without infringement of the rights of others, except in so far as any such infringement may be a demonstrably necessary consequence of doing what is authorised to be done'.[7] If, however, a public body is authorised to execute a variety of works at its discretion (many of which are likely to affect private rights) then the body will rarely be prevented from infringing those rights, for that would prevent it from doing the very task which it was set up to perform.[8]

SECTION 15.   ACTS CONNECTED WITH PARLIAMENTARY PROCEEDINGS

It is a defence that the act complained of took place in the course of parliamentary business and as part thereof[9] for each House of Parliament has a parliamentary privilege to regulate its own concerns.[10] Whether this extends to an assault committed within the Chamber on the Speaker was expressly left open in *Elliot's case*.[11]

SECTION 16.   EXECUTIVE ACTS

In general it is no defence that the act complained of is an act of the executive.[12] To this there are two exceptions.

(A)   ACT OF STATE

Neither the official responsible nor the Crown can be sued for injuries tortiously inflicted outside the territorial jurisdiction of the Crown upon aliens by authority or subsequent

---

5   *Tate and Lyle Industries Ltd v Greater London Council* [1983] 2 AC 509, [1983] 1 All ER 1159, HL.
6   *Manchester Corpn v Farnworth* [1930] AC 171, HL; *Geddis v Bann Reservoir Proprietors* (1878) 3 App Cas 430, HL.
7   *Marriage v East Norfolk Rivers Catchment Board* [1950] 1 KB 284 at 307, [1949] 2 All ER 1021, CA (per Jenkins LJ); cf *Metropolitan Asylum District Managers v Hill* (1881) 6 App Cas 193, HL.
8   [1950] 1 KB 284 at 307–8. The cases on this defence of statutory authority are very numerous but since they turn on the interpretation of the particular statutes and merely illustrate the general principle set out in the text, it seems unprofitable to discuss them here.
9   Report of Select Committee on Official Secrets Acts HC 101 of 1939.
10   *Bradlaugh v Gossett* (1884) 12 QBD 271; *R v Graham-Campbell, ex p Herbert* [1935] 1 KB 594.
11   (1629) 3 State Tr 293.
12   *Leach v Money* (1765) 19 State Tr 1001.

ratification of the Crown.[13] If the act is committed in British territory, the defence is available only where the plaintiff is an enemy alien[14] or, possibly, a friendly alien resident in British territory who has broken his duty of temporary local allegiance to the Crown.[15]

(B) PREROGATIVE

The Crown still retains a few prerogative powers to interfere with the rights of the citizen. If it takes property under prerogative powers it ordinarily has to pay compensation.[16] If, however, the power is exercised during or in contemplation of war, there is no entitlement to compensation in respect of damage to or destruction of property.[17]

SECTION 17.   AN ACT WHICH IS ALSO A CRIME

(A)   ASSAULT AND BATTERY

The ordinary principle of res judicata applies to suits in tort, with the result that it is a defence to subsequent proceedings that the same issue has previously been litigated between the same parties. It is, however, no defence that the act is also a crime for which the defendant has been convicted or acquitted.[18] To this rule section 45 of the Offences Against the Person Act 1861 furnishes an exception. In certain cases, classified by that Act as minor assaults the criminal conviction operates as a bar to subsequent proceedings in tort.[19]

SECTION 18.   PLAINTIFF A WRONGDOER

There may be cases where the plaintiff has a prima facie claim in tort but the court finds that his own wrongful conduct debars him from entitlement to a remedy. A maxim often called ex turpi causa non oritur actio is invoked.[20]

Applying the maxim is an uncertain exercise, made even more problematic by the recent judgment of the Court of Appeal in *Clunis v Camden and Islington Health Authority*.[1] The source of the maxim is straightforward. Lord Mansfield CJ declared in

---

13 *Buron v Denman* (1848) 2 Exch 167; *Walker v Baird* [1892] AC 491, PC. In *A-G v Nissan* [1970] AC 179, [1969] 1 All ER 629, the House of Lords left undecided whether in any circumstances Act of State could ever be pleaded against British subjects in respect of acts outside the realm.

14 *R v Bottrill, ex p Kuechenmeister* [1947] KB 41 at 57 (per Asquith LJ), CA; *Netz v Chuter Ede* [1946] Ch 224, [1946] 1 All ER 628.

15 *Johnstone v Pedlar* [1921] 2 AC 262, HL. It may be, however, that the Crown must indicate that it has withdrawn its protection of the alien before the defence becomes available (per Lord Atkinson at 285).

16 *A-G v Nissan* [1970] AC 179, [1969] 1 All ER 629, HL.

17 Section 1(1) of the War Damage Act 1965 reversing *Burmah Oil Co Ltd v Lord Advocate* [1965] AC 75, [1964] 2 All ER 348, HL.

18 But see *McIlKenny v Chief Constable of the West Midlands* [1980] QB 283, [1980] 2 All ER 227.

19 For examples of the application of s45 see *Solomon v Frinagan* (1866) 30 JP Jo 756; *Masper v Brown* (1876) 1 CPD 97; *Dyer v Munday* [1895] 1 QB 742, CA.

20 See doubts as to the appropriateness of the Latin tag in *Pitts v Hunt* [1990] 3 WLR 542 at 565 (per Dillon LJ).

1   [1998] 3 All ER 180, [1998] 2 WLR 902.

1775.[2] 'No court will lend its aid to a man who founds his cause of action upon an immoral or illegal act'. But does that mean that whenever a plaintiff is shown to have been engaged in criminal conduct at the time that he alleges that he suffered harm, his claim must fail? Will a plaintiff breaking the speed limit herself be denied a remedy against a defendant who collides with her when he is well over the alcohol limit and driving on the wrong side of the road? The judgment of the Court of Appeal in *Revill v Newbery*[3] suggested that criminal conduct is not an absolute bar to a claim in tort. There, a burglar, who did not threaten any personal violence, was allowed to sue the householder who fired a shotgun at him without warning after the plaintiff broke into a garden shed. The defendant's response was said to be 'disproportionate' to the evil posed by the plaintiff's criminal conduct.

Before exploring the judgment in *Clunis*, we need to examine the origins of ex turpi causa. Its origins lie in contract not tort. No court will enforce a contract arising out of an illegal transaction. If the plaintiff must rely on an illegal contract to succeed in tort, his action in tort too must fail. So in *Taylor v Chester*[4] the plaintiff deposited a £50 note with the defendant as security for his agreement to pay her for 'rent' of her brothel for an orgy. His claim in detinue for return of the pledge failed because he could only deny the validity of the pledge by showing its illegal and immoral purpose. Similarly, if to succeed in tort, the plaintiff must seek to assert an interest in property arising out of an illegal contract, he must fail if to establish that interest he must rely on the illegality.[5] If his claim can be established without reliance on the relevant illegal act, he may still succeed, despite a general taint of criminality.

A series of judgments by the Court of Appeal[6] had sought to establish a broader, more flexible test for ex turpi. Would it be an affront to the public conscience to afford the plaintiff a remedy? Thus, to put it briefly, minor illegalities could be overlooked. But more seriously culpable conduct might result in denial of redress, even though to establish his claim in contract the plaintiff did not need to rely directly on the relevant illegality. The House of Lords in *Tinsley v Milligan*[7] vigorously criticised and forthrightly rejected such a 'public conscience' test in the context of contract. A plaintiff who cannot establish a claim in contract without reliance on his own illegal or immoral conduct fails. Other evidence of illegality or immorality, not crucial to the existence of the relevant obligation, does not give rise to a defence of ex turpi. Returning to tort, the modern case law prior to *Clunis*, clearly establishes the application of a defence of ex turpi in tort beyond claims resting on illegal contracts. The conceptual basis of the defence remained unclear. In *Kirkham v Chief Constable of Greater Manchester Police*[8] the issue was perceived as a matter of public policy. Should the plaintiff be allowed to succeed in the light of his own wrongdoing? Would it affront the public conscience or shock the ordinary citizen to allow this particular plaintiff to recover compensation? In *Pitts v Hunt*[9] both Balcombe LJ and Dillon LJ condemned such a test as imprecise and difficult to apply, expressing very much the same sort of criticisms as those later articulated by the House of Lords in *Tinsley v Milligan*.

In *Pitts v Hunt* the plaintiff was injured in an accident when he was a pillion passenger on a motor cycle. He and the driver had both been drinking heavily and the plaintiff

2   *Holman v Johnson* (1775) 1 Cowp 341.
3   [1996] QB 567, CA.
4   (1869) LR 4 QB 309.
5   *Bowmakers Ltd v Barnet Instruments Ltd* [1945] KB 65.
6   *Saunders v Edwards* [1987] 1 WLR 1116; *Euro-Diam v Bathurst* [1990] 1 QB 1; *Howard v Shirlstar Container Transport Ltd* [1990] 1 WLR 1292, CA.
7   [1994] 1 AC 340, [1993] 3 All ER 65, HL.
8   [1990] 2 QB 283, CA; see also *Reeves v Metropolitan Police Comr* [1998] 2 WLR 401, CA.
9   [1991] 1 QB 24 at 50 and 57.

had been 'egging' the driver on to ride in an ever more reckless and dangerous manner. All three judges in the Court of Appeal held that the defence of ex turpi succeeded. Beldam LJ found it contrary to public policy to allow the plaintiff to succeed. Balcombe LJ[10] held that as between two drunken youths bent on a joint criminal enterprise no appropriate standard of care could be set. Dillon LJ[11] found that as the plaintiff's claim arose directly from his participation in a crime, his claim must fail.

The decision in *Clunis v Camden and Islington Health Authority*[12] supports Dillon LJ's analysis. Christopher Clunis had a history of mental illness. After his release from detention in a mental hospital, and having missed four appointments with his doctors, he made an unprovoked attack on a man at a tube station, stabbing him and killing him. Clunis was convicted of manslaughter. He sought to sue the health authority responsible for his care alleging that their failure to provide him with adequate treatment resulted in his deranged killing of his unfortunate victim and his own subsequent conviction for manslaughter. The Court of Appeal upheld a plea of ex turpi. The plaintiff's claim must fail because the very basis of his claim was injury resulting from his own criminal act. Their Lordships rejected argument by his counsel that what must be considered was whether given Clunis' mental disorder and the alleged inadequacy of his care, the public conscience would be appalled by allowing him redress. Ex turpi was not a 'wholly discretionary' defence. Where a claim in tort arises from participation in criminal conduct, no cause of action arises against the plaintiff's fellow miscreants. When the harm of which the plaintiff complains derives from his own conviction for a criminal offence, any claim must fail.

Clunis thus confirms, and explains, a series of judgments denying a remedy in tort to, among others, a burglar seeking to sue the driver of his getaway car[13], the widow of a burglar claiming loss of dependency against the driver responsible for her husband's death in a road accident[14], her dependency being the loss of his income from crime. But other judgments are now in disarray. In *Revill v Newbery*[15] the plaintiff's very presence on the defendant's property derived from his criminal conduct. But for his crime, he would not have been injured. In *Lane v Holloway*[16] an elderly man provoked an argument with the defendant who retaliated by a violent assault on him. A plea of ex turpi failed. The defendant's response was out of all proportion to the wrongful conduct of the plaintiff. Yet in both cases the plaintiff's own wrongdoing triggered the harm of which they subsequently complained. Can they be distinguished from *Clunis* on the grounds that the very injury of which Clunis complained was his crime itself, his conviction for manslaughter. And in those cases, where one criminal seeks to sue another engaged on the self-same criminal enterprise, he can rely *only* on his own criminal conduct to establish a cause of action. The plaintiffs in *Revill* and *Lane*, by contrast, may have been in the wrong place at the wrong time because of their criminal or anti-social behaviour, but they claimed in respect of injuries which were arguably not an inevitable consequence of their own wrongdoing.

Any such distinction is paper thin however and leaves open key questions. Is it now the case that any claim in tort must fall if founded on criminal conduct however gross the wrongdoing of the defendant? Is ex turpi now limited to *criminal* wrongdoing? Prior authority clearly indicated that anti-social or disgraceful conduct falling short of

10   [1991] 1 QB 24 at 46.
11   [1991] QB 24 at 50–51.
12   [1998] 3 All ER 180, [1998] 2 WLR 902, CA.
13   *Ashton v Turner* [1981] QB 137.
14   *Burns v Edman* [1970] 2 QB 541.
15   Supra.
16   [1968] 1 QB 379, CA.

criminality could suffice to raise the defence of ex turpi in certain cases[17]. Classifying just what degree of bad or immoral conduct gave rise to the defence largely depended on just the 'affront to public conscience' test so vigorously rejected in *Tinsley v Milligan* and *Clunis v Camden and Islington Health Authority*. Assuming conduct short of crime remains a source of a plea of ex turpi, any test other than a broad policy based approach to 'public conscience' seems difficult to envisage and the discretionary nature of an anti-social ex turpi plea appears inevitable. It must be noted that *if* the plaintiff's alleged wrongdoing is not criminal conduct, concepts of disgraceful or immoral conduct change with the times. In 1868 it was held that a woman seeking to sue her lover for infecting her with a venereal disease should fail on the grounds of her own flagrant immorality in engaging in extra-marital intercourse.[18] Judges today are unlikely to follow that Victorian precedent. In 1981, Lord Denning argued that suicide although no longer criminal was such an intrinsically immoral act that damages should never be awarded for the consequences of suicide or attempted suicide.[19] The Court of Appeal in *Kirkham v Chief Constable of Greater Manchester Police* disapproved his dictum. The plaintiff's husband was seriously disturbed and had attempted suicide. Police failed to tell the prison authorities of his condition and he successfully committed suicide. His widow recovered compensation for the negligence of the police. And in *Reeves v Metropolitan Police Comr*[20] it was held that where a prisoner was known to be a suicide risk, ex turpi did not apply to bar a claim by his widow even though the deceased was mentally competent. This self harm was exactly the conduct which the defendants had a duty to guard against.

It is important to note that often facts which raise the possibility of a successful plea of ex turpi may also give rise to other defences. If I throw a brick through my neighbour's window yelling 'come out and fight' and he beats me to a pulp, he may also argue I was volenti to the ensuing fight and contributorily negligent as to my safety.

SECTION 19.   SELF-HELP REMEDIES

In addition to the defences so far discussed the law sanctions a number of 'self-help' remedies enabling a person against whom some prior tort has been committed to take action to remedy the damage done which would otherwise itself be tortious. These include retaking chattels wrongly withheld from the plaintiff,[1] abatement of nuisance,[2] distress damage feasant[3] and replevin.[4] Such defences will not be discussed further

---

17   *Kirkham v Chief Constable of Greater Manchester Police* [1990] 2 QB 283.
18   *Hegerty v Shine* (1878) 14 Cox CC 145; and see *Siveyer v Allison* [1935] 2 KB 403.
19   *Hyde v Tameside Area Health Authority* (1981) 2 PN 26, CA.
20   [1998] 2 All ER 381, [1998] 2 WLR 401, CA.
1   This defence known as recaption of chattels can therefore be used where a trespass to or conversion of the plaintiff's goods has taken place. See *Blades v Higgs* (1861) 10 CBNS 713, (1865) 11 HL Cas 621; *Patrick v Colerick* (1838) 3 M & W 483; *Anthony v Haney* (1832) 8 Bing 186.
2   Eg chopping off branches of overhanging trees; see *Lemmon v Webb* [1895] AC 1, HL.
3   Seizing a chattel unlawfully on your land as 'security' until compensation is paid (eg until the bus company pays for the damage done to your rosebed by a bus which has veered off the road and into your garden). Distress damage feasant may no longer be utilised to seize animals: s 7(1) of the Animals Act 1971. For a fuller account of legitimate self-redress see *Clerk and Lindsell* §§ 21-128 et seq.
4   An action to reclaim goods taken under some wrongful judicial process; see *Clerk and Lindsell* §§ 21-128–21-129.

here. In general the courts are reluctant to allow ancient remedies to be revived to expand the freedom of the citizen to resort to self-redress. Nonetheless such remedies refuse to fade away entirely as is witnessed by an attempt to defend wheel-clamping by invoking distress damage feasant.[5]

5   *Arthur v Anker* [1997] QB 564, [1996] 3 All ER 783, CA.

Part III

Intentional interference with economic interests

CONTENTS

CHAPTERS		PAGE
7	Interference with economic interests	113
8	False representations	118
9	Unlawful interference with trade	143
10	Intellectual property interests	163

Chapter 7

Interference with economic interests

SECTION 1. 'RIGHTS' AND ECONOMIC INTERESTS[1]

The law of torts affords every member of society comprehensive protection from deliberately inflicted harm to his person, his goods and his land by means of the torts discussed in the previous part. Protection of legitimate interests in a person's livelihood, in his business and trading interests, is significantly less comprehensive. Should my, and my family's economic prosperity, be diminished because I have been physically attacked and can no longer work, my attacker must compensate us for our loss of income. Where the defendant claims some justification or authority for what he did to me, the onus lies on him to establish lawful grounds for interfering with my right to bodily security. If one workman takes the tools of the trade of another he does so at his peril. A misguided belief that the tools were his own will not avail him. Yet if a businessman motivated by pure spite against another mounts a campaign to destroy the other's business, to seduce away from him his customers, to dissuade other traders from dealing with him, the injured party may have no remedy in tort for the loss of his livelihood.

In *Keeble v Hickeringill*[2], Holt CJ enunciated a wide principle of liability for intentional harm to economic and trading interests. He held that 'he who hinders another in his trade or livelihood is liable to an action for so hindering him'. But that principle never took root in English law. In *Allen v Flood*[3] in 1896, the House of Lords, by a majority, stifled the growth of any general principle of liability in tort for intentional and malicious interference with economic and business interests. Flood and Taylor were shipwrights taken on for the day by the Glengall Iron Company to work on the woodwork of a ship. During the day other employees of the company, who were boilermakers working on the ironwork of the ship, discovered that the respondents had previously been employed by another firm working on ironwork. The boilermakers belonged to a union which objected strongly to shipwrights being employed to do ironwork. Allen, an official of the union, sought an interview with an officer of the Glengall Iron Company and told him that unless the respondents were dismissed all the boilermakers would 'knock off work'. Flood and Taylor were told at the end of the day that their services would be no longer required. They brought an action against

---

1 See generally Cane *Tort Law and Economic Interests* (1996).
2 (1706) 11 East 574n.
3 [1898] AC 1, HL.

Allen for maliciously inducing the company not to employ them on subsequent occasions, for intentionally interfering with their livelihood.

The case for the respondents depended largely on their establishing a positive right to protection of their economic interests. Expressing the minority opinion, and holding that such a right did exist, Hawkins J described it thus:[4]

> ... the legal right which each of the plaintiffs, in common with every man in this country, has to pursue freely and without hindrance, interruption or molestation that profession, trade or calling which he has adopted for his livelihood.

The majority in *Allen v Flood* refused to recognise such a right, akin to rights to bodily security, property or reputation. All the law recognises is a person's freedom to pursue his livelihood or business. Allen, in seeking to persuade the company not to re-engage the respondents, was equally exercising his freedom to arrange affairs, as he saw it, in the interests of the members of his union. The House of Lords, having found nothing intentionally unlawful in what Allen did, further rejected the contention that his motive, to 'punish' the respondents for their earlier breach of the boilermakers' desired 'monopoly' of ironwork, transformed an otherwise lawful act into an unlawful act actionable in tort.

The absence of any right to protection of economic interests in English law has several consequences. First and obviously, it restricts the scope of the law of torts in guarding plaintiffs against unfair practices by others. An English plaintiff in the equivalent circumstances of the American plaintiff in *Tuttle v Buck*[5] would be left remediless. The defendant in that case, a rich banker, set up a rival barber's shop with the sole intention of driving the plaintiff out of business by undercutting his prices. In Minnesota, the plaintiff recovered for his losses.[6]

Secondly, development of the economic torts became haphazard.[7] The prior existence of specific torts of inducing breach of contract and conspiracy was confirmed in *Allen v Flood*. The next 80 years or so saw the extension of that first tort to interference with subsisting contracts and the development of the tort of intimidation and other innominate torts of unlawful interference. Now Lord Diplock has suggested that there is a common principle linking the economic torts. There is a 'genus' tort of unlawful interference with the trade or business of another of which the traditional economic torts are 'species'.[8]

Thirdly, the restricted development of liability for deliberately inflicted harm to economic interests has necessarily had an effect on the development of negligence in relation to damage to economic interests. Can a rational system of law refuse a remedy to a businessman who suffers financial losses because of the deliberate and spiteful conduct of a rival, and grant a remedy where identical losses result from some third party's negligence? Consider this illustration. A firm of cattle auctioneers lose business because a rival firm undercut their fees and offer inducements to farmers to send cattle

4   [1898] AC 1 at 14.
5   107 Min 145 (1909).
6   On the development of rights in economic interests in the US generally, see Heydon *Economic Torts* (2nd edn).
7   See the comment that the economic torts have been at best 'a ramshackle construction for decades' in Lord Wedderburn, (1984) 46 MLR 224 at 229. For a thoroughgoing account of this area see Carty 'Intentional Violation of Economic Interests: the Limits of Common Law Liability' (1988) 104 LQR 250.
8   *Merkur Island Shipping Corpn Laughton* [1983] 2 AC 570. The boundaries of any such tort remain hazy. It is at best still an 'embryo' tort; see *Lonrho plc v Fayed* [1989] 2 All ER 65 at 71 and 73, CA. For an analysis of the implication of such a 'genus' tort and consideration of the role of tort in this area see Carty (1988) 104 LQR 250.

only to them. The firm's loss is irrecoverable. But what if that same firm suffer an identical loss of business because a neighbouring research institute negligently allows foot and mouth disease to spread to local cattle, and government restrictions on the movement of cattle stop all cattle auctions for a period of months?[9] We shall suggest a little later that it is not necessarily inconsistent to make the latter liable for his negligence while the former remains free of legal responsibility for his deliberate actions.

SECTION 2. FREE COMPETITION; UNFAIR COMPETITION[10]

What must next be considered is why the English courts rejected a general recognition of economic interests. The clearest explanation is to be found in a dictum of Atkin LJ in *Ware and de Freville Ltd v Motor Trade Association*.[11]

> The truth is that the right of the individual to carry on his trade or profession or execute his own activities, whatever they may be, without interruption, so long as he refrains from tort or crime, affords an unsatisfactory basis for determining what is actionable, in as much as the right is conditioned by a precisely similar right in the rest of his fellow men. Such co-existing rights do in a world of competition necessarily impinge upon one another ... The true question is, was the power of the plaintiff to carry on his trade etc, interrupted by an act which the law deems wrongful.

English law embraced a fundamental doctrine of free competition, which was manifestly inconsistent with any assumption that the interest in pursuing a livelihood or a trade was entitled to absolute legal protection. Acts of competitors, or others, damaging a person in his business were to be tortious only if the act causing the damage was in itself 'unlawful'. That of course is a circular statement; it begs the question of what constitutes an 'unlawful' act in the context of damaging another's trade or business.

'Unlawful' acts resulting in liability for violation of economic interests may be divided into three categories. The first, which is relatively uncontroversial, comprises those specific torts concerned with false representations.[12] Free competition does not validate the use of lies and fraud to do down your competitors. Thus the tort of deceit imposes liability for false representations in reliance on which the plaintiff suffers damage. Passing off prevents one trader falsely cashing in on the reputation of another by seeking to mislead customers by representing his goods as another's or by some other 'fraudulent' trade practice. And injurious falsehood 'punishes' the trader who falsely disparages his competitors. All these torts are in a very real sense 'unfair competition' torts, and are fully discussed in the next chapter.

Secondly, there are the classic economic torts of inducing breach of contract, conspiracy, intimidation and so on. These are the torts which Lord Diplock has now suggested belong to one 'genus' of unlawful acts interfering with trade or business. These torts, although equally capable of being utilised as 'unfair competition' torts, have suffered over the past 80 years from their embroilment in the controversy over trade union rights. They came to be seen, and often to be taught, as almost exclusively labour law torts of little interest to the tort student as such. It was the bitter and

9 See *Weller & Co v Foot and Mouth Disease Research Institute* [1966] 1 QB 569 discussed post, Ch 12.
10 See Whish *Competition Law* (2nd edn, 1989) chs 1 and 2.
11 [1921] 3 KB 40 at 79, CA. For the origins of the doctrine of free competition within the common law, see the *Case of Gloucester Grammar School* (1410) YB 11 Hen 4 fo 47 pl 21.
12 But note deceit may also be relevant in other 'classic' economic torts too: *Lonrho plc v Fayed* [1990] 2 QB 479, [1989] 2 All ER 65, CA.

long-running litigation over the takeover of Harrods that 'liberated' such torts from their labour law straightjacket.[13] Thirdly and finally, there is a growing group of torts concerned with the protection of intellectual property. Many are largely statutory - for example actions for breach of copyright and infringement of patents - but at present the (residual) action for breach of confidence remains subject to development by the common law alone.

The categories of torts concerned with economic interests will be dealt with in the order outlined above. No attempt will be made to outline or consider in any detail the immunities of trade unions in respect of torts in the second category. The emphasis will be placed on this broad function of the torts (or tort) in the context of fair competition, and the civil rights of employers and workers. Detailed examination of statutory provision for breach of copyright or infringements of patents is beyond the scope of this work. The chapter on the third category of intellectual property torts will thus be short and intended simply to complete the picture of liability in respect of interference with economic interests. What has to be assessed overall is to what extent the law of torts now imposes liability for unfair competitive practices.

SECTION 3.   ECONOMIC LOSS AND NEGLIGENCE

An attempt must now be made to answer the question posed earlier of whether the common law can rationally impose liability for negligent violation of economic interests while intentional violations remain non-actionable. Two primary issues need to be considered. Do the reasons for not imposing liability in respect of intentional violations apply with equal force to negligence? If it is now correct to explain the basic principle of liability for intentional interference with economic interests in terms of a 'genus' tort of liability for any unlawful act violating economic interests, can negligence be regarded as a further 'species' of unlawful act? The rationale for regarding the 'right' to pursue a trade or livelihood as a freedom, a power, to carry on that trade or livelihood, as opposed to a right accorded the same status as the right to bodily security, derives from the judicial perception of the demands of free competition. Just as I am free to set up in business as a greengrocer, to choose to whom I will sell and from whom I will buy my produce, so is my neighbour free to do the same. And to promote his business he may adopt any lawful strategy. To put it crudely, if that drives me out of business, tough. I have proved to be insufficiently hardy and skilled at the trade. The market economy encourages success and depends on the 'best' man or woman winning. But if my business suffers because of another's negligence, for example a negligent contractor fractures a gas main and the road leading to my shop is blocked off for several days while repairs are carried out, there is no harm done to the doctrine of free competition in imposing liability upon the negligent actor. Indeed, rather the opposite; a competitive economy requires that each enterprise should maximise its skill and so enhance its own profitability and offer the optimum service.

So, the second question is that if there is no reason derived from the principle of free and fair competition that negligent interference with economic interests should not be actionable, can negligence properly be regarded as a 'species' of unlawful act resulting in liability for invasion of economic interests? Carelessness as such can no more constitute a tort in relation to economic interests than malice or spite on their own. A negligently caused explosion in south Manchester which because of the vagaries of the city's ancient sewage system results in part of the city centre being blocked to traffic for several hours will not and should not result in liability for all the

13   See *Lonrho plc v Fayed* [1992] 1 AC 448, [1991] 3 All ER 303, HL.

consequent business losses. But where the relationship of the plaintiff and the defendant is sufficiently close to induce or require the plaintiff to rely and depend on the care and skill of the defendant to safeguard his economic interests then a failure to do so, a breach of duty, can properly be regarded as an unlawful act creating liability for the ensuing loss subject to two caveats.

The first concerns the respective roles of contract and tort.[14] Any business relying on another to provide goods or services is free to contract for those goods or services. If they fail to meet contract standards, the suppliers will be liable for breach of contract. If there is no contract, it may be argued that the law of torts should not rush in and impose liability.[15] Nor, similarly, it can be argued, should tort liability be imposed where the plaintiff relies on a contract to which he is not a party. That, it is said, would breach the rules on privity of contract. Hence, in many instances where it is alleged that negligent conduct causing economic loss is tortious, no tort can be committed because any relevant duty can arise in contract alone.

The second caveat relates to the implications of liability for negligently inflicted economic loss. Where would the limits of liability be drawn to avoid the spectre of liability 'in an indeterminable amount for an indefinite time to an indeterminate class'.[16] Both illustrate the very real problems of defining the scope of any duty to avoid negligently inflicted economic loss. Neither problem constitutes an unanswerable case that such loss should never be recoverable in tort. They do illustrate why the recent trend has been that recovery of financial loss should be the exception rather than the rule. To put it crudely, the law will always be readier to require others to protect you from physical harm than to demand that they, for no reward, look after your money and other economic interests.[17]

SECTION 4. ECONOMIC TORTS AND ECONOMIC REGULATION[18]

The discussion so far in this chapter has ignored two important elements in the debate on the role of the economic torts. The principle of free competition may be called into doubt. And even those who accept the basic premise of a competitive economy may come to wonder how much of the original notion has survived recent developments. Increasingly, Parliament has legislated to regulate the economy, to eliminate unfair practices. And the judiciary has responded[19] taking account of the emphasis now placed on free competition being fair competition. These developments must be noted as we examine the scope of the economic torts in 1999.

---

14 See further post.
15 See Cane 'Contract, Tort and Economic Loss' in Furmston (ed) *The Law of Tort* (1986); *Murphy v Brentwood District Council* [1991] 1 AC 398, [1990] 2 All ER 908, HL. But compare *White v Jones* [1995] 2 AC 207, HL.
16 *Ultramares Corpn v Touche* 255 NY 170 (1931) (per Cardozo J); *Caparo Industries plc v Dickman* [1990] 2 AC 605, [1990] 1 All ER 568, HL. See post.
17 Might one expect that the less well-off would be afforded more protection than the wealthy, or the private individual than big business? See *Smith v Eric S Bush* [1990] 1 AC 831, [1989] 2 All ER 514, HL, post.
18 See Weir *Economic Torts* (1997).
19 See, for example, '...increasing recognition by Parliament of the need for more rigorous standards of commercial honesty is a factor which should not be overlooked by a judge confronted by the choice whether or not to extend by analogy to circumstances in which it has not previously been applied a principle which has been applied in a previous case whether the circumstances although different had some features in common with those of the case which he has to decide' per Lord Diplock in *Erven Warnink BV v J Townend & Sons (Hull) Ltd* [1979] 2 All ER 927 at 933.

Chapter 8

False representations

SECTION I. DECEIT

The use of deliberately false representations on which the plaintiff is induced to, and does, rely to his detriment has for nearly 200 years been actionable by means of the tort of deceit.[1] Judicial recognition that fraud never constituted fair competition has a much longer history[2] but whether earlier authorities are founded in contract, equity or tort is a matter for the legal historian. What is still of crucial importance to the law student is that the law relating to misrepresentations cannot be understood fully by considering tort alone. A misrepresentation may concurrently create rights of action in tort and contract. A misrepresentation not actionable in tort may give rise to a right to rescind a contract and misrepresentations unconcerned with contract may create an estoppel. The interrelation of common law and equity in respect of remedies for misrepresentation further complicate the picture.[3]

The development of the separate tort of deceit, with which we are concerned in this chapter, dates from the decision in *Pasley v Freeman*.[4]

> The defendant falsely misrepresented to the plaintiff that X was a person to whom the plaintiff might safely sell goods on credit. The plaintiff suffered loss through relying on this representation and was held to have an action on the case for deceit.

The tort may be defined as:

> a false representation made by the defendant knowingly, or without belief in its truth or recklessly, careless whether it be true or false, with the intention that the plaintiff should act in reliance upon the representation, which causes damage to the plaintiff in consequence of his reliance upon it.

---

1   *Pasley v Freeman* (1789) 3 Term Rep 51.
2   From 1201 there has been a writ of deceit.
3   See Cheshire, Fifoot and Furmston's *Law of Contract* (13th edn) pp 273-316.
4   (1789) 3 Term Rep 51.

(A)   FALSE REPRESENTATION

Usually the representation will consist of written or spoken words, but it may be assumed that any conduct calculated to mislead will be sufficient[5] - for example turning back the mileage indicator on the odometer of a motor car when negotiating its sale. Furthermore, '[w]here the defendant has manifestly approved and adopted a representation made by some third person' he may himself commit the tort.[6] Where a statement is capable of bearing at once a true and a false interpretation and the defendant knows of the falsity there is a false representation for present purposes.[7]

Active concealment of the truth whereby the plaintiff is prevented from getting information which he otherwise would have got is sufficient misrepresentation although no positive misstatement is made.[8] And although mere non-disclosure is not enough, a statement which is misleading because it is incomplete may be actionable. Thus, Lord Cairns held in the House of Lords case of *Peek v Gurney*[9] that 'there must ... be some active misstatement of fact, or, at all events, such a partial and fragmentary statement of fact, as that the withholding of that which is not stated makes that which is stated absolutely false'.

Where a statement by the defendant was accurate when made but, owing to a change of circumstances of which the defendant has become aware, it ceases to be true, there is an actionable misrepresentation if the defendant, by remaining silent, induces the plaintiff to act on the basis of the original statement, as *Incledon v Watson* illustrates.[10]

> In an advertisement for the sale of his school, the defendant stated the number of scholars at that time. That statement was not proved to be inaccurate. During the course of negotiations, the number decreased. The plaintiff, who bought on the faith of the representation, and who was not informed of the reduction, was held to have an action in deceit for damages.

This case illustrates the rule that what counts is whether the statement is false at the time when the plaintiff acts upon it.[11] There is some,[12] though inconclusive, support for the view that an action lies if the defendant, though believing the statement to be true when he made it, later learns of its falsity but does not disclose this to the plaintiff who subsequently relies on that statement. There are contracts in which, because only one party can know the material facts - for example contracts of insurance - that party has a legal duty to disclose material information. Upon breach of this duty the contract is voidable. Whether that failure to disclose amounts to the tort of deceit is undecided.

---

5   Cf *R v Barnard* (1837) 7 C & P 784.
6   Per Lord Maugham in *Bradford Third Equitable Benefit Building Society v Borders* [1941] 2 All ER 205 at 211, HL.
7   Per Lord Blackburn in *Smith v Chadwick* (1884) 9 App Cas 187 at 201, HL. If the court construes documents as false, but is not satisfied that the defendant intended to give them that false meaning, he is not liable in deceit: *Gross v Lewis Hillman Ltd* [1970] Ch 445, [1969] 3 All ER 1476, CA.
8   Cf *Schneider v Heath* (1813) 3 Camp 506 (buyer of ship obtained rescission of a contract induced by seller's taking ship from slipway into water, thereby concealing its rotten timbers).
9   (1873) LR 6 HL 377 at 403. And see *Banque Financière de la Cité v Westgate Insurance Co Ltd* [1990] 2 All ER 947 at 955, HL.
10   (1862) 2 F & F 841; *Jones v Dumbrell* [1981] VR 199.
11   Cf *Briess v Woolley* [1954] AC 333, [1954] 1 All ER 909, HL.
12   Per Lord Blackburn (obiter) in *Brownlie v Campbell* (1880) 5 App Cas 925 at 950, HL.

(B)   KNOWLEDGE OF FALSITY

Derry v Peek[13] establishes that, in order to make the defendant liable, he must have made the statement 'knowingly, or without belief in its truth, or recklessly, careless whether it be true or false'. In short, the plaintiff must prove[14] that the defendant did not honestly believe it to be true; it is not deceit merely because he has no reasonable grounds for believing it. The facts of the case show how onerous this burden may be.

> A company was empowered by private Act to run trams by animal power, or, if the consent of the Board of Trade was obtained, by steam power. The directors, believing that the Board of Trade would give this consent as a matter of course (since the Board of Trade had raised no objection when the plans were laid before them), issued a prospectus saying that the company had the power to run trams by steam power. Relying on this prospectus, the respondent took up shares from the company. The Board of Trade eventually refused its consent, and later the company was wound up.

The House of Lords held that an action in deceit against the directors failed because no want of honest belief on the part of any director was established by the respondent.[15] However negligent a defendant may be, that is not sufficient to make him liable for the tort of deceit.

(C)   INTENTION TO DECEIVE

The plaintiff must prove that the statement was 'made with the intention that it should be acted upon by the plaintiff, or by a class of persons which will include the plaintiff'.[16] Thus, an action in deceit may be based on an advertisement in a newspaper if the plaintiff shows that he was one of the class of persons at whom the advertisement was directed.[17] Lord Cairns in *Peek v Gurney*[18] might be taken as saying that the plaintiff must prove that the defendant 'intended' – in the sense that he 'desired' or 'had the purpose' – that the plaintiff should act on the statement. 'Intention' is, however, best interpreted in the way in which it is normally interpreted in torts: that is, if the misrepresentation is calculated, or if its natural and necessary consequence is, to induce the plaintiff, then the defendant's conduct is 'intentional'.[19]

A misrepresentation need not be communicated to the plaintiff by the defendant, provided the defendant intended that it be communicated to him and that he rely on it. In *Pilmore v Hood*[20] the facts were as follows.

> A, who was negotiating the sale of a public house to B, made certain false statements to B concerning the takings of the public house. The transaction fell through. To A's knowledge,

13 (1889) 14 App Cas 337 at 374, HL (per Lord Herschell).
14 Although the plaintiff need not shoulder a criminal standard of proof, his burden of proving fraud is stricter than that of the ordinary civil standard: *Hornal v Neuberger Products Ltd* [1957] 1 QB 247, [1956] 3 All ER 970, CA.
15 But see now the Companies Act 1985, ss 67-69 (statutory liability for false prospectuses).
16 Per Lord Maugham in *Bradford Third Equitable Benefit Building Society v Borders* [1941] 2 All ER 205 at 211, HL.
17 *Richardson v Silvester* (1873) LR 9 QB 34 (plaintiff misled by false advertisement in Press that a farm was for sale).
18 (1873) LR 6 HL 377.
19 *Polhill v Walter* (1832) 3 B & Ad 114; *Richardson v Silvester* (supra) and dicta of Lord Chelmsford (at 399) and of Lord Colonsay (at 401) in *Peek v Gurney* (supra) lend support to this view.
20 (1838) 5 Bing NC 97. And see *Langridge v Levy* (1837) 2 M & W 519.

B passed on to C these false statements. A then sold to C without correcting these statements and was held to be liable to him in deceit.

The plaintiff must also have been influenced in the manner intended. If, therefore, company promoters issued a prospectus to the plaintiff, who bought shares (not by subscribing to this issue, but subsequently on the market), and the prospectus was not calculated to influence market dealings, no action would lie.[1] The motive of the defendant is irrelevant; it is no excuse that the defendant who made a false statement about shares of some company genuinely believed that investment in that company would be advantageous to the plaintiff,[2] and still less that the defendant did not intend the plaintiff to suffer any loss in consequence of the misrepresentation.[3] Of course, it goes almost without saying that promoters will be liable for this tort where they issue false information about a company to inflate the market value of shares in that company for their personal gain.[4]

(D) RELIANCE OF THE PLAINTIFF

The plaintiff must prove that the misrepresentation of the defendant both influenced him[5] and caused him to act to his own prejudice as he did.[6] The action lies if the misrepresentation was only one of several factors acting upon the mind of the plaintiff; if the court is satisfied that the false statement was 'actively present to his mind' when he acted, it will not readily hold that the plaintiff might, even if the false statement had not been made, nevertheless have acted as he did.[7] The courts sometimes say that the misrepresentation must be material; they mean that if the plaintiff acted in a way that a person was likely to act in reliance on the statement of the defendant, this would be prima facie evidence that he did so rely on it.[8]

It is sometimes doubted whether a misrepresentation of an opinion is actionable. Of course, there is an area of privilege to tell untruths without liability in deceit. An example is the seller who inflatedly describes his house as highly desirable and commodious - such sales talk does not constitute actionable misrepresentation. Further, if both parties have equal access to information about goods, and one falsely describes them as first class, then no action lies. When, however, the opinion purports to impart information to another who is not on an equal footing; for example, if a dealer states to a customer that a new machine of the type sold by him can lift 5,000 lbs, or if an opinion purports to be expert and accordingly derived from a background of knowledge not possessed by the plaintiff, an action will lie for such misrepresentations.[9]

1   *Peek v Gurney* (supra) had similar facts. Cf *Andrews v Mockford* [1896] 1 QB 372, CA. The Stock Exchange now makes a public advertisement of an issue a condition precedent to the grant of a market quotation, and intention to induce marketing dealings will presumably now be imputed.
2   Per Lord Blackburn in *Smith v Chadwick* (1884) 9 App Cas 187 at 201, HL.
3   *Brown, Jenkinson & Co Ltd v Percy Dalton (London) Ltd* [1957] 2 QB 621, [1957] 2 All ER 844, CA.
4   *Possfund Custodian Trustee Ltd v Diamond* [1996] 2 All ER 774.
5   *Downs v Chappell* [1996] 3 All ER 344, [1997] 1 WLR 426, CA.
6   *Smith v Chadwick* (1884) 9 App Cas 187, HL; *MacLeay v Tait* [1906] AC 24, HL. There must be some conduct of the plaintiff in reliance on the representation. Harmful effects produced directly on the plaintiff (eg if the false statement causes him to be ill) are not the subject of a claim for this tort, even though the plaintiff does not recover in the same action for loss suffered through acts performed in reliance: *Wilkinson v Downton* [1897] 2 QB 57. See ante.
7   *Edgington v Fitzmaurice* (1885) 29 Ch D 459, CA.
8   *Arnison v Smith* (1889) 41 Ch D 348 at 369 (per Lord Halsbury LC).
9   Cf *Brown v Raphael* [1958] Ch 636, [1958] 2 All ER 79, CA.

The same general principles govern statements of law.[10] If the representations refer to legal principles as distinct from the facts on which these principles operate, and the parties are on equal footing, those representations are only expressions of belief and of the same effect as expressions of opinion between parties on an equal footing. In other cases where the defendant professes legal information beyond that of the plaintiff, the ordinary rules of liability for deceit apply.

It is equally confusing to state that a misrepresentation of intention is never an actionable deceit. Certainly, if a defendant promises to do something and fails to carry out his promise, the plaintiff must ordinarily look to the law of contract for his remedy. If, however, the defendant at the time of his statement lacks either the will or the power to carry out the promise, there is a misrepresentation capable of giving rise to proceedings for deceit; the diner who orders and consumes his meal without intending to pay for it is liable in deceit. Similarly, it has been held to be actionable to state, in an invitation to the public to subscribe to an issue of debentures by a company, that the loan was being floated in order to improve buildings, when the real purpose was to discharge existing liabilities.[11]

Contributory negligence has been held to be no defence in an action for deceit. A plaintiff who relied on the statement made by the defendant about the turnover of a public house which was to be sold was successful in an action in deceit although, had he availed himself of the opportunity, afforded to him by the defendant, of examining the accounts, he would have discovered the error.[12] On the other hand, a plaintiff who is aware of the falsity,[13] and, perhaps, one who is misled by any patent defect,[14] cannot recover.

(E) LOSS

There is no cause of action unless the plaintiff proves that he has sustained loss or damage.[15] Ordinarily, the damages will be for pecuniary loss, but damages for personal injuries[16] and for loss of property[17] are also recoverable.

The plaintiff is entitled to recover all the actual damage directly flowing from the fraud, even though not foreseeable. If he is induced by fraud to buy business property he can claim not only the difference between the price and market value, but also, for example, expenses reasonably incurred in trying to run the business fraudulently sold

---

10 *West London Commercial Bank Ltd v Kitson* (1884) 13 QBD 360, CA.
11 *Edgington v Fitzmaurice* (1885) 29 Ch D 459, CA.
12 *Dobell v Stevens* (1825) 3 B & C 623.
13 He is not taken to know of facts coming to the knowledge of his agent where the agent did not acquire that knowledge in his capacity as agent for this plaintiff: *Wells v Smith* [1914] 3 KB 722.
14 Cf *Horsfall v Thomas* (1862) 1 H & C 90.
15 Damage need not be proved in order to obtain rescission: per Sargant LJ in *Goldrei Foucard & Son v Sinclair and Russian Chamber of Commerce in London* [1918] 1 KB 180 at 192, CA; *Lemprière v Lange* (1879) 12 Ch D 675 (infant, on becoming tenant, made false representation - landlord could rescind although he could not recover damages for value of use and occupation).
16 *Langridge v Levy* (1837) 2 M & W 519; *Graham v Saville* [1945] 2 DLR 489 (CA Ontario) (a plaintiff who was induced to 'marry' the defendant by his fraudulent misrepresentation that he was a bachelor, and who became pregnant by him, recovered damages in deceit for physical injuries consequent on the pregnancy and for reduced matrimonial prospects).
17 *Mullett v Mason* (1866) LR 1 CP 559: fraudulent misrepresentation that a cow was free from disease; the loss of five other infected cows was held recoverable in deceit.

to him,[18] interest on loans entered into to facilitate the purchase of the property,[19] and the loss of the profit which he might reasonably have earned but for the defendant's deceit.[20]

It is unclear whether exemplary damages can be awarded in deceit in order to teach the defendant that tort does not pay.[1] The availability of exemplary damages in this tort depends on whether Lord Devlin's decision in *Rookes v Barnard*[2] restricting exemplary damages to three classes of conduct concurrently extended the range of torts in which awards of exemplary damages may exceptionally be made. The Court of Appeal in *AB v South West Water Services Ltd*[3] somewhat tentatively suggested that that was not the case. Aggravated damages to compensate the plaintiff for the injury to his feelings and dignity may, however, be awarded in deceit.[4]

(F)   AGENCY

Agency is a concept which is generally of little relevance generally in the law of torts. But deceit is an exception to the rule. As well as being vicariously liable for false statements made by agents who are employees, a principal may also be liable for representations, made on his behalf by independent persons acting for him in relation to a particular transaction – for example an estate agent or a broker. A principal who expressly authorises a statement which he and the agent know to be untrue is liable with the agent as a joint tortfeasor. He is vicariously liable for statements known to be untrue by the agent and will further be liable where one agent passes on to another information which he knows to be false in order that the second 'innocent' agent may pass it on to the plaintiff who then acts on it to his detriment.[5] It is unclear whether, if an agent makes a statement without knowing it to be untrue and without authority to make that statement, the principal is liable in deceit if he would have known of the falsity of the statement.[6]

The key question in relation to liability for deceit by agents is generally whether the false representation was made within the scope of the agent's actual or ostensible authority. Was it a representation which the agent was actually authorised to make, or

---

18   *Doyle v Olby (Ironmongers) Ltd* [1969] 2 QB 158, [1969] 2 All ER 119, CA; *Banque Bruxelles Lambert SA v Eagle Star Insurance Co Ltd* [1997] AC 191, HL.
19   *Archer v Brown* [1985] QB 401, [1984] 2 All ER 267 (that the loss resulted from the plaintiff's impecuniosity did not prevent its recovery).
20   *East v Maurer* [1991] 2 All ER 733, [1991] 1 WLR 461, CA.
1   *Mafo v Adams* [1970] 1 QB 548, [1969] 3 All ER 1404; *Archer v Brown* (supra); *Metall und Rohstoff AG v ACLI Metals (London) Ltd* [1984] 1 Lloyds Rep 598, CA. See more generally, Law Commission *Aggravated, Exemplary and Restitutionary Damages* (Consultation Paper No 132) (1993).
2   [1964] AC 1129, [1964] 1 All ER 367, HL. On exemplary damages generally, see post.
3   [1993] QB 507, [1993] 1 All ER 609, CA.
4   *Archer v Brown* (supra); *Shelley v Paddock* [1980] QB 348, [1980] 1 All ER 1009, CA; *Saunders v Edwards* [1987] 2 All ER 651, [1987] 1 WLR 1116, CA. But note the doubts expressed re aggravated damages generally in *AB v South West Water Services Ltd* (supra).
5   *London County Freehold and Leasehold Properties Ltd v Berkeley Property and Investment Co Ltd* [1936] 2 All ER 1039, CA (as explained in *Anglo-Scottish Beet Sugar Corpn Ltd v Spalding UDC* [1937] 2 KB 607, [1937] 3 All ER 335).
6   *Armstrong v Strain* [1952] 1 KB 232, [1952] 1 All ER 139, CA (held not to be tortious); but was this decision per incuriam? See *Woyka & Co v London and Northern Trading Co* (1922) 10 HL Rep 110, CA.

which the principal's conduct of affairs allowed him to appear to be authorised to make?[7] At any rate, where the agent is also an employee[8] the fact that he sets out to deceive his employer as well as the plaintiff, and intends to benefit himself alone, will not relieve the principal from liability for the agent's deceit.[9] But the false representation must be one which the agent had ostensible authority to make. The employer-principal will not be liable simply because the agent is his employee. For the purposes of the tort of deceit the employee's course of employment is delimited by the scope of his authority.[10] Lord Keith explained the rationale of the rule governing a principal's vicarious liability for deceit thus:[11]

> In the end of the day the question is whether the circumstances under which a servant has made a fraudulent representation which has caused loss to an innocent party contracting with him are such as to make it just for the employer to bear the loss. Such circumstances exist where the employer by words or conduct has induced the injured party to believe that the servant was acting in the lawful course of the employer's business. They do not exist where such belief, although it is present, has been brought about through misguided reliance on the servant himself, when the servant is not authorised to do what he was purporting to do, when what he is purporting to do is not within the class of acts that an employee in his position is usually authorised to do and when the employer has done nothing to represent that he is authorised to do it.

A principal whose agent has been bribed to induce him to enter into a transaction on the principal's behalf has a claim in tort against the briber for damages.[12] He cannot, however, receive double compensation by pursuing both his equitable remedy to recover the bribe from the agent and his tort action against the briber. He must elect between these two remedies. Where an agent offers a bribe acting within the scope of his actual or ostensible authority, the principal will be vicariously liable for that fraud as much as for any other act of deceit.[13]

(G) STATUTE OF FRAUDS AMENDMENT ACT 1828

By section 6 of this statute:

> No action shall be brought whereby to charge any person upon or by reason of any representation or assurance made or given concerning or relating to the character, conduct, credit, ability, trade, or dealings of any other person, to the intent or purpose that such other

---

7   In *Kooragang Investments Pty Ltd v Richardson and Wrench Ltd* [1982] AC 462, [1981] 3 All ER 65, PC the fraudulent agent had been expressly prohibited from preparing valuations relating to companies in which he had an interest. Nevertheless, he prepared valuations in reliance on which the plaintiffs lent money to the companies. The defendant's corporate name did not appear on the valuations. It was held that the plaintiffs did not rely on any apparent authority granted to the agent by his employers. His authority was thus delimited by the scope of his actual authority.

8   When the agent is not a servant and the fraud is initially aimed at the principal there will be no vicarious liability to other victims of the fraud: *Kwei Tek Chao v British Traders and Shippers Ltd* [1954] 2 QB 459, [1954] 1 All ER 779.

9   *Lloyd v Grace Smith & Co Ltd* [1912] AC 716.

10   *Armagas Ltd v Mundogas SA, The Ocean Frost* [1986] AC 717, [1986] 2 All ER 385, HL. See post.

11   [1986] AC 717 at 781.

12   *Mahesan S/O Thambiah v Malaysian Government Officers' Co-operative Housing Society Ltd* [1979] AC 374, [1978] 2 All ER 405, PC.

13   *Armagas Ltd v Mundogas SA, The Ocean Frost* [1986] AC 717, [1985] 3 All ER 795, CA.

person may obtain credit, money, or goods upon, [sic] unless such representation or assurance be made in writing signed by the party to be charged therewith.

The section prevents evasion of the Statute of Frauds (which requires guarantees to be in writing) by suing in tort instead of contract, and, in interpreting it, the courts have consistently taken heed of this legislative purpose.[14]

The Act does not apply to actions for breach of contract, and in all probability is confined to 'actions upon representations as such'.[15] The signature of an agent does not satisfy the requirements of the section.[16] Even though the defendant has induced the plaintiff to give credit in order to secure a pecuniary gain for himself, it seems that the Act applies.[17]

(H)   MISREPRESENTATION ACT 1967

Section 2(1) enacts:

> Where a person has entered into a contract after a misrepresentation has been made to him by another party thereto and as a result thereof he has suffered loss, then, if the person making the misrepresentation would be liable to damages in respect thereof had the misrepresentation been made fraudulently, that person shall be so liable notwithstanding that the misrepresentation was not made fraudulently, unless he proves that he had reasonable ground to believe and did believe up to the time the contract was made that the facts represented were true.

Its very important effect is that where the misrepresentation by a party induces the plaintiff to enter into a contract with him, the plaintiff can recover damages for resulting loss without proving fraud. If all the other requirements of the tort of deceit are satisfied he will then have an action unless the defendant proves that he believed on reasonable grounds that his statement was true. A plaintiff may succeed under this Act although he fails in negligence because no duty of care in making the statement was owed to him.[18] The other rules about the tort of deceit discussed in this chapter will continue to apply, with one exception,[19] in respect of these misrepresentations to persons entering into contracts. The Act does not extend the scope of the tort of negligence. It extends the separate tort of deceit, and the rules of deceit not negligence will generally govern such issues as the measure of damages.[20] However, contributory negligence is available as a partial defence in a claim under the Act when liability under the Act is concurrent with liability in common law negligence.[1] Where the representation falls outside the

14 *Lyde v Barnard* (1836) 1 M & W 101; *Banbury v Bank of Montreal* [1918] AC 626, HL.
15 *Banbury v Bank of Montreal* [1918] AC 626, HL.
16 *Swift v Jewsbury and Goddard* (1874) LR 9 QB 301, Ex Ch. Signature on behalf of a company by its duly authorised agent is, for the purposes of s 6, the signature of the company: *UBAF Ltd v European American Banking Corpn* [1984] QB 713, [1984] 2 All ER 226, CA.
17 So held by the House of Lords when interpreting the analogous provisions of a Scottish statute in *Clydesdale Bank v Paton* [1896] AC 381, HL.
18 *Howard Marine and Dredging Co Ltd v A Ogden & Sons (Excavations) Ltd* [1978] QB 574, [1978] 2 All ER 1134, CA.
19 The Act does not apply where the representation was made by a third party, including the defendant's agent: *Resolute Maritime Inc v Nippon Kaiji Kyokai* [1983] 2 All ER 1.
20 *Royscott Trust v Rogerson* [1991] 2 QB 297, [1991] 3 All ER 294, CA. In *Watts v Spence* [1976] Ch 165, [1975] 2 All ER 528, damages awarded for innocent misrepresentation under the Act included compensation for loss of bargain. And see *Andre & Cie SA v Ets Michel Blanc et Fils* [1977] 2 Lloyd's Rep 166 at 181; affd [1979] 2 Lloyd's Rep 427, CA.
1 *Gran Gelato Ltd v Richcliff (Group) Ltd* [1992] Ch 560, [1992] 1 All ER 865, CA.

Act, as for instance where it is made by a person who is not a party to the contract, the victim of negligence will still have to rely on the tort of negligence. The 1967 Act does not impose liability on the agent personally if he makes false representations to induce the making of a contract. His liability, too, remains to be established at common law, in either deceit or negligence.[2]

Prior to the 1967 Act there were circumstances in which the victim of an innocent misrepresentation could seek rescission of a contract although he could not have sued for deceit. Section 2(2) of the Act provides that the court may, if of the opinion that it would be equitable to do so, having regard to the nature of the misrepresentation and the loss that would be caused by it if the contract were upheld, as well as to the loss that rescission would cause to the other party, declare the contract subsisting and award damages in lieu of rescission. In effect, then, the court has a discretion to require the victim of an innocent misrepresentation to accept damages in lieu of rescission. Rescission can be obtained although damage is not proved, presumably the court could award damages in lieu of rescission to a person who has not proved damage.

SECTION 2.   PASSING OFF[3] - UNFAIR TRADING

The action for deceit affords a remedy to businessmen who are the direct target of fraudulent misrepresentation. The tort of passing off protects traders against misrepresentations aimed at their customers which are calculated to damage the trader's business or goodwill. The classic tort of passing off was limited to the use, in connection with his own goods, of the trade name or trade mark of a rival intended to induce that rival's customers to believe that the goods were produced by the rival trader and so cash in on his goodwill. The House of Lords in 1915 laid the foundation for a more all-embracing tort of unfair trading practice, and in 1979 confirmed that this tort, for the sake of convenience still entitled passing-off, had a broad role to play in controlling dishonest competitive practices. In *A G Spalding & Bros v A W Gamage Ltd*,[4] Lord Parker described the right which is protected by this tort as the 'property in the business or goodwill likely to be injured by the misrepresentation'.[5]

The extent of the broader tort was tested in *Erven Warnink BV v J Townend & Sons (Hull) Ltd*.[6]

> The plaintiffs were Dutch traders who manufactured an alcoholic drink known as 'advocaat'. Its principal ingredients were eggs and spirits with an admixture of wine. The defendants had for several years manufactured another alcoholic egg drink composed of egg and fortified wine known as 'egg flip' and up to 1974 marketed it under that name. Because of the vagaries of the excise law which imposes higher duties on spirits than fortified wine 'egg flip' retailed at a lower price than 'advocaat'. In 1974 the defendants began to market their alcoholic egg drink as 'Keeling's Old English Advocaat' and captured an appreciable share of the English market in 'advocaat'.

The House of Lords held that no-one was likely to be deceived into believing that the defendants' drink was Dutch 'advocaat' (that is, that they were buying the plaintiffs' product), and so no cause of action for passing off in its classic form arose.

2   *Resolute Maritime Inc v Nippon Kaiji Kyokai* [1983] 2 All ER 1, [1983] 1 WLR 857.
3   See Wadlow *The Law of Passing Off* (2nd edn, 1995).
4   (1915) 84 LJ Ch 449.
5   Ibid, at 452.
6   [1979] AC 731, [1979] 2 All ER 927, HL. And see *Associated Newspapers plc v Insert Media Ltd* [1991] 3 All ER 535, CA; *Mirage Studios v Counter Feat Clothing Co Ltd* [1991] FSR 145; *Kimberley-Clark Ltd v Fort Sterling Ltd* [1997] FSR 877.

Nevertheless, the name 'advocaat' was generally understood to denote a distinct species of drink by virtue of which the plaintiffs had built up their reputation and goodwill, and the defendants' misrepresentation had induced the public to believe they were buying 'advocaat' causing damage to the plaintiffs' business and goodwill. On these findings a cause of action arose in tort.

Lord Diplock identified five characteristics necessary to found an action for passing off in its wider form. There must be:

(a)   a misrepresentation;
(b)   made by a trader in the course of trade;
(c)   to prospective customers of his or ultimate consumers of goods and services supplied by him;
(d)   which is calculated to injure the business or goodwill of another trader (in the sense that it is a reasonably foreseeable consequence); and
(e)   which causes actual damage to the business or goodwill of the trader by whom the action is brought or will probably do so.[7]

(A)   THE MISREPRESENTATION

The misrepresentation may take any of the following forms.[8]

(1)   MARKETING A PRODUCT AS THAT OF THE PLAINTIFF

A defendant must not market a commodity with a statement that it is the product of the plaintiff when this is not so.[9]

(2)   USING THE PLAINTIFF'S NAME

To engage in the same line of business as the plaintiff and to use a similar name may be passing off.[10] If the defendant carries on business in his own name (or one which he has assumed for some time[11]) then he does not commit this tort unless there are further special circumstances showing dishonesty:[12] he is entitled knowingly to take

---

7   [1979] 2 All ER 927 at 932. See also the slightly more restrictive definition given by Lord Fraser at 943. Both opinions are considered in *Anheuser-Busch Inc v Budejovicky Budvar NP* [1984] FSR 413. Note, however, that in some recent decisions of the Court of Appeal - such as *Reckitt & Colman Products Ltd v Borden Inc* [1990] 1 WLR 491 and *Consorzio del Prosciutto di Parma v Marks & Spencer Ltd* [1991] RPC 351, CA - have reverted to the so-called 'classic trinity' approach based on misrepresentation, goodwill and damage. For discussion of both approaches see Cornish *Intellectual Property* (1996) ch 16.

8   The list in the text is not necessarily exhaustive. For example, in *Francis Day and Hunter Ltd v Twentieth Century Fox Corpn Ltd* [1939] 4 All ER 192 at 199, PC Lord Wright thought the tort would be made out where people went to a performance of the defendant's work under the impression that they were going to witness the plaintiff's work.

9   *Lord Byron v Johnston* (1816) 2 Mer 29 (defendant publisher advertised poems as Byron's when they were written by another person with a different name); *C G Volkes Ltd v F J Evans and Marble Arch Motor Supplies Ltd* (1931) 49 RPC 140, CA: CE Ltd were sub-contractors for the plaintiff. Held: the plaintiff could restrain the defendant from passing off the wipers in question as those of the plaintiff when the defendant acquired the wires directly from CE Ltd. Because the plaintiff normally inspected the wipers, the defendant was deemed to have done so in this instance.

10   *Tussaud v Tussaud* (1890) 44 Ch D 678; *Boswell-Wilkie Circus (Pty) Ltd v Brian Boswell Circus (Pty) Ltd* [1985] FSR 434.

11   *Jay's Ltd v Jacobi* [1933] Ch 411, [1933] All ER Rep 690.

12   *Sykes v Sykes* (1824) 3 B & C 541; cf *Croft v Day* (1843) 7 Beav 84. In *Wright, Layman and Umney Ltd v Wright* (1949) 66 RPC 149, CA the defendant could use his own name, but committed passing off once he traded as 'Wright's Chemical Co'.

advantage of the benefits which may accrue to him from the trade use of his own name,[13] but if he confusingly describes his goods by his own name it is no defence that his use is bona fide.[14] A company does not, however, acquire and incorporate the individual rights of its promoters to carry on business under their own names.[15]

(3)   USING THE PLAINTIFF'S TRADE NAME

To use the plaintiff's trade name - that is, the designation adopted by the plaintiff to identify goods which he markets, or services which he renders - may constitute misrepresentation for the purposes of this tort. The following are examples.

> To describe and sell sauce as 'Yorkshire Relish' was to commit a tort against the original manufacturer of sauce under that name.[16]

> At the request of the defendant, the plaintiff used the name, 'Dr Crock and his Crackpots' when broadcasting with his band in the defendant's programme, 'Ignorance is Bliss'. When the plaintiff had left this programme, he was entitled to restrain the defendant from putting another band in the programme with the title 'Dr Crock and his Crackpots'.[17]

If the trade name merely describes the goods or their characteristics then ordinarily the plaintiff cannot prevent others from using it. For example the terms vacuum cleaner,[18] gripe water,[19] 'cellular' textiles,[20] nourishing stout[1] and shredded wheat[2] may all be used with impunity. A very heavy burden of proof is cast on the plaintiff who seeks to establish that a name which is merely descriptive of the product has acquired a technical secondary meaning, so exclusively associated with the plaintiff's own products, that its use by others is calculated to deceive purchasers. This burden was discharged by the makers of 'Camel Hair Belting' in the leading case of *Reddaway v Banham*.[3] The task is a little easier where the descriptive words connect the product with the place of its manufacture: the manufacturers of 'Glenfield Starch',[4] 'Stone Ales'[5] and 'Chartreuse' liqueurs,[6] have, for instance, succeeded in passing off actions.

The courts are much more willing to protect the use of a fanciful name, namely one that does not describe the quality of the goods - for example, 'Apollinaris'.[7] It has

---

13 *John Brinsmead Ltd v Brinsmead and Waddington & Sons Ltd* (1913) 29 TLR 237; on appeal (1913) 29 TLR 706, CA; *Burgess v Burgess* (1853) 3 De GM & G 896. There is no similar protection for a nickname: *Biba Group v Biba Boutique* [1980] RPC 413.
14 *Parker-Knoll Ltd v Knoll International Ltd* [1962] RPC 265, HL; *W H Allen & Co v Brown Watson Ltd* [1965] RPC 191 (P published a very successful, unexpurgated edition of Frank Harris's *My Life and Loves*; D committed passing off when he bought the rights of and published an expurgated, abridged version under the same title).
15 *Tussaud v Tussaud* (1890) 44 Ch D 678; nor has a foreign company a right to set up in England in competitive business with the plaintiff company of the same name: *Sturtevant Engineering Co Ltd v Sturtevant Mill Co of USA Ltd* [1936] 3 All ER 137.
16 *Powell v Birmingham Vinegar Brewery Co* [1896] 2 Ch 54, CA.
17 *Hines v Winnick* [1947] Ch 708; cf *Forbes v Kemsley Newspapers Ltd* [1951] 2 TLR 656 (*Sunday Times* could not publish articles under name of Mary Delane, unless they were written by the plaintiff, its former correspondent of that name).
18 *British Vacuum Cleaner Co Ltd v New Vacuum Cleaner Co Ltd* [1907] 2 Ch 312.
19 *Re Woodward's Trade Mark, Woodward Ltd v Boulton Macro Ltd* (1915) 85 LJ Ch 27.
20 *Cellular Clothing Co v Maxton and Murray* [1899] AC 326, HL.
1 *Raggett v Findlater* (1873) LR 17 Eq 29.
2 *Canadian Shredded Wheat Co Ltd v Kellogg Co of Canada Ltd* [1938] 1 All ER 618, PC.
3 [1896] AC 199, HL.
4 *Wotherspoon v Currie* (1872) LR 5 HL 508.
5 *Montgomery v Thompson* [1891] AC 217, HL.
6 *Rey v Lecouturier* [1908] 2 Ch 715; affd sub nom *Lecouturier v Rey* [1910] AC 262, HL.
7 *Apollinaris Co Ltd v Norrish* (1875) 33 LT 242.

been suggested that a person originally entitled to protection for a fanciful name may lose his right if the name later becomes a mere description of that type of product rather than a word associated with goods of the plaintiff.[8] This may well be so, but no case deciding it has been traced.[9] The attempt failed in *Havana Cigar and Tobacco Factories Ltd v Oddenino*.[10]

> The plaintiffs were the original manufacturers of Corona cigars. The defendants supplied other cigars as Corona cigars. The plaintiffs successfully sued in passing off, the court rejecting the argument of the defendants that the word no longer described a brand of cigar, but only a particular size of cigar.

(4)   USING THE PLAINTIFF'S TRADE MARK[11]

It may be tortious to use the plaintiff's trade mark - that is, a design, picture or other arrangement affixed by him to goods which he markets so as to identify them with him.[12]

Section 2(2) of the Trade Marks Act 1994 expressly saves the common-law action of passing off in respect of trade marks. This may be a valuable resort where the plaintiff fails to prove registration, or where the registration does not extend to the goods in question, or where it is invalid. In such cases, the statutory action for infringement of the plaintiff's trade mark will fail and it will be necessary to have recourse to the common-law action.

(5)   IMITATING APPEARANCE OF THE PLAINTIFF'S GOODS

To imitate the appearance of the plaintiff's goods (and especially where this is accompanied by other sources of confusion, such as a not dissimilar name[13]) may be passing off. So, where the plaintiffs had for over 30 years marketed lemon juice in a distinctive yellow plastic squeeze-pack shaped like a natural lemon, they could maintain an action for passing off against the defendants who produced their juice in a similar container. They were entitled to protect the distinctive 'get-up' of their product.[14]

If the appearance complained of is dictated by functional considerations - for example the purpose or performance of the goods, or simplicity in handling or processing them - the courts will be reluctant to interfere. An action to prevent the use by the defendant of the normal shape of shaving stick container accordingly failed.[15] Yet the manufacturer of laundry blue which had a knobbed stick through the middle of the container was

8   Eg *Ford v Foster* (1872) 7 Ch App 611 (obiter).
9   The cases usually said to cover the point are *Liebig's Extract of Meat Co Ltd v Hanbury* (1867) 17 LT 298 and *Lazenby v White* (1871) 41 LJ Ch 354n (on which, see the 9th edn of this work at p 128). One further case which is much more in point is *G H Gledhill & Sons Ltd v British Perforated Toilet Paper Co* (1911) 28 RPC 429, 714, CA. The Court of Appeal proceeded on the footing that the plaintiff's interest was in the tills and that they therefore had no monopoly in the provision of suitable paper for the tills. For a case where P lost the protection of a trade name in a magazine, *Today*, seven years after it had amalgamated with another magazine, see *Norman Kark Publications v Odhams Press Ltd* [1962] 1 All ER 636.
10   [1924] 1 Ch 179, CA. The same outcome was reached in *Antec International Ltd v South Western Chicks (Warren) Ltd* [1998] 18 LS Gaz R 32 ('farm fluid' was held to be trade name - derived from Antec Farm Fluid S - and not merely a generic term).
11   Compare the related wrong of infringement of a trade mark under the Trade Marks Act 1994. But note that under the Act, there is no need to prove goodwill in a trade mark: *Fisons plc v Norton Healthcare Ltd* [1994] FSR 745.
12   *Millington v Fox* (1838) 3 My & Cr 338; *Singer Machine Manufacturers v Wilson* (1877) 3 App Cas 376 at 391-2, HL (per Lord Cairns LC).
13   *Massam v Thorley's Cattle Food Co* (1880) 14 Ch D 748, CA.
14   *Reckett & Colman Products v Borden Inc* [1990] 1 All ER 873, HL.
15   *J B Williams Co v H Bronnley & Co Ltd* (1909) 26 RPC 765, CA.

able to prevent the defendant from marketing a product similar in appearance, since he satisfied the court that this appearance was more than merely functional - the defendant was at liberty to have a stick in his product, but not one of the same 'get-up' as the plaintiff's.[16] Protection will not be afforded where the defendant's product is merely similar to that of the plaintiffs in particulars which are common to all types of that manufactured product.[17]

(6)   SELLING INFERIOR GOODS TO THOSE OF THE PLAINTIFF, THEREBY MISLEADING THE PURCHASER

A defendant must not sell goods which are in fact, and which are described as, the goods of the plaintiff, but which are of a quality inferior to that of the normal new and current product of the plaintiff, in such a way as to cause prospective purchasers to believe that the goods are the normal, new and current product of the plaintiff.

Thus, the manufacturers of Gillette razor blades obtained an injunction restraining the defendant from selling used Gillette blades as 'genuine' ones.[18] On the other hand, a general dealer in a working-class area who advertised in his shop: 'All types of electric lamps and fittings at cut prices' was held not liable in passing off to the manufacturers of Osram lamps for selling old Osram lamps, because it was not established that his acts were calculated to deceive the public into thinking that new lamps were being offered for sale.[19] Judicial reluctance to settle the respective merits of various products[20] led to a denial of a remedy in *Harris v Warren and Phillips*.[1]

> The publishers of a songwriter, who had recently attained fame, were unable to restrain the defendants from passing off the writer's early work (in which the defendants had the copyright, and which, it was contended, was of greatly inferior quality to her latest work) as new work. The court held that it could draw no sharp dividing line between the quality of her early songs and that of her recent ones.

(7)   FALSE ADVERTISING

Three cases illustrate when false advertising may amount to passing off. The first is *Cadbury Schweppes Pty Ltd v Pub Squash Co Pty Ltd*.[2]

> The plaintiffs successfully launched a new canned lemon drink with a big television and radio advertising campaign. The following year, the defendants launched a similar drink with a television and radio campaign in which they imitated the slogans and visual images of the plaintiff's advertising. It was held that such advertising could be passing off, but the action failed because the plaintiffs did not prove that there had been a confusing misrepresentation.

16   *William Edge & Sons Ltd v William Niccolls & Sons Ltd* [1911] AC 693, HL.
17   *Jamieson & Co v Jamieson* (1898) 14 TLR 160, CA.
18   *Gillette Safety Razor Co and Gillette Safety Razor Ltd v Franks* (1924) 40 TLR 606; cf *AG Spalding & Bros v AW Gamage Ltd* (1915) 84 LJ Ch 449, HL (D restrained from selling P's footballs with the false inference that they were of the type currently marketed by P); *Wilts United Dairies Ltd v Thomas Robinson Sons & Co Ltd* [1958] RPC 94, CA (D sold canned milk under P's trade name without revealing that the contents were appreciably older than those habitually marketed by P); *Morris Motors Ltd v Lilley* [1959] 3 All ER 737 (defendant dealer sold a car as a 'new Morris' when he bought it from a retail customer who had taken delivery of it as a new car immediately before. Defendant was representing himself as a dealer authorised by the plaintiffs, the car manufacturers, and that passing off therefore injured the goodwill of the plaintiffs).
19   *General Electric Co and British Thomson-Houston Co v Pryce's Stores* (1933) 50 RPC 232.
20   Cf *White v Mellin* [1895] AC 154, HL.
1   (1918) 87 LJ Ch 491.
2   [1981] 1 All ER 213, PC. Cf *United Biscuits (UK) Ltd v Asda Stores Ltd* [1997] RPC 513 (launching and advertising a biscuit called 'Puffin', which was presented in a similar manner to the plaintiff's market leader, 'Penguin' was held to amount to passing off).

Secondly, in *Masson Seely & Co Ltd v Embosotype Manufacturing Co*[3] the defendants deliberately created a market for their goods by copying the plaintiffs' catalogue in such a way as to induce the public to believe that goods offered by the defendants were those of the plaintiffs - customers of the plaintiffs normally ordered goods by reference to certain coined key words in the catalogue, and the defendants used the same artificial words in their catalogue. Although the defendants' goods were inferior to those sold by the plaintiffs, this was held to be passing off.

Much more recently, in *Associated Newspapers plc v Insert Media Ltd*,[4] the defendants arranged to insert advertising material into the plaintiff's newspapers without their authority. Readers would assume that the newspaper had sanctioned the inserts, with consequent potential damage to the plaintiff's reputation and goodwill. The defendants' conduct was found to constitute a misrepresentation amounting to passing-off.

(8)   MISREPRESENTATIONS DESIGNED TO CASH IN ON ANOTHER'S GOODWILL

The examples so far given of misrepresentations constituting passing off all, in the main, concern attempts to induce consumers to believe that they are purchasing the plaintiff's products. Passing off is no longer, however, restricted to such misrepresentations alone. The process of extending the tort to more general forms of unfair trade practice gained momentum first from the famous 'Champagne' case. In *J Bollinger v Costa Brava Wine Co*[5] the facts were as follows.

The defendants marketed 'Spanish Champagne', a Spanish wine. The plaintiffs were one of several manufacturers of champagne in the Champagne region of France. The court found that members of the public bought the defendants' wine in the mistaken belief that they were buying champagne from the vineyards of Champagne. It was held that the defendants committed the tort of passing off.

Danckwerts J held that the description 'champagne' was part of the plaintiffs' goodwill and a right of property. A group of persons producing goods in a certain locality and naming those goods by reference to that locality were entitled to protection against competitors who sought to cash in on their goodwill and reputation by attaching that name to a product originating from a different locality and with which the competing product has no rational association. The limitation to goods produced in a certain locality was considered immaterial in *Erven Warnink BV v J Townend & Sons (Hull) Ltd*.[6] The Dutch traders recovered for the loss in their business resulting from the defendants' misleading appropriation of the name 'advocaat' for their different and cheaper alcoholic egg drink. The crucial issues were:
1   whether there was a 'distinctive class of goods'; and
2   that those goods were marketed in England by a class of persons whose product was genuinely indicated by the use of the name 'advocaat'.

---

3   (1924) 41 RPC 160, cf *Purefoy Engineering Co Ltd v Sykes Boxall & Co Ltd* (1955) 72 RPC 89, CA.
4   [1991] 3 All ER 535, CA.
5   [1960] Ch 262; subsequent proceedings [1961] 1 All ER 561, [1961] 1 WLR 277; followed in *Vine Products Ltd v Mackenzie & Co Ltd* [1969] RPC 1 ('Sherry' to be confined to products from Jerez in Spain); *Consejo Regulador de las Denominaciones v Matthew Clark & Sons* [1992] FSR 525 and in *John Walker & Sons Ltd v Henry Ost & Co Ltd* [1970] 2 All ER 106, [1970] 1 WLR 917 (injunction granted to one whisky blender to restrain defendant from passing off as 'Scotch Whisky', whisky mixed with cane spirit). But note also *Taittinger v Allbev Ltd* [1993] FSR 641, CA (would elderflower champagne be confused with the real thing?).
6   [1979] AC 731, [1979] 2 All ER 927, HL.

An earlier decision not confined to goods or services as such, further illustrates the protection afforded by this tort to reputation and goodwill. In *Illustrated Newspapers Ltd v Publicity Services (London) Ltd*[7] the facts were as follows.

The plaintiffs owned certain illustrated periodicals. The defendants supplied hotels with folders (bearing the name of the appropriate periodical) for them, and without the plaintiffs' permission inserted a four-page advertisement in the middle, headed 'Supplement'. The defendants justified their conduct on the ground that nobody was induced to deal with them in the mistaken belief that he was dealing with the plaintiffs. Nonetheless the plaintiffs were held to have a cause of action for the injury thus caused to their goodwill in their advertising media by the defendants' misrepresentation.

(9)   CHARACTER MERCHANDISING

The developing trade of character merchandising allows great profits to be made from exploiting the popularity of famous television characters, both real and fictional. In particular, children's cartoons have spawned industries of their own. Having seen the Teenage Mutant Ninja Turtles on television, the child viewers were pestering their parents for Turtle shirts, Turtle mugs and so on. Unlicensed distributors may try to cash in on the craze. In *Mirage Studios v Counter Feat Clothing*[8] an injunction was granted to prevent unauthorised use of the 'Turtle' connection.

(B)   IN THE COURSE OF A TRADE

The representation must be made in the course of a trade. Trade is liberally defined and includes pursuit of a profession[9] and a person's interest in his literary and performance rights.[10] The tort is not available, however, to protect the name of a political party. In 1982 an attempt to prevent the defendant calling his party the Social Democrat Party failed.[11]

(C)   A REPRESENTATION TO CUSTOMERS OR ULTIMATE CUSTOMERS

The representation must be made either to prospective customers of the plaintiff or to ultimate consumers of goods or services supplied by him.[12] If the parties have no common field of activity, that in itself does not defeat an action, provided that injury to

7   [1938] Ch 414, [1938] 1 All ER 321. And see *Associated Newspapers plc v Insert Media Ltd* (supra); *Bristol Conservatories Ltd v Conservatories Custom Built Ltd* [1989] RPC 455, CA.
8   [1991] FSR 145.
9   *Society of Incorporated Accountants v Vincent* (1954) 71 RPC 325. But note the curious decision in *Pontiac Marina Pte Ltd v CDL Hotels International Ltd* [1997] FSR 725 (H Ct, Singapore) where Chao Hick Tin J held that trading need not have actually commenced for goodwill to have arisen (and therfore be vulnerable).
10   See *Lord Byron v Johnston* (1816) 2 Mer 29; *Hines v Winnick* [1947] Ch 708, [1947] 2 All ER 517; *Illustrated Newspapers Ltd v Publicity Services (London) Ltd* [1938] Ch 414, [1938] 1 All ER 321.
11   *Kean v McGivan* [1982] FSR 119, CA.
12   *Erven Warnink BV v J Townend & Sons (Hull) Ltd* [1979] AC 731 at 742, [1979] 2 All ER 927 at 932-3, HL (per Lord Diplock). As regards foreign-based companies, the law is uncertain. According to one account, the foreign-based company must establish that it has customers in England: see the *Warnink* case per Lord Fraser at 943-4; *Athletes Foot Marketing Associates Inc v Cobra Sports Co* [1980] RPC 343. On the other hand, Maxim's, the famous Paris restaurant, succeeded in preventing a Norfolk restaurant from trading under that name despite having no trading base in England: *Maxim's Ltd v Dye* [1978] 2 All ER 55, [1977] 1 WLR 1155.

goodwill from confusion is established. In one case, a bank was held able to restrain a moneylender from setting up in trade under the same name on the ground that it would endanger its reputation if it were thought also to be a moneylender.[13] *The Times* newspaper obtained an injunction against the defendant who represented it to be his principal or business associate in his cycle dealer business.[14] On the other hand, Granada TV could not prevent Ford from calling a new model Granada, for there was neither a connection or association between the two activities, nor any proved confusion of the public.[15] A well-known children's broadcaster who used the pseudonym Uncle Mac could not prevent the defendants from marketing 'Uncle Mac's Puffed Wheat' because he failed to prove such confusion as would lead to damage to his goodwill.[16] Nor could the originator of 'The Wombles' prevent the defendants from marketing 'Wombles Skips'.[17] But in the light of the developments of a trade in 'character' itself, might these cases be decided differently today? The defendants in the latter case might not be harming the reputation of the originator of the Wombles per se but could be limiting the profit to be exploited from the character.[18]

Where the misrepresentation relates to a product produced by a group of traders, rather than one single plaintiff, the group must establish that they constitute a distinctive class of traders who have built up goodwill by the use of a particular name or description of goods. Thus, as have seen, the French producers of champagne succeeded by establishing they all operated from a particular geographical area: Champagne in France.[19] And the Dutch manufacturers of 'advocaat' proved that their product was generally recognised to share a particular and distinctive composition: eggs and spirits.[20]

(D)   CALCULATED TO INJURE GOODWILL

Proof of intention to deceive is not essential in contrast to the tort of deceit.[1] The test is rather whether a false representation has in fact been made, fraudulently or otherwise,[2] which will foreseeably result in misleading consumers.[3] It is unnecessary (though desirable, where possible) to prove that any members of the public were deceived. Thus, where the defendant had done no more than sell to middlemen, who were not themselves deceived, the action was held still to lie where it was to be expected that in due course the act of the defendant would be calculated to cause confusion in the minds of the purchasing public.[4] It is not essential that the person deceived should know the name of the plaintiff: it is enough 'if a person minded to obtain goods which are identified in

13   *Harrods Ltd v R Harrod Ltd* (1923) 40 TLR 195, CA.
14   *Walter v Ashton* [1902] 2 Ch 282.
15   *Granada Group Ltd v Ford Motor Co Ltd* [1973] RPC 49.
16   *McCulloch v Lewis A May (Produce Distributors) Ltd* [1947] 2 All ER 845.
17   *Wombles Ltd v Wombles Skips Ltd* [1977] RPC 99; cf *Annabel's (Berkeley Square) Ltd v G Schock* [1972] RPC 838, CA (Annabel's Club and Annabel's Escort Agency).
18   See *Mirage Studios v Counter Feat Clothing* (supra).
19   *J Bollinger v Costa Brava Wine Co* (supra).
20   *Erven Warnink BV v J Townend & Sons (Hull) Ltd* (supra).
1   *Baume & Co Ltd v A H Moore Ltd* [1958] Ch 907, [1958] 2 All ER 113, CA.
2   Indeed, in *Gillette UK Ltd v Edenwest Ltd* [1994] RPC 297 it was held that innocence on the part of the defendant was no defence to an action for damages against him.
3   *AG Spalding & Bros v AW Gamage Ltd* (1915) 84 LJ Ch 449 at 452, HL (per Lord Parker). For cases where there was held to be no confusion, see *Grand Hotel Co of Caledonia Springs v Wilson* [1904] AC 103, PC (P's product 'Caledonian Waters' - D found a new spring in Caledonia and marketed its product as 'from our spring at Caledonia'); *Office Cleaning Services Ltd v Westminster Office Cleaning Association* (1944) 61 RPC 133, CA; affd (1946) 63 RPC 39, HL (rival firms of office cleaners trading under the above names, respectively).
4   *Draper v Trist* [1939] 3 All ER 513, CA.

his mind with a certain definite commercial source is led by false statements to accept goods coming from a different commercial source'.[5] If the public will not be in any sense confused, there is no tort.[6] But when a cordial was marketed as 'elderflower champagne' it was held some consumers might link that drink with real champagne damaging the reputation of the genuine article.[7]

In determining whether the representation is confusing, one must take into account the experience and perceptiveness of those likely to buy the goods, as well as the purpose of the defendants. Thus, where the defendant put a design of two elephants on yarn tickets of material to be sold in rural districts of India, the fact that his design was different from that of the two elephants pictured on the plaintiff's yarn tickets did not prevent the House of Lords from finding for the plaintiff.[8] Similarly, although the ordinary standard to be applied is that of the unwary member of the public,[9] if the particular trade is exclusively with experts, the test must be whether such an expert is likely to be deceived.[10] And 'likely', in this context, means 'on the balance of probabilities'.[11]

(E) PROOF OF DAMAGE

The action lies even though no damage is proved;[12] probability of damage is enough.[13]

(F) DEFENCES

None of the general defences to torts which might apply calls for special attention. But consent is perhaps the most important in this context.[14]

---

5 Per Lord Greene MR in *Plomien Fuel Economiser Co Ltd v National School of Salesmanship Ltd* (1943) 60 RPC 209 at 214, CA. The same applies even though the drug passed off by imitating get-up was sold on prescription only so that the public had no choice of supplier: *F Hoffman-La Roche & Co AG v DDSA Pharmaceuticals Ltd* [1969] FSR 410, CA.

6 Examples of failure for this reason include *Cadbury Schweppes Pty Ltd v Pub Squash Co Pty Ltd* [1981] 1 All ER 213, PC and *Newsweek Inc v BBC* [1979] RPC 441, CA (the owners of the magazine *Newsweek* could not prevent the BBC from using the same name for a new current affairs programme for nobody would confuse a programme with a magazine).

7 *Taittinger v Allbev Ltd* [1993] FSR 641, CA.

8 *Johnston v Orr-Ewing* (1882) 7 App Cas 219, HL; cf *William Edge & Sons Ltd v William Niccolls & Sons Ltd* [1911] AC 693, HL; *Lee Kar Choo v Lee Lian Choon* [1967] 1 AC 602, [1966] 3 All ER 1000, PC.

9 *Reckitt & Colman Products Ltd v Borden Inc* [1990] 1 All ER 873 at 888, HL (per Lord Oliver).

10 *Singer Manufacturing Co v Loog* (1882) 8 App Cas 15, HL.

11 *Neutrogena Corpn v Golden Ltd* [1996] RPC 473.

12 *Draper v Trist* [1939] 3 All ER 513, CA; *Procea Products Ltd v Evans & Sons Ltd* (1951) 68 RPC 210.

13 *HP Bulmer Ltd and Showerings Ltd v J Bollinger SA* [1978] RPC 79, CA. Only want of damage prevented an action for this tort from being available in *McCulloch v Lewis A May (Produce Distributors) Ltd* [1947] 2 All ER 845. Other cases where the action failed for this reason are *A-G and General Council of Medical Education of United Kingdom Registration v Barrett Proprietaries Ltd* (1932) 50 RPC 45 (publishers of British Pharmacopoea could not recover against defendants who used letters 'BP' on cartons of drugs made by them): *Taittinger v Allbev Ltd* (supra).

14 Ex turpi causa is a defence: *Lee v Haley* (1869) 5 Ch App 155; *Ford v Foster* (1872) 7 Ch App 611 at 630-1 (per Mellish LJ).

(G)   REMEDIES

(I)   INJUNCTION

This remedy is often the most important to the plaintiff. As always, it is awarded at the discretion of the court, and the actual form of the injunction is often one of the most contested points in this class of litigation.[15] If the defendant's conduct is calculated to divert customers, even though no sale has occurred, then in accordance with general principles an injunction will lie to prevent the apprehended wrong.[16]

(2)   DAMAGES

The plaintiff recovers damages for the loss of profits which he has sustained in consequence of customers being diverted from him to the defendant. In addition, he may recover for loss of business reputation[17] and goodwill.[18] The alternative to the common law inquiry into damages is the equitable remedy of an account of the profits actually made by the defendant in consequence of the passing off.[19] There are dicta to the effect that an account of profits will not be directed for such period as the defendant's action was innocent:[20] it is uncertain whether more than nominal damages may be awarded when the defendant neither knew nor ought to have known[1] that he was committing the tort of passing off.[2]

(H)   UNFAIR TRADING AND PASSING OFF

The landmark decision of the House of Lords in *Erven Warnink BV v J Townend & Sons (Hull) Ltd*, extending, as we have seen, the classic tort of passing off to a wider class of misrepresentations resulting in damage to a rival's goodwill, leaves open the limits of the tort as a means of controlling unfair trading practices. Lord Diplock recognised that Parliament has progressively intervened to impose on traders higher standards of commercial candour.[3] He clearly indicated that the steady trend in legislation reflecting the legislative view of what is today acceptable conduct in the marketplace should be matched by the development of the common law. Consequently, earlier decisions that misleading trade practices did not amount, on their facts, to the tort of passing off, must be treated with some caution. Consider the following two cases. Would either or both now fall within the wider principle enunciated in the *Warnink* case?

15 In the absence of a threat to continue the acts complained of, the courts may grant a declaration but not an injunction (though giving liberty to apply for an injunction, eg if the defendant does continue): *Treasure Cot Co Ltd v Hamley Bros* (1950) 67 RPC 89.
16 *Reddaway v Bentham Hemp Spinning Co* [1892] 2 QB 639 at 648, CA (per Smith LJ).
17 *AG Spalding and Bros v AW Gamage Ltd* (1918) 35 RPC 101; *Treasure Cot Co Ltd v Hamley Bros* (supra).
18 *Aktiebolaget Manus v R J Fullwood and Bland Ltd* (1954) 71 RPC 243.
19 In computing this profit, sales by the defendant to middlemen can be considered, although the middlemen were not deceived, and have not yet passed the goods on to the public: *Lever v Goodwin* (1887) 36 Ch D 1, CA.
20 *Edelsten v Edelsten* (1863) 1 De GJ & Sm 185 at 199, HL (per Lord Westbury).
1 *Edward Young & Co Ltd v Holt* (1947) 65 RPC 25: held that 'innocent' bears this meaning.
2 *Draper v Trist* (supra); *Marengo v Daily Sketch and Sunday Graphic Ltd* (1948) 65 RPC 242 at 251, HL (per Lord Simonds).
3 [1979] 2 All ER 927 at 933.

In *Cambridge University Press v University Tutorial Press*[4] the plaintiff's book was the one prescribed for a matriculation examination. The defendants' conduct in deceiving the public that their book was the one prescribed afforded the plaintiffs no cause of action.

In *Sales Affiliates Ltd v Le Jean Ltd*[5] the plaintiffs marketed appliances and materials for 'Jamal' permanent waves. The defendants in business as hairdressers, when asked by their customers for 'Jamal' treatment, used materials other than those of the plaintiffs and, by misrepresenting their own process as being one associated with the name and goodwill of the plaintiffs, thereby caused damage to the plaintiffs. There seems no reason of public policy to prevent such unfair trading from amounting to passing off.

One note of caution should be struck. Does there come a point when the extension of passing off becomes a means of protecting a monopoly and excluding all competition? Lord Bridge in *Reckitt & Colman Products Ltd v Borden Inc*[6] warned of this danger.

SECTION 3.   INJURIOUS FALSEHOOD

The tort of injurious, or malicious, falsehood also operates to protect interests in goodwill and economic reputation.[7] Passing off prevents competitors from using false representations to cash in on the plaintiff's goodwill. Injurious falsehood, by contrast, affords a remedy where business reputation is maliciously disparaged even though no aspersion is made against the character of an individual sufficient to give rise to a cause of action in defamation.

The Court of Appeal has defined this tort as follows:[8]

> That an action will lie for written or oral falsehoods ... where they are maliciously published, where they are calculated in the ordinary course of things to produce, and where they do produce, actual damage...

(A)   INTERESTS PROTECTED[9]

Originally, this tort protected persons against unwarranted attacks on their title to land, by virtue of which they might be hampered in the disposal of that land. Hence, it was called 'slander of title'.[10] Later it was held equally applicable to goods, in which case the tort was usually called 'slander of goods'.[11] By 1874 it was established that disparagements of the quality of property, as well as aspersions on title to it, were tortious.[12] Before the end of the century, *Ratcliffe v Evans*[13] had decided that the tort

---

4   (1928) 45 RPC 335. Would such conduct constitute the kind of 'reverse passing off' actionable in *Bristol Conservatories Ltd v Conservatories Custom Built Ltd* [1989] RPC 455 (defendants using plaintiff's catalogues to sell their own goods)?
5   [1947] Ch 295, [1947] 1 All ER 287. And consider *Rima Electric Ltd v Rolls Razor Ltd* [1965] RPC 4 (was there any damage to the plaintiffs as opposed to misleading the customers and inducing them to spend money which they would have otherwise have spent elsewhere?)
6   [1990] 1 All ER 873 at 877.
7   *CHC Software Care Ltd v Hopkins & Wood* [1993] FSR 241.
8   *Ratcliffe v Evans* [1892] 2 QB 524 at 527, CA.
9   See Newark 'Malice in Actions on the Case for Words' (1944) 60 LQR 366.
10   Eg *Gerard v Dickenson* (1590) Cro Eliz 196.
11   *Malachy v Soper* (1836) 3 Bing NC 371; cf *Green v Button* (1835) 2 Cr M & R 707 (defendant told person who had contracted with plaintiff to sell him timber that he, the defendant, had a lien on it, and thereby prevented plaintiff from obtaining delivery).
12   *Western Counties Manure Co v Lawes Chemical Manure Co* (1874) LR 9 Exch 218.
13   [1892] 2 QB 524, CA.

could be committed whenever damaging lies about a business were uttered (hence yet another name sometimes given to this tort - 'trade libel'). Since then, the tort has been almost ubiquitously referred to as 'injurious falsehood'. The potential ambit and utility of injurious falsehood has been considerably expanded by two recent decisions of the Court of Appeal which endorse the applicability of the tort wherever any individual's economic interests are threatened,[14] and reject any suggestion that only truly *commercial* interests are protected. Consequently, to some extent, the demarcation line between injurious falsehood and defamation has been blurred.[15]

Any type of interest in land, whether vested in possession or not,[16] is protected. Trade marks,[17] patents,[18] trade names,[19] copyright[20] and company shares,[1] may all be the subject of actionable disparagements. The following random illustrations of circumstances treated by the courts as being within the scope of the tort demonstrate its extent. An untrue statement by the defendant to a customer that the plaintiff, a commercial traveller with whom the customer had formerly dealt, was now in the employment of the defendant's firm;[2] failure to delete the name of the plaintiff, a musical accompanist, from the programme of a concert series in which she was no longer to appear (because, as a result of this, others might not offer her engagements for the period covered by the advertised programme);[3] a false statement in the defendant's newspaper that the plaintiff had ceased to carry on business;[4] an erroneous statement that the plaintiff's wife (who helped the plaintiff in his drapery business) had committed adultery in the shop with the parson newly appointed to the parish.[5]

Joyce v Motor Surveys Ltd is a particularly useful example of a successful action in injurious falsehood.[6]

The plaintiff became tenant of one of defendants' lock-up garages in order to have premises at which he could be registered as a tyre dealer. The defendants subsequently wished to evict the plaintiff in order to sell the entire property with vacant possession. They therefore told the Post Office not to forward any more mail to him at that address, and told the tyre manufacturers' association that he was no longer trading there. The defendants' conduct was held to constitute injurious falsehood.

The essence of the tort is that the defendant's lies should have caused economic damage to the plaintiff. So, in 1662, depriving the plaintiff of her opportunity of marriage gave rise to liability.[7] In 1991, in *Kaye v Robertson*,[8] the plaintiff actor was photographed without his consent as he lay in a hospital bed recovering from near fatal injuries. The newspaper presented a story concerning him as though it had been obtained with his authority and thereby deprived Mr Kaye of the opportunity to market his own account.

---

14 *Kaye v Robertson* [1991] FSR 62, CA; *Joyce v Sengupta* [1993] 1 All ER 897.
15 See also Gibbons 'Defamation Reconsidered' (1996) 16 OJLS 587.
16 *Vaughan v Ellis* (1608) Cro Jac 213.
17 *Greers Ltd v Pearman and Corder Ltd* (1922) 39 RPC 406, CA.
18 *Wren v Weild* (1869) LR 4 QB 730.
19 *Royal Baking Powder Co v Wright, Crossley & Co* (1900) 18 RPC 95, HL.
20 *Dicks v Brooks* (1880) 15 Ch D 22.
1   *Malachy v Soper* (1836) 3 Bing NC 371.
2   *Balden v Shorter* [1933] Ch 427, [1933] All ER Rep 249. The action failed for a different reason.
3   *Shapiro v La Morta* (1923) 130 LT 622, CA. The action failed for other reasons.
4   *Ratcliffe v Evans* (supra); *Danish Mercantile Co v Beaumont* (1950) 67 RPC 111 (defendant's bare statement that he was the only authorised importer of certain machines).
5   *Riding v Smith* (1876) 1 Ex D 91.
6   [1948] Ch 252.
7   *Sheperd v Wakeman* (1662) 1 Sid 79.
8   [1991] FSR 62, CA.

That was held to be sufficient to constitute injurious falsehood.[9] In *Joyce v Sengupta*[10] the defendant newspaper published an article insinuating that the plaintiff had abused her position as lady's maid to the Princess Royal to steal from her employer personal letters. The plaintiff contended that the article might well prejudice her future employment prospects. Her claim in injurious falsehood was allowed to proceed.

(B) DISPARAGEMENT

It is a disparagement if there is some misstatement as to the extent of the plaintiff's interest in his property or as to the quality of his goods. Thus, a false statement by a newspaper owner that the circulation of his newspaper greatly exceeded that of the plaintiff's rival newspaper was held to be capable of being tortious.[11]

A threat of proceedings for infringement of a patent[12] or a trade mark[13] may be enough. Section 70 of the Patents Act 1977,[14] section 26 of the Registered Designs Act 1949, and section 253 of the Copyright, Designs and Patents Act 1988 make it a statutory tort for a person by circulars, advertisements or otherwise to threaten proceedings for infringement wherever the defendant is unable to prove that the plaintiff's act constitutes an infringement of the defendant's patent, registered design or design rights. On the other hand, an assertion by way of mere 'puffery' that the defendant's goods are better, either generally or in specific respects, than the plaintiff's, is not actionable.[15] The courts will not conduct advertising campaigns for businessmen by deciding on the relative merits of their competing trade products. The leading case is *White v Mellin*.[16]

> W bought, for sale in his shop, bottles of infant food made by M and affixed on them, before selling to customers, a label that Dr V's food for infants and invalids (in fact a product of W) was better in particular respects than any other. An action for injurious falsehood failed, on the ground (inter alia) that this mere puff was not a disparagement.[17]

The test is whether a reasonable man would take the claim being made in denigration of the plaintiff's goods as one made seriously.[18]

(C) FALSE STATEMENT

The plaintiff has the burden of establishing that the statement was untrue.[19] The statement must be a false one about the plaintiff or his property; it is not enough that a false statement resulted in harm to him.

9   It is also worthy of mention that the Court of Appeal was keen to offer protection against the gross invasion of the actor's privacy.
10   [1993] 1 All ER 897, CA.
11   *Lyne v Nicholls* (1906) 23 TLR 86; cf *Evans v Harlow* (1844) 5 QB 624.
12   *Mentmore Manufacturing Co Ltd v Fomento (Sterling Area) Ltd* (1955) 72 RPC 157, CA.
13   *Colley v Hart* (1890) 44 Ch D 179 at 183 (per NORTH J).
14   See *Johnson Electric Industrial Manufacturing Ltd v Mabuchi-Motor KK* [1986] FSR 280.
15   *Young v Macrae* (1862) 3 B & S 264; *Hubbuck & Sons v Wilkinson, Heywood and Clark* [1899] 1 QB 86, CA.
16   [1895] AC 154, HL.
17   Could M have succeeded on the basis of one of the other torts dealt with in this chapter?
18   *De Beers Abrasive Products Ltd v International General Electric Co of New York Ltd* [1975] 2 All ER 599; test subsequently applied in *Vodaphone Group plc v Orange Personal Communications Services Ltd* [1997] FSR 34 (per Jacob J).
19   *Royal Baking Powder Co v Wright, Crossley & Co* (1900) 18 RPC 95 at 99, HL (per Lord Davey). And see also *Joyce v Sengupta* (supra) at 901 (per Sir Donald Nicholls VC). Note that where the statement is 'not obviously untrue', no action will lie: *MacMillan Magazines Ltd v RCN Publishing Co Ltd* [1998] FSR 9 (per Neuberger J).

(D) PUBLICATION

Because the essence of the tort is the effect produced by the false statement on persons entering into relations with the plaintiff, the falsehood must be published to persons other than the plaintiff.[20] Whether a negligent or accidental publication is sufficient is undecided. However, it is clear that the defendant is liable for a republication which is the natural and probable result of his original publication.[1]

(E) MALICE

This is undoubtedly the most difficult and controversial element in this tort although, at the outset, it can asserted with confidence that good faith on the part of the defendant will always be a good defence.[2] The difficulty comes in defining what amounts to malice. There is weighty authority for the view that, until the late nineteenth century, the plaintiff had only to prove an intention on the part of the defendant to disparage. That is, only (and here the analogy to defamation is close) if the defendant had set up some prima facie privilege - for example, that he was protecting his own interest in the property disparaged - did the plaintiff, in order to succeed, have to rebut this privilege by proving malice.[3] However, the cases decided during the last 65 years[4] have so uniformly insisted on the need for the plaintiff to prove malice that the former view is no longer tenable.[5]

Even so, it is difficult to define 'malice' in this context. It has been variously defined as 'improper motive',[6] an intention to injure,[7] or want of honest belief in the truth of the statement.[8] What is significant is that, usually, the courts have not preferred any one of these definitions to the exclusion of the others.[9] Thus, the House of Lords in *White v Mellin*[10] held that either an intention to injure or knowledge of the falsity of the statement would be enough.

Lord Coleridge LCJ laid down the correct guiding principle in *Halsey v Brotherhood*.[11] He said:

> although it injures and is untrue ... it is a statement that the defendant has a right to make, unless, besides its untruth and besides its injury, express malice is proved, that is to say, want of bona fides or the presence of mala fides.

20 Cf *Malachy v Soper* (1836) 3 Bing NC 371.
1   *Cellactite and British Uralite v H H Robertson & Co* (1957) Times, 23 July.
2   *Spring v Guardian Assurance plc* [1994] 3 All ER 129, HL.
3   See Newark (1944) 60 LQR 366, and the cases there cited.
4   See, eg, *McDonald's Hamburgers v Burgerking UK* [1986] FSR 45.
5   In *Loudon v Ryder (No 2)* [1953] Ch 423, [1953] 1 All ER 1005, the plaintiff, in her action for slander of title, claimed in the usual way for relief by way of injunction or otherwise. Although her action failed for want of malice on the part of the defendant, the court nevertheless granted her a declaration that she, and not the defendant, was entitled to the property in issue. Similarly, it was held in *RJ Reuter Co Ltd v Mulhens* [1954] Ch 50 at 75, CA (per Evershed MR), that such an order might be made 'where the court may consider it appropriate to state, in the form of a declaration, its conclusion upon the title of the plaintiff which the defendant has in good faith challenged and continues to challenge'.
6   *Balden v Shorter* [1933] Ch 427 at 430, [1933] All ER Rep 249 at 250 (per Maugham J).
7   *Steward v Young* (1870) LR 5 CP 122 at 127 (per Montague Smith J).
8   *Greers Ltd v Pearman and Corder Ltd* (1922) 39 RPC 406 at 417, CA (per Scrutton LJ).
9   Indeed, *British Railway Traffic and Electric Co v CRC Co and LCC* [1922] 2 KB 260, is one of the few cases where the court has held that some particular type of these variants of malice has to be proved. No case where such a finding was essential to the decision is known.
10 [1895] AC 154 (the ratio decidendi is to be found most clearly in the opinion of Lord Herschell LC at 160); cf Atkin LJ in *Shapiro v La Morta* (1923) 130 LT 622 at 628, CA and Scrutton LJ in *Greers Ltd v Pearman and Corder Ltd* (1922) 39 RPC 406 at 417-8, CA.
11 (1881) 19 Ch D 386 at 388, CA; cf *Wren v Weild* (1869) LR 4 QB 730.

The plaintiff may discharge his burden of proving this element of bad faith in any one of several ways. He does so by proving that the defendant made the statement knowing it to be false, or that he made it recklessly, careless whether it was true or false.[12] A defendant who is shown to have been actuated by ill-will, will be held 'malicious'. He will be liable if his purpose was to damage the plaintiff's business, even, it seems, though he was also acting for the benefit of his own interests.[13] It seems that if the defendant knew his statement to be untrue this is enough: the plaintiff does not also have to prove that the defendant intended (or even knew) that the statement be disparaging.[14]

London Ferro-Concrete Co Ltd v Justicz affords a typical example of a plaintiff's successful discharge of his burden of proving malice.[15]

The defendant wrote to a firm of contractors that the plaintiff (who was his competitor for a sub-contract with the firm) used 'inadequate' methods of work. The court held that the defendant knew his statement to be untrue and he was held liable in injurious falsehood.

(F) DAMAGE

The plaintiff must prove that the false statement caused him pecuniary loss.[16] A debatable point has been whether the requirement that special damage has to be proved can be discharged by showing general loss of custom without adducing evidence that particular customers have withdrawn their business in consequence of the falsehood.[17] Whether evidence of general loss of business will be sufficient depends on 'the nature and circumstances of the falsehood'. For example, the plaintiff cannot be expected to produce individuals who have been affected by a statement in a newspaper, and evidence of general business loss will in such a case be admitted.[18] The same rule has been extended to a circular to customers, where, in the circumstances, the circular was reasonably likely to cause a falling off of business.[19] On the other hand, a plaintiff failed who complained that the defendants had stated in their newspaper that his house was haunted, but who neither produced witnesses giving evidence that the statement had influenced them to the detriment of the plaintiff, nor showed that the house had depreciated in value as a result of it.[20] The expenses of bringing litigation in order to remove a cloud on the title placed by the defendant's statement are special damages.[1]

The difficulties inherent in proving actual loss led to actions for injurious falsehood becoming extremely rare.[2] Consequently the common law rules of damage have been modified by the Defamation Act 1952, section 3 of which enacts:

12 *Kaye v Robertson* [1991] FSR 62 at 67 (per Glidewell LJ).
13 The ratio decidendi of *Joyce v Motor Surveys Ltd* [1948] Ch 252 (where the defendant wanted to make his property saleable with vacant possession) is supported by the judgment of Collins MR in *Alcott v Millar's Karri and Jarrah Forests Ltd* (1904) 91 LT 722 at 723, CA. Cf *Mentmore Manufacturing Co Ltd v Fomento (Sterling Area) Ltd* (1955) 72 RPC 157.
14 *Wilts United Dairies Ltd v Thomas Robinson Sons & Co Ltd* [1957] RPC 220; affd (but this point was not considered) [1958] RPC 94, CA.
15 (1951) 68 RPC 261, CA.
16 *Ajello v Worsley* [1898] 1 Ch 274; *Shapiro v La Morta* (1923) 130 LT 622, CA; *Allason v Campbell* (1996) Times, 8 May. When the damage complained of is physical injury, this tort is presumably not applicable and *Wilkinson v Downton* [1897] 2 QB 57 must be relied on; cf *Guay v Sun Publishing Co Ltd* [1952] 2 DLR 479; affd [1953] 3 DLR 577.
17 *Malachy v Soper* (1836) Bing NC 371 decided that the tort is not actionable per se.
18 *Ratcliffe v Evans* [1892] 2 QB 524 at 533, CA.
19 *E Worsley & Co Ltd v Cooper* [1939] 1 All ER 290; cf *Lyne v Nicholls* (1906) 23 TLR 86.
20 *Barrett v Associated Newspapers Ltd* (1907) 23 TLR 666, CA.
1 *Elborow v Allen* (1622) Cro Jac 642.
2 *Joyce v Sengupta* [1993] 1 All ER 897 at 906, CA.

In an action for slander of title, slander of goods or other malicious falsehood, it shall not be necessary to allege or prove special damage - (a) if the words upon which the action is founded are calculated to cause pecuniary damage to the plaintiff and are published in writing or other permanent form;[3] or (b) if the said words are calculated to cause pecuniary damage to the plaintiff in respect of any office, profession, calling, trade or business[4] held or carried on by him at the time of the publication.[5]

In the large majority of instances of this tort, it will now no longer be necessary to prove special damage.[6] This is especially important in view of the doubt whether an injunction could be obtained before the Act where damage was merely likely to accrue.[7] The economic damage inflicted on the plaintiff by the falsehood may be accompanied by considerable mental distress and injury to her feelings.[8] The Court of Appeal in *Joyce v Sengupta*[9] suggested that injury to feelings as such was not recoverable. But Sir Michael Kerr contended that as part of general damages, an award of aggravated damages might in part reflect the injury to the plaintiff's feelings and dignity.

(G)   DEFENCES

In those circumstances where a defendant in defamation could plead legislative immunity or absolute privilege, for example statements in judicial proceedings, the same defence would no doubt be available here. Formerly, it might have been apposite to say that the defences of qualified privilege in defamation were similarly applicable, but the present insistence on malice in this tort makes it irrelevant any longer to consider that point.

(H)   INJURIOUS FALSEHOOD AND DEFAMATION

There are clear similarities between injurious falsehood and the related tort of defamation.[10] And it is clear that there are occasions when the plaintiff has a choice of remedy. In *Joyce v Sengupta*, where the plaintiff argued that allegations that she had stolen from the Princess Royal constituted an injurious falsehood threatening her employment prospects, the defendants contended that her proper remedy lay in defamation. By electing to sue in injurious falsehood the plaintiff was able to obtain legal aid (unavailable in defamation) and the defendant lost the right to trial by jury. The Court of Appeal refused to strike out the plaintiff's claim. There is no principle of law that a plaintiff must pursue the most appropriate remedy. She is entitled to elect for

---

3   This includes broadcasting.
4   No doubt these words will have the same meaning in the present context as they do in the context of defamation
5   Note also that in *Joyce v Sengupta* (supra) the Court of Appeal made the point that s 3 is not confined to awards of nominal damages.
6   A plaintiff who relies on s 3 is not allowed to prove special damage unless he has specifically pleaded it: *Calvet v Tomkies* [1963] 3 All ER 610, CA.
7   *Dunlop Pneumatic Tyre Co Ltd v Maison Talbot* (1904) 20 TLR 579, CA; cf *White v Mellin* [1895] AC 154 at 163-4 and 167, HL. Note that *Easycare Inc v Bryan Lawrence & Co* [1995] FSR 597 establishes that the normal rules applicable to the granting of interlocutory injunctions do not apply in cases of injurious falsehood.
8   In *Fielding v Variety Inc* [1967] 2 QB 841, [1967] 2 All ER 497, CA Lord Denning stated that damages for injured feelings were not recoverable for the tort of injurious falsehood.
9   [1993] 1 All ER 897.
10 See Gibbons, (1996) 16 OJLS 587.

the remedy most beneficial to her. This is the effect of *Joyce v Sengupta*: as long as I have an arguable case that defamatory allegations about me may damage my financial prospects as well as my reputation, I may be able to choose whether to sue in defamation or injurious falsehood. And, of course, if I elect for the latter remedy I can claim legal aid. Nonetheless, other significant differences between the two torts remain.

Chapter 9

Unlawful interference with trade[1]

Allen v Flood[2] established the ground rules for liability in tort for interference with economic interests other than by way of false representations. A person has no right to pursue his trade or livelihood; he merely enjoys a freedom to promote his business and financial interests which the law must reconcile with the equivalent freedoms enjoyed by all his fellows. Where the conduct of one person damages the business interests of another or interferes with his freedom to advance his trade or livelihood, the '... existence of a bad motive, in the case of an act which is not otherwise illegal, will not convert that act into a civil wrong'.[3] For nearly a century subsequent to *Allen v Flood*, development of tort liability for interference with trade was sporadic. There appeared to be a haphazard list of torts: inducing breach of contract, interference with contracts, conspiracy, intimidation and random others. Lord Diplock has now enunciated a 'genus' tort, '... interfering with the trade or business of another person by doing unlawful acts'.[4] The other economic torts, he suggests, are merely 'species' of this 'genus' tort.

Two points should be grasped.
1 The underlying principle of English law today is undoubtedly that unlawful acts interfering with economic interests are prima facie tortious. This principle links the 'false representation' torts with the 'general' economic torts discussed in this chapter.[5] And in defining unlawful acts, the courts, over the whole spectrum of the economic torts, will take into account that while free competition still underlies our economy, fair competition is seen as equally important.
2 Not all the 'general' economic torts can be said to derive from Lord Diplock's 'genus' tort of unlawful interference (which is not yet clear). Conspiracy remains an anomalous tort in this field, and direct inducement of breach of contract is probably a separate and independent tort.[6]

---

1 See generally Cane *Tort Law and Economic Interests* (2nd edn, 1996); Carty 'Intentional Violations of Economic Interests: The Limits of Common Law Liability' (1988) 104 LQR 250.
2 [1898] AC 1, HL.
3 [1898] AC 1 at 92 per Lord Herschell.
4 *Merkur Island Shipping Corpn v Laughton* [1983] 2 AC 570 at 608, [1983] 2 All ER 189 at 196.
5 See Carty (1988) 104 LQR 250.
6 For a contrary view, see Weir *Economic Torts* (1997).

SECTION I.   CONSPIRACY

The tort of conspiracy takes two forms:

1   'unlawful means conspiracy' - when two or more persons combine to do an unlawful act, or a lawful act by unlawful means; and

2   'simple conspiracy' - when two or more persons combine wilfully to injure another in his trade, and damage to his trade results.[7]

The first form of conspiracy is probably superfluous for if unlawful means[8] are used to interfere in trade, the 'genus' tort of unlawful interference with trade will ipso facto be committed. The second is anomalous because it contradicts the fundamental assumption in *Allen v Flood* that motive alone cannot make illegal that which would otherwise be legal conduct. It can be justified only as 'a crude (and arbitrary) method of attacking an abuse of market power'.[9] In *Lonrho Ltd v Shell Petroleum Co Ltd (No 2)*[10] the House of Lords recognised conspiracy as a 'highly anomalous cause of action' but considered it too well established to be discarded.

(A)   COMBINATION

The requirement for combination poses little difficulty in the main. The 'antique fiction' that husband and wife were one person in the eyes of the common law no longer prevents spouses being liable together for the tort of conspiracy.[11] Directors and their company may conspire together since the company is a separate legal entity at law.[12] In order to establish such a conspiracy, it is essential to identify the relevant 'mind and will' of the company, which will normally be found in the director who had management or control over the particular act in question.[13] From this, it follows that the relevant alter ego of the company will be located in different people for different purposes (usually discoverable from the company's articles of association).[14]

Where the combination takes the form of a conspiracy to do an unlawful act, it is essential to establish that the act which is the aim of the conspiracy is in fact illegal. In *Marrinan v Vibart*[15] the facts were these. M pleaded that V and X - both policemen - conspired to make defamatory statements about him to the Director of Public Prosecutions, and to give false evidence at the Old Bailey and at a later enquiry by the Masters of his Inn. None of these three statements could ever form the subject of a civil action because of the absolute privilege afforded judicial proceedings. It was held that there was no cause of action in conspiracy, because the acts which allegedly caused the damage were not unlawful in any form of civil action. The decision illustrates that 'unlawful act' conspiracy is not necessarily limited to interference with economic

---

7   *Quinn v Leathem* [1901] AC 495, HL.
8   See *Lonrho plc v Fayed* [1991] 3 All ER 303 at 312, HL (per Lord Bridge). Unless there are acts sufficient to constitute unlawful means for the purposes of conspiracy but insufficient to ground an action in the 'genus' tort of unlawful interference with trade.
9   See Carty (1988) 104 LQR 250. And see *Clerk and Lindsell* para 23.78 which pertinently suggests that a combination of two street corner grocers is unlikely to be more oppressive to competitors than the actions of a supermarket chain in single ownership.
10   [1982] AC 173, [1981] 2 All ER 456, HL. And see *Lonrho plc v Fayed* (supra) at 307 (per Lord Bridge).
11   *Midland Bank Trust Co Ltd v Green (No 3)* [1982] Ch 529, [1981] 3 All ER 744.
12   *Belmont Finance Corpn Ltd v Williams Furniture Ltd* [1979] Ch 250, [1979] 1 All ER 118. And see *Taylor v Smyth* [1991] 1 IR 142 (conspiring with companies under accused's control).
13   *El Ajou v Dollar Land Holdings plc* [1994] 2 All ER 685, CA.
14   *Meridan Global v Securities Commission* [1995] 3 All ER 918 at 923, PC (per Lord Hoffmann).
15   [1963] 1 QB 528, [1962] 3 All ER 380, CA.

interests, but has little import. Had the statements not been privileged, the defendants would have been liable as joint tortfeasors without the need to add a claim in conspiracy.

Combinations with which the tort of conspiracy is concerned may take various designs: of traders in order to ward off the competition of a rival trader;[16] of trade union officials for the purpose of compelling an employer to dismiss a non-union man;[17] of wholesalers and distributors against a retailer in order to crush opposition to their policy of supplying newspapers to those setting up new businesses in areas which existing retailers thought to be adequately catered for;[18] of trade union officers and employers against a rival employer to further monopolistic conditions which would lead to better conditions for members of the union;[19] of an employers' federation and a trade union to deprive a worker belonging to another trade union of his job in order to promote collective bargaining in the industry concerned;[20] of employees against their employer threatening a strike unless he dismissed a worker belonging to another union;[1] of members of a theatre audience to hiss an actor off the stage.[2]

(B)   THE PURPOSE OF THE DEFENDANTS

Although perhaps no branch of the law of torts contains a higher proportion of House of Lords cases than conspiracy, the principles can be shortly stated. In *Crofter Hand Woven Harris Tweed Co Ltd v Veitch* the facts were as follows.[3]

> The appellants produced tweed cloth in the Outer Hebrides. Only the weaving of their cloth took place on the island; they imported yarn from the mainland. Other firms had their cloth spun as well as woven on the island. The respondents, V and M, were trade union officials of the union to which most of the spinners employed in the island mills belonged. Employers of these men informed V and M that the competition of the appellants prevented them from raising wages. The respondents (who were assumed by some of their Lordships to be acting in combination with the mill-owners) instructed dockers at the island's port to refuse to handle yarn imported from the mainland consigned to the appellants and cloth made by them which they desired to export. Without breaking their contracts of employment, the dockers obeyed. The appellants sought to stop this embargo on the ground that it was an actionable conspiracy. They failed, because the House of Lords held that the predominant purpose of the combination was the legitimate promotion of the interests of the combiners.

The tort of 'simple' conspiracy is thus committed only when the predominant purpose of the defendants' combination is deliberately to inflict damage on the plaintiff.[4] It is not enough to demonstrate that the defendants were well aware that damage to the plaintiffs was an inevitable consequence of their collective action. Until 1981, the requirement that the defendants intended to cause injury to the plaintiff was thought to apply only to 'simple' conspiracy where no unlawful means are employed to damage the plaintiff's interests. But the House of Lords in *Lonrho Ltd v Shell Petroleum Co*

---

16 *Mogul SS Co v McGregor, Gow & Co* [1892] AC 25, HL. Action failed.
17 *Quinn v Leathem* [1901] AC 495, HL. Action succeeded.
18 *Sorrell v Smith* [1925] AC 700, HL. Action failed.
19 *Crofter Hand Woven Harris Tweed Co Ltd v Veitch* [1942] AC 435, [1942] 1 All ER 142, HL. At least one member of the House of Lords (Viscount Simon, at 439) thought that the employers were not parties to the combination. Action failed.
20 *Reynolds v Shipping Federation Ltd* [1924] 1 Ch 28. Action failed.
1   *White v Riley* [1921] 1 Ch 1, CA. Action failed.
2   *Gregory v Duke of Brunswick* (1844) 6 Man & G 953. Action succeeded.
3   [1942] AC 435, [1942] 1 All ER 142, HL.
4   [1942] AC 435 at 445, 452, 478, 490 and 493.

Ltd (No 2)[5] held otherwise. The defendants breached sanctions orders against the illegal regime in Rhodesia substantially increasing their profits at the plaintiff's expense. Rejecting the claim in conspiracy, the House of Lords found that even if unlawful means were used to further the conspiracy, no liability arose in conspiracy unless the defendants acted '... for the purpose not of protecting their own interests but of injuring the interests of the plaintiff'.[6] How, then, does 'unlawful means' conspiracy differ from 'simple' conspiracy? Any significant distinction between the two would effectively have been obviated by the Court of Appeal's decision in *Metall und Rohstoff AG v Donaldson Lufkin and Jenrette*[7] when it was held that in all cases of conspiracy the *predominant* intention of the defendants must be injury to the plaintiff. Had that decision stood, any group of 'conspirators' could have justified their action by showing that their primary design was to secure their own commercial advantage. That interpretation of *Lonrho Ltd v Shell Petroleum Co Ltd* was decisively rejected by the House of Lords in *Lonrho plc v Fayed*.[8] In other words, their Lordships insisted upon distinguishing intention from motive.

In that case, the plaintiffs, who had sought to take over the House of Fraser (including Harrods), alleged that the defendants had unlawfully[9] made false and fraudulent representations to the Secretary of State for Trade and Industry, thus procuring their own successful takeover of the disputed company. There could be no doubt that the defendants' predominant intention was to advance their own interests. So the Court of Appeal struck out the plaintiffs' claim in conspiracy.[10] The Law Lords restored the claim. Lord Bridge affirmed that (1) in *any* action for conspiracy, proof of an intent to injure the plaintiff is required, (2) in 'unlawful means' conspiracy that intention need not be the defendants' primary design. If unlawful means are utilised to forward the conspiracy, the defendants cannot excuse the use of such means by proving that their predominant purpose was to protect or advance their own interests.[11] Of course, if there is now a tort of interference with trade where the unlawful means themselves render the defendants' acts tortious, a plea of 'unlawful means' conspiracy is rendered largely otiose.

In 'simple' conspiracy, when the defendants' predominant purpose is injury to the plaintiff, it will not avail them that they have the subsidiary interest of protecting their own interests. If the predominant purpose is to protect the legitimate trade interests of the defendants, then there is no actionable conspiracy although a subsidiary purpose *is* to damage the plaintiff. The defendants' legitimate interests extend beyond material ones: if trade union officers further a purpose which is not calculated to improve the financial state of their members, but which is honestly believed by them to be desirable and has in fact the support of their members - for example officers of a musicians' union opposing racial discrimination among dance-hall patrons[12] - this is a legitimate interest. Beyond that, the meaning of 'legitimate' is not clear: perhaps a combination for the purpose of making the plaintiff pay a debt owed by him to the defendant union, by securing that he should otherwise be deprived of work, is an example of an 'illegitimate'

5   [1982] AC 173, [1981] 2 All ER 456, HL.
6   [1982] AC 173 at 189 and 464 respectively. On the extent to which *Lonrho* applies to all forms of 'unlawful means' conspiracy, see *Clerk and Lindsell* para 23.81.
7   [1990] 1 QB 391, [1989] 3 All ER 14.
8   [1992] 1 AC 448, [1991] 3 All ER 303.
9   But will it be necessary at the full trial to prove that the misrepresentation on the part of the defendants constituted actionable deceit? See per Dillon LJ in *Lonrho plc v Fayed* [1989] 2 All ER 65 at 69, CA.
10   [1989] 2 All ER 65.
11   Supra, per Lord Bridge at 309-10.
12   *Scala Ballroom (Wolverhampton) Ltd v Ratcliffe* [1958] 3 All ER 220, CA. After *Rookes v Barnard*, this decision might be different unless no breach of contract was threatened.

interest.[13] Once the bona fides of the defendants is established, it is irrelevant that the damage inflicted to secure the purpose is disproportionately severe.[14] The defendants are not liable merely because they were actuated by spite or ill-will.[15] On the other hand, 'it is sufficient if all the various combining parties have their own legitimate trade or business interests to gain, even though these interests may be of differing kinds'.[16]

It is uncertain whether the burden of proving the purpose of damaging the plaintiff is on the plaintiff. Lords Wright[17] and Porter[18] held that the burden is on the plaintiff. Viscount Maugham held that the burden is on the defendant and the other two law lords were silent. It is submitted that the view of the majority is to be preferred.[19] It is in accord with earlier House of Lords decisions and with the expressed intention of the Law Lords in *Lonrho Ltd v Shell Petroleum Co Ltd* to confine the ambit of the anomalous tort of 'simple' conspiracy.[20]

(C)   JUSTIFICATION

Wherever the burden of proof lies, it is clear that the scope of justification in 'simple' conspiracy is wider than in the other 'general' economic torts. In conspiracy the defendant who proves that his object was to further his legitimate trade interests succeeds. As we shall see, that does not in itself justify procuring a breach of contract. In practice, those combining will almost always be able to satisfy the court that they were actuated by self-interest. It follows, therefore, that conspiracy is a relatively unimportant tort in this field of economic affairs: the chances of a successful action (where no alternative cause of action would have lain) are remote. This was the inevitable result of the judicial reluctance to look beyond the purposes of the parties to the economic consequences of the parties' conduct. The justification for this has been expressed by Lord Wright as follows.[1]

> ... we live in a competitive or acquisitive society, and the English common law may have felt that it was beyond its power to fix by any but the crudest distinctions the metes and bounds which divide the rightful from the wrongful use of the actor's own freedom, leaving the precise application in any particular case to the jury or judge of fact. If further principles of regulation or control are to be introduced, that is matter for the legislature.

There are indications that judicial attitudes to competition are changing. Greater emphasis is placed on fairness. Nevertheless, the House of Lords in *Lonrho* clearly indicated its distaste for the tort of simple conspiracy and its role in the sphere of

---

13   *Giblan v National Amalgamated Labourers Union of Great Britain and Ireland* [1903] 2 KB 600, CA.
14   Per Viscount Simon at 447; but see *Trollope & Sons v London Building Trades Federation* (1895) 72 LT 342, CA.
15   Per Lord Wright at 471: 'I cannot see how the pursuit of a legitimate practical object can be vitiated by glee at the adversary's expected discomfiture'; cf Viscount Simon at 444-5 and Viscount Maugham at 450. Yet the court must inquire into the state of knowledge of the defendants whenever it is relevant for the ascertainment of their purpose: *Huntley v Thorton* [1957] 1 All ER 234; *Bird v O'Neal* [1960] AC 907, [1960] 3 All ER 254, PC.
16   Per Viscount Maugham in *Crofter Hand Woven Harris Tweed Co Ltd v Veitch* [1942] AC 435, at 453 [1942] 1 All ER 142; cf the judgment of Evatt J in *McKerman v Fraser* (1931) 46 CLR 343 (High Ct Australia).
17   [1942] AC 435 at 471, HL.
18   [1942] AC 435, at 495, HL.
19   And so applied in *Huntley v Thornton* [1957] 1 All ER 234.
20   And see *Sorrell v Smith* [1925] AC 700, HL.
1   *Crofter Hand Woven Harris Tweed Co Ltd v Veitch* (supra) at 472.

economic relations is now minimal. The future role of 'unlawful means' conspiracy remains inextricably entwined with the fate of its offspring, a genus tort of unlawful interference.[2]

SECTION 2.   INDUCING BREACH OF CONTRACT

For well over a century a distinct tort of inducing breach of contract has been recognised.[3] The tort is committed when the defendant knowingly induces a third party to break his contract with the plaintiff, and loss to the plaintiff results therefrom. It is not necessary to prove that any unlawful means were employed by the defendant to induce the breach of contract where that breach was the result of direct persuasion or intervention by the defendant.[4] Hence, inducing breach of contract cannot be regarded as a 'species' of any 'genus' tort of unlawful interference with trade. But the original tort of inducing breach of contract has been extended in various ways:

1   Inducement of breach of non-contractual obligations may be actionable.
2   Indirect procurement of a breach of contract may be actionable, but only if unlawful means are used.
3   Interference with contract short of procuring an actual breach of contract may be actionable, once again on proof of unlawful means.
4   And Lord Denning has suggested that a broader tort of interfering with contractual relations may exist.[5]

It will be suggested that the second two 'extensions' of inducing breach of contract are in fact species of the genus tort of unlawful interference[6] and that the Denning 'tort' of interference with contractual relations, without the need to establish unlawful means, is non-existent.[7]

An action for enticement of a servant from his master's service was established by the sixteenth century.[8] A separate and generally applicable tort of inducing breach of contract without lawful justification or excuse dates from *Lumley v Gye*.[9] The court held, on plea of demurer, that the following facts could constitute a tort.

A singer was under a contract to sing at the plaintiff's theatre but was not the plaintiff's servant. She was induced by the defendant, who knew[10] of this contract, to break it in order to sing at his theatre instead.

This new principle was soon extended from contracts of service to contracts generally; and dicta in some cases indeed contemplated its application to advantageous business relations not embodied in contracts.[11] But *Allen v Flood*[12] restricted its scope to interferences with actual contracts, or other enforceable civil obligations. The elements of this tort must now be examined.

2   See *Lonrho plc v Fayed* (supra) at 314 (per Lord Templeman).
3   *Lumley v Gye* (1853) 2 E & B 216.
4   See *D C Thomson & Co Ltd v Deakin* [1952] Ch 646, [1952] 2 All ER 361.
5   *Torquay Hotel Co Ltd v Cousins* [1969] 2 Ch 106 at 137-8.
6   See Carty (1988) 104 LQR 250.
7   See *Clerk and Lindsell* para 23.19.
8   Separate torts of enticing and harbouring servants were abolished by the Administration of Justice Act 1982.
9   (1853) 2 E & B 216.
10 The plaintiff failed at the subsequent trial because the jury found that the defendant was unaware of the contract.
11 *Temperton v Russell* [1893] 1 QB 715, CA (eg preventing the plaintiff from making a contract); *Bowen v Hall* (1881) 6 QBD 333, CA.
12 [1898] AC 1, HL; *Sorrell v Smith* [1925] AC 700, HL.

(A) KINDS OF CONTRACT

Any valid and enforceable contract can found an action upon subsequent interference with it.[13] Meagre evidence of its terms is enough[14] but interference with void contracts is, of course, not actionable.[15]

(B) BREACH OF OTHER OBLIGATIONS

It is now established that it is tortious deliberately to procure the violation of any enforceable obligation providing violation of that obligation is itself actionable. So, on analogy with inducing breach of contract, it is a tort to induce a breach of statutory duty (if performance of that duty confers a benefit on the plaintiff),[16] even if the breach of statutory duty does not itself give rise to an action in tort.[17] It is also tortious to induce the breach of an equitable obligation.[18] As with inducing breach of contract, it is not necessary to prove any unlawful means were used to procure the breach.[19] The unlawful act is the procurement itself, the 'unjustifiable interference with legal rights'.[20]

(C) BREACH OF CONTRACT

Dicta from earlier this century[1] that the breach must be such as goes to the root of the contract are no longer supportable. Following the Court of Appeal decision in *Law Debenture Trust Corpn v Ural Caspian Oil Corpn*,[2] it is now clear that inducing breach of secondary contractual rights - such as the right to damages when a primary contractual obligation has been broken - can give rise to tortious liability.[3] Any breach of contract, even one that is not actionable in certain respects, may now be sufficient. In *Torquay Hotel Co Ltd v Cousins*[4] an injunction was granted against the defendants who, in the course of industrial action, were attempting to stop a supplier fulfilling his contract with the plaintiff. The contract expressly exempted either party from liability for events beyond their control, including labour disputes, which led to a failure to perform. The Court of Appeal interpreted the clause as '... an exception from liability

---

13 Cf *DC Thomson & Co Ltd v Deakin* [1952] Ch 646 at 677 (per Evershed MR); [1952] 2 All ER 361, CA, and *Findlay v Blaylock* 1937 SC 21.
14 *Daily Mirror Newspapers Ltd v Gardner* [1968] 2 QB 762, [1968] 2 All ER 163, CA.
15 *Shears v Mendeloff* (1914) 30 TLR 342 (infant's contract); *Said v Butt* [1920] 3 KB 497 (mistake); *Joe Lee Ltd v Lord Dalmery* [1927] 1 Ch 300 (gaming); *British Motor Trade Association v Gray* 1951 SC 586 (contract void in restraint of trade - obiter dictum of Lord Keith).
16 *Meade v Haringey London Borough* [1979] 2 All ER 1016, CA; *Associated British Ports v Transport and General Workers' Union* [1989] 3 All ER 796 CA; rev'd on other grounds [1989] 3 All ER 822, HL.
17 *Wilson v Housing Corpn* [1997] IRLR 346.
18 *Prudential Assurance Co Ltd v Lorenz* (1971) 11 KIR 78; *Lonrho plc v Fayed (No 2)* [1991] 4 All ER 961.
19 *Associated British Ports v Transport and General Workers' Union* (supra) at 812 and 816.
20 *F v Wirral Metropolitan Borough Council* [1991] Fam 69, [1991] 2 All ER 648, CA.
1   Per Porter J in *De Jetley Marks v Lord Greenwood* [1936] 1 All ER 863 at 872; doubted by Evershed MR in *D C Thomson & Co Ltd v Deakin* [1952] Ch 646 at 689-90.
2   [1995] Ch 152, [1995] 1 All ER 157, CA.
3   [1994] 3 WLR 1221 at 1235 (per Beldam LJ).
4   [1969] 2 Ch 106, [1969] 1 All ER 522, CA; and see *Clerk and Lindsell* para 12.15.

for non-performance rather than an exception from the obligation to perform'.[5] Thus, the defendant's conduct still constituted inducing a breach of that latter obligation.

Many actions of this kind are, therefore, concerned largely with interpreting the contract in order to decide whether there has been a breach. Thus, in *Hivac Ltd v Park Royal Scientific Instruments Ltd*[6] the facts were as follows.

> The plaintiffs had been the only English makers of midget valves for hearing aids. Setting up in competition, the defendants employed on this work some of the staff of the plaintiffs in their spare time. It was held that an implied term must be read by the plaintiffs into the engagement of this staff that the latter should not break their fidelity to the plaintiffs by doing an act which would injure the plaintiffs' business, and, in view of the fact that the plaintiffs had a monopoly of this type of work and those members of the staff had a monopoly of the skill, an injunction restraining the inducement of breach of contract should be granted.

On the other hand, if a contract is determinable by either party at pleasure, it is not actionable if the defendant induces a party to determine that contract,[7] for there has been no breach but merely a lawful determination of the contract.

Inducing a strike where there is a no-strike clause in the contract is inducing breach of contract.[8] Giving notice to terminate a contract lawfully cannot give rise to a tort, but most strike notices are not notices to terminate but notice of forthcoming breaches of contract. Accordingly, union officials inducing strike action are open to liability in tort.[9] The 'immunities' afforded by statute, albeit now in an attenuated form, are discussed later in this chapter.

Even though the defendant is not responsible for the initial breach of a contract, he will be liable if he is responsible for continuing the breach of a still subsisting contract.[10] So, where the defendant had engaged a servant in ignorance of an existing contract of service between the servant and the plaintiff, he was held liable for having continued to employ him after learning of the facts.[11]

But is it still necessary to prove a breach of an obligation under the contract? In *Torquay Hotel Co Ltd v Cousins*, Lord Denning contended that even if the exemption clause in the contract resulted in there being no breach of contract, the defendant remained liable for 'interfering' with the contract. 'Preventing or hindering' performance of a contract was sufficient. There is little support for a tort of such width.[12] Preventing or hindering performance of a contract by unlawful means is actionable as *Dimbleby v NUJ*[13] illustrates.

> Journalists employed by the plaintiff refused, in breach of their contracts of employment, to prepare copy. As a result, the plaintiff faced severe difficulties in fulfilling his contract with

5   [1969] 2 Ch 106 at 143, CA (per Russell LJ).
6   [1946] Ch 169, [1946] 1 All ER 350, CA.
7   *McManus v Bowes* [1938] 1 KB 98, [1937] 3 All ER 227, CA.
8   *Rookes v Barnard* [1964] AC 1129, [1964] 1 All ER 367, HL.
9   See *Clerk and Lindsell* para 23.18.
10 *Smithies v National Association of Operative Plasterers* [1909] 1 KB 310, CA; cf *Denaby and Cadeby Main Collieries Ltd v Yorkshire Miners Association* [1906] AC 384, HL. There must be a continuing obligation at the time of the breach - in what circumstances then, if any, will the tort be committed if A agrees to sell his house to B, and C (who knows that A has broken this agreement) buys it from A? For the availability of an injunction, see post.
11 *Blake v Lanyon* (1795) 6 Term Rep 221; *Fred Wilkins & Bros Ltd v Weaver* [1915] 2 Ch 322; cf *Read v Friendly Society of Operative Stonemasons* [1902] 2 KB 88 at 95 (per Darling J); on appeal [1902] 2 KB 732, CA. And see *Jones Bros (Hunstanton) Ltd v Stevens* [1955] 1 QB 275, [1954] 3 All ER 677, CA.
12 *Associated British Ports v Transport and General Workers' Union* (supra) at 806 and 812-13.
13 [1984] 1 All ER 117, [1984] 1 WLR 67; and see *Shipping Co Uniform Inc v ITWF* [1985] ICR 245, [1985] IRLR 71.

the publishing company. Nevertheless, the plaintiff managed to procure alternative copy. Sir John Donaldson MR held the NUJ liable for unlawful interference with the plaintiff's contractual obligations. Hindrance where unlawful means were employed was sufficient.

Dimbleby & Sons Ltd v NUJ should preferably be seen as an example of the 'genus' tort of unlawful interference with trade rather than an extension of the distinct tort of inducing breach of contract.[14]

(D)   KNOWLEDGE OF THE CONTRACT

The defendant must be shown to have had actual or constructive knowledge,[15] at least of the existence,[16] of the contract which has been broken.[17] The courts have in recent years been very willing to conclude that the defendant had sufficient knowledge to be aware that he was inducing a breach.[18]

(E)   'INDUCEMENT' AND 'INTERFERENCE'

The classic tort of directly inducing a breach of contract - established in *Lumley v Gye*[19] - has developed apparently into a much broader tort with the emphasis on interference with contractual relations. In *Thomson & Co Ltd v Deakin*,[20] Jenkins LJ enumerated the various forms of the tort as he saw it in 1952. These were:
1   direct procurement of a breach of a contract,
2   direct intervention in the contract, for example disabling a contracting party,
3   indirect procurement or intervention (for example, secondary industrial action preventing performance of the contract), and
4   inconsistent dealings.
  Authority establishes that 'interference' in all these four circumstances may be tortious. We shall see that direct intervention in the contract, and indirect procurement or intervention, both require proof of unlawful means. Should they better be regarded as 'species' of the 'genus' tort of unlawful interference with trade?[1]

14 Or as some sort of 'half-way' tort of unlawful interference with contract: see Carty (1988) 104 LQR 250.
15 *British Industrial Plastics Ltd v Ferguson* [1940] 1 All ER 479, HL; *Middlebrook Mushrooms Ltd v TGWU* [1993] ICR 612. But in *Lumley v Gye* Lord Campbell directed the jury that 'if the defendant bona fide believed that the agreement with the plaintiff had ceased to be binding upon Miss Wagner the *scienter* was not proved and the defendant would be entitled to the verdict'; whereupon the jury found for the defendant.
16 He need not know its terms: *J T Stratford & Son Ltd v Lindley* [1965] AC 269, [1964] 3 All ER 102, HL; *Greig v Insole* [1978] 3 All ER 449.
17 *Long v Smithson* (1918) 118 LT 678 Div Ct; *British Homophone Ltd v Kunz and Crystallate Gramophone Record Manufacturing Co Ltd* [1935] All ER Rep 627. In *D C Thomson & Co Ltd v Deakin* [1952] Ch 646 at 687, [1952] 2 All ER 361, CA (per Evershed MR), it is suggested that 'common knowledge about the way business is conducted' would be sufficient constructive knowledge; *Cunard Steamship Co Ltd v Stacey* [1955] 2 Lloyd's Rep 247, CA (official of seaman's union deemed to know seaman's contract would conform with Merchant Shipping Act 1894). It is enough if the defendant deliberately disregards means of knowledge: *Emerald Construction Co v Lowthian* [1966] 1 All ER 1013, CA.
18 *J T Stratford & Son Ltd v Lindley* [1965] AC 269 at 307, [1964] 3 All ER 102, HL.
19 (1853) 2 E & B 216.
20 [1952] Ch 646, [1952] 2 All ER 361, CA.
1   See Carty (1988) 104 LQR 250; Elias and Ewing 'Economic Torts and Labour Laws: Old Principles and New Feasibilities' [1982] CLJ 321.

(1) DIRECT PERSUASION OR PROCUREMENT

Direct persuasion or procurement or inducement applied by the defendant to the contract-breaker is sufficient.[2] If the contract-breaker is a limited company, an approach to some person in the company with actual or ostensible authority to make contracts is required.[3] The issue here seems a straightforward one of causation. There has been much discussion of what has been thought to be a significant distinction between advice and persuasion, but the problem resolves itself into nothing more than whether the breaking of the contract is 'fairly attributable to any such pressure, persuasion or procuration on the part of any of these defendants',[4] and presents just the same difficulties on the facts as other problems of causation in torts.[5] Any distinction between advice and persuasion is unimportant.[6] For example, a trade union official, who sent to managers of the plaintiffs' public houses a circular questionnaire asking, inter alia, for details of the receipts and profits of their houses, was held to have caused the managers to break their contractual obligation not to disclose confidential information. The managers were led to disclose these items because they thought that the defendant's union might ultimately secure them better wages and conditions.[7]

It is important to decide whether the inducement is direct or indirect because if indirect procurement is relied on, the breach has to be a necessary consequence, and unlawful means have to be used. An inducement may be direct even though a federation transmits it through its members to a contracting party.[8] Where the inducement is direct, it is the other party to the contract, and not the one who is induced, who alone can sue for this tort.[9]

(2) DIRECT INTERVENTION

It will be actionable if the defendant intervenes so as to prevent a contracting party from performing his contract, for example by kidnapping or otherwise restraining him,[10] or by removing from him essential tools.[11] The wrongful act against the one contractor creates a cause of action for interference in the contract of the other. In *GWK Ltd v Dunlop Rubber Co Ltd*[12] the facts were as follows.

A motor car manufacturer had contracted with the plaintiffs that, when he exhibited his car at a motor show, it would have tyres made by the plaintiffs fitted to it. The defendants

---

2   *Thomson v Deakin* [1952] Ch 646 at 681, CA (per Evershed MR); at 694 (per Jenkins LJ).
3   [1952] Ch 646 at 681, CA (per Evershed MR).
4   [1952] Ch 646 at 686, CA per Evershed MR (ratio decidendi). On the difficulty of deciding whether there is merely a transmission of information, and no inducement, see *Camellia Tanker Ltd v International Transport Workers' Federation* [1976] ICR 274, CA.
5   Eg, *Jasperson v Dominion Tobacco Co* [1923] AC 709, PC.
6   *Torquay Hotel Co Ltd v Cousins* [1969] 2 Ch 106 at 147, [1969] 1 All ER 522, CA (per Winn LJ).
7   *Bent's Brewery Co Ltd v Hogan* [1945] 2 All ER 570.
8   *Daily Mirror Newspapers Ltd v Gardner* [1968] 2 QB 762, [1968] 2 All ER 163, CA. In *J T Stratford Ltd v Lindley*, Lord Pearce alone thought the inducement direct because the employers' association had been notified.
9   *Williams v Hursey* (1959) 103 CLR 30 (H Ct Australia). And see *Brekkes Ltd v Cattel* [1972] Ch 105, [1971] 1 All ER 1031. The party induced has locus standi to obtain a declaration: *Greig v Insole* [1978] 3 All ER 449. If the procurer intentionally damages the party induced he may have a cause of action for unlawful interference: see post.
10   *D C Thomson & Co Ltd v Deakin* [1952] Ch 646 at 678 (per Evershed MR); at 694-5 (per Jenkins LJ).
11   [1952] Ch 646 at 702 (per Morris LJ).
12   (1926) 42 TLR 376; on appeal 42 TLR 593, CA.

unlawfully removed the plaintiffs' tyres and substituted their own. That trespass to the car owner's goods created liability to the plaintiffs.

In *D C Thomson & Co Ltd v Deakin*, Evershed MR[13] limited liability for direct intervention resulting in a breach of contract to tortious acts (as in *GWK Co Ltd v Dunlop*). There is some authority that a wrongful act which, if effected by the contractor, would be a breach of contract is sufficient.[14] Not every breach of a penal statute will be wrongful[15] and some form of unlawful means must always be established thus bringing direct intervention within the 'genus' tort of unlawful interference.

(3) INDIRECT PROCUREMENT

This version of the tort is frequently invoked to stop secondary industrial action. It is committed when the defendant procures a third party to do a wrongful act, normally to breach his contract of employment in order to prevent performance of the main contract. For example, union officials persuade men working for a supplier of parts to a motor car manufacturers to strike, thus preventing their employer from performing his contract with the manufacturers. That conduct, involving, as it does, an unlawful act on the part of the strikers, may be actionable at the suit of the manufacturer.

For liability to be established, more than 'general exhortations issued in the course of a trade dispute – such as "stop supplies to A" or "treat X as black"'[16] – must be proved. Such inducements do not necessarily result in a breach of contract. The object might be obtained by lawful means.[17] But the defendants in *J T Stratford & Sons Ltd v Lindley*[18] were found liable.

S Ltd let out barges on hire to customers. These customers were under a contractual obligation to return the barges to S Ltd's moorings. The defendant union officials instructed their members to break their contracts of employment with S Ltd's customers by not returning the barges. The members obeyed those instructions and did not work the barges back to S Ltd's moorings. The House of Lords held that this amounted to the tort of procuring a breach of the contract between S Ltd and their customers, that the latter should return the barges to S Ltd (for that breach of contract was a necessary consequence of the defendant's conduct).

And in *Falconer v ASLEF*[19] the defendants were held liable to the plaintiff for his hotel expenses incurred when they called railmen out on strike thus preventing the plaintiff from travelling on the ticket he had purchased for a planned journey. The interference with the performance of the contract between British Rail and the plaintiff was found to be a necessary consequence of the defendants' actions. Indirect procurement is actionable only on proof of unlawful means. While this will often consist of breaches of contract by a third party, other unlawful means may suffice.[20] Thus, the tort of nuisance committed by demonstrators hindering distribution of the plaintiffs' newspapers was held to constitute the necessary unlawful means in *News Group Newspapers v SOGAT '82*.[1]

13 Supra, at 678.
14 Supra, at 694 (per Jenkins LJ); *Statnigros v Storhaug & Partners* [1953] CLY 3556 (landlord covenanted with plaintiff tenant to leave open a particular door on Saturday mornings; landlord's agent locked it and held liable in damages on principle of *Lumley v Gye*).
15 *Lonrho Ltd v Shell Petroleum Co Ltd (No 2)* [1982] AC 173, [1981] 2 All ER 456, HL.
16 *Clerk and Lindsell* para 23.32.
17 *D C Thomson & Co Ltd v Deakin* (supra).
18 [1965] AC 269, [1964] 3 All ER 102, HL.
19 [1986] IRLR 331 (county court).
20 *Merkur Island Shipping Corpn v Laughton* [1983] 2 AC 570, [1983] 1 All ER 334, HL.
1 [1987] ICR 181.

(4)   INCONSISTENT DEALINGS[2]

In *D C Thomson & Co Ltd v Deakin*, Jenkins LJ further stated that 'there seems to be no doubt that if a third party, with knowledge of a contract between the contract breaker and another, had dealings with the contract breaker which the third party knows to be inconsistent with the contract, he has committed an actionable interference'.[3] This is correct[4] - but it is not always simple to decide whether the defendant, in making the inconsistent dealing, has merely taken advantage of the voluntary decision already made of the third party to discontinue his contract, or whether he has in fact been instrumental in bringing about the breach. *British Motor Trade Association v Salvadori* illustrates the point.[5]

> Third parties had entered into covenants with the plaintiffs not to resell motor cars except under certain conditions. The defendants had bought some cars from these third parties with a view to resale at a profit in circumstances which amounted to a breach of the covenant with the plaintiffs.

Roxburgh J held that the defendants had offered a price for a car high enough to cause a man who would not otherwise have broken his covenant to sell it in breach of covenant and that they were therefore liable.[6] He did add, however, that 'any active step taken by a defendant having knowledge of the covenant by which he facilitates a breach of that covenant is enough', and that 'a defendant by agreeing to buy, paying for and taking delivery of a motor car known by him to be on offer in breach of covenant' commits the tort.[7] This case can be contrasted with *Batts Combe Quarry Ltd v Ford*.[8]

> On selling his quarry to the plaintiffs, a father contracted not to assist in setting up any rival quarry in the neighbourhood. His son, the defendant, decided to set up such a quarry and the father financed him in this enterprise. It was held that the acceptance of this gift by the son was not an actionable interference with the contract of the plaintiff.

(F)   STATE OF MIND OF THE DEFENDANT

A defendant is liable if he intends to bring about a breach of the contract. It is irrelevant that he did not act with malice in the sense of spite or ill-will.[9] The decision of the Court of Appeal in *Exchange Telegraph Co v Gregory & Co*[10] illustrates this.

2   For critical analysis of this version of the tort see *Clerk and Lindsell* ch 23 and Carty (1988) 104 LQR 250.
3   Supra, at 694; not considered by the other judges.
4   At least if the word 'dealings' is limited to 'the making of a contract'. Jenkins LJ may have intended to include other dealings - eg accepting benefits under a contract already made. In *De Francesco v Barnum* (1890) 63 LT 438, an action succeeded against a theatrical manager, who continued to employ show girls after receiving notice of a prior inconsistent contract which they had with the plaintiff.
5   [1949] Ch 556, [1949] 1 All ER 208.
6   [1949] Ch 556 at 565.
7   *British Industrial Plastics Ltd v Ferguson* [1940] 1 All ER 479, HL.
8   [1943] Ch 51, [1942] 2 All ER 639, CA.
9   There are dicta in *Lumley v Gye* (supra) and *Bowen v Hall* (supra) that malice is essential, but later cases such as *Quinn v Leathem* [1901] AC 495 at 510, HL (per Lord Macnaughton), *South Wales Miners' Federation v Glamorgan Coal Co Ltd* [1905] AC 239, HL, *The Kalingrad and The Nadezhda Krupskaya* [1997] 2 Lloyd's Rep 35 and *D C Thomson & Co Ltd v Deakin* (supra) at 676 (per Evershed MR) have made it abundantly clear that spite or ill-will is not required. Good faith is no defence: *Greig v Insole* [1978] 3 All ER 449.
10 [1896] 1 QB 147, CA; *British Motor Trade Association v Salvadori* [1949] Ch 556, [1949] 1 All ER 208; *Emerald Construction Co v Lowthian* [1966] 1 All ER 1013.

The plaintiffs had a monopoly of information about Stock Exchange prices and circulated this information to subscribers who had contracted not to communicate it to others; they also published it in a newspaper, issued six times daily. The defendant, a stockbroker, induced a subscriber to give him information contained in the plaintiffs' circular, and posted it in his own office for the benefit of his clients. He was held liable for interfering with a contract.

If the defendant does an act, the substantially certain consequence of which is to bring about a breach of a contract of which he is aware, then he will be presumed to have intended it, and be held liable unless the presumption is rebutted.[11] A negligent interference with a contract does not constitute this tort,[12] as the current tendency of the courts in such torts is to insist upon a deliberate and intentional act aimed at the plaintiff.[13]

It remains to be clearly established whether the defendant must merely intend the act that causes a breach of contract or whether he must intend not simply the act, but also that the act will cause a breach of contract. The leading case, *Millar v Bassey*,[14] is hopelessly confused on the matter. Two Court of Appeal judges adopted diametrically opposed views, while the third was unfathomably equivocal.[15]

(G)   DAMAGE

It must be proved that the breach of the contract has caused damage, or at least that damage can be inferred from the circumstances.[16]

An illustration of this need to prove damage is furnished by *Jones Bros (Hunstanton) Ltd v Stevens*.[17]

The defendant continued to employ a servant, after learning that the servant, in entering into his employment, was breaking his contract with the plaintiffs. It was shown, however, that in any event, the servant would not have returned to the plaintiffs' employment. It was held, therefore, that the plaintiffs' action based on this tort failed: they had suffered no damage.

(H)   JUSTIFICATION

It is established that, exceptionally, circumstances may justify interference with contracts. As yet the courts have not laid down any detailed rules for this defence. The dictum of Romer LJ is, however, widely cited.[18]

11 *White v Riley* [1921] 1 Ch 1, CA. And see *Emerald Construction Co v Lowthian* [1966] 1 All ER 1013 at 1019, CA (per Diplock LJ). Dealing with a plea that the tort is not committed when the defendant has an honest doubt whether he was interfering with the contract, Browne-Wilkinson J held in *Swiss Bank Corpn v Lloyds Bank Ltd* [1979] Ch 548 at 580, [1977] 2 All ER 853 at 877-9 that, if a defendant chooses to adopt a course which to his knowledge will undoubtedly interfere with the plaintiff's contract, on one view of the law, he must at least show that he was advised and honestly believed he was legally entitled to take that course.
12 *Cattle v Stockton Waterworks Co* (1875) LR 10 QB 453; *Société Anonyme de Remorquage à Hélice v Bennetts* [1911] 1 KB 243.
13 *Bennett v Metropolitan Police Comr* [1995] 2 All ER 1; *Northern Territory v Mengel* (1995) 69 ALJR 527, (H Ct Aus).
14 [1994] EMLR 44, CA.
15 For detailed discussion, see Howarth *Textbook on Tort* (1995) pp 479-484. But see also the more recent decision in *The Kalingrad and The Nadezhda Krupskaya* [1997] 2 Lloyd's Rep 35 where Rix J emphasised (at 39) the need to intend a breach of contract to be caused.
16 *Exchange Telegraph Co v Gregory & Co* [1896] 1 QB 147, CA; *Goldsoll v Goldman* [1914] 2 Ch 603; on appeal [1915] 1 Ch 292, CA; *Bents Brewery Co Ltd v Hogan* [1945] 2 All ER 570.
17 [1955] 1 QB 275, [1954] 3 All ER 677, CA.
18 *Glamorgan Coal Co Ltd v South Wales Miners' Federation* [1903] 2 KB 545 at 574-5, CA; approved by Lord Lindley HL sub nom *South Wales Miners' Federation v Glamorgan Coal Co Ltd* [1905] AC 239 at 252, HL.

... regard might be had to the nature of the contract broken; the position of the parties to the contract; the grounds for the breach; the means employed to procure the breach; the relation of the person procuring the breach to the person who breaks the contract; and to the object of the person in procuring the breach.

In that case it was held that the defendants were not justified in calling the miners out on strike in order to keep up the price of coal by which the miners pay was regulated.[19] The breach by a plaintiff of his contract with the defendant will not justify the defendant in inducing a third party to break his contract with the plaintiff.[20]

Brimelow v Casson is one of the rare cases where the defence succeeded.[1]

> The defendants were representatives of various theatrical unions, and the plaintiff owned a touring theatrical company. The defendants induced a theatre manager to break his contract with the plaintiff because the plaintiff was paying such low wages to his company that some chorus girls were compelled to resort to prostitution. The interest which the defendants had in keeping up the standards of the theatrical profession was held to justify their procuring the breach.

It may be that, if the means whereby the breach is effected are wrongful in themselves, the defence of justification is not available.[2] In any event, it is clear that the defence is not very wide, and the facts which would absolve the defendants in the tort of conspiracy on the ground that the acts were done for the purpose of protecting the trade interests of the defendants will not constitute justification for the tort of procuring a breach of contract.[3] Similarly, an employer may subsequently 'cure' an ostensibly wrongful dismissal of an employee when facts later come to light showing that the dismissal was justified after all; but this kind of justification does not, except in exceptional circumstances, apply in the tort of procuring a breach of contract.[4] In both cases, the interest in maintaining the security of contracts is greater than the interest in protecting free trade.

On the other hand, lawfully to exercise one's own contractual rights (as against A) with the consequence that it will inevitably cause A to break his contract with B probably is justified. As Rix J explained in *The Kalingrad and The Nadezhda Krupskaya*:[5]

> [If] a shipowner enters into a time-charter on terms (which are standard) which entitles him to withdraw his vessel for late payment of hire, it seems to me that he remains entitled as is justified in validly exercising that right even if he thereby interferes knowingly and intentionally with another contract.

---

19 Cf *Temperton v Russell* [1893] 1 QB 715, CA where trade union officials were not justified in interfering in order to enforce certain conditions of labour in a particular trade: *Read v Friendly Society of Operative Stonemasons* [1902] 2 KB 88.
20 *Smithies v National Association of Operative Plasterers* [1909] 1 KB 310, CA. Of course if a contract which X has made with Y is so inconsistent with an earlier contract between X and Z that the later contract interfered with the performance of the earlier one, the very act of X in making the contract with Y constitutes a tort. And see the analysis of this defence by Goff J in *Pritchard v Briggs* [1980] 1 All ER 294 at 326 et seq.
1   [1924] 1 Ch 302; but Simonds J in *Camden Nominees Ltd v Forcey* [1940] Ch 352 at 366 treated that decision as being based on the separate ground of ex turpi causa non oritur actio.
2   *Camden Nominees Ltd v Forcey* [1940] Ch 352; cf *Green v Button* (1835) 2 Cr M & R 707.
3   See ante.
4   *SOS Kinderdorf International v Bittaye* [1996] 1 WLR 987 at 994, PC (per Lord Keith).
5   [1997] 2 Lloyd's Rep 35 at 39.

(I) REMEDIES

(1) DAMAGES

Higher damages will often be recoverable in this tort than could be obtained in an action for breach of contract against the contract-breaker.[6]

a   The damages will be assessed in the light of the facts as at the date of the breach, not when the contract was made.

b   Any damage which the defendant intended to cause is recoverable in tort, for example if the defendant intended to make the plaintiff bankrupt.[7]

c   The damages may be more extensive than those awarded in contract under the rule in *Hadley v Baxendale*.[8]

d   Damages are at large in this tort; thus in *GWK Co Ltd v Dunlop Rubber Co Ltd*,[9] the court included compensation for loss of prestige in its award of general damages. In *British Motor Trade Association v Salvadori*, holding that 'the maintenance of fixed prices and the covenant system as an integral feature of that policy is a trade interest which the plaintiffs are entitled to protect against unlawful interference', Roxburgh J held further that the expenses incurred in unravelling and detecting the devices of the defendants for evading the covenant system were recoverable.[10]

Sometimes the action in tort will succeed where one in contract would fail - for example where, if physical restraint is used, frustration might be pleaded in contract.

(2) INJUNCTION

The remedy often sought is that of an injunction. As with other torts, an injunction, being a discretionary remedy, may be refused, although the tort is established.[11] An injunction may be awarded, although an action for damages fails.[12] On the other hand, an injunction will be refused against a defendant who persuades an employee of the plaintiff to leave his employment and work for the defendant, where the effect of the injunction would be to tie a reluctant employee to the plaintiff.[13] Thus, Lumley failed to recover damages from Gye because Gye was unaware of the contract, but he obtained an injunction against him.[14] An injunction may also be granted to prevent conduct

---

6   Per Erle CJ in *Lumley v Gye* (supra) at 233-4.
7   Ibid.
8   Cf *Gunter v Astor* (1819) 4 Moore CP 12 (enticement of servants by a rival piano manufacturer; although only in breach for one half day, the court rejected a claim that the damages in tort be so restricted, and awarded two years loss of profits).
9   (1926) 42 TLR 376.
10 [1949] Ch 556 at 568-9, [1949] 1 All ER 208. (1) There may be other reasons for preferring the action in tort. Complications which arise from the plaintiff's election whether to sue his contractee in deceit or breach of contract will be avoided in this action: see post. (2) The duty of the plaintiff to mitigate his damage may be less strict when he is the victim of an intentional tort: *Carmen v Fox Film Corpn* 204 App Div 776 (1923) (NY); cf Williams *Joint Torts* at p 285: 'a plaintiff is never under a duty to mitigate intended damage'. Interesting problems about the effect of satisfaction of a judgment in contract on the claim in tort remain unsolved: *Bird v Randall* (1762) 3 Burr 1345.
11 Eg *Rely-a-Bell Burglar and Fire Alarm Co Ltd v Eisler* [1926] Ch 609, where the effect of granting an injunction would have been to prevent the servant from working at all. An injunction against the new employer who enticed him was refused.
12 In *Esso Petroleum Co Ltd v Kingswood Motors (Addlestone) Ltd* [1974] QB 142, [1973] 3 All ER 1057, a mandatory injunction was ordered requiring the reconveyance of a garage sold in breach of a solus tie agreement.
13 *Lotus Cars Ltd v Jaguar Cars Ltd* [1982] LS Gaz R 1214.
14 *Lumley v Wagner* (1852) 1 De G M & G 604.

which will lead to a breach of contract although it is not sufficient 'interference' for the tort action in damages - the basis for such an injunction is that the 'proprietary interest'[15] may be protected.[16]

The common practice has been for plaintiffs initially to apply for an injunction ex parte. Pending hearing, the court will often grant an interlocutory injunction on the basis of the plaintiffs' affidavit. This happened, for example, in *JT Stratford & Son Ltd v Lindley*[17] and *Torquay Hotel Co Ltd v Cousins*.[18] But the court must be satisfied that the balance of convenience favours granting the injunction.[19]

SECTION 3.   UNLAWFUL INTERFERENCE WITH TRADE

The precise extent to which business and trading interests are protected against actions which do not constitute either conspiracy or interference with contractual obligations remains unclear. Lord Diplock's 'genus' tort, '... interfering with the trade or business of another person by doing unlawful acts'[20], awaits clear definition and confirmation. Intimidation, the use of unlawful threats to harm the plaintiffs' business, is clearly established as a 'species' tort. The scope of the remainder of the 'genus' tort has traditionally been bedeviled by two problems. Does it embrace any harm to economic interests not adequately protected by conspiracy, interference with contract (in all its forms) or intimidation? And what constitutes unlawful means?

(A)   INTIMIDATION: UNLAWFUL THREATS

The tort of intimidation is committed whenever unlawful threats are invoked deliberately[1] to prevent another person from doing some act which he is entitled to do and harm results either to the subject of the threats[2] or to a third party.[3] To some extent, the common law tort may be of less practical importance since the entry into force of

---

15 Cf Kitto J in *A-G for New South Wales v Perpetual Trustee Co Ltd* (1951) 85 CLR 237 at 297: 'a person has a right in rem in respect of the contractual rights, the rights in personam, which he possesses as against the other party to his contract'.
16 *Manchester Ship Canal Co v Manchester Racecourse Co* [1901] 2 Ch 37, CA, applying *Lumley v Wagner* where A agreed to sell land to B, and then contracted to sell to C, injunction granted to B restraining C from performing his contract; *Earl Sefton v Tophams Ltd and Capital and Counties Property Co Ltd* [1965] Ch 1140, [1965] 3 All ER 1; revsd on other grounds, [1967] 1 AC 50, [1966] 1 All ER 1039, HL. Injunctions are freely given under this head when disclosure of trade secrets is involved: *Printers and Finishers Ltd v Holloway* [1964] 3 All ER 731 at 738. And see *Swiss Bank Corpn v Lloyds Bank Ltd* [1979] Ch 548, [1977] 2 All ER 853 and *Pritchard v Briggs* [1980] Ch 338, [1980] 1 All ER 294.
17 [1965] AC 269 at 307, HL.
18 [1969] 2 Ch 106, [1969] 1 All ER 522, CA.
19 *NWL Ltd v Woods* [1979] 3 All ER 614, [1979] 1 WLR 1294, HL. On the factors to be considered in deciding whether a court in its discretion grants an interlocutory injunction, see *Hadmor Productions Ltd v Hamilton* [1983] 1 AC 191, [1982] 1 All ER 1042, HL and *American Cyanamid Co v Ethicon Ltd* [1975] AC 396, [1975] 1 All ER 504, HL; *Dimbleby & Sons Ltd v NUJ* [1984] 1 All ER 751, [1984] 1 WLR 427, HL; *Associated British Ports v Transport and General Workers' Union* [1989] 3 All ER 796, CA.
20 *Merkur Island Shipping Corpn v Laughton* [1983] 2 AC 570 at 608, HL.
1   Intent to injure is crucial in the tort of intimidation: *Cheticamp Fisheries Co-operative Ltd v Canada* (1995) 123 DLR (4th) 121 at 127 (per Chipman JA).
2   'Two-party' intimidation.
3   'Three-party' intimidation; as to the extent to which the principles of law differ depending on whether it is a case of 'two-party' or 'three-party' intimidation see *Clerk and Lindsell* para 23.54.

the Protection from Harassment Act 1997. Under section 3(2) of that Act, '... damages may be awarded for (among other things) any anxiety caused by the harassment and any *financial loss resulting from the harassment*'.[4] We suggest that much will depend on how restrictively the courts interpret the italicised words. If indirect financial losses are not covered, then recourse to the common law tort will remain the only means of redress.

Early authorities on intimidation involved threats of violence.[5] The modern tort of intimidation is defined in *Rookes v Barnard*.[6]

> The plaintiff was an employee of BOAC who had resigned from his trade union. The defendants were union officials. They threatened BOAC that all union members employed at BOAC would strike unless the plaintiff was dismissed. BOAC consequently gave the plaintiff notice and (lawfully) dismissed him.

The House of Lords held that the unlawful threat of a breach of contract by union members contributed the unlawful means necessary to create a cause of action in intimidation. The tort requires an intent to injure coupled with threats of unlawful action. If the threat is to do something that the defendant is entitled to do the tort is not committed.[7] As Lord Reid put it in *Rookes v Barnard*[8] 'so long as the defendant only threatens to do what he has a legal right to do he is on safe ground'.

The crucial issue, then, is what for the purposes of the tort of intimidation constitutes unlawful means.[9] The commission of any tort will suffice. A breach of contract will be enough in the case of 'three-party' intimidation,[10] though not in 'two-party' intimidation (where the threatened breach is of the defendant's own contract). Breach of equitable obligations may also be sufficient.[11] A criminal act that is in breach of a penal statute may not be sufficient, however, if that statute was not intended to create private rights.[12]

(B)   UNLAWFUL CONDUCT

In *Barretts & Baird (Wholesale) Ltd v IPCS*[13] the plaintiffs were members of the Association of British Abattoir Owners and companies in the meat trade. The defendant trade union represented fatstock officers employed by the Meat and Livestock Commission (MLC) in connection with the certification of slaughtered meat among other functions. The union, on their behalf, was engaged in a dispute with the MLC over pay and conditions. The officers voted to take strike action and a one-day strike had already created considerable difficulties for the plaintiffs' business. They alleged that the defendants were liable for interfering in their business by unlawful means either by inducing breach of the officers' contracts of employment or by breach of statutory duty by the MLC. Henry J, attempting to define the tort of unlawful interference, held that four ingredients to the tort must be established. There must be:
1   interference with the plaintiff's trade or business;
2   unlawful means;

4   Emphasis added.
5   For a modern example see *Godwin v Uzoigwe* [1993] Fam Law 65, CA.
6   [1964] AC 1129, [1964] 1 All ER 367, HL.
7   *Ware and De Freville v Motor Trade Association* [1921] 3 KB 40, CA.
8   [1964] AC 1129 at 1168-9, HL.
9   See *Clerk and Lindsell* para 23.41 et seq.
10   *Rookes v Barnard* (supra).
11   *Dixon v Dixon* [1904] 1 Ch 161.
12   *Lonrho Ltd v Shell Petroleum Ltd (No 2)* [1982] AC 173, [1981] 2 All ER 456, HL.
13   [1987] IRLR 3.

3 intent to injure the plaintiff; and
4 actual injury.
He refused the plaintiffs' application for an interlocutory injunction on two grounds. The alleged breach of statutory duty by the MLC was not made out. Statute required them to provide a system of inspection, not a strike-free system. Moreover, even if the breach of their contracts of employment by the fatstock officers constituted unlawful means, no intention to injure the plaintiffs was proved.

It is around the two bones of contention in *Barretts & Baird v IPCS* - intent to injure and unlawful means - that the debate on the limits of an unlawful interference has raged. That such a tort exists now seems unchallengeable,[14] but its definition and ambit remains disputed.[15] The balance of authority appears now to require direct intent to injure the plaintiff.[16] But what will constitute the requisite unlawful means?[17] Unlawful acts which constitute torts in themselves will suffice. Breaches of contract are sufficient for the tort of intimidation. If a threatened breach of contract can ground an action, it would seem inconsistent if an actual breach cannot. Other civil wrongs may be enough in this context. It remains unclear whether for example *any* alleged tort claimed to constitute unlawful means needs to be fully actionable at the instance of the person at whom the tort is directed. At the very least, it is clear that no action lies where the defendant's unlawful means constitute the use of an arrangement that is unlawful only in the sense that it is in restraint of trade.[18] In *Lonrho plc v Fayed*[19] the unlawful means consisted of a fraud allegedly perpetrated on the Secretary of State for Trade and Industry. But as the minister suffered no damage from the fraud (the damage was inflicted on Lonrho) he could not have sued in deceit. The House of Lords left open until the full trial the question of whether the defendants' conduct amounted to the unlawful means necessary to found an action for unlawful interference with trade. Restraint of trade alone is insufficient.[20]

The central problem again revolves around criminal acts. In certain cases, policy considerations may militate against implementation of civil liability as in *Chapman v Honig*[1] where, even though the landlord maliciously evicting a tenant subpoenaed to give evidence against him acted in contempt of court, no action was found to lie in tort. The House of Lords decision in *Lonrho Ltd v Shell Petroleum Co Ltd (No 2)*[2] poses difficulties of a far more general nature.

> The plaintiffs complied with sanctions orders prohibiting the supply of oil to the illegal regime in Southern Rhodesia. The defendants in breach of the orders continued to supply oil

---

14 *Lonrho plc v Fayed* [1989] 2 All ER 65, CA; on appeal [1991] 3 All ER 303, HL; *Associated British Ports v Transport and General Workers' Union* [1989] 3 All ER 796, CA.
15 *Lonrho plc v Fayed* (supra) at 70 (per Dillon LJ).
16 See, eg, *Lonrho v Fayed* [1990] 2 QB 479, CA. But note, too, *Cheticamp Fisheries Co-operative Ltd v Canada* (1995) 123 DLR (4th) 121 where it was further stated that the tort would not accommodate any notion of 'constructive intent to injure'.
17 *Associated British Ports v Transport and General Workers' Union* (supra) at 819 (per Stuart Smith LJ).
18 *Newport Association Football Club Ltd v Football Association of Wales Ltd* [1995] 2 All ER 87.
19 [1990] 2 QB 479, [1989] 2 All ER 65, CA; on appeal [1992] 1 AC 448, [1991] 3 All ER 303, HL; and see *Associated British Ports v Transport and General Workers Union* (supra).
20 *Mogul SS Co v McGregor Gow & Co* [1892] AC 25, HL.
1 [1963] 2 QB 502; and see *Hargreaves v Bretherton* [1959] 1 QB 45, [1958] 3 All ER 122 (no cause of action arising in respect of harm resulting from the defendant's perjury); but in *Acrow (Automation) Ltd v Rex Chainbelt Inc* [1971] 3 All ER 1175, [1971] 1 WLR 1676, CA the defendants were held liable for business losses resulting from the defendant's aiding and abetting breach of an injunction not to impede the plaintiffs' manufacture of certain equipment.
2 [1982] AC 173, [1981] 2 All ER 456, HL.

to that regime. The plaintiffs alleged that those unlawful acts resulted in losses to them caused by the prolongation of the illegal regime increasing the defendants' business at the plaintiffs' expense.

The plaintiffs sought to establish liability for their business losses on three grounds: conspiracy, breach of statutory duty and interference with trade by unlawful means. Conspiracy failed because no intent to injure as opposed to promote the interests of the defendants was proved. Breach of statutory duty failed because the statutory prohibition on supplying oil was not shown to be a duty imposed for the benefit or protection of a class of which the plaintiffs were members. The plaintiffs were thus forced, in pursuit of their third claim, to rely heavily on the broad principle enunciated by Lord Denning in *Ex p Island Records*[3] that '... whenever a lawful business carried on by one individual in fact suffers damage as the consequence of a contravention by another individual of any statutory prohibition the former has a civil right of action against the latter for such damage'. Lord Diplock in *Lonrho* expressly rejected such a wide principle of liability for economic loss. The correct approach, he said, was one of 'construction' of the statute. Was it intended to create private rights? The decision in *Lonrho* received further support from the Court of Appeal in *RCA Corpn v Pollard*.[4] There, the defendants were selling bootlegged Elvis Presley records, a criminal offence in contravention of the Dramatic and Musical Performers' Protection Act 1958. The Court of Appeal refused an injunction to the plaintiffs who enjoyed exclusive recording contracts for Presley records. The loss of commercial benefits resulting to them from the defendants' statutory crime did not give rise of itself to a cause of action in tort or any right to an injunction.

It is difficult, then, to evaluate whether there remain circumstances in which a statutory crime which is not independently a civil wrong will be sufficient to constitute unlawful means for the purposes of this tort. Lord Diplock's rejection of the 'wide principle' of liability for business losses must however be seen in context. No intent to injure Lonrho was proved. That intent was said, in *Barretts & Baird v IPCS*, to be an essential ingredient of the tort of unlawful interference. It remains open to a higher court finally to establish that while liability for business losses resulting from statutory crimes does not follow automatically, where intention to injure the plaintiff is established, a statutory crime may constitute the necessary unlawful means.[5]

Two further questions await judicial clarification.

1   What precise interests are protected? Trade or livelihood is the common term used, but are economic interests more generally embraced by the tort? *Falconer v ASLEF*,[6] admittedly only a county court decision, resulted in an award to a disappointed rail traveller where a strike caused him to incur hotel expenses.

2   To what extent, if at all, does a defence of justification apply to this emergent tort?

---

3   [1978] Ch 122, [1978] 3 All ER 824, CA.
4   [1983] Ch 135, [1982] 3 All ER 771, CA. The court was careful to state that it was not pronouncing on the soundness of earlier cases such as *Springhead Spinning Co v Riley* (1868) LR 6 Eq 551 where property rights were protected by injunction.
5   A question left open by *Associated British Ports v Transport and General Workers' Union* [1989] 3 All ER 796, CA; revsd on other grounds [1989] 3 All ER 822, HL. See the discussion in Carty (1988) 104 LQR 250.
6   [1986] IRLR 331.

SECTION 4.   ECONOMIC TORTS AND TRADE UNIONS[7]

It is virtually impossible for a trade union to take effective action in the traditional manner (that is, by invoking in the last resort industrial action by way of strikes or threats of strikes) without risking liability arising from one of the economic torts discussed earlier. Calling members out on strike may constitute inducing breach of contract. Threatening a strike to preserve a 'closed shop' or to protect a demarcation agreement risks liability for intimidation. Thus, since 1906,[8] the common law has first to a greater, and now to an increasingly lesser, extent been modified by statutory immunities afforded to unions and their officials for acts done in contemplation or furtherance of a trade dispute. The extent of trade union immunities has depended on the political complexion of the government of the day and the Conservative Government elected in 1979 enacted legislation which largely eroded the liberal immunities conferred by section 13(1) of the Trade Union and Labour Relations Act 1974. That legislation was consolidated in the Trade Union and Labour Relations (Consolidation) Act 1992. Under that later Act, secondary action is excluded from protection. Unions themselves are subjected to liability with complicated rules concerning 'vicarious' liability for actions by members. And immunities which remain[9] are lost unless industrial action is supported in a ballot of the membership.[10]

The details of trade union immunities are beyond the scope and space available for a work on torts. What has to be addressed by students of tort is whether a clear definition of trade union rights - rights which enjoy equal status to the employer's interests in pursuing his trade - would be a preferable means of resolving the conflict?[11]

---

7   For full treatment of this area see *Weir*. On the Employment Act 1990 see Carty (1991) 20 ILJ 1; Simpson (1991) 54 MLR 418.
8   Trade Disputes Act 1906.
9   See ss 219-221; for action excluded from protection see ss 222-225.
10   Sections 226-235, as amended (restrictively) by the Trade Union Reform and Employment Rights Act 1993 ss 17-21.
11   See Elias and Ewing [1982] CLJ 321.

Chapter 10

Intellectual property interests[1]

SECTION I.   COPYRIGHT, PATENTS AND SIMILAR INTERESTS

Intellectual property can be roughly defined as the intangible products of a person's mind and skill. Tangible property, be it land or goods, is protected from intentional interference by trespass and conversion, and from carelessly inflicted harm by the tort of negligence. Intangible property takes several forms. Contractual rights are, as we have seen, safeguarded to a limited extent by the general economic torts. Goodwill built up in the course of a business is protected in part by the tort of passing off. But what of a person's interest in the results of his intellectual efforts? To what extent are works of literature or art, or scientific inventions afforded protection by the law of torts? Interests in such intellectual property are predominantly defined and protected by statute. The Copyright, Designs and Patents Act 1988 protects authors, artists and musicians from those who would 'pirate' their efforts.[2] The Patents Act 1977, as amended by the 1988 Act, safeguards new scientific and technological inventions.[3] The Trade Marks Act 1994 supplements the tort of passing off by enabling traders to register their mark, rendering any infringement of that mark actionable.[4] Designs are also protected by statute.[5] Legislation to protect intellectual property is therefore far from novel. The difficulty lies in ensuring that the law keeps pace with technological development. Recent legislation in this area was a response partly to technological innovations which had rendered earlier statutes redundant. It also had to take account of several European directives and international treaties.[6]

The detailed provisions of the relevant statutes are beyond the scope of this work.[7] Protection of intellectual property must inevitably be, in the main, a matter for legislation. Rules must be made to allow the 'owner' of the 'property' to register his claim. The

---

1   See Cornish *Intellectual Property* (3rd edn, 1996).
2   See further *Clerk and Lindsell* ch 24.
3   See *Clerk and Lindsell.*
4   In two difficult cases for the orthodox view of passing off - those involving plaintiffs who have no trading base in the jurisdiction but either (a) an international trading reputation or (b) a pre-trading publicity campaign in their favour - section 56(2) of the 1994 Act protects reputation alone: see Carty 'Passing Off and the Concept of Goodwill' [1995] JBL 139.
5   Registered designs by the Registered Designs Act 1949; unregistered designs by Part III of the 1988 Act.
6   For the background to the 1988 Act, for example, see *Intellectual Property and Innovation* (Cmnd 9712).
7   See *Clerk and Lindsell* ch 24; *Cornish.*

inventor of a product, for example, needs to register a patent in order to protect his intellectual property right. Complex questions bedevil copyright in the different stages of production of a book. Who has rights in the substance, in the typography, in a particular edition? All may be 'owned' by different persons. Should any rights in information be absolute? Should provision be made to override such rights, on occasion, in the public interest, or should copyright be used to conceal vital information?[8]

Scientific inventions pose equally difficult problems of principle. Are there products on which the grant of a monopoly, which is the effect of a patent, should be refused?[9] For what period should a patent be allowed? Whether rights in a novel invention accrue to an employee or his employer has to be regulated. Provision must be made to ensure that while the profits of his efforts accrue to the inventor, others can benefit from it.

Accordingly, the groundwork for the grant and regulation of intellectual property rights rests largely in statute. Those rights are, on occasion, protected by the criminal law but the equitable remedy of account of profits can be particularly useful. The action for infringement of copyright, patents or trade marks remains essentially an action in tort. The remedies available include damages, an injunction and an Anton Piller order. The potential in these areas for profit from tort has resulted in a number of judicial statements, that, in respect of infringement of patents at least, exemplary damages may be awarded.[10]

SECTION 2. BREACH OF CONFIDENCE[11]

(A) THE OBLIGATION OF CONFIDENTIALITY

The grant of a patent protects research processes only once they have concluded in a novel invention. At that stage, production of a cheaper 'copycat' version may constitute an infringement of the patent. Where details are leaked to a competitor at an earlier stage - while the idea has yet to be expressed in written or other form - how does the law of torts protect such secrets?[12] And what of other confidential information, lists of clients, special manufacturing processes and so on? The common law and equity now extend a degree of protection to all victims of breach of confidence. Where information of a confidential nature is entrusted to another in circumstances where that other is relied on to keep the confidence, an obligation of confidentiality will arise.[13]

In very many instances the confidential information is valuable as part of the plaintiff's business and economic interests. But this is not always so. Personal information is equally protected by the obligation of confidentiality. In *Argyll v Argyll*,[14] for example, the plaintiff was granted an injunction to prohibit her former husband

---

8   See *Lion Laboratories v Evans* [1985] QB 526, [1984] 2 All ER 417, CA; *Church of Scientology of California v Miller* (1987) Times, 23 October.

9   Should, for example, patents ever be granted on genetically engineered life-forms? See Curry *Patentability of Genetically Engineered Plants and Animals* (1987).

10 See *Morton-Norwich Products Inc v Intercen Ltd (No 2)* [1981] FSR 337 doubted in *Catnic Components Ltd v Hill & Smith Ltd* [1983] FSR 512.

11 For a fuller account see *Clerk and Lindsell* ch 26.

12 When a competitor seeks to induce an employee to divulge trade secrets, an action for inducing breach of contract may lie: *Hivac Ltd v Park Royal Scientific Instruments Ltd* [1946] Ch 169, [1946] 1 All ER 350.

13 See *Coco v A N Clark (Engineers) Ltd* [1969] RPC 41; *Dunford & Elliott Ltd v Johnston* [1978] FSR 143, CA, and see generally *Cornish*.

14 [1967] Ch 302; *Stephens v Avery* [1988] Ch 449, [1988] 2 All ER 477.

disclosing marital confidences. The relationship between doctors and their patients gives rise to an obligation on the doctor to keep his patient's confidences.[15]

The obligation of confidence often also arises in contract. The duty of fidelity owed by an employee not to disclose his employer's trade secrets derives from his contract of employment. But contract is not a prerequisite of the obligation of confidence. Take, for example, *Seager v Copydex Ltd.*[16]

> The plaintiff had told the defendants about a new type of carpet grip. Without conscious plagiarism the defendants developed this idea which had been given to them in confidence. The plaintiff was awarded damages to compensate him for their having used his idea without paying for it. The information must not be in the public domain; it must not be public knowledge.

An action for damages has been found to lie even in circumstances where neither breach of contract nor harm to tangible or intangible property is established. Nevertheless the precise nature of the action for breach of confidence remains unclear. Criteria used to determine the measure of damages indicate a judicial perception of the action as an emergent tort.[17] The duty of confidentiality is discussed in terms reminiscent of the more familiar duty of care. The development of a public interest defence somewhat akin to qualified privilege in defamation again suggests a tort.[18] The Law Commission has proposed clarification of the issue by creating a statutory tort of breach of confidence.[19] For the present, however, the better view remains that whatever the circumstances are which created the confidential relationship, the obligation to remain silent depends on a duty of good faith enforceable in equity.

Where breach of confidence protects personal information it protects to a limited extent an interest in privacy. It is not, however, to be equated with a tort of invasion of privacy. Privacy, so far as it is protected by the existing law of tort, is safeguarded by the Protection from Harassment Act 1997.[20] Where confidential information is obtained and disclosed without any abuse of a confidential relationship, no tort is committed.[1] Once such a relationship is established, though, the obligation binding the recipient of confidential information also binds any third party to whom that information is transmitted.[2] Should a disloyal employee or spouse propose to sell trade secrets or marital confidences to the popular press, an injunction will be granted against the newspaper as well.[3]

---

15 *X v Y* [1988] 2 All ER 648; *W v Egdell* [1990] Ch 359, [1990] 1 All ER 835, CA.
16 [1967] 2 All ER 415, [1967] 1 WLR 923.
17 See *Seager v Copydex Ltd* (supra).
18 *Initial Services Ltd v Putterill* [1968] 1 QB 396 at 405, CA; *Fraser v Evans* [1969] 1 QB 349 at 362; *Khashoggi v Smith* (1980) 124 Sol Jo 149, CA.
19 Law Com No 110 *Breach of Confidence* (Cmnd 8388).
20 Of course, once the European Convention on Human Rights and Fundamental Freedoms is enacted into English Law, Art 8 thereof will amplify this protection.
1   See, for example, *Malone v Metropolitan Police Comr* [1979] Ch 344; no tort involved in 'telephone tapping'. On the protection of privacy generally see *Reports of the Committee on Privacy and Related Matters* 1990 (Cm 1102); 1992 (Cm 2135)(the Calcutt reports). Consider how other torts incidentally protect privacy - eg trespass to land: see *Baron Bernstein of Leigh v Skyways and General Ltd* [1978] QB 479, [1977] 2 All ER 902.
2   *Printers and Finishers Ltd v Holloway* [1964] 3 All ER 731.
3   See generally *Cornish*.

(B)   PUBLIC INTEREST

Disclosure of confidential information may be justified in the public interest.[4] The competing public interests in maintaining the bond of confidence[5] and access to particular information must be weighed against each other.[6] A legitimate interest in the subject matter of the information must be proved. Curiosity is insufficient; it must, in its nature, be such that it ought to be disclosed.[7] Disclosure of evidence or 'iniquity' will always be justifiable. In *Lion Laboratories Ltd v Evans*[8] the plaintiffs sought to prevent publication of internal memoranda leaked by employees to the press. The memoranda cast doubt on the reliability of the intoximeter manufactured by the plaintiffs and used by the police to test alcohol levels in drivers. The Court of Appeal refused to grant an injunction. The public interest in the reliability of the product which could, if unreliable, result in unfair prosecutions (and thus the disclosure of this information to the proper authorities) outweighed any private rights of the plaintiff.

The existence of competing interests, the patient's right to confidentiality and the potential risk to third parties, poses acute problems for physicians. May they, for example, breach confidence to warn a patient's sexual partner that the patient is suffering from AIDS? Risk of physical harm to a third party is almost certainly sufficient to release a person from the bond of confidentiality.[9] Indeed in America, doctors who failed to warn a young woman of her ex-boyfriend's (their patient's) homicidal tendencies and threats against her were held liable in negligence to her family after her ex-boyfriend murdered her.[10] The risk of harm must, however, be proved to be a real risk. In *X v Y*,[11] publication of the names of two doctors found to be HIV positive was banned by Rose J. There was no significant risk to their patients which outweighed the doctor's right to confidentiality. Prurient interest does not equal public interest.[12] By contrast, in *W v Egdell*,[13] the defendant, a psychiatrist, had been engaged to prepare a report on W in support of his application to a Mental Health Review Tribunal. W had been detained under the Mental Health Act 1983 after being convicted of multiple manslaughter. He sought a transfer from a special hospital to a lower security unit in preparation for his ultimate discharge from hospital. Dr Egdell concluded that far from being 'cured', W remained dangerously ill with a morbid interest in explosives. The Court of Appeal held that Dr Egdell was justified in breaching W's confidence and sending a copy of his report to the hospital where W was detained, and to the Home Secretary.

4   *Initial Services Ltd v Putterill* (supra). Decisions on confidentiality and the state which suggest that the public interest in its information is accorded a low priority as against state 'secrets' should be treated with caution and confined to their special facts: see *A-G v Jonathan Cape Ltd* [1976] QB 752, [1975] 3 All ER 484, (Crossman diaries) and *A-G v Guardian Newspapers* [1987] 3 All ER 316, [1987] 1 WLR 1248, HL (*Spycatcher* affair).
5   Note that there is a public as well as a private interest in confidentiality in many contexts: *X v Y* (supra); *W v Egdell* (supra).
6   *Church of Scientology of California v Miller* (1987) Times, 23 October.
7   *Cambridge Nutrition Ltd v BBC* [1990] 3 All ER 523.
8   [1985] QB 526, [1984] 2 All ER 417, CA.
9   See Brazier *Medicine, Patients and the Law* (2nd edn, 1992) ch 3.
10 *Tarasoff v Regents of the University of California* 551 P 2d 334 (1976).
11 [1988] 2 All ER 648.
12 *Stephens v Avery* [1988] Ch 449, [1988] 2 All ER 477.
13 [1990] Ch 359, [1990] 1 All ER 835, CA.

(C)   REMEDIES[14]

The most common remedy in breach of confidence is the injunction. It is clearly preferable to anticipate and prevent the disclosure to the public at large of the relevant information. Damages may be awarded where loss resulting from an actual breach is suffered. It is unclear whether damages for mental distress may be awarded.[15] Where the confidential information is of commercial value, an account of profits is often sought.

14   See, generally, Burrows *Remedies for Torts and Breaches of Contract* (2nd edn, 1994).
15   *Stevens v Avery* (supra).

Part 1V

Negligent invasions of interests in person and property and economic interests

CONTENTS

CHAPTERS   PAGE

11 Duty of care I: the neighbour principle   171
12 Duty of care I: recognised harm   199
13 Breach of duty   231
14 Causation   264
15 Defences to negligence   281
16 Liability for defective premises and structures   303

Chapter 11

Duty of care I:
the neighbour principle

SECTION I.   INTRODUCTION

Far more people suffer damage from careless acts of others than from intentional ones, and so the provision made for them is of cardinal importance in the law of torts. English law has long recognised that, in certain circumstances, persons guilty of careless conduct were liable in damages to their victims.[1] So, the liability of those engaged in certain common callings, such as ferrymen, surgeons, smiths, innkeepers and the like, goes back to the fourteenth century. Further, many actions of nuisance and trespass were based on negligent conduct. Gradually, a large variety of situations in which negligence was the common element was subsumed under the action on the case. But not until from, perhaps, 1825 onwards was there any emergence of negligence as a separate tort; there was merely a list of situations where the victims of careless conduct might recover damages. Thereafter, actions upon the case for negligence became common, no doubt spurred on at first by the increase in negligently inflicted injuries through the use of the new mechanical inventions such as the railways, and later by the abolition of the forms of action.[2] The existence of negligence as a separate tort with a distinct set of principles became undeniable, and in practical terms it is perhaps the most important tort of all. It must be realised, however, that negligent acts do not come within the scope of the tort of negligence only. For example, negligent conduct relating to the use of land may well be actionable in nuisance.

It is essential to grasp from the start of any consideration of the tort of negligence that it is not the law that any person who suffers harm as a result of another's carelessness can sue in tort. The tort of negligence requires more '...than heedless or careless conduct'.[3] The injured party must establish that the defendant owed him a duty to take care to protect him from the kind of harm suffered, that he was in breach of that duty, and that it was the defendant's breach of duty which was found to be the cause of the plaintiff's injury. Duty, breach and causation must be established in every

---

1   For the history of the tort of negligence, see Winfield (1926) 42 LQR 184-201.
2   The main milestones were *Vaughan v Menlove* (1837) 3 Bing NC 468; *Winterbottom v Wright* (1842) 10 M & W 109; *Heaven v Pender* (1883) 11 QBD 503, CA.
3   *Lochgelly Iron & Coal Co v McMullan* [1934] AC 1, at 25 HL per Lord Wright.

successful claim in negligence.[4] This chapter seeks to identify the fundamental principles addressing the definition of duty.

SECTION 2.   PROXIMITY AND POLICY

(A)   DUTY-SITUATIONS

The concept of duty of care in negligence[5] emerged towards the end of the eighteenth century, and is now so firmly rooted that there can be no doubt that actions in negligence must fail where duty is not established.[6] There are many strands in this requirement of duty, for example there is generally no duty to intervene to rescue a stranger from peril[7] nor are soldiers under a duty of care to their comrades in battle.[8] In the particular circumstances the defendant must be proved to owe a duty at least to somebody to act or refrain from acting; there must be one of those general situations which the law recognises as being capable of giving rise to a duty; in many situations, as we shall see, it has been held that there can be no such duty. Even if the facts fall outside the 'no duty' category the plaintiff must further show that the defendant, when conducting himself in the manner complained of, owed a duty to him personally. A nurse who carelessly jolts ampoules containing fluid for an injection has broken her duty of care to the hospital. Yet she is not liable to a patient who is paralysed because phenol solution in which the ampoules are later placed seeps into the fluid (with which he is subsequently injected) through cracks, invisible to the naked eye, made in an ampoule by the jolt. She owed no duty to the patient in respect of that act.[9] Nor is it sufficient to show that the defendant owed a general duty of care to the particular plaintiff. The plaintiff must establish that the defendant owed him a duty in respect of the kind of harm of which he complains. A defendant may be under a duty to protect the plaintiff from personal injury but not from economic loss. A general practitioner advising his patient on treatment for her heart condition and high blood pressure owes a duty to safeguard that patient's health, but will not be liable for the economic loss occasioned to the patient if he gives her an unsuccessful tip for the Grand National and the horse comes in last! Even where there is clearly a duty in respect of particular harm, there may not be liability if the risk which materialises is not of a type envisaged by the law when imposing the duty on the defendant. A defendant lending a loaded rifle to her 10-year-old son may be liable to her neighbour if the boy carelessly fires the gun and injures him. Yet if the boy simply drops the rifle on the neighbour's foot there will be no liability. The duty imposed on the mother did not extend to that particular risk of injury.

In identifying the existence and scope of duties of care, the law originally developed in an empirical manner by decisions that in some particular circumstances there was a

4   However, judges by no means always clearly distinguish between the three. In *Roe v Minister of Health* [1954] 2 QB 66 at 85 Lord Denning LJ opined that the three questions were in many cases simply different ways of looking at one and the same question: 'Is the consequence fairly to be considered within the risk created by the negligence?'.
5   Duties similar to these discussed here under common law negligence may also arise under statutes or contracts.
6   *Heaven v Pender* (1883) 11 QBD 503 at 507 (per Brett MR), CA; *Thomas v Quartermaine* (1887) 18 QBD 685 at 694 (per Bowden LJ) CA; *Le Leivre v Gould* [1893] 1 QB 491 at 497 (per Lord Esher MR), CA; *Grant v Australian Knitting Mills Ltd* [1936] AC 85, PC at 101; *Hay (or Bourhill) v Young* [1943] AC 92 [1942] 2 All ER 396, HL.
7   See *Stovin v Wise* [1996] AC 923, at 930-931, HL per Lord Nicholls.
8   *Mulcahy v Ministry of Defence* [1996] QB 732, [1996] 2 All ER 758, CA.
9   *Roe v Minister of Health* [1954] 2 QB 66, [1954] 2 All ER 131, CA.

duty and that in others there was none, by identifying categories of duties. The first attempt to rationalise these cases was made in *Heaven v Pender*, by Brett MR, who produced this formula:[10]

> whenever one person is by circumstances placed in such a position with regard to another that everyone of ordinary sense who did think would at once recognise that if he did not use ordinary care and skill in his own conduct with regard to those circumstances he would cause danger or injury to the person or property of the other, a duty arises to use ordinary care and skill to avoid such danger.

In 1932 came the dictum of Lord Atkin in *Donoghue v Stevenson*,[11] his famous 'neighbour principle':

> The rule that you are to love your neighbour becomes in law, you must not injure your neighbour; and the lawyer's question, (Who is my neighbour?) receives a restricted reply. You must take reasonable care to avoid acts or omissions which you can reasonably foresee would be likely to injure your neighbour. Who, then, in law is my neighbour? The answer seems to be persons who are so closely and directly affected by my act that I ought reasonably to have them in contemplation as being so affected when I am directing my mind to the acts or omissions which are called in question.

This 'neighbour principle' is not the ratio decidendi of the case and it is probable that Lord Atkin never intended it to be an exact comprehensive statement of law.[12] The importance of *Donoghue v Stevenson* is two-fold. (1) It firmly established a new category of duties, that of manufacturers of goods to eventual users, a category which, as will be seen later,[13] has since developed far beyond the limits of the facts of that case. (2) It finally set at rest any possible doubts whether the tort of negligence was capable of further expansion or was to be rigidly tied down by existing precedents. It was a clear instance of the courts' taking account of the new conditions of mass production and complex marketing of goods wherein there are many intermediaries between manufacturer and consumer, and, by a conscious work of judicial legislation, imposing on manufacturers certain minimum standards of care in favour of the consumer.[14]

Sometimes, whether a duty exists is straightforward. There are numerous and extensive categories of situations which are treated by the courts as imposing a duty of care. By way of illustration merely, makers or repairers of goods owe a duty to those who use those goods, a teacher owes a duty to his child-pupil, an occupier of land to visitors there, doctors to their patients, those engaged in skilled occupations to their customers, those carrying out activities on a highway to other highway users. Besides broad categories such as these, there are many instances of more specific and well-established duties hence, before one falls back on general principle, on the Atkin 'neighbour' test, one must ascertain whether on similar facts the courts have already recognised a duty for, remember, whether a duty exists will be a matter of law not fact.

Then, there are other cases where the law has unequivocally denied duty: one may carelessly allow a blind man to walk over a cliff without warning him; a landowner may excavate his land in a careless manner in circumstances where he can foresee that by

---

10 (1883) 11 QBD 503 at 509.
11 [1932] AC 562, HL at 580.
12 Cf *Haseldine v CA Daw & Son Ltd* [1941] 2 KB 343 at 362 (per Scott LJ), [1941] 3 All ER 156, CA.
13 See ch 17, post.
14 The clearest exposition of this function of *Donoghue v Stevenson* is in the judgment of Lord Devlin in *Hedley Byrne & Co Ltd v Heller & Partners Ltd* [1964] AC 465, [1963] 2 All ER 575, HL.

abstracting percolating water from below he will cause a settlement of a plaintiffs adjoining buildings; he is not liable because he owes no duty of care in respect of percolating water.[15] There is no duty in respect of economic loss caused by damage to the person or property of an individual other than the injured party herself, or a person with a current proprietary interest in the damaged property.[16] So if a star footballer is injured, his club cannot claim the loss accruing to them by his inability to continue to play for them, nor can his wife sue in respect of the loss of income to her because he can no longer pay for her designer suits.

(B)   THE RISE AND FALL OF ANNS

What happens when the facts fall into neither group? Were it to be the case that the courts would hold no duty exists unless an earlier precedent establishes such a duty, the law of torts would remain frozen and static for all time. Lord Macmillan stated in *Donoghue v Stevenson* that the 'categories of negligence are never closed'[17] which means at least, as Asquith LJ said in *Candler v Crane Christmas & Co*,[18] 'that in accordance with changing social needs and standards new classes of persons legally bound or entitled to the exercise of care may from time to time emerge'. So over several decades from Lord Atkin's formulation of the 'neighbour principle' new duty-situations were readily recognised by the courts. Thus, it was held that an education authority owes a duty to the driver of a vehicle to exercise reasonable supervision of children in its nursery adjoining the highway so as to prevent them from endangering his safety on the highway, by, for example, running unattended out of the nursery through an unlocked gate on to the roadway and causing him to swerve to avoid injuring them.[19] An electricity authority which had high-voltage wires near a climbable tree was liable to the personal representatives of a child who trespassed off a nearby footpath, climbed the tree, and was killed.[20]

In each of the above examples, the defendant failed his 'neighbour'. He could have foreseen, and should have taken steps to prevent, the injury suffered by the plaintiff. So was the 'neighbour test' the sole criterion determining whether or not a duty arises? In a series of judgments from 1970 to 1982 the courts came close to such a doctrine. First, in *Home Office v Dorset Yacht Co Ltd*,[1] Lord Reid declared:

> The time has come when we can and should say that it [Lord Atkins's neighbour principle] ought to apply unless there is some justification or valid explanation for its exclusion.

Then in *Anns v Merton London Borough Council*[2], Lord Wilberforce proposed his now discredited two-stage test.

15 *Langbrook Properties Ltd v Surrey County Council* [1969] 3 All ER 1424; *Thomas v Gulf Oil Refining Ltd* (1979) 123 Sol Jo 787 (oil company had no duty to avoid fissuring its rock strata and thereby depriving neighbouring plaintiff farmer of water in his ponds); *Midland Bank v Bargrove Property Services* (1991) 24 Con LR 98.
16 *Leigh and Sillivan Ltd v Aliakmon Shipping Co Ltd* [1986] AC 785, [1986] 2 All ER 145.
17 [1932] AC 562 at 619 HL.
18 [1951] 2 KB 164 at 192, [1951] 1 All ER 426, CA.
19 *Carmarthenshire County Council v Lewis* supra (in that case the lorry struck a telegraph pole, and the driver was killed); *Barnes v Hampshire County Council* [1969] 3 All ER 746, HL (local education authority liable for letting children out of a school early before parents or others came to fetch them, when traffic accident ensued).
20 *Buckland v Guildford Gas Light and Coke Co* [1949] 1 KB 410, [1948] 2 All ER 1086.
1   [1970] AC 1004 at 1027, [1970] 2 All ER 294 at 297, HL.
2   [1978] AC 728 at 751-2, [1977] 2 All ER 492 at 498, HL.

...the position has now been reached that in order to establish that a duty of care arises in a particular situation, it is not necessary to bring the facts of that situation within those of previous situations in which a duty of care has been held to exist. Rather the question has to be approached in two stages. First, one has to ask whether, as between the alleged wrongdoer and the person who suffered damage there is a sufficient relationship of proximity or neighbourhood such that, in the reasonable contemplation of the former, carelessness on his part may be likely to cause damage to the latter, in which case a prima facie duty of care arises. Secondly, if the first question is answered affirmatively, it is necessary to consider whether there are any considerations which ought to negative, or to reduce or limit the scope of the duty of the class of person to whom it is owed or the damages to which a breach of it may give rise.

The two-stage test looked deceptively simple. Applied fairly literally, a judge ruling on a novel duty-situation might reason thus. (1) Was the harm to the plaintiff foreseeable bringing him within the 'neighbour principle'? (2) Was there any valid policy reason to deny the existence of a duty to the plaintiff?[3] In effect the plaintiff, having established foreseeability, raised a presumption of the existence of a duty which the defendant then had to rebut on policy grounds. Lord Wilberforce himself, however, recognised that policy factors had a central role to play in determining the extent of duty-situations in *McLoughlin v O'Brian*:[4]

... at the margin, the boundaries of a man's responsibilities for acts of negligence have to be fixed as a matter of policy.

Lord Scarman, in that same case, came closer to declaring foreseeability to be the *sole* test of the existence of a duty. Rejecting any policy-oriented limitations on liability for psychiatric harm (what is today popularly termed post-traumatic stress disorder), he argued:[5]

... if principle inexorably requires a decision which entails a degree of policy risk, the court's function is to adjudicate according to principle, leaving policy curtailment to the judgment of Parliament.

Both Lord Scarman and Lord Bridge[6] feared that judicial conservatism would lead to unjust rigidity in the common law. Over a period of 14 years from 1970 to 1984 the categories of negligence looked infinitely expandable. The boundaries of liability for psychiatric harm extended.[7] And more importantly the extent of liability for non-physical damage, for pure economic loss, greatly increased.[8] Indeed the tort of negligence looked

---

3   For example, to refuse a remedy to a plaintiff-burglar injured by the negligence of his drunken companion while driving the getaway car. Injury to the plaintiff was readily foreseeable but as a matter of policy no duty was recognised as owed by one participant in crime to another, *Ashton v Turner* [1981] QB 137, [1980] 3 All ER 870. And a claim by a child for 'wrongful life', that doctors acted negligently in not aborting her was rejected on policy grounds; the damage to her of the failure to diagnose that her mother had rubella was foreseeable. But the Court of Appeal held (inter alia) that such claims would undermine the sanctity of human life; *McKay v Essex Area Health Authority* [1982] QB 1166, [1982] 2 All ER 771, CA.
4   [1983] 1 AC 410 at 421, [1982] 2 All ER 298 at 303.
5   *McLoughlin v O'Brian* supra, and see *Attia v British Gas plc* [1988] QB 304, [1987] 3 All ER 455, CA.
6   Ibid at 441 and 320.
7   See for example *McLoughlin v O'Brien* supra, and see *Attia v British Gas Plc* [1988] QB 304, [1987] 3 All ER 455, CA.
8   For example, see *Ross v Caunters* [1980] Ch 297, [1979] 3 All ER 580; *Junior Books Ltd v Veitchi Co Ltd* [1983] 1 AC 520, [1983] 2 All ER 301 HL (perhaps the high water mark of foreseeability equals duty?).

set to undermine the very boundaries of contract and tort long established in the English law of obligations and, in particular, to undermine the doctrines of consideration and privity of contract.[9]

Since 1984, however, judicial caution has resurfaced and the House of Lords in particular has lead a retreat from *Anns*, bringing the tort of negligence back to a much more category-based approach once more. Their Lordships determination to restrict the unchecked expansion of the tort, to prevent the emergence of any presumption that all kinds of harm were the responsibility of someone other than the plaintiff, is trenchantly summed up by Lord Hoffmann in *Stovin v Wise*.[10]

> The trend of authorities has been to discourage the assumption that anyone who suffers loss is prima facie entitled to compensation from a person (preferably insured or a public authority) whose act or omission can be said to have caused it. The default position is that he is not.

The retreat from *Anns* began when in *Governors of the Peabody Donation Fund v Sir Lindsay Parkinson & Co Ltd*[11] Lord Keith deplored the literal manner in which the two-stage test in *Anns* had sometimes been applied. Denying a remedy to a development company who sued a local authority for the financial loss occasioned to them by an inadequate drainage system, which they alleged that the authority had negligently approved, he said of the *Anns* test[12]

> There has been a tendency in some recent cases to treat these passages as being themselves of a definitive character. This is a temptation to be resisted in determining whether or not a duty of care of a particular scope was incumbent on the defendant. It is material to take into consideration whether it is just and reasonable that it should be so.

In effect Lord Keith demanded that the *plaintiff* identify policy grounds why a duty should arise, why the defendant should be made responsible for his welfare. Judicial disapproval for the *Anns* test continued apace.[13] What is now clear beyond doubt is that foreseeability of harm alone is not enough to create a duty of care.

> It has been said almost too frequently to require repetition that foreseeability of likely harm is not in itself a sufficient test of liability in negligence. Some further ingredient is invariably needed to establish the requisite proximity of relationship between the plaintiff and defendant, and all the circumstances of the case must be carefully considered and analysed in order to ascertain whether such an ingredient is present.[14]

Exactly what constitutes the 'necessary proximity' to give rise to a duty-situation is difficult to define precisely. Foreseeability of harm to the plaintiff remains a necessary pre-condition of liability. There can be no proximity without foreseeability. But additionally the plaintiff must establish grounds on which it is proper to impose on the defendant responsibility for that harm, reasons why it is fair to expect the defendant to safeguard the plaintiff's interests rather than expecting the plaintiff to look after himself. The courts have recognised the vagueness of concepts such as proximity and fairness, and the difficulty of defining such criteria in order to give them '...utility as practical

---

9   See (1991) 54 MLR 48.
10   [1996] AC 923 at 949.
11   [1985] AC 210, [1984] 3 All ER 529, HL.
12   Ibid at 240 and 534 respectively.
13   *Yuen Kun-yeu v A-G of Hong Kong* [1988] AC 175 at 190-194, PC; *Rowling v Takaro Properties Ltd* [1988] AC 473 at 501, [1988] 1 All ER 163 at 172, PC.
14   *Hill v Chief Constable of West Yorkshire* [1988] 2 All ER 238, HL, at 241 per Lord Keith.

tests.'[15] The need to introduce some element of predictability into the development of duty-situations may be what has led us back to a more category-based approach. Lord Bridge in *Caparo Industries plc v Dickman*[16] asserted:

> Whilst recognising, of course, the importance of the underlying general principles common to the whole field of negligence, I think the law has now moved in the direction of attaching greater significance to the more traditional categorisation of distinct and recognisable situations as guides to the existence, the scope and the limits of the varied duties of care which the law imposes. We must now, I think, recognise the wisdom of the words of Brennan J in the High Court of Australia in *Sutherland Shire Council v Heyman*,[17] where he said:
>
> > 'It is preferable in my view that the law should develop novel categories of negligence incrementally and by analogy with established categories, rather than by a massive extension of a prima facie duty of care restrained only by indefinable 'consideration', which ought to negative, or to reduce or limit the scope of the duty or the class of person to whom it is owed.'

Lord Bridge was not contending for a return to a pre-*Donoghue v Stevenson* approach. A plaintiff in an action for negligence will not fail simply because the duty-situation he relies on has never previously been recognised. The House of Lords have not closed the categories of negligence.[18] A plaintiff seeking recognition of a novel duty situation *will* have to argue his case in the context of existing authority, to persuade the court that to extend liability into this new situation accords with previous analyses of policy and justice in analogous cases. Moreover a finding of no duty in analogous cases will tell against the plaintiff. So, in *X v Bedfordshire County Council*,[19] it was sought to establish that local authorities owe a duty of care in relation to their powers to protect children from abuse and neglect. There was no precedent in relation to a public authority's administration of a social welfare scheme. However Lord Browne-Wilkinson[20] looked at analogous powers vested in the police to protect society from crime, in the financial regulatory bodies to protect investors from fraud and, finding no duty in either of those contexts, suggested that establishing a duty in relation to child protection would be an onerous task.

How difficult a task the plaintiff faces will vary depending on the kind of harm he has suffered. The courts are more ready to impose responsibility to safeguard others from physical injury and damage to their property, than from economic losses. Lord Bridge in *Caparo* continued:[1]

> One of the most important distinctions always to be observed lies in the law's essentially different approach to the different kinds of damage which one party may have suffered in consequence of the acts or omissions of another. It is one thing to owe a duty to avoid causing injury to the person or property of others. It is quite another to avoid causing others to suffer purely economic loss.

15 *Caparo Industries plc v Dickman* [1990] 1 All ER 568 at 574 (per Lord Bridge); Lord Oliver declared '... to search for any single formula which will serve as a general test of liability is to pursue a will-o' the wisp', at 585.

16 [1990] 1 All ER 568 at 574; and see *Murphy v Brentwood District Council* [1990] 2 All ER 908 at 915.

17 (1985) 60 ALR 1 at 43-44.

18 See, for example, *Spring v Guardian Assurance plc* [1995] 2 AC 296, [1994] 3 All ER 129, HL.

19 [1995] 2 AC 633, [1995] 3 All ER 353, HL.

20 Ibid at 751.

1 Supra at 574.

Where physical damage is caused to one person by another's carelessness, establishing that the defendant *ought* to be responsible for avoiding inflicting that damage is generally less problematic. As Lord Oliver put it in *Caparo*[2] in the context of loss caused by physical damage '... the nexus between the defendant and the injured plaintiff can rarely give rise to any difficulty.' The same judge declared in *Murphy v Brentwood District Council*.[3] 'The infliction of physical injury to the person or property of another universally requires to be justified'.

Nonetheless the House of Lords made it crystal clear in *Marc Rich & Co AG v British Rock Marine Co Ltd*[4] that, even in claims in relation to physical damage, foreseeability alone is insufficient to create a duty of care. Citing Saville LJ in the Court of Appeal, Lord Steyn confirmed[5] that *whatever the nature of the relevant harm* (our emphasis) the court must consider, not only the foreseeability of such harm, but address the relationship between the parties and in every case be '... satisfied that in all the circumstances it is fair, just and reasonable to impose a duty of care'. The facts of the case were as follows:

> The plaintiffs' cargo had been loaded on the first defendant's vessel under contracts incorporating the usual terms and conditions of international shipping contracts. Mid-voyage, the ship put into port with a crack in her hull. A surveyor employed by the third defendant, a classification society (an organisation responsible for checking the safety of ships at sea) inspected the vessel and certified that after some temporary repairs it should proceed on its voyage. A few days later the ship sank and the cargo worth £6m was lost. The plaintiff recovered some of that sum from the first defendants, but their liability was limited by the terms of the shipping contracts. The plaintiffs then attempted to recover the balance of their loss from the classification society. They had suffered readily foreseeable physical damage to their property as a result of the society's negligent inspection of the ship and the 'green light' the society's surveyor had given to carry on with the voyage.

Giving the majority judgment in the House of Lords and finding no duty to the cargo owners, Lord Steyn acknowledged that where one person's carelessness *directly* caused physical damage to another, the law will more readily impose a duty. The infliction of loss to the plaintiffs in this case was however, he argued, indirect. There was no contract between the plaintiff and the society; no direct reliance by the plaintiffs on the expertise of the society. Imposing a duty would undermine the framework of contracts within which cargo is carried at sea. Classification societies are independent non-profit-making bodies who act in the public interest to promote the collective welfare of people and property on the seas. Faced with litigation of this sort, such societies might act defensively, refusing to carry out urgent or problematic inspections carrying high risk of liability. Resources would be diverted from the societies' fundamental work to confront complex litigation. It would thus be unfair and unjust to impose a duty in respect of the plaintiff's lost cargo. The societies' responsibility was primarily towards the collective welfare of those at sea. Individual cargo owners should be left to their contractual remedies.

Lord Lloyd dissented. He perceived the facts as little more than a straightforward application of *Donoghue v Stevenson*. The surveyor certifying the ship as fit to sail de facto controlled its fate. Had he refused a certificate, the shipowners would not have continued the voyage. He argued that in cases of physical damage proximity it goes without saying that where the facts cry out for a duty of care as they did in this case

2   Ibid at 585.
3   [1990] 2 All ER 908 at 935.
4   [1996] AC 211, [1995] 3 All ER 307, HL.
5   Ibid at 235.

'..it would require an exceptional case to refuse to impose a duty on the grounds that it would not be fair, just and reasonable'. In other words, for Lord Lloyd, in case of physical harm to people or property, once foreseeability of harm is proven there should be a strong presumption of liability. He concluded thus:[6]

> Otherwise there is a risk that the law of negligence will disintegrate into a series of isolated decisions without any coherent principles at all, and the retreat from *Anns* will turn into a rout.

One crucial question is left unanswered. Had lives been lost when the ship sank, would the classification society have owed a duty to the dead sailors? Counsel for the society appeared to concede a duty in relation to personal injury. Lord Steyn's robust judgment finding it unreasonable to attach legal consequences to the society's carelessness makes it difficult to judge whether had that issue been moot, a duty to individuals personally at risk would indeed have been found.

(C)   LIMITING THE CATEGORIES OF NEGLIGENCE

Judicial conservatism and the adoption by the House of Lords of Brennan J's dictum in *Sutherland Shire Council v Heyman* may not close the categories of negligence. It does of course restrict their growth. First, by demanding that new duty-situations develop incrementally, it becomes harder to establish a new category of negligence significantly different from, or wider in scope, than its predecessors.[7] Second, it may be that where a duty-situation is not entirely novel, but analogous to a category or case where earlier authorities refused to recognise a duty, the door is indeed closed to expansion of the classes of duty-situations.

In *Leigh and Sillivan Ltd v Aliakmon Shipping Co Ltd*[8] a consignment of steel coils was damaged while being shipped from Korea to England. The buyers under the terms of their contract with the sellers had not become the owners of the coils at the time the damage was suffered but they had accepted the risk. So the sellers still owned the coils, but the buyers stood to lose from the damage. A line of authority before 1980[9] denied the existence of any duty in respect of damage to property to any person without a proprietary interest in that property. However in 1982,[10] in two similar cases, judges at first instance found that the risk of such a loss to buyers was readily foreseeable by the carriers. They would know that it was highly likely that if goods were damaged in transit on the sea, contractual and credit arrangements often resulted in buyers being forced to accept and pay for damaged goods. Applying the *Anns* test there were no policy considerations that suggested the defendants should not be responsible for that kind of loss. The House of Lords in *Leigh and Sillivan Ltd v Aliakmon Shipping Co Ltd* condemned those judgments. Lord Brandon[11] denied the applicability of the neighbourhood principle at all in circumstances where clear authority ruled out recognition of a duty-situation. Even before its effective demise, the *Anns* test was inapplicable where what was in issue is '... the existence of a duty of care in

6   Ibid at 230.
7   Note the reliance placed by Lord Steyn in *Marc Rich & Co AG v British Rock Marine Co Ltd* (supra) on the absence of precedent for shipowners suing classification societies.
8   [1986] AC 785, [1986] 2 All ER 145, HL.
9   See *Margarine Union v Cambay Prince Steamship Co Ltd* [1969] 1 QB 219, [1967] 3 All ER 775; *The Mineral Transporter* [1986] AC 1, [1985] 2 All ER 935, PC.
10   *The Irene's Success* [1982] QB 481, [1982] 1 All ER 218; *The Nea Tyhi* [1982] 1 Lloyd's Rep 606.
11   Supra at 815 and 153 respectively.

a factual situation in which the existence of such a duty had been repeatedly held not to exist'.

Well-established authority had settled the matter[12]. Only a person with a proprietary interest in property was owed any duty in respect of damage to that property. However easily foreseeable consequential loss to others might be, that kind of loss was irrecoverable. Similar principles apply to injury to persons too. If either of us is injured in a road accident we may recover our loss. Our employer cannot recover the cost of hiring a replacement to give tort lectures, nor can our families claim the cost of engaging a chauffeur or cook.[13] The concept of 'neighbourhood' cannot be invoked to breathe new life into a context where authority has already deemed it inappropriate to recognise a duty-situation.

Judicial refusal to review proposed categories of negligence previously ruled 'out of court' does to some extent fossilise the tort of negligence. But consider some of the reasons justifying such an approach. Principles in tort need to be reasonably predictable. Otherwise litigation proliferates often fruitlessly. Tort defines those obligations imposed on us. We know what our contractual obligations entail because we chose to enter into them. Justice demands that we have some means of knowing what obligations to others we must honour. And then there is the question of insurance. In a number of tort claims the dispute is not really between the plaintiff and defendant but between their insurers. The decision as to when a person should insure against loss to himself and when he should insure against liability to others depends on an understanding of the circumstances in which a duty of care will arise. If you know it is highly likely a certain kind of loss will be left to lie where it falls, you, as a prudent person, insure yourself against that loss. If you know it is very probable that a particular sort of careless conduct will give rise to liability to another, you insure against that liability. Until recently, only rarely did judges openly address the issue of insurance.[14] The fact that one party might be insured was supposed to be irrelevant to liability.[15] However, *who*, given the economic and social realities of the parties' relationship, *ought* sensibly to have insured against the relevant loss is now on occasion openly used to determine whether it is just, fair and reasonable to impose a duty on the defendant.[16] Or should the plaintiff have shouldered the responsibility of ensuring that he protected himself, at least from the financial consequences of the relevant harm? Lord Lloyd in his dissent in *Marc Rich & Co AG v Bishop Rock Marine Co Ltd*[17] sounds a note of caution. Judicial statements on insurance are not necessarily based on empirical factual evidence. They may too often be no more than assumptions about common practice unsupported by conclusive evidence.

(D)   THE UNFORESEEABLE PLAINTIFF

Albeit foreseeability alone is insufficient to create a duty of care, it must never be forgotten that the defendant can only be held subject to a duty of care if he should

12 See also *Stephens v Anglian Water Authority* [1987] 1 WLR 1381, CA (refusal to reverse long established rule re abstraction of water from land whatever the consequences).

13 If either of us is killed our families will be able to claim for the loss of income and services our death occasions but only because statute (the Fatal Accidents Act) amended the common law to allow claims for loss of dependency; see post at p 554 et seq.

14 An early example can be seen in the judgment of Lord Denning MR in *Spartan Steel and Alloys Ltd v Martin & Co (Contractors) Ltd* [1973] QB 27 at 38.

15 *Capital and Counties plc v Hampshire County Council* [1997] 2 All ER 865 at 891 CA.

16 See *Murphy v Brentwood District Council* [1990] 2 All ER 908 at 923; *Marc Rich & Co AG v British Rock Marine Co Ltd* [1996] AC 211 at 241; *Stovin v Wise* [1996] AC 923 at 954.

17 Supra at 228.

have foreseen injury of the kind that actually materialised to the plaintiff, or to a defined class of persons to which the plaintiff belongs. 'English law does not recognise a duty in the air, so to speak; that is, a duty to undertake that no one shall suffer from one's carelessness.'[18] But suppose that the plaintiff is in breach of his duty of care to Z, but that Y also has suffered damage as the result of the same careless act. In the early days of the development of this tort of negligence, there was much support for the view that Y could also recover. In one leading case the view was canvassed by the Court of Exchequer Chamber that where the defendant railway company could have foreseen that sparks from their engine would set fire to an adjoining field, they were liable to the owner of a cottage 200 yards away across a road when the fire, fanned by a strong wind, destroyed the cottage, although they could not have foreseen harm to the plaintiff's cottage.[19] In the classic American case, *Palsgraf v Long Island Railroad Co*:[20]

> An employee of the defendant railway company, in helping a passenger on to a train, negligently dislodged a parcel which the passenger was carrying. Unknown to the employee, it contained fireworks. These exploded and the shock upset some scales at the other end of the platform. The scales struck the plaintiff, who was standing on the platform. The majority of the court held that the action failed because, although the conduct was careless, no duty was owed to the plaintiff to protect him against this hazard. The minority dissented on the ground that the plaintiff's injuries were the proximate result of the negligent act of the defendant.

This view of the majority, contained in the judgment of Cardozo CJ, a judge of international reputation, that there was no liability to a plaintiff towards whom harm could not be anticipated, was to have great influence on English judicial thought. The decisive moment came in 1943, in the House of Lords decision in *Hay (or Bourhill) v Young*.[1] A motor-cyclist carelessly collided with another vehicle. The plaintiff who was outside the area of foreseeable danger suffered nervous shock as a result of hearing the noise of the collision. The House of Lords held that the fact that the plaintiff was outside the area of foreseeable danger in itself prevented her from succeeding; the House explicitly rejected the argument that because the defendant violated his duty of care to a third party he was responsible for the damage which he inflicted on the plaintiff.

In *Goodwill v British Pregnancy Advisory Service*[2], the defendants had performed a vasectomy on a man who three years later became the plaintiff's lover. Knowing that he had had a vasectomy, the couple did not use contraception and the plaintiff became pregnant and gave birth to a child. The vasectomy had, as a tiny number of such procedures do, spontaneously reversed. The plaintiff claimed that the defendants owed her a duty and were negligent in failing to warn her lover of the possibility that he might regain his fertility. Her claim was struck out. Had her lover, to the knowledge of the defendant, been married at the time of the vasectomy, a duty might have been owed to his wife. The plaintiff was merely one of an indeterminate large class of women with whom the man in question might have sexual intercourse during his lifetime. The relationship with the defendant was so tenuous that no duty to her should be contemplated.

18   *Bottomley v Bannister* [1932] 1 KB 458 at 476 (per Greer LJ).
19   *Smith v London and South Western Rly Co* (1870) LR 6 CP 14, Ex Ch.
20   284 NY 339 (1928).
1   [1943] AC 92, [1942] 2 All ER 396. And see p 204, post.
2   [1996] 1 WLR 1397, CA; and see *Roe v Minister of Health* [1954] 2 QB 66, CA.

SECTION 3.   OMISSIONS

Where there is no prior relationship between the parties, an omission to act will not constitute actionable negligence, however readily foreseeable the harm to the plaintiff. A passer-by who stands and watches a child drown in a shallow pool is not liable for failing to intervene to save her, even though he could do so at minimal risk to himself. A 'Bad Samaritan', who neglects even to summon aid to the victims of a road accident, prioritising getting to work on time, is not liable for his omission. English law imposes no duty to rescue.[3] Lord Nicholls elegantly summed up the distinction between acts and omissions declaring it to be:[4]

> ... one matter to require a person to take care if he embarks on a course of conduct which may harm others. It is another matter to require a person, who is doing nothing to take positive action to protect others from harm for which he is not responsible.

A pure omission will not give rise to liability. However, when the defendant's earlier act creates a duty to take care the fact that an omission is the immediate cause of harm will not prevent the defendant from being liable. So, if the plaintiff is a passenger in a car driven by the defendant, and is hurt because the defendant fails to apply the brake, he has a claim in negligence.[5] In other cases there may be an existing relationship which imposes a positive duty to act, and so a liability for an omission: for example the relationship of education authority and pupil.[6] The general practitioner who has accepted a patient onto his NHS list may be liable if he negligently omits to treat the patient, refusing to visit or turning him away from the surgery. Accepting responsibility for the patient's NHS care imposes a positive duty to act.

SECTION 4.   THE LIABILITY OF PUBLIC AUTHORITIES

(A)   GENERAL

There is no general principle granting public authorities immunity from liability in negligence just because they are public, not private, bodies.[7] A pedestrian knocked down by a council truck can sue the local council. A schoolgirl injured by a dilapidated ceiling collapsing on her in the classroom can sue the education authority. Difficulties arise in relation to the liability of a public authority when the alleged negligence on the part of the authority derives from its exercise, or failure to exercise, statutory powers conferred on it by Parliament, very often powers to provide some public service. The

---

3   Such a duty is imposed in a number of civil law systems; see *Smith v Littlewoods Organisation Ltd* [1987] 1 All ER 710 at 729, HL per Lord Goff.

4   *Stovin v Wise* [1996] AC 923 at 930, HL.

5   In *Johnson v Rea Ltd* [1962] 1 QB 373, [1961] 3 All ER 816, CA, the defendant stevedores (without lack of care) dropped soda ash on a surface over which they subsequently invited the plaintiff to pass. Held they had a duty to take care that the surface was safe, and their failure to remove the ash was actionable; this also may be regarded as an omission in the course of the performance of their operation of unloading the bags of soda ash.

6   See *X v Bedfordshire County Council* [1995] 2 AC 633 at 735. Another illustration is where the conduct of the defendant lulls the plaintiff into a false state of dependence on the defendant. A railway company which omitted to lock a crossing on the approach of a train was held liable to a person injured because of its previous regular practice (on which the plaintiff reasonably relied) of locking the crossing at the train's approach. *Mercer v South Eastern and Chatham Rly Co's Managing Committee* [1922] 2 KB 549.

7   *Mersey Docks and Harbour Board Trustees v Gibbs* (1866) LR 1 HL 93; *Allen v Gulf Oil Refining Ltd* [1981] AC 1001, [1981] 1 All ER 353, HL.

essence of the plaintiff's claim is that he has suffered damage because the public authority has provided an inadequate service. Any such claim today will confront formidable obstacles in establishing a duty of care owed by the authority to the individual plaintiff. A number of reasons explain the particular complexities inherent in negligence claims against public authorities.

(1) Many statutory powers enabling public authorities to provide public services confer on the authority a measure of discretion as to how, or even *if,* the relevant power should be exercised.

(2) Very often, what the plaintiff alleges is not that the authority itself negligently created the danger which befell him, but that it failed to protect him from that danger.

(3) Consequently, a proportion of action against public authorities relates to the authority's failure to act at all, to an omission to exercise the relevant power.

(4) The nature of some public services, for example the investigation and prevention of crime, has been held to require that in the public interest special immunities should protect the authority from liability in negligence.

(5) Judges have become increasingly concerned about the financial burden claims in negligence may make on the public purse.

Just as the decision in *Anns v Merton London Borough Council*[8] appeared to trigger a radical expansion of the tort of negligence generally, so in its specific consideration of the liability of public authorities, *Anns* looked set to extend the liability of public bodies. What is now crystal clear is that a retreat from *Anns* in relation to the liabilities of public authorities is, if anything, even more marked than the general retreat outlined above. The decisions of the House of Lords in *X v Bedfordshire County Council*[9] and *Stovin v Wise*[10] operate to place stringent limits on any such liability.

Any earlier suggestion that the ability of public authorities to pay out compensation justifies a liberal imposition of liability was first roundly condemned by Lord Bridge in *Murphy v Brentwood District Council*:[11]

> ... the shoulders of a public authority are only broad enough to bear the cost because they are financed by the public at large. It is pre-eminently for the legislature to decide whether those policy reasons should be accepted as sufficient for imposing on the public the burden of providing compensation for private financial losses.

In *Stovin v Wise*[12] Lord Hoffman reiterated that it was one thing to provide a public service at public expense and quite another '... to require the public to pay compensation when a failure to provide the service has resulted in loss'.

(B) EXERCISE OF A DISCRETIONARY POWER

The facts and arguments rehearsed in the famous case of *Home Office v Dorset Yacht Co Ltd*[13] neatly illustrate the problems inherent in a claim for negligent exercise of statutory powers.

> A group of borstal trainees were working and staying overnight in a training party on Brownsea Island in Poole Harbour, Dorset. They were in the custody of three borstal officers, servants

---

8 [1978] AC 728, [1977] 2 All ER 492, HL.
9 [1995] 2 AC 633, [1995] 3 All ER 353, HL.
10 [1996] AC 923, [1996] 3 All ER 801, HL.
11 [1990] 2 All ER 908 at 931, HL.
12 Ibid at 952.
13 [1970] AC 1004, [1970] 2 All ER 294, HL.

of the Home Office. One night in breach of their instructions, the officers simply went to bed failing altogether to supervise the boys. Several trainees attempted to escape boarding and damaging the plaintiffs' yacht which was moored offshore.

The likelihood of the damage in these circumstances was readily foreseeable. But the Home Office had a wide statutory discretion as to how borstals be managed, whether open or closed institutions should be operated, and how much freedom should be given to trainees. If the Home Office were held to owe a duty to private individuals injured by escaping trainees it might he inhibited in exercising that discretion properly for the benefit of the boys and the community generally. The House of Lords held that the Home Office could owe a duty of care to the yachtowners. An error of judgment in the exercise of the discretionary power to care for and control the trainees would not of itself have enabled an aggrieved member of the public to sue. However, if the discretion were exercised so carelessly and unreasonably that '... there has been no real exercise of the discretion which Parliament has conferred'[14] then the defendant would have acted quite outside the power conferred on him and Parliament would not '... be supposed to have granted immunity to persons who do that ...'.[15] So, if, as was assumed for the purpose of establishing the preliminary point of law, borstal officers did simply disregard instructions to supervise the trainees, their conduct was clearly outside the discretion conferred on them and the Home Office. Had the facts been different, if, for example, the trainees as part of a pre-release plan had been quite deliberately allowed to roam free around the island, a decision based on a judgment of their reliability and the need to prepare them for release, that decision would have been well within the discretion granted the Home Office.[16] Even if the exercise of discretion proved with hindsight to be erroneous, no duty of care would be owed to the individuals suffering damage when the trainees sought to flee the island.

Elaborating on the principles relating to discretionary powers in *Anns v Merton London Borough Council*[17] Lord Wilberforce sought to distinguish policy and operational decisions. Where the exercise of a discretionary power involved a high level of broad policy-making, for example judgments about resource allocation, or priorities for action, establishing that a public authority had acted beyond the limits of the power conferred on it by Parliament would be difficult. Very convincing evidence would be required to persuade a court that what was decided was quite beyond the jurisdiction of the authority. Broad policy-making would *rarely* be the business of the courts. However once broad policy was decided, and further decisions had to be made how to implement that policy, establishing that an authority acted outside its powers in the 'operational' arena might be easier. Many 'operational' powers retained an element of discretion, but identifying the boundaries of that discretion would be more straightforward. Borstal officers simply going to bed and making no attempt to supervise trainees as they were supposed to do might be seen as 'operational' negligence.

---

14   Ibid at 1031 per Lord Reid.
15   Ibid: note that in *X v Bedfordshire County Council*, supra, Lord Browne-Wilkinson relies heavily on the judgment of Lord Reid regarding Lord Diplock's more complex analysis requiring any decision to be shown to be ultra vires in the public law sense as neither 'helpful or necessary' (at 735-736). Lord Browne-Wilkinson also makes it clear that it is not the case that an action for negligence arising out of the exercise of statutory powers needs for procedural purposes to be classified as a public law claim and brought by way of judicial review. If the relevant conduct of the public authority is beyond the ambit of their statutory discretion, the common law governs their liability. Students of tort can now thankfully forget about the complexities of *O'Reilly v Mackman* [1983] 2 AC 237.
16   See per Lord Diplock [1970] AC 1004 at 1066-67.
17   [1978] AC 728, [1977] 2 All ER 492, HL.

The policy/operational dichotomy proposed in *Anns* was to come under constant fire from both fellow judges[18] and academic commentators.[19] In *X v Bedfordshire County Council*[20] Lord Browne-Wilkinson sought to rationalise the principles which had evolved via *Dorset Yacht* and *Anns* to determine liability for the exercise of statutory powers.[1] The case dealt with two groups of appeals relating to failures in public services. The facts are complex.

The first group of cases, the 'child care' appeals comprised two rather different allegations that local authorities had acted negligently in relation to statutory powers to protect children from abuse. (1) Five plaintiffs, children of the same parents, alleged that *Bedfordshire* council acted negligently in failing to take them into care after it had received reports of parental abuse and gross neglect. (2) A mother and daughter alleged that their local council, *Newham*, acted negligently when on the basis of a mistaken identification of the mother as the child's abuser, the child was removed from home. Both claimed that their enforced separation caused them psychiatric harm.

The second group of cases, the 'education' cases involved once again three rather different claims that education authorities acted negligently in the exercise of their powers to provide the plaintiffs with appropriate education. (1) The plaintiff who had learning difficulties, had been placed in a local mainstream school. He claimed that *Dorset* failed to diagnose his learning disorder, to refer him to an educational psychologist, and to ensure that he received appropriate schooling. (2) In a broadly similar case, the second plaintiff alleged that *Hampshire* had failed to assess his educational needs and remove him from mainstream schooling. He additionally alleged that his headmaster was negligent in failing to refer him for assessment by educational psychologists, and so his learning difficulties were never addressed or adequately treated. In effect, in both the *Dorset* and the *Hampshire* cases, the plaintiffs sued because they were *not* placed in special schools. (3) In the third education case, *Bromley* council was sued because the plaintiff alleged the council placed him in a special school, having negligently failed to assess his real needs and potential, and provide appropriate mainstream schooling for him.

Lord Browne-Wilkinson acknowledged the factual diversity of the several claims before their Lordships. Nonetheless, all raised fundamental questions as to what extent authorities charged with statutory duties are liable to individuals injured by failure to perform such duties. Addressing the imposition of a common law duty of care on public authorities,[2] he set out the following principles.

A distinction should be made between (a) *decision-making* cases, where it is contended that the defendant owes a duty of care in the manner in which it exercises a statutory discretion and (b) *implementation* cases, where what is in issue is the manner in which a statutory discretion has been exercised in practice. In education, a decision to close a school clearly falls into the decision-making category and the day-to-day running of a school falls into the implementation category. In the latter category, an ordinary duty of care is clearly owed in relation to pupils' safety. The fact that the service is provided pursuant to statute is not necessarily incompatible with a normal relationship of proximity between school and pupils.[3] Indeed in implementation claims, claims relating to the practical manner in which decisions are put into practice, the usual

18   Most recently, see Lord Hoffmann in *Stovin v Wise* [1996] AC 923 at 951.
19   See for example Bailey and Bowman 'The Policy/Operational Dictionary: A Cuckoo in the Nest' [1986] CLJ 430.
20   [1995] 2 AC 633, [1995] 3 All ER 353, HL.
1   See Brodie 'Public authorities - negligence actions - control devices' (1998) 18 Legal Studies 1.
2   His Lordship offers a comprehensive analysis of the potential liability in tort in general in relation to the public authorities' performance of statutory duties. This analyses and that part of the judgment in *X* dismissing related claims for breach of statutory duty is discussed post at p 423 et seq.
3   [1995] 2 AC 633 at 735.

principles of foreseeability and proximity apply albeit '...profoundly influenced by the statutory framework within which those acts were done'.[4]

Wherever a claim relates to the exercise of a statutory discretion Lord Browne-Wilkinson confirmed that 'nothing which an authority does within the ambit of that discretion can be actionable at common law'.[5] If a decision complained of falls outside the statutory discretion '...it *can* (but not necessarily will) give rise to common law liability.'[6] *But*, retreating from *Dorset Yacht* and *Anns*, if the exercise of discretion includes matters of policy the courts cannot adjudicate on such policy matters, and cannot determine that the decision is outside the statutory discretion vested in the authority by Parliament. His Lordship offers no comprehensive definition of policy matters acknowledging difficulty in identifying whether and when a discretionary judgment includes a 'policy' decision. He gives examples including matters of resource allocation and decision involving balancing conflicting social aims. So, for example, perhaps decisions by the Home Office to offer prisoners in general family leave after five years of their sentence to maintain family links and so improve chances of rehabilitation on release might fall within Lord Browne-Wilkinson's policy area as involving balancing public safety against the rehabilitation of offenders.

Before any common law duty can be imposed in relation to the exercise of a statutory discretion, a court must resolve three questions:[7] (a) Is the negligence relied upon negligence in the exercise of a statutory discretion involving policy considerations? If so the claim will fail pro tanto as being non justiciable; (b) Were the acts alleged to give rise to the cause of action within the ambit of the discretion conferred on the local authority? If not (c) Is it appropriate to impose on the local authority a duty of care?

Applying those general principles to the actual cases before him, Lord Browne-Wilkinson struck out the whole of the 'child care' claims finding no duty of care could lie in those cases. The allegations of negligence did not necessarily involve broad policy considerations, such as how much money should be allocated to various child care services, or balancing conflicting aims of child protection and family stability. It might just be possible that a full hearing on the facts would establish that in either the *Bedfordshire* or the *Newham* claim, the local authority acted outside the ambit of its proper discretion, that they were so unreasonable in the decision they took in relation to the children that no reasonable council could have arrived at such decisions.[8] The plaintiffs fell at the third hurdle. Was it appropriate to impose a duty of care in the circumstances? Should the courts superimpose a duty of care on the statutory framework of duties and remedies created by Parliament? He concluded that they should not.[9] The statutory framework involved co-operation between many individuals and agencies concerned in child welfare. To impose a duty of care on the local authority could disrupt that partnership. Child protection is an area of great sensitivity inevitably even in its implementation phase involving conflicts of interests. Other remedies were available to redress grievances. Most importantly no analogous case in relation to a statutory social welfare scheme had been identified where a common law duty had been imposed. Such schemes were essentially designed to protect vulnerable individuals from harm done by others. The courts '... should proceed with great care before holding

4   Ibid at 739.
5   Ibid at 738.
6   Ibid.
7   Ibid at 740.
8   A possible hypothetical example might involve social workers who asserted that they always listened only to parents because children were 'unreliable', or vice versa.
9   Ibid   at 748-751.

liable in negligence those who have been charged by Parliament with the task of protecting society from the wrongdoing of others'.[10]

The plaintiffs in the 'education' cases fared a little better. In so far as the three claims complained of decisions taken by the local authorities as to assessment and placement of the children, they failed again at the third hurdle. The statutory framework for providing for children with special needs contained alternative grievance procedures and like the 'child care' cases involved sensitive decision-making issues. However, in the *Dorset* and *Bromley* cases, the allegations relating to inadequacies in the provision made by the council for advice from educational psychologists could be pursued, as could the claim in the *Hampshire* case relating to the alleged inadequacy of the advice provided by the boy's headmaster. If a local authority offers a professional service it owes a duty to those using the service. A headmaster assumes responsibility not only for the physical safety of his pupils but also for their educational needs. Such duties were not incompatible with the successful operation of the statutory scheme to protect the interests of children with special needs.

One further issue needs to be addressed in relation to *X v Bedfordshire County Council*. So far we have looked only at the direct liability[11] of the council for its failure to deliver adequate services. As will have been apparent from the facts of both the 'child care' and the 'education' cases, questions also arise as to an authority's vicarious liability for the negligence of its employees. In the *Newham* case it was alleged that both a social worker employed by Newham and a psychiatrist employed by the local health authority were negligent in their conduct of the inquiry as to the identity of the child's abuser. In all the 'education' cases it was claimed that educational psychologists and/or teachers employed by the council were negligent. The House of Lords said of the vicarious liability of public service employees generally[12] that (1) the employee would only owe a duty of care to the individual member of the public where the existence of such a duty is '... consistent with the proper performance of his duties to the ... authority' and (2) it is appropriate to impose such a duty on the employee. The psychiatrist and the social worker in the *Newham* case were engaged to advise the council, not to treat mother or child. No duty to the family arose. Moreover given the strong policy reasons militating against liability being imposed on local councils at all in this area of child protection, Lord Browne-Wilkinson suggested that even if it might be argued that there was sufficient proximity to give rise to a duty, it would not be just and reasonable to impose a duty on individual social workers and psychiatrists.[13] By contrast in the context of the 'education' cases, the relevant employees, psychologists and teachers were employed within a framework where their duties required them to provide advice directly to children and their parents. Their potential duty to the families in receipt of 'education' services in no way conflicted with their duty to the authority. A duty of care was incumbent on the individual professionals for which the council were vicariously liable.[14]

Subsequently to the decision in *X*, which appeared to limit the potential for litigation against local authorities failing to exercise their powers of child protection adequately, the Court of Appeal in *W v Essex County Council*[15] refused to strike out a claim by

10 Ibid at 751.
11 As to the distinction between direct and vicarious liability in this context see per Lord Browne-Wilkinson at 739-740.
12 Ibid at 739-740. And note *Barrett v Enfield London Borough Council* [1997] 3 All ER 171, CA.
13 Ibid at 751-754; the decision in *X* casts doubt on the judgment in *Everett v Griffiths* [1920] 3 KB 163 that a psychiatrist conducting an assessment leading to compulsory admission to hospital under the Mental Health Act 1983 owes any duty of care to the patient to be detained.
14 Ibid at 763, 766, 770.
15 [1998] 3 All ER 111, CA.

children abused by a foster child placed in their family home by the authority. The plaintiffs alleged that their parents had been assured that the foster child was not suspected of abuse albeit the local authority knew that the child had been cautioned for abusing other children. The action was allowed to continue because the alleged duty of care did not arise from the authority's exercise (or failure to exercise) their statutory powers but rather, as in the education cases in *X*, from the authority's negligent advice.

(C)   FAILURE TO EXERCISE A STATUTORY POWER

To put it crudely, the defendant authorities in *X v Bedfordshire County Council* were exercising their several statutory powers to protect children from abuse and meeting education needs, but allegedly doing so incompetently. They provided a service which was claimed to be inadequate. What of the case where a public authority simply does not exercise its powers at all? In *Stovin v Wise*[16], the facts were refreshingly simple. The plaintiff suffered serious injuries when his motor cycle collided with a car driven by the first defendant who came out of a junction. The junction was dangerous because a bank on adjoining land obscured roadusers' views. Accidents had occurred at the junction on at least three earlier occasions. The local council, the authority responsible for the highway, was joined as a second defendant. It was alleged that the council owed a common law duty of care to road users. The council was aware of the danger posed by the junction. At a meeting prior to the accident in which the plaintiff was injured, the council had acknowledged the visibility problems and recommended removal of at least part of the bank providing the owners of the land, British Rail, agreed. The owners simply did not respond to the council's proposal despite a further meeting between representatives of the council and themselves eight months before Mr Stovin's accident. No further contact between the council and British Rail took place. No reminder was sent. The council simply let the matter lie. They did however have statutory powers had they so wished to issue a notice compelling British Rail to act to eliminate the danger to the highway. On the facts of the case, however, the council, had they acted more diligently, would not have needed to resort to such powers. British Rail appeared to have no active objection to removing part of the bank. It was just that no-one got on with the job.

Could the council be liable for their failure to act, their omission to exercise their statutory powers? Giving the judgment of the majority in the House of Lords, Lord Hoffmann once again attacked *Anns v Merton London Borough Council*. Foreseeability of harm to another generated by the defendant's acts or omission does not create any presumption of a duty to prevent that harm, particularly where to do so requires that the defendant engage in positive action to prevent harm he did not create. Looking at Lord Wilberforce's arguments in *Anns* that statutory powers, in *Anns* itself to inspect buildings, generated a duty to act, a duty to exercise their responsibilities to the public and make decisions responsibly, Lord Hoffmann was equally dismissive. Public law demands that councils exercise their power responsibly. By way of application for judicial review, an order of mandamus may be obtained to enforce *consideration* of the proper exercise of statutory powers but it does not follow that an authority '... necessarily owes a duty of care which may require that the power should actually be exercised'.[17] A public authority exercising its statutory powers so as to cause independent or additional damage might be liable in negligence. Reverting to the pre-*Anns* decision in

16 [1996] AC 923, [1996] 3 All ER 801, HL.
17 Ibid at 950.

East Suffolk Rivers Catchment Board v Kent[18] he declared that the fundamental principle remained that an authority entrusted with a power to intervene is not liable simply because someone is harmed by their failure to do so. Lord Hoffmann addressed the existence of claims to breach of statutory duty. In determining whether such a claim lay, the court must examine the policy of the relevant statute to see if Parliament intended to confer a private right to sue for breach of that statutory *duty*. He opined that where no such intent to provide compensation, to create a statutory liability to compensate for loss of a benefit or service was found '... the same policy should ordinarily exclude the existence of a common law duty of care'.[19]

Where only a power to act was imposed, the additional argument that Parliament had entrusted discretion to the authority militated against a common law duty. Nonetheless *Stovin v Wise* does not entirely close the door to actions in negligence for failure to exercise a statutory power. The minimum preconditions for any duty of care based on a statutory power were (1) that it would be irrational not to have exercised the power so that there would be a public law duty to act and (2) there are '...exceptional grounds for holding that the policy of the statute requires compensation to be paid to persons who suffer loss because the power was not exercised'. Such exceptional grounds will normally have to be based either on evidence of general reliance within the community on the provision of the service by the local authority, or a particular reliance on the service by the plaintiff. In the context of general reliance it should be established that patterns of behaviour depended on a near universal and reasonable expectation that the public authority would deliver protection from particular kinds of harm almost as a matter of routine. The service would be one which was much the same whomsoever it was provided for. Thus to offer it to one and not another might easily be seen as irrational. Giving examples, Lord Hoffmann suggests that routine building inspections (the defective service in *Anns* itself) might be such an example. Reliance on the fire brigade Lord Hoffmann regards as an interesting example of the issues. Private individuals do rely on the fire brigade because they cannot protect themselves against a raging fire. Yet all prudent individuals carry insurance to protect themselves against the consequences of fire.[20] In the absence of such general community reliance on the provision of a service, a plaintiff must show a particular reliance arising out of the conduct of the defendant and/or the relationship of the parties. He gives the example of the maintenance of a lighthouse on which mariners necessarily rely.

Applying his key principles of irrationality and reliance to the facts before him he found[1], first, that given the multiplicity of other demands on the council's resources the delay in getting on with the job to minimise the danger at this particular junction did not establish irrationality. Moreover, even were irrationality proven, this was not a case where the policy of the statute indicated a duty of care to individuals at special risk should lie. Imposing a duty of care and the consequent threat of litigation could distort council priorities. Councils eager to avoid personal injury claims might switch money from schools to road maintenance; nor were the courts well placed to act as a deterrent to bad practice among highway authorities. Courts know little about highway improvement. The primary responsibility for safety on the roads lies with road users. Hazardous conditions can never be eliminated. Highway authorities should not be made primarily responsible for minimising such hazards.

18   [1941] AC 74, HL; and see *Sheppard v Glossop Corpn* [1921] 3 KB 132.
19   [1996] AC 923 at 953.
20   See *Capital and Counties plc v Hampshire County Council* [1997] 2 All ER 865, CA.
1   [1996] AC 923 at 956-958.

(D)   PUBLIC SERVICE IMMUNITIES?

The decisions of the House of Lords in *X v Bedfordshire County Council* and *Stovin v Wise* illustrate the reluctance of the judiciary to impose a duty in tort in respect of the exercise, or failure to exercise, statutory powers to deliver public services. They fall short nonetheless of granting public authorities outright immunity from liability akin, say, to that enjoyed by judges in the exercise of judicial powers.[2] Something apparently closer to immunity is accorded to the police at least in relation to their duties to investigate and prevent crime, and maintain public safety on the roads and in conditions of disorder. In *Hill v Chief Constable of West Yorkshire*[3] the facts were as follows:

> A young woman was murdered by the infamous 'Yorkshire Ripper'. Her estate sued the police alleging a catalogue of errors and incompetence which it was claimed prevented the Ripper's earlier arrest and thus failed to prevent the deceased's murder.

The House of Lords held that there was insufficient proximity between the defendant police force and the deceased. Unlike the trainees in *Dorset Yacht*, the defendants had no control over, no special relationship with the primary wrongdoer. And the deceased was simply a member of the general public. There could be no general duty to prevent crime owed to all of us, or every victim of a burglary or mugging might seek to sue. But their Lordships also advanced more wide-ranging reasons of public policy justifying police immunity from suit in such cases.
(1)   Fear of liability to particular individuals might promote defensive policing. So one might ask, would there be a risk that the police would prioritise the protection of wealthy businesses because a successful lawsuit based on such a burglary would cost more in damages than a burglary of a council flat?
(2)   Defending court cases could lead to undesirable diversion of police resources from their job of preventing crime.
(3)   And, finally, courts are not equipped to judge 'the reasonableness of discretionary policing'.

Developing such public interest immunity, subsequent decisions have held (inter alia) that failure to respond adequately to a 999 call could not give rise to a duty of care.[4] In *Ancell v McDermott*[5] failure to warn road users of dangers posed by an oil spillage did not create a duty in tort. In *Hughes v National Union of Mineworkers*[6] no duty arose in the policing of a riot. In *Osman v Ferguson*[7] the plaintiffs were well known by the police to be targets of harassment by a disturbed individual. Unlike the unfortunate victim in *Hill*, police were aware of their special vulnerability to assault and had told them not to 'worry' about being protected. There was sufficient proximity to the plaintiffs. Yet again no duty lay. A number of further cases followed *Osman* which in general[8] held that policy considerations militated against imposition of a duty of care to the individual.[9] So in *Daly v Chief Constable of Merseyside Police*[10]

2   See ante at p 102; note also immunity afforded to advocates in *Rondel v Worsley* [1969] 1 AC 191, HL; and witness immunity discussed in *X v Bedfordshire County Council* [1995] 2 AC 633.
3   [1989] AC 53, [1988] 2 All ER 238, HL.
4   *Alexandrou v Oxford* [1993] 4 All ER 328, CA.
5   [1993] 4 All ER 355, CA.
6   [1991] 4 All ER 278, CA.
7   [1993] 3 All ER 344, CA.
8   For a case that finds in favour of the plaintiff see *Swinney v Chief Constable of Northumbria* [1997] QB 464, [1996] 3 All ER 449, CA.
9   See *W v Metropolitan Police Comr* (1997) Times, 21 July; *Daly v Chief Constable of Merseyside Police* unreported.
10   Supra.

arguments that police assumed a duty to people submitting themselves to an identification parade were rejected. Such procedures are routine practice and reasons against imposing liability were said to be 'overwhelming'. The English courts' evaluation of the competing interests of the safety of the individual and the efficient operation of the police service, however, was rejected by the European Court of Human Rights when the plaintiffs in *Osman*[11] took their case to that court. That judgment of the Human Rights Court illustrates just how, potentially, the Human Rights Act may affect the development of the tort of negligence and is explored further in the final section of the next chapter.

Even at common law, police immunity was not absolute. The series of events resulting in the horrific events at the Hillsborough football ground, when police allowed crowds of fans to pour into the ground resulting inevitably in the crushing to death and devastating injury of a large number of fans attracted no 'immunity'.[12] Police who negligently discharged a CS canister could be sued,[13] as could officers who failed to warn prison authorities that the plaintiff's husband was mentally disturbed and a suicide risk.[14]

The extent of public interest immunity in the context of policing and other analogous public services is addressed in *Capital and Counties plc v Hampshire County Council*[15] analysing the potential liability in negligence of the fire brigade. Three cases were consolidated before the Court of Appeal. In the first, the firefighters attended the scene of the fire and, before locating the source of the fire, a senior officer ordered that the sprinkler system be switched off. This resulted in the rapid spread of the fire and the destruction of the building. Switching off sprinklers before the source of a fire is identified is acknowledged to be a highly dangerous procedure. In the second case, fire officers were called after the plaintiffs' premises were showered with sparks after a controlled explosion on nearby land. Firefighters established that all visible fires had been put out, but left without inspecting the plaintiffs' premises indoors. Subsequently a fire did break out severely damaging those premises. In the third case, fire broke out at the plaintiffs' chapel, but water hydrants nearby were insufficient to provide the water supply necessary to extinguish the fire. Maintaining an adequate water supply to fight fires is the responsibility of the fire service authority.

A duty was found to arise in the first case only. In switching off the sprinklers, the defendants created the danger resulting in the damage complained of, the destruction of the building. There was no reason to grant immunity in respect of such an error. Liability for such a failure to do the job the firefighters were engaged on would not impact on the overall operation of the force. In the second and third cases, there was insufficient proximity with the plaintiffs. There is no general duty of care owed to individual members of the public to fight fires. Mere attendance at the scene is insufficient to create such a duty actionable in tort. Stuart-Smith LJ drew a line between (1) incompetent fire-fighting creating risks additional to those engendered by the fire itself and so causing injury to the very individuals whom the defendants intervened to protect, and, (2) erroneous decisions about when or how to intervene, or inadequate provision to fight fires. A duty exists in the first set of circumstances but not in the latter cases.

11 *Osman v United Kingdom* [1999] 1 FLR 193
12 *Alcock v Chief Constable of South Yorkshire* [1992] 1 AC 310 HL; *Frost v Chief Constable of West Yorkshire Police* [1998] QB 254, [1997] 1 All ER 540, CA.
13 *Rigby v Chief Constable of Northamptonshire* [1985] 2 All ER 985, [1985] 1 WLR 1242; and see *Knightley v Johns* [1982] 1 WLR 349, CA.
14 *Kirkham v Chief Constable of Greater Manchester* [1990] 2 QB 283, [1990] 3 All ER 246, CA.
15 [1997] QB 1004, [1997] 2 All ER 865, CA.

Stuart-Smith LJ's analysis strongly resembles the approach taken in relation to the police by Henry LJ in *Frost v Chief Constable of Yorkshire Police*[16]. *Frost* involved claims arising out of the Hillsborough disaster. Officers at Hillsborough created the danger (overcrowding) which engulfed the ground. There were no policy or priority decisions inherent in their decision-making and no reason to exempt them from ordinary liability for professional negligence. Reverting to the language of *Anns*, Henry LJ spoke of the operational negligence responsible for the disaster at Hillsborough. The emphasis in *Capital and Counties* and in *Frost* was very much on distinguishing complaints that a service designed to protect the public from danger has failed to do so resulting in damage to an individual member of the public, from complaints that in purporting to deliver such a service the negligence of the defendants has become the *operative* (or at least a significant) cause of the damage to the plaintiff.

However analyses of proximity and causation are not sufficient of themselves to explain the series of decisions on public service 'immunities'. Consider *Mulcahy v Ministry of Defence*.[17] The plaintiff was a soldier in the Gulf War based in Saudi Arabia. While obeying orders to fetch water, he was injured when an officer negligently ordered the firing of a gun knocking the plaintiff off his feet and ultimately damaging his hearing. Statutory immunity previously afforded to the armed forces was repealed in 1987.[18] The Secretary of State had powers to restore such immunity in times of war but had not done so. Nonetheless, the plaintiff's claim failed. Common sense and public policy dictated that in 'battle conditions' no duty of care should be owed to individuals. Citing the 'police immunity' cases[19] the Court of Appeal held that imposition of a duty to one individual could prejudice a critical decision-making process, a process which necessarily left little time for reflection.

The outcome of the recent avalanche of jurisprudence on exercise of statutory powers remains uncertain. We would tentatively suggest the following criteria are currently used by the courts. (1) Beyond the traditional limits of judicial, advocate and witness immunity, no public authority is granted immunity from claims in negligence as such. The defendants (be they police, army, or local council) cannot plead that *no* claim can ever lie because of the nature of their public duties. (2) However, where those public duties involve making decisions of extreme sensitivity,[20] weighing the conflicting needs of different individual members of the public,[1] or, where decisions are necessarily taken under extreme pressure of events,[2] or, where litigation and its pressures might diminish the quality of the public service overall,[3] in respect of those duties (that part of their 'job') a public authority may be accorded 'immunity' in the public interest. It will necessarily be easier for authorities such as police forces to fall within such a category. (3) That 'immunity' however may be conferred in a variety of ways. Courts may declare that the decision or conduct under attack falls within the policy arena now out of bounds to judicial scrutiny via a claim in negligence.[4] The judge may as in *Hill* and *Mulcahy* overtly invoke public interest immunity, or, as in *X v Bedfordshire County Council*,[5]

16   [1997] 1 All ER 540 at 566; revsd on a different point sub nom *White v Chief Constable of South Yorkshire Police* [1999] 1 All ER 1, HL.
17   [1996] 2 All ER 758, CA.
18   Crown Proceedings (Armed Forces) Act 1987.
19   In particular, *Hughes v National Union of Mineworkers* [1991] 4 All ER 278, CA.
20   As with powers to protect children from abuse see *X v Bedfordshire County Council* (supra) and see *H v Norfolk County Council* [1997] 1 FLR 384.
1   Eg police and fire-services faced with several emergency calls for help.
2   Battle conditions or riots?
3   Because public authorities might distort spending priorities to protect against lawsuits but not necessarily for the public good.
4   See *X v Bedfordshire County Council* [1995] 2 AC 633 at 740, HL (ante at p 185).
5   [1995] 2 AC 633, HL.

the court may use the test of what is just and reasonable to exclude a particular area of activity (in that case child protection) from the ambit of the tort of negligence. Diverse reasons are advanced to answer what is essentially the same question. Will granting a special duty, imposing a particular responsibility, to this individual who claims harm resulting from inadequate public service, damage the service overall?

In attempting to answer that question, it is increasingly clear that the economic consequences of imposing a duty of care now influence judicial decision-making. Economic analysis permeates Lord Hoffmann's judgment in *Stovin v Wise*.[6] He analyses liability for omissions in general in terms of efficient allocation of resources.[7] He looks at the impact on public finances of imposing liability in the police cases.[8] In assessing reliance on public services, he engages with socio-economic patterns of behaviour and in ultimately dismissing any duty of care to the injured road users, more openly than any of his judicial colleagues, he concludes that the cost to the community outweighed any benefits to the individual.[9] Whether such a balance of cost and benefit will survive the Human Rights Act is explored at the end of the next chapter.

SECTION 5.   DUTY AND THIRD PARTIES

Examination of principles governing the exercise of statutory powers have shown that only rarely will a public authority be liable for failing to prevent harm occasioned by some third party's deliberate wrongdoing or carelessness. Individuals too are not subjected to any general duty to protect their 'neighbours' from others' tortious conduct.

There is in general, apart from circumstances of vicarious liability,[10] no duty imposed on one person in respect of loss or injury occasioned to another by a third party, even if that loss or injury is readily foreseeable and preventable.[11] An omission to warn a next door neighbour that she has left a door open, or a failure to telephone the police when you see a suspicious person in her garden, results in no liability on your part for the burglary committed by that person. For a positive duty to act to be imposed in respect of the consequences of third parties' actions two conditions must be met over and above the foreseeability of those actions:

1   There must exist either between the defendant and the third party, or between the defendant and the plaintiff, some special relationship which properly demands of the defendant that he safeguard the plaintiff from the wrongful conduct of the third party.
2   The damage done by the third party must be closely related to, and a very probable result of, some failure in care by the defendant.

Whether both these issues go to the existence of a duty, or the first to duty, and the second to remoteness of damage, is a nice point. We shall so divide them for convenience and deal with the second condition later in the chapter on causation. However it illustrates that, while analysis of the tort of negligence into component parts of duty, breach and remoteness is useful for an understanding of the tort, the three are nevertheless closely inter-related. Oliver LJ put the question thus:[12]

6   [1996] AC 923, [1996] 3 All ER 801, HL.
7   Ibid at 944.
8   Ibid at 952.
9   Ibid at 958.
10 See post ch 25.
11 *Weld-Blundell v Stephens* [1920] AC 956 at 986, HL per Lord Sumner; *Smith v Leurs* (1945) 70 CLR 256 at 261-262 per Lord Dixon CJ.
12 *Perl (P) (Exporters) Ltd v Camden London Borough Council* [1983] 3 All ER 161 at 167.

...I think that the question of the existence of duty and that of whether the damage brought about by the act of a third party is too remote are simply two facets of the same problem: for if there be a duty to take reasonable care to prevent damage being caused by a third party then I find it difficult to see how damage caused by that third party consequent on the failure to take such care can be too remote a consequence of the breach of duty. Essentially the answer to both questions is to be found in answering the question: in what circumstances is a defendant to be held responsible at common law for the independent act of a third person whom he knows or ought to know may injure his neighbour?

There is alas, for the student, no principle applicable to all cases where a duty may arise in respect of the wrongdoing of others. Three categories may be suggested but they are by no means exhaustive.[13]

(1) Where the defendant has the right to control the conduct of the third party, a failure of control resulting in the very kind of damage likely to result from lack of control may be actionable by the injured plaintiff. So where parents or teachers fail to supervise young children adequately, they may be in breach of duty not only to the child if she injures herself, but also to any other person injured by intentional or negligent wrongdoing by that child.[14] Cases previously noted on public authorities are illustrative. In *Home Office v Dorset Yacht Co Ltd*[15] the Home Office's contention that no duty could arise in the case of a wrong committed by a person of full age and capacity, who was not the servant of or acting on behalf of the defendant, failed. The statutory right to control the trainees conferred on the borstal authorities imported a duty of care to those who were at immediate risk of loss or damage from negligent failure to control the trainees. Their 'special relationship' with the trainees and the existence of an identifiable and determinate class of potential victims (the yacht owners) created the duty owed to the latter.[16] As we have seen such proximity was absent in *Hill v Chief Constable of West Yorkshire*[17] where the mother of the Yorkshire Ripper's last victim sought on behalf of her daughter's estate to sue the police for negligence in failing to apprehend Sutcliffe earlier. Unlike the Home Office in *Dorset Yacht*, there was, before his arrest, no right vested in the West Yorkshire police to control his conduct; there was no 'special relationship' either between the police and Sutcliffe or the police and his unfortunate final victim. There was nothing to distinguish Miss Hill from any other member of the public.[18] There was neither a special responsibility for the wrongdoers nor an assumption of responsibility to protect the plaintiff.

By contrast, in a Canadian case, a father was held liable for the conduct of his qualified but inexperienced son when he allowed the youth to drive his (the father's) car in treacherous icy conditions. He enjoyed sufficient control to make him responsible for

---

13 See in particular the speech of Lord Goff in *Smith v Littlewoods Organisation Ltd* [1987] 1 All ER 710 at 728 et seq.

14 For example when lack of supervision leads to a child straying onto the road where a driver is injured swerving to avoid him; see *Carmarthenshire County Council v Lewis* [1955] AC 549, [1955] 1 All ER 565.

15 [1970] AC 1004, [1970] 2 All ER 294, HL.

16 Had the trainees made good their escape from the island it is clear that the Home office would not have been held liable for subsequent crimes committed by them on the mainland even though a presumption of general criminal activity by the boys is more than foreseeable.

17 [1988] QB 60, [1987] 1 All ER 1173, CA; affd [1989] AC 53, [1988] 2 All ER 238, HL; see above at p 190.

18 *Hill v Chief Constable of West Yorkshire,* supra at 243-44. Would the police have been under a duty to a victim attacked after Sutcliffe's arrest had negligence by officers guarding him at the police station allowed him to escape? Would the identity of the victim have to be foreseeable? Note *Osman v Ferguson* [1993] 4 All ER 344, CA (discussed above at p 190).

inadequate driving of the youth.[19] In *Barrett v Ministry of Defence*[20] a sailor drank himself insensible, and later asphyxiated on his own vomit after being put in his bunk at a remote base. The Court of Appeal held that the Navy had no duty in tort to prevent him abusing alcohol. But when colleagues put him in his bunk they assumed responsibility for his welfare once he could not longer care for himself.

(2) Where the defendant has created some special source of danger, or presented a third party with the means of committing a tort, he may be under a duty to those placed at risk by his folly. For example, handing a loaded gun to a small boy in the street, who then shoots the next passer by, will result in liability on the part of the foolish adult who created the danger. But this is a category which must be carefully confined. Do you owe a duty of care to road users placed at risk by a student whom you know to be drunk, but to whom you lend your car to drive home? Do you owe a similar duty in respect of the conduct of guests at your dinner party, when you are aware they came by car, but whom you continue to ply with alcohol?[1] Note that mere knowledge of a source of danger created by someone else is insufficient to give rise to a duty to remove that source of danger.[2]

(3) Most hotly disputed has been the scope of the duty imposed on owners of adjoining property in respect of the security of their property. For there clearly is a duty to take care that property you occupy is not a source of danger to adjoining premises so that, for example, failure to maintain the property in good repair, allowing fire to spread from one to the other, may all in appropriate circumstances be actionable. In *Perl (P) (Exporters) Ltd v Camden London Borough Council*[3] the facts were these:

> The local authority owned a block of flats the basement flat of which was unoccupied. The plaintiffs were tenants of an adjoining flat. The empty flat was left unsecured and there had been several burglaries in the area. Burglars entered the empty flat, knocked a hole through the 18-inch common wall and burgled the plaintiffs' property.

The Court of Appeal found that the authority owed the plaintiffs no duty of care in respect of the loss inflicted by the burglary. The relationship of neighbouring property owners was of itself insufficient to impose on one the duty to guard the other against the foreseeable risk of burglary by way of an unsecured property. And in *Smith v Littlewoods Organisation Ltd*[4] the House of Lords rejected a claim for damage caused by a fire started by vandals in a disused cinema owned by the defendants which spread to the plaintiffs' property. Of crucial importance in both judgments was the issue of, if a duty were imposed, how could it be fulfilled? If the only effective precaution was a twenty-four hour guard on the premises, was this an obligation which could fairly be laid on the defendant, or did responsibility for securing his own premises, albeit in difficult circumstances, remain with the plaintiff? And the policy implications of extending the duty to neighbouring owners to embrace the conduct of thieves and vandals were clearly of the highest relevance.

> Is every occupier of a terraced house under a duty to his neighbours to shut his windows or lock his door when he goes out, or to keep access to his cellars secure, or even to remove his

19   *LaPlante v LaPlante* (1995) 125 DLR (4th) 569.
20   [1995] 3 All ER 87, [1995] 1 WLR 1217, CA.
1   See *Paterson Zochonis & Co Ltd v Merfarken Packaging Ltd* [1986] 3 All ER 522 per Robert Goff LJ at 540-542.
2   See *Stovin v Wise* [1996] AC 923 (discussed above at p 188).
3   [1984] QB 342, [1983] 3 All ER 161.
4   [1987] 1 All ER 710.

fire escape, at the risk of being held liable in damages if thieves thereby obtain access to his own house and thence to his neighbour's house? I cannot think that the law imposes any such duty.[5]

Two notes of caution must be mentioned. In relation to the duties of neighbouring property owners consideration must always be given to potential duties created by the torts of nuisance and *Rylands v Fletcher*, as well as negligence. None of the series of decisions excludes the possibility of either an exceptional case imposing a duty of care on neighbouring property owners in respect of damage done by third parties, nor of some other new category of special relationship imposing liability for third parties arising in an appropriate case in the future. However, given Lord Hoffmann's trenchant support in *Stovin v Wise*[6] for rigorously limiting liability for omissions, essentially on the grounds of why should A pay to safeguard B's interests, if A is not engaged in any activity economically beneficial to himself, such an exceptional case seems less and less likely to manifest itself. Why should a neighbour put himself to expense (in time or money) to protect someone else's property, Lord Hoffmann might inquire?

SECTION 6. DUTIES IN TORT AND CONTRACT

There are many circumstances when liability for negligence could arise concurrently in tort and contract. An implied duty of care derives from the contract between the parties.[7] The proximity of the parties creates a concurrent duty in tort. Concurrent liability has always been recognised where the defendant exercised a 'common calling', for example a blacksmith, innkeeper or common carrier. Those 'callings' imposed a duty to show the degree of skill normally expected of a person exercising that particular 'calling', irrespective of contract. But in the case of many professionals, such as solicitors and architects, it was traditionally held that, where there was a contract between the parties, the plaintiff was confined to his remedy in contract alone.[8] A number of Court of Appeal decisions sought to destroy any such restrictive rule. Where the defendant undertook to provide a service, and the plaintiff relied on the careful performance of that service, a duty of care should normally arise from the parties' relationship concurrent with any duty implied into a contract.[9]

Lord Scarman sought to resurrect the traditional rule and exclude concurrent liability in contract and tort in *Tai Hing Cotton Mill Ltd v Liu Chong Hing Bank Ltd*:[10]

> Though it is possible as a matter of legal semantics to conduct an analysis of the rights and duties inherent in some contractual relationships either as a matter of contract law when the question will be what, if any, terms are to be implied or as a matter of tort law when the task will be to identify a duty arising from the proximity and character of the relationship between the parties, their Lordships believe it to be correct on principle and necessary for the avoidance of confusion in the law to adhere to the contractual analysis, on principle because it is a relationship in which the parties have, subject to a few exceptions, the right to determine their obligations to each other, and for avoidance of confusion because different consequences

5 *Perl (P) (Exporters) Ltd v Camden London Borough Council* [1984] QB 342, [1983] 3 All ER 161 at 360 and 172.
6 [1996] AC 923 at 944, HL.
7 For an example of a duty of care implied by statute into a contract for services see the Supply of Goods and Services Act 1982, s 13 discussed post at p 339.
8 *Bagot v Stevens, Scanlan & Co Ltd* [1966] 1 QB 197, [1964] 3 All ER 577, CA.
9 *Esso Petroleum Co Ltd v Mardon* [1976] QB 801, [1976] 2 All ER 5, CA; *Midland Bank Trust Co Ltd v Hett, Stubbs & Kemp* [1979] Ch 384, CA; *Batty v Metropolitan Property Realisations Ltd* [1978] QB 544, [1978] 2 All ER 445, CA.
10 [1986] AC 80 at 107, HL.

do follow according to whether liability arises from contract or tort, eg in the limitation of action.

A series of conflicting decisions from the Court of Appeal followed *Tai Hing*.[11] At the heart of the matter lay an essentially practical question. When a person enters into a contract, in circumstances where, were there no contract, there would nonetheless be a duty in tort, should he forfeit the potential advantages suing in tort may have over contract? Such advantages most regularly relate to the rules of limitation of actions. By electing to sue in tort the plaintiff may have longer in which to bring his claim. In contract the limitation period begins to run from the date of the breach of contract. In tort that start may be delayed until the date when the plaintiff could reasonably have become aware of the breach of the duty.[12] The Latent Damage Act 1986 applies only to actions in tort.[13]

The House of Lords in *Henderson v Merrett Syndicates Ltd*[14] has finally resolved the issue. Concurrent liability in contract and tort is generally applicable. The old restrictive rules Lord Scarman sought to resurrect in *Tai Hing* remain dead and buried. Providing that a duty in tort is not contrary to the terms of the contract agreed between them, a duty in tort arising out of the special relationship between the parties lies concurrently with the obligations imposed by the contract. Lord Goff declared:[15]

> … the common law is not antipathetic to concurrent liability, and there is no sound basis for a rule which automatically restricts the plaintiff to either a tortious or contractual remedy. The result may be untidy; but given that the tortious duty is imposed by the general law, and the contractual duty is attributable to the will of the parties, I do not find it objectionable that the claimant may be entitled to take advantage of the remedy which is most advantageous to him, *subject only to ascertaining whether the tortious duty is so inconsistent with the applicable contract that, in accordance with ordinary principle the parties must be taken to have agreed that the tortious remedy is to be limited or excluded.*

A plaintiff who has either expressly or implicitly agreed to give up any remedy in tort cannot go back on his word. He cannot assert a duty in tort quite contrary to the framework of agreed contractual terms. However, where a contract deals with only part of the relationship between the parties, a duty of care wider than the contractual duty may arise from the circumstances of the case. Such duties may be concurrent but not co-extensive.[16] Thus, if we entrust our portfolio of shares in US companies to a paid financial adviser, our contract will govern his professional liability to us. If that contract excludes a duty in tort, we cannot elect to sue in tort in respect of those dealings between us. If that same defendant also gives us general advice on how to reinvest our US profits elsewhere, no bar exists to a duty of care in respect of those aspects of our relationship not governed by contract.

It must not be assumed that tort always offers advantages over contract. The limits of a tort action in comparison with contract must be noted in this context. A surgeon treating an NHS patient can owe him no obligation higher or stricter than that of reasonable care. He does not contract with his patient to 'guarantee' success. In *Thake*

---

11 Contrast for example, *Forsikringsaktieselskapet Vesta v Butcher* [1988] 2 All ER 43, CA with *Lee v Thompson* (1989) 6 PN 91, CA; and see the disagreement within the Court of Appeal in *Johnstone v Bloomsbury Health Authority* [1992] QB 333, [1991] 2 All ER 293.
12 See post at 572.
13 *Iron Trades Mutual Insurance Ltd v Buckingham (JK) Ltd* [1990] 1 All ER 808.
14 [1995] 2 AC 145, HL. See Whitaker 'The application of the "broad principle" in Hedley-Byrne as between parties to a contract' (1997) 17 Legal Studies 169.
15 Ibid at 193-194.
16 *Holt v Payne Skillington* [1996] PNLR 179, CA.

v Maurice[17] the plaintiff paid for a private vasectomy. The operation was carefully and competently performed. Some time later the minute risk of natural reversal of the surgery materialised. The plaintiff's wife conceived again. In his action for breach of contract the plaintiff's counsel argued thus. The surgeon never mentioned the possibility of the vasectomy 'failing'. Therefore, he contracted to render Mr Thake sterile. When he failed to do so he was in breach of contract. The Court of Appeal finally dismissed that claim holding that in such a contract a term 'guaranteeing' success could not reasonably be implied.[18] But the argument could never even have been attempted in tort.

Consider also the famous American case of *Hawkins v McGee*.[19] The plaintiff severely burned his hand. The defendant, a plastic surgeon, undertook to treat the hand and restore it to perfect condition. After treatment the hand was in fact much worse than before. The measure of damages awarded in contract was the difference between the hand after treatment and a perfect hand. In tort it would have been the difference between the burned hand and the hand after surgery. In contract the plaintiff is awarded damages for his expectation losses, for not obtaining the result he contracted for. In tort he is generally[20] awarded only compensation for the consequences of any lack of care, to return him to the position he enjoyed prior to the tort.

The relationship between tort and contract is relevant not only to questions of concurrent liability but also to cases where a third party seeks to establish that A who owes a duty in contract to B also owes a duty in tort to him. *Donoghue v Stevenson*[1] dismisses the fallacy that privity of contract per se prevents such a duty to the third party ever arising. If there is the necessary proximity between the parties then a duty in tort may arise independently of any contract between A and B. Nonetheless courts will be wary of extending a liability in tort to third parties where the defendant's primary duty rests on a contractual obligation to someone else. They will seek to ensure that a duty in tort to the third party does not conflict with the primary contractual duty. The judgment of the House of Lords in *White v Jones*[2] (discussed fully in the next chapter) however confirms that liability in tort for breach of an obligation owed in contract to another party can arise in appropriate circumstances. Indeed in *Williams v Natural Life Health Foods Ltd*[3] their Lordships acknowledge tort may play a 'gap filling role' where contract fails to achieve justice. Privity of contract with A is not a bar to liability to B; it is a consideration which should not be overlooked.

17 [1986] QB 644, [1986] 1 All ER 497, CA.
18 The plaintiff lost 2-1 in the Court of Appeal. See though the judgment at first instance [1984] 2 All ER 513. Peter Pain J held for the plaintiff in contract and his judgment is instructive on the relationship between tort and contract.
19 84 NH 114, 146 A 641 (1929).
20 For an example of expectation losses recovered in tort see *White v Jones* [1995] 1 All ER 691, HL; discussed post at p 222.
1   [1932] AC 562; see ante at p 173.
2   [1995] 1 All ER 691.
3   [1998] 2 All ER 577, HL; discussed post at p 224.

Chapter 12

Duty of care II: recognised harm

SECTION I. INTRODUCTION

'The rule that you are to love your neighbour becomes in law, you must not injure your neighbour'

Lord Atkin's famous and elegant phrase begs one vital question. What kinds of injury must you take care to avoid inflicting on your neighbour? Failing to return his love may hurt him deeply. No-one would suggest that he can sue you for his distress. The previous chapter examined how subsequent judgments have sought to develop a broad framework within which the parameters of duties of care in tort may be defined. The elevation of the Atkin neighbour principle to a quasi-statutory formula and its recent demotion from any such status has been considered. This chapter concentrates on what is perhaps the most crucial issue in the process of defining duty-situations. What kinds of harm give rise to a duty of care in tort?

Restrictive interpretations of the Atkin principle in the years immediately following *Donoghue v Stevenson* sought to limit its application to personal injuries alone.[1] Over 30 years passed before it was considered applicable to claims for economic loss at all.[2] Today, in principle, recognition is accorded in an appropriate case to duties to avoid physical damage to persons and property, including psychiatric injury to persons and damage to real property, and to duties to avoid inflicting economic loss alone. Without doubt it is much easier to obtain recognition of a duty to avoid physical damage than a duty to avoid 'pure' economic loss. But that does not mean that determining the scope of a duty to avoid personal injuries is in all instances free of controversy. Problems arise in relation to the foreseeability of injury to a particular plaintiff, the limits of liability for emotional harm and whether social policy requires that certain types of harm to persons go uncompensated in the 'public interest'. Nor does the more ready recognition of physical damage as a source of duty mean that the distinction drawn between physical damage and 'pure' economic loss is clear and undisputed. And the case law illustrates, too, the artificiality of attempting systematically to define exact and immoveable boundaries between questions of duty, breach and remoteness of damage. The essence of the issue of what kinds of harm are remediable in tort is the determination of the

---

1   Eg *Deyong v Shenburn* [1946] KB 227, [1946] 1 All ER 226, CA.
2   *Hedley Byrne & Co v Heller & Partners Ltd* [1964] AC 465, [1963] 2 All ER 575, HL.

limits of the tort of negligence. The umbrella of the scope of the duty of care provides a convenient, but not always satisfactory, mechanism within which to explore those limits.[3]

The following principles must be borne in mind throughout this chapter.

1   There are kinds of harm which are currently irremediable in English law even if intentionally and maliciously inflicted. Invasion of privacy and interference with business, without otherwise unlawful means, are just two examples. When the harm of which the plaintiff complains does not give rise to a tort if committed intentionally, the courts will be naturally reluctant to say that such harm gives rise to a cause of action if inflicted carelessly.

2   Liability for careless acts and omissions has to be confined within manageable proportions. The courts will strive to avoid liability 'in an indeterminable amount for an indefinite time to an indeterminate class[4]'. As Lord Steyn put it in *White v Chief Constable of South Yorkshire Police*[5]:

> [We] do not live in Utopia: we live in a practical world where the tort system imposes limits to the classes of claims that rank for consideration as well as to the heads of recoverable damages. This results, of course, in imperfect justice but it is by and large the best that the common law can do.

3   Once again the proper functions of tort and contract and the borderline between them are in issue. Where the substance of the plaintiff's claim is that the defendant failed to provide value for money for services performed, and no contract existed between them, is imposing a duty of care in such circumstances trespassing on the sanctity of privity of contract? Does it matter?[6]

4   Once the Human Rights Act 1998 comes into force (sometime in 2000) courts will be required to re-assess some of the existing boundaries of the tort of negligence too. Judges will need to reflect whether limitations on duties of care founded on pragmatic policy reasons violate rights to life under Article 2, to privacy under Article 8, to access to justice under Article 6, or indeed to peaceful possession of property under the First Protocol to the Convention. Students must not conclude that the impact of the European Convention on Human Rights is limited to the intentional torts. The possible impact of the Act on the boundaries of duty of care is briefly strictly reviewed at the conclusion to this chapter.

SECTION 2.   HARM TO PERSONS

(A)   DUTY TO THE UNBORN

Whether a duty of care was owed to a child damaged by another's negligence before its birth remained unresolved at common law until 1992. In *Burton v Islington Health Authority*[7] the Court of Appeal finally held that a duty is owed to the unborn child which crystallises on the live birth of the child. But prior to 1992 the question of any duty prior to the birth remained unresolved albeit that the potential for and horror of

---

3   For powerful criticism of the concept of duty of care in negligence see J C Smith *Liability in Negligence* (1984) Carswell and read in particular ch 1 'The Mystery of Duty'.
4   *Ultramares Corpn v Touche* 255 NY 170 (1931) at 444 per Cardozo CJ.
5   [1999] 1 All ER 1, HL.
6   See *White v Jones* [1995] 2 AC 207 at 262-265 per Lord Goff, HL.
7   [1993] QB 204, [1992] 3 All ER 833; and see *De Martell v Merton and Sutton Health Authority* [1992] 3 All ER 820, CA.

injury to the foetus had been graphically illustrated by the thalidomide tragedy when children all over the world were born with serious deformities caused by a sedative taken by their mothers in early pregnancy. Public opinion was not prepared to wait patiently for judicial resolution of the matter, so Parliament intervened. The Congenital Disabilities (Civil Liability) Act 1976 provides that a child who is born alive but disabled as a result of an occurrence before its birth may in certain circumstances have a cause of action in negligence against the person responsible for that occurrence.[8] Section 4(5) provides that the 1976 Act supersedes the common law in respect of births after its passing and so it has generally been thought that the common law duty eventually recognised in *Burton v Islington Health Authority* only applies to a claim by a plaintiff born *before* 1976.[9] The duty imposed under the Act relates to any occurrence, whether it be one affecting the reproductive capacity of either parent before conception (for example toxic chemicals which damage the father's sperm so as to cause him to beget disabled children), or one affecting the mother during pregnancy (such as a drug causing deformities to the foetus in the womb). The peculiarity of the duty to the child is that it is derivative only. The relevant occurrence must have resulted in liability in tort to the affected parent although it is no answer that the parent suffered no actionable injury '... if there was a breach of legal duty which, accompanied by injury, would have given rise to the liability.'[10] But if there was no injury, wherein lies the breach of duty? It can only be argued that it lies in the breach of duty to the parent to avoid inflicting on her the harm naturally resulting from giving birth to a damaged child. The 1976 Act in general imposes a duty towards parents to avoid inflicting injury to their reproductive functions. The cause of action conferred on the child when born is simply a by-product of the breach of duty to the affected parent.

Not surprisingly then, mothers[11] are expressly immune from general liability under the Act. How could a mother damaging her baby by smoking or drinking too much be in breach of duty to herself? Or would she be in breach of duty to the father in damaging his child? But section 2 does expressly provide for the only direct duty owed to the unborn child under the 1976 Act. A woman may be liable for damage to her child inflicted by her negligent driving of a motor vehicle when she knows or ought to know herself to be pregnant. The reasoning behind such maternal liability is perhaps that, in reality, her insurers will meet the cost of the child's claim.

The complexity of the 1976 Act has to be seen to be believed. Its failure to address the issue of causation, the greatest problem in any case of pre-natal injury, has resulted in it being a largely useless and unused piece of legislation. Ironically the common law duty owed to those born before 1976 has, too late, provided a more effective and comprehensive remedy than the statutory solution adopted in some haste.

One crucial question in relation to pre-natal injury and the scope of recognition of harm to persons has been ventilated in the courts. In *McKay v Essex Area Health Authority*[12] the Court of Appeal held that in England the common law recognised no claim for 'wrongful life'. The plaintiff was born, before the passing of the 1976 Act, with terrible disabilities resulting from her mother having contracted rubella (German measles) in pregnancy. The mother had undergone tests when she realised that she had been in contact with the disease and had been negligently told that the tests were negative. She would have opted for an abortion had tests proved positive. The child,

---

8   Section 1(1). Note that s 44 of the Human Fertilisation and Embryology Act 1990 extends the 1976 Act to cover negligently inflicted disability in the course of licensed fertility treatment.
9   For an elegant argument to the contrary see Murphy (1994) 10 PN 94.
10   Section 1(3).
11   See s 1. Fathers are not so immune. But what sorts of circumstance could create paternal liability - infecting mother and baby with AIDS?
12   [1982] QB 1166, [1982] 2 All ER 771, CA.

through its parents, sued in respect of the harm caused to her by her birth encumbered by her manifold disability. The Court of Appeal held that it was impossible to measure the harm resulting from entry into a life afflicted by disability where the only alternative was no life at all. Nor were they prepared to impose on doctors a duty of care which was in essence a duty to abort.

In respect of births subsequent to the 1976 Act Ackner LJ[13] said that the Act gave a cause of action only in respect of occurrences causing disabilities which would otherwise not have afflicted the child. It did not afford a remedy to a child whose birth, afflicted by pre-existing disability, was caused by the defendant's alleged negligence. His Lordship's finding that the Act was inapplicable to a claim for 'wrongful life' was seen by him as preventing such claims arising in future. However, one alternative result of Ackner LJ's finding that the 1976 Act does not allow 'wrongful life' suits is that that Act is irrelevant to such suits and that the issue of 'wrongful life' with all its ethical and moral implications remains open for review by the House of Lords.[14]

(B)   DUTY TO RESCUERS

Recognition of a duty owed in respect of physical and emotional injury to rescuers raises two important questions about the ambit of the duty to avoid harm to persons. The rescuer is only indirectly at risk from the negligent conduct. Is he then a foreseeable plaintiff? As a rescuer 'elects' to undertake the rescue can he properly claim that the originator of the danger owes him any obligation in respect of his safety which he has 'chosen' to imperil?

In 1935 the Court of Appeal held for the first time that a defendant who owed a duty to another also owed a duty to those who might foreseeably attempt to rescue him from the acute peril in which the defendant's negligence had placed him.[15] Subsequent case law consistently confirmed a judicial policy to encourage and commend rescue attempts. 'Danger invites rescue. The cry of distress is a summons to relief.'[16] Consequently arguments that no duty is owed to the rescuer electing to imperil his own safety have fallen on deaf ears. Whether the rescuer is a member of the emergency services, whose public duty it is to embark on the rescue mission, or a well-meaning member of the public,[17] the courts will now hold that a duty is owed to him.

The duty owed to rescuers is independent of proof of any breach of duty to another person. In *Videan v British Transport Commission*[18] it was held that a duty was owed to a stationmaster rescuing his small son who had been trespassing on the lines. Albeit that, at that time, no duty was owed to the child trespasser, the stationmaster's presence on the tracks dealing with an emergency was foreseeable thus creating a duty to him directly and personally. The independent duty to a rescuer is now imposed, not only on those who endanger other people or their property so as to invite rescue, but also on anyone endangering himself or his own property so as to create the likelihood of rescue. A householder whose negligent use of a blowlamp resulted in his setting his roof on fire was held liable to the fireman injured fighting the blaze.[19]

13 Ibid at 1187 and 786.
14 See Symmons 'Policy Factors in Actions for Wrongful Birth' (1987) 50 MLR 269; Fortin (1987) JSWL 306.
15 *Haynes v Harwood* [1935] 1 KB 146, CA.
16 *Wagner v International Rly Co* 232 NY Rep 176 (1921).
17 *Baker v T E Hopkins & Son Ltd* [1959] 3 All ER 225, CA (damages awarded to the widow of a doctor rescuer); *Chadwick v British Transport Commission* [1967] 2 All ER 945, [1967] 1 WLR 912 (nearby resident coming to the aid of victims of a rail disaster and suffering nervous shock).
18 [1963] 2 QB 650, [1963] 2 All ER 860, CA.
19 *Ogwo v Taylor* [1988] AC 431 [1987] 3 All ER 961, HL.

Arguments that members of the emergency services should not, as a matter of policy, receive compensation for undertaking the very duty which they are engaged to perform have received scant consideration from the English courts. The rescue cases in England are marked by an emphatic desire by the judiciary to 'reward' desirable conduct and encourage in this limited sphere 'Good Samaritanism'. The economic issues behind the imposition of liability to firemen and police officers are ignored. What the courts are in fact doing on one interpretation is transferring the loss from the public purse to the shoulders of the negligent citizen, imposing a tax on carelessness.[20]

In the context of liability to members of 'professional rescue' services, such as the police, firefighters and ambulance workers, controversy has raged about awarding such rescuers damages for psychiatric injury triggered by the trauma of their work. It is entirely clear that the courts will award compensation to the ordinary citizen who puts himself in danger trying to help the victims of some horrific disaster.[1] The controversial claims brought by police officers present at the Hillsborough disaster when nearly a hundred spectators at a football match were crushed to death are discussed in the following section when we address the decision of the House of Lords in *White v Chief Constable of South Yorkshire Police.*[2]

(C) LIABILITY FOR PSYCHIATRIC HARM

Damages cannot be awarded, at common law, for ordinary grief and sorrow experienced when a relative or friend is killed or injured,[3] or when a person is distressed by some dreadful incident or disaster. The courts have traditionally been cautious about awarding damages for any non-physical harm to the person, even when that harm goes well beyond normal distress resulting in some cases in obvious physical symptoms. The reasons for caution are easy to catalogue. They are the difficulties of putting a monetary value on such harm, the risk of fictitious claims and excessive litigation ('opening the floodgates'), and the problems of proving the link between the defendant's negligence and the injury to the plaintiff. Gradual, if belated, judicial recognition that psychiatric evidence can establish that link between mind and body led to the abandonment of the nineteenth century attitude that non-physical harm was always irrecoverable.[4] The courts began to be prepared to award damages for what was for many years called nervous shock.[5] A plaintiff who became mentally ill because of the shock to his nervous system of an incident which either threatened his own safety[6] or involved witnessing

---

20 See the American judgments cited in *Ogwo v Taylor* [1987] 1 All ER 668 at 674-675, CA.
1 *Chadwick v British Transport Commission* [1967] 2 All ER 945, [1967] 1 WLR 912.
2 [1999] 1 All ER 1, HL.
3 But note that statute allows for the limited provision of bereavement damages for spouses and parents of children under 18 in the Fatal Accidents Act 1976, s 1A. See post at p 557.
4 For the nineteenth century view see *Victoria Railways Comrs v Coultas* (1888) 13 App Cas 222, PC. For an analysis of how in the author's view law has always 'limped behind medicine' see Sprince 'Negligently inflicted psychiatric damage: a medical diagnosis and prognosis' (1998) 18 Legal Studies 55.
5 The phrase can be misleading and should be regarded as no more than a customary means of grouping together cases where the plaintiff becomes mentally ill as a consequence of an assault upon his nervous system; see *Alcock v Chief Constable of South Yorkshire* [1991] 4 All ER 907 at 923 (per Lord Oliver); and see *McLoughlin v O'Brian* [1982] 2 All ER 298 at 301 (per Lord Wilberforce).
6 See *Dulieu v White & Sons* [1901] 2 KB 669 (plaintiff suffered a miscarriage after just missing being run over).

exceptionally distressing injuries to others[7] would in certain circumstances[8] recover compensation for psychiatric harm.[9] It will become apparent that what the law labels nervous shock or psychiatric harm, often but not invariably, describes the condition known to psychiatrists and the media as post-traumatic stress disorder (PTSD).[10] Psychiatric illness can follow from an incident in which negligence results in injury, or threatened injury, in a number of ways. Principally, first, and very obviously, a plaintiff who suffers severe physical injury, for example in a road accident, may well also succumb to mental illness triggered by the terror of the accident and his or her consequent pain and suffering. Second, an accident may take place causing the plaintiff shock and fear for his or her own safety but not resulting in any bodily harm. Nonetheless, the shock may cause the victim to succumb to psychiatric illness.

Third, the plaintiff may not be directly involved in the original accident, and be at no personal risk of physical injury. Such a plaintiff suffers psychiatric harm because of the effect that injuries to others have on him or her. The classic example would be a mother who witnesses horrific injury to her children.[11] The majority of the early 'nervous shock' cases belong in this third category. The plaintiff is classified as a *secondary* victim of the defendant's negligence. A series of judgments set limits, – 'control mechanisms' – on who may claim as such a secondary victim of psychiatric harm.[12] We will discuss these limits fully a little later. They are of course designed to keep the floodgates closed. In essence, and very briefly, to recover damages, a *secondary* victim must generally establish (1) a close tie of love or affection with the primary victim, such ties of affection will generally be presumed to exist between, for example, spouses and parents and children and (2) a proximity in time and place to the scene of the accident. He must show special reasons why the defendant ought to foresee that he might suffer injury by shock.

Victims of psychiatric illness in our first two categories are *regarded as primary* victims of the defendant's negligence. A person who suffers psychiatric illness as well as physical injury causes us no problems. Post-traumatic stress disorder is part and parcel of his claim for injury. *Page v Smith*[13] deals with plaintiffs in the second category.

The plaintiff was involved in a collision with a car negligently driven by the defendant. He suffered no physical injury. However, almost immediately he succumbed to a revival in an acute form of the chronic fatigue syndrome (ME) which he had suffered from at various times earlier in life. He became so ill that he was unable to work. The defendant argued that, as the plaintiff suffered no physical injury, he was not liable for injury through shock. A normal person with no previous history of psychiatric illness would not be expected to become ill as a result of a minor collision.

The House of Lords found for the plaintiff. In cases involving 'nervous shock' they held that a clear distinction must be made between primary and secondary victims. In claims by the latter certain 'control mechanisms' do limit potential liability for psychiatric harm. Shock in a person of normal fortitude must be foreseeable. But Mr Page, the

---

7 See *Hambrook v Stokes Bros* [1925] 1 KB 141, CA (plaintiff saw driverless lorry career down the road in the direction of her children).

8 Note refusal of damages to the plaintiff in *Hay (Bourhill) v Young* [1943] AC 92, HL (plaintiff heard but did not see accident involving a cyclist unrelated to her).

9 The term now preferred to nervous shock; see *Attia v British Gas plc* [1987] 3 All ER 455 at 462, CA (per Bingham LJ).

10 See *Vernon v Bosley* [1997] 1 All ER 577, CA; *White v Chief Constable of South Yorkshire Police* [1999] 1 All ER 1 at 30-31, HL per Lord Steyn.

11 Eg *Hambrook v Stokes Bros*, supra.

12 *Bourhill v Young*, supra; *McLoughlin v O'Brian*, supra. The leading case is now in *Alcock v Chief Constable of South Yorkshire Police* [1992] 1 AC 310, [1991] 4 All ER 907, HL.

13 [1996] AC 155, [1995] 2 All ER 736, HL.

plaintiff, was a primary victim of the defendant's negligence. It was readily foreseeable that he would be exposed to personal injury, and physical and psychiatric harm were not to be regarded as different kinds of damage. Once injury to a *primary* victim is foreseeable; he can recover both for any actual physical harm that he suffers and for any recognised psychiatric illness ensuing from the defendant's breach of duty. Even so, in the case of both primary and secondary victims of psychiatric harm, damages are available only in relation to a recognised psychiatric illness.

So just what kind of psychiatric disorder will give rise to a claim for damages in negligence? Until the decision in *Vernon v Bosley (No 1)*[14] the plaintiff who was a secondary victim of psychiatric harm had to show that his illness resulted from the shock to him, the trauma of witnessing or coming upon the immediate aftermath of the events injuring the primary victim. He had to establish that he suffered from post-traumatic stress disorder (PTSD). In *Vernon v Bosley* the facts were as follows:

> The plaintiff's two young children were passengers in a car driven by their nanny, the defendant, when it veered off the road and crashed into a river. The plaintiff did not witness the original accident, but was called to the scene immediately afterwards and watched unsuccessful attempts to salvage the car and rescue his children. These efforts failed and the children drowned. The plaintiff became mentally ill and his business and his marriage both failed. The defendant accepted that his illness resulted from the tragic deaths of his children but contended that his illness was caused not by the shock of what he experienced at the riverside, but by pathological grief at the loss of his family resulting in an illness called pathological grief disorder (PGD not PTSD).

The Court of Appeal held that although damages for ordinary grief and bereavement remain irrecoverable,[15] a secondary victim was entitled to recover damages for psychiatric illness where he could establish that he met the general pre-conditions for such a claim, that is a close relationship with the primary victim and proximity to the accident, and that the negligence of the defendant caused or contributed to his mental illness. The plaintiff could recover compensation regardless of whether in part his illness consisted of an abnormal grief reaction as much as post traumatic stress disorder.

A note of caution must be sounded here. The decision in *Vernon v Bosley* does not mean that every person who loses a loved one and becomes ill through grief can sue the defendant responsible for the death of the primary victim. Should a child die in a car crash in Cornwall and the news of her death, the misery of her loss, result in her grandmother in Newcastle becoming ill, no claim will lie. The grandmother cannot establish the requisite conditions limiting any claim by secondary victims. It is to these conditions, the 'control mechanisms', to which we must now turn.

The conditions for liability to a secondary victim established by analysis of the case law up to 1982 generally required that the plaintiff should be present at the scene of the accident, or very near to it, so that with his unaided senses he realised what had happened, and that generally he must be very closely related to the person suffering physical injury. Indeed in the vast majority of cases the plaintiff has been the parent of a young child.

In *McLoughlin v O'Brian*[16] the facts were as follows:

> The plaintiff's husband and three children were in a car which was involved in an accident caused by the defendants' negligence. All four of her family were injured, one so seriously that she died almost immediately. An hour afterwards a friend told her of the accident at her

14   [1997] 1 All ER 577, CA.
15   See also *Alcock v Chief Constable of South Yorkshire Police* [1991] 4 All ER 907 at 917, 925, HL.
16   [1983] 1 AC 410, [1982] 2 All ER 298, HL.

home two miles away. He drove her to the hospital where she was told of the death and saw the three injured. The plaintiff, a woman of reasonable fortitude, suffered severe shock, organic depression and a change of personality; there were numerous symptoms of a physiological character.

The Court of Appeal rejected her claim limiting the duty to avoid shock to those at or very near the scene of the accident. The House of Lords unanimously overturned their ruling. They held that the plaintiff had to establish proximity to the traumatic events but coming as she did upon the 'immediate aftermath' of the accident in which her family had been so grievously injured she was well within the scope of the duty to avoid nervous shock. Beyond that there are distinct differences of approach among their Lordships as to where to set the limits of the duty to avoid inflicting shock and in particular whether the test should be foreseeability alone or whether policy limits should be used to confine the scope of recovery for shock.

Lord Bridge and Lord Scarman appeared to favour an approach which simply relied on foreseeability.[17] If in all the circumstances, harm resulting from shock should have been reasonably foreseeable by the defendant, damages should be recoverable. There should be no special rules for nervous shock dependent either on the relationship of the plaintiff to the victim of the original physical injury or the plaintiff's own physical proximity to the accident. Policy limitations on recovery for nervous shock should be avoided. Lord Edmund-Davies disagreed, holding policy factors to be justiciable but not relevant to Mrs McLoughlin's claim.[18] Lord Wilberforce recognised '... a real need for the law to place some limit on the extent of admissible claims.'[19] He stressed the importance of the tie between the accident victim and the plaintiff and the plaintiff's proximity to the scene of the accident. In what is now the leading case on liability for psychiatric harm, *Alcock v Chief Constable of South Yorkshire Police*,[20] it was Lord Wilberforce's opinion which held sway. The facts were as follows:

> In April 1989, 95 people died and over 400 were injured when South Yorkshire police allowed an excessive number of spectators to crowd into the football ground at Hillsborough. People were quite literally crushed to death. The plaintiffs claimed damages for psychiatric illness ensuing from the horror of what had happened to their relatives (or in one case fiance). Before the House of Lords two issues were pre-eminent. Could relatives other than parents or spouses bring an action for psychiatric harm? Could those who were not at the football ground but witnessed coverage of the disaster on television recover?

(1) Their Lordships refused to prescribe rigid categories of potential plaintiffs in nervous shock claims. They held that there must generally be a close and intimate relationship between the plaintiff and the primary victim of the sort generally enjoyed by spouses and parents and children.[1] Siblings and other more remote relatives would normally fall outside such a relationship in the absence of special factors. But for instance a grandmother who had brought up a grandchild since infancy might qualify. Consequently claims by brothers, sisters and brothers-in-law failed in *Alcock*, while the claim on the part of a fiancee was allowed. Lord Ackner suggested that in cases of exceptional horror where even a reasonably strong nerved individual might suffer shock-induced psychiatric injury, even a bystander unrelated to the victim might recover.[2]

17   Ibid at 429 and 310, and 431 and 311 respectively.
18   Ibid at 428-9 and 309-10.
19   Ibid at 423 and 305.
20   [1992] 1 AC 310, [1991] 4 All ER 907, HL.
1   Ibid at 914 (per Lord Keith) at 919-20 (per Lord Ackner), at 930 (per Lord Oliver) and at 935 (per Lord Jauncey).
2   Ibid at 919. And see per Lord Oliver at 930.

(2) A degree of proximity in time and space between the plaintiff and the accident is required. The plaintiff must normally either witness the accident himself or come upon the aftermath in a very short period of time.[3] Identifying a relation several hours after death was not sufficient. Witnessing the accident via the medium of television will not generally be sufficient.[4] Parents who watched the Hillsborough disaster on television had their claims rejected. Television pictures could not normally be equated with actual sight or hearing at the event or its aftermath. The television company's code of ethics prohibits graphic coverage of individual suffering.[5] Once again there might be exceptional cases where simultaneous broadcasts of a disaster did equate to personal presence at the accident.[6] In the Court of Appeal, Nolan LJ gave the example of a balloon carrying children at some live broadcast event suddenly bursting into flames.[7]

(3) The relevant harm, the psychiatric illness must be shown to result from the trauma of the event or its immediate aftermath.[8] Psychiatric illness resulting from being informed of a loved one's death, however grisly the circumstances, is not recoverable.[9] So if a young child is crushed by falling masonry at school, and within an hour, her mother comes to her deathbed at the hospital, the mother may recover from the trauma of coming upon the immediate aftermath of the accident. But if the child's father has a heart attack when told of the girl's fate, his loss remains irrecoverable.[10] Their Lordships in *Alcock* adopted an avowedly pragmatic approach to psychiatric harm. They rejected a simplistic approach based on immovable categories of who could recover and in what circumstances. They also refused to extend liability for psychiatric harm indefinitely. Lord Oliver expressly conceded that he could not '... regard the present state of the law as either satisfactory or logically defensible'[11] and suggested Parliamentary intervention might be timely.[12] One nice point was left open. Can the primary victim himself be liable for harm caused by shock? If my daughter negligently walks in front of a two-ton lorry while shopping with me, can I sue her for my consequent illness?[13] The answer may well be yes, however unmotherly such an action might be. If, as we saw in *Ogwo v Taylor*,[14] a negligent householder is liable to firefighters injured in the fire his carelessness occasioned, why should a foolhardy *adult* daughter escape liability to horrific shock and illness she causes her mum?

Alcock might at first sight appear to have settled some firm principles delimiting liability for psychiatric harm. Alas their Lordships in reality provoked as many questions as they answered. Let us look first at liability to bystanders. Lord Ackner, as we have noted, suggested that a truly horrific disaster might entitle even unrelated bystanders

3   Ibid at 914-15 (per Lord Keith) at 920-1 (per Lord Ackner), at 930-2 (per Lord Oliver) and at 936 (per Lord Jauncey).
4   Ibid at 937.
5   Ibid at 921 (per Lord Ackner).
6   Ibid at 921 (per Lord Keith) and at 931 (per Lord Oliver).
7   [1991] 3 All ER 88 at 122.
8   After *Vernon v Bosley*, supra, it is no longer necessary that it be exclusively shock which triggered the plaintiff's illness.
9   At 914-15 (per Lord Keith) disapproving, first instance judgments in *Hevican v Ruane* [1991] 3 All ER 65; *Ravenscroft v Rederiaktieblaget Transatlantic* [1991] 3 All ER 73; revsd [1992] 2 All ER 470n, CA.
10 As it would be if his illness were precipitated by identifying his daughter at the mortuary next day.
11 Ibid at 932.
12 Ibid at 931.
13 At 932 per Lord Oliver.
14 [1988] AC 431.

to recover damages for psychiatric illness. Yet in *McFarlane v E E Caledonia Ltd*[15] the facts were as follows:

> The plaintiff witnessed the destruction of an oil rig, the Piper Alpha, from aboard a support vessel involved in attempts to rescue survivors of the explosion which tore apart the Piper Alpha. He was not himself involved in the rescue effort and was far enough away from the burning rig to avoid any personal danger. However a more horrifying spectacle than watching fellow humans burn to death on an exploding oil rig is difficult to imagine.

The Court of Appeal overturned a decision in his favour awarding him damages. A rescuer in such circumstances would have been entitled to compensation. The plaintiff was not a rescuer nor was he a participant in the terrifying event at risk himself.[16] As a bystander only, it was not foreseeable that he would suffer such shock. Stuart-Smith LJ effectively sought to close the door, left ajar in *Alcock*, on liability to bystanders. Practical and policy reasons militated against such liability – reactions to horrific events were 'entirely subjective'.[17]

White v Chief Constable of South Yorkshire Police[18] further explored the boundaries of *Alcock*. The plaintiffs were police officers who claimed damages for psychiatric illness resulting from their professional involvement in events at the Hillsborough football ground when so many died or were seriously injured in the crush at the ground. Five of the six plaintiffs assisted the injured and sought to ensure that, subsequent to the full height of the disaster, no further danger ensued to those leaving the ground. The sixth plaintiff was on duty at the mortuary. None of the plaintiffs were exposed to any personal risk of physical injury. Claims by police officers who had actually dragged dead and injured spectators from the melee and risked injury themselves had earlier been conceded and settled by the defendants. The Court of Appeal held by 2-1 that a duty of care was owed to the officers actually present at the ground.[19] First, it was said that the officers were *primary victims* of the Chief Constable's negligence. They were participants in the event, present at the ground in pursuit of their duties who were required to be there by the Chief Constable. They were (save for one of the plaintiffs) directly involved in the negligent consequences of their 'employer's'[20] failure to provide safe crowd control. Second, even if (as Henry LJ conceded) there was doubt as to the plaintiffs' status as primary victims, they could recover as secondary victims. The police officers were not there bystanders in the same category as the oilman who witnessed the Piper Alpha tragedy. They should be classified as rescuers. All the officers actually at the ground involved in assisting the injured victims might be regarded as rescuers because public policy requires a 'wide rather than a narrow definition'[1] of rescue. Only the officer on duty at the mortuary failed to qualify either as a primary victim (she was not directly involved in the initial horror) or as a rescuer. The decision provoked outrage from the many relatives of those killed and injured at Hillsborough who had been refused compensation by the judgment in *Alcock*. The House of Lords in *White v Chief Constable of South Yorkshire Police*[2] reversed the findings of the appeal court openly

15 [1994] 2 All ER 1, CA; (1995) 46 NILQ 18; (1995) 15 Legal Studies 415 and see *Hegarty v E E Caledonia Ltd* [1996] 1 Lloyd's Rep 413.
16 Ibid at 13.
17 Ibid at 14.
18 [1999] 1 All ER 1, HL overturning the judgment of the Court of Appeal sub nom *Frost v Chief Constable of South Yorkshire Police* [1997] 1 All ER 540, CA.
19 *Frost v Chief Constable of South Yorkshire Police* [1997] 1 All ER 540, CA.
20 Police officers are not technically 'employees' of the Chief Constable but for all relevant purposes their relationship with the Chief Constable may be regarded as a quasi-employment.
1   Ibid at 567.
2   [1999] 1 All ER 1.

acknowledging the argument that it would be perceived as unacceptable to compensate police officers at the ground in the course of their job and yet deny any remedy to brothers and sisters who saw their relatives die horrifically[3].

First, by a majority of 4-1,[4] their Lordships ruled that the plaintiffs were not to be classified as primary victims of the defendants' negligence. Employers' duties to safeguard their employees from personal injury form part of the ordinary rules of tort. It does not follow that a duty to avoid causing physical harm to employees necessarily imports a duty not to cause psychiatric injury. Such a duty may arise where an employee imposes such a burdensome workload that stress-related illness is readily foreseeable[5]. In such circumstances the employee is indeed a primary victim of his employer's negligence. However where the psychiatric harm results, not from anything directly done to the employee-plaintiff, but from his traumatic experience of what is done to others, he is a secondary victim, just like any other plaintiff not endangered himself but witnessing injury to others. He can thus recover only if he meets conditions set by the 'control mechanisms' in *Alcock*.[6] The Hillsborough police officers witnessed the disaster, but lacked the requisite close ties of love or affection with the victims.

Second, by a majority of only 3-2, their Lordships ruled that the plaintiff could not recover within some special broad category of 'rescuers'. Rescuers, who succumb to psychiatric illness, must meet the same conditions as other witnesses of injury to third parties. They can recover only if their illness results either from the fear of foreseeable physical injury to themselves or they meet the other conditions limiting recovery by secondary victims.

It appears, then, that *White* has attempted to close the door on further expansion of liability for psychiatric harm. Caution has become the judicial watchword once again. However, one important issue of the extent of liability to psychiatric harm has never much troubled even the more 'cautious' of the judiciary. It must be noted that the 'eggshell skull' rule applies in claims for psychiatric harm, just as it does in cases of physical injury.[7] For a claim to lie, psychiatric harm to a normal, reasonably mentally tough individual must be foreseeable. If a child is knocked off her cycle suffering minor injuries and a complete stranger, because of some pre-existing neurosis, suffers a mental breakdown, he cannot recover damages. But once some effect on a normal person is foreseeable, the fact that the degree of that effect, the extent of the illness suffered by a psychologically vulnerable plaintiff is greater than would be expected will not deny the plaintiff full compensation.[8]

As Lord Steyn admits in *White v Chief Constable of South Yorkshire*[9] '... the law on the recovery of compensation for pure psychiatric harm is a patchwork quilt of distinctions which are difficult to justify'. No student is likely to disagree with his Lordship. Even after judicial attempts to clarify the principles governing liability for psychiatric harm and package claims neatly into primary and secondary claims, loose ends remain. Reflect on the following examples.

(1) A final year student arrives home to witness her hall of residence burning to the ground. In her room are all her revision notes and the only copy of her dissertation. Unsurprisingly she succumbs to clinical depression. Can she recover damages? If the fire is caused by faulty

3   Ibid at 48 per Lord Hoffmann.
4   As in *Walker v Northumberland County Council* [1995] 1 All ER 737, (1996) 59 MLR 296.
5   See also *Hunter v British Coal Corpn* [1998] 2 All ER 97, CA (plaintiff's claim failed after he became psychiatrically ill as a result of his involvement in an incident in which an explosion killed a colleague).
6   Though see Weir [1993] CLJ 520.
7   *Brice v Brown* [1984] 1 All ER 997. And note *Vernon v Bosley* supra.
8   *Brice v Brown* [1984] 1 All ER 997.
9   [1999] 1 All ER 1 at 38.

wiring and the university can be shown to be negligent in its maintenance of the residence, could she argue she is a primary victim because her psychiatric illness is consequent on the damage to her property in respect of which she will certainly have a claim in negligence? Might she assert, if a secondary victim, 'a close tie of love and affection to her notes'. In *Attia v British Gas plc*[10], decided before *Alcock*, a woman did win damages after suffering a nervous breakdown caused by witnessing her home burn down.

(2) A second, equally unlucky, student is working in a university laboratory when an explosion rocks the building. He feels the shockwaves and hears the blast, but only minimal damage ensues in the laboratory where he is at the time. However it is immediately clear that the neighbouring laboratory has been completely destroyed and his four closest friends were working there. His fears are justified.[11] All four were killed in the blast. The surviving student succumbs to psychiatric illness. If he shows that his illness resulted from reasonable fear to himself, does he recover as a primary victim? If he admits that it was the shock of his friends' fate which triggered his illness, does he fail because of the absence of the requisite 'close tie of love and affection'.[12]

The student may be forgiven for finding this whole area of law confusing and contradictory. Reform is often called for. Three very different solutions have been advanced. Stapleton[13] advocates the abolition of recovery in tort for pure psychiatric harm. She argues the case for a return to the harsh, but clear and equitable rules, of the Victorian judges contending that 'no reasonable boundaries for the cause of action [can] be found and this [is] an embarrassment to the law'. Mullany and Handford[14] contend that no special rules should limit claims for psychiatric illness. Foreseeability of psychiatric injury should be the only condition of recovery of compensation. The Law Commission recommends a 'middle way'[15]. The condition that secondary victims enjoy a close tie of love or affection with the individual who suffers physical harm would stay. All other 'control mechanisms' would go.

SECTION 3.   POLICY AND PUBLIC INTEREST

The ebb and flow of judicial readiness to limit liability for foreseeable harm by invoking 'public policy' is at the core of the discussion in both this and the previous chapter. Let us clarify one issue first. The concept of public policy applied by the courts to limit duties of care in tort has in many cases little to do with the public interest in the sense of public morality. Policy, as we have seen it in operation so far in tort, is concerned far more with the following factors:

1   Is the imposition of a duty in the relevant circumstances feasible and enforceable? Harm to my neighbour's person or property is easily foreseeable if I leave my home so insecure that a burglar or a rapist can use my house to gain a concealed exit to hers. But what steps am I required to take to secure her safety?

2   Is the imposition of a duty fair? When is the law properly to demand that X safeguards the interests of Y rather than requiring Y to take care of himself? So both in the judgments relating to liability for vandals and burglars obtaining entry

10   [1988] QB 304, [1987] 3 All ER 455, CA.
11   For a case on broadly analagous facts, where the plaintiff succeeded see *Dooley v Cammell Laird & Co Ltd* [1951] 1 Lloyd's Rep 271.
12   Unless perhaps one of the dead students is his fiancée?
13   'In restraint of tort' in P Birks (ed) *Frontiers of Liability* (1994) 83.
14   *Tort Liability for Psychiatric Damage: The Law of Nervous Shock* (1993); and see 'Hillsborough Replayed' (1998) 113 LQR 410. A similar case is eloquently advanced by Teff in 'Liability for Negligently Inflicted Psychiatric Harm; Justifications and Boundaries' (1998) 57 CLJ 91.
15   *Liability for Psychiatric Illness* Law Com No 249 (1998).

to neighbouring property, and the decisions on the exercise of statutory powers, judicial policy has come down on the side of individual responsibility rather than promoting a broad duty of 'community care' for each other.

3   What are the implications for insurance cover of extending the scope of duty situations?

This factor is rarely voiced publicly but is crucial. Extending duties of care to cover deserving cases is all very well in the abstract, but futile if the defendant lacks funds to pay any damages. Insurance cover requires some certainty in defining the scope of potential liability in order to set realistic premiums and to delineate the conditions of the policy. So as we have seen in claims for psychiatric harm the range of possible victims suffering grief or distress as a result of a relative or friend's injury or death is more or less unlimited. The law to a greater or lesser extent, dependent on the current judicial trends, imposes arbitrary limits.[16] Feasibility, fairness and stability are the key policy issues usually invoked by the courts in tort. They are criteria designed to attempt to create a balanced framework defining the relationships between individuals in society. They are concerned with where X stands in relation to his 'neighbour' Y. Of course in utilising concepts of fairness, of what is 'just and reasonable' social judgments are made. For example, the promotion of the virtue of self-reliance is taken for granted. But in general in the majority of cases so far considered no obvious and fundamental moral or ethical issues have been at stake.

How will the courts approach the issue of the imposition of a duty of care where genuinely moral questions are posed? Two examples of denying the existence of a duty in such cases have already been touched on. The courts have refused to recognise a duty of care owed by one participant in crime to another. In *Clunis v Camden and Islington Health Authority*[17] the Court of Appeal went further and said that a remedy in tort can never arise from the plaintiff's own criminal act. And in *McKay v Essex Area Health Authority*[18] the Court of Appeal refused to impose a duty to a child to terminate her existence before her birth.

Yet in a number of other decisions the courts have shown themselves unwilling to mount the unruly horse of public policy in claims where the policy factors raised were essentially matters of public morality and society's values. The applicability of this sort of public interest limitation on the scope of the tort of negligence has been tested in a series of cases concerning whether damages are recoverable in respect of the birth of an unplanned baby subsequent to a negligently performed sterilisation. At first, in *Udale v Bloomsbury Area Health Authority*,[19] Jupp J refused the mother compensation towards the upkeep of the child despite the defendant's admission of negligence. He limited her damages to compensation for the discomfort of her pregnancy. The birth of a child was, he said, a 'blessing' and the financial cost of such a 'blessing'[20] was irrecoverable. It offended society's notions of what is right and the value afforded to human life, and the knowledge that his parents had claimed damages in respect of his birth might distress and damage the child emotionally as he grew to maturity.

A year later the Court of Appeal in *Emeh v Kensington Area Health Authority*[1] overruled Jupp J on the policy issue. They were unconvinced that the policy objections should prevent recovery of damages. There might be an incentive to late abortions. The unity of the family and the welfare of the child might well be strengthened not

---

16 See *White v Chief Constable of South Yorkshire Police*, supra at 48-49 per Lord Hoffmann.

17 [1998] QB 978, [1998] 3 All ER 180; discussed supra at p 105.

18 [1982] QB 1166, [1982] 2 All ER 771, CA supra at p 196.

19 [1983] 2 All ER 522, [1983] 1 WLR 1098.

20 '... I would have to regard the financial disadvantages as offset by her gratitude for the gift of a boy after four girls'! ibid per Jupp J at 531 and 1109 respectively.

1   [1985] QB 1012, [1984] 3 All ER 1044.

harmed by financial help with his upkeep. Above all their Lordships expressed a disinclination to place limits on the scope of the duty owed to the mother by reference to what was 'socially unacceptable'. That exercise, echoing Lord Scarman in *McLoughlin v O'Brian*, they preferred to leave to Parliament.[2]

The decision in *Emeh* prompts a number of questions. Will the judicial tendency manifested in *Emeh* to avoid questions of social policy as devices to limit duty-situations survive the new activist tendency to invoke policy more readily, recently exhibited by the House of Lords in *White*[3]? How should the loss of which Mrs Emeh complained properly be classified? Was it harm to the person, simply another consequence of the bungled sterilisation along with the discomfort and danger of her unwanted pregnancy? Or is it more properly to be regarded as economic loss on a par with wasted expenditure and/or loss of profits? In *Goodwill v British Pregnancy Advisory Service*[4] the plaintiff sued the clinic which she alleged failed to warn her lover of the potential failure rate of vasectomy. Their relationship began some time after his surgery. Nonetheless she contended that, had he been adequately advised by the defendant, he would have communicated the relevant information to her so that she would then have taken appropriate contraceptive precautions. She contended that the birth of her child was a consequence of the defendants' negligence. Holding that the defendants owed no duty of care to the plaintiff, the Court of Appeal treated her claim as a claim for economic loss, for the financial loss occasioned to her by unplanned maternity. The defendants were not liable because the plaintiff was not a person whom they could be expected to identify as immediately affected by the services they rendered to her lover. The man's future sexual partners were not persons for whose benefit the vasectomy was performed. Classifying failed sterilisation as economic loss to the parent(s), whether that claim succeeds or not, has a certain logic to it. The main purpose of compensation will be to meet the costs of raising the child. Yet the question also highlights the fragile boundary between different types of loss. Were a woman to become pregnant, subsequent to a failed sterilisation, and that pregnancy makes her so ill she could not resume her previous paid work how ought we to classify her loss? Were the birth of the child to trigger such a profound psychosis that for several years she had to employ nannies around the clock to care for the child, would the ensuing loss be physical injury, psychiatric harm, or economic loss?

SECTION 4.   PHYSICAL DAMAGE TO PROPERTY

Recognition of a duty to avoid proximate physical damage to another's property, as much as to his person, raises no unique problem of principle.[5] Should a negligent driver manage by the narrowest of margins to prevent his vehicle actually injuring the first named author, but the impact does ruin her new Parisienne dress, she may recover the cost of the dress without problems. Should the careless driver, swerving to avoid her, crash into the second named author's front wall, he may recover the cost of repairing the wall. Whether the damaged property comprises chattels or real property, a duty not to inflict that kind of harm arises in appropriate circumstances although quite often

2   At 1021 and 1053 respectively and see *Scuriaga v Powell* (1979) 123 Sol Jo 406 (damages in contract for birth of child after failed abortion); and *Thake v Maurice* [1986] QB 644, [1986] 1 All ER 497, CA; *Gold v Haringey Health Authority* [1988] QB 481, [1987] 2 All ER 888, CA.
3   Particularly in their frank admission that compensating police officers but not relatives was unacceptable.
4   [1996] 2 All ER 161, [1996] 1 WLR 1397, CA.
5   But note foreseeability alone is not enough; see *Marc Rich & Co AG v British Rock Marine Co Ltd* [1996] AC 211, [1995] 3 All ER 307, HL discussed supra at p 178.

where the parties are literally neighbours the source of the action may lie in nuisance rather than negligence simpliciter.[6]

The class of persons to whom a duty in respect of damage to property is owed and the manner in which harm is classified as physical damage to property as opposed to 'pure' economic loss do however call for careful consideration. The House of Lords in *Leigh and Sillivan Ltd v Aliakmon Shipping Co Ltd*[7] confirmed the rule that a duty in respect of loss or damage to property is owed only to a person having '… legal ownership of or a possessory title to the property concerned at the time when the loss or damage occurred'. Should an old house in the process of conversion to flats be destroyed by a fire caused by negligence, only the owner of the house, or a tenant, may recover compensation. The builders, the plumbers, the decorators all of whom lose out on valuable contracts to convert the property are left remediless. Contractual rights in relation to property may well be adversely affected by loss or damage to that property, but they are insufficient to give rise to a duty of care.

Where the plaintiff has the necessary title to the damaged property the further question arises of how harm is classified. All harm, be it personal injuries or physical damage to property, is quantified in economic terms. What loss of earnings did the plaintiff's injuries occasion him? How much is it going to cost to repair or replace a damaged wall? What test then can be applied to determine if harm is primarily physical, or solely economic, so taking it into the problematic field of the limited scope of the duty to avoid 'pure' economic loss?

It has always been clear that physical damage to, or defects in, property which simply render it less than value for money, but *not* dangerous, will be classified as economic loss. So if you buy a central heating boiler which heats the house inefficiently and at vast expense the loss you suffer is economic loss alone, readily recoverable in contract, but subject to restrictive rules in tort. Where the defective property is dangerous, however, a line of authority relating to buildings contended that if there was imminent danger of damage to person or other property, the cost of rectifying the defect and avoiding the danger could be categorised as physical damage, albeit that no tangible physical damage had yet materialised.[8] The decision of the House of Lords in *Murphy v Brentwood District Council*[9] rejected that line of authority as close to heresy. Physical damage means just what it says, actual physical harm to persons or other property such as wounds, disease, or crumbling masonry shattering furniture. Where no such damage has materialised the loss caused by the need to repair defective property, to obviate the danger, constitutes economic loss.

In *Murphy* itself the plaintiff had purchased a house built on an in-filled site over a concrete raft foundation. In 1981 he discovered cracks in the house threatening the whole fabric of the property. Had he done nothing the house might have collapsed on top of him. He sued the local council for negligently approving the plans for the foundations. The House of Lords held (inter alia) that the council could not be liable unless the builder would have been so liable.[10] The first question to address was what was the nature of the plaintiff's loss. Their Lordships conceded that a builder of premises

6   [1986] AC 785, [1986] 2 All ER 145; and see *The Mineral Transporter* [1986] AC 1, [1985] 2 All ER 935, PC; *Tate and Lyle Industries Ltd v Greater London Council* [1983] 2 AC 509, [1983] 1 All ER 1159, HL.
7   Ibid at 149; *Simaan General Contracting Co v Pilkington Glass Ltd (No 2)* [1988] QB 758, [1988] 1 All ER 791, CA.
8   *Batty v Metropolitan Property Realisations Ltd* [1978] QB 554, [1978] 2 All ER 445, CA; *Anns v Merton London Borough Council* [1978] AC 728, [1977] 2 All ER 492, HL.
9   [1991] 1 AC 398, [1990] 2 All ER 908.
10   For direct authority on the liability of builders see *Department of the Environment v Thomas Bates & Son Ltd* [1991] 1 AC 499, [1990] 2 All ER 943, HL.

is subject to the same duty of care in tort as the manufacturers of chattels to 'avoid injury through defects in the premises to the person or property of those whom he should have in contemplation as likely to suffer such injury if care is not taken'.[11] So, to illustrate the points made, if the ceiling had actually collapsed on Mr Murphy, injuring him, his family and his dinner guests or destroying his piano, all might have had a claim for personal injuries (or property damage) against the builder. However unless and until such actual physical damage has occurred the cost of making the house safe and/ or any diminution in the value of the property is purely economic.

One matter must be made clear. Mr Murphy's house at the time of his action was already suffering from serious cracks in the internal walls. Physical damage, you might have thought. Not so. For that damage was damage to, and defects in, the very property in question; it was not a case of the defective property causing damage to quite separate property. In an earlier judgment of the House of Lords it had been suggested that where there was a 'complex structure', defects in one part of the structure causing damage to some other part might be regarded as having damaged 'other property.[12] In *Murphy* any such doctrine is abandoned.[13] Be it premises or chattels, property is to be regarded as an integral whole. You cannot argue that the damage done when defects in the roof cause cracks in the bedroom walls constitutes damage to other property. Only if some distinct and separate item, not part and parcel of the overall structure, causes damage is the requirement of damage to other property satisfied. An example may help. You purchase a house built by X. The central heating system was installed by Y. Some months after you move in (but while fortunately you are not at home) an explosion damages the house. You retain a right of action against Y for his negligently manufactured item has damaged a separate property, the house itself.[14]

There can be some strange consequences in applying the *Murphy* doctrine. Assume an impecunious houseowner becomes aware of the worsening condition of her property. But she does nothing about it because she cannot afford to pay for the necessary repairs. Several months later the house collapses injuring her and damaging her priceless set of Law Reports. It seems she may then sue to recover compensation for that physical damage.[15] But the 'imminent danger' doctrine suffered from a similar anomaly as Lord Bridge pointed out.[16] If you became aware of defects in the house at an early stage, before they posed any danger, the cost of repair was irrecoverable. The longer you waited to carry out repairs, the greater the cost. Did you have to wait till conditions were so bad that the 'imminent danger' conferred a right of action? It should be noted that for the most part Commonwealth jurisdictions have declined to follow the *Murphy* 'doctrine' and allowed plaintiffs in circumstances analogous to Mr Murphy's to succeed.[17]

---

11   Supra at 916 (per Lord Keith). Note that the question of the liability of the council even for physical injury was left open.
12   In *D & F Estates Ltd v Church Comrs for England* [1988] 2 All ER 992 at 1006-7 (per Lord Bridge).
13   Supra at 926-8 (per Lord Bridge himself); at 932-3 (per Lord Oliver); at 942 (per Lord Jauncey).
14   Ibid at 928 (per Lord Bridge).
15   See *Nitrigin Eireann Teoranta v Inco Alloys Ltd* [1992] 1 All ER 854; would the defendant be able to plead contributory negligence?
16   Supra at 429.
17   See eg *Invercargill City Council v Hamlin* [1996] AC 624, [1996] 1 All ER 756.

SECTION 5. 'PURE' ECONOMIC LOSS

Classifying the plaintiff's loss as purely economic does not preclude recovery of that loss, but will require that the plaintiff convince the court that the defendant owed him a duty to safeguard him against just that sort of loss. And as we have noted earlier,[18] the courts are generally much less willing to find the existence of such a duty than a duty to protect others from physical injury or damage. As Lord Fraser put it in *The Mineral Transporter Ltd*[19] '... some limit or control mechanism has to be imposed on the liability of a wrongdoer towards those who have suffered economic damage as a consequence of his negligence.' This restrictive approach to economic loss means this today in practice. Economic loss is recoverable only when the plaintiff can establish that within a 'special relationship' between them, the defendant assumed responsibility for the plaintiff's economic welfare.[20] The defendant must be proven to have undertaken responsibility for the plaintiff from the financial loss of which he complains. Where no such 'special relationship' exists, a stream of case law makes it clear that economic loss is irrecoverable however readily foreseeable that loss may be and however 'unfair' the plaintiff's plight may seem. Within the magic 'special relationship', liability may arise just as readily from the performance of services for the benefit of the plaintiff as the making of statements or giving of advice. However historical development of the law in this area makes it simpler to begin by examining economic loss resulting from inaccurate statements and information.

(A) STATEMENTS AND 'SPECIAL RELATIONSHIPS'

Two difficulties beset the imposition of any duty to avoid making careless statements. There is, first, the difference between words and acts. As Lord Reid put it in *Hedley Byrne & Co Ltd v Heller & Partners Ltd*:[1]

> Quite careful people often express definite opinions on social or informal occasions, even when they see that others are likely to be influenced by them; and they often do that without taking that care which they would take if asked for their opinion professionally, or in a business connection.

And moreover, while negligent acts will generally have a limited range of impact, negligent words may be widely broadcast without the consent or foresight of the speaker.

Where physical damage has resulted from careless statements the courts have shown less reluctance to impose a duty of care.[2] So a doctor whose negligent certification of the plaintiff as a person of unsound mind led to his detention in a mental hospital was held liable in negligence as long ago as 1927.[3] Nevertheless, whenever it is contended

18 At pp 177-178. And see generally (1991) 107 LQR 249; [1993] CLJ 437; (1995) 111 LQR 301.
19 [1985] 2 All ER 935 at 945; and note *White v Chief Constable of South Yorkshire Police* [1999] 1 All ER 1 at 31 (per Lord Steyn).
20 *Williams v Natural Life Health Foods Ltd* [1998] 2 All ER 577, HL; *Henderson v Merrett Syndicates Ltd* [1995] 2 AC 145, [1994] 3 All ER 506, HL.
1 [1964] AC 465 at 487, [1963] 2 All ER 575 at 580.
2 See *Sharp v Avery and Kerwood* [1938] 4 All ER 85, CA (defendant cyclist negligently performed his undertaking to guide the vehicle in which the plaintiff was a passenger; liable to the plaintiff for his ensuing injuries); and see *Bird v Pearce* (1979) 77 LGR 753, CA; *Clayton v Woodman & Son (Builders) Ltd* [1961] 3 All ER 249 (revsd on other grounds [1962] 2 All ER 33, CA) (careless instruction on how to proceed with building work resulting in physical harm to the bricklayer).
3 *De Freville v Dill* (1927) 96 LJKB 1056.

that a duty lies in respect of careless words, spoken or written, the criteria more usually invoked to limit liability for words inflicting economic loss must sometimes also be borne in mind in relation to physical damage. Should a colleague, late at night at a University party, complain to the Professor of Surgery of giddiness and nausea, she cannot sue if he mistakenly suggests that she has had too much to drink rather than diagnosing the heart disease of which she dies a couple of days later. That said, the problems of liability for careless statements resulting in economic loss are still much more substantial.

The development of the duty to avoid statements causing pecuniary loss is inextricably linked to the troubled history of liability for economic loss in general. The original difficulty relating to pecuniary loss resulting from careless statements was this. A person suffering economic loss through relying on a fraudulent statement could sue in the tort of deceit. In *Derry v Peek*[4] the House of Lords had held that to establish deceit the plaintiff must prove fraud—that the defendant knew that his statement was untrue, or was reckless as to its untruth. Negligence was insufficient. In *Candler v Crane, Christmas & Co*[5] the Court of Appeal relied on *Derry v Peek* to refuse a remedy to the plaintiff who had invested funds in a company on the basis of accounts negligently prepared by the defendant. Without evidence of fraud they held that economic loss resulting from misstatement was irrecoverable.

The fallacy inherent in *Candler v Crane, Christmas & Co* was exposed by the House of Lords in the landmark judgment in 1963, *Hedley Byrne & Co Ltd v Heller & Partners Ltd*.[6]

> The plaintiffs asked their bankers to inquire into the financial stability of a company with which they were having business dealings. Their bankers made inquiries of the company's bankers, who carelessly gave favourable references about the company. Reliance on these references caused the plaintiffs to lose £17,000. The plaintiffs sued the defendants for their careless statements. The action failed because the defendants had expressly disclaimed any responsibility.

Nevertheless all five Law Lords proceeded to re-examine the authorities on liability for careless statements. They rightly limited the rule in *Derry v Peek* to its proper function of defining the limits of the tort of deceit and thus held it to be irrelevant to the issue of whether a duty of care arose in negligence. Nor did the absence of a contract deny the plaintiff a remedy. As Lord Devlin said:[7]

> A promise given without consideration to perform a service cannot be enforced as a contract by the promisee, but if the service is in fact performed and done negligently the promisee can recover in an action in tort.

But their Lordships were not prepared simply to recognise a duty of care in respect of statements on the basis of the *Donoghue v Stevenson* neighbour principle alone. For liability for statements resulting in economic loss to be imposed, some narrower test than the foreseeability of the loss must be satisfied.[8] The House of Lords was not prepared to formulate rules which might expose a maker of careless statements to liability to a large indeterminate class of plaintiffs. For instance, newspapers were not to be accountable to everybody who read their advice columns and suffered loss through relying on their negligent advice.[9] The plaintiff to recover for negligent misstatements,

4   (1889) 14 App Cas 337, HL and see p 120, ante.
5   [1951] 2 KB 164, [1951] 1 All ER 426, CA (but see the powerful judgment of Denning LJ).
6   [1964] AC 465, [1963] 2 All ER 575, HL.
7   Ibid at 526 and 608 respectively.
8   See per Lord Reid at 483 and 580 and per Lord Pearce at 537 and 616.
9   [1971] AC 793, [1975] 1 All ER 150, PC.

must establish that the statement was made within a relationship where the plaintiff could reasonably rely on the skill and care of the defendant in making the statement. He must show some 'special relationship' with the defendant which properly resulted in the defendant undertaking responsibility for the accuracy of the statements made.

What sorts of relationships did later case-law find to be sufficiently special? Lord Diplock in the Privy Council case of *Mutual Life and Citizens' Assurance Co Ltd v Evatt*[10] made an early attempt to narrow the scope of liability for misstatements. Liability should arise only in the context of certain professional relationships where giving advice was the primary purpose of the relationship. So solicitors would be responsible for legal advice offered to clients, and stockbrokers for financial guidance, but an insurance company volunteering financial advice to a policy holder should not be liable. The Court of Appeal largely ignored *Evatt*. So in *Chaudhry v Prabhakar*[11] the defendant who considered himself something of an expert on motor cars was held liable to his friend whom he agreed to assist with the purchase of the car when his advice proved woefully inadequate and negligent. The trend up until 1989 appeared to be to allow a liberal interpretation of what constituted a special relationship.

Two decisions of the House of Lords outline the parameters of liability for economic loss arising from negligent advice, *Caparo Industries plc v Dickman*[12] and *Smith v Bush*.[13] Although *Caparo* was actually decided subsequently to *Smith v Bush*, it may help to consider *Caparo* first.

> The defendants were the auditors who acted for Fidelity plc. They had prepared annual accounts on the strength of which Caparo (the plaintiff) bought shares in Fidelity and then mounted a successful takeover bid. Caparo alleged that the accounts were inaccurate and misleading showing a pre-tax profit of £1.3m when they should have recorded a loss of £400,000. Had Caparo been aware of the true state of affairs they would never have bid for Fidelity.

The House of Lords found against Caparo on a preliminary point of law. The auditors owed no duty of care in respect of the accuracy of the accounts either to members of the public who relied on the accounts to invest in the company or to any individual existing shareholder who similarly relied on those accounts to increase his shareholding.[14] Auditors prepare accounts, not to promote the interests of potential investors, but to assist the shareholders collectively to exercise their right to control over the company.[15] Four conditions must be met for a defendant to be liable for economic loss resulting from negligent advice or information. (1) The defendant must be *fully* aware of the nature of the transaction which the plaintiff had in contemplation as a result of receipt of the information. (2) He must either have communicated that information to the plaintiff directly, or well know that it will be communicated to him (or a restricted class of persons of which the plaintiff is an identifiable member). (3) He must specifically anticipate that the plaintiff will *properly* and *reasonably* rely on that information when deciding whether or not to engage in the transaction in question. (4) Finally, the purpose for which the plaintiff does rely on that information must be a purpose connected with interests which it is reasonable to demand that the defendants protect.

---

10 [1971] AC 793, [1975] 1 All ER 150, PC.
11 [1988] 3 All ER 718, CA; and see also *Esso Petroleum Co Ltd v Mardon* [1976] QB 801, CA.
12 [1990] 2 AC 605, [1990] 1 All ER 568, HL.
13 [1990] 1 AC 831, [1989] 2 All ER 514, HL.
14 The Court of Appeal had held that existing shareholders were owed such a duty distinguishing the shareholder investors from other members of the public: [1989] 1 All ER 798.
15 [1990] 1 All ER 568 at 580-1 (per Lord Bridge); at 600-1 (per Lord Oliver).

No duty is owed to all potential investors for such a duty would in truth result in unlimited liability. If auditors were liable to *any* investor who relied on the published accounts to deal with the company simply because such conduct is foreseeable, they would equally be liable to anyone else who dealt with the company to his detriment, for example, to banks lending the company money or tradesmen extending credit terms.[16] Caparo sought to argue that the vulnerability of Fidelity to takeover should have alerted the auditors to the likelihood of a company, such as Caparo, mounting a takeover bid, and that they were not just *any* potential investor, but existing shareholders. Their Lordships held that the defendants were under no duty to safeguard the economic interests of predators,[17] and that the statutory duty imposed on them by Parliament was to protect the interests, and existing holdings of, the shareholders in the client company,[18] and not to facilitate investment decisions whether by existing shareholders or others.

A positive avalanche of cases on the limits of *Hedley Byrne* liability followed *Caparo*. We give just a few examples[19] to illustrate the application of the *Caparo* principles. Thus it was held (inter alia) that directors of a company who issued a prospectus to invite shareholders to take up a rights issue were not under a duty to those shareholders who relied on the prospectus to make further investments.[20] Nor were accountants advising a creditor company on the appointment of a receiver liable to that company's debtors.[1] In both cases the relationship between the parties lacked the necessary proximity. The defendants had done nothing to make themselves responsible for the financial welfare of the plaintiffs. But what if some express representation has been made directly to the plaintiff on the basis of which he argues he then decided to go ahead with a particular transaction? Much may turn on the facts of the case. In *James McNaughton Paper Groups v Hicks Anderson*[2] the defendant accountants became aware that the plaintiffs were considering a takeover of their clients. At a meeting between the two companies the defendants were asked to confirm the accuracy of draft accounts which they did in very general terms. The Court of Appeal found that no duty was owed to the plaintiffs. The draft accounts were not prepared for their benefit, and the defendants would reasonably expect a party to a takeover bid to take independent advice and not rely exclusively on draft accounts. However, where it was pleaded that the defendants had prepared profit forecasts expressly designed to induce the plaintiffs to increase their bid for a company at risk of takeover the Court of Appeal refused to strike out the claim, and ordered a full trial on the facts.[3]

Perhaps the key question in this sort of case is whether advice given by the defendant has been given in a context in which the assumption that plaintiffs should generally look after their own financial interests can be displaced. Have the defendants in effect induced the plaintiffs to place faith in their judgment? Thus in *Henderson v Merrett Syndicates Ltd*[4] managing agents at Lloyds who placed monies entrusted to them by Names at Lloyds in underwriting contracts owed a duty of care to 'their' Names.

16 See *Al Saudi Banque v Clark Pixley* [1990] Ch 313, [1989] 3 All ER 361.
17 Why should auditors be responsible for the success of those actively seeking to destroy their client?
18 As to whether an existing shareholder might sue if his existing proprietary interest was damaged by negligence on the part of the auditors (ie be sold at an undervalue) see Lord Bridge [1990] 1 All ER 568 at 580-1 (probably yes) and Lord Oliver at 601 (leaving the question open).
19 See further *Clerk & Lindsell* paras 7-61-7-87.
20 *Al-Nakib Investments (Jersey) Ltd v Longcroft* [1990] 3 All ER 321.
1   *Huxford v Stoy Hayward & Co* (1989) 5 BCC 421.
2   [1991] 2 QB 113, [1991] 1 All ER 134, CA.
3   *Morgan Crucible v Hill Samuel Bank Ltd* [1991] 1 All ER 148, CA.
4   [1995] 2 AC 145 HL, see (1997) 17 Legal Studies 169. As to concurrent liability in tort and contract see supra at p 196.

The agents undertook responsibility for advising the plaintiff and finding appropriate investments for their money. They in effect 'took over' the plaintiffs financial affairs. *Williams v Natural Life Health Food Ltd*[5] is an instructive case. The second defendant set up a company to franchise health food business and run his own shop. The plaintiffs approached the company to obtain a franchise. Having received a glowing brochure and prospectus which included testimonies to the second defendant's experience and success, the plaintiffs went ahead and obtained a franchise. At no stage in the pre-contractual negotiations did they have any contact with the second defendant personally. The enterprise was a disaster and the plaintiffs' shop failed to make money, resulting in severe financial loss to the plaintiffs. They sued the company and the second defendant. The company went into liquidation so the action proceeded against the second defendant alone. The House of Lords found that there was no special relationship between him and the plaintiffs because there were no personal dealings between them and neither directly nor indirectly did the second defendant convey to the plaintiffs that he assumed personal responsibility for their affairs nor was there evidence that the plaintiffs relied on his personal undertakings to safeguard their economic well-being as franchisers. The dealings were all with the company. Unlike the Lloyds' agents, the defendant took no role as an individual in 'managing' the plaintiffs' business interests.

We move now to look at *Smith v Bush*. Note that in *Caparo*[6] Lord Oliver described *Smith v Bush*[7] as the outer limit of *Hedley Byrne* liability.

> The defendant surveyors acting for the mortgagees gave favourable reports on properties to be purchased by the plaintiff mortgagors. Express disclaimers denied any liability to the mortgagors.[8] Nonetheless the evidence was that 90% of house purchasers do in fact rely on the mortgagees' report[9] and do not engage their own surveyor. The mortgagor paid the surveyor's fee and the defendants were well aware that the mortgagors (of whose identity they were apprised) would rely on the report and would suffer loss if that report were negligently prepared.

The House of Lords unanimously found that in such circumstances a duty of care is owed to the mortgagors. Unlike in *Caparo* the defendants were well aware of the identity of the plaintiffs, knew that their advice would be transmitted to the plaintiffs and appreciated exactly how the plaintiffs would act in reliance on that advice. There was no element of uncertainty relating to the transaction consequent on that advice. There was no question of liability other than to one identifiable plaintiff.[10] There was no conflict between the interests of the surveyors' client and the mortgagors. If the surveyors did

5   [1998] 2 All ER 577, [1998] 1 WLR 830, HL.
6   [1998] 2 All ER 577 at 598.
7   [1990] 1 AC 831, [1989] 2 All ER 514, HL.
8   The disclaimers were found to fall foul of ss 2, 11 and 13 of the Unfair Contract Terms Act 1977; scc post at p 300.
9   *Smith v Bush* was a consolidated appeal concerning two separate plaintiffs. In one case the mortgagee showed the actual report to the plaintiff. In the other, the report itself was not disclosed to the plaintiff.
10   The likelihood that *a* purchaser may emerge in the future who will suffer loss if a survey is carelessly conducted is insufficient. A particular individual who will almost inevitably place faith in the report and act to his detriment must be within the defendant's contemplation: see *The Morning Watch* [1990] 1 Lloyd's Rep 547. Contrast *Smith v Bush* with *Goodwill v British Pregnancy Advisory Service* [1996] 2 All ER 161, CA (no liability to a subsequent partner of a man whose vasectomy failed; the plaintiff argued had her lover been properly advised of the risk of failure she would have been told and taken suitable precautions; Gibson LJ doubted that she could be considered an identifiable plaintiff; 'The defendants could know nothing about the likely course of action of future sexual partners').

the job properly and produced a proper valuation they discharged their duty to both mortgagee and mortgagor. The plaintiffs who paid their fees were properly entitled to rely on their professional skill and advice.[11] It is important of course to remember that proof of a duty to act carefully in giving advice or information is only the first stage in the claim. Claims will fail for the same reason as other actions in negligence. Want of care may not be proved.[12] Or the plaintiff may fail to show that his loss resulted from the defendant's carelessness.[13] If the plaintiff, albeit he believed the information, would have acted as he did regardless of the defendant's negligence his loss is not caused by that negligence.[14] One peculiarity relating to the duty to avoid careless statements is the immunity afforded to one class of professionals. Barristers are on policy grounds immune from liability for negligent advice given in the course of litigation.[15]

(B)   THE EXTENDED *HEDLEY BYRNE* PRINCIPLE

What then is the basis of *Hedley Byrne* liability? Lord Griffiths, in *Smith v Bush*, dismissed as unhelpful the notion that liability rests on an assumption of responsibility by the defendant.[16] Indeed the defendants in *Smith v Bush* manifested every intention to the contrary attempting expressly to disclaim liability. A duty, Lord Griffiths argued, can arise, not only where the defendant either expressly or implicitly undertakes responsibility to the plaintiff for advice or information, but also where the particular relationship between the two is such that it is just that the defendant be subject to such responsibility.[17] Lord Griffiths' criticism of any principle of assumption of responsibility was strongly supported by a number of academic commentators.[18] However subsequent decisions of the House of Lords forcefully endorse assumption of responsibility as the basis of an extended *Hedley Byrne* principle which embraces negligent performance of services as much as negligent statements and advice.[19] Subsequently other Law Lords have given more credence to assumption of responsibility as the fundamental basis of *Hedley Byrne* liability. Lord Goff in *Henderson v Merrett Syndicates Ltd*[20] rested his finding of liability on the part of the managing

---

11 Lord Griffiths and Lord Jauncey both make references to the reasonableness of purchasers at the lower end of the market relying on the building society survey rather than facing the additional expense of an independent report. Yet *Smith v Bush* has been applied to a property worth £100,000 in *Beaumont v Humberts* [1990] 49 EG 46, CA. Is the value of the property perhaps more relevant to the validity and reasonableness of any disclaimer rather than whether a duty is owed at all? See post at p 301.

12 *Stafford v Conti Commodity Services Ltd* [1981] 1 All ER 691; *Argy Trading Developments Co Ltd v Lapid Developments Ltd* [1977] 3 All ER 785, [1977] 1 WLR 444.

13 *Banque Financière de la Cité v Westgate Insurance Ltd* [1991] 2 AC 249, [1990] 2 All ER 947, HL (note that their Lordships also found no duty in that case).

14 *J E B Fasteners Ltd v Marks, Bloom & Co* [1983] 1 All ER 583, CA (plaintiff failed to prove that he relied on negligently prepared accounts when making his investment). And see *Williams v Natural Life Health Foods Ltd* supra at 836.

15 *Rondel v Worsley* [1969] 1 AC 191, [1967] 3 All ER 993, HL; *Saif Ali v Mitchell (Sydney) & Co* [1980] AC 198, [1977] 3 All ER 1033, HL (immunity extends to pre-trial work intimately connected with the case in court and extends to solicitor-advocates too).

16 At 865 confirming the judgment of the Court of Appeal in *Ministry of Housing and Local Government v Sharp* [1970] 2 QB 223, [1970] 1 All ER 1009.

17 See *Al Saudi Banque v Clark Pixley* [1989] 3 All ER 361 at 367 (per Millet J) (there should either be an assumption of responsibility or a relationship 'equivalent to contract').

18 See, for example, Barker 'Unreliable Assumptions in the Modern Law of Negligence' (1993) 109 LQR 461; Hepple 'The Search for Coherence' (1997) 50 Current Legal Problems 69; Cane *Tort Law and Economic Interests* (2nd edn, 1996).

19 *Williams v Natural Life Health Foods Ltd* [1998] 2 All ER 577, HL.

20 [1995] 2 AC 145 at 182.

agents on their assumption of responsibility towards those who relied on their special expertise in underwriting. In *White v Jones,*[1] Lord Browne-Wilkinson affirmed the importance to *Hedley Byrne* liability of discovering whether the defendant had assumed responsibility for the advice or task undertaken to benefit the plaintiff. He stressed that what is crucial is a '… a conscious assumption of responsibility for the *task* rather than a conscious assumption of legal responsibility to the plaintiff for its careful performance' (our emphasis). Lord Browne-Wilkinson's analysis may help to clarify the apparent paradoxes of *Hedley Byrne* liability. The defendants in *Caparo* neither did, nor could be expected to, assume responsibility for the profitability of the plaintiffs' takeover bid. The defendants in *Smith v Bush* might well have wished to avoid *legal* responsibility to the purchasers but their relationship with the purchasers was such that they did undertake responsibility to provide an accurate valuation of the property and it was readily foreseeable and just what might be expected that the purchasers would rely on that valuation.

Case law since *Hedley Byrne,* in particular the three recent decisions of the Law Lords in *Henderson v Merrett Syndicates Ltd, White v Jones* and *Williams v Natural Life Ltd,* has confirmed that *Hedley Byrne* opened the doors to much greater availability of redress for economic loss in tort than had previously been available. In *Hedley Byrne* itself Lord Devlin stated:

> Cases may arise in the future in which a new and wider proposition, quite independent of contract, will be needed. There may, for example, be cases in which a statement is not supplied for the use of any particular individual.[2]

Seeking to extend yet further the boundaries of a duty to avoid inflicting financial loss on others, a robust approach was taken by Megarry V-C in *Ross v Caunters.*[3]

> The defendant solicitor negligently drew up a will so that he failed to carry out his client-testator's instruction to benefit the plaintiff. The plaintiff sued the solicitor in negligence.

The plaintiff could in no sense be said to have relied on the solicitor yet his action succeeded. The judge held that the law had by 1979 so developed that he should apply the neighbour principle in *Donoghue v Stevenson* in the absence of any policy factors negativing or limiting the scope of such a duty. There was close proximity between the plaintiff and the defendant. His contemplation of her was 'actual, nominate and direct' and that proximity arose out of the duty he undoubtedly owed to the testator. It was in no way 'casual, accidental or unforeseen'. The liability arising from the duty was to one person alone[4] so that spectre of indeterminate liability was of no assistance to the defendant. The House of Lords in *Caparo* signalled clearly that economic loss is not recoverable simply on the basis of foreseeability. Yet in *White v Jones*[5], the House of Lords nonetheless found for the plaintiff on facts closely analogous to *Ross v Caunters.*

> After a family quarrel the testator (aged 78) disinherited his two daughters, the plaintiffs. A few months later the family was reconciled and on 17 July the testator instructed his solicitors,

1   [1995] 2 AC 207 at 274.
2   At 530 and 611 respectively.
3   [1980] Ch 297, [1979] 3 All ER 580. And see *Al-Kandari v JR Brown & Co* [1988] QB 665, [1988] 1 All ER 833, CA.
4   See *Caltex Oil (Australia) Pty Ltd v Dredge Wellenstad* (1976) 136 CLR 529 (High Court of Australia) (note the importance in relation to economic loss of there being one identifiable plaintiff and not a diffuse class of potential plaintiffs).
5   [1995] 2 AC 207, HL. See Murphy 'Expectation Losses, Negligent Omissions and the Tortious Duty of Care' (1996) 55 CLJ 43.

the defendants, to draw up a new will including legacies of £9,000 to each of the plaintiffs. The defendants failed to act on those instructions and on 14 September the testator died. As a result of the defendants' negligent delay in acting on their client's (the testator's) instructions, the plaintiffs 'lost' their legacies.

The House of Lords held that the plaintiffs' economic loss was recoverable. Lord Goff made it clear that their Lordships did not endorse Megarry V-C's simplistic approach basing liability to the disappointed beneficiaries on the neighbour principle alone.[6] The claim by the plaintiffs in *White v Jones,* as in *Ross v Caunters,* posed a number of conceptual difficulties,[7] principally the following. (1) The defendants' duty was owed only to his client (the testator) under the contract between them. No third party could benefit under that contract. Privity of contract excluded any duty to the disappointed beneficiaries. (2) The plaintiffs' claims, being claims for pure economic loss, could succeed only within a narrow interpretation of *Hedley Byrne*, that is the plaintiffs must be able to show that the defendants entered into a special relationship with the plaintiff to provide advice and/or services for them, and, that the plaintiff *relied* on the defendants' expertise. Establishing reliance in such a case where intended beneficiaries might know nothing of their expectations under a will would be problematic. (3) If liability were imposed, establishing sensible boundaries to such liability would be impossible.

The majority in the House of Lords found these difficulties could be surmounted.[8] However the conceptual grounds on which their Lordships established liability in *White v Jones* must be read with some caution. Lord Goff is entirely frank in admitting that in this case he is strongly motivated by an impulse to do practical justice. He points out the 'extraordinary fact' that if no duty in tort were owed to the plaintiffs, the only persons who might have a valid claim (the testator and his estate) suffered no loss, and the only persons who suffered a loss (the disappointed beneficiaries) have no claim.[9] The defendants would escape scot-free despite their admitted negligence. Lord Browne-Wilkinson warned that his analysis of liability was only what was necessary for the purposes of this case he was '… not purporting to give any comprehensive statement of this aspect of the law. '[10]

So what does *White v Jones* decide? (1) The existence of a contract between the defendants and a third party (the testator) did not by virtue of the rules on privity of contract exclude a duty in tort to the plaintiff. (2) Such a duty could arise, if quite apart from the contract, the circumstances of the case gave rise to a special relationship between the parties. (3) On the facts of *Hedley Byrne* itself, proof that the plaintiff relied on the advice given, or statements made, by the defendants, and that the defendants should have foreseen such reliance, was an 'inevitable' condition of liability. However reliance is *not* in every case a necessary condition for the creation of a special relationship giving rise to a duty to safeguard the plaintiff from economic loss. (4) A special relationship will arise when the defendant assumes responsibility for providing services knowing and accepting that 'the future economic welfare of the intended beneficiary is dependent on his careful execution of the task'[11]. When A knows that B's economic well-being is dependent on his careful conduct of affairs, that may be sufficient to create a *Hedley Byrne* relationship. (5) On the facts of *White v Jones* itself, there were no reasons of policy why such a duty should not be imposed on the defendants. Despite their Lordship's strictures about its conceptual basis, the actual outcome of the decision in *Ross v Caunters* imposing liability on solicitors for negligently

---

6   [1995] 2 AC 207 at 268.
7   Detailed in full [1995] 2 AC 207 at 260-262.
8   Note the powerful dissent of Lord Mustill.
9   Ibid at 259-260.
10   Ibid at 274.
11   Ibid at 275 (per Lord Browne-Wilkinson).

executed wills had worked well and had not given rise to unlimited claims. In such cases there was no conflict of interest[12] between the duty owed to the testator in contract, and the duty owed to the plaintiffs in tort. Fulfilling the contractual obligation to the defendant at one and the same time would have discharged the duty of care owed to the plaintiffs.

White v Jones does, at a minimum, establish three crucial principles governing liability for pure economic loss. (1) A duty to avoid causing such loss is confined to special relationships within which the defendant has assumed responsibility for protecting the plaintiff's economic welfare. (2) Such a relationship will arise only where the plaintiff is readily identifiable as an individual or a member of a class of persons for whom the defendant undertakes responsibility in the performance of a particular task. (3) *Hedley Byrne* relationships are not confined to negligent misstatements and careless advice. Provision of services, including services provided at the behest of a third party, may create a special relationship in appropriate conditions[13]. Reliance is not an essential ingredient of a special relationship.

To sum up, *White v Jones* endorses the wider interpretation of *Hedley Byrne* prophesied by Lord Devlin, albeit equally clearly rejecting any suggestion that liability for economic loss can simply be equated with liability for physical harm.

A willingness to give a liberal, extended interpretation to *Hedley Byrne* liability married to an apparent impetus to do justice to a hard done by plaintiff is once again apparent in *Spring v Guardian Assurance plc*.[14] The plaintiff sued his former employers for breach of contract, malicious falsehood and negligence. The reference the defendants provided for him when he sought to be appointed as an agent for another insurance company was so unfavourable that the company refused to appoint him. The reference suggested that the plaintiff was dishonest. The trial judge found that there was no evidence to support any allegation of dishonesty and that the reference was carelessly prepared, albeit that the defendants did not act maliciously. As there was no malice, the plaintiff's claim in malicious falsehood failed. The judge dismissed the action for breach of contract but found for the plaintiff in negligence. Both parties appealed and the Court of Appeal rejected both claims. In the House of Lords, the majority held that it was an implied term of the former contract of employment that any subsequent reference be supplied with due care. The Law Lords also ruled in the plaintiff's favour in tort. In supplying a reference, at least in circumstances where as in this case references were required as a matter of regulation,[15] the defendants assumed responsibility to the subject of the reference to prepare the reference with care. That they owed such a duty to the recipient of the reference is already established by *Hedley Byrne* itself. The employee (if only indirectly) relies on his former employer to carry out this service with appropriate care. His interests are 'entrusted' to the skill of the referee. His financial prospects are largely in their hands.

However in *Spring*, as in *White v Jones*, there was present a major policy issue, arguably militating against liability. Allegations of dishonesty are clearly defamatory. Yet had the plaintiff sued in defamation, given that the judge held that that no malice was proven, his claim would have been met by a defence of qualified privilege. Defendants are protected against liability for defamation on grounds of qualified privilege where information is communicated in discharge of a duty to supply that information.

12 Compare *White v Jones* with *Clarke v Bruce Lance & Co* [1988] 1 All ER 364 (no duty to beneficiary in advising the testator in another transaction which ultimately reduced the value of the plaintiff's legacy under the will).
13 And see *Williams v Natural Life Health Foods Ltd* [1998] 2 All ER 577, [1998] 1 WLR 830, HL; *Carr-Glynn v Frearsons* [1998] 4 All ER 225, CA.
14 [1995] 2 AC 296, [1994] 3 All ER 129, HL.
15 The regulatory authority (LAUTRO) which governs the conduct of insurance companies required both that the company seeking to appoint the plaintiff seek a reference and that the defendants supply such a reference.

The giving of references is a classic example of qualified privilege. In defamation that privilege is defeated only by evidence that the defendants *knew* that what they said was untrue. To allow the plaintiff's claim in negligence would (it was contended) undermine the protection afforded by defamation. Employers and others supplying references would be inhibited in what they were prepared to say and/or possibly refuse to supply references at all. Their Lordships were perhaps surprisingly dismissive of such arguments. Lord Woolf acknowledged that public policy required that references be full and frank but countered that public policy also required that references '... should not be based upon careless investigations'. A negligently favourable reference can give rise to liability; hence his Lordship saw no problem in imposing liability for a negligently written adverse reference. The law should encourage referees to act carefully with proper regard for the interests of both the recipient and the subject of the reference.

A strong desire to offer the plaintiff redress for a perceived injustice can be seen in the opinions of the Law Lords.[15a] Addressing the need to prove malice to succeed in defamation Lord Woolf declared that

> The result of this requirement is that an action for defamation is a wholly inadequate remedy for an employee who is caused damage by a reference which due to negligence is inaccurate. This is because it places a wholly disproportionate burden on the employee. Malice is extremely difficult to establish... Without an action for negligence, the employee may, therefore, be left with no practical prospect of redress even though the reference may have permanently prevented him from obtaining employment in his chosen vocation.

Williams v Natural Life Health Foods Ltd[16] perhaps encapsulated the present state of play on extended *Hedley Byrne* liability in the relatively brief speech delivered by Lord Steyn. He made three crucial points. (1) Once it is established that a case falls within the extended *Hedley Byrne* principle, that there is a special relationship between the parties[17] '... there is no need to embark on any further inquiry whether it is "fair just and reasonable" to impose liability for economic loss'. (2) He acknowledged, and commended, the 'essential gap-filling role' of the law of tort. While rules of privity of contract prevent substantial justice being done in contract, Lord Steyn saw torts as moving in to fill that gap. *Spring* illustrates that that gap-filling role may operate between different torts as well. There, negligence is utilised to correct what their Lordships regarded as a deficiency in defamation. (3) However, outside those relationships blessed by the extended *Hedley Byrne* principle, plaintiffs suffering economic loss will not it seems recover that loss in tort. Lord Steyn declares:[18]

> The extended *Hedley Byrne* principle is the rationalisation or technique adopted by English law for the recovery of damages in respect of economic loss caused by the negligent performance of services.

It is to the claims by plaintiffs unable to bring themselves within that principle that we now turn.

(C) BEYOND *HEDLEY BYRNE*?

Self-evidently, there are several other ways in which one person's negligence can cause another economic loss very different from the situations giving rise to *Hedley Byrne* liability. In 1966 three years after *Hedley Byrne* the difficult but instructive case of *Weller*

15a But contrast *Spring* with *Kapfunde v Abbey National plc* [1999] ICR 1, CA.
16 [1998] 2 All ER 577, [1998] 1 WLR 830, HL.
17 At 581.
18 At 581.

& Co v Foot and Mouth Disease Research Institute[19] was decided. The defendants had carelessly allowed cattle to become infected by foot and mouth disease. The plaintiffs were auctioneers whose business suffered badly when quarantine restrictions prevented them holding auction sales of cattle. Widgery J said that no duty of care was owed to the plaintiffs for their loss of profits. The scope of any duty owed was limited to cattle owners who suffered physical damage to their property when cattle had to be destroyed. The loss occasioned to the auctioneer was readily foreseeable but so was economic loss to countless other enterprises: the pubs, the cafes, the car parks, the shops who would benefit from the influx into the town of crowds on market day. Policy required that a cut-off point be set. Widgery J set it at those suffering physical harm and, on the facts of *Weller,* it is easy to understand why.

A series of judgments on the damages recoverable when services such as water, gas or electricity were negligently interrupted confirmed Widgery J's finding that economic loss unrelated to physical damage was irrecoverable. In *British Celanese Ltd v Hunt*[20] and *S C M (UK) Ltd v W J Whittall & Son Ltd*[1] the cutting off of electricity supplies damaged the plaintiff's machines and materials resulting in a loss of production. The plaintiffs recovered both their additional expenditure in replacing and repairing machinery and their loss of profits on the lost production run. The Court of Appeal in the latter case held that the economic loss, the loss of profits, was recoverable as it was immediately consequent on physical damage to the plaintiff's property. In 1973 the Court of Appeal again considered economic loss in *Spartan Steel and Alloys Ltd v Martin & Co (Contractors) Ltd.*[2] The defendants' negligence caused the cable carrying electricity to the plaintiff's factory to be cut through interrupting the supply for $14\frac{1}{2}$ hours. To avoid molten metal solidifying in the furnaces the plaintiffs used oxygen to melt it and pour it out of the furnaces. This reduced the value of the metal and lost the plaintiffs the £400 profit they would have expected to make on that melt. The plaintiff also lost a further £1,767 on the other four melts which they would normally have completed in the time that the electricity was cut off. The majority of the Court of Appeal held that they could recover only the loss in value of the metal actually in the furnaces and the loss of profit on that melt. The remaining loss was pecuniary loss unrelated to any physical damage and irrecoverable. Edmund-Davies LJ dissenting considered that such foreseeable and direct economic loss should be recoverable. For him the occurrence or non-occurrence of physical damage was a fortuitous event with no relevance in legal principle. In language similar to that later employed by Megarry V-C in *Ross v Caunters*, he argued that if that very kind of economic loss to that plaintiff was a reasonably foreseeable and direct consequence of want of care, a duty to avoid that kind of loss arose.

The decision of the House of Lords in *Junior Books Ltd v Veitchi Co Ltd* in 1982[3] appeared, for a very short time, to vindicate such a liberalised approach to recovery for economic loss, potentially liberating economic loss from the shackles of *Hedley Byrne.*

The plaintiffs contracted with main contractors to build a new factory in Scotland. The defendants were nominated sub-contractors, specialist flooring experts, who laid the floor in

---

19 [1966] 1 QB 569, [1965] 3 All ER 560. And see *Cattle v Stockton Waterworks Co* (1875) LR 10 QB 453 (plaintiff could not recover for loss on contract to tunnel on land belonging to another after that land had been flooded by the defendant's negligence).
20 [1969] 2 All ER 1252, [1969] 1 WLR 959.
1 [1971] 1 QB 337, [1970] 3 All ER 245, CA.
2 [1973] QB 27, [1972] 3 All ER 557, CA and see *Electrochrome Ltd v Welsh Plastics Ltd* [1968] 2 All ER 205; *The Kapetan Georgis* [1988] 1 Lloyd's Rep 352.
3 [1983] 1 AC 520, [1982] 3 All ER 201, HL (although this case originated in Scotland (like *Donoghue v Stevenson*) it is authoritative on English law).

the main production area. Due to the defendants' negligence the floor was so defective that it had to be taken up and relaid. The plaintiffs sought to recover (a) their expenditure in replacing the floor and (b) loss of profits caused by disruption to their business.

No allegation was made in the pleadings that the floor was dangerous. No information was provided as to the terms of either the main or the sub-contract in particular as to whether there was any relevant exemption clause in either contract. The House of Lords nevertheless held by a majority of 4–1 that the plaintiffs' losses were recoverable. Lord Roskill described the parties' relationship as 'almost as close a commercial relationship as it is possible to envisage short of privity of contract.'[4] He further disapproved the drawing of the boundary of liability in tort on the basis of 'somewhat artificial distinctions between physical and economic or financial loss', and the concomitant contention that liability for financial loss of the type suffered by Junior Books lay in contract alone. He left open the issue of whether in the light of the majority's application of the proximity and policy approach to economic loss *Spartan Steel*[5] could any longer be regarded as correctly decided. The prospect of a new dawn signalled by *Junior Books* evaporated swiftly. A trio of appellate decisions reaffirmed the majority opinions in *Spartan Steel*. There is no general liability for pecuniary loss dissociated from physical damage however foreseeable that pecuniary loss may be.[6] *Junior Books* it was said was a case which on its special facts created such close proximity between the parties as to provide an exception to the rule[7]. In *Muirhead v Industrial Tank Specialties Ltd* the facts were these. The plaintiff, a fish merchant, devised a plan to buy lobsters in the summer when prices were low and store them to sell at profit on the Christmas market. The lobsters had to be stored in tanks through which seawater was constantly pumped, filtered and recirculated. The pumps proved to be defective because the electric motors were not suitable for use in the UK. The plaintiff sued the manufacturers of the electric motors for (1) the loss of several lobsters who died in the tanks, (2) expenditure on attempts to correct the fault, and (3) loss of profits on the enterprise.

The Court of Appeal affirmed *Spartan Steel*. The plaintiff could recover only for the loss of his property (dead lobsters) and any loss of profit consequent on those dead lobsters. Only that economic loss directly consequent on physical damage could be recovered in tort. In the absence of any evidence of express reliance on, or close proximity to, the defendants, the defendants owed no duty to protect the plaintiff against financial loss whether that loss be wasted expenditure or loss of profit. Manufacturers owe no duty in tort to ensure products are value for money.

Outside the extended *Hedley Byrne* principle, it seems that no duty to protect others from pure economic loss will arise however predictable that loss may be, however 'just and reasonable' it might appear that the defendant should bear that loss. The judicial sympathy for the plaintiff abundantly evidenced in *White v Jones* was singularly absent in *Murphy v Brentwood District Council*.[8]

First in *Murphy v Brentwood District Council*, as we have seen, their Lordships classified the loss suffered by the plaintiff, a subsequent purchaser of a defective

---

4 Ibid at 542 and 211 respectively.
5 *Muirhead v Industrial Tank Specialties* [1986] QB 507, [1985] 3 All ER 705, CA; *Simaan General Contracting Co v Pilkington Glass Ltd (No 2)* [1988] QB 758, [1988] 1 All ER 791, CA; *Greater Nottingham Co-operative Society v Cementation Piling and Foundations Ltd* [1989] QB 71, [1988] 2 All ER 971, CA.
6 *Simaan General Contracting Co v Pilkington Glass Ltd (No 2)* supra.
7 Arguably creating the necessary *Hedley Byrne* relationship?
8 [1991] 1 AC 398, [1990] 2 All ER 908, HL; and see *Department of the Environment v Bates* [1991] 1 AC 499, [1990] 2 All ER 943, HL; *D & F Estates Ltd v Church Comrs for England* [1989] AC 177, [1988] 2 All ER 992, HL.

dwelling, as pure economic loss, albeit that his home, if not repaired, would ultimately have collapsed. Such pecuniary loss is irrecoverable in tort whether it be the builder or the local council who approved the original building plans who is the defendant. In the absence of a special relationship of proximity such as arguably was present in *Junior Books v Veitchi*,[9] neither manufacturers of chattels nor builders of property are subject to a duty of care in relation to the quality of their work. To impose any such general duty would introduce into the law of tort transmissible warranties of quality.[10] Such guarantees are provided for only in contract. Nor in *Murphy* would their Lordships contemplate any gap-filling role for tort[11]

The simplicity of the above statement is marred somewhat by a *dictum* of Lord Bridge. He tentatively suggests that even in the absence of a special relationship with the builder

> ... if a building stands so close to the boundary of the building owner's land that after discovery of the dangerous defect it remains a potential source of injury to persons or property on neighbouring land or the highway, the building owner ought, in principle, to be entitled to recover in tort ... the cost of obviating the danger ... *to protect himself from potential liability to third parties.*[12]

The Bridge exception, doubted by Lord Oliver,[13] could theoretically drive a coach and horses through the *Murphy* rule. Assume Mr Murphy had children. The cracks in the walls of his house, if left unrepaired and the family remained in the house, posed a danger, a potential source of injury to them. Could Mr Murphy argue he should recover the cost of protecting himself against liability to the children or his visitors? Lord Bridge's hesitation illustrates a judicial dilemma. Beyond *Hedley Byrne* judges strive to provide predictability and restrict claims for economic loss. Yet they want to retain the ability to meet the really 'hard case'.

A *second* category where the House of Lords have declared economic loss is *never* recoverable is more straightforward and explicable. A plaintiff who suffers economic loss consequent on physical damage to another person, or to property in which at the time damage is suffered he has no proprietary interest, cannot recover that loss in tort.[14] In *Leigh and Sillivan Ltd v Aliakmon Shipping Ltd*[15] the plaintiffs had contracted to buy a cargo of steel coils to be shipped from Korea. The cargo was damaged at sea. The contractual and credit arrangements between the plaintiffs and the sellers of the steel coils were such that, although the risk in the cargo had passed to the plaintiffs, they did not own the coils. They ended up having to pay for damaged goods. Such arrangements where the party likely to suffer loss was not the owner of a cargo is not uncommon. Loss to the plaintiffs was readily foreseeable to the defendant shippers.

9 [1990] 2 All ER 908 at 919 (per Lord Keith), at 930 (per Lord Oliver). Might Mr Murphy's claim have succeeded against the buildings at least had he contacted them directly and been assured 'The foundations of the house you propose to buy are A1'?
10 *D & F Estates Ltd v Church Comrs for England* supra at 1010 (per Lord Oliver).
11 See *Williams v Natural Life Health Foods Ltd* supra at p 224.
12 [1990] 2 All ER 908 at 926.
13 [1990] 2 All ER 908 at 936.
14 For a statutory exception to that rule see the Fatal Accidents Act 1976. Note also the Latent Damage Act 1986, s 3 post.
15 [1986] AC 785, [1986] 2 All ER 145. Note that in this case as in others, an essential difficulty in imposing a duty in tort derives from the relationship between the defendants' contractual duty to a third party and the purported tortious duty to the plaintiff. If the defendant shippers had excluded or limited their duty in contract to the sellers, how would that exclusion or limitation affect their duty in tort? See the judgment of Robert Goff LJ in the Court of Appeal [1985] QB 350 at 399, and note the contrasting approaches of Lord Fraser and Lord Roskill in *Junior Books v Veitchi* supra.

Nonetheless it was irrecoverable at common law. Two powerful reasons may explain the refusal to countenance recovery of economic loss in such circumstances. (1) As in *Weller v Foot & Mouth Institute,* defining a cut-off point for liability where claims relate to consequential losses arising from a primary injury to a third party is nigh on impossible. An international football star is injured in a road accident. His leg is broken and his sportscar is irreparably damaged. In the absence of the star, his team lose valuable sponsorship and fail to win the FA Cup. His favourite charity loses the money they would have gained because he had promised to let them auction his car. His mum does not get the house he promised her when he won his next bonus. The list is endless. (2) The plaintiffs in *Leigh & Sillivan* suffered damage to their *business* interests. True the defendants 'caused' that damage but on what grounds should they have undertaken responsibility for protecting the plaintiffs' business? The risk was foreseeable to the plaintiffs as readily as to the defendants. It was for the plaintiffs to protect themselves against that risk. Nothing was said or done by the defendants to take that responsibility on themselves.

For the present, extended *Hedley Byrne* liability marks the limits of recovery for economic loss. Nonetheless a note of caution must be struck. Look again at the decisions denying liability for economic loss. Consider *Muirhead v Industrial Tank Specialities*[16]. Imagine Mr Muirhead had personally telephoned the defendants and expressly inquired about the compatibility and suitability of their electric motors for his fish tank. Had they assured him that the motors met his needs, would he have established a *Hedley Byrne* relationship? If there was evidence of previous dealing between them, and/or Mr Muirhead had shown he expressly selected and nominated the motor supplies because of their special expertise and that the defendants were well aware this was the case would that be enough to contend that the defendants assumed responsibility for the service provided for Mr Muirhead? *Junior Books* was excoriated immediately after it was decided but never overruled on its facts. Is there any less evidence of the defendants assuming responsibility for the service provided than in *White v Jones*? The cynic may conclude that if you look hard enough and you want to find it, a *Hedley Byrne* relationship may often be discovered.

SECTION 6.   HUMAN RIGHTS AND THE DUTY OF CARE

It is readily apparent that in setting the boundaries of the duty of care, the courts have sought to balance the interests of the individual suffering loss or harm against the cost of imposing liability on the defendant. That exercise is transparent in cases addressing the liability of public authorities, but is not confined to those kinds of cases alone. The common law's exclusion of liability for pure omissions, the very limited duty to protect others from the acts of third parties, the rules on liability for psychiatric harm and the strict restriction on recovery for pure economic loss all derive from that self-same balancing exercise. The process often appears to suggest that what the law has to do is to weigh the *private* interests of the plaintiff against competing *public* interests, which may be endangered if liability in tort is imposed on the defendant. So, for example, in *X v Bedfordshire County Council*[17] it was suggested that imposing a duty of care on local authorities charged with protecting children from abuse might paradoxically disrupt the service. Children generally might suffer if the particular children suing the council won their case. In claims against the police, the courts have voiced concerns about defensive policing and diversion of resources. The 'patchwork quilt' of liability

16 [1986] QB 507, CA.
17 [1995] 2 AC 633, HL; discussed supra at p 185.

for psychiatric harm is justified on grounds of pragmatism. The public good in its diverse forms trumps private interests, even interests as basic as freedom from injury.

Have the English courts given sufficient weight to the individual's rights? Has the individual's claim to protection of certain basic interests been properly regarded as a public interest, an interest which the state has a duty to safeguard as much as, say, the state should support the integrity and efficiency of the police service? At the time of writing, *X v Bedfordshire County Council* is under attack before the European Court of Human Rights. That court's judgment in *Osman v United Kingdom*[18] is instructive in casting light on how the Human Rights Act 1998 may prompt a review of the boundaries of duty of care as perceived at common law.

A teacher at a school attended by the second plaintiff developed an obsession with the boy. A series of disturbing incidents took place including a petrol attack on the family home. Several meetings were held with the police. Ultimately the teacher shot and wounded the boy and shot and killed his father (the first plaintiff's husband). The plaintiffs sued the police in negligence alleging that officers failed to take adequate preventive measures to protect the family. Their claim was struck out, the Court of Appeal holding that, on *policy* grounds, no duty of care was owed to the plaintiffs.[19] Following the decision of the House of Lords in *Hill v Chief Constable of West Yorkshire*,[20] the appeal court refused to allow the case to proceed with the consequence that no English Court ever investigated the facts of the case. Effectively, as was illustrated in the previous chapter, a public service immunity prevailed.

The plaintiffs alleged breaches of three articles of the European Convention, Article 2, protecting the right to life, Article 8, relating to respect for private and family life, and Article 6, which guarantees access to justice. The Court found no violation of Articles 2 and 8. They ruled that while Articles 2 and 8 may impose on states positive obligations to take measures to protect both individual lives and freedom from harm and harassment, the judges (in the majority) were not persuaded that the police had failed to take such measures. The European Court of Human Rights, unlike the English courts, reviewed the facts of the claim in depth. Nonetheless the plaintiffs' claim for breach of Article 6 succeeded.

The Court unanimously held that the exclusionary rule which prevented a full hearing of the plaintiffs' suit against the police denied them their fundamental right of access to a fair and public hearing. The Court acknowledged that the police service was not granted an absolute immunity. However in the balancing exercise conducted by the Court of Appeal insufficient weight was given to the competing public interests of the plaintiffs as opposed to the interests of the community. In a case involving the protection of a child and the right to life, public policy could not dictate that the police should be immune from liability.

The ECHR decision in *Osman* does not mean that policy considerations can never exclude a duty of care. States enjoy a 'margin of appreciation' in regulating access to the courts. Limitation based on national policy objectives may be articulated but any limitation on access to justice must not destroy the very essence of the right and policy considerations excluding a duty of care must bear '… a reasonable relationship of proportionality between the means employed and the aim sought to be achieved'. In *Osman v United Kingdom* where, proximity between the police and the family was clear, and a child's life was at stake, the exclusionary rule protecting the police lacked that proportionality.

18 [1999] 1 FLR 193, ECHR.
19 See *Osman v Ferguson* [1993] 4 All ER 344, CA.
20 [1989] AC 53, HL; discussed supra at p 190.

What does the ECHR decision in *Osman v United Kingdom* mean for the student of torts? Once the Human Rights Act 1998 comes into force remember that the English courts will have to implement Article 6 themselves.[1] The case law previously discussed in these two chapters on duty of care, will need to be reviewed. Where the harm of which the plaintiff complains involves fundamental rights guaranteed by the relevant articles of the European Convention, any exclusionary rule denying a duty of care on policy grounds must be shown to be *proportional* to the nature of the harm suffered and the strength of the plaintiff's claim. Consider just two possible examples where established case law might be challenged from a human rights perspective.

(1) The absolute exclusion of any duty to rescue others in peril is not shared by civil law traditions. French law, and other civil law systems, imposes a limited duty to aid fellow citizens in danger.[2] Does a common law rule that effectively denies any protection to the victim's right to life (Article 2) violate Article 6 in denying access to justice by an exclusionary rule which does not even begin to assess the proportionality of the parties' competing interests.

(2) Are the rules on recovery for psychiatric harm adequately proportional? The House of Lords in *Alcock v Chief Constable of South Yorkshire*[3] denied compensation to siblings suffering psychiatric illness after witnessing the terrible fate of their brothers and sisters. Is the justification for excluding liability proportional to the victims' rights under Article 8?

---

1   On which see generally supra at p 6.
2   See *Smith v Littlewoods Organisation Ltd* [1987] 1 All ER 710 at 729 HL per Lord Goff.
3   [1992] 1 AC 310, [1991] 4 All ER 907, HL.

Chapter 13

Breach of duty

SECTION I.   THE STANDARD OF CARE

(A)   LAW, NOT FACT

So far, only the range of persons to whom the defendant owes a duty of care and the types of harm to which the duty of care extends have been considered. Although it is not uncommon for the standard of care to be treated as part of the 'duty', it seems preferable to confine 'duty' to the question of whether the defendant is under an obligation to the plaintiff and to treat separately the question of the extent of the duty owed. The conduct of the defendant, and especially the nature of the duty of care imposed on him or her, must next be looked at. It is a matter of law and not fact to decide the rules to be applied in deciding whether the defendant has broken a duty of care which was owed to the plaintiff. It will be seen that the standard required of the defendant is that of the reasonable person, which is a legal standard.

In *Glasgow Corpn v Muir*, Lord Thankerton explained, after deciding that the appellants owed a duty to take reasonable care for the safety of children on the premises, that the further question had to be settled: 'the test by which … the standard of care is to be judged'.[1] In *Paris v Stepney Borough Council*,[2] where the House of Lords considered a claim in negligence brought by a one-eyed workman whose good eye was injured in the course of work which involved risk to the eyes while not wearing goggles, Lord Oakley first held that 'the duty of an employer towards his servant is to take reasonable care for the servant's safety in all the circumstances of the case' and then defined the standard of care required. Similarly, in *Bolton v Stone*, Lord Normand commenced his judgment as follows:[3]

> My Lords, it is not questioned that the occupier of a cricket ground owes a duty of care to persons on an adjacent highway or on neighbouring property who may be in the way of balls driven out of the ground by the batsman. But it is necessary to consider the measure of the duty owed.

It is a matter of law that if A owes B a duty of care A must attain the standard of a reasonable person 'a reasonable man'(as it has traditionally been put). A further

1   [1943] AC 448 at 454, [1943] 2 All ER 44, HL.
2   [1951] AC 367 at 384, [1951] 1 All ER 42, HL.
3   [1951] AC 850 at 860, [1951] 1 All ER 1078, HL.

examination of the legal meaning of this phrase will be made later.[4] There are other principles of law relating to the standard of care. The fundamental issue is how to strike a balance between the utility of the activities of the defendant and the threat of harm to the plaintiff which these activities engender. One must take into account these two basic factors in deciding whether one who owes a duty to another has shown reasonable care.[5]

The function of the courts in ascertaining the balance between the individual's right to freedom from harm and the social utility of the defendant's activity can be seen to involve determinations of the general public interest. This can mean that matters extraneous to the specific issues in dispute between the plaintiff and the defendant may be taken into account in assessing the standard of care required of the defendant. A good illustration of such an approach can be found in the case law concerning the standard of care demanded of doctors counselling patients on the risks of proposed medical treatment. In *Sidaway v Bethlem Royal Hospital*[6] the House of Lords held by a majority of 4–1 that the test should be whether the doctor conformed to a practice of disclosure sanctioned by responsible medical opinion. In rejecting the contention that the standard of care ought to be what the reasonable patient would want to know,[7] rather than what the reasonable doctor was prepared to tell, their Lordships made several references to what they saw as undesirable social consequences of adopting a patient-centred standard. These included that patients might irrationally reject necessary treatment, that, in general,[8] lay people would not understand further information if they were given it, and their Lordships' view that most people were in any case content to leave the decision on the risk versus benefit equation of proposed treatment to their doctors.

In *Budden v BP Oil Ltd*[9] the Court of Appeal struck out the following claim.

> An action was brought on behalf of a child alleging that the child had suffered brain damage caused by excessive lead in his blood. The high level of lead was assumed to result from lead particles emitted from vehicles using petrol supplied by the defendants. The lead had been deliberately added to the petrol. Parliament was progressively phasing down the permitted lead content in petrol. At the time of the damage to the child the level of lead in petrol complied with the permitted limits but would not have done later. The relevant legislation did not provide that it was a defence to any action that the limit was not exceeded—it merely made it a crime to exceed the limit.

The appeal court found that Parliament in setting the limit must be regarded as having conclusively determined in the public interest, taking into account all factors of which health risk was only one, that at the relevant time it was reasonable to add that amount of lead to petrol. Should the courts have felt themselves precluded by Parliament in that instance from making an independent judgment on the standard of care in a negligence action? The legislation was silent on civil liability for lead-induced injury. Compare *Budden v BP Oil Ltd* with *Froom v Butcher*.[10] In the latter case the key issue

4   See p 237 et seq, post.
5   Eg per Pearson J in *Donaldson v McNiven* [1952] 1 All ER 1213 at 1216; affd [1952] 2 All ER 691, CA.
6   [1985] AC 871, [1985] 1 All ER 643, HL.
7   The 'prudent patient' is the standard adopted in a number of American states; see *Canterbury v Spence* 464 F 2d 772 (1972) at 780; this was the approach endorsed by Lord Scarman in his dissenting opinion in *Sidaway*. And note the very different analysis of public interest by the High Court of Australia in *Rogers v Whitaker* [1993] 4 Med LR 78.
8   But not where the lay person happened to be a highly educated Law Lord: see per Lord Diplock at 659.
9   (1980) 124 Sol Jo 376, CA.
10   [1976] QB 286, [1975] 2 All ER 520. See further post at p 287.

was whether the plaintiff was contributorily negligent in not wearing a seatbelt. At the time of the accident legislation to make wearing seatbelts compulsory and not wearing them a crime had not yet passed through Parliament. The Court of Appeal felt free to find that failing to wear a seatbelt clearly constituted contributory negligence.

(B) THE GUIDING PRINCIPLES OF LAW

(1) THE LIKELIHOOD OF HARM

Lord Wright in *Northwestern Utilities Ltd v London Guarantee and Accident Co Ltd* said[11]

> The degree of care which that duty involves must be proportioned to the degree of risk involved if the duty of care should not be fulfilled.

The amount of caution required tends to increase with the likelihood that the defendant's conduct will cause harm. Of course, in certain instances, the chance of harm may be so small that a person is held to be taking reasonable care although he does not guard against such remote possibilities. The degree of risk of harm is merely one factor to be taken into account, along with the other factors now to be enumerated, in deciding whether in all the circumstances reasonable care has been taken.[12]

(2) THE SERIOUSNESS OF THE RISK AND THE RISK OF SERIOUS INJURY

Not only is it a principle of law that a greater risk of injury is a material factor in framing the standard of care, but it is equally a legal rule that the gravity of the injury is material. In *Paris v Stepney Borough Council*[13] the Court of Appeal had held that, where the disability of a workman did not increase the risk of an accident, but only increased the risk of serious injury if such an accident did befall him, the disability was irrelevant in determining the standard of care. The House of Lords reversed this, holding that the gravity of the consequences if an accident did occur had to be taken into account in fixing the measure of care.[14]

(3) THE UTILITY OF THE ACT OF THE DEFENDANT

In *Paris v Stepney Borough Council* the House of Lords was also careful to point out that 'the seriousness of the injury or damage risked and the likelihood of its being in fact caused may not be the only relevant factors'.[15] The reference was plainly to that

11 [1936] AC 108 at 126, PC, approved by Lord Normand in *Paris v Stepney Borough Council*, [1951] AC 367 at 381, [1951] 1 All ER 42, HL; cf Cardozo J, in *Palsgraf v Long Island Railroad Co* 248 NY 339 (1928): 'The risk reasonably to be perceived defines the duty to be obeyed', and Lord Macmillan in *Glasgow Corpn v Muir* [1943] AC 448 at 456, [1943] 2 All ER 44, HL: 'the degree of care required varies directly with the risk involved'.
12 *The Wagon Mound (No 2)* [1967] 1 AC 617 at 642–3, [1966] 2 All ER 709, PC (per Lord Reid).
13 [1950] 1 KB 320, [1949] 2 All ER 843, CA.
14 [1951] AC 367, [1951] 1 All ER 42; but see *Withers v Perry Chain Co Ltd* [1961] 3 All ER 676, CA (the health risk to the plaintiff had to be balanced against her interest in keeping her job), p 296, post.
15 Ibid at 382 per Lord Normand.

other basic consideration mentioned earlier, the utility of the act of the defendant. *Daborn v Bath Tramways Motor Co Ltd*, illustrates this point well:[16]

> The relevant issue was whether the driver, in wartime, of a left-hand-drive ambulance had been negligent in turning into a lane on the off-side of the road without giving a signal.

Holding that she had not broken her duty of care, Asquith LJ said:[17]

> In determining whether a party is negligent, the standard of reasonable care is that which is reasonably to be demanded in the circumstances. A relevant circumstance to take into account may be the importance of the end to be served by behaving in this way or that. As has often been pointed out, if all the trains in this country were restricted to a speed of five miles an hour, there would be fewer accidents, but our national life would be intolerably slowed down. The purpose to be served, if sufficiently important, justified the assumption of abnormal risk. The relevance of this applied to the present case is this: during the war which was, at the material time, in progress, it was necessary for many highly important operations to be carried out by means of motor vehicles with left-hand drives, no others being available. So far as this was the case, it was impossible for the drivers of such cars to give the warning signals which could otherwise be properly demanded of them. Meanwhile, it was essential that the ambulance service should be maintained. It seems to me, in those circumstances, it would be demanding too high and an unreasonable standard of care from the drivers of such cars to say to them: 'Either you must give signals which the structure of your vehicle renders impossible or you must not drive at all.'

Similarly, what might be want of care towards an employee in a commercial enterprise will not necessarily be want of care towards a fireman, for 'one must balance the risk against the end to be achieved', and 'the commercial end to make profit is very different from the human end to save life or limb'.[18] And the extent of the duty owed by a police officer to a suspect whom he is pursuing must similarly be judged in the light of the end to be attained—that is the lawful arrest of the suspect.[19]

(4)   THE COST OF AVOIDING THE HARM

It is relevant to consider how extensive and costly the measures necessary to eliminate the risk would be. In *Latimer v AEC Ltd*[20] Denning LJ said:

> In every case of foreseeable risk, it is a matter of balancing the risk against the measures necessary to eliminate it.

In this case an exceptional storm had caused a factory floor to become flooded; when the water receded, the floor was found to be covered with a slimy mixture of oil and water so that its surface was slippery. The issue was the liability of the factory owners

---

16   [1946] 2 All ER 333, CA.
17   [1946] 2 All ER 333 at 336. Cf *Quinn v Scott* [1965] 2 All ER 588 at 593 (per Glyn Jones J): 'the safety of the public must take precedence over the preservation of the amenities and [I] cannot hold that the [National] Trust's duty to care for the countryside diminishes to any degree the duty not to subject users of this highway to unnecessary danger'.
18   *Watt v Hertfordshire County Council* [1954] 2 All ER 368, CA at 371 per Denning LJ.
19   *Marshall v Osmond* [1983] QB 1034; and see *Rigby v Chief Constable of Northamptonshire* [1985] 2 All ER 985, [1985] 1 WLR 1242 (police firing CS gas canister into a shop to flush out a dangerous psychopath).
20   [1952] 2 QB 701 at 711, [1952] 1 All ER 1302 at 1305, CA; cf *Watt v Hertfordshire County Council* [1954] 2 All ER 368, CA (duty of fire authority to firemen in respect of equipment) where the dictum of Asquith LJ, in *Daborn v Bath Tramways Motor Co Ltd* supra, was also approved.

to a workman who, some hours later, was injured through slipping on the floor. The House of Lords affirmed the decision of the Court of Appeal that there was no negligence at common law, Lord Tucker saying:[1]

The only question was: Has it been proved the floor was so slippery that, remedial steps not being possible, a reasonably prudent employer would have closed down the factory rather than allow his employees to run the risks involved in continuing work?

In *The Wagon Mound (No 2)* the Judicial Committee stated:[2]

A reasonable man would only neglect ... a risk [of small magnitude] if he had some valid reason for doing so, eg that it would involve considerable expense to eliminate the risk.

But just how far can this principle be stretched? In the case of a private individual or enterprise there must come a point where if the defendant lacks the resources to minimise a significant risk of injury to others, he should cease to engage in the relevant activity. If a football club cannot afford to replace a wooden stand constituting a fire risk, they should not allow spectators to use that stand.[3] Where the defendant is a public enterprise, however, the position may differ. In *Knight v Home Office*[4] the plaintiff's husband committed suicide while detained in a prison hospital wing. The judge accepted that the standard of care and supervision for suicidal prisoners may well have fallen below that to be expected in an NHS psychiatric facility. Yet he dismissed the plaintiff's claim. He said:[5]

In making the decision as to the standard demanded the court must, however, bear in mind as one factor that resources available for the public service are limited and that the allocation of resources is a matter for Parliament.

Similarly in *Walker v Northumberland County Council*[6] the judge warned that:

The practicability of remedial measures must clearly take into account the resources and facilities at the disposal of the person or body owing the duty of care and the purpose of the activity giving rise to the risk of injury.

(C)   THE RELATION BETWEEN STANDARD OF CARE AND DUTY

Accepting, then, that it is a matter of law that the considerations just discussed are to be taken into account in determining whether the defendant has been negligent, one must ask the further question whether the standard of care has to be particularised in detail in terms of 'duty'. A motorist fails to sound his horn at a crossing and is held liable in negligence to another motorist with whom he collides, the court holding that he should have sounded his horn. Would such a decision thenceforth be authority for the proposition that a motorist has a duty at law to sound his horn when approaching an intersection? It has been argued:[7]

1   [1953] AC 643 at 659, [1953] 2 All ER 449 at 445, HL.
2   [1967] 1 AC 617 at 642, [1966] 2 All ER 709. For the relevance of the defendant's financial resources, see *Goldman v Hargave* [1967] 1 AC 645 at 663, PC.
3   See *Latimer v AEC* [1953] AC 643 at 659.
4   [1990] 3 All ER 237.
5   [1990] 3 All ER 237 at 243.
6   [1995] 1 All ER 737.
7   *Charlesworth.*

... situations tend to repeat themselves, persons find that if they do what was found to be reasonable under similar circumstances they will themselves be free from liability, and accordingly the general rule of reasonable conduct tends to be split up into a number of branches, each of which contains directions as to the way in which a reasonable man would behave under the circumstances in question. This result is both inevitable and beneficial. One of the objects of law is to prescribe rules of conduct so that the individual will know how to act in any given set of circumstances, and to direct him to act as a reasonable man without telling him in more detail how a reasonable man is found by experience to act under those circumstances is to give him very little guidance. When new sets of circumstances arise, it is necessary to fall back on the general test of reasonable conduct viewed in the light of such of the existing rules of conduct as seem most nearly appropriate to the case.

However, is the assumption on which this superficially attractive argument is based well founded? Is it really the case that the situations of fact in negligence are usually the same as some case previously decided, and not infinitely various? So, in running down cases, it will usually be relevant to consider the speed of the vehicles, visibility, the state of the road, the distance within which the vehicles pulled up—but how often in any given case will these factors exactly correspond with those of a previously decided case? Are not the special circumstances of each case almost always unique, so different in at least one material point, that a catalogue of duties based on conduct can hardly be compiled?

What, then, is the judicial practice in the matter? In general,[8] the higher courts have forcefully rejected attempts to particularise duties. For instance, in *Baker v E Longhurst & Sons Ltd*,[9] Scrutton LJ appeared to lay down a principle that a person driving in the dark must be able to pull up within the limits of his vision. Shortly afterwards, in another road traffic case, Lord Wright said of cases such as *Baker v Longhurst*:[10]

> ... that no one case is exactly like another, and no principle of law can in my opinion be extracted from those cases. It is unfortunate that questions which are questions of fact alone should be confused by importing into them as principles of law a course of reasoning which has no doubt properly been applied in deciding other cases on other sets of facts.

When counsel again relied on the dictum of Scrutton LJ, in *Morris v Luton Corpn*, Lord Greene adopted the dictum of Lord Wright 'in the hope that this suggested principle [of Scrutton LJ] may rest peacefully in the grave in future'.[11] Most important of all is the 1959 decision of the House of Lords in *Qualcast (Wolverhampton) Ltd v Haynes*.[12] The House went out of its way to stress that a judge's reasons for finding want of reasonable care are matters of fact, not law, for otherwise 'the precedent system will die from a surfeit of authorities'.[13] That judges now give reasons for conclusions formerly arrived at by juries without reasons must not be allowed to elevate these decisions of fact into propositions of law.

Naturally, in certain common kinds of claim, notably those arising out of road traffic accidents, factual situations do repeat themselves. Judges may properly refer to earlier decisions for guidance as to how to apply the standard of reasonableness. The infinite

8   Though, for the contrary approach see, for example, *Caminer v Northern and London Investment Trust Ltd* [1951] AC 88, [1950] 2 All ER 486, HL.
9   [1933] 2 KB 461 at 468, CA.
10   *Tidy v Battman* [1934] 1 KB 319 at 322, CA; cf *SS Heranger (Owners) v SS Diamond (Owners)* [1939] AC 94, HL at 101 (per Lord Wright).
11   [1946] KB 114 at 116, [1946] 1 All ER 1 at 3, CA. And see *Easson v London and North Eastern Rly Co* [1944] KB 421, [1944] 2 All ER 425, CA.
12   [1959] AC 743, [1959] 2 All ER 38.
13   [1959] 2 All ER 38 at 43–4 (per Lord Somervell).

variability of human conduct however makes it undesirable to express such a standard in terms of inflexible legal duty. In *Worsfield v Howe*:[14]

> The defendant car driver edged blind from a side road across stationary tankers and collided with a motorcyclist approaching on the main road past the tankers. Because the Court of Appeal had held in a previous case that a driver so edging out was not negligent the trial judge felt bound to absolve the defendant from liability.

The Court of Appeal held that the previous decision laid down no legal principle, that such decisions were to be treated as ones of fact, and held the defendant negligent. In *Foskett v Mistry*[15] the Court of Appeal reinforced that attitude. They ruled that in running down claims whether reasonable care had been taken must be judged in the light of all the facts of that particular incident. Citation of authorities could rarely be justified.

SECTION 2.   THE 'REASONABLE MAN'

> Negligence is the omission to do something which a reasonable man, guided upon those considerations which ordinarily regulate the conduct of human affairs, would do, or doing something which a prudent and reasonable man would not do.[16]

The legal standard is not that of the defendant himself but that of 'a man of ordinary prudence',[17] a man using 'ordinary care and skill',[18] a 'hypothetical' man.[19] Lord Macmillan has said:[20]

> The standard of foresight of the reasonable man ... eliminates the personal equation and is independent of the idiosyncrasies of the particular person whose conduct is in question.

Yet it is inadequate, not to say question-begging, to say that the standard then is an objective one. The definition of the reasonable person is not complete unless the words 'in the circumstances' are embodied. Plainly, these words may prevent the test from being wholly objective, for the boundary between the external facts and the qualities of the actor is ill-defined. How far, then, is the standard of the 'reasonable man' an objective one?

(A)   CHILDREN

In *Mullin v Richards*[1] the Court of Appeal confirmed that, in relation to a child, the test is what degree of care and foresight can reasonably be expected of a child of the age of the defendant. Two 15-year-old girls were fooling about during a mathematics lesson, fencing with plastic rulers. One of the rulers snapped and a fragment of plastic entered

14   [1980] 1 All ER 1028, [1980] 1 WLR 1175, CA.
15   [1984] RTR 1.
16   *Blythe v Birmingham Waterworks Co* (1856) 11 Exch 781 at 784 per Alderson B.
17   *Vaughan v Menlove* (1837) 3 Bing NC 468 at 475 (per Tindal CJ).
18   *Heaven v Pender* (1883) 11 QBD 503 at 507 (per Brett MR).
19   *King v Phillips* [1953] 1 QB 429 at 441, [1953] 1 All ER 617, CA per Denning LJ.
20   *Glasgow Corpn v Muir* [1943] AC 448 at 457, [1942] 2 All ER 44, HL; cf the earlier dictum of Holmes J in *The Germanic* 196 US 589 (1904): 'The standard of conduct ... is an external standard, and takes no account of the personal equation of the man concerned'.
1   [1998] 1 All ER 920; and see re contributory negligence *Yachuk v Oliver Blais Co Ltd* [1949] AC 386, PC; *Gough v Thorne* [1966] 3 All ER 398, CA; *Morales v Ecclestone* [1991] RTR 151, CA.

the plaintiff's eye ultimately causing her to lose any effective sight in that eye. Adopting the judgment of the High Court of Australia in *McHale v Watson*,[2] the Court of Appeal held that the plaintiff had failed to establish that her schoolfriend was negligent. A 15-year-old, unlike an adult, might well not foresee the risk of her behaviour, particularly as the practice had not been banned at school nor had any similar accident occurred. Some degree of irresponsibility may be expected of children playing together.[3] In *McHale v Watson* itself, a 12-year-old boy threw a spike at a post. Unfortunately the spike ricocheted off the post and hit the plaintiff (a girl of nine) in the eye. The High Court of Australia held that the standard of care to be demanded of the boy must be judged by the 'foresight and prudence of an ordinary boy of 12'. An unresolved question, in relation to the standard of care demanded of children, is whether the test is entirely objective or will take into account the child's actual mental ability, maturity and experience.[4]

(B)   ADULTS AFFECTED BY DISABILITY OR INFIRMITY

It is unclear to what extent if at all the standard of the reasonable person will be adjusted to allow for the incapacities and infirmities of individual adults. Consider whether the standard of care is (or should be) affected if the defendant is elderly, or deaf, or minus a limb. In *Daly v Liverpool Corpn*[5] it was held that in deciding whether a 67 -year-old woman was guilty of contributory negligence in crossing a road, one had to consider a woman of her age, not a hypothetical pedestrian. The point will be in issue only rarely in respect of the standard required of defendants for the following reason. A person who causes an injury to another because he suffers from some disability or infirmity will nonetheless usually be negligent, not because of want of care at the time of the accident, but because, being aware of his disability, he allowed himself to be in the situation; a motorist with seriously impaired eyesight who collides with another car because she fails to see an approaching vehicle is not negligent because she is partially sighted, but because, given her defective vision, she is negligent in electing to drive so as to endanger others.

In *Roberts v Ramsbottom*[6] the defendant suffered a slight stroke just before getting into his car. He was completely unaware that he had had a stroke although he admitted that he felt somewhat dizzy. A few minutes after starting his journey he was involved in a collision injuring the plaintiff. It was held that even though his carelessness resulted from impaired consciousness of which the defendant was at the time of the collision unaware, he was liable in negligence.

Neill J offered two grounds to support the finding of negligence. He held that the defendant was liable because he '...continued to drive when he was unfit to do so and when he should have been aware of his unfitness'. But he also contended that any disability affecting a defendant's ability to drive could only exempt him from the normal, objective standard of care where that disability placed his actions 'wholly beyond his control', where the defendant was in effect in a state of automatism. The Court of Appeal in *Mansfield v Weetabix Ltd*[7] rejected that second approach as coming close to equating liability in negligence with strict liability. A lorry driver was involved in a collision when

2   (1964) 111 CLR 384.
3   *Mullins v Richards*, supra at 928 per Butler-Sloss LJ.
4   *Yachuk v Oliver Blais Co Ltd* supra at 396; *McHale v Watson* supra per Owen J, 'child of the same age, intelligence and experience'.
5   [1939] 2 All ER 142.
6   [1980] 1 All ER 7, [1980] 1 WLR 823.
7   [1998] 1 WLR 1263.

he partially lost consciousness as a result of a hypoglycaemic state induced by a malignancy of which he was completely unaware. Overruling the trial judge's finding of negligence, the Court of Appeal held that where a disability or infirmity prevented the defendant from meeting the objective standard of care, and the defendant was not, and could not reasonably have been, aware of his condition, that condition must be taken into account in determining whether or not the defendant was negligent.

(C) INTELLIGENCE AND KNOWLEDGE

The defendant's actions must conform to certain criteria expected of a person of normal intelligence in a given situation. It is no defence that someone acted 'to the best of his own judgment', if his 'best' is below that of the reasonable man.[8] A man whose reactions are slower than average is not thereby excused. A woman whose intelligence is superior or whose reactions are quicker than average is not liable for failing to use those above-average qualities,[9] unless she has professed to have some special skill or expertise in which case the law demands that she must manifest that skill or expertise.

Two branches of knowledge must be considered separately: the first, that of memory and experience. If X had been on a certain highway several times, and a reasonable man who had been there as often would know that it was busy, then X also is expected to know, even though his memory is so poor that he does not remember it. Similarly, people are deemed to know those things which adults from their experience are expected to know: that some things easily explode, that others burn, that there is a law of gravity—this minimum amount of knowledge of matters of everyday experience they are deemed to possess.[10] There is one refinement of this rule: where, in the circumstances, the status of the defendant is relevant then the standard is that of a person in that position.[11] Thus, in *Caminer v Northern and London Investment Trust* the knowledge required of a landowner with regard to elm trees on his estate, their proneness to disease, lack of wind resistance and the like, was of a standard between that of an urban observer and a scientific arboriculturist.[12] In *The Wagon Mound (No 2)* case the Judicial Committee of the Privy Council said that the shipowner was liable for a fire caused by discharging oil in Sydney harbour because the chief engineer should have known that the discharge created a real risk of the oil on the water catching fire.[13] Moreover if someone elects to take on a particular task, albeit he is not an expert or professional, in the field, he will be expected to have the necessary degree of knowledge to complete the task competently.[14]

Secondly, what knowledge of the facts and circumstances surrounding him must the defendant have? He will not be excused for failing to observe what a reasonable man would have observed—a dock authority who did not know, but ought to have known, that the dock was unsafe, was negligent.[15] Further, even if a reasonable man himself could not be expected to know, he may be required to get and follow expert advice: the landlord of flats must therefore consult a specialist engineer about the safety

8   *Vaughan v Menlove* (1837) 3 Bing NC 468 at 474 (per Tindal CJ).
9   See *Woodridge v Sumner* [1963] 2 QB 43, [1962] 2 All ER 978, CA, infra.
10 *Caminer v Northern and London Investment Trust* [1951] AC 88, [1950] 2 All ER 486, HL carries the point: cf *Haynes v Harwood* [1935] 1 KB 146, at 153 CA (per Greer LJ).
11 Supra and see *Clarke v Holmes* (1862) 7 H & N 937, Ex Ch (employer required to know more about the dangers of unfenced machinery than workman).
12 [1951] AC 88 at 100 (per Lord Normand), [1950] 2 All ER 486, HL. And see *Quinn v Scott* [1965] 2 All ER 588, [1965] 1 WLR 1004.
13 [1967] 1 AC 617, [1966] 2 All ER 588.
14 See *Chaudry v Prabhakar* [1989] 1 WLR 29, CA (friend agreeing to act as gratuitous agent in connection with the purchase of a car).
15 *Mersey Docks and Harbour Board Trustees v Gibbs* (1866) LR 1 HL 93.

of his lift.[16] It is clear that actual knowledge of the circumstances on the part of the defendant increases the standard of care imposed,[17] but it is less clear that the greater one's memory or experience the greater is the measure of the care imposed.

Knowledge, in particular expert knowledge, does not remain static over the years. Scientific and technological advances lead to constant revision of and improvements in safety standards. In an action in negligence the defendant must always be judged in the light of the state of scientific, technological or other expert knowledge which should have been available to him at the time of the alleged breach of his duty of care. Concrete evidence that a drug damages the foetus is not conclusive evidence that either the doctor prescribing the drug, or the pharmaceutical company marketing the drug, were negligent.[18] The test in negligence[19] must be, at the time when the drug was prescribed or marketed, should the risk of injury to the foetus have been foreseen. As Lord Denning put it, when a plaintiff claimed in respect of a medical accident which had never occurred before in *Roe v Minister of Health*[20] 'We must not look at the 1947 accident with 1954 spectacles'.

(D) SKILL

It has been seen that a person's conduct must conform to the standard of a person of normal intelligence. When a person has held himself out as being capable of attaining standards of skill either in relation to the public generally, for example by driving a car,[1] or in relation to some person for whom he is performing a service, he is required to show the skill normally possessed by persons doing that work. A doctor failing to diagnose a disease cannot excuse himself by showing that he acted to the best of his skill if a reasonable doctor would have diagnosed it.[2] Nor can a young hospital doctor plead that he is inexperienced or overworked if he fails to attain the level of competence to be expected from a person holding his 'post' and entrusted with his responsibilities.[3] The same principle presumably applies to newly qualified solicitors.[4] One must, in this class of case, be careful to ascertain exactly what skill the defendant held himself out to have.

> Where the plaintiff had her ears pierced by a jeweller in order to wear earrings and subsequently contracted a disease that might have been avoided had the work been done with normal medical

16 *Haseldine v Daw & Son Ltd* [1941] 2 KB 343 at 356, [1941] 3 All ER 156, CA (per Scott LJ).
17 *Brooks v London and North Western Rly Co* (1884) 33 WR 167, Div Ct.
18 The drug thalidomide undoubtedly caused serious deformities in babies whose mothers took the drug in early pregnancy. One of the major obstacles confronting claims for compensation by the damaged children was doubt whether at the time the drug was first available, as opposed to after the births of several deformed babies, doctors and embryologists appreciated that drugs could cross the placental barrier and injure the foetus. Another example is just *when* should the dangers of using asbestos in buildings have been understood by construction firms.
19 Hence the argument that product liability at least should be strict. See ch 17, post, and in particular the effect of incorporating the 'development risks' defence into the new strict liability regime.
20 [1954] 2 QB 66 at 84.
1   *Nettleship v Weston* [1971] 2 QB 691, [1971] 3 All ER 581, CA.
2   In *Bolam v Friern Hospital Management Committee* [1957] 2 All ER 118, it was held that a doctor who conforms to practices accepted as proper by some responsible members of his profession is not liable merely because other members would take a different view.
3   *Wilsher v Essex Area Health Authority* [1987] QB 730, [1986] 3 All ER 801; revsd on a different point [1988] AC 1074, [1988] 1 All ER 871, HL.
4   *Nettleship v Weston* [1971] 2 QB 691 at 709 per Megaw LJ.

skill, the jeweller was required only to show the skill of a jeweller doing such work, not that of a doctor.[5]

In *Wells v Cooper*:[6]

A householder fitted a new door handle so insecurely that the plaintiff, when pulling it, lost his balance and was injured.

The Court of Appeal held that the householder was required to show the standard of care, not of a professional carpenter nor of a person having such skill as the defendant actually possessed, but that of a reasonably competent carpenter doing such a trifling domestic job.[7] Where someone has not held himself out as having special skill, he is not liable when he shows average skill in the circumstances although he has special skill.[8] One of the main reasons why the courts insist on applying a uniform standard of skill is the practical difficulty of assessing a particular person's actual skill or experience.[9]

Skill, just like every other aspect of the standard of care, has to be assessed in the light of all the circumstances surrounding the alleged breach of duty. No defendant will be expected to attain the same degree of skill under pressure in an emergency, 'in the heat of the moment', as would be demanded in less stressful circumstances.[10] Thus police chasing a suspect must still drive carefully but the hot pursuit of the offender will be taken into account in ascertaining whether the officers concerned fell below the appropriate standard of driving competence.[11] Where negligence is alleged in the course of playing a sport, the fact that the object of competitive sport is to win and that spectators attend sporting occasions to see competitors exhibit their skill at the game will be relevant. So in *Wooldridge v Sumner*[12] Diplock LJ held that where a showjumper was concentrating his attention and exerting his skill to complete his round of the showjumping circuit this must be taken into account in determining whether a momentary misjudgment constituted negligence. By contrast in *Condon v Basi*[13] a footballer sued in negligence when he suffered a broken leg as a result of a tackle by the defendant found by the referee to be serious foul play. The defendant was held liable and upholding the judgment at first instance, the Court of Appeal held that a clear breach of the rules of the game would be a relevant but not conclusive consideration in deciding whether there had been actionable negligence. The overall test was whether the defendant showed that degree of reasonable regard for the safety of others to be expected of a competent player of his class?

5   *Philips v William Whiteley Ltd* [1938] 1 All ER 566.
6   [1958] 2 QB 265, [1958] 2 All ER 527, CA. And see *Chaudhry v Prabhakar* [1988] 3 All ER 718, [1989] 1 WLR 29, CA.
7   If the householder employed a professional carpenter no doubt the latter would be under a contractual duty to him to use the skill of a professional, but what standard would the professional owe to members of the public?
8   *Wooldridge v Sumner* [1962] 2 All ER 978 at 989 (per Diplock J).
9   That was one reason why the Court of Appeal in *Nettleship v Weston* supra, held that a learner-driver has to reach the standard of any other driver even towards his instructor-passenger.
10 Many of the cases on the standard of care in emergencies deal with contributory negligence: see *Jones v Boyce* (1816) 1 Stark 493 discussed post at p 287; on primary liability and emergency see *Parkinson v Liverpool Corpn* [1950] 1 All ER 367, CA; *Ng Chun Pui v Lee Chuen Tat* [1988] RTR 298, PC.
11 *Marshall v Osmond* [1983] QB 1034, [1983] 2 All ER 225.
12 [1963] 2 QB 43, [1962] 2 All ER 978, CA.
13 [1985] 2 All ER 453, [1985] 1 WLR 866.

(E)   THE CIRCUMSTANCES OF THE PLAINTIFF

The defendant's actual knowledge of the circumstances may affect his measure of care. The standard owed to a woman known to be pregnant,[14] or to a workman with one eye,[15] may, according to particular circumstances, be greater. If the defendant neither knows nor ought to know of these circumstances, they do not affect the measure of his duty. As Lord Sumner put it[16]

> ... a measure of care appropriate to the inability or disability of those who are immature or feeble in mind or body is due from others, who know of or ought to anticipate the presence of such persons within the scope and hazard of their own operations.

In *Haley v London Electricity Board*[17] the House of Lords applied Lord Sumner's dictum when they held that a body conducting operations on a city highway should foresee that blind persons would walk along the pavement, and that it owes a duty to take those precautions reasonably necessary to protect them from harm; on the facts it was held liable although a sighted person would not have been injured in consequence of its operations.

Where the injured party is, or should be, known to the defendant, and the latter has some responsibility for his welfare, the defendant should have in mind the particular needs of that person. So in *Johnstone v Bloomsbury Health Authority*[18] discussing the duty owed by the employer-authority to junior doctors required to work excessive hours Stuart Smith LJ said:

> ... it must be remembered that the duty of care is owed to an individual employee and different employees may have a different stamina. If the authority in this case knew or ought to have known that by requiring him to work the hours they did, they exposed him to risk of injury to his health, then they should not have required him to work in excess of the hours that he safely could have done.

It is no answer to a claim in negligence to respond that you did not appreciate the risk that your conduct would injure the plaintiff, if the reasonable defendant with your knowledge of the plaintiff and the circumstances would have perceived that risk. Human frailty must be taken into account and defendants cannot shift their duty to plaintiffs by arguing in all circumstances that it is for the plaintiff to look out for himself. So in *Pape v Cumbria County Council*[19] it was found to be insufficient for employers to supply their workers with rubber gloves. They must warn them of the risk of dermatitis unless the gloves are worn. The prudent employer takes all reasonable steps to ensure that safety equipment is properly understood and used by employees. By contrast in *Eastman v South West Thames Regional Health Authority*[20] the defendants were held not liable when the plaintiff was thrown out of her seat in an ambulance and injured when the driver braked hard. She claimed that the driver was negligent in not expressly

14   *Hay (or Bourhill) v Young* [1943] AC 92 at 109, [1942] 2 All ER 396 per Lord Wright.
15   *Paris v Stepney Borough Council* [1951] AC 367, at 385, 386, HL (per Lord Oakley and Lord Morton, respectively).
16   *Glasgow Corpn v Taylor* [1922] 1 AC 44 at 67. Of course, there are numerous cases where defendants have not been held in breach of duty to infants (eg *Donovan v Union Cartage Co Ltd* [1933] 2 KB 71, Div Ct) or to blind persons (eg *Pritchard v Post Office* (1950) 114 JP 370, CA).
17   [1965] AC 778, [1964] 3 All ER 185, HL.
18   [1992] QB 333, [1991] 2 All ER 293, CA.
19   [1992] 3 All ER 211.
20   [1991] 2 Med LR 297, CA.

instructing her to wear her seat-belt. A notice in the ambulance carried just that instruction. The plaintiff was not herself a patient, but was accompanying her mother-in-law to hospital. The Court of Appeal found that the ambulance staff had done all that was reasonable in the circumstances. Passengers could choose whether or not to wear the belt provided and a clear notice advised them to do so. Had the plaintiff been herself a sick and confused elderly lady the outcome might well have been different.

(F) THE 'HURLY BURLY OF LIFE'

The tort of negligence does not demand perfection, does not require that those to whom a duty of care is owed are safeguarded against every conceivable risk. The 'reasonable man' test largely rests on common sense and the exigencies of everyday life must be recognised. A good example of the allowance made by the law for the 'hurly burly of life' can be seen in cases relating to parental and quasi-parental duties. In *Carmarthenshire County Council v Lewis*[1] the defendant council were held liable when a small boy wandered out of his nursery school and onto a nearby road causing an accident in which the plaintiff's husband died. The council were negligent because premises where small children are should be designed to ensure that children cannot wander off endangering themselves or others. But Lord Reid said[2] that the teacher who had not noticed the boy leave her classroom while she attended to a child with a cut knee was not negligent. Those in charge of small children cannot have eyes in the back of their heads.

In *Surtees v Kingston-upon-Thames Borough Council*[3] a child was scalded when her foster mother left her for a moment or two by a wash-basin and she somehow managed to turn on the hot tap and ran scalding water over her foot. The majority of the Court of Appeal held that the foster mother's arguable oversight was not negligence. Courts should be slow to characterise incidents in family life as negligence 'given the rough and tumble of home life'. Beldam LJ dissented. He argued that it would have required only momentary thought to remove the child from the vicinity of the tap. Was the majority decision fair to the injured child or does it go rather further than simply acknowledging the realities of life and its conflicting demands? Was the court in effect saying reasonable mothers make mistakes and should not be penalised for them? In other contexts, such as professional liability, no such allowance is made. Perhaps the concept of children suing their parents is seen as unedifying? Or was the Court of Appeal simply acknowledging that a risk-free existence is not feasible nor in all circumstances desirable. In *Porter v Barking and Dagenham London Borough Council*[4] a 14-year-old boy, injured when he and a friend were allowed to practise shotput unsupervised, failed in his action for negligence against the school authorities. The standard of care in relation to children should not be framed so as to stifle initiative.

(G) REASONABLE ANTICIPATION

In all the varied cases relating to the standard of care there is a recurrent emphasis on what could reasonably be anticipated or foreseen as constituting the standard of the

1   [1955] AC 549, [1955] 1 All ER 565, HL.
2   [1955] AC 549 at 564.
3   [1991] 2 FLR 559.
4   (1990) Times, 9 April.

reasonable man.[5] This serves to emphasise both that one must not look at the circumstances in the light of what has in fact happened[6] and that it is immaterial that, since the accident, the defendant has taken precautions against a further such accident.[7] It is elementary law that someone cannot be expected to take precautions against dangers which he cannot reasonably be expected to anticipate.'[8]

(H)   FORESEEABLE ACTS OF THIRD PARTIES

Even where the courts are prepared to find a duty in respect of the act of third parties, it will often be difficult to decide, when there has been an intervening act of a third party, whether the defendant's act has caused the damage suffered by the plaintiff. It is important to note that the issue of causation becomes material only after the failure of the defendant to take due care has been proved. Whether the defendant has shown that standard of care will frequently depend on what acts or omissions of another he could reasonably have anticipated. If the plaintiff is injured because a third party has done something which the defendant could not reasonably foresee that he would do, the defendant is not liable.[9] Yet, in *London Passenger Transport Board v Upson*,[10] the House of Lords reversed the ruling of Lord Greene MR, in the court below that 'drivers are entitled to drive on the assumption that other users of the road, whether drivers or pedestrians, will behave with reasonable care'.[11] Lord Uthwatt added:[12]

It is common experience that many do not. A driver is not, of course, bound to anticipate folly in all its forms, but he is not, in my opinion, entitled to put out of consideration the teachings of experience as to the form those follies commonly take.

Nor can one excuse oneself by relying on another to do an act unless that reliance was reasonable. *Manchester Corpn v Markland* illustrates this:[13]

The appellants were the statutory authority for the supply of water to the borough of Eccles. One of the appellants' service pipes in a road in Eccles burst; three days later, the resulting pool of water froze, and a car skidded on the ice knocking down and killing a man. In an action of negligence by the dependants of the deceased against the appellants, it was held to be no defence that the appellants chose to rely on Eccles Corporation to notify them of bursts— they should themselves have taken proper precautions.

---

5   *Glasgow Corpn v Muir* [1943] AC 448, [1943] 2 All ER 44, HL; *Paris v Stepney Borough Council* [1951] AC 367, [1951] 1 All ER 42, HL.
6   'Nothing is so easy as to be wise after the event' per Bramwell B, in *Cornman v Eastern Counties Rly Co* (1859) 4 H & N 781 at 786. This principle serves to re-emphasise the point that negligence must be judged on the state of scientific and technological knowledge at the time of the alleged carelessness, discussed ante at p 239.
7   *Hall v Brooklands Auto-Racing Club* [1933] 1 KB 205 at 225, CA (per Greer LJ).
8   *Tilley v Stevenson* [1939] 4 All ER 207 at 210, CA per Slesser LJ.
9   *Donaldson v McNiven* [1952] 2 All ER 691, CA.
10   [1949] AC 155, [1949] 1 All ER 60, HL.
11   [1947] KB 930 at 938.
12   [1949] AC 155 at 173; cf *Grant v Sun Shipping Co Ltd* [1948] AC 549 at 567 (per Lord Du Parcq), [1948] 2 All ER 238, HL.
13   [1936] AC 360, HL.

(I)   GENERAL PRACTICE OF THE COMMUNITY

Commonly, a defendant will support his claim to have shown due care by showing that he conformed to the common practice of those engaged in the activity in question. The evidence is obviously relevant. And, as we shall see in the next section, conforming to the practice of the profession will often be conclusive in claims against professionals. So a specialist who failed to diagnose the complaint of the plaintiff was held not to have been negligent when he used the normal methods of British medical specialists, although the use of an instrument usually employed in the United States might have resulted in a correct diagnosis.[14] Yet evidence of general practice is not always decisive. In *Cavanagh v Ulster Weaving Co Ltd*:[15]

> The plaintiff slipped coming down a roof ladder. Despite unchallenged evidence that the 'set-up' was in perfect accord with established practice, the House of Lords restored the jury's verdict that the defendants were negligent.

In *Brown v Rolls Royce Ltd*:[16]

> The defendants failed to provide the plaintiff with barrier cream commonly supplied by employers to workmen doing work like this. They had relied on proper medical advice in not providing the cream. They further maintained that the plaintiff had not proved that the cream would have prevented him from contracting dermatitis. Held that the plaintiff had not discharged his burden of proving that negligence by the defendants caused his dermatitis.

Commercial enterprises must take steps to keep abreast of scientific developments. Growing understanding of the effects of industrial noise and its role as a causative factor in deafness was not matched by action by employers. In *Thompson v Smith's Shiprepairers (North Shields) Ltd*[17] it was held that once there was general awareness of the dangers of noise and protective equipment became available from about 1963 onwards that defendants were liable for impairment of hearing caused after that date.

Failure to conform to a standard imposed by a statute, although of course it may constitute a breach of statutory duty, is not in itself conclusive evidence of negligence:[18] it may, however, sometimes be prima facie evidence.[19]

14   *Whiteford v Hunter* (1950) 94 Sol Jo 758, HL; cf *Vancouver General Hospital v McDaniel* (1934) 152 LT 56, PC; *Wright v Cheshire County Council* [1952] 2 All ER 789, CA.
15   [1960] AC 145, [1959] 2 All ER 745, HL.
16   [1960] 1 All ER 577, HL. And see *Stokes v Guest Keen and Nettlefold (Bolts and Nuts) Ltd* [1968] 1 WLR 1776, where the negligence of a works doctor in not instituting medical examinations and in not warning of the risks was held to have caused the scrotal cancer of the plaintiff workman.
17   [1984] QB 405, [1984] 1 All ER 881.
18   In *Powell v Phillips* [1972] 3 All ER 864, CA, it was held that breach of the *Highway Code*, despite s 37(5) of the Road Traffic Act 1972, creates no presumption of negligence calling for an explanation; it is just one relevant circumstance. In *Trotman v British Railways Board* [1975] ICR 95, it was held that breach of a regulation in British Railways' Rule Book created a rebuttable inference of negligence. A breach of a navigational bye-law is particularly cogent evidence of negligence, eg *Cayzer, Irvine & Co v Carran Co* (1884) 9 App Cas 873 at 880–1 (per Lord Blackburn), HL, sed quaere whether it is conclusive.
19   *Blamires v Lancashire and Yorkshire Rly Co* (1873) LR 8 Exch 283; *Phillips v Britannia Hygienic Laundry Co* [1923] 1 KB 539 at 548 (per McCardie J); affd [1923] 2 KB 832, CA; *Anglo-Newfoundland Development Co Ltd v Pacific Steam Navigation Co* [1924] AC 406 at 413, HL (per Lord Dunedin); see also *Harrison v National Coal Board* [1951] AC 639, [1951] 1 All ER 1102, HL; *National Coal Board v England* [1954] AC 403, [1954] 1 All ER 546, HL. And compliance with a statutory requirement does not exclude liability in negligence. *Bux v Slough Metals Ltd* [1974] 1 All ER 262, CA. And see *Budden v BP Oil Ltd* (1980) 124 Sol Jo 376, CA, p 232, ante.

Before we proceed to examine how negligence may be proven, we briefly need to explore two particularly common kinds of breach of duty: professional negligence and breach of the employer's duty of care.

SECTION 3.   PROFESSIONAL NEGLIGENCE[20]

(A)   THE BACKGROUND

There is in terms of fundamental principle no distinction between the guidelines ascertaining the standard of care of professionals from those applicable to any other person. Whether the defendant is a plumber or an architect or a consultant surgeon, the primary question is whether in all the circumstances the defendant acted with the skill and competence to be expected from a person undertaking his particular activity and professing his specific skill. The problems which arise in actions against professionals include these:

1   There may be disputes within the profession as to what constitutes proper practice.
2   The implications of professional negligence are likely to be more far flung. When a carpenter makes an error fixing a new door, damage may be inflicted on the fabric of the house, the householder may suffer personal injury if the door falls off, but the range of potential harm is limited. Should an architect designing blocks of tower flats make an error in design, hundreds of people are at risk, and the financial cost of correcting the error in several blocks of flats may be astronomic.
3   The potentially high cost of professional negligence has resulted in massive increases in insurance premiums in particular for architects, solicitors, and accountants. Many professions are now calling for statutory limits on damages awards for professional negligence, for provision to be made for 'capping' damages.
4   Particularly acute difficulties affect doctors. Cutbacks in the NHS mean doctors may often be overworked and hospitals under-resourced. Junior doctors may be forced to do tasks beyond their competence in the absence of sufficient consultant cover. And patients may wish to play a greater part in decision-making these days.
5   Finally, and rather obviously, a professional defendant will be worth suing. The rules of the profession are likely to oblige him to take out professional indemnity cover. For these and many other reasons in practice actions for professional negligence tend to be fraught with difficulty for the plaintiff and to be fought vigorously by the professional backed by his insurers. Some further guidelines are therefore now given on the current state of the law in England relating to professional negligence.

(B)   DUTY AND BREACH

Very often the duty of care will arise concurrently in tort and within the contract between the professional and his client. Save where an NHS professional is treating a patient, most professional/client relationships are founded on a contract for services. The client pays the solicitor or the accountant for her advice. A duty of care will be implied into that contract,[1] but will a duty in tort arise concurrently allowing the client to opt whether to sue in contract or tort? After years of conflicting judgments, the House of Lords in

---

20   For full treatment of this important topic, see Dugdale and Stanton *Professional Negligence* (3rd edn); *Jackson and Powell on Professional Negligence* (3rd edn).
1   See s 13 of the Supply of Goods and Services Act 1982.

Henderson v Merrett Syndicates Ltd[2] ruled in favour of concurrent liability providing that imposing a duty in tort does not conflict with the contractual terms agreed between the parties. When duties of care do arise concurrently, whether there has been a breach of duty will generally be determined on exactly the same principles regardless of whether the action is brought in tort or contract. However, contract may impose duties higher than those of the duty of care. In *Thake v Maurice*[3] a surgeon failed to warn a private patient of the risk that a vasectomy may be reversed by nature restoring the patient's fertility. The patient argued that the surgeon contracted to render him sterile. He was therefore liable for that breach of contract regardless of whether or not he was negligent when the patient's wife conceived again. The Court of Appeal eventually held by 2–1 that no reasonable man would infer from his contract with a doctor that the doctor guaranteed success.[4] But *Thake v Maurice* graphically illustrates the separate roles of tort and contract where the plaintiff seeks to establish a liability independent of classic negligence. The argument pursued by the plaintiff could not even have been attempted had he been an NHS patient with no contract with the defendant.

In a number of professional relationships the core of the professional's duty is to offer advice. Liability in negligence will depend largely on the principles governing liability for negligent statements. May the professional find himself liable to a third party, to someone other than the client, who relies on, or suffers loss as a result of that advice? The professions trembled in the early 1980s at the prospect of ever-increasing liabilities. If an auditor negligently gave a favourable report on a company, and a flood of investors lost their life savings by rushing to invest in the company, where would the auditors' liability end? The judicial retrenchment on liability for economic loss has to a large extent dissipated this particular professional nightmare. In *Caparo Industries plc v Dickman*[5] auditors prepared a report on a company on the basis of which the plaintiff mounted a successful takeover bid of that company. The plaintiffs alleged that the report negligently suggested pre-tax profits of £1.2m when in fact there had been losses of £400,000. The House of Lords held that no duty was owed to the plaintiffs. Mere foreseeability of financial loss to a third party was insufficient to create a duty on the part of the professional. For a duty to arise to a third party the professional: (1) must be aware that his advice will be transmitted to the plaintiff, or to an identifiable class of persons of whom the plaintiff is one; (2) that advice must be transmitted in order to forward a specific purpose of transaction of the plaintiffs, and (3) it must be reasonable in all the circumstances for the plaintiff to rely on that advice, rather than to seek independent advice of his own, and the professional must be well aware that the plaintiff will so rely on his advice.

Two examples of where professionals did owe duties to third parties can be seen in *Smith v Bush* and *White v Jones*. In *Smith v Bush*[6] the plaintiff mortgagees relied on survey reports obtained by the mortgagors as assurances that the properties which they wished to buy were structurally sound and worth more or less the agreed purchase price. The House of Lords held it was well known that over 90% of house-buyers relied on the building society survey report for which they ultimately paid. The defendant surveyors should have appreciated that the plaintiffs reasonably entrusted them with

---

2   [1995] 2 AC 145, [1994] 3 All ER 506, HL.
3   [1986] QB 644, [1986] 1 All ER 497. And see *Eyre v Measday* [1986] 1 All ER 488 (female sterilisation).
4   But the appeal court unanimously held the surgeon liable in negligence. The failure to warn was held to be negligent and as a result the wife failed to recognise the symptoms of pregnancy soon enough to be able to opt for an abortion.
5   [1990] 2 AC 605, [1990] 1 All ER 568, HL.
6   [1990] 1 AC 831, [1989] 2 All ER 514, HL.

responsibilities for safeguarding their interests. In *White v Jones*,[7] a solicitor negligently delayed to act on his client's instructions to draw up a new will including legacies to the client's daughters. The client was elderly and in poor health and died before the defendant drew up the new will. The plaintiffs thus 'lost' their legacies. The solicitor was found liable for their disappointed expectations. But note that the solicitor's duty is only to act on his client's instructions[8] and no duty to a third party will lie if the solicitor's primary duty to her client conflicts with any responsibility to the third party.[9]

(C) THE REASONABLE 'PROFESSIONAL'

The basic test of whether the defendant conformed to the standard of the reasonable man, the reasonable 'professional', must be elaborated a little.

The defendant must exhibit the degree of skill which a member of the public would expect from a person in his or her position. Pressures on him, even pressures for which he is in no way responsible will not excuse an error on his part. Negligence is not to be equated with moral culpability or general incompetence. In *Wilsher v Essex Area Health Authority*,[10] a premature baby was admitted to a specialist neo-natal unit. An error was made in that medical staff failed to notice that the baby was receiving too much oxygen and the baby became blind. The Court of Appeal held that the doctors were negligent and by a majority that they must be judged by reference to their 'posts' in the unit. It would be irrelevant that they were inexperienced, or doing a job which should have been done by a consultant, or just grossly overworked. The dissenting judge argued that the doctors should be assessed individually. If a particular doctor was too junior for his 'post' then it should be the health authority who were directly liable to the plaintiff for providing inadequate staffing and resources.[11]

In determining the standard demanded in a particular 'post', be it surgical registrar or partner in a firm of solicitors, expert evidence of proper practice must be called. Where practice is disputed, conformity with a responsible body of opinion within the profession will generally suffice.[12] Nonetheless the courts remain the ultimate arbiter of what constitutes reasonable and responsible professional practice. In *Edward Wong Finance Co Ltd v Johnson, Stokes v Master*[13] the defendant solicitors followed a uniform practice among the profession in Hong Kong of paying the purchase price to the vendor in return for their promise to ensure that the property was free of encumbrance. The vendors fraudulently failed to do so, and the plaintiff thus failed to obtain an unencumbered title to the property. The Privy Council held that, while evidence of the practice of the profession went a long way to show that the defendant was not negligent, it was not conclusive. The risk of fraud should have been foreseen and precautions taken to avoid that risk. In claims against doctors, until recently judges seemed more than unusually unwilling to challenge expert professional opinion. Lord Scarman castigated a trial judge for presuming to prefer one body of distinguished professional opinion to another.[14] However, in *Bolitho v City and Hackney Health Authority*,[15] Lord Browne-Wilkinson stressed that to constitute evidence of proper, non-negligent,

7   [1995] 2 AC 207, HL; and see *Ross v Caunters* [1980] Ch 297, [1979] 3 All ER 580.
8   *Clarke v Bruce Lance & Co* [1988] 1 All ER 364, [1988] 1 WLR 881.
9   [1988] 1 All ER 364; and see *Clerk & Lindsell* 8–77 to 8–79.
10   [1987] QB 730, [1986] 3 All ER 801; revsd on the issue of causation [1988] AC 1074, [1988] 1 All ER 871, HL.
11   On the direct liability of health authorities to patients see post.
12   *Bolam v Friern Hospital Management Committee* [1957] 2 All ER 118, [1957] 1 WLR 582.
13   [1984] AC 296, PC.
14   *Maynard v West Midlands Regional Health Authority* [1984] 1 WLR 634 at 639.
15   [1998] AC 232, HL; and see *Hucks v Cole* [1993] 4 Med LR 393, CA.

practice expert opinion must be shown to be reasonable and responsible '…the court has to be satisfied that the exponents of the body of opinion relied on can demonstrate that such opinion has a logical basis'.[16] If 'in a rare case' it can be shown that professional opinion cannot withstand logical analysis, then in a claim against a doctor, as much as in a claim against any other professional, a judge is entitled to find that expert opinion is not reasonable or responsible.

Errors of judgment are often the essence of professional negligence. An error of itself is not negligence. The issue in all cases is whether the error in question evidenced a failure of professional competence. The virtual immunity offered to doctors for errors of clinical judgment was firmly condemned by the House of Lords in *Whitehouse v Jordan*.[17] As Lord Edmund Davies put it:

> The test [of negligence] is the standard of the ordinary skilled man exercising or professing to have that special skill. If a surgeon fails to measure up to that standard in any respect ('clinical judgment') or otherwise he has been negligent.

Care must be taken in assessing that standard to relate what is expected of the professional to the expertise he claims to hold and not to demand unrealistic standards of skill and knowledge. In *Luxmoore-May v Messenger May-Baverstock*[18] the plaintiff took a painting to a local auctioneers for valuation and sale. The defendants were held not liable for failing to discover that it was a painting by a well-known artist of the 18th century.[19] A general practitioner consulted by a patient complaining of stomach trouble is not expected to have the same level of knowledge as the consultant gastro-enterologist, but he must as a reasonable general practitioner know when he ought to refer the patient on to a gastro-enterologist.

(D)   PATIENTS AND DOCTORS

Two factors militate to accentuate the problems of an action against a professional where the professional is a medical practitioner.

First, there is the fear that a flood of successful litigation against doctors will trigger the practice of 'defensive' medicine. Your doctor will opt for the treatment least likely to lead to you suing him rather than the treatment which may be best for you medically. Patients will be subjected to unnecessary tests to protect the doctors and the NHS will thus incur unnecessary expenses. No judge has expressly found against a patient plaintiff on this basis[20] but the spectre of defensive medicine haunts the growing avalanche of often unsuccessful medical litigation.[1]

Second, there is the thorny problem of 'informed consent'. We saw earlier that failure by a doctor to advise a patient on the risks of treatment does not invalidate the patient's consent so as to give rise to an action in trespass.[2] But counselling a patient so as to aid him to make a sensible decision on whether or not to agree to proposed treatment

16 [1997] 3 WLR 1151 at 1159.
17 [1981] 1 WLR 246 at 258, HL.
18 [1990] 1 All ER 1067 (they met the 'GP' standard).
19 Or probably was a painting by George Stubbs: this 'fascinating' question was left open by the Court of Appeal; at 1083 (per Slade LJ).
20 Do you think that this was a factor in *Whitehouse v Jordan* [1981] 1 All ER 267, [1981] 1 WLR 246? (obstetrician held not liable for failing to proceed more swiftly to Caesarean section: did the judges fear a rise in the rate of Caesarean births to protect obstetricians from liability to brain damaged babies?)
1   But it is a spectre which on investigation often proves to lack substance; see Jones (1987) 3 Professional Negligence 43.
2   See ante at p 85.

is part and parcel of the doctor's duty of care.[3] How should the issue of breach of that duty be determined? The House of Lords in *Sidaway*[4] held that the normal test of professional negligence must apply, that is accepted professional practice. In *Gold v Haringey Health Authority* the treatment involved was non-therapeutic sterilisation. The plaintiff chose to be sterilised as a means of permanent contraception. A further pregnancy would not have endangered her health. The judge at first instance[5] said the doctor's duty in counselling her on the risks and disadvantages of sterilisation should be judged by what she, as a reasonable woman, would want to know. She was not receiving therapeutic treatment needed for her health and so *Sidaway* could be distinguished. The Court of Appeal quashed his decision. The test in all cases, they proclaimed, should be accepted professional practice.[6] Only if professional practice in informing patients of risks of treatment effectively negates any notion of patient choice will the doctor be found negligent. So in *Smith v Tunbridge Wells Health Authority*,[7] a surgeon who failed to warn a young married man that the proposed surgery might render him impotent was held to be negligent, even though other surgeons testified that they too chose not to warn of that risk.

The debate on 'informed consent' illustrates that negligence, like trespass, could have a role in defining our individual rights, and promoting individual autonomy. Who should decide whether the benefits of proposed treatment outweigh the risks? That is the question of principle. The courts have so far generally refused to distinguish between negligent treatment as such, and a failure by the doctor in his delicate task of assisting his patient to make his own choices on treatment,[8] and to exercise his right to self-determination.[9] Judicial fear of a flood of medical litigation, as has happened in the US, and fraternal regard to the medical profession, have induced the English courts so far to be cautious about the use of the law of torts to uphold patients' rights.

SECTION 4. EMPLOYERS' LIABILITY TO THEIR EMPLOYEES

The risk of personal injury either suffered in an accident at work, or by contracting an industrial disease, is particularly acute in certain types of employment. The general liability[10] of employers remains liability in negligence alone but it is one of the most highly developed and thoroughly litigated areas of the law of negligence. Compensation for industrial injuries is provided for by way of the state scheme relating to industrial injuries. Nonetheless the higher level of common law damages ensure that many employees continue to elect for the common law remedy in negligence. In order to ensure

3 *Chatterton v Gerson* [1981] QB 432, [1981] 1 All ER 257.
4 *Sidaway v Governors of Bethlem Royal Hospital and the Maudsley Hospital* [1985] AC 871, [1985] 1 All ER 643.
5 [1986] 1 FLR 125.
6 [1988] QB 481, [1987] 2 All ER 888, CA.
7 [1994] 5 Med LR 334.
8 See in particular the judgment of Lord Diplock in *Sidaway* supra.
9 See H Teff 'Consent to Medical Procedures: Paternalism, Self Determination, or Therapeutic Alliance' (1985) 101 LQR 432; M Brazier 'Patient Autonomy and Consent to Medical Treatment' (1987) 7 LS 169.
10 Of course in certain cases specific statutory duties in respect of safety are imposed on employers and in such cases an action for breach of statutory duty may lie; see post at ch 21. Breach of the general statutory code on safety provided for by the Health and Safety at Work Act 1974 is not actionable as a breach of statutory duty. Section 17(1) expressly provides that breach of the code of practice under the Act is not of itself tortious. But it may be that in assessing negligence judges may tend to treat conformity with the code as evidence that reasonable care has been taken; and vice versa?

that an employee awarded compensation for negligence against his employer receives the money due to him the Employers' Liability (Compulsory Insurance) Act 1969 requires employers to insure against liability for injury sustained by employees in the course of their employment. Despite the massive volume of material on employers' liability the basic principles can be stated here quite succinctly. Lord Wright summed up the employer's duty thus in the leading case of *Wilsons and Clyde Coal Co Ltd v English*:[11]

> a duty which rests on the employer and which is personal to the employer, to take reasonable care for the safety of his workmen, whether the employer be an individual, a firm, or a company, and whether or not the employer takes any share in the conduct of the operations.

As will be seen, some of the language deployed to analyse employers' responsibility for the safety of their employees, is the language of duty. Employers are said to owe a tripartite duty of care to take reasonable care to provide competent staff, adequate equipment and a safe system of working. Despite the language, perhaps the core of the majority of cases on employers' liability relates to standard of care. The central question discussed in this section then, is just what degree and kinds of safeguards must employers put in place to discharge their responsibility in tort for the health and safety of their workers?

(A)   A PERSONAL, NON-DELEGABLE DUTY

The duty is a personal one of a general nature. As will be seen later,[12] there is another form of tortious liability, known as vicarious liability, where a person is liable not for breach of his own personal duty, but for the tort of an employee. Because, until the Law Reform (Personal Injuries) Act 1948, an employer sued by a workman on account of the employer's vicarious liability for the tort of a fellow-workman could successfully raise the defence of common employment, the personal duties of employers have been kept strictly separate from those for which their responsibility is vicarious. It is true that, since that Act abolishes the defence of common employment, this strict marking off of personal duty has become less important in circumstances where the plaintiff can in any event prove fault by a fellow-employee. Yet, it would be misleading to state that the distinction can now be ignored; for there will still be many cases where the employer is in breach of his personal duty and yet no employee is at fault;[13] further, the distinction remains the basis of judicial thinking on the subject, and the development and implications of the cases cannot be understood if this is not grasped.

Employers' responsibilities fall naturally into three divisions: (1) personnel, (2) those concerned with place of work, machinery, tools and raw materials, (3) the general management or system of work—how to use machinery, organise the detailed working, and supervision.

Once breach of the employer's duty is established, liability will follow even in the absence of any primary negligence by the employer or his employees. The duty of care

11   [1938] AC 57 at 84, [1937] 3 All ER 628, HL. Where a workman is hired to another employer that employer who would be vicariously liable for his torts according to the principles of *Mersey Docks and Harbour Board v Coggins and Griffith (Liverpool) Ltd* [1947] AC 1, [1946] 2 All ER 345, HL, p 506, post, is also the 'employer' who owes him this duty of care: *O'Reilly v Imperial Chemical Industries Ltd* [1955] 2 All ER 567, [1955] 1 WLR 839.
12   Chapter 25, post.
13   It may be that there is an inadequate system for when culpability can be attached to no one person; or it may be that the individual at fault is not an employee of the employer sued as in *McDermid v Nash Dredging and Reclamation Co Ltd* [1987] AC 906, [1987] 2 All ER 878, HL.

owed to the employee is non-delegable. In *McDermid v Nash Dredging and Reclamation Co Ltd*[14] the plaintiff was employed by the defendants as a deckhand. He was sent to work on a rig owned by a Dutch company under the control of a Dutch captain employed by that Dutch company. The plaintiff of course had no idea he was not continuing to work on one of his employer's boats under one of 'their' captains. The plaintiff suffered serious injuries when as a result of the Dutch captain's carelessness a rope that the plaintiff was untying as the rig moved off snaked round his legs. The employers denied responsibility because quite rightly they contended they were not vicariously liable for the conduct of someone else's employee. The House of Lords held the defendants liable on these very simple grounds. The evidence showed that the plaintiff was injured because no safe system of work was in operation. The duty incumbent on his employers to devise and operate such a system was not performed. The essential characteristic of the employer's non-delegable duty '... is that, if it is not performed, it is no defence for the employer to show that he delegated its performance to a person, whether his servant or not his servant, whom he reasonably believed to be competent to perform it. Despite such delegation the employer is liable for the non-performance of the duty'.[15]

Although the duty is personal, and is not discharged by entrusting it to competent delegates, it is still a liability for negligence, not a liability imposed regardless of fault. 'The obligation is fulfilled by the exercise of due care and skill' and Lord Tucker has stressed[16] the importance of not enlarging the employer's duty until it is barely distinguishable from his absolute statutory obligations. An employer may be liable for a mere omission;[17] actual knowledge on his part of a danger is not insisted on if he ought to have known of it.[18] It is a question of fact whether there has been a breach of the duty;[19] precedents relating to industrial practice form guidance as to an employer's breach of duty but no more.[20] Evidence of compliance with common practice will be strong but not conclusive evidence that the employer has discharged his duty. Nevertheless once a substantial risk of, for example, industrial disease, is well known, failure to protect employees against that disease will be actionable even if it is the 'customary practice' of the trade to go on ignoring the risk.[1]

The same defences are available as in other forms of negligence; contributory negligence is, of course, important in reducing damages. Although it will be recalled that it is very difficult to establish assumption of risk because the courts are reluctant to find that a workman has voluntarily encountered the danger,[2] yet, if the employment necessarily involves particular risks, for example a cinema stunt man, the employer has then no duty to remove these risks, and a workman injured in consequence of

14 [1987] AC 906, [1987] 2 All ER 878, HL. And see *Kondis v State Transport Authority* (1984) 154 CLR 672 (Aust HC).

15 Ibid at 223 per Lord Brandon.

16 *Latimer v AEC Ltd* [1953] AC 643 at 658, [1953] 2 All ER 449, HL. *Cook v Square D* [1992] ICR 262, sub nom *Square D v Cook* [1992] IRLR 34, CA (employee injured working on a site in Saudi Arabia; no evidence of any negligence by the employer). In *Richardson v Stephenson Clarke Ltd* [1969] 3 All ER 705, the employers left it to the plaintiff employee to choose his equipment. He chose carelessly and was hurt. *Held*, the employers had discharged their duty by providing safe equipment and leaving the selection of the equipment to the plaintiff; the plaintiff's negligence alone caused the accident. On a difficult problem of causation, see *McGhee v National Coal Board* [1972] 3 All ER 1008, [1973] 1 WLR 1, HL.

17 *Williams v Birmingham Battery and Metal Co* [1899] 2 QB 338, CA.

18 *Baker v James* [1921] 2 KB 674 at 681 (per McCardie J).

19 *Latimer v AEC Ltd* [1953] AC 643 at 655 (per Lord Oaksey); further, res ipsa loquitur applies— *Ballard v North British Rly Co* 1923 SC (HL) 43 at 53 (per Lord Dunedin), HL.

20 *King v Smith* [1995] ICR 339, CA.

1 *Thompson v Smiths Shiprepairers (North Shields) Ltd* [1984] QB 405, [1984] 1 All ER 881.

2 *Smith v Baker & Sons* [1891] AC 325, HL.

undertaking them will not recover in negligence. However, it must be remembered that the three-fold formulation of the employer's duty by Lord Wright[3] is not exclusive. It may be that the employer's duty further embraces warning and counselling prospective employees of inherent risks of the work before the employee accepts the job.[4]

In one respect a distinction has to be made between defective equipment and failure to provide competent staff or a proper system of working. The Employers' Liability (Defective Equipment) Act 1969 applies only to defective equipment, including plant and machinery, vehicles, aircraft and clothing provided by the employer for the purpose of his business.[5] Even though the defect is attributable to the negligence of an independent contractor or other third party the employer is still liable to his employee for personal injuries suffered in consequence in the course of his employment. It was uncertain when an employer would be liable to his workmen for other types of negligence on the part of his independent contractor.[6] The effect of the decision of the House of Lords in *McDermid v Nash Dredging & Reclamation Co Ltd* would seem to be (although the point is not fully discussed in the judgments) that 'non-delegable' means just what it says and that in respect of any of the components of the duty owed by the employer delegation of the duty to any third party will be no defence if breach of that duty is proved.

Remembering always that the basic question is whether the employer has failed to take reasonable care for the safety of his employee[7] and that the tripartite division is not necessarily exhaustive of the area of liability in negligence of employers to their workforce, it is convenient now to examine shortly the three categories.

(B) THE PROVISION OF COMPETENT STAFF

Before 1948, an employee injured by the incompetence of his fellow-employee could recover damages in negligence from his employer only by establishing that the employer was himself negligent in employing the fellow-employee in the circumstances. Now that common employment no longer absolves the employer from vicarious liability, clearly this head is of much less importance. This category of case will now only be relevant where the plaintiff cannot prove any fault on the part of the other employee and yet can show that his injury results from negligent staffing provision—the commonest case will be where the employer appoints an insufficiently qualified or experienced person for a particular task.[8]

---

3   In *Wilsons and Clyde Coal Co Ltd v English* (supra).
4   See *White v Holbrook Precision Castings* [1985] IRLR 215, CA.
5   The Act will not apply, for example where a domestic cleaner is injured because an electrician has carelessly installed a plug in her employer's home; nor is the employer liable at common law if he has carefully chosen the electrician: *Cook v Broderip* (1968) 206 Estates Gazette 128.
6   *Davie v New Merton Board Mills Ltd* [1959] AC 604, [1959] 1 All ER 346, HL (an employer who bought a tool from a reliable source was not liable for a latent defect caused by the negligence of the independent contractor). *Sumner v William Henderson & Sons Ltd* [1963] 2 All ER 712n, [1963] 1 WLR 823, CA.
7   Emphasised again by the House of Lords in *General Cleaning Contractors Ltd v Christmas* [1953] AC 180, [1952] 2 All ER 1110, HL; cf *Drummond v British Building Cleaners Ltd* [1954] 3 All ER 507, [1954] 1 WLR 1434, CA.
8   *Black v Fife Coal Co Ltd* [1912] AC 149, HL (employment of a colliery manager without experience of carbon monoxide in a pit where its presence was a possible danger); especially per Lord Shaw at 170. In *Hudson v Ridge Manufacturing Co Ltd* [1957] 2 QB 348, [1957] 2 All ER 229, knowingly to employ a workman continually indulging in horseplay was held to violate this duty.

(C) ADEQUATE PREMISES AND PLANT

The employer must take care to provide safe premises[9] and plant for his workers. Both failure to provide some necessary equipment and the provision of defective appliances constitute breaches of this duty. So, the failure of ship-owners to provide essential spare ropes for a voyage was actionable negligence.[10] There is probably a duty not merely to provide the material, but also to maintain it.[11]

(D) A PROPER SYSTEM OF WORKING

The scope of this requirement was considerably increased by the decision of the Court of Appeal in *Speed v Thomas Swift & Co Ltd*:[12]

> The plaintiff was engaged in loading a ship from a barge. Normally, the particular part of this loading operation, which required the port and starboard winches to be used together, was carried out while the ship's rails were left in position; only when one winch was being used was it ordinarily necessary to remove a section of the rails in order to prevent their being caught by the hook. The following special circumstances however, made it dangerous on that occasion to load with two winches without removing the section of the rail. Other sections of the rail had been damaged by accident and had had to be removed; timber was lying against the rails so that it was likely easily to be dislodged; the port winch was not in perfect order. A hook caught in the rail, and the rail and timber fell into the barge, and injured the plaintiff. It was held that he could recover in negligence because the defendants had not, in these particular circumstances, laid out a safe system of work.

Lord Greene MR, approved the following description of 'system of work'.[13]

> What is system and what falls short of system may be difficult to define ... but, broadly stated, the distinction is between the general and the particular, between the practice and method adopted in carrying on the master's business of which the master is presumed to be aware and the insufficiency of which he can guard against, and isolated or day to day acts of the servant of which the master is not presumed to be aware and which he cannot guard against; in short, it is the distinction between what is permanent or continuous on the one hand, and what is merely casual and emerges in the day's work on the other hand.

He added:[14]

---

9   'Whether the servant is working on the premises of the master or on those of a stranger, that duty is still the same; but ... its performance and discharge will probably be vastly different in the two cases. The master's own premises are under his control: if they are dangerously in need of repair he can and must rectify the fault at once if he is to escape the censure of negligence. If, however, a master sends his plumber to mend a leak in a respectable private house, no one could hold him negligent for not visiting the house himself to see if the carpet in the hall creates a trap': per Pearce LJ in *Wilson v Tyneside Window Cleaning Co* [1958] 2 QB 110 at 121, [1958] 2 All ER 265 at 271, CA.
10 *Vaughan v Roper & Co Ltd* (1947) 80 Ll J L Rep 119, CA.
11 Dicta in *Wilsons and Clyde Coal Co Ltd v English* [1938] AC 57, [1937] 3 All ER 628, HL, and the much cited judgment of Sir Arthur Channel in *Toronto Power Co Ltd v Paskwan* [1915] AC 734 at 738, PC.
12 [1943] KB 557, [1943] 1 All ER 539; approved by the House of Lords in *Colfar v Coggins and Griffith (Liverpool) Ltd* [1945] AC 197, [1945] 1 All ER 326, HL, where, however, Viscount Simon LC suggested that the principles there laid down marked the limit of the duty (at 202).
13 [1943] KB 557 at 562, citing *English v Wilsons and Clyde Coal Co Ltd* in the Court of Session 1936 SC 883, at 904.
14 [1943] KB 557 at 563.

It ... may include ... the physical lay-out of the job—the setting of the stage, so to speak—the sequence in which the work is to be carried out, the provision in proper cases of warnings and notices, and the issue of special instructions. A system may be adequate for the whole course of the job or it may have to be modified or improved to meet circumstances which arise. Such modifications or improvements appear to me equally to fall under the head of system.

On the other hand, in *Winter v Cardiff RDC*,[15] the House of Lords held that a workman, who was injured because a rope provided by the employer for that purpose had not in fact been used to lash a regulator being carried on a lorry in which he was travelling, could not complain of the system of work. Lord Porter said:[16]

The difference ... is between a case where sufficient and adequate provisions have been made, which will, if carried out, protect the workman unless one of his fellows does not use proper care in carrying out the system, and a case where the system itself makes no such provision.

Does this suggest that, provided a safe system is devised, any failure in operation of the system will not be actionable as a breach of the employer's personal duty? This proposition must be treated with caution after *McDermid v Nash Dredging and Reclamation Co Ltd*. Lord Brandon asserted unequivocally that the duty extended to the operation of the system,[17] the crucial factor being in that case perhaps that the relevant carelessness in operating the system was that of the man in control of the operation and not just a fellow employee of the plaintiff.

The House of Lords has also laid down that in considering whether the employers are negligent, regard must be had to their knowledge of physical defects of particular workmen, so that it was relevant, in deciding whether the employers had taken reasonable care to protect a workman from flying metal by providing him with goggles, that the employers knew him to be one-eyed.[18]

Many of the decided cases on employers' liability focus on responsibility for physically dangerous work environments. The risk to the employee is of crude injury whether by a mechanical device or via industrial disease. Other sorts of risk, too, come within the employers' duty. Claims for stress-related illness are rapidly becoming commonplace. In *Johnstone v Bloomsbury Area Health Authority*[19] the Court of Appeal refused to strike out a claim by a junior doctor that the excessive hours which he was required to work had damaged his health. And in *Walker v Northumberland County Council*[20] a social worker recovered damages after his employers failed to reduce his workload on his return from sick leave after suffering a nervous breakdown. The continued stress triggered a second bout of illness. The court held that, given the obvious risk of further mental injury to the plaintiff, the employer should have taken steps to reduce the level of stress to which the plaintiff was exposed by his work.

However, it must not be forgotten that employers' liability is not unlimited. He does not have to 'insure' his personnel against all work-related risk. In *Reid v Rush & Tompkins Group plc*[1] an employer was held not liable for failing to provide his employee posted abroad with insurance against risks encountered in that posting.

15 [1950] 1 All ER 819, HL.
16 [1950] 1 All ER 819 at 822.
17 [1987] 3 WLR 212 at 223.
18 *Paris v Stepney Borough Council* [1951] AC 367, [1951] 1 All ER 42, HL. On the other hand in *Charlton v Forrest Printing Ink Co Ltd* [1980] IRLR 331, CA, it was held that an employee attacked by robbers after collecting wages from the bank could not sue his employers on the ground that they neglected his safety by not employing a security firm instead.
19 [1992] QB 333, [1991] 2 All ER 293, CA.
20 [1995] 1 All ER 737.
1   [1989] 3 All ER 228, [1991] 1 WLR 212.

Consider too the rights of workmen on premises. If the workman is merely employed by an independent contractor of the occupier he will, of course, have the rights of a visitor against the occupier. He will only have the greater rights of an employee against an employer in respect of the defect on the premises if he shows that the defect was tantamount to a failure on the employer's part to take reasonable care to protect his safety as, for instance, in *General Cleaning Contractors Ltd v Christmas*,[2] where the employee of a firm of window cleaners was held to be entitled to recover from the firm for failure to lay out a safe system on the premises of a customer whose windows he was cleaning. Subject to that, he will be limited to the rights of a visitor as laid down in the Occupiers' Liability Act 1957 and to any right of action for breach of statutory duty that there may be. If he is the employee of the occupier, he will then not be limited to the rights of a visitor, but will have those further rights considered here. For example, his employer will be liable for defective equipment negligently provided by a third party in circumstances, where under the Occupiers' Liability Act, an occupier would not be liable for that independent contractor's fault—and moreover his employer must insure against this risk.[3] Particular difficulty may arise where the employee at the time of the accident is actually working on a site abroad. In *Cook v Square D*[4] the plaintiff suffered injury while working in Saudi Arabia. The Court of Appeal held that the employers did not have a duty to guarantee the safety of premises occupied by third parties. The question must be whether in the light of all the circumstances the employer had done enough to take reasonable steps to protect his staff.

Finally it should be noted that negligence by an employer can result in liability to the employee's family as well as the employee himself. If the employee is exposed to toxic substances at work, or to transmissible disease,[5] so that unwittingly he endangers his wife who washes his workclothes or his family who contract the disease, the employer may owe a duty of care to the family as well. But there must be adequate proof that the level of toxicity, or the risk of infection, did endanger the employee so as to create a real risk to the family.[6]

SECTION 5.   PROVING NEGLIGENCE

(A)   LAW AND FACT

The law of negligence and, even more so, the reported cases cannot be fully understood unless something of the background of procedure is appreciated. Actions of negligence are now tried by a judge sitting without a jury; the judge himself tries issues of both law and fact: it will not therefore be surprising if the judgments in such cases do not meticulously mark off matters of law and fact from one another. Most of these actions were once tried by a judge sitting with a jury; it was then sufficiently accurate to say that matters of law were for the judge and matters of fact for the jury.

Where does the boundary between law and fact properly lie? The following are matters of law:

---

2   [1953] AC 180, [1952] 2 All ER 1110, HL; *Drummond v British Building Cleaners* [1954] 3 All ER 507, CA; *Smith v Austin Lifts Ltd* [1959] 1 All ER 81, [1959] 1 WLR 100, HL.

3   The Employers' Liability (Compulsory Insurance) Act 1969.

4   [1992] IRLR 34, CA (compare the outcome of this decision with *McDermid v Nash Dredging and Reclamation Ltd* [1987] AC 906, [1987] 2 All ER 878, HL).

5   Consider the potential liability if a health worker became infected with hepatitis B and passed on the disease to her husband/other sexual partners.

6   *Hewett v Alf Brown's Transport* [1992] ICR 530, CA (no evidence levels of lead waste to which the husband was exposed were sufficient to cause wife's lead poisoning).

1   all questions of duty—was the duty owed to the plaintiff, was it within the hazard,
      and the like;
2   the standard of care—what the standard is, and whether there is any evidence of
      failure to conform to it;
3   the principles to be applied in determining whether the damage was too remote,
      and whether there was any evidence of such damage; whether any recognised
      heads of damage have not been taken into account.
Matters of fact are:
1   resolving conflicts in the evidence and determining what the circumstances were
      and what the parties did;
2   evaluating the conduct of the parties in the light of the facts found and deciding
      whether it constituted a failure to take care, having regard to the standard of care
      required of the defendant;
3   deciding, in the light of the facts found, whether the damage was caused by the
      defendant and the extent of the damage;[7] assessment of damages.[8]

When appellate courts largely heard appeals from judges sitting with a jury, they
were concerned solely with those matters defined as matters of law. Today the appellate
jurisdiction from the judge sitting alone is much broader. '[It] has... jurisdiction to review
the record of the evidence in order to determine whether the conclusion originally
reached upon that evidence should stand; but this jurisdiction has to be exercised with
caution.'[9] The court should be 'satisfied that any advantage enjoyed by the trial judge
by reason of having seen and heard the witnesses, could not be sufficient to explain or
justify the trial judge's conclusion',[10] before it disturbs his findings of fact. On the
other hand, where, as often happens, the facts are not in dispute, but the case rests on
the inference to be drawn from them, an appellate court is in as good a position as the
trial judge to decide the case.[11]

(B)   ONUS OF PROOF

Whether what is in issue is the veracity of primary facts or the validity of the inferences
to be drawn from those facts, the burden of establishing:
a   that the defendant was negligent, and
b   that his negligence resulted in the plaintiff's loss or injury
rests on the plaintiff. Should the evidence be equally balanced so that the accident
might have been the result of lack of care or competence, but might just as easily have
occurred without carelessness, the plaintiff fails. He has not established negligence.
Thus in *Ashcroft v Mersey Regional Health Authority*[12] the plaintiff suffered a partial
paralysis in her face when in the course of surgery on her left ear the surgeon cut into
a facial nerve. Expert evidence showed that this was often an inherent risk of such

7   These and (2) are matters of inference from (1).
8   See ch 29.
9   Per Viscount Simon in *Watt v Thomas* [1947] AC 484 at 486, [1947] 1 All ER 582, HL.
10   Per Lord Thankerton, *Watt v Thomas* supra at 488.
11   *Powell v Streatham Manor Nursing Home* [1935] AC 243 at 267, [1935] All ER Rep 58 at 67
      (per Lord Wright), HL. See also *Benmax v Austin Motor Co Ltd* [1955] AC 370, [1955] 1 All
      ER 326, HL. Appellate courts are now exercising this power so freely that many appellate
      decisions now turn solely on matters of inference from facts. *Morris v West Hartlepool Steam
      Navigation Co Ltd* [1956] AC 552, [1956] 1 All ER 385, HL is a typical example of the House
      of Lords substituting its own evaluation of the facts for that of the trial judge: nothing else is in
      issue, yet the case appears in the Law Reports. And see *Whitehouse v Jordan* [1981] 1 All ER
      267, [1981] 1 WLR 246, HL.
12   [1983] 2 All ER 245; affd [1985] 2 All ER 96n.

surgery even when performed with the greatest skill, but all the experts accepted it also sometimes happened because of a failure in skill. The plaintiff's claim failed.

At least Mrs Ashcroft knew what had happened even though her counsel failed to establish that the facts proved constituted negligence. In many cases of alleged negligence the plaintiff knows only that he has been injured. How he came to be hit on the head by a falling object or a collapsing wall, why a swab remained in his abdomen after surgery, is a closed book to him. In a number of cases the plaintiff may be able to invoke the principle of res ipsa loquitur.

(C)   RES IPSA LOQUITUR

In *Scott v London and St Katherine's Docks Co*[13] the facts were:

> The plaintiff, a customs officer, while near the door of the defendants' warehouse, was injured by some sugar bags falling on him. The judge directed the jury to find a verdict for the defendants on the ground of lack of evidence of negligence by the defendants, who called no evidence. On appeal a new trial was directed.

The court justified this direction of a new trial in the following terms, which have since become known as res ipsa loquitur:[14]

> There must be reasonable evidence of negligence. But where the thing is shown to be under the management of the defendant or his servants, and the accident is such as in the ordinary course of things does not happen if those who have the management use proper care, it affords reasonable evidence, in the absence of explanation by the defendants, that the accident arose from want of care.

In the past there has been a tendency to elevate res ipsa loquitur to the status of a principle of substantive law or of at least a doctrine. In the 1970s the Court of Appeal decisively swung away from that approach. In *Lloyde v West Midlands Gas Board*, Megaw LJ said:[15]

> I doubt whether it is right to describe res ipsa loquitur as a 'doctrine'. I think that it is no more than an exotic, although convenient, phrase to describe what is in essence no more than a common-sense approach, not limited by technical rules, to the assessment of the effect of evidence in certain circumstances. It means that a plaintiff prima facie establishes negligence where: (i) it is not possible for him to prove precisely what was the relevant act or omission which set in train the events leading to the accident, but (ii) on the evidence as it stands at the relevant time it is more likely than not that the effective cause of the accident was *some* act or omission of the defendant or of someone for whom the defendant is responsible, which act or omission constitutes a failure to take proper care for the plaintiff's safety.

It is still necessary to examine the content of res ipsa loquitur, but always with that warning in mind.

Three separate requirements must be satisfied, as follows.

---

13   (1865) 3 H & C 596, Ex Ch.
14   Per Erle CJ at 601. It is not necessary to plead the doctrine; it is enough to prove facts which make it applicable; *Bennett v Chemical Construction (GB) Ltd* [1971] 3 All ER 822, CA.
15   [1971] 2 All ER 1240 at 1246. The Court of Appeal in *Turner v Mansfield Corpn* (1975) 119 Sol Jo 629 unanimously affirmed that judgment. And see *Ng Chun Pui v Lee Chuen Tat* [1988] RTR 298, PC.

(1)   'THE DOCTRINE IS DEPENDENT ON THE ABSENCE OF EXPLANATION'[16]

This merely means that if the court finds on the evidence adduced how and why the occurrence took place then there is no room for inference. So, in *Barkway v South Wales Transport Co Ltd*[17] where the tyre of an omnibus burst and the omnibus mounted the pavement and fell down an embankment, res ipsa loquitur did not apply because the court had evidence of the circumstances of the accident and so was satisfied that the system of tyre inspection in the garage of the defendants was a negligent one. Yet the word 'explanation' must be qualified by the adjective 'exact'.[18] This is to make it clear that a plaintiff who is able to present a partial account of how an accident happened is still not precluded from relying on res ipsa loquitur for further inferences essential to the winning of his case. The partial explanation may make it more obvious that an inference of negligence can be drawn. Of course, as in the *Barkway* case, even if res ipsa loquitur is inapplicable because all the material facts are proved, those facts may be found to constitute negligence.[19]

(2)   THE HARM MUST BE OF SUCH A KIND THAT IT DOES NOT ORDINARILY HAPPEN IF PROPER CARE IS BEING TAKEN

The courts have applied the doctrine to things falling from buildings,[20] and to accidents resulting from defective machines, apparatus or vehicles.[1] It applies where motor cars mount the pavement,[2] or where aircraft crash on taking off.[3] On the other hand, it was held inapplicable where a fire having been left by a lodger in his grate, neighbouring rooms were damaged by fire spreading from his room.[4]

It will be recalled that the classic definition of Erle CJ referred to accidents happening 'in the ordinary course of things'. *Mahon v Osborne*[5] raised the issue whether this means that it must be a matter of common experience, so that the experience of the expert is irrelevant. Goddard LJ held that the doctrine applied where swabs had been left in the body of a patient after an abdominal operation[6] but Scott LJ thought that where the judge could not, as with surgical operations, have enough knowledge of the circumstances to draw an inference of negligence, the doctrine did not apply.[7] Since

---

16   *Barkway v South Wales Transport Co Ltd* [1950] 1 All ER 392 at 394, HL per Lord Potter.
17   [1950] 1 All ER 392. And see *Swan v Salisbury Construction Co Ltd* [1966] 2 All ER 138, PC. In *Richley v Faull* [1965] 3 All ER 109 D's car hit P's car when D's car was on the wrong side of the road. D proved that he skidded. Without mentioning res ipsa loquitur, the court reached the solution supported by common sense that D was liable unless he showed that the skid occurred through no fault of his. Similarly in *Henderson v Henry E Jenkins & Sons* [1970] AC 282, [1969] 3 All ER 756, HL, the sudden failure of brakes on a lorry owing to a corroded pipe in the hydraulic braking system was held to impute negligence to the owners.
18   Per Lord Dunedin in *Ballard v North British Rly Co* 1923 SC 43 at 54, HL.
19   Conversely, a defendant is not liable for an unexplained accident, to which res ipsa loquitur might otherwise apply, if he establishes that he himself was not negligent: *Barkway v South Wales Transport Co Ltd* [1948] 2 All ER 460 at 463 (per Bucknill LJ).
20   *Byrne v Boadle* (1863) 2 H & C 722 (flour barrel falling from upper window on to plaintiff, walking on the street below); *Kearney v London and Brighton Rly Co* (1870) LR 5 QB 411.
1   *Ballard v North British Rly Co* 1923 SC 43, HL (defective coupling on train); *Kealey v Heard* [1983] 1 All ER 973, [1983] 1 WLR 573 (collapsing scaffolding).
2   *McGowan v Stott* (1923), in (1930) 143 LT 219n, CA; *Ellor v Selfridge & Co Ltd* (1930) 46 TLR 236; *Laurie v Raglan Building Co Ltd* [1942] 1 KB 152, [1941] 3 All ER 332, CA.
3   *Fosbroke-Hobbes v Airwork Ltd and British-American Air Services Ltd* [1937] 1 All ER 108.
4   *Sochacki v Sas* [1947] 1 All ER 344.
5   [1939] 2 KB 14, [1939] 1 All ER 535, CA.
6   [1939] 2 KB 14 at 50.
7   [1939] 2 KB 14 at 23. It is impossible to be certain of the view of MacKinnon LJ, in view of the conflicting reports, perhaps the fullest of which is (1939) 108 LJKB 567.

then, the Court of Appeal has held it to be prima facie evidence of negligence that a man, on leaving hospital after a course of radiography treatment to his hand and arm, had four stiff fingers and a useless hand;[8] and a court of first instance has been influenced by expert evidence in rejecting the application of res ipsa loquitur to a case where a patient sustained a fractured jaw as a result of a dental extraction.[9] It is suggested that where an unexplained accident occurs from a thing under the control of the defendant, and medical or other expert evidence shows that such accidents would not happen if proper care were used, there is at the very least strong evidence of negligence.

(3)   THE INSTRUMENTALITY CAUSING THE ACCIDENT MUST BE WITHIN THE EXCLUSIVE CONTROL OF THE DEFENDANT

(a)   The meaning of 'control'
If the defendant is not in control res ipsa loquitur does not apply. In *Turner v Mansfield Corpn*:[10]

> The plaintiff driver of the defendant's dust cart was injured when its back raised itself up as the plaintiff drove it under a bridge. It was held that since the plaintiff was in control it was for him to explain the accident and since he could furnish no evidence from which negligence could be inferred, he failed.

McGowan v Stott[11] is an important case in that it called a halt to previous attempts to insist on complete control of all the circumstances before the rule could apply. Previously, Fletcher Moulton LJ had indicated[12] that the scope of res ipsa loquitur was severely limited in highway accidents because all the essential surrounding circumstances were seldom under the defendant's control, but the court in *McGowan v Stott* refused to follow this, and declared the doctrine applicable to accidents on the highway where the defendant was in control of the vehicle causing the damage. Two actions brought against railway companies by plaintiffs who had fallen out of trains illustrate the degree of control essential for the doctrine to apply.

> In *Gee v Metropolitan Rly Co*,[13] a few minutes after a local train had started its journey, the plaintiff leaned against the offside door, which flew open. This was held evidence of negligence on the part of the railway company.

> In *Easson v London and North Eatern Rly Co*,[14] the plaintiff's claim failed, Goddard LJ holding that 'it is impossible to say that the doors of an express corridor train travelling from Edinburgh to London are continuously under the sole control of the railway company'.

8   *Cassidy v Ministry of Health* [1951] 2 KB 343, [1951] 1 All ER 574, CA. *Saunders v Leeds Western Health Authority* [1993] 4 Med LR 355 (child suffering cardiac stoppage under anaesthetic).
9   *Fish v Kapur* [1948] 2 All ER 176; contra, if the patient swallows a throat pack; *Garner v Morrall* (1935) Times, 31 October.
10   The case is briefly reported at (1975) 119 Sol Jo 629, CA, but Street based the text on a full Court of Appeal transcript.
11   (1923) in (1930) 143 LT 219n, CA. Where the apparatus is in the plaintiff's house, eg gas apparatus, the onus is on the plaintiff to show that it was improbable that persons other than the defendant could have interfered with it—only then can he invoke res ipsa loquitur: *Lloyde v West Midlands Gas Board* [1971] 2 All ER 1240, CA. In *Ward v Tesco Stores Ltd* [1976] 1 All ER 219, CA, the plaintiff slipped on yoghurt spilled on the floor of the defendants' supermarket. Even though there was no evidence as to how long the yoghurt had been on the floor it was held to be a case of prima facie negligence.
12   *Wing v London General Omnibus Co* [1909] 2 KB 652 at 663–4, CA.
13   (1873) LR 8 QB 161.
14   [1944] KB 421 at 424, [1944] 2 All ER 425, CA.

(b) Where one of two or more persons is in control
If the instrumentality is in the control of one of several employees of the same employer, and the plaintiff cannot point to the particular employee who is in control, the rule may still be invoked so as to make the employer vicariously liable: thus, a hospital authority has been held answerable for negligent treatment where the plaintiff could not show which of several members of the staff was responsible.[15]

Further, if a surgeon is shown to be in general control of an operation, and the patient cannot establish whether it was the malpractice of the surgeon or one of the theatre staff which inflicted damage on him in the course of that operation, it seems that res ipsa loquitur applies in an action of negligence against the surgeon.[16] If, on the other hand, the surgeon is not in control of all the relevant stages of the treatment, and if the plaintiff cannot prove that the act complained of took place at a time when the defendant surgeon was in control, res ipsa loquitur cannot be relied on.[17] *Walsh v Hoist & Co Ltd*[18] extends the doctrine further: when the defendant's duty is so extensive that he is answerable for the negligence of his independent contractor, and an accident occurs while the independent contractor is performing the work delegated to him, the plaintiff can invoke res ipsa loquitur against both the defendant and his independent contractor.[19]

A related, though distinct, problem is the position of a plaintiff who establishes, without invoking the rule of res ipsa loquitur, that the damage to him was caused either by the negligence of A or the negligence of B. If he is merely able to show that only A or B but not both must have been negligent then he is not entitled to a judgment against both unless the defendants have refused to give evidence, in which case adverse inferences against them may be drawn.[20] It is, however, the duty of the trial court to come to a definite conclusion on the evidence—it must not dismiss the action because of uncertainty as to which party was free from blame.[1] If the inference is that one or other or both have been negligent the plaintiff has made out a prima facie case against either A or B, or both.[2] Of course, if the circumstances do not warrant the inference that one or other has been negligent, the plaintiff fails.[3]

Beyond setting out the above guidance, it is submitted that one cannot define the circumstances where the doctrine applies. As usual in negligence, some writers list all the circumstances where res ipsa loquitur has been applied as if they were precedents

---

15 *Cassidy v Ministry of Health* [1951] 2 KB 343, [1951] 1 All ER 574, CA. For more detailed examination of this from the standpoint of vicarious liability, see p 512, post.
16 *Mahon v Osborne* [1939] 2 KB 14, [1939] 1 All ER 535, CA. So held by Goddard LJ, with whom Mackinnon LJ, appeared to agree, Scott LJ, dissenting.
17 *Morris v Winsbury-White* [1937] 4 All ER 494; perhaps Somervell LJ disagreed with this statement of law in *Roe v Minister of Health* [1954] 2 QB 66 at 80, [1954] 2 All ER 131 at 135, CA.
18 [1958] 3 All ER 33, CA; *Kealey v Heard* [1983] 1 All ER 973, [1983] 1 WLR 573.
19 Apparently, the employer conceded that he is liable even though the plaintiff had not established that the act did not occur within that area of the independent contractor's operations for which the employer is not answerable, viz, acts of collateral negligence.
20 *Baker v Market Harborough Industrial Co-operative Society Ltd* [1953] 1 WLR 1472, CA; *Cook v Lewis* [1952] 1 DLR 1 decides that where either A or B has committed a tort against P and it is the careless act of both of them which prevents P from knowing which caused the harm, both are liable (A and B were hunters, one or other of whom fired the shot which hit P).
1 *Bray v Palmer* [1953] 2 All ER 1449, [1953] 1 WLR 1455, CA.
2 *Roe v Minister of Health* [1954] 2 QB 66, [1954] 2 All ER 131, CA per Denning LJ (ratio); *France v Parkinson* [1954] 1 All ER 739, CA; where vehicles collide either at cross roads or on the brow of a hill, and both drivers are dead, a passenger has a prima facie case, in the absence of other evidence, against both drivers or either of them; *Davison v Leggett* (1969) 133 JP 552, CA, (head-on collision centre lane, negligence by both drivers inferred), and more fully reported in *Knight v Fellick* [1977] RTR 316, CA.
3 *Knight v Fellick* [1977] RTR 316, CA.

on points of law. But the Court of Appeal has held[4] that these cases do not lay down any principles of law; they are merely a guide to the kind of circumstance where the doctrine might successfully be invoked.

(D)   THE EFFECT OF RES IPSA LOQUITUR[5]

In some cases the inference to be drawn by resorting to the rule is twofold: that the defendant caused the accident, and that he was negligent. In others, the cause is known, and only the inference of negligence arises.[6]

As has been seen above, on the proved facts it may be just as likely that the event happened without negligence as that it happened in consequence of negligence, in which case there is no evidence of negligence. If, however, in such circumstances, res ipsa loquitur applies, its effect is to make it 'relevant to infer negligence'[7] from the fact of the accident—that simply means that there is in law evidence on which the judge may properly find for the plaintiff.[8] The distinctive function of the rule is to permit an inference of negligence from proof of the injury and the physical instrumentality causing it, even though there is no proof of the facts identifying the human agency responsible. Looked at this way, its affinity to the ordinary rule of evidence that circumstantial evidence is admissible to prove negligence is clear. As Atkin LJ has said:[9]

> ... all that one wants to know is whether the facts of the occurrence do as a matter of fact make it more probable that a jury may reasonably infer that the damage was caused by want of care on the part of the defendants than the contrary.

It is clear then that at least the effect of res ipsa loquitur is to afford prima facie evidence of negligence. It does not shift the burden of proof to the defendant[10] in the sense that in the absence of rebutting evidence from him the courts must find for the plaintiff.[11]

Once res ipsa loquitur has been successfully invoked to raise an inference of negligence against the defendant its effect is simply this. There is sufficient evidence for the judge to find for the plaintiff—in the old days he could not have withdrawn the case from the jury. It may be on certain facts that the inference of negligence is so cogent that the judge must rule in favour of the plaintiff but this will by no means always be the case. As Du Parcq LJ said:[12]

> The words res ipsa loquitur, ... are a figure of speech, by which sometimes is meant that certain facts are so inconsistent with any view except that the defendant has been negligent

4   *Easson v London and North Eastern Rly Co* [1944] KB 421 at 423, [1944] 2 All ER 425, CA per Goddard. LJ
5   For the clearest judicial statement, see the eight rules laid down by Evatt J in *Davis v Bunn* (1936) 56 CLR 246 at 267–8.
6   *Barkway v South Wales Transport Co Ltd* [1950] 1 All ER 392 at 399–400 (per Lord Normand), HL.
7   *Ballard v North British Rly Co* 1923 SC (HL) 43 at 54.
8   *Cole v De Trafford (No 2)* [1918] 2 KB 523 at 528 (per Pickford LJ).
9   *McGowan v Stott* (1923), in (1930) 143 LT 219n, CA; cf Greer LJ in *Langham v Governors of Wellingborough School and Fryer* (1932) 101 LJKB 513 at 518, CA.
10 On burden of proof generally see *Wilsher v Essex Area Health Authority* [1988] AC 1074, [1988] 1 All ER 871, HL
11 Despite some suggestions to this effect in older authorities eg Lord Evershed MR in *Moore v R Fox & Sons Ltd* [1956] 1 QB 596, [1956] 1 All ER 182, CA. (The Court of Appeal in *Turner v Mansfield Corpn* (1975) 119 Sol Jo 629 held that this case should no longer be regarded as an authority on res ipsa loquitur.) *Ludgate v Lovett* [1969] 2 All ER 1275, CA.
12 *Easson v London and North Eastern Rly Co* [1944] KB 421 at 425, [1944] 2 All ER 425.

that any jury [or judge] which, on proof of these facts, found that negligence was not proved would be giving a perverse verdict. Sometimes, the proposition does not go as far as that, but is merely that on proof of certain facts an inference of negligence may be drawn by a reasonable jury [or judge] …

To sum up, the effect of res ipsa loquitur depends on the cogency of the inference to be drawn, and will vary from case to case: if, for instance, a vehicle mounts the pavement, this is evidence of negligence, but reasonable people may differ about the inference to be drawn from it, so that a verdict of no negligence would not be upset—yet something may fall from the defendant's window in such circumstances that only an inference of negligence can be drawn, whereupon a verdict of no negligence might be set aside.

The effect of res ipsa loquitur where the defendant gives evidence must also be considered. Plainly the effect of the doctrine is to shift the onus to the defendant in the sense that the doctrine continues to operate unless the defendant calls credible evidence which explains how the accident may have occurred without negligence, and it seems that the operation of the rule is not displaced merely by expert evidence showing theoretically possible ways in which the accident might have happened without the defendant's negligence. But beyond this the courts describe the effect in two different ways. Sometimes they state that once the defendant has furnished evidence of the cause of the accident consistent with his having exercised due care it becomes a question whether, upon the whole of the evidence, the defendant was negligent or not and the defendant will succeed unless the court is satisfied that he was negligent.[13] On other occasions they state that the defendant loses unless he proves that the accident resulted from a specific cause which does not connote negligence on his part but on the contrary points to its absence as more probable.[14] Probably there is no inconsistency in these judicial utterances; all may depend on the context of the cases and the cogency of the rebutting evidence in the particular case. A useful example of how a defendant can rebut an inference of res ipsa loquitur can be seen in *Ng Chun Pui v Lee Chuen Tat*.[15] A coach veered across the road colliding with a bus coming in the opposite direction. The plaintiff called no evidence and the Privy Council ruled that the facts of themselves raised an inference of negligence. But the defendants testified that an unidentified car cut across their coach causing the driver to brake suddenly and skid across the road. They were found to have rebutted any inference of negligence since the driver's reaction to an emergency beyond his control did not constitute any breach of duty.

---

13 Eg *Ballard v North British Rly Co* 1923 SC (HL) 43 at 54 (per Lord Dunedin); *The Kite* [1933] P 154, [1933] All ER Rep 234; *Colvilles Ltd v Devine* [1969] 2 All ER 53, HL.
14 Eg *Moore v R Fox & Sons Ltd* [1956] 1 QB 596, [1956] 1 All ER 182, CA.
15 [1988] RTR, PC.

Chapter 14

Causation[1]

Causation is relevant in all torts. Problems may arise in relation to proof that the defendant's wrongful conduct did in fact cause the plaintiff's damage and to what extent the defendant *ought* to be held responsible for the full extent of such damage. Causation is often analysed in two stages.[2] Factual causation relates to the issue of whether and how the plaintiff can establish that the defendant's conduct did result in the harm of which he complains. Remoteness of damage concerns the extent of the consequences of his wrongful conduct for which the defendant ought to be accountable. Unfortunately for the student, there is no crystal clear boundary between the two. In this chapter we will look first at evidence of causation and its difficulties, then analyse complex issues of concurrent and consecutive causes, and finally explore the rules relating to remoteness of damage. The student must be warned however that, especially in relation to consecutive and concurrent causes, questions of factual causation and remoteness are often inextricably intertwined.

We deal with causation in this part on negligence for two reasons. First, very many, though not all, of the more complex cases in causation arise in negligence. Secondly, in negligence, unlike those torts actionable per se such as trespass, damage must be proved for liability to be established at all. Causation in relation to a tort actionable per se relates only to the extent of the defendant's liability. In negligence, in the absence of proof of damage, no action lies. What is said in this chapter about proving an evidential relationship between the defendant's conduct and the plaintiff's damage is generally applicable in tort. Principles governing remoteness of damage are individual to each tort and dealt with in the relevant analysis of each tort in this work.

SECTION I.   CAUSE AND EFFECT

Establishing cause and effect in law can be far from easy. Every occurrence is the result of a combination of several different events. The history of an incident resulting in injury to a plaintiff will include a series of acts and omissions which combined with the conditions in which those events took place culminate in the harm occasioned to the plaintiff. This series of events include both events prior to and subsequent to the

---

1   There is an excellent analysis of the general principles of causation in Hart and Honoré *Causation in the Law* (2nd edn, 1985).
2   See, for example, *Winfield & Jolowicz* (1998) ch 6.

allegedly tortious conduct of the defendant. Consider the facts of *Wright v Lodge*.[3] The second defendant was driving her Mini at night along a dual carriageway in the fog. The road was unlit. Her engine failed and the car came to a stop in the near side lane. A few minutes later, as the driver was trying to restart her car, an articulated lorry being driven at 60 mph by the first defendant crashed into the Mini virtually destroying the car and seriously injuring a passenger in the back seat of the car. After hitting the Mini, the lorry careered across the central reservation. The lorry fell on its side blocking the road and four oncoming vehicles collided with it. One driver died of his injuries and another was seriously injured.

What or who caused those injuries? Had the second defendant not chosen to go out that evening, or had it not been foggy, or had the road been lit, the accident might never have happened. In one sense each of those factors is a cause without which (causa sine qua non) the accident would not have occurred. The law, of course, first looks to the human actors. The unlit road and the fog are part of the complex of conditions which produced the accident, but not causes of it in law. However, not all human acts constitute in law the cause of an event. No-one would suggest that by driving out that night, the driver of the Mini (or the lorry) were responsible for the three plaintiffs' injuries. What must be identified is the operative cause or causes.

The lorry driver argued that it was not only his negligence in driving so fast on a foggy night which caused the dreadful pile-up on the road. The driver of the Mini should have pushed her car off the road before trying to restart it. Had she done so, he would not have collided with her. 'But for' her failure to ensure that her car did not block the road the whole disaster would have been avoided? The Court of Appeal disagreed. While the judges accepted that the driver of the Mini was negligent in some degree in not moving her car, and liable for the injuries to her passenger, jointly with the lorry driver, they held that she was not liable to the drivers of the cars involved in the second collision across the other side of the carriageway. Her initial negligence was not a legally operative cause of those injuries which were solely the responsibility of the lorry driver who had driven so grossly carelessly that night. Not every cause 'without which'— 'but for'— an accident would not have occurred is a relevant cause in law. Causation in such complex cases should be decided by invoking at least a degree of common sense.

SECTION 2.   EVIDENCE OF CAUSATION

In *Wright v Lodge* there was at least no doubt that what was done, or rather not done, by the second defendant contributed as a matter of fact to the injuries of all three plaintiffs. Other cases are less straightforward. It is clear beyond doubt the plaintiff must advance sufficient evidence that it is more likely than not that the alleged cause (the wrongful conduct of the defendant) did occasion his loss or injury. Where a man was sent home without treatment from a casualty department after complaining of acute stomach pains and sickness and later died of arsenical poisoning, his widow's claim against the hospital failed even though the hospital admitted negligence.[4] The court found that even had he been given prompt and competent treatment, the man would still have died as a result of the arsenic.

Where there is some evidence that the defendant's conduct may have contributed to the plaintiff's injury the burden remains with the plaintiff to establish on the balance

3   [1993] 4 All ER 299, CA.
4   *Barnett v Chelsea and Kensington Hospital Management Committee* [1969] 1 QB 428, [1968] 1 All ER 1068.

of probabilities that it did so.[5] Particularly when the injury is a disease, the plaintiff's task may be formidable.[6] Consider the example of a man claiming that he developed dermatitis because of contact with substances at work and that his employer negligently failed to supply him with protective clothing. The likelihood is that the medical evidence will indicate that contact with the substances at work is just one possible cause but that several other hypotheses are also possible. He may have an allergy to some food or the washing powder used to launder his clothes and so on. The issue of whether the plaintiff has produced sufficient evidence of causation, sufficient evidence that 'but for' the defendant's conduct he would not have suffered injury is a question of law not fact. And the essence of the exercise in which the courts are engaged is once again, as in *Wright v Lodge,* the legally operative cause, selecting from among the plethora of possible causes the 'responsible cause', of the plaintiff's loss or injury.

Where the plaintiff has proved a breach of duty by the defendant and can further prove that that breach of duty materially increased the risk of the injury to which the plaintiff succumbed, the defendant will be held liable. Thus in *McGhee v National Coal Board*[7] it was found that failure to provide adequate washing facilities substantially increased the danger to the plaintiff of his developing dermatitis. He recovered damages from his employers, the National Coal Board, even though he could not prove via conclusive medical evidence that his affliction resulted from the absence of washing facilities alone. Furthermore defendants may also be liable on an extension of the *McGhee* principle if it can be shown that their conduct materially enhanced an existing risk of injury, albeit it cannot be conclusively proved that the defendant's negligence was actually the sole cause of that risk materialising. The logic of the principle enunciated by the House of Lords in *McGhee* was accepted by their Lordships as being far from faultless. Lords Reid and Wilberforce expressly stated that the decision was essentially a matter of common sense and policy rather than principle. In effect were their Lordships were attempting to ease the plaintiffs' burden of proving causation. The Court of Appeal in *Page v Smith (No 2)*[8] also seemed to seek to assist a plaintiff beset by evidential difficulties. The plaintiff had suffered for several years from chronic fatigue syndrome (popularly known as ME). When the disease appeared to be in remission, he was involved in a collision with a car negligently driven by the defendant. The plaintiff suffered no physical harm, but within hours of the accident he succumbed to a revival of his earlier disease. The Court of Appeal upheld the judge's finding that medical evidence that stress *could* contribute to chronic fatigue syndrome, together with the juxtaposition of the accident and the plaintiff's renewed symptoms, were sufficient to establish that the defendant's negligence materially contributed to the plaintiff's illness.

However a series of decisions of the House of Lords appear to disapprove of such a 'robust' 'common sense' approach to causation. In *Hotson v East Berkshire Area Health Authority*[9] the House of Lords refused to extend the *McGhee* 'rule' any further. The plaintiff fell several feet from a tree injuring his hip. He was rushed to hospital but his injury was not diagnosed until five days later. The hospital admitted negligence and responsibility for the pain which the boy suffered during the five days while treatment was negligently delayed. They denied liability for the condition (avascular necrosis) which the boy developed as a result of a failure in the blood supply to the

5   *Hotson v East Berkshire Area Health Authority* [1987] AC 750, [1987] 2 All ER 909, HL. And see *Kay v Ayrshire and Arran Health Board* [1987] 2 All ER 417, HL.
6   Though it is not only cases relating to disease which can be complex, see *Allied Maples Group Ltd v Simmons & Simmons* [1995] 4 All ER 907, [1995] 1 WLR 1602, CA.
7   [1972] 3 All ER 1008, [1973] 1 WLR 1, HL. *Clowes v National Coal Board* (1987) Times, 23 April.
8   [1996] 3 All ER 272, [1996] 1 WLR 855.
9   [1987] AC 750, [1987] 2 All ER 909. And see (1991) 54 LQR 511.

injured hip. The trial judge found[10] that there was a 75% chance that avascular necrosis would have developed as a result of the injury even if promptly treated, and a 25% chance that the delay contributed to the development of the condition. He held that the hospital were liable for loss of that chance and awarded damages assessed at 25% of the compensation which would have been payable had the defendants been 100% liable for the plaintiff's condition. The House of Lords, quashing the judgment[11] for the plaintiffs, held that the finding that the accident itself was more likely than not to have caused the avascular necrosis concluded the issue in the defendants' favour.[12] The House of Lords in *Hotson* held that there was no basis in tort for the judge's decision to award the plaintiff 25% damages to represent the lost 'chance' of complete recovery. If the alleged cause could be proved or be inferred to be more likely than not the cause of the damage the plaintiff was entitled to full compensation. Otherwise he was entitled to nothing. It was left open whether when a lost chance of recovery, or avoiding loss, could be proved to result from a breach of duty, compensation for that lost chance is recoverable in tort at all.

In *Allied Maples Group Ltd v Simmons & Simmons*[13] the Court of Appeal held that such compensation was recoverable at least where the plaintiff's loss depends on the hypothetical action of a third party.

The plaintiffs had been advised by the defendant solicitors in negotiations to purchase certain businesses from another furniture company. At one stage the proposed contract included an undertaking by the vendor company that there were no outstanding liabilities in respect of their properties. In the course of negotiations that undertaking was deleted. After purchasing the business, the plaintiffs found themselves liable for substantial sums arising from leases previously held by the vendor company. The original undertaking would have protected them from such liabilities. The plaintiffs argued that the defendants were negligent in not advising them to approach the vendors and to seek to retain the original clause in the contract. The issue was whether the vendors would have agreed to do so.

The Court of Appeal held that the plaintiff's must prove that it was more likely than not that properly advised they would have approached the vendors, but need not prove that it was more probable than not that the latter would have agreed. The plaintiffs need only establish that there was a 'substantial chance' that the vendors would have provided them with the protection requested. Evaluating the value of that lost chance was a matter of quantification of damage. In *Spring v Guardian Assurance plc*[14] an employer was found liable for negligently giving the plaintiff a bad reference. The plaintiff recovered for his lost chance of employment. He could not prove he would have got the job.

Evidential problems, however, again defeated the plaintiff in *Kay v Ayrshire and Arran Health Board*[15]. A small boy suffering from meningitis was negligently given a massive overdose of penicillin. Fortunately he recovered both from the toxic overdose and the disease but he was left profoundly deaf. Meningitis, even when entirely properly treated, can result in deafness. There was hardly any evidence available about the effect of the level of overdose of penicillin the child received because fortunately such errors are rare. The trial judge elected to 'infer' that the effect of the overdose on the boy's system was likely to increase the risk that he would succumb to complications from

10 [1985] 3 All ER 167, [1985] 1 WLR 1036.
11 The judgment of Simon Brown J was upheld by the Court of Appeal [1987] AC 750, [1987] 1 All ER 210.
12 See per Lord Mackay at 240 and per Lord Ackner at 248.
13 [1995] 1 WLR 1602. See Lunney 'What Price a Chance' (1996) 15 Legal Studies.
14 [1995] 2 AC 296, [1994] 3 All ER 129, HL.
15 [1987] 2 All ER 417, HL.

meningitis (ie deafness). So he found for the plaintiff, albeit there was little scientific evidence for his theory. The House of Lords sympathised with the child's family, but held that no sufficient evidence that the admitted and gross negligence caused the boy's deafness had been advanced. Paucity of evidence could not be prayed in aid to assist a plaintiff.

In *Pickford v Imperial Chemical Industries plc*[16] the plaintiff suffered from a disease involving cramp of the hand, a condition often referred to, if incorrectly, as repetitive strain injury. She had worked as a secretary for the defendants spending between 50-75% of her time on typing duties. To succeed in her claim for negligence against her employers, she had to establish that the cause of her condition was organic, not psychogenic. The trial judge held that he was unable to decide between the conflicting medical evidence and that other lay evidence about the plaintiff's work patterns led him to conclude that the cause was not organic. The onus of proving that the cause was organic lay on the plaintiff. The Court of Appeal overruled his judgment, but were themselves overruled by the Law Lords. Where expert evidence of causation is inconclusive, the plaintiff must lose. She had not satisfied the burden of proof of causation established in *Wilsher v Essex Area Health Authority*.[17] That was the case (discussed earlier in relation to breach of duty) in which junior doctors negligently administered excess oxygen to a premature infant. He later developed retrolental fibroplasia (RLF) a condition that ultimately left him completely blind. Medical practice required careful monitoring of infants receiving oxygen because of evidence that excess oxygen might cause RLF in premature babies. But there were said to be five other possible causes of RLF in very sick, very premature babies. The trial judge ruled that the plaintiff having proved a breach of duty arising from a failure to protect the plaintiff from the risk of the very sort of damage which in fact materialised, the onus moved to the defendants to prove that some other cause actually resulted in that damage. He sought to shift the burden of proof of causation to the defendant. He was severely rebuked by the House of Lords for his presumption. Nor could their Lordships accept the argument of the majority in the Court of Appeal[18] that the principle in *McGhee* could extend to the facts of *Wilsher*. The plaintiffs had not established that it was more probable than not that excess oxygen rather than any of the other possible causes caused the plaintiff to succumb to RLF.[19] Indeed by virtue of his ruling that having proved breach of duty the burden of disproving causation shifted to the defendant, the judge failed to address the issue of the conflicting scientific evidence. Their Lordships made it crystal clear that in no circumstances did the burden of proof so shift and ordered a retrial on the issue of causation. Lord Bridge warned against the dangers of allowing sympathy for the plaintiff to overrule the established principles of proof.

> [W]hether we like it or not, the law, which only Parliament can change, requires proof of fault causing damage as the basis of liability in tort. We should do society nothing but disservice if we made the forensic process still more unpredictable and hazardous by distorting the law to accommodate the exigencies of what may seem hard cases.[20]

16 [1998] 3 All ER 462, [1998] 1 WLR 1189, HL.
17 [1988] AC 1074, [1988] 1 All ER 871.
18 [1987] QB 730, [1986] 3 All ER 801; see the dissenting judgment of Sir Nicholas Browne-Wilkinson V-C.
19 Confirming the judgment in *Bonnington Castings Ltd v Wardlow* [1956] AC 613, [1956] 1 All ER 615.
20 At 833.

One final point needs to be noted in relation to establishing evidence of causation. In the overwhelming majority of cases the evidential difficulties centre solely on the question 'what would have happened if?'. *Bolitho v City and Hackney Health Authority*[1] offers an example where the question 'what *should* have happened' also has to be addressed. A doctor negligently failed to respond to a nurse's request to attend a sick child. A little later the child stopped breathing and suffered a cardiac arrest. However it was disputed among the expert witnesses at the trial whether, had the doctor attended, good medical practice would have suggested that she intubate the child (to assist him to breathe). The House of Lords held that to establish that the negligent failure to attend the child caused his cardiac arrest, the plaintiff needed to prove, not just that the doctor did not intubate the child, but that in not doing so she was negligent. They needed to establish that the negligent failure to attend the child resulted in his being deprived of a treatment which he should have received and which would have prevented his cardiac arrest.

SECTION 3.   MULTIPLE CAUSES

(A)   NOVUS ACTUS INTERVENIENS

In many instances, subsequent to the negligence of the defendant a contingency may arise resulting in further injury to the plaintiff. For example, the plaintiff may initially suffer minor injuries at the hands of the defendant, but die as a result of bungled medical treatment. Such harm may be described as 'ulterior harm'. The defendant is not liable for all ulterior harm. In marking off the limits of his liability it will not ordinarily matter whether we use the language of risk or cause. The man run down by the defendant's negligence cannot recover for the extra damage sustained when a tile falls off a roof on to his head while he is on his way to hospital. This is because the defendant's conduct did not create a special risk of harm from that kind of contingency, or because the falling tile was a coincidence. The original negligent driving and the subsequent fall of the tile were independent acts; the conjunction of the two events was abnormal and not contrived by human agency. The falling of the tile broke the chain of causation; it constituted a novus actus interveniens, an intervening act sufficient to relieve the defendant of further liability for the consequences of his own conduct.

A few examples will illustrate the courts' general approach to the problem of intervening acts. In *Scott v Shepherd*[2] it was held to be no defence to the man who first threw a firework into the crowd that the plaintiff would have suffered no loss had not a third party picked it up and thrown it again after the defendant had thrown it, because the third party, in throwing it, was acting for his self-preservation. In short, where the act of the defendant has placed a third party or the plaintiff in a situation of 'alternative danger', if that person acts reasonably in the agony of the moment, his act will not break the chain of causation from the act of the defendant. In another case the plaintiff's ship lost her compass and charts when the defendant's ship negligently collided with it; and consequently the plaintiff's ship ran aground while trying to make for port: the defendant was liable for this further harm.[3] Damage incurred in rescuing a person imperilled by the act of the defendant or by his own folly[4] is not too remote where the

---

1   [1998] AC 232, [1997] 4 All ER 771.
2   (1773) 2 Wm Bl 892.
3   *The City of Lincoln* (1889) 15 PD 15, CA.
4   *Ogwo v Taylor* [1988] AC 431, [1987] 3 All ER 961, HL.

possibility of such rescue could have been anticipated;[5] A night watchman, injured while trying, in the course of his duty, to extinguish a fire in the premises of his employer, may recover.[6] Where the injuries negligently inflicted by the defendant on a plaintiff's husband induced a state of acute anxiety neurosis which persisted for 18 months and caused him to take his own life, the defendant was held liable to the plaintiff.[7] In each of these cases the ulterior harm was within the foreseeable risk; the subsequent events were not sufficiently abnormal responses to the situation created by the defendant's negligence; the kind of happening 'was on the cards'. In *Reeves v Metropolitan Police Comr*[8] the plaintiff's husband hanged himself in his prison cell. There was no evidence that the deceased had been diagnosed as suffering from any mental disorder but he had been identified as a 'suicide risk'. The Court of Appeal held that his suicide did not constitute a novus actus interveniens breaking the chain of causation. The evidence available to the defendants of his emotionally disturbed state and suicidal tendencies imposed on them a duty to protect the deceased, effectively from himself. Suicide was a kind of harm which the defendants should have contemplated and guarded against. It was harm within the ambit of the duty imposed on the defendants—a risk which it was the defendants' duty to prevent from materialising.

In all the above examples, the defendant failed to establish that the intervening event constituted a novus actus interveniens. When might such a claim succeed? Three rather different kinds of novus actus must be considered.

(1)   The intervening event may be an act of nature[9] (Act of God as it sometimes described)[10]. For example, a child is injured playing football at school, and, as she is wheeled across the playground to the waiting ambulance she is struck by lightning. The injury inflicted by the lightning is not in any sense a consequence of her sports injury. However note that the act of nature must be overwhelming, unpredictable and in no sense linked to the defendant's negligence. Change the facts of our example a little. Imagine that the injured child is left lying in the playground uncovered and unattended, in January. A sudden hailstorm erupts chilling the girl to the bone and the sharp hailstones aggravating her injury. Would the storm then be a novus actus?

(2)   The plaintiff's own conduct may constitute a novus actus.

(3)   The act of a third party may be argued to break the chain of causation.

We consider these two latter cases in more detail now. There is no doubt that the plaintiff's own conduct can constitute a novus actus in appropriate circumstances. In *McKew v Holland and Hannens and Cubitts (Scotland) Ltd*[11] the plaintiff had suffered an injured leg owing to the defendants' negligence. Yet he was denied compensation when he subsequently broke his ankle attempting, while still suffering from the effects of the first injury, to descend a steep staircase unaided. His own imprudence, his unreasonable conduct, constituted a fresh and separate cause of the second injury. Contrast *McKew* with *Wieland v Cyril Lord Carpets Ltd*.[12] The plaintiff suffered neck injuries and had to wear a collar. She later fell downstairs because, as a result of the

5   *Haynes v Harwood* [1935] 1 KB 146, [1934] All ER Rep 103, CA. The court did, of course, first decide that the careless defendant owed a duty of care to this would-be rescuer, *Baker v TE Hopkins & Sons Ltd* [1959] 3 All ER 225, [1959] 1 WLR 966, CA.
6   *D'Urso v Sanson* [1939] 4 All ER 26.
7   *Pigney v Pointer's Transport Services Ltd* [1957] 2 All ER 807; see also *Kirkham v Chief Constable of Greater Manchester Police* [1990] 2 QB 283, [1990] 3 All ER 246, CA.
8   [1998] 2 All ER 381, CA.
9   *Carslogie Steamship Co Ltd v Rogal Norwegian Government* [1952] AC 292, [1952] 1 All ER 20.
10   *Nichols v Marsland* (1876) 2 ExD 1.
11   [1969] 3 All ER 1621, HL.
12   [1969] 3 All ER 1006.

initial injury and the neck collar, she could not use her bifocal lenses with her usual skill. Her further injury was found to be attributable to the defendants' original negligence. Unlike the rash Mr McKew, Mrs Wieland suffered a further injury triggered by her original disability, despite taking all reasonable care of herself. Unreasonable conduct on the part of the plaintiff acts as a novus actus interveniens breaking the chain of causation. Even if readily foreseeable, the courts, as a matter of policy, will not impose liability on one man for the calculated imprudence of another. Defining unreasonable conduct will not always be easy. In *Emeh v Kensington, Chelsea and Westminster Area Health Authority*[13] the plaintiff conceived again after an operation to sterilise her carried out by the defendant. The defendant admitted negligence but denied liability for the cost of the upkeep of the child. That loss to the plaintiff, he contended, resulted from her 'unreasonable' decision not to seek an abortion, and the judge at first instance agreed with him. The Court of Appeal held that as, by the time the plaintiff realised she was pregnant, she was well into the second trimester of pregnancy, it was not unreasonable for her to refuse the trauma and risk of late abortion. Slade LJ[14] made it clear that save in exceptional circumstances he would never regard it as unreasonable to refuse abortion even earlier in pregnancy when the procedure is relatively simple and free of risk. Waller LJ[15] was less clear on this point. Do you think it can be held to be 'unreasonable' to refuse an operation (however simple) which is not necessary for your health and to which many people still have moral objections?[16]

When will an intervening act on the part of a third party constitute a novus actus interveniens? The relevant principles are flexible and their application is sometimes difficult. It is, for instance, uncertain when, if at all, the plaintiff can recover for prolongation of his incapacity resulting from careless medical treatment of his initial injuries.[17] What if a road accident victim who should have largely recovered from his original injuries contracted AIDS from a contaminated transfusion?[18] It must be admitted that considerations of policy will affect judicial thinking in such cases. This conclusion is the more acceptable when it is understood that in marginal cases the courts have felt free to hold the defendant liable by the risk approach where the ultimate harm was causally irrelevant. For example, a decorator who carelessly left unlocked the house in which he had been working while he went to fetch more wallpaper was liable to the owner in contract for thefts from the house perpetrated by a thief while the defendant had left the house empty and unlocked.[19] The courts can more easily take policy considerations into account when they are free, as in that case, to hold the defendant liable within the doctrine of risk although the defendant could not be said to have caused a loss such as this, which resulted from the deliberate, subsequent and independent conduct of a third party. Take the case of the pedestrian who is knocked down in the dark by the defendant's car—application of either risk or causative principles will result in holding the defendant answerable for the further harm inflicted by another motorist who runs over him within seconds of the first incident as he lies in the roadway.[20] But

13   [1985] QB 1012, [1984] 3 All ER 1044 CA.
14   Ibid 1053.
15   Ibid 1048.
16   On the related issue of the duty to minimise damages by accepting medical treatment see *Selvanayagam v University of the West Indies* [1983] 1 All ER 824, [1983] 1 WLR 585, PC (discussed post at p 530).
17   In Ireland the courts have held that the plaintiff can recover the whole of his loss from the original tortfeasor: the negligent treatment does not constitute a novus actus: *Conley v Strain* [1988] IR 628.
18   Does the injury become different in type or only in extent?
19   *Stansbie v Troman* [1948] 2 KB 48, [1948] 1 All ER 599.
20   But see *Knightley v Johns* [1982] 1 All ER 851, [1982] 1 WLR 349 discussed post at p 272 and *Wright v Lodge* [1993] 4 All ER 299 discussed ante at p 265.

only application of the doctrine of risk could make the defendant answerable for the pickpocket who steals the pedestrian's wallet as he lies unconscious.

The central issue in any case becomes whether the defendant's negligence was responsible in law for the materialisation of their particular risk. Issues of remoteness will arise but before addressing the question of remoteness two prior matters must not be overlooked. Did the defendant owe any duty to the plaintiff to safeguard his person or property?[1] If he did, was he negligent? Were there any practicable measures which he could have taken which would have avoided or minimised the risk of the ulterior harm?[2] Only if duty and breach are proved do problems of remoteness arise.

In *Lamb v Camden London Borough Council*[3] the defendants carelessly broke a water main outside the plaintiff's Hampstead house. The escaping water undermined the foundations and the house subsided so that until repaired it was uninhabitable. Squatters moved into the unoccupied house, and by the time they were evicted had done damage totalling £30,000. The only issue was whether that damage was too remote.

Lord Denning MR held that it was a question of policy whether the damage was too remote. Considering that the plaintiff could readily have insured against the risk and could have taken more steps to guard against squatting, and that the defendants had no right to enter the premises, policy dictated that the damage be held too remote even though it was foreseeable.[4] Oliver LJ wrestled with the contention that the ratio of Lord Reid's judgment in *Home Office v Dorset Yacht Co Ltd*[5] was that the subsequent act was too remote unless that act was likely to happen. He found Lord Reid's statement to be obiter and that the subsequent act was neither likely nor even reasonably foreseeable. He added that he did not dissent from the view of Lord Denning that on grounds of policy foreseeable acts could still be too remote. Watkins LJ held that words such as 'possibility' or 'unlikely' did not assist him. Even though the act was reasonably foreseeable it was too remote.[6] He reached this conclusion by taking 'a robust and sensible approach'. His conclusion was:[7]

> I have the instinctive feeling that squatters' damage is too remote. I could not possibly come to any other conclusions, although on the primary facts I, too, would regard the damage or something like it as reasonably foreseeable in these times.

These judgments eloquently demonstrate the flexibility and inherent uncertainty surrounding the issue of whether a particular subsequent act is to be adjudged too remote a consequence of the defendant's negligence.[8]

1   *Maloco v Littlewoods Ltd* [1987] AC 241, sub nom *Smith v Littlewoods Organisation Ltd* [1987] 1 All ER 710, HL; *Hill v Chief Constable of West Yorkshire* [1988] QB 60, [1987] 1 All ER 1173, CA discussed ante at p 190.
2   *King v Liverpool City Council* [1986] 3 All ER 544, [1986] 1 WLR 890, CA.
3   [1981] QB 625, [1981] 2 All ER 408, CA.
4   At 637 and 414 respectively.
5   [1970] AC 1004 at 1030, [1970] 2 All ER 294 at 300, HL.
6   Supra at 644 and 419 respectively.
7   Supra at 647 and 421 respectively.
8   And see *Knightley v Johns* [1982] 1 All ER 851, CA, where the defendant negligently overturned his car in a road tunnel and the plaintiff, a police cyclist, riding the wrong way in the tunnel was then injured in a collision with another car, a police inspector having carelessly failed to order the closure of the tunnel. The plaintiff's injuries were held to be too remote because they were not reasonably foreseeable.

(B)   CONCURRENT CAUSES

Various types of act which may be described as 'concurrent' must be looked at separately. If two tortious acts result in damage, and either one would have produced the same damage, as when two fires are started and merge to fires burn out a building, then the perpetrator of each act is responsible for the whole damage, because each act is a substantial factor in producing the result. Similarly, if two independent acts simultaneously bring about the same damage, as where two ships negligently collide, injuring a third party,[9] those responsible for the respective negligent acts are each fully liable.

If the defendant commits a tort (or an act which will become a tort if non-remote damage ensues) and, before his act spends its force, some later tortious act combines with it to produce a particular result which would not have been produced without the operation of the second act, then the defendant will be liable if, and only if, it is found, by applying the rules already stated, that his act caused the damage.[10] In *Hale v Hants and Dorset Motor Services Ltd* and another, the facts were:[11]

> P Corporation negligently allowed tree branches to overhang a highway. H was a passenger in a bus negligently driven by a servant of the defendant omnibus company in such a way that a branch struck the window of the bus with the result that he was blinded by broken glass.

It was held that the corporation and the bus company were each liable in full to H: each was negligent in not foreseeing that this harm was likely to result in combination with the negligence of the other.

In *Fitzgerald v Lane*[12] the plaintiff was crossing a pelican crossing when he was hit by a car driven by D1. The collision threw him up on the bonnet of the car and back onto the road where he was struck by a car driven by D2. He suffered severe injuries including damage to his neck resulting in partial tetraplegia. Whether it was contact with the car driven by D1 or D2 which caused the injury to the neck could not be established. Both were held jointly liable, and the plaintiff was held contributorily negligent.

(C)   CONSECUTIVE CAUSES

In *Baker v Willoughby*[13] the defendants admitted negligently injuring the plaintiff in the leg. Before the action came to trial, burglars shot the plaintiff in that same leg and it had to be amputated. The House of Lords held that the defendants remained liable for the loss of amenity occasioned by the injury inflicted by them. The fortuitous event

9   *The Koursk* [1924] P 140, CA. Should the first defendant remain liable if the other 'cause' is the non-tortious act of another person, or a natural cause, or the act of the plaintiff himself? Cf *Cummings (or McWilliams) v Sir William Arrol & Co Ltd* [1962] 1 All ER 623.

10   *Rouse v Squires* [1973] QB 889, [1973] 2 All ER 903, CA, at 898 (per Cairns LJ). 'If a driver so negligently manages his vehicle as to cause it to obstruct the highway and constitute a danger to other road users, including those who are driving too fast or not keeping a proper lookout, but not those who deliberately or recklessly drive into the obstruction, then the first driver's negligence may be held to have contributed to the causation of an accident of which the immediate cause was the negligent driving of the vehicle which because of the presence of the obstruction collides with it or with some other vehicle or some other person.'

11   [1947] 2 All ER 628, CA; *Robinson v Post Office* [1974] 2 All ER 737 discussed post at p 279.

12   [1989] AC 328, [1988] 2 All ER 961, HL.

13   [1970] AC 467, [1969] 3 All ER 1528.

of the second tort did not relieve them of liability. But in *Jobling v Associated Dairies Ltd*[14] the plaintiff was partially incapacitated by an accident at work. Later, but before the trial, he became incapacitated by a supervening illness. The House of Lords, distinguishing *Baker v Willoughby* held that the defendants were only responsible for the plaintiff's loss of earnings up until the time he succumbed to illness. Justification for this distinction between a second tort and supervening illness rests on the flimsy ground that the second tortfeasor would have been liable only for the additional damage inflicted by him and not the whole of the plaintiff's incapacity. It must never be forgotten that the object of damages in tort is to put the plaintiff as far as possible in the position which he would have been 'but for' the tort. Plaintiffs are not supposed to profit. Hence the principle of common law that a widow's damages for loss of her husband would be calculated taking into account her prospects of re-marriage![15] The plaintiff in *Jobling* would eventually have been unable to work even if the tort had never happened. Disease is a vicissitude of life. The House of Lords on policy grounds refused to make the defendants responsible for that vicissitude.

SECTION 4.   REMOTENESS OF DAMAGE

Rules which make the wrongdoer liable for all the consequences of his wrongful conduct are exceptional and need to be justified by some special policy. Normally the law limits liability to those consequences which are attributable to that which made the act wrongful.[16]

There are torts, deceit is one example,[17] where imposing liability for all the damage factually related to the relevant wrongdoing is considered justifiable. Such extensive liability is exceptional. In negligence[18] certain consequences of the defendant's tortious conduct will be considered too remote from his wrongdoing to impose on him responsibility for those consequences. It simply thought to be unjust to make the defendant answerable for events far removed from his original breach of duty. Accordingly, we must now consider the content of such rules on remoteness of damage.

(A)   *RE POLEMIS* AND *THE WAGON MOUND*

In relation to remoteness of damage the two most discussed cases remain, even after all these years, *Re Polemis and Furness, Withy & Co* and *The Wagon Mound*. In *Re Polemis*:[19]

> Stevedores employed by the charterers of a ship negligently caused a plank to fall into the hold of the ship, which contained a cargo of petrol in tins. In this hold was petrol vapour from the tins. The ship was destroyed by the fire which at once ensued. Arbitrators found that a spark caused by the plank's coming in contact with something in the hold ignited the petrol vapour and caused the fire, and that the causing of the spark could not reasonably have been anticipated from the falling of the plank, though some damage to the ship might reasonably have been anticipated.

14   [1982] AC 794, [1981] 2 All ER 752.
15   No longer, thanks to Parliament. See post at p 559.
16   *Banque Bruxelles Lambert SA v Eagle Star Insurance Co Ltd* [1997] AC 191 per Lord Hoffman at 213.
17   See above at p 122.
18   As is also the case in (inter alia) nuisance, *Rylands v Fletcher*, and breach of statutory duty.
19   [1921] 3 KB 560, CA.

The Court of Appeal unanimously held that the charterers were liable for the loss of the ship because it was a direct, although not a foreseeable, consequence of the negligent act of their employees.

In *The Wagon Mound*:[20]

> The defendants carelessly discharged oil from their ship into Sydney Harbour. About six hours later the ship set sail and left the harbour. The oil was carried by wind and tide beneath the plaintiff's wharf, 200 yards away. After being advised that they could safely do so, the plaintiffs continued welding operations on their wharf. Some 55 to 60 hours after the original discharge of the oil, molten metal from the welding operations on the wharf, when fanned by the wind, set fire to some cotton waste or rag floating in the oil beneath the wharf. The waste set fire to the oil whereupon the flames quickly developed into a conflagration which severely damaged the wharf. The oil also congealed upon the slipways adjoining the wharf and interfered with the plaintiff's use of the slips. The defendants neither knew nor ought to have known that the oil was capable of being set afire when spread on water.[1]

The Judicial Committee of the Privy Council held that the defendants were not liable in negligence because they could not reasonably have foreseen that the plaintiff's wharf would be damaged by fire when they carelessly discharged the oil into the harbour.

There is room for argument how far *Polemis* and *Wagon Mound* are truly in conflict. On the assumption that they are, strict adherence to precedent should have required that as a decision of the English Court of Appeal, *Re Polemis* governed the development of rules of remoteness of damage. However, that is not the case and *The Wagon Mound* has become the fount of wisdom on remoteness of damage.

(B) FORESEEABLE TYPE OF HARM

The *Wagon Mound* held that if the damage which materialises is damage by fire, then for the defendant to be liable he must have been able to anticipate damage by fire; that he could anticipate damage by fouling the wharf's slipways was not enough. An unbroken succession of subsequent cases at all levels, House of Lords,[2] Privy Council,[3] Court of Appeal[4] and first instance,[5] has accepted that the harm suffered must be of a kind, type or class foreseeable as a result of the defendant's negligence. So, the test of liability for shock is foreseeability of injury by shock.[6] If a person suffers personal harm through contact, then it must be shown that harm through contact was foreseeable.

20 *Overseas Tankship (UK) Ltd v Morts and Dock & Engineering Co Ltd* [1961] AC 388, [1961] 1 All ER 404, PC. See (1960) 76 LQR 567; (1961) 77 LQR 467; (1962) 25 MLR 1.
1 Some of these facts can only be gleaned from the reports in the courts below, [1958] 1 Lloyd's Rep 575, [1959] 2 Lloyd's Rep 697. In subsequent proceedings arising out of the same discharge of oil the owners of other damaged ships recovered damages in negligence on the ground that the damage was foreseeable; *Overseas Tankship (UK) Ltd v Miller Steamship Co Pty, The Wagon Mound (No 2)* [1967] 1 AC 617, [1966] 2 All ER 709, PC. The plaintiffs in *The Wagon Mound* dared not advance the evidence suggesting it was foreseeable the oil would ignite on water for fear they would be held contributorily negligent in continuing welding operations. At that time contributory negligence was a complete defence in New South Wales.
2 *Hughes v Lord Advocate*, [1963] AC 837, [1963] 1 All ER 705, HL; *Donaghey v Boulton and Paul Ltd* [1968] AC 1 at 26 (per Lord Reid); *Banque Financière de la Cité SA v Westgate Insurance Co Ltd* [1991] 2 AC 249, [1990] 2 All ER 947, HL.
3 *The Wagon Mound (No 2)* [1967] 1 AC 617.
4 *Stewart v West African Terminals Ltd* [1964] 2 Lloyd's Rep 371 at 375 (per Lord Denning MR); *Doughty v Turner Manufacturing Co Ltd* [1964] 1 QB 518 at 529.
5 *Wieland v Cyril Lord Carpets Ltd* [1969] 3 All ER 1006 at 1009 (per Eveleigh J); *Tremain v Pike* [1969] 3 All ER 1303 at 1308 (per Payne J).
6 *The Wagon Mound* at 426.

Bradford v Robinson Rentals Ltd is a typical illustration of the working of these principles.[7]

> The defendant employers carelessly exposed the plaintiff van driver to extreme cold in the course of his duties. In consequence he suffered frost-bite. The court held that the defendants exposed him to severe cold and fatigue likely to cause a common cold, pneumonia or chilblains, and that frost-bite was of the same type and kind as the harms foreseeable, so that the defendants were held liable.

Where a wife sustained foreseeable psychological damage the fact that some of it resulted from the effect of her husband's changed behaviour (he also was injured in the accident) did not prevent her from claiming – the damage was of a foreseeable type and 'the fact that it arises or is continued by reason of an unusual complex of events does not avail the defendant'.[8]

Suppose that we give a loaded gun to a 14-year-old boy, which he drops on his foot. We are careless in handing him the gun, we owe him a duty of care, and an injured foot is the consequence, and yet we are not liable. The risk against which we had to guard was him shooting himself, but the harm which materialised was of a totally different kind: damage by impact of the gun is different from damage by the shooting of a bullet from it.

There are areas of uncertainty in defining 'kind' of damage, as *Tremain v Pike* illustrates:[9]

> The plaintiff herdsman, while working for the defendant farmers, contracted a rare condition, Weil's disease, through coming in contact with rats' urine. Weil's disease was not foreseeable, though other diseases arising from the presence of rats were foreseeable. The defendants were held not liable.

Payne J stated:[10]

> [Weil's disease] was entirely different in kind from the effect of a rat bite, or food poisoning by the consumption of food or drink contaminated by rats. I do not accept that all illness or infection arising from an infestation of rats should be regarded as of the same kind.

Would a defendant who knew of the risk that blood supplied for transfusion might be contaminated (eg by hepatitis B) be exculpated if he was at the relevant time unaware of the possibility of contamination by the AIDS virus (HIV)? It is submitted he would not. He was aware of the risk of blood-borne disease—the very kind of damage inflicted. The damage inflicted by HIV differed only in its greater extent.

(C)   THE MEANS BY WHICH THE HARM WAS CAUSED

Since *The Wagon Mound,* the courts have frequently reiterated that the defendant may be liable even though he could not envisage that precise set of circumstances which produced harm of the foreseeable kind. In *Hughes v Lord Advocate*,[11] H, aged 8, and

---

7   [1967] 1 All ER 267, [1967] 1 WLR 337.
8   *Malcolm v Broadhurst* [1970] 3 All ER 508 at 511 (per Geoffrey Lane J). *Brice v Brown* [1984] 1 All ER 997 (foreseeability of shock therefore liable for plaintiff's acute mental illness-no need to foresee exact mental process leading to the ultimate result).
9   [1969] 3 All ER 1303, [1969] 1 WLR 1556.
10   At 1308.
11   [1963] AC 837, [1963] 1 All ER 705, HL.

another boy aged 10 were playing on an Edinburgh highway. Near the edge of the roadway was a manhole some nine feet deep, over which a shelter tent had been erected. Post Office workmen working on underground cables left the area after dark, placed red paraffin warning lamps there and took the ladder from the manhole and laid it on the ground. The boys came up and started meddling with this equipment and H, while swinging one of the lamps by a rope over the hole, stumbled over the lamp, and knocked it into the hole. An explosion followed. H was thrown into the manhole and severely burned. The explosion occurred because paraffin from the lamp escaped, vaporised and was ignited by the flame. This particular development of events was not foreseeable, but the defendant was held liable for the negligence of the workmen.

The defendant was liable because H was injured as a result of the type or kind of accident or occurrence that could reasonably have been foreseen, even though the workmen could not have foretold the exact way in which H would play with the alluring objects that had been left to attract him or the exact way in which in so doing he might get hurt. The workmen's conduct created a risk of the kind of harm, personal injuries by fire, which materialised.

If harm of a foreseeable kind occurs, it will normally be no defence that the precise mechanics of the way in which the negligent act results in the harm could not be foreseen.[12] Since it was foreseeable that a defendant's pack of terrier dogs would bowl over and scratch children, he was liable when one of them bit the plaintiff child without bowling him over.[13] The fact that an explosion much greater in magnitude than was foreseeable resulted in damage to the plaintiff will be no defence.[14] In general, it is only when the accident is caused by the intrusion of some new and unforeseen factor that the way in which the damage was caused is relevant. Lord Reid in *Hughes v Lord Advocate* discussed *Glasgow Corpn v Muir*, where the facts were as follows:[15]

Two picnickers were allowed to carry a tea urn through a passage of the defendants' tea house. For a reason which was not explained, one of them slipped, and children buying sweets at a counter in the passage were scalded. An action by the children in negligence against the defendants failed.

Lord Reid said of this case that a person carelessly carrying a hot tea urn near children would not be liable if it were upset and caused damage because the ceiling collapsed; the fall of the ceiling would be an extraneous cause. Yet one case is particularly difficult to reconcile with the principles set out in this subsection, *Doughty v Turner Manufacturing Co Ltd*.[16]

The defendants placed an asbestos cement cover over a heat treatment bath containing sodium cyanide as a very hot molten liquid. The defendants' employees carelessly dislodged this cover so that it slid into the bath. The molten liquid exploded, erupted from the bath, and injured the plaintiff workman nearby. Although it was foreseeable that damage by splashing would result from dislodging the cover it was not foreseeable that an explosion would ensue.

The defendants were held not liable, even though the kind of harm, damage by burning, was foreseeable. They would have been liable for damage by splashing; the risk of damage by explosion was not foreseeable and this risk which materialised differed from the one which was foreseeable so substantially that *Hughes v Lord Advocate* was

---

12 *Draper v Hodder* [1972] 2 QB 556, [1992] 2 All ER 510, CA.
13 *Wieland v Cyril Lord Carpets Ltd* [1969] 3 All ER 1006 (per Eveleigh J).
14 *Vacwell Engineering Co Ltd v BDH Chemicals Ltd* [1971] 1 QB 88, [1969] 3 All ER 1681; on appeal [1971] 1 QB 111n, [1970] 3 All ER 535n.
15 [1943] AC 448, [1943] 2 All ER 44 HL.
16 [1964] 1 QB 518 [1064] 1 All ER 98,CA.

distinguished. The distinction drawn between a burn caused by a splash and one caused by an explosion is a fine one. But if the current trend to restrict the ambit of duty is considered together with the refusal of the House of Lords in *Wilsher v Essex Area Health* Authority[17] to take an unmoveable approach to factual causation, may such fine distinctions become the norm?[18]

(D) EXTENT OF THE DAMAGE

Where the very kind of harm which is foreseeable has occurred, it has always been the case that the defendant cannot plead that the plaintiff was earning more than the average victim, or that goods were exceptionally valuable. Damages are not restricted to the average loss of earnings or average value of goods in the circumstances, even supposing that such a sum was calculable. Similarly, if the facts can be proven, the shop assistant who usually earns £100 week will recover her full loss if she is knocked down on her way to fulfil a once-only lucrative television contract. The extent and limitations of this approach are illustrated by *Liesbosch (Dredger) v Edison*.[19]

> The plaintiffs' dredger, the *Liesbosch,* was sunk owing to the negligence of the defendants. The plaintiffs' poverty prevented them from buying a replacement immediately, and so, to fulfil an existing contract, they had to hire another dredger at an exorbitant rate. The plaintiffs recovered compensation for: (1) the market price of a comparable vessel; (2) the cost of adapting and insuring such a vessel; (3) expenses occasioned by their liability to fulfil their contract for the period between the loss of the *Liesbosch* and when a replacement could reasonably have been in service (expenses caused by penalty clauses in the contract).

However, the House of Lords refused to award the plaintiffs compensation for the additional cost to them of hiring a replacement dredger which was considerably greater than the additional cost of buying a dredger. That additional loss was held to result from an 'extraneous' cause,[20] the plaintiff's poverty, and so was too remote from the defendants negligence. The judgment in the *Liesbosch* is difficult to reconcile with the line of authority to be discussed in the next section requiring that normally you 'take the plaintiff as you find him'. It may be seen perhaps as a judgment less truly related to remoteness than concerning a failure to mitigate loss where it would be reasonable to do so.[1] Perhaps ultimately all that can be said is that the *Liesbosch* represents yet another policy decision motivated by judicial concern to limit the extent of liability for economic loss[2].

---

17 [1988] AC 1074, [1988] 1 All ER 871 HL.
18 And see *Crossley v Rawlinson* [1981] 3 All ER 674. The defendant carelessly started a fire on his lorry on the highway. It was foreseeable than an AA patrol man 100 yards away would run down a path to help put out the fire. He slipped in a concealed hole on the path while running to the fire and was injured. The court held that no injury while running along the path was foreseeable and so no action lay. The case seems wrongly decided.
19 [1933] AC 449, cf *The Daressa* [1971] 1 Lloyd's Rep 60.
20 Ibid at 460 per Lord Wright.
1 See *Dodds Properties (Kent) Ltd v Canterbury County Council* [1980] 1 All ER 928.
2 For the same reason an injured wife cannot recover further damages because her husband, incapacitated in the same accident, and so not requring a secretary, is no longer able to employ her as a part-time secretary: *Malcolm v Broadhurst* [1970] 3 All ER 508. Nor can injured children recover more because the hysterical obsession of their mother aggravates their symptoms: *McLaren v Bradstreet* (1969) 113 Sol Jo 471. See also *Schneider v Eisovitch* [1960] 2 QB 430, [1960] 1 All ER 169.

(E)   THE 'THIN SKULL' RULE

Before *The Wagon Mound*, it was established law that, in relation to personal injury, the defendant had to 'take the plaintiff as he found him' so that the victim could claim damages for the entire harm to his person, even though, owing to some special bodily sensitivity, it was greater than would have been suffered by the ordinary individual. Thus, the haemophiliac[3], or the extreme neurotic[4], who sustained greater damage than the ordinary person have recovered the full extent of their damage, even though the defendant could not have foreseen such extensive harm. The courts have held that *The Wagon Mound* has not affected this principle, commonly described as the 'thin skull' rule (or sometimes the 'eggshell skull' rule). In *Smith v Leech Brain & Co Ltd*:[5]

A negligently inflicted burn on P's lip resulted in his dying of cancer, for the tissues of the lip in which the cancer developed were in a pre-malignant condition at the time when the burn made the cancer develop.

The defendants were held liable for the damage resulting from the death.

In *Robinson v Post Office*,[6] the defendants carelessly lacerated the plaintiff's leg; a doctor's subsequent anti-tetanus injection caused encephalitis because the plaintiff was allergic to the injected serum. The defendants were held liable.

There is no authoritative ruling whether the same principle applies to property damage in tort. In *Parsons v Uttley Ingham*[7], the defendants negligently failed to install proper ventilation in a hopper used to feed the plaintiff's pigs. The ground nuts fed to the pigs went mouldy and the pigs died of a rare disease. Some mild 'food poisoning' might have been foreseen as a consequence of feeding pigs mouldy nuts. Death was a highly unusual consequence. The Court of Appeal held that the defendants must in effect 'take the pigs as they found them, and awarded full compensation for the loss of the plaintiffs' property, the pigs. The decision resulted from a claim for breach of contract but the Court of Appeal acted on the basis that in this respect the rules of remoteness in contract and tort were the same.

Presumably, the defendant takes as he finds them, not only the physical state of the damaged person or property, but also the surrounding external physical circumstances. This is the crux of *Great Lakes Steamship Co v Maple Leaf Milling Co*:[8]

The defendants negligently failed to lighten the plaintiffs' ship at the time stipulated. When the water level fell the ship grounded and was damaged. This damage was more extensive because the ship settled on a large submerged anchor which the defendants neither knew nor could have expected to be there. The defendants were liable for all the damage to the ship.

The decision is correct: the damage was of a foreseeable type; it was of greater extent than foreseeable, not because of internal characteristics of the property, but because of special external circumstances. No doubt the same rule applies to personal injuries: the defendant who negligently causes the plaintiff to stumble, so that he slides off the

---

3   *Bidwell v Briant* (1956) Times, 9 May.
4   *Love v Port of London Authority* [1959] 2 Lloyd's Rep 541; or exacerbation of pre-existing nervous disturbance: *Malcolm v Broadhurst* [1970] 3 All ER 508. *Brice v Brown* [1984] 1 All ER 997.
5   [1962] 2 QB 405, [1961] 3 All ER 1159.
6   [1974] 2 All ER 737, [1974] 1 WLR 1176, CA.
7   [1978] QB 791, [1978] 1 All ER 525, CA.
8   (1924) 41 TLR 21—on the generally held view that it matters not that the case was in contract, not tort. On remoteness in contract and tort see Cartwright 'Remoteness of Damage in Contract and Tort' (1996) 55 CLJ 488.

edge of a precipice concealed from view, will be liable for those consequences of the risk of stumbling, either before or after *The Wagon Mound*. Once the 'stage is set', the defendant's liability is adjudged accordingly; the defendant must 'take the plaintiff as he finds him'.

Chapter 15

Defences to negligence

SECTION I.   CONTRIBUTORY NEGLIGENCE

At common law, it was a complete defence if the defendant proved that the plaintiff was guilty of contributory negligence. The Law Reform (Contributory Negligence) Act 1945 now provides that contributory negligence no longer affords a complete defence, but merely reduces the damages to the extent to which the plaintiff has been contributorily negligent. In the leading case of *Butterfield v Forrester* the facts were as follows.[1]

> The defendant partially obstructed the highway by putting a pole across part of it. The plaintiff, riding violently at dusk, did not observe the pole and ran into it and suffered injuries, but would have seen it had he been using ordinary care.

Holding that the plaintiff failed, despite the wrongful act of obstruction by the defendant, Lord Ellenborough said:[2]

> One person being in fault will not dispense with another's using ordinary care for himself. Two things must concur to support this action, an obstruction in the road by the fault of the defendant, and no want of ordinary care to avoid it on the part of the plaintiff.

In order to establish contributory negligence the defendant must plead[3] and prove that:
(a)   the injury of which the plaintiff complains resulted from the particular risk to which the plaintiff exposed himself by virtue of his own negligence;
(b)   the negligence of the plaintiff contributed to his injury;
(c)   there was fault or negligence on the part of the plaintiff.
We then have to consider:
(d)   the scope of the Law Reform (Contributory Negligence) Act 1945;
(e)   apportionment of damages between the plaintiff and defendant.

---

1   (1809) 11 East 60.
2   (1809) 11 East 60 at 61.
3   *Fookes v Slaytor* [1979] 1 All ER 137, [1978] 1 WLR 1293, CA.

(A) RISK

This is a requirement which may be compared with the rule that the plaintiff, in an action based on negligence, must prove that the risk which in fact materialises is the one against which the defendant was under a duty to guard.[4] Here the defendant must show that the harm sustained by the plaintiff belongs to that general class of perils to which the plaintiff was exposed by his own negligent conduct. The important, yet difficult, case of *Jones v Livox Quarries Ltd* illustrates this point.[5]

> The plaintiff was riding down a slope leading to the bottom of a quarry on the back of the defendants' vehicle, contrary to their orders, when another vehicle of the defendants was negligently driven into the back of the first vehicle. As a result, the plaintiff was injured. By so riding, the plaintiff exposed himself not only to the risk of falling off the vehicle but also to the risk of being injured in the particular way in which he was injured. The court therefore found that he was contributorily negligent.

It is plain from the judgments delivered that, if the damage sustained by the plaintiff had been foreign to the risk to which his negligent conduct subjected him, the defence would have failed.[6] So, for example, had the driver of the vehicle negligently set fire to it thus causing the plaintiff injury by burns, the plaintiff would have suffered just the same injury regardless of his own lack of care.

Interestingly, the risk to which the plaintiff subjects himself may be one of his own creation, so long as the defendant's negligence consists of a duty to care for the plaintiff after the risk has materialised. In *Barrett v Ministry of Defence*,[7] a naval airman drank himself unconscious and subsequently died by choking on his own vomit. His widow sued the defendants for negligence on the basis that, as his employer, they owed him a duty of care to prevent him from becoming so drunk that he may cause himself injury. The Court of Appeal held that once the deceased had collapsed, and the defendants had taken steps to care for him, the defendants had thereby undertaken a duty of care in respect of the plaintiff. Since the steps taken were inadequate, the defendants were liable in negligence. But the damages payable were reduced because the plaintiff's *preceding* folly in subjecting himself to harm through drunkenness amounted to contributory negligence.

(B) THAT THE PLAINTIFF'S NEGLIGENCE WAS A CONTRIBUTORY FACTOR

This is undoubtedly the aspect of the defence of contributory negligence which calls for the most careful examination. The key to the proper understanding of the development of the case law on this subject is the full appreciation of the seriousness of the absolute rule of common law which deprived the plaintiff of a remedy if he himself was guilty of any fault, however slight, contributing to the damage which he suffered.

The essence of the matter is causation. As Lord Atkin put it:[8]

4   See ch 11 ante.
5   [1952] 2 QB 608, CA.
6   [1952] 2 QB 608, CA. Singleton LJ took the view (at 612) that there would be no defence where a plaintiff negligently sat upon an unsafe wall, and a driver negligently ran into the wall and injured the plaintiff. By contrast, Denning LJ thought (at 616) that the plaintiff would succeed, if, while riding on the vehicle, he had been hit in the eye by a shot from a gun fired by a negligent sportsman.
7   [1995] 3 All ER 87, [1995] 1 WLR 1217, CA.
8   *Caswell v Powell Duffryn Associated Collieries Ltd* [1940] AC 152 at 165, [1939] 3 All ER 722, HL.

... if the plaintiff were negligent but his negligence was not a cause operating to produce the damage there would be no defence. I find it impossible to divorce any theory of contributory negligence from the concept of causation.

Not unnaturally, the courts sought to mitigate the harshness of this doctrine of contributory negligence.[9] In doing so they evolved various tests to cover different sets of circumstances. The best-known test was the so-called 'last opportunity rule' on which *Davies v Mann*[10] is the leading case.

The plaintiff negligently left his ass, fettered by its forefeet, in a highway. The defendant drove his wagon and horses into it at a rapid pace, thereby killing it. Had he used proper care, the defendant could have avoided injuring the ass, but he was driving too fast. It is uncertain when he saw the ass, if indeed he saw it at all.

It was held that, notwithstanding his own negligence, the plaintiff could recover damages because the defendant, had he been driving properly, could still have avoided the consequences of that negligence.[11] Subsequent attempts were made to apply this rule of law to analogous cases. In each case, two things were crucial: first, the time of both the plaintiff's and the defendant's acts and, second, the respective knowledge of the parties.[12]

In the maritime context, the Maritime Conventions Act 1911 had authorised the court, in the case of collisions at sea, to apportion the loss according to the degree to which each party was at fault, and this principle was made generally applicable by the Law Reform (Contributory Negligence) Act 1945.[13] Since the passing of these Acts, the need for the courts to select some particular cause as the predominant one has disappeared. A plaintiff whose own acts contributed to his injury or damage is no longer completely defeated, he merely has his damages proportionately reduced to the extent to which he was at fault. The courts are free to look for all the causes and apportion accordingly. As Lord Porter put it:[14]

It [the 1945 Act] enables the court (be it judge or jury) to seek less strenuously to find some ground for holding the plaintiff free from blame, or for reaching the conclusion that his negligence played no part in the ensuing accident, in as much as, owing to the change in the law, the blame can now be apportioned equitably between the two parties.

Plainly, the courts are no longer concerned with the subtleties and refinements of the 'last opportunity' rule and the like. In order to decide whether the plaintiff's negligent conduct is contributory, one applies exactly those rules of causation set out in chapter 12. The earliest important case, and, moreover, the one on which the courts still rely, was *Admiralty Comrs v SS Volute*.[15] It was actually decided under the Maritime Conventions Act, but the key principles are the same.

The Volute, a convoy leader, changed her course without signalling. *The Radstock*, on discovering that she was thereby endangered, negligently put on full steam ahead. Although this negligence

---

9   *Stapley v Gypsum Mines Ltd* [1953] AC 663 at 677, [1953] 2 All ER 478, HL (per Lord Porter).
10 (1842) 10 M & W 546.
11 Perhaps the most important of the cases following it is *Radley v London and North Western Rly Co* (1876) 1 App Cas 754, HL.
12 Especially *British Columbia Electric Rly Co Ltd v Loach* [1916] 1 AC 719, PC; *The Eurymedon* [1938] P 41 at 49–50, [1938] 1 All ER 122, CA (per Greer LJ).
13 Maritime Conventions Act 1911, s 1; Law Reform (Contributory Negligence) Act 1945, s 1.
14 *Stapley v Gypsum Mines Ltd* [1953] AC 663 at 677, [1953] 2 All ER 478, HL.
15 [1922] 1 AC 129, HL.

was subsequent to that of *The Volute*, both vessels were held to blame for their ensuing collision, and apportionment under the Act was directed.

In a speech warmly supported by the other Law Lords, Viscount Birkenhead pointed out that, despite the fact that cases of 'strictly synchronous negligence' were rare, the courts could, nevertheless, still find that the negligence of both parties contributed to the resulting injury even though their acts were not 'synchronous'. He added:[16]

> Upon the whole I think that the question of contributory negligence must be dealt with somewhat broadly and upon commonsense principles as a jury would probably deal with it. And while, no doubt, where a clear line can be drawn, the subsequent negligence is the only one to look at, there are cases in which the two acts come so closely together, and the second act of negligence is so much mixed up with the state of things brought about by the first act, that the party secondly negligent, while not held free from blame under the *Bywell Castle* rule, might, on the other hand, invoke the prior negligence as being part of the cause of the collision so as to make it a case of contribution. And the Maritime Conventions Act with its provisions for nice qualifications as to the quantum of blame and the proportions in which contribution is to be made may be taken as to some extent declaratory of the Admiralty rule in this respect.

The test, he pointed out, is whether the plaintiff 'in the ordinary plain common sense of this business ... contributed to the accident'. This does not mean, of course, that whenever the negligence of the defendant is preceded by negligence on the part of the plaintiff, there is always contributory negligence; the acts may be so severable that only that of the defendant can be said to have caused the damage, but there is no need to retain a separate rule of 'last opportunity' in order to reach this conclusion. Evershed LJ explained this clearly in *Davies v Swan Motor Co (Swansea) Ltd*.[17]

> As I understand the *Davies v Mann* principle ... it is this: in that case the plaintiff's negligence or fault consisted in placing the donkey upon the highway; but it having been observed in due time by the defendant ... the negligence of the plaintiff had really ceased to be an operating factor in the collision ... the plaintiff ... as a negligent actor, was at the material time, *functus officio*, one might say *functus culpa*.[18]

The difficulties encountered in determining whether the plaintiff's negligence is contributory are usually not of law but of fact: there is room for difference of opinion on whether, in any particular case, the negligence of the plaintiff has ceased to be an operating factor. But only if this inference is made does the plaintiff's conduct cease to be contributory negligence.

Since *The Volute*, the House of Lords has frequently stressed this test of causation in contributory negligence. Thus, in *Swadling v Cooper*[19] (where the Court of Appeal had attempted to frame elaborate classifications),[20] the House of Lords reversed the decision and upheld the direction of the trial judge to the jury, which in substance was: 'Whose negligence was it that substantially caused the injury?'.[1] The Privy Council

16 [1922] 1 AC 129 at 144.
17 [1949] 2 KB 291 at 317, [1949] 1 All ER 620, CA.
18 Cf *Boy Andrew (Owners) v St Rognvald (Owners)* [1948] AC 140 at 149, HL where Viscount Simon opined: 'The negligence of the donkey-owner was therefore a fault not contributing to the collision: it was merely a *causa sine qua non*'.
19 [1931] AC 1, [1930] All ER Rep 257, HL (collision at crossroads between defendant's car and the motorcycle of the plaintiff's husband, who was killed).
20 [1930] 1 KB 403.
1   See *Stapley v Gypsum Mines Ltd* [1953] AC 663, [1953] 2 All ER 478, HL (especially the speech of Lord Reid).

has also followed *The Volute* and issued a forceful warning against the dangers of 'attempts to classify acts in relation to one another with reference to time or with regard to the knowledge of one party at a particular moment of the negligence of the other party'.[2]

These principles may be clarified by an examination of some of the more important cases decided since the passing of the Act of 1945. In *Henley v Cameron*[3] the facts were as follows.

The defendant chose to leave his car unlighted on the highway at night, and the husband of the plaintiff, riding a motorcycle, carelessly collided with it and was killed. An apportionment under the 1945 Act was made.

Applying the rule laid down in *The Volute*, Tucker LJ pointed out that 'it must always remain a question of fact whether the negligence of B is "so mixed up" with the state of things brought about by A's negligence as to make the negligence of both contributory causes to the accident'.[4] He also pointed out the illogicality of asserting that the rules of contributory negligence differ from those of causation, saying:[5]

I cannot understand how, when considering whether the negligence of A or B or of both has been the effective cause of an accident, the answer can depend on whether A or B happens to be the plaintiff in the action or whether they are both defendants.

In *Boy Andrew (Owners) v St Rognvald (Owners)*,[6] as one vessel negligently overtook another, the latter negligently changed course, collided with the first vessel, and sank. The House of Lords followed *The Volute* and found both parties blameworthy. Viscount Simon said:[7]

The suggested test of 'last opportunity' seems to me inaptly phrased and likely in some cases to lead to error, as the Law Revision Committee said in their report (Cmd 6032 of 1939, p 16):

'In truth, there is no such rule – the question, as in all questions of liability for a tortious act, is, not who had the last opportunity of avoiding the mischief, but whose act caused the wrong?'.

In *Davies v Swan Motor Co (Swansea) Ltd* the facts were these.[8]

Contrary to orders, the plaintiff was standing on steps at the off-side of a dust lorry. The driver of the lorry turned to the right without warning just as a following vehicle was overtaking him, and the plaintiff was injured in the ensuing collision. Both drivers were negligent, but it was also held that the plaintiff was contributorily negligent.

Evershed LJ, after considering separately the *Davies v Mann* type of case (where the negligence of the defendant alone, in his opinion, caused the accident), said of the 'last opportunity' rule:[9]

2 *Marvin Sigurdson v British Columbia Electric Rly Co Ltd* [1953] AC 291 at 299, PC.
3 [1949] LJR 989, CA; cf *Harvey v Road Haulage Executive* [1952] 1 KB 120, CA; *Rouse v Squires* [1973] QB 889, [1973] 2 All ER 903, CA.
4 [1949] LJR 989 at 992–3, CA.
5 [1949] LJR 989 at 993, CA.
6 [1948] AC 140, HL.
7 [1948] AC 140 at 149, HL.
8 [1949] 2 KB 291, [1949] 1 All ER 620, CA.
9 [1949] 2 KB 291 at 318, CA.

Now that as a doctrine I venture to think has suffered a demise independently altogether of the Act of 1945 ... No doubt, in practice, such a rule was found useful by judges who were anxious in the interests of justice to avoid coming to a conclusion wholly adverse to a plaintiff merely because, at the material time, the plaintiff was still a negligent actor to some perhaps quite trivial extent. Now the Law Reform (Contributory Negligence) Act 1945, has rendered it no longer necessary to resort to devices of that kind.

Denning LJ stressed that the matter is purely one of causation. Of the *Davies v Mann* type of case where the plaintiff negligently leaves an obstruction in the highway and the defendant negligently runs into it, he said that the fact that the defendant sees the obstruction 'may mean in some cases that the obstruction is not the cause of the accident': in short, one does not apply a mechanical rule of 'last opportunity', but one asks whether 'his conduct would be so powerful a factor in producing the damage that the presence of the parked vehicle would not be itself a cause of the damage'.[10] Similarly, in *Jones v Livox Quarries Ltd*,[11] Denning LJ said:

> There is no clear guidance to be found in the books about causation. All that can be said is that causes are different from the circumstances in which, or on which, they operate. The line between the two depends on the facts of each case. It is a matter of common sense more than anything else ... The man's negligence here was so much mixed up with his injury that it cannot be dismissed as mere history. His dangerous position on the vehicle was one of the causes of his damage.

(C) THE NEGLIGENCE OF THE PLAINTIFF

There is an important difference between the defence of contributory negligence and the tort of negligence. To set up this defence, the defendant need not prove that the plaintiff owed the defendant a duty of care. As was said in *Nance v British Columbia Electric Rly Co Ltd*:[12]

> ... all that is necessary to establish such a defence is to prove to the satisfaction of the jury that the injured party did not in his own interest take reasonable care of himself and contributed, by this want of care, to his own injury.

So far as proving this is concerned, it is well established that the lack of care on the part of the plaintiff must be proved by the defendant according to the usual civil standard of proof: the balance of probabilities.[13]

It may be assumed that decisions on the standard of reasonable care required of the *defendant* in negligence apply equally to determine whether the *plaintiff* has taken reasonable care for his own safety.[14] Many of the problems relating to the standard of reasonableness discussed with reference to the standard of care in the tort of negligence

10   [1949] 2 KB 291 at 323, CA.
11   [1952] 2 QB 608 at 616, CA.
12   [1951] AC 601 at 611, [1951] 2 All ER 448, PC (per Viscount Simon); cf *Jones v Livox Quarries Ltd* [1952] 2 QB 608 at 615, CA (per Denning LJ).
13   *Owens v Brimmell* [1977] QB 859, [1976] 3 All ER 765; *Limbrick v French* [1993] PIQR P 121.
14   Whereas a workman suing for breach of statutory duty is not necessarily 'contributorily negligent' because his conduct would have been sufficiently careless to make his employer vicariously liable, the standard of care required of a workman who sues in negligence is apparently the same as that required of him as a defendant in negligence: *Staveley Iron and Chemical Co Ltd v Jones* [1956] AC 627, [1956] 1 All ER 403, HL.

arise here also. This is especially the case in relation to children (where, it will be recalled, the age of the child is considered material[15]), and in relation to the rule that 'a prudent man will guard against the possible negligence of others when experience shows such negligence to be common'.[16] The warning issued when we discussed breach of duty in negligence must be repeated in the present connection: viz, that decisions on particular facts ought not too readily to be regarded as establishing legal principles.[17] The Court of Appeal is as free to infer contributory negligence – and thereby reverse the trial judge – as it is to infer negligence.[18]

A few examples of contributory negligence include the following: a moped driver who does not wear a crash helmet,[19] or simply fails to fasten it securely;[20] a car passenger who does not wear a seat belt,[1] or who knows that the car's foot-brake does not work;[2] a passenger injured by negligent drunken driving (so long as he either travelled knowing that his driver was so drunk that his capacity to drive carefully was impaired, or that he was later going to be a passenger with a driver he accompanied on a drinking bout which affected both the driver's capacity to drive safely and his own capacity to appreciate the danger);[3] a pedestrian who crosses a pelican crossing with the lights on green.[4] On the other hand, a house buyer who relies on the valuation of his building society's surveyor is not contributorily negligent in not having his house independently surveyed.[5] But if the survey undervalues the premises and a loan to purchase is made on the strength of that valuation, the lender will be contributorily negligent if the borrower defaults in repayment and the lender incurs losses by virtue of the negligent undervaluation. In such circumstances the lender is expected independently to verify the borrower's ability to repay the loan.[6]

If the negligence of the defendant puts the plaintiff in a position of imminent personal danger, conduct by the plaintiff which in fact operates to produce harm to him (but which is nevertheless reasonable in the agony of the moment) does not, on the authority of *Jones v Boyce*,[7] amount to contributory negligence.

> There, a passenger in a coach reasonably believed that the coach was about to overturn through the negligent driving of the defendant, the coach proprietor. He therefore jumped off, breaking

15 See *Gough v Thorne* [1966] 3 All ER 398, CA; *Mullin v Richards* [1998] 1 All ER 920, CA; *Morales v Eccleston* [1991] RTR 151, CA. Where a workman's contributory negligence lay in not complying with instructions, the court refused, with respect to this issue of contributory negligence, to take account of his known low intelligence but agreed that it was relevant in measuring the standard of care required of the defendant employer: *Baxter v Woolcombers Ltd* (1963) 107 Sol Jo 553, CA.
16 *Grant v Sun Shipping Co Ltd* [1948] AC 549 at 567, [1948] 2 All ER 238, HL (per Lord Du Parcq).
17 *SS Heranger (Owners) v SS Diamond (Owners)* [1939] AC 94 at 101, HL.
18 *Hicks v British Transport Commission* [1958] 2 All ER 39, [1957] 1 WLR 493, CA.
19 *O'Connell v Jackson* [1972] 1 QB 270, [1971] 4 All ER 129, CA.
20 *Capps v Miller* [1989] 2 All ER 333, [1989] 1 WLR 839, CA.
1 *Froom v Butcher* [1976] QB 286, [1975] 3 All ER 520, CA. Although in *Mackay v Borthwick* 1982 SLT 265 (Scotland) it was held that a woman with a hiatus hernia who did not wear a seatbelt on a short journey was not contributorily negligent. Failure to wear a seatbelt is now a criminal offence: Motor vehicles (Wearing of Seat Belts) Regulations 1982, SI 1982 No 1203.
2 *Gregory v Kelly* [1978] RTR 426.
3 *Owens v Brimmell* [1977] QB 859, [1976] 3 All ER 765.
4 *Fitzgerald v Lane* [1989] AC 328, [1988] 2 All ER 961, HL; cf *Tremayne v Hill* [1987] RTR 131, CA.
5 *Yianni v Edwin Evans & Sons* [1982] QB 438, [1981] 3 All ER 592.
6 *Legal and General Mortgage Services Ltd v HPC Professional Services* [1997] PNLR 567; *Platform Home Loans Ltd v Oyston Shipways Ltd* [1998] Ch 466, CA; *UCB Bank plc v David J Pinder plc* [1998] PNLR 398.
7 (1816) 1 Stark 493.

his leg. As things transpired, the coach did not overturn, but the passenger was adjudged not to be contributorily negligent and he successfully recovered in full from the defendant.

The critical question in such cases is whether the plaintiff behaved reasonably in the dilemma in which the defendant had placed him, due account being taken of the alarm which such a situation would engender in the prudent plaintiff.[8] The rule was subsequently extended in *Brandon v Osborne, Garrett & Co*.[9]

The plaintiff and her husband were in the defendants' shop as customers. Owing to the negligence of the defendants, broken glass falling from the roof imperilled the husband of the plaintiff, who instinctively clutched her husband to try to bring him to a place of safety and was herself injured. Had she remained in her original position she would not have been injured. Her injury was held not to be the result of her own contributory negligence.

These cases mark the limits to which the courts have taken the doctrine. Whether it extends to instinctive acts to protect strangers, or interests other than personal safety, is undecided.

Where the plaintiff is exercising some right – such as passage along a highway, or some common approach to his premises which the landlord has retained – his deliberately encountering a risk of danger created by the defendant is not necessarily contributory negligence. It will only amount to contributory negligence if, after making due allowance for his right to be there, the plaintiff is showing an unreasonable neglect of his own safety.[10]

Just as the defendant employer may be answerable for the negligence of his employee, so in principle should the contributory negligence of an employee of the plaintiff afford the defendant a good defence where that employee was acting in the course of his employment. So in one case, where A, driving B's van for B was struck by C, but A's careless driving contributed to the damage to the van, B's damages were reduced accordingly.[11] On the other hand, the contributory negligence of an independent contractor is not imputed to the principal, and that of a driver is not imputed to a passenger,[12] nor is that of a spouse imputed to the wife or husband.[13] When a child is

8   For accidents in the shipping law context, the rule is known as the 'rule in *The Bywell Castle*': (1879) 4 PD 219, CA.
9   [1924] 1 KB 548.
10 *Clayards v Dethick and Davis* (1848) 12 QB 439 (the plaintiff, a cabman, was prevented from taking his horse out of a mews by the only access to the highway because the defendants had dug and negligently fenced a trench at the junction of the mews and highway. In trying to get his horse out, he injured it. His action for damages succeeded despite the defendant's plea of contributory negligence); *Behrens v Bertram Mills Circus Ltd* [1957] 2 QB 1, [1957] 1 All ER 583.
11 *Kenfield Motors v Hayles and Rees* [1998] CL 429.
12 *Mills v Armstrong, The Bernina* (1888) 13 App Cas 1, HL (same principle was held to apply in the case of ships).
13 *Mallett v Dunn* [1949] 2 KB 180, [1949] 1 All ER 973; *Berrill v Road Haulage Executive* [1952] 2 Lloyds Rep 490 (wife driving husband's car not as his servant or agent; her contributory negligence did not prevent husband recovering in full for damage to car). Both the case last cited and *France v Parkinson* [1954] 1 All ER 739, CA, decide that the contributory negligence of a bailee is not to be imputed to a bailor. *Lampert v Eastern National Omnibus Co Ltd* [1954] 2 All ER 719n, decided that where a wife is injured in a collision between her car (driven by her husband) and another car, in which the two drivers are equally to blame, the wife's damages are to be reduced to one half. Although the wife would be liable to the other driver for her husband's negligence (see ch 29 post) why should her liability to third parties be equated with failure to take care for her own safety? Cf *Dawrant v Nutt* [1960] 3 All ER 681.

accompanied by an adult, the contributory negligence of the adult is not imputed to the child.[14] Consider *Oliver v Birmingham and Midland Motor Omnibus Co Ltd.*[15]

> The plaintiff, an infant in the care of his grandfather, was crossing a road when he was injured by the negligent driving of the defendant's omnibus by their servant. Although his grandfather was also negligent, the infant was held entitled to recover in full.

(D)   THE SCOPE OF THE LAW REFORM (CONTRIBUTORY NEGLIGENCE) ACT 1945[16]

The primary object of the 1945 Act is to provide that, where the defence of contributory negligence was previously available, the courts may now, instead of exonerating the defendant from liability, reduce the damages awarded against him to the extent to which the plaintiff was contributorily negligent. But the detailed provisions of the Act call for further study. Section 1(1) reads as follows:

> Where any person suffers damage as the result partly of the fault of any other person or persons, a claim in respect of that damage shall not be defeated by reason of the fault of the person suffering the damage, but the damages recoverable in respect thereof shall be reduced to such extent as the court thinks just and equitable having regard to the claimant's share in the responsibility for the damage.

Section 4 defines 'damage' as including loss of life and personal injury, and thus probably embraces any loss for which damages can at common law be awarded.[17] The use of the word 'result' is a neutral term regarded by the courts as leaving them free to continue to treat contributory negligence as a matter of causation.[18] What is clear, then, is that under the Act contributory negligence which contributes to the injuries suffered by the plaintiff is as relevant as contributory negligence contributing to the incident in which the injuries are suffered. Thus, a passenger failing to wear a seat belt cannot be said to be in any way responsible for the collision in which he is thrown against the steering wheel. But he is nonetheless responsible for those injuries that would have been avoided had he worn a belt.[19] The correct question is not 'what was the cause of the accident?' but rather, 'what was the cause of the damage?'.[20] In *Capps v Miller*[1] a young man suffered devastating brain injury when he was knocked off his moped by a drunken driver. He had not fastened the chin strap of his helmet and the

14   Where a disabled child's action rests on the Congenital Disabilities (Civil Liability) Act 1976 his damages are reduced if it is shown that the parent affected shared the responsibility for his being born disabled: s 1(7).
15   [1933] 1 KB 35, [1932] All ER Rep 820, Div Ct; cf *Murray v Harringay Arena Ltd* [1951] 2 KB 529, [1951] 2 All ER 320n, CA. Note, however, that if the parent is in breach of his duty to safeguard the child's safety the defendant may seek a contribution from the negligent parent under the Civil Liability (Contribution) Act 1978.
16   See (1986) 49 MLR 102.
17   In *Drinkwater v Kimber* [1951] 2 All ER 713, the trial judge held that it excluded pecuniary loss, but the Court of Appeal [1952] 2 QB 281 at 290 (per Singleton LJ), though affirming the decision, did so on other grounds and disagreed with this narrow interpretation of 'damage'.
18   Thus, where the plaintiff's own negligence prior to his act of rescue contributed to his injuries, his damages were reduced. The plaintiff (a train guard) went to the rescue of the defendant, who was negligently trying to board a moving train, without first applying the emergency brake: *Harrison v British Railways Board* [1981] 3 All ER 679.
19   See post.
20   *Froom v Butcher* [1976] QB 286, [1975] 3 All ER 520, CA; *O'Connell v Jackson* [1972] 1 QB 270, [1971] 3 All ER 129 (injured motorcyclist not wearing helmet).
1   [1989] 2 All ER 333, [1989] 1 WLR 839, CA.

helmet came off before he hit the road. The trial judge held that the plaintiff's failure to secure his helmet increased his injuries by 'some incalculable degree' and that, the defendant being 100% responsible for the accident, no reduction for any contributory negligence should be made. The Court of Appeal reversed his ruling. The judge had fallen into error in focusing on responsibility for the accident rather than the injury. Failure to wear a securely fastened helmet is now a criminal offence. That failure did in fact exacerbate the plaintiff's injuries and thus constituted contributory negligence.

The definition of 'fault' in the 1945 Act has proved to be very problematic. 'Fault' is defined in section 4 as 'negligence, breach of statutory duty or other act or omission which gives rise to liability in tort or would, apart from this Act, give rise to the defence of contributory negligence'. The first limb of the definition of 'fault' thus makes the partial defence of contributory negligence apparently applicable to all torts. Section 11 of the Torts (Interferences with Goods) Act 1977 expressly excludes contributory negligence as a defence to conversion or intentional trespass to goods. As far as other intentional torts are concerned the balance of authority now favours the availability of the contributory negligence defence; at any rate in relation to trespass to the person.[2] In the context of product liability, contributory negligence is expressly included as a defence under the Consumer Protection Act 1987. It is not, however, a defence to an action for deceit,[3] and is conceptually difficult to apply in the context of negligent misstatements (which presuppose that the plaintiff's contribution to his loss – his reliance – be reasonable, and therefore not negligent[4]).

A still more problematic question is whether the defence of contributory negligence can be invoked in an action for breach of contract.[5] Despite earlier dicta to the effect that where the parties have defined their mutual obligations in a contract, a concurrent duty in tort should not arise,[6] it is now clear that where a duty of care arises within a contractual relationship, or where one party assumes responsibility to perform carefully a professional service (and the other party relies upon that assumption of responsibility) the plaintiff may opt to sue in contract or tort.[7] It has even been held by the Court of Appeal that the tortious duty can be wider than the contractual one.[8] From this, it follows that a private patient suing in respect of the negligent delivery of her baby has a choice of contractual or tortious damages.[9] Furthermore, it has been held at first instance that the client of a negligent solicitor may make a similar choice whether to sue in contract or in tort.[10] On the other hand, an NHS patient has no such choice; nor does a disappointed legatee suing a solicitor for negligence in respect of the preparation of a will.[11] In relation to the hospital patient, it would scarcely accord with common

2 *Murphy v Culhane* [1977] QB 94, [1976] 3 All ER 533, CA; *Barnes v Nayer* (1986) Times, 19 December; *Wasson v Chief Constable of the Royal Ulster Constabulary* [1987] 8 NIJB 34.

3 *Alliance and Leicester Building Society v Edgestop Ltd* [1994] 2 All ER 38.

4 *JEB Fastners Ltd v Marks, Bloom & Co* [1981] 3 All ER 289.

5 See, eg, *De Meza and Stuart v Apple, Van Straten, Shena and Stone* [1975] 1 Lloyd's Rep 498, CA.

6 *Tai Hing Cotton Mill Ltd v Liu Chong Hing Bank Ltd* [1986] AC 80 at 107, PC; *National Bank of Greece SA v Pinios Shipping Co* [1989] 1 All ER 213, CA; *Lee v Thompson* (1989) 6 PN 91, CA; *Johnstone v Bloomsbury Health Authority* [1992] QB 333, [1991] 2 All ER 293, CA.

7 *Henderson v Merrett Syndicates Ltd* [1994] 3 All ER 506, HL. Note also that if a concurrent tortious duty was held not to exist, the Latent Damage Act 1986 could never be applied to contractual negligence for that Act has been held not to apply in relation to breach of contract: *Iron Trade Mutual Insurance Co Ltd v J K Buckenham Ltd* [1990] 1 All ER 808.

8 *Holt v Payne Skillington (a firm)* [1996] PNLR 179.

9 See *Kralj v McGrath* [1986] 1 All ER 54.

10 *Midland Bank Trust Co Ltd v Hett, Stubbs and Kemp* [1979] Ch 384, [1978] 3 All ER 571; doubted by Lloyd LJ in *Lee v Thompson* (1989) 6 PN 91, CA.

11 See *Ross v Caunters* [1980] Ch 297, [1979] 3 All ER 580; *White v Jones* [1995] 2 AC 207, [1995] 1 All ER 691, HL.

sense to say that the NHS patient who was contributorily negligent should suffer a reduction in damages but that her wealthier sister, who paid for treatment, should not.[12]

Equally, since there may be concurrent duties in tort and contract, is it any more sensible to assert that the defence of contributory negligence should, on a single set of facts, be available only so long as the plaintiff frames his action in tort? Although it has no place where the action may *only* be framed in contract,[13] the Court of Appeal has nonetheless held that where the defendant's liability in contract is concurrent with a breach of duty in tort – that is, where he is *negligently in breach* of contract – the 1945 Act *can* be applied.[14] On the other hand, where the defendant is in breach of a contractual term that is framed in terms of exercising reasonable care,[15] the 1945 Act cannot be applied to reduce the award of damages, if he owes no concurrent common law duty of care.[16] In these cases, of course, the difficulty lies in answering the far from obvious questions of where and why no concurrent common law duty exists.

(E)   APPORTIONMENT OF DAMAGES

The 1945 Act directs courts to reduce the award of damages as they think 'just and equitable having regard to the claimant's share in responsibility for the damage'. If the plaintiff's lack of care is found to have contributed to his damage, some reduction must be made. His carelessness cannot be totally disregarded on the ground that that course of action would be 'just and equitable',[17] nor may a judge evade apportionment by pleading the difficulty of ascertaining the precise degree to which the plaintiff's own carelessness exacerbated his injury.[18] Decisions on apportionment will generally be reached on a commonsense basis; and the Court of Appeal will only interfere with the trial judge's conclusions on apportionment if he or she can be shown plainly to be wrong.[19] Lord Reid summed up the basic guidelines for apportionment in *Stapley v Gypsum Mines Ltd*:[20]

> A court must deal broadly with the problem of apportionment, and, in considering what is just and equitable, must have regard to the blameworthiness of each party, but the claimant's share in the responsibility for the damage cannot, I think, be assessed without considering the relative importance of the acts in causing the damage apart from his blameworthiness.

Two factors, therefore, have to be considered: the causative potency of the act,[1] and the extent to which the plaintiff deviates from the standard of the reasonable man who

---

12 Unless you contend that by providing consideration for the duty undertaken by the defendant, the plaintiff 'buys' protection from her own as well as his lack of care.
13 *AB Marintrans v Comet Shipping Ltd* [1985] 3 All ER 442, [1985] 1 WLR 1270. See also *Barclays Bank plc v Fairclough Building Ltd* [1995] 1 All ER 289, CA: P's fault is an irrelevancy where D is 'guilty' of a breach of strict contractual duty *unless* P's conduct, rather than D's breach, was the true cause of P's loss.
14 *Forsikringsaktieselskapet Vesta v Butcher* [1989] AC 852, [1988] 2 All ER 43, HL. See also *Gran Gelato Ltd v Richcliff (Group) Ltd* [1992] Ch 560, [1992] 1 All ER 865, CA stating that contributory negligence can apply to a claim under s 2(1) of the Misrepresentation Act 1967 where the claim lies concurrently with a claim in negligence.
15 For example, Supply of Goods and Services Act 1982, s 13.
16 *Forsikringsaktieselskapet Vesta v Butcher* [1989] AC 852, [1988] 2 All ER 43, HL.
17 *Boothman v British Northrop Ltd* (1972) 13 KIR 112, CA.
18 *Capps v Miller* [1989] 2 All ER 333, [1989] 1 WLR 839, CA.
19 *Hannam v Mann* [1984] RTR 252.
20 [1953] AC 663 at 682, HL.
1   *Davies v Swan Motor Co (Swansea) Ltd* [1949] 2 KB 291 at 326.

shows care for his own safety.[2] Where there are two or more defendants, the extent of the plaintiff's contributory negligence must be assessed before addressing the respective responsibilities of the defendants.[3] So where a plaintiff walked across a pelican crossing when the lights were on green and was hit first by D1 and then by D2, the House of Lords ruled that the first stage of the apportionment exercise should be to determine the extent to which his own folly contributed to his injuries, so as to assess the totality of the damages due to him. Only after completion of this exercise should the respective contributions to those damages of the two tortfeasors be settled.

One common example of contributory negligence – failing to wear a seat belt – provides a useful illustration of how apportionment ought to work in practice. Lord Denning in *Froom v Butcher*[4] suggested norms of a 25% reduction if wearing the seat belt would have prevented the injury, and 15% where it would simply have reduced the severity of the injuries. In *Gregory v Kelly*,[5] however, where the plaintiff not wearing his seat belt knew that the car also had a faulty foot-brake, a reduction of 40% was made. Of course, if the plaintiff would have still suffered injuries of equal severity (albeit of a different type), even if he had worn his seatbelt, no reduction at all would be ordered.[6] In each case, the judge must exercise his discretion to determine just what share of responsibility for the accident the plaintiff should, in fairness, bear. But it is not an unlimited discretion. In *Pitts v Hunt*, Beldam LJ commented, obiter, that it was not possible for a court to order a 100% contribution from the plaintiff under the 1945 Act.[7] The terms in which the Act is framed presuppose at least *some* element of fault on the part of the defendant, and thus any notion of 100% contributory negligence, necessarily falls outwith the purview of the Act. To order a 100% reduction of damages (and thus negate D's liability) would be to make a nonsense of the Act talking in terms of shared responsibility.

SECTION 2.   VOLUNTARY ASSUMPTION OF RISK

(A)   IS ASSUMPTION OF RISK PROPERLY REGARDED AS A DEFENCE?

It has been explained previously that the consent of the plaintiff may take two forms, consent to the actual invasion of his interest – for example, where he invited someone to walk on to his land – or consent to the risk of a tort being committed. Only the latter is discussed here, for although it is not solely concerned with negligence, the risk assumed by the plaintiff is usually that of the defendant's negligent conduct. The Latin

2   The expression 'blameworthiness' used by Lord Reid suggests a moral term. It is submitted that the High Court of Australia in *Pennington v Norris* (1956) 96 CLR 10, rightly rejected this standard in favour of the standard of the 'unreasonable man'. Further, *Quintas v National Smelting Co Ltd* [1961] 1 All ER 630, [1961] 1 WLR 401, CA, could on one reading suggest that if the trial judge finds the defendant liable for breach of statutory duty, and the Court of Appeal reverses that finding, but holds the defendant liable for negligence, this is a ground for reducing the amount deducted from the plaintiff's damages for his contributory negligence.
3   *Fitzgerald v Lane* [1989] AC 328, [1988] 2 All ER 961, HL; reversing [1987] QB 781, [1987] 2 All ER 455, CA.
4   [1976] QB 286, [1975] 3 All ER 520, CA. See also *O'Connell v Jackson* [1972] 1 QB 270, [1971] 3 All ER 129, CA (motorcyclist; 15% reduction for not wearing a crash helmet); *Capps v Miller* [1989] 2 All ER 333, [1989] 1 WLR 839, CA (10% where the plaintiff was wearing his helmet but had not fastened it securely); consider *Owens v Brimmell* [1977] QB 859, [1976] 3 All ER 765 (where the passenger accepted a lift knowing the driver was drunk). See Symmons (1977) 40 MLR 350; Gravells (1977) 93 LQR 581.
5   [1978] RTR 426.
6   [1978] RTR 483.
7   [1990] 3 WLR 542 at 547, CA.

maxim volenti non fit injuria is commonly used to embrace both these aspects of consent. Assumption of risk has been summarised thus:[8]

> If the defendants desire to succeed on the ground that the maxim *volenti non fit injuria* is applicable, they must obtain a finding of fact that the plaintiff freely and voluntarily, with full knowledge of the nature and extent of the risk he ran, impliedly agreed to incur it.

Assumption of risk is looked at by the courts in two different ways. On one view it suggests that the defendant has not in the circumstances broken a duty of care. On the other, there is a breach of duty, but a plea of assumption of risk removes the effect of that negligence. Whichever of these two judicial approaches is taken, the consequences are likely to be the same, although a conceptual grasp of the application of the volenti principle is somewhat easier under the first.

Examples illustrate the two different judicial techniques. Suppose that X is walking along a busy highway when he is hit by a golf ball struck from a tee placed dangerously near to that highway. If X is an ordinary pedestrian, he may be able to sue the golf club in negligence, but if, on the other hand, he is a golfer who is crossing the highway in order to reach the next tee he would fail. One could say that the plaintiff fails if the defendant shows that the plaintiff assumed the risk of the defendant's negligence. On the other hand, the fact that the plaintiff is a golfer is merely one of the circumstances pertinent to the question of whether the defendant took reasonable care in respect of *this* plaintiff. Sometimes it will not emerge from the plaintiff's evidence that the plaintiff comprehended the risk, and then of course the defendant will himself have to prove that fact if he seeks thereby to rebut the plaintiff's claim. For example, a plaintiff who has been injured while riding in the defendant's car may make out a prima facie case without revealing that the defendant was, to the plaintiff's knowledge, drunk. If the defendant wishes to rely on that further factor, he must prove it. On one view he is merely adducing evidence of matters which are material in deciding whether, in all the circumstances of the case, there has been a breach of the duty to take care.[9] Alternatively, one could say that the plaintiff consented to the risk of negligent driving.

By contrast, a case such as *Murray v Harringay Arena Ltd* is more easily understood by treating it as one where there was no breach of duty.[10]

> A six-year-old boy was injured when the puck at an ice hockey match was hit out of the rink in the course of play and landed among the spectators. The Court of Appeal held that his claim in negligence failed.

It would be straining logic to say that the child concerned had in fact assumed the risk. Indeed, it may be regarded as a policy decision that organisers of sporting events owe no duty to any spectators to guard against certain dangers incidental to the ordinary conduct of the game.

8   *Letang v Ottawa Electric Rly Co* [1926] AC 725 at 731, PC (citing *Osborne v London and North Western Rly Co* (1888) 21 QBD 220).

9   *Insurance Comr v Joyce* (1948) 77 CLR 39 (H Ct Australia). *Nettleship v Weston* [1971] 2 QB 691, [1971] 3 All ER 581, CA shows both techniques in use: Salmon LJ applied this one to the question whether a learner driver was liable for injuring his car passenger whereas Lord Denning MR adopted the standard volenti approach. See also *Morris v Murray* [1990] 3 All ER 801 at 806–7, CA (per Fox LJ) and *Watt v Hertfordshire County Council* [1954] 2 All ER 368, CA. (P was a fireman injured because a jack on the back of the lorry on which he was travelling in the course of his duties slewed forward when the driver had to apply his brakes suddenly. Held that volenti non fit injuria was irrelevant; the issue was whether, in the circumstances, the employers were negligent in requiring the plaintiff to travel on the back of a lorry together with an unlashed heavy jack and found that there was no failure to take reasonable care.)

10   [1951] 2 KB 529, [1951] 2 All ER 320, CA.

Some judges clearly favour the 'no duty' approach. Thus Asquith J has said that:[11]

> As a matter of strict pleading it seems that the plea volenti is a denial of any duty at all, and, therefore, of any breach of duty, and an admission of negligence cannot strictly be combined with the plea.

The 1962 decision of the Court of Appeal in *Wooldridge v Sumner* is also important.[12] In that case, the facts were as follows.

> A non-paying spectator, a photographer, was injured by a horse competing at a jumping show. It was held that the rider was not liable in negligence even though he was guilty of an error of judgment.[13]

The court explained that volenti non fit injuria in English law 'presupposes a tortious act by the defendant'.[14] This does not mean, however, that there can never be actionable negligence within a sporting context. Where, as in *Smolden v Whitworth*,[15] for example, the referee neglects to officiate a rugby game so as to keep it within the rules (which are designed, in part, to ensure the players' safety), it is quite possible for an injured competitor to sue the referee for his negligence without being met by the defence of volenti.

In an employment context, however, the courts appear to favour the assumption of risk approach. In *ICI Ltd v Shatwell*,[16] the House of Lords eschewed the *Wooldridge* interpretation. Instead, their Lordships held that an injured shot-firer could not sue his employer for the conduct of a fellow shot-firer because he had, in the special circumstances of the case,[17] assumed the risk of his fellow shot-firer's negligence. We submit that the House of Lords found it more convenient to exempt the employer by finding a defence of consent to negligence than it might have done had it asked whether there was in the circumstances a breach of duty. That is why the survival of both approaches to the assumption of risk defence are to be expected. And this perhaps explains why, in *Morris v Murray*,[18] the Court of Appeal declined to enter into the niceties of which theoretical argument was correct preferring simply to judge the merits of the case before them.

(B)   ILLUSTRATIONS OF WHEN THE PLAINTIFF IS DEEMED TO HAVE ASSUMED THE RISK

(1)   SUITS BY EMPLOYEES AGAINST EMPLOYERS

The defendant is not liable whenever the plaintiff is deemed to have absolved him from liability for the consequences. The rule used to be especially important in actions by

11   *Dann v Hamilton* [1939] 1 KB 509 at 512, [1939] 1 All ER 59.
12   [1963] 2 QB 43, [1962] 2 All ER 978. *Baker v T E Hopkins & Son Ltd* [1959] 3 All ER 225 at 243, CA (per Willmer LJ) provides another sound exposition on the principle, when it said of a claim by an injured rescuer 'that, once it is determined that the act of the rescuer was the natural and probable consequence of the defendant's wrongdoing, there is no longer any room for the application of the maxim volenti non fit injuria'.
13   He would be liable if he failed to take the care expected of a reasonable competitor in a sporting event: *Wilks v Cheltenham Home Guard Motor Cycle and Light Car Club* [1971] 2 All ER 369, CA.
14   [1962] 2 All ER 978 at 990, CA (per Diplock LJ).
15   [1997] PIQR P133.
16   [1965] AC 656, [1964] 2 All ER 999, HL.
17   See post.
18   [1990] 3 All ER 801 at 806.

workmen alleging negligence by their employers. Nineteenth-century cases in which workmen sued employers for injuries sustained at work held, in effect, that if the employee knew of the danger, this would be enough, regardless of whether in reality the employee had any choice but to obey his 'boss'. The House of Lords (no doubt reflecting the changing social and economic attitudes) changed this approach by disapproving of the latest of these cases, *Thomas v Quartermaine*,[19] in *Smith v Baker & Sons* where the facts were as follows.[20]

> The plaintiff, an employee of the defendants who were railway contractors, was employed in drilling holes in a rock cutting, and was aware of the danger caused by a crane continually swinging crates of stones above his head. A stone fell out of a crate and injured him. He brought an action in negligence against the defendants, who pleaded volenti non fit injuria.

The House of Lords held that, notwithstanding the plaintiff's knowledge of the risk, the evidence justified a finding by the jury that he had not voluntarily undertaken it. Although the House of Lords accepted that 'a particular consent may be inferred from a general course of conduct',[1] it was held that knowledge alone is not enough: the jury must affirm 'that he consented to the particular thing being done which would involve the risk, and consented to take the risk upon himself'. Lord Watson said:[2]

> The question which has most frequently to be considered is not whether he voluntarily and rashly exposed himself to injury, but whether he agreed that, if injury should befall him, the risk was to be his and not his master's. [Whether continuing at work knowing of the danger is an assumption of the risk] depends ... upon the nature of the risk, and the workman's connection with it, as well as upon other considerations which must vary according to the circumstances of each case.

Since then, there has been a series of employer-employee cases in which this defence has been negatived on the ground of the employee's want of consent. *Bowater v Rowley Regis Corpn* is typical.[3]

> The plaintiff carter was ordered by the defendants, his employers, despite his protests, to take out a horse known by them to be unsafe. Eventually, he took out the horse, but was thrown off the cart when the horse bolted. He sued in negligence in respect of his injuries.

The Court of Appeal rejected the defence of volenti non fit injuria. Goddard LJ said:[4]

> ... it can hardly ever be applicable where the act to which the servant is said to be '*volens*' arises out of his ordinary duty, unless the work for which he is engaged is one in which danger is necessarily involved.

Yet where the plaintiff was susceptible, to her and her employer's knowledge, to dermatitis, and her employer found work for her which entailed a slight risk of the disease, the employer was held not liable for her then contracting it. He was not obliged either to dismiss her or to make the work safe for her with her particular susceptibility;

---

19   (1887) 18 QBD 685, CA.
20   [1891] AC 325, HL; cf *Yarmouth v France* (1887) 19 QBD 647, CA.
1   [1891] AC 325 at 338, HL (per Lord Halsbury LC).
2   [1891] AC 325 at 355, HL.
3   [1944] KB 476, [1944] 1 All ER 465, CA.
4   [1944] KB 476 at 480–1.

she took the risk and could not then complain.[5] In *ICI Ltd v Shatwell*,[6] the House of Lords expressly supported the general principle that assumption of risk will not ordinarily defeat a claim by an employee against his employer. At the same time, it recognised that where the claim rested on vicarious liability for joint and flagrant disobedience of a safety rule by the plaintiff and his wrongdoing fellow-servant, and where the latter was not the superior of the plaintiff (or one whose orders he was bound to obey), the employer would, exceptionally, be able to invoke the defence against the plaintiff employee.

(2)   DRUNKEN DRIVERS[7] /DRUNKEN PILOTS

In what other sorts of circumstances may a defence of volenti apply? Remember it is not enough simply to show that the plaintiff was well aware that he ran a risk of injury. In *Nettleship v Weston*[8] the friend teaching the plaintiff how to drive naturally knew that as a brand new learner she was more likely to cause an accident endangering him than an experienced driver. But he had expressly asked for reassurance that she was properly insured. He did not in effect take on himself full responsibility for whatever befell him. He neither undertook not to sue her nor to absolve her from any duty otherwise owed to him.

Where no pre-existing relationship exists between the parties volenti can rarely apply. In such cases, the defence will only be relevant only in strictly defined and fairly exceptional circumstances. Cases relating to drunken drivers and their passengers are instructive. We look first at *Dann v Hamilton*.[9]

> The plaintiff voluntarily accompanied the defendant as a passenger in a car driven by him, knowing that the defendant was under the influence of drink to such an extent that the chances of a collision from negligent driving were substantially increased. She was injured by his negligent driving and her action was held not to be barred by the defence of volenti non fit injuria.

Asquith J held that the maxim applied 'where a dangerous physical condition has been brought about by the negligence of the defendant, and, after it has arisen, the plaintiff, fully appreciating its dangerous character, elects to assume the risk thereof'.[10] Although he doubted whether the defence could lie where the consent of the plaintiff preceded the subsequent act of negligence complained of, the ratio decidendi of his judgment probably is no more than a finding of fact that:

> [T]he plaintiff, by embarking in the car ... with knowledge that through drink the driver had materially reduced his capacity for driving safely, did not impliedly consent to, or absolve the driver from, liability for any subsequent negligence on his part whereby she might suffer harm.[11]

---

5   *Withers v Perry Chain Co Ltd* [1961] 3 All ER 676, CA. (But might this decision be better explained in terms of no breach of duty in the circumstances?); cf *Paris v Stepney Borough Council* [1951] AC 367, [1951] 1 All ER 42, HL.

6   [1965] AC 656, [1964] 2 All ER 999, HL.

7   Cases of drunken drivers are useful to illustrate the underlying principles but must now be dealt with subject to the Road Traffic Act 1988. See post.

8   [1971] 2 QB 691, [1971] 3 All ER 581, CA.

9   [1939] 1 KB 509, [1939] 1 All ER 59.

10   [1939] 1 KB 509 at 517.

11   [1939] 1 KB 509 at 518; approved in *Slater v Clay Cross Co Ltd* [1956] 2 QB 264, [1956] 2 All ER 625, CA. But note the partial defence of contributory negligence may be available to the drunken driver: *Owens v Brimmell* [1977] QB 859, [1976] 3 All ER 765.

Indeed, in our submission, the preferable view is that volenti is crucially concerned with consent to *future* risks. This notion of the defence is supported by a considerable body of case law.[12] It has also received weighty academic support.[13] But are the two notions mutually exclusive? Only if they are is it necessary to select between one or other of the interpretations just outlined. According to Diplock LJ, they would indeed appear to be antithetical on the basis that volenti only applies where the plaintiff consents to future risks. He stated forthrightly that it would make a nonsense to say that the plaintiff 'agreed to run the risk that the defendant might be negligent ... [where] the plaintiff would only play his part after the defendant had already been negligent'.[14]

For several years in England, though not in other Commonwealth jurisdictions,[15] *Dann v Hamilton* was accepted as authority for the proposition that accepting a lift from an obviously inebriated driver would almost certainly constitute contributory negligence[16] but would not give rise to a successful plea of volenti. Indeed, it might almost be said that volenti went out of fashion. But half a century later, in *Pitts v Hunt*,[17] the material facts were as follows.

> The plaintiff was a pillion passenger on a motorcycle ridden by the defendant. He knew that the defendant was uninsured and had no licence. After four hours of drinking together in a disco, the plaintiff 'egged-on' the defendant in 'reckless, irresponsible and idiotic' riding of the motorcycle culminating in a disastrous accident. Section 148(3) of the Road Traffic Act 1972 (now section 149 of the Road Traffic Act 1988) prevented the defence of volenti from applying in road traffic cases, but apart from that provision the Court of Appeal judged that, notwithstanding *Dann v Hamilton*, a plea of volenti would have defeated the plaintiff's claim. (In the event they held that the plaintiff's grossly irresponsible conduct and participation in several road traffic offences gave rise to a successful defence of *ex turpi causa non oritur actio*.[18])

Then came *Morris v Murray*[19] in which the facts were these.

> The plaintiff and the deceased spent the afternoon drinking together. The latter, the plaintiff agreed, had consumed about 17 whiskies! The plaintiff then agreed to the deceased's proposal that he take him up for a flight in a light aircraft. At the aerodrome, the plaintiff helped to prepare the aeroplane. Soon after take-off, the plane crashed killing the pilot and severely injuring the plaintiff who brought an action against the deceased's estate.

The Court of Appeal upheld the plea of volenti: accepting a flight with an obviously drunken pilot was held to be akin to confronting deliberately some dangerous physical condition brought about by the defendant. Whether you said that the plaintiff could not have supposed that the defendant was capable of discharging any normal duty of care, or that the plaintiff, impliedly by his conduct, waived any duty towards him, the result was the same. A person voluntarily co-operating in a flight with an intoxicated

12 See, eg, *Wooldridge v Sumner* [1962] 2 All ER 978 at 990 (per Diplock LJ); *Baker v T E Hopkins & Son Ltd* [1959] 1 WLR 966 at 983 (per Willmer LJ) and *Morris v Murray* [1991] 2 QB 6 at 17, 28 and 32 (per Fox, Stocker and Waller LJJ respectively).
13 See, eg, Jaffey 'Volenti Non Fit Injuria' [1985] CLJ 87; Kidner 'The Variable Standard of Care, Contributory Negligence and *Volenti*' (1991) 11 Legal Studies 1 and Murphy 'Negligently Inflicted Psychiatric Harm – A Re-appraisal' (1995) 15 Legal Studies 415. Compare Jones *Textbook on Torts* pp 525–527.
14 *Wooldridge v Sumner* [1962] 2 All ER 978 at 990 (per Diplock LJ). See also *Nettleship v Weston* [1971] 3 All ER 581 at 587 (per Lord Denning MR) and *ICI v Shatwell* [1965] AC 656.
15 See in particular *Insurance Comr v Joyce* (1948) 77 CLR 39.
16 *Owens v Brimmell* [1977] QB 859, [1976] 3 All ER 765.
17 [1991] 1 QB 24, [1990] 3 All ER 344.
18 See ch 6 ante.
19 [1991] 2 QB 6, [1990] 3 All ER 801, CA.

pilot takes the risk upon himself. Flying is of a different order of danger to driving on the roads.

Morris v Murray raises two further, wider questions about volenti. The first is whether the test for volenti is an objective or subjective one. Earlier (slight) authority suggested an objective test,[20] but Stocker LJ[1] later cast doubt on this approach. On the facts of *Morris v Murray*, such an answer would require that a drunken plaintiff be excused from the consequences of his own actions. (No sober person would have done as the plaintiff did!) The question must be answered on the facts of the case: did the plaintiff appreciate the danger he faced and was he capable of accepting responsibility for what happened to him? The second question is one of policy. One might argue that to allow a defence of volenti in some circumstances, runs counter to the public interest because the defendant is allowed to escape the consequences of his own *gross irresponsibility*. Fox LJ answered the point in this way:[2]

> It seems to me ... that the wild irresponsibility of the venture is such that the law should not intervene to award damages and should leave the loss where it falls.

(3)   DANGEROUS ACTIVITIES

A final context in which volenti may be applicable concerns participation in dangerous activities, including sport. Before volenti can arise, of course, the defendant must show that the plaintiff consented not only to some risk of harm but also to that particular risk which culminated in injury to him. *Gillmore v LCC* illustrates this point.[3]

> The plaintiff was a member of a physical training class run by the defendants. During an exercise in which the members of the class were lunging at each other, he was injured through losing his balance on a floor which was slippery due to the negligence of the defendants.

Du Parcq LJ held[4] that the plaintiff had not consented to the risk incidental to doing physical training on a slippery floor (although, of course, he had consented to the physical contacts which might occur in the course of the lunging exercise) and therefore the defence of assumption of risk failed.[5]

(C)   VOLUNTARY ACT

Not only must the plaintiff consent to the risk, he must also assume the risk freely and voluntarily. The decision on claims by employees constitute, in effect, judicial recognition that economic pressures negative voluntary conduct in the sense indicated by Scott LJ in *Bowater v Rowley Regis Corpn*.[6] There, his Lordship opined that:

> For the purposes of the rule ... a man cannot be said to be truly 'willing' unless he is in a position to choose freely, and freedom of choice predicates, not only full knowledge of the

---

20   *Bennett v Tugwell* [1971] 2 QB 267, [1971] 2 All ER 248.
1   [1990] 3 All ER 801 at 817, CA.
2   [1990] 3 All ER 801 at 807, CA.
3   [1938] 4 All ER 331.
4   [1938] 4 All ER 331 at 336.
5   *Cleghorn v Oldham* (1927) 43 TLR 465 is also explicable on this ground. It involved a plaintiff who recovered damages against her golf companion who had injured her with a golf club on the course.
6   [1944] KB 476, [1944] 1 All ER 465.

circumstances on which the exercise of choice is conditioned, so that he may be able to choose wisely, but the absence from his mind of any feeling of constraint so that nothing shall interfere with the freedom of his will.[7]

Accordingly, the courts have, with one early exception,[8] consistently refused to allow the defence of volenti non fit injuria to lie against rescuers.[9] They are not genuine volunteers. Nor do they, in responding to the call for rescue (even if their job requires them to go to a citizen's aid[10]), take upon themselves the risk of injury and impliedly waive any duty owed to them.[11] An analogous case obtains with respect to suicides who are owed a protective duty by either hospital or prison authorities. The question that arises is whether such authorities may raise the defence of volenti non fit injuria when a patient/inmate attempts or commits suicide. At one level the self-harmer appears to act voluntarily. But where that person has been suffering from a degree of mental illness or impaired judgement, classifying the act thus is not quite so easy. To such problem cases the courts have reached a pragmatic solution. If the act takes place without there being any duty incumbent upon the defendant to prevent a suicide attempt, it would seem that the volenti may be raised; yet where, however, the defendant was under such a duty, recourse to the defence is not permitted.[12] It may be said, too, that if the defendant places the plaintiff on the horns of a dilemma, this deprives the plaintiff of his freedom of action with the result that his reaction is not truly voluntary.[13]

In rare instances, mere knowledge of a risk will bar the plaintiff, for example, if he is the gratuitous bailee of a defective chattel. The defendant can say to the plaintiff: 'Take it or leave it'. Conversely, reasons of policy – it will be obvious that one cannot speak of some constant, rigid defence of assumption of risk – sometimes dictate that a plaintiff will not fail even though he has freely encountered a known risk (for example, where the plaintiff has a right to face the risk, such as where he walks along a highway or exercises a right of access[14]).

This last class of case illuminates the relationship between assumption of risk and the defence of contributory negligence.[15] Although the defendant cannot maintain that the plaintiff has assumed the risk, he may show that, nonetheless, the plaintiff's conduct was so unreasonable in the light of the risk that it constituted contributory negligence. Because the effect of establishing the defence of contributory negligence used to be the same as that of setting up assumption of risk, the courts have sometimes,

---

7   Cf Hodson LJ in *Christmas v General Cleaning Contractors Ltd* [1952] 1 KB 141 at 151, [1952] 1 All ER 39, CA; affd sub nom, *General Cleaning Contractors Ltd v Christmas* [1953] AC 180, [1952] 2 All ER 1110, HL.
8   *Cutler v United Dairies (London) Ltd* [1933] 2 KB 297, [1933] All ER Rep 594, CA.
9   *Haynes v Harwood* [1935] 1 KB 146, [1934] All ER Rep 103, CA.
10 *Ogwo v Taylor* [1988] AC 431, [1987] 3 All ER 961, HL (fireman).
11 *D'Urso v Sanson* [1939] 4 All ER 26 (night-watchman extinguishing fire on employers' premises); cf *Merrington v Ironbridge Metal Works Ltd* [1952] 2 All ER 1101; *Baker v T E Hopkins & Son Ltd* [1959] 3 All ER 225, CA (doctor-rescuer); *Sylvester v Chapman Ltd* (1935) 79 Sol Jo 777: plaintiff mauled by leopard at an animal show of the defendants when he crossed the barrier to extinguish a cigarette smouldering in the straw between the barrier and the cage, 'was not rescuing anyone from imminent danger of death, nor even preventing damage to property, since there were people who could easily have done with precautions what he did' (per Lord Wright MR); therefore he had no cause of action against the defendants.
12 *Reeves v Metropolitan Police Comr* [1998] 2 All ER 381, CA.
13 See the cases on alternative danger discussed ante.
14 *Clayards v Dethick and Davis* (1848) 12 QB 439. In *Burnett v British Waterways* [1973] 2 All ER 631 a lighterman was injured in the defendant's dock having read a notice that he entered at his own risk. Held volenti did not apply because he had not agreed to be bound by its terms and had no choice in the matter.
15 See further Kidner 'The Variable Standard of Care, Contributory Negligence and *Volenti*' (1991) 11 Legal Studies 1.

in the past, not been careful to heed the distinctions between them. But, since the passing of the Law Reform (Contributory Negligence) Act 1945 the distinction has become more important. Now, if the defence of assumption of risk is made out, the plaintiff still recovers nothing,[16] whereas, as has been seen, a plaintiff guilty of contributory negligence alone has his damages reduced to the extent to which he was responsible for the damage.

Section 149 of the Road Traffic Act 1988 applies where vehicles are being used in circumstances where third party insurance is compulsory. It provides:

> ... if any other person is carried in or upon the vehicle while the user is so using it, any antecedent agreement or understanding between them (whether intended to be legally binding or not) shall be of no effect so far as it purports or might be held to negative or restrict any such liability of the user ... [to passengers] ... and the fact that a person so carried has willingly accepted as his the risk of negligence on the part of the user shall not be treated as negativing any such liability of the user.

This provision rules out the defence of volenti non fit injuria in any action brought by a passenger against the driver of a vehicle on a public road.[17]

The theoretical basis for the defence of volenti non fit injuria excites great academic interest and debate.[18] Current judicial attitudes are perhaps most clearly expressed by Lord Herschell in *Smith v Baker & Sons*. He said:

> The maxim is founded on good sense and justice. One who has invited or assented to an act being done towards him cannot, when he suffers from it, complain of it as a wrong.[19]

SECTION 3. EXCLUDING LIABILITY

The already limited application of the defence of volenti is further restricted by the operation of the Unfair Contract Terms Act 1977. That Act, unhappily for the student, misrepresents itself by its title. It is in fact as crucial to tort as it is to contract where there is a purported unilateral exclusion of liability by the defendant. To make matters worse, on occasion, the Act must be read in tandem with the Unfair Terms in Consumer Contracts Regulations 1994[20] which impose even greater restrictions on the ability to exclude liability than those discussed below where (i) the tortious duty co-exists beside a contractual obligation in a *consumer contract* and (ii) the terms of that contract have not been individually negotiated.[1]

The Act applies[2] to 'business liability' only. That term refers to liability arising from 'things done or to be done by a person in the course of a business' and the occupation of premises used for 'business purposes'. Section 2 prohibits altogether exclusion or limitation of liability for death or personal injury resulting from negligence.[3] Any contract

---

16 As in *Morris v Murray* [1991] 2 QB 6, [1990] 3 All ER 801, CA.
17 *Pitts v Hunt* [1990] 3 All ER 344 at 356–7, 359 and 366 (but note applicability of defence of ex turpi causa).
18 See Jaffey 'Volenti Non Fit Injuria' [1985] CLJ 87; Kidner 'The Variable Standard of Care, Contributory Negligence and *Volenti*' (1991) 11 Legal Studies 1 and Murphy 'Negligently Inflicted Psychiatric Harm – A Re-appraisal' (1995) 15 Legal Studies 415.
19 [1891] AC 325 at 360, HL. Cited with approval by Fox LJ in *Morris v Murray* [1990] 3 All ER 801 at 807, CA.
20 SI 1994 No 3159.
1 For a full discussion of the effect of these regulations see Beatson *Anson's Law of Contract* (1998) pp 196–198.
2 Section 1. On the Act generally see Palmer and Yates [1981] CLJ 108.
3 Section 2(1).

term or notice purporting so to do is invalid. In the case of loss other than death or personal injury, or death or personal injury resulting from a tort other than negligence, an exclusion or limitation of liability is invalid 'except in so far as the term of notice satisfies the requirement of reasonableness'.[4] Finally section 2(3) provides:

> Where a contract term or notice purports to exclude or restrict liability for negligence a person's agreement to or awareness of it is not of itself to be taken as indicating his voluntary acceptance of any risk.

Several questions must be asked about the operation of the 1977 Act. Business liability is nowhere comprehensively defined. Professions[5] and central and local government are expressly included within the term. But what of the work of a charity? Is the NSPCC a business? We submit that it probably is. The test does not appear to be whether the defendant is a profit-making commercial enterprise. The distinction is one between the domestic and the business sector of life. In view of section 2(3), can volenti ever now operate against a business? There is as yet no conclusive authority on the point. Clearly, knowledge of the unilateral exclusion of liability by notice will be insufficient, but so would it be at common law. An agreement per se will not be binding. In *Johnstone v Bloomsbury Area Health Authority*[6] a junior hospital doctor brought an action against his employers alleging damage to his health caused by the unreasonable hours he was required to work. Refusing to strike out the claim, the Court of Appeal took the view that a clause in his contract imposing those hours of work could only constitute volenti or an attempt to limit the employer's duty of care. If it was the latter, it might well fall foul of the 1977 Act. It remains to be seen whether there are residual circumstances – perhaps when the plaintiff took the initiative – where volenti might still operate.

The crux of the question in many cases where the operation of the 1977 Act is in issue will often be twofold. Has a breach of duty been proved and purportedly excluded? In the case of loss other than death or personal injury, was the exclusion of liability reasonable? The first question may be difficult to answer. Consider a lecturer asked by a student to advise him on a lease for a flat saying to the student 'This is only general advice ... I am not a practising solicitor ... I cannot accept liability for what I say'. Is the lecturer excluding liability, or limiting the duty owed to the student (if any), or simply indicating the standard of care to be expected from him?

What is now clear is that the effect of sections 11(3)[7] and 13(1)[8] of the Act ensure that where, 'but for' a purported disclaimer, a common law duty of care would have arisen, the Act operates to strike down or limit the extent of that disclaimer. In *Smith v Eric S Bush*,[9] surveyors were instructed by the building society to inspect and report on a house the plaintiff wished to buy. The surveyors expressly excluded any liability

---

4   Section 2(2). And for a definition of reasonableness see s 11.
5   See *Smith v Eric S Bush* [1990] 1 AC 831, [1989] 2 All ER 514, HL.
6   [1992] QB 333, [1991] 2 All ER 293, CA.
7   Section 11(3) provides: '... the requirement of reasonableness under the Act is that it should be fair and reasonable to allow reliance [on the disclaimer], having regard to all the circumstances obtaining when the liability arose or (but for this notice) would have arisen'.
8   Section 13(1) provides: 'To the extent that this Part of this Act prevents the exclusion or restriction of any liability it also prevents – (a) making liability or its enforcement subject to restrictive or onerous conditions; (b) excluding or restricting any right or remedy in respect of the liability, or in subjecting a person to any prejudice in consequence of his pursuing any such right or remedy; (c) excluding or restricting rules of evidence or procedure; and (to that extent) ss 2 and 5 to 7 also prevent excluding or restricting liability by reference to terms and notices which exclude or restrict the relevant obligation or duty'.
9   [1990] 1 AC 831, [1989] 2 All ER 514, HL.

to the plaintiff herself. The House of Lords found: (1) that the close relationship between the surveyor and the plaintiff was such that, in the absence of the purported disclaimer, a duty of care was owed to the plaintiff,[10] and, (2) that in the circumstances, the disclaimer was unreasonable. In the vast majority of cases, house purchasers did, as the surveyors well knew, rely on the report commissioned by the building society, a report for which they in fact paid. Lord Griffiths[11] suggested four factors by which to gauge reasonableness under the Act: (1) whether the parties were of equal bargaining power; (2) whether it was practicable to expect the plaintiff to obtain independent advice; (3) the complexity of the task which formed the subject of the disclaimer; (4) the practical consequences of striking down the disclaimer.[12]

The operation of the 1977 Act and the 1994 Regulations both in practice still require further elaboration and interpretation. What is crystal clear, however, is that there is no longer any foolproof exclusion notice or agreement.

---

10 At 839–841.
11 Had the 1977 Act been then in force, would the disclaimer in *Hedley Byrne & Co v Heller and Partners* [1964] AC 465, [1963] 2 All ER 575 have survived judicial scrutiny?
12 Would such action increase the cost/availability of the service?

Chapter 16

Liability for defective premises and structures

Liability for defective premises,[1] to those who suffer loss or damage on those premises,[2] may in general rest with two main types of defendant. First, the person actually occupying the premises may be held responsible for their condition; and here responsibility is generally for personal injuries such as a broken ankle sustained when a rotten floorboard gives way. Secondly, someone other than the occupier may be liable for defects in the premises. This latter category of potential defendants is broad in scope and includes landlords, builders and professionals such as architects and consulting engineers. While in some cases the relevant defect once again gives rise to personal injury – perhaps an employee's broken ankle is caused by a landlord's failure to repair the premises rented by his employer – in many non-occupier cases, what the plaintiff complains of is economic loss. This might be the case if you were to discover that the house which you bought from a development company is falling apart after the development company has gone into liquidation. If you wish to sue the original builder or the architect, you would be seeking to recover the financial loss occasioned by your property's diminished value and/or the cost of repair. In line with the general trend to limit liability for economic loss, we shall see that liability of non-occupiers for defective premises is now significantly restricted in scope.

SECTION I. OCCUPIERS' LIABILITY

Occupiers' liability is nowadays predominantly defined by statute, but there remains (at least according to the decided cases) a small, residual role for the common law in relation to certain negligently performed activities that take place on the defendant's premises.[3] For this reason, it is necessary to consider the liability of occupiers under three headings. We deal first with the rules embodied in the Occupiers' Liability Act 1957, which operates with respect to visitors to the defendant's premises. Secondly,

1 For the purposes of this chapter, the term 'premises' shall be used for convenience to connote not just any building owned by the defendant, but also any land owned by him, regardless of whether there are any buildings on it. A plaintiff's action is equally viable, under the statutory regimes to be discussed, in either case.
2 A plaintiff who was elsewhere than on the defendant's premises when he was injured must frame his action either in negligence, in nuisance (whether private or public) or under the rule in *Rylands v Fletcher* (as to which see the 9th edition of this work at pp 303–6).
3 See *Revill v Newbery* [1996] 1 All ER 291 at 298, CA (obiter); *Fowles v Bedfordshire County Council* [1995] PIQR P 386, CA..

we consider the Occupiers' Liability Act 1984, which governs liability to non-visitors. Finally, we consider the residual common law rules that apply both to visitors and non-visitors where they are injured by particular activities on the defendant's premises.

(A) LIABILITY TO VISITORS: THE OCCUPIERS' LIABILITY ACT 1957

(1) WHO IS AN OCCUPIER?

The first precondition of a defendant's liability under the Occupiers' Liability Act 1957 is that he be the occupier of the premises on which the plaintiff's loss occurs. The 1957 Act supplies no statutory definition of occupier but instead states that those who would be treated as occupiers at common law should be treated likewise for the purposes of the Act.[4] The leading definition of 'occupier' is that of the House of Lords in *Wheat v E Lacon & Co Ltd*.[5]

> The defendants owned a public house of which Mr R was their manager. Mr R and his wife were allowed by agreement to live in the upper floor, access to which was by a door separate from the licensed premises. Mrs R was allowed to take paying guests on the upper floor. An accident was sustained by a paying guest on the staircase leading to the upper floor. It was held that although the plaintiff was injured in the private area of the premises, the defendants (along with Mr and Mrs R) were still liable. They had retained enough residuary control over that part of the premises to be treated as occupiers.

The case thus decides that there may be two or more occupiers simultaneously; that exclusive occupation is not required; that the test is whether a person has some degree of control associated with, and arising from his presence in and use of, or his activity in the premises. A good example of the scope for multiple occupancy can be seen in the case of *AMF International Ltd v Magnet Bowling Ltd*[6] where a contractor, together with the owner, was held to be an occupier of the premises in which the plaintiff's equipment was damaged by rainwater that entered the building via a leaking doorway. Both the contractor and the owner of the premises were considered to have sufficient control over the whole building to be regarded as its joint occupiers.[7]

On the question of who may qualify as a sole occupier for the purposes of the Act, it is clear that the following earlier decisions remain sound. A concessionaire without

---

4   Occupiers' Liability Act 1957, s 1(2).
5   [1966] AC 552, [1966] 1 All ER 582, HL.
6   [1968] 2 All ER 789. See also *Fisher v CHT Ltd (No 2)* [1966] 2 QB 475, [1966] 1 All ER 88, CA (the owners of a club and the defendants who ran a restaurant in the club under licence from the club were both held to be occupiers). It is doubtful (but unsettled) whether someone who has granted a private right of way occupies that right of way: *Holden v White* [1982] QB 679, [1982] 2 All ER 328, CA; *McGeown v Northern Ireland Housing Executive* [1995] 1 AC 233, [1994] 3 All ER 53, HL (obiter). Further, a highway authority which has a statutory obligation to maintain a footpath which lies on land owned by another is not the occupier of that footpath: *Whiting v Hillingdon London Borough Council* (1970) 68 LGR 437. Nor is it the occupier of a highway which has not been adopted, even if the occupier owns the relevant land: *Holmes v Norfolk County Council* (1981) 131 NLJ 401. On the other hand, where the occupier has adopted the highway, there will be liability for both negligent misfeasance and nonfeasance under s 58 of the Highways Act 1980 (save where the loss is pure economic loss: *Wentworth v Wiltshire County Council* [1993] 2 All ER 256).
7   In such cases, the degree of care that the plaintiff may expect from each occupier is determined by the degree of control held by each: *Wheat v Lacon* (supra) at 581 and 595 (per Lord Denning) and 601 and 590 (per Lord Pearson).

a lease in a fairground is an occupier,[8] a local authority which has requisitioned a house[9] is an occupier (even in respect of those parts of the house in which it allows homeless persons to live),[10] and a contractor converting a ship into a troopship in dry dock occupies the ship.[11] On the other hand, a decorator who has undertaken to do no more than paint a house does not have sufficient control to be regarded as its occupier.[12]

(2)   SCOPE OF THE ACT

Prior to the enactment of the Occupiers' Liability Act 1957, the duty owed by an occupier to entrants upon his land varied according to their common law status.[13] The highest standard of care was owed to those, such as hotel guests, who were on his land by virtue of contract. Next, a lesser duty was owed to his invitees.[14] A still lower duty was owed to mere licensees (ie those permitted but not requested to be there), while in relation to trespassers the occupier's obligation was merely to refrain from deliberately or recklessly causing them injury.[15] A further complexity lay in the fact that the content of the duty varied according to the manner in which the plaintiff's injury was sustained: a distinction was drawn between injuries sustained by virtue of something done on the defendant's premises and those caused merely by the dangerous state of the premises.[16] The 1957 Act was enacted to give effect to the recommendations contained in the Law Reform Committee's Third Report[17] designed to eliminate the confusion that clouded the common law rules on liability to entrants on premises. The rules enacted by sections 2 and 3 of the Act 'have effect, in place of the rules of the common law, to regulate the duty which an occupier of premises owes to his visitors in respect of dangers due to the state of the premises or to things done or omitted to be done on them'.[18]

(a)   Visitors
The 1957 Act imposes a duty in respect only of 'visitors'.[19] And 'visitors', for the purposes of the Act, are those persons who were invitees or licensees at common law:[20] that is, anyone to whom an occupier gives any invitation or permission to enter or use his premises. Accordingly, in terms of the level of duty owed, the common law distinction between invitees and licensees is no longer of any real importance.[1] It does, however, remain important to distinguish between visitors on the one hand, and other entrants on the other, because the duties of an occupier to those other entrants are

---

8   *Humphreys v Dreamland (Margate) Ltd* [1930] All ER Rep 327, HL.
9   *Hawkins v Coulsdon and Purley UDC* [1954] 1 QB 319, [1954] 1 All ER 97, CA.
10 *Greene v Chelsea Borough Council* [1954] 2 QB 127, [1954] 2 All ER 318, CA; *Harris v Birkenhead Corpn* [1976] 1 All ER 341, CA (a local authority, having acquired a house by compulsory purchase, occupies it even before its staff enter it).
11 *Hartwell v Grayson Rollo and Clover Docks Ltd* [1947] KB 901, CA.
12 *Page v Read* (1984) 134 NLJ 723.
13 See *Clerk and Lindsell* (1995) paras 10.01–10.03.
14 That is, those who had a mutual business interest with the occupier, such as customers in a shop.
15 *Robert Addie & Sons (Collieries) Ltd v Dumbreck* [1929] AC 358, HL.
16 These were termed, respectively, the 'activity duty' and the 'occupancy duty'.
17 Cmd 9305.
18 Section 1.
19 In doing so, it envisages not only personal injury suffered by a visitor, but also any property damage he may suffer: s 1(3)(b).
20 Section 1(2). It is also provided that contractual entrants, in so far as they have not legitimately provided otherwise in their contract, shall also be afforded the common duty of care.
1   *Campbell v Northern Ireland Housing Executive* [1996] 1 BNIL 99. For an argument that it ought, in a limited set of circumstances, to have importance see Murphy 'Public Rights of Way and Private Law Wrongs' (1997) Conveyancer 362.

governed not by the 1957 Act but by the later 1984 Act.[2] This raises the interesting
question of whether, where there is more than one occupier, a person could be a visitor
in relation to Occupier A but a trespasser in relation to Occupier B? Lord Goff answered
this question in *Ferguson v Welsh*:

> If it be the case that one only of such occupiers authorises a third person to come onto the
> land, then plainly the third person is vis à vis that occupier, a lawful visitor. But he may not
> be a lawful visitor vis à vis the other occupier. Whether he is so or not must, in my opinion,
> depend on the question whether the occupier who authorised him to enter had authority,
> actual (express or implied) or ostensible authority, from the other occupier to allow the third
> party onto the land ... if he had not, then the third party will be, vis à vis that other occupier,
> a trespasser.[3]

Those entrants covered by the 1984 Act are often called trespassers, but the class is
not confined only to persons whose presence constitutes a trespass to premises. If
they are on the premises of the defendant without his permission, even though they
have not gone there voluntarily[4] – eg if they have been thrown there or chased there
– then they fall within this group, just as much as if they have committed the tort of
trespass. Similarly, although he is not a trespasser:

> ... a person entering any premises in exercise of rights conferred by virtue of an access agreement
> or order under the National Parks and Access to the Countryside Act 1949, is not, for the
> purposes of this [1957] Act, a visitor of the occupier of those premises.[5]

A more complex situation exists with respect to persons who sustain injury on a public
right of way. At one time it was thought that no-one using a public right of way could
be classified as a visitor for the purposes of the 1957 Act.[6] However, following the
House of Lords decision in *McGeown v Northern Ireland Housing Executive*,[7] the
matter appeared to be rather less straightforward.

> The plaintiff's husband was the tenant of a house on the defendants' housing estate. The
> house was accessed by a path over which the public had acquired a right of way. It was upon
> this path that the plaintiff tripped and sustained a broken leg. She argued that the defendants
> were liable to her as a visitor under the Occupiers' Liability Act (Northern Ireland) 1957.[8]
> The House of Lords held that she was not a visitor and therefore could not sue under the
> statute.

The complexity in this case stems from the fact that their Lordships confined their
decision to persons using a public right of way qua member of the general public (eg

2   *Stone v Taffe* [1974] 3 All ER 1016, CA is one of the few cases since the 1957 Act to turn on
     this distinction. (Pub manager in breach of contract allowed P and others to have a party after
     hours. P, who was unaware of that restriction in the contract, was held to be a visitor, not a
     trespasser, vis à vis the brewery employer.)
3   [1987] 3 All ER 777, 785, HL.
4   If the defendant's negligence causes a licensee involuntarily and unpremeditatedly to encroach
     slightly on land where he has no permission to go, he retains the rights of a licensee: *Braithwaite
     v Durham Steel Co Ltd* [1958] 3 All ER 161.
5   Occupiers' Liability Act 1957, s 1(4).
6   *Greenhalgh v British Railways Board* [1969] 2 QB 286 at 292–3, [1969] 2 All ER 114 at 117,
     CA (per Lord Denning MR). On the other hand, though no action will lie for nonfeasance
     according to *McGeown v Northern Ireland Housing Executive* [1995] 1 AC 233, [1994] 3 All
     ER 53, HL (cf *Thomas v British Railways Board* [1976] QB 912, [1976] 3 All ER 15, CA), an
     action can of course be brought in respect of any injury caused by the defendant's misfeasance
     (eg digging, and leaving uncovered, a hole in the right of way into which the plaintiff later falls).
7   [1995] 1 AC 233, [1994] 3 All ER 53, HL.
8   The same, in all material respects, as the English Act of that name and year.

a moorland hiker who neither knows nor is interested in who owns the *solum* of the right of way). As Lord Keith put it: 'Once a public right of way is established, there is no question of permission being granted by [sic] those who choose to use it'.[9] The notion of using a right of way by virtue of 'permission' is similar to that of using it qua licensee. But what, Lord Browne-Wilkinson wondered, of those who are expressly invited onto the land?

> In the case of an invitee there is no logical inconsistency between the plaintiff's right to be on the premises in exercise of the right of way and his actual presence there in response to the express or implied invitation of the occupier. It is the invitation which gives rise to the occupier's duty of care to an invitee.[10]

This obiter proposition has since been dismissed by the decision of the Court of Appeal in *Campbell v Northern Ireland Housing Executive*[11] in which case a plaintiff who was injured on a public right of way, on the way to the shops (ie as a licensee), was held to be outside the scope of the 1957 Act. Despite this rejection of Lord Browne-Wilkinson's distinction, it is submitted that there was much to be said for the impeccable logic underscoring his view, even though it would have meant giving new life, in the limited context of persons using public rights of way, to the significance of invitee/licensee dichotomy.[12]

Whether one accepts the thrust of Lord Browne-Wilkinson's proposition or not, the pre-Act cases which determined when an invitation of the occupier might be implied remain in full force. They remain relevant because those who were invitees under the old law are now to be treated as visitors rather than trespassers under the Act. In *Edwards v Railway Executive* the House of Lords held that permission should not be implied merely because the occupier knows of the plaintiff's presence or because he has failed to take the necessary steps to prevent his entry. Rather, '[t]here must be evidence either of express permission or that the land-owner has so conducted himself that he cannot be heard to say that he did not give it'.[13]

In each case, it is a question of fact whether permission to enter can be implied and the burden of proving the existence of such a permission rests with the plaintiff seeking to rely on it.[14] The rules are the same for children, but must be applied with a degree of common sense. In relation to children, for instance, permission might be implied on the basis of an 'allurement' that would present no temptation to an adult. In *Glasgow Corpn v Taylor*,[15] for example, shiny red berries growing in the open on the defendant's land were held to be an allurement to a child aged seven, to whom the berries looked like cherries or blackcurrants. On the other hand, the mere fact that the occupier has on his premises a dangerous object which is alluring to children does not make him liable to every child who comes onto his land, although the presence of the object in a place which is accessible to children may aid the inference of permission to enter.[16] But if the child can be shown to be a trespasser – perhaps because he was aware from a notice that the owner did not want him to be present there – then he shall be afforded only the

---

9   [1995] 1 AC 233 at 246, [1994] 3 All ER 53 at 62, HL. Presumably, his Lordship meant to say 'granted *to* those who choose to use it'.
10   [1995] 1 AC 233 at 248 and 64.
11   [1996] 1 BNIL 99.
12   For a fuller account of the arguments see Murphy 'Public Rights of Way and Private Law Wrongs' (1997) 61 Conveyancer 362.
13   [1952] AC 737 at 747, [1952] 2 All ER 430 at 437, HL (per Lord Goddard).
14   [1952] AC 737.
15   [1922] 1 AC 44, HL.
16   *Hardy v Central London Rly Co* [1920] 3 KB 459, CA; *Latham v R Johnson and Nephew Ltd* [1913] 1 KB 398, CA.

level of protection afforded to trespassers under the 1984 Act. Moreover, in some circumstances occupiers are deemed only to permit young children onto their land subject to the condition that they are accompanied by a responsible adult.[17]

Of course, in cases concerning adults, an implied permission will seldom if ever depend upon the existence of an allurement. Instead, permission will have to be implied on the basis of rather different facts. But, as Lord Porter pointed out in the *Edwards* case:

> ... an open pathway, as in *Cooke v Midland Great Western Rly of Ireland*,[18] or a knowledge that a track is and has long been constantly used, coupled with a failure to take any steps to indicate that ingress is not permitted, as in *Lowery v Walker*,[19] may well amount to a tacit licence.[20]

Persons entering as of right, such as police with search warrants and the host of officials empowered by statute to enter premises, are specifically deemed by the 1957 Act to be present with the occupier's permission.[1]

(b) Against what risks does the Act afford protection?

The Act plainly regulates the duty of the occupier in relation to structural defects or other dangers due to the state of the premises themselves, or indeed 'things' on the premises such as vicious dogs roaming free in the garden.[2] That this is not the limit of its scope is made clear by the fact that in addition to dangers arising from the state of the premises the Act refers also to dangers due to 'things done or omitted to be done on them'. At the very least, then, the Act covers acts or omissions which have created a dangerous condition of a continuing nature which later causes harm.

A more difficult question is whether the Act also extends to acts (whether of the occupier or others) which cause harm to the visitor. Section 1(2) provides that the Act 'shall regulate the nature of the duty imposed by law in consequence of a person's occupation or control of premises'. At common law an occupier had a duty not to permit others to use his premises in such a way that would foreseeably harm other persons on those premises.[3] Regardless of whether such cases previously fell within that sub-head

17 *Latham v R Johnson and Nephew Ltd* [1913] 1 KB 398, CA; *Bates v Stone Parish Council* [1954] 3 All ER 38, CA (no circumstances to qualify the permissions given by the defendants to infant children to enter their playground; three-year-old child held to be a licensee). In *Phipps v Rochester Corpn* [1955] 1 QB 450, [1955] 1 All ER 129, Devlin J criticised this rule on the ground that it was lacking in precision: eg, what degree of incapacity on the part of the child and what qualifications on the part of his companion are called for? Nevertheless, the rule stands on the authority of the Court of Appeal.

18 [1909] AC 229, HL (defendant railway company kept an unlocked turntable close to a public road; children were in the habit of playing with it, having gained access through a well-worn gap in a fence of the defendants – held that the defendants were liable to such a child, a licensee, for injuries sustained while playing on the turntable).

19 [1911] AC 10, HL.

20 Supra, per Lord Porter at 744. See also *Robert Addie & Sons (Collieries) Ltd v Dumbreck* [1929] AC 358 at 372–3, HL (per Viscount Dunedin); cf *Gough v National Coal Board* [1954] 1 QB 191, [1953] 2 All ER 1283, CA.

1 Section 2(6). Police officers pursuing inquiries without a warrant may take advantage of the generally implied licence to approach a front door via the garden path: *Robson v Hallett* [1967] 2 QB 939, [1967] 2 All ER 407. But like other visitors they will cease to have visitor status if they fail to leave immediately the licence is expressly withdrawn: *Snook v Mannion* [1982] RTR 321.

2 *Hill v Lovett (OH)* 1992 SLT 994. At common law, if the danger confronted the visitor while on the premises, although he actually suffered the harm off the premises – eg, falling off an unfenced cliff into the sea – the rules regulating the duties of occupiers towards visitors applied: *Perkowski v Wellington Corpn* [1959] AC 53, [1958] 3 All ER 368, PC. The wording of s 1(1) of the Act is also wide enough to cover this situation.

3 *Glasgow Corpn v Muir* [1943] AC 448, [1943] 2 All ER 44, HL.

of the law of negligence creating special duties of occupiers to invitees or licensees, it is submitted that the joint effect of subsections (1) and (2) is to bring those situations within the Act – the duty of care arises in consequence of the fact that the defendant is an occupier.[4] On the other hand, activities not directly associated with occupation – such as firing arrows – which at the time of their commission caused harm to the visitors, were governed by ordinary principles of negligence, and not by the special rules relating to occupiers.[5] It has been stated (obiter) that the Act does not apply to such activities (regardless of whether the act in question was the occupier's, a contractor's or a visitor's), for the duty of care is imposed on the actor because he is himself performing an act foreseeably likely to cause harm to others present on the premises, and not because the actor occupies the land.[6]

Before the 1957 Act, some cases had held that a plaintiff might sometimes have the choice of suing either in ordinary negligence or by virtue of the special duty owed by occupiers.[7] Since the Act only displaces the common law rules imposed in consequence of occupation, it follows that if some other duty is imposed by common law or an alternative statute (for some reason independent of occupation of the premises) the plaintiff may rely on either the 1957 Act *or* the other cause of action (or both). For example, a workman injured on his employer's premises may rely either on the common duty of care laid down in the Act or on the duty of the employer to provide a safe system of work or on some statutory duty of the employer to provide safe access or the like.[8]

(3) The common duty of care

(a) General principles

The common duty of care is a duty to take such care as in all the circumstances of the case is reasonable to see that the visitor will be reasonably safe in using the premises for the purposes for which he is invited or permitted by the occupier to be there.[9]

If the entrant does not use the premises for that purpose which entitles him to be there, no duty is owed to him under the 1957 Act and any remedy which he might have would be afforded by the 1984 Act. Scrutton LJ neatly encapsulated the principle when he said: 'When you invite a person into your house to use the stairs, you do not invite

---

4 All three judges in *Videan v British Transport Commission* [1963] 2 QB 650, [1963] 2 All ER 860, CA were of this same opinion (obiter).
5 See *Ferguson v Welsh* [1987] 3 All ER 777, [1987] 1 WLR 1553, HL.
6 *Revill v Newbery* [1996] 1 All ER 291, CA. The rationale here is that the restrictive wording of s 1(2) – 'The rules so enacted shall regulate the nature of the duty imposed by law *in consequence of a person's occupation or control* of premises' – excludes this class of acts. Thus, when premises were set alight by their occupier, this was clearly a negligent act performed otherwise than *in consequence of occupation or control*. It is unsurprising that damages in such a case should be awarded on the basis of the general law of negligence rather than the 1957 Act: *Ogwo v Taylor* [1988] AC 431, [1987] 3 All ER 961, HL.
7 Eg *Slade v Battersea and Putney Group Hospital Management Committee* [1955] 1 All ER 429 where a relative visiting a sick patient in the state hospital was injured because polish had recently been spread on the floor, and she had not been warned of it, she was able to sue in ordinary negligence. Also, in *Thompson v Bankstown Municipal Council* (1953) 87 CLR 619 (H Ct Australia) a boy was electrocuted as a result of the negligent maintenance by the defendants of their overhead electric wires. It was held that although he was a trespasser, he could nonetheless invoke the separate duty in negligence of a statutory undertaker supplying electric power to take care in the maintenance of that equipment.
8 Eg *Ward v Hertfordshire County Council* [1970] 1 All ER 535, CA (duties of local authority both as education authority and occupier considered when child hurt by playground flint wall, though defendants held not liable under either head because the wall was not dangerous).
9 Occupiers' Liability Act 1957, s 2(2).

him to slide down the bannisters'.[10] To the extent that the visitor to premises exceeds the permission he has been granted to be there, he is to be treated, in relation to any injury he then suffers, as a trespasser.

Those entering as of right are not 'invited or permitted' by the occupier for any purpose. Section 2(6) of the Act nonetheless extends the common duty of care to them by providing that 'persons who enter premises for any purpose in the exercise of a right conferred by law are to be treated as permitted by the occupier to be there for that purpose, whether they in fact have his permission or not'. Section 2(6) does not extend the category of visitors beyond the common law definition. It merely extends the circumstances when an entrant will be owed the common duty of care by providing that those who enter for any purpose in the exercise of a right conferred by law are to be treated as permitted by the occupier to be there for that purpose.[11]

Whether the standard required by the common duty of care has been attained is a question of fact; and the matters to which the court will pay regard will vary from case to case.[12] One important point, however, is that the defendant's failure to discharge the common duty of care need not amount to negligent misfeasance. Thus, a football club that can anticipate crowd trouble from visiting supporters, yet fails to make the game all-ticket or ban those visiting supporters, may still be liable in respect of injuries sustained by a policeman when they use loose pieces of concrete as projectiles.[13] Equally, liability will not depend on the failure to take preventive measures otherwise amounting to actionable nonfeasance at common law.[14] If, on the other hand, injury to the plaintiff is of a kind that is too unforeseeable, no liability will attach for failure to take precautions. This is because, as was held in *Jolley v Sutton London Borough Council*,[15] the same test for the remoteness of damage that applies in negligence applies also under the Act.[16] In determining what is foreseeable, section 2(3) offers a measure of assistance. There, the Act states:

> The circumstances relevant for the present purpose include the degree of care, and of want of care, which would ordinarily be looked for in such a visitor, so that (for example) in proper cases -
> (a) an occupier must be prepared for children to be less careful than adults; and
> (b) an occupier may expect that a person, in the exercise of his calling, will appreciate and guard against any special risks ordinarily incident to it, so far as the occupier leaves him free to do so.

---

10 *The Carlgarth* [1927] P 93 at 110.
11 *Greenhalgh v British Railways Board* [1969] 2 QB 286, [1969] 2 All ER 114, CA, see especially per Lord Denning MR at 292–3.
12 Although its recommendations do not have the force of law, where minimum safety standards have been recommended by the British Standards Institution, they will amount to strong evidence on the question of whether an occupier has taken sufficient precautions: *Ward v Ritz Hotel (London)* [1992] PIQR P 315, CA.
13 *Cunningham v Reading Football Club* [1992] PIQR 141.
14 Sed quaere? It is difficult to see why the failure of the football club to take preventive steps would *not* be actionable as common law negligence. The events had been pre-echoed at earlier games (making the injury to the policeman foreseeable) and the contractual nexus between the parties would presumably satisfy the proximity requirement.
15 [1998] 3 All ER 559, [1998] 1 WLR 1546, CA.
16 The decision on the facts (but not the ratio) in this case is highly questionable. A boy had jacked up an old and rotten boat on D's land with a view to repairing it. It later collapsed on him. The Court of Appeal categorised the harm – injury caused by a an 'alluring', dangerous old boat – as too remote on the basis that the injury was caused in an unforeseeable fashion. This reasoning is difficult to square the *Wagon Mound* principle that it is the *type* of harm (not the manner in which it is occasioned) which determines remoteness.

These two examples restate existing rules of common law, and therefore support the view that in deciding the countless issues of fact which will arise in applying the 'common duty of care' it will be proper to consider cases decided before the Act as guides (but no more than that) in interpreting the duty where no unambiguous rule is laid down in the Act itself.

The following common law principles remain important. In deciding whether there is a danger, regard must be had to the physical and mental powers of a child visitor;[17] in short, what is not a danger to an adult may be a danger to a child. And this may be so because of the allurement to a child of some condition on the land.[18] In determining the standard of care owed to a child who is not accompanied by a guardian, it will be material to inquire whether, in the circumstances, the occupier could reasonably have expected the presence of the unaccompanied infant.[19] If the unaccompanied child cannot be expected by the occupier, he will inevitably be a trespasser. But since the passage of the 1984 Act, it is of much less significance that he cannot sue for his injuries qua visitor.[20]

The significance of section 2(3)(b), which deals with the care to be shown to visitors possessed of a particular profession, may be illustrated by decisions at common law concerning window cleaners. A window cleaner injured through the insecurity of some part of the exterior of the premises which he uses as a foothold or handhold for the purpose of cleaning the outside of the windows is expected by the occupier to have guarded against this special risk which is ordinarily incident to the calling of a window cleaner.[1] But there is no reason why the occupier should not be liable if the window cleaner is injured through some defect in the staircase which leads to his injury when he is going upstairs, in the ordinary way, to reach the windows on an upper floor.[2] Similarly, an occupier is entitled to expect that a chimney sweep will guard against dangers from flues.[3] But a self-employed plasterer injured when scaffolding collapsed beneath him recovered damages from the occupier since the risk was inherent in the defective state of the premises and not an expected risk of his employment as a plasterer.[4] In short, though special skills of the entrant are *relevant* to the determination

---

17 *Cooke v Midland Great Western Rly of Ireland* [1909] AC 229 at 238, HL per Lord Atkinson; cf *Gough v National Coal Board* [1954] 1 QB 191, [1953] 2 All ER 1283, CA. The cases are legion but they all turn on their particular facts eg *Williams v Cardiff Corpn* [1950] 1 KB 514 [1950] 1 All ER 250, CA (a grassy slope with broken glass at the foot is a trap for a four-year-old child). The principle stated in the text also applied at common law in the case of adults suffering from mental or physical handicap, and, it is submitted, will continue to apply to them under the Act.

18 Eg *Glasgow Corpn v Taylor* [1922] 1 AC 44, HL (brightly coloured poisoned berries in a park and within easy reach of the child). But contrast with *D (a minor) v Department of Environment (NI)* [1992] 4 BNIL 117 (no liability when a six-year-old climbed a tree and fell out!).

19 See *Phipps v Rochester Corpn* [1955] 1 QB 450, [1955] 1 All ER 129, containing a thoroughgoing review by Devlin J of the rights of child visitors. Applied in *Simkiss v Rhondda Borough Council* (1982) 81 LGR 460, CA.

20 The 1984 Act replaced the harsh rules of common law that had traditionally been applied to trespassers. The difference in the child's protection is therefore the limited discrepancy in the duties imposed by the 1957 and 1984 Acts.

1   *Christmas v General Cleaning Contractors Ltd* [1952] 1 KB 141, [1952] 1 All ER 39, CA, affirmed on other grounds, [1953] AC 180, [1952] 2 All ER 1110, HL. Similarly, a deliveryman injured when making deliveries cannot sue for the inherent dangers in handling heavy goods; he may reasonably be expected by the occupier to use his expertise in making those deliveries: *Phillips v Perry* (1997) unreported, CA.

2   See *Bates v Parker* [1953] 2 QB 231, [1953] 1 All ER 768, CA.

3   *Roles v Nathan* [1963] 2 All ER 908, CA. A factory occupier owes a lesser standard of care to a fireman trying to put out a fire than to his employees and has no duty to provide alternative escape facilities: *Bermingham v Sher Bros* 1980 SLT 122, HL.

4   *Kealey v Heard* [1983] 1 All ER 973, [1983] 1 WLR 573.

of whether the occupier is in breach of the common duty of care, they will not automatically absolve him from responsibility (especially where the risk is not one ordinarily encountered by a person possessed of the particular entrant's skills).

(b)   Warning

At common law an occupier discharged his duty to a visitor by a warning sufficient to convey to the visitor full knowledge of the nature and extent of the danger. That rule was changed by section 2(4)(a) of the Act which now provides that:

> ... where damage is caused to a visitor by a danger[5] of which he had been warned by the occupier, the warning is not to be treated without more as absolving the occupier from liability, unless in all the circumstances it was enough to enable the visitor to be reasonably safe.

So, for example, the farmer who warns the veterinary surgeon whom he has summoned to the farm at night to attend a sick cow, 'Be careful how you go down the yard or you may fall into a tank', or the railway company which warns of the dangerous roof over what is the sole approach to the ticket office, no longer absolve themselves from liability by that warning alone. In *Roles v Nathan*[6] Lord Denning provided a further example of where the mere fact of providing a warning would not discharge the duty of care owed under the Act. He opined that merely warning visitors of the danger of a footbridge over a stream would be insufficient to ensure a visitor's safety if there was only one footbridge and it was essential to use that bridge to enter the defendant's land. But he added that if there were two bridges and one of them was safe, a warning about the unsafe bridge would then exclude liability.[7]

Where, on the other hand, a warning is given, but the visitor declines to heed it – eg where a customer fails to observe the warning of a shopkeeper not to go to the far end of the shop because there is a dangerous hole – a court would probably hold that, in all the circumstances, the common duty of care had been discharged. If the defendant does not know of the danger it is obvious that he cannot rely on section 2(4)(a), although he may still have a defence under section 2(1).[8]

(c)   Assumption of risk

The common duty of care does not impose on an occupier any obligation to a visitor in respect of risks willingly accepted as his by the visitor (the question whether a risk is so accepted to be decided on the same principles as in other cases in which one person owes a duty of care to another).[9]

It has already been seen that according to the ordinary principles of negligence a defendant has broken no duty of care towards a plaintiff who has voluntarily assumed the risk. Section 2(5) of the 1957 Act makes it clear that this principle also applies to the common law duty of care.

At common law no duty of care was owed to a visitor who had full knowledge of the nature and extent of the danger.[10] Case law confirms that a similar approach is to be taken with respect to the common duty of care owed under the Act, although at one time it was thought that the visitor's knowledge of the danger was merely a relevant factor in deciding whether, in all the circumstances, it was enough to enable him to be

---

5   Does 'danger' mean the peril or the thing which creates the peril, or both?
6   [1963] 2 All ER 908, [1963] 1 WLR 1117, CA.
7   [1963] 2 All ER 908 at 913.
8   *White v Blackmore* [1972] 2 QB 651, [1972] 3 All ER 158, CA.
9   Occupiers' Liability Act 1957, s 2(5). But where the occupier occupies the premises for business purposes note the application of s 2(3) of the Unfair Contract Terms Act 1977.
10   *London Graving Dock Co Ltd v Horton* [1951] AC 737, [1951] 2 All ER 1, HL.

reasonably safe.[11] In recent years the courts have had occasion to revisit the issue and have taken the view that knowledge of self-evident dangers relieves the occupier of his duty under section 2(2). In *Cotton v Derbyshire Dales District Council*,[12] for example, the Court of Appeal held that the owner of a path which lay adjacent to cliffs and presented an obvious danger was under no duty to visitors who were injured by falling from those cliffs. Similarly, in *Staples v West Dorset District Council*,[13] damages were refused where the plaintiff slipped and was injured on the defendant council's algae-covered rocks. To begin with, he had full knowledge of the danger; secondly, it was proven that even if there had been a warning, he would have ignored it in any case.

(d) Contributory negligence

Section 2(3) of the 1957 Act states that in deciding whether the occupier has discharged his common duty of care, the want of care which would ordinarily be looked for in such a visitor is a relevant circumstance. In other words, the plaintiff cannot by his own carelessness enlarge the duty of care owed to him by the defendant. It is therefore implicit in section 2(3) that the apportionment provisions of the Law Reform (Contributory Negligence) Act 1945 apply to an action for breach of the common duty of care exactly as they do to any action for negligence simpliciter. And indeed a number of cases under the 1957 Act have applied these apportionment provisions.[14]

(e) Liability for independent contractors

Section 2(4)(b) of the Act provides that where damage is caused to a visitor by a danger due to the faulty execution of any work of construction, maintenance or repair[15] by an independent contractor employed by the occupier, the occupier is not to be treated without more[16] as answerable for the danger if in all the circumstances he had acted reasonably in entrusting the work to an independent contractor and had taken such steps (if any) as he reasonably ought in order to satisfy himself that the contractor was competent and that the work had been properly done. To a large extent, this provision replicates the common law position whereby there is not normally any vicarious liability for torts committed by independent contractors. However, the provision warrants further analysis.

First, in applying this subsection, the courts must consider whether, initially, it was reasonable for the occupier to engage an independent contractor to undertake the construction, maintenance or repair work. It is by no means obvious what this entails for it is difficult to envisage a situation in which the court would expect the occupier to have performed construction work himself in preference to an independent contractor. No doubt, then, it will be presumptively reasonable for an occupier to engage a

---

11 *Bunker v Charles Brand & Son Ltd* [1969] 2 QB 480, [1969] 2 All ER 59.
12 (1994) Times, 20 June, CA.
13 (1995) 93 LGR 536, CA.
14 Eg *Bunker v Charles Brand & Son Ltd* [1969] 2 QB 480, [1969] 2 All ER 59; and see *McMillan v Lord Advocate* 1991 SLT 150n.
15 This expression covers work incidental to construction: *AMF International Ltd v Magnet Bowling Ltd* [1968] 2 All ER 789. It also extends, curiously, to demolition work: *Ferguson v Welsh* [1987] 3 All ER 777 at 783, [1987] 1 WLR 1553, HL.
16 In *Coupland v Eagle Bros Ltd* (1969) 210 Estates Gazette 581, the plaintiff was electrocuted by a live wire which the electrical contractor had not switched off while carrying out electrical work. The occupier knew that the wire was dangerous and had not warned anyone; the 'without more' provision did not absolve him from liability, for he was concurrently careless with the contractor. Even though the cause of harm falls outside these words – eg, the stowing of cargo by a stevedore – the defendant occupier may still discharge his common duty of care by relying on the stevedore as his independent contractor: *Mullis v United States Lines Co* [1969] 1 Lloyd's Rep 109. This is because s 2(4)(b) is only an 'example' of the common duty of care.

contractor wherever, as in *Haseldine v C A Daw & Son Ltd*,[17] the work to be done necessitates special skill or equipment not possessed by the occupier. Delegation should also be reasonable where it is the normal commercial practice to employ contractors, for example for office cleaning.

Secondly, the Act stipulates that the occupier *may* have to check the competence of the employee. Here, it would seem that, if the work is of a fairly routine nature the contractor may be trusted.[18] Where, however, the work entrusted to a contractor is of a kind that, after its completion, necessarily involves a risk to future visitors if it has been carelessly executed,[19] the occupier *will* be under a duty to check the competence of the contractor. Thirdly, the occupier may need 'to take such steps as he reasonably ought in order to satisfy himself that the work had been competently done'. It is unclear from the statute whether this involves a subjective test or an objective one. If the former were adopted, it would mean that limited financial resources might provide a sufficient reason for not having engaged, say, an architect to assess the quality of the work. If an objective test were employed, the only relevant factor would be the degree of risk inherent in the kind of work done.

Since the Act uses the past tense in relation to work done it is clear that section 2(4)(b) does not envisage the occupier employing a suitable professional to supervise the ongoing work of an independent contractor. However, section 2(4)(b) simply provides an example of how the common duty of care might be discharged. Thus, in some circumstances it may be expected of the occupier that he will have the contractor's work supervised. In *AMF International Ltd v Magnet Bowling Ltd*,[20] for example, it was said that if the occupier was going to invite a third party, the plaintiff, to bring valuable timber on to the site during construction, then to escape liability he may have to employ a supervising architect to ensure that the contractors had made the premises sufficiently safe for that timber safely to be brought there. On the other hand, it was said in *Ferguson v Welsh*[1] that an occupier will not normally be liable to the contractor's employee for injuries sustained because the premises were unsafe by virtue of the dangerous system of work adopted by the independent contractors. But Lord Keith also stated that, in circumstances in which the occupier knows or has reason to know that the contractor is using an unsafe system of work, he might be liable for not ensuring that a safe system was employed.[2]

(4)   SOME SPECIAL CASES WITHIN THE ACT

(a)   Fixed or movable structures
Section 1(3) provides that:

> The rules so enacted in relation to an occupier of premises and his visitors shall also apply, in like manner and to the like extent as the principles applicable at common law to an occupier of premises and his invitees or licensees would apply, to regulate –

17   [1941] 2 KB 343, [1941] 3 All ER 156, CA.
18   In *Cook v Broderip* (1968) 206 Estates Gazette 128, the occupier of a flat was not liable to his domestic help who was injured because a contractor had negligently put a new switch fuse in the flat; he was entitled to trust the contractor.
19   Eg the repair of a lift which, if carelessly done, clearly poses a risk to subsequent visitors. In one such case, it was central to the court's decision that the occupier was under a duty 'to obtain and follow good technical advice': *Haseldine v Daw & Son Ltd* [1941] 2 KB 343, 356, [1941] 3 All ER 156, 168.
20   [1968] 2 All ER 789, [1968] 1 WLR 1028.
1   [1987] 3 All ER 777 at 783, HL.
2   Ibid. Note however, that any such liability would not arise qua occupier but rather qua joint tortfeasor with the contractor: see ibid per Lord Goff at 786.

(a) the obligations of a person occupying or having control[3] over any fixed or movable structure, including any vessel, vehicle or aircraft'.

The expression 'movable structures' will cover such appliances as gangways and ladders, as well as vessels, vehicles and aircraft. The criterion is probably whether one might go into or upon the 'structure'. It is, however, much more difficult to interpret the expression 'fixed structure', for 'fixed structure' (mentioned in section 1(3)) and 'premises' (mentioned in section 1(1)) must be mutually exclusive terms for the purposes of the Act. It is clear that the term 'premises' is confined simply to land: it also includes permanent buildings erected on the land. Accordingly, 'fixed structures' must be taken to connote some non-movable chattels constructed on land. No doubt the draftsmen doubted whether docks or erections on part of the land such as garden sheds, or swings in a playground, or even scaffolding or lifts were 'premises' and yet thought that movable structures might not cover them. Beyond doubt, all of these are within the Act, but it is important whether a structure falls within section 1(1) or section 1(3) because different duties of care may be owed under these respective subsections. If A provides a defective ladder for his independent contractor to repair A's premises, the Act does not apply for the benefit of the injured contractor, for A has ceased to have enough control of the ladder to be an occupier of it.[4] By contrast, A may still be liable either as the bailor of goods or as an occupier of premises who intends that the plaintiff should use A's appliances on his land.[5]

(b) Damage to property[6]
In the same way as it has been seen to extend to fixed or movable structures, section 1(3) discussed in the preceding section, also covers:

(b) the obligations of a person occupying or having control over any premises or structure in respect of damage to property, including the property of persons who are not themselves his visitors.

This subsection will impose a duty on the occupier to prevent damage to goods on the premises arising from the defective physical condition of the premises. The injured visitor would, for example, be able to recover damages for her torn clothes and presumably for damage to her property, even if she is herself uninjured.[7] Where the entrant is carrying the goods of a third party, it is doubtful whether the Act gives the third party an action.[8] Furthermore, the expression 'damage to property' is not apt to cover loss of property so that the section will not cover the duty of boarding-house keepers to keep safe custody of visitors' goods. Still less will it reverse the common law decision that a publican owes no duty of care to prevent a customer's motorcycle

---

3 Not that an engineering firm did not abandon control of a machine roller when they called in a specialist contractor to modify it, and so they retained the obligations of occupiers within s 1(3)(a): *Bunker v Charles Brand & Son Ltd* [1969] 2 QB 480, [1969] 2 All ER 59.
4 *Wheeler v Copas* [1981] 3 All ER 405.
5 *Wheeler v Copas* [1981] 3 All ER 405.
6 See North 'Damage to Property and the Occupiers' Liability Act 1957' (1966) 30 Conveyancer 264.
7 *AMF International Ltd v Magnet Bowling Ltd* [1968] 2 All ER 789. It would also seem that loss consequential on the damage to property is also recoverable, so that a car-hire firm could recover loss of earnings when their car was damaged after having been driven onto the defendant's land by the *owner* of the car.
8 Thus, if the visitor's car is damaged he has a remedy, but the finance company, from whom he has it on a credit agreement, does not.

from being stolen from the yard of the public house.[9] On the other hand it seems consistent with what was said in the preceding section that, whenever the occupier would have a duty at common law to prevent damage to goods on his land (whether due to the state of the premises or acts or omissions thereon), the common duty of care will apply.[10]

(c)   Liability in contract

At common law, contracts for the use of premises were deemed to contain various implied terms relating to the safety of the premises.[11] In lieu of those implied terms,[12] section 5 enacts:

> (1)   Where persons enter or use, or bring or send goods to, any premises in exercise of a right conferred by contract with a person occupying or having control of the premises, the duty he owes them in respect of dangers due to the state of the premises or to things done or omitted to be done on them, in so far as the duty depends on a term to be implied in the contract by reason of its conferring that right, shall be the common duty of care.
>
> (2)   The foregoing subsection shall apply to fixed and movable structures as it applied to premises.

The effect of this section is as follows. Where a person enters the occupier's premises under a contract between himself and the occupier, the occupier is obliged to extend the common duty of care to that entrant, subject to a contrary term in their contract. It is, of course, open to the occupier specifically to increase the level of care by express provision in the contract. On the other hand, the extent to which he may exclude or limit his responsibilities towards contractual entrants is governed by the operation of the rules discussed in the next section.

Section 5 is not limited in its operation to personal injury caused by the defective state of the occupier's premises; it also covers damage to goods. What is less clear is whether an action by a contractual entrant must be based solely on contract – on the basis of the term implied into the agreement by virtue of section 5 – or whether he has the alternative of suing in tort. In *Sole v W J Hallt Ltd*[13] a tradesman who had come onto the occupier's premises to perform some plaster work was injured when he fell down an unprotected stair-well. It was held by Swanick J that contractual entrants had the option of suing in either contract – under section 5(1) – or in tort under section 2(1).[14]

What happens where the contract is silent but of a kind that, at common law, traditionally attracted a different implied term? Does section 5(1) operate in such circumstances? An example would be a passenger on a railway platform who, at common law, was historically protected by a duty on the railway company to make the railway

---

9   *Tinsley v Dudley* [1951] 2 KB 18, [1951] 1 All ER 252, CA. It would seem that, whatever the common law position, the combined effect of s 1(3)(b) and s 1(1) is to deny the visitor a remedy for loss of property if she is injured and, for example, her valuable necklace falls off her person to be carried away in an adjoining stream.

10   Supported by *AMF International Ltd v Magnet Bowling Ltd* [1968] 2 All ER 789.

11   See especially *Francis v Cockrell* (1870) LR 5 QB 501; *Gilmore v LCC* [1938] 4 All ER 331.

12   The expression 'the duty...shall be the common duty of care' shows that the duty replaces, and is not merely alternative to, the terms implied at common law.

13   [1973] 1 All ER 1032. Quaere the effect of any contributory negligence.

14   This decision is almost certainly wrong since the Act specifically limits visitors (to whom s 2(1) refers) to those who were either invitees or licensees at common law. The whole purpose of s 5 is to ensure some protection to contractual entrants where no such protection is mentioned in the contract. Since it is a decision at first instance, there is no obligation for any future court to follow it.

platform reasonably safe.[15] Others present on the platform, such as relatives waving someone off, were afforded the usual duty extended to licensees. The question is, therefore, whether fare-paying passengers are now protected by the common law implied term which, apart from the statute, would form part of the contract of carriage, or whether they are afforded, instead, the common duty of care by virtue of section 5(1). It is submitted that the statutory implied term applies. The Act does not say that the term is to be implied where, otherwise, the contract would be silent on the matter. Instead, the statutory implied term is to be included in the contract wherever 'the duty depends upon *a term* to be implied in the contract'. We suggest that the statutory term should, therefore, be implied in preference to the common law term.[16]

(5)   EXCLUSION OF LIABILITY

Section 2(1) provides:

> An occupier of premises owes the same duty, the 'common duty of care', to all his visitors, except in so far as he is free to and does extend, restrict, modify or exclude his duty to any visitor or visitors by agreement or otherwise.

The occupier therefore has two options if he wishes to modify the common duty of care owed to his visitors. First, where the visitor enters by virtue of a contract – for example, a contractor who enters to carry out work on premises or a tenant granted access to the common parts of a block of flats – an express term of the contract can be drafted to modify the common duty of care. Secondly, in respect of non-contractual entrants, a clear and unequivocal notice,[17] either affixed at the point of entry to the land,[18] or included in a programme or ticket giving access to the land,[19] will suffice. These two broad options must, however, be read subject to section 3 of the Act which sets out some important limits on the occupier's freedom to limit or exclude his liability.

Section 3(1) provides that the duty of care owed by an occupier to those visitors he is bound to admit onto his premises by virtue of a contract, who are nonetheless 'strangers to the contract',[20] cannot be excluded or restricted.[1] On the other hand, the subsection also provides that any term of the contract which obliges him to increase the level of care shown to such entrants will be effective in determining the standard of care to be shown. Section 3(1) is designed to ensure the protection of employees of the person with whom the occupier contracts. If the occupier contracts with A for work to be done on his premises by A's employees, it would be a nonsense for him, on the one hand to be bound to admit those employees, yet, on the other, be free to exclude any potential liability to them.

Section 3(2) further enacts:

---

15 *Protheroe v Railway Executive* [1951] 1 KB 376, [1950] 2 All ER 1093.
16 Cf the analysis in the 9th edition of this work at p 297.
17 Note the difference between a notice (excluding or restricting liability) and a warning (alerting entrants to a danger present on the premises).
18 *Ashdown v Samuel Williams & Sons Ltd* [1957] 1 QB 409, [1957] 1 All ER 35, CA.
19 *White v Blackmore* [1972] 2 QB 651, [1972] 3 All ER 158, CA.
20 Defined as 'a person not for the time being entitled to the benefit of the contract as a party to it or as the successor by assignment or otherwise of a party to it, and accordingly includes a party to the contract who has ceased to be so entitled'(s 3(3)).
1   A similar effect is achieved in relation to contractors who enter premises under a contract with the landlord, where the tenant has agreed with the landlord (extra-contractually) to allow such contractors to enter the premises.

A contract shall not by virtue of this section have the effect, unless it expressly so provides, of making an occupier who has taken all reasonable care answerable to strangers to the contract for dangers due to the faulty execution of any work of construction, maintenance or repair or other like operation by persons other than himself, his servants and persons acting under his direction and control.

On reflection, it is apparent that the burden on the defendant under section 3 appears to be greater than that imposed by the common duty of care because he is unable to delegate to independent contractors any part of his duty to take care.[2] Furthermore, while section 3 of the 1957 Act places some restrictions on the ability of an occupier to limit or exclude his liability, further restrictions upon his freedom so to do are also imposed under the Unfair Contract Terms Act 1977. This Act drastically reduces the latitude granted to a person who occupies premises for 'business purposes' to exclude or restrict his liability.[3]

The Unfair Contract Terms Act 1977 renders invalid any contract term or notice purporting to exclude or restrict liability for death or personal injury[4] resulting from breach of the common duty of care under the 1957 Act where the premises are occupied for the business purposes of the occupier.[5] In the case of other loss or damage, any attempted contract term or notice restricting or excluding liability is subject to the requirement of reasonableness.[6] If the exclusion is in the form of a contract term, its reasonableness is to be gauged by reference to 'the circumstances which were, or ought reasonably to have been, known to or in the contemplation of the parties when the contract was made'.[7] If the exclusion of liability is in the form of a notice, then its reasonableness is to be judged in the light of 'all the circumstances obtaining when the liability arose'.[8] Of the two tests, the former is the more plaintiff-friendly, for in respect of notices, 'all the circumstances' presumably include, and extend beyond, those in the actual or imputed contemplation of the parties. The more lenient test, applied to a contractual term, might be justified on the basis that the plaintiff had an opportunity, at the time of contracting, to bargain against the inclusion of any such exclusion of liability.

Agreement to, or knowledge of, the term or notice will not be evidence that the visitor has assumed the risk of injury giving rise to the defence of volenti non fit injuria.[9] Equally, oral stipulation of any such term or notice, made at the time of the entrant's visit will similarly fail necessarily to render the entrant volens; for under the 1977 Act, any such announcement itself constitutes a notice.[10]

The 1977 Act quite clearly leaves an occupier free (via a notice on a front gate) to exclude liability to most of his visitors since its operation is limited to those entering in

2   The duty in respect of independent contractors now imposed by s 3(1) and (2) is not exactly the same as the common duty of care imposed by s 2(4)(b). First, s 3(2) limits the liability not only in respect of, as in s 2(4)(b), 'the faulty execution of any work of construction, maintenance or repair' but additionally in respect of any 'other like operation'. Secondly, whereas s 2(4)(b) specifies in detail what would be reasonable care by the occupier in relation to the conduct of the independent contractor, s 3(2) states that he shall take 'all reasonable care' without further particularising this standard – it cannot be assumed that the two standards are identical.
3   Note that the 1977 Act and s 3 of the 1957 Act will often work in tandem since most, if not all, of s 3 cases are likely to involve an occupier for 'business purposes'.
4   Unfair Contract Terms Act 1977, s 2(1).
5   Unfair Contract Terms Act 1977, s 1(1)(c).
6   Unfair Contract Terms Act 1977, s 2(2).
7   Unfair Contract Terms Act 1977, s 11(1).
8   Unfair Contract Terms Act 1977, s 11(3).
9   Unfair Contract Terms Act 1977, s 2(3).
10   Unfair Contract Terms Act 1977, s 14.

connection with business purposes[11] and the Act makes clear that it is the purposes of the occupier alone which are relevant.[12] Some cases are clear; consider *Ashdown v Samuel Williams & Sons Ltd*.[13]

> By licence of the defendants, the plaintiff crossed the defendants' land. A notice board purported to curtail the liabilities of the defendants to licensees. The Court of Appeal held that because the defendants had taken reasonable steps to bring the conditions of the notice to the attention of the licensee, these conditions (which were interpreted by the court to exclude liability for damage sustained in the way in which the plaintiff's injuries were caused) excluded the defendants' liability in the same way that conditions in a contract, which the defendant has taken reasonable steps to bring to the notice of the other party, exclude liability.

If the case had arisen after 1977 the defendant would not have been able to exclude his liability under the Occupiers' Liability Act. But what if the facts of *White v Blackmore*[14] were repeated now? Notices at the entrance to the track and in the programme handed to spectators and competitors excluded liability for injuries occurring in 'jalopy' races. The races were being run to raise money for charity. In 1972 the notices sufficed to exclude the organisers' and occupiers' liability. Today, a preliminary question would be whether the track was occupied for business purposes. Similarly, is a Sunday school within the 1977 Act when a bazaar or jumble sale is being held there, but not on Sunday mornings? Are churches and synagogues occupied for business purposes? What of the housewife who does some part-time hairdressing at home and whose customer is hurt coming downstairs from the bathroom?

The only further attempt at clarification of the definition of 'business purposes' is to be found in section 2 of the Occupiers' Liability Act 1984. That particular section amends the Unfair Contract Terms Act to provide:

> but liability of an occupier of premises for breach of an obligation or duty toward a person obtaining access to the premises for recreational or educational purposes, being liability for loss or damage suffered by reason of the dangerous state of premises is not a business liability of the occupier unless granting that person such access for the purposes concerned falls within the business purposes of the occupier.[15]

The purpose of this tortuously worded provision appears to be to allow farmers and owners of countryside areas to exclude liability to day-trippers. The land is occupied for 'business purposes', namely farming or forestry. But any duty owed to entrants coming to the land to picnic and so on can now, once again, be excluded by agreement or notice. And the confused wording of the section may result in it having even more widespread implications.[16]

---

11 Section 14 defines 'business' so as to include 'a profession and the activities of any government department or public or local authority'. So if I invite students for a tutorial, or a postgraduate for supervision, at my home, do I then occupy my home for 'business purposes'?
12 What happens, however, if I let a room of my house to a postgraduate student? Should the premises as a whole be treated as business premises? Equally, what if the premises are under dual control, and only one of the occupiers is a business occupier? On both these matters see Mesher 'Occupiers, Trespassers and the Unfair Contract Terms Act 1977' (1979) 43 Conveyancer 58.
13 [1957] 1 QB 409, [1957] 1 All ER 35.
14 [1972] 2 QB 651, [1972] 3 All ER 158, CA.
15 Unfair Contract Terms Act 1977, s 1(3)(b).
16 See Bragg and Brazier 'Occupiers and Exclusion of Liability' (1986) 130 Sol Jo 251 and 274.

(B)   LIABILITY TO NON-VISITORS: THE OCCUPIERS' LIABILITY ACT 1984

Liability to trespassers and all other uninvited entrants is now regulated by section 1 of the Occupiers' Liability Act 1984.[17] The Act there provides that it:

> shall have effect in place of the rules of common law[18] to determine –
> (a)   whether any duty is owed by a person as occupier of premises to persons other than his visitors in respect of any risk of their suffering injury on the premises by reason of any danger due to the state of the premises or to things done or omitted to be done on them.
> (b)   if so, what that duty is.

Although the Act avowedly replaces the rules of common law in relation to occupiers' liability towards uninvited entrants, three exceptional instances fall outwith the Act because of the terms in which it is drafted. First, section 1(8) expressly confines that liability to personal injuries. It follows that common law liability for damage to trespassers'[19] (and other uninvited entrants') property survives the 1984 Act. Secondly, the Act's remit is further limited in that no duty is owed by the occupier of the *solum* of a public right of way to persons using that right of way.[20] (It is arguable, however, that since the Act specifically provides that nothing in its provisions affects any duty otherwise owed to such persons, that users of public rights of way are owed the duty of common humanity formulated in *British Railways Board v Herrington.*[1]) Finally, it was held in *Revill v Newbery*[2] that acts of the occupier that are not done in connection with the occupation fall outside the purview of the Act. That is to say, acts which do not, in themselves, affect the safety of the premises fall under the common law.[3]

A duty to uninvited entrants in respect of any danger due to the state of the premises arises only when three conditions are met:[4]
(a)   The occupier must be aware of the danger or have reasonable grounds to believe it exists.
(b)   He must have known, or had reasonable grounds to know, that the uninvited entrant either was in, or might come into, the vicinity of the danger. (So, where occupiers had no reason to expect that trespassers were taking shortcuts across their land, no duty arose.[5])
(c)   The risk of injury to an uninvited entrant resulting from that danger was one against which, in all the circumstances of the case, the occupier might reasonably be expected to offer the uninvited entrant some protection.

---

17   The Act is based on proposals from the Law Commission Report No 75 'Liability for Damage or Injury to Trespassers and Related Questions of Occupiers' Liability' (Cmnd 6428).
18   As to which see *British Railways Board v Herrington* [1972] AC 877, [1972] 1 All ER 749, HL.
19   That such common law liability did arise on the principle in *British Railways Board v Herrington* (supra) is clear from *Tutton v A D Walter Ltd* [1986] QB 61, [1985] 3 All ER 757 where there was liability for negligently spraying crops so as to kill a neighbour's bees. The judge held that the bees were probably not trespassers but that liability to their keeper would arise even if the bees were trespassing.
20   Occupiers' Liability Act 1984, s 1(7).
1   [1972] AC 877, [1972] 1 All ER 749, HL. See further Buckley 'The Occupiers' Liability Act 1984 – Has *Herrington* Survived?' (1984) 48 Conveyancer 413; Murphy 'Public Rights of Way and Private Law Wrongs' (1997) Conveyancer 362.
2   [1996] 1 All ER 291, CA.
3   However, in *Revill*, Neill LJ said that in applying the common law the same principles as those contained in the 1984 Act should be applied: [1996] 1 All ER 291 at 298, CA.
4   Occupiers' Liability Act 1984, s 1(3).
5   *White v St Albans City and District Council* (1990) Times, 12 March, CA.

The test for the existence (as opposed to substance) of the duty of care imposed by the Act comprises a curious admixture of objective and subjective elements. The first and second limbs of the test introduce a subjective element – they focus on the *individual occupier's* actual or imputed knowledge.[6] As regards this imputed knowledge, however, it is important to distinguish the notion of constructive knowledge. The occupier will only fall within section 1(3)(a), for example, if he actually knows of the danger on his premises, or has actual knowledge of the state of affairs in which the danger could reasonably be foreseen (even if he does not foresee it).[7] If he neither knows of the danger, nor of the state of affairs, then he will not be liable just because a reasonable occupier would have known of that state of affairs. Thus a landowner who never once looks round his grounds could not be held liable; but a landowner who does survey his land and turns a blind eye to something which is an obvious source of danger would be caught by the subsection. The third limb is more objective in focusing on all the circumstances of the case. It is not entirely objective, however, in that it only demands protection be commensurate with what can reasonably be expected of the individual occupier. 'All the circumstances' will include the nature of the entrant's presence on the premises. On this basis, burglars and thieves can expect little or no protection under the Act where they are injured because of the *dangerous state of the premises*.[8] On the other hand, where such persons are injured because of a *negligent act* performed by the defendant, the common law will still afford them a measure of protection. *Revill v Newbery* illustrates this point. There, a burglar whom the defendant negligently shot was able to sue in negligence even though the case fell outside the 1984 Act. Furthermore, the court was unprepared to entertain the defendant's claim that the defence of ex turpi causa should apply.

'All the circumstances', for the purposes of section 1(3) of the Act, will also include the age and capabilities of the entrant. Accordingly, where occupiers are aware that children often trespass on their land, there will be an expectation that some protection should be extended to those children, however mischievous they may be.[9] Other relevant circumstances may include personal characteristics of the occupier and the limits on his financial resources.

Once the *existence* of the duty has been established, the matter of the *substance* of the duty then arises. The content of the duty is governed by section 1(4) of the Act which provides that: 'the duty is to take such care as is reasonable in all the circumstances of the case to see that he [the uninvited entrant] does not suffer injury on the premises by reason of the danger concerned'. One significant difference between the 1984 and 1957 Acts is provided for in section 1(5) of the former. There it is stipulated that any duty arising under the 1984 Act can:

> ... in an appropriate case, be discharged by taking such steps as are reasonable in all the circumstances of the case to give warning of the danger concerned or to discourage a person from incurring the risk.

---

6   In *White v St Albans City and District Council* (1990) Times, 12 March, the court failed both to confirm or negate the suggestion made here when it considered the meaning of s 1(3)(b). It simply held that all the facts of the case are relevant to determining whether an occupier should be deemed to have knowledge that trespassers would come into the vicinity of the danger.

7   *Swain v Natui Ram Puri* [1996] PIQR P 442.

8   See *Murphy v Culhane* [1977] QB 94 at 98 where Lord Denning MR suggested (obiter) that the defence of ex turpi causa non oritur actio might be available in any event.

9   See Jones 'The Occupiers' Liability Act 1984 – The Wheels of Law Reform Turn Slowly' (1984) 47 MLR 713, 721.

The warning does not have to be sufficient to enable the uninvited entrant to remain safely on the land. If the occupier of a building site with dangerous concealed trenches puts up notices[10] around the perimeter of the site '*Danger: Keep Out! Concealed Trenches*', that warning would be insufficient to discharge the occupier's duty towards his visitors. But since it makes specific mention, as the Act demands, of 'the danger concerned', it would almost certainly suffice vis à vis an uninvited adult entrant.[11] The fact that a warning notice has been read by an uninvited entrant will not, of itself, render that person volens,[12] but the Act does provide for the operation of a very similar defence in this context. It states:

> No duty is owed by virtue of this section to any person in respect of risks willingly accepted as his by that person (the question of whether a risk was so accepted to be decided on the same principles as in other cases in which one person owes a duty of care to another).[13]

Finally, under section 1(8), it is specifically provided that non-visitors are not entitled to sue in respect of property damage. Accordingly, a trespasser who, due to the perilous state of the premises, trips and falls on the occupier's land while snooping there may sue in respect of his personal injuries but not for the damage caused to his camera.

(C)   COMMON LAW LIABILITY AND ACTIVITIES ON LAND

Naturally, an occupier who intentionally harms a person whom he has permitted to be on his premises is answerable for so doing. Further, regardless of whether the plaintiff has an alternative remedy under the Act of 1957, an occupier also owes a common law duty of care not to conduct activities on his land foreseeably likely to harm persons other than trespassers of whose presence he ought to be aware.[14]

The following cases illustrate typical acts within ordinary negligence. In *Gallagher v Humphrey*,[15] through the defendant occupier's negligent maintenance of a crane, goods carried by it fell on the plaintiff, whom the defendant had permitted to be on the land. The defendant was held liable in negligence. Also, in 1966, the Privy Council held in *Railways Comr v McDermott* that a railway body was liable in negligence for not taking reasonable care to make a level crossing safe.[16] And, in another case, a plaintiff who, having seen off friends on a train, was injured by the open door of the guard's van as the train moved away from the platform. It was held this person was owed a

10 The Unfair Contract Terms Act 1977 does not apply to the duty created by the Occupiers' Liability Act 1984.

11 In relation to a young child, unable to read, who is allured onto the premises, it is less likely that such a notice would suffice. In any event, such a child might be classified as a visitor by virtue of an implied licence.

12 *Titchener v British Railways Board* [1983] 3 All ER 770.

13 Occupiers' Liability Act 1984, s 1(6). The difference between this statutory version of volenti and its common law cousin lies in the fact that at common law the plaintiff, to be *volens*, must accept both the risk of injury *and* the fact that any resulting loss should be his own. Under the 1984 Act, the defendant can raise the defence in s 1(6) on proof of the former alone. Furthermore, properly understood, *volenti* is to be confined to the assumption of risk in relation to future rather than extant dangers: *Morris v Murray* [1991] 2 QB 6 (per Fox, Stocker and Waller LJJ at 17, 28 and 32 respectively). See also Murphy (1995) Legal Studies 415, 428–9.

14 In *Chettle v Denton* (1951) 95 Sol Jo 802, CA, the defendant, while shooting game on private land, hit the plaintiff who was a licensee on the land. The defendant was held liable in negligence in that he would have seen the plaintiff if he had taken reasonable care.

15 (1862) 6 LT 684. And see *Tolhausen v Davies* (1888) 57 LJQB 392 at 394–5; affd 58 LJQB 98, CA.

16 [1967] AC 169, [1966] 2 All ER 162, PC; *Thomas v British Railways Board* [1976] QB 912, [1976] 3 All ER 15, CA.

duty of reasonable care by the railway company and was entitled to sue in negligence.[17] Similarly, a passenger on a ship recovered for the injuries she suffered when seamen failed to keep passengers clear of flailing ropes while unmooring.[18] And likewise, where hospitals are negligently administered,[19] or schools badly supervised,[20] the liability is in the ordinary law of negligence. Furthermore, it follows from what has been said above that the setting in motion of machinery may also be within the ambit of these acts of misfeasance.[1]

Common law rules relating to the duties of occupiers of premises have also ordinarily been held to extend to movable structures. Consequently, the question arises whether a trespasser on a vehicle driven by the servant of the owner of the vehicle, and of whose presence the driver is aware, can sue in ordinary negligence or whether he is subject to the special rules about trespassers injured by defective premises. In *Conway v George Wimpey & Co Ltd*[2] the Court of Appeal held that the plaintiff was a trespasser and therefore failed (counsel having conceded that, if he was a trespasser, he lost the case). It is submitted that this decision is erroneous, however. The injury was sustained not by reason of any defect in the lorry but because of the negligent way in which it was driven.[3] In that event, as Denning LJ rightly held in *Young v Edward Box & Co Ltd*,[4] the liability of the defendant rests on whether the driver drove the vehicle negligently within the scope and course of his employment – the ordinary rules of negligence and no others apply, unless the injury is caused by the defective condition of the vehicle.

It will be recalled that it is an open question as to what extent these rules remain unaffected by the Occupiers' Liability Act 1957. So far as the 1984 Act is concerned, there are no words equivalent to those located in the 1957 legislation, which might be construed to restrict statutory liability for activities performed in consequence of the defendant's occupation. Accordingly, as regards the physical injury of non-visitors, it is extremely doubtful that any of the pre-existing common law survived the passage of the Act.

(D) LIABILITY TO THOSE OUTSIDE THE PREMISES

The risk created by dangers caused by the defective state of premises is not confined to entrants to those premises. Slates falling from roofs, crumbling walls and dangerous

---

17 *Thatcher v Great Western Rly Co* (1893) 10 TLR 13, CA. In *Dunster v Abbott* [1953] 2 All ER 1572, CA, a canvasser when leaving premises in the dark was injured, allegedly because the defendant occupier turned off a light too soon. This, too, was held to be a problem in general negligence, and not of invitees/licensees.
18 *Daly v General Steam Navigation Co Ltd, The Dragon* [1980] 3 All ER 696, [1981] 1 WLR 120, CA.
19 Eg *Collins v Hertfordshire County Council* [1947] KB 598, [1947] 1 All ER 633; and *Cassidy v Ministry of Health* [1951] 2 KB 343, [1951] 1 All ER 574, CA.
20 Eg *Rich v LCC* [1953] 2 All ER 376, CA; *Jauffir v Akhbar* (1984) Times, 10 February (negligent parental supervision); *Slade v Battersea and Putney Group Hospital Management Committee* [1955] 1 All ER 429; *Slater v Clay Cross Co Ltd* [1956] 2 QB 264, [1956] 2 All ER 625, CA (plaintiff hit by train while walking in a tunnel through which defendants knew persons habitually passed). Cf *Thompson v Bankstown Municipal Council* (1953) 87 CLR 619 (H Ct Australia).
1 *Excelsior Wire Rope Co Ltd v Callan* [1930] AC 404, [1930] All ER Rep 1, HL; but not the continued running of a moving staircase: *Hardy v Central London Rly Co* [1920] 3 KB 459, CA.
2 [1951] 2 KB 266, [1951] 1 All ER 363, CA; cf *Twine v Bean's Express Ltd* [1946] 1 All ER 202.
3 This vital fact is not stated in the Law Reports – see [1950] 2 All ER 331 at 332.
4 [1951] 1 TLR 789. And see *Rose v Plenty* [1976] 1 All ER 97, [1976] 1 WLR 141, CA.

activities carried out on premises are just a few examples of risks just as likely to endanger passers by, or persons on adjoining premises. The circumstances in which the occupier of premises owes a duty to such persons ought therefore to be considered briefly.

As will be seen,[5] an action in public nuisance often lies at the instance of those injured on a highway as a result of harmful conditions on adjoining land. Because of this historical anomaly, in a large number of situations a plaintiff may sue for personal injuries either in negligence or nuisance, or both. Indeed, in several House of Lords cases, it has been a matter of indifference whether the case was decided in negligence or nuisance.[6] Often, it is quite fortuitous which tort is relied on. *Holling v Yorkshire Traction Co Ltd*[7] is a typical example.

> The defendants emitted so much steam and smoke onto the highway from their adjoining factory that the view of drivers was obscured so that a fatal collision between two vehicles occurred. It was held to be negligence on the part of the defendant to fail to post an employee at each end of the affected area.

There is no doubt, then, that the ordinary principles of negligence can be applied where highway users are injured because of harmful operations being carried out there.[8]

(E) LIABILITY TO THOSE ON ADJOINING PREMISES

Occupiers are under a general duty to take reasonable care to prevent dangers on their premises damaging persons or property on adjoining premises.[9] This is so whether the danger arises from disrepair on the premises, or some man-made or natural hazard such as fire caused by lightning striking a tree.[10] Also, where adjoining properties have mutual rights of support, negligently allowing a property to fall into dereliction so as to damage the adjoining premises is actionable in negligence as well as in nuisance.[11]

There are two issues of particular difficulty affecting the duties of care owed to each other by occupiers of adjoining premises. First, where a plaintiff tenant sues his landlord for damage resulting from the defective state of repair of premises retained by the landlord, the case law is confused. Take first *Cunard v Antifyre Ltd*.[12]

5   See ch 18, post.
6   See, eg, *Longhurst v Metropolitan Water Board* [1948] 2 All ER 834, HL; *Caminer v Northern and London Investment Trust Ltd* [1951] AC 88, [1950] 2 All ER 486, HL; *Bolton v Stone* [1951] AC 850, [1951] 1 All ER 1078, HL. Sometimes, it is not even clear upon which tort the decision is based, see, eg, Denning LJ in *Mint v Good* [1951] 1 KB 517 at 526, [1950] 2 All ER 1159 at 1168, CA.
7   [1948] 2 All ER 662; cf *Wheeler v Morris* (1915) 84 LJKB 1435, CA.
8   Eg *Hilder v Associated Portland Cement Manufacturers Ltd* [1961] 3 All ER 709, [1961] 1 WLR 1434 (defendant occupiers of field allowed children to play football there; liable to motor-cyclist who, when driving along adjoining highway, was knocked off his vehicle by a ball kicked by the children from the field).
9   *Hughes v Percival* (1883) 8 App Cas 443, HL: the premises for the benefit of which the present rule applies are those in respect of which someone other than the defendant has a vested interest in possession. And note *Murphy v Brentwood District Council* [1990] 2 All ER 908 and 926 (per Lord Bridge).
10 *Goldman v Hargrave* [1967] 1 AC 645, [1966] 2 All ER 989, PC. Water normally percolates from the defendant's land to the plaintiff's and the defendant pumps out the water from his land, and by so stopping the subterranean flow causes settlement damage to the plaintiff's land. The plaintiff has no remedy because the defendant has no duty to adjoining occupiers in respect of percolating water: *Langbrook Properties Ltd v Surrey County Council* [1969] 3 All ER 1424, [1970] 1 WLR 161.
11 *Bradburn v Lindsay* [1983] 2 All ER 408.
12 [1933] 1 KB 551; the principle on which this case was based was approved, obiter, by du Parcq J in *Bishop v Consolidated London Properties Ltd* (1933) 102 LJKB 257 at 262.

Some defective roofing and guttering, which formed part of the premises retained by the defendant landlord, fell into a part of the premises let by him to the plaintiff tenant. As a result, his wife was injured and his goods were damaged. Damages in general negligence were awarded to both the tenant and his wife.

Yet in *Cheater v Cater*[13] the Court of Appeal held that a landlord, who had let a field to a tenant at a time when there was a yew tree on the adjoining premises retained by the landlord, was not liable in negligence when the tenant's horse died through eating leaves from the tree which was then in the same state as at the date of the lease. Then, in *Shirvell v Hackwood Estates Co Ltd*,[14] the court doubted *Cunard v Antifyre Ltd* holding that the workman of a tenant could not recover in negligence from the landlord whose tree on adjoining land fell on him. Finally, the facts in *Taylor v Liverpool Corpn* were as follows.[15]

The plaintiff, the daughter of a tenant of one of the defendant landlords' flats, was injured by the fall of a chimney stack belonging to these flats into the yard adjoining the premises. The landlords had negligently maintained this chimney, which formed part of the building retained by them.

Stable J found for the plaintiff in negligence, following *Cunard v Antifyre Ltd*, and distinguishing *Cheater v Cater* on the ground that the tenant had there impliedly agreed to take the risk in respect of danger existing on the premises at that time, and treating the observations in *Shirvell's* case as obiter on the ground that no negligence had in any event occurred. The principle in *Cunard v Antifyre Ltd* would seem to be preferable to the one which affords landlords' blanket immunity in respect of retained premises in disrepair.[16]

The second area of difficulty in delimiting the duty owed by an occupier to those on adjoining premises relates to damage inflicted on those adjoining premises by third parties. No duty will generally[17] be found to lie where damage is inflicted on a neighbour's property by vandals or burglars even though the wrongdoers' conduct may have been facilitated by disrepair or lax security on the part of the occupier.[18] This is in line with the general reluctance on the part of the courts to impose on a person, who has no special relationship with a third party, liability for the conduct of that party.

SECTION 2.   LIABILITY OF NON-OCCUPIERS

The occupier of premises may have immediate control over the state of those premises, and the capacity to repair defects in them, but in a number of instances, particularly in relation to structural defects, nothing he has done will have caused the relevant defect. Cracks in a house resulting from inadequate foundations will often be the result of the negligence of the builder and endanger the occupier as much as any visitor to the property. Parliament passed the Defective Premises Act in 1972 to impose on persons providing dwellings some limited responsibility to subsequent purchasers and their

13 [1918] 1 KB 247, CA (not cited in *Cunard v Antifyre Ltd*).
14 [1938] 2 KB 577 at 594–5 (per Green LJ), [1938] 2 All ER 1, CA.
15 [1939] 3 All ER 329.
16 It is submitted that the Court of Appeal in *Shirvell's* case wrongly thought that the decisions where a landlord, having no control of the defective premises, had been held not liable, applied in the case before them: see post.
17 In *P Perl (Exporters) Ltd v Camden London Borough Council* [1984] QB 342, [1983] 3 All ER 161 the Court of Appeal did not entirely rule out special circumstances which might give rise to such a duty to adjoining occupiers.
18 *Smith v Littlewoods Organisation Ltd* [1987] AC 241, [1987] 1 All ER 710, HL.

families, and to clarify the responsibilities of landlords. As will be seen, the Act is a far from perfect example of legislation. Shortly after the Act came into force, however, the judiciary sought to extend the common law by, in effect, imposing a duty of care on builders, local authorities and others involved in construction work wherever it was reasonably foreseeable that any negligence on their part would cause loss or injury to subsequent purchasers or visitors to the property.[19] The courts virtually by-passed the Defective Premises Act, invoking the *Donoghue v Stevenson* neighbour principle in order to remedy what was then perceived to be a gap in the 'consumer protection' provided for property owners. That trend in judicial innovation attracted extensive criticism from the House of Lords from 1984 onwards,[20] and met its ultimate end in *Murphy v Brentwood District Council*.[1]

Lord Mackay in *Murphy* considered that, as Parliament had in the Defective Premises Act made provision for imposing statutory duties on those involved in providing dwellings, it was not 'a proper exercise of judicial power' for the courts to create a large new area of responsibility at least in relation to local authorities.[2] Radical extensions of consumer protection laws should, it was thought, be left to Parliament. Most importantly, *Murphy* represents the high-water mark of judicial retreat from extensive liability for economic loss. It also attempted to reassert a firm boundary between contract and tort. If a person has a contract with the builder of her new house, that contract imposes obligations on the builder to ensure that the house is both safe and value for money. Should structural defects diminish the value of the property, or require her to incur expenditure on repairs, she can recover that loss in contract. But if she is a subsequent purchaser with no contractual relationship with the builder, that economic loss[3] is irrecoverable in tort against the builder or indeed any other third party,[4] save where she had entered into some special relationship with that third party.[5] Warranties of quality are confined to contractual relationships.[6]

(A)   THE DEFECTIVE PREMISES ACT 1972

One key feature of the *Murphy* case is the repeated insistence by their Lordships that the courts should not seek to impose common law rules of liability where Parliament, via the Defective Premises Act 1972, had already done so. Since *Murphy*, therefore, the primacy of the Act has been put beyond question, especially since, under section 6(3) its provisions are made non-derogable.

---

19 *Batty v Metropolitan Property Realisations Ltd* [1978] QB 554, [1978] 2 All ER 445, CA; *Anns v Merton London Borough Council* [1978] AC 728, [1977] 2 All ER 492, HL.
20 For example, *Governors of the Peabody Donation Fund v Sir Lindsay Parkinson & Co Ltd* [1985] AC 210, [1984] 3 All ER 529, HL and see ch 11 ante.
1   [1991] 1 AC 398, [1990] 2 All ER 908, HL; and see *Department of the Environment v Thomas Bates & Son Ltd* [1991] 1 AC 499, [1990] 2 All ER 943, HL.
2   Ibid at 918. For similar sentiments see 923 (per Lord Keith), 930 (per Lord Bridge) and 938 (per Lord Oliver).
3   The loss is economic because once the plaintiff discovers the defect, he is on his guard and will not suffer physical injury. The only loss that he sustains is the cost of making the premises safe and habitable.
4   Eg, a local authority.
5   Such as a surveyor I instruct to inspect or value the house. A further potential exception was adverted to by Lord Keith who thought that 'if a building stands so close to the boundary of the building owner's land that after discovery of the dangerous defect it remains a potential source of injury to persons or property on neighbouring land or on the highway, the building owner ought, in principle, to be entitled to recover in tort from the negligent builder': [1991] AC 398 at 475.
6   *D & F Estates v Church Comrs for England* [1989] AC 177, [1988] 2 All ER 992, HL.

Section 1 of the Act imposes on any 'person taking on work for or in connection with the provision of a dwelling' a strict liability to ensure that the work he takes on is 'done in a workmanlike, or, as the case may be professional manner, with proper materials and so that as regards that work the dwelling will be fit for habitation when completed'.[7] Thus, a builder who reasonably believing that his materials were suitable, used asbestos in roofing materials at a time before the dangers of asbestos were appreciated, would still be in breach of his duty under section 1. Section 1 covers all those involved in building new homes; not just builders, but also contractors, architects and developers.[8] Alas, while splendid in theory, section 1 is in practice more or less a dead letter.[9] First, houses built under the National House Building Council scheme, and covered by a National House Building Registration Council Certificate, are exempted from the strict liability regime created by section 1.[10] Secondly, and much more importantly, the limitation period under the Act begins to run as soon as the dwelling is completed, which may be a very considerable time before a structural defect finally manifests itself.[11] By contrast, in a negligence action, by virtue of the Latent Damage Act 1986,[12] the limitation period begins to run only when the plaintiff should reasonably have known of the relevant damage (subject to a long-stop of 15 years after which any action in respect of property damage is barred completely). Defects in timbers, foundations and other parts of the fabric of a building rarely become apparent for several years.

Other provisions of the Defective Premises Act – sections 3 and 4 – concerning the survival of a duty of care after disposal of the premises, and landlords' duties of care where there is an obligation to repair are, as we shall see, rather more useful.

(B)   BUILDERS AND CONTRACTORS: PHYSICAL DAMAGE

A builder or contractor actually engaged in construction or repair work on land and premises affixed to that land owes a duty of care[13] to the occupier of the premises, her visitors, and, where their presence is foreseeable, probably to trespassers as well.[14] Any universal exemption from a duty of care in respect of real property did not survive the decision in *AC Billings & Sons Ltd v Riden*[15] where B Ltd, building contractors,

---

7   The section applies to omissions as much as to acts: *Andrews v Schooling* [1991] 3 All ER 723, [1991] 1 WLR 783, CA; but it is confined to defects rendering the dwelling (but not, importantly, commercial properties) uninhabitable: *Thompson v Clive Alexander and Partners* (1992) 59 BLR 77.

8   See Defective Premises Act 1972, s 1(3) (including local authorities). The fact that all such persons might be liable creates the potential for difficulties in establishing causation. The test to be applied is whether the defendant's breach of the section is a 'significant cause' of the unfitness of the dwelling: *Bayoumi v Protim Services Ltd* [1996] EGCS 187.

9   See Spencer 'The Defective Premises Act 1972 – Defective Law and Defective Law Reform' (1974) CLJ 307 and (1975) CLJ 48.

10   Defective Premises Act 1972, s 2. For a time most new houses built were erected within the NHBC scheme, but since the latter part of the last decade, opting out in this way has not occurred: see Wallace '*Anns* Beyond Repair' (1991) 107 LQR 228.

11   See for an example of the theoretical scope of s 1 made futile by the limitation provisions: *Rimmer v Liverpool City Council* [1985] QB 1, [1984] 1 All ER 930, CA.

12   See post.

13   *Miller v South of Scotland Electricity Board* 1958 SC (HL) 20, HL.

14   The contractor may of course also be the occupier in which case his liability to trespassers will be regulated by the Occupiers' Liability Act 1984. In other circumstances ordinary principles of negligence apply: *Railway Comr v Quinlan* [1964] AC 1054, [1964] 1 All ER 897, PC; *Miller v South of Scotland Electricity Board* (supra) (defendants liable to child trespasser when they carelessly disconnected electricity in a building about to be demolished so that a child suffered a shock from a live cable).

15   [1958] AC 240, [1957] 3 All ER 1, HL.

were employed to make an alteration to the front of part of a house. In the course of this work B Ltd failed to take reasonable care to make access to the house safe and R, a visitor, was injured when leaving the house in the hours of darkness. B Ltd were held liable in negligence.

Subsequent decisions found the original builders of a property liable for personal injury (or physical damage to other property) resulting from the negligent construction or repair of buildings both to subsequent occupiers and to their visitors.[16] Thus, if the defendant contractor negligently erects an unsafe roof which some time later collapses injuring the occupier and her dinner party guests, the victims have a claim against the contractor for those injuries. And if the collapse of the roof also smashes the windows in the next door property, the neighbours may also sue the contractor.

The fact that the contractor at the time of the erection of the property was also the landowner no longer affords him immunity from liability in negligence. Most of the content of the maxim caveat emptor in relation to sale of land in this context has now been eroded.

First, '[a] landowner who designs or builds a house or flat is no more immune from personal responsibility for faults of construction than a building contractor, or from personal responsibility than an architect, simply because he has disposed of his house or flat by selling or letting'.[17] But this principle covers only negligence in the original construction of the building, not inadequate repairs or maintenance by the original owner and vendor.

Section 3 of the Defective Premises Act goes further, providing that where 'work of construction, repair, maintenance or demolition or any other work is done on or in relation to premises, any duty of care owed because of the doing of the work to persons who might reasonably be expected to be affected by defects in the state of the premises by the doing of the work shall not be abated by the subsequent disposal of the premises by the person who owed the duty'. Thus, a botched job in repairing floorboards will create liability to visitors while the owner remains the occupier; and that liability will survive for the benefit of subsequent occupiers and their visitors when the owner sells or lets the house.

But section 3 is not comprehensive. It does not cover all possible sources of danger on premises, particularly those caused by omissions. Leaving dangerous refuse on premises and failing to remedy or warn the subsequent occupier of a ruinous defect existing before the vendor came into occupation are probably not covered by the words used in section 3, 'work of construction, repair, maintenance[18] or demolition or any other work'. Thus, the common law principle that there is no duty not to sell or let a ruinous house probably survives albeit in a much attenuated form. Only the House of Lords can finally take up Lord Denning's invitation in *Dutton v Bognor Regis UDC*[19] that the old cases should be overruled.[20]

It is suggested that today the crucial point is not whether the defendant contractor is or was the landowner, but what kind of damage resulted from his negligence. If actual physical injury to some person, or separate property, is inflicted as a consequence of his incompetence, that injury is likely to be recoverable just as it would be if the 'guilty' cause of the injury were a negligently manufactured chattel.[1]

16 *Gallagher v N McDowell Ltd* [1961] NI 26; *Sharpe v ET Sweeting & Sons Ltd* [1963] 2 All ER 455, [1963] 1 WLR 665.
17 *Rimmer v Liverpool City Council* [1984] 1 All ER 930 at 938, CA.
18 Could omissions to remove or repair pre-existing defects be caught by this word 'maintenance'?
19 [1972] 1 QB 373 at 394.
20 Eg, *Otto v Bolton and Norris* (supra).
1   See *Murphy v Brentwood District Council* [1990] 2 All ER 908, HL at 917 (per Lord Keith) at 925–6 (per Lord Bridge).

(C) BUILDERS AND CONTRACTORS: OTHER LOSS

As we have already observed, no duty of care will be imposed on a builder or contractor in respect of economic loss occasioned by negligent work of construction or repair, save where some special relationship is found to exist between him and the plaintiff. Thus, contractors and development companies owe no duty in tort in respect of financial losses occasioned to subsequent occupiers of property with whom they have no contractual relationship. Authority to the contrary – notably *Batty v Metropolitan Property Realisations Ltd*[2] and *Anns v Merton London Borough Council*[3] – has been overruled.

> In *D & F Estates Ltd v Church Comrs for England*,[4] the defendants were the builders of a block of flats of which the plaintiffs subsequently became the occupiers. Crumbling plasterwork caused by the defendants' negligence forced the plaintiffs to expend some considerable sums of money on repairs. The House of Lords found that the defendants were not liable for the plaintiffs' loss.

On analogy with liability for chattels, the defendants owed a duty to safeguard the plaintiffs against physical damage to persons or property caused by negligent construction of the property, but not against loss caused by a defect in the quality of the property itself. Damage to the property itself constituted a defect in quality – the property was not value for money. Recoverable physical damage must be occasioned to separate property. The House of Lords left open the question of the 'complex structure' of buildings. If a defect in the foundations threatens the structure of a particular flat in a block of flats, or a dwelling house threatens damages to the garden wall, is there damage to separate property?[5]

Some of the questions left open in *D & F Estates* are at least partially answered by the House of Lords in *Murphy v Brentwood District Council*.[6] *Murphy*, strictly speaking, relates to the liability of local authorities, but its applicability to builders and contractors was expressly confirmed in the short judgment in *Department of the Environment v Thomas Bates & Son Ltd*.[7] The plaintiff in *Murphy* had purchased from a construction company a semi-detached dwelling constructed on a concrete raft foundation over an in-filled site. Eleven years later the plaintiff noticed cracks in the house which proved to be caused by serious defects in the concrete raft. Repairs which were essential to make the house safe and habitable would have cost £45,000. The plaintiff could not afford that sum and had to sell the house for £35,000 less than he would have received but for the damage caused by the defective foundations. He sued the local council whom he alleged had negligently approved the plans for the foundations.

The House of Lords rejected his claim, classifying the damage he suffered as irrecoverable economic loss. The plaintiff argued that the nature of the damage to his home posed an immediate and imminent danger to his and his family's health and safety, and so ought to be classified as physical damage. The Law Lords unanimously rejected

---

2   [1978] QB 554, [1978] 2 All ER 445, CA.
3   [1978] AC 728, [1977] 2 All ER 492, HL.
4   [1989] AC 177, [1988] 2 All ER 992, HL.
5   Ibid per Lord Bridge at 1006–7.
6   [1991] 1 AC 398, [1990] 2 All ER 908.
7   [1991] 1 AC 499, [1990] 2 All ER 943, HL.

that contention.[8] Lord Bridge described the distinction between physical damage and financial loss in this way:[9]

> If a builder erects a structure containing a latent defect which renders it dangerous to persons or property, he will be liable in tort for injury to persons or property resulting from that dangerous defect. But, if the defect becomes apparent before any injury or damage has been caused, the loss sustained by the building owner is purely economic.

The effect of *Murphy* would seem to be this. Outside a contractual relationship, negligent construction (and presumably also repair and extension) of a building only results in liability if actual physical damage is caused to a person, or to property that is not part and parcel of the building. If defective foundations cause cracks in the walls or threaten damage to any fixture in the building installed by the defendant, the cost of remedying the damage is irrecoverable economic loss. By contrast, if A negligently installs a defective central heating boiler in a building erected by B and later bought and occupied by C, then that boiler explodes damaging the building, that loss is recoverable by C against A. A's negligence has caused actual damage to property quite separate from the inherently defective structure he installed. Lord Bridge, in *Murphy*, also suggested a new exception to refusal of recovery for economic loss. He opined that where the defect in the building requiring repair threatens damage to adjoining land or the highway:

> ... the building owner ought, in principle, to be entitled to recover in tort from the negligent builder the cost of demolition, so far as that cost is necessarily incurred in order to protect himself from potential liability to third parties.[10]

Consideration of the decision in *Murphy* prompts a number of questions.[11]
(1) Is it just to leave the occupier to bear the loss? Lord Keith maintained that in reality it was not ordinary home-owners who suffered. Disputes such as the one in *Murphy* were essentially quarrels between insurers.[12]
(2) Just how far can Lord Bridge's caveat concerning third party liability be stretched? If you may recover that economic loss occasioned by the need to ensure your crumbling house does not damage your neighbour's house or crash onto a passer-by on the highway, why may you not recover the loss occasioned by the need to ensure that you do not incur similar liability to your visitors?[13]
(3) Finally, is this the logical result of *Murphy*? You discover that your house has a latent defect which you have no funds to repair, three months later the ceiling falls in injuring you, your spouse and smashing the grand piano. Do you then recover for that loss and all its consequences or are you guilty of contributory negligence

---

8   In the Commonwealth courts the slavish adherence to the irrecoverability of economic loss caused by defective building work has been, to varying degrees, rejected. In Australia and New Zealand, the negligent builder enjoys no such immunity: *Bryan v Moloney* (1994) 128 ALR 163; *Invercargill City Council v Hamlin* [1994] 3 NZLR 513. In Canada, an intermediate position, depending on a threat to health and safety, has been adopted: *Winnipeg Condominium No 36 v Bird Construction Co* (1995) 121 DLR (4th) 513.
9   [1990] 2 All ER 908 at 926, HL.
10   [1990] 2 All ER 908, HL.
11   See Howarth 'Negligence after *Murphy* – Time to Re-think' (1991) 50 CLJ 58.
12   [1990] 2 All ER 908 at 923, HL. No evidence is advanced to support the proposition.
13   One difference is that I could of course 'obviate' that danger by having no visitors. Another is that I can reasonably warn my visitors but I cannot practically warn all passers-by who walk beneath a dangerous overhanging gable, for example.

for not minimising the loss you suffer, or for not rectifying the defect at your own expense?[14]

Leaving aside economic loss, it has also been held, in *Smith v Drumm*,[15] that builders are liable under section 1 of the 1972 Act if their work leaves the premises in a state that is not fit for habitation. In this case, the converted flat was left without either electricity or gas, and on that basis deemed to be unfit for habitation. Had the work simply been rectification work – instead of 'construction, conversion or enlargement (as per the Act) – no duty under section 1 would have been owed.[16]

(D)   PROFESSIONAL ADVISERS

The strict liability imposed by section 1 of the Defective Premises Act 1972 in respect of the construction of buildings is equally incumbent on architects and other professionals involved in the design of the building as upon the building contractors. Additionally those professionals owe a duty of care to any person who may be injured on the site in the course of the building work,[17] and to subsequent occupiers of the premises in respect of both their personal safety and damage to property separate from the original property itself. The reasoning in *Murphy* relating to builders applies equally to architects and engineers. The professional will not be liable in tort for economic loss arising from the defective nature of the building whether that cost is occasioned by the need to carry out repairs to make the building safe or diminution in the value of the property. On subsequent disposal of the premises, surveyors engaged to inspect the property will be liable for any failure to value the property competently or to discover and report on relevant defects in the property. Where the surveyor has been engaged by the building society contemplating financing the plaintiff's house purchase he will generally be liable, not only to his client (ie the society), but also to the purchasers where they have relied on his survey rather than commissioned an independent surveyor.[18] But where a surveyor is expressly commissioned only to value property he is not under any duty to report on defects generally or advise on possible difficulties with resale of the property.[19]

(E)   LOCAL AUTHORITIES

Local authorities owe duties to tenants and subsequent purchasers of local authority dwellings as builders and contractors. In *Rimmer v Liverpool County Council*[20] the defendants were held liable to a council tenant injuring himself when he fell against a negligently used, thin glass panel and the glass shattered.

14 For a partial answer see *Nitrigin Eireann Teoranta v Inco Alloys Ltd* [1992] 1 All ER 854. See also *Targett v Torfaen Borough Council* [1992] 3 All ER 27 (where one rents property, it may in some circumstances be unreasonable to expect a tenant to do repairs that the landlord is obliged to perform).
15 [1996] EGCS 192.
16 *Jacobs v Morton and Partners* (1994) 72 BLR 92.
17 In *Clay v A J Crump & Sons Ltd* [1964] 1 QB 533, [1963] 3 All ER 687, CA, an architect was held liable for directing a wall to be left standing during demolition whereupon it collapsed on the plaintiff who was working on the site. The court rejected the argument that the architect's only duty was his contractual one to his employer. This decision was followed in *Driver v William Willett (Contractors) Ltd* [1969] 1 All ER 665 (consulting engineer liable to workman for failing to advise builder about unsafe hoist which caused plaintiff's injuries).
18 *Smith v Eric S Bush* [1990] 1 AC 831, [1989] 2 All ER 514, HL.
19 *Sutcliffe v Sayer* [1987] 1 EGLR 155.
20 [1985] QB 1, [1984] 1 All ER 930, CA.

The decision of the House of Lords in *Murphy* removes from local authorities the greatest potential area of liability for defective premises. Local authorities are entrusted with the function of inspecting and approving all building work. Negligent exercise of these powers may result in local people purchasing and living in defective, even dangerous, property. *Murphy* makes clear that the local authority will not be liable in tort for any economic loss occasioned by the defects in the property. But would the authority be liable if actual injury was caused to a resident or his property – property not an integral part of the premises? The House of Lords contended that the builder would be so liable – but what if the builder has gone into liquidation? That question was left open by their Lordships.[1] In the current climate, where restrictions on the duty of care owed by public authorities are prevalent, even actual injury may be irrecoverable.[2] True, the purpose for which local authorities are granted inspection powers is to protect the health and welfare of local people.[3] But is this a duty owed to individuals or merely a collective public duty? And why should the local council be liable for what is, at bottom, the negligence of a third party, the builder?

(F) LANDLORDS

The liability of landlords for defects arising from disrepair on premises let by them was originally largely limited to contractual liability. A person other than the tenant had no remedy even if the landlord was in breach of a contractual duty to carry out maintenance and repairs. And like vendors, he owed no duty in respect of defects arising before the tenancy was granted. As we have seen, landlords are now liable just like anyone else for *their* negligent installations or repairs in premises let by them.[4] That tortious liability covers tenants, their families and others injured on the premises.

Section 4 of the Defective Premises Act established important duties in respect of landlords under an obligation[5] to carry out repairs or maintenance on the premises, or who are empowered to carry out repairs.[6] A landlord owes to all persons who might reasonably be expected to be affected by defects in the state of the premises a duty to take such care as is reasonable in all the circumstances to see that they are reasonably safe from personal injury or from damage to their property caused by relevant defects. The landlord is liable although he did not know of the defect, if he ought to have known of it.[7] A defect is relevant if it is one in the state of the premises arising from, or continuing because of, an act or omission by the landlord which constitutes or would, if he had had notice of the defect, have constituted a failure by him to carry out his obligation to

---

1   [1990] 2 All ER 908 at 912 and 917, HL.
2   See *Ephraim v Newham London Borough Council* (1992) 25 HLR 207, CA.
3   See the powerful arguments to this effect in the speech of Lord Wilberforce in *Anns v Merton London Borough Council* [1978] AC 728, [1977] 2 All ER 492, HL. Note *Anns* was only overruled as far as recovery for economic loss is in issue.
4   *Rimmer v Liverpool City Council* (supra). Where the defective work has been performed by a third party, however, the landlord remained immune at common law. Cf the position in Australia in respect of defects caused by another that were capable of reasonable discovery by the landlord: *Northern Sandblasting Pty Ltd v Harris* (1997) 71 ALJR 1428.
5   This includes statutory obligations.
6   Defective Premises Act 1972, s 4(4). This extension to the case where the tenant cannot legally insist on a repair but where the landlord has a power to repair is important in view of cases like *Mint v Good* [1951] 1 KB 517, [1950] 2 All ER 1159, CA, which decides that landlords of small houses let on periodic tenancies, have such a power. For application of this principle resulting in liability under the Act see *McAuley v Bristol City Council* [1992] QB 134, [1992] 1 All ER 749, CA.
7   Defective Premises Act 1972, s 4(2).

the tenant for the maintenance or repair of the premises.[8] The duty is wide; it extends to trespassers and those outside the premises. It also applies where the landlord merely has a right to enter to carry out maintenance or repairs.

The liability of non-occupiers for actual physical damage is now fairly extensive. Nonetheless, it is not yet by any means comprehensive. If an owner knows of a defect in his premises (not created by him) before he sells or lets them but neither repairs it nor gives warning of the defect, the Act imposes no liability on him for harm which results after he has disposed of them by sale or lease, and there is no liability at common law.[9] A landlord who fails to repair where he has no obligation or power to do so has no liability either under the Act or at common law.

8 Defective Premises Act 1972, s 4(3). Failures to remedy such defects are actionable, alternatively, on the basis of negligence *simpliciter*: *Targett v Torfaen Borough Council* [1992] 3 All ER 27.
9 *Cavalier v Pope* [1906] AC 428, HL; *Bromley v Mercer* [1922] 2 KB 126; *Davis v Foots* [1940] 1 KB 116, [1939] 4 All ER 4, CA (although because of housing legislation this case would now be decided differently; the principle is unaffected).

Invasions of interests in person and property where intentional or negligent conduct need not always be proved

CONTENTS

CHAPTERS   PAGE

17   Product liability   337
18   Nuisance   357
19   *Rylands v Fletcher*   395
20   Animals   413
21   Violation of interests protected by statute, or action for breach of
     statutory duty   417

The common element in the torts discussed in this Part is that a defendant who has not committed the act complained of either intentionally or negligently, and who is not merely being held accountable for the acts of an employee or an independent contractor, may nevertheless sometimes be liable for the tort. These are often called torts of 'strict liability'. As Lord Macmillan has observed, 'strict liability' is an ambiguous term.[1] Moreover, it suggests that there is some set of circumstances common to a series of torts where liability arises for acts which are neither intentional nor negligent:[2] it might even imply that, in this particular class of circumstances, the defendant is liable for all his acts. In fact, the rules differ from tort to tort – therefore the nature and extent of the liability in each of them must be considered separately.[3] 'Strict liability' cannot be assigned a constant meaning.

---

1   *Read v J Lyons & Co Ltd* [1947] AC 156 at 171, [1946] 2 All ER 471, HL.
2   Cf the view of Winfield [1931] CLJ 193-4 that it may be taken to mean liability for the torts of independent contractors, or of anyone except a stranger.
3   Cf Lord Porter in *Read v J Lyons*, supra, at 178.

Chapter 17

Product liability[1]

SECTION I. INTRODUCTION

The complex history of liability for loss or injury caused by defective products illustrates well the gradual development and changing perceptions of the role of the law of torts and its inter-relationship with the law of contract. The classical common law stance towards faulty or useless goods was caveat emptor (buyer beware). The individual buying goods was expected either to take steps to ensure that the goods were safe for use and value for money, or to make contractual arrangements which would provide him with a remedy should the goods prove to be defective. If he failed to protect himself, any loss would lie where it fell, with him. In 1893 Parliament intervened to give protection to purchasers of goods via the first Sale of Goods Act. Conditions were implied into contracts of sale that goods should be merchantable and, if the purpose for which the goods were bought had been made known to the retailer, the goods must be fit for that purpose. Where goods had been bought by the person to whom they occasioned loss or injury, the burden of liability shifted to the retailer.

The Sale of Goods Act 1893 offered comfort only to the purchasers of goods. A person suffering food poisoning from contaminated tinned fish bought for him by someone else was not assisted by that legislation. But in 1932 in *Donoghue v Stevenson*,[2] the House of Lords held that the ultimate user of a product might in certain circumstances have an action in negligence against the manufacturers of a product causing injury to his person or his property. The liability of manufacturers in negligence in respect of defective products developed gradually over the next 50 years. Parliament intervened to strengthen the contractual rights of purchasers of goods[3] and services[4] with increasingly interventionist consumer protection laws.[5] And in respect of certain types of goods the criminal law was invoked to protect safety standards, and an action for breach of statutory duty[6] was expressly created to allow individuals injured by goods

---

1   See generally Stapleton *Product Liability* (London: Butterworths, 1994).
2   [1932] AC 562, [1932] All ER Rep 1, HL.
3   See the Sale of Goods Act 1979.
4   See the Supply of Goods and Services Act 1982 (as amended by the Sale and Supply of Goods Act 1994) and note also the Unfair Contract Terms Act 1977.
5   Domestic consumer protection legislation has been strengthened further by the 1993 European Directive on Unfair Terms in Consumer Contracts.
6   Consumer Protection Act 1961, s 3 and Consumer Safety Act 1978, s 6; both these provisions are now repealed and replaced by the Consumer Protection Act 1987, s 41.

in the specified categories to recover compensation from the manufacturers without recourse to an action in negligence.

Thus it can be seen that by 1987 little survived of the principle of caveat emptor. The social climate which gave birth to that principle had altered. The conditions in which goods are manufactured and marketed had changed so as to make unrealistic the underlying assumption that a prudent individual could, if he wished, ensure he got a fair bargain. But the plethora of potential remedies remained confusing and discriminated between purchasers and other users. The difficulty of proving negligence became especially problematic in relation to products. Throughout the 1970s several official bodies[7] advocated that manufacturers should be made strictly liable for defective products. It was considered that where a product carried some inherent risk of injury that risk should be borne by the manufacturer who put the product on the market. He benefits by the enterprise; he should bear its burdens. Moreover, while for every individual to insure himself against any form of personal accident would be costly and impracticable for many members of our community, it was said that manufacturers could simply and conveniently insure against liability or, where necessary, pass the cost on to the consumer.

The final victory for proponents of strict liability was won in Europe. On 25 July 1985 the Council of the European Communities issued a Directive[8] requiring member states to implement a regime of strict liability for defective products. The UK Government responded by enacting the Consumer Protection Act 1987. The Act applies only to goods put on the market after March 1988, but both the Directive and the Act leave existing actions in respect of defective products unaffected. Contractual claims against the retailer, the action in negligence and, where appropriate, actions for breach of statutory duty, remain available side by side with the new rules on strict liability. The Act is further limited in its effect in that it provides only for claims in relation to personal injury and damage to private property. Damage to business property and economic loss resulting from defective products are outside the new regime of strict liability. Tragically for advocates of strict liability the UK Government exercised its option to provide for a 'development risks' defence to strict liability claims by consumers[9] whereby manufacturers who can prove that the state of scientific and technical knowledge at the time the product was put on the market was not such that they could be expected to have discovered the relevant defect, are exempt from liability. We shall have to see, therefore, whether the effect of the introduction of strict liability does more in reality than simply reverse the burden of proof demanded by common law negligence.

SECTION 2.   CONSUMER PROTECTION AND THE CHANGING COMMON LAW

(A)   THE LIMITATIONS OF CONTRACT

The primary means invoked to protect consumers against faulty goods was the law of contract. The original Sale of Goods Act 1893 has now been replaced by the Sale of

7   See Law Commission Report on Liability for Defective Products (1977) Law Com No 82, Cmnd 6381; Strasbourg Convention on Products Liability in regard to Personal Injury and Death 1977 (reproduced as Annex A in Law Com No 82); Royal Commission on Civil Liability and Compensation for Personal Injury (Pearson Report) (1978) Cmnd 7054, Vol 1.
8   85/374/EEC. On the implementation of the Directive in the EC generally see Kelly and Attree *Product Liability in Europe* (1992).
9   See s 4(1)(e) of the Consumer Protection Act 1987 discussed post.

Goods Act 1979 (itself amended by the Sale and Supply of Goods Act 1994). It is that 1979 Act (as amended) which now incorporates into every contract of sale terms of satisfactory quality[10] and fitness for purpose.[11] Identical terms are implied into any contract for services in the course of which goods are supplied by the Supply of Goods and Services Act 1982.[12] Thus, if in the course of private dental treatment a dentist provides her patient with dentures which crumble within the week, it matters not whether any contract of sale for the dentures exist. She clearly had a contract for services with the dentist and she supplied her with dentures that were not of satisfactory quality. Terms implied into contracts of sale or service by virtue of the 1979 and 1982 Acts cannot be excluded against the consumer.[13]

The protection given by statute to purchasers is thus considerable. The liability is strict. It is irrelevant that the retailer is in no way to blame for the defect and may lack any opportunity to discover the defect. Nor is it limited to protection against injury to person or property. Satisfactory quality is defined as meeting 'the standard that a reasonable person would regard as satisfactory taking into account any description of the goods, the price (if relevant) and all the other relevant circumstances'. So, providing you buy your own electric blanket, you can sue the retailer both if it is not of satisfactory quality because it is faultily wired and you suffer an electric shock and if it is useless and fails to heat your bed.

The limitations on the effectiveness of contract as a means of general consumer protection against defective goods arise from the rules of privity of contract.[14] A person who is not a party to a contract cannot benefit from that contract. So if your mother bought your electric blanket and gave it to you as a present, you cannot sue the retailer in contract if it proves to be faulty. Equally, where you purchase the faulty blanket yourself, if the retailer has gone out of business, you have no claim in contract against the wholesalers or the manufacturers. Vertical privity denies you the benefit of conditions of merchantability and fitness for purpose in the first example where you have no contract with the retailer. Horizontal privity denies me a remedy in contract where your contract with the retailer is practically valueless.

A number of devices have occasionally been used to evade the consequences of rules of privity. In *Lockett v Charles*[15] a husband and wife took a meal together in a restaurant. The husband ordered the food and paid the bill. The wife contracted food poisoning from contaminated food. The court held that the husband acted as his wife's agent and contracted on her behalf. Thus she could sue on the contract for the food. But the circumstances which allow an inference of agency will be strictly limited. A mother buying goods for her child cannot be said to act as the child's agent. She may be able to recover any loss to her caused by injury to the child. So if a small child is scalded by a faulty hot water bottle purchased by his mother, the mother may sue on her contract with the retailer.[16] She will recover the cost to her of caring for her injured child, but the child will be unable to recover in contract for his pain and suffering. Any action by the child must lie in negligence, breach of statutory duty, or under the Consumer Protection Act 1987 against the manufacturers.

---

10   Section 14(2)A.
11   Section 14(3).
12   Section 4.
13   Unfair Contract Terms Act 1977, s 6; Supply of Goods and Services Act 1982, s 13.
14   See *Cheshire, Fifoot and Furmston's Law of Contract* (12th edn) ch 14.
15   *Lockett v A & M Charles Ltd* [1938] 4 All ER 170.
16   See *Preist v Last* [1903] 2 KB 148.

(B)   THE ACTION FOR NEGLIGENCE

The development of liability in negligence for defective goods enjoyed a chequered history in the nineteenth century. In *Dixon v Bell*,[17] a master who entrusted a loaded gun to his young servant was found liable to a third party injured by the servant firing the gun on the ground that the goods 'were in a state capable of doing mischief'. The court in *Langridge v Levy*[18] declined an invitation to deduce from *Dixon v Bell* a general principle for putting into circulation things 'of a dangerous nature'. In *Winterbottom v Wright*,[19] the driver of a coach was seriously injured as a result of a defect in the coach. His action against the defendant who supplied his employers with coaches and horses failed. The court held that as the plaintiff had no contract with the defendant, the defendant owed him no duty in respect of the coach's calamitous state of disrepair. It was, and remains, correct that the plaintiff could not take advantage of express terms in the contract as to the repair and maintenance of the coach. What the court in *Winterbottom v Wright* failed to analyse was the possibility of a separate and independent obligation arising within the tort of negligence.

Case law between 1851 and 1932 continued to deny or ignore any general duty to take care in the manufacture and distribution of goods, but to create exceptional cases where a duty did lie. Liability was eventually recognised in respect of goods 'dangerous in themselves',[1] in respect of known defects of which no warning of the defect was given by the supplier.[2] And occupiers were held liable to their invitees in respect of appliances on their premises which proved to be defective.[3] The boundaries of these instances of liability for defects were unclear and the need to prove knowledge of the defect in the second category was often fatal to the success of a claim.

The decision of the House of Lords in *Donoghue v Stevenson*[4] heralded a new age.

> D drank a bottle of ginger beer, manufactured by S, which a friend bought from a retailer and gave to her. The bottle allegedly contained the decomposed remains of a snail which were not, and could not be, detected (as the bottle was opaque) until the greater part of the contents of the bottle was consumed. She alleged that she was ill as a result, and sued S. The House of Lords had to decide whether these averments disclosed a cause of action, and they found for the plaintiff by a majority of 3 to 2.

Lord Atkin first discussed the difficulties of finding a general principle of negligence in English law, and then set forth that doctrine of duty to one's neighbour which has already been examined.[5] He then considered the cases which might seem to stand in the way of the plaintiff's winning, and found that all could be distinguished, either because the relationship of the parties was so much more distant that no duty arose, or because the dicta went further than was necessary for the determination of the particular issues. He then concluded that, by finding for the plaintiff, the following proposition was being enunciated:[6]

---

17   (1816) 5 M & S 198.
18   (1837) 2 M & W 519. The court nevertheless found for the plaintiff on the ground of fraud.
19   (1842) 10 M & W 109.
1   See *Longmeid v Holliday* (1851) 6 Exch 761.
2   *Heaven v Pender* (1883) 11 QBD 503 at 517, CA; *Clarke v Army and Navy Co-operative Society* [1903] 1 KB 155, CA.
3   *Heaven v Pender*, supra.
4   [1932] AC 562, HL.
5   See ch 11 ante.
6   [1932] AC 562 at 599, HL. This proposition will henceforth be called the 'narrow rule' in the case and the 'neighbour principle', the broad rule.

a manufacturer of products, which he sells in such form as to show that he intends them to reach the ultimate consumer in the form in which they left him with no reasonable possibility of intermediate examination, and with the knowledge that the absence of reasonable care in the preparation or putting up of the products will result in an injury to the consumer's life or property, owes a duty to the consumer to take that reasonable care.

Lord Thankerton found for the plaintiff on the ground that the manufacturer in cases like this brought himself into such a direct relationship with the consumer that a duty of care was imported. Lord Macmillan also distinguished earlier cases, stressed that the categories of negligence could be extended, and held that there was a duty of care towards the intended consumer on the part of those who manufacture food and drink intended for consumption by members of the public in the form in which he issued them.

Donoghue v Stevenson has since been extended in its range of application to goods. The principles of negligence derived from that decision remain of the utmost importance even after the introduction by the Consumer Protection Act of strict liability for defective products. They must be examined carefully and the following matters considered:

1   Are there persons who may be liable in negligence in respect of defective goods who would not be classified as 'producers', who are under the Act the categories of persons classified as liable for the purposes of strict liability?
2   Are there kinds of loss remediable in negligence but not under the Act?
3   What is the nature of the special limitation rules under the Act?
4   How radical a departure from common law negligence is the strict liability regime introduced by the 1987 Act?

(1)   THE NARROW RULE IN *DONOGHUE V STEVENSON* – DEFECTIVE PRODUCTS

It will be recalled that Lord Atkin stated the 'narrow rule' as follows:

> ... a *manufacturer of products*, which he sells in such a form as to show that he intends them to reach the *ultimate consumer* in the form in which they left him with no reasonable possibility of intermediate examination and with the knowledge that the absence of reasonable care in *the preparation or putting up* of the products will result in an injury to the consumer's *life or property*, owes a duty to the consumer to take that reasonable care.

The courts have not been content to keep within this definition: the italicised key words have been extended in later cases; sometimes the liability in respect of products has been increased, not by a liberal interpretation of these key phrases, but rather by having recourse to the broad rule in *Donoghue v Stevenson*.

(2)   RANGE OF DEFENDANTS

Lord Atkin imposed liability on manufacturers. Later case law extended liability to, among others, assemblers[7] and repairers[8] and to suppliers of drinking water.[9] Suppliers of goods, whether retailers or wholesalers, have been held liable where their function went beyond mere distribution. For example, a car dealer selling vehicles reconditioned by him,[10] and a retail chemist[11] failing to observe the manufacturers' instructions to test the product

---

7   *Malfroot v Noxal Ltd* (1935) 51 TLR 551 (fitting sidecar).
8   *Haseldine v C A Daw & Son Ltd* [1941] 2 KB 343, CA (lift repairer).
9   *Read v Croydon Corpn* [1938] 4 All ER 631; *Barnes v Irwell Valley Water Board* [1939] 1 KB 21, [1938] 2 All ER 650, CA.
10 *Herschtal v Stewart and Ardern Ltd* [1940] 1 KB 155, [1939] 4 All ER 123.
11 *Kubach v Hollands* [1937] 3 All ER 907.

before labelling it, were both found liable to injured users. Indeed, wherever the circumstances are such that a supplier would normally be expected to check a product, then a duty to do so may be imposed. Second-hand car dealers will be expected to check the steering on used cars.[12] Wholesalers who fail to test for themselves a hair dye of dubious provenance will be held negligent.[13]

A number of categories of persons owing a duty of care will also be categorised as 'producers' for the purposes of strict liability but by no means all are. For example, in the case of suppliers failing to carry out tests their strict liability may, as we shall see, be discharged simply by naming the person who supplied the goods to them. Producers of primary agricultural produce are excluded from the strict liability regime altogether. And repairers are beyond the scope of the new rules as well.

(3) PRODUCTS

'Products' includes today not only food and drink[14] but quite clearly any product in normal domestic use. Underwear,[15] hair dye,[16] motor cars,[17] computer software,[18] houses[19] and installations in,[20] and staircases outside[1] houses have all been treated as proper subjects of a duty of care.[2] Pre-*Donoghue v Stevenson* distinctions[3] between products 'dangerous in themselves' and other goods can now be largely disregarded.[4] The distinction remains relevant only in that the greater the potential danger inherent in a product the more stringent the precaution to protect the user against those dangers must be.[5]

(4) ULTIMATE CONSUMER

It follows from what has been said about products that 'consumer' now covers any user of products. The child scalded by the faulty hot water bottle purchased by her mother can sue in negligence. But less obvious persons at risk may also be within the scope of the manufacturers' duty. In *Barnett v H and J Packer & Co*,[6] the proprietor of a sweet shop was injured by a piece of metal protruding from a sweet. He recovered

---

12 *Andrews v Hopkinson* [1957] 1 QB 229, [1956] 3 All ER 422; and see *Fisher v Harrods Ltd* [1966] 1 Lloyd's Rep 500 (defendant retailer liable to donee of customer for harm to eyes caused by a jewellery cleaning fluid).
13 *Watson v Buckley, Osborne Garrett & Co Ltd* [1940] 1 All ER 174.
14 *Barnes v Irwell Water Board*, supra (water).
15 *Grant v Australian Knitting Mills Ltd* [1936] AC 85, PC.
16 *Watson v Buckley, Osborne, Garrett & Co Ltd,* supra.
17 *Herschtal v Stewart and Ardern Ltd*, supra
18 *St Albans City Council v International Computers Ltd* [1996] 4 All ER 481.
19 *Anns v Merton London Borough Council* [1978] AC 728, [1977] 2 All ER 492 and 758-9, HL; *Batty v Metropolitan Property Realisations Ltd* [1978] QB 554 (land and fixtures on land – ie houses – are not subjected to the new strict liability rules).
20 *Haseldine v C A Daw Son Ltd* [1941] 2 KB 343, [1941] 3 All ER 156, CA.
1   *Targett v Torfaen Borough Council* [1992] 3 All ER 27.
2   See generally Miller *Product Liability and Safety Encyclopedia.*
3   See *Dominion Natural Gas Co Ltd v Collins and Perkins* [1909] AC 640, PC.
4   See *Billings (AC) & Sons Ltd v Riden* [1958] AC 240, [1957] 3 All ER 1, HL.
5   But that must not be construed as a rule distinct from negligence that there is a separate class of dangerous things which the defendant must keep safe at his peril. See *Read v J Lyons & Co Ltd* [1947] AC 156 at 172-3, [1946] 2 All ER 471, HL per Lord Macmillan.
6   [1940] 3 All ER 575; cf *Mason v Williams and Williams Ltd* [1955] 1 All ER 808 (manufacturers of chisel liable to the plaintiff when a splinter flew off the negligently made chisel supplied to the plaintiff's employers by them and injured his eye).

damages from the sweet's manufacturers. And in *Stennett v Hancock and Peters*[7] a bystander was held to be within the rule in *Donoghue v Stevenson*.

> The defendant garage owner negligently reassembled the flange on the wheel of X's lorry. When, later, X was driving the lorry on the highway, the flange came off the lorry, mounted the pavement and injured the plaintiff, a pedestrian. The defendant was held liable for his negligent repair.

(5) SALE

There seems no reason why the rule should not apply even where there is no sale of goods distributed in the course of business, for example free samples provided by manufacturers.[8] The liability for goods supplied in a domestic or social context is more disputable. Would a housewife who baked a fish pie for a charity fair be liable to the family who bought it and ate the pie and succumbed to food poisoning? Would she be liable to her own children who ate the pie's twin for their tea?[9]

(6) INTERMEDIATE EXAMINATION

> ... *which he sells in such a form as to show that he intends them to reach the ultimate consumer in the form in which they left him with no reasonable possibility of intermediate examination.*

If the rule is to apply, 'the customer must use the article exactly as it left the maker, that is in all material features, and use it as it was intended to be used'.[10] The effect of intermediate examination seems to be this: if someone in the place of the manufacturer would reasonably contemplate that the defect in the goods would remain there at the time of their use by the plaintiff despite their passing through the hands of intermediaries, he is still liable.[11] The test is not whether intermediate examination is possible.[12]

This test with respect to goods is stricter than that for the general conception of negligence under the 'neighbour principle'. In *Clay v A J Crump & Sons Ltd*[13] the facts were as follows.

> Under the supervision of the defendant architect, demolition contractors were demolishing a building, and builders were to construct a new one. On his advice a wall was left standing on the site. It subsequently fell on the plaintiff, an employee of the builders.

---

7 [1939] 2 All ER 578.
8 See *Hawkins v Coulsdon and Purley UDC* [1954] 1 QB 319 at 333, [1954] 1 All ER 97, CA per Denning LJ.
9 The 'narrow rule' in *Donoghue v Stevenson* is probably inapplicable to gratuitous transfers. There are cases where liability has been established in respect of dangers known to the transferor: see *Hodge & Sons v Anglo-American Oil Co* (1922) 12 Ll L Rep 183; and see *Hurley v Dyke* [1979] RTR 265, HL. Where the defect is not known to the transferor there seems no reason in principle why the 'broad rule' should not apply to impose liability on a gratuitous transferor. What would be the standard of care demanded of the housewife in the example in the text?
10 *Grant v Australian Knitting Mills Ltd* [1936] AC 85 at 104, PC.
11 Ibid at 105; *Haseldine v C A Daw & Co Ltd* [1941] 2 KB 343 at 376, CA. And see *Nitrigin Eireann Teoranta v Inco Alloys* [1992] 1 All ER 854 (fractured pipe would not have been discovered with reasonable care).
12 *Dransfield v British Insulated Cables Ltd* [1937] 4 All ER 382, which is to the contrary, is to be regarded as wrongly decided. It would appear from *Vacwell Engineering Co Ltd v BHD Chemicals Ltd* [1971] 1 QB 88, [1969] 3 All ER 1681 that in other respects the rules of remoteness for this tort are the same as in the general law of negligence.
13 [1964] 1 QB 533, [1963] 3 All ER 687, CA.

The defendant pleaded that the demolition and building contractors and their employees had the opportunity of intermediate examination. This was held to be a case not of the narrow products rule but of the broad principle, so that the intermediate examination principle did not apply to defeat the plaintiff's claim against the architect.

(7) PREPARATION OR PUTTING UP

The defect may be in the design[14] or in the container and, probably, in the labelling of the package.[15]

(8) CONTINUING DUTY OF CARE

What if the product when first put on the market was not manufactured with any lack of care? At that time, on all the reasonably available evidence, the manufacturers could have discovered no defect in their product, but later evidence of risks to person or property posed by a latent defect becomes available. Do the manufacturers owe any duty

a   to attempt to recall the goods, and

b   to warn affected consumers of the danger?

It is clear beyond doubt that even though originally the design of a product may have complied with all due care, once a design defect becomes patent the manufacturer is liable in negligence if he continues to produce and market the unsafe product.[16] In respect of unsafe products already in circulation, a continuing duty of care is owed to do whatever is reasonable to recall the defective product and warn users of the risk the defect may pose to their health and/or property.[17] As regards the duty to warn, it may be sufficient, according to Canadian authority, if the manufacturer passes the warning on to the doctor who supplied the patient with the product rather than warning the patient herself.[18] So far as the duty to recall the product goes, it is clear that the recall procedure must itself be conducted non-negligently if further liability is to be avoided.[19]

(9) ECONOMIC LOSS

The duty of care in respect of defective products remains, in general, limited to a duty to avoid inflicting injury to the ultimate consumer's life or property.[20] Economic loss occasioned by defective goods, whether it takes the form of wasted expenditure on the useless product itself, or loss of profits caused by the defective product not doing the job for which it was acquired, is irrecoverable in the tort of negligence save in the most exceptional circumstances.[1]

---

14 *Hindustan Steam Shipping Co Ltd v Siemens Bros & Co Ltd* [1955] 1 Lloyd's Rep 167.

15 *Kubach v Hollands* [1937] 3 All ER 907.

16 *Wright v Dunlop Rubber Co Ltd* (1972) 13 KIR 255, CA.

17 *Hobbs (Farms) v Baxenden Chemicals* [1992] 1 Lloyd's Rep 54; *Walton v British Leyland UK Ltd* (1978) Times, 13 July; see Miller & Lovell *Product Liability and Safety Encyclopedia*; *Rivtow Marine Ltd v Washington Ironworks* (1974) 40 DLR (3d) 530 (Canada).

18 *Dow Corning v Hollis* (1995) 129 DLR (4th) 609.

19 *McCain Foods Ltd v Grand Falls Industries Ltd* (1991) 80 DLR (4th) 252.

20 The property damage must arise from a use to which the defendant might reasonably have expected the property to be put. There was no liability where waterproofing compound was lost when pails manufactured by the defendant melted in the intense heat of Kuwait: *Aswan Engineering Establishment Co v Lupdine Ltd* [1987] 1 All ER 135, [1987] 1 WLR 1, CA.

1   *Simaan General Contracting Co v Pilkington Glass Ltd (No 2)* [1988] QB 758, [1988] 1 All ER 791, CA.

In *Junior Books Ltd v Veitchi Co Ltd*,[2] the plaintiffs recovered damages for their wasted expenditure on defective flooring laid by the defendants and additionally recovered for their loss of profits during the time that their business was disrupted while a new floor was being laid. The defendants were sub-contractors expressly nominated for the task by the plaintiffs because of their expertise and reputation as flooring specialists. The House of Lords held that:

a   the broad neighbour principle in *Donoghue v Stevenson* was applicable to economic loss as much as to injury to persons or property, and

b   the very close relationship between the parties in *Junior Books* gave rise to a duty of care to avoid defects in the product likely to result in financial loss.

Subsequent decisions of the House of Lords have declared *Junior Books* to be a case to be confined to its own 'special facts'.[3] That is judicial shorthand for declaring a previous decision to be largely wrong. But *Junior Books* on those 'special facts' has not been expressly overruled. Proposition (a) that the 'neighbour principle' in *Donoghue v Stevenson* applies to economic loss clearly has been overruled. Otherwise the current position is this. Economic loss, whether it be wasted expenditure on the product or loss of profits, is generally irrecoverable in tort.[4] The manufacturer is not subject to a warranty of quality save in contract. Where a product conceals a latent defect capable of causing injury to persons or separate property, if that defect is discovered prior to the risk of injury materialising, the loss occasioned to the user in the costs of repairing or jettisoning the product still constitutes irrecoverable economic loss.[5] The only possible exception would be if the damage to the item in question was not due to a fault in an integral part of that product but instead in a separate item, made by a third party, that had been incorporated into it. This is the so-called 'complex structure' exception which was applied in *Jacobs v Moreton and Partners*[6] where D constructed faulty foundations to remedy the existing defects in the foundations of P's property. There had always been problems with the foundations but the further damage to P's property was attributable to the defects in D's 'remedial' foundations.[7]

(10) PROVING NEGLIGENCE

The scope of liability for negligent manufacture, distribution and repair evolved from the rule in *Donoghue v Stevenson* can thus be seen to be considerable. It is in the formidable task of proving negligence in the narrow sense that plaintiffs confront the greatest difficulty. In the classic application of the narrow rule in *Donoghue v Stevenson* – where the ultimate consumer is suing the man at the far end of the chain, the manufacturer – it is often verging on impossible to prove by direct evidence absence of reasonable care. The consumer's difficulties may be compounded by problems of causation especially, for example in claims relating to drug induced injury. Yet the burden of proof remains with the plaintiff. Lord Macmillan said in *Donoghue v Stevenson*:[8]

2   [1983] 1 AC 520, [1982] 3 All ER 201, HL.
3   See ch 12 ante.
4   *Murphy v Brentwood District Council* [1991] 1 AC 398, [1990] 2 All ER 908, HL; *Simaan General Contracting Co v Pilkington Glass Ltd (No 2)* [1988] QB 758, [1988] 1 All ER 791, CA; *Muirhead v Industrial Tank Specialities Ltd* [1986] QB 507, [1985] 3 All ER 705, CA; *Aswan Engineering Establishment Co v Lupdine Ltd* [1987] 1 All ER 135, [1987] 1 WLR 1, CA.
5   *Murphy v Brentwood District Council*, supra.
6   (1994) 72 BLR 92.
7   But note that the decision in *Jacobs v Moreton* has since been doubted, obiter, in *The Orjula* [1995] 2 Lloyd's Rep 395.
8   [1932] AC 562 at 622, HL.

The burden of proof must always be upon the injured party to establish that the defect which caused the injury was present in the article when it left the hands of the party whom he sues, that the defect was occasioned by the carelessness of that party ... There is no presumption of negligence in such a case at present, nor is there any justification for applying the maxim res ipsa loquitur.

The Privy Council modified this unbending approach in *Grant v Australian Knitting Mills Ltd*[9] where the plaintiff was concerned to prove that the dermatitis he contracted was caused by the presence of invisible excess sulphites in the underwear that he purchased which was made by the defendants. It was explained that the test was whether, on the balance of probabilities, it was a reasonable inference to be drawn from the evidence that the harm was so caused.[10] On the issue of negligence, it was said:[11]

if excess sulphites were left in the garment, that could only be because someone was at fault. The appellant is not required to lay his finger on the exact person in all the chain[12] who was responsible, or to specify what he did wrong. Negligence is found as a matter of inference from the existence of the defects taken in connection with all the known circumstances ...

This approach is eminently practical and good law,[13] and is to be preferred to the obiter dicta of Lord Macmillan, in so far as the two are in conflict.[14] Where the presence of the defect in combination with the known circumstances gives rise to an inference of negligence against the manufacturers the burden shifts to the defendant to rebut that inference. That may be done either by pinpointing the exact cause giving rise to the defect and establishing that it does not arise from any want of care, or by the manufacturer producing evidence as to his system and establishing that the system was consistent with all due care. In *Daniels and Daniels v R White & Sons Ltd*,[15] the plaintiff was seriously injured when he drank lemonade containing a large quantity of carbolic acid. The acid presumably came from the washing process used by the defendant manufacturer. The judge accepted evidence of the precautions taken by the defendants to avoid such a contingency and found that the plaintiffs had failed to prove negligence.

The problems faced by the plaintiff are compounded where the relevant defect is not a construction defect but a design defect. Construction defects occur where the product properly put together and packaged is harmless. But, as we have seen, a number of products are wrongly constructed: for example, a snail got into ginger beer, carbolic acid got into lemonade. Design defects occur where the basic design of the product proves to be inherently dangerous. Because it follows that with a construction defect something has gone wrong which normally does not go wrong, construction defects allow the possibility of the court inferring negligence. By contrast, an inference of negligence in respect of a design defect is impossible. The plaintiff has to prove that:

a   the manufacturer should have been aware of the risk of the defect, and
b   he could reasonably have avoided the defect.

---

9   [1936] AC 85, PC.
10 Ibid, at 96-7.
11 Ibid, at 101.
12 What if the plaintiff does not know whether the negligence is that of the manufacturer, the bottler, the wholesaler, the carrier or the retailer?
13 For a lucid and similar explanation of the burden of proof see *Mason v Williams and Williams* [1955] 1 All ER 808 at 810, CA per Finnemore LJ.
14 This was exactly the approach of the House of Lords in the Scottish case of *Lockhart v Barr* 1943 SC 1 where the purchaser of aerated water contaminated with phenol recovered from the manufacturer although he could not prove how the phenol came to be in the aerated water.
15 [1938] 4 All ER 258.

The issue all too often becomes one of whether at the time that the product was put on the market scientific and technical knowledge available to the manufacturer should have enabled him to have identified the danger.

The classic example of the difficulties posed in proving negligence can be found in the thalidomide case. All over the world children whose mothers had taken the drug thalidomide were born with serious deformities. But at the time the drug was first marketed embryology was a little understood science. Whether or not drugs crossed the placental barrier was not then known. Animal tests for risks to the foetus were far from routine and their usefulness was disputed.[16] An action in negligence required parents to prove that in the state of scientific knowledge at the time of marketing the drug, before the tragic births of the thalidomide babies taught us all an unforgettable lesson, the manufacturers should have recognised the risk. They had to make their case in the dark. Every attempt to gain discovery of records of tests and expert reports was fought to the last degree. The thalidomide tragedy became the spur for those who advocated reform of the law.[17]

(11)   PROVING CAUSATION

The next problem faced by the plaintiff is that of proving causation. Normally, this is done in the usual way in accordance with the 'but for' test.[18] But in relation to certain types of product – especially pharmaceutical products – great difficulties can arise. In the case of such products the plaintiff will necessarily already be suffering from some form of illness. Where the plaintiff's condition deteriorates or he suffers the onset of another, related illness, the question is whether the drug caused the worsened condition or whether it would have happened in any event. Similarly, it is one thing to allege that a drug has caused injurious side-effects, it is another to prove that it has done so. Thus, in *Loveday v Renton*[19] the action failed because it could not be proved, on the balance of probabilities, that the plaintiff's brain damage had been caused by the administration of the pertussis vaccine. And this was despite the fact that it was known that the pertussis vaccine *could* cause brain damage in children.

This is not to say that causation can never be established in such cases. In *Best v Wellcome Foundation Ltd*,[20] for example, the Irish Supreme Court held that causation could be inferred on the basis of common sense from the fact that the first sign of the plaintiff's brain damage followed closely on the heels of the administration of the pertussis vaccine. In such an instance, it was held, there was no other plausible explanation of its cause. It satisfied the balance of probabilities threshold.

(C)   ACTION FOR BREACH OF STATUTORY DUTY

Before moving on to examine the outcome of the campaign to reform the general law of product liability by introducing strict liability, brief mention must be made of the possibility of an action for breach of statutory duty in respect of certain limited categories of goods. Since 1961, the Secretary of State has had power to make safety regulations prescribing detailed rules as to, among other things, the design, manufacture and

16 For an account of the legal issues arising from the thalidomide tragedy see Teff and Munro *Thalidomide: The Legal Aftermath* (1976).
17 While very difficult to establish negligence in relation to a design defect it is not impossible: see *Independent Broadcasting Authority v EMI Electronics and BICC Construction Ltd* (1980) 14 BLR 1.
18 See ch 14, ante.
19 [1990] 1 Med LR 117.
20 [1994] 5 Med LR 81.

packaging of specified classes of goods.[1] The minister's powers are now provided for by Part II of the Consumer Protection Act 1987. Breach of safety regulations is a criminal offence but section 4 of the 1987 Act expressly provides that an individual injured by a breach of regulations has an action for breach of statutory duty. The regulations cover only a limited class of goods and the action for damages lies only where the defect in the goods derives from breach of the regulations and is subject to the defence of due diligence provided for by section 39. There are no reported decisions on the action for breach of safety regulations provided for by earlier consumer protection legislation.

SECTION 3. THE STRICT LIABILITY REGIME

(A) THE EUROPEAN DIRECTIVE AND THE CONSUMER PROTECTION ACT 1987

It can be seen then that where no contractual remedy was available to an English plaintiff injured by a defective product he confronted formidable difficulties in establishing negligence, and where no negligence could be proved the loss continued to lie where it fell. The inequity of leaving the person least well equipped to bear, or protect himself against, the loss, and lack of any logical reason for discriminating between purchasers of goods and other users convinced all those august bodies[2] who reviewed liability for products that strict liability should extend to manufacturers as well as retailers and that any user of the product should be able to invoke strict liability against the manufacturer.

Industry was unsurprisingly generally less enthusiastic about calls for reform. It was strenuously argued[3] that while individual consumers who suffered injury from defective products might benefit from the introduction of strict liability, consumers as a whole would be adversely affected by such a change. The cost of products would rise to cover increased insurance premiums required by the need to insure against strict liability. The variety of goods available would decrease, limiting consumer choice of goods. Companies would protect themselves by sticking to well-known and well-tried products and not take risks with minor variations. Finally, and most cogently, it was contended that research and technological innovation in England would be seriously impeded. Risk is an inextricable component of new developments on the frontiers of knowledge. If companies had to bear the risk of some unknown defect themselves, rather than leaving it with the unfortunate victims, they would simply shut down on research and development. British industry would suffer.

Only when the new rules have been in force for some considerable time can we evaluate whether the gloomy forecasts of sections of industry were correct. Two important features of the implementation of strict liability must be borne in mind. First, the regime provided for in the Consumer Protection Act 1987 derives from the European Community Directive of 12 July 1985.[4] Although the Directive allows for some variation

---

1 The original statutory powers (contained in the Consumer Protection Act 1961, s 3) have been repealed and replaced by the Consumer Protection Act 1987, s 41. Note that it is only breach of specific safety regulations which gives rise to an action for breach of statutory duty and not infringement of the new general safety duty provided for by s 10 of the 1987 Act.
2 Law Commission, see Report No 82 on Liability for Defective Products (1977) Cmnd 6381; Council of Europe, see Strasbourg Convention on Products Liability in regard to personal Injury and Death (1977); and the Pearson Commission on Civil Liability and Compensation for Personal Injury (1978) Cmnd 7054, Vol 1.
3 See Law Com No 82 Cmnd 6381.
4 85/374.

in the rules throughout member states, the basic regime throughout the Community is the same. British industry is subjected to the same rules as the European competitors. Indeed one of the aims of the Directive was to harmonise national laws because as it is put in the preamble:

... the existing divergences may distort competition and affect the free movement of goods within the common market and entail a differing degree of protection of the consumer against damage caused by a defective product to his health or property.

Secondly, in the UK, industry, in particular the pharmaceutical industry, has persuaded the government to adopt the 'development risks' defence albeit that every official report on product liability advised against such a course of action.

The detailed provision for strict liability made by the 1987 Act must now be examined. It would have been possible, and would certainly have made life easier for students, to give statutory force in the UK to the Directive. As it is, however, where the interpretation of the Consumer Protection Act is doubtful it should be construed in the light of the Directive. Should there be any obvious conflict between the provisions of the Act and the Directive, any dispute will ultimately have to be decided by the European Court of Justice in Brussels.[5] There is some oblique authority that, despite section 2(1) of the European Communities Act 1972, the wording of the Act should prevail.[6]

(B) WHO CAN SUE UNDER THE ACT?

Wherever a defect in a product wholly or partly causes personal injury or death the victim or his dependants may invoke the rules of strict liability to sue under the Act.[7] The injured individual need not be a purchaser or even a direct user of the faulty goods. If defective brakes in a new car bought by A suddenly fail causing a road accident in which A, his passenger B, and C a pedestrian are seriously injured, all three can sue the car's manufacturer. Where a defective product causes damage to a baby before birth, the baby may sue in respect of its disabilities.[8] The prime aim of the Directive and the Act is to provide protection against personal injuries and death but consumers can also sue under the Act where a defect in a product results in damage to private property (including land) providing the amount to be awarded to compensate for that damage exceeds £275.[9] Damage to property used for business purposes[10] is expressly excluded under both the Act and the Directive, as is the loss of or any damage to the product itself.[11] Nor is economic loss arising from defective products within the scope of the new strict liability rules.[12]

---

5   Interestingly, in *EC Commission v United Kingdom, C-300/95* [1996] ECR I-6765, the Commission refused to accept that the UK's adoption of the development risk defence is, despite plausible arguments to the contrary, compatible with Art 7 of the Directive.
6   *Faccini Dori v Recreb Srl*: C-91/92 [1995] All ER (EC) 1.
7   Section 2(1).
8   Section 6(3).
9   See s 5. See generally Bell 'Product Liability Damages in England and Wales' (1992) 20 Anglo-American Law Review 371.
10   Section 5(3).
11   Section 5(2).
12   For the very limited circumstances in which damages for economic loss might be recoverable in negligence see ch 12 ante.

(C)   ON WHOM IS STRICT LIABILITY IMPOSED?

Liability is not limited to manufacturers alone. The Directive imposes liability on 'producers'[13] and defines producers so as to ensure that plaintiffs should almost always be able to identify easily and swiftly an organisation or individual deemed responsible for putting the product into circulation. The Act adopts a different formula but identifies the same classes of person as responsible for products. Essentially, all those involved in the primary production and marketing of goods are made liable. Repairers and distributors who may owe the consumers a duty of care at common law are generally outside the scope of the new strict liability regime.

Section 2 of the Act imposes liability on the following categories of persons.

1   Liability is imposed on 'producers'.[14] Producers are defined as:
    a   manufacturers[15]
    b   in the case of products which are not made, but won or abstracted (for example coal and minerals) the person who won or abstracted the product,[16] and
    c   in respect of products which are neither made, nor won or abstracted (for example crops), but where essential characteristics of the product are attributable to an industrial or other process, the person carrying out that process.[17] The cumbersome nature of (c) is, as we shall see, explained by the exemption of primary agricultural produce from the regime instituted by the Act.

2   Liability is imposed on any person who brand names a product or by other means holds himself out as a producer.[18] Should you buy a food processor at Marks & Spencer which bears the brand name 'St Michael' and a part flies out of the machine and injures you, you may sue Marks & Spencer and it is no defence against you that the processor was actually made by a third party.

3   Liability is imposed on any person importing a product into the European Community from outside.[19] Had you bought a Japanese food processor you need not concern yourself with the intricacies of suing in Japan; you can proceed against whichever European Community firm brought the product into the community.

4   The problems of the consumer at the end of a long chain of distributors have been discussed earlier. The ultimate consumer may well not know the identity of the manufacturer. Section 2(3) provides that any supplier of a product will be liable to the injured person unless he complies with a request to name, within a reasonable time, the person supplying him with the product. Distributors may thus be deemed to be subject to strict liability unless they can and do name the next organisation up the chain of distribution. A duty of care when imposed on a distributor cannot be otherwise shifted up the chain.

5   The Directive expressly defines manufacturers of component parts as 'producers' and so they, too, are subject to strict liability.[20] The Act achieves the same end by more tortuous means defining 'product' so as to embrace component parts.[1] The effect is simply illustrated. Should defective brakes in a new car fail causing personal injuries, the injured person may sue both the 'producer' of the finished product, the car manufacturers, and the 'producer' of the defective component,

13 Article 3.
14 Section 2(2)(a).
15 Section 1(2)(a).
16 Section 1(2)(b).
17 Section 1(2)(c).
18 Section 2(2)(b).
19 Section 2(2)(c). Note that a person importing a product into the UK from another member state is not made strictly liable under the Act. He may, however, be liable in negligence.
20 Article 3(1).
1   See s 1(2).

the manufacturers of the brakes. Section 1(3), however, provides that a supplier of the finished product shall not be deemed to be liable for defects in all component parts because he cannot name the actual manufacturer of each and every component.

(D) PRODUCTS

'Products' are defined in the Act as 'any goods or electricity' and include component parts and in certain cases raw materials.[2] Primary agricultural produce is excluded from strict liability unless it has been subject to some industrial process[3] ('initial process' is the term used in the Directive[4]). A consumer injured by contaminated beefburgers can clearly sue the person responsible for processing the beef from beef into burger. If the contamination existed in the cattle before processing, for example the cattle had been affected by fallout from a nuclear incident such as Chernobyl, he cannot invoke strict liability against the farmer who originally sold the cattle. But what if the beef were contaminated by BSE attributable to the way the cattle were fed by the farmer to fatten them up? Would that constitute an 'industrial process'?

In earlier drafts of the Directive, blood and human tissues were expressly excluded from the Directive. No express mention is now made of these in the Directive or the Act. So it is unclear whether a patient infected with some disease by a contaminated blood transfusion can hold the transfusion service strictly liable. It seems unlikely that human tissues would be classified as 'goods'. Immovable property, that is land and fixtures on land, is beyond the scope of the Act'.[5] Goods which become fixtures within immovable property, for example central heating boilers installed in private houses are probably within the scope of the Act.[6]

(E) DEFINING 'DEFECT'

Strict liability must not be confused with 'no-fault' liability. Proof that a product resulted in injury is not sufficient to establish liability. 'Fault' must still be proved by the plaintiff but the relevant fault becomes that a 'defect' in the product resulted in injury, rather than want of care. If 'defect' can be proved then carelessness as such is irrelevant. Thus, if a housewife is badly cut about the face when the blade from her new food processor flies off the machine, she will succeed in her claim for compensation simply on proof of the obvious, that the processor is unsafe and defective. A child drinking lemonade contaminated by carbolic acid will recover damages without problems: contaminated lemonade is defective. Evidence that this was inexplicable in view of the system designed by the manufacturers to guard against such a catastrophe is irrelevant.[7]

Defect[8] is defined in section 3 of the Act in terms that there is a defect in a product if the safety of that product is not such as persons generally are entitled to expect. In assessing what persons generally are entitled to expect, all the circumstances are to be taken into account including:

2 Section 1(2).
3 See the Directive, Article 2 and s 1 of the 1987 Act.
4 Are the terms 'industrial' and 'initial' synonymous? Does combine-harvesting count as an industrial (or initial) process?
5 Liability for defectively constructed buildings remains subject to the general rules of negligence and the Defective Premises Act 1972.
6 See Article 2 of the Directive.
7 See *Daniels and Daniels v R White & Sons Ltd* [1938] 4 All ER 258.
8 See generally Stoppa 'The Concept of Defectiveness in the Consumer Protection Act 1987' [1992] Legal Studies 210.

(a) the manner in which, and purposes for which, the product has been marketed, its get-up, the use of any mark in relation to the product and any instructions for, or warnings with respect to, doing or refraining from doing anything with or in relation to the product;

(b) what might reasonably be expected to be done with or in relation to the product; and

(c) the time when the product was supplied by its producer to another;

and nothing in this section shall require a defect to be inferred from the fact alone that the safety of a product which is supplied after that time is greater than the safety of the product in question.

It remains for the plaintiff to prove that taking into account the criteria outlined in section 3 the product is defective. No product on earth is entirely safe and free of risk. The test is whether the risk to person and property posed by the product in the context of its common use or uses exceeds what is generally acceptable. Take the example of a sharp knife marketed as a kitchen knife for chopping vegetables and packaged so as to be reasonably child proof on display. If the knife cuts off the tip of my finger I cannot claim that my injury resulted from a defect in the product. Its cutting edge was a risk I accepted as the 'price' for a knife which did its job. But if the self-same knife were marketed as 'Marvellous Magic Dagger' and a child cut himself or his playmate then the defect would be easily provable. The risk to children would be generally unacceptable. Ultimately, the question here is one of whether the manufacturer ought to issue a warning as to dangers one would not expect the product to present. In this regard, there is persuasive Canadian authority to suggest that there is no duty to warn of an obvious danger.[9]

The test of 'defect' is likely to involve the courts in risk/benefit analysis. This can best be illustrated by examples of liability for drugs.[10] A new and effective antibiotic is put on the market. In 99.5% of cases it works well with fewer side-effects than other antibiotics. Alas, 0.5% of consumers develop serious kidney damage caused by the drug. If an identifiable group of persons should or could have been foreseen as susceptible to damage, then the failure to warn doctors of the potential allergic reaction may conclude the issue of defect. Failure to give adequate instructions is a presentational failure and relevant to defining defect. If the allergic reaction is unforeseeable, so that no liability in negligence could arise, then the issue is whether the general benefit conferred by the drug outweighs the risk to the few. A new minor tranquilliser posing a risk of kidney damage to however small a group would probably be found defective. The benefit of yet another mild sedative would not in society's evaluation justify any significant risk. A drug to combat AIDS to prolong victims' lives by contrast would, by contrast, be likely to justify a very high degree of risk to life and health. Where the consumer of the drug faces a prospect of almost certain and painful death any product offering realistic hopes of cure or palliation is generally acceptable, albeit the product itself may be inherently dangerous to some of its users.

The application of the broad criteria laid down in section 3 to guide the courts in interpreting 'defect' will have to be worked through on a case-by-case basis. The presentation of the product and the likely use or uses of the product which are specifically designated as relevant guidelines in defining 'defect' by section 3(2)(a) and (b) are inextricably bound up together with the risk/benefit analysis discussed above. Section 3(2)(c) demands further and separate considerations. It has two implications.

First, the time when the product was put into circulation is obviously relevant to determine whether the defect was inherent in the product or the result of 'fair wear and tear'. When a child's seat belt in a car is eight years old and has been used by three ebullient children, can it be expected to be as safe as when new? Will cost be relevant?

9 *Deshane v Deere & Co* (1993) 106 DLR (4th) 385 (Ont CA).
10 See Newdick 'Liability for Defective Drugs' (1985) 101 LQR 405.

Should I expect a food processor which I buy very cheaply to become not just less useful but less safe too?[11] Second, section 3(2)(c) provides that safety standards must be judged by the generally acceptable standards at the time at which the product was put on the market, and not with hindsight by the standards of the time when the relevant claim comes to court. Take a hypothetical example of lung cancer induced by cigarettes. A claim against the cigarettes' manufacturers comes to trial in 2003. In 2001 cigarettes were banned outright save for special provision for addicts to be prescribed nicotine on the NHS. The medical evidence shows the cancer was well established by 1993. The test must be whether the product was below generally acceptable safety standards in 1993. That cigarettes are regarded as absolutely unacceptable in 2001 is irrelevant. Nor would it be conclusive if by 2001 'safer' (non- carcinogenic) cigarettes had been invented.[12]

The likelihood is that in relation to construction and presentation defects strict liability will be easy to prove. Where the manufacturing process breaks down, eg where snails get into ginger beer, or an automated process suffers an unnoticed power failure running out ten cars in a batch of a thousand with defective steering, the product will be patently defective. Where instructions on use are inadequate, or warnings as to use fail to make the consumer safe, again a defect will be easily established. The need to engage in a rigorous examination of risks and benefits of a product will generally be reserved for design defects. And of course the implication for industry of design defects is much more traumatic. Compensating 10 unlucky victims of a freak construction defect is a less daunting enterprise than compensating the hundreds or thousands who may have suffered injury before a design defect became patent.

(F)   GENERAL DEFENCES

Section 4 of the Act provides several defences to strict liability. They include the following:
1   The defect is attributable to compliance with any statute or European Community rule prescribing how the product is made. The defence is not available where there are no statutory rules on how the product is made but there are rules requiring licensing of the product by a public body before it can be marketed.[13]
2   The defendant can prove that he never supplied the product to another,[14] for example experimental drugs are stolen from the research laboratory of a drug company and sold by the thieves.
3   The defendant did not supply the goods in the course of business.[15] Thus, I am not strictly liable for defects in the food I serve my colleagues at a dinner party.
4   The defect did not exist in the product when the defendant supplied the product to another.[16] Accordingly, a chocolate manufacturer would not be liable for poisoned chocolates injected with acid by some third party on the supermarket shelves.

---

11   Consider the conceptual basis for product liability discussed by Clark at (1985) 48 MLR 325.
12   Section 3 states: '...nothing in this section shall require a defect to be inferred from the fact alone that the safety of a product which is supplied after that time is greater than the product in question'. Where the plaintiff was himself a smoker, any damages awarded would in any case be substantially reduced on the ground of his contributory negligence: s 6(4). On current safety standards what are the chances of success for a plaintiff who did not himself smoke but contracted cancer from passive smoking? Is alcohol a defective product within s 3?
13   Section 4(1)(a). For example, drugs which must be licensed under the Medicines Act 1968.
14   Section 4(1)(b).
15   Section 4(1)(c).
16   Section 4(1)(d).

5   Manufacturers of components will not be liable where the defect arose in the finished product and was caused by faulty design of the finished product or inadequate installation in the finished product by the manufacturers of that product.[17]

In addition to the defences provided for by section 4, section 6(4) provides that the contributory negligence[18] of the consumer shall be available as a defence to strict liability under the Act. Two difficult questions are posed. The Law Reform (Contributory Negligence) Act 1945 provides that when a finding of contributory negligence is made, apportionment between the plaintiff and defendant of responsibility (and thus damages) is on the basis of relative fault. Where the plaintiff has been careless of his own safety and the defendant is strictly liable, will this mean that the plaintiff will generally have to bear the lion's share of responsibility for his injury? Or will the courts at this stage have to revert to considering any evidence of want of care on the part of the defendant?

More problematic to resolve in practice, however, will be defining the circumstances in which if a product is put to an improper or imprudent use this is simply evidence of contributory negligence or whether it goes to the fundamental issue of whether the plaintiff's injuries were wholly or partly caused by a defect in the product. A stepladder is bought for cleaning windows by a family. The 20-year-old son of the household used it to build an assault course. After 10 of his 14-stone friends have thundered across it, the wood cracks as the young man himself is on the ladder. He falls and breaks a leg. Is he simply guilty of a degree of contributory negligence, or was the ladder put to a use that it would not generally be expected to withstand?

(G)   THE 'DEVELOPMENT RISKS' DEFENCE[19]

The incorporation of the 'development risks' defence into the Act via section 4(1)(e) is without doubt the most controversial part of the legislation. Permitting member states to incorporate such a defence was a compromise by the European Community in order to end the long drawn-out process of agreeing to implement strict liability at all.

Section 4(1)(e) provides that a defendant shall not be liable where he can show:

> that the state of scientific and technical knowledge at the relevant time was not such that a producer of products of the same description as the product in question might be expected to have discovered the defect if it had existed in his products while they were under his control.

The effect of the defence is this. Consider the example of drug-induced injury. A plaintiff establishes that the product fails to comply with society's general expectations for the safety of that type of product. That means he proves that the risks created by the drug outweigh the potential benefit of the product. The defendant may still escape liability by virtue of the 'development risks' defence if he can prove that the nature of the defect was such that at the time he marketed the drug[20] available scientific and technical knowledge[1] would not have revealed the defect. Had the Consumer Protection

---

17   Section 4(1)(f).
18   Section 6(4).
19   See generally Newdick 'Risk, Uncertainty and "Knowledge" in the Development Risk Defence' (1992) 20 Anglo-American Law Review 309.
20   It will not be enough to establish that at the time the design was first put on the market the defect was not discoverable. Once the defect becomes apparent, any further marketing of batches of the drug will engage liability both under the Act and in negligence: see *Wright v Dunlop Rubber Co Ltd* (1972) 13 KIR 255 on this issue.
1   The 'development risks' defence as defined in the Directive (Article 7(e)) is worded thus: 'the state of scientific and technical knowledge at the time when he put the product into circulation was not such as to enable the existence of the defect to be discovered'. There is no reference to

Act 1987 been in force at the time of the thalidomide tragedy, the crucial question would have been this: given the limited understanding of embryology at that time, and the lack of knowledge as to whether drugs did cross the placental barrier, could the manufacturers on the basis of the then current scientific knowledge have foreseen the risk to the foetus? The answer might well have been no.

The new rules would have conferred one significant advantage on the parents of the damaged babies. In negligence they would have had to prove that the defendants should have foreseen the risk. By contrast, under the statute, the onus is on the defendants to prove that they could not have anticipated the danger. As such, self-interest impels manufacturers to disclose all reports of tests on the product and expert opinion made available to them.

The regime of strict liability introduced by the Consumer Protection Act 1987 significantly benefits plaintiffs by:
a   ensuring liability for construction defects in all circumstances, and
b   requiring the defendant to provide an explanation for a design defect consonant with his having designed the product in order to exclude all known and knowable defects.

The risk of the unknown defect in the UK continues to be borne by the injured individual. Both the Law Commission and the Pearson Commission regarded the incorporation of a 'development risks' defence which results in this effect as unacceptable. The Pearson Report put it this way:[2]

> ... to exclude development risks from a regime of strict liability would be to leave a gap in the compensation cover, through which, for example, the victims of another thalidomide disaster might slip.

As case law fleshes out the bare bones of the rules for liability introduced by the 1987 Act we shall have to see whether in practice the form of 'strict' liability adopted has done much more than reverse the burden of proof demanded by the tort of negligence.

(H)   CAUSATION

The burden of proving that:
a   there was a 'defect' in the product, and
b   the relevant injury or damage was wholly or partly caused by that defect.[3]
rests with the plaintiff. This in turn often presents a problem in establishing causation where an improper or unexpected use of the product leads to the plaintiff's injury: is it the improper use or the defect which is responsible for the injury? Consider the following hypothetical examples.
1   A new antibiotic is marketed. Information to doctors includes a warning not to prescribe the drug to pregnant women. The drug is only available on prescription. Dr Stone prescribes the drug for Tom. Tom feels better the next day. He discontinues the tablets and gives the remainder to his colleague Jane who is 10

---

whether a 'producer of products of the same description might have been expected to have discovered the defect' as in s 4(1)(e) of the Act. The test in the Directive refers to knowledge in general and would embrace evidence from research scientists. The test in s 4(1)(e) appears to be the traditional negligence test of what could reasonably be expected from companies in that line of business. Yet in *EC Commission v United Kingdom*: C-300/95 [1997] 3 CMLR 923, the ECJ held that there was no inconsistency between s 4(1)(e) and Art 7. And this was in spite of the fact that Art 7 appears to involve a narrower test.
2   Pearson Report (1978) Cmnd 7054, Vol 1, para 1259.
3   See s 2(1) of the Act and Art 4 of the Directive.

weeks' pregnant. She takes the tablets and her baby is born seriously damaged.[4]

2   A trendy student buys a lurid pink dye in a dressmaking shop. He uses it to dye his hair and suffers acute dermatitis as a result.[5]

3   A wealthy businessman buys domestic gas convector heaters and installs them in his swimming pool to heat the pool. One heater explodes destroying the pool.

One causation issue is, however, somewhat clearer. Intermediate examination of the product will no longer exculpate the manufacturer from liability for defects in the product existing at the time that he put the product into circulation. That some third party may share liability for the injury to the plaintiff is relevant only to the issue of contribution between the tortfeasors.[6]

Factual difficulties with causation for the consumer seeking to identify and sue the manufacturer will largely be alleviated by the obligation on each supplier to name his supplier or be deemed strictly liable himself for the defective goods.[7] Only where the last party identified is bankrupt will problems arise.

In the US claims have been litigated where the actual manufacturer of the product injuring the plaintiff cannot be traced. Injury is proved to be the result of a drug now identified as defective. The drug may have been prescribed several years ago and the identical chemical compound marketed by several companies. There is no way of determining which branch of the drug was prescribed to individual plaintiffs. Courts in the US have held that liability should be apportioned between all companies manufacturing the drug in proportion to their share in the market for that drug.[8]

(I)   LIMITATION

Actions under Part I of the Consumer Protection Act 1987 introducing strict liability for defective products are subject to two periods of limitation:

1   The action must be brought within three years of the date on which injury or damage was suffered by the plaintiff, or, if later, the date on which the plaintiff becomes aware of the injury or damage.[9] Only in the case of personal injuries does the court have a discretion to override that three-year period.

2   No action may be brought in any circumstances more than ten years from the date on which the defendant supplied the relevant product to another.

Claims such as those which came before the courts in the US for cervical cancer which several young women in their late teens developed as a result of a drug (DES) taken by their mothers in pregnancy could not thus be brought under the 1987 Act. In this country, the young women would have had to fall back on the common law action for negligence.

---

4   Questions of causation can be seen from this example to be inextricably bound up with the definition of a 'defect'. The defendants could argue that the manner in which the product was marketed as a 'prescription only' drug with appropriate information supplied to GPs rendered it acceptably safe.

5   Should dye intended for use on materials be marked 'Not to be used on the hair'?

6   See Art 8(1) of the Directive. Contribution is not limited to tortfeasors but is available between all persons liable for the same damage: see the Civil Liability (Contribution) Act 1978 discussed in ch 29 post. Retailers liable to purchasers for breach of the implied conditions of the contract of sale may also seek a contribution from the manufacturers.

7   See s 2(3) discussed ante.

8   See *Sindell v Abbott Laboratories* 26 Cal 3d 588 (1980); discussed by Newdick 'Liability for Defective Drugs' (1985) 101 LQR 405.

9   For example, a person who took a particular drug in 1999 but only became aware of the kidney damage caused by that drug in 2004.

Chapter 18

Nuisance

SECTION I.   NUISANCE AS A SEPARATE TORT

(A)   SCOPE OF THE LAW OF NUISANCE

This chapter deals with two torts: public nuisance and private nuisance. Though both may be actionable under the civil law, the commission of a public nuisance, such as obstructing a public highway, also amounts to a criminal offence.[1] We therefore deal with public nuisance separately, later in this chapter. To begin with, however, and for the greater part of this chapter, we are concerned only with the more prevalent tort of private nuisance.

A nuisance is usually defined as any activity or state of affairs causing a substantial and unreasonable interference with a plaintiff's land or his use or enjoyment of that land. From this definition we can discern three kinds of interests to which nuisance law affords protection.[2] As regards the third of these – the protection of rights in connection with the *enjoyment* of land – it is possible to make an important observation about nuisance law: namely, that it recognises the value of the enjoyment of land,[3] whether

---

1   Whether there is, in truth, anything much left of the common law offence of public nuisance is a moot point. On the one hand, many of the established forms of public nuisance are now proscribed as *statutory nuisances*. On the other hand, the flexibility of the common law offence – which has historically outlawed a miscellany of public 'mischiefs' – may be the only available means of punishing activities not yet outlawed by Parliament (albeit at the cost of transgressing the *nulla poena sine lege* principle): see further Spencer 'Public Nuisance – a Critical Examination' (1989) 48 CLJ 55, and section 8 post.

2   Though the enjoyment of land and the use of land may, at one level, be seen as distinct interests, it is important to recognise that they are inter-related and that it is not uncommon for more than one to be violated at any one time. See, for example, *Dodds Properties v Canterbury City Council* [1980] 1 All ER 928, CA (interruption to *use of*, and *damage to*, a garage used for business purposes, caused by the defendants' pile-driving operations). Furthermore, in the important decision in *Hunter v Canary Wharf* [1997] 2 All ER 426, HL it was held (obiter) by Lord Lloyd (at 442) and Lord Hoffmann (at 451–2) that the enjoyment of land was only a protected interest in so far as the destruction of that enjoyment represents a diminution in the value of the property affected. Cf Lord Cooke, ibid (at 463), and Gearty 'The Place of Nuisance in the Modern Law of Torts' [1989] CLJ 214.

3   In *Hunter* (supra at 452), Lord Hoffmann sought to equate 'sensible discomfort' with an injury to the land rather than to the person. However, it should be noted that (a) he was only speaking obiter and (b) the distinction, apart from being inherently vague, is difficult to sustain: see Oliphant 'Unblurring the Boundaries of Nuisance' (1998) 6 Tort Law Review 21 and O'Sullivan 'Nuisance in the House of Lords – Normal Service Resumed' [1997] CLJ 483, 485.

belonging to the plaintiff or the defendant. It follows from this that not every interference with B's land caused by A will amount to an actionable nuisance. Instead, the law calls for reasonable tolerance between neighbours vis à vis the respective uses to which each puts his land.[4] Indeed, from time to time, it is almost inevitable that each neighbour will put his land to a use that causes some irritation to the other.[5] It would be absurd for the law to allow an action in nuisance for every minor irritation so caused for it would unjustifiably circumscribe the freedom to enjoy one's own land. It is for this reason that the law of nuisance insists not simply that there be an interference with the plaintiff's land, or any right or interest in that land, but also that the interference be both *substantial* and *unreasonable*.

The range of activities that may give rise to an action in nuisance are manifold. They commonly include the emission of noxious fumes, smoke, noise and heat or the generation of violent vibrations. But not every instance of smoke or noise emission will sustain a nuisance action: it is impossible to characterise any of the activities just listed as inevitably and incontrovertibly a nuisance. At most, all that can be said about them is that they each have the *potential* to constitute a nuisance. Imagine, for example, that a neighbour's very young child manages to turn the volume on a CD player full on. Naturally, the noise will create a disturbance until the neighbour turns it back down again. In such an instance it would be a very unjust law that characterised such a fleeting disturbance as an actionable nuisance. Instead, the law insists that the plaintiff must demonstrate not simply that an interference has occurred but that the interference was both substantial and unreasonable.[6] In our example, it would be difficult to say that the disturbance caused by a momentary increase in the volume of a CD was either of these.

While the rigours of the law of nuisance are tempered by the requirement that interferences must be both unreasonable and substantial, it is important to appreciate that there are no precise thresholds beyond which any such disturbances achieve either status. The concepts of magnitude and unreasonableness are context-dependent.[7] Gauging each depends upon a series of factors that we explore in depth later in this chapter. One cautionary note that should be entered here, however, is that, unlike the law of negligence, reasonableness in nuisance refers not to the defendant's conduct but instead to the *outcome* of his conduct. We are not concerned, per se, with whether the defendant passes the 'reasonable man test' (in the sense of taking reasonable care to avoid causing harm) that is central to the tort of negligence. Rather, we are concerned to assess the reasonableness of *the harm* occasioned to the plaintiff.[8] Thus, as Lindley LJ observed in *Rapier v London Tramways Co* – where the nuisance emanated from too many horses crammed into the defendant's stable – 'If I am sued for nuisance, and nuisance is proved, it is no defence to say and to prove that I have taken all reasonable

4   In *Bamford v Turnley* (1862) 3 B & S 66, 122 ER 25, for example, Bramwell B described nuisance as 'A rule of give and take, live and let live'; and the give and take principle was echoed by Lord Goff in *Cambridge Water Co Ltd v Eastern Counties Leather plc* [1994] 2 AC 264, [1994] 1 All ER 53, HL.
5   Eg, a 21st birthday celebration that goes on until late at night.
6   The *magnitude* and *unreasonableness* of an interference should not be assumed to be mutually exclusive: the existence of the former is often a precondition to the existence of the latter. See post.
7   *Sturges v Bridgman* (1879) 11 Ch D 852.
8   *Walter v Selfe* (1851) 4 De G & Sm 315. See also, Gearty [1989] CLJ 214, at 231–3.

care to prevent it'.[9] On the other hand, it would be wrong to assume that the reasonableness of the defendant's conduct is an irrelevant consideration, for there exists an important inter-relationship between the reasonableness of what the defendant does and the reasonableness of the interference it causes to the plaintiff. Disturbances caused by malice[10] or reckless disregard for one's neighbour – such as persistently playing a musical instrument in the small hours of the morning – as opposed to those caused innocently and unavoidably,[11] are manifestly less easy to justify.

As originally conceived, the law of nuisance was not designed to cover personal injuries. It was exclusively concerned with acts or omissions[12] causing violations of land or interests in or over land.[13] For a time it was thought that such injuries were actionable in nuisance. In *Hunter v Canary Wharf Ltd*, however, the House of Lords stated (obiter) that such injuries are not recoverable in private nuisance but rather, if at all, in negligence.[14] The fact that the law has fluctuated on this point, while on the one hand a source of confusion, serves to demonstrate that the boundaries of the law of nuisance are by no means fixed or easy to identify.[15] This is in large part because the tort of negligence has, to a considerable extent, eclipsed (or, at least, subsumed) important elements of nuisance.[16]

(B)   NUISANCE AND ENVIRONMENTAL LAW

Nuisance law – whether private or public – plays only a limited role in the protection of the environment.[17] The fact that there has been a steady growth in popular concern for the protection of the environment has resulted in the implementation of a number of statutes that impose a regulatory regime that renders the common law very much a secondary means of protection. As Lord Goff put it:

---

9   [1893] 2 Ch 588 at 600. Similarly, in *Halsey v Esso Petroleum Co Ltd* [1961] 2 All ER 145, Veale J held the defendants liable in nuisance for the noise generated by lorries driving in and out of their depot at night, causing disturbance to the plaintiff who lived opposite. And this was despite their endeavours to do everything feasible to keep the noise to a minimum. See also *Read v Lyons & Co Ltd* [1947] AC 156 at 183, [1946] 2 All ER 471 at 482 (per Lord Simmonds, obiter) and *Cambridge Water Co Ltd v Eastern Counties Leather plc* [1994] 2 AC 264 at 298, [1994] 1 All ER 53 at 71, HL (per Lord Goff, obiter).

10   Eg, *Hollywood Silver Fox Farm Ltd v Emmett* [1936] 2 KB 468, [1936] 1 All ER 825.

11   Eg, *Moy v Stoop* (1909) 25 TLR 262. In *Hunter v Canary Wharf* [1997] 2 All ER 426 at 465, HL, Lord Cooke expressed the view (obiter) that the 'malicious erection of a structure for the purpose of interfering with television reception should be actionable in nuisance'.

12   Nuisance is actionable not just on the basis of misfeasance, but also nonfeasance. See, eg, *Goldman v Hargrave* [1967] 1 AC 645, [1966] 2 All ER 989, PC. Note also that the *positive* duty to prevent harm to others is more pronounced in nuisance than it is in negligence: see Markesinis 'Negligence, Nuisance and Affirmative Duties of Action' (1989) 105 LQR 104.

13   For a brief account of the genesis of private nuisance, see the 9th edition of this work at p 345. See also *Hunter* (supra) per Lord Goff at 435ff and Gearty [1989] CLJ 214.

14   [1997] 2 All ER 426, HL, per Lord Goff (at 438) and Lord Lloyd (at 442).

15   In *Sedleigh-Denfield v O'Callaghan* [1940] AC 880 at 903, [1940] 3 All ER 349 at 364, HL, Lord Wright commented that 'The forms which nuisance may take are protean ... many reported cases are no more than illustrations of particular matters of fact which have been held to be nuisances'. See also, Gearty [1989] CLJ 214.

16   See Newark 'The Boundaries of Nuisance' (1949) 65 LQR 480.

17   See Murphy 'Noxious Emissions and Common Law Liability – Tort in the Shadow of Regulation' in Lowry and Edmunds *Environmental Protection and the Common Law* (1999); Steele 'Private Law and the Environment: Nuisance in Context' (1995) 15 Legal Studies 236; Ogus and Richardson 'Economics and the Environment: A Study in Private Nuisance' [1977] CLJ 284.

[S]o much well-informed and carefully structured legislation is now being put in place to effect environmental protection ... there is less need for the courts to develop a common law principle to achieve the same end, and indeed it may be undesirable that they should do so.[18]

The point is this. Many of the sorts of conduct that would formerly have sounded in nuisance (and nuisance alone!) are now also covered by statutes such as the Clean Air Act 1993 and the Environmental Protection Act 1990.[19] The implementation of such legislation has meant that it is easier and more effective to pursue a grievance via the local environmental health officers (who can prosecute such 'statutory nuisances') than through the courts where the costs of funding, especially in the light of recent cut-backs on the availability of legal aid, may be prohibitively high.

A further, related cause of the diminution in the number of nuisance actions has been the effect of planning legislation. Essentially, the requirement that planning permission be obtained prior to a change in use of existing premises, or the construction of new ones, has meant that some potential nuisances can be avoided prospectively. Thus, where a person is denied the planning permission to turn his house into a small printing works, the obvious potential for disturbance to a neighbour caused by vibrations is avoided in advance. In such cases, nuisance law, which operates retrospectively – that is, in response to an *extant* interference, or potentially injurious state of affairs – is clearly denied any role. It would be wrong, however, to assume that nuisance is now a completely redundant tort in the environmental context.[20] On the contrary, it retains the potential to perform at least two useful functions. First, it can operate as an enforcement procedure supplemental to those contained in the relevant statutes (yet where a particular activity has been authorised by planning permission, the courts will naturally be hesitant in finding that it has caused an actionable nuisance to the plaintiff).[1] Secondly, whenever such a case is decided in favour of the plaintiff, the effect of the judgment may be to establish standards in relation to, say, pollution control which are additional to those contained in the relevant statute.[2]

(C)   NUISANCE AND OTHER TORTS

As Erle CJ once remarked, the law of nuisance is 'immersed in undefined uncertainty'.[3] This uncertainty, according to one commentator, is mainly attributable to the fact that 'the boundaries of the tort of nuisance are blurred'.[4] Undoubtedly, there is much force in this contention. To begin with, there is a considerable overlap and inter-relationship between nuisance and negligence. As Lord Wilberforce remarked in *Goldman v Hargrave*, a nuisance 'may comprise a wide variety of situations, in some of which negligence plays no part, in others of which it is decisive'.[5] Not only does this dictum

18   *Cambridge Water Co Ltd v Eastern Counties Leather plc* [1994] 2 AC 264 at 305, [1994] 1 All ER 53 at 76, HL. Cf Gearty [1989] CLJ 214.
19   For a good account of these and other Acts creating statutory nuisances see Buckley *The Law of Nuisance* (1996) chs 10–12.
20   See Murphy 'Noxious Emissions and Common Law Liability – Tort in the Shadow of Regulation' in Lowry and Edmunds *Environmental Protection and the Common Law* (1999).
1   *Gillingham Borough Council v Medway (Chatham) Dock Co Ltd* [1993] QB 343, [1992] 3 All ER 923. See also the supportive comments of Lord Goff in *Hunter v Canary Wharf Ltd* [1997] 2 All ER 426, HL (at 433) that 'it will usually be open to local people to raise the possibility of [nuisance] ... at the stage of the application for planning permission'.
2   The extent to which nuisance can presently achieve these functions is discussed at length in Steele 'Private Law and the Environment: Nuisance in Context' (1995) 15 Legal Studies 236.
3   *Brand v Hammersmith and City Rly Co* (1867) LR 2 QB 223 at 247.
4   Newark (1949) 65 LQR 480.
5   [1967] 1 AC 645 at 657, [1966] 2 All ER 989, PC.

reveal that the overlap is ill-defined and partial, it also forces us to ask one of the most vexed questions in the whole of the law of nuisance: whether nuisance liability is strict or fault-based. We defer consideration of this matter until later in the chapter. For now, we are concerned only to note that concurrent liability in nuisance and negligence can arise out of a single set of facts. For example, if I were to light a fire next to my neighbour's fence and then leave it unattended, I might be held liable in either negligence or nuisance if the fire were to spread to his fence or shrubs. In such a case, not only would the factual basis of the liability be shared, so too would be the *legal* basis of liability. Thus, in one decided case where the action was framed both in negligence and nuisance, on dismissing the negligence action, the judge also stated that he 'need not discuss the alternative claim based on nuisance .. [since the latter] cannot be established unless negligence is proved'.[6] On a practical level, then, there is frequently a choice in terms of the way in which a plaintiff may frame his action. But on a jurisprudential level, the question that remains is why, when nuisance protects interests in the enjoyment of land, it is necessary to extend the boundaries of negligence to cover similar situations – especially at a time when the judicial trend is to restrain the growth of negligence.[7]

While the interface between negligence and nuisance leads to some very problematic questions about the nature of nuisance liability, it should also be noted that there is also a considerable overlap between the rule in *Rylands v Fletcher*[8] – which imposes liability for the escape from land of things that will foreseeably cause mischief if they escape[9] – and nuisance.[10] In juridical terms, the two torts can be distinguished.[11] Yet they share a number of common features which is in large part due to the fact that the rule in *Rylands v Fletcher* was (avowedly) derived from the law of nuisance.[12] Trespass to land, on the other hand, concerns direct rather than consequential harm and may therefore be distinguished from nuisance in both juridical and factual terms. Equally, being actionable per se, trespass does not require the plaintiff to prove damage.[13] Thus, in *Kelsen v Imperial Tobacco Co (of Great Britain and Ireland) Ltd* where a sign erected by the defendants projected into the air space above the plaintiff's shop, it was held that the erection of the sign constituted a trespass but not a nuisance since 'the presence of this sign ... caused no inconvenience and no interference with the plaintiff's use of his air'.[14] On the other hand, where damage does occur, 'it makes no difference to the result' whether the action is framed in trespass or in nuisance.[15]

The fact that there exists an overlap between nuisance and the other torts mentioned in the preceding paragraph makes it difficult to classify any of them purely on the basis of the interest protected. If, for example, a neighbour's land is damaged because of an

---

6   *Bolton v Stone* [1951] AC 850 at 860, [1951] 1 All ER 1078 at 1082, HL (per Lord Porter). This point was later endorsed by Lord Reid in *The Wagon Mound (No 2)* [1967] 1 AC 617, [1966] 2 All ER 709, HL: 'the similarities between nuisance and [negligence] ... far outweigh any differences' (at 640 and 717 respectively).

7   See Gearty [1989] CLJ 214.

8   (1866) LR 1 Exch 265.

9   Chapter 19 post.

10 *Cambridge Water Co Ltd v Eastern Counties Leather plc* [1994] 2 AC 264, [1994] 1 All ER 53, HL.

11 For some insight into the distinction, see *Leakey v National Trust* [1980] QB 485, [1980] 1 All ER 17, CA.

12 See *Cambridge Water Co Ltd v Eastern Counties Leather plc* [1994] 2 AC 264 at 298, [1994] 1 All ER 53 at 69–70, HL. See also Newark (1949) 65 LQR 480.

13 *Stoke-on-Trent Council v W & J Wass Ltd* [1988] 3 All ER 394, [1988] 1 WLR 1406.

14 [1957] QB 334 at 343, [1957] 2 All ER 343 and 349, CA (per McNair J). Cf *Smith v Giddy* [1904] 2 KB 448 where it was held to be a nuisance when the defendant allowed his trees to overhang the plaintiff's land and thus stymie the growth of the plaintiff's fruit trees.

15 *Home Brewery Co v William Davies & Co (Loughborough) Ltd* [1987] QB 339 at 354 (per Piers Ashworth QC). See also Hudson 'Trespass or Nuisance' (1960) 19 MLR 188.

overflow of water, much will depend upon the directness of the invasion (central to trespass[16]); the role of fault (crucial in 'state of affairs' nuisance cases[17]), and whether the invasion was attributable to a foreseeably injurious escape (which lies at the heart of *Rylands v Fletcher* liability[18]).

A final characteristic of the tort of nuisance that should be noted is that the normal remedy sought by the plaintiff is an injunction rather than damages. His main concern, when subjected to the persistent late-night trumpet playing of his neighbour, for example, is that his neighbour should desist. But, as we shall see, injunctions are granted on a discretionary basis. They may therefore be refused even though an actionable nuisance can be proven. The courts' right to refuse an injunction despite the commission of an actionable nuisance enables them to pursue economic[19] or social objectives. For example, in one case concerning cricket balls being struck from a village green onto the plaintiffs' land, it was stated that:

> it does not seem just that a long-established activity, in itself innocuous, should be brought to an end because someone else chooses to build a house nearby and so turn an innocent pastime into an actionable nuisance.[20]

The extent to which the courts refuse an injunction where a nuisance has been established should not, however, be exaggerated. In the vast preponderance of cases where the plaintiff can prove the commission of a nuisance, he will also succeed in obtaining an injunction. Later in this chapter we shall see that the courts have developed a series of factors to which they will have regard before denying injunctive relief to those who can prove the commission of a nuisance.

SECTION 2.   THE BASIS OF NUISANCE LIABILITY

According to the definition of nuisance offered here, it is apparent that the successful plaintiff must show a substantial interference either with his land or with the use or enjoyment of his land. He must also demonstrate that the interference was an unreasonable one. Yet, thus stated, the basis of nuisance liability is grossly over-simplified. As we shall see, the factors taken into account by the courts in assessing both the magnitude and reasonableness of an interference are manifold, inter-related and, at times, notionally complex.

(A)   SUBSTANTIAL INTERFERENCE

Before a plaintiff can succeed in a nuisance action, he must first be able to prove that he has suffered damage, for as we noted when distinguishing nuisance from trespass, nuisance is not a tort which is actionable per se.[1] Since the law of nuisance protects not just against physical damage to land, but also against interferences with the use or enjoyment of it, it is immediately apparent that we require a definition of damage that

---

16   *Preston v Mercer* (1656) Hard 60.
17   *Sedleigh-Denfield v O'Callaghan* [1940] AC 880, [1940] 3 All ER 349, HL; see post.
18   (1868) LR 3 HL 330.
19   Ogus and Richardson 'Economics and the Environment: A Study in Private Nuisance' (1977) 36 CLJ 284.
20   *Miller v Jackson* [1977] QB 966 at 986, [1977] 3 All ER 338 at 349, CA (per Geoffrey-Lane LJ). Cf *Kennaway v Thompson* [1981] QB 88, [1980] 3 All ER 329, CA.
1   For a very few limited exceptions to this rule, see the 9th edition of this work.

embraces both tangible and intangible interferences. In addition to physical harm to land, our concept of damage must also embrace those cases in which the plaintiff's complaint related to, say, the emission of unpleasant smells, or the generation of loud noise; in short, with things that represented 'sensible discomfort',[2] being interferences with the amenities associated with land ownership.

Although, for the purposes of nuisance, both physical damage and disturbances to the enjoyment of land are actionable, it does not follow that we need not distinguish between the various kinds of interference. Indeed, as we shall see, the case law requires us to treat material harm differently from interferences with amenities.

(1)   INTERFERENCE WITH THE USE OR ENJOYMENT OF LAND

Where interference with the use or enjoyment of land (amenity nuisance) is concerned, the law requires give and take on the part of neighbouring land owners. This principle is neatly encapsulated in the words of Lord Wright in *Sedleigh-Denfield v O'Callaghan* where he said that '[a] balance has to be maintained between the right of the occupier to do what he likes with his own [land], and the right of his neighbour not to be interfered with'.[3] From this it is implicit that, as between neighbours, some measure of interference with the use and enjoyment of each other's land is permissible. It is only a *substantial* interference with a plaintiff's amenities that the law will deem to be a nuisance. Thus, in *Gaunt v Fynney* Lord Selbourne stated that '[a] nuisance by noise ... is emphatically a question of degree ... Such things to offend against the law, must be done in a manner which, beyond fair controversy, are to be regarded as excessive'.[4] The same rule, that the nuisance must be substantial, applies equally in respect of other amenities. Thus, for example, an interference with the right to the free passage of light – acquired by grant or prescription,[5] and sometimes referred to as the right to 'ancient lights' – only amounts to a nuisance where it deprives the plaintiff of 'sufficient light, according to the ordinary notions of mankind, for the comfortable use and enjoyment of his house'.[6]

The key issue, then, is determining when an interference with amenities amounts to a substantial infringement of the plaintiff's interests. It is certainly the case that the plaintiff's health need not be shown to have suffered.[7] Indeed, the loss of a single night's sleep has been held to be sufficiently substantial to constitute a nuisance.[8] So, too, has using adjoining premises for the purposes of prostitution (despite the fact that this fails to impinge directly upon the senses of the plaintiff in the way that, for example, noxious fumes do[9]). The question of whether an interference is sufficiently substantial to amount to an actionable nuisance is one of fact and is to be determined on a case-by-case basis. But not every interference will constitute a nuisance, and an interference that comprises a nuisance in one context may not do so in another.[10] The

---

2   *Hunter v Canary Wharf,* supra (per Lord Hoffmann at 452).
3   [1940] AC 880 at 903, HL.
4   (1872) 8 Ch App 8 at 11–12.
5   The acquisition of this right is a technical matter of land law (see further Gray *Elements of Land Law* (2nd edn, 1993) ch 17). English common law recognises no automatic right to light, and such a right can only be acquired in connection with a building: *Harris v de Pinna* (1886) 33 Ch D 238, CA.
6   *Colls v Home and Colonial Stores* [1904] AC 179, HL at 208 (per Lord Lindley).
7   *Crump v Lambert* (1867) LR 3 Eq 409 at 412 (per Lord Romily MR).
8   *Andreae v Selfridge & Co Ltd* [1938] Ch 1, [1937] 3 All ER 255, CA.
9   *Thompson-Schwab v Costaki* [1956] 1 All ER 652. See also *Laws v Florinplace Ltd* [1981] 1 All ER 659 (sex shop established in a residential area).
10 *Sturges v Bridgman* (1879) 11 Ch D 852.

most commonly cited formulation of the rule by which the interference is to be adjudged substantial is that supplied by Knight Bruce VC in *Walter v Selfe*:[11]

> ought this inconvenience to be considered in fact as more than fanciful, more than one of mere delicacy or fastidiousness, as an inconvenience materially interfering with the ordinary comfort physically of human existence, not merely according to elegant or dainty modes and habits of living, but according to plain and simple notions among the English people?

Over the years, the courts have tended to gauge the seriousness of an interference by reference to two main considerations: the sensitivity of the plaintiff and the locality in which the alleged nuisance occurs. Neither of these factors is conclusive of whether an interference is sufficiently substantial to constitute a nuisance; they are merely *relevant* considerations which ought to be taken into account in all amenity nuisance cases.

(a)   The sensitivity of the plaintiff
If the activity of which the plaintiff complains only disturbs the use or enjoyment of his land because he carries on there a 'delicate trade', heightening his sensitivity to interference, then the interference complained of will not amount to an actionable nuisance. The disturbance must be such that it would substantially inconvenience a plaintiff of ordinary sensitivities, for the courts will not allow a plaintiff to turn an ordinarily innocuous activity into a nuisance. For example:

> In *Robinson v Kilvert*,[12] a landlord who remained in occupation of the cellar let the superjacent floor to the plaintiff. Because of the landlord's business it was necessary for the cellar to be dry and hot. The heat of the cellar passed through the ceiling to the floor above which was used by the plaintiff as a paper warehouse and caused damage to a stock of brown paper kept there. The court rejected the plaintiff's application for an injunction to restrain the landlord from keeping his cellar so hot since the heat transfer would not have caused a problem for anyone other than the plaintiff.

It was only the fact that he was engaged in an 'exceptionally delicate trade' that caused him to suffer loss. Similarly, in *Bridlington Relay Ltd v Yorkshire Electricity Board* the defendants' power line was interfering with the plaintiff's business of providing a radio and television relay service to subscribers. It was said, obiter, that because interference with the recreational amenity of television viewing was not a *substantial* interference, the plaintiffs could not sue for the business interference complained of: 'the plaintiffs could not succeed in a claim for damages for nuisance if ... an ordinary receiver of television by means of an aerial mounted on his house could not do so'.[13] It may be of importance that this case was decided in 1965 when television ownership was rare, rendering viewers exceptionally sensitive plaintiffs. In the 1990s, television viewing is far more common and less easily classified as a hypersensitive activity. Indeed, if the same facts were to arise today, it is possible that the court would hold there to be a nuisance.[14]

Such a possibility was certainly not ruled out in *Hunter v Canary Wharf Ltd* where the House of Lords suggested that, in certain circumstances, an action for this kind of

---

11   (1851) 4 De G & Sm 315 at 322.
12   (1889) 41 Ch D 88, CA.
13   [1965] Ch 436 at 446, [1965] 1 All ER 264 at 270 respectively (per Buckley J).
14   Such is the case in Canada: see *Nor-Video Services Ltd v Ontario Hydro* (1978) 84 DLR (3d) 221, 231 where Robins J, in the Ontario High Court, stated that: 'an inability to receive [a television broadcast] ... would undoubtedly to my mind detract from the beneficial use and ownership of property'.

interference might lie. However, in refusing to award damages to the plaintiffs in *Hunter*, Lord Goff stated that while interferences with television reception 'might in appropriate circumstances be protected', it was also the case that 'more is required than the mere presence of a neighbouring building to give rise to an actionable private nuisance'.[15] Following *Hunter*, then, it is unclear exactly if and when interferences with television viewing (and, by analogy, other such 'luxury' amenities) might form the basis of a nuisance action. Would there, for example, be an actionable nuisance where the interference is caused by the operation of an existing power station rather than by the construction of a tall building?[16] Bear in mind that the decision in *Hunter* is premised *only* by a long-standing concern to allow landowners the freedom to build on their land (subject, of course, to planning restrictions).[17]

Although it is well-established that '[a] man cannot increase the liabilities of his neighbour by applying his own property to special uses',[18] it does not follow that he will not be compensated in full for all the damage that he does suffer where a plaintiff of ordinary sensitivity would also have been able to found a nuisance action in respect of the interference complained of. So, in *McKinnon Industries Ltd v Walker*,[19] damage to the plaintiff's commercially grown orchids caused by the emission of sulphur dioxide gas from the defendant's factory was held to be actionable since it amounted to a non-remote consequence of what had already been proved to be a nuisance. On the other hand, the fact that the plaintiff has suffered appreciable financial loss should not be taken, of itself, to amount to a substantial interference[20] (although the infliction of such business losses may be taken into account in deciding whether the interference as a whole was substantial[1]).

(b)   Location of the plaintiff's premises
The locality in which the plaintiff's premises are situated is a second factor which assists the courts in determining whether the interference complained of is sufficiently substantial to amount to a nuisance. The expectations of the plaintiff, in terms of comfort, peace and quiet, will naturally vary according to the location of his house or business. The point was succinctly made in *Sturges v Bridgman*,[2] in which case a physician complained about the noise generated by a neighbouring confectioner who was operating a pestle and mortar. There, Thesiger LJ held that the court should take account of the fact that the area consisted largely of medical specialists' consulting rooms since:

---

15   [1997] 2 All ER 426 at 432, HL. Much was made in the case of the fact that the defendants had obtained planning permission to build the tower and the fact that the construction of buildings with such permission was a normal use of land. Qualifying this, however, Lord Cooke observed (at 465), that he could 'see no reason why neighbours prejudicially affected should not be able to sue in nuisance if a building does exceed height, bulk or location restrictions. For then the developer is not making either a lawful or a reasonable use of his landowning rights'.
16   See, on this question, the view of the Court of Appeal in *Hunter* [1996] 1 All ER 482.
17   See *A-G (Ex rel Gray's Inn Society) v Doughty* (1752) 2 Ves Sen 453, HL. One answer might be to alow the construction of tall buildings, allow a nuisance action but restrict a remedy to one of damages: see O'Sullivan 'A Poor Reception for Television Nuisance' [1996] CLJ 184.
18   *Eastern and South African Telegraph Co Ltd v Cape Town Tramways Companies Ltd* [1902] AC 381 at 393, PC (per Lord Robertson).
19   [1951] 3 DLR 577, PC.
20   See, eg, the Australian decision in *Victoria Park Racing and Recreation Grounds Ltd v Taylor* (1937) 58 CLR 479.
1   *Thompson-Schwab v Costaki* [1956] 1 All ER 652, [1956] 1 WLR 335, CA.
2   (1879) 11 Ch D 852. See also, *Murdoch v Glacier Metal Co Ltd* [1998] 07 LS Gaz R 31 (loud, night-time factory noise held not to be actionable in all the circumstances of the case (including P's proximity to a busy bypass)).

[w]hether anything is a nuisance or not is a question to be determined, not merely by an abstract consideration of the thing itself, but in reference to its circumstances; what would be a nuisance in Belgrave Square would not necessarily be so in Bermondsey; and where a locality is devoted to a particular trade … [the courts] would be justified in finding, and may be trusted to find, that the trade … is not an actionable wrong.[3]

Though locality is relevant in deciding amenity cases, it is not necessarily a conclusive consideration. Thus, although locality provides a compelling reason for the decision in *Adams v Ursell*[4] – where a fish and chip shop established in a fashionable street was held to be a nuisance – it was not determinative in *Rushmer v Polsue and Alfieri Ltd*[5] where printing presses were used at night in a printing district. Equally, it should be noted that the character of a locality is susceptible to change over time. Thus, the fact that an area was at one time wholly residential does not mean that the residents will always be entitled to a very high standard of peace and quiet. In *Gillingham Borough Council v Medway (Chatham) Dock Co Ltd*,[6] for example, it was held that planning permission which had been granted to change the use of an old naval dockyard into a commercial port (which turned out to be very noisy at night) should be taken to have effected a change in the character of the neighbourhood. As Buckley J put it: 'where planning permission is given … the question of nuisance will thereafter fall to be decided by reference to a neighbourhood with … [the new] development or use and not as it was previously'.[7]

On the other hand, obiter dicta in a decision of the Court of Appeal appears to constrain the effect of Buckley J's judgment to cases in which the interference complained of occurs *after* the character of the neighbourhood has already changed. The Court of Appeal took the view, in *Wheeler v JJ Saunders Ltd*,[8] that the simple grant of planning permission cannot be taken, ipso facto, to license what would otherwise be a nuisance. In other words, the court was chary of allowing administrative decisions (not susceptible to appeal) to be taken simply to extinguish existing private rights. But where planning permission has been obtained, it will play a part in the court's decision-making.[9]

(2) MATERIAL DAMAGE TO LAND

So far we have only been concerned with what amounts to a substantial interference with the use or enjoyment of land (otherwise known as 'amenity nuisance'). In this section we consider cases in which the activity complained of causes actual physical damage to the plaintiff's land. The kinds of nuisance that concern us here include collapses of the defendant's property onto the plaintiff's land,[10] drenching or

---

3 (1879) 11 Ch D 852 at 865.
4 [1913] 1 Ch 269. See also *Thompson-Schwab v Costaki* [1956] 1 All ER 652 in which a brothel was set up in a high class street.
5 [1906] 1 Ch 234; affd [1907] AC 121, HL. Equally, the smell of oil on the border of an industrial area can constitute a nuisance: *Halsey v Esso Petroleum Co Ltd* [1961] 2 All ER 145.
6 [1993] QB 343, [1992] 3 All ER 923.
7 [1993] QB 343 at 361.
8 [1995] 2 All ER 697 at 711, CA.
9 The rationale here was explained by Lord Goff in *Hunter* when he observed (at 433) that: 'it will usually be open to local people to [complain]… at the stage of the application for planning permission'.
10 *Wringe v Cohen* [1940] 1 KB 229, [1939] 4 All ER 241, CA. Cf *Sack v Jones* [1925] Ch 235 (not a nuisance where the plaintiff's house caused the defendant's house to collapse).

flooding,[11] vegetation damage caused by the emission of noxious fumes,[12] the encroachment of roots[13] and vibration damage.[14] In such instances, the courts will approach the question of substantial interference rather differently than where the plaintiff complains of amenity nuisance.

To begin with, where physical damage to property is concerned, the character of the district in which the plaintiff's land lies is *not* a material factor in assessing the gravity of the interference. In *St Helen's Smelting Co v Tipping*[15] – a case in which the plaintiff's shrubs had been damaged by fumes emitted from the defendants' copper-smelting plant – Lord Westbury held that:

> It is a very desirable thing to mark the difference between an action brought for a nuisance upon the ground that the alleged nuisance produces material injury to the property, and an action ... on the ground that the thing alleged ... is productive of personal discomfort. With regard to the latter ... a nuisance must undoubtedly depend greatly on the circumstances of the place where the thing complained of actually occurs. But where [physical damage is caused] ... there unquestionably arises a very different consideration.[16]

One difficulty that arises from the fact that the plaintiff's location is irrelevant in physical damage cases is that physical damage and interference with amenities can often arise simultaneously, without there being any clear distinction between the two. If, for example, vibrations cause plaster to break off my walls, those same vibrations will probably also adversely affect the comfort and enjoyment of my home. Furthermore, the fact that the defendant engages in such a disturbing enterprise is likely to cause a diminution in the value of my house which is not easy to classify as either an amenity nuisance or an instance of physical damage.[17] Notwithstanding these problems, some attempts have been made by the courts to clarify the meaning of 'material damage'. In respect of the former, a dictum of Lord Selbourne suggests that it is enough if science can trace a deleterious physical change in the property.[18] However, in the light of the scope for difficulty distinguishing between amenity nuisances and those involving physical damage,[19] it is probably better not to ignore the locality issue in all but the most clear-cut cases.

Just as in the case of interferences with the use or enjoyment of land, it is important to establish that the physical damage complained of is substantial in nature. Hence, in

11 *Sedleigh-Denfield v O'Callaghan* [1940] AC 880, [1940] 3 All ER 349, HL; *Hurdman v North Eastern Rly Co* (1878) 3 CPD 168; *Broder v Saillard* (1876) 2 Ch D 692.
12 *St Helen's Smelting Co v Tipping* (1865) 11 HL Cas 642, 11 ER 1483; *Manchester Corpn v Farnworth* [1930] AC 171, HL.
13 *Masters v Brent London Borough Council* [1978] QB 841, [1978] 2 All ER 664.
14 *Grosvenor Hotel Co v Hamilton* [1894] 2 QB 836.
15 (1865) 11 HL Cas 642.
16 (1865) 11 HL Cas 642 at 650.
17 Although the drop in value of the property (absent the cost of repairs to the walls) is, in fact, a purely economic loss, it is arguably implicit from *Bone v Seale* [1975] 1 All ER 787, CA that such loss should be treated as property damage insofar as, in that case, the court treated it separately from the award for the amenity nuisance. Does this mean that diminution in value is to be regarded, in nuisance, as physical damage? If so, since in *Halsey v Esso Petroleum Co Ltd* [1961] 2 All ER 145 it was presumed that the value of property will be affected wherever a substantial interference with enjoyment occurs, it could be argued that *all* amenity cases involve at least some element physical damage according to this conception. Problematic though this conception is, it is the one favoured in *Hunter*. Cf *Mayo v Seaton UDC* (1903) 68 JP 7 (the erection of public lavatories which depreciated the value of the plaintiff's premises held not to amount to a private nuisance) and *Clerk and Lindsell* (1995) at p 894.
18 *Gaunt v Fynney* (1872) 8 Ch App 8 at 11–12.
19 See Oliphant (1998) 6 Tort Law Review 21.

Darley Main Colliery Co v Mitchell[20] it was held that minor subsidence (though identifiable and tangible) caused the plaintiff no appreciable harm and was therefore not an actionable nuisance.

(3) INTERFERENCE WITH SERVITUDES

For the sake of completeness we mention here a final category of damage that can, technically, form the basis of a nuisance action. It involves interferences with servitudes such as the right to light and air, and the right to support of land and buildings. The rules in relation to these rights are complex and more suitably the subject-matter of a textbook on property law than one on tort.

(B) UNREASONABLENESS

There is perhaps no more confusing matter in the whole of the law of private nuisance than the role played by unreasonableness in the ascription of liability. Conceivably, unreasonableness could relate to one or both of two inter-related issues: the conduct of the defendant and the nature of the interference with the plaintiff's land. Properly understood, it is the interference, rather than the defendant's conduct, which must be unreasonable.[1] This does not mean, however, that the nature of the defendant's conduct is irrelevant, since the unreasonableness of the defendant's user will often influence the court's characterisation of the interference as unreasonable. Imagine, for example, that I regularly fire a gun on my land in order to control vermin that poses a threat to my crops. The noise made by the gun is precisely the same as if I were firing it out wantonness. In both cases, the sound level remains constant and so, therefore, does the degree of disturbance that I cause to my neighbour. In the latter case, however, a judge might declare there to be a nuisance on the basis that the shooting was completely unwarranted. In the former case, by contrast, where the shooting was reasonable in order to effect pest control, she could easily reach the opposite conclusion.

The difference between the two cases lies in the way in which we characterise the nature of the interference (albeit by reference, in part, to the nature of the defendant's conduct). Not in every case in which the defendant acts unreasonably will he be liable in nuisance; for it is the unreasonableness of the interference (coupled, of course, with its gravity) which matters. So, for example, if I play my CDs late at night and at full volume, I will not be liable in nuisance to my neighbour if she is almost entirely deaf and hears virtually nothing. The interference in such a case will be regarded as de minimis and, as McNeill J stated in *Tetley v Chitty*, the plaintiff must be able to demonstrate 'a *real* interference with his use and enjoyment of his premises'.[2]

There are several factors that the courts typically will take into account in deciding whether the interference is unreasonable. We consider each in turn.

---

20 (1886) 11 App Cas 127.
1   See *Sampson v Hodson-Pressinger* [1981] 3 All ER 710, for example, where the ordinary use of premises which, as a result of their being poorly constructed, caused intolerable noise to be perceived in adjoining premises was held to be a nuisance. See also *Toff v McDowell* (1993) 25 HLR 650.
2   [1986] 1 All ER 663 at 665. In *Bradford Corpn v Pickles* [1895] AC 587 at 601, HL, Lord Macnaghten stated that no action would lie '[i]f the act ... gives rise merely to damage without legal injury'. See also *Crown River Cruises v Kimbolton Fireworks Ltd* [1996] 2 Lloyd's Rep 533.

(1)   THE SERIOUSNESS OF THE INTERFERENCE

Generally, the more serious an interference with the plaintiff's interests, the more likely it is that the interference will be regarded by the court as unreasonable. And the seriousness of the interference is influenced by four factors: the duration of the harm, the extent (or degree) of the harm, the character of the harm and the social value of the use interfered with.

(a)   The duration of the harm

We have already seen that before a nuisance action will succeed, regardless of whether the plaintiff complains of physical damage or simply a disturbance to the peaceful enjoyment of his land, he must always show that he has suffered a substantial interference.[3] Apart from being a threshold requirement in its own right, the persistence of an interference has a direct bearing on its reasonableness. In general terms, the more persistent an interference, the more likely it is that the courts will deem it to be unreasonable. Self-evidently, it is much less reasonable to expect one's neighbours to tolerate a nauseating smell that is more or less permanent than one that lasts for just a few moments. Accordingly it is much more readily considered a nuisance. It follows from this that nuisances normally involve ongoing interferences rather than ones which are only transitory or isolated.[4]

In some circumstances, however, even isolated or transitory interferences are actionable. For example, if the interference complained of is an isolated event but it causes physical damage, the courts appear willing to tolerate claims in nuisance so long as the damage arose out of a dangerous 'state of affairs'.[5] In *Spicer v Smee*[6] – a case in which defective electrical wiring in the defendant's premises resulted in the plaintiff's bungalow being destroyed by fire – Atkinson J put the matter thus: '[a] private nuisance arises out of a state of things on one man's property whereby his neighbour's property is exposed to danger'. Similarly, in *Midwood & Co Ltd v Manchester Corpn*,[7] where an accumulation of inflammable gas caused an explosion to occur which set fire to the plaintiff's premises, the court again held there to be a nuisance by focusing upon the prevailing state of affairs,

Though it is a precondition of liability in respect of an isolated event that it arose from a dangerous state of affairs on the defendant's land, it is important to be clear that damages are only awarded for the harm caused. Nothing can be recovered in connection with the menacing state of affairs for this is merely a prerequisite for, and not the basis of, the defendant's liability. Nuisance law insists that the plaintiff must demonstrate

---

3   See *Walter v Selfe* (1851) 4 De G & Sm 315 in respect of amenity nuisance, and *Darley Main Colliery Co v Mitchell* (1886) 11 App Cas 127 in relation to nuisances involving physical damage.

4   Thus, in *Cunard v Antifyre Ltd* [1933] 1 KB 551 (where some of the defendant's roofing fell into the plaintiff's premises) Talbot J stated (at 557) that: 'nuisances, at least in the vast majority of cases, are interferences for a substantial length of time'.

5   *Midwood & Co Ltd v Manchester Corpn* [1905] 2 KB 597, CA; *Spicer v Smee* [1946] 1 All ER 489. Note, also, that where there is a short-term interference the courts will allow claims for amenity nuisance: *Matania v National Provincial Bank Ltd and Elevenist Syndicate Ltd* [1936] 2 All ER 633, CA (plaintiff successfully sued on the basis of the excessive dust and noise generated by the defendant's building work); *Crown River Cruises Ltd v Kimbolton Fireworks Ltd* [1996] 2 Lloyd's Rep 533 (plaintiff bothered by a 20-minute firework display). One possible explanation of why isolated events causing interferences with the enjoyment of land are not actionable is that there is no quantifiable loss to compensate.

6   [1946] 1 All ER 489 at 493.

7   [1905] 2 KB 597, CA. See also *Stone v Bolton* [1949] 2 All ER 851, CA (pedestrian struck by a cricket ball hit out of the cricket ground); *British Celanese Ltd v A H Hunt (Capacitors) Ltd* [1969] 2 All ER 1252 (isolated escape of metal foil causing a short-circuit at a nearby electricity sub-station).

that he has suffered actual damage – whether in the form of physical damage to land or in the form of an interference with his amenities.

(b)   The extent of the harm

Whether an interference is serious (and hence unreasonable) must be assessed in the light of its impact on the defendant. Whenever I play my piano, I generate a level of noise that may be moderately irksome to my neighbour, but he may easily drown it out by turning on his television or radio. On the other hand, if I were to play my trombone, it would generate much more noise and be likely to remain heard and cause disturbance no matter what steps my neighbour might take. The relationship between the degree of interference and its unreasonableness is therefore clear: the louder I play an instrument, or the more odious the smell that my business generates, the more likely it is that the court will find the interference thereby caused to be not only substantial, but also unreasonable.

In addition, the gravity of the harm caused must not be gauged on a purely objective basis (eg by reference only to the loudness of my trumpet playing). There is also an important role for a subjective element in the assessment of whether the interference was unreasonable. Although there is usually a correlation between the magnitude of an interference and its unreasonableness, this is not always the case. Where, for example, I play my trombone late at night generating, say, 20 decibels of noise, this would, nine tines out of ten, be considered a very substantial (and hence unreasonable) disturbance to my next-door neighbour. Where, however, my neighbour is practically deaf, she may only faintly hear the trombone. Accordingly, despite the *objective* loudness of my playing, it will not *subjectively* be perceived to be an unreasonable interference. And, as we have already seen, the plaintiff must show substantial damage, for 'the law does not regard trifling and small inconveniences, but only regards sensible inconveniences which sensibly diminish the comfort … *of the property which is affected*'.[8] Inherent in this is the fact that nuisance liability is not fault-based, for I may wholly unreasonably play my CDs very loudly and every night, but the fact that it does not diminish my neighbour's enjoyment of her land negates any prospect of my being successfully sued for nuisance.

(c)   The character of the harm

Harm, for the purposes of nuisance law, as we have already seen, may take the form either of physical damage to land or an interference with the use or enjoyment of it. Although all three forms are actionable, physical injury is generally regarded as being inherently a more serious kind of harm than an interference with a the plaintiff's amenities. Indeed, the distinction drawn in *St Helen's Smelting Co v Tipping* between physical damage and amenity nuisance[9] has been taken by some commentators to support the proposition that physical injury is actionable regardless of whether the defendant's user of his land was objectively reasonable.[10] This proposition probably goes too far,

---

8   Per Lord Wensleydale in *St Helen's Smelting Co v Tipping* (1865) 11 HL Cas 642 at 654 (emphasis added). See also *Sturges v Bridgman* (1879) 11 Ch D 852 at 863, CA where Thesiger LJ observed that, where the interference is of 'so trifling a character, that, upon the maxim *de minimis non curat lex*, we arrive at the conclusion that the defendant's acts would not have given rise to [liability]'.

9   (1865) 11 HL Cas 642 at 650 (per Lord Westbury).

10   See, eg, Ogus and Richardson 'Economics and the Environment: a Study of Private Nuisance' (1977) 36 CLJ 284, 297.

especially in the light of what was said (obiter) in *Ellison v Ministry of Defence*.[11] Nonetheless, it does draw to attention to the fact that, even in the context of nuisance, the English courts remain chary of protecting personal discomforts falling short of physical injury.[12] The central issue is whether the interference is unreasonable.[13] So, in cases of physical injury – which can easily be proven and quantified in terms of damages – it is simpler for the courts to find that the interference complained of was unreasonable than in cases of personal discomfort or annoyance.[14] Consequently, physical violations of the plaintiff's land have become less readily tolerated than disruptions to the peaceful enjoyment of it.

(d)   Social value of the use interfered with
The final factor that can affect the seriousness of the harm is the nature of the use to which the plaintiff puts his land. Where the plaintiff uses his land in such a way that it can be classified as socially useful, it is more likely that the disruptive interference complained of will be regarded by the court as serious. In *Smith v Giddy*,[15] for example, branches on the defendant's trees which overhung the plaintiff's land and prevented his commercially cultivated fruit trees from growing properly were held to be a nuisance whereas it was stated obiter that, had the plaintiff not been growing such trees, the mere blockage of light would not have been actionable.

(2)   REASONABLE USER OF THE DEFENDANT'S LAND

Strictly, as we have noted at several points, nuisance liability depends upon there being an unreasonable interference with the plaintiff's interests rather than there being unreasonable conduct on the part of the defendant. However, there is an immutable and fundamental inter-relationship between the reasonableness of the interference and the reasonableness of the user or activity. The fact that one is engaged in an unreasonable user will, ipso facto, render any interference thereby caused equally unreasonable: an interference that is caused by an unjustifiable activity cannot itself be justified.[16] The converse, as Lord Goff noted in *Cambridge Water Co Ltd v Eastern*

---

11   (1996) 81 BLR 101 (the defendants constructed large fuel containers on their land. These trapped a large amount of rainwater which eventually flooded the plaintiff's land. It was said that there was a reasonable use of land for the purposes of nuisance law and that the damage was not actionable in nuisance). See also Steele 'Private Law and the Environment: Nuisance in Context' (1995) 15 Legal Studies 236, 252.

12   See the observations of Lord Hoffmann in *Hunter* noted at the beginning of this chapter.

13   See, eg, *Watt v Jamieson* 1954 SC 56 at 58 where Lord President Cooper held that though the defendant's ventpipe had caused plaster damage and dry-rot to occur in a neighbouring flat, the key question was 'whether what he [the plaintiff] was exposed to was *plus quam tolerabile*'. In short, his concern was with the unreasonableness of the harm rather than with its form.

14   As Lord Selborne put it in *Gaunt v Fynney* (1872) 8 Ch App 8 at 1–12: '[amenity nuisance] is much more difficult to prove than when the injury complained of is the demonstrable effect of a visible or tangible cause'. See also *Hunter v Canary Wharf* [1997] 2 All ER 426, HL where Lord Lloyd opined (at 442) that 'Damages for loss of amenity value cannot be assessed mathematically. But this does not mean that such damages cannot be awarded'; and *Ruxley Electronics and Construction Ltd v Forsyth* [1995] 3 All ER 268, HL.

15   [1904] 2 KB 448, 451.

16   Though the unreasonableness of the user will confirm the unreasonableness of the interference, it does not follow that all unreasonable users will result in liability. For example, an unreasonable user that causes minimal interference will not be actionable: the interference needs to be substantial as well as unreasonable. Cf Cross 'Does only the Careless Polluter Pay? A Fresh Examination of the Nature of Private Nuisance' (1995) 111 LQR 445, at fn 32.

Counties Leather plc, is also true: 'if the user is reasonable the defendant will not be liable for consequent harm to his neighbour's enjoyment of his land'.[17]

In assessing the reasonableness of the defendant's user the courts have resort to a series of factors which are relevant to the determination.

(a) The defendant's motive

In judging what constitutes a nuisance, the courts will take into account the main object of the defendant's activity. Thus, for example, in *Harrison v Southwark and Vauxhall Motor Co*[18] the useful nature of the defendants' construction work was part of the reason why the plaintiff's action was dismissed. Where, however, the defendant's primary aim is to injure his neighbour, there is considerable authority that his malicious motives may render the interference unreasonable. In *Christie v Davey*,[19] the plaintiffs' action lay in respect of noises being made by their defendant neighbours. Central to North J's judgment that the noises were a nuisance was the fact that they were made 'deliberately and maliciously for the purpose of annoying the plaintiffs'.[20] Similarly, in *Hollywood Silver Fox Farm Ltd v Emmett*[1] the court held the firing of guns to be actionable where they were fired out of spite, with the object of interfering with the breeding of silver foxes by the plaintiff. The defendant's malicious purpose was again emphasised. What needs to be appreciated here is that if nuisance is a strict liability tort, as Lord Goff proclaimed it to be in the *Cambridge Water* case, then it is not the unreasonableness of the defendant's conduct, per se, that is of concern. Rather, it is the fact that this has a direct impact on the reasonableness of the interference. This is consistent with the definition of nuisance offered at the beginning of this chapter which does not stipulate unreasonable conduct – for this would blur the distinction between negligence and nuisance – but instead, an unreasonable interference.

An important, and seemingly anomalous, case in this context is that of *Bradford Corpn v Pickles*.[2] There, the defendant was exercising his legal right to abstract water percolating beneath his land thereby preventing it from reaching the plaintiff's adjoining reservoir. In dismissing the plaintiff's nuisance action, Lord Macnaghten held that:

> it is the act, not the motive for the act, that must be regarded. If the act, apart from motive gives rise merely to damages without legal injury, the motive, however reprehensible it may be, will not supply that element.

At first sight, this short passage from his lordship's dictum would appear difficult to square with *Christie v Davey* and the *Hollywood Silver Fox Farm* case. Indeed, a number of commentators have been at pains to reconcile the cases on the basis that *Bradford Corpn v Pickles* is a sui generis type of case concerning, as it does, rights in respect of servitudes.[3] But this argument, turning on the plaintiff's *absolute* right to extract water, is unconvincing, for there is a no less absolute right to use one's land for

---

17 [1994] 2 AC 264 at 299, [1994] 1 All ER 53 at 71, HL. See also *Sanders-Clark v Grosvenor Mansions Co Ltd* [1900] 2 Ch 373 at 375–6 (per Buckley J); *Bamford v Turnley* (1862) 3 B & S 66 at 83 (per Bamford B.) On the other hand, a reasonable user that causes physical damage rather than an amenity nuisance will almost certainly be actionable: see *Halsey v Esso Petroleum Co Ltd* [1961] 2 All ER 145.
18 *Harrison v Southwark and Vauxhall Water Co* [1891] 2 Ch 409 at 414 (per Vaughan Williams LJ).
19 [1893] 1 Ch 316.
20 [1893] 1 Ch 316 at 326.
1 [1936] 2 KB 468, [1936] 1 All ER 825.
2 [1895] AC 587, HL.
3 See, eg, the 9th edition of this work.

lawful purposes even where a substantial interference is caused to one's neighbour.[4] What the argument fails to recognise is that Lord Macnaghten's focus is not so much on the *reasonableness* of the interference, but rather upon its *gravity*. His concern is primarily with whether the act complained of has occasioned a substantial interference, since the notions of *factual* and *legal* interference are not necessarily coextensive. His point is that, in the absence of substantial harm, any action in nuisance based on the malicious conduct of the defendant must fail![5] This accords with the principle *de minimis non curat lex*, long since deemed to be applicable to nuisance cases.[6] At all events, in *Hunter v Canary Wharf Ltd*, Lord Cooke reasserted the principle that the defendant actuated by malice may incur liability where the same interference, innocently caused, would not lead to this result.[7]

Wanton ill-conduct serves no socially useful function. Accordingly, it has the effect of rendering unreasonable practically any interference which the defendant thereby caused. Where, however, the defendant's activity does possess some social utility, and it is this social utility that motivates the defendant, the court will naturally be less inclined to declare any resulting interference to be unreasonable. The country must have power stations, factories and smelting works. But the need for motorcycle speedway tracks or racecourses is much less pressing and, consequently, such activities much more readily form the basis of successful nuisance actions.[8]

(b)   Location of the defendant's enterprise

Just as the location of the *plaintiff's* premises is important in determining what constitutes a 'substantial interference' in cases of amenity nuisance, so too is the location of the *defendant's* premises important in assessing the reasonableness of the defendant's conduct (which, in turn, affects the reasonableness of the interference he causes). Put simply, we are concerned with the question 'what is it reasonable to do?' and not with the question (relevant when considering the location of the plaintiff's premises), 'what is it reasonable to put up with?'. Thus, in addition to considering the usefulness of the defendant's activity, we must also consider whether it is being carried on in a suitable locality. In this connection, the courts have recognised the national policy of segregating different uses of land and have furthered this policy by taking into account whether the defendant is putting his land to a use which is compatible with the main use to which land in that area is usually put. To take an example, the operation of a chemicals works would not, per se, be considered to be an unreasonable use of land. But if it was operated in a residential area, it could be so regarded. If, however, the factory was located in an industrial area, the activity would probably be considered lawful.[9]

---

4   See, eg, *Hunter v Canary Wharf Ltd* [1997] 2 All ER 426, HL where Lord Goff refused to accept that the lawful construction of a tall building constituted nuisance when its construction caused interference to the plaintiffs' television reception. For an interesting account of various (unnecessary) attempts at reconciling these cases see Cross 'Does only the Careless Polluter Pay? A Fresh Examination of the Nature of Private Nuisance' (1995) 111 LQR 445, 453–5.

5   His dictum is nonetheless misleading in so far as it appears to suggest that D's motive may *always* be disregarded. This is manifestly not the case as the *Christie* and *Silver Fox* cases amply demonstrate.

6   *Sturges v Bridgman* (1879) 11 Ch D 852.

7   [1997] 2 All ER 426 at 465ff.

8   See, eg, *A-G v Hastings Corpn* (1950) 94 Sol Jo 225, CA and *Dewar v City and Suburban Racecourse Co* [1899] 1 IR 345, respectively.

9   It was decided in *Ball v Ray* (1873) 8 Ch App 467 that converting part of a house in a residential street into stables caused an unreasonable interference. By contrast, a similar degree of interference caused by piano being played, or crying children, would not be a nuisance. Cf *Moy v Stoop* (1909) 25 TLR 262.

(c) Fault

The undoubted role that fault can play in determining nuisance liability raises one of the most difficult questions in the whole of the law of tort: is nuisance liability strict or fault based? To answer this question, we must first identify the function served by identifying fault on the part of the defendant and secondly the limits to the role it plays in the ascription of nuisance liability. Much of the confusion that surrounds these issues stems from one famous passage in Lord Reid's Privy Council speech in *The Wagon Mound (No 2)* where he said:

> Nuisance is a term used to cover a wide variety of tortious acts or omissions and in many negligence in the narrow sense is not essential. An occupier may incur liability for the emission of noxious fumes or noise although he has used the utmost care in building and using his premises ... [And yet] although negligence may not be necessary, fault of some kind is almost always necessary and fault generally involves foreseeability.[10]

At first sight, this passage may appear either intractable or inherently self-contradictory. Negligence is the archetypal fault-based tort. How then can it be asserted that while negligence is not required, fault is almost invariably a precondition of liability? The answer lies in Lord Reid's qualification that it is only *negligence in the narrow sense* that need not be shown. The first point to note is that 'negligence in the narrow sense' refers to no more than a breach of a duty of care (ie, failure to meet the standard of conduct of the reasonable man). The second point is that, though one undertakes an enterprise with all possible caution, one can seldom guarantee that certain, *foreseeable*, adverse consequences will not arise. I may, for example, drive my car with all due care but be unable to prevent a collision with another car caused by my skidding on a patch of 'black ice'. In such a case, though I could not be found negligent, it might still be said that I was at fault in the rather different sense that I knowingly took the risk of such an occurrence by deciding to drive in the first place. The element of fault in this second sense derives from the foreseeability of an accident even though I drive to an exemplary standard. It is submitted that it is this notion of fault that Lord Reid considered to be crucial to nuisance liability.

The question of whether nuisance involves strict or fault-based liability was revisited by the House of Lords in *Cambridge Water Co Ltd v Eastern Counties Leather plc*.[11] There, Lord Goff, with whom the other four Law Lords agreed, offered a similar interpretation to ours on the role of fault in nuisance liability. He said:

> [T]he fact that the defendant has taken all reasonable care will not of itself exonerate him ... But it by no means follows that the defendant should be held liable for damage of a type which he could not reasonably foresee; and the development of the law of negligence in the past 60 years points strongly towards a requirement that such foreseeability be a prerequisite of liability in damages for nuisance, as it is of liability in negligence.[12]

This passage makes it clear that liability in nuisance is strict in the sense that a defendant may be found liable regardless of the care he took to avoid causing harm. Nonetheless, his Lordship reserved a residual role for fault (in the second sense) in that liability will only attach to those users of land that involve a foreseeable risk of harm.[13]

---

10 [1967] 1 AC 617, 639; [1966] 2 All ER 709, 716.
11 [1994] 2 AC 264, [1994] 1 All ER 53, HL.
12 [1994] 2 AC 264 at 300, [1994] 1 All ER 53 at 71–2, HL.
13 For a fuller account of the role of foreseeability in nuisance and *Rylands and Fletcher* see Wilkinson '*Cambridge Water Company v Eastern Counties Leather plc*: Diluting Liability for Continuing Escapes' (1994) 57 MLR 799.

(d)   The kind of user
A final factor that can influence the court's view of the reasonableness of the defendant's user is the kind of activity in which he is engaged. Here, the concern is simply with the actual use to which the defendant puts his land. If my neighbour disturbs me by operating a noisy printing press in order to produce illegal, pornographic literature, his activity can never be justified, for the activity is illegal and thus unreasonable. It follows that any substantial disturbance thereby caused can also never be justified. Put bluntly, illegal and extremely dangerous enterprises[14] are, by definition, unreasonable users of land and, apart from the criminal aspects of such activities, any disturbances they cause will, ipso facto, be regarded as unreasonable, *regardless* of motive.[15]

The kinds of activity likely to be deemed unreasonable per se will commonly overlap with those which, for the purposes of liability under the rule in *Rylands v Fletcher*,[16] constitute 'non-natural' users of land. Though the two notions are related, it is also clear that they are not co-extensive. Accordingly, in the case of *Fay v Prentice*,[17] the defendant was found liable in nuisance in respect of water dripping from the eaves of his building although such a user would not be termed non-natural for the purposes of *Rylands v Fletcher* liability. On the other hand, the fact that a given user could be regarded as 'non-natural' for *Rylands* purposes might be material in deciding whether it was also an 'unreasonable user' for the purposes of nuisance.[18] We return to the question of what constitutes a non-natural user in the next chapter.

(e)   Impracticability of preventing or avoiding the interference
It will always be material whether the defendant, by taking reasonable, practicable steps to prevent the interference, could still have achieved his purpose without interfering with the plaintiff's use of his land. If, without excessive expenditure, a factory owner could install equipment that would prevent him causing a disturbance to his neighbours, the courts might treat this as conclusive that the defendant's user was unreasonable. In *Andreae v Selfridge & Co Ltd*, for example, where building operations that were generating noise and dust interfered with the comfortable enjoyment of a neighbour's hotel, it was held that the defendants who had undertaken an ostensibly reasonable user of the land were nonetheless under a duty:

> to take proper precautions, and to see that the nuisance is reduced to a minimum. It is no answer for them to say: 'But this would mean that we should have to do the work more slowly than we would like to do it, or it would involve putting us to some extra expense'.[19]

Similarly, in *Leeman v Montagu*[20] a poultry farmer who made no attempt to rearrange his farm was held liable in nuisance in respect of 750 cockerels that crowed between the hours of 2.00 and 7.00 am. On the other hand, in one case involving young children whose crying often caused a disturbance to the plaintiff, it was held that there was no liability as there was no evidence that the children had been neglected or suffered from

14   Eg, the storing of large quantities of high explosives in a private, terraced house.
15   In *Cambridge Water Co Ltd v Eastern Counties Leather plc* [1994] 2 AC 264 at 298, [1994] 1 All ER 53 at 71, HL, Lord Goff identified that unreasonable land use is not necessarily to be equated with negligent land use, though wherever there is evidence of a negligently conducted activity, the courts may well conclude that it amounts to an unreasonable user.
16   (1868) LR 3 HL 330; see also chapter 19, post.
17   (1845) 1 CB 828, CA.
18   On the relationship between the two notions, see Murphy 'Noxious Emissions and Common Law Liability – Tort in the Shadow of Regulation' in Lowry and *Edmunds Environmental Protection and the Common Law* (1999).
19   [1938] Ch 1 at 9–10, [1937] 3 All ER 255 at 267, CA.
20   [1936] 2 All ER 1677.

a want of care.[1] What was crucial to this finding was the actual ability of the defendant to eradicate or minimise the interference. This principle was endorsed in *Leakey v National Trust* where, despite ultimately being found liable in respect of an earth-slide from their land, the Court of Appeal expressly declared that '[t]he extent of the defendant's duty [to minimise any interference], and the question of whether he has or has not fulfilled that duty, may ... depend on the defendant's financial resources'.[2]

SECTION 3.   WHO CAN SUE?

(A)   OWNERS AND RESIDENT OCCUPIERS

Reflecting the fact that nuisance law has traditionally protected interests in land, the conventional approach adopted by the English courts was to allow only those who own the land to bring an action in nuisance. As Lord Simmonds put it in *Read v Lyons*: 'he alone has a lawful claim who has suffered an invasion of some proprietary or other interest in land'.[3] It was this insistence on the existence of a proprietary interest that underpinned the decision of the Court of Appeal in *Malone v Laskey*.[4] In that case, a wife was injured when vibrations created by the defendant caused a lavatory cistern to fall off the wall and onto her head. Her claim for personal injuries failed because she had no legal or equitable interest in the property,[5] and the same reasoning was employed by the courts in a string of subsequent cases.[6]

The requirement of a proprietary or possessory interest in land in order to bring an action in nuisance was, for a time, cast in doubt by the Court of Appeal in *Khorasandjian v Bush*.[7] Since then, however, the principle that a proprietary interest is required to found an action in private nuisance has been put beyond doubt by the House of Lords in *Hunter v Canary Wharf Ltd.* There Lord Goff stated that:

> an action in private nuisance will only lie at the suit of a person who has a right to the land affected. Ordinarily such a person can only sue if he has the right to exclusive possession of the land, such as a freeholder or tenant in possession, or even a licensee with exclusive possession ... But a mere licensee on the land has no right to sue.[8]

Other than those rights to property explicitly recognised in this short passage, Lord Goff also recognised a further instance in which the right to sue would be afforded. Though exceptional, his lordship considered the decision in *Foster v Warblington UDC*[9] to be good law and, as such, a person in actual possession (with no right to be

1   *Moy v Stoop* (1909) 25 TLR 262.
2   [1980] QB 485 at 526, [1980] 1 All ER 17 at 37, CA.
3   [1947] AC 156 at 183, [1946] 2 All ER 471 at 482, HL (obiter).
4   [1907] 2 KB 141, CA.
5   Perhaps ironically, this reasoning would not apply today in respect of *a spouse* with no proprietary interest, for under s 30 of the Family Law Act 1996 a spouse with no such interest is afforded a statutory right to occupy the matrimonial home (so long as the other spouse has a proprietary right to it). Such 'matrimonial home rights', as they are known, were recognised as a sufficient interest in the property to sue in *Hunter v Canary Wharf* [1997] 2 All ER 426 at 440, HL (per Lord Goff).
6   See, eg, *Tate & Lyle Industries Ltd v Greater London Council* [1983] 2 AC 509, [1983] 1 All ER 1159, HL; *Cunard v Antifyre Ltd* [1933] 1 KB 551 and *Metropolitan Properties Ltd v Jones* [1939] 2 All ER 202, CA.
7   [1993] QB 727, [1993] 3 All ER 669, CA.
8   [1997] 2 All ER 426 at 438, HL.
9   [1906] 1 KB 648, CA.

there) is allowed a right of action against a third party (ie someone other than the true owner).[10] Apart from these instances, it is unlikely that anyone else – such as a squatter – would be entitled to bring a nuisance action.[11]

(B) REVERSIONERS

Where a landowner is not in occupation at the time of the interference complained of, but where he retains a reversionary interest in the land, he may sue in respect of the nuisance so long as he can prove that *his* (the reversionary) interest in the land has been affected. If the damage is of a temporary, rather than a permanent, nature, then he has no basis upon which to sue, and this is so even if the reversioner can show that it is likely that a similar, temporary interference will take place in the future.[12] In this context, a 'permanent' interference has been described as one that:

> will continue indefinitely unless something is done to remove it. Thus a building which infringes ancient lights is permanent within the rule ... On the other hand, a noisy trade and the exercise of an alleged right of way, are not in their nature permanent within the rule, for they cease of themselves, unless there be someone to continue them.[13]

In accordance with this principle, a reversioner may sue where an adjoining landowner constructs a house, the eaves of which project over his land and discharge rainwater onto it.[14] Similarly, physical damage caused to the reversioner's buildings will afford the reversioner a cause of action.[15] Conversely, no such action will lie where the nuisance complained of comprises merely temporary annoyance caused by the emission of smoke.[16]

(C) PLAINTIFFS SUFFERING PERSONAL INJURIES, DAMAGE TO CHATTELS OR ECONOMIC LOSS

It was held in *Hunter v Canary Wharf*[17] that personal injuries are not, per se, recoverable in an action for private nuisance. Nonetheless, an action will lie where 'the injury to the amenity of the land consists in the fact that persons on it are liable to suffer inconvenience, annoyance or illness'.[18] The point is one of emphasis. The personal injury, to be recoverable, must be seen in terms of a diminution in the capacity of the land to be enjoyed. As such, where defective wiring in a neighbouring house causes a fire that spreads to the plaintiff's house, the plaintiff should be allowed to recover not only for the damage caused to his house but also for any burns he sustains because it is not only the land, but also the amenity of the land (characterised in terms of the ability to live there free from burns) that has been affected. The matter has resonance at the stage of quantifying damages: 'the reduction in amenity value is the same whether the land is occupied by the family man or the bachelor ... the quantum of damages in private nuisance does not depend on the number of those enjoying the land in

10 [1906] 1 KB 648 at 659–60 (per Vaughan-Williams LJ).
11 Cf the speech of Lord Hoffmann in *Hunter v Canary Wharf* [1997] 2 All ER 426, HL where he suggested (at 449) that it is sufficient if the plaintiff 'was de facto in exclusive possession'.
12 *Simpson v Savage* (1856) 1 CBNS 347 (smoke discharged from a fire).
13 *Jones v Llanrwst UDC* [1911] 1 Ch 393 at 404 (per Parker J).
14 *Tucker v Newman* (1839) 11 Ad & El 40.
15 *Meux's Brewery Co v City of London Electric Lighting Co* [1895] 1 Ch 287.
16 *Simpson v Savage* (1856) 1 CBNS 347.
17 [1997] 2 All ER 426 at 442, HL (per Lord Lloyd).
18 *Hunter v Canary Wharf Ltd* [1997] 2 All ER 426 at 452, HL (per Lord Hoffmann).

question'.[19] In other words, there will be no multiplication of damages just because more than one person is affected.

Whatever the state of the law in connection with private nuisance, it is well established that personal injuries are recoverable in public nuisance.

So far as damage to chattels is concerned, it is also reasonably well established that private nuisance will afford a remedy. In *Midwood & Co Ltd v Manchester Corpn*,[20] for example, damages were awarded by the Court of Appeal for loss of stock in trade; while in *Halsey v Esso Petroleum Co Ltd*[1] they were awarded for damage to washing on a clothes line. Notwithstanding the fact that in *Hunter* their Lordships staunchly reasserted the principle that nuisance was a tort to *land*, it was also explicitly stated that an action in respect of *consequential* damage to chattels was recoverable.[2]

Finally, let us consider economic loss. In this context, it is clear, as Lord Hoffmann recognised in *Hunter*, that consequential economic loss in the form of the plaintiff's inability to use the land for the purposes of his business is recoverable.[3] Beyond this, it is worth noting that two cases[4] decided according to the rule in *Rylands v Fletcher*[5] have accepted, in principle, the recoverability of pure economic losses. Since Lord Goff's view in the *Cambridge Water* case was that *Rylands* was a tort derived from nuisance, it could be argued that there should be no objection to pure economic losses being recovered in nuisance *so long as* they arise out of an interference with land or its amenity value.

SECTION 4.   WHO CAN BE SUED?

A person is liable in nuisance only if he bears 'some degree of personal responsibility'.[6] Such persons can conveniently be identified under three main headings: creators of the nuisance, occupiers and landlords.

(A)   CREATORS

If the actual wrongdoer is invested with the management and control of the premises from which the nuisance emanates, then he is liable irrespective of whether he is an occupier of those premises in the normal sense of the word.[7] Even though the person who created the interference was neither at the time of the proceedings, nor at the time when he created the interference, in occupation or control of the premises from which it emanated, but merely created it with the authority of the occupier of the premises, he may still be liable. Nor will he be excused simply because he lacks the right to enter

---

19   [1997] 2 All ER 426 at 442, HL per Lord Lloyd.
20   [1905] 2 KB 597, CA.
1   [1961] 2 All ER 145. Though an award in respect of damaged furniture was denied in *Cunard v Antifyre Ltd* [1933] 1 KB 551, it should be noted that the case was ultimately decided in negligence.
2   [1997] 2 All ER 426, at 452, HL (per Lord Hoffmann). For critique, see Oliphant (1998) 6 Tort Law Review 21.
3   [1997] 2 All ER 426.
4   *British Celanese Ltd v A H Hunt (Capacitors) Ltd* [1969] 2 All ER 1252; *Ryeford Homes Ltd v Sevenoaks District Council* [1989] 2 EGLR 281.
5   (1868) LR 3 HL 330.
6   Per Lord Atkin in *Sedleigh-Denfield v O'Callaghan* [1940] AC 880 at 897, [1940] 3 All ER 471, HL.
7   *Hall v Beckenham Corpn* [1949] 1 KB 716, [1949] 1 All ER 423.

onto the premises in order to abate it.[8] In accordance with ordinary principles of tortious liability, anyone who authorises another to commit a nuisance is himself also liable. So, for example, a local authority is liable where it authorises the use of its land as a go-kart circuit, where a nuisance is the known and inevitable consequence of go-kart racing taking place there.[9] If, however, land is let by a local authority to persons who may or may not cause a nuisance, no such liability will attach as the eventuality of a nuisance is not inevitable.[10] It is the act of authorising conduct that will cause a nuisance that enables the courts to treat the landowner as though he had caused the interference himself.

Where the interference complained of arises from a 'state of affairs' that was created by the defendant,[11] he will again be held liable (even though his initial conduct does not, of itself, amount to a nuisance) so long as harm to the plaintiff is a foreseeable consequence of that initial conduct. Thus, he who plants poplar trees – itself an innocuous act – is liable in nuisance in respect of the indirect harm caused by their roots spreading under neighbouring land.[12] Equally, maintaining defective electric mains gives rise to liability for foreseeable damage that in fact ensues.[13] Where, on the other hand, the defendant creates a state of affairs that will not foreseeably result in a nuisance, the courts will refuse to attach liability.

In *Ilford UDC v Beal*,[14] the defendant erected a retaining wall along the bank of a river. Because the wall was not constructed in accordance with the best engineering practice it was later completely undermined by the river. This undermining caused the wall to move forward a foot or two where it came to press against, and cause damage to, the plaintiff's sewer. The plaintiff neither knew, nor ought to have known, about the presence of the sewer. The damage to the sewer was therefore unforeseeable and the defendant was held not liable in nuisance.

Although the key to liability in such cases is indubitably the remoteness of the injurious consequences of the defendant's initial conduct, it is not always easy to distinguish those cases in which the defendant genuinely created the dangerous state of affairs from those in which he merely failed to remedy it. The point can be illustrated by reference to *Goldman v Hargrave*:[15]

A redgum tree that was growing on the defendant's land caught fire when it was struck by lightning. The defendant took measures to fell the tree but because of changes in the weather

8   *Thompson v Gibson* (1841) 7 M & W 456. In *Southport Corpn v Esso Petroleum Co Ltd* [1953] 2 All ER 1204 at 1207, Devlin J said (obiter): 'I can see no reason why ... if the defendant as a licensee or trespasser misuses someone else's land, he should not be liable for a nuisance in the same way as an adjoining occupier would be'. Despite this dictum, there has been no English case in which liability was imposed upon a person who had never been in occupation or control of the relevant premises in respect of conduct which was not authorised by someone who was in occupation. In Australia, there is direct authority that a trespasser is not liable in nuisance: *Beaudesert Shire Council v Smith* (1966) 40 ALJR 211 (H Ct Australia).

9   *Tetley v Chitty* [1986] 1 All ER 663.

10 *Smith v Scott* [1973] Ch 314, [1972] 3 All ER 645. In this case undesirable tenants were always likely to annoy their neighbours by noise and vandalism, but that they would do so was not guaranteed. See also *Rich v Basterfield* (1847) 4 CB 783 and *Hussain v Lancaster City Council* (1998) 77 P & CR 89.

11 Contrast those circumstances in which the defendant only inherits or continues a state of affairs produced by a third party. In such cases, considered in the next section, the defendant's liability attaches (if at all) because of his failure to remedy the potentially injurious state of affairs.

12 *Butler v Standard Telephones and Cables Ltd* [1940] 1 KB 399, [1940] 1 All ER 121; followed in *McCombe v Read* [1955] 2 QB 429, [1955] 2 All ER 758.

13 *Midwood & Co Ltd v Manchester Corpn* [1905] 2 KB 597, CA.

14 [1925] 1 KB 671.

15 [1967] 1 AC 645, [1966] 2 All ER 989, PC. See also *Radstock Co-operative and Industrial Society Ltd v Norton-Radstock UDC* [1968] Ch 605, [1968] 2 All ER 59, CA.

conditions (including a strengthening in the wind) the tree which had not been completely extinguished, rekindled. The fire then spread to the plaintiff's land. One of the Privy Council's findings of fact was that the defendant's method of dealing with the fire gave rise to a foreseeable risk of the fire reviving and spreading.

It is not wholly clear whether the defendant's wrongdoing amounted to misfeasance (in that he dealt inappropriately with a burning tree thereby creating a risk to his neighbour) or nonfeasance (in that he failed to avert an extant risk of fire spreading). Had the tree not been felled in the manner adopted by the defendant, the fire may never have rekindled and spread to the defendant's land. On the other hand, had the tree not been struck by lightning in the first place, a hazardous state of affairs would never have arisen on the defendant's land. Whether cases such as this are better seen as involving misfeasance or nonfeasance is by no means easy to decide.[16]

(B)   OCCUPIERS

As we noted in the previous section, the occupier of premises will be liable in respect of nuisances that he has himself created. But he may also be liable where he fails to take reasonable steps to remedy a dangerous state of affairs on the land that he occupies. In determining what amounts to the reasonable steps he might be expected to take, the court, for reasons of justice, may, as we shall see, have regard to his limited financial and other resources; especially if the plaintiff has had the state of affairs involuntarily thrust upon him.

So far as the liability of occupiers for misfeasance is concerned, there are essentially four ways in which a problem scenario might arise.

(1)   ACTS OF A TRESPASSER

If the dangerous state of affairs on the defendant's land is created by a trespasser, so long as the occupier knows or ought to know about it, he is liable in nuisance in respect of damage thereby caused to his neighbour. The leading case is *Sedleigh-Denfield v O'Callaghan*.[17] There, the drainage system on the defendant's land became blocked because of the negligent acts of a trespasser. The defendant's servant who had been responsible for periodically cleansing the drainage system over a period of three years ought to have noticed the risk of flooding and for this reason the defendant was held liable for the flood damage that the blockage had caused to the plaintiff. In finding the defendant liable, the House of Lords stressed the importance of his (constructive) knowledge of the risk:

> An occupier is not prima facie responsible for a nuisance created without his knowledge and consent. If he is to be liable a further condition is necessary, namely, that he had knowledge or means of knowledge, that he knew or should have known, of the nuisance in time to correct it.[18]

It is important to distinguish cases such as *Sedleigh-Denfield*, from two further kinds of case. First, from those such as *Smith v Littlewoods Organisation Ltd*[19] where the House of Lords held that there was no liability where the trespassers had, *in the absence*

16 In the eventuality, the Privy Council treated *Goldman* as a nonfeasance case.
17 [1940] AC 880, [1940] 3 All ER 349, HL.
18 [1940] AC 880 at 904 and 365 respectively.
19 [1987] AC 241, [1987] 1 All ER 710, HL.

of actual or constructive knowledge on the part of the defendants, caused a fire in the defendants' disused cinema which spread to the plaintiff's property. Secondly, from those where the third party merely uses the defendant's land as a means of gaining access to the plaintiff's land rather than, as in *Sedleigh-Denfield*, where the third party's mischievous act or omission actually occurs on the defendant's land. In such cases the Court of Appeal has held that the defendant will be free of any general liability in respect of the acts of such third parties.[20]

A final point that ought to be noted is that, where the defendant's failure to abate a nuisance can be attributed to a pre-existing duty to consult the interested parties before any remedial steps can permissibly be taken, the defendant's inaction will not be taken by the courts to be an unreasonable failure to erase the menacing state of affairs.[1]

(2) ACTS OF NATURE

If a dangerous state of affairs arises on the defendant's land due to an act of nature of which the occupier knows or ought to know, he is liable in nuisance if damage occurs to a neighbouring landowner. In *Goldman v Hargrave*, the facts of which we noted when considering the liability of the creator of a nuisance, the Privy Council extended the rule in *Sedleigh-Denfield v O'Callaghan* – that an occupier must take reasonable steps to remedy a potentially hazardous state of affairs – to cases in which the danger arises by an act of God. However, Lord Wilberforce added the important qualification that the unreasonableness of the defendant's attempts to avert such a danger must be judged in the light of his financial and other resources. He said:

> [T]he law must take account of the fact that the occupier on whom the duty is cast has, ex hypothesi, had this hazard thrust upon him through no seeking or fault of his own. His interest and his resources, whether physical or material, may be of very modest character ... A rule which required of him in such unsought circumstances in his neighbour's interest a physical effort of which he is not capable, or an excessive expenditure of money, would be unenforceable or unjust.[2]

Although *Goldman* is, strictly, an Australian decision, its underlying rationale was adopted in the English case of *Leakey v National Trust for Places of Historic Interest or Natural Beauty*.[3] There, the defendants owned land on which there stood a large mound of earth which the defendants knew to be prone to subsidence. When, following a particularly dry summer which caused cracks in the earth to appear, the mound finally gave way causing damage to the plaintiff's houses, it was held by the Court of Appeal that the defendants were liable in respect of the land-slip. Although the defendants had given permission to the plaintiff to abate the cause of the nuisance, they had themselves done nothing to remove the danger.[4]

20 *Perl (P) Exporters Ltd v Camden London Borough Council* [1984] QB 342, [1983] 3 All ER 161.
1 *Page Motors Ltd v Epsom and Ewell District Council* (1981) 80 LGR 337, CA.
2 [1967] 1 AC 645 at 663, [1966] 2 All ER 989 at 996, PC. This might be seen as undermining the supposed strictness of nuisance liability. On the other hand, it might be seen as being a not unreasonable user of the land (and, therefore, a not unreasonable ensuing interference).
3 [1980] QB 485, [1980] 1 All ER 17, CA. See also *Davey v Harrow Corpn* [1958] 1 QB 60, [1957] 2 All ER 305, CA (a landowner who allows the branches or roots of trees to encroach on a neighbour's land will be liable in nuisance).
4 But note that it is doubtful whether liability arises for the presence of animals *ferae naturae* or failure to remove them: *Farrer v Nelson* (1885) 15 QBD 258; *Seligman v Docker* [1949] Ch 53, [1948] 2 All ER 887.

(3)   Nuisances created by independent contractors

An employer, naturally enough, is vicariously liable for nuisances created by an employee in the course of his employment.[5] But as regards independent contractors, the defendant is only liable in respect of their failure to take precautions if, as Slesser LJ held in *Matania v National Provincial Bank and Elevenist Syndicate Ltd*,[6] 'the act done is one which in its very nature involves a special danger of nuisance being complained of'. In that case, the occupier of the first floor of a building was held liable to the superjacent occupiers, in respect of the dust and noise generated by the alteration works carried out by the independent contractors he had employed.

The nature of an occupier's liability for independent contractors was more widely stated by Cockburn CJ in *Bower v Peate*,[7] when holding a principal liable for his independent contractor's withdrawing support from the buildings of the plaintiff:

> a man who orders a work to be executed, from which, in the natural course of things, injurious consequences to his neighbour must be expected to arise ... is bound to see to the doing of that which is necessary to prevent the mischief, and cannot relieve himself of his responsibility by employing someone else.

(4)   Acts of a previous occupier

If the predecessor of the defendant occupier created a hazardous state of affairs and the defendant knows or ought to know of its existence then, according to the obiter dictum of Scrutton LJ in *St Anne's Well Brewery Co v Roberts*,[8] the defendant is liable in respect of any damage to which it gives rise.

(C)   LANDLORDS

We have already seen that a landlord who authorises his tenant to commit a nuisance is treated, in law, as the creator of the nuisance, and will himself be liable for that nuisance. But there are three further situations that call for discussion in which the landlord *may* be held liable qua landlord (as opposed to qua creator).

First, if at the date of letting the landlord knows or ought to know of the condition giving rise to the actionable nuisance, he will be liable despite the tenancy if he has not taken a covenant to repair the premises from the tenant.[9] According to Goddard J in *Wilchick v Marks and Silverstone*, it was held that a landlord ought to know not only of those defects that are patently obvious but also of those that are capable of being discovered by use of reasonable care.[10] Secondly, a landlord will also be liable for dangerous conditions that arise from want of repair during the currency of the tenancy

---

5   *Spicer v Smee* [1946] 1 All ER 489 at 493 (per Atkinson J, obiter).

6   [1936] 2 All ER 633 at 646, CA.

7   (1876) 1 QBD 321 at 326. Cf Atkinson J, following *Bower v Peate* in *Spicer v Smee*, supra at 495: 'where danger is likely to arise unless work is properly done, there is a duty to see that it is properly done'. For a fuller discussion of liability for the acts of independent contractors, see ch 25, post.

8   (1928) 140 LT 1, CA (part of an ancient wall collapsed damaging the plaintiff's inn but, on the facts, the defendant was found not liable because of the lack of (constructive) knowledge that the wall was likely to collapse). Followed in *Wilkins v Leighton* [1932] 2 Ch 106.

9   *Todd v Flight* (1860) 9 CBNS 377; *Gandy v Jubber* (1864) 5 B & S 78; revsd 9 B & S 15, Ex Ch (undelivered judgment); *Bowen v Anderson* [1894] 1 QB 164.

10   [1934] 2 KB 56 at 67–8.

if he has covenanted to perform such repairs,[11] reserves the right to enter and repair,[12] or has an implied right to enter and repair.[13] Furthermore, where the landlord's premises are situated on a highway, he will be liable to passers-by or neighbouring landowners regardless of whether the want of repair is attributable to his (ie, the landlord's) want of care.[14] Finally, where a landlord does something to the premises, that leads inevitably to a nuisance if the premises are occupied, then he, rather than the tenants, will be liable. In *Toff v McDowell*,[15] for example, the tenants had used the premises in a perfectly normal fashion but, because the landlord had taken up the floor covering, anyone occupying the premises would sound unbearably loud to the subjacent plaintiff. The landlord was held liable and directed to replace the flooring.

As regards the liability of a tenant, it is well established that if he has covenanted to repair the premises, he is liable in nuisance for damage arising from a failure to effect those repairs.[16] On the other hand, the mere fact that the landlord has covenanted to repair the premises, will not, ipso facto, exonerate the tenant from nuisance liability.[17] As Lawrence LJ explained in *St Anne's Well Brewery Co v Roberts*:[18]

> Any bargain made by the person responsible [ie the occupier] to his neighbour or to the public that another person should perform that obligation may give rise to rights as between the two contracting parties, but does not, in my judgment, in any way affect any right of third parties, who are not parties or privy to such contract.

SECTION 5.   MUST THE INTERFERENCE EMANATE FROM THE DEFENDANT'S LAND?

The land from which the interference has its source will normally be in the ownership or control of the defendant. Indeed, in so far as nuisance law is designed to provide a means of regulating competing land uses, it might even be argued that land ownership on the part of the defendant is as important as the classic requirement that the plaintiff have a proprietary interest.[19] Nonetheless, dicta abounds to the effect that the defendant

11 *Payne v Rogers* (1794) 2 Hy Bl 350.
12 *Wilchick v Marks and Silverstone* [1934] 2 KB 56; *Heap v Ind Coope and Allsopp Ltd* [1940] 2 KB 476, [1940] 3 All ER 634, CA; *Spicer v Smee* [1946] 1 All ER 489.
13 *Mint v Good* [1951] 1 KB 517, [1950] 2 All ER 1159, CA.
14 *Wringe v Cohen* [1940] 1 KB 229, [1939] 4 All ER 241, CA (followed in *Mint v Good* [1951] 1 KB 517, [1950] 2 All ER 1159, CA). The importance of the rule in *Wringe v Cohen* has since been amplified by the imposition on landlords of onerous obligations to maintain houses, let for fewer than seven years, in a state of good repair (see ss 11–16 of the Landlord and Tenant Act 1985, as amended by the Housing Act 1988). On the other hand, the rule in *Wringe v Cohen* does not apply to premises that do not lie on a highway, nor does it apply to nuisances arising from acts of trespassers or processes of nature: *Cushing v Peter Walker & Son (Warrington and Burton) Ltd* [1941] 2 All ER 693.
15 (1993) 25 HLR 650.
16 *Brew Bros Ltd v Snax (Ross) Ltd* [1970] 1 QB 612, [1970] 1 All ER 587, CA. But note that the tenant's covenant to repair does not exonerate the landlord from liability for, as Sachs LJ observed (at 638 and 601 respectively): 'the test of an owner's duty to his neighbour depends on the degree of control exercised by the owner in law or in fact for the purpose of repairs'. And in this context it should be noted that the repair obligations placed upon landlords under ss 11–16 of the Landlord and Tenant Act 1985 are made immutable.
17 *Wilchick v Marks and Silverstone* [1934] 2 KB 56; cf the obiter view of Heath J in *Payne v Rogers* (1794) 2 Hy Bl 350 that to hold the tenant liable would encourage circuity of action.
18 (1928) 140 LT 1 at 8, CA.
19 In *Miller v Jackson* [1977] QB 966 at 980, [1977] 3 All ER 338 at 344, CA Lord Denning MR proclaimed that, '[i]t is the very essence of a private nuisance that it is the unreasonable use by a man of *his land* to the detriment of his neighbour' (emphasis added).

need not be the owner of the land from where the nuisance emanates. Thus, in *Sedleigh-Denfield v O'Callaghan* Lord Wright declared 'the ground of responsibility' to be merely 'the possession and control of the land from which the nuisance proceeds'.[20]

SECTION 6.   DEFENCES

(A)   STATUTORY AUTHORITY

The fact that the activity giving rise to the interference complained of is authorised by statute is the single most important defence in the law of private nuisance.[1] Many activities which interfere with the enjoyment of land are carried out by public or private enterprises in pursuance of an Act of Parliament. But if the statute merely confers a permissive power, then it has been established that the power must be exercised so as not to interfere with private rights.[2] Whether the activity complained of is explicitly authorised by statute, and whether any potential nuisance action is thereby defeated is a matter of statutory interpretation.

> In *Allen v Gulf Oil Refining Ltd*[3] the defendant company was authorised by statute compulsorily to acquire land near Milford Haven for the purpose of constructing and operating an oil refinery. The plaintiffs complained that the smell, noise and vibrations made by the refinery constituted a nuisance. The company pleaded the defence of statutory authority.

The House of Lords held that the plaintiffs would first have to establish a nuisance, and that the change in the local environment caused by authorising the operation of the refinery was relevant to that issue.[4] If a nuisance could be established, then the company had the onus of proving that it was an inevitable result of carrying on a refinery there.[5]

It follows from this that the defendant must use all due diligence in performing the activity authorised by statute. If he fails so to do, he will be held to have exceeded the level of damage for which he was granted immunity under the statute. So, in *Tate & Lyle Industries Ltd v Greater London Council*,[6] the defendants were held liable in public nuisance where reasonable care in the design and erection of new ferry terminals,

---

20   [1940] AC 880 at 903, [1940] 3 All ER 349 at 364, HL. See also *J Lyons & Sons v Wilkins* [1899] 1 Ch 255, CA; *Hubbard v Pitt* [1976] QB 142, [1975] 3 All ER 1, CA; *Ward Lock & Co Ltd v Operative Printers' Assistants' Society* (1906) 22 TLR 327, CA; *Thomas v National Union of Mineworkers (South Wales Area)* [1986] Ch 20, [1985] 2 All ER 1 and most recently *Khorasandjian v Bush* [1993] QB 727, [1993] 3 All ER 669, CA.

1   Statutory authority is a general defence in tort, but enjoys most *practical significance* in the context of private nuisance.

2   *Metropolitan Asylum District Managers v Hill* (1881) 6 App Cas 193, HL.

3   [1981] AC 1001, [1981] 1 All ER 353, HL.

4   This point was endorsed by Buckley J in *Gillingham Borough Council v Medway (Chatham) Dock Co Ltd* [1993] QB 343 at 360, [1992] 3 All ER 923 at 934 in relation to the (broadly) analogous defence of authorisation by planning permission: 'Prior to 1984 [these] roads had been relatively quiet roads ... [but] I must judge the present claim in nuisance pursuant to the planning permission for use of the dockyard as a commercial port'. But note that an injunction can exceptionally be obtained to restrain the defendant from engaging in a land use authorised by planning permission: *Wheeler v JJ Saunders* [1995] 2 All ER 697. Cf the general position set out in *Hunter* and discussed ante.

5   In this respect the House of Lords followed its earlier decision in *Manchester Corpn v Farnworth* [1930] AC 171, HL where a power station established under statute emitted poisonous fumes that damaged the plaintiff's fields.

6   [1983] 2 AC 509, [1983] 1 All ER 1159, HL. See also *Department of Transport v North West Water Authority* [1984] AC 336, [1983] 1 All ER 892, HL.

which they had been authorised to build by statute, would have at least partially avoided the siltation of the River Thames which damaged the plaintiffs' business. As some degree of siltation would have been inevitable, even with properly designed terminals, the plaintiffs were awarded only 75% of their total loss.

One further matter that bedevils the defence of statutory authority occurs where the defendant is a public authority. More particularly, the problem surfaces where the public body is invested with a *discretionary* statutory power. Generally, that body will not be liable in respect of its formulation of policy *within* the statutory power, but it may be liable in respect of the negligent implementation of the policy finally settled upon.[7]

(B) PRESCRIPTION

The right to commit a private nuisance may be acquired as an easement by prescription. In order to decide whether this defence avails, one must look to the law of real property to identify whether the right claimed is capable of constituting an easement. The most common way of acquiring an easement is by 20 years' overt and undisturbed user. One may, for example, acquire the right to pour effluent into a stream, but not if it is done secretly.[8] Equally, one may acquire the right do such things as discharge surface water,[9] or rainwater from the eaves of one's house,[10] onto a neighbour's land. It is also well established that the user must be continual. So, where there is a perpetual change in the amount of inconvenience caused – as in the case of fumes or noise – it is doubtful whether an easement can be obtained.[11]

One matter that is beyond doubt is that if the user is prohibited by statute, it cannot be claimed as a prescriptive right.[12] Furthermore, 'acts which are *neither preventable nor actionable* cannot be relied upon to found an easement'.[13] Thus, where a defendant confectioner had for more than 20 years made certain noises on his land, which then, for the first time, interfered with the plaintiff doctor's user of his land, the defendant could not plead a prescriptive right.[14] It was held that as there had been no invasion of a legal right before the consulting room was built, there were no steps that the plaintiff could, or might, have taken to prevent the interference.

(C) THE PLAINTIFF'S CONDUCT[15]

It is no defence that the plaintiff came to the nuisance by occupying the land adjoining it.[16] Nor is it a defence that the nuisance has only arisen because the plaintiff has chosen

---

7   The distinction between policy making and operational errors was first adverted to in *Anns v Merton London Borough Council* [1978] AC 728, [1977] 2 All ER 492. Whether such a distinction is juridically tenable has since, however, been subjected to rigorous judicial challenge: see *Rowling v Takaro Properties Ltd* [1988] AC 473 at 501, [1988] 1 All ER 163 at 172, PC (per Lord Keith).

8   *Liverpool Corpn v H Coghill & Son* [1918] 1 Ch 307.

9   *A-G v Copeland* [1902] 1 KB 690.

10 *Thomas v Thomas* (1835) 2 Cr M & R 34.

11 *Hulley v Silversprings Bleaching Co* [1922] 2 Ch 268.

12 *Liverpool Corpn v H Coghill & Son* [1918] 1 Ch 307.

13 *Sturges v Bridgman* (1879) 11 Ch D 852 at 863, CA (per Thesiger LJ, emphasis added).

14 (1879) 11 Ch D 852 at 863.

15 See also ante where we discuss the inability of the plaintiff to heighten his sensitivities in order to sue in nuisance.

16 *Bliss v Hall* (1838) 4 Bing NC 183; *Miller v Jackson* [1977] QB 966, [1977] 3 All ER 338, CA (no defence to cricket club that the ground first became a nuisance when the plaintiff built premises close to it).

to use a particular part of his land: the law only protects the man in the reasonable use of his land against those nuisances which the defendant has not acquired a prescriptive right to commit.[17] Moreover, it may be assumed that the plaintiff has the normal duty in tort to take reasonable steps to mitigate his loss. He should, for instance, take reasonable steps to minimise the damage when his land is flooded in consequence of his neighbour's tortious conduct. The ordinary principles of causation apply in nuisance law and, if the nuisance is caused by the plaintiff's own acts, he cannot recover.[18] The defences of consent and assumption of risk are also available. *Pwllbach Colliery Co Ltd v Woodman*[19] illustrates the operation of the consent defence in this context.

> A lessor allowed his lessee to carry on the business of coal mining. The issue was whether he could complain when the lessee's non-negligent operations caused coal dust to be deposited on other land owned by the lessor. The House of Lords held that only if the terms of the lease could be construed as authorising a nuisance was there any defence. Their lordships then pointed out that, since the nuisance was not a necessary consequence of carrying on that trade, in the absence of an express authorisation of the nuisance in the lease, the defence of consent failed.

As regards the assumption of risk defence, *Kiddle v City Business Properties Ltd*[20] is a case in point. There, the plaintiff complained of the damage caused to his shop when flooding from the gutter carrying water from a part of the premises retained by the defendant landlord occurred without negligence on the defendant's part. It was held that the tenant took the premises as he found them and must be deemed to have run this risk. Accordingly, his action in nuisance failed.

Contributory negligence on the part of the plaintiff might also, in principle, be raised as a defence to an action in nuisance; at least where the nuisance arises out of negligent conduct.[1] There is certainly obiter dictum to this effect in the public nuisance case of *Trevett v Lee*.[2]

(D)   OTHER DEFENCES

The Fires Prevention (Metropolis) Act 1774 provides that, in an action brought in respect of a fire, it is a defence to prove that the fire began accidentally.[3] But, as Atkinson J decided in *Spicer v Smee*,[4] the defence has no application where the fire was caused by the negligence of the defendant, or was intentionally created by him or by those for whom he was responsible. Even when a fire starts accidentally, if the defendant negligently allows it to grow into a raging fire, the Act will not afford him a defence for the damage it later causes.[5] Accordingly, the defence has no application in nuisance law except, perhaps, where a person would be liable in nuisance even though his conduct was neither intentional nor negligent.

---

17   *Sturges v Bridgman* (1879) 11 Ch D 852, CA; *Elliotson v Feetham* (1835) 2 Bing NC 134.
18   Cf the case in public nuisance: *Almeroth v Chivers & Sons Ltd* [1948] 1 All ER 53, CA.
19   [1915] AC 634, HL.
20   [1942] 1 KB 269, [1942] 2 All ER 216.
1   Query whether the courts would accept this defence where the nuisance was caused by the defendant's deliberate and malicious conduct?
2   [1955] 1 All ER 406, CA at 412 (per Evershed MR).
3   Note that the Act applies generally, not merely to London: *Filliter v Phippard* (1847) 11 QB 347.
4   [1946] 1 All ER 489.
5   *Goldman v Hargrave* [1967] 1 AC 645, [1966] 2 All ER 989, PC.

As we saw earlier,[6] an occupier who unreasonably fails to avert a danger to his neighbour arising out of an act of God will be liable in nuisance. Where, however, there is an occurrence alleged by the plaintiff to be a nuisance, which in truth is an inevitable accident, it is well established that no liability will attach.[7] But it is no defence that the act of the defendant would not have been a nuisance but for the acts also of others, provided that the defendant knew what the others were doing.[8]

SECTION 7. REMEDIES

(A) DAMAGES

The measure of damages in nuisance is similar to that awarded for trespass to land.[9] The plaintiff is entitled to full reparation for his loss. Where, for instance, a house (or crops, or the like[10]) is destroyed or damaged, then the plaintiff will recover the difference between the monetary value to him of his interest (whether he be landlord, tenant or otherwise) before and after the event.[11] Where business loss is suffered in consequence of the interference, whether by loss of custom[12] or the cost of moving elsewhere,[13] this is also recoverable in nuisance. Where, however, a hotel owner complained of loss of custom caused by nearby building operations, the Court of Appeal reversed an award of damages to the full extent of loss of custom, holding that a certain amount of the interference was, in the circumstances, reasonable although likely to lead to some loss of custom. The court therefore assessed what proportion of the business loss was attributable to that excess of noise and dust which alone was actionable.[14] In 1966, in *Overseas Tankship (UK) Ltd v Miller Steamship Co Pty Ltd, The Wagon Mound (No 2)*,[15] the Privy Council held that, in public nuisance, it is not enough that the damage complained of is a direct consequence of the wrongful act; it must be a foreseeable consequence. Obiter dicta in the case stated this rule to be applicable also to private nuisance.

The amount to be awarded by way of damages increases the longer the nuisance continues. Curiously, the law does not treat this as the continuance of the original nuisance complained of, but rather as a new and distinct nuisance. Thus, in one case where a defendant imposed a strain on the plaintiff's wall by piling earth against it and was sued in nuisance, it was stated that 'a fresh cause of action arises as each brick topples down, and that there is a continuing cause of action until the root of the trouble is eradicated'.[16] Whether the continuance of the interference is characterised as a fresh nuisance or as a prolongation of the original one is largely immaterial so far as the

---

6 See section 4, ante.
7 *Tennent v Earl of Glasgow* (1864) 2 M 22, HL.
8 *Thorpe v Brumfitt* (1873) 8 Ch App 650.
9 See ch 5, ante. For an argument in favour of exemplary damages in private nuisance see Murphy 'Noxious Emissions and Common Law Liability – Tort in the Shadow of Regulation' in Lowry and Edmunds *Environmental Protection and the Common Law* (1999).
10 See *Marquis of Granby v Bakewell UDC* (1923) 87 JP 105 for a detailed calculation on this basis of the value of fish destroyed by pollution of a stream.
11 *Moss v Christchurch RDC* [1925] 2 KB 750, Div Ct. And not the cost of restoring it to its original state: *Lodge Holes Colliery Co Wednesbury Corpn* [1908] AC 323, HL; *C R Taylor (Wholesale) Ltd v Hepworths Ltd* [1977] 2 All ER 784 (plaintiff not entitled to recover the cost of reinstating his destroyed billiard hall which he did not intend to use for that purpose again – the basis of assessment was simply the reduced value of the premises).
12 *Fritz v Hobson* (1880) 14 Ch D 542.
13 *Grosvenor Hotel v Hamilton* [1894] 2 QB 836 at 840, CA (per Lindley LJ).
14 *Andrae v Selfridge & Co Ltd* [1938] Ch 1, [1937] 3 All ER 255, CA.
15 [1967] 1 AC 617, [1966] 2 All ER 709, PC.
16 *Maberley v Peabody & Co of London Ltd* [1946] 2 All ER 192 at 194 (per Stable J).

plaintiff is concerned. He is much more interested in having the nuisance abated and will, in most cases, seek an injunction. However, as we shall see in the next section, an injunction is a discretionary remedy and the court has a statutory power[17] to grant damages in lieu of an injunction (thus enabling it to make an award that takes account of future as well as past harm). The principles governing the exercise of the court's discretion were set out by Smith LJ in the leading case of *Shelfer v City of London Electric Lighting Co*.[18] There it was stated that the court has jurisdiction to grant damages in lieu where (i) the injury to the plaintiff is small, (ii) it is quantifiable in money, (iii) it is capable of being adequately compensated in money, and (iv) it would be oppressive to the defendant to grant an injunction.[19] The insistence that the harm complained of be small places an important restriction on the court's ability to grant damages instead of an injunction.[20] In addition, it seems from *Elliott v London Borough of Islington*[1] that a restrictive definition of what amounts to a small degree of harm should be applied. In that case, the pressing of the defendant's tree against the plaintiff's wall – causing it to move only a very few inches – was regarded as 'very considerable harm'. Furthermore, in relation to the fourth limb of the *Shelfer* test, as Bingham MR observed in *Jaggard v Sawyer*, '[i]t is important to bear in mind that the test is one of *oppression*, and the court should not slide into application of a general balance of convenience test'.[2]

(B) INJUNCTION

An injunction is an order from the court directing the defendant to desist from the future commission of any tortious act. It is the remedy most often sought in nuisance cases and is granted on a discretionary basis. Thus, even where the plaintiff can establish an actionable claim, he may nonetheless be refused an injunction. Broadly, there are two factors which influence the courts in deciding whether or not to grant an injunction: the gravity of the interference and the public interest.[3] As regards the first of these, the courts tend to view occasional interferences as insufficiently substantial to warrant the grant of an injunction.

> In *Cooke v Forbes*, for example, the plaintiff used a certain bleaching chemical in making cocoa-nut matting. Occasionally, emission of sulphuretted hydrogen from the defendant's plant damaged the plaintiff's manufactures. Without prejudice to a claim in damages, the court refused an injunction because the interference was only occasional.[4]

17 Supreme Court Act 1981, s 50. This power is discussed at some length in Buckley *The Law of Nuisance* (1996) pp 148–152.
18 [1895] 1 Ch 287 at 322–323. In this case the court was dealing with the equivalent provision to s 50 of the 1981 Act (Lord Cairns' Act, s 2). The principles enunciated have since been reiterated, however, in relation to the 1981 Act by Bingham MR in *Jaggard v Sawyer* [1995] 2 All ER 189 at 203, CA (a trespass case).
19 This means, in effect, that the defendant buys the right to commit the nuisance: see Tromans 'Nuisance – Prevention or Payment' [1982] CLJ 87 and O'Sullivan 'A Poor Reception for Television Nuisance' [1996] CLJ 184.
20 *Wood v Conway Corpn* [1914] 2 Ch 47.
1 [1991] 1 EGLR 167, CA.
2 [1995] 2 All ER 189 at 203, CA.
3 For a full account of the principles governing the exercise of this discretion see Buckley *The Law of Nuisance* (1996) ch 8.
4 (1867) LR 5 Eq 166. Once the plaintiff has established that a substantial interference has occurred, and is likely to recur, the burden is on the defendant to adduce evidence of special circumstances why an injunction should not be granted: *McKinnon Industries Ltd v Walker* (1951) 3 DLR 577 at 581, PC (per Lord Simonds).

An example of the role that can be played by the public interest is evident in the judgment of Peter Gibson LJ in *Wheeler v JJ Saunders Ltd*.[5] In that case, the nuisance was caused by the defendant running a pig farm. In relation to the application for an injunction, his Lordship said: 'I can well see that in such a case the public interest must be allowed to prevail and that it would be inappropriate to grant an injunction'.[6]

The fact that the plaintiff's chief concern is with the future abatement of the nuisance does not mean that he will not also seek damages (as we have seen) in respect of the past harm that he has suffered. In consequence, the law of nuisance is complicated by the fact that the plaintiff may often seek two remedies at once. Of particular note in this context is the Canadian decision that, where both remedies are granted, any damages must not include an element in respect of permanent depreciation in the plaintiff's land: it is to be presumed that the injunction will be obeyed, and that the land will not so depreciate.[7]

SECTION 8. PUBLIC NUISANCE

(A) NATURE OF PUBLIC NUISANCE

Public nuisance is not susceptible to any precise definition. The term covers a miscellany of acts and omissions which 'endanger the life, health, property, morals or comfort of the public' or, alternatively, 'obstruct the public in the exercise or enjoyment of rights common to all Her Majesty's subjects'.[8] Despite this definitional obscurity, two general observations about the nature of public nuisance can be made. To begin with, it is clear that, at least in principle, a public nuisance is first and foremost a criminal offence at common law.[9] Secondly, and on the other hand, it is equally clear that a public nuisance may form the basis of a civil action in two ways: by a relator action for an injunction, brought in the name of the Attorney-General on behalf of a private citizen, to suppress the criminal activity of the defendant, or by an action in tort brought a by a private citizen who can show that he has suffered 'special damage' beyond that suffered by the others of Her Majesty's subjects affected by the defendant's interference.

In this book we are not concerned with the criminal law aspects of public nuisance, merely with the civil law actions which may be brought by either the Attorney-General or the private individual who establishes special damage.

(I) THE RELATOR ACTION

If the defendant is responsible for a nuisance that affects a large number of citizens but fails to occasion any of them special damage, then an individual citizen may seek to persuade the Attorney-General to suppress the defendant's activity on his behalf, by way of a relator action for an injunction. To do so, the elements of the crime of public nuisance must be established. In practice, this method of obtaining injunctive relief is

5 [1995] 2 All ER 697 at 711. See also the similar view expressed by Buckley J in *Gillingham Borough Council v Medway (Chatham) Docks Co Ltd* [1993] QB 343 at 364, [1992] 3 All ER 923 at 937–938.
6 Cf the earlier Court of Appeal decision in *Kennaway v Thompson* [1981] QB 88, [1980] 3 All ER 329, CA.
7 *Macievich v Anderson* [1952] 4 DLR 507 (Manitoba Court of Appeal).
8 *Archbold's Criminal Practice* (1985) paras 27–44.
9 Most established public nuisances are now prohibited by statutes such as the various Public Health Acts, the Food Act 1984 and the Highways Act 1980. See further Spencer 'Public Nuisance – A Critical Examination' [1989] CLJ 55, 76–80.

very seldom used.[10] This is in large part explained by the fact that the Attorney-General is unlikely to entertain an application for a relator action where the victim has not experienced special harm, and where such harm has been suffered, the victim is entitled to bring a civil action in his own name.

(2) CIVIL ACTIONS FOR 'SPECIAL DAMAGE'

There are two situations in which a private citizen may mount a civil action for public nuisance. The first concerns cases where the defendant is responsible for an interference which bears the characteristics of a private nuisance *except* that it affects a much greater number of people.[11] And here, just as in private nuisance, it is not a prerequisite that the act itself be unlawful: the nuisance derives from the detrimental effect of the act complained of. The second concerns cases where the interference would not bear the key characteristics of a private nuisance in that it does not affect the plaintiff's land, or his use or enjoyment of it. Instead, the nuisance in such cases amounts to an inconvenience occasioned to the public generally, but causes special damage to the plaintiff (ie damage beyond that suffered by other members of the public). Such nuisances typically involve obstructing, or creating a danger on the highway.

Crucial to both kinds of public nuisance is the requirement that the plaintiff must suffer, or be at risk of, 'special damage'. Special damage – sometimes referred to as 'particular damage' – is a term almost as obscure in its meaning as public nuisance itself.[12] Nonetheless, what is at least clear is that special damage must not be confused with 'special damages', which latter term is used in personal injury negligence actions to describe pecuniary losses incurred up to the date of the trial which must be specifically pleaded and proved.

While it is difficult to supply a precise definition of special damage, it is possible to advert to a number of established categories of such loss. Pecuniary loss stemming from loss of business or custom, where the injury was of a 'substantial character, not fleeting or evanescent' has long been recognised as such a category.[13] But where other

10 Spencer, in his thoroughgoing account of the modern usage of public nuisance, supplies evidence that in a five year span between 1978 and the end of 1982 only two applications for relator actions were received by the Attorney-General: 'Public Nuisance – A Critical Examination' [1989] CLJ 55, fn 14.

11 Examples of such nuisances include driving heavy lorries through residential streets: *Gillingham Borough Council v Medway (Chatham) Dock Co Ltd* [1993] QB 343, [1992] 3 All ER 923; blasting from a quarry causing vibrations, dust and noise: *A-G v PYA Quarries Ltd* [1957] 2 QB 169, [1957] 1 All ER 894, CA; holding 'acid-house parties': *R v Shorrock* [1994] QB 279, [1993] 3 All ER 917, CA.

12 See Kodilinye 'Public Nuisance and Particular Damage in the Modern Law' [1986] Legal Studies 182. See also Scholl J's earlier review of the authorities in *Walsh v Ervin* [1952] VLR 361; *Harper v G N Haden & Sons* [1933] Ch 298, [1932] All ER Rep 59; *Benjamin v Storr* (1874) LR 9 CP 400; *Wilkes v Hungerford Market Co* (1835) 2 Bing NC 281 and *Ricket v Directors etc of the Metropolitan Rly Co* (1867) LR 2 HL 175.

13 *Benjamin v Storr* (1874) LR 9 CP 400 at 407, per Brett J (plaintiff's coffee shop lost custom when the defendant parked horse-drawn vans outside his premises); *Lyons, Sons & Co v Gulliver* [1914] 1 Ch 631, CA; *Blundy Clark & Co Ltd v London and North Eastern Rly Co* [1931] 2 KB 334, [1931] All ER Rep 160. See also *Caledonian Rly Co v Walker's Trustees* (1882) 7 App Cas 259, HL (depreciation in the value of land) and *Tate and Lyle Industries Ltd v Greater London Council* [1983] 2 AC 509, [1983] 1 All ER 1159, HL (cost of dredging silted-up river in order to continue use of a ferry). In relation to economic loss, a curious anomaly exists where the loss is caused by negligence on the part of the defendant. Take, for example, the defendant whose lorry breaks down and blocks the highway because he has failed properly to maintain it. If the action is framed in public nuisance it is likely to succeed, but if it is framed in negligence, it will almost certainly fail for want of sufficient proximity to establish a duty of care: *Caparo Industries plc v Dickman* [1990] 2 AC 605, [1990] 1 All ER 568. For criticism, see the comments of Ambrose J in *Ball v Consolidated Rutile* [1991] Qd 524 at 546.

members of the public have also suffered economic loss, it is more difficult for the plaintiff to establish special damage, for he is able only to show the same kind of damage as that suffered by the others.[14] The plaintiff's problem in such a case is that the difference between his loss and that suffered by other citizens is merely one of degree and not one of kind. Since the plaintiff's loss, albeit greater in degree than that suffered by the generality of the public, is of the same kind, his action for public nuisance will fail.[15] In addition to pecuniary loss, personal injury[16] and property damage[17] have also been held to constitute special damage. So, too, have causing inconvenience and delay, provided that the harm thereby caused to the plaintiff is substantial and appreciably greater in degree than any suffered by the general public.[18] Thus, a plaintiff could recover in public nuisance both for damage to his vehicle on the highway and for interference with peaceful sleep in his adjoining house.[19]

The majority of public nuisance cases arise where the defendant either creates a danger on, or obstructs,[20] the highway.[1] As far as rendering the highway unsafe is concerned, there is a long line of cases that establishes liability in public nuisance in respect of walls,[2] fences,[3] windows[4] etc that fall onto the highway from adjoining premises. But other examples include leaving dangerous articles such as defective cellar flaps or unlighted scaffolding there,[5] or conducting operations off the highway which menace the safety of those upon it.[6]

Cases involving a creation of danger on the highway help illustrate the rigid categorisation of the law of torts. If someone falls over a projection on the forecourt (not forming part of the public footpath) leading to a shop, then his rights are merely those owed in negligence to visitors to premises – he has no action in public nuisance.[7] Should this happen on the footpath, however, it becomes a case derived from public nuisance. And, if one deviates only slightly from the footpath in order to pass an obstruction, and is injured while thus off the highway, this might be within the area of public nuisance.[8]

As regards obstructing the highway, it is well established that temporary and reasonable obstructions of the highway will not attract liability.

14 *Martin v LCC* (1899) 80 LT 866.
15 *Ricket v Directors etc of the Metropolitan Rly Co* (1867) LR 2 HL 175 at 190 and 199, HL (per Lord Chelmsford and Lord Cranworth respectively).
16 *Castle v St Augustine's Links Ltd* (1922) 38 TLR 615.
17 *Halsey v Esso Petroleum Co Ltd* [1961] 2 All ER 145, [1961] 1 WLR 683.
18 *Walsh v Ervin* [1952] VLR 361; *Boyd v Great Northern Rly Co* [1895] 2 IR 555.
19 *Halsey v Esso Petroleum Co Ltd* [1961] 2 All ER 145. But was Veale J correct in holding that the plaintiff recovered even though he was unlawfully using the road to park his car when it was damaged?
20 Whether there is an obstruction is a question of fact: *Harper v G N Haden & Sons* [1933] Ch 298.
1   The same principles apply to navigable waterways: *Tate & Lyle Industries Ltd v Greater London Council* [1983] 2 AC 509, [1983] 1 All ER 1159, HL; *Rose v Miles* (1815) 4 M & S 101.
2   *Mint v Good* [1951] 1 KB 517, [1950] 2 All ER 1159.
3   *Harrold v Watney* [1898] 2 QB 320, 67 LJQB 771, CA.
4   *Leanse v Lord Egerton* [1943] KB 323, [1943] 1 All ER 489.
5   *Penny v Wimbledon UDC and Iles* [1899] 2 QB 72.
6   *Castle v St Augustine's Links* (1922) 38 TLR 615 (plaintiff lost an eye when a golf ball smashed the window of his car). Cf *Stone v Bolton* [1950] 1 KB 201, [1949] 2 All ER 851 (cricket ball escaping the cricket ground not a public nuisance as it was an isolated event).
7   *Jacobs v LCC* [1950] AC 361, [1950] 1 All ER 737, HL; in *Bromley v Mercer* [1922] 2 KB 126, CA, an unsafe wall adjoining a highway which amounted to a public nuisance, collapsed, not onto the highway, but onto a child playing on private land – the child was held to have no cause of action derived from public nuisance; *Creed v John McGeoch & Sons Ltd* [1955] 3 All ER 123 (road merely under construction, neither dedicated nor taken over by local authority; therefore not highway nuisance).
8   *Barnes v Ward* (1850) 9 CB 392; *Barker v Herbert* [1911] 2 KB 633, CA.

In *Trevett v Lee*,[9] the defendant, who had no mains connection, laid a hosepipe across the highway in a time of drought in order to obtain a water supply from the other side of the road. The plaintiff, who tripped over it and suffered injury, failed in an action for public nuisance since the defendant's user of the highway was reasonable 'judged both from their own point of view and from the point of view of the other members of the public'.[10]

Though an obstruction of the highway is only partial, it may nonetheless give rise to liability in public nuisance. As Lord Evershed MR explained in *Trevett v Lee*, '[a]n obstruction is something which permanently or temporarily removes the whole *or part of the highway* from public use'.[11] Accordingly, where a vehicle is parked in such a way as to narrow significantly the width of the road, its owner may be held liable in public nuisance.[12] The obstruction need not, of course, be caused by vehicles. A crowd – such as men picketing an employer's premises – may just as easily obstruct the highway and form the basis of an action in public nuisance.[13] But where a demonstration or picket takes place peacefully, could it not be argued that the obstruction was nonetheless a reasonable use of the highway?[14]

(B) THE RELATIONSHIP BETWEEN PUBLIC NUISANCE AND PRIVATE NUISANCE

Though many of the decided cases on public nuisance – especially those involving obstructions to, and dangers on, the highway – are clearly incapable of founding an action in private nuisance, there are nonetheless, in certain respects, several important points of connection between the two torts. First, where an interference is of a kind capable of constituting a private nuisance – such as a disturbance caused by vibrations or noise – and it affects a sufficiently large class of Her Majesty's subjects, the action becomes curiously metamorphosed from being one in private, to one in public nuisance. The difference, as Denning LJ explained in *A-G v PYA Quarries Ltd*,[15] lies in the fact that:

> a public nuisance is a nuisance which is so widespread in its range or so indiscriminate in its effect that it would not be reasonable to expect one person to take proceedings on his own responsibility to put a stop to it, but that it should be taken on the responsibility of the community at large.

Unfortunately, dicta in the case was unhelpful on identifying what amounts to a sufficiently large class of Her Majesty's subjects: it was merely stated that it was a question of fact whether the number of persons affected was sufficiently large.[16]

A second connection between private and public nuisance occurs where the invasion of the plaintiff's interest arises from the defendant adopting or continuing a nuisance that was begun by a third party: the rules on who is deemed to be responsible

9   [1955] 1 All ER 406, CA (applying the dictum of Romer LJ in *Harper v G N Haden & Sons* [1933] Ch 298 at 320, CA). Whether it is a defence to say that the obstruction is reasonable because it is for the public benefit is unsettled. In *R v Russell* (1827) 6 B & C 566 it was held to be defence, but the decision in this case was later doubted in *R v Ward* (1836) 4 Ad & El 384.
10 [1955] 1 All ER 406 at 412, CA (per Lord Evershed MR).
11 [1955] 1 All ER 406 at 409, CA (emphasis added).
12 *A-G v Gastonia Coaches Ltd* [1977] RTR 219; *Dymond v Pearce* [1972] 1 QB 496, [1972] 1 All ER 1142, CA.
13 *News Group Newspapers v SOGAT '82 (No 2)* [1987] ICR 181, [1986] IRLR 337.
14 See Carty 'The Legality of Peaceful Picketing on the Highway' [1984] PL 600.
15 [1957] 2 QB 169 at 190–191, [1957] 1 All ER 894 at 908, CA.
16 [1957] 2 QB 169 at 184, CA (per Romer LJ).

for such an interference are the same.[17] Thirdly, as we have seen, the courts will consider the reasonableness of the defendant's conduct in determining whether an action derived from public nuisance may lie. Thus, whether one who has collided with a vehicle left standing without lights at night and obstructing a highway can sue will depend in part on whether the vehicle has been there for a long time, and whether there was good excuse for its being there.[18]

Despite these affinities,[19] public and private nuisance are quite separate torts: the former is concerned with the protection of those who have a proprietary interest in the land affected while the latter only exists where an inconvenience is caused to the public generally. Equally, the distinction between the two torts is marked by the unavailability of the defence of prescription in public nuisance[20] and by the fact that victims of private nuisances, able to demonstrate a substantial interference, need not prove more loss than their fellows. Finally, though it is well established that pure economic loss is recoverable in public nuisance, there is, to date, no authoritative statement on its recoverability in private nuisance. In *Dunton v Dover District Council*[1] it was suggested by Griffiths J that economic loss consequent upon an extant nuisance action – for hotel bookings that were lost because of the nuisance – might be recoverable. Where economic loss is the only loss, however, there are only obiter statements to the effect that it *may* be recovered in private nuisance.[2]

One particular case in which it is necessary to distinguish private and public nuisances concerns interferences with access to a highway or waterway. If the case is framed in terms of the landowner's inability to access the highway, the relevant tort will be private nuisance. Where, however, the action is framed in terms of the loss of custom – because access to the plaintiff's premises has been obstructed – the action will lie in public nuisance. The distinction is important, because in the former case, the private nuisance preventing the plaintiff's access, is treated as analogous to trespass and is actionable per se.[3]

(C) REMEDIES IN PUBLIC NUISANCE

(I) Injunction

As we have already seen, where the victim of a public nuisance cannot establish special damage, a relator action for an injunction may be brought by the Attorney-General on his behalf. Where, however the victim is able to demonstrate that he has suffered special

---

17 *Sedleigh-Denfield v O'Callaghan* [1940] AC 880 at 893, 899 (per Lord Atkin) and 907 (per Lord Wright), [1940] 3 All ER 349, HL. Similarly, constructive (as opposed to actual) knowledge is sufficient to secure a criminal conviction for public nuisance: *R v Shorrock* [1994] QB 279, [1993] 3 All ER 917, CA (applying *Sedleigh-Denfield* to convict a landowner who, before he went away for the weekend, let his field to three people to hold a 15 hour 'acid-house party').

18 *Trevett v Lee* [1955] 1 All ER 406; *Ware v Garston Haulage Co Ltd* [1944] 1 KB 30, [1943] 2 All ER 558, CA; *Maitland v Raisbeck and R T and J Hewitt Ltd* [1944] KB 689, [1944] 2 All ER 272, CA.

19 Interestingly, the Privy Council drew no distinction between public and private nuisance in *Overseas Tankship (UK) Ltd v Miller Steamship Co Pty Ltd, The Wagon Mound (No 2)* [1967] 1 AC 617, [1966] 2 All ER 709, PC.

20 *Mott v Shoolbred* (1875) LR 20 Eq 22.

1 (1977) 76 LGR 87.

2 See *British Celanese Ltd v A H Hunt (Capacitors) Ltd* [1969] 2 All ER 1252; *Ryeford Homes Ltd v Sevenoaks District Council* [1989] 2 EGLR 281.

3 *Nicholls v Ely Beet Sugar Factory Ltd* [1936] Ch 343, CA (exclusive fishery rights alleged, but not proven, to be interfered with by the plaintiff depositing refuse in the river in which those fishery rights existed).

damage, an injunction is just as much available to him in public nuisance as it is in private nuisance.[4]

(2) DAMAGES

Most commonly, a claim in public nuisance will be for personal injuries or for pecuniary losses sustained by people using a public highway. In addition, however, occupiers of premises adjoining the highway may also recover in an action based on public nuisance when they suffer special damage as a result of a nuisance on a highway. And this is the case notwithstanding that the damage complained of is not suffered by them qua users of the highway. For example, shopkeepers have succeeded in this tort where access to their premises has been interfered with,[5] or where their customers have been subjected to noxious smells and darkened rooms as a result of the parking of horses and carts outside their premises.[6]

It is clear from the decision of the Privy Council in *Overseas Tankship (UK) Ltd v Miller Steamship Co Pty Ltd, The Wagon Mound (No 2)*[7] that damages are available subject to the same principle of remoteness of damage as applies in negligence. That is, the plaintiff will only recover so far as the defendant ought to have foreseen the type of loss suffered by the plaintiff.

> There the plaintiffs' ship was damaged in a fire caused by the defendants carelessly allowing oil to overflow from their ship into the waters of Sydney Harbour. The defendants were held liable in public nuisance, but only because the fire on the plaintiffs' ship was held to be a foreseeable consequence of the defendants' wrongful act.

Two further limitations exist with respect to the quantum of damages the plaintiff may expect to receive. First, it was decided by the Court of Appeal in *AB v South West Water Services Ltd* – a case in which the a public water supply in Cornwall was seriously polluted – that no matter how reprehensible the public nuisance, exemplary damages will never be available. An important element in the court's decision was the following question (which it was unable to answer):

> [I]n the case of a public nuisance affecting hundreds or even thousands of plaintiffs how can the court assess the sum of exemplary damages to be awarded to any one of them to punish or deter the defendant without knowing at the outset the number of successful plaintiffs and the approximate size of the total bill for exemplary damages?[8]

Secondly, the plaintiff's damages can be reduced by operation of the defences of contributory negligence or volenti non fit injuria.[9]

---

4   *Spencer v London and Birmingham Rly Co* (1836) 8 Sim 193.
5   *Fritz v Hobson* (1880) 14 Ch D 542.
6   *Benjamin v Storr* (1874) LR 9 CP 400.
7   [1967] 1 AC 617, [1966] 2 All ER 709, PC.
8   [1993] QB 507 at 531, [1993] 1 All ER 609 at 627 (per Sir Thomas Bingham MR), CA. Law Commission Consultation Paper No 132, *Aggravated, Exemplary and Restitutionary Damages* (1993).
9   *Dymond v Pearce* [1972] 1 QB 496, [1972] 1 All ER 1142, CA (motorcyclist collided with a lighted lorry parked on a straight, wide section of the highway but he was held to be the sole author of his injuries).

Chapter 19

Rylands v Fletcher

SECTION I. INTRODUCTION

The rule in *Rylands v Fletcher*[1] is probably the best known example of a strict liability tort in English law and it derives from the 19th century case of that name.

> The defendants employed independent contractors to build a reservoir on their land. Through the negligence of the independent contractors, disused shafts upon the site which communicated with the plaintiff's mine beneath the reservoir were not blocked up. On the filling of the reservoir, the water escaped down the shafts and flooded the plaintiff's mine.

Although the defendants were neither themselves negligent nor vicariously liable for the negligence of their independent contractors,[2] they were held liable both by the Court of Exchequer Chamber and the House of Lords. Blackburn J, delivering the judgment of the Court of Exchequer Chamber, said:[3]

> We think that the true rule of law is that the person who for his own purposes brings on his lands and collects and keeps there anything likely to do mischief if it escapes, must keep it in at his peril, and if he does not do so, is prima facie answerable for all the damage which is the natural consequence of its escape.

Lord Cairns in the House of Lords broadly agreed with this judgment, but he restricted the scope of the rule to instances where the defendant made 'a non-natural use' of the land.[4] Though seemingly innocuous, this addition to Blackburn J's formulation of the rule gave rise to one of the most vexed questions in relation to *Rylands v Fletcher* liability: what is the essence of 'a non-natural use' of land. As we shall see in part four of this chapter, there remains no clear answer to this question.

One instructive point, though not always made, is that Blackburn J did not consider himself to be making new law. The following quotation encapsulates his thinking.

> The general rule, as above stated, seems on general principle just. The person whose grass or corn is eaten down by the escaping cattle of his neighbour, or whose mine is flooded by the

1 (1866) LR 1 Ex 265; affd (1868) LR 3 HL 330.
2 For discussion of vicarious liability and liability in relation to independent contractors, see ch 25 post.
3 (1866) LR 1 Ex 265 at 279–80.
4 (1866) LR 1 Ex 265 at 338–40.

water from his neighbour's reservoir, or whose cellar is invaded by the filth of his neighbour's privy, or whose habitation is made unhealthy by the fumes and noisome vapours of his neighbour's alkali works, is damnified without any fault of his own; and it seems but reasonable and just that the neighbour, who has brought something on his own property which was not naturally there, harmless to others so long as it is confined to his own property, but which he knows to be mischievous if it gets on his neighbour's, should be obliged to make good the damage which ensues if he does not succeed in confining it to his own property.[5]

Yet, close though the analogy with nuisance may appear,[6] the fact remains that *Rylands v Fletcher* was the starting point of a form of liability which, as developed by the courts in subsequent decisions, was wider and quite different in kind to any that preceded it.

This extension of liability gave rise to speculation whether or not some comprehensive theory of strict liability for harm caused to persons by ultra-hazardous things was being formulated. Such a theory, whatever attraction it may once have had, is certainly no longer tenable after the interpretation put upon *Rylands v Fletcher* by the House of Lords in *Read v J Lyons & Co Ltd*.[7] The facts were as follows.

The appellant, while working in the respondent's factory, was injured by an explosion there. No allegation of negligence was made by her against the respondents, whom she sued in respect of her injuries. The basis of her claim was that the defendants carried on the manufacture of high-explosive shells, knowing that they were dangerous things.

The ground for the decision of the House of Lords in favour of the respondents was that *Rylands v Fletcher* does not apply unless there has been an escape from a place where the defendant has occupation or control over land to a place outside his control.[8] But the importance of the case does not end there. The decision in *Read v Lyons* constituted a denial of a general theory of strict liability for ultra-hazardous activities: there is only liability for non-negligent escapes where the several preconditions for *Rylands v Fletcher* liability (considered in the following sections) are satisfied. Where these preconditions are not met, the plaintiff's case can only be predicated on the intentional or negligent conduct of the defendant.

Perhaps the most remarkable characteristic of this rule has been its fluidity. Stated in very broad terms by Blackburn J, it was at once modified in the case itself by the House of Lords, who confined it to instances involving a 'non-natural user'. There followed a widespread application of the rule: often cases properly sounding in nuisance only were brought within the fold of *Rylands v Fletcher*. The rule was given a greater measure of elasticity by the interpretation of 'non-natural use' by the Privy Council in 1913, who defined it as 'some special use bringing with it increased danger to others, and [which] must not merely be the ordinary use of the land or such a use as is proper

5   (1866) LR 1 Ex 265 at 280.
6   For an excellent, if somewhat dated, account of the relationship between liability in nuisance and liability under the rule in *Rylands v Fletcher* see Newark 'The Boundaries of Nuisance' (1945) 65 LQR 480. See also *Cambridge Water Co Ltd v Eastern Counties Leather plc* [1994] 2 AC 264 at 298, [1994] 1 All ER 53 at 69–70, HL (per Lord Goff).
7   [1945] KB 216, CA; affd, [1947] AC 156, [1946] 2 All ER 471, HL.
8   There are obiter dicta to the effect that the escape of a dangerous thing from the defendant's chattel, located on a highway (*Rigby v Chief Constable of Northamptonshire* [1985] 2 All ER 985 at 996) or his vessel, situated on a navigable waterway (*Crown River Cruises Ltd v Kimbolton Fireworks Ltd* [1996] 2 Lloyd's Rep 533 is sufficient to give rise to *Rylands* liability. These dicta are, however, difficult to sustain both in principle, and in the light of existing authority: see *Jones v Festiniog Rly Co* (1868) LR 3 QB 733; *Powell v Fall* (1880) 5 QBD 597; *West v Bristol Tramways Co* [1908] 2 KB 14. Such actions, it is submitted, should sound in negligence, not *Rylands v Fletcher* – which has always been a land based tort – *unless*, as in the three cases cited, the defendant has a statutory right to occupation of the public thoroughfare.

for the general benefit of the community'.[9] Although this concept may not be quite so wide as that of the 'unreasonable user' germane to private nuisance, it was fluid enough to enable the House of Lords in *Read v Lyons* to doubt whether the operating of a munition works in wartime was a non-natural user, and this, despite the fact that the House of Lords had held, 26 years earlier, that *Rylands v Fletcher* did apply to an explosion from a munitions factory in wartime.[10] Even after 1913, *Rylands v Fletcher* continued to be invoked freely, and often it was not sufficiently sharply distinguished from nuisance.[11] And then in 1947 came the reaction in *Read v Lyons*. Following this decision, the emphatic warning must be given that those pre-1948 decisions of the lower courts which appeared to have extended the original rule must now be closely scrutinised before they are accepted as good authorities.

SECTION 2. 'THINGS' WITHIN THE RULE

Blackburn J spoke of 'anything likely to do mischief if it escapes'. These things must not be summarily described as 'dangerous' and then be equated (and, in turn, confused) with those things which have been styled 'dangerous' in the context of negligence. It would be wise to eschew the word 'dangerous' since it is an inherently protean concept. A simple example of the need for caution in this context can be supplied by reference to the mischievous 'thing' in *Rylands v Fletcher* itself – water. Water is, of course, not 'dangerous' per se, yet, as Du Parcq LJ observed in *Read v Lyons*,[12] what matters here is whether the thing is likely to do damage on escaping to other land.[13] Whether or not this involves personal danger is quite irrelevant. Thus, filth and water are both 'things' within the rule.

It is equally true that the ultra-hazardous quality of the thing (in the sense that the thing in question is inherently dangerous – like dynamite) is of no moment. In *Cambridge Water Co Ltd v Eastern Counties Leather plc*[14] – the leading case on *Rylands v Fletcher* liability – it was held by Lord Goff that:

[T]here is much to be said for the view that the courts should not be proceeding down the path of developing such a theory [of liability for ultra-hazardous activities] … I incline to the view that, as a general rule, it is more appropriate for strict liability in respect of operations of high risk to be imposed by Parliament, than by the courts.[15]

In *Read v Lyons*,[16] counsel argued that the thing must have 'capacity for independent movement' as well as being a potential cause of harm – so that glass, for example, would be outside the rule. Provided that an extension is made to include a thing likely to give off something such as a gas, which itself has capacity for independent movement, this

9 *Rickards v Lothian* [1913] AC 263 at 280, PC.
10 *Rainham Chemical Works Ltd v Belvedere Fish Guano Co* [1921] 2 AC 465, HL. It has also been held that the construction of (essential) large fuel installations on an airfield were a natural use of the land because they, as integral to the airfield, were of benefit to the '*national* community as a whole': *Ellison v Ministry of Defence* (1996) 81 BLR 101, 119 (Judge Bowsher QC, emphasis added).
11 The most authoritative statement of the continuing affinity between the two torts is set out by Lord Goff in *Cambridge Water Co Ltd v Eastern Counties Leather plc* [1994] 2 AC 264 at 298–9, [1994] 1 All ER 53 at 69–71, HL.
12 [1945] KB 216 at 247, CA.
13 Cf Lord Porter in *Read v J Lyons & Co* [1947] AC 156 at 176, [1946] 2 All ER 471, HL.
14 [1994] 2 AC 264, [1994] 1 All ER 53, HL.
15 [1994] 1 All ER 53 at 76, HL.
16 [1947] AC 156 at 158, [1946] 2 All ER 471, HL.

contention has much to commend it, and there is some, though hardly adequate, support for it in the cases.[17]

Things which have been held to be capable of giving rise to *Rylands v Fletcher* liability include electricity,[18] gas likely to pollute water supplies,[19] explosives,[20] fire and things likely to cause, and which in fact cause, fires (including a motor vehicle whether the tank contains,[1] or be emptied of,[2] petrol),[3] things likely to give off noxious gases or fumes,[4] water,[5] sewage,[6] and slag heaps.[7] Cases holding planted yew trees[8] and chair-o-planes[9] to be within the rule are also probably sound so long as there is movement of the mischievous thing beyond the boundary of the land under the defendant's control. Whether a decayed rusty wire fence[10] and a flag-pole,[11] have been rightly regarded as being within the rule is doubtful.

A final, and interesting illustration of the kind of 'things' that may fall within the rule is supplied by the case of *A-G v Corke*.[12] There it was held that the owner of land who allowed caravan dwellers to live on that land was answerable on this principle for the interferences which they perpetrated on adjoining land.

The last characteristic of those 'things' whose escape may give rise to liability under the rule is that they must have been brought onto the land by the defendant. This final characteristic applies only to 'things artificially brought or kept upon the defendant's land'.[13]

SECTION 3.   PARTIES

(A)   WHO MAY BE SUED?

Blackburn J said that the rule applies to a 'person who for his own purposes brings on his lands and collects and keeps there' the thing in question. The thing may or may not be something which in its nature is capable of being naturally there: what matters is

---

17 Eg *Wilson v Newberry* (1871) LR 7 QB 31 at 33 (per Mellor J): 'things which have a tendency to escape and to do mischief'.
18 *National Telephone Co v Baker* [1893] 2 Ch 186.
19 *Batchellor v Tunbridge Wells Gas Co* (1901) 84 LT 765.
20 *Rainham Chemical Works Ltd v Belvedere Fish Guano Co* [1921] 2 AC 465, HL and CS gas canisters: *Rigby v Chief Constable of Northamptonshire* [1985] 2 All ER 985.
1   *Musgrove v Pandelis* [1919] 2 KB 43, CA.
2   *Perry v Kendricks Transport Ltd* [1956] 1 All ER 154, [1956] 1 WLR 85, CA.
3   *Jones v Festiniog Rly Co* (1868) LR 3 QB 733 (sparks from railway engine); *Balfour v Barty-King* [1956] 2 All ER 555 (blowlamp), affd on other grounds [1957] 1 QB 496, [1957] 1 All ER 156, CA.
4   *West v Bristol Tramways Co* [1908] 2 KB 14, CA; *Halsey v Esso Petroleum Co Ltd* [1961] 2 All ER 145, [1961] 1 WLR 683 (acid smuts).
5   *Rylands v Fletcher* (1868) LR 3 HL 330, HL; *Western Engraving Co v Film Laboratories Ltd* [1936] 1 All ER 106, CA.
6   *Humphries v Cousins* (1877) 2 CPD 239.
7   *Kennard v Cory Bros & Co Ltd* [1921] AC 521, HL.
8   *Crowhurst v Amersham Burial Board* (1878) 4 Ex D 5.
9   *Hale v Jennings Bros* [1938] 1 All ER 579, CA.
10 *Firth v Bowling Iron Co* (1878) 3 CPD 254.
11 *Shiffman v Grand Priory in British Realm of Venerable Order of the Hospital of St John of Jerusalem* [1936] 1 All ER 557.
12 [1933] Ch 89. In *Smith v Scott* [1973] Ch 314, [1972] 3 All ER 645 undesirable tenants were held to be outside the rule, because a landlord has no 'control' over tenants.
13 *Bartlett v Tottenham* [1932] 1 Ch 114 at 131, CA (per Lawrence LJ). It is probable that, by analogy with nuisance, a defendant who has not himself brought the thing on to the premises is within the rule.

whether the particular thing has in fact been accumulated there. If, therefore, water flows from A's underground tunnels into B's mines, whether by force of gravitation or by percolation, A is not liable in *Rylands v Fletcher* for that escape if the water was naturally on A's land and he did nothing to accumulate it there.[14] On the other hand, there was liability in *Rylands v Fletcher* itself because steps had been taken by the defendants to accumulate the water on their land by constructing the reservoir.[15] The cases where flooding of neighbouring land results from pumping or diverting water from the land of the defendant to that of the plaintiff may be nuisance, or even perhaps trespass. But they cannot be within *Rylands v Fletcher* if the defendant has not artificially accumulated the water.[16] Similarly, the escape of rocks is outside the rule since there has been no accumulation.[17] If, however, rocks are blasted in quarrying, there may then be liability for accumulating the explosives.[18]

In the case of vegetation, assuming the other elements of the rule to be satisfied, it will be important to consider whether that vegetation was planted there deliberately, for the planting of it will constitute an accumulation.[19] *Giles v Walker*,[20] always assuming that the case was decided on *Rylands v Fletcher*, which is not clear, may be a relevant authority in this context.

> The defendant, in order to redeem some of his forest land, ploughed it up. Thereafter, thistles grew all over the ploughed land. Thereafter, thistle-down escaped from the defendant's land to the plaintiff's, where it seeded itself.

Finding that the thistles were 'the natural growth of the soil', the court held that this was no tort.[1] Yet it seems, from an interjection of Lord Esher MR, during the argument, that the result would have been different had the court found that the defendant had been responsible for the thistles having come onto his land. Had there been a finding of fact that the ploughing up of the land had caused the thistles to come on to the defendant's land and grow there, the requirement of artificial accumulation would have been satisfied.[2]

Problems of responsibility for accumulation were also considered by the House of Lords in *Rainham Chemical Works Ltd v Belvedere Fish Guano Co*.[3]

> A and B contracted with the Ministry of Munitions to manufacture explosives on their land. They formed a limited company, C Ltd, and arranged for C Ltd to perform this contract for them on the land of A and B. Thus, C Ltd were, quoad A and B, licensees. Neighbouring landowners suffered damage to their land caused by an explosion on the land of A and B while C Ltd were using it, and they sued A and B, and C Ltd.

---

14 *Wilson v Waddell* (1876) 2 App Cas 95, HL.
15 And in *Broder v Saillard* (1876) 2 Ch D 692, where the water was brought onto the land in connection with the stabling of the horses of the defendant.
16 Eg *Baird v Williamson* (1863) 15 CBNS 376; *Whalley v Lancashire and Yorkshire Rly Co* (1884) 13 QBD 131, CA; cf *Hurdman v North Eastern Rly Co* (1878) 3 CPD 168, CA.
17 *Pontardawe RDC v Moore-Gwyn* [1929] 1 Ch 656.
18 *Miles v Forest Rock Granite Co (Leicestershire) Ltd* (1918) 34 TLR 500, CA. Sed quaere, if it is not the explosives, but the rocks which have escaped.
19 *Crowhurst v Amersham Burial Board* (1878) 4 Ex D 5.
20 (1890) 24 QBD 656, Div Ct, and see 62 LT 933. Cf *Seligman v Docker* [1949] Ch 53.
1   But note the limited liability imposed in nuisance for damage resulting from the naturally occurring dangerous condition of land: *Leakey v National Trust* [1980] QB 485, [1980] 1 All ER 17.
2   62 LT at 934. Observations by the Court of Appeal in *Davey v Harrow Corpn* [1958] 1 QB 60, [1957] 2 All ER 305, CA, support the view taken in the text.
3   [1921] 2 AC 465, HL.

It was decided that a licensee who himself accumulates something on the land of another is liable for the consequences of that accumulation.[4] Further, the House of Lords held that those who remain in occupation of land are also liable to landowners injured by the escape of that which their licensee accumulates in discharge of a contractual duty owed by the occupiers to a third party.

Lord Sumner further stated (obiter) that if 'they [A and B] ... simply suffered others to manufacture upon the site which they nevertheless continued to occupy' they would be liable for the consequences of an escape.[5] On the other hand, Eve J in *Whitmores (Edenbridge) Ltd v Stanford*[6] held that a landowner, upon whose land some other person had a prescriptive right to accumulate water for his own purposes, would not be liable under the rule. The extent to which an occupier is liable in respect of the accumulations of his licensees cannot be regarded as settled, but it is relevant to observe that in *Rylands v Fletcher* Blackburn J spoke only of a person who 'for his own purposes' brings things on his land.[7] Thus, a local authority which is required by statute to permit the discharge of sewage into its sewers is treated as responsible for the accumulation of that sewage.[8]

A person who authorises another to commit a tort is normally also himself liable for that tort. Thus, a lessor, who lets land for a particular purpose in such circumstances that he is necessarily taken to have authorised the interference which the lessee in consequence causes, is liable in nuisance.[9] There were obiter dicta in *Rainham Chemical Works Ltd v Belvedere Fish Guano Co* to the effect that the same rule applies in *Rylands v Fletcher* – in short, that a defendant may be liable although he does not occupy the land, if he has authorised another to accumulate something on it, when the thing so accumulated later escapes.[10]

What happens where the accumulation is not on the land owned or occupied by the defendant? In *Rigby v Chief Constable of Northamptonshire*, Taylor J relying on a passage in the then current edition of *Clerk and Lindsell on Torts*, suggested (obiter) that there was, so far as he could see, 'no difference in principle between allowing a man-eating tiger to escape from your land onto that of another and allowing it to escape from the back of your wagon parked on the highway'.[11] The same view is held by other leading commentators[12] but is, it is submitted, wrong. How can the requirements that

4   Where, however, over 20 years had elapsed since the licensee had the right to enter and accumulate water there, he was held not to be accountable for the escape of water, if he no longer had control of the land: *Westhoughton Coal and Cannel Co Ltd v Wigan Coal Corpn Ltd* [1939] Ch 800, [1939] 3 All ER 579, CA.
5   [1921] 2 AC 465 at 480.
6   [1909] 1 Ch 427.
7   (1866) LR 1 Exch 265 at 279. But see *Humphries v Cousins* (1877) 2 CPD 239 where an occupier who was bound to receive sewage into drains on his land in circumstances where it was presumably not collected for his own purposes was nonetheless held liable for an escape. On the other hand, in *Read v Lyons*, Viscount Simon doubted ([1947] AC 156 at 170) whether a defendant making munitions in his factory at the Government's request in wartime brought things onto his land 'for his own purposes'. Gas, water and electricity boards, and inland waterways authorities carrying out statutory duties, do not accumulate for their own purposes. Accordingly, *Rylands v Fletcher* does not apply: *Dunne v North Western Gas Board*, [1964] 2 QB 806, [1963] 3 All ER 916, CA; *Boxes Ltd v British Waterways Board* [1971] 2 Lloyd's Rep 183, CA.
8   *Smeaton v Ilford Corpn* [1954] Ch 450, [1954] 1 All ER 923.
9   See previous chapter.
10   [1921] 2 AC 465 at 476 (per Lord Buckmaster); at 489 (per Lord Parmoor); cf *A-G v Cory Bros & Co* (1918) 34 TLR 621, but not considered at [1921] 1 AC 521, HL. Contra the obiter dicta of Scrutton and Greer LJJ in *St Anne's Well Brewery Co v Roberts* (1928) 140 LT 1, CA (at 5 and 9 respectively).
11   [1985] 2 All ER 985 at 996. There is further recent obiter dictum to similar effect in *Crown River Cruises Ltd v Kimbolton Fireworks Ltd* [1996] 2 Lloyd's Rep 533 (per Potter J).
12   See *Salmond & Heuston* (1996) 311; Rogers *Winfield & Jolowicz on Tort* (1998) 451.

there be an artificial accumulation on, and a non-natural use of, the defendant's land be satisfied if both the accumulation and escape take place elsewhere? The preferable view, we suggest, is that such cases should be actionable, if at all, as negligent omissions.[13] The rule in *Rylands v Fletcher* has long since been stated by the House of Lords to be no more than 'a principle applicable between *occupiers* in respect of *their land*'.[14]

(B)   WHO MAY SUE?

It is clear that this rule permits a landowning plaintiff, as in *Rylands v Fletcher* itself, to sue in respect of damage to land. Similarly, in relation to damage to chattels, Blackburn J later allowed a claim where sparks from a railway engine set fire to a haystack;[15] and several other cases bear out that liability for damage to chattels is recoverable.[16] But what of those who suffer no such property damage (whether to personalty or realty), but merely personal injuries? It would appear that the question needs to be addressed in two stages.

First, where the plaintiff is an occupier of land, *Hale v Jennings Bros* is binding Court of Appeal authority for the proposition that an occupier can recover in respect of personal injuries.[17]

A tenant of a stall at a fair suffered personal injuries as the result of an escape of the defendant's chair-o-plane. She was held to have a good cause of action based on *Rylands v Fletcher*.

Secondly, what of the plaintiff who suffers personal injury but has no such proprietary interest? Here, the law is less clear. In both *Perry v Kendricks Transport Ltd*[18] and *British Celanese Ltd v AH Hunt (Capacitors) Ltd*[19] it was suggested, obiter, that even those with no proprietary interests are able to bring an action for personal injuries on the basis of *Rylands v Fletcher*. Furthermore, there is nothing in Blackburn J's judgment in *Rylands* which appears to prohibit such a possibility. Indeed, to the contrary, his lordship envisaged liability in respect of '*all the damage* which is the natural consequence of its escape'.[20] On this basis, it might by argued that a proprietary interest in land is not (and never has been) a prerequisite to recovery under this tort.[1] On the other hand, however, it might be argued that, following the *Cambridge*

---

13   Negligent omissions, however, are only infrequently actionable: see Murphy 'Expectation Losses, Negligent Omissions and the Tortious Duty of Care' [1996] CLJ 43. On the other hand, creating an obvious source of danger, that is liable to be 'sparked off' by a third party may give rise to negligence liability: *Haynes v Harwood* [1935] 1 KB 146; *Smith v Littlewoods Organisation Ltd* [1987] AC 241 at 272, HL (per Lord Goff, obiter); *Topp v London Country Bus* [1993] 1 WLR 976 (noted in Murphy 'An Accident Waiting to Happen?' [1994] Tort Law Review 77).
14   *Read v Lyons* [1947] AC 156 at 173, HL (per Lord Macmillan, emphasis added).
15   *Jones v Festiniog Rly Co* (1868) LR 3 QB 733; cf *Cattle v Stockton Waterworks Co* (1875) LR 10 QB 453 at 457 (per Blackburn J).
16   Eg *Midwood & Co Ltd v Manchester Corpn* [1905] 2 KB 597, CA; *Musgrove v Pandelis* [1919] 2 KB 43, CA; *Collingwood v Home and Colonial Stores Ltd* [1936] 3 All ER 200, CA; cf *Read v J Lyons & Co* [1947] AC 156 at 169, HL (per Viscount Simon).
17   [1938] 1 All ER 579, CA. See also the Australian case of *Benning v Wong* (1969) 43 ALJR 467 to like effect.
18   [1956] 1 All ER 154, [1956] 1 WLR 85, CA.
19   [1969] 2 All ER 1252, [1969] 1 WLR 959.
20   (1866) LR 1 Exch 265 at 279.
1   Contrast the position in nuisance where such an interest is a precondition of entitlement to sue: *Hunter v Canary Wharf Ltd* [1997] 2 All ER 426, HL. Cf Jones *Textbook on Torts* (1998) p 356; *Winfield and Jolowicz* p 456.

Water case – where Lord Goff was at pains to stress the fact that *Rylands* liability was historically derived from private nuisance – the rule, like nuisance,[2] should be available only to those who possess an interest in land affected by the escape. The trouble with combining the decisions in *Hunter* and *Cambridge Water* in this way is that it overlooks that in nuisance the emphasis is placed on the plaintiff having a proprietary interest: central to locus standi. By contrast, in *Rylands v Fletcher*, the emphasis is upon the defendant's property – it is there that there must be an accumulation, and from there that there must be an escape.

In the absence of clear authority, it is submitted that the view that anyone suffering personal injury may recover is to be preferred since the similarities between nuisance and *Rylands v Fletcher* are, as we shall see later in this chapter, apt to be overstated. On the other hand, it should be pointed out that several of their Lordships in *Read v Lyons* expressed powerfully the view, albeit obiter, that personal injuries were irrecoverable under *Rylands*.[3] To some extent, however, the distinction between personal injuries and property damage is not always easy to sustain since, especially in the case of personal injury to the occupier or holder of a proprietary interest, injury to the person might be seen to merge into a general injury to the proprietary interest as a whole.[4]

A final question in this context is whether the plaintiff who suffers pure economic loss is able to claim for his losses under the rule in *Rylands v Fletcher*. Here, too, the law is somewhat uncertain. It was held in *Weller & Co v Foot and Mouth Disease Research Institute*[5] that the escape of a virus was not actionable by the plaintiff, a cattle auctioneer, when it caused a loss of profit to his business after making a third party's cattle unsaleable. But in the case of *Ryeford Homes v Sevenoaks District Council*,[6] the possibility of recovery for pure economic loss was again mooted, as a preliminary issue, and not ruled out. Judge Newey QC expressed the view that pure economic loss was, *in principle*, recoverable under the rule in *Rylands v Fletcher* so long as it was 'a sufficiently direct result of an escape of water from sewers'.[7] This view is thought to be correct, and it is entirely consistent both with Blackburn J's judgment in *Rylands v Fletcher* and the decision in the *Weller* case.[8]

SECTION 4.   THE NON-NATURAL USE OF LAND

Blackburn J said that the rule applied only to a thing 'which was not naturally there'.[9] In the House of Lords, Lord Cairns used more ambiguous words which have since

---

2   Though it was suggested in *Khorasandjian v Bush* [1993] QB 727, [1993] 3 All ER 669, CA that a proprietary interest was not required to bring an action in private nuisance, this view has now been authoritatively rejected by the House of Lords in *Hunter v Canary Wharf* [1997] AC 655, [1997] 2 All ER 426, HL.

3   [1947] AC 156, HL at 173 (per Lord Macmillan), at 178 (per Lord Porter) and at 180–1 (per Lord Simonds).

4   See the analysis of *Hunter v Canary Wharf* (supra) in the previous chapter.

5   [1966] 1 QB 569, [1965] 3 All ER 560. See also, in similar vein, *Cattle v Stockton Waterworks Co* (1875) LR 10 QB 453 (escape of water which made it more expensive for the plaintiff to carry out his contract to construct a tunnel; not actionable).

6   [1989] 2 EGLR 281.

7   On the facts of this case, however, the defendants were able to invoke the defence of statutory authority (on which, see infra).

8   The fact that the auctioneer's loss in *Weller* was contingent upon the cattle owners' loss rendered the loss of profit from the would-be auctions an *indirect*, and hence irrecoverable, economic loss.

9   Viscount Simon in *Read v Lyons* [1947] AC 156 at 166, [1946] 2 All ER 471, HL, described this as 'a parenthetic reference to' the test of Lord Cairns.

been construed as meaning[10] that the defendant is only answerable if, in bringing the thing onto his land,[11] he is making 'a non-natural use' of the land. The expression 'non-natural use' is very flexible and the courts are afforded a great deal of latitude in construing whether the defendant has engaged in a 'non-natural use'. The form in which Lord Moulton, on behalf of the Privy Council, expressed this rule in *Rickards v Lothian* emphasised this flexibility.[12] He said that '[i]t must be some special use bringing with it increased danger to others, and must not merely be the ordinary use of the land or such a use as is proper for the general benefit of the community'.[13] Viscount Simon in *Read v Lyons* thought this statement to be 'of the first importance'[14] and Lord Porter said:[15]

> each seems to be a question of fact subject to a ruling of the judge as to whether ... the particular use can be non-natural, and in deciding this question I think that all the circumstances of the time and place and practice of mankind must be taken into consideration so that what might be regarded as ... non-natural may vary according to those circumstances.

The current tendency is to interpret 'non-natural use' narrowly, and many earlier cases may be no longer followed. For instance, in *Read v Lyons*, despite the contrary previous decision of the House of Lords in *Rainham Chemical Works Ltd v Belvedere Fish Guano Co*,[16] it was doubted whether building and running a munitions factory on land in wartime was a non-natural user.[17] Similarly, despite the words of Lord Moulton in *Rickards v Lothian*, concerning uses that bring a 'general benefit to the community', Lord Goff emphatically denied the fact that the generation of employment for a local community was sufficient to transform the storage of chemicals used in the tanning industry into a natural use of the land. He said:

> I myself, however, do not feel able to accept that the creation of employment as such, even in a small industrial complex, is sufficient of itself to establish a particular use as constituting a natural or ordinary use of land.[18]

Beyond this, his Lordship offered little to clarify the meaning of the term 'non-natural use'. Instead of taking the opportunity to do so in *Cambridge Water*, he declined to say more than that he did not consider it necessary to redefine the phrase in that context as 'the storage of chemicals on industrial premises should be regarded as *an almost classic case* of non-natural use'.[19]

Notwithstanding the crepuscular haze that continues to overhang the meaning of non-natural use of land, the following instances can confidently be stated to be natural uses of land: water-pipe installations in buildings;[20] growing trees, even though planted by the defendant (at least if they are not poisonous);[1] working mines and minerals on

---

10 (1868) LR 3 HL 330 at 337–40. See Williams 'Non-natural use of land' [1973] CLJ 310.
11 What matters is whether the accumulation (as distinct from the escape) is a non-natural use: *Read v Lyons*, supra at 186 (per Lord Uthwatt).
12 [1913] AC 263 at 280, PC.
13 [1913] AC 263 at 280, PC. It has since been qualified that this means the 'national community as a whole': *Ellison v Ministry of Defence* (1996) 81 BLR 101, 119 (per Judge Bowsher QC).
14 [1947] AC 156 at 169, HL.
15 Ibid at 176.
16 [1921] 2 AC 465, HL.
17 [1947] AC 156 at 169–70 (per Viscount Simon) and 173–4 (per Lord Macmillan), HL.
18 [1994] 1 All ER 53 at 79, HL.
19 [1994] 1 All ER 53, emphasis added.
20 *Rickards v Lothian* [1913] AC 263, HL; *Tilley v Stevenson* [1939] 4 All ER 207, CA.
1   *Noble v Harrison* [1926] 2 KB 332, Div Ct.

land;[2] building or pulling down walls;[3] lighting a fire in the fireplace of a house;[4] installing necessary wiring for electric light;[5] storing metal foil in a factory.[6] The provision for sewage disposal by a local authority,[7] and the escape from a ship of generated steam are probably also natural uses.[8] By contrast, it has been held that the storing of water, gas and electricity in bulk in mains, and the like,[9] the operation of a chair-o-plane,[10] the use of a blowlamp to thaw pipes in a loft[11] and the storage of ignitable material in a barn[12] constitute non-natural uses of the land. It is difficult to resist the conclusion that the notion of 'non-natural user' is presently a narrow one, and that the current interpretation of the term is likely to restrict the scope of application of the rule in *Rylands v Fletcher*.

SECTION 5.   ESCAPE

According to the orthodox view, an explosion which injures a plaintiff within the factory where the explosion occurs is outside the rule since there must be an 'escape from a place where the defendant has occupation of, or control over, land to a place which is outside his occupation or control'.[13] Equally, a yew tree that poisons a horse which eats its leaves by reaching its head over onto the land of the defendant is outside the rule since the 'dangerous' leaves never go beyond the boundary of the defendant's land.[14] By contrast, where something escapes from one place of entertainment in a fairground to a stall tenanted by another fairground operative (but still within the fairground), there *is*, apparently, a sufficient escape.[15]

In *Midwood & Co v Manchester Corpn*[16] one of the two grounds of liability was *Rylands v Fletcher*.

2   *Rouse v Gravelworks Ltd* [1940] 1 KB 489, [1940] 1 All ER 26, CA.
3   *Thomas and Evans Ltd v Mid-Rhondda Co-operative Society Ltd* [1941] 1 KB 381, [1940] 4 All ER 357, CA; *St Anne's Well Brewery Co v Roberts* (1928) 140 LT 1, CA.
4   *Sochaski v Sas* [1947] 1 All ER 344; and also holding a torch at the top of the opening of a grate in order to test chimney draught: *J Doltis Ltd v Isaac Braithwaite & Sons (Engineers) Ltd* [1957] 1 Lloyd's Rep 522.
5   *Collingwood v Home and Colonial Stores Ltd* [1936] 3 All ER 200, CA.
6   *British Celanese Ltd v A H Hunt (Capacitors) Ltd* [1969] 2 All ER 1252; *Mason v Levy Auto Parts of England Ltd* [1967] 2 QB 530, [1967] 2 All ER 62 (storage of spare motor parts and engines; having regard to quantities of combustible material, manner of storage and character of neighbourhood).
7   *Pride of Derby and Derbyshire Angling Association v British Celanese Ltd* [1953] Ch 149 at 189, [1953] 1 All ER 179 at 203, CA (per Denning LJ); contra, *Smeaton v Ilford Corpn* [1954] Ch 450 at 470, [1954] 1 All ER 923 (per Upjohn J) and *Ryeford Homes v Sevenoaks District Council* [1989] 2 EGLR 281.
8   *Howard v Furness Houlder Argentine Lines Ltd and A and R Brown Ltd* [1936] 2 All ER 781.
9   *Northwestern Utilities v London Guarantee and Accident Co Ltd* [1936] AC 108, PC; *Western Engraving Co v Film Laboratories Ltd* [1936] 1 All ER 106, CA: water in unusual quantities brought onto land for manufacturing purposes of defendant occupier.
10   *Hale v Jennings Bros* [1938] 1 All ER 579, CA.
11   *Balfour v Barty-King* [1956] 2 All ER 555; affd on other grounds [1957] 1 QB 496, [1957] 1 All ER 156, CA.
12   *E Hobbs (Farms) v Baxendale Chemical Co* [1992] 1 Lloyd's Rep 54.
13   *Read v J Lyons & Co* [1947] AC 156 at 168, [1946] 2 All ER 471, HL (per Viscount Simon).
14   *Ponting v Noakes* [1894] 2 QB 281.
15   This point was essential to the decision in *Hale v Jennings Bros* [1938] 1 All ER 579, CA, although it may not have been argued. Similarly, an escape to the lower part of the same building is sufficient: *J Doltis v Isaac Braithwaite & Sons (Engineers) Ltd* [1957] 1 Lloyd's Rep 522. The key to these cases appears to be an escape onto land under another's control, regardless of property ownership.
16   [1905] 2 KB 597, CA.

After an explosion in a cable belonging to and laid by the defendants in the highway, inflammable gas escaped into the plaintiff's nearby house and set fire to its contents.

In *Charing Cross West End and City Electric Supply Co v Hydraulic Power Co*,[17] the Court of Appeal, relying on this case, held that there was a sufficient escape when water from a main, laid by the defendants under the highway, escaped and damaged the plaintiff's electric cable which was near to it and under the same highway. The House of Lords in *Read v Lyons* did not overrule these cases, and pointed out that there was in each of them an escape onto property, over which the defendant had no control, from a container which the defendant had a licence to put in the highway.[18] On the other hand, the proposition that the rule also extends to cases where the defendant has no such licence in respect of a public thoroughfare is thought to be wrong.[19]

The actual harm wrought by the escape need not be immediately caused by the thing accumulated. So, for example, it was held in *Kennard v Cory Bros & Co* that where parts of a coal slag heap escaped and their pressure on a third party's quarry spoil caused that spoil to damage the plaintiff's land, the escape requirement of *Rylands v Fletcher* was satisfied.[20]

SECTION 6.   FORESEEABILITY OF HARM

Since the important decision in the *Cambridge Water* case, it is clear that foreseeability of harm is required if a plaintiff is to succeed in an action based on *Rylands v Fletcher*. The facts were as follows.

Solvents which had been used by the defendants in their tannery for many years had a history of being spilt onto the floor of the defendants' factory. From there, they seeped into a natural groundwater source drawn upon by the plaintiff in order to fulfil their statutory duty to supply drinking water to the inhabitants of Cambridge. The seepage caused the water to become contaminated to the extent that it was unwholesome according to European Community standards. No-one had supposed that this contamination would take place, mainly because of the volatility of the solvents which it had been thought had simply evaporated from the defendants' factory floor.

A unanimous House of Lords held the defendants not to be liable on the basis of the unforeseeability of the harm caused to the plaintiff's water supply. Lord Goff, who delivered the only full speech in the case, stated that: 'foreseeability of damage of the relevant type should be regarded as a prerequisite of liability in damages under the rule'.[1] What his Lordship failed to make clear, however, is whether damage had to be foreseeable (a) in terms of the *kind* of harm alone or (b) in terms of *both* an escape occurring *and* harm being thereby caused. In relation to the former notion of foreseeability of harm, the test would be akin to the one used to determine the remoteness

---

17   [1914] 3 KB 772, CA.
18   [1947] AC 156 per Lord Porter at 177, HL; cf Viscount Simon at 168 and Lord Simonds at 183. *Hillier v Air Ministry* (1962) Times, 8 December (cows electrocuted by underground electric cable; liable within rule).
19   See the obiter suggestion of Taylor J in *Rigby v Chief Constable of Northamptonshire* [1985] 2 All ER 985 at 996 to this effect (police fired CS gas canisters into the plaintiff's shop in order to flush out a psychopath who had entered those premises). See also *Crown River Cruises Ltd v Kimbolton Fireworks Ltd* [1996] 2 Lloyd's Rep 533 (escape from a vessel on a navigable waterway).
20   [1921] AC 521 at 538, HL (per Viscount Finlay).
1   [1994] 1 All ER 53 at 75, HL.

of damage in negligence and nuisance.[2] If the second test were used – that is, if the foreseeability of harm were not simply gauged by reference to the potentially injurious nature of the accumulated substance, but also by reference to the likelihood of its escape – then foreseeability in this sense would undermine the strictness of *Rylands* liability by introducing a fault requirement: to insist on the foreseeability of *the escape* is to hinge liability upon the defendant's failure to confine something the escape of which he ought to have anticipated and exercised due diligence to contain.[3] Thus, even though his Lordship failed to make absolutely clear which model of foreseeability he favoured, it has since been suggested, obiter,[4] that it was the former, especially in the light of his Lordship pointing out, elsewhere in his speech, that the rule is one of strict liability in that liability may attach 'notwithstanding that [the defendant] ... has exercised all reasonable care and skill to prevent the escape'.[5]

SECTION 7. DEFENCES

(A) STATUTORY AUTHORITY

Sometimes, public bodies storing water, gas, electricity and the like, are by statute exempted from liability so long as they have taken reasonable care. It is a question of statutory interpretation whether, and, if so, to what extent, liability under *Rylands v Fletcher* has been excluded. Only if there is a statutory *duty* (as opposed to a mere *permission*) to perform the hazardous activity will there be a defence. Thus, in *Green v Chelsea Waterworks Co*,[6] there was no liability when a water main burst because the Waterworks Company was under an obligation to keep the main charged at high pressure making a damaging escape an inevitable consequence of any non-negligent burst. By contrast, the mere statutory permission to provide a water supply was not enough to afford the defendants immunity.

Smeaton v Ilford Corpn provides a further example of the statutory authority defence in operation.[7]

> Sewage accumulated by the defendants in their sewers overflowed onto the land of the plaintiff in circumstances which were held to constitute neither nuisance nor negligence. According to section 31 of the Public Health Act 1936, under which the defendants had acted in receiving the sewage: 'A local authority shall so discharge their functions ... as not to create a nuisance'. In interpreting this to mean that the defendants were absolved from liability provided they did not create a nuisance, the court held that the defendants had a defence under the statute to an action based on *Rylands v Fletcher*.

A final point in this context is that the defence only operates in respect of *Rylands v Fletcher* liability. So, if the reason for the escape is the defendant's negligence, the presence of a statutory duty to perform the hazardous activity will not afford a defence.

---

2   *Overseas Tankship (UK) Ltd v Morts Dock & Engineering Co Ltd, The Wagon Mound* [1961] AC 388, [1961] 1 All ER 404, PC. For an argument that it may be a broader test in *Rylands* see McIntyre 'Liability for Asbestos Related Injury' (1997) 4 Irish Planning and Environmental Law Journal 83.

3   See, eg, *Bolton v Stone* [1951] AC 850, [1951] 1 All ER 1078, HL.

4   *Ellison v Ministry of Defence* (1996) 81 BLR 101. See also the excellent account provided by Wilkinson, '*Cambridge Water Company v Eastern Counties Leather plc*: Diluting Liability for Continuing Escapes' (1994) 57 MLR 799.

5   [1994] 1 All ER 53 at 71.

6   Eg *Green v Chelsea Waterworks Co* (1894) 70 LT 547.

7   [1954] Ch 450, [1954] 1 All ER 923.

This begs the question: who is to prove the absence of negligence, the plaintiff or the defendant? There is no English authority on the point but a majority decision of the High Court of Australia has held the onus to lie with the plaintiff.[8] It is submitted that this decision has little to commend it, for, according to Blackburn J's famous dictum in *Rylands v Fletcher*, a defendant is 'prima facie answerable for all the damage which is the natural consequence of [the thing's] ... escape'.[9]

(B) CONSENT OF THE PLAINTIFF

If the plaintiff has permitted the defendant to accumulate the thing the escape of which is complained of, then he cannot sue if it escapes.[10] For the purposes of this defence, implied consent will clearly suffice. Thus, a person becoming the tenant of business premises at a time when the condition or construction of adjoining premises is such that an escape is likely to ensue, is deemed to have consented to the risk of such an event actually happening. This defence was the crux of *Kiddle v City Business Properties Ltd*,[11] where an overflow of rainwater from a blocked gutter at the bottom of a sloping roof in the possession of the landlord, and above the tenant's premises, damaged the stock in the tenant's premises.[12]

If the accumulation benefits both plaintiff and defendant, this is an important element in deciding whether the plaintiff is deemed to have consented.[13] Where, therefore, for the benefit of the several occupants of a building, rainwater is collected on the roof,[14] or a water-closet is installed,[15] or water pipes are fitted,[16] the several occupants are presumed to have consented. On the other hand, the defence does not seem to be available as between a commercial supplier of gas (in respect of gas mains under the highway) and a consumer in premises adjoining the highway.[17] In any event, an occupier will not be presumed to have consented to installations being left in a dangerously unsafe state.[18]

(C) CONTRIBUTORY NEGLIGENCE

Where the plaintiffs worked a mine under the canal of the defendant, and had good reason to know that they would thereby cause the water from the canal to escape into this mine, it was held that the plaintiffs could not sue in *Rylands v Fletcher* when the water actually escaped and damaged their mine. Cockburn CJ described the matter thus:

8   *Benning v Wong* (1969) 43 ALJR 467.
9   (1866) LR 1 Exch 265 at 280.
10 *Kennard v Cory Bros & Co* [1921] AC 521, HL.
11 [1942] 1 KB 269, [1942] 2 All ER 216.
12 The principle of implied consent does not apply, however, where the plaintiff and the defendant are not in a tenant-landlord relationship: *Humphries v Cousins* (1877) 2 CPD 239.
13 *Peters v Prince of Wales Theatre (Birmingham) Ltd* [1943] KB 73, [1942] 2 All ER 533, CA. Where the plaintiff by inference has consented to having the benefit of the defendant's watercourse, but contends that he has not consented to a negligent accumulation of water, the onus is on the plaintiff to allege and prove negligence: *Gilson v Kerrier RDC* [1976] 3 All ER 343, [1976] 1 WLR 904, CA.
14 *Carstairs v Taylor* (1871) LR 6 Exch 217.
15 *Ross v Fedden* (1872) LR 7 QB 661.
16 *Anderson v Oppenheimer* (1880) 5 QBD 602, CA (the reasoning is muddled, but this is the most likely basis of the decision).
17 *Northwestern Utilities Ltd v London Guarantee and Accident Co Ltd* [1936] AC 108 at 120, PC.
18 *A Prosser & Sons Ltd v Levy* [1955] 3 All ER 577, [1955] 1 WLR 1224, CA.

'the plaintiffs saw the danger and may be said to have courted it'.[19] Where the plaintiff is contributorily negligent, the apportionment provisions of the Law Reform (Contributory Negligence) Act 1945 will now clearly apply. Further, as was said in *Eastern and Southern African Telegraph Co Ltd v Cape Town Tramways Co Ltd*, 'a man cannot increase the liabilities of his neighbour by applying his own property to special uses, whether for business or pleasure'.[20] In that case, the plaintiff, who complained that the tramways of the defendant caused electrical interference with the receipt of messages through his submarine cable, failed in their action because no damage to the cable itself was caused. The plaintiff suffered loss only because he relied on the cable for the transmission of messages.[1]

(D) ACT OF THIRD PARTIES: *RYLANDS V FLETCHER* OR NEGLIGENCE?

What must next be considered is whether it is a defence that, although the defendant brought the thing onto his land, it has only escaped through the act of a third party. It is evident from *Rylands v Fletcher* itself that the defendant is liable for an escape attributable to his independent contractors.[2] Further, there is weighty support for the proposition that the defendant is liable for escapes caused by any other third party where the defendant ought reasonably to have foreseen the act of that third party and had enough control of the premises to be able to prevent it. The proprietor of a chair-o-plane was accordingly held liable for the escape of a chair caused by a passenger's tampering with it;[3] the owner of a flag-pole was also liable when small children caused the pole to fall and injure the plaintiff.[4] Similarly, a gas company laying a main in a highway were liable for damage caused by an explosion of gas when the surrounding earth subsided due to a third party's subjacent mines.[5]

On the other hand, in *Rickards v Lothian*, the defendant was not liable where flooding of the plaintiff's premises was caused by an unknown third party who had maliciously turned on a water tap in the defendant's premises and blocked the waste pipe of the lavatory basin.[6] So, too, was there immunity in *Box v Jubb* where the defendant's reservoir overflowed when a third party, conducting operations higher up the stream supplying it, discharged downstream an unusually large volume of water without any warning.[7]

There has been a tendency for these two cases to be taken to support the view that once the defendants have proved that the escape was the act of a stranger 'they avoid liability, unless the plaintiff can go on to show that the act which caused the escape

---

19 *Dunn v Birmingham Canal Navigation Co* (1872) LR 7 QB 244 at 260; affd LR 8 QB 42. (Note that at the time of this decision contributory negligence was a *complete* defence.)
20 [1902] AC 381, at 393, PC; cf *Hoare & Co v McAlpine* [1923] 1 Ch 167, which left open the question whether a plaintiff who complained that his buildings had been damaged could be met by the plea that they were damaged only because they were dilapidated buildings having insecure foundations.
1   This decision may, however, be better understood in terms of the plaintiff's loss not being a sufficiently direct consequence of the escape.
2   See ch 25, post for separate treatment of independent contractors.
3   *Hale v Jennings Bros* [1938] 1 All ER 579, CA.
4   *Shiffman v Grand Priory in British Realm of Venerable Order of the Hospital of St John of Jerusalem* [1936] 1 All ER 557 at 561 (per Atkinson J, obiter on *Rylands v Fletcher*).
5   *Hanson v Wearmouth Coal Co Ltd and Sunderland Gas Co* [1939] 3 All ER 47, CA.
6   *Rickards v Lothian* [1913] AC 263.
7   (1879) 4 Ex D 76; cf *Black v Christchurch Finance Co* [1894] AC 48, PC. Analogous cases to those last cited are those suggesting that there is no liability where an unobservable defect of nature causes the escape, or where there is flooding because a rat gnaws through a water cistern: *Carstairs v Taylor* (1871) LR 6 Exch 217.

was an act of the kind which the owner could reasonably have contemplated and guarded against'.[8] It is our submission, however, that, although the case law itself clearly supports such a proposition, it has nonetheless been erroneously decided (and supported by academics[9]). We do not suggest the final decisions in the two cases to be wrong. Rather, it is our contention that the legal doctrine according which they ought have been decided is mistaken: they are negligence, not *Rylands* cases. The reasoning for this assertion is as follows.

Since *Rylands v Fletcher* is a strict liability tort, it follows that negligence in the narrow sense (ie the breach of a duty of care) plays no part in determining liability. This much was made abundantly clear by Lord Goff in *Cambridge Water v Eastern Counties Leather plc* when he said: 'the defendant will be liable for harm caused to the plaintiff by the escape, notwithstanding that he has exercised all reasonable care and skill to prevent the escape from occurring'.[10] In other words, and contrary to the view in *Perry v Kendricks*,[11] just quoted, it should not matter whether the defendant 'could reasonably have contemplated and guarded against' the intervention of a third party. The better approach is to say that such cases have nothing to do with *Rylands v Fletcher*. In essence, they do not involve a failure to control (that is, keep in) a dangerous thing (*Rylands*); they centre, instead, upon a failure to control the reasonably foreseeable harmful acts of a third party (negligence). The distinction between these two classes of negligent omission was staunchly made by the House of Lords in *Smith v Littlewoods Organisation Ltd*.[12]

It is also quite clear that *Rylands v Fletcher* (which is concerned with escapes) is to be contrasted with deliberate discharges of the dangerous thing onto another's land. Those cases, at least where the discharge is by the person who accumulated the thing, should sound in trespass.[13] In short then, it is submitted that *Rylands v Fletcher* should not accommodate the defence of the unforeseeable act of a stranger since it is inconsistent with the juridical foundations of the tort – such a defence necessarily runs counter to the unanimous decision of the House of Lords as to its strict liability basis.

(E) ACT OF GOD

This defence has received a prominence out of all proportion to its practical importance. It arises only where an escape is caused through natural causes and without human intervention, in 'circumstances which no human foresight can provide against, and of which human prudence is not bound to recognise the possibility'.[14]

In *Nichols v Marsland*[15] the defence succeeded where a most violent thunderstorm caused flooding. Yet the defence was put in its proper perspective by the House of

8 Per Parker LJ in *Perry v Kendricks Transport Ltd* [1956] 1 All ER 154 at 161; likewise Jenkins LJ held (at 160) that once the act of a stranger is made out, 'one reaches the point where the claim based on *Rylands v Fletcher* merges into the claim in negligence'.

9 See, eg, all previous editions of this work.

10 [1994] 1 All ER 53 at 71, HL. In Australia, where the strictness of *Rylands* liability has not been recognised, the tort has been abandoned in favour of actions based on a 'non-delegable duty' in negligence: *Burnie Port Authority v General Jones Pty Ltd* (1994) 120 ALR 42, High Court.

11 [1956] 1 All ER 154 at 161, CA.

12 [1987] 1 All ER 710. See also *Topp v London Country Bus (South West) Ltd* [1993] 1 WLR 976.

13 *Rigby v Chief Constable of Northamptonshire* [1985] 2 All ER 985 at 996 (per Taylor J).

14 A definition of Lord Westbury in *Tennent v Earl of Glasgow* (1864) 2 M 22, HL at 26–7, approved and followed by the House of Lords in *Greenock Corpn v Caledonian Rly Co* [1917] AC 556, HL.

15 (1876) 2 Ex D 1.

Lords in *Greenock Corpn v Caledonian Rly Co*[16] where an extraordinary and unprecedented rainfall was held in similar circumstances not to be an Act of God: the explanation of *Nichols v Marsland* was that there, the jury found that no reasonable person could have anticipated the storm and the court would not disturb this finding of fact.

The problem with the way in which the defence has been constructed by the courts is that they make its incidence referable to reasonable foresight of the cause of an escape. This, on one construction, tends to undermine the strictness of *Rylands* liability because it makes the defendant's liability depend, in part, upon the existence of fault.[17] A second (and preferable) construction of the defence is possible. This involves requiring that an Act of God be beyond all human foresight. According to this construction, we are not excusing the defendant because the natural event causing the escape was beyond reasonable foresight; instead, we are concerned with identifying the truly unique and freak occurrence (which should be distinguished from the highly unusual (but not unknown) event[18]).

On this basis, in this country at least, it might be argued that few phenomena beyond earthquakes and tornadoes are likely to constitute this defence to *Rylands v Fletcher*. Certainly, the paucity of occasions on which the defence has succeeded would tend to vindicate this view.

(F) NECESSITY

It has been held[19] that if an intentional release of a substance can ground liability in *Rylands v Fletcher* – in this instance the firing of CS gas canisters by police officers intent on flushing out a psychopath from the defendant's shop – then the defence of necessity ought to be available in this tort. However, an intentional invasion of the plaintiff's property in this fashion is actionable only in trespass.

SECTION 8. NUISANCE AND *RYLANDS v FLETCHER*

Apart from the fact that the *Cambridge Water* case continues the trend towards bringing *Rylands v Fletcher* closer to nuisance, there still remain important differences between the two torts. To begin with, the category of things coming under *Rylands v Fletcher* is narrower than that in nuisance. In *Rylands v Fletcher*, a tangible thing must be accumulated which, in its nature, is likely to cause mischief, either upon its own escape or upon its giving off fumes, gas, electricity, or possibly odours, which themselves escape. In nuisance, on the other hand, no physical object having that quality need be

---

16 [1917] AC 556, HL.
17 If this construction is accepted, the failure to prevent the escape thus caused ought, instead, to sound in negligence.
18 To allow reasonable foreseeability of the abnormal event to play a part in defining the defence is also, and inescapably, to suggest that foresight of such events is a factor which determines prima facie liability. And while, in the wake of the *Cambridge Water* case, it is clear that foreseeability is a relevant factor in a *Rylands* action, it is important to appreciate that it only operates to characterise a kind of harm, for which D would otherwise be prima facie liable, as too remote (see supra). If foreseeability of the 'freak' event were to play a part in defining this defence, however, it would operate at the level of the *definition* (as opposed to *limitation*) of prima facie liability. (For (obiter) judicial support for our view see *Ellison v Ministry of Defence* (1996) 81 BLR 101.)
19 *Rigby v Chief Constable of Northamptonshire* [1985] 2 All ER 985 at 996.

on the defendant's land.[20] Thus, in *Christie v Davey*,[1] a defendant who beat a tray against the wall of his house was held liable in nuisance to his neighbour for the interference caused by the noise; but because a tray is likely neither in itself to escape (nor to give off fumes, smells, or even noise), the defendant in that case could not have been liable in *Rylands v Fletcher*. More doubtfully, the list of mischief-making things giving rise to *Rylands* liability may be shorter than that for which liability in nuisance may be imposed. Whereas trees likely to fall may give rise to actions in nuisance, it was held in *Noble v Harrison*[2] that beech tree branches, which actually broke off causing damage, were not sufficiently likely to cause damage upon their 'escape' as to be within *Rylands v Fletcher*.

The justification for such a distinction may very well be that since the scope of liability in *Rylands v Fletcher* is wider, the propensity of the thing to cause harm on escaping must be the more obvious. Likewise, although it is not in itself a defence to this tort that the defendant was unaware that the thing was likely to do harm, proof that it was not, according to the common experience of humanity, likely to cause harm on escaping will absolve the defendant.[3]

In addition, *Rylands v Fletcher* must still be examined separately because it will afford a remedy where nuisance will not in the following circumstances.

1   If the defendant has accumulated 'a thing' which escapes, then, regardless of whether he was negligent in allowing it to escape or of whether it was foreseeable that it would in the particular circumstances escape, he will be liable: 'the principle is one of strict liability in the sense that the defendant may be held liable notwithstanding that he has exercised all due care to prevent the escape from occurring'.[4] In nuisance, the defendant is liable for damage resulting from a state of affairs on his land where the negligent management of that state of affairs makes it foreseeable that a substantial interference with the plaintiff's use of his land will result.[5] Foresight of the escape, however, is not necessary in *Rylands v Fletcher*. Indeed, to insist on foresight of the escape is to introduce the requirement of fault into something that the *Cambridge Water* case makes clear is a strict liability tort.[6]

2   The occupier is liable in *Rylands v Fletcher* for the accumulation of, and the escape caused by, independent contractors. In nuisance, the liability for independent contractors is less extensive.[7]

20 The only case apparently inconsistent with this is *Hoare & Co v McAlpine* [1923] 1 Ch 167, a decision at first instance, treating vibrations caused by a pile-driver as being within the rule (see Pollock's criticism, (1923) 39 LQR 145). But note that the case might more appropriately have been decided in nuisance. It was disapproved of in *Barrette v Franki Compressed Pile Co of Canada Ltd* (1955) 2 DLR 665 (pile-driving vibrations not within *Rylands v Fletcher*, but held to be nuisance).
1   [1893] 1 Ch 316.
2   [1926] 2 KB 332 at 342 (per Wright J); there were other reasons why an action based on *Rylands v Fletcher* failed.
3   *West v Bristol Tramways Co* [1908] 2 KB 14 at 20–1, CA (per Lord Alverstone).
4   *Cambridge Water Co Ltd v Eastern Counties Leather plc* [1994] 2 AC 264 at 306, [1994] 1 All ER 53 at 73, HL (per Lord Goff).
5   This explains why *quia timet* injunctions lie for a 'state of affairs' in nuisance but not necessarily for an 'accumulation' in *Rylands v Fletcher*.
6   See further Wilkinson '*Cambridge Water Company v Eastern Counties Leather plc*: Diluting Liability for Continuing Escapes' (1994) 57 MLR 799 at 803–7. Cf *Bolton v Stone* [1951] AC 850, HL on the role of foreseeability of an escape in determining the existence of *negligence* (in the narrow sense).
7   See ch 18, ante.

3   In nuisance the plaintiff must possess a proprietary interest in the land affected;[8] the same is apparently not true in *Rylands v Fletcher*.[9]

4   Damage by fire may sometimes be the subject of a claim in trespass or negligence, or the separate action on the case for fire.[10] It may also give rise to a claim in nuisance or in *Rylands v Fletcher*. It will be recalled that the Fires Prevention (Metropolis) Act 1774 provides that the person on whose land a fire 'shall accidentally begin' has a defence.[11] This defence is not available to suits based on *Rylands v Fletcher*[12] although it is sometimes a defence in nuisance.[13]

5   Although the *Rylands v Fletcher* concept of 'non-natural use' is closely related to the nuisance concept of 'unreasonable user', the two are not (yet) co-extensive.[14] Indeed, it has long been recognised that a use may be natural and yet give rise to liability in nuisance.[15] Equally, the reasonableness of the defendant's user is merely one factor that may be taken into account in assessing nuisance liability; but it is not a precondition of liability since it is only the unreasonableness of the interference that counts.[16]

Beyond these five heads it is difficult to state with confidence further circumstances where the distinction between nuisance and *Rylands v Fletcher* is clear. It is sometimes it is said that in *Rylands v Fletcher* liability lies in respect of an isolated escape, whereas the interference required in nuisance must have a certain degree of permanence.[17] But this distinction cannot be accepted as an accurate mark of demarcation since it does not take account of the 'state of affairs' cases in nuisance. Recall that provided there is a threatening state of affairs on the defendant's land, an action in nuisance may still lie even though only an isolated escape of something causes the plaintiff's loss.[18]

---

8   *Hunter v Canary Wharf* [1997] AC 655, [1997] 2 All ER 426, HL.

9   *Hale v Jennings Bros* [1938] 1 All ER 579, CA. But if *Rylands* derives from nuisance, why not?

10   *Balfour v Barty-King* [1957] 1 QB 496, [1957] 1 All ER 156, CA; *Mason v Levy Auto Parts of England Ltd* [1967] 2 QB 530, [1967] 2 All ER 62. In *H & N Emanuel Ltd v Greater London Council* [1971] 2 All ER 835, CA, it was held than an occupier is liable for an escape of fire caused by the negligence of anyone other than a stranger.

11   See ante.

12   *Musgrove v Pandelis* [1919] 2 KB 43, CA; *Mulholland and Tedd Ltd v Baker* [1939] 3 All ER 253; *Perry v Kendricks Transport Ltd* [1956] 1 All ER 154, CA; *Balfour v Barty-King*, supra, at first instance.

13   See ante.

14   See *Cambridge Water v Eastern Counties Leather plc* [1994] 1 All ER 53 at 71, HL where Lord Goff indicated that they were different but closely related concepts with similar functions. See also *Ellison v Ministry of Defence* (1996) 81 BLR 101 and *Graham and Graham v ReChem International Ltd* [1996] Env LR 158 (suggesting that they are virtually interchangeable concepts). Cf Cross 'Does only the Careless Polluter Pay? A Fresh Examination of the Nature of Private Nuisance' (1995) 111 LQR 445 and Murphy 'Noxious Emissions and Common Law Liability: Tort in the Shadow of Regulation' in Lowry and Edmunds *Environmental Regulation and the Common Law* (1999). See also Layard 'Balancing Environmental Considerations' (1997) 113 LQR 254.

15   Eg *Leakey v National Trust* [1980] QB 485, [1980] 1 All ER 17, CA; *Sedleigh-Denfield v O'Callaghan* [1940] AC 880 at 888, [1940] 3 All ER 349 at 354 (per Viscount Maugham), HL; *British Celanese Ltd v A H Hunt (Capacitors) Ltd* [1969] 2 All ER 1252, [1969] 1 WLR 959.

16   See *Sampson v Hodson-Pressinger* [1981] 3 All ER 710, for example, where the ordinary use of premises which, as a result of their being poorly constructed, caused intolerable noise to be perceived in adjoining premises was held to be a nuisance. See also *Toff v McDowell* (1993) 25 HLR 650.

17   Cf Newark 'The Boundaries of Nuisance' (1949) 65 LQR 480 at 488.

18   *Midwood & Co Ltd v Manchester Corpn* [1905] 2 KB 597, CA.

Chapter 20

Animals

SECTION I. NEGLIGENCE AND STRICT LIABILITY

Persons who own or control animals are subject to the same duty of care in respect of the care and control of those animals as those responsible for any other chattels.[1] Thus, in *Aldham v United Dairies (London) Ltd*[2] the defendant was held liable when his unattended pony became restive and jabbed at a passing pedestrian knocking her down. And in *Draper v Hodder*[3] the owner of a pack of terriers was found liable when the dogs bit a neighbour's child. He was negligent in failing to control and/or train the pack adequately. An occupier of premises may be liable under the Occupiers' Liability Acts for breach of the common duty of care in respect of injuries inflicted by dogs on his premises.[4] But liability for damage inflicted by animals extends beyond mere failure to control them properly.[5] The Animals Act 1971 provides a strict liability regime that covers a range of circumstances in which damage might be caused by both dangerous and non-dangerous animals.

SECTION 2. DAMAGE DONE BY DANGEROUS ANIMALS

(A) DANGEROUS SPECIES

Section 2(1) of the Animals Act 1971 imposes strict liability where any damage is caused by an animal which belongs to a dangerous species. A dangerous species, for these purposes, is one which is not commonly domesticated in the British Isles, and whose fully grown animals have such characteristics that they are likely, unless restrained, to

1 *Fardon v Harcourt-Rivington* [1932] All ER Rep 81 at 83; *Birch v Mills* [1995] 9 CL 354.
2 [1940] 1 KB 507, [1939] 4 All ER 522. And see *Brock v Richards* [1951] 1 KB 529, CA.
3 [1972] 2 QB 556, [1972] 2 All ER 210, CA (the defendant's contention that while bowling over or scratching by the excited dogs was foreseeable, biting was harm of a distinct and unforeseeable type, was rejected).
4 *Hill v Lovett (OH)* 1992 SLT 994. Consider also whether an action for breach of statutory duty might lie for failing to muzzle a pit bull terrier as required by the Dangerous Dogs Act 1991 which fails expressly to create a civil cause of action.
5 For example, liability may sound in nuisance for the smell emanating from animals kept by the defendant (*Wheeler v JJ Saunders* [1995] 2 All ER 697, CA), or in *Rylands v Fletcher* for an animal that escapes (*Behrens v Bertram Mills Circus Ltd* [1957] 2 QB 1, [1957] 1 All ER 583).

cause severe damage or that any damage they may cause is likely to be severe.[6] A species is dangerous if it is likely to cause damage either to persons or to property, so the list is not confined to animals likely to attack man, such as bears, tigers, lions etc. An action lies under the Act even though the damage caused is not of the kind in respect of which the species is known to be dangerous. Similarly, liability arises even though the animal has not escaped from control: so a keeper would be liable if his elephant slips or stumbles and thereby causes damage. Under the Act, 'damage' includes the impairment of any mental condition.[7] So, for example, if someone suffered nervous shock with resulting physical illness at the sudden appearance of a cobra, there would be liability.

(B) NON-DANGEROUS SPECIES

Section 2(2)[8] of the Animals Act 1971 imposes liability in certain circumstances for an animal which does not belong to a dangerous species. Three requirements must be met. First, the damage must be of a kind which the animal, unless restrained, was likely to cause[9] or which, if caused by the animal, was likely to be severe. There is no need to show that the severity of the potential damage ensues from any abnormal characteristics in the animal.[10] Severity may simply be an inevitable consequence of the size of an animal's jaw! This formulation covers not only, say, a dog which attacks a man, but also an animal with a dangerous disease that spreads the infection to other animals.

The second requirement of section 2(2) of the Animals Act 1971 is that the likelihood of the damage, or of its being severe, must be due to characteristics of the animal which are not normally found in animals of the same species[11] or are not normally so found except at particular times or in particular circumstances.[12] In this connection, the Court of Appeal has rejected the contention that horses ushered onto a road by a mischievous third party display an unusual characteristic when they gallop along that road out of blind panic. Instead, their Lordships held that the true cause of the injury to the plaintiff car driver coming in the other direction was the deliberate release of the horses onto the highway and not an unusual characteristic in them.[13] On the other hand, a bitch

---

6   Animals Act 1971, s 6(2).
7   Animals Act 1971, s 11.
8   Note that this provision is extremely convoluted and has variously been described as 'very cumbrously worded' (per Lord Denning MR in *Cummings v Granger* [1977] QB 397 at 404, CA) and of 'somewhat tortuous wording' (per Slade LJ in *Curtis v Betts* [1990] 1 All ER 769 at 771, CA).
9   In *Smith v Ainger* [1990] CLY 3297, CA it was held that it is enough to prove merely that the injurious occurrence *might* happen. Sed Quaere?
10 *Curtis v Betts* [1990] 1 All ER 769 at 772 and 778, CA.
11 The keeper in one case was liable where a horse of unpredictable and unreliable behaviour crushed its groom against the bar of its trailer even though it had no previous tendency to injure people, for that was a characteristic unusual in a horse: *Wallace v Newton* [1982] 2 All ER 106. 'Species' is defined in s 11 of the Animals Act 1971 to include sub-species. It seems that different breeds of dogs are treated as sub-species: *Curtis v Betts* [1990] 1 All ER 769, CA.
12 In *Cummings v Granger* [1977] QB 397, CA, the plaintiff was bitten by the defendant's Alsatian dog which was used as a guard dog in his scrapyard. The dog used to bark and run around when coloured people like the plaintiff approached. This characteristic is not normally found in Alsatian dogs except when used as guard dogs. This was held to be a particular circumstance within the Animals Act 1971 s 2(2)(b).
13 *Jaundrill v Gillett* (1996) Times, 30 January.

with a litter of pups which was prone at such a time only to bite strangers, or a bull mastiff defending his 'territory' are covered by section 2(2).[14]

The third requirement of this subsection is that the animal's unusual characteristics must have been known to the keeper or to his servant or member of his household under the age of 16, and a causal link between the 'abnormal' characteristic and the injury caused by the animal must be established.[15]

(C)   LIABILITY FOR EITHER KIND OF DANGEROUS ANIMAL

Liability under the Animals Act 1971 is imposed on the keeper regardless of whether the animal in question belongs to a dangerous or a non-dangerous species. And a keeper for the purposes of the Act is defined in terms of the person who owns the animal or has it in his possession, or who is head of the household of which a member under the age of 16 owns the animal or has it in his possession.[16] This last provision prevents evasion of liability by making a child in the family the nominal owner. If a person ceases to keep, own or possess it, he continues to be liable until another person owns or possesses it.[17] Liability is imposed regardless of fault. The defendant is not liable for any damage which is due wholly to the fault of the person suffering it[18] and damages will be reduced under the Law Reform (Contributory Negligence) Act 1945 where the plaintiff's fault merely contributes to his damage.[19] It is a defence under the Act that the damage was suffered by a person who has voluntarily accepted the risk.[20] An employee who accepts a risk incidental to his employment shall not be treated as accepting it voluntarily.[1] It is also a defence that the damage occurred on property where the plaintiff was a trespasser if it is proved either that the animal was not kept there for the protection of persons or property or (if the animal was kept there for the protection of persons or property) that keeping it there for that purpose was not unreasonable.[2] Presumably it would be difficult to maintain this defence in respect of a dangerous species being kept for protection only, because that might well be unreasonable. Trespassers will never have a remedy when attacked by an animal of a dangerous species not kept for protection.

14   *Curtis v Betts* [1990] 1 All ER 769, CA.
15   *Jaundrill v Gillett* (1996) Times, 30 January.
16   Animals Act 1971, s 6(3).
17   Animals Act 1971, s 6(3). But a person who takes possession only for the purpose of preventing damage or restoring it to its owner is not thereby made liable: s 6(4).
18   Animals Act 1971, s 5(1). In *Cummings v Granger* [1977] QB 397 at 404, CA, Lord Denning MR appeared to hold that even though the plaintiff trespassed in the defendant's yard, the fact that the dog bit the plaintiff showed that the damage was not wholly due to the plaintiff's fault, but only partly so, with the result that this defence was not available. Yet since the question of a defence could not arise unless the dog had bitten the plaintiff, it is difficult to see how, if Lord Denning is right, that defence could ever succeed.
19   Animals Act 1971, s 10.
20   Animals Act 1971, s 5(2). In *Cummings v Granger* [1977] QB 397, CA the court found that when the plaintiff knew of the dog she must be taken to have voluntarily accepted the risk. The court, especially Ormrod LJ (at 408), treated this defence as being wider than the common law defence of volenti.
1   Animals Act 1971, s 6(5); *Canterbury City Council v Howletts & Port Lympne* [1997] ICR 925 (tiger keeper killed by one of the zoo's tigers; the zoo especially encouraged 'bonding' between the tigers and their keepers (which necessitated entering the cage regularly; keepers dependents entitled to sue)).
2   Animals Act 1971, s 5(3); *Cummings v Granger* [1977] QB 397, CA (reasonable to keep an Alsatian dog, known to be ferocious, to protect old cars in a locked yard). Had the Guard Dogs Act 1975 been in force, Lord Denning MR would have held that failure to comply with the requirement of that Act that the dog had to be in the control of the handler would have made the keeping of the dog unreasonable.

SECTION 3.   LIABILITY FOR STRAYING LIVESTOCK

Section 4 of the Animals Act 1971 imposes liability on a person in possession of livestock which stray onto another's land. Under the Act, 'livestock' means cattle, horses, asses, mules, hinnies, sheep, pigs, goats, poultry and deer not in the wild state.[3] The liability is for damage done by the livestock to the land or to any property on it.[4] Presumably, 'property' includes other animals as well as goods, but the plaintiff cannot recover under the Animals Act 1971, section 4 for his personal injuries. Either the person in possession or the owner (even though not in possession) can recover for damage to his land or property.

A plaintiff may incur expense in keeping livestock while it cannot be restored to its owner or while it is detained in pursuance of the power conferred by the Act to detain it.[5] He can recover any such expenses reasonably incurred.[6] Liability is strict under this section, so no fault need be proved. The defendant is not liable for any damage due wholly to the fault of the plaintiff.[7] This defence applies where the plaintiff could have prevented the damage by fencing[8] so long as the plaintiff was under a duty to fence, owed to a person having an interest in the land from which the livestock strayed and the straying would not have occurred but for that breach.[9] The Law Reform (Contributory Negligence) Act 1945 applies in respect of damage in part caused by the plaintiff's own fault.[10] It is also a defence that the livestock strayed from a highway and its presence there was a lawful use of the highway, for the owner of property adjoining a highway is presumed to have accepted risks incidental to such ownership.[11]

SECTION 4.   LIABILITY FOR INJURY DONE BY DOGS TO LIVESTOCK

Section 3 of the Animals Act 1971 provides that where a dog causes damage by killing or injuring livestock[12] its keeper is liable for the damage, even though he was not negligent. A person is not liable if the livestock was killed or injured on land onto which it had strayed and either the dog belonged to the occupier or its presence on the land was authorised by the occupier.[13] It is a defence that the damage was due wholly to the fault of the person suffering it.[14]

---

3   Animals Act 1971, s 11.
4   This would not cover the case when there is no damage, only loss. For example, the Ministry of Agriculture, Food and Fisheries makes a foot and mouth order restricting movement of cattle, but none of P's cattle are destroyed.
5   Animals Act 1971, s 7. See *Matthews v Wicks* (1987) Times, 25 May, CA; *Morris v Blaenau Gwent District Council* (1982) 80 LGR 793.
6   Animals Act 1971, s 4(1)(b).
7   Animals Act 1971, s 5(1); *Nelmes v Chief Constable of Avon and Somerset Constabulary* (9 February 1993, unreported), CA (P kicked a police dog, before his arrest, provoking it into biting him).
8   Fencing includes the construction of any obstacle designed to prevent animals from straying.
9   Animals Act 1971, s 5(6). In the absence of any such duty to fence, there is no defence under the Act.
10   Animals Act 1971, ss 10 and 11.
11   Animals Act 1971, s 5(4), (5).
12   Livestock for this purpose is slightly wider than under s 4 in that it includes pheasant, partridges and grouse while in captivity: s 11.
13   Animals Act 1971, s 5(4).
14   Animals Act 1971, s 5(1). If the plaintiff by his fault has contributed to the damage, the Law Reform (Contributory Negligence) Act 1945 applies to permit a reduction of the damages awarded.

Chapter 21

Breach of statutory duty

SECTION I. INTRODUCTION[1]

Exceptionally now, a person suffering damage as a result of a violation of a statute may have an action in tort in respect of that damage, commonly styled an action for breach of statutory duty. For the plaintiff the great advantage of a claim for breach of statutory duty is that in many cases all he need prove is that the defendant failed to fulfil his statutory obligation. There is no requirement to establish that the breach was either intentional or negligent. The early cases on the tort rested on a broad principle that whenever a violation of a statute caused damage to an individual's interests a right of action in tort arose.[2] Leading nineteenth-century decisions[3] markedly restricted the scope of the tort, requiring that any person claiming for breach of a statutory duty must first establish that the legislature intended that violation of his right or interest be tortious.

Lord Denning MR attempted(ultimately unsuccessfully) to resurrect the broader principle in *Ex p Island Records Ltd*.[4] He contended that if '… a private right is being interfered with by a criminal act, thus causing or threatening to cause him special damage over and above the generality of the public, then he can come to the court as a private individual and ask that his private right be protected.'[5] Thus, he held that whenever a lawful business carried on by a private person suffered damage as a result of contravention of a statutory prohibition an action for breach of statutory duty would lie.

This 'broad Denning principle', had it taken root, would have transformed the action for breach of statutory duties and opened up the way for greater protection of individual interests by the law of torts in two crucial respects. First in respect of damage to economic and business interests, plaintiffs could have taken advantage of the extensive provision made by statute to regulate the economy to obtain compensation for losses which the classic economic torts left irremediable.[6] Second, citizens aggrieved by the

---

1 See generally K M Stanton *Breach of Statutory Duty in Tort* (1986), R A Buckley 'Liability in Tort for Breach of Statutory Duty' (1984) 100 LQR 204.
2 *Couch v Steel* (1854) 3 E & B 402 was the last important case resting on the old broad principle.
3 See *Atkinson v Newcastle and Gateshead Waterworks Co* (1877) 2 Ex D 441, CA; *Groves v Lord Wimborne* [1898] 2 QB 402, CA.
4 [1978] Ch 122, [1978] 3 All ER 824, CA.
5 Ibid at 139.
6 See ante ch 9.

failure of public authorities to fulfil obligations designed to protect their welfare could have sought extensive redress from central and local government. The decisions of the House of Lords in *Lonrho Ltd v Shell Petroleum Co Ltd (No 2)*[7] and *X v Bedfordshire County Council*[8] appear, however, to have stifled the further development of the action for breach of statutory duty.

Relying on *Ex p Island Records* the plaintiffs in *Lonrho Ltd v Shell Petroleum Co Ltd (No 2)*, an oil company which had suffered heavy losses because they complied with government sanctions orders prohibiting trade with the illegal regime in Rhodesia while competitors flagrantly violated those orders, sought to sue their competitors for breach of the orders. The House of Lords firmly rejected and condemned the 'broad Denning principle', reasserting that the general rule in a claim for breach of statutory duty is that 'where an Act creates an obligation and enforces performance in a specified manner ... that performance cannot be enforced in any other manner'.[9] Where the only manner of enforcing performance for which the Act provides is the criminal process, there are only two classes of exception to this general rule. The first is '... where on the true construction of the Act it is apparent that the obligation or prohibition was imposed for the benefit of a particular class of individuals'.[10] And the second arises where statute creates a public right and an individual member of the public suffers 'particular, direct and substantial damage other and different from that which is common to the rest of the public'.[11] Lonrho's claim fell outside either exception. Sanctions orders prohibiting trade with Rhodesia were intended to end all trade and bring down the illegal regime. They were not imposed for the benefit or protection of any class of business, but to create public rights enjoyable by all citizens wishing to avail themselves of such rights.[12]

In *X v Bedfordshire County Council* the House of Lords held that no action for breach of statutory duty arose out of *either* legislation imposing duties on local authorities to safeguard the welfare of children in their area and protect them from chuld abuse, *or* legislation requiring local authorities to meet the educational needs of children in their district. Lord Browne-Wilkinson acknowledged that legislation to protect children at risk and to provide for education was undoubtedly designed to benefit those children, but found that it was not Parliament's intention to allow individual children harmed by a local authority's failure to meet its statutory obligations to recover compensation for that harm from the public purse. His Lordship noted that no case had been cited before the court where statutory provisions creating a general regulatory scheme to promote social welfare had been held to give rise to a private law claim for damages. He went on to say.[13]

> Although regulatory or welfare legislation affecting a particular area of activity does in fact provide protection to those individiuals particularly affected by that activity, the legislation is not to be treated as being passed for the benefit of those individuals *but for the benefit of society in general.* [Our emphasis.]

---

7   [1982] AC 173, [1981] 2 All ER 456, HL; and see *RCA Corpn v Pollard* [1983] Ch 135, [1982] 3 All ER 771, CA.

8   [1995] 2 AC 633, [1995] 3 All ER 353.

9   *Doe d Bishop of Rochester v Bridges* (1831) 1 B & Ad 847 at 859.

10   Per Lord Diplock at 186 and 461 respectively.

11   *Benjamin v Storr* (1874) LR 9 CP 400 at 407.

12   As to this second exception to the general rule see post and see *Stanton* at pp 50–51. Is Lord Diplock himself creating a new category of action for breach of statutory duty?

13   Supra at 731–732. And see *Capital and Counties plc v Hampshire County Council* [1997] QB 1004, [1997] 2 All ER 865, CA.

To succeed in a claim for breach of statutory duty after the decisions in *Lonrho* and *X* the plaintiff must satisfy a two-part test. He must establish that *when*[14] Parliament enacted the relevant statute (1) it was intended to protect a class of persons to which he belongs and (2) Parliament envisaged that in providing that protection of his interests he should be enabled to claim compensation for any failure to protect those interests. The matter is in theory entirely one of construction of the statute in question, but as Lord Browne-Wilkinson in *X* candidly admitted while the principles of breach of statutory duty may be clear '…the application of those principles in any particular case remains difficult'.[15]

SECTION 2.   ELUSIVE PARLIAMENTARY INTENT

The success or failure then of any attempt to frame an action for breach of statutory duty will turn on identifying the elusive intention of Parliament. In reality, in a number of cases, the legislature probably never addressed the issue of whether individuals should be able to claim damages for breach of the obligations embodied in the relevant statute. Only rarely does Parliament expressly declare that any breach of the statute should,[16] or should not,[17] be actionable in tort. Now that courts may refer to Hansard, some glimmering of the Parliamentary intent may on occasion be gained from perusal of Parliamentary debate.[18] In the majority of instances, the judges struggle with principles and policy developed over the years.

It cannot be stressed too forcefully that an action for breach of statutory duty can only lie if the court finds Parliament intended to confer a right to compensation on an individual injured by breach of that duty.[19] It is not enough to show simply that a statute was designed to protect the plaintiff in some general sense.

First, loss or injury of a recognised type must be shown. Unauthorised publication of information about the plaintiff in breach of Mental Health Tribunal Rules was insufficient.[20] Invasion of privacy was not a recognised head of damage.

Second, the plaintiff must convince the court that if he did suffer some injury as a consequence of violation of the statute, Parliament envisaged that he should be entitled to monetary compensation for that violation. In *Hague v Deputy Governor of Parkhurst Prison*[1] prisoners alleged that they had suffered injury as a result of (inter alia) being held in solitary confinement in breach of the Prison Rules. The House of Lords held that evidence that the Rules were in part designed to protect prisoners was insufficient to show Parliament intended that prisoners should be able to sue for breach of the Rules.

Lord Jauncey put it this way:[2]

The Prison Act 1952 is designed to deal with the administration of prisons and the management and control of prisoners. It covers such wide-ranging matters as central administration, prison officers, confinement and treatment of prisoners, release of prisoners on licence. Its objects

14 See *Issa v Hackney Borough Council* [1997] 1 All ER 999, [1997] 1 WLR 956, CA.
15 Supra at 730.
16 For two examples where Parliament expressly created a civil remedy for breach of statutory duty see the Protection from Harassment Act 1997, s 3; the Consumer Protection Act 1987, s 41.
17 See Health and Safety at Work Act 1974, s 47(2).
18 See *Richardson v Pitt-Stanley* [1995] QB 123. [1995] 1 All ER 460, CA.
19 *Hague v Deputy Governor of Parkhurst Prison* [1991] 3 All ER 733 at 750 (per Lord Jauncey).
20 *Pickering v Liverpool Daily Post and Echo Newspapers plc* [1991] 1 All ER 622, HL.
1   [1991] 3 All ER 733, HL.
2   [1991] 3 All ER 733 at 750–1.

are far removed from those of legislation such as the Factories and Coal Miners Acts whose prime concern is to protect the health and safety of persons[3] who work therein.

The priority afforded to interests in bodily security by the law of torts (particularly within an employment context) is reflected in the willingness of the courts to interpret industrial safety legislation so as to confer a right of action on injured workmen. Breaches of statutory rules to fence machinery in the Factories Act[4] and regulations made for miners safety by the Mines and Quarries Acts[5] represent classic examples of the statutory provisions traditionally held enforceable in tort. In such cases, the courts readily found that Parliament, in enacting rules to protect workers, envisaged that an injured employee should be able to claim compensation from any employer who failed to provide his workforce with the protection Parliament demanded. Strict liability for injury to employees both offered an overwhelming incentive to employers to ensure that safety rules were compiled with, and meant the cost of any injury which befell a worker fell on the employer, not the luckless individual. Piecemeal legislation on industrial safety was originally intended to be replaced by a new all-embracing statutory regime introduced by the Health and Safety at Work Act etc 1974. Sections 2–9 of the Act imposed general safety duties on all employers. Breach of those general duties are expressly stated not to be actionable in tort.[6] Section 15 of the Act empowered the Secretary of State to make specific health and safety regulations for particular industries.[7] Breach of such regulations will be actionable, unless the regulation in question provided otherwise.[8]

The making of such regulations to replace earlier legislation proceeded at snail's pace until reinvigorated by European legislation. A series of European Community directives require implementation of an ambitious and coherent scheme for industrial safety across Europe. A 'framework' directive[9] is given effect by the Management of Health and Safety at Work Regulations 1992[10] which provide for general safety duties akin to those imposed by sections 2–9 of the 1974 Act. No claim in tort lies for breach of such duties.[11] More specific regulations address different aspects of workers' safety[12] and a claim in tort will lie for breach of such regulations.[13] For example, the Workplace (Health, Safety and Welfare) Regulations 1992[14] impose duties in respect of ventilation and cleanliness at all workplaces. The duties imposed by such regulations vary in form. Some are absolute requiring that employees' safety be guaranteed. Others demand only that the employer do what is reasonably practicable. In the interpretation of these modern 'European' regulations, case law on their predecessors such as the Factories Act may remain relevant, and most importantly the principle that employees injured at work should have generous access to compensation for industrial injury remains intact.

---

3   Note that Lord Bridge suggests (at 741) an action might lie for breach of those of the Prison Rules concerned with industrial safety in prison workshops.
4   *Groves v Lord Wimborne* (supra).
5   *Black v Fife Coal Co Ltd* [1912] AC 149; *National Coal Board v England* [1954] AC 403, [1954] 1 All ER 546.
6   Health and Safety at Work etc Act 1974, s 47(1)(a).
7   Replacing earlier legislation such as the Factories Acts.
8   Health and Safety at Work etc Act 1974, s 47(2).
9   EC 89/391.
10   SI 1992 No 2051.
11   SI 1992 No 2051, reg 15.
12   Unlike the regulations originally made under the 1974 Act, these regulations address the different aspects of employees' safety common to all employments, rather than addressing particular industries separately.
13   Because they continue to be made under s 47(2) of the Health and Safety at Work etc Act 1974.
14   SI 1992 No 3004.

There are precedents for the protection of interests in land and goods against violation of a statute. A mine owner recovered damages from a neighbouring mine owner in breach of his statutory duty to pump water out of the mine.[15] Economic losses too have exceptionally been found recoverable where protection from that kind of loss is within the ambit of the statute. In *Monk v Warbey*[16] the plaintiff suffered bodily injuries in a road accident. Alas, the driver of the car was uninsured and impecunious. The plaintiff recovered his consequent financial loss by successfully suing the owner of the car who, in breach of his statutory duty, had allowed his friend to drive the vehicle uninsured against third party risks. Yet in the recent case of *Richardson v Pitt-Stanley*[17] a claim against the plaintiff's employer-company and its directors for failure to comply with provisions of the Employers' Liability (Compulsory Insurance) Act 1969 requiring employers to insure against liability for accidents at work failed. The Court of Appeal held that in respect of the company, the employee already enjoyed a range of remedies at common law enforceable against company assets. If there were no such assets (and there were not because the company had gone into liquidation), and no insurance policy, no additional claim for breach of statutory duty under the 1969 Act would avail the plaintiff. The substantial criminal penalties under the Act militated against the existence of a civil claim and some slight indication that Parliament did not intend to create such a private right was to be found in Hansard. If no action for breach of statutory duty was intended against the company, their lordships thought it unlikely that Parliament intended a claim to lie against individual directors. The Act was not designed to guarantee that the plaintiff received the compensation that an effective insurance policy would have provided.

In *Rickless v United Artists Corpn*[18] the plaintiffs won a massive award of damages for the defendants' unauthorised use of clips from old Peter Sellers films. The Court of Appeal found that violation of section 2 of the Dramatic and Musical Performers' Protection Act 1958, prohibiting use of such material without the performer's consent, did create a civil right of action. The purpose of the Act was protection of performers' rights and correlative financial interests. In the light of the current judicial trend to restrict liability for economic loss, clear evidence that that was the very type of loss protected by the statute will be required. In *Richardson v Pitt-Stanley*[19] Stuart-Smith LJ signalled fairly clearly that only exceptionally would such losses be recoverable in an action in breach of statutory duty.

> In my opinion, the court will more readily construe a statutory provision so as to provide a civil cause of action where the provision relates to the safety and health of a class of persons rather than where they have thereby suffered economic loss.

So in *Wentworth v Wiltshire County Council*[20] a plaintiff seeking to recover for damage to his business caused by disrepair of the adjacent highway failed in his claim. The duty to maintain the highway existed to protect users against personal injury not to safeguard the profits of traders. A number of further factors will impact on the courts' readiness to find that Parliament intended that one of the class of persons for whose benefit an Act was passed should have a private action for compensation for its breach.

15 *Ross v Rugge-Price* (1876) 1 Ex D 269.
16 [1935] 1 KB 75, CA.
17 [1995] QB 123, [1995] 1 All ER 460, CA.
18 [1988] QB 40, [1987] 1 All ER 679, CA.
19 [1995] QB 123 at 132.
20 [1993] QB 654, [1993] 2 All ER 256, CA.

(1)   There is a great reluctance to allow a claim for breach of statutory duty against a public authority for failure to provide adequate public services. Claims against health[1] and education ministers[2] for failure to meet their statutory obligations to ensure adequate health care to patients and education for the nation's children failed. In *X v Bedfordshire County Council*,[3] Lord Browne-Wilkinson, addressing claims in respect of the child care protection system had no doubt that the relevant statutes were intended to protect children from abuse, but that the language and framework of the legislation was not designed to allow individual children or families to sue. Local authorities, their officers and professional advisers were required to make judgments of 'peculiar sensitivity', striking an almost impossible balance between the harm to a child of abuse and the harm of being removed from its home. His lordship doubted whether a claim for breach of statutory duty could ever lie where the relevant duty required the defendant first to arrive at a subjective judgment on disputed facts in the exercise of broad discretionary powers conferred by Parliament. Unsurprisingly, then, the House of Lords[3a] later overruled an earlier judgment of the Court of Appeal, *Thornton v Kirklees Metropolitan Borough Council*,[4] where an action for breach of statutory duty had been held to lie to enforce the local authority's duty to house homeless persons.

Perhaps Lord Bridge summed up the heart of the case against imposing liability for breach of statutory duty on public bodies when he issued this ringing warning against too great a readiness to find an action for breach of duty against any public authority:[5]

> …. the shoulders of a public authority are only broad enough to bear the loss because they are financed by the public at large. It is pre-eminently for the legislature to decide whether these policy reasons should be accepted as sufficient for imposing on the public the burden of providing compensation for financial losses. If they do so decide, it is not difficult for them to say so.

(2)   If the alleged breach of duty derives not from a breach of a statute itself, but a breach of regulation made under a statute, this tricky question arises. Did the enabling Act empower the minister to make regulations conferring private rights of action on individuals?[6]

(3)   The statutory duty itself must be precise in its terms so as to make enforcing it by way of action fair to the defendant.[7]

(4)   Finally, it must be shown that to intend that a private right of action should lie for violation of a statute, Parliament could have envisaged the circumstances in which the plaintiff came to suffer harm. In *Olotu v Home Office*[8] the plaintiff was remanded in custody for a period exceeding the 112-day limit set by the Prosecution of Offences (Custody Time Limits) Regulations. The court found that those Regulations were

---

1   *R v Secretary of State for Social Services, ex p Hincks* (1979) 123 Sol Jo 436.
2   *Watt v Kesteven County Council* [1955] 1 QB 408, [1955] 1 All ER 473.
3   [1995] 2 AC 633, [1995] 3 All ER 353, HL.
3a   *O'Rourke v Camden London Borough Council* [1988] AC 188.
4   [1979] QB 626, [1979] 2 All ER 349, CA.
5   *Murphy v Brentwood District Council* [1990] 2 All ER 908 at 931.
6   *Hague v Deputy Governor of Parkhurst Prison* [1991] 3 All ER 733, HL. Note the rather different answers to the question from Lords Bridge and Jauncey. And see *Olotu v Home Office* [1997] 1 WLR 328, 339, C.A.
7   *Cutler v Wandsworth Stadium Ltd* [1949] AC 398, [1949] 1 All ER 544, HL; *X v Bedfordshire County Council* [1995] 2 AC 633, [1995] 3 All ER 353, HL.
8   [1997] 1 WLR 328, CA; and see *Issa v Hackney London Borough Council* [1997] 1 All ER 999, [1997] 1 WLR 956, CA.

designed to achieve expedition in the prosecution of crime and to ensure that accused persons did '…not languish in prison for excessive periods awaiting trial'. Protecting accused persons, the class to which the plaintiff belonged, was clearly an object of the Regulations. However no claim for breach of statutory duty lay because, the Appeal Court found, neither Parliament nor the secretary of state laying the Regulation would have foreseen a scenario where *both* the Crown Prosecution Service failed to comply with its duty under the Regulations *and* the accused person failed to apply for immediate bail.

SECTION 3.   THE NATURE OF THE ACTION

Care must be taken to avoid confusion between this tort and negligence, albeit in practice plaintiffs will often make concurrent claims in breach of statutory duty and negligence. Lord Browne-Wilkinson offers an instructive analysis in *X v Bedfordshire County Council*.[9] Addressing the extent of the defendant local authorities' liabilities in tort generally for failure in child care and educational provision he distinguished between three possible causes of action in tort.

(1)   *Breach of statutory duty simpliciter*. Such a claim, in the tort which this chapter centrally addresses '…depends neither on any breach of the plaintiffs' common law rights nor on any allegation of negligence by the defendants'. If a private right of action lies for violation of a statute, the plaintiff has no need to prove negligence.

(2)   *The common law duty of care*. It may be that the performance of a statutory duty gives rise to a common law duty of care. The ordinary rules of the tort of negligence then apply.

(3)   *The careless performance of a statutory duty*. If it is not established that in respect of a particular statutory duty, Parliament did intend to confer on the plaintiff a private right of action for breach of statutory duty, nor, that the circumstances of the plaintiff's relationship with the defendant gave rise to a common law duty of care, no claim in tort lies simply for the careless performance of a statutory duty per se.

A classic claim for breach of statutory duty then, once a private right of action has been found to lie, requires only that the plaintiff prove that breach of duty, that the statutory obligation was not fulfilled. In many cases, liability is truly strict. In others the statute may prescribe that some degree of negligence be proven or allow a defence if the defendant shows that avoiding injury to the plaintiff was not 'reasonably practicable'. In all cases the nature of the conduct constituting violation of the statute is prescribed by the statute itself, not principles of common law negligence.

The rules (often imprecise because of the ever-present problem of statutory interpretation) governing this tort are now further examined.

SECTION 4.   WHAT THE PLAINTIFF MUST PROVE

(A)   AN OBLIGATION ON THE DEFENDANT

A mandatory duty must be imposed on the defendant if the action is to lie. The imposition of a criminal offence prohibiting members of the public from engaging in

---

9   [1995] 2 AC 633 at 731–736; and see *London Passenger Transport Board v Upson* [1949] AC 155 at 168.

certain conduct is insufficient.[10] The conferral of a power to act is not enough. The statute must create a positive obligation incumbent on the defendant. Such an obligation will normally be found in a statute, or in regulations made under a statute. A number of cases have considered whether an action lies for breach of provisions of the European Community treaties. In *Garden Cottage Foods Ltd v Milk Marketing Board*[11] it was held that an action lay for breach of the duty imposed by Article 86 not to abuse a dominant position in the common market. Construing Article 30, on the legality of the imposition of import restrictions by the UK Government, the majority of the Court of Appeal in *Bourgoin SA v Ministry of Agriculture*[12] refused to award damages in breach of statutory duty. The judgments establish the availability in principle of the action for breach of community legislation. The distinction between them was said to lie in that Article 86 imposes a directly applicable duty on individuals, whereas Article 30 concerns the discretionary powers of public authorities. Oliver LJ vigorously dissented and the majority desision on breach of statutory duty and Article 30 has been questioned[13] by the House Of Lords. The impact of European Community law on tort is only just beginning to be teased out. All too often, the problem is trying to squeeze an indubitable right under European law into an inappropriate common law pigeon hole.[14] The implications for the protection of economic interests, which are heavily regulated by community rules to eliminate unfair competition, of the availability of claims in tort for breach of those rules, will be far-reaching. But is an action based on a right directly conferred by EC law properly styled an action for breach of *statutory* duty?

(B) THE STATUTE MUST IMPOSE THE BURDEN ON THE DEFENDANT

This issue has been raised most frequently in actions by workers (who have been injured by some act or omission of fellow workers) against their employers. It is not always easy to decide whether the duty is imposed on the employer or on the worker. Thus, it was held by the House of Lords in *Harrison v National Coal Board* that duties relating to mines, when expressed impersonally, are imposed on the mine owner, but that the duties relating to shot-firing, since they are expressly imposed on the shot-firer, are not duties of the mine owner.[15] Obviously, the present tort does not lie against the employer unless the duty imposed on him has been broken.[16]

Once the statute has been interpreted to impose a duty on the employer, the general principle is clear. The House of Lords has held:[17]

> ... the owner cannot relieve himself of his obligation by saying that he has appointed reasonably competent persons and that the breach is due to negligence on their part ...

It would therefore be no defence to an employer of a workman injured by an unfenced machine that the foreman has failed to carry out the instructions to fence which the employer issued to him. The rule is the same where the duty of the employer has been

10 *Lonrho Ltd v Shell Petroleum Co Ltd (No 2)* [1982] AC 173, [1981] 2 All ER 456 at 462, HL.
11 [1984] AC 130 [1983] 2 All ER 770, HL.
12 [1986] QB 716, [1985] 3 All ER 585, CA. See post on the tort of misuse of power at p 499.
13 *Kirklees Metropolitan Borough Council v Wickes Building Supplies Ltd* [1993] AC 227 at 280–282.
14 See above at pp 9–10.
15 [1951] AC 639, [1951] 1 All ER 1102, HL.
16 See p 523, post, for a discussion of whether the employer is vicariously liable for breach by the employee of a statutory duty imposed on the employee.
17 *Lochgelly Iron and Coal Co Ltd v M'Mullan* [1934] AC 1 at 13 HL (per Lord Warrington).

neglected by the independent contractor[18] of the employer.[19] Other problems, however (which will be discussed later),[20] are raised when the defendant has delegated the duty to the plaintiff himself, and the plaintiff is injured as a result of his own failure to perform the delegated duty.

(C)   THE STATUTE PROTECTS THE PLAINTIFF'S INTEREST BY WAY OF A CAUSE OF ACTION IN TORT

The fundamental issue, as the courts time and time again insist, is simply whether the Act intended to give a right of action in tort.[1] Everything else is subordinate to that. The following considerations are no more than guides, deducible from decided cases, to the principles which the courts utilise in seeking that (usually unexpressed) legislative intention: they must not be elevated to the status of inflexible rules of law overriding the paramount question of the purpose of the statute. As Lord Simonds has said:[2]

> The only rule which in all circumstances is valid is that the answer must depend on a consideration of the whole Act and the circumstances, including the pre-existing law, in which it was enacted.

(1)   THE STATE OF THE PRE-EXISTING COMMON LAW

Sometimes, the law of torts in force before the passing of the Act[3] is considered to afford adequate compensation to victims in circumstances also covered by the statute,[4] the object of the statute being to regulate certain activities in order to prevent the occurrence of that loss which the existing law of tort would redress:[5] then the statute will not usually confer an additional cause of action for damages. For instance, the ordinary law of negligence affords adequate protection for the victims of road accidents: yet the need to reduce these accidents is so urgent that there is much legislation regulating road traffic—the construction and use of vehicles and the carrying of lights during hours of darkness are random illustrations. But the courts do not generally allow persons injured by motorists in breach of such statutory duties to sue in reliance on the relevant statute: they leave them to pursue their remedy in negligence, and regard the sanctions of the statute as limited to the imposition of the penalty there prescribed.[6]

---

18 See p 509, post.
19 *Hosking v De Havilland Aircraft Co Ltd* [1949] 1 All ER 540; *Braham v J Lyons & Co Ltd* [1962] 3 All ER 281, CA; cf *Hole v Sittingbourne and Sheerness Rly Co* (1861) 6 H & N 488.
20 See p 432, post.
1   Eg *Hague v Deputy Governor of Parkhurst Prison* [1991] 3 All ER 733, (per Lord Jauncey at 705), HL. *Atkinson v Newcastle and Gateshead Waterworks Co* (1877) 2 Ex D 441 at 448 (per Lord Cairns LC), CA; *Pasmore v Oswaldtwistle UDC* [1898] AC 387 at 397 (per Lord Halsbury LC), HL.
2   *Cutler v Wandsworth Stadium Ltd* [1949] AC 398 at 407, [1949] 1 All ER 544, HL.
3   So in *Issa v Hackney London Borough Council* [1997] 1 WLR 956, no claim lay in respect of a statutory nuisance because *in 1936* when the relevant Act was passed virtually all victims of such a nuisance would have been able to recover compensation from their landlords.
4   See *Richardson v Pitt-Stanley* [1995] QB 123, CA. (If it is argued there should be a claim for breach of statutory duty additional to common law remedies, it must be shown that the private action for breach of the statute will actually be effective.)
5   Sometimes, as in *Square v Model Farm Dairies (Bournemouth) Ltd* [1939] 2 KB 365, [1939] 1 All ER 259, CA (sale of infected milk), the court might decide that no tort was intended to be created because existing contractual remedies were adequate.
6   *Phillips v Britannia Hygienic Laundry Co* [1923] 2 KB 832, CA (defective axle on lorry, in breach of Motor Cars (Use and Construction) Order 1904; no action available to owner of another vehicle damaged in consequence of breach); *Clarke v Brims* [1947] KB 497, [1947] 1

If, however, the statute merely affirms an interest of the plaintiff which the common law already recognises, and does not purport to be giving that interest statutory protection for some quite different purpose, then the plaintiff may be free to sue for breach of the statute.[7] Thus, in *Ashby v White,* where the right to vote, a common law right, had been confirmed by statute, Holt CJ said:[8]

> And this statute ... is only an enforcement of the common law; and if the parliament thought the freedom of elections to be a matter of that consequence, as to give their sanction to it, and to enact that they should be free; it is a violation of that statute, to disturb the plaintiff in this case in giving his vote at an election, and consequently actionable.

(2)   ALTERNATIVE REMEDIES PROVIDED BY STATUTE

It has been suggested that where a statute fails to provide any alternative means of enforcement in the event of breach of the relevant duty, the plaintiff's task to establish that an action in tort was intended by the statute may be eased.[9] But the absence of an alternative remedy is not by any means irrefutable evidence that Parliament intends to grant the plaintiff redress via an action for breach of statutory duty. Counsel for prisoners claiming damages for breaches of the Prison Rules sought to argue that the absence of any other remedy available to them necessarily meant that an action lay. The House of Lords forcefully rejected that contention.[10] Equally the availability of an alternative remedy is not fatal to the case: '...the mere existence of some other statutory remedy is not necessarily decisive'.[11] Administrative remedies and criminal penalties must be considered separately.

Provision is made in many cases where public authorities fail to carry out their duties for administrative machinery to secure compliance with those duties. Representations may be made to the secretary of state who can order a recalcitrant local authority to fulfil its responsibilities for public health or education. An aggrieved citizen may find that the provision of such an administrative remedy is found to prevent any action in tort arising.[12] This will not be so in all cases. Pupils injured as a result of dangerous school premises have been allowed to sue in tort for breach of statutory regulations[13]

All ER 242 (failure to carry a red rear light on a car gave no right of action under this head to plaintiff who collided with the car); *Balmer v Hayes* 1950 SC 477 (failure of driver to disclose in an application for a driving licence, that he was epileptic, gave no cause of action to a passenger injured when an attack of epilepsy caused the driver to collide with another vehicle); *Verney v Wilkins* (1962) 106 Sol Jo 879 (learner-driver not liable for passenger's injuries merely because in breach of Act he was unaccompanied by qualified driver); *Coote v Stone* [1971] 1 All ER 657, CA (parking on clearway not actionable in itself).

7   *Wolverhampton New Waterworks Co v Hawkesford* (1859) 6 CBNS 336 at 356 (per Willes J). He may then have the choice of the action for breach of statutory duty or the existing common-law remedy, eg *Simon v Islington Borough Council* [1943] 1 KB 188 at 193, [1943] 1 All ER 41, CA (neglect of abandoned tramway).

8   (1703) 2 Ld Raym 938 at 954.

9   *Thornton v Kirklees Metropolitan Borough Council* [1979] QB 626, CA; but overruled on its facts in *O'Rourke v Camden London Borough Council* [1998] AC 188, HL. And see *Booth & Co (International) Ltd v National Enterprise Board* [1978] 3 All ER 624.

10 *Hague v Deputy Governor of Parkhurst Prison* [1991] 3 All ER 733.

11 *X v Bedfordshire County Council* [1995] 2 AC 633 at 731.

12 *Wyatt v Hillingdon London Borough Council* (1978) 76 LGR 727 (no action lay by disabled person alleging breach of the duty under s 2 of the Chronically Sick and Disabled Persons Act 1970 in failing to meet her need for home help; she had a statutory remedy of making representations to the Secretary of State).

13 *Reffell v Surrey County Council* [1964] 1 All ER 743, [1964] 1 WLR 358 (was this because representations after the event would be futile?).

despite the provision in the Education Act empowering the secretary of state to compel local authorities to carry out their statutory duties, including their safety obligations.

Where the 'alternative remedy' is the imposition of a criminal penalty, the onus will be on the plaintiff to establish that his claim falls within one of the two exceptions to the general rule of non-actionability in such a case reasserted by Lord Diplock in *Lonrho*.[14] He must show that the interest of the statute was not just to regulate a particular activity in the general public interest but to benefit a class of persons to which he belongs.[15] The existence of criminal penalties in the Factories Acts did not bar concurrent remedies in tort. The duties imposed by those Acts were specifically designed to protect workmen.[16] But breach of statutory rules regulating the operation of greyhound tracks and betting thereon did not enable an aggrieved bookmaker to sue.[17] The statute was not passed to safeguard or enhance the business of bookmakers.

(3)   PUBLIC AND PRIVATE RIGHTS

The plaintiff seeking to sue in this tort must establish that a right or interest of his has been violated by the breach of duty. It will be easier for him to do this where the duty is imposed for the benefit of a defined and ascertainable group of persons to whom he belongs. It is submitted that he is not precluded merely because the statute is shown by the defence to be designed for the protection of the public. In a dictum followed since,[18] Atkin LJ stated the law as follows:[19]

> ... the question is not to be solved by considering whether or not the person aggrieved can bring himself within some special class of the community or whether he is some designated individual. The duty may be of such paramount importance that it is owed to all the public. It would be strange if a less important duty, which is owed to a section of the public, may be enforced by an action, while a more important duty owed to the public at large cannot. The right of action does not depend on whether a statutory commandment or prohibition is pronounced for the benefit of the public, or for the benefit of a class. It may be conferred on anyone who can bring himself within the benefit of the Act, including one who cannot be otherwise specified than as a person using the highway.

Lord Browne-Wilkinson in *X v Bedfordshire County Council*[20] appears in his overview of breach of statutory duty simpliciter to endorse a view that only where a duty was imposed to protect '...a limited class of the public' will an action for breach of statutory duty arise. He does not, however, address the issues outlined by Atkin LJ above nor cast doubt on the authority of *Monk v Warbey* in which the only class designed to benefit was indeed the public at large.

Note too Lord Diplock's second exception[1] to the general rule of non-actionability where alternative criminal remedies were provided by the statute related to special damage resulting to the plaintiff in his enjoyment of a public right (a right available to

---

14 See ante at p 418.
15 See *Atkinson v Newcastle and Gatehead Waterworks Co* (1877) 2 Ex D 441, CA.
16 *Groves v Lord Wimbourne* [1898] 2 QB 402; breach of the duty to stop at a pedestrian crossing is a rare example of road safety regulations being interpreted so as to create a right of action in tort; *London Passenger Transport Board v Upson* [1949] AC 155, [1949] 1 All ER 60, HL; is this perhaps because pedestrians at (zebra) crossings constitute a defined class of person intended to be protected by the statutory rules?
17 *Cutler v Wandsworth Stadium Ltd* [1949] AC 398, [1949] 1 All ER 544, CA.
18 See *Monk v Warbey* [1935] 1 KB 75, CA; *cf Richardson v Pitt-Stanley* [1995] QB 123, CA.
19 *Phillips v Britannia Hygenic Laundry Co* [1923] 2 KB 832 at 841, CA.
20 [1995] 2 AC 633 at 731.
1   *Lonrho Ltd v Shell Petroleum Co Ltd (No 2)* [1982] AC 173, [1981] 2 All ER 456, HL; see ante at p 418.

all Her Majesty's subjects). It is somewhat difficult to discern whether Lord Diplock was simply endorsing the approach of Atkin LJ (quoted earlier) that certain duties might be designed to benefit each and every member of the public individually, or initiating a new category of breach of statutory duty. Such a new category might on its face enable a person suffering special damage to sue without establishing a specific intention to protect his individual interest. The wording used by his lordship is obscure and one of the authorities relied on is a leading judgment on public nuisance.[2] Thus any extension of the tort seems unlikely.[3]

(D)   THE HARM SUFFERED BY HIM IS WITHIN THE SCOPE OF THE GENERAL CLASS OF RISKS AT WHICH THE STATUTE IS DIRECTED

The leading case is *Gorris v Scott*:[4]

> A statutory order required that those parts of a ship which were occupied by animals were to be divided into pens of a specified size by substantial divisions. The defendant violated this order in respect of a ship on which he was transporting sheep belonging to the plaintiff. This violation caused the plaintiff's sheep to be washed overboard. The statute was designed to prevent the spread of disease, not to prevent animals from being drowned: an action for breach of statutory duty therefore failed.

In similar vein the duty imposed on highway authorities to repair the roads in order to protect users from injury was held not to embrace loss of profit to a local trader.[5]

The House of Lords has held that the statutory duty on an employer to fence every dangerous part of a machine was confined to the prevention of a workman coming into contact with moving parts of the machine and did not envisage protecting him from injury caused by ejected or flying pieces of the machine itself, or of the material on which the machine was working.[6] On the other hand, when a bogie was derailed by a stone that had been allowed to fall from the roof of a mine in breach of the defendants' statutory duty, and the plaintiff was injured thereby, the House of Lords held that 'where the object of the enactment is to promote safety there can be no implication that liability for a breach is limited to one which causes injury in a particular way'.[7] And in *Gerrard v Staffordshire Potteries*[8] the defendant was found in breach of regulations requiring eye protection against any 'reasonably foreseeable risk engaged in the work from particles of fragments thrown off' where a foreign body flew out of a jar the plaintiff was glazing. The statute was designed to safeguard the worker from any object dangerous to the eye dislodged in the course of her work.

2   *Benjamin v Storr* (1874) LR 9 CP 400.
3   See *Stanton* at pp 49–51.
4   (1874) LR 9 Exch 125.
5   *Wentworth v Wiltshire County Council* [1993] 2 All ER 256, CA; and see *Merlin v British Nuclear Fuels plc* [1990] 2 QB 557, [1990] 3 All ER 711 (damage to property means actual damage not diminished value through risk of contamination). Contrast the finding in *Merlin* with *Blue Circle Industries plc v Ministry of Defence* [1996] EGCS 190 (contamination requiring an intensive cleansing operation does constitute damage to land).
6   *Close v Steel Co of Wales* [1962] AC 367, [1961] 2 All ER 953; cf *Wearing v Pirelli Ltd* [1977] 1 All ER 339, HL (the defendant employer was liable when the unfenced dangerous part of the machine jerked his employee's hand against the materials being worked upon).
7   *Grant v National Coal Board* [1956] AC 649 at 664, [1956] 1 All ER 682, HL (per Lord Tucker); *Donaghey v Boulton and Paul Ltd* [1968] AC 1, [1967] 2 All ER 1014, HL; *Millard v Serck Tubes Ltd* [1969] 1 All ER 598, [1969] 1 WLR 211, CA.
8   [1995] ICR 502.

(E)   THE PLAINTIFF WAS ONE OF THE PERSONS PROTECTED BY THE STATUTE

Breach of a statute may give rise to an action in tort, but not necessarily at the instance of the particular plaintiff, as *Knapp v Railway Executive* shows:[9]

> The Brighton & Chichester Railway Act 1844 provided for the erection of gates at level crossings, and the general supervision and maintenance thereof. K had stopped his car slightly short of a level crossing governed by this Act because it was closed against road traffic. Somehow, the brake of the car was released; the car moved forward and struck the gate. The gate had not been maintained in accordance with the Act, so that it swung back and injured the driver of an oncoming train. It was held that the purpose of these provisions was to protect road users against danger from the railway only, and that an engine driver on the railway was thus not within the scope of the Act.

(F)   WHEN DAMAGE MUST BE PROVED

In general the plaintiff must prove the relevant damage ensuing from the alleged breach of duty. The question is: what is the nature of the right or interest protected by the statute? If, for example, it is an interest in personal safety, then the courts will grant a remedy in tort only if the plaintiff shows that he has sustained personal injury in consequence of a breach of the statutory duty.[10]

There are judgments in which it has been held that where, from its context, it is clear that the statute created a right in the plaintiff so absolute in its content that the plaintiff was to be protected against a violation, even though it caused no damage, then the tort is actionable per se. Thus, in *Ashby v White*,[11] interference with the statutory right to vote was held actionable per se, and in *Ferguson v Earl Kinnoull*[12] the refusal on the part of the defendant, in the face of a statute, to determine the suitability of the plaintiff, a minister of religion, for a living to which he had been presented, was held actionable per se. Yet in *Pickering v Liverpool Daily Post and Echo Newspapers plc*[13] Lord Bridge declared that an action could lie only on proof of '... loss or injury of a kind for which the law awards damages'. Neither *Ashby* nor *Ferguson* were cited in that judgment.

(G)   THE CONDUCT OF THE DEFENDANT WAS OF SUCH A CHARACTER AS TO VIOLATE THE STATUTE

Whether a defendant is liable for a breach, even though his act is neither intentional nor negligent, depends on the statute. Liability is strict in many cases. For instance, non-negligent failure properly to maintain a lift in efficient working order has been held by the House of Lords to be an actionable breach of the Factories Act 1937.[14] On the other hand, other statutes require the defendant only to do what is 'reasonably practicable'. So, regulation 11 of the provision and use of Work Equipment Regulations

9   [1949] 2 All ER 508, CA; cf *Lavender v Diamints Ltd* [1949] 1 KB 585, [1949] 1 All ER 532, CA.
10 Eg *Watts v Enfield Rolling Mills (Aluminium) Ltd* [1952] 1 All ER 1013, CA.
11 (1703) 2 Ld Raym 938; cf *Simmonds v Newport Abercarn Black Vein Steam Coal Co* [1921] 1 KB 616, CA.
12 (1842) 9 Cl & Fin 251, HL.
13 [1991] 1 All ER 622 at 632.
14 *Galashiels Gas Co Ltd v Millar* [1949] AC 275, [1949] 1 All ER 319, HL.

1992[15] requires the use of fixed guards for dangerous machinery *if practicable* and, if not, sets in place a graded hierarchy of safety measures employers must take. There is a mass of case law on the interpretation of statutory provisions laying down standards of conduct: the point to note here is that one must always turn to the statute imposing the duty to discover against what types of conduct on the part of the defendant the plaintiff will be protected by an action in tort.

(H)   A BREACH OF THE DUTY

This presents no further problem: the burden of proof is on the plaintiff.

(I)   CAUSATION

As with other torts, heads of damage are recoverable only when the breach of the defendant 'caused' them: moreover, as we have seen in many actions, especially those by workers for breach of safety requirements, success depends on proof that injury to the plaintiff has been so 'caused'. In this tort 'the employee must in all cases prove his case by the ordinary standard of proof in civil actions: he must make it appear at least that on a balance of probabilities the breach of duty caused or materially contributed to his injury'.[16] Where the plaintiff steel erector would not have worn a safety belt had it been provided, the House of Lords held that his employers were not liable to him for breach of their statutory duty to provide one.[17]

SECTION 5.   DEFENCES

(A)   THE RELATION BETWEEN CRIMINAL AND TORTIOUS LIABILITY

Breaches of particular statutory duties may give rise both to criminal and tortious proceedings. It must not, however, be assumed that the defences in each case are identical. For example, the defences open to mine owners under the Coal Mines Act 1911 were held to be wider in criminal proceedings than in actions for breach of statutory duty.[18]

(B)   ASSUMPTION OF RISK

Wheeler v New Merton Board Mills Ltd[19] decided that volenti non fit injuria is not a defence to an action brought by a workman for breach by an employer of his statutory duty—at least where the statute makes the employer liable whether or not his conduct

---

15 SI 1992 No 2392.
16 *Bonnington Castings Ltd v Wardlaw* [1956] AC 613 at 620, [1956] 1 All ER 615 at 618, HL (per Lord Reid); cf *McGhee v National Coal Board* [1972] 3 All ER 1008, HL (an action in common-law negligence). Even though the plaintiff has proved the employer's breach of statutory duty with regard to a machine and that he has sustained injury from the machine, the onus of proving causation remains with the plaintiff; *Lineker v Raleigh Industries Ltd* [1980] ICR 83, CA.
17 *Cummings (or McWilliams) v Sir William Arrol & Co Ltd* [1962] 1 All ER 623, HL.
18 [1933] 2 KB 669, CA.
19 [1965] AC 656, [1964] 2 All ER 999, HL.

was intentional or negligent. In *ICI Ltd v Shatwell*,[20] the House of Lords approved the *Wheeler* case so far as employers' statutory duties are concerned, but it added that the defence of volenti 'should be available where the employer was not himself in breach of statutory duty and was not vicariously in breach of any statutory duty through the neglect of some person who was of superior rank to the plaintiff and whose commands the plaintiff was bound to obey'.[1] The grounds for the *Wheeler* decision are not discoverable: this makes it all the harder, in the absence of any decision outside the sphere of such duties of employers to workers, to know whether the defence is generally inapplicable to actions for breach of statutory duty.[2] It may well be contrary to public policy for anybody, and not merely employers, to contract out of a duty imposed by Act of Parliament: if this is so, assumption of risk may never be a defence to this action.

(C) CONTRIBUTORY NEGLIGENCE

At common law, contributory negligence on the part of the plaintiff was a defence.[3] Apportionment of damages is now possible under the Law Reform (Contributory Negligence) Act 1945.[4] The principles of the defence are the same as those already discussed, subject to this exception.[5] Legislation and regulations designed to protect health and safety are often expressly designed to protect workers against acts of inattention; accordingly, a 'risky act due to familiarity with the work or some inattention resulting from noise or strain' will not be contributory negligence, although it might be sufficient negligence to make the employer vicariously liable to a third party negligently injured thereby.[6] Frequently the employer has delegated to his employee responsibility for the performance of the statutory duty and that employee is negligent. The House of Lords held in *Boyle v Kodak Ltd*[7] that 'once the plaintiff has established that there was a breach of enactment which made the employer absolutely liable, and that that breach caused the accident, he need do no more.'[8] 'But if the employer can prove that

20 [1965] AC 656, [1964] 2 All ER 999, HL.
1 [1965] AC 656 at 687.
2 See an obiter dictum of Lord Normand in *Alford v National Coal Board* [1952] 1 All ER 754 at 757, HL.
3 *Casewell v Powell Duffryn Associated Collieries Ltd* [1940] AC 152, [1939] 3 All ER 722, HL (unanimous but obiter).
4 *Cakebread v Hopping Bros (Whetstone) Ltd* [1947] KB 641, [1947] 1 All ER 389, CA.
5 It is difficult to accept the view of Denning J, in *Lavender v Diamints Ltd* [1948] 2 All ER 249 (not considered on appeal, [1949] 1 KB 585, [1949] 1 All ER 532, CA) that a contributorily negligent plaintiff in an action for non-negligent violation of statutory duty must be awarded no damages.
6 *Staveley Iron and Chemical Co Ltd v Jones* [1956] AC 627 at 648, [1956] 1 All ER 403 at 410, HL (per Lord Tucker), explaining the similar decision of the House of Lords in *Caswell v Powell Duffryn Associated Collieries Ltd* [1940] AC 152, [1939] 3 All ER 403 at 410, HL (per Lord Tucker). In *Mullard v Ben Line Steamers Ltd* [1971] 2 All ER 424, CA, the deduction for contributory negligence was reduced because the plaintiff's conduct 'was a monetary error, not to be judged too harshly when balanced against the defendants' flagrant and continuous breach of statutory duty' (per Sachs LJ at 428). On the difficulty of proving contributory negligence in this tort as distinct from that of negligence, see *Westwood v Post Office* [1974] AC 1, [1973] 3 All ER 184, HL, and especially the statements by Lord Kilbrandon at 17, that a workman's disobedience is not the same as contributory negligence.
7 [1969] 2 All ER 439. This decision applied *Ross v Associated Portland Cement Manufacturers Ltd* [1964] 2 All ER 452, HL, and *Ginty v Belmont Building Supplies Ltd* [1959] 1 All ER 414.
8 [1969] 2 All ER 439 at 441 (per Lord Reid).

the only act or default of anyone which caused or contributed to the non-compliance was the act or default of the plaintiff himself, he establishes a good defence.'[9]

In *Boyle v Kodak Ltd* the statutory duty to fix a ladder securely while a storage tank was painted was imposed on both the employers and the employee who was injured through its breach. The Court of Appeal dismissed the action on the ground that the plaintiff was the sole cause of the accident, but the House of Lords allowed his appeal. The employers had not proved that they had instructed the plaintiff on how to comply with the regulations; therefore their breach of statutory duty was a cause of the damage. The significance of the plaintiff's also being in breach of his statutory duty was that it constituted a ground for apportionment of the damages: he was awarded one half. Had the statute imposed the duty on the employers alone, the plaintiff's damages would not have been reduced (although performance of the duty was delegated to him by his employers) unless the employers proved that the plaintiff failed to take care for his own safety and so was contributorily negligent.

(D)   ACT OF THIRD PARTY

This is not a defence where the statute is deemed to impose a liability so strict that the defendant is responsible for such acts: as usual, all depends on the interpretation of the Act.[10]

SECTION 6.   PROPOSALS FOR REFORM

The case law determining when an action in tort will lie for violations of a statute cannot be represented as consistent or in the main well-reasoned; hence the difficulty in ascertaining a body of principles governing the tort. In 1969 the Law Commission recommended a single reform.[11] The following provision should be enacted.

> Where any Act passed after this Act imposes or authorises the imposition of a duty, whether positive or negative and whether with or without a special remedy for its enforcement, it shall be presumed, unless express provision to the contrary is made, that a breach of the duty is intended to be actionable (subject to the defences and other incidents applying to actions for breach of statutory duty) at the suit of any person who sustains damage in consequence of the breach.

---

9   [1969] 2 All ER 439 at 446 (per Lord Diplock).
10   *Cooper v Railway Executive (Southern Region)* [1953] 1 All ER 477 at 478.
11   Law Com Report No 21 'The Interpretation of Statutes' para 38, App A(4)1.

Part VI

Interests in reputation – defamation

CONTENTS

CHAPTER		PAGE
22	Defamation	435
23	Defences and Remedies	457

Chapter 22

Defamation

SECTION I. INTRODUCTION

(A) BACKGROUND ISSUES

There are two types of defamation: libel which, in general, is written, and slander which, in general, is oral.[1] In some respects, different rules are applicable to each.[2] Both, however, protect the interest in the reputation of the plaintiff. There is, therefore, no tort unless there has been a communication of the defamatory matter to a third party, for it is the opinion held of the person defamed by others that matters.[3] Insults directed to the plaintiff himself do not in themselves constitute defamation; the tort is not primarily concerned with the plaintiff's wounded feelings. Instead, the gist of the action is that the defendant either lowers the plaintiff in the estimation of reasonable, right-thinking members of society, or causes such citizens to shun or avoid him.

In many ways defamation is unique among torts, and it is best understood in the context of its historical development.[4] Until the sixteenth century, general jurisdiction over defamation was exercised by ecclesiastical courts. Thereafter, the common law courts developed an action on the case for slander where 'temporal', as distinct from 'spiritual', damage could be established. This progress became too rapid for the judges, who proceeded to hedge the action around with tight restrictions. In the Stuart period, the Court of Star Chamber assumed criminal jurisdiction over all types of libels. The common law courts succeeded to this jurisdiction on the abolition of that court in 1641. The upshot of this was that the common law courts then established a distinction between libel and slander on the basis that damage would be presumed in libel, but

---

1   It is inaccurate, however, to say that slander is always oral and that libel is always visual. The use of sign language as between two deaf persons, for example, is probably capable of constituting slander. Equally, television broadcasts and public theatre performances of a defamatory nature are, by statute, libelous rather than slanderous: see post p 452.
2   For a full account, see Section 5, post.
3   For a powerful argument that it is not reputation, per se, that matters, but rather the concern that persons ought not wrongly to be judged by false information see Gibbons 'Defamation Reconsidered' (1996) 16 OJLS 587.
4   See Veeder *Select Essays in Anglo-American History* (1909) vol 446-73; *HEL* vol v 205-12, vol vii 333-78.

that the plaintiff would have to prove 'special damage'[5] before an action for slander would lie.

In the late nineteenth and early twentieth centuries, liability in defamation was extended because of the menace to reputations occasioned by the new, popular press with its mass circulation. The recent history of defamation is marked by continuing conflict between the need to protect individuals from unjustifiable character assassination and the right to freedom of speech:[6] the press maintains that the latter is often disregarded at the expense of open and honest criticism of those in authority. But in *Derbyshire County Council v Times Newspapers Ltd*[7] the press scored a notable victory. The House of Lords ruled that public authorities and governmental bodies were not entitled to sue in defamation. As Lord Keith put it:

> It is of the highest public importance that a democratically elected governmental body, or indeed any governmental body, should be open to uninhibited public criticism. The threat of a civil action for defamation must inevitably have an inhibiting effect on freedom of speech.[8]

Since that case was decided, two further cases have confirmed the fundamentality of the right to freedom of speech conferred by Article 10 of the European Rights Convention. In the first, *Tolstoy Miloslavsky v United Kingdom*,[9] the European Court of Human Rights issued a declaration that a libel damages award of £1.5m granted by an English jury had been a violation of the defendant's freedom of speech in that case (but it also recognised that practice had changed since *Rantzen v Mirror Group Newspapers (1986) Ltd*[10]). In the second, *Reynolds v Times Newspapers Ltd*,[11] the Court of Appeal was mindful of the fact that the Convention was destined to become part of English law and suggested that, in the spirit of that provision English common law ought to allow the defence of qualified privilege to be raised by the press when commenting on public figures.

The political import of the tort of defamation means that many changes in the law have been effected by legislation, some of it ill-considered and badly drafted. The tort is also notable for many detailed and complex rules – some substantive, others procedural – which have been developed by the courts over the years. Despite these statutory and common law complexities, defamation actions have proved to be a popular recourse for wealthy public figures seeking, with the aid of expensive lawyers, to vindicate their reputations publicly in the law courts.[12] Indeed, the tort is to some extent a wealthy person's tort, for legal aid is available neither to pursue, nor to defend, a

---

5   The phrase 'special damage' is to some extent misleading; 'actual damage' is a more accurate term to capture the sense of that which must be proved: see Jolowicz 'The Changing use of "Special Damage" and its Effects on the Law' [1960] CLJ 214.
6   See, eg, Barendt 'Libel and Freedom of Speech in English Law' [1993] PL 449. See also, *Rantzen v Mirror Group Newspapers (1986) Ltd* [1994] QB 670, [1993] 4 All ER 975, CA.
7   [1993] AC 534, [1993] 1 All ER 1011, HL. Note, too, their Lordship's references to (but not reliance on) Art 10 of the European Convention on Human Rights.
8   Ibid at 547. The principle was extended to political parties in the course of an election campaign in *Goldsmith v Bhoyrul* [1997] 4 All ER 268. But what if an individual party member sues qua individual?
9   (1995) 20 EHRR 442.
10 [1994] QB 670, [1993] 4 All ER 975, CA.
11 [1998] 3 All ER 961, CA.
12 Note that some of the scope for litigation has been removed by the Defamation Act 1996 which, inter alia, reduces the limitation period from three years to one: Defamation Act 1996, s 5. Also, the new summary procedure, which confers considerable powers of disposal upon the courts (under ss 8-10), helps to streamline procedure and avert the possibility of protracted litigation, so long as adequate compensation can be achieved by an award not exceeding £10,000.

defamation action.[13] On the other hand, in the past, a number of libel actions have, on occasion, been supported by private funds set up by wealthy individuals with an axe to grind who have themselves suffered at the hands of the popular press.

Another notable facet of defamation actions in recent years is the very high level of damages that have been awarded. These damages have not simply compensated the plaintiffs for their loss of reputation, they have also included very sizeable amounts of exemplary (or punitive) damages. The amount of damages is normally set by a jury,[14] and until recently the Court of Appeal had no power to reduce any award made by the jury. It could only order a new trial if it found the damages to be excessive. Rules of the Court, made under section 8 of the Courts and Legal Services Act 1990, now empower the appeal court to substitute for an excessive award 'such sum as appears to the court to be proper'. Such a substitution occurred in *John v MGN Ltd*[15] where a famous pop singer's libel action initially won him £350,000. The damages were subsequently reduced by the Court of Appeal to £50,000. In addition, Sir Thomas Bingham MR suggested that, in future, the courts could provide guidance to juries on the level of awards either substituted or approved by the Court of Appeal in previous cases; that awards in personal injury cases might be looked at by jurors by way of comparison, and that the judge and the parties' respective counsel could indicate to the jury the award they consider to be appropriate.[16]

Defamation has become a lucrative specialism for lawyers, too. Even a brief trawl of the decided cases reveals that a good many cases reach the appeal courts, most of which concern not the essence of the claim itself, but rather, complex arguments on pleading and particulars. In consequence, legal costs consume large proportions of many claims. For instance, the headline-grabbing *McLibel* case[17] saw an award of £60,000 made to McDonald's (which they stated they would pursue from the joint defendants whose joint annual income was less than £7,500) while the costs had soared to £10m. Against this background, the Defamation Act 1996 which, inter alia, simplified some aspects of defamation procedure,[18] diverted a number of cases away from the courts[19] and provided for a summary procedure to dispose of claims under £10,000,[20] was very much to be welcomed.

13   Legal Aid Act 1974, s 7; Sch I, Pt II, para 1. The Faulks Report recommended that legal aid be made available with safeguards. On this and other considerations see *Gatley* ch 20. But note the judgment in *Joyce v Sengupta* [1993] 1 All ER 897 allowing the plaintiff to sue in malicious falsehood (for which legal aid is available) in respect of newspaper stories claiming that she had stolen personal letters from her employer.
14   Exceptionally, under the summary procedure introduced by s 8 of the Defamation Act 1996, a judge may determine the level of damages that the plaintiff is to receive.
15   [1996] 2 All ER 35. See also *Rantzen v Mirror Group Newspapers (1986) Ltd* [1994] QB 670, CA and *Jones v Pollard* [1997] EMLR 233, CA (award of £100,000 reduced to one of £40,000).
16   Ibid, at 51-2. As a limit to such guidance, on the other hand, the defendant is not permitted to mention to the jury any of the amounts he may have offered to the plaintiff in their pre-trial correspondence: *Kiam v Neil* [1995] EMLR 1, CA.
17   *McDonald's Corpn v Steel* (1997) Times, 20 June.
18   Sections 8-10. In addition RSC Ord 82, r 3A introduced a new procedure allowing either party to apply to a judge in chambers for a 'ruling on meaning' to identify whether a word or phrase is capable of (as opposed to, formerly, 'arguably capable of') bearing a defamatory connotation. This rule is confirmed by s 7 of the 1996 Act.
19   Section 5, for example, reduces the limitation period in defamation actions from three years to one.
20   Sections 8(3), 9(1)(c). To use this summary procedure the court must primarily be satisfied that 'there is no defence to the claim which has a reliable prospect of success' there being no other reason why the case should be tried: s 8(3). If there is no such prospect of success, and no other reason why the case should be tried, the court may dismiss the case: s 8(2).

Since no cause of action survives the defamed person's death,[1] it is clear that reputation is merely a transitory interest. It is an interest which, by way of the defences available, has to be balanced against the public interest. So, should we inform the police of our suspicion that a neighbour is abusing his child, so long as our suspicion is honestly held, we have a defence of qualified privilege (even if our allegations prove to be unfounded). Similarly, fair comment protects the press when expressing their views on the actions of politicians, public servants and others in the public eye. But there is no general public interest in information such as to protect the press if their basic facts are untrue. An article correctly reporting the conduct of a minister may criticise that conduct with vigour. But no defence will avail the newspaper if it gets its basic facts wrong. In the US, by contrast, criticism of a public figure will normally only constitute an actionable defamation if it was activated by malice, even if parts of the allegations are untrue.[2]

The debate on how to achieve the correct balance between the individual's interest in his good name and freedom of speech is a vital attribute of a democratic society.[3] In attempting to resolve that debate via the development of the tort of defamation, however, the courts are hindered by the elaborate procedural 'game' which characterises many libel actions, the unpredictability of the jury, and the absence of developed torts of invasion of privacy and breach of confidence.[4] All too often, the latter lie at the heart of libel actions. If you were on a jury hearing evidence that a newspaper tapped a person's telephone, 'set him up' with a meeting with a prostitute, and hounded his young family, could you discount that behaviour when assessing the truth or falsity of the allegations made?

Defamation certainly has constitutional significance, but its role as a protection against the abuse of freedom of speech is apt to be overestimated. To begin with, there is an ancient rule that protects would-be defamers from court actions in respect of their criticism of the Parliamentary conduct of MPs.[5] This rule served to deny Neil Hamilton (a then MP) the right to sue *The Guardian* newspaper in respect of allegations it had made about Mr Hamilton being corrupt in receiving cash in return for asking Parliamentary questions.[6] Additionally, there is nowadays almost a sense in which defamation itself has become a side issue. Arguably, protection of privacy and prevention of press harassment have a higher profile.[7] Both questions came under intensive review by a committee established under the chairmanship of Sir David Calcutt QC which, in 1990, made initial representations to improve and strengthen press self-regulation and to criminalise certain sorts of intrusive behaviour.[8] The committee

---

1   See Law Reform (Miscellaneous Provisions) Act 1934, s 1(1). However, defaming a dead person may still constitute a criminal libel.

2   *New York Times v Sullivan* 376 US 254 (1964). Proposals for a '*Sullivan*' defence were expressly rejected by the Neill Committee which reported in 1991 and whose recommendations, in part, formed the basis for the Defamation Act 1996. See *Report on Practice and Procedure in Defamation* (1991).

3   See Gibbons 'Defamation Reconsidered' (1996) 16 OJLS 587.

4   See Cane *Anatomy of Tort Law* (1997) pp 72ff.

5   Bill of Rights 1689, Art 9.

6   (1995) The Guardian, 22 July (per May J: following *Prebble v Television New Zealand* [1995] 1 AC 321). Since that case, s 13 of the Defamation Act 1996 has enabled MPs to waive the Art 9 privilege pertaining to parliamentary debates. But this waiver operates only at the behest of an individual MP (not automatically) and it does not apply to Parliament as whole: s 13(1), (2). See further Sharland and Loveland 'The Defamation Act 1996 and Political Libels' [1997] PL 113.

7   For instance, under the Protection from Harassment Act 1997, s 3, a course of conduct that amounts to, and ought reasonably to be apprehended as amounting to, harassment is made tortious and permits actions both for injunctive relief as well as for damages.

8   *Report of the Committee on Privacy and Related Matters* Cm 1102 (1990).

reconvened in 1993 and recommended both a statutory press tribunal and the introduction of a new tort of infringement of privacy.[9] The calls for a Protection of Privacy Bill were echoed by the National Heritage Committee of the House of Commons[10] and those calls have to some extent been answered in the form of the Protection from Harassment Act 1997. Leaving these developments aside, however, it should be noted that the tort of defamation has an ancient history and a capacity for survival which may outlive more topical concerns.

SECTION 2. ELEMENTS OF DEFAMATION

Regardless of whether a defamation action is framed in libel or slander, the plaintiff must always prove that the words, pictures, gestures etc are defamatory. Equally, the plaintiff must show that they refer to him. Finally, he must also prove that they were maliciously published. These are the three essential elements in a defamation action.

(A) THE MEANING OF DEFAMATORY

(1) INJURY TO REPUTATION

The classic definition of a defamatory statement is one 'which is calculated to injure the reputation of another, by exposing him to hatred, contempt or ridicule'.[11] It is clear that being made a laughing stock is not sufficient. In *Blennerhassett v Novelty Sales Services Ltd*[12] a newspaper advertisement was headed 'Beware of Yo Yo' and went on to imply that Mr Blennerhassett, a worthy man, had now been placed under supervision in a quiet place in the country by reason of his fascination at the defendant's toy, the Yo Yo. Although the plaintiff, a stockbroker, showed that his arrival at the Stock Exchange on the day after the publication was greeted with 'jeers, ribaldry and laughter', the statement was held not to be capable of a defamatory meaning.[13] The inadequacy of this definition is now generally recognised, especially in that it does not embrace injury to trading reputation.[14]

Lord Atkin proposed the alternative test: '[do] the words tend to lower the plaintiff in the estimation of right-thinking members of society generally?'[15] This test cures some of the defects of the earlier one, yet the expression 'right-thinking members of society' is intrinsically ambiguous. For while it is established that it is defamatory to

9   *Second Report of the Committee on Privacy and Related Matters* Cm 2135 (1993).
10 Fourth Report of the National Heritage Committee, *Privacy and Media Intrusion* 1992-3 HC 294-1.
11 *Parmiter v Coupland* (1840) 6 M & W 105 at 108 (per Parke B); *Emerson v Grimsby Times and Telegraph Co Ltd* (1926) 42 TLR 238, CA.
12 (1933) 175 LT Jo 393.
13 On the other hand, so long as it inspires contempt or ridicule, even a caricature has been held to constitute defamation: *Dunlop Rubber Co Ltd v Dunlop* [1921] 1 AC 367, HL; cf *Dolby v Newnes* (1887) 3 TLR 393.
14 Eg, *Capital and Counties Bank v George Henty & Sons* (1882) 7 App Cas 741 at 771, HL (per Lord Blackburn); *Tournier v National Provincial and Union Bank of England* [1924] 1 KB 461 at 477 and 486-7 (per Scrutton and Atkin LJJ), CA.
15 *Sim v Stretch* [1936] 2 All ER 1237 at 1240, HL. In *Rubber Improvement Ltd v Daily Telegraph Ltd* [1964] AC 234 at 285, [1963] 2 All ER 151 at 174, HL, Lord Devlin said that the test was the effect on the 'ordinary' man, not the 'logical' man. See also *Skuse v Granada Television* [1996] EMLR 278 and *Berkoff v Burchill* [1996] 4 All ER 1008, CA (to describe someone as 'hideously ugly' held by a majority of their Lordships to be capable of lowering the plaintiff's public standing).

say that a person is insane,[16] or that she has been raped,[17] do right-thinking persons think less well of those unfortunates? On the other hand, that one's associates (being themselves an ordinary cross-section of a respectable part of the community) think less well of one in consequence of a statement does not necessarily make that statement defamatory. Thus, in *Byrne v Deane* it was held that to impute that a member of a golf club had informed the police about an illegal fruit-machine kept in the club, was not defamatory, even though it lowered him in the esteem of his fellow members.[18] A certain class of society may think badly of police informers, but to impute this practice to anyone is nonetheless not defamatory.[19]

Certain sections of society would be scandalised by an imputation that a person is a member of the National Front Party, but can right-thinking citizens be so affected when that individual belongs to a political party which the law in no way prohibits? Would it be defamatory to say that someone is impotent, poverty-stricken, the daughter of a murderer or pictured in an advertisement for whisky? Is it defamatory to say of a worker who stayed at work during a strike that he was a 'scab' or a 'blackleg'?[20] No confident answers to these questions can be given because English law has not defined 'defamatory' precisely.[1] With diffidence it is suggested that the 'right-thinking' person test (which has yet to be subject to an appellate court's close scrutiny) must be understood in one of two ways. First, if most citizens would shun or avoid a person in consequence of the statement, then it will be classed as defamatory. Secondly, and alternatively, if a substantial and respectable proportion of society would think less well of a person then, again, the statement will be construed as defamatory provided that their reaction is not plainly anti-social or irrational.[2]

These interpretations accord with *Byrne v Deane* and they also support the view that to say that someone is a 'scab' or that a bank manager is in the National Front are defamatory remarks, even though such persons do not go down in the esteem of 'right-thinking' people.

(a) Words of abuse

To say that abuse is not defamatory is misleading. The cases relied on for this erroneous statement are cases of slander deciding that special damage must ordinarily be proved.[3] The test to be applied to words of abuse is exactly the same as for other allegedly defamatory statements. Thus, it has been held that it may be defamatory to call a man

16 *Morgan v Lingen* (1863) 8 LT 800.
17 *Youssoupoff v Metro-Goldwyn-Mayer Pictures Ltd* (1934) 50 TLR 581, CA.
18 [1937] 1 KB 818, [1937] 2 All ER 204, CA.
19 *Sim v Stretch* [1936] 2 All ER 1237, HL. On the other hand, not merely the golfing fraternity, but right-thinking persons will (it has been held) think worse of an amateur golfer who allows his name to be used in the advertising of chocolates: *Tolley v JS Fry & Sons* [1931] AC 333, HL. Yet, in *Gibbings v O'Dea & Co Ltd* (1948-9) Macgillivray & Le Quesne Copyright Cases 31 it was held not to be libel for the defendants to use the name of the plaintiff, who was an author, on an advertisement for mattresses in the *Irish Times*.
20 McCardie J thought not in *Myroft v Sleight* (1921) 90 LJKB 883.
1 Gibbons' answer would be to change the basis of the action from damage to reputation to awarding a remedy for unsubstantiated allegations: 'Defamation Reconsidered' (1996) 16 OJLS 587.
2 If the words would not in themselves convey to the ordinary person the meaning which a special group of experts would give to them, then this interpretation would not apply (unless an innuendo were pleaded: see post) because the basic rule that words must be defamatory in their ordinary meaning would not be satisfied: *Mollo v BBC* (1963) Times, 2 February. Nor is it defamatory, without more, for D to say that P is Mr X, even though others have published defamatory articles about Mr X, for the libel complained of must be in the statement published by the defendant: *Astaire v Campling* [1965] 3 All ER 666, [1966] 1 WLR 34.
3 Eg *Thorley v Lord Kerry* (1812) 4 Taunt 355. But in that case, it was explicitly stated (at 365) that, 'for mere general abuse spoken, no action lies'.

a villain,[4] a black-sheep,[5] an habitual drunkard[6] or a pansy.[7] What matters is the context and manner in which the words are uttered. Only if they amount to a vituperative expostulation will they not be regarded as, prima facie, defamatory (always assuming they are spoken within the earshot of third parties).

(b)   Words of opinion

A statement may be defamatory, even though the maker states it, not as fact, but as mere opinion.[8] One must take into account circumstances of time and place.[9] Thus, in *Slazengers Ltd v Gibbs & Co*,[10] it was defamatory to state during the war with Germany that the plaintiffs were a German firm likely to be closed down. For this reason, earlier authorities on what is defamatory must be treated with caution. Consider *Youssoupoff v Metro-Goldwyn-Mayer Pictures Ltd*[11] where, in 1934, it was held defamatory to say of the plaintiff that she had been raped. Would that still be defamatory today? Are allegations of pre-marital sex, illegitimacy or even adultery likely to damage reputation today?

(c)   Other examples of injured reputation

Several further examples may help to illustrate what is, and what is not, defamatory. To say that a motorist drove negligently is defamatory,[12] but not (in itself) that a trader has been put on a stop-list.[13] Nor is it defamatory to announce in a newspaper that the plaintiff was married on the day before the date fixed for the wedding.[14] On the other hand, it is defamatory to impute to a trader, businessman or professional man a lack of qualification, knowledge, skill, capacity, judgment or efficiency in the conduct of his trade or business or professional activity such as a severe attack on the special anaesthetising technique of a practising dental surgeon.[15] But it is not defamatory merely to criticise a trader's goods; the trader himself must be attacked. If, however, one can read into a criticism of the product a criticism of its maker, then that criticism may be defamatory.[16] To say that a baker's bread is *always unwholesome* is, for instance, defamatory.[17] But to say that a product does not answer its purpose is not.[18] To say that a trader is bankrupt or insolvent is defamatory;[19] but to say that he has ceased to be in business is not, for it does not reflect on his reputation.[20]

4   *Bell v Stone* (1798) 1 Bos & P 331.
5   *M'Gregor v Gregory* (1843) 11 M & W 287.
6   *Alexander v Jenkins* [1892] 1 QB 797 at 804, CA (per Kay LJ).
7   *Thaarup v Hulton Press Ltd* (1943) 169 LT 309, CA. For an example of a particularly abusive alleged libel see *Cornwell v Myskow* [1987] 2 All ER 504, [1987] 1 WLR 630, CA.
8   *Braddock v Bevins* [1948] 1 KB 580 at 598, [1948] 1 All ER 450, CA.
9   *Dolby v Newnes* (1887) 3 TLR 393 (a statement, although not defamatory at a private dinner party, may become so if repeated in a magazine).
10   (1916) 33 TLR 35.
11   (1934) 50 TLR 581, CA. (Could the risk of her having contracted AIDS or disease from her attacker be relevant, cancelling our changed social attitudes to rape victims?)
12   *Groom v Crocker* [1939] 1 KB 194, [1938] 2 All ER 394, CA.
13   *Ware and De Freville Ltd v Motor Trade Association* [1921] 3 KB 40, CA.
14   *Emerson v Grimsby Times and Telegraph Co Ltd* (1926) 42 TLR 238, CA.
15   *Drummond-Jackson v British Medical Association* [1970] 1 All ER 1094, CA.
16   *Evans v Harlow* (1844) 5 QB 624.
17   *Linotype Co Ltd v British Empire Type-Setting Machine Co Ltd* (1899) 81 LT 331, HL (per Lord Halsbury LC).
18   *Evans v Harlow* (1844) 5 QB 624.
19   *Shepheard v Whitaker* (1875) LR 10 CP 502.
20   *Ratcliffe v Evans* [1892] 2 QB 524, CA. Nor is it defamatory to say that his business is suffering as a result of competition: *Stephenson v Donaldson & Sons* (1981) 262 Estates Gazette 148. In some circumstances it may be the separate tort of injurious falsehood.

(2)   WHO MAY BE DEFAMED

Words, pictures or gestures can never be defamatory unless they disparage the reputation of either a living person[1] or the commercial reputation of a trading corporation.[2] Accordingly, it is defamatory of a trading company to assert that it indulges in black-market activities.[3]

The fact that the law allows commercial enterprises to sue for defamation is seen by the press as a powerful inhibition of vigorous criticism of such entities. The threat to sue for libel has a 'chilling effect' on investigations by the media and may allow corrupt practices to remain hidden from the public. The late Robert Maxwell used the libel laws to good effect to protect his dubious empire. Yet, the right of companies to sue for libel is now so well established that only Parliament could alter the law. But can public authorities invoke the tort of defamation to protect their 'governing reputation'? The House of Lords unanimously rejected any such proposition in *Derbyshire County Council v Times Newspapers Ltd*.[4]

> The defendants had published articles questioning the propriety of the plaintiffs' management of pension funds. The House of Lords struck out the claim holding that democratically elected government bodies and public authorities should be open to uninhibited public criticism. The 'chilling effect' of libel might prevent publication of matters about which the public ought to be informed.

In effect, the right of free speech and freedom of the press (enshrined in Article 10 of the European Convention on Human Rights) outweighed the Council's claim to protect its reputation.[5] Note that much of what their Lordships said about libel and public authorities could apply with equal force to other classes of plaintiff. Moreover, the limitation on the authority suing in libel, be it a local council or government ministry, does not apply to any individual who can show that he personally has been defamed. The Prime Minister is just as much entitled to sue for defamation as anyone else, regardless of whether the alleged defamatory statement concerns his personal or professional conduct.

---

1   In the absence of any decision by English courts on the point, it may be presumed that they will follow decisions in other common law jurisdictions to the effect that words defamatory of dead persons will not sustain an action by relatives who cannot prove that their reputation is besmirched; cf *Porter Report*, § 27. A trade union cannot be defamed: *Electrical, Electronic, Telecommunication and Plumbing Union v Times Newspapers Ltd* [1980] QB 585, [1980] 1 All ER 1097, CA, because the Trade Union and Labour Relations (Consolidation) Act 1992, ss 10-12 deprive trade unions of legal personality.

2   In relation to companies, the statement 'must attack the corporation or company in the method of conducting its affairs, must accuse it of fraud or mismanagement, or must attack its financial position': *South Hetton Coal Co v North-Eastern Association Ltd* [1894] 1 QB 133 at 141, CA (per Lopes LJ).

3   *D and L Caterers Ltd and Jackson v D'Anjou* [1945] KB 364, [1945] 1 All ER 563, CA; cf *Holdsworth Ltd v Associated Newspapers Ltd* [1937] 3 All ER 872, CA (actionable to say that limited company refused to accept interim wages award of joint conciliation board for the industry). A company may recover substantial damages even though it suffers no financial loss: *Selby Bridge (Proprietors) v Sunday Telegraph Ltd* (1966) 197 Estates Gazette 1077.

4   [1993] 1 All ER 1011, overruling *Bognor Regis UDC v Campion* [1972] 2 QB 169, [1972] 2 All ER 61.

5   For critique see Loveland 'Defamation and "Government": Taking Lessons from America' [1994] LS 206. Recall, also, that the Convention was formally incorporated into English law in the Human Rights Act 1998.

(3) THE INTERPRETATION OF DEFAMATORY STATEMENTS

It has so far been assumed that the meaning of the statement complained of is readily ascertainable. But this is not always so. There are, therefore, certain rules of interpretation which must now be considered.

(a)   Innuendo

The initial question in any defamation action is whether the words complained of are capable of bearing a defamatory meaning. In the absence of an allegation that those words possess an extended meaning, words must be construed by the judge[6] in their ordinary and natural sense.[7] The whole of the statement must be looked at, not merely that part which the plaintiff alleges to be defamatory (although, of course, it may be relevant to take account of the greater importance of some part of a statement – for example the headlines of an article in a newspaper[8]). In *Charleston v News Group Newspapers*,[9] for instance, two soap opera stars sued in respect of material published in the defendants' newspaper which depicted the plaintiffs' faces superimposed upon two near-naked torsos. The article printed beneath the picture castigated the makers of a pornographic computer game. It was held that, taken as a whole, the picture and the article were not capable of being defamatory. There may be circumstances, too, where the context in which the words were uttered must be taken into account. In *Bookbinder v Tebbit*,[10] for example, the alleged slander was made at a political meeting. The Court of Appeal said that the meaning to be attached to the defendant's words could be affected, among other things, by the form of the question to which the words were an answer or the general course of the speech in issue.

Similarly, there may be circumstances where the plaintiff alleges that the statement is defamatory because specific facts known to the reader give to the statement a meaning other than, or additional to, its ordinary meaning; this is known as a 'true' or 'legal' innuendo. In such cases the plaintiff must plead and prove such facts,[11] for the defendant is entitled to know the meaning of the statement on which the plaintiff seeks to rely so that he is able to argue either that, even thus construed, the statement is not defamatory or that it is true of the plaintiff.

There is also a third possibility: that the words may have a meaning beyond their literal meaning which is inherent in them and arises by inference or implication. This is sometimes known as the 'false innuendo'. The plaintiff has to plead separately any such 'false innuendo'. A 'false innuendo' differs from a 'true innuendo' in that the

---

6   *Turner v Metro-Goldwyn-Mayer Pictures Ltd* [1950] 1 All ER 449 at 465, HL (per Lord Greene).
7   *Capital and Counties Bank Ltd v George Henty & Sons* (1882) 7 App Cas 741 at 772, HL (per Lord Blackburn); *Skuse v Granada Television* [1996] EMLR 278, CA; *Gillick v BBC* [1996] EMLR 267, CA. In *Mitchell v Faber & Faber Ltd* [1998] EMLR 807 Hirst LJ stated that, '[i]n deciding whether words are capable of carrying a defamatory meaning the court will reject those meanings which can only emerge as the product of some strained or forced or utterly unreasonable interpretation'. Similarly, in *Edwards v Times Newspapers Ltd* (1997) unreported it was held that the ordinary meaning of words used must be construed in the light of the meaning that would be attached to them by 'the ordinary reader'.
8   *Shipley v Todhunter* (1836) 7 C & P 680.
9   [1995] 2 AC 65, [1995] 2 All ER 313, HL.
10   [1989] 1 WLR 640 at 647.
11   Ord 82 r 3(1) provides that 'where the plaintiff alleges that the words or matter complained of were used in a defamatory sense other than their ordinary meaning, he shall give particulars of the facts and matters on which he relies in support of such sense'. Case law adds that the plaintiff must prove that those facts were actually known to some people (*Fullam v Newcastle Chronicle and Journal Ltd* [1977] 1 WLR 651, CA) and that these facts were in existence and known to those people at the time of the publication (*Grappelli v Derek Block (Holdings) Ltd* [1981] 2 All ER 272, CA).

pleader of a 'false innuendo' does not generally need set out any extrinsic facts in support of his plea. However, if there is no obvious ordinary or natural meaning to be ascribed to the words complained of, then this, in turn, obscures the sense in which the words bear a 'false innuendo'. It has therefore been held, in *Allsop v Church of England Newspaper Ltd*,[12] that in such circumstances the plaintiff must plead the particular meaning upon which he relies.

(i) True innuendoes Here are some typical examples of 'true', or 'legal', innuendoes. In one case, the defendant, having engaged the plaintiff, a well-known singer, to perform at a concert, printed her name third in the order on the programme. The court accepted evidence that in the musical world the best singer was placed at the head of the programme and those of lesser reputation in the middle, so that the programme constituted a defamatory innuendo of the plaintiff.[13] In another case, a caption under a newspaper photograph of a man and a woman to the effect that it was Mr C and his fiancée conveyed to those who knew that the plaintiff lived with Mr C as his wife the defamatory meaning that she had done so without being married to him.[14] Finally, in a further case it was held that to include a cartoon of a well-known amateur golfer in an advertisement for chocolate implied that he was being paid for the advertisement and was thus prostituting his amateur status.[15]

In *Hough v London Express Newspaper Ltd*,[16] the question that arose was whether a plaintiff relying on an innuendo has to prove that it was published to somebody who interpreted the matter in the defamatory sense alleged.

The defendants published an account and photograph of the 'curly-headed wife' of a named boxer. The plaintiff, the boxer's wife, produced witnesses who gave evidence that they had read the statement to mean that the plaintiff was not the wife of the boxer. In the event, they were not misled into thinking that she was not his wife, nor was any person produced as a witness so misled.

It was held that one need only prove that there are people who *might* understand the words in a defamatory sense, but there is no need for 'evidence that some person did so understand them'.[17] On the basis of this objective test, the plaintiff succeeded even though no-one was shown to have believed in the imputation in question.

(ii) False innuendoes Problems also arise with regard to false innuendoes. In the House of Lords case of *Rubber Improvement Ltd v Daily Telegraph Ltd*,[18] the defendants published an article which stated that the Fraud Squad of the City of London Police were investigating the affairs of the plaintiff's company. The article was found to be defamatory in its ordinary meaning because the simple statement that the Fraud Squad are inquiring into his affairs may damage his reputation even though it is consistent with his innocence. However, since what was said was true – the Fraud

---

12 [1972] 2 QB 161, [1972] 2 All ER 26, CA.
13 *Russell v Notcutt* (1896) 12 TLR 195, CA.
14 *Cassidy v Daily Mirror Newspapers Ltd* [1929] 2 KB 331, CA.
15 *Tolley v JS Fry & Sons Ltd* [1931] AC 333, [1931] All ER Rep 131, HL.
16 [1940] 2 KB 507, [1940] 3 All ER 31, CA.
17 Ibid, at 515 (per Goddard LJ). See also *Theaker v Richardson* [1962] 1 All ER 229, CA (defendant liable for publishing a libel to plaintiff's husband although no evidence that husband believed the accusation made against his wife) and *Shanson v Howard* [1997] CLY 2037.
18 [1964] AC 234; sub nom *Lewis v Daily Telegraph* [1963] 2 All ER 151, HL. But see *Hyams v Peterson* [1991] 1 NZLR 711 where the New Zealand Court of Appeal found a statement containing words of suspicion could impute guilt.

Squad were conducting the investigations mentioned – no action lay.[19] The plaintiff also alleged that the words were defamatory in a second way: by imputing that there was ground for suspicion about the way in which their business was conducted. The thrust of this plea was that imputation of reasonable suspicion (while consistent with their innocence) was nonetheless equally capable of diminishing the plaintiffs' trading reputation.

On the facts, the House of Lords held that the words were not defamatory in this second sense. Their Lordships distinguished, on the one hand, imputing reasonable grounds for suspicion and, on the other, simply reporting the fact of suspicion. As Lord Devlin put it: '[l]oose talk about suspicion can very easily convey the impression that it is a suspicion that is well-founded'.[20] This crucial distinction between a statement and imputation of suspicion has since been reasserted by the Court of Appeal in *Mapp v News Group Newspapers Ltd*.[1] However, for present purposes, the main point is that the second plea in *Rubber Improvement Ltd v Daily Telegraph Ltd* constituted the allegation of a false innuendo and therefore did not require the plaintiffs to adduce evidence of any extrinsic facts which had to be particularised in the pleading.

When a defendant newspaper described a well-known broadcaster as 'bent' the plaintiff had to set out the meaning of the word on which he relied.[2] If a statement is capable of many different meanings and the plaintiff does not specify those on which he relies the defendant is entitled to justify the statement on any meaning which it reasonably bears.[3] If, in a long article which contains many different meanings in relation to him, the plaintiff fails to plead the meaning(s) on which he relies, the defendant is entitled to have the plaintiff's statement of claim struck out on the ground that it discloses no reasonable cause of action.[4]

(b)   The roles of judge and jury in construing what is defamatory

The judge decides whether a statement is capable of bearing a defamatory meaning, whether in its normal meaning or by innuendo.[5] That being resolved in the affirmative, the jury then decides whether it did bear a defamatory meaning on the occasion complained of.[6] The judge has to construe the words used, to decide whether they are capable of a defamatory meaning; once he decides that they are so capable, the jury decide the meaning of the words in finding whether they are defamatory.[7] The plaintiff may contend that the statement has different defamatory meanings. In such instances, the judge decides which of those the statement is capable of conveying, and the jury then decides which particular meaning within that category the words do bear.[8] In *Aspro*

---

19 There is an important difference between something being defamatory *simpliciter* and something being defamatory and *actionable*. To be defamatory, the statement must merely diminish P's reputation; but to be actionable, the statement must also be untrue. In short, both true and false statements may be defamatory, but only the latter may be actionable.

20 [1964] AC 234 at 285, HL.

1 [1998] QB 520, CA.

2 *Allsop v Church of England Newspaper Ltd* [1972] 2 QB 161, [1972] 2 All ER 26, CA.

3 *London Computer Operators Training Ltd v BBC* [1973] 2 All ER 170, CA.

4 *DDSA Pharmaceuticals Ltd v Times Newspapers Ltd* [1973] QB 21, [1972] 3 All ER 417, CA.

5 *Adam v Ward* [1917] AC 309 at 329, HL (per Lord Dunedin); *Lloyd v David Syme & Co Ltd* [1986] AC 350, [1986] 2 WLR 69, PC; *Mapp v News Group Newspapers Ltd* [1997] EMLR 397, CA. By virtue of s 7 of the Defamation Act 1996, the judge must consider whether the statement is capable (as opposed to being merely 'arguably capable') of bearing a particular meaning.

6 *Cassidy v Daily Mirror Newspapers Ltd* [1929] 2 KB 331 at 340, CA (per Scrutton LJ).

7 *Jones v Skelton* [1963] 3 All ER 952, [1963] 1 WLR 1362, PC.

8 *Slim v Daily Telegraph* [1968] 2 QB 157, [1968] 1 All ER 497, CA.

9 [1995] 4 All ER 728, [1996] 1 WLR 132, CA.

Travel v Owners Abroad Group plc,[9] for example, the court was faced with the question of whether allegations that the plaintiffs' family company was 'going bust' were capable of bearing a defamatory meaning. Among other things, the court had to consider the alleged false innuendo that it was defamatory in the sense that such allegations would lower the directors of such a company in the estimation of the public by implicitly suggesting that, notwithstanding the company's insolvency, the directors were nonetheless allowing it to continue trading.

If an appellate court holds that the words are incapable of a defamatory meaning where a jury, having been entrusted with the decision by the trial judge, has found for the plaintiff, the court will set aside the verdict and enter judgment for the defendant. Conversely, on the very rare occasions when an appellate court holds that a jury could not reasonably have found that the words were not defamatory, it will set aside the verdict and order a new trial.[10] Where the judge has misdirected the jury on the law, its verdict will also be set aside.[11]

The courts seek to ensure that the issues which come to trial are clean cut in order to erode the advantage one party might obtain by clever tactics. It is a fundamental principle in an action for defamation that:[12]

> the trial of the action should concern itself with the essential issues and the evidence relevant thereto and that public policy and the interests of the parties require that the trial should be kept strictly to the issues necessary for a fair determination of the dispute between the parties.

Moreover, what is sauce for the plaintiff is also sauce for the defendant. Defendants pleading the defence of justification must do so in a manner which makes it quite clear what meaning or meanings they seek to justify.[13] Time and again the Court of Appeal has deplored attempts to take advantage of the rules of pleading in order to acquire an unfair advantage at the actual trial.[14]

(4)   IMMATERIALITY OF THE DEFENDANT'S KNOWLEDGE

The general common law position is that '[a] person charged with libel cannot defend himself by showing that he intended in his breast not to defame'.[15] Nor is it a defence that a person has no actual knowledge that his statement is defamatory. It is usually stated that liability at common law is absolute: it matters not whether the defendant could have taken steps to discover that the statement was defamatory. The leading case is *Cassidy v Daily Mirror Newspapers Ltd*.[16]

> With the authority of Mr C, the defendants published a photograph, taken at a race meeting, with the following words underneath: 'Mr C, the racehorse owner, and Miss X, whose

---

10 *Lockhart v Harrison* (1928) 139 LT 521 at 523, HL (per Lord Buckmaster); *Australian Newspaper Co v Bennett* [1894] AC 284, PC, is a good example of judicial reluctance to do this. Cf *Broome v Agar* (1928) 138 LT 698, CA. (Court of Appeal refused to direct new trial because jury had decided that it was not defamatory for mistress to say that her chauffeur was a rotter who went out joy-riding in her car.)

11 *Tournier v National Provincial and Union Bank of England* [1924] 1 KB 461, CA; cf *Dakhyl v Labouchere* [1908] 2 KB 325n, HL.

12 *Polly Peck (Holdings) plc v Trelford* [1986] 2 All ER 84 at 94, [1986] 2 WLR 845 at 945, CA (per O'Connor LJ).

13 *Lucas-Box v News Group Newspapers Ltd* [1986] 1 All ER 177, CA; *Morrell v International Thomson Publishing Ltd* [1989] 3 All ER 733 at 734-5, CA (per May LJ).

14 *Morrell v International Thomson Publishing Ltd* (supra) at 733-5.

15 *E Hulton & Co v Jones* [1910] AC 20 at 23, HL (per Lord Loreburn LC).

16 [1929] 2 KB 331, CA.

engagement has been announced'. The defendants published the photograph, not knowing that the plaintiff was married to Mr C, and having taken no steps whatever to find out whether Mr C was already married. The defendants were held liable to the plaintiff.

The case provides clear authority for the proposition that, at common law, one may be liable for a statement which one does not actually know to be defamatory. To this general rule about absolute common law liability there are two exceptions – one statutory, one rooted in the common law. These exceptions can be viewed in two ways: either as 'chinks' in the general rule or as defences to the application of the rule. We prefer to deal with them in second of these two ways and they are discussed in depth in the next chapter.

(B)   REFERENCE TO THE PLAINTIFF

'In order to be actionable the defamatory words must be understood to be published of and concerning the plaintiff.'[17] The plaintiff need not be mentioned in the statement, nor need everyone reading it know that he was referred to; it is sufficient if ordinary sensible people, proved to have special knowledge of the facts, might reasonably believe that the statement referred to the plaintiff.[18] The damages will be lower where only a small proportion of those who read the article would know that it was defamatory of the plaintiff.

(1)   CLASS LIBELS

Where a statement defamatory of a class of persons is made, the same test is applied to determine whether individuals within the class may sue. If the class is so small that persons would reasonably believe that every member of it is targeted, then each individual member may sue. Thus, where proceedings were pending against 17 persons, it was held that one of them could sue a third party who said of them all that 'these defendants helped to murder HF'.[19] A similar rule applies to directors of a small company,[20] and, presumably, also to trustees of an institution. But a statement that 'all estate agents are rogues' would not enable any one member of such a large class to sue.

Even where the class is too large to permit every member to sue, an individual within the class may still be able to sue if he can show that the statement was especially referable to him. Often this will rest on an innuendo, which must then be specifically

---

17 *Knupffer v London Express Newspaper Ltd* [1944] AC 116 at 121, [1944] 1 All ER 495, HL (per Lord Atkin). Cf *Farrington v Leigh* (1987) Times, 10 December, CA.

18 *Morgan v Odhams Press Ltd* [1971] 2 All ER 1156, HL. *Cassidy v Daily Mirror Newspapers Ltd* [1929] 2 KB 331, CA. If the defendant publishes a statement defamatory on its face about someone described but not named, and a later publication by the defendant names the plaintiff so as to identify to readers of the first newspaper article, for the first time, the person written about, the second publication may be relied on to support the allegation that the first one referred to the plaintiff: *Hayward v Thompson* [1982] QB 47, [1981] 3 All ER 450, CA.

19 *Foxcroft v Lacy* (1613) Hob 89; cf *Browne v D C Thomson & Co Ltd* 1912 SC 359 (defendants' newspaper published article stating that, in Queenstown, the Roman Catholic religious authorities had instructed that all Protestant shop assistants were to be dismissed. The seven persons who alone exercised religious authority on behalf of the Roman Catholic Church in Queenstown were able to sue in libel).

20 *Aspro Travel v Owners Abroad Group plc* [1995] 4 All ER 728, CA (defamation of directors of a family company). But cf *Chomley v Watson* [1907] VLR 502 where the true statement 'Either you or Jones stole the money' was held not to be actionable by the innocent party, Jones.

pleaded, and the court will order the plaintiff to give full particulars of the facts on which the claim rests.[1]

Two cases illustrate the position. First, *Le Fanu v Malcomson*.[2]

The defendants published an article suggesting that in some of the Irish factories cruelties were practised upon employees. There were circumstances in the article as a whole, including a reference to Waterford, which enabled the jury to identify the plaintiffs' Waterford factory as the one at which the article was aimed. The plaintiffs' action succeeded.

Secondly, *Knupffer v London Express Newspaper Ltd*.[3]

During the war, the defendants' newspaper referred to the quisling activities of the Young Russian party. Although the party was international, and had a British branch of 24 members headed by the plaintiff, the article referred only to the party's activities in France and the US. Since the total membership was several thousands, each member could not be said to be identified. No facts were proved in evidence that could identify the plaintiff as being singled out in the article, and therefore his action failed.

(2) UNINTENTIONAL REFERENCES TO THE PLAINTIFF

The plaintiff may be defamed although the defendant did not intend it. Where the defamation is intentional, however, a greater level of damages may be awarded.[4] In several cases, newspaper proprietors who did not intend to defame the plaintiff have been held liable. In *Hulton v Jones*,[5] for example, the defendants published a fictional article about 'Artemus Jones'. The writer of the article did not know of the plaintiff, of that name, who was a former contributor to the newspaper. But the managing editor, on reading the article in proof, had thought at first that the plaintiff was intended. The defendants were held liable.

In *Newstead v London Express Newspaper Ltd*,[6] the defendants published an account of the trial for bigamy of 'Harold Newstead, thirty-year-old Camberwell man'. The reporter had included the address and occupation of the Harold Newstead of whom this was a correct report, but the sub-editor deleted it; this want of particularity caused readers to think that the plaintiff – another Harold Newstead of Camberwell, of about the same age – was meant. It was held to be no defence that the words were true of, and intended to refer to, another: the jury was justified in finding that the words referred to the plaintiff. No English appellate decision has been traced, however, where a defendant who could not possibly have known that the words were referable to the plaintiff, has been held liable.

(C) 'MALICIOUS' PUBLICATION

Though always referred to as the need for 'malicious publication', in truth, the requirement is for there to have been mere publication; the adjective 'malicious' is in

---

1   *Bruce v Odhams Press Ltd* [1936] 1 KB 697, [1936] 1 All ER 287, CA.
2   (1848) 1 HL Cas 637, HL.
3   [1944] AC 116, [1944] 1 All ER 495, HL.
4   *Bridgmont v Associated Newspapers Ltd* [1951] 2 KB 578, [1951] 2 All ER 285, CA.
5   [1910] AC 20, HL.
6   [1940] 1 KB 377, [1939] 4 All ER 319, CA. And see *Grappelli v Derek Block (Holdings) Ltd* [1981] 2 All ER 272, [1981] 1 WLR 822, CA and *Hayward v Thompson* [1982] QB 47, [1981] 3 All ER 450 (effect of later publications identifying the person defamed).

practice otiose, save that the presence of malice serves to defeat the defences of fair comment and qualified privilege (on both of which, see the next chapter).

Publication is 'the making known the defamatory matter after it has been written to some person other than the person of whom it is written'.[7] This requirement of publication to a third party merely underlines that the tort protects not an individual's opinion of himself but the estimation in which others hold him. Because of this rule, it is often important to know when the defendant, who perhaps addressed his remarks to the plaintiff alone, can be held responsible for the fact that third parties have learnt of the defamation. The rule is that if he intended that it should be published to them, or ought to have foreseen such publication, he is liable, but not otherwise.[8] A defendant is not liable for an 'unsuspected overhearing of the words' spoken by him to the plaintiff.[9] He is not liable where a father opens his son's letter,[10] or the butler opens even the unsealed letter of his employer.[11] A correspondent should expect that clerks of a businessman-plaintiff might, in the ordinary course of business, open letters addressed to him at his place of business but not marked 'personal', 'private', etc. He is therefore responsible for the publication to them where the correspondence is not so marked.[12] It is also to be expected that a husband will open an unstamped manila envelope lying on the door-mat looking like a circular, even though it is sealed and addressed to his wife.[13]

In general, the original maker of a statement is not liable for its republication by another, but that other will be responsible even though he expressly states that he is merely reproducing what he has been told from a specified source.[14] So the writer, newspaper proprietor and printer of a defamatory article in a newspaper are each liable for its publication.[15] In accordance with ordinary principles, however:

> where a man who makes a request to another to publish defamatory matter, of which, for the purpose, he gives him a statement, whether in full or in outline, and the agent publishes the matter, adhering to the sense and substance of it, although the language be to some extent his own, the man making the request is liable to an action as the publisher.[16]

A man who knows that reporters are present when he is making a speech is not thereby responsible for its publication in the press, but he is answerable if he gives the information to them with a view to publication.[17] On the other hand, when a television

---

7   *Pullman v Walter Hill & Co* [1891] 1 QB 524 at 527, CA (per Lord Esher MR).
8   *Huth v Huth* [1915] 3 KB 32 at 38, CA (per Lord Reading CJ); *Slipper v BBC* [1991] 1 All ER 165. Note also *McNichol v Grandy* [1932] 1 DLR 225 (S Ct Canada): held that the burden of proving that it would not be expected that a statement would be overheard lies with the defendant.
9   *White v J and F Stone (Lighting and Radio) Ltd* [1939] 2 KB 827, [1939] 3 All ER 507, CA.
10 *Powell v Gelston* [1916] 2 KB 615.
11 *Huth v Huth* [1915] 3 KB 32, CA. Cf the case if the sender knew that the plaintiff was blind, and that the butler often opened letters for her.
12 *Pullman v Walter Hill & Co* [1891] 1 QB 524, CA. But what if one sent a letter marked 'private' to, say, the Prime Minister, or even to any other busy public figure? Might there not be publication to the secretary who opened it?
13 *Theaker v Richardson* [1962] 1 All ER 229, [1962] 1 WLR 151, CA.
14 *M'Pherson v Daniels* (1829) 10 B & C 263.
15 And distributors. In *Goldsmith v Sperrings Ltd* [1977] 2 All ER 566, CA, it was held not to be an abuse of process for Sir James Goldsmith to pursue a claim arising from an article in *Private Eye* against 37 different distributors with a view to making them settle his claim on the basis of their undertaking to cease distributing the magazine. Note, too, that distributors may require the original publisher to indemnify them against liability. Thus, the original defamer may have to pay out damages several times over.
16 *Parkes v Prescott* (1869) LR 4 Exch 169 at 179 (per Montague Smith J).
17 *Adams v Kelly* (1824) Ry & M 157; *McWhirter v Manning* (1954) Times, 30 October.

broadcast foreseeably invites comment in the next day's newspapers, the maker of the original defamatory statement will be liable for its repetition by the press.[18]

The requirement of publication to a third party is satisfied by dictating a letter to one's typist,[19] and probably also when office staff press-copy it.[20] A judge at first instance in Northern Ireland has held that a printer does not, by the very act of handing back in a parcel the printed handbills to the customer-author, publish those handbills.[1] The defendant's publication to his own wife is not enough[2] but publication to the wife of the plaintiff is.[3]

Difficulties of proving publication are eased by certain rebuttable presumptions. Proof of proper addressing and posting of a letter gives rise to a presumption of publication to the addressee.[4] And a postcard and a telegram[5] (but not an unsealed letter[6]) are presumed to have been published to Post Office officials. On the other hand, in one case,[7] there was held to be no publication where the defendant handed to X a folded unsealed letter which X, without reading or showing to others, handed to the plaintiff.

There is no publication to a person unless the defamatory meaning of the communication would be understood by that third person – a postcard defamatory of, but not known to be referable to the plaintiff (by persons unaware of the special facts), has been held not to be published to Post Office staff.[8]

On occasion, there may be publication by omission. Failure by a defendant who is authorised and able to remove or amend defamatory matter which is the work of another amounts to publication by him. Thus, those in charge of a club will be accountable for defamatory matter placed by another on the noticeboard of the club if they do not remove it within a reasonable time.[9]

18 *Slipper v BBC* [1991] 1 All ER 165. In effect, this decision is no more than an application of the general law of causation; the foreseeable repetition of the statement by the press is too probable to be regarded as a novus actus interveniens.

19 *Pullman v Walter Hill & Co* [1891] 1 QB 524, CA. The circulation of inter-departmental memoranda within a company is also sufficient publication: *Riddick v Thames Board Mills Ltd* [1977] QB 881, [1977] 3 All ER 677, CA.

20 The reports of *Pullman v Walter Hill & Co* [1891] 1 QB 524 do not expressly state that the press-copying in that case was held to be a publication, but Lord Esher MR said in *Boxsius v Goblet Frères* [1894] 1 QB 842 at 849, CA that the case had so decided, and he was a judge in both cases.

1 *Eglantine Inn Ltd v Isaiah Smith* [1948] NI 29 (the printer was nevertheless held jointly liable for the subsequent distribution of the handbills by the author's agents).

2 *Wennhak v Morgan* (1888) 20 QBD 635, Div Ct.

3 *Wenman v Ash* (1853) 13 CB 836.

4 *Warren v Warren* (1834) 1 Cr M & R 250.

5 *Sadgrove v Hole* [1901] 2 KB 1, CA.

6 *Huth v Huth* [1915] 3 KB 32, CA. (It was stated, obiter, that had Post Office officials in fact read the letter to check whether it was properly stamped, that would have been publication. Does this mean that it is foreseeable that any mail will be thus opened – for example, to see whether prohibited articles are sent – or is it limited to unsealed mail?)

7 *Clutterbuck v Chaffers* (1816) 1 Stark 471.

8 *Sadgrove v Hole* [1901] 2 KB 1, CA. The same applies to cipher messages and messages in a foreign language.

9 *Byrne v Deane* [1937] 1 KB 818, [1937] 2 All ER 204, CA. Compare those cases where the matter is carved in stone, or the defendant is not in control of the place where the libel is exhibited. Here the impracticability/impossibility of avoiding the publication negates any prospect of liability.

SECTION 3. DISTINGUISHING LIBEL AND SLANDER

(A) CRITERIA FOR DISTINGUISHING LIBEL FROM SLANDER

Any medium whereby thought and ideas can be expressed or conveyed may constitute the publication of a defamation – words, pictures, gestures,[10] music and statues are all examples.[11] It is, however, the choice of medium which determines whether the defamation is libel or slander; and it is because the rules relating to the two torts differ in some important particulars that it is necessary to distinguish between them.

There can be no doubt that anything communicated in the form of a permanent character and visible to the eye is libel, and that anything temporary and merely audible is slander. Thus, books, newspapers, letters and even effigies[12] are libels, and spoken words are slander. What is more difficult, however, is how to characterise things which are in permanent form but only audible, and things which are visible but not in permanent form. In *Youssoupoff v Metro-Goldwyn-Mayer Pictures Ltd*,[13] the scenes depicted on the screen in a talking film were held to constitute libel. Yet, at most, the case supports the view that permanency is an important element in the test for libel. It does not establish that permanency is the sole criterion. Slesser LJ stated the ratio decidendi of the case as follows:

> There can be no doubt that, so far as the photographic part of the exhibition is concerned, that is a *permanent matter to be seen by the eye*, and is the proper subject of an action for libel, if defamatory. I regard the speech which is synchronised with the photographic reproduction and forms part of one complex, common exhibition as an ancillary circumstance, part of the surroundings explaining that which is to be seen.[14]

The case, however, does not settle authoritatively whether a defamatory anecdote in a film is libel. Nor does it tell us whether defamatory remarks on a compact disc are slander. Although there are obiter dicta in other cases suggesting that permanency is a sufficient criterion,[15] technically, the point remains undecided. It follows, therefore, that it is not possible to say into which category the following fall: tape recordings, talking parrots that have learnt certain phrases from their owners and sky-writing.

The dictation of a letter to a typist is only slander.[16] The forwarding of the typed letter itself is undoubtedly libel, and, it is thought, a libel for which the dictator is accountable because he authorised his agent to forward it. The reading aloud of a letter written by another, where those to whom it was read were aware that the speaker was

---

10 See *Cook v Cox* (1814) 3 M & S 110 at 114 (per Lord Ellenborough).

11 Even the lighting of a lamp in the day-time in the plaintiff's garden, thereby inferring that he keeps a brothel, is caught: *Jefferies v Duncombe* (1809) 2 Camp 3; and perhaps also so is police shadowing of a plaintiff's house.

12 *Monson v Tussauds Ltd* [1894] 1 QB 671, CA (placing of a waxwork effigy of the plaintiff holding a gun in a room next to another room in which there was a representation of a murder scene for which the plaintiff was tried but acquitted).

13 (1934) 50 TLR 581, CA.

14 Ibid, at 587 (emphasis added).

15 Eg, in *Monson v Tussauds Ltd* [1894] 1 QB 671, CA, Lopes LJ stated (at 692) that: 'Libels are generally in writing or printing, but this is not necessary; the defamatory matter may be conveyed in some other permanent form. For instance, a statue, a caricature, an effigy, chalk marks on a wall, signs, or pictures may constitute a libel'.

16 In *Osborn v Thomas Boulter & Son* [1930] 2 KB 226, [1930] All ER Rep 154, CA, this appeared to Scrutton and Slesser LJJ to be slander only, but Greer LJ was inclined to think it libel. When the typist listens to a dictaphone a libel is probably being published.

reading from the document, was held to be libel in *Forrester v Tyrrell*.[17] The short report of this case does not, however, mention whether the point was argued.[18] In *Osborn v Boulter*,[19] Scrutton and Slesser LJJ thought that the reading aloud of a document was slander, yet it is submitted that the approach in *Forrester v Tyrrell* is to be preferred as the defamatory material is both visible and in permanent form; the reading of it simply constitutes the means of publication. This uncertainty at common law has prompted statutory intervention to cover mass media communications. Section 166 of the Broadcasting Act 1990 now provides that the publication of any words in the course of any broadcast programme, on television or radio, shall be treated as publication in a permanent form. It no longer matters whether the broadcast is for general public reception or otherwise. Similarly, the Theatres Act 1968 provides that the publication of words in the course of a performance of a play shall also be treated as publication in a permanent form.[20]

(B) JURIDICAL DIFFERENCES BETWEEN LIBEL AND SLANDER

There are two major juridical differences between libel and slander. First, a libel of sufficient seriousness may be punished as a crime whereas slander is always only tortious.[1] Secondly, libel is actionable per se whereas slander, subject to the exceptions discussed in the next section, is actionable only upon proof of actual damage.[2]

(C) EXCEPTIONAL CASES WHERE SLANDER IS ACTIONABLE PER SE

(1) IMPUTATION OF CRIME

The limits of this exception cannot precisely be defined because it is not settled whether the reason for it is the social ostracism resulting from such a slander, or the putting of the plaintiff in jeopardy, or even some other matter.

At the very least, the following points are incontrovertible. The crime must be one for which the plaintiff could be made to suffer corporally – that is, by punishment with at least imprisonment in the first instance. The statement 'I know enough to put you in gaol' is therefore actionable per se.[3] If the perpetrator, having been arrested, can only

---

17 (1893) 57 JP 532, CA. MacDermott J followed this decision with obvious reluctance in *Robinson v Chambers (No 2)* [1946] NI 148 in which the audience was aware that the defendant was reading out a letter.

18 If the secretary simply hands or reads the letter back to the person who dictated it, then there can be no defamation, for there has been no publication.

19 [1930] 2 KB 226, [1930] All ER Rep 154, CA. Slesser LJ left open (at 236) whether 'the circumstance of dictation, and the dictated matter being brought back and considered by the dictator, may constitute in certain cases a libel'. What of the office cleaner who unintentionally sets off the dictaphone?

20 Section 4. But note that performances given 'on a domestic occasion in a private dwelling' are exempted by s 7 of the Act.

1 Of course, spoken words may constitute a crime where the other elements of that crime are present: eg blasphemy or sedition. Earlier views that to constitute a crime a libel must be calculated to provoke a breach of the peace were rejected by the House of Lords in *Gleaves v Deakin* [1980] AC 477, [1979] 2 All ER 497.

2 Although the term 'special damage' is used frequently, this is misleading, as noted earlier, since the phrase has other meanings in other contexts. In fact, the use of the term 'special damage' in this context is to be attributed to the dictum of Lord Wensleydale in *Lynch v Knight* (1861) 9 HL Cas 577.

3 *Webb v Beavan* (1883) 11 QBD 609; this illustration also shows that a general imputation of criminality without reference to a specific offence is sufficient.

be punished by a fine for the offence in question (and not by imprisonment) the imputation of the commission of the crime remains outside the exception.[4] And this is the case even though there is a power to commit for non-payment of the fine.[5]

The words used must also be clear and unambiguous. If they convey a mere suspicion – of murder, for example – they do not fall within the exception and the slander is not actionable per se.[6] In addition, in construing the meaning of the words, it is firmly established that they must be looked at in context in order to discover what was imputed. This rule is made clear by *Thompson v Bernard.*[7]

> The words 'T is a damned thief, and so was his father before him; and I can prove it' seem clear enough, but because they were followed in this case by the statement, 'T received the earnings of the ship, and ought to pay the wages', the court directed a non-suit, because only breach of contract was in fact imputed.

This case also illustrates the obvious point that difficult problems of criminal law may have to be solved in order to determine whether the facts imputed constituted a crime punishable by imprisonment or otherwise corporally. If the plaintiff has to rely on some secondary meaning of the words spoken, he must, according to *Gray v Jones,*[8] prove that they were reasonably capable of being so interpreted. That case also lends support to the view that social ostracism is at least one of the reasons for this exception. Having found that the words 'You are a convicted person' might reasonably mean that a crime punishable corporally was imputed, Atkinson J, in a closely reasoned judgment, held them to be within the exception because, although they would not place the plaintiff in jeopardy,[9] they would tend to make him ostracised socially. On the other hand, there have been several cases where something criminal in character, but for technical reasons not punishable in the requisite way, has been held to be outside the rule – presumably because the plaintiff was not in jeopardy. In *Lemon v Simmons,*[10] for instance, to say that a husband stole from his wife while the couple were living together was held not to impute a crime, because husbands were not at that time punishable for such thefts.

(2) IMPUTATION OF CERTAIN TYPES OF DISEASE

To impute that a person has a contagious venereal disease is also to commit a slander actionable per se.[11] Whether the exception has any greater scope is doubtful. There is weak authority that leprosy is within the exception;[12] and it has sometimes (unconvincingly) been asserted that scarlet fever and the plague are also covered.[13] Yet, even if it *is* defamatory to impute a communicable disease, such as scarlet fever or tuberculosis, it is submitted that, unless suffering from the particular disease induces

---

4 *Hellwig v Mitchell* [1910] 1 KB 609; *Ormiston v Great Western Rly Co* [1917] 1 KB 598.
5 *Michael v Spiers and Pond Ltd* (1909) 101 LT 352.
6 *Simmons v Mitchell* (1880) 6 App Cas 156, PC.
7 (1807) 1 Camp 48.
8 [1939] 1 All ER 798.
9 On which see *Jackson v Adams* (1835) 2 Bing NC 402.
10 (1888) 57 LJQB 260. *D and L Caterers Ltd and Jackson v D'Anjou* [1945] KB 364, [1945] 1 All ER 563, CA, raised, but did not decide, the point whether trading, as well as social ostracism, will be deemed sufficient, for there, a crime punishable by imprisonment was imputed to a limited company engaged in trade.
11 *Bloodworth v Gray* (1844) 7 Man & G 334. Even if AIDS is not strictly speaking a venereal disease, an imputation that a person has that disease would probably also be actionable per se.
12 *Taylor v Perkins* (1607) Cro Jac 144: the words 'Thou art a leprous knave' were held to be actionable per se.
13 See *Gatley*, § 166.

moral condemnation or loathing, it is probably not now actionable per se. Even in the case of venereal disease, it is not actionable per se to say that the plaintiff has suffered from it in the past.[14]

The rationale for making the imputation of contagious venereal diseases actionable per se was, historically, that it might dissuade people from associating with the victim. Nowadays, when so many cures are easily available for many, if not most, infectious or contagious diseases, it might be questioned whether this exception ought to survive. Indeed, the last reported case within this exception was *Bloodworth v Gray* in 1844.[15]

(3) SLANDER IN RESPECT OF OFFICE, PROFESSION, CALLING, TRADE OR BUSINESS

At common law, a slander in respect of an office, profession, trade or business was actionable per se if, first, it was calculated to disparage him in his office, and, secondly, it was spoken in relation to his office. Section 2 of the Defamation Act 1952 now recasts this most important of circumstances in which slander is actionable per se. It provides:

> In an action for slander in respect of words calculated to disparage the plaintiff in any office, profession, calling, trade or business held or carried on by him at the time of the publication, it shall not be necessary to allege or prove special damage, whether or not the words are spoken of the plaintiff in the way of his office, profession, calling, trade or business.

The provision thus removes the second common law requirement. The words are actionable even though they are not said of the plaintiff in the conduct of his profession so long as the imputation they carry is designed to disparage him in his particular calling. Section 2 also nullifies decisions such as *Jones v Jones*[16] where the House of Lords held that an allegation that a headmaster had committed adultery with a school cleaner did not relate to his conduct in his profession. Today, such an allegation would certainly be actionable simply because it had prejudicial effects on his employment.

Words are also actionable per se if they impute some want of integrity or some corrupt or dishonest conduct in the office, whether of profit or honour.[17] At common law, if allegations merely imputed incompetence, a distinction was drawn between offices of profit and offices of honour. An imputation of incompetence in the discharge of an office of profit was actionable per se at common law, and continues to be so under the Act. In respect of an office of honour, a mere imputation of incompetence was not actionable per se unless the charge, if true, would have been a ground for removing the plaintiff from his office.[18] Following the Act, a slander relating to an office of honour is actionable per se only if it imputes either dishonesty or want of integrity, or such incompetence as would be a ground for removal from office.[19]

(4) IMPUTATION OF THE UNCHASTITY OF A WOMAN

The loosely-worded Slander of Women Act 1891 provides that 'words spoken and published … which impute unchastity or adultery to any woman or girl, shall not require special damage to render them actionable'. Imputation of 'unchastity' has been held to include the imputation of lesbianism;[20] and it is assumed, though the Act does not say

---

14 *Taylor v Hall* (1742) 2 Stra 1189.
15 (1844) 7 Man & G 334.
16 [1916] 2 AC 481.
17 *Booth v Arnold* [1895] 1 QB 571, CA.
18 *Alexander v Jenkins* [1892] 1 QB 797, CA.
19 *Robinson v Ward* (1958) 108 L Jo 491.
20 *Kerr v Kennedy* [1942] 1 KB 409, [1942] 1 All ER 412.

so expressly, that it confers the right to sue upon the woman alone, and not her alleged male partner in the act of unchastity. Slang expressions of unchastity are probably enough, but gestures and other media of communication, not being 'words', fall outside the Act.[1]

(D)   SPECIAL DAMAGE AND REMOTENESS OF DAMAGE

The question of what 'special damage' must be proved in respect of those forms of slander which are not actionable per se seems so intertwined with the problem of remoteness of damage in defamation that both these topics will be considered under the one heading.

Some material loss is required if an allegation of special damage is to be substantiated. So, for instance, loss of employment,[2] the refusal of persons to enter into contracts with the plaintiff,[3] the loss of hospitality from friends proved to have provided food or drink on former occasions would all qualify.[4] A mere threat of material loss is insufficient,[5] but it is uncertain whether loss of consortium,[6] either by husband or wife, is special damage. Consider *Lynch v Knight*.[7]

> The defendant told the plaintiff's husband that the plaintiff had almost been seduced before their marriage, whereupon the husband made her leave their home. Her action in slander claiming loss of consortium as special damage failed.

The ground of the decision was not that loss of consortium is not special damage, but rather that the damage was too remote. We suggest that Lord Campbell was correct in his assertion in that case that loss of consortium may constitute special damage.[8]

In *Allsop v Allsop*,[9] a plaintiff suffered physical illness as a result of the mental suffering she sustained following the slander. This was held not to be special damage. Noting that mental distress and bodily harm may be taken account of by way of aggravation in assessing damages in defamation,[10] *Allsop* must be taken as deciding that special damage in slander must be damage in respect of a primary interest – that is, loss of esteem or association – and that the primary purpose of the law of defamation is not to protect against psychiatric harm resulting from the apprehension of the effects of defamatory matter being published to third persons.

The extent to which, if at all, the law of remoteness in defamation differs from that in the remainder of the law of torts has historically raised difficulties. In the first half of the nineteenth century, any damage caused by the wrongful act of a third party was too remote a consequence of the defamation of the defendant. Thus, a person *wrongfully* dismissed by his employer in consequence of the defendant's slander failed

1   Sign-language is a probable exception.
2   *Coward v Wellington* (1836) 7 C & P 531.
3   *Storey v Challands* (1837) 8 C & P 234.
4   *Davies v Solomon* (1871) LR 7 QB 112. The rationale is that the loss of food and drink represents a loss of material value.
5   *Michael v Spiers and Pond Ltd* (1909) 101 LT 352.
6   Spousal support.
7   (1861) 9 HL Cas 577.
8   Ibid, at 589-91. His dictum was approved by Lord Goddard CJ in *Best v Samuel Fox & Co Ltd* [1952] AC 716 at 732, [1952] 2 All ER 394, HL. And see also *Wright v Cedzich* (1930) 43 CLR 493 at 530, H Ct of Australia (per Rich J), and *Lampert v Eastern National Omnibus Co* [1954] 2 All ER 719n, [1954] 1 WLR 1047.
9   (1860) 5 H & N 534.
10   Ibid at 539 (per Bramwell B).

in his attempt to sue his employer in *Vicars v Wilcocks*.[11] Crucially, his dismissal was not 'the legal and natural result' of the defendant having defamed him to his employer. The rule that defamers were liable only for the natural and necessary consequences of their acts[12] does not, however, survive the decision of the Court of Appeal in *Slipper v BBC*.[13] It is clear that the ordinary principles of remoteness of damage now apply as much to defamation as to any other tort.[14] Thus, the key question is now: was the kind of damage suffered by the plaintiff a reasonably foreseeable consequence of the defendant's act?[15] Accordingly, if a tabloid newspaper charges a distinguished law professor with sexual harassment and the university suspends him, and his publishers cancel his book contract, he may claim compensation for the whole of that loss.

Particular problems arise in defamation where additional loss results from a repetition of the libel. In *Slipper v BBC* itself, allegations in the original broadcast were given even wider publicity in newspaper reviews of the programme. The Court of Appeal refused to strike out the part of the claim dealing with that damage. While unauthorised repetition might, on occasion, constitute a novus actus interveniens – breaking the chain of causation – there has never been an absolute rule that the defamer cannot be liable for the consequences of such a repetition. Thus, if we write to the Students' Union claiming a colleague is embezzling the Student Law Society's funds, it is very much foreseeable that this allegation will be repeated. If the letter had not been sent, but another colleague took it from one our desks and sent it to the *Sun* newspaper, there would be a break in the chain of causation, in just the same way as in any other tort.[16]

---

11 (1806) 8 East 1.
12 *Ward v Weeks* (1830) 7 Bing 211.
13 [1991] 1 QB 283, [1991] 1 All ER 165, CA. See also *Sutcliffe v Pressdram* Ltd [1991] 1 QB 153.
14 In *Lynch v Knight*, Lord Wensleydale stated that '[t]o make the words actionable ... the consequence must be such as ... might fairly and reasonably have been anticipated and feared would follow': (1861) 9 HL Cas 577, 600.
15 On this test, the *decision* in *Vicars v Wilcocks* would probably still be the same. The illegality of the employer's action would give it an element of independence from the defendant's defamation and thus render it unforeseeable.
16 See *Weld-Blundell v Stephens* [1920] AC 956, HL.

Chapter 23

Defences and remedies

Some of the defences already discussed in relation to other torts may also be available in defamation. The same rules apply so, except for consent and assumption of risk, they are therefore not dealt with here. But several other defences, peculiar to defamation, must also be discussed. To a large extent these defences, particularly the ones based on privilege, reflect the fact that defamation law recognises the vital interest in freedom of speech. At its extreme – in cases attracting an absolute privilege – the law will allow comment to be made regardless of whether it is true, and regardless of the defendant's malicious motive.

SECTION I. CONSENT AND ASSUMPTION OF RISK

The better opinion is that consent is an independent defence in defamation.[1] Someone who telephones a newspaper with false information about himself will not be able to sue in defamation when the newspaper publishes it; but he does not consent to the publication in a newspaper of a story about himself that he told at a parish vestry meeting.[2] Consent need not always be implied. Where consent is explicitly supplied on a contractual basis, for example, this too will defeat a defamation action.[3]

It is sometimes a difficult question of fact to decide whether a plaintiff has consented to the repetition of a defamatory statement. If, for instance, the plaintiff asked the defendant to repeat it, so as to abandon the privilege attaching to the occasion of the original publication, or because he did not properly understand on the first occasion, he would not be consenting.

The defence of assumption of risk was upheld in *Chapman v Ellesmere*.[4] The plaintiff maintained that even if he had consented to the publication of a report of an inquiry by the Jockey Club, he had not consented to its publication in such a form as to contain an innuendo against him. The Court of Appeal rejected this plea on the ground that, in effect, the plaintiff had agreed to run the risk of the particular form that the statement might take.[5]

---

1 But see *Russell v Duke of Norfolk* [1949] 1 All ER 109 at 120, CA (per Denning LJ). This issue may be crucial if, for example, A asks B for a reference and B is actuated by malice in providing one, unless the consent is deemed to be to a non-malicious reference only.
2 *Cook v Ward* (1830) 6 Bing 409.
3 *Cookson v Harewood* [1932] 2 KB 478n, [1931] All ER Rep 533, CA.
4 [1932] 2 KB 431, [1932] All ER Rep 221, CA.
5 Ibid, at 464 (per Slesser LJ).

SECTION 2.   JUSTIFICATION

It is no part of the plaintiff's case to establish that the defendant's statement was untrue: the plaintiff has merely to prove the publication of a statement defamatory of him. If, however, the defendant can prove that his statement was true, he has a complete defence even if he made the statement maliciously. The rationale is that 'the law will not permit a man to recover damages in respect of an injury to a character which he does not... possess'.[6] The defendant does not discharge this burden by proving that he honestly believed it to be true. Rather, he must prove that it was true.[7] Nor will it avail him to show that he repeated accurately to a third party what he heard from another, even though he told that third party that it was a mere repetition.[8] If the words impute the commission of a specific offence, it is not enough to prove that the plaintiff was suspected of the alleged offence.[9] These restrictions on the defence are clearly necessary to prevent it from being abused.

Before deciding whether the defendant can successfully plead justification, one must first discover, in accordance with the rules discussed above, what the statement complained of has been interpreted to mean.[10] If the statement contains an innuendo, that too must be justified.[11] And even if the defendant justifies the innuendo, he will still fail unless he also justifies the primary meaning of the words used; for they form a separate head of claim.[12] If the defendant enters a plea of justification and a denial of the innuendo, success on the first plea but a failure to deny the innuendo means that the defence fails. And just as the plaintiff must specifically plead the meanings he relies on as defamatory, so must the defendant pleading justification 'make it clear to the plaintiff what is the case he is seeking to set up'.[13]

Obviously, then, many problems on justification are merely points of interpretation where the material question is: 'Does that which is proved to be true tally with that which the defendant's statement is interpreted to mean?'. *Wakley v Cooke* is a typical case.[14]

> The defendant called the plaintiff a 'libellous journalist'. He proved that a judgment against the plaintiff for libel had once been obtained. Because the defamatory statement complained of meant that the journalist habitually libelled people, the defendant had not justified it.

---

6   *M'Pherson v Daniels* (1829) 10 B & C 263.
7   *Peters v Bradlaugh* (1888) 4 TLR 414, Div Ct. Has the defendant merely to adduce a preponderance of evidence that the crime has been committed, or to prove it beyond reasonable doubt? The former test would appear to be sufficient: *Laurence v Chester Chronicle* (1986) Times, 8 February; cf *Hornal v Neuberger Products Ltd* [1957] 1 QB 247, [1956] 3 All ER 970, CA.
8   *M'Pherson v Daniels* (1829) 10 B & C 263. On the other hand, repetition of a prevalent rumour may be justified following *Aspro Travel v Owners Abroad plc* [1995] 4 All ER 728 where the Court of Appeal refused to strike out the defendants' plea of justification on this basis.
9   *Rubber Improvement Ltd v Daily Telegraph Ltd* [1964] AC 234 at 274-5, HL (per Lord Hodson).
10   See ch 22 ante.
11   *Prior v Wilson* (1856) 1 CBNS 95.
12   *Watkin v Hall* (1868) LR 3 QB 396 at 402 (per Blackburn J); *Rubber Improvement Ltd v Daily Telegraph Ltd* [1964] AC 234, [1963] 2 All ER 151, HL.
13   *Lucas-Box v Associated Newspaper Group* [1986] 1 All ER 177, [1986] 1 WLR 147, CA. And see *Morrell v International Thomson Publishing Co Ltd* [1989] 3 All ER 733, CA.
14   (1849) 4 Exch 511. On the question of whether it is more defamatory of a woman to allege that she has had an extra-marital affair with one man rather than another see *Khashoggi v IPC Magazines Ltd* [1986] 3 All ER 577, [1986] 1 WLR 1412, CA.

The opposite result prevailed in *Bookbinder v Tebbit*.[15] The defendant had alleged at an electoral meeting that the plaintiff had squandered public money on a campaign to print 'Support Nuclear Free Zones' on council stationery. He sought to justify his claim by advancing evidence of general financial mismanagement on the part of the plaintiff, the leader of the local council. The Court of Appeal struck out those particulars of justification. They did not pertain to the very specific 'sting' of the libel. One cannot justify an express claim of misconduct by generalised evidence of the plaintiff's behaviour.

The defence will not fail if the statement is substantially true: if it is inaccurate only in minor points of detail, the defendant succeeds.[16] Similarly, 'it is unnecessary to repeat every word which might have been the subject of the original comment. As much must be justified as meets the sting of the charge, and if anything be contained in a charge which does not add to the sting of it, that need not be justified'.[17] In *Clarke v Taylor* the facts were as follows.[18]

The defendant accused the plaintiff, C, of taking part in a 'grand swindling concern' at Manchester, and added that 'C had been at Leeds for one or two days before his arrival in [Manchester]… and is supposed to have made considerable purchases there. It is hoped, however, that the detection of his plans in Manchester will be learnt in time to prevent any serious losses from taking place'. The defendant justified the statement that the plaintiff had swindled at Manchester, but not the remainder of the statement. It was held that this was a sufficient plea of justification because the remaining words did not allege any further act of criminality.

Many statements contain both statements of fact and opinion: for example, 'X was drunk again last night; his behaviour is disgusting'. If the defendant relies on a plea of justification in respect of this, he must prove not only that X was drunk but also that the statement that his behaviour was disgusting (in so far as that comment adds to the sting of the libel) was accurate. If the further statement introduces new matter, or implies the existence of further facts, he must prove those further facts which justify the terms in which he has described the plaintiff.[19]

At common law, every material statement had to be justified. If, therefore, the defendant could prove the truth of three charges but not that of a distinct fourth charge, the defence failed, although these circumstances would be relevant in assessing damages. This rule is modified by section 5 of the Defamation Act 1952 which stipulates:

In an action for libel or slander in respect of words containing two or more distinct charges against the plaintiff, a defence of justification shall not fail by reason only that the truth of every charge is not proved if the words not proved to be true do not materially injure the plaintiff's reputation having regard to the truth of the remaining charges.[20]

It is now therefore important to know when there are several charges. The section can only apply when the defendant has proved first, that at least one charge, itself incapable of further division, is substantially true, after having been separated from the remaining

15 [1989] 1 All ER 1169, [1989] 1 WLR 640, CA.
16 *Alexander v North Eastern Rly Co* (1865) 6 B & S 340 (defendants published notice that plaintiffs had been sentenced to a fine of £1 with alternative of three weeks' imprisonment: in fact, the alternative was only two weeks' imprisonment).
17 *Edwards v Bell* (1824) 1 Bing 403 at 409 (per Burrough J).
18 (1836) 2 Bing NC 654.
19 *Cooper v Lawson* (1838) 8 Ad & El 746. There is sometimes another possible defence; that of fair comment (as to which see post).
20 A defendant who relies on s 5 must plead it as a defence: *Moore v News of the World* [1972] 1 QB 441, [1972] 1 All ER, 915, CA.

charges and secondly, that it is itself incapable of further severance. At common law, the courts had also to consider when charges were severable, because any severable charge could be separately justified with a view to reducing damages or, perhaps, establishing some other defence in respect of other charges. Presumably, the common law rules on what is a severable charge apply also under the Act.[1]

The effect of the Act is illustrated by considering its application to the facts of the pre-Act decision in *Goodburne v Bowman*.[2]

> The plaintiff was alleged by the defendant to have made, in each of his two periods of office as mayor, a small secret profit from the corporation on selling coals to the poor. The defendant justified the statement by pleading that the plaintiff did this in one of these terms of office only. This plea failed because it did not establish the truth of all the material statements in the libel.

Under the 1952 Act, it would be open to the jury, on similar facts, to find that, in view of the truth of one of the two charges, the other did not separately, materially injure his reputation. The plaintiff cannot evade the section by basing his cause of action, in the first place, solely on those residuary parts of the defendant's statement which are not true; if the different parts of an article are not plainly severable the defendant can base a defence of justification on the whole of the article.[3] Where several defamatory allegations have a common 'sting' they are not to be regarded as separate and distinct. The defendant must justify the 'sting' and 'it is fortuitous that what is in fact similar fact evidence is found in the publication'.[4]

If a defendant persists in a plea of justification and thereby prolongs the period in which the damage from the publication continues to spread, a greater sum by way of aggravated damages may be awarded against him.[5]

Before the enactment of the Human Rights Act 1998, the completeness of the defence of justification required great emphasis. Even if the defendant was inspired by malice, or even if, when he made the statements, he did not believe them to be true, his defence was sound so long as they were true. Defamation law offers no protection against even the most gross invasion of privacy per se. However, once the 1998 Act comes into force,[6] some degree of protection for privacy in its own right will be introduced. It may then be the case that newspapers in this country will no longer be able to rake up someone's forgotten past, and ruin them, without risking tortious liability. Whether this will be the effect of the Act depends upon the construction that will be placed on Article 8 of the Convention.[7] For under section 6(3)(b) of the Act – which provision prohibits public bodies acting inconsistently with Convention rights – a public body is defined as 'any person certain of whose functions are functions of a public nature'.

A further curb on the freedom of the press to dig up aspects of a person's past is contained in the Rehabilitation of Offenders Act 1974. In relation to 'spent' convictions of 'rehabilitated persons', the Act specifies that after the expiry of certain defined periods – the duration of which differs according to the length of sentence – convictions (other

---

1 See *Clarkson v Lawson* (1830) 6 Bing 587; *Davis v Billing* (1891) 8 TLR 58, CA; *Fleming v Dollar* (1889) 23 QBD 388, CA.
2 (1833) 9 Bing 667.
3 *S and K Holdings v Throgmorton Publications Ltd* [1972] 3 All ER 497, CA, distinguishing *Plato Films Ltd v Speidel* [1961] AC 1090, HL.
4 *Polly Peck (Holdings) plc v Trelford* [1986] 2 All ER 84 at 102; *Khashoggi v IPC Magazines Ltd* [1986] 3 All ER 577, [1986] 1 WLR 1412, CA.
5 *Cassell & Co Ltd v Broome* [1972] AC 1027 at 1125, HL (per Lord Diplock). As to late entry of a plea of justification see *Atkinson v Fitzwalter* [1987] 1 All ER 483, [1987] 1 WLR 201, CA.
6 At the time of writing, it is expected that the Act will come into force in the year 2000.
7 Article 8 of the Convention protects respect for private and family life.

than a sentence of life imprisonment or one of more than two-and-a-half years, or one of preventive detention) become spent and the convicted person becomes rehabilitated. Section 8 provides that where a plaintiff sues for defamation because a spent conviction has been dug up against him, proof that the matter complained of was true will not avail the publisher of a defence if the publication is proved to have been made with malice. The onus of establishing the presence of malice – defined as 'some spiteful, irrelevant or unproper motive' – lies with the plaintiff.[8]

SECTION 3.   INNOCENT DISSEMINATORS

(A)   INNOCENT PUBLICATION: THE COMMON LAW

Although, as we saw in the previous chapter, a person is normally deemed to have published defamatory matter even if he did not know it to be defamatory, an exception to this rule exists where the defendant did not play a primary part in its publication. Such defendants typically include newsvendors, booksellers and the like. They may be referred to by the generic term 'innocent disseminators' and it is well established that such distributors are not liable for their acts of publication if they are 'innocent' in the following sense.

The leading case is *Vizetelly v Mudie's Select Library Ltd* where the proprietors of a circulating library were held to be distributors to whom this special rule would apply if they were proved to be 'innocent'. The rule was clearly set out by Romer LJ in that case. He stated that a defence would lie in respect of 'a person who is not the printer or the first or main publisher of a work which contains a libel, but [who] has only taken, what I may call, a subordinate part in disseminating it'.[9] To determine whether the defendant was such a person, he must succeed in showing:

(1) that he was innocent of any knowledge of the libel contained in the work disseminated by him, (2) that there was nothing in the work or the circumstances under which it came to him or was disseminated by him which ought to have led him to suppose that it contained a libel[10] and (3) that, when the work was disseminated by him, it was not by any negligence on his part that he did not know that it contained the libel.[11]

Whether he does so succeed is a question of fact for the jury.[12] In *Vizetelly's* case, the jury found that the proprietors had not established their 'innocence': in a publication taken by the defendants, the publishers had circulated a notice asking for the return of copies of a certain book in order to withdraw a particular page containing defamatory matter. The defendants ignored the circular, and, moreover, failed to employ a reader to peruse the novels in their library. On the other hand, libraries need not have scholarly works read before circulating them.[13] Nor, more surprisingly, it seems, need the importers of publishers' remainders of American detective stories read them.[14]

---

8   *Herbage v Pressdram Ltd* [1984] 2 All ER 769, [1984] 1 WLR 1160, CA.
9   [1900] 2 QB 170 at 180, CA. See also *Emmens v Pottle* (1885) 16 QBD 354, CA; *Goldsmith v Sperrings Ltd* [1977] 2 All ER 566, [1977] 1 WLR 478, CA (newsvendor).
10 In *Goldsmith v Sperrings* (supra) attempts to strike out actions against several vendors of *Private Eye* as an attempt to suppress that journal altogether failed. There was evidence that the vendors ought to have been aware of alleged libels.
11 [1900] 2 QB 170 at 180, CA.
12 Cf *Sun Life Assurance Co of Canada v W H Smith & Sons Ltd* [1933] All ER Rep 432, CA.
13 *Weldon v Times Book Co Ltd* (1911) 28 TLR 143, CA.
14 *Bottomley v F W Woolworth & Co Ltd* (1932) 48 TLR 521, CA.

Besides newsvendors, booksellers and circulating libraries, a porter delivering parcels has been held to be within the exception.[15] No doubt persons lending books gratuitously, persons making gifts of them, and record dealers are also protected. It is irrelevant to determine whether the Post Office, when delivering mail, or British Telecommunications operating its telephone services, are within it, because legislation exempts both of them and their employees from any liability in tort in respect of postal packets or the telephone service.[16]

(B) DEFAMATION ACT 1996, s 1

The common law defence of innocent dissemination was largely subsumed within, but not technically repealed by, section 1 of the 1996 Act. Accordingly, it is unlikely that the *Vizetelly* defence will be much relied upon in future. The statutory defence is a broader one that is (normally) no less onerous to invoke. Under section 1(1), a person has a defence if he shows that he was not the 'author, editor or publisher'[17] of the matter complained of; that he took reasonable care in relation to its publication, and that he did not know (or have reason to believe) that what he did caused or contributed to the publication of defamatory matter.

The defence is wider than the common law defence of innocent dissemination in that a much wider class of persons may avail themselves of it.[18] It largely mirrors the *Vizetelly* test in that the defendant has a burden and standard of proof that require him to show his innocence as regards knowledge of the defamatory nature of the statement,[19] and that he took reasonable care in relation to his part in its publication. So far as the reasonable care test is concerned, under section 1(5) of the Act, the court is directed to have regard to three specific factors: (a) the degree of the defendant's responsibility for the content of the statement complained of, or for the decision to publish it; (b) the nature or circumstances of the publication;[20] and (c) the previous conduct or character of the author, editor or publisher.[1]

---

15 *Day v Bream* (1837) 2 Mood & R 54. And so presumably is the girl who delivers the morning paper.

16 Post Office Act 1969 and British Telecommunications Act 1981.

17 The notion of publisher, for the purposes of the Act, is confined to that of 'commercial publisher'; that is, 'a person whose business is issuing material to the public': s 1(2).

18 Under s 1(3)(a) of the Act, those involved in the production process or printing of books, newspapers and magazines are also covered. So, too, are those who distribute information by way of electronic media such as Internet users (s 1(3)(c)), those, such as chat-show and phone-in hosts, who broadcast information in live programmes (s 1(3)(d)) and those, such as Internet service providers, who operate communications systems which are used to transmit defamatory statements (s 1(3)(e)).

19 Strictly, *Vizetelly* required ignorance of *a libel* (a narrower concept than that of a defamatory remark). To this extent, the defence is more restrictive than its common law equivalent in that knowledge of a defamatory statement (eg, one known to be defamatory, but believed to be true) will defeat the defence.

20 The Act is unclear on what is meant by 'the circumstances of the publication'. Presumably, however, remarks made about infamous or notorious persons would require greater concern than remarks about less well-known people.

1 Presumably, here, the standard of care demanded is greater in relation to publishers with a history of producing defamatory material.

(C) OFFER OF AMENDS: DEFAMATION ACT 1996, ss 2-4

Section 4 of the Defamation Act 1952 formerly provided a little used and widely criticised, technical defence in cases of innocent publication.[2] This section has now been repealed by Schedule 2 to the 1996 Act. In its stead, a more modern, revamped defence of 'offer to make amends' has been introduced.[3] The availability of the new defence is confined to those defendants who did not know, or had no reason to believe, that the statement in question referred to the plaintiff and was untrue and defamatory of him.[4]

The new defence may only be invoked where the offer to make amends is in writing and states that it is such an offer under the 1996 Act.[5] In addition, the offer must satisfy three further prerequisites: it must contain a correction to, and apology for, the original statement; it must state a willingness to publish that correction and apology; it must make clear that the publisher agrees to pay to the aggrieved party such sum as may be agreed between them, or, otherwise, judicially determined.[6] If the offer of amends is accepted, section 3(2) prohibits the aggrieved party from subsequently bringing or continuing defamation proceedings. If, on the other hand, the offer is not accepted, the offer may nonetheless be invoked as a defence in any subsequent defamation proceedings brought by the plaintiff.[7] For this reason, we submit that it would normally be unwise for a plaintiff to reject an offer of amends. Should he instead pursue an action in the courts, in order for the offer not to constitute a defence, the plaintiff would have to show, first, that the defendant knew or had reason to believe that the statement referred to the plaintiff and, secondly, that it was both false and defamatory.[8]

The offer of amends defence may prove to be much more widely used than the former defence under the Defamation Act 1952 that it replaces. It no longer requires the alleged defamer to prove his innocence: this is now presumed under section 4(3).[9] Accordingly, it effects a significant change in the location of the burden of proof. On the other hand, any defendant who wishes to use this defence is debarred from resorting to any other defence (such as justification).[10] This means that he is forced to choose between, on the one hand, definitely paying moderate damages (that he either agrees with the plaintiff, or are judicially determined), or, on the other hand, risking paying damages in full if another defence – such as justification – were held not to be available.[11]

---

2 The principal problem with s 4 of the 1952 Act was that it placed the onus on the defendant to demonstrate his innocence by proving the absence of negligence. (For further details see the 9th edition of this work.)
3 Defamation Act 1996, ss 2-4.
4 Ibid, s 4(3).
5 Ibid, s 2(3).
6 Ibid, s 2(3), (4).
7 Ibid, s 4(2).
8 This imposition of the burden of proof upon the plaintiff occurs by virtue of s 4(3) which introduced a statutory presumption of the publisher's innocence, thus giving him the right to invoke his offer of amends as a defence. Furthermore, even where the offer is rejected, the offer may be used to mitigate any subsequent award of damages: s 4(5).
9 Another difference between this provision and s 4 of the 1952 Act is as follows. If the offer is refused, the case will proceed but D may still use the making of the offer as a defence where he knew (a) that the publication was defamatory of P but (b) D reasonably believed that what was said was true. This was not the case under the old law.
10 Defamation Act 1996, s 4(4).
11 See further Milmo 'The Defamation Bill' (1995) 145 NLJ 1340.

SECTION 4.   ABSOLUTE PRIVILEGE

Certain occasions are deemed to be so important that those making statements upon them are not liable in defamation despite their statements being untrue and even malicious. These occasions, where the public interest in freedom of communication is paramount, are called cases of absolute privilege.

(A)   PARLIAMENTARY PROCEEDINGS

By the law of Parliament, the courts for centuries had no jurisdiction to hear evidence of proceedings in Parliament.[12] This immunity extended beyond all statements made in the course of parliamentary proceedings to all reports, papers, votes, and proceedings published by, or under the authority of, either House.[13] This assertion of 'Parliamentary privilege' meant not only that parliamentary proceedings could not found an action in defamation but also that such proceedings could not be relied on in relation to a claim arising out of a non-parliamentary publication. Thus, in one case, the court would not admit evidence of statements contained in *Hansard* that the plaintiff sought to introduce in order to demonstrate malice.[14]

Section 13 of the Defamation Act 1996 introduced a significant change in the law on parliamentary privilege.[15] It permits an MP to waive the prohibition on adducing evidence of parliamentary proceedings enshrined in Article 9 of the Bill of Rights 1688.[16] It also permits, by virtue of section 13(5), evidence contained in such documents as reports produced by parliamentary committees to be adduced. Section 13 therefore represents an important (and not uncontroversial) constitutional change.[17]

(B)   EXECUTIVE MATTERS

In the leading case of *Chatterton v Secretary of State for India*,[18] it was held that a letter from the Secretary of State for India to his Parliamentary Under-Secretary providing

---

12   Bill of Rights 1688 Art 9; *Ex p Wason* (1869) LR 4 QB 573 at 576 (per Cockburn CJ). Hence, the frequent challenge by the victim to the MP to repeat outside the House his attacks on the victim's reputation. Petitions addressed to Parliament are within the immunity: *Lake v King* (1670) 1 Wms Saund 131. But there is no general immunity for letters written to MPs: *Rivlin v Bilainkin* [1953] 1 QB 485, [1953] 1 All ER 534. Letters from MPs to the Speakers do fall within the immunity: *Rost v Edwards* [1990] 2 QB 460, [1990] 2 All ER 641 at 650.

13   Parliamentary Papers Act 1840, s 1, offsetting *Stockdale v Hansard* (1839) 9 Ad & El 1. Significantly, the section does not confer absolute privilege; it orders the judge to 'stay', whereby the suit 'shall be deemed and taken to be finally put an end to'. Since Command Papers are outside this immunity, the method of bringing them within it is to use an unopposed return under the Parliamentary Paper, but that cannot be done if Parliament is not sitting.

14   *Church of Scientology of California v Johnson-Smith* [1972] 1 QB 522, [1972] 1 All ER 378. Compare *Rost v Edwards* [1990] 2 QB 460, [1990] 2 All ER 641 where Popplewell J did allow evidence drawn from the *Register of Members' Interests* on the basis that this was a public document.

15   Cf the common law rule in *Prebble v Television New Zealand* [1995] 1 AC 321, [1994] 3 All ER 407.

16   Section 13 operates *in favour* of MPs only. The waiver enables an MP to vindicate his character in a defamation action by adducing evidence of Parliamentary proceedings. It does not, by contrast, allow the defendant to adduce evidence from a similar source in order to substantiate his argument: s 13(4).

17   For comment see Sharland and Loveland 'The Defamation Act 1996 and Political Libels' [1997] PL 113.

18   [1895] 2 QB 189, CA. The Parliamentary Commissioner Act 1967, s 10(5) also gives an absolute privilege to the Parliamentary Commissioner for his reports to Parliament and for certain of

the material for the answer to a parliamentary question was absolutely privileged. It is impossible to say how high in the hierarchy of civil servants a defendant must be before he enjoys this privilege, but a message from the High Commissioner for Australia to his Prime Minister about a matter of commerce which concerned the Government of Australia has also been held to be privileged.[19] Communications with the European Commission relating to enforcement of competition proceedings similarly fall within absolute privilege.[20]

It has been doubted whether those below the status of minister may claim the privilege.[1] If it were not for the cases relating to military communications, to be considered next, one might confidently submit that routine communications between persons not in charge of government departments are outside the privilege. Indeed, one might even doubt whether the courts would willingly extend it at all beyond the limits reached in the decisions above.

In *Dawkins v Lord Paulet*[2] it was held that a report on the plaintiff from his superior officer to his commander-in-chief could not form the basis of an action for libel. The rationale of the case is not clear, however. Cockburn CJ dissented; Lush J based his judgment on the principle that the army was outside the jurisdiction of the courts,[3] but one of the three grounds of Mellor J's judgment was that such letters were absolutely privileged.[4] It is submitted that this is not strong enough authority for the proposition that communications within the civil service generally that relate to the character and ability of personnel are absolutely privileged. Nor does the case decide that civil servants below ministerial rank enjoy this absolute privilege; but such communications, as we shall see, would be adequately protected by the qualified privilege which doubtless attaches to them.

A final point in this context is that absolute privilege must not be confused with the procedural rule that the Crown, whether or not it is a party, cannot be compelled in any litigation, to produce or disclose the existence of any documents the production or disclosure of which would be contrary to the public interest.[5] In practice, because the Crown could decide at its discretion whether to produce the document, this rule has

---

his communications to MPs; the Local Commissioners have a similar absolute privilege under the Local Government Act 1974, s 32, as does the Legal Services Ombudsman under s 23 of the Courts and Legal Services Act 1990.

19 *M Isaacs & Sons Ltd v Cook* [1925] 2 KB 391.
20 *Hasselblad (GB) Ltd v Orbinson* [1985] QB 475, [1985] 1 All ER 173, CA. But should this more properly be regarded as 'judicial privilege'?
1 *Szalatnay-Stacho v Fink* [1946] 1 All ER 303 at 305 (per Henn Collins J); not considered, [1947] KB 1, CA; *Richards v Naum* [1967] 1 QB 620, [1966] 3 All ER 812, CA. On grounds of public policy, arising out of international comity, English courts will concede to foreign governments immunities similar to those accorded by way of privilege to the UK government. Thus, no action for libel lies in respect of an internal memorandum from a foreign embassy: *Fayed v Al-Tajir* [1988] QB 712, [1987] 2 All ER 396, CA.
2 (1869) LR 5 QB 94.
3 But see *Dawkins v Lord Rokeby* (1873) LR 8 QB 255, Ex Ch; affd (1875) LR 7 HL 744.
4 In *Gibbons v Duffell* (1932) 47 CLR 520, the High Court of Australia was confronted with the argument that the police were to be equated with the army, so that communications within the force were absolutely privileged. In *Merricks v Nott-Bower* [1965] 1 QB 57, [1964] 1 All ER 717, CA, the report by one high ranking police officer to another about a third police officer was held not to be so clearly the subject of absolute privilege that a claim in libel should be struck out.
5 Crown Proceedings Act 1947, s 28. And see *Schneider v Leigh* [1955] 2 QB 195, [1955] 2 All ER 173, CA.

effectively prevented plaintiffs from maintaining libel suits, even for communications within the civil service, which were not absolutely privileged.[6]

(C) JUDICIAL PROCEEDINGS

Statements made in proceedings before superior and inferior courts of record and magistrates' courts are privileged. The privilege extends to other tribunals recognised by law,[7] provided they are 'exercising functions equivalent to those of an established court of justice'.[8] In cases of doubt, 'the overriding factor is whether there will emerge from the proceedings a determination the truth and justice of which is a matter of public concern'.[9] Thus, an enquiry before an Inn of Court into the conduct of a barrister was absolutely privileged,[10] even though the body had no power to issue a subpoena, or to take evidence on oath, and sat in private. The disciplinary committee of the Law Society,[11] courts-martial[12] and select committees of the House of Commons[13] are also within the privilege. If the functions are merely administrative, or determine neither the rights, nor the guilt, nor the innocence of anyone, there is no absolute privilege, even though judicial procedures such as hearing evidence or summoning witnesses are used.[14] Justices dealing with applications for liquor licensing,[15] a meeting of the London County Council for the grant of music and dancing licences,[16] official industrial conciliation processes[17] and complaints to social security adjudication officers,[18] have all been held to be outside the scope of the privilege. Competition proceedings before the European Commission, by contrast, have been held to attract absolute privilege despite the administrative nature of their procedures: the public interest in the Commission's duty to enforce European competition law was held to outweigh the private interests of litigants seeking to vindicate their reputations.[19]

---

6   *Home v Bentinck* (1820) 2 Brod & Bing 130, Ex Ch, *Beatson v Skene* (1860) 5 H & N 838 and *West v West* (1911) 27 TLR 476, CA, are examples of cases where the rule was successfully used for that purpose. The House of Lords in *Conway v Rimmer* [1968] AC 910, [1968] 1 All ER 874 invested the courts with a residual power to demand production when the public interest does not demand non-disclosure. To this extent the Crown's discretion to withhold documents is curtailed. The House of Lords has suggested that only in very clear cases will that residual power be invoked: *Air Canada v Secretary of State for Trade (No 2)* [1983] 2 AC 394, [1983] 1 All ER 161, CA.

7   Either under statute or royal prerogative of justice: *Lincoln v Daniels* [1962] 1 QB 237, [1961] 3 All ER 740, CA.

8   *O'Connor v Waldron* [1935] AC 76 at 81, [1934] All ER Rep 281 at 283, PC. And see *Trapp v Mackie* [1979] 1 All ER 489, HL (a Scottish case on the privilege of a witness at an inquiry, but not one on defamation).

9   *Lincoln v Daniels* [1962] 1 QB 237 at 255-6, [1961] 3 All ER 740, CA (per Devlin LJ).

10 Ibid.

11 *Addis v Crocker* [1961] 1 QB 11, [1960] 2 All ER 629, CA.

12 *Dawkins v Lord Rokeby* (1873) LR 8 QB 255; affd (1875) LR 7 HL 744.

13 On principle, these would seem to have been more properly within the 'legislative' privilege, but this is not the basis of *Goffin v Donnelly* (1881) 6 QBD 307. But see now *Rost v Edwards* [1990] 2 QB 460, [1990] 2 All ER 641.

14 *O'Connor v Waldron* [1935] AC 76, [1934] All ER Rep 281, PC.

15 *Attwood v Chapman* [1914] 3 KB 275.

16 *Royal Aquarium and Summer and Winter Garden Society v Parkinson* [1892] 1 QB 431, CA.

17 *Tadd v Eastwood* [1985] ICR 132, [1985] IRLR 119, CA.

18 *Purdew and Purdew v Seress Smith* [1993] IRLR 77.

19 *Hasselblad (GB) Ltd v Orbinson* [1985] QB 475, [1985] 1 All ER 173, CA.

The privilege is enjoyed by judges, parties, witnesses,[20] counsel[1] and solicitors,[2] and presumably also jurors. Judges are protected although their statements are malicious or irrelevant.[3] Whether others than these who are engaged in the proceedings are privileged is doubtful.[4] They are certainly not protected where the statement is so irrelevant that it is no longer made by a person qua participant in the proceedings.[5] It is usually stated that the privilege is lost when the court has no jurisdiction.[6]

Finally, it should be noted that the privilege extends to documents initiating,[7] or made in the course of the proceedings (for example, pleadings and affidavits).[8] However, documents prepared prior to proceedings that do not have any *necessary* link with those proceedings are not privileged in this way. Accordingly, in one case where a defamatory letter was written by the defendant council to the plaintiff's solicitor in the course of pre-hearing negotiations, it was held that, since the letter's contents did not have any necessary import for any future legal proceedings, it was inappropriate to allow the defendant to claim a privilege.[9]

(D)   SOLICITOR-CLIENT COMMUNICATIONS

Closely related to the privilege just discussed is the question of how far statements to solicitors by either clients or witnesses before trial, are protected. If the purpose of not restricting the prosecution of judicial proceedings is to be attained, it would be unrealistic to deny to a witness privilege in respect of a proof of his evidence made immediately before trial. The House of Lords has therefore held in *Watson v M'Ewan* that a witness making a proof after the issue of a writ, but before trial, is absolutely privileged.[10] This extension by the House of Lords of the privilege surrounding judicial proceedings is restricted to matters outside the proceedings which are necessary for the administration of justice. It does not extend to a complaint to the Bar Council, even though that is a recognised channel for complaints by the public about members of the Bar.[11]

20   *Seaman v Netherclift* (1876) 2 CPD 53, CA.
1   *Munster v Lamb* (1883) 11 QBD 588, CA.
2   *Mackay v Ford* (1860) 5 H & N 792.
3   *Scott v Stansfield* (1868) LR 3 Exch 220.
4   The doubt arises because judicial immunity may derive from the separate defence of judicial act (see ante) not from privilege in defamation: *Hamilton v Anderson* (1858) 3 Macq 363 at 375, HL; cf, *Law v Llewellyn* [1906] 1 KB 487, CA.
5   In answer to the question: 'Were you at York on a certain day?', a statement by a witness: 'Yes, and AB picked my pocket there', would not be made qua witness (per Cockburn CJ, in *Seaman v Netherclift* (1876) 2 CPD 53 at 57, CA) if the proceedings were entirely unconnected with AB.
6   Eg *Gatley* § 391.
7   But not, if the initiating document is wrongly sent to the Bar Council, instead of to an Inn of Court: *Lincoln v Daniels* [1962] 1 QB 237, [1961] 3 All ER 740, CA.
8   See *Lilley v Roney* (1892) 61 LJQB 727; *Revis v Smith* (1856) 18 CB 126; *Mahon v Rahn* [1997] 3 All ER 687; *Taylor v Serious Fraud Office* [1997] 4 All ER 887. *Veal v Heard* (1930) 46 TLR 448, Div Ct (which held that a notice of objection to the renewal by a judicial body of a licence is not privileged) is wrongly decided on this point. For the pre-trial statements of witnesses, see infra. What of a false oath leading to a warrant of arrest? The privilege confers a general defence to all torts, eg conspiracy, and not merely to defamation: *Marrinan v Vibart* [1963] 1 QB 528, [1962] 3 All ER 380, CA.
9   *Waple v Surrey County Council* [1998] 1 All ER 624, CA. See also *Daniels v Griffith* [1998] EMLR 489, CA (no privilege in respect of a defamatory statement (relating to P) given by D to the police which was later used by a parole board considering P's parole because the parole board was not a court of law); cf *Mond v Hyde* [1998] 3 All ER 833, CA (official receiver covered by privilege in respect of statements made in bankruptcy proceedings in so far as those statements were made for the purpose of court proceedings).
10   [1905] AC 480, HL.
11   *Lincoln v Daniels* [1962] 1 QB 237, [1961] 3 All ER 740, CA.

Whether all communications between solicitor and client should be so privileged is clearly a different matter. Yet consider *More v Weaver*.[12]

> In a discussion between solicitor and client on whether a loan should be called in, the plaintiff was defamed. Importantly, the discussion bore no relation to any actual or prospective litigation. The statement was held to be absolutely privileged.

In *Minter v Priest*, the House of Lords expressly left open the question of whether *More v Weaver* had been rightly decided.[13] We suggest that *More v Weaver* was wrongly decided, in that, in the cases which it purported to follow,[14] solicitor-client communications were only held to be absolutely privileged because they referred to judicial proceedings actually pending. There is, in our view, little to no justification for absolute privilege except in relation to those solicitor-client communications relating to potential judicial proceedings.

(E) REPORTS OF JUDICIAL PROCEEDINGS

A fair and accurate report of judicial proceedings heard in public and published contemporaneously with those proceedings, is absolutely privileged under section 14 of the Defamation Act 1996. For the purposes of this section, 'contemporaneous' publications include those that appear 'as soon as practicable after publication is permitted'.[15] And the 'judicial proceedings' to which the Act refers are specified to mean any proceedings in a UK court, the European Court of Justice or the European Court of Human Rights.[16] Unlike the corresponding provision in the previous legislation[17] – which confined privilege to newspaper, television and radio reports – section 14 confers absolute privilege upon contemporaneous reports that appear by virtue of *any* medium of publication.

Reports of such interruptions to judicial proceedings as may be regarded as taking place in the course of the proceedings (although they may be applications with which the judge has no power to deal) were protected under the old law.[18] Presumably, they remain so protected under the 1996 Act. Similarly, nothing in the new legislation changes the common law rule that it is for the jury to decide whether the report is a fair and accurate one.[19]

Once any absolute privilege is established, it extends to consequential communications in the ordinary course of things to clerks, typists and the like.[20]

SECTION 5. QUALIFIED PRIVILEGE

In certain circumstances, it is thought desirable that reflections on the reputation of another, although untrue, should not give rise to tortious liability, provided those

---

12 [1928] 2 KB 520, CA.
13 [1930] AC 558 at 579, [1930] All ER Rep 431, HL (per Lord Atkin).
14 Eg *Browne v Dunn* (1893) 6 R 67, HL.
15 Defamation Act 1996, s 14(2).
16 Ibid, s 14(3).
17 Law of Libel Amendment Act 1888, s 3 (as to which see the 9th edition of this work).
18 *Farmer v Hyde* [1937] 1 KB 728 at 743, [1937] 1 All ER 773, CA (per Slesser LJ).
19 Although legal precision is not required, a report of a conviction for stealing a car was held not to be a fair report of a conviction for taking it without the owner's consent: *Mitchell v Hirst, Kidd and Rennie Ltd* [1936] 3 All ER 872.
20 *M Isaacs & Sons Ltd v Cook* [1925] 2 KB 391.

reflections were not published with 'malice'. These are occasions of qualified privilege. This is the most widely used defence in defamation actions and its use is underpinned, as we shall see, by the notion that defendant was under a duty – whether legal, social or moral – to make the communication complained of.[1] For the purposes of this defence, the concept of 'malice' is used as a formula subsuming several matters, proof of any one of which by the plaintiff will defeat the privilege.[2] 'Malice' will be discussed before the occasions of qualified privilege are set out.

(A) MALICE

(1) ESTABLISHING MALICE

Qualified privilege is defeated if the plaintiff proves 'malice'. Malice, for the purposes of defeating this defence, bears a special meaning and the presence of malice may be established in any of the following ways.[3]

(a) The defendant does not believe in the truth of his statement
By far the most important way of establishing malice (and thereby rebutting the privilege) is to show that the defendant did not believe in the truth of his statement or that he was reckless as to whether the statement was true or false. Thus, '[i]f a man is proved to have stated that which he knew to be false, no one need inquire further'.[4] Accordingly, a solicitor who writes that his client has admitted his negligence when he knows that he has not admitted it has abused the privilege.[5] Similarly, in *Fraser v Mirza*,[6] proof that the defendant had quite blatantly and deliberately lied in parts of the statement complained of was sufficient to establish malice and defeat his claim of privilege. On the other hand, the mere proof that the defendant had no reasonable grounds for believing his statement to be true is not enough to rebut the qualified privilege.[7] In the leading case of *Horrocks v Lowe*,[8] the House of Lords held that if the defendant honestly believed his statement to be true, his privilege is not lost merely because his conclusion that his statement was true resulted from unreasoning prejudice, or was irrational with regard to the subject matter.

There is probably one exception to the rule that a person who does not believe in the truth of a statement forfeits the privilege. Lord Bramwell stated this exception as follows:[9]

---

1 See *Adam v Ward* [1917] AC 309 at 334, HL (per Lord Atkinson).
2 Malice is used in another sense in pleading in defamation. The plaintiff normally sets out in his statement of claim that the defendant published 'maliciously', but malice in its ordinary sense need not be demonstrated.
3 By RSC Ord 82, r 3(3), the plaintiff who is seeking to defeat a plea of privilege or fair comment by proof of malice must give particulars in his reply of the facts and matters from which malice is to be inferred.
4 *Clark v Molyneux* (1877) 3 QBD 237 at 247, CA (per Brett LJ).
5 *Groom v Crocker* [1939] 1 KB 194, [1938] 2 All ER 394, CA. See also *Royal Aquarium and Summer and Winter Garden Society v Parkinson* [1892] 1 QB 431, CA, where the defendant had stated that a male and a female had performed in an indecent manner at a place of entertainment.
6 1993 SLT 527, HL.
7 *Clark v Molyneux* (1877) 3 QBD 237, CA; cf *Pitt v Donovan* (1813) 1 M & S 639. The plaintiff may, however, be able to circumvent a plea of qualified privilege by suing in negligence: see *Spring v Guardian Assurance plc* [1995] 2 AC 296, [1994] 3 All ER 129, HL.
8 [1975] AC 135, [1974] 1 All ER 662, HL.
9 *Clark v Molyneux* (1877) 3 QBD 237 at 244, CA; cf *Botterill v Whytehead* (1879) 41 LT 588 at 590 (per Kelly CB).

A person may honestly make on a particular occasion a defamatory statement without believing it to be true; because the statement may be of such a character that on that occasion it may be proper to communicate it to a particular person who ought to be informed of it.

Although authority is scanty, we submit that this exception is sound law. There may well be circumstances where the obligation to communicate the defamatory matter is so pressing that the defendant should be free to do so: this is particularly true where such information as the defendant has, is properly requested by another, or where an important interest is subjected to a serious risk of harm if the defendant does not publish the information. A good example might be informing a school that the caretaker is a paedophile. Even if the maker of the statement does not believe it of the caretaker, although she heard it from another, she might nonetheless be excused from liability for erring on the side of caution and informing the school authorities.

(b)   Abuse of the purpose of the privilege

If the defendant does not act for the purpose of protecting that interest for which the privilege is given, he loses it.[10] Even though the defendant did believe his statement to be true, if the court is satisfied that his dominant motive was an improper purpose, the privilege is lost.[11] He must use the occasion in accordance with the purpose for which the occasion arose.[12] Thus, the House of Lords was prepared to hold to be 'malicious' a letter sent to the BBC by a film company about a film critic if its purpose were proved to be to stifle criticism.[13]

The courts normally use, with reference to this class of malice, such expressions as 'wrong motive', 'personal spite' or 'ill-will'. If the defendant is actuated by such a motive, then he abuses the privilege. But where he honestly believed in the truth of his statement, the court should be very slow to draw the inference that he was activated by improper motives.[14] The language occasionally used by the courts, and more often by writers, might seem to suggest that whenever, on a privileged occasion, the defendant has exhibited an improper motive, the privilege is rebutted. This is not quite correct: not only must there be an improper motive, that motive must have been a causative factor in the publishing of the defamation. The courts usually express it as follows: 'the defendant was actuated by motives of personal spite or ill-will'.[15] Thus, in *Winstanley v Bampton*, a creditor who wrote a defamatory letter to the commanding officer of the plaintiff debtor, and believed what he wrote, forfeited his privilege because his indignation and anger had led him to defame the plaintiff.[16] If, however, the defendant was using the occasion for its proper purpose, but incidentally happened to have feelings of resentment or wrath towards the plaintiff, this would not deprive him of the privilege: the privilege is not lost if the ill-will is not the defendant's primary purpose, but merely one purpose.[17]

In deciding whether there is the requisite ill-will, it is relevant to consider the violence of the language of the communication. Yet judges have firmly laid down the rule that

---

10   Ibid, at 246 (per Brett LJ).

11   *Horrocks v Lowe* [1975] AC 135 at 149, [1974] 1 All ER 662 at 669, HL (per Lord Diplock).

12   *Royal Aquarium and Summer and Winter Garden Society v Parkinson* [1892] 1 QB 431, CA (per Lopes LJ).

13   *Turner v Metro-Goldwyn-Mayer Pictures Ltd* [1950] 1 All ER 449 at 457-8, HL (per Lord Porter).

14   *Horrocks v Lowe* [1975] AC 135 at 149-50, HL (per Lord Diplock).

15   *Wright v Woodgate* (1835) 2 Cr M & R 573, approved by Lord Shaw in *Adam v Ward* [1917] AC 309 at 349, HL.

16   [1943] KB 319, [1943] 1 All ER 661.

17   Per Lord Diplock in *Horrocks v Lowe* [1975] AC 135 at 149, [1974] 1 All ER 662, HL. See also *Fraser v Mirza* 1993 SLT 527, HL.

the courts must be very reluctant to infer malice from such evidence alone. In *Adam v Ward* Lord Atkinson said:[18]

> a person making a communication on a privileged occasion is not restricted to the use of such language merely as is reasonably necessary to protect the interest or discharge the duty which is the foundation of his privilege; but that, on the contrary, he will be protected, even though his language should be violent or excessively strong, if, having regard to all the circumstances of the case, he might have honestly and on reasonable grounds believed that what he wrote or said was true...

(c) The inclusion of extraneous matter

The introduction of extraneous matter in a communication may afford evidence of malice which will take away that privilege which would otherwise attach to the communication.[19]

(d) Unreasonable publication to persons outside the scope of the privilege

Where a defendant deliberately slanders the plaintiff in the presence of persons to whom he had no privilege to communicate the matter (although he may have a privilege to inform some of those present), or when he publishes in the press, when he could have protected his interest by a private communication, this is evidence of 'malice' which may rebut the privilege.[20]

(2) JUDGE AND JURY AND THE BURDEN OF PROOF IN RESPECT OF MALICE

The respective functions of judge and jury were summarised by Lord Finlay as follows:[1]

> It is for the judge, and the judge alone, to determine as a matter of law whether the occasion is privileged, unless the circumstances attending it are in dispute, in which case the facts necessary to raise the question of law should be found by the jury. It is further for the judge to decide whether there is any evidence of express malice fit to be left to the jury – that is, whether there is any evidence on which a reasonable man could find malice.

The burden of proving to the jury that the defendant was 'malicious' rests with the plaintiff. He discharges this burden if he proves the defendant malicious in any of the senses discussed above. In pleas of express malice, as in every other aspect of defamation, questions may arise of exactly what meaning or meanings the defamatory statement properly bore. In *Fraser v Mirza*,[2] for example, the respondent alleged, in a complaint to the Chief Constable, that the appellant police officer had acted against him on racist motives. He expressly claimed that when questioned about two television sets he gave them up without hesitation and that a friend of his in the Pakistani community had been threatened by the officer. The House of Lords held that the whole substance of the complaint was intended to convey that the plaintiff had been charged with offences relating to the television sets without any evidence. His express allegations were shown to be deliberate untruths and constituted sufficient evidence of absence of belief in the overall sting of the libel, that is, that DC Fraser charged the plaintiff on solely racist grounds.

---

18 [1917] AC 309 at 339, HL; cf *Spill v Maule* (1869) LR 4 Exch 232 for a good illustration of judicial refusal to deprive the defendant of his privilege on the ground that he used extravagant language.
19 *Adam v Ward* [1917] AC 309 at 318, HL (per Lord Finlay LC).
20 *Oddy v Lord Paulet* (1865) 4 F & F 1009.
1 *Adam v Ward* [1917] AC 309 at 318, HL.
2 1993 SLT 527, HL.

(3)   Excess of privilege and malice

It might perhaps have been sufficient to consider, as we have already done, excess of privilege in relation to 'malice'. In *Adam v Ward*, however, the House of Lords held that there are two separate questions to be answered: whether the privilege has been exceeded, and whether there is evidence of malice.[3] Proof of excess of privilege has the same effect as proof of malice: it deprives the defendant of his defence. The importance of the distinction lies in the fact that the judge decides whether the privilege is exceeded, but the jury decides whether there is 'malice'. And observations made by judges in directing juries on what is evidence of malice are not necessarily applicable when they have to rule as to excess of privilege.[4] There may be such an excess where statements quite unconnected with the main statement are introduced.[5] Take *Tuson v Evans*,[6] for example.

> In a letter to the plaintiff's agent setting out the basis of his claim against the plaintiff for arrears of rent, the defendant added: 'This attempt to defraud me of the produce of land is as mean as it is dishonest'. This 'wholly unnecessary' addition deprived him of his qualified privilege.

The privilege is also lost by publishing to more persons than is necessary. It was exceeded, for example, when the minutes of a *preliminary* inquiry by a committee of a local authority into alleged petrol thefts by employees were placed in the public library: at that stage the body of ratepayers had not the necessary common interest.[7] On the other hand, an occasion does not cease to be privileged simply because the defendant publishes to clerks or others in the reasonable and ordinary course of business practice.[8] The fact that persons are present other than those to whom there is a duty to make the statement will not end the privilege if the ordinary 'business of life could not well be carried on' were such restrictions to be imposed.[9] So, for example, a company does not forfeit its protection if, in order to have circulated a copy of the auditor's report, it sends it to printers, for that is 'reasonable and necessary'.[10]

(4)   Joint publishers and malice

Some difficult problems relating to the abuse of privilege are raised when there is a publication by joint tortfeasors or the employees of the defendant.

An agent through whom a person publishes a privileged communication enjoys the same privilege as his principal; for instance, a solicitor has the defence of qualified

---

3   [1917] AC 309, HL (per Lord Finlay at 318, Earl Loreburn at 320-1, Lord Dunedin at 327, and Lord Shaw at 348).

4   Ibid, at 321 (per Earl Loreburn).

5   If the statement, though not in strict logic relevant to the privileged occasion, is reasonably germane to the subject matter, then it is material only as evidence of malice to take the case out of the privilege: *Horrocks v Lowe* [1975] AC 135 at 151, HL (per Lord Diplock).

6   (1840) 12 Ad & El 733.

7   *De Buse v McCarthy* [1942] 1 KB 156, [1942] 1 All ER 19, CA; cf *Williamson v Freer* (1874) LR 9 CP 393 (privilege to publish by letter lost when sent by telegram).

8   *Boxsius v Goblet Frères* [1894] 1 QB 842, CA; *Edmondson v Birch & Co Ltd and Horner* [1907] 1 KB 371, CA; *Bryanston Finance Co Ltd v De Vries* [1975] QB 703, [1975] 2 All ER 609, CA. The last cited case, following *Toogood v Spyring* (1834) 1 Cr M & R 181, decides that where the publication is made only to the plaintiff, and not to third parties, there is then a qualified privilege for the publication to clerks if it is fairly warranted by any reasonable occasion (not, as in that case, for a threatening improper letter). And see also *White v J and F Stone (Lighting and Radio) Ltd* [1939] 2 KB 827, [1939] 3 All ER 507, CA.

9   *Toogood v Spyring* (1834) 1 Cr M & R 181 at 194 (per Parke B).

10   *Lawless v Anglo-Egyptian Cotton and Oil Co* (1869) LR 4 QB 262 (per Mellor J).

privilege when he publishes on behalf of his client some matter which his client had a privilege to publish.[11] Correspondingly, if a servant in the course of his employment publishes with malice, the fact that his master was not personally malicious will not exempt the master from vicarious liability: the servant has forfeited the privilege because of his malice, but he committed the tort in the course of his employment.[12] Where each party responsible for a joint publication has an individual right to publish the statement – for example, trustees or members of a committee – each has an independent privilege which is not affected by the malice of one or more of the other joint publishers. Thus, if committee man A is malicious while B and C are not, A loses his defence of qualified privilege but B and C do not.[13] Sometimes, one of the persons sued for the publication is a mere ancillary, for example, a printer or a typist. The law is probably that such an ancillary publisher may still plead qualified privilege even though all his principals published maliciously, provided that he himself was not actuated by malice.[14]

(B) INSTANCES OF QUALIFIED PRIVILEGE

(1) GENERAL PRINCIPLE

All the instances of qualified privilege now to be considered can be subsumed within the one general principle: they exist where the defendant has an interest or duty (whether legal, social or moral) to communicate intelligence about the plaintiff to a third party who has a corresponding interest or duty to receive such information.[15] The underlying rationale for the existence of a qualified privilege, in certain circumstances (discussed below), has also been summarised thus: it exists for 'the common convenience and welfare of society'.[16] Thus, 'originally and in principle there are not many different kinds of privilege, but rather for all privilege there is the same foundation of the public interest'.[17] The classic statement on the matter is that of Parke B.[18]

> [The defendant is liable for a defamatory statement] unless it is fairly made by a person in the discharge of some public or private duty, whether legal or moral, or in the conduct of his own affairs, in matters where his interest is concerned. If fairly warranted by any reasonable occasion or exigency, and honestly made, such communications are protected for the common convenience and welfare of society; and the law has not restricted the right to make them within any narrow limits.

It is convenient to group the examples of statements afforded qualified privilege – and they are examples only – as follows: privileged reports, statements which protect an interest and those made under a legal, moral or social duty.

---

11 *Baker v Carrick* [1894] 1 QB 838, CA.
12 *Citizens' Life Assurance Co v Brown* [1904] AC 423, PC; *Riddick v Thames Board Mills Ltd* [1977] QB 881, [1977] 3 All ER 677, CA.
13 *Egger v Viscount Chelmsford* [1965] 1 QB 248, [1964] 3 All ER 406, following *Longdon-Griffiths v Smith* [1951] 1 KB 295, [1950] 2 All ER 662 and *Meekins v Henson* [1964] 1 QB 472, [1962] 1 All ER 899.
14 This was the view of the majority of the Court of Appeal in *Egger v Viscount Chelmsford* [1965] 1 QB 248, [1964] 3 All ER 406 who took the bold step of disregarding statements to the contrary of the House of Lords in *Adam v Ward* [1917] AC 309 because their Lordships had not heard argument on the point.
15 *Adam v Ward* [1917] AC 309, HL.
16 *Perera v Peiris* [1949] AC 1 at 20, PC (per Lord Uthwatt).
17 *Webb v Times Publishing Co Ltd* [1960] 2 QB 535 at 563, [1960] 2 All ER 789 at 800 (per Pearson J).
18 *Toogood v Spyring* (1834) 1 Cr M & R 181 at 193, approved by Lord Shaw in *Adam v Ward* [1917] AC 309 at 349, HL.

(2) Privileged reports

Fair and accurate reports of proceedings in Parliament or in committees thereof, or a fair summary or sketch of that part of those proceedings which is of special interest,[19] are privileged at common law.[20] These, and other such common law privileges, are expressly preserved by the Defamation Act 1996,[1] even though section 15 of that Act – read in conjunction with Schedule 1 – endeavours to establish a comprehensive range of reports that attract a statutory qualified privilege.[2] The printing or broadcasting[3] of copies of, or extracts from, reports,[4] papers, votes or proceedings published by authority of either House of Parliament are also privileged independently of the 1996 Act.[5]

Judicial reports, too, remain privileged at common law, so long as they are both fair and accurate.[6] The question of whether such reports meet the criteria of fairness and accuracy falls to the jury. In view of the different rationale for this privilege, these 'judicial proceedings' (a report of which acquires a qualified privilege) are not the same as those 'judicial proceedings', a report of which, attracts an absolute privilege.[7] The former is a much broader class of reports. Yet on the authority of *Stern v Piper*,[8] qualified privilege does not stretch to a report of proceedings that are merely 'pending'. On the other hand, although a tribunal for the purposes of qualified privilege need not perform 'judicial functions' (in the narrow sense of the term), reports of its proceedings may be privileged, provided the public are admitted and the tribunal is not a mere domestic one, such as the Jockey Club.[9] The privilege still applies where the tribunal is simply considering the case in order to discover whether it has jurisdiction, even though in fact it has no such jurisdiction.[10]

By far the most comprehensive list of those reports and statements which are afforded a qualified privilege is contained in Schedule 1 to the Defamation Act 1996. Importantly, however, there are limits to this statutory privilege. The Act offers no protection in the instance of a 'publication to the public, of matter which is not of public concern and the publication of which is not for the public benefit'.[11] Nor does it confer

---

19 *Cook v Alexander* [1974] QB 279, [1973] 3 All ER 1037, CA.
20 *Wason v Walter* (1868) LR 4 QB 73.
1   Defamation Act 1996, s 15(4)(b).
2   This list, contained in Sch 1 to the 1996 Act is reproduced as the second Annex to this book.
3   Defamation Act 1952, s 9(1) extends this privilege to those forms of broadcasting to which the Act applies.
4   Parliamentary Papers Act 1840, s 2.
5   Including blue books and reports of Royal Commissions presented to Parliament: *Mangena v Edward Lloyd Ltd* (1908) 98 LT 640; on appeal (1909) 99 LT 824, CA.
6   *Furniss v Cambridge Daily News Ltd* (1907) 23 TLR 705 at 706, CA (per Sir Gorell Barnes P). In *Stern v Piper* [1997] QB 123, [1996] 3 All ER 385, CA it was said that blasphemous or obscene material would not be privileged; nor would pre-trial reporting of allegations in court documents not yet in the public domain.
7   For the judicial proceedings covered by absolute privilege see s 14(3) of the Defamation Act 1996.
8   [1997] QB 123, [1996] 3 All ER 385, CA.
9   *Chapman v Lord Ellesmere* [1932] 2 KB 431, [1932] All ER Rep 221, CA. Cf *Allbutt v General Council of Medical Education and Registration* (1889) 23 QBD 400, CA, and see especially per Lopes LJ at 410. The privilege applied to foreign courts where the subject-matter was of legitimate interest to the English newspaper-reading public (eg, where it was closely connected with the administration of justice in England – as in *Webb v Times Publishing Co Ltd* [1960] 2 QB 535, [1960] 2 All ER 789 – but not otherwise).
10 *Usill v Hales* (1878) 3 CPD 319. This case is not an authority on absolute privilege for judicial acts done without jurisdiction.
11 Defamation Act 1996, s 15(3). In *Kelly v O'Malley* (1889) 6 TLR 62, for example, irrelevant, defamatory comments made at a public meeting were afforded no privilege.

a qualified privilege in respect of the publication of anything published with malice,[12] or published illegally.[13]

So far as it relates to qualified privilege, the protection provided by section 15 of the 1996 Act is broadly similar to its now repealed predecessor, section 7 of the Defamation Act 1952. That, in turn, was little more than a reiteration of section 3 of the Law of Libel Amendment Act 1888 and, importantly, there is authority under that nineteenth century statute that what has become section 15 is to be construed conjunctively – that is, that *both* public concern *and* public benefit must be shown. Furthermore, the burden of proving this lies with the defendant.[14] The ratio decidendi of Slesser LJ in *Chapman v Lord Ellesmere*[15] was that matters of interest to a mere section of the public – for example, racing men – are not of general public interest. If, as seems likely, the same rule applies under the 1996 Act, then significant caveats must be read into some of the instances of privilege listed in Schedule 1 to the 1996 Act.[16] Both the questions of what constitutes a matter of public concern, and what constitutes a matter of public benefit, are for the jury to decide.[17]

Reports protected by the Act fall into two distinct groups: (a) those privileged without any explanation or contradiction[18] and (b) those privileged subject to explanation or contradiction.[19] In relation to the former category, protection is conferred, broadly, on a world-wide basis, in respect of reports of judicial, legislative and international organisation proceedings conducted in public, and reports on official publications. Unlike the absolute privilege that is conferred in relation to reports of judicial proceedings, the protection conferred under section 15 of the Act applies without requiring the report to be contemporaneous with the judicial proceedings. In *Tsikata v Newspaper Publishing plc*,[20] for example, it was alleged that a newspaper account of a case heard 10 years previously was in no sense a report of the case because it was not contemporaneous with the actual proceedings. The Court of Appeal rejected this contention on the basis that the statute spoke merely of 'reports' without requiring that they be contemporaneous with the proceedings upon which they centre.

In relation to the second class of reports covered by section 15 – those which are privileged subject to explanation or contradiction – no protection will be afforded if the plaintiff proves that the defendant, despite a request to publish a letter or statement of explanation or contradiction in a suitable manner,[1] has refused or neglected so to do.[2] The kinds of reports and statements that fall into this second class include those concerning official parliamentary or judicial notices to the public, meetings of public or quasi-public bodies in this country and general meetings of UK public companies.

The essential difference between the first and second class of reports is that those in the latter category tend to be based on notices issued, and meetings held, in the UK or European Union. For this reason it is much more reasonable to expect, say, a newspaper

---

12 Ibid, s 15(1).
13 Ibid, s 15(4)(a).
14 *Kelly v O'Malley* (1889) 6 TLR 62 at 64 (per Huddleston B); *Sharman v Merritt and Hatcher Ltd* (1916) 32 TLR 360.
15 [1932] 2 KB 431 at 469, [1932] All ER Rep 221 at 236, CA.
16 The broader language of the 1996 Act, though not wholly clear, would appear, however, to point the other way: see Sch 1, para 14.
17 *Kingshott v Associated Kent Newspapers Ltd* [1991] 1 QB 88, [1991] 2 All ER 99, CA.
18 Defamation Act 1996, Sch 1, Part I.
19 Ibid, Sch 1, Part II.
20 [1997] 1 All ER 655, CA (case concerned 'reports' privileged under s 7 of the 1952 Act, but since the 1996 Act also covers such reports, the authority of the case remains intact).
1   Ie, in the same manner as the publication complained of or, alternatively, in a manner that is both reasonable and adequate in the circumstances: Defamation Act 1996, s 15(2).
2   Ibid.

to print a correction or explanation relating to the initial report. By contrast, it is seen as too much of an imposition to expect the newspaper to publish such explanations or corrections when the initial report was on an item of World news.

(3)   STATEMENTS TO PROTECT AN INTEREST

(a)   The public interest

(i)   Statements by way of help in discovering criminals   Information given to the police[3] in order to detect crime is privileged.[4] Statements made by policemen in the course of their inquiries into suspected crimes are presumably also privileged. And statements made in the course of complaints about police conduct have also been held to be privileged.[5]

(ii)   Statements about the misconduct of public officers   When a member of the public brings to the notice of the proper authority any misconduct or neglect of duty on the part of public officers, his doing so is afforded qualified privilege.[6] However, when the defendant, acting in good faith, complains to the wrong official, he is not privileged.[7] But a defendant who first addresses his complaint about misconduct to his MP will almost certainly be privileged.[8] One unanswered question in this context is whether the privilege in relation to the misconduct of public officers includes those persons employed in one of the privatised public services? We suggest that it probably does.

(b)   The interest of the publisher

Just as self-defence and protection of property are defences in torts affecting the person and property, so also is a statement made to protect or advance the defendant's interests a matter of qualified privilege in defamation.[9] For instance, a creditor may write to an auctioneer to protect his security.[10] Equally, a man who replied to a letter demanding payment of fees for medical services to his wife (who died from scarlet fever) saying, 'I shall never pay him unless the law compels me, and that I do not fancy it can, as I could more easily indict Dr S for manslaughter', was held to be privileged.[11] Privilege will also extend to reasonable steps taken by the publisher to collect money owing to him,[12] warnings issued to servants about the bad character of their associates,[13] and replies to attacks on the publisher's reputation.[14]

---

3   But not to the wife of the accused: *Wenman v Ash* (1853) 13 CB 836.
4   *Padmore v Lawrence* (1840) 11 Ad & El 380.
5   *Fraser v Mirza* 1993 SLT 527, HL.
6   Eg *Harrison v Bush* (1856) 5 E & B 344 (statement to Home Secretary about county magistrate). But see *Blackshaw v Lord* [1984] QB 1, [1983] 2 All ER 311, CA: suspicions must be aired to the proper authority and not the public at large unless public safety is at risk.
7   *Hebditch v MacIlwaine* [1894] 2 QB 54, CA; *Beach v Freeson* [1972] 1 QB 14, [1971] 2 All ER 854. Cf the dictum of Lord Atkinson in *London Association for Protection of Trade v Greenlands Ltd* [1916] 2 AC 15 at 34, HL: answers to an inquiry in the genuine mistaken belief that the inquirer had a legitimate interest, held to be privileged.
8   *R v Rule* [1937] 2 KB 375, [1937] 2 All ER 772, CA.
9   *Toogood v Spyring* (1834) 1 Cr M & R 181 at 193 (per Parke B); *Aspro v Owners Abroad plc* [1995] 4 All ER 728, CA.
10   *Blackman v Pugh* (1846) 2 CB 611.
11   *Stevens v Kitchener* (1887) 4 TLR 159.
12   *Winstanley v Bampton* [1943] KB 319, [1943] 1 All ER 661.
13   *Somerville v Hawkins* (1851) 10 CB 583.
14   *Laughton v Bishop of Sodor and Man* (1872) LR 4 PC 495. But may a representative of the press, theatre, or other section of the community create a privilege by replying to an attack on

(c)   Instances of common interest

There are cases of privilege based on interest where neither the public nor the publisher *alone* has a sufficiently defensible interest for the case to be brought within either of the preceding groups. These cases concern instances in which both the publisher and the recipient of the communication have a 'common interest' in the subject matter of the communication.

A common interest of this kind exists between an employer and his employees as *Hunt v Great Northern Rly Co* illustrates.[15] There, the defendants had posted up a circular in such of their premises as would be frequented by their employees, stating (amongst other things) that the plaintiff, another former employee, had been dismissed for neglect of duty. The privilege of common interest was held to extend to the defendants.

The range of matters privileged because they are of common interest are manifold as the following examples demonstrate: a bishop replying before an assembly of his clergy to an attack on him in the legislature,[16] communications within a family on matters affecting the welfare of a member of that family,[17] a letter by a parishioner to the bishop about an incumbent,[18] a report of a member of a trade protection society to its secretary about the trading conduct of another member,[19] speeches by a company shareholder at a shareholders' meeting[20] or a trustee at a friendly society meeting,[1] a statement made by a creditor to another creditor about their debtor[2] and an invigilator informing the examinees of cheating by one of them.[3]

In one respect the scope of this privilege has been curtailed by section 10 of the Defamation Act 1952 which provides that publications, even to a qualified voter, by or on behalf of a candidate at a parliamentary or local government election, are not privileged on the ground that they are material to a question in issue in the election.[4]

(4)   STATEMENTS IN PURSUANCE OF A LEGAL, SOCIAL OR MORAL DUTY

It must be made clear that there is no general defence of publication of 'fair information on a matter of public interest'. Legitimate interest in the subject matter of a report is, alone, an insufficient basis upon which to grant that report a qualified privilege.[5] Common law had incrementally imposed certain preconditions to the acquisition of this privilege. These were consolidated into a tripartite test, enunciated in *Reynolds v Times Newspapers*.[6] There, the Court of Appeal said that first, the newspaper must owe a legal, moral or social duty to the public to publish the material concerned.

that section as a whole by the plaintiff? 'No', held Dixon J in *Penton v Caldwell* (1945) 70 CLR 219 (whose decision was reversed by the High Court of Australia on the ground that the defendant newspaper had itself been attacked by the plaintiff).

15   [1891] 2 QB 189, CA. See also *Bryanston Finance Ltd v De Vries* [1975] QB 703.
16   *Laughton v Bishop of Sodor and Man* (1872) LR 4 PC 495.
17   *Todd v Hawkins* (1837) 8 C & P 88.
18   *James v Boston* (1845) 5 LTOS 152.
19   *White v Batey & Co Ltd* (1892) 8 TLR 698.
20   *Parsons v Surgey* (1864) 4 F & F 247.
1   *Longdon-Griffiths v Smith* [1951] 1 KB 295, [1950] 2 All ER 662.
2   *Spill v Maule* (1869) LR 4 Exch 232.
3   *Bridgman v Stockdale* [1953] 1 All ER 1166, [1953] 1 WLR 704.
4   *Braddock v Bevins* [1948] 1 KB 580, [1948] 1 All ER 450, CA, must now be read in the light of this section. See also *Plummer v Charman* [1962] 3 All ER 823, CA.
5   The 'public interest' of qualified privilege is narrower in scope than the 'public interest' of fair comment (see post). *Chapman v Lord Ellesmere* [1932] 2 KB 431, CA, illustrates its strictness, which is explained by the fact that in qualified privilege, unlike fair comment, the defence will succeed although the facts are untrue.
6   [1998] 3 All ER 961, CA.

Secondly, the public must have a corresponding interest to receive that information. Finally, the nature, status, source, and circumstances surrounding acquisition of the material should be such as warrant the protection of qualified privilege.

The absence of any one of these three elements is fatal so that no defence of privilege at common law is available if a story is published speculating that the plaintiff is responsible for losses of public money on grants wrongly paid out to North Sea oil companies.[7] The information may be of interest to the public but that, of itself, does not create a duty to publish it. Indeed, a duty to publish matters of speculation and suspicion to the public at large will arise only in exceptional cases such as those where public safety is endangered.[8]

A trend that appears to be emerging is that the courts are becoming increasingly tolerant of claims about what is in the public interest – particularly where a public official is the person who is defamed. So, for example, in *Tsikata v Newspaper Publishing plc*[9] it was held that there was a public interest in information about a Ghanaian government official who had been involved with certain human rights abuses. This was so despite the fact that the official was not British and the human rights abuses had occurred abroad.

It has never been directly decided whether the moral duty to publish an apology after having published a defamatory statement attracts a qualified privilege. (Certainly, the requirement of reciprocity is satisfied in that the plaintiff, naturally, has a correlative interest in the publication of the apology for it re-establishes his good name.) In *Watts v Times Newspapers Ltd*,[10] however, the Court of Appeal failed to supply an authoritative answer to this question. The facts of the case were that the defendant published a defamatory account of the plaintiff and then subsequently apologised in terms that reiterated the initial libel. Instead of stating generally that such apologies attract qualified privilege, their Lordships merely held that no such claim to privilege could be sustained in the present case for want of a reciprocal interest in publishing the apology on the part of the defendant.

As regards the social duty on Employer A to provide a reference on behalf of one of his (former) employees to Employer B, it is clear that such a reference would be afforded qualified privilege. On the other hand, in the light of the House of Lords decision in *Spring v Guardian Assurance plc*,[11] this immunity may be of little use, since their Lordships held, in that case, that subject to the usual requirements of the tort, the employee would be entitled to frame an action in negligence (based on the contents of the reference) rather than defamation.[12]

The fact that the defendant's duty to make a statement about the plaintiff is sometimes only a moral or social one – for example, to supply a third party with a warning about the plaintiff[13] – does not prohibit his statement attracting a qualified privilege. That said, in the absence of a legal or contractual duty to make such a statement, the court may be wary of granting a privilege unless the defendant can show a strong relationship

---

7   *Blackshaw v Lord* [1984] QB 1, [1983] 2 All ER 311, CA.
8   *Camporese v Parton* (1983) 150 DLR (3d) 208.
9   [1997] 1 All ER 655, CA.
10 [1997] QB 650, [1996] 1 All ER 152, CA.
11 [1995] 2 AC 296, [1994] 3 All ER 129, HL.
12 But note that the remedy in negligence would be assessed by the judge and might well be lower than that awarded by a jury in a defamation action.
13 See, eg, *Amann v Damm* (1860) 8 CBNS 597; *S v London Borough of Newham* (1998) 96 LGR 651 (defendant council warned the Department of Health of the potential danger its employee, the plaintiff, represented to young children).

– such as friendship – between himself and the third party to whom he feels obliged to make the statement.[14]

If, however, the duty is imposed by statute, the general defence of statutory authority will apply.[15] Otherwise, the list of moral and social duties is endless. The following examples do not, therefore, purport to be an exhaustive list of the situations of fact under this head. They are merely illustrative and include the following: answers to confidential inquiries about servants;[16] supplying information about credit;[17] protection by a solicitor of his client's interests;[18] a host informing his guest of suspicions about the latter's servant.[19] A member of a woman's family may warn her about the character of her fiancé (or vice versa),[20] but the privilege stops short of protecting idle gossip or officious intermeddling by strangers.[1] *Watt v Longsdon* is a much-cited case on this point.[2]

> A company director was held to be privileged in passing on to the chairman a report that an employee was associating with another woman and otherwise misconducting himself during his employment overseas, but he was not protected in informing the wife of the employee, although she had an interest in receiving that information.

SECTION 6.   FAIR COMMENT

This defence may be defined as criticism of matters of public interest, in the form of comment upon true or privileged statements of fact, such comment being made honestly by a person who did not believe the statements to be untrue and who was not otherwise actuated by malice.

(A)   MATTERS OF PUBLIC INTEREST

The first requirement of this defence is that the statement in question must be made upon a matter of public interest. In this connection, the defence has been held to cover the public conduct of people in public offices,[3] but not their private conduct (except in so far as it throws light on whether they possess qualities such as integrity and honesty which are thought to be essential to a man in public life).[4] Matters of government and public administration,[5] including local government,[6] are also within its scope. The management of institutions of substantial public concern, such as the media itself,[7] or religious institutions, is also a matter for fair comment.[8]

14 *Todd v Hawkins* (1837) 8 C & P 88.
15 Eg *Moore v Canadian Pacific Steamship Co* [1945] 1 All ER 128 (duty of captain under Merchant Shipping Act 1894 to record in the ship's log details of all desertions from ship).
16 *Kelly v Partington* (1833) 4 B & Ad 700.
17 *London Association for Protection of Trade v Greenlands Ltd* [1916] 2 AC 15, HL.
18 Cf *Baker v Carrick* [1894] 1 QB 838 at 841, CA (per Lopes LJ).
19 *Stuart v Bell* [1891] 2 QB 341, CA.
20 *Todd v Hawkins* (1837) 8 C & P 88.
1   *Coxhead v Richards* (1846) 2 CB 569.
2   [1930] 1 KB 130, CA.
3   *Seymour v Butterworth* (1862) 3 F & F 372 (Recorder and MP).
4   Ibid, at 382 (per Cockburn CJ).
5   Eg *Henwood v Harrison* (1872) LR 7 CP 606 (the method by which defendant converted a naval vessel).
6   *Purcell v Sowler* (1877) 2 CPD 215, CA.
7   *Telnikoff v Matusevitch* [1992] 2 AC 343, [1991] 4 All ER 817, HL (recruiting policy for the BBC Russian service).
8   *Kelly v Tinling* (1865) LR 1 QB 699.

Anything submitted to the public for its appraisal is of public interest. Books,[9] articles in periodicals and newspapers,[10] plays[11] and radio broadcasts (themselves being film criticisms),[12] are examples. The work of an architect[13] and the performance of actors in public entertainments[14] are also within the defence.

Any other circumstances which may fairly be said to invite comment are also within its scope. Traders who publish handbills,[15] or those who issue public advertisements, invite comment on them. Important though the question is, how far the quality of goods offered for sale to the public is, ipso facto, the object of fair comment, remains undecided. Yet, it would be artificially restrictive if the answer depended on the extent of the manufacturer's advertising campaign.

(B)   COMMENT ON TRUE FACTS

A second part of the defence is that the comment must, with one exception,[16] be made upon true facts. The rules relating to this part of the defence are unnecessarily complicated by many technical rules. It is important to distinguish this defence from that of justification. Fair comment is available only in respect of expressions of opinion; justification is available in respect of both statements of fact and opinion. In fair comment, it is not necessary to prove the truth of the comment, merely that the opinion was honestly held. If justification is pleaded in respect of matters of opinion, the defendant must prove not merely that he honestly held the views expressed, but that they were correct views. Thus, if the statement complained of was: 'X's speech last night was inconsistent with his professions of Socialism', then, on a plea of justification, the defendant would have to prove that it was inconsistent; in fair comment, he would need to show only that he honestly held this opinion on X's speech.

Naturally, in many statements, it will be very difficult to unravel fact from comment. Yet they must be separated in due course by the court, for the defence of fair comment only lies in relation to facts that are proved to be true and statements of fact (not proved to be true) which were made on a privileged occasion.[17] If the facts are untrue, the defendant will not succeed in fair comment merely by proving that his comment is honestly made. Thus, in one case, a defendant who implied that a play was adulterous could not rely on fair comment where the court found as a fact that adultery was not dealt with in the play.[18] The words 'X is a disgrace' led the hearer to believe that they were based on unstated facts. Accordingly, the defendant could not plead fair comment in respect of those words alone. If, however, he had added 'he has deserted his wife

---

9   *Thomas v Bradbury, Agnew & Co Ltd* [1906] 2 KB 627, CA.
10   *Kemsley v Foot* [1952] AC 345, [1952] 1 All ER 501, HL.
11   *Merivale v Carson* (1887) 20 QBD 275, CA.
12   *Turner v Metro-Goldwyn-Mayer Pictures Ltd* [1950] 1 All ER 449, HL.
13   *Soane v Knight* (1827) Mood & M 74.
14   *Dibdin v Swan* (1793) 1 Esp 27; *Cooney v Edeveain* (1897) 14 TLR 34, CA; *London Artists Ltd v Littler* [1969] 2 QB 375, [1969] 2 All ER 193, CA; *Cornwell v Myskow* [1987] 2 All ER 504, [1987] 1 WLR 630, CA.
15   *Paris v Levy* (1860) 9 CBNS 342.
16   A comment on a statement of fact, not proved to be true, but itself privileged, will also found the defence.
17   *Mangena v Wright* [1909] 2 KB 958; *Grech v Odhams Press Ltd* [1958] 1 QB 310, [1957] 3 All ER 556; on appeal, [1958] 2 QB 275, [1958] 2 All ER 462, CA. It is not necessary for the defendant to justify the facts contained in a privileged statement or report but he must establish that he has given a fair and accurate report of the proceedings in question: *Brent Walker Group plc v Time Out Ltd* [1991] 2 QB 33, [1991] 2 All ER 753, CA. The facts must exist at the time of the comment: *Cohen v Daily Telegraph Ltd* [1968] 2 All ER 407, CA.
18   *Merivale v Carson* (1887) 20 QBD 275, CA.

and family' then the original words would probably be regarded as a comment on the stated facts.

The full details of the procedural complexities germane to a plea of fair comment are beyond the scope of this work. Suffice it to say that defendants will attempt, whenever they can, to cloud the distinction between facts, which they must prove, and comment which may be permissible if fair.[19] Just as the Court of Appeal has striven to force plaintiffs to set out quite clearly the meanings in the publication which they allege to be defamatory, and defendants pleading justification to spell out the meanings they seek to justify, so they have also demanded that, in a plea of fair comment, the defendant must plead his case 'with sufficient precision to enable the plaintiff to know what case he has to meet'.[20] Plaintiffs can require particulars to be given of the facts that constitute the basis of the comment.[1] In *Kemsley v Foot*,[2] the House of Lords held that if the facts on which the comment is based, though not mentioned in the alleged defamatory statement, are adequately pointed to the defendant, he may set out those facts in his pleadings and base a defence of fair comment on them. The facts were as follows.

The defendants attacked a newspaper by publishing an article headed 'Lower than Kemsley'. Kemsley, a newspaper proprietor not connected with the newspaper which had been attacked, sued the defendants. The House of Lords held that the fact that Kemsley was responsible for the Kemsley Press was sufficiently clear, and that a defence of fair comment would succeed if an honest man would have complained that the Kemsley Press was low.

The case also established that 'where the facts relied on to justify the comment are contained only in the particulars it is not incumbent on the defendant to prove the truth of every fact so stated in order to establish his plea of fair comment, but... he must establish sufficient facts to support the comment to the satisfaction of the jury'.[3]

A rather different question arose in *Telnikoff v Matusevitch*.[4] There, the defendant had written an angry and critical letter to the *Daily Telegraph* in response to an article written by the plaintiff. The key issue was whether in determining which parts of the letter constituted allegations of fact, and which were merely comment, the letter could be read alongside the offending article. The House of Lords held that only the contents of the letter itself could be considered: there were likely to be several readers who saw the letter but not the article and the publication in question must be judged on its own merits. Lord Keith advised both those writing to newspapers and the editors thereof to take care to use language distinguishing sufficiently clearly between fact and comment.[5]

Just as a plea of justification may run into difficulties where the defendant can prove some, but not every one, of his factual allegations, so too may a plea of fair comment. Hence, it is provided in section 6 of the Defamation Act 1952 that:

a defence of fair comment shall not fail by reason only that the truth of every allegation of fact is not proved if the expression of opinion is fair comment having regard to such of the facts alleged or referred to in the words complained of as are proved.[6]

---

19 For the demise of the old 'rolled-up' plea see now RSC Ord 82, r 3(2).
20 See *Control Risks Ltd v New English Library Ltd* [1989] 3 All ER 577, CA.
1   *Cunningham-Howie v F W Dimbleby & Sons Ltd* [1951] 1 KB 360, [1950] 2 All ER 882, CA.
2   [1952] AC 345, [1952] 1 All ER 501, HL.
3   Ibid, at 362 (per Lord Tucker).
4   [1992] 2 AC 343, [1991] 4 All ER 817, HL.
5   Ibid, at 823. Note, however, the spirited dissent of Lord Ackner at 826-832.
6   The Faulks Report, para 172, takes the view that where a plaintiff relies only on part of the defendant's statement, the defendant cannot support his defence of fair comment by justifying other facts in his statement. It is possible, however, that the courts could pray in aid *Kemsley v Foot* (supra) to avoid that undesirable conclusion. Where separate allegations have a common

This provision has been held not to afford a defence where the facts on which the comment is based materially add to the harm to reputation. In that event, the defendant must also prove those facts; the defence of fair comment will not assume their existence.[7]

An imputation of corrupt or dishonourable motives will render the comment unfair, unless such an imputation is an inference which a fair-minded man might reasonably draw from such facts and it also represents the honest opinion of the writer.[8]

(C)   COMMENT MUST BE HONEST AND NOT ACTUATED BY MALICE

There is only a prima facie case of fair comment when the comment in question is shown to be one which the defendant made honestly.[9] The matter has been lucidly put By Lord Esher as follows.

> Every latitude must be given to opinion and to prejudice, and then an ordinary set of men with ordinary judgment must say whether any fair man[10] would have made such a comment on the work... Mere exaggeration, or even gross exaggeration, would not make the comment unfair. However wrong the opinion expressed may be in point of truth, or however prejudiced the writer, it may still be within the prescribed limit. The question which the jury must consider is this – would any fair man, however prejudiced he may be, however exaggerated or obstinate his views, have said that which this criticism has said of the work which is criticised?[11]

When assessing whether the comment could honestly have been made by a fair-minded man, evidence of the plaintiff's standing and reputation among his fellows at the time of publication is clearly relevant but evidence of enhanced reputation by the time of the trial is not. The vital issue is whether, at the time of publication, the comment could be considered fair.[12]

Surprisingly, perhaps, if the comment is objectively fair the defendant does not have to prove that he actually believes it to be fair.[13] It is for the plaintiff to establish that the relevant criticism was not an opinion honestly held by the defendant, or that it was motivated by some improper motive. So, if a newspaper publishes a defamatory letter from a reader expressing opinions which could reasonably be justified, the publishers

---

'sting', O'Connor LJ has suggested that it is permissible in fair comment, as it is in justification, to rely on other uncomplained of parts of the relevant statement: *Polly Peck (Holding) plc v Trelford* [1986] 2 All ER 84 at 102, CA.

7   So held in *Truth (NZ) Ltd v Avery* [1959] NZLR 274, on an identical New Zealand statute; and approved obiter in *Broadway Approvals Ltd v Odhams Press Ltd* [1965] 2 All ER 523, CA.

8   *Campbell v Spottiswoode* (1863) 3 B & S 769 (where Cockburn CJ variously uses the expressions 'well-founded', 'not without cause', and 'not without foundation'); *Walker v Hodgson* [1909] 1 KB 239 at 253, CA (per Buckley LJ), approved in *Harris v Lubbock* (1971) Times, 21 October, CA.

9   *Plymouth Mutual Co-operative and Industrial Society Ltd v Traders' Publishing Association Ltd* [1906] 1 KB 403 at 418, CA (per Fletcher Moulton LJ).

10   This dictum was approved by Lord Porter in *Turner v Metro-Goldwyn-Mayer Pictures Ltd* [1950] 1 All ER 449 (except for the substitution of 'honest' for 'fair').

11   *Merivale v Carson* (1887) 20 QBD 275 at 280-1, CA. Note also that a comment may be unfair because a medical fact was omitted from the defamatory statement: *Dowling v Time Inc* (1954) Times, 25 June, CA.

12   *Cornwell v Myskow* [1987] 2 All ER 504, [1987] 1 WLR 630, CA.

13   *Telnikoff v Matusevitch* [1991] 1 QB 102, [1990] 3 All ER 865, CA; affd on this point [1992] 2 AC 343, [1991] 4 All ER 817, HL.

and editor are not required to prove they concurred in the comment.[14] Lack of belief in what was published goes to the question of malice and the onus of proving malice lies with the plaintiff. For even if the defendant survives this objective test of 'fair comment', his defence will still fail if he is shown to have been actuated by malice in the making of the comment.[15] As with qualified privilege, there is 'malice' if the defendant had no genuine belief in the truth of his comment.[16] If the purpose of the maker of the fair comment is not to give the public the benefit of his comment but to injure the plaintiff, then the defence does not lie.[17] The defendant 'is the person in whose motives the plaintiff in the libel action is concerned, and if he, the person sued, is proved to have allowed his view to be distorted by malice, it is quite immaterial that somebody else might without malice have written an equally damnatory criticism.[18] Yet '[i]t is of course, possible for a person to have a spite against another and yet to bring a perfectly dispassionate judgment to bear upon his literary merits, but, given the existence of malice, it must be for the jury to say whether it has warped his judgment'.[19]

If an employee is malicious so as to lose his defence of fair comment, then in accordance with the ordinary principles of vicarious liability, his employer will also be deprived of the defence. It will be seen later that vicarious liability in defamation may also extend to a principal-agent relationship. Thus, the publisher of a periodical could not establish fair comment when the writer of a book review was himself malicious as the court found that the writer was an agent.[20] On the other hand, the publisher's defence of fair comment is not affected when the writer of a letter in the correspondence column of his newspaper is malicious.[1] A joint publisher probably does not lose his defence of fair comment because of the malice of another joint publisher unless he is vicariously liable for that other.[2]

(D)   BURDEN OF PROOF AND THE FUNCTIONS OF JUDGE AND JURY

The defendant has the onus of proving that the matter is of public concern, that the facts on which the comment is based are true, and that the comment is such as an honest man might make. The plaintiff must then prove that the defendant was actuated by malice in publishing the matter. It is for the judge to decide whether the matter commented on is one of public interest.[3] Lord Porter has said:

---

14 For a contrary judgment from Canada see *Cherneskey v Armadale Publishers* [1979] 1 SCR 1067 (Supreme Court of Canada).
15 The separateness of these two matters was emphasised in *McQuire v Western Morning News Co* [1903] 2 KB 100, CA.
16 RSC Ord 82, r 6 prohibits interrogatories as to the defendant's source of information or grounds of belief where qualified privilege or fair comment is pleaded.
17 *Merivale v Carson* (1887) 20 QBD 275 at 281-2, CA (per Lord Esher).
18 *Thomas v Bradbury, Agnew & Co Ltd* [1906] 2 KB 627 at 638, CA (per Collins MR).
19 Ibid, at 642.
20 *Gros v Crook* (1969) 113 Sol Jo 408; doubted by Faulks Reports, para 272(a).
1   *Lyon v Daily Telegraph Ltd* [1943] KB 746, [1943] 2 All ER 316, CA. Contra *Gatley*, § 730.
2   In *Gros v Crook* (supra) the court held that it would not have found the defendant liable for the writer's malice had he not been vicariously liable. To the same effect, see per Lord Denning in *Egger v Viscount Chelmsford* [1965] 1 QB 248 at 265, CA; contra Davies LJ at 269, and *Gatley* § 787.
3   *South Hetton Coal Co v North-Eastern News Association* [1894] 1 QB 133 at 141, CA (per Lopes LJ).

It is for the jury in a proper case to determine what is comment and what is fact; but a prerequisite to their right is that the words are capable of being a statement of a fact or facts. It is for the judge alone to decide whether they are so capable, and whether his ruling is right or wrong is a matter of law for the decision of an appellate tribunal.[4]

Finally, the defence of fair comment resembles that of qualified privilege in so far as the defendant, in order to raise a prima facie defence, must establish certain facts, and both defences fail if it is shown that the defendant was 'actuated by malice' in publishing the statement.

SECTION 7.   APOLOGY

The offer or the making of an apology is not a defence at common law, although it may be given in evidence in mitigation of damages. Under statute, however, it is a defence. Section 2 of the Libel Act 1843 enacts that:

> In an action for a libel contained in any public newspaper or other periodical publication, it shall be competent to the defendant to plead that such libel was inserted in such newspaper or other periodical publication without actual malice, and without gross negligence, and that before the commencement of the action, or at the earliest opportunity afterwards, he inserted in such newspaper or other periodical publication a full apology for the said libel, or, if the newspaper or periodical publication ... should be ordinarily published at intervals exceeding one week, had offered to publish the said apology in any newspaper or periodical publication to be selected by the plaintiff in such action.

Every such defence must be accompanied by a payment of money into court by way of amends.[5] The issues of malice, gross negligence, and the adequacy of the apology are to be decided separately by the jury.

This defence is very little used, and for three reasons. If the defendant fails in his plea, the jury must assess the damages without regard to the payment into court, and the plaintiff is entitled to a judgment for the sum awarded by the jury plus costs, even though the sum awarded does not exceed the sum paid into court. Secondly, since the Neill recommendations of an extended defence of offer of amends has been introduced for unintentional defamation,[6] this ancient statutory defence has been rendered all the less likely to be used. Finally, even where the 1996 Act does not apply – that is, where the defamatory statement was made negligently but not innocently[7] – it is still better for a defendant to pay into court under the general provisions of RSC Ord 22, for, by virtue of that rule, if the award of the jury does not exceed the amount paid into court, judgment will be given for the defendant together with his costs since the date of the payment into court (unless the judge in the exercise of his discretion orders otherwise).

---

4   *Turner v Metro-Goldwyn-Mayer Pictures Ltd* [1950] 1 All ER 449 at 461, HL.
5   Libel Act 1845, s 2.
6   Defamation Act 1996, ss 2-4; see ante.
7   Section 4 of the 1996 Act prohibits the use of the offer of amends defence in cases where the defendant 'knew or had reason to believe that the statement complained of referred to the aggrieved part ... and was both false and defamatory'.

SECTION 8.   REMEDIES

(A)   DAMAGES

The main function of the tort of defamation is to compensate the plaintiff for his loss of reputation: that is, the extent to which he is held in less esteem and respect and suffers loss of goodwill and association.[8]

Damages for this loss of reputation are at large in respect both of libel and slander actionable per se. The principles ordinarily applicable to damages at large,[9] apply equally here. Accordingly, by way of parasitic damages, compensation may be given for insult or injury to feelings.[10] Likewise, circumstances of aggravation and mitigation are important. Damages may be aggravated by such matters as the mode, circumstances and extent of publication and the conduct of the defendant from publication to verdict.[11] By contrast, the defendant's belief in the truth of his statements,[12] the fairness of his reports[13] and his being provoked by the plaintiff[14] may all mitigate the level of damages.

Where partial justification is proved, although the defendant may be unable to prove sufficient facts to establish justification at common law or to bring himself within section 5 of the Defamation Act 1952, the defendant may nonetheless be able to rely on the facts proved to reduce damages.[15] Indeed, in an exceptional case, he may do so to reduce the damages almost to vanishing point.[16] Persistence in an unsubstantiated plea of justification will lead to a higher award of damages.

Exemplary – that is, punitive – damages may be awarded in one circumstance: where the defendant calculated that the money to be made out of his wrongdoing would probably exceed the compensation payable for the defamation, and where he defamed the plaintiff either knowing his conduct to be illegal, or was reckless as to its illegality.[17] Where several plaintiffs are libelled, the amount of exemplary damages may properly take account of the fact that the defendant has libelled more than one person, but the total should not exceed the total representing a proper sum by way of punishment for the defendant.[18]

A spate of exceptionally high awards in libel claims led to concern about excessive levels of damages. Awards of hundreds of thousands of pounds were made which did not expressly include any element of exemplary damages. Comparisons were drawn between huge awards for damaged reputations and the relatively low sums awarded to

---

8   The best judicial survey is in the judgment of Devlin LJ in *Dingle v Associated Newspapers Ltd* [1961] 2 QB 162, [1961] 1 All ER 897, CA; affd sub nom *Associated Newspapers Ltd v Dingle* [1964] AC 371, [1962] 2 All ER 737, HL.
9   See ch 27 post.
10 *Goslin v Corry* (1844) 7 Man & G 342; *Ley v Hamilton* (1935) 153 LT 384 at 386, HL (per Lord Atkin). Query: are damages recoverable for injuries to the plaintiff's feelings caused by publishing the libel to him? See *Hayward v Thompson* [1982] QB 47, CA.
11 *Praed v Graham* (1889) 24 QBD 53, CA. For a recent review on the punitive *versus* compensatory function of aggravated damages see the Law Commission Consultation Paper No 132, *Aggravated, Exemplary and Restitutionary Damages* (1993) para 2.7.
12 *Bryce v Rusden* (1886) 2 TLR 435; *Forsdike v Stone* (1868) LR 3 CP 607 (bona fide mistake of identity).
13 *Smith v Scott* (1847) 2 Car & Kir 580; *East v Chapman* (1827) Mood & M 46.
14 *Moore v Oastler* (1836) 1 Mood & R 451n.
15 *Atkinson v Fitzwalter* [1987] 1 All ER 483, [1987] 1 WLR 201, CA.
16 *Pamplin v Express Newspapers Ltd (No 2)* [1988] 1 All ER 282, [1988] 1 WLR 116n.
17 *Cassell & Co Ltd v Broome* [1972] AC 1027, [1972] 1 All ER 801, HL.
18 *Riches v News Group Newspapers Ltd* [1986] QB 256, [1985] 2 All ER 845, CA.

victims of personal injury.[19] The turning point came in *Sutcliffe v Pressdram Ltd*[20] when the Court of Appeal set aside a £600,000 award. Their Lordships warned that in assessing any element of aggravated damages, misconduct by the defendant is relevant only in so far as it increases the injury to the plaintiff: the jury's own indignation at that conduct was irrelevant in arriving at a proper quantum of compensatory damages.

In addition, section 8 of the Courts and Legal Services Act 1990 empowers the Court of Appeal to substitute 'such sum as appears to be proper' for the award of a jury where that award is quashed as excessive.[1] In relation to the meaning of 'excessive' in this context, the Court of Appeal has held the test to be whether a reasonable jury would have thought the award proposed necessary to compensate the plaintiff and re-establish his reputation.[2] And finally, even beyond section 8 of the 1990 Act, it has since been held in *John v MGN Ltd*[3] that damages might permissibly be controlled in two further ways. First, by the court drawing the jury's attention to the levels of awards made in personal injuries cases (while recognising that no direct analogy can be drawn because of the different nature of the 'injury' involved) and, secondly, by allowing the court and counsel to mention to the jury what they consider to be an appropriate award and its appropriate bracket. In particular, this last development may help to curtail the huge amounts that have been awarded by juries in the past.

On occasion, the loss of reputation suffered by the plaintiff will cause him a knock-on pecuniary loss – for example, loss of business – and that loss, in addition to general damages, will also be recoverable.

In the case of slanders not actionable per se, actual damage must be proved. It is doubtful, therefore, whether any other damages other than those for actual damage are recoverable for such slanders.[4] If this is correct, the rules in relation to aggravated and exemplary damages just discussed, do not apply.

Evidence of the bad reputation of the plaintiff will be a ground for mitigating the level of damages since a reputation already largely lost is, ipso facto, of less value. The rules governing evidence of reputation are complex and, in practice, a trial often resolves itself into a tactical battle over this issue. The governing principle is that general evidence alone is permitted (and then, only after prior notice and particulars have been given).[5] Evidence of specific facts to show the disposition of the plaintiff is not admissible at present.[6] The court is concerned with the esteem in which the plaintiff is in fact held –

19 See Law Commission Report No 225, *Personal Injury Compensation: How Much is Enough?* (1994).

20 [1991] 1 QB 153, [1990] 1 All ER 269, CA.

1   In *Rantzen v Mirror Group Newspapers Ltd* [1993] 4 All ER 975 the Court of Appeal made use of this section and reduced a jury award of £250,000 to one of £110,000.

2   Ibid.

3   [1997] QB 586, [1996] 2 All ER 35, CA.

4   Spencer Bower, *Actionable Defamation* (1st edn) p 174, states that no other damages may be given; there is an obiter dictum by Williams J in *Brown v Smith* (1853) 13 CB 596 to the same effect. In *Dixon v Smith* (1860) 5 H & N 450, the plaintiff doctor claimed a guinea, being the loss of a particular patient in consequence of the slander, together with damages for general decline in business, and deterioration of goodwill. After denying, on the grounds of remoteness, such general damages as resulted from repetition of the slander, the court held the damages not to be limited to the guinea. Whether the further damages were at large, or for some non-remote business loss other than the loss of the patient, is not clear, but an observation by Martin B (at 452), supports the latter interpretation.

5   RSC Ord 82, r 7.

6   *Scott v Sampson* (1882) 8 QBD 491, Div Ct; *Hobbs v C T Tinling & Co Ltd* [1929] 2 KB 1, CA. The Neill Committee recommended abolition of this rule which it regarded as offering comfort to 'gold-diggers'.

with his established reputation[7] – and not with his actual character, or with the reputation which he deserves. Thus, where, on a privileged occasion, a newspaper published extracts from a parliamentary report, and then embellished this report with details not found in the report, it could not mitigate its damage by asserting that the plaintiff's reputation was already tarnished by the privileged publication of the parliamentary report.[8] Where the defendant has persisted in a plea of justification, in assessing damage to reputation, it is the plaintiff's reputation at the time of the trial which is in issue.[9] Of course, the ordinary rule of evidence applies: if the plaintiff gives evidence, he may be cross-examined as to credit, although evidence to rebut his answers is forbidden. The jury should be directed to disregard this cross-examination when fixing damages.[10]

(B)   INJUNCTION

Plaintiffs in defamation actions often seek interlocutory injunctions as soon as they have served the writ so as to prevent further publication. The courts, conscious of the need not to interfere unduly with press freedom, normally do not grant such interim injunctions when the case is contested and the plaintiff is unable to show that a defence of justification, fair comment or privilege is likely to fail at the eventual trial.[11] But where the Attorney-General sought an injunction to prevent further publication of an alleged contempt, it was said that in that instance the interest in the protection of justice (as perceived by the Attorney-General) prevailed over the interest in free speech.[12] The courts will readily grant injunctions to successful plaintiffs where further publication is apprehended.[13]

Where publication of a libel is threatened but has not yet occurred, according to the Court of Appeal in *British Data Management plc v Boxer Commercial Removals plc*,[14] a quia timet injunction may be awarded if the plaintiff is able to set out with reasonable certainty the gist of the libel.[15]

7   *Plato Films Ltd v Speidel* [1961] AC 1090, [1961] 1 All ER 876, HL, approving *Scott v Sampson* (1882) 8 QBD 491 and *Hobbs v C T Tinling & Co Ltd* [1929] 2 KB 1, CA.
8   *Associated Newspapers Ltd v Dingle* [1964] AC 371, [1962] 2 All ER 737, HL.
9   *Cornwell v Myskow* [1987] 2 All ER 504 at 508, CA.
10 *Hobbs v C T Tinling & Co Ltd* [1929] 2 KB 1, CA.
11 *Bonnard v Perryman* [1891] 2 Ch 269, CA. For recent illustrations see *Crest Homes Ltd v Ascott* [1980] FSR 396; *Harakas v Baltic Mercantile and Shipping Exchange Ltd* [1982] 2 All ER 701, CA and *Al-Fayed v The Observer Ltd* (1986) Times, 14 July.
12 *A-G v News Group Newspapers Ltd* [1987] 2 All ER 833, CA (rule in *Bonnard v Perryman* (supra) does not apply to an action for conspiracy).
13 *Monson v Tussauds Ltd* [1894] 1 QB 671, CA.
14 [1996] 3 All ER 707, CA.
15 Note that the plaintiff need not prove *verbatim* the wording of the threatened libel.

Part VII

Misuse of process

CONTENTS

CHAPTER   PAGE

24   Misuse of process   491

Chapter 24

Misuse of process

The nature of the motive with which an act is done does not in general make that act unlawful and a tort.[1] The torts discussed in this chapter represent limited exceptions to that general rule. The essence of the wrongful conduct becomes the misuse of a right conferred on individuals for the public good. Abuse of that right for private benefit or other improper ends gives rise to tortious liability. The tort of malicious prosecution is long established and in recent years seems to have revived from the degree of torpor which affected the development of the tort in the middle of this century. The evolution of the tort of misfeasance in public office looks set to expand the role tort plays in controlling the conduct of public officials.

SECTION I. MALICIOUS PROSECUTION AND RELATED CLAIMS

It is a tort maliciously and without reasonable and probable cause to initiate against another judicial proceedings which terminate in favour of that other and which result in damage to reputation, person, freedom or property.

The torts considered in this section are concerned with protecting the interest in freedom from unjustifiable litigation. Their function comes very close to that of defamation, the protection of reputation. The difference is that institution of proceedings will sometimes cause pecuniary loss or loss of personal liberty without damaging reputation—when that happens, there may be malicious prosecution but there cannot be defamation.

It is also necessary to distinguish this branch of the law of torts from false imprisonment. It is of the essence of false imprisonment that the initial act in itself is wrongful, for example the wrongful use of a form of judicial process when an arrest is made upon a warrant which is in fact invalid. Malicious prosecution presupposes that the proper procedural formalities have been carried out, and is concerned with the purposes for which they were used. Obviously, false imprisonment does not cover all the ground covered by malicious prosecution, because interference with freedom of movement is required in false imprisonment.

As is the case in any claim for false imprisonment, in this tort too the plaintiff has a prima facie right to trial by jury.[2]

1 *Bradford Corpn v Pickles* [1895] AC 587; *Allen v Flood* [1898] AC 1, HL.
2 *Cropper v Chief Constable of South Yorkshire Police* [1990] 2 All ER 1005, CA.

The delicate balance of public interests involved in malicious prosecution must not be underestimated. As Fleming so eloquently explains:[3]

> The tort of malicious prosecution is dominated by the problem of balancing two countervailing interests of high social importance: safeguarding the individual from being harassed by unjustifiable litigation and encouraging citizens to aid in law enforcement.

(A)   INSTITUTION OF PROCEEDINGS

The defendant must have been 'actively instrumental' in instigating the proceedings.[4] In *Martin v Watson*,[5] the House of Lords addressed just what that requirement involved. Their lordships confirmed that merely giving information to a police officer,[6] or a magistrate,[7] on which that official bases his or her own *independent* judgement to launch a prosecution, does not render the original complainant responsible for the prosecution. The decision to prosecute, the responsibility for launching proceedings against the plaintiff, rests with the public officials who determine that a prosecution should go ahead.[8] However, in *Martin v Watson* the defendant, who had a history of ill-feeling against the plaintiff, deliberately set out to deceive police officers, making an entirely false allegation that the plaintiff had exposed himself to her. The trial judge found that she had acted maliciously, intending that the police act on her lies and prosecute the plaintiff. The Court of Appeal held that, nonetheless, the defendant was not responsible for the prosecution of the plaintiff.[9] The Law Lords unanimously reversed that judgement.[10]

A defendant who complains to police or magistrates will be regarded as the 'prosecutor' and liable in malicious prosecution if the following conditions are met. (1) The defendant falsely and maliciously gave information to the police, making it clear that he or she is prepared to be a witness for the prosecution and in circumstances where it can be inferred that the defendant desires and intends that the plaintiff be prosecuted. (2) The facts of the alleged offence are such that they are exclusively within the knowledge of the defendant, so that it is practically impossible for police officers to make any independent judgement whether or not to proceed with the prosecution. Not to impose liability in such cases would, Lord Keith declared,[11] '...stultify completely

---

3   *The Law of Torts* (8th ed, 1992) p 609, quoted in *Martin v Watson* [1994] 2 All ER 606 at 614 and 616, CA.
4   *Danby v Beardsley* (1880) 43 LT 603 at 604 (per Lopes J). In *Evans v London Hospital Medical College* [1981] 1 All ER 715, it was held that a hospital which provided pathology reports for the police did not institute proceedings.
5   [1996] AC 74, [1995] 3 All ER 559.
6   *Danby v Beardsley* (1880) 43 LT 603; nor will supplying information to police, on the basis of which officers decide to make an arrest engage liability for false imprisonment; *Davidson v Chief Constable of North Wales* [1994] 2 All ER 597, CA; see above p 42.
7   *Cohen v Morgan* (1825) 6 Dow & Ry KB 8.
8   In direct contrast to circumstances where the defendant initiates a private prosecution. However, note there may be cases where a public prosecution is brought, but on the facts of the case the defendant has effectively required that the prosecution go ahead formally accepting responsibility for the initiation of the relevant proceedings: see *Mohamed Amin v Jogendra Kumar Bannerjee* [1947] AC 322, PC, considered in *Casey v Automatic Renault Canada Ltd* (1966) 54 DLR (2d) 600 Sup Ct Canada; *Malz v Rosen* [1966] 2 All ER 10, [1966] 1 WLR 1008.
9   [1994] 2 All ER 606.
10 [1996] AC 74, [1995] 3 All ER 559.
11 [1995] 3 All ER 559 at 568.

the tort of malicious prosecution and deny any remedy to victims of baseless and malicious accusations.'[12]

(B)   NATURE OF PROCEEDINGS

Where the plaintiff has been subjected to a criminal prosecution as a consequence of which he lost, or risked losing,[13] his liberty and/or his reputation, a remedy in the tort of malicious prosecution is clearly available. However, not all criminal prosecutions give rise to a claim in malicious prosecution, and, in limited cases, maliciously instituting non-criminal proceedings may afford a remedy for maliciously instituting proceedings.

In 1698 Holt CJ delivered a judgment in *Savile v Roberts*[14] which required that the proceedings must be such as to inflict one of the following:

> 1. The damage to a man's fame, as if the matter whereof he is accused be scandalous ... 2. ... such [damages] as are done to the person; as where a man is put in danger to lose his life, or limb, or liberty ... 3. Damage to a man's property, as where he is forced to expend his money in necessary charges, to acquit himself of the crime of which he is accused.

Since that time the courts have regarded this judgment as marking the outer limits of the tort.

A prosecution for an infringement of parking regulations which resulted in acquittal and no financial loss for the plaintiff would thus be unlikely to form the basis of a successful claim for malicious prosecution. A civil action can only rarely do so for it will be assumed that when the plaintiff loses his suit, the defendant's reputation is restored and he recovers his costs in defending the action.[15] Malicious proceedings in bankruptcy and winding up, however, do generate a remedy.[16] The very institution of proceedings may wreck the plaintiff's business, destroying confidence in his competence, integrity and his company's goodwill.

An action will lie for maliciously procuring a warrant of arrest.[17] Maliciously procuring a search warrant is an actionable wrong long '...recognised though rarely successfully prosecuted.'[18] Generally, the damage to the plaintiff ensues from the execution of the warrant, the entry into his premises, or the seizure of the property. Exceptionally the issue of a warrant may cover actionable harm.[19]

In *Gregory v Portsmouth City Council*[20] the plaintiff sued the defendant for maliciously instituting disciplinary proceedings against him. He argued that the disciplinary process was analogous to the criminal process. The charges against him hurt his reputation and put him to expense in defending himself. The Court of Appeal held that there were no grounds to extend the scope of a tort of maliciously instituting

---

12   As to liability where the defendant continues proceedings after learning of facts which negate the basis of the prosecution, see *Tims v John Lewis & Co Ltd* [1951] 2 KB 459 at 472 CA; revised on another point sub nom *John Lewis & Co Ltd v Tims* [1952] AC 676 HL. A lawyer who does more than advise his client in good faith may be deemed responsible for the prosecution! *Johnson v Emerson and Sparrow* (1871) LR 6 Exch 329.

13   *Berry v British Transport Commission* [1962] 1 QB 306, [1961] 3 All ER 65, CA.

14   (1698) 1 Ld Raym 374.

15   *Quartz Hill Consolidated Gold Mining Co v Eyre* (1883) 11 QBD 674 at 689–690 per Bowen LJ.

16   *Chapman v Pickersgill* (1762) 2 Wils 145; and see *Clerk & Lindsell* para 15-42.

17   *Roy v Prior* [1971] AC 470, [1970] 2 All ER 729, HL.

18   *Gibbs v Rea* [1998] 3 WLR 72 at 80; and see *Reynolds v Metropolitan Police Comr* [1985] QB 881, [1984] 3 All ER 649.

19   *Gibbs v Rea* (supra).

20   (1997) 96 LGR 569, CA.

proceedings beyond criminal prosecutions and exceptional cases such as bankruptcy and winding up. And in *Gizzonio v Chief Constable of Derbyshire*[1] the Court of Appeal also rejected an attempt to construct a tort of malicious refusal of bail.

(C)   TERMINATION IN FAVOUR OF PLAINTIFF

The proceedings must have terminated in favour of the plaintiff.[2] Even though the plaintiff has been convicted of a lesser offence,[3] or has had his conviction quashed on appeal,[4] or has been acquitted on a technicality, for example a defect in the indictment,[5] this requirement is satisfied. If the conviction of the plaintiff stands, then even though there is no right of appeal from it and although he can satisfy the court in the instant proceedings that the conviction was grossly unjust, there is no cause of action in this tort.[6] The plaintiff seems to satisfy the present requirement if he proves that the defendant has discontinued the proceedings;[7] the plaintiff cannot sue, it seems, while the proceedings are still pending.[8]

(D)   ABSENCE OF REASONABLE AND PROBABLE CAUSE

Malicious prosecution is treated with some caution by the courts, fearful of discouraging the enforcement of the law against suspected offenders and anxious to protect the interest in bringing litigation to a close.[9] This judicial attitude is reflected in the development of the requirement that there must be an absence of reasonable and probable cause.

The plaintiff has the difficult task of proving a negative – a burden which he does not discharge merely by proving malice on the part of the defendant,[10] and the court will not order the defendant to give particulars of the grounds on which he prosecuted.[11]

The House of Lords has approved the following definition of reasonable and probable cause:[12]

an honest belief in the guilt of the accused based upon a full conviction, founded upon reasonable grounds, of the existence of a state of circumstances, which, assuming them to be true, would reasonably lead any ordinary prudent and cautious man, placed in the position of the accuser, to the conclusion that the person charged was probably guilty of the crime imputed.

1   (1998) Times, 29 April, CA.
2   This requirement is not imposed where, for example, an arrest or search warrant is procured, *supra*. But it was considered fatal in an attempt to construct a tort of malicious refusal of bail: *Gizzonio v Chief Constable of Derbyshire*, *supra*.
3   *Boaler v Holder* (1887) 51 JP 277, Div Ct.
4   *Reynolds v Kennedy* (1748) 1 Wils 232.
5   *Wicks v Fentham* (1791) 4 Term Rep 247.
6   *Basébé v Matthews* (1867) LR 2 CP 684; nor can a plaintiff sue who is merely ordered to enter into recognizances to keep the peace: *Everett v Ribbands* [1952] 2 QB 198, [1952] 1 All ER 823, CA.
7   *Watkins v Lee* (1839) 5 M & W 270.
8   Per Willes J (obiter) in *Gilding v Eyre* (1861) 10 CBNS 592 at 604.
9   See for example the decision of the Court of Appeal in *Martin v Watson* [1994] 2 All ER 606; revsd [1995] 3 All ER 559, HL.
10   *Johnstone v Sutton* (1786) 1 Term Rep 510, Ex Ch.
11   *Stapley v Annetts* [1969] 3 All ER 1541, [1970] 1 WLR 20, CA.
12   *Hicks v Faulkner* (1881) 8 QBD 167 at 171 (per Hawkins J); affd 46 LT 130 CA, approved in *Herniman v Smith* [1938] AC 305, [1938] 1 All ER 1.

The House of Lords has held that, in order that the plaintiff may succeed on the issue of reasonable and probable cause, he must prove one or other of the following.[13] *Either—*

1   The defendant did not believe that the plaintiff was probably guilty of the offence. Evidence should be given by the plaintiff of some fact or facts which, either inherently or coupled with other matters proved in evidence, would permit the inference that the defendant did not believe in the plaintiff's guilt. The Privy Council has recently held (Lords Goff and Hope trenchantly dissenting) that where there was powerful circumstantial evidence, the silence of the defendant in the face of allegations made against him might afford some evidence of absence of reasonable and probable cause.[14] If such evidence is given, the question must be left to the jury, whether it has been proved to their satisfaction that the defendant did not believe in the plaintiff's guilt. But unless such evidence is given it is not proper to put a question to the jury as to the defendant's belief.[15] This question to the jury must be formulated precisely and should not refer to reasonable cause. It should be either: 'Did the defendant honestly believe in the plaintiff's guilt?' or 'Did he honestly believe in the charges he was preferring?' It must not be: 'Did he honestly believe that there were reasonable grounds for the prosecution?' for that would cause the jury to determine on the whole issue of reasonable and probable cause.[16] Merely to prove that the defendant had before him information which might or might not have led a reasonable man to form an opinion that the plaintiff was guilty is not evidence that the defendant did not believe him to be guilty. If this ground is relied on, the older cases suggest that the plaintiff must give some evidence from which an inference may be drawn as to what the defendant's belief actually was: it is not sufficient to give evidence from which a guess may be made as to what it was. Nor is it sufficient merely to supply evidence of reasons for non-belief. If such evidence is relied on there must also be evidence that these reasons were in fact operative; but if silence affords some inference of absence of belief in cause the heavy burden of proof on the plaintiff may now be somewhat eased.[17] *Or—*

2   That a person of ordinary prudence and caution would not conclude, in the light of the facts in which he honestly believed, that the plaintiff was probably guilty. It is for the judge and not the jury to determine whether a man of ordinary prudence would have so concluded. It is for the judge alone to determine whether there is reasonable and probable cause.[18] The trouble experienced in splitting the functions of judge and jury in consequence of this rule accounts for most of the complexities of this tort. There is the ever-present danger that the questions addressed to the jury will be so general that the ultimate question left to the judge of reasonable cause is instead improperly decided by the jury. In conducting the trial the judge has two alternatives: he may direct the jury that, if they find certain facts, or arrive at certain answers to specific questions which he puts to them, there is reasonable and probable cause, leaving it to the jury to find a general verdict on this hypothetical direction; his alternative – and this is the

---

13   *Glinski v McIver* [1962] AC 726, [1962] 1 All ER 696, HL; *Reynolds v Metropolitan Police Comr* (supra).
14   *Gibbs v Rea* [1998] AC 786, PC.
15   *Herniman v Smith* [1938] AC 305 at 317, HL (per Lord Atkin); *Ward v Chief Constable of West Midlands Police* (1997) Times, 13 December, CA.
16   *Tempest v Snowden* [1952] 1 KB 130, [1952] 1 All ER 1, CA.
17   See *Gibbs v Rea*, supra.
18   *Lister v Perryman* (1870) LR 4 HL 521.

better course – is to direct the jury to settle the facts in dispute, whereupon he decides, upon the whole case, whether there is reasonable and probable cause.[19]

It is impossible to enumerate all the factors which may be relevant in deciding whether there was reasonable and probable cause. Particularly important points would be that the defendant acted in good faith on the advice of counsel[20] (although that he did so act is not conclusive[1]), or on the advice of the police,[2] where the defendant, however honest his act, had taken reasonable care to inform himself of the facts,[3] whether the defendant's mistake was one of fact or law (obviously a plaintiff cannot treat a mistake on a difficult legal point as evidence of lack of reasonable cause).[4]

(E) MALICE: IMPROPER PURPOSE

In addition, the plaintiff must prove malice on the part of the defendant,[5] that is 'any motive other than that of simply instituting a prosecution for the purpose of bringing a person to justice'.[6]

The judge decides whether there is any evidence of malice and the jury decides whether there is malice in fact.[7] There was, for instance, evidence of malice where the defendant landlord made the charge in order to evict the plaintiff tenant from his house,[8] and where the defendant accused the plaintiff of exposing himself to her as part of a long-running vendetta between neighbours.[9] The question is not whether the defendant is angry or inspired by hatred,[10] but whether the defendant has a purpose other than bringing an offender to justice. There is malice, for instance, if he uses the prosecution as a means of blackmail or any other form of coercion. Where the motives of the defendant are mixed, the plaintiff will fail unless he establishes that the dominant purpose is something other than the vindication of the law.[11] However, it is crucial to note that a plaintiff who proves malice but not want of reasonable and probable cause still fails.[12] Should a tenant, therefore, establish that his landlord has instituted

---

19 *Abrath v North Eastern Rly Co* (1883) 11 QBD 440 at 458 (per Bowden LJ), CA; affd (1886) 11 App Cas 247, HL. And see *Green v De Havilland* (1968) 112 Sol Jo 766.
20 *Ravenga v Mackintosh* (1824) 2 B & C 693; cf *Bradshaw v Waterlow & Sons Ltd* [1915] 3 KB 527, CA.
1 *Abbott v Refuge Assurance Co Ltd* [1962] 1 QB 432, [1961] 3 All ER 1074, CA.
2 *Malz v Rosen* [1966] 2 All ER 10, [1966] 1 WLR 1008.
3 *Abrath v North Eastern Rly Co* (1833) 11 QBD 440 at 451 (per Brett MR), CA.
4 *Philips v Naylor* (1859) 4 H & N 565. In *Riches v DPP* [1973] 2 All ER 935, CA, it was held that allegations of malice and want of reasonable cause in an action against the DPP stood no chance of success when the committing magistrate, the trial judge and the jury all shared the view of the evidence held by the DPP.
5 *Brown v Hawkes* [1891] 2 QB 735, CA. In *Wershof v Metropolitan Police Comr* [1978] 3 All ER 540, the plaintiff proved absence of reasonable cause, but failed because he could not prove malice.
6 Per Alderson B in *Stevens v Midland Counties Rly Co* (1854) 10 Exch 352.
7 *Brown v Hawkes* [1891] 2 QB 718.
8 *Turner v Ambler* (1847) 10 QB 252.
9 *Martin v Watson* [1995] 3 All ER 559, HL.
10 *Brown v Hawkes* supra at 722 (per Cave J).
11 Not malice when the defendants' motive was to recoup themselves in a civil action, so that they first prosecuted in order to conform to the rule that prosecution for felony must precede civil actions relating thereto: *Abbott v Refuge Assurance Co Ltd*, ante.
12 *Silcott v Metropolitan Police Comr* [1996] 8 Admin LR 633, CA; *Gizzonio v Chief Constable of Derbyshire* (1998) Times, 29 April, CA.

proceedings against him for stealing the landlord's fixtures, with the object of determining his tenancy, the tenant's action in this tort will still fail if absence of reasonable cause is not also proved by him.[13]

(F) THE CROWN PROSECUTION SERVICE

As will be obvious, the vast majority of precedents establishing this tort predate the Prosecution of Offences Act 1985, albeit there has been a flurry of more recent cases. Under the 1985 Act, the Crown Prosecution Service, headed by the Director of Public Prosecutions, took over responsibility for prosecutions initiated by the police. Several questions relating to the potential liability of the CPS and the police remain unanswered as yet.[14] Assume the plaintiff is originally charged and remanded in custody at the instigation of the police. The CPS reviews the evidence and decides to discontinue proceedings. He cannot sue for false imprisonment in respect of the period when he was detained by judicial order. But is discontinuance of the proceedings termination of those proceedings in his favour? If the CPS continue proceedings, thus endorsing the judgment of police officers, proving absence of reasonable and probable cause will be a mammoth task.

The CPS and its officers enjoy no general immunity in tort, in particular against claims for malicious prosecution or misfeasance in office.[15] However, the CPS owes no *general*[16] duty of care in relation to the conduct of prosecutions. The Court of Appeal found that such a liability in negligence might have an 'inhibiting effect on the discharge by the CPS of its central function of prosecuting crime.'[17] Moreover, courts will be vigilant to ensure that any action in malicious prosecution brought against the CPS is not in reality a disguised claim for negligence. Incompetence is not evidence of malice.[18]

(G) DEFENCES

No questions on defences call for special comment other than that of whether it is a defence to establish that the plaintiff was guilty of the offence for which he was prosecuted. Obviously, in the rare case where a defendant had no reasonable cause and was malicious, and the proceedings terminated in the plaintiff's favour, and yet, at the trial for malicious prosecution the defendant is able to establish the guilt of the plaintiff, the plaintiff would recover at best a very small sum of damages; there is, indeed, some authority for the view that in such a case the action fails altogether.[19]

---

13 *Turner v Ambler* supra.
14 See *Clerk and Lindsell* 15-38 to 15-39.
15 *Elguzouli-Daf v Metropolitan Police Comr* [1995] QB 335, CA.
16 But where prosecutors had undertaken a particular responsibility to provide information to magistrates, a duty of care was exceptionally owed to the plaintiff; *Welsh v Chief Constable of Merseyside Police* [1993] 1 All ER 692.
17 *Elguzouli-Daf v Metropolitan Police Comr*, supra, at 183.
18 *Thacker v Crown Prosecution Service* (1997) Times, 29 December, CA.
19 *Heslop v Chapman* (1853) 23 LJQB 49 at 52 (per Jervis CJ and Pollock CB); cf *Shrosbery v Osmaston* (1877) 37 LT 792 at 794 (per Lindley J); contra Wightman J in *Williams v Banks* (1859) 1 F & F 557 at 559.

SECTION 2.   ABUSE OF PROCESS

It may be a tort to use legal process in its proper form in order to accomplish a purpose other than that for which it was designed and thereby cause damage.

The leading case is *Grainger v Hill*:[20]

> The defendant was held liable when he had the plaintiff arrested, ostensibly for non-payment of a debt, but in fact in order illegally to compel him to surrender the register of a vessel, without which the plaintiff could not take the vessel to sea.

The case decided that in this tort the plaintiff need not prove want of reasonable and probable cause; nor need the proceedings have terminated in his favour.[1] The plaintiff must show that the predominant purpose of the other party in using the legal process has been one other than that for which it was designed.[2] Thus, a defendant who issued by mistake a plaint note for a debt which had already been paid was held not liable.[3] In contrast with malicious prosecution, damage to fame, person or property need not be proved; any special damage is enough.[4] It should be noted that in *Metall und Rohstoff AG v Donaldson Lufkin & Jenrette Inc*[5] the Court of Appeal, while somewhat grudgingly accepting the tort of abuse of process recognised in *Grainger v Hill*, doubted the existence of any more general tort of maliciously instituting civil proceedings.

SECTION 3.   WITNESS IMMUNITY

It is a fundamental principle of the common law that no-one can be civilly liable for evidence given in court;[6] thus no action lies in defamation for words spoken as a witness in court,[7] nor will conspiracy lie against policemen who conspire to defame the plaintiff at a criminal trial.[8] A plaintiff who is imprisoned in consequence of the defendant's giving false evidence on oath at the plaintiff's trial has no cause of action;[9] perjury is

---

20   (1838) 4 Bing NC 212; *Gibbs v Pike and Wells* (1842) 9 M & W 351 (maliciously registering a court order); *Speed Seal Products Ltd v Paddington* [1986] 1 All ER 91, [1985] 1 WLR 1327, CA; and see W Wells 'The Abuse of Process' (1985) 102 LQR 9.

1   *Speed Seal Products Ltd v Paddington* (supra).

2   *Metall und Rohstoff AG v Donaldson Lufkin & Jenrette Inc* [1989] 3 All ER 14 at 50, CA; *Clissold v Cratchley* [1910] 2 KB 244, CA.

3   *Corbett v Burge, Warren and Ridgley Ltd* (1932) 48 TLR 626. It was also said in this case that loss of business profits is not a recoverable head of damage, sed quaere.

4   Eg if a suit in deceit was instituted for the purpose of damaging the plaintiff's credit. In *Smith v East Elloe RDC* [1956] AC 736, [1956] 1 All ER 855, HL, the House of Lords held there to be jurisdiction to hear a claim that a clerk to a council knowingly and in bad faith wrongfully procured a compulsory purchase order to be made and confirmed by a minister, even though a statute precluded the courts from challenging the validity of the order itself on the grounds of bad faith.

5   [1989] 3 All ER 14 at 51.

6   *Roy v Prior* [1971] AC 470, [1970] 1 All ER 729, HL.

7   Chapter 24 ante.

8   *Marrinan v Vibart* [1963] 1 QB 528, [1962] 3 All ER 380, CA.

9   *Hargreaves v Bretherton* [1959] 1 QB 45, [1958] 3 All ER 122, approved obiter in *Roy v Prior* supra at 477 (per Lord Morris of Borth-y-Gest). In *Evans v London Hospital Medical College* [1981] 1 All ER 715, it was held that this immunity extends to statements made before the issue of a writ or the institution of a prosecution, distinguishing *Saif Ali v Sydney Mitchell & Co* [1980] AC 198, [1978] 3 All ER 1033. But note *Palmer v Durnford Ford (a firm)* [1992] QB 483, [1992] 2 All ER 122 (restricting immunities of expert witnesses).

a crime but not a tort. Witness immunity extends to the preparation as well as the presentation of evidence and so a claim for fabrication of evidence made outside the tort of malicious prosecution will generally fail.[10] Any remedy then for alleged attempts to 'frame' the plaintiff can lie only in malicious prosecution where absence of reasonable and probable cause must be proved. A claim that police lied to the court must fail, if despite the untruths there was due cause to prosecute.[11] It has been held that in proceedings for malicious arrest the plaintiff can rely on statements made by the defendant in court when seeking the warrant: the wrong is the arrest with malice, of which the statement in court provides evidential support.[12]

SECTION 4.   MISFEASANCE IN PUBLIC OFFICE

A successful application for judicial review of administrative action which results in an administrative process being quashed as invalid or unlawful does not[13] of itself create any liability in tort for loss or damage suffered by the applicant. The developing tort of misfeasance in public office may, however, be set to offer a remedy in damages for misuse of administrative process.[14] Certainly there are growing numbers of claims brought in misfeasance. Where an individual suffers loss or damage consequent upon administrative action which the relevant officer knows to be unlawful that loss or damage is recoverable in tort.[15] The plaintiff in *Roncarelli v Duplessis*[16] lost his liquor licence after the defendant, the then Prime Minister of Quebec, ordered the Quebec Licensing Commission to revoke the licence. Duplessis acted against the plaintiff as part of his campaign against Jehovah's Witnesses. He recovered damages in tort for the malicious abuse of the licensing process.

In *Bourgoin SA v Ministry of Agriculture*[17] the plaintiffs were French turkey producers who had been banned by the defendants from exporting turkeys to England. The reason given was risk of disease but, for the purposes of the preliminary point of law, the ministry admitted that the true grounds were protection of British turkey producers and that they acted accordingly in breach of Article 30 of the EEC Treaty in imposing unjustifiable import restrictions. They contended that they were nevertheless not liable for misfeasance in public office because there was no intent to injure the plaintiffs but, rather, to protect British interests. Mann J held, and the Court of Appeal confirmed, that proof of malice is not essential to the tort. It is sufficient that the plaintiff prove that the defendant knew that he acted unlawfully[18] and that his act would injure the plaintiff. Malice is a possible but not essential ingredient of the tort.[19]

An action for misfeasance in public office will lie against a local authority, or similar public body, as much as against an individual. When the relevant decision is collective (for example a resolution by a local council) it is enough to show that the majority of

10 *Silcott v Metropolitan Police Comr* [1996] 8 Admin LR 633, CA; *Docker v Chief Constable of West Midlands Police* [1998] 17 LS Gaz R 31, CA.
11 *Silcott v Metropolitan Police Comr*, supra.
12 *Roy v Prior* supra.
13 *Dunlop v Woollahra Municipal Council* [1982] AC 158, [1981] 1 All ER 1202, PC.
14 *Jones v Swansea City Council* [1990] 3 All ER 737, HL.
15 *David v Abdul Cader* [1963] 3 All ER 579, [1963] 1 WLR 834; *Davis v Bromley Corpn* [1908] 1 KB 170, CA.
16 (1959) 16 DLR (2d) 689.
17 [1986] QB 716, [1985] 3 All ER 585, CA.
18 *Three Rivers District Council v Bank of England (No 4)* (1998) Times, 10 December, CA.
19 *Elguzouli-Daf v Metropolitan Police Comr* [1995] 1 All ER 833 at 840; though note that in *Bennett v Metropolitan Police Comr* [1995] 2 All ER 1 at 13–14 it was suggested an express intent to harm the plaintiff must be established.

those supporting the resolution did so with intent to damage the plaintiff and knowledge of the unlawful nature of their act.[20] In *Racz v Home Office*[1] the extent of a public authority's vicarious liability for misfeasance was ventilated. The plaintiff claimed that prison officers unjustifiably removed him to a strip cell knowing they had no lawful grounds to do so and/or acting maliciously. The Court of Appeal struck out the claim against the Home Office holding that, were the individual officers liable in misfeasance, they must have acted ultra vires and thus outside the scope of their employment. The House of Lords overruled that decision. Unauthorised, unlawful conduct by employees does not necessarily take an employee outside the scope of his employment. To do so, and thus relieve the employer of his vicarious liability for the employee's tortious conduct, the unlawful conduct must be so far beyond the authorised duties of the employee as to amount to a 'frolic of his own'. A full trial of the nature of the prison officers' alleged misfeasance was required. So, for example, if prison officers deliberately set out to teach a difficult prisoner a lesson, their misfeasance might well be within the scope of their employment, even though an entirely improper mode of carrying out their duties. But if a prison officer were to act entirely on the basis of personal spite, perhaps because the prisoner was having an affair with her lover, a contrary result might ensue.[2]

Fabrication of evidence by police officers and malicious refusal of bail are further examples of possible misfeasance in office. However, witness immunity prevails in the tort of misfeasance and no claim can thus be based on evidence given in, or prepared for, the courts.[3] Misfeasance cannot be used to circumvent the requirements in malicious prosecution of proof of absence of reasonable and probable cause.

---

20 *Jones v Swansea City Council* [1990] 3 All ER 737, HL. And on misfeasance in office generally, see *Three Rivers District Council v Bank of England (No 3)* [1996] 3 All ER 558; and *(No 4)* (1998) Times, 10 December, CA
1   [1994] 2 WLR 23, HL.
2   Though the abuse of the officer's position of authority by virtue of which she has access to the plaintiff may be sufficient even in this case to keep her within the scope of her employment.
3   *Silcott v Commissioner of Police for the Metropolis* (1996) 8 Admin LR 633, CA; *Gizzonio v Chief Constable of Derbyshire* (1998) Times, 29 April, CA.

Part VIII

Remedies and parties

CONTENTS

CHAPTER		PAGE
25	Vicarious liability	503
26	Remedies	525
27	Compensation for personal injuries	539
28	Extinction of remedies	566
29	Parties	579

Chapter 25

Vicarious liability[1]

SECTION I. IMPORTANCE OF THE DISTINCTION BETWEEN EMPLOYEES AND INDEPENDENT CONTRACTORS

For the present purpose the law divides emplyed persons into two groups:

1   those employed to perform services in connection with the affairs of the employer, and over whom the employer has control in the performance of those services. In tort, these persons have traditionally been termed 'servants'. That word, in modern parlance, tends to be taken to refer to domestic help alone. Hence, save when discussing older case law, the term 'employee' will be used hereafter;

2   those who do work for another, but who are not controlled by that other in the performance of that work. Normally, such work will be carried out in pursuance of a contract for services, and the persons doing it are therefore called 'independent contractors'.

The distinction is important for the following reason. If an employee commits a tort in the course of his employment, then the employer is liable regardless of whether he himself has committed a tort: 'every act which is done by a servant in the course of his duty is regarded as done by his master's orders, and consequently is the same as if it were the master's own act. ...'[2] This, of course, is the clearest case of a strict tortious liability, and it may be regarded as a judicial decision of policy that the employer is to bear the financial responsibility for those torts committed by his employees in the course of his enterprise – both because he is better able to stand the loss (or insure against it),

---

1   On this chapter generally, see Atiyah *Vicarious Liability in the Law of Torts* and *Clerk & Lindsell* ch 5.
2   *Bartonshill Coal Co v McGuire* (1858) 3 Macq 300 at 306, HL (per Lord Chelmsford LC).

because he can pass it on to the public in the form of increased prices, and because he will thereby be encouraged to maintain higher standards of conduct in the running of his business.

If the act complained of is not that of an employee, then the employer is not, without more, liable: he can be sued only if he himself has, in the circumstances, committed a tort (or if he was in breach of a non-delegable duty).[3] An employer may be vicariously liable for the torts of his employees, but he is not liable for the torts of those who are his independent contractors. For this reason, it is vital to distinguish the two classes of persons.

SECTION 2.   CRITERIA FOR DISTINGUISHING EMPLOYEES AND INDEPENDENT CONTRACTORS[4]

(A)   CONTROL

The formula most often used by the courts in the past to mark the distinction is 'control': 'The final test … lies in the nature and degree of detailed control over the person alleged to be a servant'.[5] A person is an employee where the employer 'retains the control of the actual performance' of the work.[6]

In a simple industrial society, as England was until this century, where work was done largely by agricultural labourers or craftsmen under the directions of employers who had the same or even greater technical skill than their workmen, it would ordinarily be enough to say that the employer could tell the man not merely what task he was to perform, but also how he should perform it. If the employer could do both these things, the man was a servant. Nowadays, when a new class of managers, as distinct from owners, has arisen in industry, and when so many employees have some technical skill which is often not possessed by any of their employers, the relationship has become more subtle and hardly capable of exact definition: the control dimension will not, by itself, be adequate.[7] Put simply, it is no longer a cast iron test for the existence of an employer/employee relationship.[8] Note also that the courts may, for policy reasons, hold someone to be an employee though aspects of his work suggest more that he is an independent contractor. In *Lane v Shire Roofing*,[9] for example, the Court of Appeal drew attention to the policy reasons that exist within the field of health and safety at work to decide a borderline case in favour of classifying the worker as an employee.

In deciding whether enough 'control' is exercised over another to make him an employee one must take into account several factors, no single one of which is conclusive. The criteria include the extent to which the employer can control the details of the work, whether the method of payment is on a time or a job basis,[10] whose tools, equipment and premises are to be used,[11] the skill called for in the work, the intention

---

3   *Bull v Devon Area Health Authority* [1993] 4 Med LR 117.
4   See Kidner 'Vicarious Liability: For whom should the Employers be Liable?' (1995) 15 LS 47.
5   *Performing Right Society Ltd v Mitchell and Booker (Palais de Danse) Ltd* [1924] 1 KB 762 at 767 (per McCardie J).
6   *Honeywill & Stein Ltd v Larkin Bros (London's Commercial Photographers) Ltd* [1934] 1 KB 191 at 196, [1933] All ER Rep 77 at 81, CA (per Slesser LJ).
7   *Short v J and W Henderson Ltd* (1946) 62 TLR 427 at 429, HL (per Lord Thankerton). The inadequacy of this test was expressly stated in *Cassidy v Ministry of Health* [1951] 2 KB 343 at 352, [1951] 1 All ER 574, CA (per Somerville LJ).
8   For alternative tests see *Clerk and Lindsell* para 5-05 et seq.
9   [1995] IRLR 493, CA.
10   Employees are generally paid by the hour whereas independent contractors are normally paid for the complete job.
11   *Quarman v Burnett* (1840) 6 M & W 499.

of the parties,[12] the freedom of selection of labour by the employer,[13] and the power to dismiss. All these matters, and many more, but especially and increasingly that mentioned in the quotation below from Denning LJ, must be considered in order to decide whether this right of control can be inferred. His Lordship said:[14]

> It is often easy to recognise a contract of service when you see it, but difficult to say wherein the difference [between a contract of service and a contract for services] lies.[15] A ship's master, a chauffeur, and a reporter on the staff of a newspaper are all employed under a contract of service; but a ship's pilot, a taxi-man, and a newspaper contributor are employed under a contract for services. *One feature which seems to run through the instances is that, under a contract of service, a man is employed as part of the business, and his work is done as an integral part of the business; whereas, under a contract for services, his work, although done for the business, is not integrated into it but is only accessory to it.*[16]

Another approach to the question is to ask 'is the worker in business on his own account?[17] Where a building worker neither hired his own help, nor provided his own equipment, and had no say in the control of the site, the Privy Council found his position to be that of an employee rather than an independent contractor selling his services to site owners.

(B)   SOME PARTICULAR CASES EXAMINED

In the majority of cases, there is no difficulty in determining the status of the person.[18] Factory employees, office clerical staff, agricultural workers and the like are clearly employees; whereas garage proprietors, house builders, and dry-cleaners are the independent contractors of the members of the public who employ them. A typical instance where someone might fall into either group, depending on the circumstances, is that of a sales representative.[19] Similarly, a chauffeur is an employee, but a taxi driver is not.[20]

Those who work ad hoc, on temporary contracts acquired through an employment agency, may, on occasion, be treated as employees of the agency for the purposes of

12 *Johnson v Coventry Churchill International Ltd* [1992] 3 All ER 14.
13 At common law the owner of a ship was not liable for the negligence of a compulsory pilot: *The Halley* (1868) LR 2 PC 193 (see now Pilotage Act 1987; *Oceangas (Gibraltar) Ltd v Port of London Authority* [1993] 2 Lloyd's Rep 292). The statutory obligation that watermen on Thames barges shall be licensed does not prevent a waterman from being a servant since there are many from which to choose, and the barge owner can dismiss: *Martin v Temperley* (1843) 4 QB 298.
14 *Stevenson, Jordan and Harrison Ltd v MacDonald and Evans* [1952] 1 TLR 101 at 111, CA. Cf somewhat similar observations by Lord Wright in *Montreal v Montreal Locomotive Works* [1947] 1 DLR 161 at 169, PC.
15 Contract of service/contract for services are here merely synonymous with employee/independent contractor.
16 Our italics. Cf *Bank Voor Handel en Scheepvart NV v Slatford* [1953] 1 QB 248 at 295, [1952] 2 All ER 956, CA (per Denning LJ): 'It depends on whether the person is part and parcel of the organisation'; reversed on other grounds [1954] AC 584, [1954] 1 All ER 969, HL (sub nom *Bank Voor Handel en Scheepvaart v Administrator of Hungarian Property*).
17 *Lee Tin Sang v Chung Chi-Keung* [1990] 2 AC 374, [1990] 2 WLR 1173, HL; *Lane v Shire Roofing* [1995] IRLR 493, CA.
18 For the special statutory provisions defining when a trade union is vicariously liable for various torts involving industrial action, see the Trade Union and Labour Relations (Consolidation) Act 1992, s 15.
19 Or the holder of a university research fellowship who is required also to act as a part-time demonstrator.
20 When is a director an employee?

each separate engagement.[1] Whether the general arrangement – that is the worker being registered on the agency's books – could amount to a contract of employment would appear to turn on the question whether there is a mutuality of obligation between the worker and agency.[2] When such mutuality will be deemed to exist, however, is a difficult question to which, as yet, there is no authoritative answer.[3]

(1) HOSPITAL STAFF

The courts were once much concerned to decide which members of hospital staff are employees. This issue exposed the problems of the 'control' test. How could lay members of a hospital board be said to 'control' a Nobel prize-winning neurosurgeon? After much uncertainty it is now settled that nurses, radiographers,[4] house surgeons,[5] and assistant medical officers[6] in the full-time service of hospitals are employees. Part-time anaesthetists have also been held to be employees on the ground that they are members of the organisation of the hospital.[7] Surgeons and consultants working under the National Health Service, even though only engaged part-time, will for the same reason be employees of the hospital authority. They are all operating as part and parcel of the NHS enterprise. It is only when the surgeon or consultant treats the patient under a private contract between himself and the patient that the hospital trusts is not answerable for his torts.

(2) BORROWED EMPLOYEES

It is often difficult to decide whose employee a person is when he is lent by his employer to another. The authoritative decision here is *Mersey Docks and Harbour Board v Coggins and Griffiths (Liverpool) Ltd.*[8]

> The board owned many mobile cranes, each handled by skilled workmen engaged and paid by it. In the ordinary course of its business, it hired out a crane to the respondents, a stevedoring company, for use in unloading a ship. The power to dismiss remained with the board, but the contract provided that the driver was to be the servant of the hirers. While loading the cargo, the driver was under the immediate control of the hirers in the sense that the hirers could tell him which boxes to load and where to place them, but they could not tell him how to manipulate the controls of the crane. Through the negligent handling of the crane by the driver while loading, a third party was injured. The House of Lords was called upon to decide from which of the two, the board or the hirers, the plaintiff was to recover his damages: that is, whose servant was he at the time of the accident?

1 *McMeechan v Secretary of State for Employment* [1997] IRLR 353, CA.
2 *Clark v Oxfordshire Health Authority* [1998] IRLR 125, CA. 'Mutuality' is used here simply to connote a reciprocal agreement.
3 But see *Carmichael v National Power plc* [1998] IRLR 301, CA (a majority of the Court of Appeal stated that mutuality exists where there is an implied term in the global arrangement whereby the agency commits itself to providing a reasonable amount of work while the employee commits himself to doing a reasonable amount of work).
4 *Gold v Essex County Council* [1942] 2 KB 293, [1942] 2 All ER 237, CA.
5 *Collins v Hertfordshire County Council* [1947] KB 598, [1947] 1 All ER 633; *Cassidy v Ministry of Health* [1951] 2 KB 343, [1951] 1 All ER 574, CA.
6 *Cassidy v Ministry of Health* (supra).
7 *Roe v Minister of Health* [1954] 2 QB 66, [1954] 2 All ER 131, CA.
8 [1947] AC 1, [1946] 2 All ER 345, HL; *Karuppan Bhoomidas v Port of Singapore Authority* [1978] 1 All ER 956, PC (even though a byelaw provided that those loading and discharging vessels shall be under the superintendence of the ship's officers, stevedores were held to remain employees of the port authority, which was vicariously liable for their torts).

It was held that the board was solely liable. There is a very strong presumption indeed[9] that someone remains the employee of the general or permanent employer although another employer borrows his services. Where cranes or vehicles were let out on hire with a driver, the owner was responsible for his employee's negligence unless he had divested himself of all possession and control.[10] But if the system of work that is used is unsafe, according to *Morris v Breaveglen Ltd*[11] it is the general employer who is liable (on the basis of his non-delegable duty to this effect).

SECTION 3.   IS THERE A SEPARATE CATEGORY OF AGENTS?

We have seen that a person who does work for another may be either an employee or an independent contractor. Such a person may also, at the same time, be an agent: that is, the category of 'agent' partially overlaps with the categories of both 'servant' and 'independent contractor'. It is submitted that this category of agents, although of great importance in other branches of the law, such as contract, has little relevance in the present context (subject to the exceptions discussed below). An agent may or may not be subject to that degree of control which will make him an employee: the law of torts is here concerned only to know in any particular case whether or not he is an employee. A person employed on a weekly wage to sell vacuum cleaners and under orders as to his times and place of employment will be at once an agent (in contracting to sell cleaners) and an employee. On the other hand, no one would suggest that, if the defendant employed a chartered accountant to settle his liability for income tax, the defendant would be liable if the accountant negligently knocked down a pedestrian while driving to the tax office in order to discuss the matter. The accountant would be an agent and an independent contractor of the defendant, but not his employee.[12]

One tort, namely that of deceit, affords an important exception to the rule that the law of torts is not concerned with the separate category of agents. Where a principal delegates authority to another person to negotiate a contract on his behalf, he may be liable for the fraud of his 'agent'. So, for example, if an estate agent, in the course of negotiating the sale of a house of his principal, knowingly makes untrue statements about that house to a third party who acts on them to his detriment, in some circumstances, the principal will be liable in deceit. And yet the estate agent is not the principal's employee. This liability exists only where the principal can be said to have held out this estate agent as one authorised to make such representations in the course of making the contract.[13] This provides a valuable clue to solving the problem – such misrepresentations, though capable of giving rise to tortious liabilities, are so intimately associated with, and inseparable from, the contractual relation to which end the agency

---

9   For an example where the company 'borrowing' employees did become vicariously liable for their acts, see *Sime v Sutcliffe Catering Scotland Ltd* [1990] IRLR 228 (Court of Session).

10   And the original employer will of course be primarily liable if he hires out an incompetent driver: *McConkey v Amec plc* (1990) 27 Con LR 88, CA.

11   [1993] PIQR P294, CA.

12   The obiter dicta of the House of Lords in *Heatons Transport (St Helens) Ltd v Transport and General Workers Union* [1973] AC 15 at 99, HL, that the test to be applied in determining the responsibility of a master or principal for the act of a servant or an agent 'is the same: was the servant or agent acting on behalf, and within the scope, of the authority conferred by the master or principal?' must not (it is submitted) be taken to apply in tort so as to refute the propositions advanced in this section. See also *Watkins v Birmingham City Council* (1975) 126 NLJ 442, CA (a schoolboy distributing milk to classrooms in his school was not a servant of the local education authority, although he might well have been an agent).

13   Cf *Uxbridge Permanent Benefit Building Society v Pickard* [1939] 2 KB 248 at 254–5, [1939] 2 All ER 344, CA (per Lord Greene MR).

is directed that they assume the quality of contract, where agency as such, of course, is important.[14]

The concept of agency is applicable also to negligent statements made by an estate agent.[15] But it is an essential prerequisite of liability of the principal that the agent acted within the scope of the authority which the principal's acts led the plaintiff to believe the agent enjoyed. Where the agent is at the same time an employee of the principal, the agent cannot act beyond the scope of his authority and still remain within the general course of his employment.[16]

The other area which demands special attention is the liability of the owner of a vehicle when it is driven by someone else. Of course the owner is liable if his employee drives it negligently in the course of his employment. The courts have not stopped there and the House of Lords in *Morgans v Launchbury*[17] affirmed that if the vehicle is driven by the owner's agent and the user is driving as the owner's agent, for the owner's purposes, the owner is again liable. The facts in *Morgans v Launchbury* were as follows.

> The defendant wife owned the car and with her permission her husband took it on a pub crawl. When he was too drunk to drive, he asked his drinking companion to drive. The wife was held not liable for the companion's negligent driving.

The court held that the driver was not the agent of the owner and that a car owner is liable only if the driver is his employee acting in the course of his employment or is his authorised agent driving for and on behalf of the owner. Lord Wilberforce added that 'agency' in such a context was merely a concept the meaning and purpose of which is that the owner ought to pay.[18] The House rejected the argument that it was so desirable to find someone liable who was covered by compulsory third-party insurance, that it should hold the owner liable for anyone who drove with his permission: only Parliament, not the courts, could make that extension of liability.[19] It is submitted that *Morgans v Launchbury* does not upset the general rule in vicarious liability that a principal is not liable merely because his agent commits a tort while acting as agent.[20]

---

14 Whether this exception will be restricted to deceit because of the need for a contractual element, or whether the parallel concept of 'holding out' will permit its extension to any tort where the defendant has held out a person to represent him in performing a transaction with others, is doubtful. The High Court of Australia has held an insurance company liable when its agent (not a servant) defamed a rival company while soliciting business: *Colonial Mutual Life Assurance Society Ltd v Producers and Citizens Assurance Co of Australia* (1931) 46 CLR 41; dicta in *Houldsworth v City of Glasgow Bank* (1880) 5 App Cas 317 at 326, HL (per Lord Selbourne) and *Lloyd v Grace, Smith & Co* [1912] AC 716 at 734–5, HL (per Lord Macnaghten) lean towards the Australian position. But was Blain J right in *Gros v Crook* (1969) 113 Sol Jo 408 in holding, in a libel action, that a book reviewer in *The Times Literary Supplement* was an agent, and not an independent contractor?

15 *Kooragang Investments Pty Ltd v Richardson and Wrench Ltd* [1982] AC 462, [1981] 3 All ER 65, PC. In that case, therefore, the principal was held not liable for the agent's negligent statement because the agent was not authorised to make the valuations, the subject of the negligent statements.

16 *Armagas Ltd v Mundogas SA, The Ocean Frost* [1986] AC 717, [1985] 3 All ER 795, HL.

17 [1973] AC 127, HL; approving *Hewitt v Bonvin* [1940] 1 KB 188, CA.

18 [1973] AC 127 at 135, HL.

19 In *Norwood v Navan* [1981] RTR 457, CA, a husband was held not liable for the negligence of his wife when driving his car for family shopping. In *Nelson v Raphael* [1979] RTR 437, the seller of a car asked a friend to hand over the car to the buyer and collect his cheque. When the friend demonstrated the controls to the buyer, the seller was vicariously liable for the friend's negligence while doing so.

20 *Nottingham v Aldridge* [1971] 2 QB 739, [1971] 2 All ER 751.

SECTION 4. LIABILITY IN RESPECT OF AN INDEPENDENT CONTRACTOR

The employer is not normally liable merely because an independent contractor commits a tort in the course of his employment; he is liable only if he himself is deemed to have committed a tort. This may happen in one of three ways.

(A) AUTHORISING HIM TO COMMIT A TORT

In many circumstances the law will attribute to a man the conduct of another being, whether human or animal, if he has instigated that conduct. If X sets his dog upon Y it is as much a battery as if X had struck Y with his fist. He who instigates or procures another to commit a tort is deemed to have committed the tort himself;[1] it matters not whether that other was an employee, an independent contractor or an agent (human or otherwise). In *Ellis v Sheffield Gas Consumers Co* the facts were:[2]

> Having no legal power to do so, the defendants' gas undertaking employed an independent contractor to dig up a part of a street. The plaintiff fell over a heap of earth and stones made by the contractor in the course of digging, and the defendants were held liable on the ground that they had authorised this nuisance.

It is not always easy, however, to decide whether the defendant can be said to have authorised the tortious act. Where a lessee was empowered to erect certain structures, but the lease reserved to the lessor the right to approve the plans for such structures (which right the lessor is not reported to have exercised), this was not enough to make the lessor answerable for the lessee's negligence in the course of building the structure.[3] On the other hand, although a taxi driver is certainly not an employee, if his fare orders him to drive fast or to take other risks, he is jointly responsible for any ensuing tort.[4]

If a person commits a tort while purporting to act on behalf of another, but in fact without his authority, and that other later ratifies the act which amounted to a tort, he thereby becomes answerable for the tort in the same way as if he had given authority prior to commission. The principal must know, at the time when he ratifies,[5] of the commission of the act which constitutes a tort, but he is not excused because he was unaware that the ratified act was a tort if he would have been liable in tort had he done the act himself with such ignorance. Thus, if he ratifies the purchase of goods which the vendor had no right to sell, he is liable in conversion, although he is unaware that the sale was unlawful.[6]

---

1   Even if that other had a defence, the principal may still be liable: *Barker v Braham* (1773) 3 Wils 368 (defendant authorised sheriff to arrest plaintiff on an illegal warrant; although the sheriff was protected from liability by reason of acting under the warrant, the defendant was still liable in false imprisonment).
2   (1853) 2 E & B 767.
3   *Hurlstone v London Electric Rly Co* (1914) 30 TLR 398, CA.
4   Cf *M'Laughlin v Pryor* (1842) 4 Man & G 48. Mere failure to object or other passive acquiescence would not be enough.
5   *Freeman v Rosher* (1849) 13 QB 780.
6   *Hilbery v Hatton* (1864) 2 H & C 822.

(B)   TORTS WHERE INTENTIONAL OR NEGLIGENT CONDUCT NEED NOT ALWAYS BE PROVED

The torts of 'strict liability' previously discussed are characterised not only by the fact that, in some instances, there is a liability where no intentional or negligent act has been committed by one's independent contractors. Thus we have seen that in nuisance,[7] *Rylands v Fletcher*[8] and breach of statutory duty[9] that the employer may in some circumstances be liable for the conduct of his independent contractor.

(C)   NEGLIGENCE

An employer may be liable in negligence for damage caused by the acts of his independent contractors in the following circumstances:[10]

(1)   PERSONAL NEGLIGENCE ON THE PART OF THE EMPLOYER

First, there may be such an element of personal negligence on the part of the employer as to make him liable for the acts of his independent contractor, and this may be so even though the duty of care owed by the employer in a particular case is not so extensive as to make the employer liable merely because his independent contractor has been negligent. Thus, the employer is liable where he carelessly appoints an incompetent contractor. Equally, where, without precautions, the risk of harm is foreseeable, failure by the employer to provide in the contract for those precautions, is actionable negligence.[11] *Robinson v Beaconsfield RDC*[12] furnishes another example of personal negligence on the part of the employer.

> The defendants employed contractors to clean out cesspools in their district. No arrangements were made for the removal of the deposits of sewage upon their being taken from the cesspools by the contractors. The contractors deposited sewage on the plaintiff's land. The defendants were held liable for their failure to take proper precautions to dispose of the sewage.

It probably follows from the decision in *Robinson* that failure to inspect after a job has been completed would constitute negligence.

(2)   NON-DELEGABLE DUTIES

In some categories of negligence, the duty to take care has been so widely drawn that it is not discharged by properly instructing and supervising a competent contractor: there is a positive duty not to act, even by a contractor, without taking due care. Such duties are often termed non-delegable duties. It must be emphasised that this is not

---

7   Eg *Matania v National Provincial Bank Ltd* [1936] 2 All ER 633, CA; cf *Hole v Sittingbourne and Sheerness Rly Co* (1861) 6 H & N 488; *Dalton v Angus* (1881) 6 App Cas 740, HL (the right of support); *Bower v Peate* (1876) 1 QBD 321; *Alcock v Wraith* (1991) 59 BLR 20, CA.
8   (1868) LR 3 HL 330.
9   *Hosking v De Havilland Aircraft Co Ltd* [1949] 1 All ER 540.
10   But for these purposes, a sub-contractor who himself engages a sub-sub-contractor will not be treated in law as an employer: *MTM Construction Ltd v William Reid Engineering Ltd* 1998 SLT 211n, OH.
11   Cf *Hughes v Percival* (1883) 8 App Cas 443, HL.
12   [1911] 2 Ch 188.

true of all duty situations,[13] and it is, of course, a question of law whether such a wide duty is owed.

Where the activity is particularly hazardous, such as the lighting of open fires on bush land,[14] or re-roofing in a row of terraced houses where difficulties with the 'joins' between the properties were well known,[15] or the taking of flash-light photographs in a cinema,[16] the duty of care has been held not to be delegable. Where employers are carrying out inherently dangerous operations on or near a highway which may foreseeably harm highway users, and the negligence of their independent contractors does cause such harm, the employers are again liable. Consider *Holliday v National Telephone Co.*[17]

> The defendants, in laying telephone wires along a street, employed an independent contractor to solder the tubes in which these wires were carried. In negligently using a benzolene lamp, he injured a passer-by. The defendants were held liable.

On the other hand removing a hawthorn tree from a garden adjoining a highway is not an inherently dangerous activity. Accordingly, its owner is not liable for harm caused to the plaintiff by his contractor removing it negligently.[18] Structural operations damaging neighbouring premises are, however, also within the rule.[19] Similarly, a railway company owes a duty to passengers to see that bridges along its lines are carefully built.[20]

The categories of non-delegable duties are not closed. NHS authorities may well owe such a duty. With the setting up of a nationalised health service, hospital treatment all too often assumes an impersonalised and institutional form. A patient whose success in an action for negligence depends on his establishing negligence on the part of a particular employee of a hospital often has an impossible burden of proof to discharge; he may, while anaesthetised, be the victim of negligence in the operating theatre and not be able to show whether the senior surgeon, his assistant or the theatre sister, was responsible. And with cutbacks in the number of permanent staff employed in the NHS it may be that one or more of these is not an employee of the hospital, but an agency doctor or nurse brought in on an ad hoc basis. One obvious solution is to hold that hospital authorities have a duty to provide proper treatment at all stages, a duty which they do not throw off by entrusting it to competent staff. *Lindsey County Council v Marshall,*[1] *Gold v Essex County Council*[2] and *Collins v Hertfordshire County*

---

13 This is the flaw in Chapman 'Liability for Negligence of Independent Contractors' (1934) 50 LQR 71. For the liability of occupiers of land to their visitors for the acts of independent contractors under the Occupiers' Liability Act 1957, see ch 16 ante.
14 *Black v Christchurch Finance Co* [1894] AC 48, PC. And see *Balfour v Barty-King* [1957] 1 QB 496, [1957] 1 All ER 156, CA (owner liable for fire when independent contractor plumber used blowlamp in loft to thaw defendant's frozen pipes).
15 *Alcock v Wraith* (1991) 59 BLR 20, CA.
16 *Honeywill and Stein Ltd v Larkin Bros (London's Commercial Photographer) Ltd* [1934] 1 KB 191, CA.
17 [1899] 2 QB 392, CA; cf *Hardaker v Idle District Council* [1896] 1 QB 335, CA (damaging gas pipe while laying sewer under highway); *Penny v Wimbledon UDC and Iles* [1899] 2 QB 72 (heap of soil left unlighted on highway); *Walsh v Holst & Co Ltd* [1958] 3 All ER 33, CA. In *Pickard v Smith* (1861) 10 CBNS 470, the same principle was applied to hold a railway refreshment room proprietor liable to a passenger who fell down a hole which the servant of the defendant's independent contractor negligently left on the platform.
18 *Salsbury v Woodland* [1970] 1 QB 324, [1969] 3 All ER 863, CA.
19 *Hughes v Percival* (1883) 8 App Cas 443, HL (party wall negligently cut into while contractor was rebuilding part of adjoining premises); *Alcock v Wraith* (supra).
20 *Grote v Chester and Holyhead Rly Co* (1848) 2 Exch 251.
1   [1937] AC 97, [1936] 2 All ER 1076, HL.
2   [1942] 2 KB 293 at 301, [1942] 2 All ER 237, CA (per Lord Greene MR).

Council[3] pointed the way, and that there was such a non-delegable duty formed the basis of Denning LJ's judgement in *Cassidy v Ministry of Health*.[4]

There it was held that a hospital authority which ran a casualty department had a duty to provide proper medical and nursing attention for those who presented themselves there, complaining of illness or injury.[5] A direct non-delegable duty to patients would have several consequences in today's health service. Perhaps until about 1980 it did not matter too much whether Denning LJ was right in *Cassidy*.[6] If all the professionals caring for a patient were employees and it could be proved that someone was negligent, the hospital authority was necessarily vicariously liable for the tort of one of their employees. With increasing use of agency staff, however, the hospital, if its liability is solely vicarious, may be able to turn round to the patient and contend that she cannot prove a person for whom the hospital is vicariously responsible is at fault. On the other hand, the hospital may be liable for failure to implement a reliable system of work, such as one to deal with emergencies.[7] Consider, too, the following scenarios. A child falls ill in the night and a doctor from the deputising service engaged by the family GP fails to diagnose meningitis. An elderly lady finally gets a date for a hip replacement. The health authority contracts her operation out to a private clinic. If the GP and health authority are subject to '*Cassidy*' non-delegable duties, they are responsible for any negligence on the part of their independent contractors, the deputising services and the private clinic.[7a]

The Employer's Liability (Defective Equipment) Act 1969 applies when, for the purposes of his business, an employer provides equipment (which includes any plant and machinery, vehicle, aircraft and clothing) for his employee and the employee suffers personal injury in the course of his employment in consequence of a defect in that equipment. The injury is then deemed also to be attributable to the negligence of the employer if the defect is attributable wholly or partly to the negligence, or other tort, of an independent contractor or other third party. This Act therefore imposes an extensive statutory duty on employers. It leaves unchanged the common law duty of the employer to provide a safe system in respects other than the provision of equipment.[8]

> In *McDermid v Nash Dredging and Reclamation Co Ltd*,[9] the plaintiff was employed as a deck-hand by the defendants. He was instructed to go and work on another tug owned by a different company within the same group as the defendants. As a result of the negligence of that tug master, who was not an employee of the defendants, the plaintiff suffered severe injuries. The House of Lords held the defendants liable for failing to provide a safe system of work.

The breach of their non-delegable duty in respect of their employee's, the plaintiff's safety, was not discharged by delegating that duty to the master of the tug. The duty

3 [1947] KB 598, [1947] 1 All ER 633.
4 [1951] 2 KB 343 at 362–3, [1951] 1 All ER 574, CA (but probably not of the other two judges). And see *Wilsher v Essex Area Health Authority* [1987] QB 730, [1986] 3 All ER 801, CA. Cf *Jones v Manchester Corpn* [1952] 2 QB 852 at 869, [1952] 2 All ER 125, CA (per Denning LJ); *Razzel v Snowball* [1954] 3 All ER 429, CA; *MacDonald v Glasgow Western Hospitals Board of Management* 1954 SLT 226.
5 *Barnett v Chelsea and Kensington Hospital Management Committee* [1969] 1 QB 428, [1968] 1 All ER 1068.
6 For a view that he was wrong see *Yepremian v Scarborough General Hospital* (1980) 110 DLR (3d) 513 (Ontario CA).
7 *Bull v Devon Area Health Authority* [1993] 4 Med LR 117.
7a See *M v Calderdale Health Authority* [1998] Lloyd's Med Rep 157.
8 Note the obligation to insure under the Employers' Liability (Compulsory Insurance) Act 1969.
9 [1987] AC 906, [1987] 2 All ER 878, HL; and see *Davie v New Merton Board Mills Ltd* [1959] AC 604 at 646, HL (per Lord Reid).

to devise and operate a safe system of work was finally held to be non-delegable. But it must be stressed that that duty remains a duty to take reasonable care, not an absolute duty to ensure the employee's safety. In *Cook v Square D Ltd*,[10] for example, an employee working in Saudi Arabia was injured falling over an unguarded raised tile. The Court of Appeal held that the employers 8,000 miles away could not be responsible for every day-to-day event in the workplace. The real question was whether they had done what a reasonable employer should do in order to set up, operate and monitor a safe system of work.

The grounds of social policy for imposing non-delegable duties on employers and health authorities may explain the development of such duties in those areas. But in one or two other instances the courts have also been prepared to extend the categories of non-delegable duties. In *Rogers v Night Riders*,[11] for example, the plaintiff's mother telephoned the defendants for a taxi to take her daughter to the station and the mother paid for the cab. During the journey, a door flew open and the plaintiff was injured. The taxi driver was not an employee but an independent contractor for the defendants. Nevertheless the defendants were held to be in breach of their primary duty to the plaintiff. As far as she knew, it was the defendants who undertook to convey her safely and carefully to her destination. What has to be considered now is whether the courts are moving towards the development of a principle that, where one person or organisation undertakes to provide a service for another, albeit independently of any contract, he has a duty not only to exercise care personally, but also to ensure that, whoever actually carries out the service, the service is performed carefully.

SECTION 5.   WHERE THE EMPLOYER IS NOT LIABLE FOR THE ACTS OF AN INDEPENDENT CONTRACTOR

(A)   NO BREACH BY EMPLOYER OF ANY DUTY IMPOSED ON HIM BY THE LAW OF TORTS

An employer is liable for damage caused by tortious acts of his independent contractor only where there is a breach by the employer of a duty owed by him: the question is always what is the extent of the risk against which the employer has the duty to guard.[12] In the case of all other duty situations (and they are very numerous), the employer discharges his duty by taking care in the appointment of an independent contractor. No catalogue of instances falling within this last-mentioned group will be attempted: one example only is given. In *Phillips v Britannia Hygienic Laundry Co*,[13] the owner of a lorry was held not liable when a third party's vehicle was damaged in consequence of the negligent repair of his lorry by a garage proprietor.

---

10   [1992] ICR 262; but note that the incident in *McDermid* also took place abroad. Are you convinced by the distinctions made between the two cases: see ibid per Farquhason LJ at 270–1.

11   [1983] RTR 324, CA; and see *Cynat Products Ltd v Landbuild (Investment and Property) Ltd* [1984] 3 All ER 513.

12   *Dalton v Angus* (1881) 6 App Cas 740 at 831, HL (per Lord Watson).

13   [1923] 1 KB 539, affd [1923] 2 KB 832, CA; followed in *Stennett v Hancock and Peters* [1939] 2 All ER 578. But would the garage be liable for the negligent repair by its independent contractor? And see *Taylor v Rover Co Ltd* [1966] 2 All ER 181. A more recent example is *Rivers v Cutting* [1982] 3 All ER 69, CA (a policeman arranged, under powers given by the Removal and Disposal of Vehicles Regulations 1968, for a garage to tow away a car broken down on the M1 motorway; he was not liable for the garage's negligent towing).

(B)   COLLATERAL NEGLIGENCE

Employers of independent contractors are never liable for, as it is commonly stated, the 'collateral negligence' of their contractors. *Padbury v Holiday & Greenwood Ltd*[14] at once furnishes facts which illustrate the principle and contains what, it is submitted, is the soundest statement of the principle.

> A employed B to fit casement windows into certain premises. B's servant negligently put a tool on the sill of the window on which he was working at the time. The wind blew the casement open and the tool was knocked off the sill on to a passer-by.

Holding the employer not liable, Fletcher Moulton LJ said:[15]

> before a superior employer could be held liable for the negligent act of a servant of a sub-contractor it must be shown that the work which the sub-contractor was employed to do was work the nature of which, and not merely the performance of which, cast on the superior employer the duty of taking precautions.

In short, the employer is liable for those risks of harm created by the work itself which the employer is having done. 'Collateral' means collateral to the risk which marks the limit of the duty of the employer. If the employer is to be liable, the danger must be inherent in the work; it is not enough that the contractor chooses a negligent way of performing it where the normal manner of performance would create no reasonably foreseeable peril to the plaintiff.[16]

The negligence must be 'in the employer's department of duty'.[17] A householder who employs a contractor to repair his lamp over the highway is liable if the contractor repairs it in such a way that it falls on to a passer-by, for that is the very risk in respect of which the duty of the householder is imposed on him, but he is not liable if the contractor, while repairing it, allows a hammer to drop on to the passer-by, for that act would be outside the employer's range of duty. If hospitals do owe non-delegable duties to patients in respect of their treatment, it does not follow that the hospital is liable when an agency doctor negligently backs his car into yours when driving from one part of the hospital site to another. That act is not within the non-delegable duty to patients. *Wilson v Hodgson's Kingston Brewery Co*[18] also shows how liability for the acts of independent contractors falls short of vicarious liability for the torts of an employee.

---

14   (1912) 28 TLR 494, CA.
15   Ibid, at 495. Cf *Hardaker v Idle District Council* [1896] 1 QB 335 at 342, CA (per Lindley LJ). *Thompson v Anglo-Saxon Petroleum Co Ltd* [1955] 2 Lloyd's Rep 363 is another example.
16   Many of the old cases state the rule rather differently by saying that the employer is not liable where the contractor does something collateral to the contract, eg *Hole v Sittingbourne and Sheerness Rly Co* (1861) 6 H & N 488 at 497 (per Pollock CB); *Penny v Wimbledon UDC and Iles* [1899] 2 QB 72, CA. The formulation in this text is preferred because the contract cannot affect the scope of the duty of the employer – the contractor may do an act within the area of his duty in tort. Conversely, the employer may be liable for acts or omissions collateral to the contract if they are within the scope of his duty; cf *Robinson v Beaconsfield RDC* [1911] 2 Ch 188.
17   *Cassidy v Ministry of Health* [1951] 2 KB 343 at 365, [1951] 1 All ER 574, CA (per Denning LJ). This judgment contains a lucid statement of the nature of collateral negligence. For the difficulty in ascertaining exactly the defendant's duty for the purpose of this rule: see *Salsbury v Woodland* [1970] 1 QB 324 at 349, CA (per Sachs LJ).
18   (1915) 85 LJKB 270, Div Ct.

The defendants employed X, an independent contractor, to deliver beer at a public house. X delivered it through a cellar flap on the highway which he negligently left open, causing the plaintiff, who was passing along the pavement, to be injured. Pointing out that X could have delivered it through the front door, the court held that the incident was not within the scope of any duty on the part of the defendant to take care.

SECTION 6.   LIABILITY IN RESPECT OF EMPLOYEES

(A)   THE COMMISSION OF A TORT BY THE EMPLOYEE

An employer is liable whenever his employee commits a tort in the course of his employment. All the elements of the particular tort[19] must subsist during the employer-employee relationship, except that the employer may be answerable even though the relationship has ceased when the damage occurs.[20]

Where a duty of care imposed on the employer has been broken, but the plaintiff cannot prove which employee of the employer is responsible for the breach, as would be expected, the employer is liable:[1] the burden of proving that due care was taken is shifted on to the employer.

In *Roe v Minister of Health* all three judges in the Court of Appeal stated (obiter) that where a plaintiff established negligence on the part of one or more of several employees of the defendant hospital authority, the defendant authority was vicariously liable although the plaintiff could not prove which of those employees committed the negligent act.[2] Further, the ratio decidendi of *Cassidy v Ministry of Health* is that where the plaintiff has been injured as a result of some operation in the control of one or more employees of a hospital authority (and he cannot identify the particular employee who was in control), and in all other respects the requirements of the res ipsa loquitur rule in respect of the act are satisfied, the hospital authority is vicariously liable unless it proves that there has been no negligent treatment by any of its employees.[3] These two decisions were arrived at on the basis of vicarious liability,[4] not on the basis of a breach of duty of the employer. There seems no reason, therefore, why they should not be regarded as generally applicable to the principle of vicarious liability; there are no special rules relating to hospital authorities.

19   A procedural bar against suing the servant will not prevent the master from being vicariously liable: *Staveley Iron and Chemicals Co Ltd v Jones* [1956] 1 All ER 403, HL; *Broom v Morgan* [1953] 1 QB 597, [1953] 1 All ER 849, CA.
20   *Briess v Woolley* [1954] AC 333, [1954] 1 All ER 909, HL.
1   *Grant v Australian Knitting Mills Ltd* [1936] AC 85 at 101, PC; *Olley v Marlborough Court Ltd* [1949] 1 KB 532, [1949] 1 All ER 127, CA (guest left bedroom key at hotel office; upon the key being taken and the bedroom burgled, onus cast on defendant hotel to prove that they and their staff took reasonable care of the key).
2   [1954] 2 QB 66, [1954] 2 All ER 131, CA.
3   [1951] 2 KB 343, [1951] 1 All ER 574, CA.
4   Although Denning LJ would have founded liability in *Cassidy's* case on breach of duty, he agreed with his brethren, Somervell LJ and Singleton LJ, in respect of the statement in the text.

(B) THE COURSE OF EMPLOYMENT

Everything depends on whether the employee did the act 'in the course of his employment'.[5] This is an issue of law to the extent that judges have devised certain principles which must be applied, even when a court has a power of appellate review only on matters of law and not of fact.[6] The applicability of these rules of law to a particular case is, of course, a matter of fact, and the diversity of employment relationships is so great that it will not be surprising to discover that these issues of fact are frequently of exceptional difficulty. The legal element of which 'course of employment' is composed must now be examined.

(C) RELEVANT FACTORS IN DETERMINING WHETHER THE ACT WAS COMMITTED IN THE COURSE OF EMPLOYMENT

(I) MODE OF DOING THE WORK THAT AN EMPLOYEE IS EMPLOYED TO DO

One must distinguish a employee's wrongful mode of doing authorised work – for which the employer is liable – from an act of the kind which the employee is not employed to perform.[7] The possible variations of fact here are endless, but one or two examples will explain the working of the rule.

> In *Century Insurance Co Ltd v Northern Ireland Road Transport Board*,[8] the driver of a petrol lorry, while transferring petrol from the lorry to an underground tank at a garage, struck a match in order to light a cigarette and then threw it, still alight, on the floor. An explosion and a fire ensued.

His employers were held liable for the damage caused, for he did the act in the course of carrying out his task of delivering petrol: it was an unauthorised way of doing what he was employed to do. Similarly, in *Bayley v Manchester, Sheffield and Lincolnshire Rly Co*,[9] erroneously thinking that the plaintiff was in the wrong train, a porter of the defendants forcibly removed him. The defendants were held liable.

And in *Harrison v Michelin Tyre Co Ltd*:[10]

> The plaintiff was injured when an employee of the defendants deliberately steered the truck which he was driving a few inches off the designated passageway and knocked the plaintiff over as he stood at his machine. The defendants were held liable. The momentary horseplay engaged in by the defendant's servant did not take him outside the course of his employment.

Cases of the class now being examined illustrate how much wider is the employer's vicarious liability for the torts of his employee than his personal liability for those of his independent contractor. The facts in very many instances, for example those in the case last cited, would constitute mere 'collateral negligence' in the case of independent contractors, and yet are 'in the course of employment' for the purposes of the doctrine

---

5   Even though the act is outside the scope of employment the employer may still be liable for breach of his own duty to provide a safe system of work: in *Hudson v Ridge Manufacturing Co Ltd* [1957] 2 QB 348, [1957] 2 All ER 229, an employer was held liable to an employee for failure to prevent horseplay by one workman known to be likely to harm other workmen. It seems that a claim based on vicarious liability would have failed.

6   Eg *LCC v Cattermoles (Garages) Ltd* [1953] 2 All ER 582, CA.

7   *Goh Choon Seng v Lee Kim Soo* [1925] AC 550, PC.

8   [1942] AC 509, [1942] 1 All ER 491, HL.

9   (1873) LR 8 CP 148.

10 [1985] 1 All ER 918; and see *Duffy v Thanet District Council* (1984) 134 NLJ 680.

of vicarious liability. But where the line lies between the employee within and outside her course of employment can be difficult to determine. Compare the previous case with *Aldred v Nacanco*.[11] An employee knowing a basin in the washroom to be unsteady shoved it against a colleague causing her injury. The Court of Appeal held her act to be quite unrelated to her work and so outside her course of employment. And consider the following three cases. A transport company is not liable when the conductor, instead of the driver, on his own initiative turns round an omnibus at the terminus and negligently injures a third party.[12] On the other hand, a bus company is liable for the negligence of a driver who allows a conductor to drive the omnibus.[13] And an employer is liable for the racist taunts of, and assaults upon, employee A by employees B, C and D.[14]

(2) Authorised limits of time and space

The conduct of an employee is within the scope of his employment only during his authorised period of work or a period which is not unreasonably disconnected from the authorised period. Thus, someone paid for working until 6 pm who stays on for a few minutes in order to finish a job will still be within the scope of his employment, but not a man who comes into his employer's premises without permission during his holiday.[15] In *Ruddiman & Co v Smith*,[16] the facts were as follows.

> The defendants provided a washroom for their clerks. After office hours had ended, and preparatory to going home, a clerk used the washroom, and left a tap running. His act was held to be within the scope of his employment so as to make the defendants liable for the ensuing flooding of adjoining premises.

It follows that, ordinarily, employees travelling to and from their place of work are not within the course of their employment. But there are instances where travel is so closely connected with a person's work that the ordinary principle cannot apply. In *Smith v Stages*,[17] an employee had been working away from his home and his usual workplace. He was involved in a road accident driving home, in his own car, so that he could resume work at his usual place of employment the next day. He was paid for the day he needed to drive back as a normal working day. The House of Lords held that he remained within the course of his employment. His journey from A to B was part and parcel of his job in those circumstances, and his employers, in effect, directed that he make the journey.

There are of course many jobs where travel is itself the essence of the employment. For example, sales representatives and employed mini-cab drivers all make journeys to do the job. What if such employees make a detour from their set pattern of work for their own purposes, to visit a boyfriend or do their own shopping perhaps?

---

11 [1987] IRLR 292, CA. Their Lordships expressed some disapproval of *Harrison v Michelin Tyre Co Ltd*. Yet perhaps the judgments can be reconciled? The driver in *Harrison* was still doing what he was employed to do, driving. In *Aldred*, nothing relating to the employee's act was concerned with the job she was engaged to do.
12 *Beard v London General Omnibus Co* [1900] 2 QB 530, CA; cf *Kay v ITW Ltd* [1968] 1 QB 140, [1967] 3 All ER 22, CA; *Iqbal v London Transport Executive* (1973) 16 KIR 329, CA.
13 *Ricketts v Thos Tilling Ltd* [1915] 1 KB 644, CA. And see *Ilkiw v Samuels* [1963] 2 All ER 879, CA.
14 *Tower Boot Co Ltd v Jones* [1997] 2 All ER 506, CA (the importance of the Race Relations Act 1976 demanded that the provisions governing vicarious liability be given a broad interpretation).
15 *Compton v McLure* [1975] ICR 378.
16 (1889) 60 LT 708, Div Ct.
17 [1989] AC 928, [1989] 1 All ER 833, HL; see also *Vandyke v Fender* [1970] 2 QB 292; *Elleanor and Cavendish Woodhouse Ltd v Comerford* [1973] 1 Lloyd's Rep 313, CA.

The courts have often been called upon to decide whether a detour by a servant is within the scope of his employment. The classical ruling is that of Parke B in *Joel v Morrison*.[18]

If he was going out of his way, against his master's implied commands when driving on his master's business, he will make his master liable; but if he was going on a frolic of his own, without being at all on his master's business, the master will not be liable.

Whether the detour by the employee is a 'frolic of his own' is clearly a matter of degree. Here are two cases, one on each side of the line.

A carter was in charge of a horse and cart during the day. Without permission he drove them home, a ¼-mile out of his way, for his midday dinner, and left the horse unattended outside his home. His employer was held liable for damage done by the horse when it ran away.[19]

A carman, having delivered wine, was to bring back some empties directly to the shop of his employers. On the return journey, before reaching the shop, he deviated from his route in order to pick up a cask at the home of the clerk accompanying him and take it somewhere else for that clerk's private purposes. While on the way to the clerk's home he drove the cart negligently and injured the plaintiff. His employers were held not liable.[20]

Consider carefully, in each case, exactly what job the employee was engaged to do. If an employee is found to have gone on a frolic of his own, can he be deemed to have re-entered his employer's service? An attempt to establish such a resumption failed in *Rayner v Mitchell*.[1]

X was employed to deliver beer and pick up empties. He took out the cart on an unauthorised trip and on his return picked up some empties. This was held not enough to constitute a resumption of his employment, and his master was held not liable for his negligent driving while returning with the empties on board to the premises of his master.

(3) EXPRESS PROHIBITION

Often, of course, an employer expressly forbids certain acts. But it does not follow from this that an act done in defiance of the prohibition is thereby placed outside the scope of employment. If it were so, the employer would only have to issue specific orders not to be negligent in order to escape liability for his employee's negligence. The House of Lords has laid down the rule as follows:[2]

[T]here are prohibitions which limit the sphere of employment, and prohibitions which only deal with conduct within the sphere of employment. A transgression of a prohibition of the latter class leaves the sphere of employment where it was, and consequently will not prevent recovery of compensation. A transgression of the former class carries with it the result that the man has gone outside the sphere.

---

18 (1834) 6 C & P 501 at 503.
19 *Whatman v Pearson* (1868) LR 3 CP 422.
20 *Storey v Ashton* (1869) LR 4 QB 476.
1 (1877) 2 CPD 357.
2 *Plumb v Cobden Flour Mills Co Ltd* [1914] AC 62 at 67, HL (per Lord Dunedin) (a workmen's compensation case, but the principles are the same).

Again, a few illustrative examples are helpful. First, *Canadian Pacific Rly Co v Lockhart*.[3]

> The defendants prohibited their staff from driving uninsured cars on the company's business. In breach of this instruction, S drove an uninsured car negligently, while engaged on the company's business, and injured the plaintiff.

Holding the defendants liable, the Judicial Committee advised:[4]

> [I]t was not the acting as driver that was prohibited, but that non-insurance of the motor car, if used as a means incidental to the execution of the work which he was employed to do. It follows that the prohibition merely limited the way in which, or by means of which, the servant was to execute the work which he was employed to do, and that breach of the prohibition did not exclude the liability of the master to third parties.

Likewise, a garage hand employed to move vehicles in a garage, but forbidden to drive them, was acting in the course of his employment when he drove a van out of the garage on to the highway (in order to make room in the garage for another vehicle), and collided on the highway with the plaintiff's van.[5] These cases may be contrasted with *Rand v Craig*.[6]

> The defendant employed his servants to carry rubbish from X to Y. Instead they deposited some of this rubbish on the land of the plaintiff.

The defendant was held not liable for this trespass because they were employed, not to carry rubbish generally but only to carry it from X to Y: the act was therefore of a kind that they were impliedly forbidden to do.

If a driver gives a lift to a third party in breach of his employer's instructions and tortiously injures that passenger through careless driving, the courts approach the question of the employer's liability as follows. The issue does not turn on the fact that the passenger is a trespasser.[7] The employer is not liable if his prohibition has marked the limits of the scope of employment, so that giving the lift was outside that scope. On the other hand, if the prohibition affected only the mode in which the employee was to perform his duties, the employer may be vicariously liable. Two cases show the distinction.

In *Twine v Bean's Express Ltd*,[8] the facts were as follows.

> The employer had a contract to employ his vans on Post Office business. Contrary to his express instruction his driver gave a lift to a third party.

It was held that giving the lift was outside the scope of employment. Operating what was in effect a 'free taxi service' was not the job the driver was employed to do.

---

3 [1942] AC 591, [1942] 2 All ER 464, PC.
4 [1942] AC 591 at 601, PC.
5 *LCC v Cattermoles (Garages) Ltd* [1953] 2 All ER 582, CA; cf *Limpus v London General Omnibus Co* (1862) 1 H & C 526, Ex Ch (bus driver, contrary to instructions, raced a rival bus in order to get custom – a direction to the jury that these instructions defined the scope of employment were held wrong in law). Contrast with *Iqbal v London Transport Executive* (1973) 16 KIR 329, CA.
6 [1919] 1 Ch 1, CA.
7 *Young v Box & Co* [1951] 1 TLR 798, CA; *Rose v Plenty* [1976] 1 All ER 97, [1976] 1 WLR 141, CA.
8 (1946) 175 LT 131, CA.

Contrast *Rose v Plenty*.[9]

A milkman employed a 13-year-old to deliver and collect milk bottles on his milk round contrary to his employer's order that children were not to be employed by roundsmen in the performance of their duties. The driver negligently injured the boy.

The employer was held vicariously liable because the prohibition affected only the manner in which the roundsman was to perform his duties of delivering milk and did not limit the scope of those duties. He was still delivering milk, and the boy he had wrongly recruited to assist him was part of that enterprise.

(4)   CONNECTION WITH EMPLOYER'S WORK

Frequently, employees do acts which they have no express authority to do, but which are nevertheless calculated to further some proper objective of their employer. Unless the means of accomplishing this objective is so outrageous that no employer could reasonably be taken to have contemplated such an act as being within the scope of employment, the employer will be liable for torts thus committed, as the following cases show.

Poland v John Parr & Sons is the leading case.[10]

H, a servant of the defendants, while going home to dinner, reasonably believed that a boy was stealing sugar from a bag on a passing lorry of his employers. He struck the boy, who fell and, in consequence, had to have a leg amputated. Although his act in defence of his master's property was so unreasonable as to be tortious, it was not sufficiently excessive to be outside the scope of his employment.

Holding that 'a servant has an implied authority upon an emergency to endeavour to protect his master's property if he sees it in danger or has reasonable ground for thinking that he sees it in danger',[11] the Court of Appeal found the defendants liable. Atkin LJ did, however, point out that:[12]

[W]here the servant does more than the emergency requires, the excess may be so great as to take the act out of the class. For example, if H had fired a shot at the boy, the act might have been in the interest of his employers, but that is not the test.

With this may be contrasted *Warren v Henlys Ltd*.[13]

A garage attendant employed by the defendants accused the plaintiff, in violent language, of leaving the garage without paying for his petrol. After paying, the plaintiff called the police and said that he would report him to his employers. At this the attendant assaulted the plaintiff.

It was held that there was no evidence to go to the jury that 'this assault ... was so connected with the acts which the servant was expressly or impliedly authorised to do

9   [1976] 1 All ER 97, [1976] 1 WLR 141, CA. As to principles applicable when a prohibition is statutory, see *Alford v National Coal Board* [1952] 1 All ER 754, HL.
10   [1927] 1 KB 236, CA.
11   [1927] 1 KB 236 at 240, CA (per Bankes LJ).
12   [1927] 1 KB 236 at 245, CA.
13   [1948] 2 All ER 935. In *Keppel Bus Co Ltd v Sa'ad bin Ahmad* [1974] 2 All ER 700, PC, a bus conductor struck a passenger after a quarrel. Although the conductor's duties extended to keeping order, his employer was not vicariously liable because there was no evidence of disorder.

as to be a mode of doing those acts'.[14] A very obvious example of conduct unconnected with the employer's work is seen in *Makanjuola v Metropolitan Police Comr*.[15] A police officer extracted sexual favours from the plaintiff in return for a promise not to report her to the immigration authorities. It was held that his act was entirely for his own purposes and not an act his employer in any sense authorised. Of course, were the officer's proclivities known to senior officers it might be argued there was a breach of a primary duty of care to the public. Finally, where the acts of prison officers are broadly in furtherance of the interests of the Home Office, the Home Office remains liable even though the officers acts amount to misfeasance in a public office.[16]

(5)   DELIBERATE CRIMINAL CONDUCT

Evidence that the employee's conduct was a criminal or otherwise wilful wrongdoing will not of itself take that conduct outside the scope of the employee's employment.[17] So an employer may be liable where an over-enthusiastic defence of his interests results in an assault which is in the circumstances a crime as well as a tort.[18] Similarly, in *Vasey v Surrey Free Inns*,[19] an employer was held liable in respect of an assault upon the plaintiff committed by two doormen in his employ. The doormen's acts were, crucially, in response to the plaintiff having caused damage to the employer's premises by kicking them. Accordingly, the doormen's actions were construed as being in furtherance of the employer's interests.

There may be cases, however, where albeit the wrongful conduct is in no sense in the employers' interests it is so much part and parcel of the job that the employee is engaged to do that the employers remain liable for that conduct. In *Bracebridge Engineering Ltd v Darby*,[20] in a sex discrimination claim under the Sex Discrimination Act 1975, supervisors sexually harassed a woman employee in the context of warnings about poor time-keeping. The employers were found vicariously liable for that harassment which constituted a wrongful mode of doing just what they were employed to do. Even where the act is not so much part and parcel of what the employee is employed to do, it is tolerably clear that a generous approach to the notion of vicarious liability will be taken where the acts of the employee are contrary to anti-discrimination legislation.[1]

Finally, in another case, *Morris v C W Martin & Sons Ltd*, a firm of cleaners to whom a furrier had entrusted the cleaning of the plaintiff's mink stole were liable for the theft of the stole by the very employee whose job it was to clean the stole.[2]

---

14 Ibid, at 938 (per Hilbery J).
15 [1992] 3 All ER 617, CA.
16 *Racz v Home Office* [1994] 2 AC 45, HL.
17 *Barwick v English Joint Stock Bank* (1867) LR 2 Exch 259; *Lloyd v Grace, Smith & Co* [1912] AC 716 HL.
18 *Poland v Parr* (supra).
19 [1996] PIQR P 373, CA.
20 [1990] IRLR 3, EAT; compare with *Makanjuola v Metropolitan Police Comr* (supra).
1   *Tower Boot Co Ltd v Jones* [1997] ICR 254, CA (racist taunts and physical assaults of some employees upon another were considered to be inside the scope of their contracts of employment).
2   [1966] 1 QB 716, [1965] 2 All ER 725, CA. Even a gratuitous bailee has the burden of proving that he was not negligent if the bailed goods are lost: *Port Swettenham Authority v T W Wu & Co Sdn Bhd* [1979] AC 580, [1978] 3 All ER 337, PC. A bailee is also liable for the negligence of the servants of his independent contractor: *British Road Service Ltd v Arthur Crutchley & Co Ltd* [1967] 2 All ER 785. In *Fairline Shipping Corpn v Adamson* [1975] QB 180, [1974] 2 All ER 967, a director who was not himself a bailee, assumed responsibility for refrigerated goods and was held liable for carelessly allowing them to defrost.

A dishonest or criminal act is no bar, per se, to the employer's vicarious liability.[3] The crucial question is whether that act was committed in the course of employment.[4] Thus, the theft of the mink stole in *Morris* by the man entrusted with the job of cleaning it constituted an unlawful mode of doing his job.[5] The theft of the stole by a cook in the canteen at the firm's factory would, however, be an act unrelated to his employment there. Accordingly, the employer would not be held vicariously liable in the absence of personal negligence – for example, in employing persons known to be dishonest – he will not be liable simply for supplying the opportunity to commit a crime.

Fraud

In *Barwick v English Joint Stock Bank*,[6] fraudulent misrepresentations by a bank manager were held to be made in the course of employment. Before 1912 it had been thought that the employer would only be liable for wilful wrongdoing where, as in *Barwick's* case, the act was done for his benefit. In that year, however, *Lloyd v Grace, Smith & Co*[7] was decided by the House of Lords.

> In an action to recover title deeds by the plaintiff (who was a client of the defendant firm of solicitors), the material point was whether the firm were liable for the act of their managing clerk, who, when the plaintiff consulted him about selling her property and realising a mortgage, fraudulently induced her to sign documents transferring those properties to him. The managing clerk was employed, among other things, to carry out conveyancing transactions. Although the firm derived no benefit from these frauds, perpetrated by their employee for his own purposes, they were held liable for his acts.

But the issue of vicarious liability for fraud must be approached cautiously. The liability of an employer for a fraud perpetrated by an employee is not to be treated identically with liability for other forms of wrongdoing. Lord Keith put it this way:[8]

> [D]ishonest conduct[9] is of a different character from blundering attempts to promote the employer's business interests involving negligent ways of carrying out the employer's work or excessive zeal and errors of judgment in the performance of it. Dishonest conduct perpetrated with no intention of benefiting the employer but solely with that of procuring a personal gain or advantage to the servant is governed, in the field of vicarious liability, by a set of principles and a line of authority of particular application.

The key question where it is sought to make an employer liable for a fraud committed by the employee, for his own benefit, is whether the plaintiff relied on ostensible authority with which the employer had clothed the employee. Was it anything said or done by the employer which induced the plaintiff to trust the untrustworthy servant?

> In *Kooragang Investments Pty Ltd v Richardson & Wrench Ltd*,[10] the respondents had instructed their employee, a valuer, not to act for a particular group of companies in which the valuer had a financial interest. He nonetheless did so act and submitted valuations to the

3   *Port Swettenham Authority v TW Wu & Co* [1979] AC 580, [1978] 3 All ER 337, PC
4   *T v North Yorkshire County Council* (1998) Times, 10 September, CA.
5   As did a burglary by a porter in a block of flats when the porter burgled the flat using keys entrusted to him by his employers, the management company who ran and maintained the flats: *Nahhas v Pier House (Cheyne Walk) Management Ltd* (1984) 270 Estates Gazette 328.
6   Supra.
7   Supra.
8   *Armagas Ltd v Mundogas SA, The Ocean Frost* [1986] AC 717, [1985] 3 All ER 795, HL.
9   Will Lord Keith's comments be equally applicable to theft by a servant?
10   [1982] AC 462, [1981] 3 All ER 65, PC.

appellants on the strength of which they lent money to the group. The valuer stamped the valuations with the respondents' corporate name. His own name did not appear on the paper.

The Privy Council held that the appellants did not rely on any ostensible authority granted to the valuer by his employers and that he acted beyond the scope of his actual authority which was limited by the prohibition against acting for the group. Similarly, the absence of any actual or ostensible authority was the key factor in refusing to hold the defendants liable in *Generale Bank Nederland NV v Export Credit Guarantee Department*[11] where the employee (together with a third party) defrauded the plaintiff.

A rather different point was canvassed in *Armagas Ltd v Mundogas SA, The Ocean Frost*.[12] The vice-president of the defendant company had negotiated, via a broker, a deal with the plaintiffs from which he received a secret profit. He had no authority to arrange the deal, nor did anything done by the defendants induce the plaintiffs to believe that he had such authority. The plaintiffs argued that even though the vice-president acted beyond the scope of his authority as the defendants' agent, he remained within the course of his employment as their employee. The House of Lords reasserted that, as far as the tort of deceit was concerned, the parameters of the employee's course of employment were determined by the scope of his authority.

(D)   STATUTORY DUTY AND VICARIOUS LIABILITY

It remains undecided to what extent an employer may be vicariously liable for breach by an employee of a statutory duty imposed directly on him and not on his employer. In *Stanbury v Exeter Corpn*, the local authority which appointed a sanitary inspector was held not liable for the negligence of that inspector in carrying out public duties imposed on him by authority of statute.[13] Both the House of Lords and Court of Appeal have considered (obiter) whether employers are liable for breaches of statutory duty by miners employed by them. The point was left open in *Harrison v National Coal Board*[14] and *England v National Coal Board*,[15] although in the latter case it was held that the employer was vicariously liable for the breach (because it was still open for the court to regard the act as negligent at common law despite the fact that the statute covered the same ground). It is thought that the question is one of statutory interpretation: does the statute intend to create not only a liability on the servant on whom the duty is expressly imposed, but also on his employer?[16] So far as the Crown is concerned, it seems that the rather obscurely worded section 2(3) of the Crown

---

11   [1998] 1 Lloyd's Rep 19, CA.
12   [1986] AC 717, [1985] 3 All ER 795, HL.
13   [1905] 2 KB 838, Div Ct.
14   [1951] AC 639, [1951] 1 All ER 1102, HL.
15   [1953] 1 QB 724, [1953] 1 All ER 1194, CA; on appeal sub nom *National Coal Board v England* [1954] AC 403, [1954] 1 All ER 546, HL; and in *ICI Ltd v Shatwell* [1965] AC 656, [1964] 2 All ER 999, HL.
16   *Darling Island Stevedoring Co Ltd v Long* (1956) 97 CLR 36 (H Ct Australia), especially the judgment of Fullagar J. It may well be that those statutes which impose some duties expressly on employers and other duties on employees do not impliedly make the employers liable in respect of those duties expressly imposed only on employees.

Proceedings Act 1947 has the effect of making the Crown liable for breaches of statutory duty by its employees.[17]

---

17 It reads: 'Where any functions are conferred or imposed upon an officer of the Crown as such either by any rule of the common law or by statute, and that officer commits a tort while performing or purporting to perform those functions, the liabilities of the Crown in respect of the tort shall be such as they would have been if those functions had been conferred or imposed solely by virtue of instructions lawfully given by the Crown'. Section 2(2) provides that the Crown can be liable only for those breaches of statutory duty which bind persons other than the Crown and its officers. But since s 2(3) makes the Crown liable, not as if for breach of its own statutory duty, but as if it had instructed its servant to perform the work, it seems that s 2(3) is unaffected by s 2(2). Contra, the relations of public officers with public authorities other than the Crown, on which *Stanbury v Exeter Corpn* [1905] 2 KB 838 probably remains the law.

Chapter 26

Remedies

SECTION 1.   EXTRA-JUDICIAL

The availability of a limited number of self-help, extra judicial, remedies has been touched on earlier.[1] The person invoking self-help should remember that he acts at his peril.

SECTION 2.   JUDICIAL

(A)   DAMAGES[2]

(1)   Nominal

Some interests, for example, one's freedom of movement, the exercise of a vote at an election and the possession of one's property are considered to be so important that any violation of them is a tort.[3] The damages are said to be at large in respect of all these torts – that is, although the interest protected may not have a precise cash value, the court is free, on proof of the commission of the tort, to award substantial damages.[4] Nominal damages will be awarded where the court decides in the light of all the facts that no damage has been sustained.[5] The function of nominal damages, then, is to mark the vindication, where no real damage has been suffered, of a right which is held to be so important that infringement of it is a tort actionable per se. Nominal damages are given only in respect of torts actionable per se[6] and are not to be confused with a small sum of substantial damages.

One case runs counter to these principles – *Constantine v Imperial Hotels Ltd.*[7]

1   See ch 6 ante in the contexts of self-defence and recaption, abatement etc.
2   Burrows *Remedies for Torts and Breach of Contract* (2nd ed).
3   For the difficulties involved in deciding whether an action on the case is actionable per se, see the opinion of Viscount Haldane in *Hammerton v Earl of Dysart* [1916] 1 AC 57, HL.
4   Eg £5 damages were awarded to the plaintiff in *Ashby v White* (1703) 2 Ld Raym 938 (right to vote); £50 damages were treated as appropriate in *Nicholls v Ely Beet Sugar Factory Ltd* [1936] Ch 343 (interference with fishery).
5   *The Mediana* [1900] AC 113 at 116, HL (per Earl of Halsbury LC); *Neville v London Express Newspaper Ltd* [1919] AC 368 at 392, HL (per Viscount Haldane).
6   Cf *Embrey v Owen* (1851) 6 Exch 353 at 368 (per Parke B).
7   [1944] 1 KB 693, [1944] 2 All ER 171.

The plaintiff, a famous black cricketer, was improperly refused accommodation at the defendants' hotel. This was a tort derived from the former action on the case, and actionable per se. Birkett J held that he could not grant substantial damages.

The decision is wrong because damages were at large in accordance with the above principles and he found that the plaintiff suffered unjustifiable humiliation and distress; he should therefore have made an award of damages which reflected the injury to feelings.[8]

(2)   Contemptuous

These are derisory damages, marking the court's low opinion of the claim of the plaintiff, or its disapproval of his conduct in the matter. They differ from nominal damages in that they may be awarded in respect of any tort, whether actionable per se or not. Moreover, the fact that they have been awarded might be material in deciding whether to allow costs to the plaintiff.

(3)   General and special damages distinguished

These expressions have various meanings but the basic principle is this. General damages are such damages as the law will presume to have resulted from the defendant's tort; special damages are awarded for a loss that will not be presumed by the law. Thus, to avoid injustice to the defendant, the plaintiff must give notice in his pleadings of, and substantiate any claim for, 'special damages'.[9] The expenses which the defendant has actually incurred up to the date of the hearing – such as expenses for medical treatment in personal injury cases – constitute special damages. The substantial damage capable of pecuniary assessment which must be proved in the case of all torts not actionable per se is called 'special damage'; all other heads of damage – eg, mental distress – are sometimes called general damage.

(4)   Personal injuries

Detailed discussion of the principles governing compensation for personal injuries and their relationship to other compensation systems can be found in the next chapter.

(5)   Damages and tax

If the award of damages is not subject to income tax and damages are calculated by reference to income which would be taxable, then tax must be deducted in calculating damages. Therefore, tax must be deducted in calculating loss of earnings,[10] or, in awarding damages in trespass, for loss of rent[11] (rent is taxable but the damages are not). On the other hand, tax is not deducted from damages for loss of use of a taxi, for the damages take the form of the income which they represent and are taxable.[12]

---

8   And see post for general confirmation by the House of Lords of this approach in *Cassell & Co Ltd v Broome* [1972] AC 1027, [1972] 1 All ER 801.
9   See, for example, *Domsalla v Barr* [1969] 1 WLR 630, CA.
10   *British Transport Commission v Gourley* [1956] AC 185, [1955] 3 All ER 796, HL. For an assessment of the *Gourley* principle see *Burrows*, at pp 132-5.
11   *Hall & Co Ltd v Pearlberg* [1956] 1 All ER 297n. *Gourley* has also been applied to awards for libel: *Rubber Improvement Ltd v Daily Telegraph* [1964] AC 234, HL.
12   *Morahan v Archer* [1957] NI 61.

(6)   'PARASITIC' DAMAGES

There is no general rule that simply because a particular head of damage is recoverable in one tort, the same head of damage is recoverable in any other tort. In that sense, English law does not recognise any principle of 'parasitic' damages.[13] At the same time, pecuniary loss may be recovered even though the tort is not concerned to protect that pecuniary loss suffered and even though no other tort affords such protection; for example, loss of hospitality may be recovered in slander.[14] And in *Campbell v Paddington Corpn* the facts were as follows.[15]

> A nuisance on the highway (stands erected by the defendant for viewing a procession) obstructed the plaintiff's house. The plaintiff was thereby deprived of a view from his windows, and suffered pecuniary loss through not being able to charge for the viewing of the procession from the windows. Although the right to view is not a tort-protected interest, this pecuniary loss was held to be recoverable in the tort derived from public nuisance.[16]

(7)   AGGRAVATED AND EXEMPLARY DAMAGES

The object of an award of damages in tort is normally to compensate the plaintiff for what he has lost and/or suffered as a consequence of the tort. Nonetheless, in certain torts, an award of compensatory damages may take into account the motives and conduct of the defendant where they aggravate the injury done to the plaintiff. There may be malevolence or spite, or the manner of committing the wrong may be such as to injure the plaintiff's proper feelings of dignity and pride.[17] Such damages are traditionally called 'aggravated damages' and they are said to be awarded in respect of conduct which outrages the plaintiff. They have commonly been awarded in actions for defamation and trespass. Their availability in other torts has been restricted by the decision of the Court of Appeal in *A B v South West Water Services Ltd*.[18] Striking out a claim for aggravated damages in a claim for public nuisance and negligence by the victims of contaminated water supplies, their Lordships endorsed Woolf J's earlier rejection of aggravated damages in personal injuries actions founded on negligence.[19] If as a result of the defendants' tortious acts the plaintiffs suffered distress and anxiety, that injury fell to be compensated in the award of compensatory damages. Should that distress be 'magnified or exacerbated' by the defendants' conduct, that too would be reflected in the ordinary measure of damages. But no further sum, over and above full compensation for what has been suffered by the plaintiff, should be added to the

---

13   *Spartan Steel and Alloys Ltd v Martin & Co (Contractors) Ltd* [1973] QB 27 at 35, CA (per Lord Denning MR).

14   *Davies v Solomon* (1871) LR 7 QB 112.

15   [1911] 1 KB 869. And see especially the clear statement of the principle by Lush J at 879. Followed in *Owen v O'Connor* [1964] NSWR 1312 (loss of sunlight). The pecuniary loss resulting from the public nuisance has to be foreseeable: *Overseas Tankship (UK) Ltd v Miller Steamship Co Pty Ltd* [1967] 1 AC 617, [1966] 2 All ER 709, PC.

16   Damages for loss of reputation have been held recoverable in replevin (*Smith v Enright* (1893) 63 LJQB 220), and conversion (*Thurston v Charles* (1905) 21 TLR 659) and it seems that a wife can recover damages for loss of consortium in a negligence action (*Lampert v Eastern National Omnibus Co Ltd* [1954] 2 All ER 719n) even though she has no action against a person whose negligent conduct in relation to her husband deprives her of consortium. This decision seems unaffected by s 2 of the Administration of Justice Act 1982, but that section prevents a husband from claiming damages for loss of his wife's consortium.

17   *Rookes v Barnard* [1964] AC 1129 at 1221, HL.

18   [1993] QB 507, [1993] 1 All ER 609.

19   *Kralj v McGrath* [1986] 1 All ER 54 at 61 (a claim arising out of horrific mismanagement of childbirth).

compensatory damages to condemn the defendants' conduct. At that point, such an award ceases to be compensatory and becomes punitive in function. The fundamental difficulty is that, despite Lord Devlin's attempt in *Rookes v Barnard*, distinguishing between aggravated (but still supposedly compensatory) damages and exemplary (purely punitive) damages is nigh on impossible.[20] Indeed, in *A B v South West Water Services Ltd*, Sir Thomas Bingham MR came close to suggesting that aggravated damages should cease to be recognised as a distinct class of *non-compensatory* damages. Speaking of damages in defamation in which awards termed 'aggravated damages' have traditionally been common he argued:[1]

> I know of no precedent for awarding damages for indignation aroused by the defendant's conduct. Defamation cases in which a plaintiff's damages are increased by the defendant's conduct of the litigation (as by aggressive cross-examination of the plaintiff or persistence in a groundless plea of justification) are not in my view a true exception, since injury to the plaintiff's feelings and self-esteem is an important part of the damage for which compensation is awarded.

From this dictum it appears that aggravated damages should be available only if the 'injury to the plaintiff's feelings and self-esteem' are integral to the cause of action. And confirmation of this interpretation was offered in *Appleton v Garrett*[2] where a dentist had subjected a number of his patients to unnecessary and painful dental treatment. Dyson J held that aggravated damages should be available since, in an action for trespass to the person, the arousal of feelings of anger and indignation in the patients was a relevant head of damage to be compensated.

By contrast, exemplary damages (which in theory turn upon conduct which outrages the court) may be seen as an anomaly in the law of torts. Their object is to punish and deter. The preponderance of opinion until relatively recently has been that exemplary damages should be abolished.[3] Their continued existence arguably confuses the functions of the civil and criminal law. The defendant is 'punished' without being afforded the safeguards provided for accused persons in criminal proceedings. And the plaintiff who benefits from the award of exemplary damages receives an unwarranted windfall. Those who defend exemplary damages, most notably Lord Wilberforce,[4] stress that the objects of the law of tort have never been exclusively compensatory. Tort retains a deterrent function and, most importantly, in relation to the categories in which exemplary damages remain available, a role in reinforcing the civil liberties of the individual.[4a]

The practical problems in applying the present judge-made rules on exemplary awards have led to judicial disquiet.[5] In *Rookes v Barnard*, Lord Devlin limited exemplary damages awards to those categories of cases:

---

20   See also *John v MGN Ltd* [1997] QB 586; *Thompson v Metropolitan Police Comr* [1997] 2 All ER 762.
1   Ibid, at 629.
2   [1996] PIQR P1.
3   See (inter alia) the proposals for abolition of exemplary damages in defamation in the *Faulks Report – Report of the Committee in Defamation* Cmnd 5609 (1975); Burrows, at pp 283-5. See also Law Commission Consultation Paper No 132, *Aggravated, Exemplary and Restitutionary Damages* (1993); Law Commission Report *Exemplary, Aggravated and Restitutionary Damages* Law Com No 247 (1997).
4   See his forceful opinion in *Cassell & Co Ltd v Broome* [1972] AC 1027, [1972] 1 All ER 801, HL.
4a   This has been supplied by the decision in *Lancashire County Council v Municipal Insurance Ltd* [1997] QB 897 (even exemplary damages may be claimed from the tortfeasor's insurers).
5   Consider the *cri de coeur* from Stephenson LJ in *Riches v News Group Newspapers Ltd* [1985] 2 All ER 845 at 850; endorsed by the Court of Appeal in *AB v South West Water Services Ltd* [1993] 1 All ER 609 at 624. But cf *Lancashire County Council v Municipal Insurance Ltd*.

1. 'Where the plaintiff has been the victim of oppressive, arbitrary or unconstitutional action by servants of government'. The latter term embraces central and local government and includes police officers[6] and prison officers guilty of misfeasance in public office.[7] Where unlawful conduct by a police officer is proved, it is not additionally necessary to prove that it was also arbitrary or oppressive.[8] Publicly-owned utilities such as the electricity and water boards fall outside this category, as will privatised monopoly suppliers, even though they are endowed with statutory powers and obligations.[9]

2. 'Where the defendant's conduct has been calculated by him to make a profit for himself which may well exceed the compensation payable to the plaintiff.' Thus, publishers who, as in *Broome v Cassell & Co Ltd*,[10] calculate that a libel may well sell so many copies that they will still profit despite having to pay compensatory damages to the victim may learn that 'tort does not pay'.[11] In this context, it is important to stress that 'carelessness alone, however extreme, is not enough' unless the inference may be drawn 'that the publisher had no honest belief in the truth of what he published'.[12] Awards of exemplary damages are also commonly made against landlords committing torts against tenants to drive them out of their property in order to profit from selling the property or letting it to someone else at a higher rent.[13]

3. 'Where authorised by statute'.[14]

What remained unclear from Lord Devlin's purported restriction of exemplary awards in *Rookes v Barnard* was whether the range of torts in which exemplary damages were available, if the defendant's conduct fell into one of the above three categories, was greater than that established by previous authority. Could exemplary damages be awarded, say, against a producer cynically disregarding the risk posed by a defective product? Are exemplary damages available in torts protecting against the exploitation of intellectual property?[15] The Court of Appeal has ruled, albeit somewhat tentatively,[16] that exemplary damages cannot be awarded save in respect of a tort where such damages were available prior to *Rookes v Barnard*. Thus, in actions for negligence, breach of statutory duty and public nuisance,[17] no matter how gross the defendant's misconduct, he cannot be 'punished' via the law of tort. Should more emphasis be placed on tort's deterrent function? If a newspaper which sets out to profit from libel risks an award of

---

6 *Casssell & Co v Broome* [1972] AC 1027, [1972] 1 All ER 801, HL (at 1130); *Thompson v Metropolitan Police Comr* [1998] QB 498.

7 *Racz v Home Office* [1994] 2 WLR 23, HL.

8 *Holden v Chief Constable of Lancashire* [1987] QB 380, [1986] 3 All ER 836, CA.

9 *AB v South West Water Services Ltd* [1993] 1 All ER 609 at 622 and 628, CA.

10 Supra.

11 But could an action for unjust enrichment achieve the same laudable aim? See *McGregor on Damages* (14th edn) paras 324-325. And note limits of this argument exposed in *AB v South West Water Services* (supra).

12 *John v MGN Ltd* [1996] 2 All ER 35 at 57, CA (per Thomas Bingham MR).

13 *Drane v Evangelou* [1978] 2 All ER 437, [1978] 1 WLR 455, CA.

14 See the Reserve and Auxiliary Forces (Protection of Civilian Interests) Act 1951, s 3(2).

15 *Morton Norwich Products v Intercen Ltd (No 2)* [1981] FSR 337 (yes); *Catnic Components v Hill* [1983] FSR 512 (no).

16 *AB v South West Water Services Ltd* (supra).

17 Quaere whether exemplary damages are available in private nuisance: *Guppy's (Bridport) Ltd v Brookling* (1983) 14 HLR 1, CA.

exemplary damages against it, why should a drug company marketing a dangerous drug to maximise profit and recklessly ignoring its danger escape similar retribution?[18]

(8)   MITIGATION OF DAMAGE

This expression covers two separate rules in the law of torts.

a   There is the situation which is the converse of the circumstances in which aggravated damages may be awarded - evidence may be given of circumstances which justify a lesser award of damages at large.[1] For example, damages in defamation will be reduced where the defendant has been provoked by the plaintiff.[2]

b   The discussion of causation showed that it is the policy of the law not to allow a plaintiff to recover to the extent to which he has brought the loss upon himself by his own act.[3] Similarly, where the plaintiff is negligent after the commission of the tort against him, he cannot recover further damages caused by that carelessness. *The Flying Fish*[4] illustrates the point.

> The plaintiff's ship was damaged by the negligence of those in charge of the defendant's vessel. The plaintiff's captain showed want of nautical skill in that he refused aid after the collision; in consequence of this negligent refusal the ship was destroyed. The plaintiff was able to recover the damage caused by the collision but not that additional damage accruing when the ship was destroyed by the negligence of the captain.

In short, contributory negligence is concerned with negligence of the plaintiff before the cause of action has matured by the occurrence of some damage; after damage has occurred and an action in tort is vested in the plaintiff, he has a duty to take care to mitigate his loss. So an injured plaintiff should generally seek medical attention. Where a plaintiff refuses treatment or surgery which could have lessened the consequences of his injury, the onus lies on him to prove that his refusal was reasonable.[5]

Even if the plaintiff shows that the refusal of treatment is presently reasonable, there may still be a discount if it can be shown that there is a chance both (a) that the plaintiff will accept the treatment in the longer term *and* (b) that there is a chance that the treatment might succeed.[6]

---

18   See generally Anderson (1992) CJQ 233.
1   *Peruvian Guano Co Ltd v Dreyfus Bros & Co Ltd* [1892] AC 166 at 174, HL (per Lord Macnaghten); *Drane v Evangelou* [1978] 2 All ER 437, CA.
2   *Moore v Oastler* (1836) 1 Mood & R 451n.
3   See ch 14 ante. In *Dodd Properties Ltd v Canterbury City Council* [1980] 1 All ER 928, CA the plaintiff's premises were damaged in 1970, but when he repaired them in 1978 the cost of repairs was much greater. He was allowed the 1978 repair costs on the ground that in deciding what it was reasonable for a plaintiff to do in mitigation it was relevant to ask whether he could afford to repair sooner; distinguishing *Liesbosch Dredger v SS Edison* [1933] AC 449, HL; *Perry v Sidney Phillips & Son* [1982] 3 All ER 705, CA also distinguished *Liesbosch Dredger v SS Edison* in the same way.
4   (1865) 2 Moo PCCNS 77.
5   *Selvanayagam v University of West Indies* [1983] 1 All ER 824, [1983] 1 WLR 585; for criticism see (1983) 46 MLR 754, 758. But note that a woman's refusal of an abortion after the defendants' negligence resulted in an unplanned pregnancy did not constitute an unreasonable failure to mitigate damages: *Emeh v Kensington Area Health Authority* [1985] QB 1012, [1984] 3 All ER 1044, CA.
6   *Thomas v Bath District Health Authority* [1995] PIQR Q19, CA.

The distinction between avoidable and unavoidable consequences is important since the Law Reform (Contributory Negligence) Act 1945 does not extend to these avoidable consequences of a tort.[7]

Where the plaintiff does take reasonable steps to minimise the consequences of the defendant's tort, he can recover for the harm sustained by him in consequence of his action[8] or expenses thereby incurred,[9] regardless of whether his total loss would have been less had he not acted at all. Thus, in *Rogers v Austin*[10] it was held to be reasonable to hire a replacement car at above the market rate for such a vehicle where the basis of the hire agreement was that no hire payment would be required of the plaintiff until completion of her legal proceedings against the defendant.

(9)   Successive actions on the same facts

The difficulties presented by this topic are of the same character as those arising from the undefined stand of English law with regard to parasitic damages. The following principles may be gleaned from the decided cases.

The guiding rule can be stated shortly (the difficulty is in defining its terms): if one and the same act produces two different heads of damage, but does not give rise to two separate causes of action, the plaintiff cannot bring successive actions but must recover in respect of all his damage in the first proceedings. The policy is to avoid excessive litigation. The leading case is *Fitter v Veal*.[11]

> The plaintiff recovered £11 damages from the defendant for assault and battery. Some years later, he discovered that his injuries were much more serious than he had at first thought, and he underwent a surgical operation for removal of part of his skull. He was held to be unable to recover any damages in a second action for his additional injuries.

(a)   Violation of two rights separately protected

If one and the same act violates two rights which are accorded separate protection by the law of torts, then there are two separate causes of action, the pursuit of one of which will not bar proceedings in respect of the other. In *Brunsden v Humphrey*[12] the facts were as follows:

> A cab driven by the plaintiff collided with the defendant's van through the negligent driving of the defendant's servant. In county court proceedings, the plaintiff recovered compensation for the damage to his cab. He then brought a second action in the High Court for personal injuries sustained by him in the same collision, and the Court of Appeal held that this action was not barred by the earlier one.

The interest in bodily security is separate from that in one's goods – hence there were two separate causes of action.[13] Likewise, the following interests are distinct for

7   The 1945 Act applies if the plaintiff's negligence before the accident increased the harm even though it did not contribute to the accident: *Froom v Butcher* [1976] QB 286, [1975] 3 All ER 520, CA (plaintiff passenger not wearing seat belt).

8   *The Oropesa* [1943] P 32, [1943] 1 All ER 211, CA.

9   *Kirkham v Boughey* [1958] 2 QB 338, [1957] 3 All ER 153.

10   [1997] CLY 1791.

11   (1701) 12 Mod Rep 542.

12   (1884) 14 QBD 141, CA. *Brunsden v Humphrey* was accepted as correct in *O'Sullivan v Williams* [1992] 3 All ER 385 at 388, CA and *Barrow v Bankside Members Agency Ltd* [1995] 2 Lloyd's Rep 472.

13   But does a man have distinct interests in, say, a leg, and an arm? Coleridge CJ, dissenting in *Brunsden v Humphrey*, said that was the logical consequence of the decision in the case, but one of the judges who constituted the majority subsequently said that the case 'is no authority for

the present purpose: interests in land, in reputation, in freedom of the person and freedom from excessive litigation (ie malicious prosecution).[14] Where one and the same act caused a shortened expectation of life and damaged goods, two actions lay.[15] On the other hand, the interest in length of life and in freedom from pain are deemed to be subsumed under the one interest, namely that in bodily security. Accordingly, only one action may be brought.[16]

(b)   Consequential damage where two torts protect the same interest
If the primary purpose of two different torts is to protect the same interest, merely consequential damage which could have been recovered in proceedings for the first tort cannot be claimed in an action on the second tort. *Gibbs v Cruikshank*[17] decides this.

> The defendant executed an illegal distress on the land of the plaintiff. In an action of replevin the plaintiff recovered the goods and the replevin expenses. This action did not preclude a subsequent suit in trespass to land. It did, however, preclude a later action in trespass to goods for consequential business loss, for both replevin and trespass to goods primarily protect one's interest in goods and, parasitically, business interests.

It would seem that if the chief purpose of the second tort is to protect an interest different from that primarily protected by the first, then damages for the violation of the main interest protected by the second tort can be recovered in proceedings for the second tort even though those damages could have been recovered consequentially in the first action. If, as is supposed, damages for interference with land are recoverable in replevin, *Gibbs v Cruikshank* would be authority for this.[18] Suppose, for instance, that X took from Z letters which were in Z's possession and which were defamatory of Z, and gave them to Y. Suppose further that in proceedings in conversion against X, Z recovered damages for his loss of the letters qua goods, but did not claim or recover (as he could by way of consequential damages[19]) damages for loss of reputation – it is submitted that he would be able to bring a further action for defamation against X (because defamation protects mainly the interest in reputation which is a different interest from that covered by conversion, namely an interest in goods).

(c)   Successive acts
Successive actions are barred only in respect of one and the same act. If, then, A assaults B today and again tomorrow, two actions lie. Should he, however, in one and the same fight break B's nose and knock out some of his teeth, then no doubt B has only one cause of action. In less straightforward cases, one must presumably look to the

---

holding that if there be an actionable injury to the person one action may be brought for injury to one part of the body and another action for injury to another part' (per Lord Esher MR in *Macdougall v Knight* (1890) 25 QBD 1 at 8, CA). And note the power to strike out an unreasonable claim as an abuse of process: *The Indian Grace* [1992] 1 Lloyd's Rep 124.

14 *Guest v Warren* (1854) 9 Exch 379. And see *Ash v Hutchinson & Co (Publishers) Ltd* [1936] Ch 489, [1936] 2 All ER 1496, CA, for a further addition to the list.
15 *The Oropesa* [1943] P 32, [1943] 1 All ER 211, CA.
16 *Derrick v Williams* [1939] 2 All ER 559, CA; cf *Chant v Read* [1939] 2 KB 346.
17 (1873) LR 8 CP 454.
18 See also *Guest v Warren* (1854) 9 Exch 379.
19 See *Thurston v Charles* (1905) 21 TLR 659.

pleadings of the first action to discover whether the facts there relied on do or do not include those later complained of.

(d)   One tortious act causing damage on different occasions
Sometimes, however, one and the same act may cause the same damage over and over again. If X digs a hole in Y's land, Y's cattle may fall into it and suffer injury both before and after Y has sued X for trespass to land. There is, however, only one act of a tortious nature, namely digging the hole – it follows, therefore, that only one suit in trespass to land can be brought. If, on the other hand, A throws an object on B's land and B recovers in trespass to land, and thereafter B's cattle stumble over it and are injured, B can bring a second action, for leaving an object on the land of another is an act of trespass in itself, separate from the earlier trespass constituted by throwing the object on to the land.[20]

(B)   TORT AND CONTRACT

For a time the Court of Appeal, in a series of decisions,[1] gave support to dicta by Lord Scarman in *Tai Hing Cotton Mills Ltd v Liu Chong Hing Bank Ltd*[2] to the effect that where the relationship between two parties is contractual, no concurrent duty should lie in tort. Yet it has since been authoritatively determined that concurrent duties in contract and tort may in fact lie.[3] Furthermore, the plaintiff is at complete liberty to choose whichever course of action – whether in contract or tort – he thinks will be most advantageous to him.[4] That choice may be crucial for the following reasons.

1   Causes of action for liquidated damages may perhaps be assignable if they lie in contract,[5] but not if they lie in tort.[6]
2   Although the plaintiff may not freely evade the contractual immunities of minors and mentally disordered persons by suing in tort, in some circumstances he can sue them for torts committed in the course of a contractual relationship.[7]
3   There are circumstances in which an action in contract will give greater damages than one under the Fatal Accidents Acts.[8] Although the Fatal Accidents Acts may perhaps bind the Crown in tort proceedings, they do not bind the Crown in contract actions (to which they also extend).

20   In principle the same rules should apply to torts not actionable per se. *Maberley v Henry W Peabody & Co London Ltd* [1946] 2 All ER 192 decides that where two separate torts are committed, here also two successive actions may be brought. One opinion only (that of Lord Bramwell) in *Darley Main Colliery Co v Mitchell* (1886) 11 App Cas 127, HL does, however, hold that two actions also lie where the one tortious act causes damage on two different occasions, but no support for this isolated judgment has been found in other decisions.
1   *National Bank of Greece SA v Pinios Shipping Co* [1990] AC 637, [1989] 1 All ER 213, HL; *Lee v Thompson* (1989) 6 PN 91; *Johnstone v Bloomsbury Area Health Authority* [1992] QB 333, [1991] All ER 293, CA.
2   [1985] 2 All ER 947 at 957.
3   *Henderson v Merrett Syndicates Ltd* [1995] 2 AC 145, [1994] 3 All ER 506, HL
4   Ibid, at 194 and 533, HL (per Lord Goff).
5   *County Hotel and Wine Co v London and North Western Rly Co* [1918] 2 KB 251 at 258 (per McCardie J), not considered on appeal when affirmed on other grounds: [1919] 2 KB 29, CA, [1921] 1 AC 85, HL.
6   See Marshall *Assignment of Choses in Action* p 59.
7   See post.
8   *Sellars v Best* [1954] 2 All ER 389, [1954] 1 WLR 913.

4   The Crown is answerable in tort for the acts of a restricted class of 'servants'.[9] That restricted definition does not apply to actions against the Crown for breaches of contracts made by servants of the Crown.

5   Trade unions are partially immune from tortious liability but are liable for breach of contract.[10]

6   Most importantly, the rules relating to limitation of actions differ depending on whether the plaintiff sues in contract or tort. In contract, time starts to run from the date of the breach of contract; in negligence it runs only from the date damage was suffered, or the date when the plaintiff had the necessary knowledge of the facts to sue, if that be later. The plaintiff-friendly provisions of the Latent Damage Act 1986 do not apply to an action for breach of a contractual duty of care.[11] Note that the availability of a defence of contributory negligence no longer depends on which remedy the plaintiff seeks, where the essence of his claim is breach of a duty of care rather than of a strict contractual obligation.[12]

(C)   TORT AND RESTITUTION

(I)   ELECTION OF REMEDIES

It sometimes happens that a plaintiff has the choice of suing either in tort or in restitution.[12a] For example, if the defendant wrongfully takes the plaintiff's goods and sells them, the plaintiff has the choice of suing in conversion or bringing an action for restitution of an unjust enrichment for the price received by the defendant. It is not proposed to make that detailed examination of the law of restitution which would be necessary if every possible circumstance which could give rise to an action both in tort and restitution were to be considered.[13] Suffice to note that the torts which will most commonly be an alternative to an action in restitution are conversion,[14] trespass to goods,[15] trespass to land by removing minerals,[16] and deceit.[17] In principle, the rule is capable of applying to any tort, but of course where the defendant has merely damaged the plaintiff without benefiting himself, restitution will not be an alternative remedy.[18]

This election by the plaintiff to sue in restitution has sometimes been erroneously described as a 'waiver' of the tort. The plaintiff does not 'waive' the tort if he elects to sue in restitution.[19] He is free at any time before he has signed judgment to abandon his suit in restitution and pursue his alternative remedy in tort instead. And his suit in

9   Crown Proceedings Act 1947, s 2.
10   See post.
11   *Iron Trades Mutual Insurance Co Ltd v J K Buckenham Ltd* [1990] 1 All ER 808, CA; and see post.
12   *Forsikringsaktieselskapet Vesta v Butcher* (supra).
12a For a good account of the interrelationship between tort and restitution, see Cane *The Anatomy of Tort Law* (1997) ch 5.
13   On this, see Goff and Jones *The Law of Restitution* (3rd edn) ch 32.
14   *Lamine v Dorrell* (1705) 2 Ld Raym 1216; *Thomas v Whip* (1715) cited in 1 Burr 458.
15   *Oughton v Seppings* (1830) 1 B & Ad 241; *Rodgers v Maw* (1846) 15 M & W 444; *Neate v Harding* (1851) 6 Exch 349.
16   *Powell v Rees* (1837) 7 Ad & El 426.
17   *Hill v Perrott* (1810) 3 Taunt 274; *Mahesan S/O Thambiah v Malaysian Government Officers' Co-operative Housing Society* [1979] AC 374, [1978] 2 All ER 405, PC.
18   And see *Phillips v Homfray* (1883) 24 Ch D 439, CA.
19   Hedley 'The Myth of Waiver of Tort' (1984) 100 LQR 653. And see *Maheson S/O Thambiah v Malaysian Government Officers' Co-operative Housing Society* [1979] AC 374, [1978] 2 All ER 405, PC, where the court also held that a principal whose agent had received a bribe could either sue for deceit or recover the bribe in restitution, but that he could not be compensated twice over.

restitution will not bar proceedings in tort on the same facts against another wrongdoer unless the plaintiff has not merely obtained judgment but has also had satisfaction of it. It is true that if he signs judgment in restitution, his claim in tort against that defendant is barred,[20] but that is merely an illustration of the rule that where the plaintiff has succeeded in one cause of action he has no further cause of action in respect of that very violation of a particular interest for which the first cause of action lay.

These rules are clearly illustrated by the leading case of *United Australia Ltd v Barclays Bank Ltd*.[1]

A cheque payable to the plaintiffs was wrongfully endorsed by M & Co, presented by M & Co for payment to, and collected for it, by its bankers, the defendants. The plaintiffs discontinued an action against M & Co in restitution for money had and received without obtaining final judgment. The plaintiffs then sued the defendants for conversion of the cheque. The House of Lords held that the plaintiffs could not be said to have 'waived' their right to sue the defendants by having instituted proceedings against M & Co – nothing less than satisfaction of a judgment in the first proceedings would have barred this action in tort for the same damage. The plaintiffs, therefore, were not precluded from bringing the present action in tort.

(2) ADVANTAGES OF PROCEEDINGS IN TORT OR RESTITUTION

The crucial difference between proceedings in tort or restitution today lies in the different measure of damages.[2] For example, if A converts B's watch valued £10, then in a suit in conversion B will recover £10; but if A sells it to C for £15, B can recover £15 in restitution as money had and received by A. Some of the differences between contract and tort mentioned in the previous section are also relevant here: for example, the disabling effect of infancy or insanity[3] and the operation of the Crown Proceedings Act 1947.

(D) ACCOUNT

Sometimes it is more advantageous for the plaintiff to seek an account of the defendant's profits resulting from the tort rather than to claim damages. Frequently, the victim of a tort such as passing off will obtain an injunction and an account of the defendant's profits, but the remedy is not confined to these torts.[4]

(E) INJUNCTIONS

(1) AS A REMEDY PER SE, OR AS AN ADDITION TO DAMAGES

A remedy in damages alone may sometimes be inappropriate or insufficient to vindicate the plaintiff's rights. Where there is a risk a tort may be repeated, what the plaintiff wants is an order to prohibit that repetition – that is, an injunction. An injunction is a

---

20　*United Australia Ltd v Barclays Bank Ltd* [1941] AC 1 at 30, HL (per Lord Atkin).
1　[1941] AC 1, [1940] 4 All ER 20, HL.
2　In *Universe Tankships Inc of Monrovia v International Transport Workers' Federation* [1983] 1 AC 366, [1982] 2 All ER 67, the House of Lords held that by bringing an action in restitution (instead of inducing breach of contract) against a trade union, the immunity of trade unions under s 13 of the Trade Union and Labour Relations Act 1974 was evaded by the plaintiff.
3　See *Morriss v Marsden* [1952] 1 All ER 925 at 927 (per Stable J).
4　See *Goff and Jones*.

crucial weapon in the plaintiff's armoury in many tort claims. It can be dealt with only briefly here.

There are two kinds of injunctions, viz, prohibitory and mandatory. A prohibitory injunction may, for example, be issued against someone who has committed a trespass or a nuisance, that is he will be restrained from committing or repeating the act. A mandatory injunction requires the defendant to undertake a positive act so as to put an end to a state of affairs which amounts to a tort – for example, a mandatory injunction may require him to pull down a wall which interferes with the plaintiff's right to light.

Where an injunction is granted before the trial of an action, pending that fuller investigation into the case which will take place at the trial, to prevent the commission or continuance of an act alleged to be tortious, it is called an interlocutory injunction. Such an injunction is commonly applied for in respect of alleged economic torts such as interference with contract, where the plaintiff contends that the state of affairs resulting from the defendant's act is so serious that the defendant ought not to be allowed to continue to create that state of affairs pending the hearing.

At one level, the granting of an interlocutory injunction might seem to be a prejudgement of the case because it is, of course, a remedy granted to plaintiff who has yet to prove that he has had his legal right infringed by the defendant. This begs the question whether such injunctions should, in justice, ever be granted. So far as the courts are concened, the matter is clear: there is no offence caused in considering the respective strength of both parties cases and, if the plaintiff has a strong prima facie case, in granting such orders.[5] Where, however, such an injunction would effectively ruin the defendant's livelihood, the courts will be loathe to grant such an order without a hearing having taken place.[6]

Two highly important forms of the interlocutory injunction are the Anton Piller order and the Mareva injunction.[7] An Anton Piller order[8] is a mandatory injunction which requires the defendant to allow the plaintiff entry to premises to search for property infringing the plaintiff's rights, or documents relevant to his claim. In actions for breach of intellectual property rights, such orders are crucial to ensure the defendant cannot destroy incriminating documents prior to the trial of the action. A Mareva injunction prohibits the defendant from moving his assets abroad or from disposing of assets within the jurisdiction.[9] Thus the plaintiff ensures that if he obtains judgment against the defendant, there will be property in England against which to enforce that judgment. Both Anton Piller orders and Mareva Injunctions are draconian measures[10] and plaintiffs will always be required to justify their claim for such interlocutory injunctions and to give undertakings to return property seized and compensate the defendants should their suit ultimately fail.

A perpetual injunction is a final one, issued after the hearing of the action. A quia timet injunction may be issued to restrain a tort which has not yet been committed, but commission of which is threatened, so long as substantial damage is very probable and imminent.[11]

The jurisdiction of the High Court[12] to grant injunctions is discretionary. An interlocutory injunction may be granted even though the plaintiff has not made out a

5   *Series 5 Software Ltd v Clarke* [1996] 1 All ER 853.
6   Ibid.
7   See further *Clerk & Lindsell* para 28-28 *et seq*.
8   *Anton Piller KG v Manufacturing Processes Ltd* [1976] Ch 55.
9   *Mareva Cia Naviera SA v International Bulkcarriers SA* [1975] 2 Lloyd's Rep 509; and see *Practice Direction* [1997] 1 All ER 288.
10   See *Columbia Pictures Industries Inc v Robinson* [1987] Ch 38, [1986] 3 All ER 338.
11   *Lemos v Kennedy Leigh Development Co Ltd* (1961) 105 Sol Jo 178.
12   Supreme Court Act 1981, s 37(1).

prima facie case. Provided there is a 'serious question', the court decides on the balance of convenience.[13] The courts exercise sparingly their discretion to grant mandatory injunctions, and will refuse unless very serious damage would otherwise occur.[14] A prohibitory injunction will be granted to a plaintiff on proof that the wrongful act is continuing, unless special circumstances exist.[15] An injunction will not be refused because it is against the public interest to restrain the activity; the courts are reluctant to leave the victim of a serious interference with merely a remedy in damages. The leading case is *Shelfer v City of London Electric Lighting Co.*[16] The most that the courts are willing to do to mitigate the consequences of their granting these injunctions as a matter of course is occasionally to suspend the coming into force of the injunction for a short period,[17] or to impose time restrictions on the injunction.[18]

(2)   INJUNCTION AND DECLARATORY JUDGMENT AS A REMEDY WHERE AN ACTION IN TORT DOES NOT LIE

One final matter which should be noted is whether, even if all the elements of a tort required for an action in damages are not made out, an injunction may still be granted to protect the plaintiffs' interest. In general the answer must be 'no'. So if the defendant successfully mounts a campaign of persecution against the plaintiff avoiding any actually tortious conduct she cannot be granted an injunction against him.[19] But the courts have, on occasion, granted injunctions to protect title to property, even where no tort is established.[20]

13   *American Cyanamid Co v Ethicon Ltd* [1975] AC 396, [1975] 1 All ER 504, HL. Lord Diplock enumerated at length the factors to be weighed in deciding where the balance of convenience lay. See also *Garden Cottage Foods Ltd v Milk Marketing Board* [1982] QB 1114, [1982] 3 All ER 292, CA where Sir John Donaldson MR preferred the phrase 'balance of justice' to balance of convenience (at 413). It is clear that public policy considerations enter the equation and not simply factors relating to the convenience of the parties: *Department of Social Security v Butler* [1995] 1 WLR 1528, CA.
14   *Redland Bricks Ltd v Morris* [1970] AC 652, [1969] 2 All ER 576, HL, where detailed rules governing the exercise of this discretion are set out. And see *Locobail International Finance Ltd v Agroexport* [1986] 1 All ER 901, CA; cf *Films Rover International Ltd v Cannon Film Sales Ltd* [1986] 3 All ER 772.
15   *Pride of Derby & Derbyshire Angling Association Ltd v British Celanese Ltd* [1953] Ch 149, [1953] 1 All ER 179, CA.
16   [1895] 1 Ch 287, CA. There have been recent attempts to extend the situations where the plaintiff will be left to his remedy in damages, especially *Miller v Jackson* [1977] QB 966, [1977] 3 All ER 338, CA, but the later case of *Kennaway v Thompson* [1981] QB 88, [1980] 3 All ER 329, CA held the *Shelfer* case to be binding, applied its rules strictly, refused to consider the public interest and held *Miller v Jackson* not to be binding.
17   In *Woollerton and Wilson Ltd v Richard Costain Ltd* [1970] 1 All ER 483, the defendant building contractors operated a crane in the plaintiffs' air space. The court suspended the injunction until the defendants completed the building, because the plaintiffs had refused reasonable compensation and the air space had become valuable only because of the defendants' activities. In *Charrington v Simons & Co Ltd* [1971] 2 All ER 588, CA, the soundness of that decision about the injunction was left open by the court and in *John Trenberth Ltd v National Westminster Bank Ltd* (1979) 253 Estates Gazette 151, the court held that the *Woollerton* case was wrongly decided and refused to follow it.
18   Eg *Dunton v Dover District Council* (1977) 76 LGR 87, CA (the use of a playground was confined to children under 12 and between 10 am and 6.30 pm).
19   See *Burnett v George* [1993] 1 FCR 1012, CA.
20   See *Loudon v Ryder (No 2)* [1953] Ch 423; *Springhead Spinning Co v Riley* (1868) LR 6 Eq 551.

Examples need not be confined to economic interests. In *Gee v Pritchard*,[1] the plaintiff obtained an injunction to prevent the defendant from disclosing confidential and private material contained in letters (which had already been returned to the plaintiff, but of which the defendant had kept copies) written by the plaintiff to the defendant – because, said the court, an injunction lies to protect the plaintiff's right of property in the letters. The English law of torts does not protect privacy as such, but it is interesting that this English case has been the cornerstone of the development in the US of the tort of infringement of privacy.

Until 1982 it seemed that the injunction was available to protect victims of criminal violations of statutes even though no action for breach of statutory duty lay. We have seen earlier how *RCA Corpn v Pollard*[2] has ruled against the availability of injunctions in such cases.[3]

The possibility of a remedy by way of injunction, even though no tort has been committed, is doubly important when it is noted that Lord Cairns' Act of 1858 enables the court to grant damages in addition to, or in substitution for, an injunction.[4]

---

1   (1818) 2 Swan 402. In *Savoy Hotel Plc v BBC* (1982) Times, 28 December the BBC filmed a barman in the Savoy bar allegedly giving short measure. Because this was without permission, the court granted an interlocutory injunction forbidding the televising of the film.
2   [1983] Ch 135, [1982] 3 All ER 771, CA and holding that *Ex p Island Records Ltd* [1978] Ch 122, [1978] All ER 824, CA was overruled by *Lonrho Ltd v Shell Petroleum Co Ltd* (No 2) [1982] AC 173, [1981] 2 All ER 456, HL.
3   Ch 21, ante.
4   Now s 50 of the Supreme Court Act 1981.

Chapter 27

Compensation for personal injuries

SECTION I. INTRODUCTORY

The function and the anomalies of torts as a system of loss distribution in society are well illustrated when we consider the overall provision made for compensation of personal injuries today.[1] The victim's financial future turns on whether he is successful in establishing that his injuries are someone else's 'fault'; essentially, that a tort was committed. Should he succeed, he and his family will receive a level of compensation, which while its method of assessment may be criticised, will help to meet his material needs and will far exceed the total of social welfare benefits available to an equally severely injured person unable to prove 'fault'[2] on the part of another.

Consider this rough example. No liability is accepted for the accuracy of the figures! X, Y and Z all aged 25 suffer severe brain damage rendering them incapable of continuing paid employment. X's accident happens when he is swimming in a cold lake. He gets into difficulties and by the time he is rescued from drowning and resuscitated, the brain damage inflicted by lack of oxygen is irreversible. Y suffers brain damage in the course of surgery to remove his appendix. Proceedings are started on his behalf but allegations of negligence against the hospital are not substantiated. Z's injuries are inflicted in a road accident for which the driver of the other car accepts liability. All three victims, before their misfortunes, were earning £13,000 a year.

Providing X and Y are successful in obtaining the maximum available social security benefits they may hope for a basic weekly income of £151.85.[3] A further £38.70[4] may also be paid to a relative caring for them. They may also be able to apply for housing benefit, for help from the local authority in converting living accommodation and for some financial help with invalid aids. Z, the only victim to benefit from the torts system, can realistically expect an award of damages of, at the most conservative estimate,

---

1   For full treatment of the topics treated briefly here, see Cane *Atiyah's Accidents, Compensation and the Law* (5th edn) (hereafter, *Atiyah*).
2   For an indictment of the 'fault' principle see *Atiyah* at pp 415–437.
3   At April 1998–9 rates. Basic incapacity allowance £64.70; disability living allowance £87.15 (care component £51.30; mobility component £35.85).
4   Invalid care allowance.

£394,000[5] providing him with an approximate weekly income[6] once invested of about £378.[7]

How can the discrepancy be justified? In the case of X, is it that his accident was his own 'fault'? Did he take the risk upon himself? What about Y? Anaesthesia is a dangerous enterprise. Risk cannot be entirely eliminated however careful doctors are. Does Y have to accept the risk to attain the benefit of the surgery? After all, X and Y could have insured themselves against their respective injuries. But then so could Z and, as we shall see later, if he has so done he will receive his insurance monies in addition to his award of damages. They will not be set off against that award. Consideration of the discrepancies in compensation for personal injuries forces reconsideration of the operation of the 'fault' system and torts.[8] Is the deterrent function of the law of torts more fundamental to the continuance of torts than was first suggested?[9] After all, if there is no moral imperative justifying why Z should be so much better off than X and Y, are there good moral and/or economic grounds, why the negligent tortfeasor who injured Z be made to pay for that injury?[10]

We shall see that the debate on compensating for personal injuries has raged for well over two decades now. Proposals for replacing torts relating to personal injuries by a comprehensive social welfare system have so far gained little ground in the UK,[11] although they have been implemented in New Zealand[12] and partially implemented elsewhere in the Commonwealth.[13] The overall context of compensation for personal injuries must be borne in mind as we examine the intricacies of the rules for assessment of damages for victims who are (comparatively) lucky enough to be able to prove a tort.

SECTION 2.   AWARDS OF DAMAGES TO LIVING PLAINTIFFS

It must not be forgotten that the overwhelming majority of claims for damages for personal injuries never come to court.[14] And save for one very limited exception,[15] damages can at present only be awarded on a once and for all basis. This results in less than perfect rules on how damages should be assessed. Predictability is at a premium often at the expense of individual justice. Lord Diplock explained the traditional approach to awards of damages for personal injuries in *Wright v British Railways Board*.[16]

5   Made up as follows: loss of earnings £133,840 (multiplicand £9,560: multiplier 14); pain and suffering and loss of amenity £50,000; cost of future care £150,000; provision for holidays and mobility £30,000; alterations to house £30,000.
6   Invested at 5%. See *Auty v National Coal Board* [1985] 1 All ER 930, [1985] 1 WLR 784.
7   Of course not all the capital sum will be invested. A proportion will be used for immediate needs such as conversion of accommodation, special wheelchairs etc. However, where these are specific needs their cost will generally be added to the total damages award: see the computations in *Housecroft v Burnett* [1986] 1 All ER 332 at 334, CA.
8   See Stapleton 'Tort, Insurance and Ideology' (1995) 58 MLR 820.
9   See the 'Report of the Royal Commission on Civil Liability and Compensation for Personal Injury' (Pearson Report) paras 1716–7 (Cmnd 7054–1).
10   See Calabresi *The Cost of Accidents* (1970).
11   See the Pearson Report.
12   See *Atiyah* at p 415 et seq. But note that the New Zealand system had to be revised for reasons of cost.
13   Eg Australia.
14   See *Atiyah* ch 8; Genn *Hard Bargaining* (1987) and *Compensation and Support for Illness and Injury* (1984).
15   Where a provisional award may be made enabling the plaintiff to re-apply for further damages if a risk of further damage (eg epilepsy) does in fact materialise: see s 32A of the Supreme Court Act 1981.
16   [1983] 2 AC 773 at 776–8, HL.

... claims for damages in respect of personal injuries constitute a high proportion of civil actions that are started in the courts in this country. If all of them proceeded to trial the administration of civil justice would break down; what prevents this is that a high proportion of them are settled before they reach the expensive and time-consuming stage of trial, and an even higher proportion of claims, particularly the less serious ones, are settled before the stage is reached of issuing and serving a writ. This is only possible if there is some reasonable degree of predictability about the sum of money that would be likely to be recovered if the action proceeded to trial and the plaintiff succeeded in establishing liability. The principal characteristic of actions for personal injuries that militate against predictability as to the sum recoverable are, first, that the English legal system requires that any judgment for tort damages, not being a continuing tort, shall be for one lump sum to compensate for all loss sustained by the plaintiff in consequence of the defendant's tortious act whether such loss be economic or non-economic, and whether it has been sustained during the period prior to the judgment or is expected to be sustained thereafter. The second characteristic is that non-economic loss constitutes a major item in the damages. Such loss is not susceptible of measurement in money. Any figure at which the assessor of damages arrives cannot be other than artificial and, if the aim is that justice meted out to all litigants should be even-handed instead of depending on idiosyncrasies of the assessor, whether jury or judge, the figure must be 'basically a conventional figure derived from experience and from awards in comparable cases'.

The practice of awarding damages in a once and for all lump sum has attracted increasingly vociferous criticism in recent years. The whole process sometimes appears to consist of little more than judicial 'guesstimates'. How long would the plaintiff live? Would she develop epilepsy in five years' time? Would injury to her back lead ultimately to disabling arthritis? Lump sums can never of their nature provide comprehensively for all the contingencies of an uncertain future. A plaintiff whose condition deteriorates after the award is finalised may end up drastically under-compensated. But a plaintiff whose medical prognosis is over-pessimistic may gain a bonus. That factor may of itself lead accident victims awaiting trial or settlement of their claim to put off rehabilitation. The worse you are when the award is made, the more compensation you win. Moreover, with a lump sum award, there is the additional risk that the fund provided by the award may be dissipated unwisely by the plaintiff or his family. Periodic payments which could be adjusted over time to meet the plaintiff's current needs were perceived as being, in certain cases, a more effective and just compensation mechanism.

More recently, the provision of flexible periodic payments to severely injured plaintiffs has become possible through the medium of the structured settlement.[17] The complexity of the structured settlement would require a chapter of its own to do the topic full justice. Yet the basic pattern of such a settlement is relatively simple.[18] The defendant's liability insurers make an immediate payment to cover losses already incurred[19] (sometimes termed the 'upfront monies'). They then use the balance of the award due to the plaintiff to purchase a package of annuities from a life insurance company to provide a flexible income for the plaintiff for the rest of his life. The payments can be indexed to increase at regular intervals, make provision for intermittent lump sum payments to meet capital needs, and have a built-in contingency provision against unexpected requirements on the part of the plaintiff or his carers.

17 See Damages Act 1996, s 2. And for a statutory definition of a structured settlement, see Damages Act 1996, s 5.
18 See Lewis 'Pensions Replace Lump Sum Damages' (1988) J Law Soc 392; Allen 'Structured Settlements' (1988) 104 LQR 448.
19 Eg loss of income and medical expenses up to the trial and past pain and suffering.

Structured settlements initially entered our legal process on a voluntary basis (albeit with judicial blessing[20]), but later, by virtue of legislation.[1] The formal introduction of structured settlements does not, however, mean that they can be imposed upon the parties by the court without the parties' consent.[2] Nor do they remove the need to forecast future losses. Equally, drawing up the necessary schedule to devise the settlement can prove as complex as the current traditional process.

Awards of damages to living plaintiffs can be broken down into three main components:

1   pecuniary losses – primarily but not exclusively those resulting from loss of earnings or earning capacity;

2   cost of further care such as medical and hospital expenses. (The aim of compensation under both these preliminary heads will be to restore the plaintiff, as far as money alone ever can, to the position which he would have enjoyed had the tort never been committed.[3]);

3   non-pecuniary loss – that is, pain and suffering and loss of amenity – forms the third head of damage.[4]

The Court of Appeal exercises overall supervision over the level of awards and sets the 'tariff' for non-pecuniary losses. Itemisation of awards is now encouraged to enable awards from individual High Court judges to be scrutinised properly.[5]

(A)   PECUNIARY LOSSES[6]

(I)   LOSS OF EARNINGS

A number of years is likely to elapse between the infliction of the relevant injuries and the trial.[6a] Loss of earnings up to the date of the trial are part of the plaintiff's 'special damages' and must be specifically pleaded.[7] All claims for loss of earnings (including business profits[8]) are computed after taking into account deductions which would have been made by way of tax.[9] Loss of perquisites, such as a 'company car', will also be taken into account.[10]

---

20 See *Practice Note (structured settlements: court's approval)* [1992] 1 WLR 328.
1   Damages Act 1996. The impetus for this statute was provided largely by the Law Commission in its review of such settlements: Consultation Paper No 125, *Structured Settlements and Interim and Provisional Damages* (1992). See also Law Com No 224 *Structured Settlement and Interim Provisional Damages* (1994).
2   Damages Act 1996, s 2.
3   See further Stapleton 'The Normal Expectancies Measure in Tort Damages' (1997) 113 LQR 257.
4   For a detailed account of the composition of non-pecuniary loss see Law Commission Consultation Paper 140, *Damages for Personal Injury: Non-pecuniary Loss* (1995).
5   *George v Pinnock* [1973] 1 WLR 118 at 126. For an example see *Housecroft v Burnett* [1986] 1 All ER 332 at 334, CA. And see also *Practice Direction (personal injuries actions: particulars of claim)* [1984] 3 All ER 165, [1984] 1 WLR 1127.
6   See Burrows *Remedies for Torts and Breaches of Contract* (2nd edn) at pp 156–86.
6a Matters are, however, expected to improve after the implementation of the changes to the legal aid system foreshadowed in the Consultation Paper *Accesss to Justice with Conditional Fees* (1998).
7   *Ilkiw v Samuels* [1963] 2 All ER 879.
8   *Kent v British Railways Board* [1995] PIQR Q42.
9   *British Transport Commission v Gourley* [1956] AC 185, [1955] 3 All ER 796, HL. The case sets out in detail how the notional tax liability is to be calculated.
10 *Clay v Pooler* [1982] 3 All ER 570. Where a director is able to show that his company suffered a loss of profits through his incapacity, so that his earnings fell, damages for this loss were awarded: *Lea v Sheard* [1956] 1 QB 192, [1955] 3 All ER 777.

Prospective loss of earnings is also recoverable. The court estimates the plaintiff's future employment prospects, his future incapacity and the number of working years of which he has been deprived.[11] The traditional judicial method is to arrive at a multiplicand derived from the estimate of his net annual loss and multiply that by a multiplier, the starting point for which is the remaining years in his working life. That multiplier is reduced to take account of contingencies such as unemployment and sickness and, above all, the fact that he receives a capital sum which he is expected to invest in some interest-bearing securities. In the important House of Lords decision in *Wells v Wells*[12] it was held that there is expectation that the prudent plaintiff will take advantage of index-linked government securities which yield a low but safe average net return. The relatively low return associated with such securities has to be reflected in a higher initial lump sum than would formerly have been made.[13] The award is calculated on the basis that he will spend the income and part of the capital annually so that the capital will be exhausted at the age which the court has assessed as the appropriate age having regard to all the contingencies. Currently, the courts assume a 3% rate of interest which is net after tax.[14] In practice the experience of the court has resulted in a multiplier which, for example, in the case of a 30-year-old, would ordinarily be about 17, reducing to about 14 in the case of a man of about 40.[15] Practitioners are familiar with current judicial trends and out of court settlements are negotiated on the basis of the current 'going rate'.[16]

Until *Wells v Wells* actuarial evidence was discouraged by the courts despite the fact that actuaries are accustomed to using statistical tables to work out expectancies and to 'discount' capital awards so as to reflect contingencies and the immediate receipt of the capital sum.[17] The main criticism levelled against actuarial tables was that, being produced for insurers, they were designed to deal with average expectancies within *groups* rather than with the actual expectancies of particular individuals (with which latter, the courts had to deal). Put thus, this criticism is somewhat misleading, for it takes no account of the fact that actuarial tables can be drawn up more specifically – for example on an occupation-specific basis – than the criticism suggests. Furthermore, it fails to indicate why a judicial guesstimate in accordance with the precedent-based approach would be any more accurate than such tables. In recognition of this fact, there was endorsement in *Wells v Wells* for the practice of counsel endeavouring to calculate their clients' claims in accordance with the most well-known set of such tables – the 'Ogden Tables'. Furthermore, when it comes into force, section 10 of the Civil Evidence Act 1995 will afford statutory recognition to the use of the Ogden Tables.

11 This paragraph is based mainly on the speeches of the House of Lords in *Taylor v O'Connor* [1971] AC 115, [1970] 1 All ER 365, HL and *Cookson v Knowles* [1979] AC 556, [1978] 2 All ER 604, HL.
12 [1998] 3 All ER 481, HL.
13 In terms of presumed rates of return, *Wells* was decided on the basis of 3% return (compared with something in the region of 4.5% which had previously been the expectation. Furthermore, received wisdom – see Lewis (1997) 60 MLR 230, at 234 – has it that the Lord Chancellor will endorse the 3% figure for the purposes of s 1 of the Damages Act 1996. This provision permits the Lord Chancellor to prescribe 'from time to time' a rate of return which serves as an official guide to the courts (though they will retain a discretion to apply a different rate where appropriate).
14 *Wells v Wells* (supra).
15 See *Pritchard v J H Cobden Ltd* [1988] Fam 22, [1987] 1 All ER 300, CA.
16 Relying heavily on publications such as *Kemp and Kemp*.
17 *Mitchell v Mulholland (No 2)* [1972] 1 QB 65, [1971] 2 All ER 1205, CA. In *Auty v National Coal Board* [1985] 1 All ER 930 at 939, CA, Oliver LJ commented '... the predictions of an actuary can only be a little more likely to be accurate (and will almost certainly be less entertaining) than those of an astrologer'. The courts seem to take a very different attitude to actuarial evidence when approving structured settlements: see Law Com 125 at pp 53–4.

Nor will the courts hear evidence from economists on future inflationary trends.[18] The House of Lords considers such evidence highly speculative[19] and takes the view that by prudent investment the plaintiff can offset the effects of inflation.[20] Only in very exceptional cases will any allowance be made for inflation to offset the effect of higher rate tax on very large awards.[1] Lord Oliver declared:[2]

> ... the incidents of taxation in the future should ordinarily be assumed to be satisfactorily taken care of in the conventional assumption of an interest rate applicable to a stable currency and the selection of a multiplier appropriate to that rate.

The courts generally continue to show touching faith in the efficacy of fine tuning the multiplicand and multiplier in order to provide an award which is both just and meets the plaintiff's needs.[3] But considerable problems have been encountered. As we have noted, several years may elapse between the accident causing injury and the trial. The plaintiff receives his actual loss of earnings up to the trial. The defendants in *Pritchard v J H Cobden Ltd*[4] sought to argue that the multiplier, which is fixed by reference to the period likely to elapse between the date of the trial and the end of the plaintiff's working life, should be reduced to allow for the actual loss recovered as special damages and to discourage delay in bringing personal injuries actions to trial. Their contentions were rejected. The Court of Appeal stressed the need that the plaintiffs had for a certain and predictable sum in lost earnings to defray their immediate post-injury expenses.

A further difficulty is encountered in fixing a multiplier where the medical evidence suggests that the plaintiff will die early as a result of his injuries. Can he recover compensation for his 'lost years' when, but for the eventually fatal injury, he would have continued to earn? Loss of income in the 'lost years' is now recoverable[5] subject to deduction of the plaintiff's own living expenses.[6] For plaintiffs injured in the middle of their working life when they have families and dependants, such income should clearly be recoverable. It is needed to ensure that even after the plaintiff's premature death his family do not suffer and the plaintiff himself can enjoy some relative peace of mind in what remains of his life. Section 3 of the Damages Act 1996 now provides for this eventuality, allowing dependants to claim those losses not compensated by the original award of damages.

It is now clear that the courts will compensate loss of earning capacity[7] as readily as loss of earnings. So a married woman who at the time of her injuries is engrossed in child rearing will be compensated for any loss of earning capacity when she would be likely to return to work outside her home.[8] Children and young people who have not

18 *Mitchell v Mulholland* (supra). But see again Law Com 125 at pp 12–14 deploring this stance.
19 See *Lim Poh Choo v Camden and Islington Area Health Authority* [1980] AC 174 at 193, HL (per Lord Scarman).
20 *Cookson v Knowles* [1979] AC 556, [1978] 2 All ER 604, HL; *Wells v Wells* [1998] 3 All ER 481, HL.
1   *Hodgson v Trapp* [1989] AC 807, HL (overruling *Thomas v Wignall* [1987] QB 1098, CA).
2   [1989] AC 807 at 835, HL.
3   For an exception see *Read v Harries* [1995] PIQR Q25.
4   [1988] Fam 22, [1987] 1 All ER 300, CA.
5   *Pickett v British Rail Engineering Ltd* [1980] AC 136, [1979] 1 All ER 774, HL (overruling *Oliver v Ashman* [1962] 2 QB 210, [1961] 3 All ER 323, CA).
6   Including a pro rata sum for his consumption of housing, electricity costs etc: *Harris v Empress Motors Ltd* [1983] 3 All ER 561, CA.
7   *Smith v Manchester Corpn* (1974) 17 KIR 1, CA; *Dhaliwal v Personal Representatives of Hunt* [1995] PIQR Q56. But what of the plaintiff who elects to paint unprofitably rather than do well-paid commercial work? See *Keating v Elvan Reinforced Concrete Co Ltd* [1967] 3 All ER 611.
8   *Daly v General Steam Navigation Co Ltd, The Dragon* [1980] 3 All ER 696, [1981] 1 WLR 120, CA.

started earning will receive compensation for the damage to, or destruction of, their employment prospects. The older the child and the more evidence there is of her prospects of remunerative work, the larger the award will be.[9] With a very young child the speculative nature of assessing his loss of earning capacity will not disentitle him from such an award but may mean a relatively small amount is received under this head of damage. In *Croke v Wiseman*,[10] for example, a 21-month old boy was permanently incapacitated in a medical accident. He was seven at the date of the trial and likely to survive until he was 40. To compensate him for loss of earnings a multiplicand of £5,000 and a multiplier of five were set by the Court of Appeal. No award was made in respect of loss of earnings in the 'lost years', and this now seems standard for children and young people.[11]

(2) MEDICAL, NURSING AND HOSPITAL EXPENSES[12]

A plaintiff is entitled to recover as special damages those medical, nursing and hospital expenses which he has reasonably incurred up to the date of trial. His predicted future expenses will then be estimated and awarded as general damages. Where the plaintiff has received private health care or plans to arrange future treatment privately, the possibility that the plaintiff could have avoided these expenses by using the facilities of the National Health Service is to be disregarded.[13] Yet if it is clear that private medical care will not be used, the courts will refuse to entertain any claim that the plaintiff makes in respect of such care that he *might have elected* to use.[14] In other respects, the expenditure must be reasonable both in relation to the plaintiff's condition and the amount paid. If he has to live in a special institution or in special accommodation, the additional expense is recoverable.[15] He cannot claim the capital cost of acquiring special accommodation, for he continues to own that accommodation.[16] But he can claim the additional annual cost over his lifetime of providing that special accommodation and the capital cost of any alterations or conversions needed to meet his disability which do not enhance the value of the property.[17] Any saving to the plaintiff which is attributable to his maintenance at public expense in a hospital, nursing home or other institution is set off against any loss of earnings.[18]

The plaintiff is able to claim his nursing expenses. If the court finds, however, that at some future time he will be unable to obtain all the private nursing services required, and will have to enter an NHS hospital, an appropriate deduction from future nursing expenses is made.[19]

---

9   See *Housecroft v Burnett* [1986] 1 All ER 332, CA (award of £56,000 for loss of earnings capacity to intelligent 16-year-old girl).
10 [1981] 3 All ER 852, [1982] 1 WLR 71, CA.
11 See *Housecroft v Burnett* (supra).
12 See the Law Commission's radical proposals in this context in Consultation Paper 144, *Damages for Personal Injury: Medical, Nursing and Other Expenses* (1996).
13 Section 2(4) of the Law Reform (Personal Injuries) Act 1948. If the plaintiff does make use of the National Health Service he cannot recover what he would have had to pay if he had had private treatment: *Cunningham v Harrison* [1973] QB 942, [1973] 3 All ER 463; *Lim Poh Choo v Camden and Islington Area Health Authority* [1980] AC 174, [1979] 2 All ER 910, HL.
14 *Woodrup v Nicol* [1993] PIQR Q14, CA.
15 *Shearman v Folland* [1950] 2 KB 43, [1950] 1 All ER 976; *George v Pinnock* [1973] 1 All ER 926, CA.
16 *Cunningham v Harrison* [1973] QB 942, [1973] 3 All ER 463, CA.
17 *Roberts v Johnstone* [1989] QB 878, [1988] 3 WLR 1247, CA.
18 Section 5 of the Administration of Justice Act 1982.
19 *Cunningham v Harrison* (supra).

Where the burden of caring for the plaintiff is largely shouldered by relatives or friends, the plaintiff's right to compensation to pay for such services is normally unaffected.[20] He is entitled to receive a sum sufficient to recompense his wife, mother or friend.[1] That the carer has given up gainful employment must be taken into account and generally her loss should be made good although the total cost of care should not exceed current commercial rates for professional nursing care.[2] Recompense is available even though the relative is caring for the plaintiff voluntarily, out of love.[3] There is no need for the parties to enter into any contractual agreement, and any agreement made for the purpose of increasing the award for care will be treated as a sham.[4] The need for additional help for the family by way of night sleepers to help a paralysed plaintiff, and substitute help to give family members a holiday, must not be overlooked.

Exceptionally, nursing care cannot be recouped in the case where the carer was also the tortfeasor who inflicted the injury. In *Hunt v Severs*,[5] a wife had run over her husband in a car but no award was made in relation to the nursing care she later provided since the House of Lords stated that this head of damage was only to be awarded in circumstances where the plaintiff had a moral duty to account for those damages to the carer. In other words, such damages were seen as an award 'compensating the carer'.[6]

(3) ADDITIONAL PECUNIARY LOSSES AND EXPENSES

Loss of earnings or earning capacity, and medical and nursing expenses commonly form the bulk of the pecuniary loss resulting from personal injuries. But other losses and expenses which can be shown to flow from the plaintiff's injuries will also generally be recoverable. These include obvious additional costs of coping with a life of disability,[7] expenses of removal to a specially adapted dwelling,[8] a specially built invalid car or some other means of giving the plaintiff mobility,[9] a telephone for emergencies[10] and so on. Similarly, losses resulting from no longer being able to pursue a profitable hobby will also be recoverable. A married woman whose injuries impaired her capability to do housework received an award for that impairment based on the cost of obtaining

---

20 *Hunt v Severs* [1994] 2 AC 350, [1994] 2 All ER 385, HL; *Donnelly v Joyce* [1974] QB 454, [1973] 3 All ER 475, CA (mother gave up job to care for six-year-old plaintiff); *Cunningham v Harrison* (supra) (wife gave up job to nurse husband); *Roberts v Johnstone* (supra) (care provided by adoptive mother).

1   In *Croke v Wiseman* [1981] 3 All ER 852, [1982] 1 WLR 71, CA the plaintiff had a life expectancy of 33 years, throughout which he would need continuous nursing by professional nurses and his parents. In awarding £119,000 for the future cost of nursing care the court took account of the mother losing her teacher's pension rights, valued at £7,000, on giving up her post.

2   *Housecroft v Burnett* (supra). Where, however, the carer's net loss of earnings is a lesser amount than the commercial rate for caring, the amount will nonetheless be confined to the carer's net loss: *Fitzgerald v Ford* [1996] PIQR Q72, CA.

3   But here, it has been suggested that the amount should be equal to 75% of the commercial rate for help: *Fairhurst v St Helens and Knowsley Health Authority* [1995] PIQR Q1.

4   [1995] PIQR Q1.

5   [1994] 2 AC 350, [1994] 2 All ER 385, HL.

6   Ibid, at 394 (per Lord Bridge). But why should the loss be so seen? Why is it not to be regarded in terms of the plaintiff's need for such care? For criticism see Matthews and Lunney 'A Tortfeasor's Lot is not a Happy One' (1995) 58 MLR 395; Law Commission Consultation Paper 144 at para 3.55. Note also the fact that the Australian Courts have refused to follow the *Hunt* approach: *Kars v Kars* (1996) 141 ALR 37.

7   In *Kroeker v Jansen* (1995) 123 DLR (4th) 652 an award was made to a woman 'disabled from some of her housework beyond the level that her husband ought reasonably to do for her'.

8   *Moriarty v McCarthy* [1978] 2 All ER 213, [1978] 1 WLR 155 (paraplegic moving to a bungalow).

9   *Housecroft v Burnett* (supra).

10 *Moriarty v McCarthy* (supra).

household help.[11] In principle, such an award should generally be available: housework is no longer the preserve of married women.

But certain 'losses' resulting from injury are more problematic. Traditionally, young unmarried women have received an award for loss of marriage prospects where they have suffered disabling or disfiguring injuries. That award was generally regarded as part of the plaintiff's recompense for loss of amenity. But it was paid for by young female plaintiffs in that, in assessing the multiplier for loss of future earnings, account was taken of the likelihood of marriage and motherhood reducing the number of years in which the plaintiff was likely to be earning.[12] In *Hughes v McKeown*[13] the judge made no award for loss of marriage prospects and consequently then, correctly, declined to reduce the multiplier used to calculate the award for loss of earnings from that appropriate to a young man of similar age. The Court of Appeal has suggested that either approach is equally acceptable.[14] Bearing in mind the change in women's status and lifestyle, the time would seem to have come for a young woman's award for loss of earnings to be unaffected by speculation that she will marry and become dependent on her husband. The personal tragedy of loss of marriage and parenthood should be reflected solely in the award for loss of amenity and be equally available to young men.

A second problematic 'loss' occurs where injuries lead to the breakdown of the plaintiff's marriage. Can he recover the additional expenditure involved in running two homes and maintaining his former wife? The Court of Appeal[15] has held such expenses to be irrecoverable. They are not 'losses' resulting from the injuries but rather a redistribution of assets. And in any case, such 'losses' should be excluded as a matter of policy: the spectre of sham 'divorces' clearly cannot be ignored.

The exclusion of certain heads of potential damage on policy grounds has concerned the courts in two other very different kinds of cases. Arguments that the unplanned birth of a healthy child should never be recoverable as a matter of policy have been firmly rejected by the Court of Appeal.[16] And an attempt by a rapist, who had earlier recovered damages for the change of personality he suffered after traumatic injury, to obtain indemnity for the damages which he was then ordered to pay to his victims unsurprisingly failed.[17]

Where a plaintiff was permanently incapacitated and, in addition to loss of earnings, there was a 'cost of care' claim, the House of Lords sought to avoid any duplication of damages as follows.[18] A full award for loss of earnings was made in the usual way with no deduction for living expenses except in respect of the 'lost years'. In calculating the award for cost of care, however, a deduction was made for the living expenses which the plaintiff would have incurred in any event had she not been injured.

---

11 The award was made regardless of whether it was actually used to obtain domestic help: *Daly v General Steam Navigation Co Ltd* [1980] 3 All ER 696, [1981] 1 WLR 120.
12 *Moriarty v McCarthy* (supra).
13 [1985] 3 All ER 284, [1985] 1 WLR 963.
14 *Housecroft v Burnett* (supra); but what of the 20-year-old law student who has a training contract at a London firm? Her prospective earnings may be higher than her speculative 'husband's' and she today may well never give up paid work. And what about the financial loss to a young man deprived of the chance of winning a high earning 'bride'?
15 *Pritchard v J H Cobden Ltd* [1988] Fam 22, [1987] 1 All ER 300, CA.
16 *Emeh v Kensington and Chelsea and Westminster Area Health Authority* [1985] QB 1012, [1984] 3 All ER 1044, CA. The damages payable in such circumstances may vary considerably. If the parents' policy was to send any son to Eton, must the award include those school fees? Probably: see *Allen v Bloomsbury Health Authority* [1993] 1 All ER 651 at 662.
17 *Meah v McCreamer (No 2)* [1986] 1 All ER 943. See also *Clunis v Camden and Islington Health Authority* [1998] 3 All ER 180, CA (discussed in ch 6, ante).
18 *Lim Poh Choo v Camden and Islington Area Health Authority* [1980] AC 174, [1979] 2 All ER 910, HL.

(4) DEDUCTION FOR BENEFITS RECEIVED

The pecuniary losses and expenses resulting from injury may on occasion be offset by benefits received whether from social security, insurance provision or charity. How far should such benefits be set-off against the award to be made to the plaintiff? Social security benefits are now dealt with in the Social Security (Recovery of Benefits) Act 1997.[19] That Act provides[20] protection for damages awards made in respect of pain, suffering and loss of amenity against the recoupment of social security benefits. Taken together, section 8 and Schedule 2 of the 1997 Act permit recoupment only as against compensation for loss of earnings, the cost of care and loss of mobility. The scheme affects the defendant in the following way. As regards those damages that represent the amount payable in respect of pain, suffering and loss of amenity, the defendant is directly liable to the plaintiff. As regards the amount now paid to the plaintiff by way of state benefits in respect of loss of earnings etc, the defendant is, instead, liable to the Secretary of State. The principle is simple: the state shall not bear the pecuniary cost of the defendant's tort, while the plaintiff at the same time should not be compensated twice over.[1] However, one possible exception to this principle is contained in Part II of Schedule 1 to the 1997 Act which allows regulations to be made for the disregarding of small payments.[2] Here it is possible that the state will not recover the pecuniary element of the damages award from the defendant.

Social security benefits are not the only collateral benefits which may result from the plaintiff's injury and disablement. Few general principles can be deduced from the authorities on when such benefits should be deducted from the award of damages for loss of earnings and additional expenditure. Any attempt to present a rational picture of the rules is likely to fail.[3] The courts make every effort to encourage benevolence so that charitable payments made to the plaintiff, for example, from a disaster fund, will not be deducted,[4] nor generally will ex gratia payments made by employers.[5] Proceeds of personal insurance policies provided for by the plaintiff or his family will not be deducted.[6] But where, even despite his sickness or disability, the plaintiff receives sick pay as part of his contract of employment, he must account for those monies[7] unless the contract provides that sick pay must be refunded in the event of a successful tort claim.[8] In *Parry v Cleaver*[9] the House of Lords held that an occupational disability pension was not deductible regardless of whether it was contributory or discretionary. The test, their lordships held, was twofold: was the money received of the same nature as what was lost, and if not, was it a benefit still intended to be paid even if the plaintiff were to be reimbursed from another source. Thus, statutory sick pay payable by the

---

19 Originally the Social Security Act 1989, s 22 and Sch 4 and the Social Security Administration Act 1992 (which had to be read in conjunction with the Social Security (Recoupment) Regulations 1990, SI 1990 No 322.
20 Section 8, Schedule 2.
1   For a fuller account of the operation of the 1997 Act, see *Clerk and Lindsell* § 27-17.
2   'Small payments' are those of £2,500 or less.
3   See the discussion in Burrows *Remedies for Tort and Breach of Contract* (2nd edn) ch 2.
4   *Redpath v Belfast and County Down Rly* [1947] NI 167 approved in *Parry v Cleaver* [1970] AC 1, [1969] 1 All ER 555, HL.
5   *Cunningham v Harrison* [1973] QB 942, [1973] 3 All ER 463; but see *Hussain v New Taplow Paper Mills Ltd* [1987] 1 All ER 417, [1987] 1 WLR 336 (where the employer was the defendant).
6   *Bradburn v Great Western Rly Co* (1874) LR 10 Exch 1 approved in *Parry v Cleaver* (supra). See also *Longden v British Coal Corpn* [1995] PIQR Q48.
7   *Turner v Ministry of Defence* (1969) 113 Sol Jo 585, CA.
8   *Browning v War Office* [1963] 1 QB 750, [1962] 3 All ER 1089, CA.
9   [1970] AC 1, [1969] 1 All ER 555, HL; followed in *Longden v British Coal Corpn* [1997] 3 WLR 1336, HL.

employer under the Social Security and Housing Benefits Act 1982 was later held to be deductible[10]. It was essentially the same as a contractual entitlement for sick pay.

In *Hussain v New Taplow Paper Mills Ltd*[11] the injured plaintiff received long-term sickness benefit provided for by a permanent health insurance scheme arranged by his employers and taken out for their (the employers') benefit. The monies received were held to be indistinguishable from contractual sick pay as opposed to analogous to a disability pension or private insurance monies. The defendants in this case were the plaintiff's employers but the Appeal Court[12] tentatively expressed the view that the result would have been the same had the tortfeasor been a third party. They further suggested that as between plaintiff employees and their employers, ex gratia benefits ought to be accounted for. The decision in *Hussain* suggested judicial approval of a policy ensuring that the plaintiff generally recovered only his net loss. The difficulties arise, of course, because two basic principles of compensatory damages conflict. On the one hand, as *Hussain* affirmed, the plaintiff should receive only his actual estimated loss, and not gain a net benefit from his injuries; on the other, the tortfeasor should not benefit either from the plaintiff's own prudence in insuring himself or from the benevolence of others.

'Victory' for the net loss principle in *Hussain* appears to have been short-lived.[13] In *Smoker v London Fire and Civil Defence Authority*,[14] the House of Lords affirmed *Parry v Cleaver*. A contributory disability pension remains non-deductible even if provided for and partly paid for by the employer. In *McCamley v Cammell Laird Shipbuilders Ltd*[15] the defendant employers took out and paid for personal accident policies on behalf of all employees. The proceeds of the policy were held to be non-deductible. The policy operated whenever an employee suffered a qualifying injury regardless of fault. It was a product of the employers' benevolence not a consequence of the tort which later materialised. The temptation is to regard *Hussain* as the 'odd man out' and to confine it to its own special facts.[16]

(B)   NON-PECUNIARY LOSSES[17]

(1)   PAIN AND SUFFERING

The plaintiff is entitled to compensation for the pain and suffering, both actual and prospective, which is caused by the injury or subsequent surgical operations.[18] If his

---

10 *Palfrey v Greater London Council* [1985] ICR 437.
11 [1988] AC 514, [1988] 1 All ER 541, HL. And see *College v Bass Mitchells and Butlers Ltd* [1988] 1 All ER 536, CA (redundancy payments).
12 [1987] 1 All ER 417, [1987] 1 WLR 336, CA.
13 But see *Hodgson v Trapp* [1989] AC 807, [1988] 3 All ER 870 on deduction of social security benefits prior to the Social Security Act 1989.
14 [1991] 2 AC 502, [1991] 2 All ER 449, HL.
15 [1990] 1 All ER 854, CA.
16 Tentatively suggested in *McCamley v Cammell Laird Shipbuilders Ltd* (supra) at 860.
17 For a full review of the current law and potential reforms in respect of amenity loss, quantum of damage and interest on awards see Law Commission Consultation Paper 140, *Damages for Personal Injury: Non-pecuniary Loss* (1995).
18 *H West & Son Ltd v Shephard* [1964] AC 326, [1963] 2 All ER 625, HL; *Cutler v Vauxhall Motors Ltd* [1971] 1 QB 418, [1970] 2 All ER 56, CA. In *Sutton v Population Services Family Planning Programme Ltd* (1981) Times, 7 November, damages were awarded for the premature onset of the menopause. And in *Kralj v McGrath* [1986] 1 All ER 54 the plaintiff received damages for her trepidation concerning a further wanted pregnancy after an obstetric 'nightmare'.

expectation of life has been reduced by his injuries, an award of damages for pain and suffering shall take account of any suffering caused or likely to be caused to him by awareness that his expectation of life has been shortened.[19] A permanently unconscious plaintiff has no claim for pain and suffering.[20] Nor, according to *Kerby v Redbridge Health Authority*,[1] is mere sorrow or upset at the loss of a child actionable.

(2)   LOSS OF AMENITIES

Compensation is also recoverable for loss of faculty. Even though the accident has converted the plaintiff into a human vegetable so that he is unaware of his injuries, he is still entitled to claim for any loss of bodily function.[2] Damages cannot be refused because the plaintiff will be unable to enjoy the damages in view of the severity of his injuries.[3] Damages are awarded for the fact of deprivation – a substantial loss. The award for loss of amenities must be made on the basis of amenities lost; it is irrelevant that the plaintiff is unaware of his deprivation. The court will take into account deprivation of sexual pleasures,[4] loss of a holiday,[5] inability to fish,[6] disfigurement,[7] as well as more obvious losses, such as inability to play games or to walk. In short, damages under this head may be increased by taking into account subjective factors, but they are not reduced because the plaintiff has been rendered unconscious or unable to appreciate his loss.

(3)   ASSESSING THE QUANTUM

Non-pecuniary damages differ from pecuniary damages in that there is no scientific method of deciding what sum should be awarded. Damages for loss of amenity and pain and suffering are normally awarded as an aggregate lump sum. This is a conventional sum which is taken to be the sum which society deems fair (fairness being interpreted by the courts in the light of previous decisions). There has evolved a set of conventional principles providing a provisional guide to the comparative severity of different injuries, and introducing a bracket of damages into which a particular injury will currently fall. In other words, loss is generally[8] compensated according to a tariff – eg £X for the loss of an arm, £Y for the loss of an eye.[9] The particular circumstances of the plaintiff, including his age and any unusual deprivation which he suffers, are taken into account. So too, it seems, must it be taken into account that the injuries were

---

19 Section 1(1)(b) of the Administration of Justice Act 1982. Damages for loss of expectation of life as such and as a separate head of damage were abolished by this Act.
20 *Wise v Kaye* [1962] 1 QB 638, [1962] 1 All ER 257, CA.
1   [1994] 3 PIQR Q1.
2   *H West & Son Ltd v Shephard* (supra), HL; *Lim Poh Choo v Camden and Islington Area Health Authority* [1980] AC 174, [1978] 2 All ER 910, HL.
3   *H West & Son Ltd v Shephard* (supra).
4   *Cook v J L Kier & Co Ltd* [1970] 2 All ER 513, CA.
5   *Ichard v Frangoulis* [1977] 2 All ER 461.
6   *Moeliker v A Reyrolle & Co Ltd* [1977] 1 All ER 9, CA.
7   Where a husband's disfigurement caused his wife to leave him and his children, £7,000 was awarded to him under that head in *Oakley v Walker* (1977) 121 Sol Jo 619. Financial losses resulting from divorce are generally irrecoverable see *Pritchard v J H Cobden Ltd* (supra).
8   The courts may depart from the standard tariff where the circumstances of a particular case require it. See, eg, *Griffiths v Williams* (1995) Times, 24 November, CA (court took account of fact that plaintiff was a rape victim).
9   This tariff is, however, somewhat out of date: see Law Commission Consultation Paper 140 at para 4.34 et seq.

inflicted in the context of a rape.[10] The fall in the value of money leads to a continuing reassessment of these awards.[11] What happens in practice is that practitioners' books and periodicals[12] regularly publish judicial awards under all the relevant heads – for example, blindness, loss of a leg, loss of an arm or paraplegia – with brief details of the plaintiff's circumstances. This enables the plaintiff's lawyers and the defendant's insurers to assess likely awards, and judges to conform to the current levels of awards made by their brethren.

The intrinsic difficulty of awarding a sum of money as compensation for the loss of amenity resulting from catastrophic injury and the problem of updating awards to compensate for the fall in the value of money are well illustrated in *Housecroft v Burnett*.[13] The injuries sustained by the 16-year-old plaintiff resulted in tetraplegia. The life which she could have expected with its pleasures, career prospects and the hope of a family was replaced by complete dependence on her mother for every aspect of her care. The court recognised the imprecise nature of the task but stressed the need for uniformity where possible. The bracket of acceptable awards should be set by reference to recent decisions. No attempt to backtrack to, and then allow for inflation on, pre-1980 awards should be encouraged. £75,000 (we estimate £130,000 today[14]) was set as the tariff for tetraplegia where the plaintiff was fully aware of her disability but not in pain. Physical pain, impairment of speech or hearing would justify an award above the average. Lack of awareness of the disability might justify an award at the lower end of the range. The difficulty of comparing levels of injury is well illustrated in *McCamley v Cammell Laird Shipbuilders Ltd*.[15] The plaintiff in that case lost most of an arm and a leg on one side. He continued to suffer great pain and regained very little mobility. The trial judge awarded him £85,000, equivalent to the then going rate for tetraplegia. The Court of Appeal judged the award generous but refused to overturn it.

(4)   PROVISIONAL AWARDS[16]

Frequently the courts are called upon to award prospective damages where the medical prognosis is imprecise. For example, the injury may have created a risk of epilepsy or osteoarthritis developing later in life. The courts used to estimate the percentage change of such a condition developing and award an equivalent proportion of damages for the results of that condition. Plaintiffs were consequently over-compensated if the risk did not materialise and under-compensated if it did. The Administration of Justice Act 1982 has accordingly provided an alternative. Where there is a chance that the plaintiff at some definite or indefinite time in the future will, as a result of the tortious act or omission, develop some serious disease or suffer some serious deterioration in his physical or mental condition, the Act provides as follows: rules may be made, and have now been made, to enable the court to assess damages on the assumption that the development or deterioration will not occur and to award further damages at a future date if it does occur on an application by the plaintiff.[17]

10 In *Griffiths v Williams* (1995) Times, 24 November, the Court of Appeal stated that the consequences of injuries incurred in such cases placed them in a distinct category from the generality of personal injuries cases.
11 *Birkett v Hayes* [1982] 2 All ER 710, CA.
12 Especially Kemp and Kemp *Quantum of Damages* and the monthly publication, *Current Law*, under the heading of 'Damages'.
13 [1986] 1 All ER 332, CA.
14 The figure was stated to be equivalent to £111,000 in 1993: *Fitzgerald v Ford* [1996] PIQR Q72.
15 [1990] 1 All ER 854, CA.
16 See generally Law Com 125 at 73–84.
17 Section 32(A)(i) and (ii) of the Supreme Court Act 1981. And see RSC Ord 37, rr 8–10.

Applying the rules on provisional damages has proved to be problematic. In *Wilson v Ministry of Defence*,[18] the plaintiff injured his ankle. He suffered continuing disability and pain, and medical reports suggested that progressive deterioration of the ankle joint might cause arthritis in years to come. Scott Baker J held that this was not an appropriate case for an order for provisional damages. Such an order required that there be a chance of a clear-cut event occurring causing a separate, additional risk to the health of the plaintiff and not merely evidence of progressive deterioration of the original injury. Such contingencies should be reflected in the lump sum award; so the plaintiff who fractures a hip with the possibility of arthritis later in life cannot take advantage of the provision for provisional damages, but the road accident victim, whose brain injuries create a risk of epilepsy developing later, may so do.

What if the condition that may develop later is life-threatening? If it is, it has been suggested that the potential injustice to the defendant in such cases outweighs the potential injustice to the plaintiff of a conventional award, hence the propriety of a conventional rather than provisional award in such cases.[19]

(5) INTEREST

The courts have power to award interest on all or any part of an award of damages and should do so on awards for personal injuries or death unless there are 'special reasons' not to do so.[20] Detailed exposition of the rules on interest is beyond the scope of this work.[1] The general rule is that interest on pre-trial pecuniary loss will be payable at half the average rate on short-term investment accounts for that period.[2] Interest payable on non-pecuniary loss will be low – not more than 2% at present.[3]

(C) DAMAGE OR DESTRUCTION OF GOODS

Claimants in personal injury actions often also have a claim for damage to goods – especially to their cars – so that it is convenient to outline here the relevant law for assessing compensation for that loss. Where the car or other goods are destroyed, damages are made up of the cost of buying a replacement, together with compensation for loss of use pending replacement, with a deduction for the salvage value of the destroyed goods.[4] Where there is damage to goods, the measure is the diminution in value, normally based on the cost of repair.[5] Damages are also given for loss of use, even though the goods were non-profit earning and not replaced during repair. Thus a motorist who has a car for pleasure can claim repair costs and compensation for loss of use while it is off the road.[6] If a substitute has been hired then the cost can be claimed, provided that the goods hired and the price paid are reasonable.[7]

18   [1991] 1 All ER 638.
19   See *Molinari v Ministry of Defence* [1994] PIQR Q33.
20   Supreme Court Act, s 34A inserted by the Administration of Justice Act 1982.
1   See *Burrows* at pp 256–62; Law Commission Consultation Paper No 140.
2   *Jefford v Gee* [1970] 2 QB 130, [1970] 1 All ER 1202, CA.
3   *Birkett v Hayes* [1982] 2 All ER 710, [1982] 1 WLR 816, CA; *Wright v British Railways Board* [1983] 2 AC 773, [1983] 2 All ER 698, HL. The reasons are (1) damages should take into account inflation up to the time of judgment and (2) damages for non-pecuniary loss are often difficult to quantify until the plaintiff's condition has stabilised. In the interests of legal consistency, however, it has been argued that the rate should now be 3% to sit more comfortably with the House of Lords decision in *Wells v Wells* (supra); see *Clerk and Lindsell* § 27-25.
4   *Moore v DER Ltd* [1971] 3 All ER 517, CA; *Thatcher v Littlejohn* [1978] RTR 369, CA. And see also *Liesbosch Dredger v SS Edison* [1933] AC 449, HL.
5   *Dodd Properties (Kent) Ltd v Canterbury City Council* [1980] 1 All ER 928, CA.
6   *The Mediana* [1900] AC 113, HL; *H L Motorworks (Willesden) Ltd v Alwahbi* [1977] RTR 276, CA.
7   *H L Motorworks (Willesden) Ltd v Alwahbi* (supra) (reasonable to hire a Rolls Royce till plaintiff's Rolls Royce repaired).

SECTION 3.   DEATH

It has been assumed so far that the tortious injuries have not proved fatal. When death ensues two issues arise. First, the deceased's estate may wish to proceed with the cause of action which the deceased himself would have had if he had not died. Secondly, others, especially relatives, may claim that they have suffered a loss in consequence of the death. In the main, two statutes need to be examined: the Law Reform (Miscellaneous Provisions) Act 1934 (which deals with survival of actions), and the Fatal Accidents Act 1976 (with respect to death giving rise to a cause of action).

(A)   SURVIVAL OF CAUSES OF ACTION

The Law Reform (Miscellaneous Provisions) Act 1934 provides that, subject to three significant exceptions, on the death of any person, all causes of action vested in him survive for the benefit of his estate.[8] Actions for defamation do not survive. The right of a person to claim under section 1A of the Fatal Accidents Act 1976 for bereavement[9] does not survive for the benefit of his estate.[10] Nor are exemplary damages available to an estate.[11] All of these are regarded as claims personal to the deceased.

The effect of the 1934 Act is that where the death of the deceased has been caused by the act or omission giving rise to the cause of action, this Act enables his estate to bring proceedings in tort against the defendant.[12] His estate may claim damages according to the usual principles for the period between when the cause of action arose and the death. Thus, damages may be awarded for pain and suffering[13] and loss of amenity[14] for that period during which the deceased actually suffered such deprivations. Damages may also be awarded for earnings lost[15] and medical expenses incurred up to the time of death.[16]

The damages awarded to his estate 'shall be calculated without reference to any loss or gain to his estate consequent on his death'.[17] For example, if the deceased loses an annuity to which he was entitled, or if insurance monies become payable upon his death, these losses and gains are disregarded in estimating the damages under the Act of 1934. The rights conferred by the 1934 Act are in addition to, and not in derogation of, any rights conferred by the Fatal Accidents Act 1976.[18] The award of damages under the 1934 Act is the same whether or not an award is also made under the 1976 Act.

No damages may now be awarded to the estate in respect of loss of income in the deceased's 'lost years'.[19] The potential overlap between claims by dependants under

---

8   Section 1(1).
9   See post.
10 Administration of Justice Act 1982, s 4(1).
11 Section 4(2) of the Administration of Justice Act 1982, replacing s 1(2)(a) of the Law Reform (Miscellaneous Provisions) Act 1934 Act.
12 For the limitation periods within which these proceedings must be brought, see s 11(5)–(7) of the Limitation Act 1980.
13 *Andrews v Freeborough* [1967] 1 QB 1, [1966] 2 All ER 721, CA (£2,000 awarded to the estate of a child of 8 who remained unconscious for a year between the accident and death); *Murray v Shuter* [1976] QB 972, [1975] 3 All ER 375, CA (£11,000 awarded to the estate of a man of 36 in respect of pain and suffering and loss of amenity during the four years he survived the accident in a coma).
14 *Rose v Ford* [1937] AC 826, [1937] 3 All ER 359, HL (£2 awarded for loss of leg amputated two days before death).
15 *Murray v Shuter* [1976] QB 927, [1975] 3 All ER 375, CA.
16 *Rose v Ford* [1937] AC 826, [1937] 3 All ER 359, HL.
17 Law Reform (Miscellaneous Provisions) Act 1934, s 1(2).
18 Law Reform (Miscellaneous Provisions) Act 1934, s 1(5); *Yelland v Powell Duffryn Associated Collieries Ltd (No 2)* [1941] 1 KB 519, [1941] 1 All ER 278, CA.
19 Law Reform (Miscellaneous Provisions) Act 1934, s 1(2)(a).

the Fatal Accidents Act for loss of dependency and an estate's claims for lost income from the 'lost years' is thus avoided.[20]

Technically, the Act of 1934 applies even though death follows instantaneously upon the commission of the tort (thus removing the possibility that the victim experiences any pain and suffering).[1] But since the Administration of Justice Act 1982 came into force, there is only one circumstance in which a claim may, in reality, be made under the 1934 Act where death is immediate.[2] And even that is of restricted application. Whether the deceased dies immediately or not, a claim for funeral expenses may be made.[3] But if a dependant has already incurred funeral expenses in respect of the deceased, and even though he is unable to prove any loss of pecuniary advantage consequent on the death, a claim in respect of those funeral expenses lies under the Fatal Accidents Act 1976.[4]

Finally, where a plaintiff was awarded provisional damages under section 32A of the Supreme Court Act 1981, if he subsequently dies due to a deterioration in his physical condition, his dependants may now claim those losses that were not compensated by the initial award of damages.[5]

(B)   DEATH AS A CAUSE OF ACTION[6]

(1)   HISTORICAL INTRODUCTION

Historically, at common law, no action in tort could be brought by third parties who suffered loss through the killing of another.[7]

Fatal accidents became so frequent with the development of railways, however, that in 1846 Parliament had to pass the Fatal Accidents Act (commonly called Lord Campbell's Act), which made considerable inroads into the common law rule. This Act, now the Fatal Accidents Act 1976, must now be looked at in detail. The Act only benefits certain dependants. Except as thereby provided, the law of torts still does not recognise the interest of one person in the life of another. An employee, therefore, can never sue if his employer is killed and he loses his job; a church may have the prospect of large financial support for many years from a wealthy member, but will have no action if he is killed; an insurance company has no cause of action because it has to discharge its obligations under a life policy sooner than it otherwise would. In short, interests beyond those of the family have no recognition when death occurs.

Section 1(1) of the Fatal Accidents Act 1976 provides:

If death is caused by any wrongful act, neglect or default which is such as would (if death had not ensued) have entitled the person injured to maintain an action and recover damages in

20   See *Gammell v Wilson* [1982] AC 27, [1980] 2 All ER 557, CA.
1   In *Hicks v Chief Constable of South Yorkshire* [1992] 1 All ER 65 it was held that momentary pain was merely part of the dying process and not an independent period of pain prior to death.
2   The problem is that, with immediate death, there is no time for the victim to appreciate pain, suffering etc and for the cause of action to vest. The better view, according to *Clerk and Lindsell* (at para 27–37), is that 'the cause of action is completed by the injuries and is vested in the deceased at the moment of death'.
3   Law Reform (Miscellaneous Provisions) Act 1934, s 1(2)(c).
4   Law Reform (Miscellaneous Provisions) Act 1934, s 3(5); *Stanton v Ewart F Youlden Ltd* [1960] 1 All ER 429.
5   Damages Act 1996, s 3.
6   Note that the law on fatal accidents is currently under review by the Law Commission: see Law Commission Consultation Paper No 148 (1997).
7   *Baker v Bolton* (1808) 1 Camp 493; *Admiralty Comrs v SS Amerika* [1917] AC 38, HL.

respect thereof, the person who would have been liable if death had not ensued shall be liable to an action for damages, notwithstanding the death of the person injured.[8]

(2)   WHO MAY SUE?

The action is brought in the name of the executor or administrator[9] of the deceased, and lies for the benefit of the following relatives:[10] wife, husband (or former wife or husband[11]), children, grandchildren, father, mother, stepparents, grandparents, brothers, sisters, uncles, aunts and their issue, adopted and illegitimate dependants and step-children of the several categories.[12] If there is no executor or administrator, or if he fails to bring the action within six months after the death of the deceased, any dependant may bring the action.[13] The Administration of Justice Act 1982 responded to social changes by including for the first time any person who was living with the deceased in the same household[14] for at least two years before that date, and was living during the whole of that period as the husband or wife of the deceased.[15]

(3)   NATURE OF THE ACT COMPLAINED OF

It must first be proved that the act caused the death.[16] Thereafter, it must be shown that there was a 'wrongful act, neglect or default' by the defendant. These words presumably embrace any tort.[17] Consequently, if the defendant's act was never actionable because he would have had a defence to any action brought by the deceased in his lifetime, no action will lie.[18] Where the deceased died as the result partly of his own fault and partly of the fault of any other person, damages are reduced to a proportionate extent[19] in the same way as under the Law Reform (Contributory Negligence) Act 1945.[20] If a dependant's contributory negligence is a cause of the

---

8   For transport accidents in the course of an international journey see the Carriage by Air Act 1961, Carriage of Passengers by Road Act 1974, the Merchant Shipping Act 1995 and the International Transport Conventions Act 1983.
9   Fatal Accidents Act 1976, s 2(1).
10 Fatal Accidents Act 1976, s 1(2)–(5).
11 An addition by the Administration of Justice Act 1982 to s 1(3)(a) of the Fatal Accidents Act 1976. By s 1(4) of the Fatal Accidents Act 1976, a former spouse includes a person whose marriage has been annulled or declared void as well as a divorced person. This provision still applies even if the surviving former spouse has remarried: *Shepherd v Post Office* (1995) Times, 15 June, CA.
12 Fatal Accidents Act 1976, s 1(5)(a): 'any relationship by affinity shall be treated as a relationship by consanguinity, any relationship of the half-blood as a relationship of the whole blood, and the stepchild of any person as his child'. The defendant must be given particulars of the dependants for whom a claim is made and of the nature of this claim: s 2(4) of the Fatal Accidents Act 1976.
13 Section 2(2) of the Fatal Accidents Act 1976.
14 Note that it is possible for a person to be living in more than one household at any one time: *Pounder v London Underground Ltd* [1995] PIQR P217.
15 Section 1(3)(b) of the Fatal Accidents Act 1976. But note that the Act is not so progressive as to recognise same-sex cohabitational relationships. Cf Family Law Act 1996, s 62.
16 In *Pigney v Pointer's Transport Services Ltd* [1957] 2 All ER 807, the deceased committed suicide while in a depressive state induced by the defendant's negligent act; the death was held to have been caused by that act, so that an action under the Fatal Accidents Act 1976 was successful (as was a similar claim in *Watson v Willmott* [1991] 1 QB 140, [1991] 1 All ER 473).
17 And a negligent breach of contract: *Grein v Imperial Airways Ltd* [1937] 1 KB 50, [1936] 2 All ER 1258, CA.
18 *Murphy v Culhane* [1977] QB 94, [1976] 3 All ER 533, CA (if the deceased had failed because of the defence of ex turpi causa – see ch 6, ante – no action would lie under the Act).
19 Fatal Accidents Act 1976, s 5.
20 See ch 15 ante.

deceased's death, that dependant's damages are reduced but the awards to other dependants are unaffected.[1]

At the time of his death the deceased must have been in a position to sue the defendant had he not died because of the wrongful act. If the limitation period expired between the injury and his death, the Limitation Act 1980 enacts that no Fatal Accidents Act claim can come into existence.[2] This ordinarily[3] means that if more than three years have elapsed between the injury and death, the claim is barred.[4] The 1980 Act also provides that if the deceased had settled his own claim,[5] no action lies under the Fatal Accidents Act,[6] but an action still lies (and without any limit on the damages) if the plaintiff had merely agreed beforehand that no more than, say, £X damages should be recoverable in the event of his being the victim of this tort.[7]

(4)   THE NATURE OF THE INTERESTS PROTECTED

In certain restricted circumstances, an action under the Fatal Accidents Act may consist of, or include, a claim for damages for bereavement.[8] This claim may be brought for the benefit of the wife or husband of the deceased.[9] It is not available for former spouses, or where the parties, though living together as husband and wife, were not married. The only other case in which a claim may be made is where the deceased was a minor (ie under the age of 18) who was never married and the claim is on behalf of his parents (if he was legitimate), or on behalf of his mother (if he was illegitimate).[10]

Apart from the claim for bereavement, a claim by a dependant lies only on proof of pecuniary loss.[11] The language ordinarily used by the courts is that there must be a loss of 'prospective pecuniary advantage' and that a 'speculative possibility' of pecuniary gain is not enough.[12] A parent could recover, therefore, when his 16-year-old daughter died, having almost completed her unpaid dressmaking apprenticeship;[13] but the parent of a three-year-old child has been held to have no cause of action.[14] Although it is not essential that the dependant should have a legal right to that aid[15] (the loss of

---

1   *Dodds v Dodds* [1978] QB 543, [1978] 2 All ER 539. The negligent dependant may also be required to make a contribution (under the Civil Liability (Contribution) Act 1978) towards the damages which the defendant has to pay for the benefit of the dependants.
2   Limitation Act 1980, s 12(1).
3   The three-year period can be extended if the deceased did not have 'relevant knowledge' of his cause of action.
4   Limitation Act 1980, s 11(1).
5   *Pickett v British Rail Engineering Ltd* [1980] AC 136 at 146–7, HL (per Lord Wilberforce) and 152 (per Lord Salmon), [1979] 1 Al ER 774 at 780 and 787 respectively.
6   Section 12(1).
7   *Nunan v Southern Rly Co* [1924] 1 KB 223, CA.
8   Fatal Accidents Act 1976, s 1A(1).
9   Fatal Accidents Act 1976, s 1A(2)(a).
10   Fatal Accidents Act 1976, s 1A(2)(b).
11   *Duckworth v Johnson* (1859) 4 H & N 653.
12   *Davies v Taylor* [1974] AC 207, [1972] 3 All ER 836, HL: wife deserted husband five weeks before his death; shortly before his death he instructed a solicitor to begin divorce proceedings. The deserting wife had no claim, for she had to show a reasonable expectation of pecuniary benefit – there had to be a significant prospect, not a mere speculative possibility, of reconciliation with the husband had he lived, and this she failed to prove. In *Kandalla v British Airways Board* [1981] QB 158, [1980] 1 All ER 341, elderly parents of two young women doctors were awarded damages on proof that the doctors intended to flee from Iraq (where they had been working) to England where they would have supported their parents.
13   *Taff Vale Rly Co v Jenkins* [1913] AC 1, HL.
14   *Barnett v Cohen* [1921] 2 KB 461.
15   *Stimpson v Wood & Son* (1888) 57 LJQB 484, the mere fact that a wife by her adultery had lost her legal right to maintenance did not bar her claim.

services gratuitously rendered is enough[16]), so long as the pecuniary benefit to the dependant would have accrued, not qua family relationship, but qua business relationship, no action lies. Thus, a father could not sue in respect of the loss of business contracts occasioned by the death of his son, who worked for the father's firm.[17] On the other hand, in *Pym v Great Northern Rly Co*[18] it was held that younger children of the deceased had sustained loss of pecuniary advantage because most of the income from the settlement of which the deceased had been tenant for life passed on his death to his widow and eldest child.

For public policy reasons, where the pecuniary loss is attributable to an illegal enterprise in which the deceased was engaged, no action will lie under the 1976 Act. Thus, in *Hunter v Butler*[19] it was held that no claim would lie where the deceased had been earning wages while, simultaneously, fraudulently claiming social security benefits. The court was concerned not to allow monies illegally gained to form the basis of a claim for dependency.

(5) PERIOD OF LIMITATION

The action must be brought within three years from either the date of the death, or 'knowledge' of the person for whose benefit it is brought, whichever is the later.[20] Where there are several potential claimants, the limitation period runs separately against each. If one had the required knowledge more than three years before the action, the action is barred against him but not against the others. Where the dependant's limitation period has expired before an action was brought on his behalf, the court has a further discretionary power to extend the period.[1]

(6) ASSESSMENT OF DAMAGES

The sum to be awarded as damages for bereavement is £7,500.[2] Where both parents claim this sum, it is divided equally between them.[3] Damages other than damages for bereavement are such as are proportioned to the injury[4] resulting from the death to the dependants respectively.[5] The actual pecuniary loss resulting to each dependant from

---

16 *Berry v Humm & Co* [1915] 1 KB 627.
17 *Sykes v North Eastern Rly Co* (1875) 44 LJCP 191. The decision was followed in *Burgess v Florence Nightingale Hospital for Gentlewomen* [1955] 1 QB 349, [1955] 1 All ER 511 (husband could not recover for loss of services of wife as dancing partner). And see *Behrens v Bertram Mills Circus Ltd* [1957] 2 QB 1, [1957] 1 All ER 583; and *Malyon v Plummer* [1964] 1 QB 330, [1963] 2 All ER 344, CA.
18 (1863) 4 B & S 396.
19 [1996] RTR 396, CA. See also *Burns v Edman* [1970] 2 QB 541, [1970] 1 All ER 886: no claim could be made by a widow who knew that her support came from the proceeds of her husband's crimes.
20 Section 12(2) of the Limitation Act 1980. And see post, for a detailed examination of 'knowledge'.
1   Section 33 of the Limitation Act 1980.
2   Damages for Bereavement (Variation of Sum) Order 1990, SI 1990 No 2575.
3   Fatal Accidents Act 1976, s 1A(4). Query whether this would be so where one parent was the tortfeasor who caused the death?
4   'Injury' includes any disease and any impairment of a person's physical or mental condition: Fatal Accidents Act 1976, s 1(6).
5   Fatal Accidents Act 1976, s 3(1).

the death is ascertained[6] and separately assessed.[7] Where an award is made to a widow and her children it is suggested that the proportion awarded to the children should represent their genuine dependency,[8] and not follow the practice of awarding the bulk of the money to the widow on the assumption that she will provide for her children.[9] Among other things, the children need protection against the risk of their mother dying and the money passing into the hands of a stepfather.

Lord Wright has explained the traditional method of measuring the damages.[10]

> The starting point is the amount of wages which the deceased was earning, the ascertainment of which to some extent may depend on the regularity of his employment. Then there is an estimate of how much was required or expended for his own personal and living expenses. The balance will give a datum or basic figure which will generally be turned into a lump sum by taking a certain number of years' purchase. That sum, however, has to be taxed down by having due regard to uncertainties...

The House of Lords elaborated this in *Taylor v O'Connor*.[11] The damages to a widow must make available to her, to spend each year, a sum free of tax equal to the amount of the dependency – an award sufficient to buy an annuity of that amount is not enough because part of the annuity will be taxable. The multiplier must be calculated from the date of the victim's death[12] and should be such that the capital sum awarded, together with the income earned by its investment, will be exhausted by the end of the period intended to be covered. It is supposed that the dependants will spend each year a part of the capital as well as the whole of the income they receive from so much of the capital as remains.[13] The multiplier of the annual loss of dependency is seldom fixed at more than 16 times that annual figure; so if the dependants have lost £2,000 a year from the death, the award will rarely exceed £32,000.

In assessing future earnings, probable deductions for income tax are to be made.[14] No account may be taken of the fact that the dependant is of independent means, except in so far as it shows what pecuniary aid to that dependant was made by the deceased.[15] So if a female Professor of Common Law loses her husband, also a law professor, it will be no answer to say that she could well support herself and her children. The crucial question is simply how much of her income did the deceased husband expend on his

---

6 *Davies v Powell Duffryn Associated Collieries Ltd* [1942] AC 601 at 612, [1942] 1 All ER 657, HL (per Lord Wright). A dependant's damages are not reduced because his mother was contributorily negligent: *Dodds v Dodds* [1978] QB 543, [1978] 2 All ER 539. When assessing a claim by a mother for the death of her son, the court must take account of the possibility of the son's marriage: *Dolbey v Goodwin* [1955] 2 All ER 166, CA. Where husband and wife with either separate incomes or a joint income share their living expenses, the amount by which their joint living expenses are less than twice the expenses of each one living separately is a benefit arising from the relationship, and may be the subject of a claim under the Fatal Accidents Acts by the husband in respect of the death of this wife: *Burgess v Florence Nightingale Hospital for Gentlewomen* [1955] 1 QB 349, [1955] 1 All ER 511.

7 *Dietz v Lennig Chemicals Ltd* [1969] 1 AC 170 at 183, HL (per Lord Morris of Borth-y-Gest). Court directs how the award be divided: s 3(2) of the Fatal Accidents Act 1976.

8 *Benson v Biggs Wall & Co Ltd* [1982] 3 All ER 300 at 303.

9 *Clay v Pooler* [1982] 3 All ER 570 at 578 (the children merely received pocket money).

10 *Davies v Powell Duffryn Associated Collieries Ltd* (supra) at 617.

11 [1971] AC 115, [1970] 1 All ER 365, HL.

12 *Graham v Dodds* [1983] 2 All ER 953, [1983] 1 WLR 808, HL.

13 *Young v Percival* [1974] 3 All ER 677, CA; and see *Taylor v O'Connor* (supra).

14 *Bishop v Cunard White Star Co Ltd* [1950] P 240 at 250, [1950] 2 All ER 22 (per Hodson J).

15 *Shiels v Cruikshank* [1953] 1 All ER 874, HL, a Scottish case, but presumably also applicable to England.

family rather than himself. In *Cookson v Knowles*,[16] the House of Lords refined further the method of calculation. As a general rule, damages up to the date of trial are to be assessed separately from those after that date. For the first part, the loss of dependency will be multiplied by the actual period between accident and trial; interest on that sum will be awarded at half the short-term investment rate current during that period. For the second part, the court will arrive at the amount of dependency (the multiplicand) by estimating the probable rate of earnings of the deceased at the date of the trial. It will calculate the multiplier in the usual way. The multiplier will be fixed by reference to the date of the death and the number of years actually elapsing between the death and the trial will then be deducted.[17] Interest is not awarded on the second sum.[18] Inflation is disregarded except in estimating earnings at the date of trial.

If the dependants have incurred funeral expenses in respect of the deceased, damages may be awarded in respect of those expenses.[19]

In assessing damages payable to a widow in respect of the death of her husband, there shall not be taken into account the remarriage of the widow or her prospects of remarriage.[20]

It will be recalled that subject to certain conditions, persons living together as man and wife, though not married, are treated as 'dependants'.[1] In assessing their damages the court has to take into account the fact that the dependant had no enforceable right to financial support by the deceased as a result of their living together.[2]

To what extent can the courts take account of events occurring between the death and trial? If such an event enables the courts to fix more precisely that which they are otherwise called upon to estimate, they must have regard to that event.[3] Thus, they have taken into account that, before trial, the defendant has died;[4] that war had broken out (reducing the deceased's life expectancy);[5] that tax rates had been reduced.[6] Each of these events enables the courts to quantify more precisely a dependant's loss of contribution from the deceased. Hypothetical events which would, but for the deceased's death, have increased the dependant's dependency will not be taken into account. So the plaintiff widow's greater prospective loss had she, as she would have so desired, given up work to have a family, was rightly disregarded in *Malone v Rowan*.[7] Also to be disregarded under the 1976 Act are benefits which have accrued or will, or may, accrue to any person from his estate, or otherwise, as a result of the death.[8]

The assessment of damages in a Fatal Accidents Act claim can thus be seen to be relatively straightforward where what is in issue is the loss of a family breadwinner.

16 [1979] AC 556, [1978] 2 All ER 604, HL; *Corbett v Barking, Havering and Brentwood Health Authority* [1991] 2 QB 408, [1991] 1 All ER 498, CA (but multiplier should be adjusted to take account of known facts).
17 *Graham v Dodds* (supra).
18 For the award of interest generally on damages where the award exceeds £200 see s 35A of the Supreme Court Act 1981.
19 Section 3(5) of the Fatal Accidents Act 1976.
20 Section 3(3) of the Fatal Accidents Act 1976. Her remarriage prospects might affect awards to her children: *Thompson v Price* [1973] QB 838, [1973] 2 All ER 846.
1 See ante. If an unmarried father is killed, even if the mother of his children has no claim, their children recover the loss of all the benefits which their father had provided for them, including such benefits given to the mother for the children's advantage – eg the cost of her air fares for a family holiday: *K v JMP Co Ltd* [1976] QB 85, [1975] 1 All ER 1030, CA.
2 Section 3(4) of the Fatal Accidents Act 1976.
3 *Corbett v Barking, Havering and Brentwood Health Authority* (supra) at 514 and 528.
4 *Williamson v John I Thorneycroft & Co Ltd* [1940] 4 All ER 61, CA.
5 *Hall v Wilson* [1939] 4 All ER 85.
6 *Daniels v Jones* [1961] 3 All ER 24, CA.
7 [1984] 3 All ER 402.
8 Fatal Accidents Act 1976, s 4.

The dependent family seek to replace the lost income of the deceased parent. In recent years the courts have recognised that the death of a parent gives rise to other pecuniary losses over and above any loss of earned income. A series of cases have considered how damages should be assessed where a mother is tortiously killed. It may be that at the time of her death she is not working outside her home or does so only on a part-time basis. The fundamental principle is that the widower and children are entitled to compensation based on the reasonable cost to them of replacing the mother's services in the home.[9] The starting point for that assessment, where children are under school age,[10] will be the national cost of hiring a nanny/housekeeper.[11] Allowance will be made for the fact that mothers do not work fixed hours and do not limit themselves to cooking, cleaning and routine tasks. They provide more general care and moral guidance and those wider 'motherly services'[12] should be reflected in the award of damages. Where the father,[13] or another relative,[14] has given up work to take over the mother's duties, and in the light of the children's needs, that is a reasonable course of action to follow, compensation may be based on that person's loss of earnings rather than the cost of a nanny.

What is said above assumes the existence of a nuclear family where the mother stays at home providing 100% of child care and the father earns 100% of the family income. That, of course, is often not the case. If the mother, too, is in regular employment, the children will suffer a loss of family income which they can obviously claim. They may also lose her 'motherly services' and the Court of Appeal has held that in such cases the compensation for the latter must be subject to a 'modest' discount because the mother did not provide full-time care.[15] But what about 'fatherly' services? Child care is not a solely female preserve and much of what a mother does can equally well be done by a father. In *Hayden v Hayden*[16] the Court of Appeal held that if the father in effect undertook most of the mother's responsibilities after his partner's death there was no loss to the child in this respect. Yet *Hayden v Hayden* must be contrasted with *Stanley v Siddique*[17] where the child's parents were not married. On the death of the mother the father undertook full responsibility for his son and soon remarried. The evidence suggested that the stepmother was likely to make a much better parent than the deceased mother. The defendants argued that the benefit conferred by the acquisition of a stepmother more than cancelled out the loss of the original mother's services. The Court of Appeal held that section 4 of the Fatal Accidents Act 1976 prevented any such 'benefit' being taken into account.

Can the two judgments be reconciled? It can only be done by understanding that in every case assessment of damages in a fatal accidents claim revolves around the special facts of a particular family. In *Stanley v Siddique* the boy had been solely cared for by his mother, however inadequately. He lost that care and the benefit conferred by an excellent stepmother could not be set off against that loss. In *Hayden v Hayden* the father had shared in the care of his daughter. When his wife was killed he simply continued to act as a loving father, increasing his parenting role to make up for the loss

---

9   *Hay v Hughes* [1975] QB 790; *Corbett v Barking, Havering and Brentwood Health Authority* [1991] 2 QB 408, [1991] 1 All ER 498, CA.

10   The Court of Appeal in *Spittle v Bunney* [1988] 3 All ER 1031 assumed a diminishing need for 'motherly services' once a child is settled at school.

11   Based on the net rather than the gross wage payable: *Spittle v Bunney* (supra).

12   *Regan v Williamson* [1976] 2 All ER 241.

13   *Mehmet v Perry* [1977] 2 All ER 529 (note the special needs of these children who suffered from the hereditary disease thalassaemia).

14   *Cresswell v Eaton* [1991] 1 All ER 484 (aunt gave up job as a traffic warden).

15   *Cresswell v Eaton* (supra).

16   [1992] 4 All ER 681, CA.

17   [1992] QB 1, [1991] 1 All ER 529, CA.

of the mother. The child, it was held, suffered a much lesser loss. In *Watson v Willmott*[18] both parents ultimately died as the result of a road accident and the infant plaintiff was adopted by his aunt. He recovered for his loss of financial dependency on both parents.[19] But he recovered nothing for loss of 'motherly services'. The adoption imposed a legal obligation on the adoptive mother to provide such care, thus in effect ensuring the boy suffered no loss in that respect.

Much as the decisions in *Hayden v Hayden* and *Watson v Willmott* may appear objectionable, they are certainly consistent with the House of Lords' approach to the non-recoverability of the gratuitous services provided by a tortfeasor to the victim of that tort in *Hunt v Severs*.[20]

SECTION 4. ALTERNATIVE COMPENSATION SYSTEMS[1]

(A) RESPONSIBILITY AND THE WELFARE STATE[2]

Public responsibility for the victims of personal injury is recognised in the existence of a safety net of benefits and provisions made for accident victims in a number of ways. The plethora of systems created leads to confusion and inequality and can only be explained here in outline.[3]

(1) The welfare state provides essential services for accident victims in two main respects. Medical advice and treatment for injury and disease are largely available free within the National Health Service. The victim of a tort, however, retains the option to elect for private treatment and to charge the cost of that treatment to the tortfeasor.[4] Where long-term care is required, that advantage may be substantial in nature. The Chronically Sick and Disabled Persons Act 1970 empowers local authorities to provide benefits and services for the disabled. In theory, that Act should ensure that all accident victims may be provided with home helps, holidays and assistance in adapting their homes. In practice, however, pressure on local authority budgets means that only minimal benefits and services may now be available. The tort victim can, as we have seen, claim the total estimated cost of such services as part of his proper measure of damages.

(2) A wide range of social security benefits are available to persons incapable of work by reason of accident or disease.[5] The level of payments made is at a subsistence rate, in general, and in no way equates with the loss of earnings suffered by the incapacitated victim. Certain of the non-means-tested benefits are also payable to tort victims but the Social Security (Recovery of Benefits) Act 1997 now provides that the state recovers these payments from the tortfeasor.[6]

18 [1991] 1 QB 140, [1991] 1 All ER 473 (note the judge's finding that the child's right of action survived the adoption).
19 Based on the difference between the level of support his natural and adoptive parents could provide.
20 But for criticism see Matthews and Lunney 'A Tortfeasor's Lot is not a Happy One' (1995) 58 MLR 395. See also Law Commission Consultation Paper 144.
1 See Stapleton 'Tort, Insurance and Ideology' (1995) 58 MLR 820.
2 See generally Oxford Socio-Legal Studies *Compensation and Support for Illness and Injury* (1984); McLean (ed) *Compensation for Damage: an International Perspective* (1993).
3 See further *Atiyah* pp 270ff.
4 Law Reform (Personal Injuries) Act 1948, s 2(4).
5 For examples of the kinds of benefit available, see the 9th edition of this work.
6 Section 6. Note that this provision requires that the 'compensator', who will usually be the defendant's insurer, must pay the *full amount* of recoverable benefits which may exceed the sum that would have been payable as compensation. This means that the state never loses out although, plainly, the defendant might (as might the plaintiff, depending on future contingencies).

Just a few examples of relevant social security benefits are given here. A person incapable of work because he is sick or disabled may claim statutory sick pay for the first 28 weeks that he is incapacitated providing that he has previously been in work and paying national insurance contributions. In 1998–9 the rate of statutory sick pay is £57-70. After 28 weeks, if he is still incapacitated, the accident victim may be able to claim various allowances for invalidity and disablement but these are unlikely to amount to more than £160 or so a week at best.

Should the accident victim need a great deal of care by others, he may be able to claim an attendance allowance. He must establish that he is so severely disabled that he requires from another person either assistance with bodily functions or constant supervision. The higher rate of attendance allowance for 24-hour attention is £51-30 per week and the lower rate for persons needing only day or night time help is £34-30. A friend or relative spending at least 35 hours a week caring for a severely disabled person may be able to claim an invalid care allowance of £38-70. Other social security benefits for the disabled include mobility allowances and, where needed, income support to top up other allowances to meet the basic requirements of life.

Such a brief survey illustrates one issue with clarity. The better off you are to start with, the more you will suffer from an incapacity in respect of which you have no remedy in tort. The university professor who succumbs to an inherent risk of surgery stands to lose a great deal more than the single mother on social security benefits before she is incapacitated. However, if the state has limited resources to compensate for disability it might be argued that high earners have no special claim for special treatment. The professor could, after all, have taken out an insurance policy covering her against all forms of personal injury or disease. There is a sense in which one could argue that social provision for disability merely reflects the inherent inequities in our society.

(3) Certain groups of the disabled may, in addition, receive extra payments related to their disability. The Vaccine Damage Payments Act 1979 provides for payments of £30,000 to persons suffering 80% disablement consequent on vaccination. The Act resulted from one of the few proposals of the Pearson Report to be implemented. Vaccination of children against diseases such as whooping cough, measles and diphtheria benefits the community as a whole. The rationale of the Act is that it is unjust to leave one family to bear alone the burden of any damage resulting from vaccination. Haemophiliacs who have contracted AIDS from the contaminated transfusions, sought similar special treatment. They successfully argued that they entrusted themselves to the National Health Service. They should not shoulder the total cost of the unknown danger lurking in the blood products which they relied on for continued life and health. The Department of Health agreed to set up a fund to compensate haemophiliacs who had contracted AIDS from blood products. Only several months later did the government reluctantly agree to a similar scheme to cover patients contracting AIDS from whole blood transfusions. They feared that they might be seen as opening the door to a general no-fault compensation scheme for medical accidents within the NHS.

(B) OTHER COMPENSATION SYSTEMS

(1) Criminal Injuries Compensation Scheme

The Criminal Injuries Compensation Board administers from government funds a statutory scheme[7] for compensating victims of crimes of violence. If they suffer personal

---

7   The basis for this scheme is the Criminal Injuries Compensation Act 1995. For background on the legislation see *R v Secretary of State for the Home Department, ex p Fire Brigades Union* [1995] 2 All ER 244.

injury as a result of violent crime or while apprehending (or seeking to apprehend) a suspect, the Board may award compensation according to a statutory tariff.

(2)   OCCUPATIONAL SICK PAY

In 1978, two-thirds of those in employment were entitled to continued payments from their employer in replacement of loss of earnings at least in part, for a limited absence from work through sickness or injury.[8] Moves towards 'casualising' labour have reduced this percentage.

(3)   OCCUPATIONAL PENSIONS

Many millions are members of pension schemes run by their employers, which entitle them to compensation beyond social security in the event of personal injury compelling their early retirement.[9]

(4)   INDUSTRIAL INJURIES SCHEME

Where injury occurs at work as a result of an industrial accident, a much more generous scheme provides higher levels of disability benefit than that available within the basic social security provision.

(5)   TRADE UNIONS

A small percentage of employees receive some payment from trade unions or friendly societies during absence from work owing to sickness or accident. Many charities also support the sick and disabled.

(6)   INSURANCE

In many cases, the person killed or injured will have taken out an insurance policy providing for benefits in the event of his death or personal injury.[10] There are three main forms of this first-party insurance. The most common is a life policy providing a guaranteed minimum sum on death. Personal accident policies cover death, loss or disablement resulting from accidents for a prescribed period. Permanent health policies provide periodic payments if the insured person becomes unable to follow his usual occupation because of sickness or accident. Sometimes these forms of insurance are provided by employers for their staff.

The Pearson Report estimated that about one-half of the total compensation for personal injury and death comes from social security and a quarter from the tort system. The remaining quarter comes from the other sources listed above. These figures show how limited a view of accident compensation is obtained if one examines only tort, and ignores these other sources of compensation.

(C)   THE PEARSON REPORT

It was against this background that in 1974 the Royal Commission on Civil Liability and Compensation for Personal Injury was set up under the chairmanship of Lord Pearson. It reported in 1978.

---

8   Pearson Report, para 137.
9   For details, see Pearson Report, para 145 et seq.
10   Much more widespread is insurance against fire or damage to one's buildings, homes, furniture and to one's car, where the insured has a right of subrogation against tortfeasors.

The fundamental issue confronting the Commission was the respective merits of a tort system and a social welfare system. New Zealand has, for instance, abandoned a system based on fault and replaced it by a social welfare scheme making compensation for injury by accident a state responsibility, like our existing social security schemes.[10a] The criticism made of the UK system is that, as we have seen, it is a blend of tort, insurance and social security.[11] The two systems have been fashioned independently, and no attempt has been made by Parliament to harmonise them.

Advocates of a social welfare approach argue that there is no justification for singling out for special treatment areas like industrial accidents. They contend that the present divide between tort and social security is illogical. If I spike my foot with a garden fork while working in my garden, I might claim sickness benefit, free treatment under the National Health Service, payment by my employer while off sick, perhaps a claim under a personal accident insurance policy or, if hospitalised, perhaps a claim on a medical protection policy. But I would have no tort claim. If we alter the facts a little so that I am hurt by a defect in my powered lawn mower, I now have a claim against my retailer in contract (and possibly also in tort), and conceivably a negligence and/or a strict liability claim against the manufacturer, whereupon all the problems of duplicating benefits, and issues of whether some or all must be offset against my tort damages arise. Does the distinction make any sense?

Critics also deplore the emphasis on the cause of the accident, rather than on the injuries to victims. They then demonstrate how costly to administer the tort system is. The Report showed that in the 1970s it cost £175m per annum to collect and distribute tort payments of £202m, so expensive are the judicial process and administering private insurance third party liability. For every £1 of insurance premium, 45p went in costs and 55p to tort victims. In contrast, under the social security system it cost £47m per annum to distribute £421m to accident victims.[12] They complain further that two-thirds of damage awards are for pain and suffering. They criticise, too, the long delays in obtaining tort compensation and the forensic lottery that any system of fault liability must inevitably be.[13]

Nonetheless, the Report rejected widespread adoption of a social welfare system, in part, especially, because it lacked data on the probable cost of a comprehensive accident and disease scheme and because it saw justice in having those at fault make reparation. Its basic proposal was to retain the mixed system of tort law and social security, with a gradual swing towards social security. It made 188 detailed proposals of which one of the most interesting was a proposal to bring road traffic accidents[14] within social security schemes on the model of industrial injuries.

A wholesale change to a social welfare system which abandons 'fault' is unlikely in England in the immediate future. In particular categories of accident, there is increasing pressure for limited 'no-fault' compensation systems. For example, the Pearson Report in its chapter on medical injury[15] recommended against immediate implementation of a 'no-fault' scheme for medical accidents, but expressly accepted that 'changing circumstances' might cause that decision to be reviewed. But on what rational grounds

10a However, owing to the fact that it ran out of money, the New Zealand system was revised considerably.
11 See Stapleton (1995) 58 MLR 820.
12 For the cost of the tort system in medical litigation see Ham et al *Medical Negligence – Compensation and Accountability* (1988).
13 See *Compensation and Support for Illness and Injury* ch 3.
14 For the problems of such a scheme actually implemented in France see Redmond-Cooper, 'No Fault Liability on French Roads' in McLean (ed) *Compensation for Damage: an International Perspective* at p 115.
15 Chapter 24.

should victims of medical accidents be singled out for special treatment? The damage done to good medical practice and doctor/patient relationships by the increasing pace of medical litigation are cited by proponents of a 'no fault' scheme for medical injuries. And the concept of 'fault' may seem especially unjust when applied to a junior doctor making an error after a 48-hour shift in an under-resourced hospital.[16] Nevertheless, a cautious approach to piecemeal implementation of 'no fault' schemes must be adopted. Otherwise, we simply add to the plethora of present compensation systems.

The impetus towards wholesale reform of compensation for personal injuries and its replacement by an accident compensation scheme has faded. A no-fault scheme could not provide tort level damages for all. Maximum levels of compensation for loss of earnings would have to be set, and compensation for pain and suffering would be minimal. The high-earning accident victim able to establish fault would lose out. Other accident victims would benefit from substantial enhancement of what the social security system now provides. There would be greater equality in suffering.[17]

16 See Brazier *Medicine, Patients and the Law* (1992) ch 10.
17 Except, of course, for victims of disease.

Chapter 28

Extinction of remedies

In this chapter, we consider the various ways in which remedies in tort may be extinguished so as to free the defendant from any (continuing) liability.

SECTION I. WAIVER

The circumstances in which waiver will extinguish liability in tort are neatly summarised by Lord Atkin:[1]

> if a man is entitled to one of two inconsistent rights it is fitting that when with full knowledge he has done an unequivocal act showing that he has chosen the one he cannot afterwards pursue the other, which after the first choice is by reason of the inconsistency no longer his to choose.

Thus, a lessor who has brought ejectment proceedings by way of forfeiture for breach of covenant cannot afterwards sue for rent.[2] Similarly, when an act is done professedly on behalf of a principal but in fact without his authority, the election by the principal to ratify deprives him of a later action alleging breach of authority.[3]

'It is essential to bear in mind the distinction between choosing one of two alternative remedies, and choosing one of two inconsistent rights.'[4] It has been seen that merely to choose one remedy is not inconsistent with the continued availability of another remedy. For instance, misdelivery by a carrier gives alternative remedies for breach of contract and conversion; a buyer who has failed in an action for rescission may subsequently recover damages in deceit.[5] In many of these cases of alternative remedies 'the plaintiff has never the slightest intention of waiving, excusing or in any kind of way palliating the tort'.[6] Obviously, then, where there is no evidence of waiver, and no inconsistency, the plaintiff will not be deprived of his alternative remedy – if someone finds that a thief has stolen his jewellery, he does not, by maintaining an action in restitution for the proceeds, thereby say in effect: 'It is my intention to abandon my claim against you for the tort of conversion'.

1   *United Australia Ltd v Barclays Bank Ltd* [1941] AC 1 at 30, [1940] 4 All ER 20, HL.
2   *Jones v Carter* (1846) 15 M & W 718.
3   *Verschures Creameries Ltd v Hull and Netherlands Steamship Co Ltd* [1921] 2 KB 608, CA.
4   Per Lord Atkin in *United Australia Ltd v Barclays Bank Ltd* [1941] AC 1 at 29, HL.
5   *Clarke v Dickson* (1858) EB & E 148; subsequent proceedings (1859) 6 CBNS 453.
6   Per Lord Atkin in *United Australia Ltd v Barclays Bank Ltd* [1941] AC 1 at 28–9, HL.

Nor will the intention to waive a tort be imputed to a plaintiff merely because he receives back part of what he has lost, and still less because he demands from the defendant the price of goods of which he has been deprived.[7] *Burn v Morris*[8] is illustrative.

The plaintiff lost a £20 note. X found it, and the defendant bought it from her for £18, knowing that it was a lost note. When it became known that X had merely found the note, she was brought before the Mayor of London's Court where she surrendered £7, being all of the £18 she then retained. Acceptance by the plaintiff of this sum of £7 did not prevent him from recovering the balance from the defendant.

Nor is it likely that the plaintiff will be held to have waived unless he has full knowledge of the material facts.[9]

Lastly, in those circumstances (which we examined in chapter 26) where more than one action can be brought on the same facts, suing in respect of one of those causes of action will not be waiver of the remainder.[10] A claim may be pursued under parallel causes until such time as liability is established. An election need normally only be made between alternative causes at the time of judgment.[11] *Island Records Ltd v Tring International plc*[12] introduced a caveat to this general rule, however: an election *ought* to be made sooner than judgment where any delay is both unreasonable and prejudicial to the defendant.

SECTION 2. SATISFACTION

Where judgment for a sum of money has been given for the plaintiff against the defendant and the defendant has satisfied that judgment by payment in full of that money, this discharges the claim of the plaintiff arising out of the same facts, not merely against the defendant, but against any other tortfeasor. Thus, in *United Australia Ltd v Barclays Bank Ltd*, Viscount Simon stated that if the plaintiffs had obtained judgment in restitution against the converters of the cheque, and if the latter had then satisfied that judgment, the plaintiffs could not subsequently have sued the bank for the tort of conversion.[13] Judgment, not followed by satisfaction, would not, however, have barred a claim against the bank.

SECTION 3. JUDGMENT

Final judgment in a suit has two principal effects. First, the original cause of action is terminated by its merger in the judgment. Where, therefore, the plaintiff elects to sue in

---

7 *Valpy v Sanders* (1848) 5 CB 886.
8 (1834) 2 Cr & M 579.
9 [1941] AC 1 at 30, HL (per Lord Atkin). Cf Lord Porter (at 54) who left open this point.
10 *Caxton Publishing Co Ltd v Sutherland Publishing Co* [1939] AC 178 at 199, [1938] 4 All ER 389, HL (*per* Lord Porter).
11 *United Australia Ltd v Barclays Bank Ltd* [1941] AC 1, [1940] 4 All ER 20, HL. In *Tang Min Sit v Capacious Investments Ltd* [1996] 2 WLR 192, PC, Lord Nicholls said (at 196-197): 'The law frequently affords an injured person more than one remedy for the wrong he has suffered. Sometimes the two remedies are alternative and inconsistent ... Faced with alternative and incosistent remedies a plaintiff must choose, or elect between them ... He is asked to choose when, but not before, judgment is given in his favour'.
12 [1995] 3 All ER 444, [1996] 1 WLR 1256.
13 [1941] AC 1 at 21, HL. Contra, if the parties merely arrive at a settlement, which, though embodied in a judge's order, is not a judgment: *Rice v Reed* [1900] 1 QB 54, CA.

conversion rather than for money had and received, although that election does not amount to a waiver of his alternative remedy, judgment in that suit of conversion, even if unsatisfied, will bar a further action against the same defendant in restitution.[14] And, of course, in those cases where successive actions on the same facts may not be brought[15] one judgment bars any further proceedings.

Secondly, by virtue of the rule known as res judicata, judgment also operates to terminate certain other claims by either of the parties against the other. Suppose that A sues B for trespass to land, and the court decides that A was in possession of the land and returns a verdict in his favour: if B later sues A for assault in ejecting him from the land on that occasion, and A raises the defence that he used reasonable force for the purpose of ejecting a trespasser, B will be estopped by the earlier judgment from denying that he was a trespasser.

Finally, it should be noted that where A causes harm to both B and C simultaneously, B's successful action does not bar C from bringing an action in her own right, later. And this is so where C, a child, is dependant upon B.[16]

SECTION 4.   RELEASE

Any surrender of a cause of action may legitimately be called a release. But the term is usually reserved for surrenders by deed. Surrender by deed discharges the cause of action even though there is no consideration.[17] Moreover, release may discharge tortious liability regardless of whether it is given before or after the commencement of the action.[18]

SECTION 5.   ACCORD AND SATISFACTION

The terminology used in connection with this method of discharge is confusing, but the law is clear. If the plaintiff enters into a valid contract with the defendant to settle a cause of action, and the defendant performs this contract, the defendant has a defence to any proceedings by the plaintiff based on that cause of action. The agreement is the 'accord'; satisfaction is used both to mean the 'consideration' given for the plaintiff's promise, and the 'performance' of that promise.

Whether the cause of action will be discharged by mere agreement – that is, before the terms of the agreement have been performed – is a matter of interpretation of the agreement. The burden is probably on the defendant to prove that the tort has been discharged even without performance of the agreement.[1]

---

14 *Buckland v Johnson* (1854) 15 CB 145; approved in *United Australia Ltd v Barclays Bank Ltd* [1941] AC 1 at 16–17, HL (per Viscount Simon LC).
15 See ch 22 ante.
16 *C (a minor) v London Borough of Hackney* [1996] 1 WLR 789, CA.
17 For an example of a release of an action in tort, see *Phillips v Clagett* (1843) 11 M & W 84.
18 *Apley Estates Co Ltd v De Bernales* [1946] 2 All ER 338; affd [1947] Ch 217, [1947] 1 All ER 213, CA, where the point was not discussed.
1 The judgment of Greer LJ in *British Russian Gazette and Trade Outlook Ltd v Associated Newspapers Ltd* [1933] 2 KB 616, [1933] All ER Rep 320, CA is a very clear judicial exposition of the law; cf Lord Atkinson in *Morris v Baron & Co* [1918] AC 1 at 35, HL, and the alternative ratio decidendi of Holroyd J in *Brewer and Gregory v Sparrow* (1827) 7 B & C 310 at 313. See also *Lee v Lancashire and Yorkshire Rly Co* (1871) 6 Ch App 527; *Ellen v Great Northern Rly Co* (1901) 17 TLR 453.

SECTION 6.   LIMITATION[2]

(A)   PERIOD OF LIMITATION

At common law there was no time limit restricting the right to sue. Successive statutes from 1623 onwards introduced limitation periods after the expiry of which an action in tort is time-barred. The victim of an alleged tort must serve his writ within a specified number of years or forfeit his remedy. The need for limitation periods is self-evident. Potential defendants would otherwise face years of uncertainty not knowing whether or not they will be sued. A fair trial becomes increasingly difficult as witnesses' memories fade and in some cases witnesses even die or leave the country. Accordingly, even if the plaintiff begins his cause of action within the statutory limitation period, his claim may still be struck out if he prosecutes it in a dilatory manner on the basis that this will amount to an abuse of process of the court.[3]

Very short and rigid time limits, however, also result in injustice to the plaintiff. He may not discover for some years that he has been the victim of a tort. Consider the common examples of persons contracting industrial disease, and the owners of negligently constructed buildings. Damage to the body from working conditions is likely to be stealthy and progressive. Definitive symptoms of disease may manifest themselves years after the disease was in fact well established.[4] When a building is erected on defective foundations, cracks may begin to ruin the fabric of the building years before they become apparent to even the most prudent homeowner.[5] It would scarcely be fair to deny the worker suffering from disease or the unfortunate homeowner any remedy at all because a rigid limitation period had expired before they could have realised that they might have a right to compensation.

The relevant and complex law on limitation is now mainly contained in the Limitation Act 1980 as amended by the Latent Damage Act 1986. In the case of actions for injury caused by negligence, nuisance or breach of duty (whether the duty exists by virtue of a contract, a statute or independently of either a contract or a statute) when the damages claimed by the plaintiff consist of, or include, damages in respect of personal injuries to the plaintiff or any other person, the period of limitation is three years.[6] In cases of actions for negligence, other than for personal injuries or death, the Latent Damage Act 1986[7] introduced a primary limitation period of six years (with provision in special circumstances for a further period of three years to run from the 'starting date' set by that Act, subject to a final 'long-stop' of 15 years).

An action for libel and slander must be brought within one year, with a discretion to allow the action to proceed despite the expiry of the one-year period.[8] Where the plaintiff sues, invoking strict liability for defective products, under the Consumer Protection

---

2   See further, Oughton, Lowry and Merkin *Limitation of Actions* (1998). See also the Law Commission Consultation Paper No 151 *Limitation of Actions* (1998).

3   *Grovit v Doctor* [1997] 1 WLR 640 at 647, HL (per Lord Woolf); *Arbuthnot Latham Bank Ltd v Trafalgar Holdings Ltd* [1998] 2 All ER 181, [1998] 1 WLR 1426, CA.

4   See *Cartledge v E Jopling & Sons Ltd* [1963] AC 758, [1963] 1 All ER 341, HL (pneumoconiosis from inhaling dust); *Thompson v Smiths Shiprepairers (North Shields) Ltd* [1984] QB 405, [1984] 1 All ER 881 (industrial deafness); *Brooks v J and P Coates (UK) Ltd* [1984] 1 All ER 702.

5   See *Anns v Merton London Borough Council* [1978] AC 728, [1977] 2 All ER 492, HL; *Pirelli General Cable Works Ltd v Oscar Faber & Partners* [1983] 2 AC 1, [1983] 1 All ER 65, HL. But note that both decisions must now be read subject to *Murphy v Brentwood District Council* [1991] 1 AC 398, [1990] 2 All ER 908, HL.

6   Limitation Act 1980, s 11(1).

7   By inserting a new s 14A into the 1980 Act.

8   Section 4A of the Limitation Act 1980 (as amended by the Defamation Act 1996, s 5).

Act 1987 he must normally bring his action within three years of suffering the relevant damage, or within three years of acquiring the necessary knowledge of the facts to sue if that date be later.[9] No action may be brought under the 1987 Act more than 10 years after the product was first put into circulation.[10] The plaintiff may still have an action in negligence after that date where, even by then, he has not discovered his injury or damage or other relevant facts pertaining to his right of action in negligence. The limitation period for other tort actions remains six years.[11]

The three-year period of limitation for personal injuries applies only to 'any action for negligence, nuisance or breach of duty (whether the duty exists by virtue of a contract or of a provision made by or under a statute or independently of any contract or any such provision)'.[12]

The term 'personal injuries' includes any disease and any impairment of a person's physical or mental condition.[13] But what exactly is meant by the broad phrase breach of duty? In *Letang v Cooper*,[14] Lord Denning MR held those words apt to include any breach of any duty imposed by the law of tort. Thus where a plaintiff sought to sue in trespass to the person more than three years after the commission of the alleged trespass,[15] her action was barred. However, the House of Lords has now ruled in *Stubbings v Webb*[16] that Lord Denning was wrong. Availing themselves of their new freedom to consult *Hansard*,[17] their Lordships held that Parliament never intended the three-year limitation period to apply to deliberate torts such as trespass to the person. Such torts were governed by the standard six-year period of limitation.

Any apparent advantage to the victim of a trespass action is however misleading. For although trespass does not fall within the three-year personal injuries rule, the plaintiff cannot take advantage of the special provisions permitting a claim exceptionally to be brought well after the original limitation period has expired.[18] *Stubbings v Webb* itself illustrates the plaintiff's dilemma. The plaintiff claimed that she had been sexually abused in childhood by her adoptive father and stepbrother. She sought to sue them in battery when she was 35 years old and came to appreciate the link between her ongoing psychiatric problems and that childhood abuse. The House of Lords ruled that her suit was subject to an absolute six-year limitation period. But had she, for example, been able to sue social workers whom she might have contended had negligently ignored her plight, the personal injuries rules would have come into play giving the court the discretion to allow her to proceed even after such a long period of time. This is certainly true where the action is brought against a mother for failure to prevent paternal abuse.[19]

---

9   Consumer Protection Act 1987, s 5(5) and Sch I.
10 Consumer Protection Act 1987, s 5(5) and Sch I.
11 Limitation Act 1980, s 2 (except in the case of proceedings for loss of postal packets under s 30(1) of the Post Office Act 1969 where the period is 12 months).
12 Limitation Act, s 11.
13 Limitation Act, s 38(1).
14 [1965] 1 QB 232, [1964] 2 All ER 929, CA.
15 Even where the trespass was intentional, see *Long v Hepworth* [1968] 3 All ER 248.
16 [1993] AC 498, [1993] 1 All ER 322, HL.
17 See *Pepper (Inspector of Taxes) v Hart* [1993] AC 593, [1993] 1 All ER 42, HL.
18 If, however, the gist of P's action is that D was under a duty to prevent a third party from committing trespass against P, then the case does not fall to be dealt with as a (six-year) trespass case: *S v W* [1995] 3 FCR 649, CA.
19 *S v W* [1995] 1 FLR 862, CA.

(B) WHEN DOES A CAUSE OF ACTION ACCRUE?

The period of limitation begins from the date on which the cause of action accrued. A cause of action accrues at that moment in time when a potential plaintiff is entitled to succeed in an action against a potential defendant.[20] There must, then, be in existence such a plaintiff and defendant. If a tort is committed against the estate of a deceased person, for example, if his goods are taken away, the cause of action does not accrue until an executor or administrator is appointed.[1] A cause of action against an ambassador does not accrue until his diplomatic immunity ends.[2] On the other hand, a plaintiff whose car has been stolen by a thief whom he does not know and cannot trace has a cause of action against that thief from the time of the theft.[3] When a cause of action lies without proof of damage, clearly time always runs from the wrongful act.

However, in negligence the cause of action accrues only when damage is suffered. And this is the case in all torts where damage is essential to the cause of action. But ascertaining when damage occurs may be difficult. The crucial date is the date of the damage not its discoverability.[4] So a claim in respect of negligent construction of a building prima facie accrues when cracking and subsidence begin,[5] not when the physical damage becomes patent. Similarly, when a negligently constructed security gate is the reason for a burglary's commission, the time runs from the date of the burglary, not the time of the negligent construction of the gate.[6] Where the relevant negligence consists of negligent advice, the question arises whether the damage founding the cause of action is suffered when the plaintiff relies on that advice,[7] or when the subsequent financial loss is suffered. On one argument, loss occurs as soon as the advice is relied upon because the plaintiff would not have acted in the way that he went on to act. A different (but not inconsistent) argument is that, in negligent valuation cases, no loss can be established until the negligent inaccuracy of the valuation can be demonstrated, necessarily, at a later stage.[8] However, the leading case of *Nykredit Mortgage Bank plc v Edwards Erdman Group Ltd (No 2)*[8a] held that a purchaser's course of action accrues at the time of the purchase for, as Lord Nicholls explained, '[h]e suffers damage by parting with his money and receiving in exchange property worth less than the price he paid.'[8b] The injustice to a plaintiff who would otherwise lose his right to a remedy before he could know of its existence explains why in the tort

---

20 More than one cause of action may arise from a single set of circumstances: in *Duke of Brunswick v Harmer* (1849) 14 QB 185, the defendant's newspaper had published a statement defamatory of the plaintiff. Seventeen years later an agent of the plaintiff purchased a copy at the defendant's office. The plaintiff's cause of action accrued upon the sale of this copy, not when the newspaper was first published. Was any other defence open to the defendant?

1   *Murray v East India Co* (1821) 5 B & Ald 204; *Pratt v Swaine* (1828) 8 B & C 285.

2   *Musurus Bey v Gadban* [1894] 2 QB 352, CA.

3   *R B Policies at Lloyd's v Butler* [1950] 1 KB 76, [1949] 2 All ER 226.

4   *Pirelli General Cable Works Ltd v Oscar Faber & Partners* [1983] 2 AC 1, [1983] 1 All ER 65, HL. Cf the position in New Zealand, established by the Privy Council, which renders uncertain the authority of *Pirelli: Invercargill City Council v Hamlin* [1996] 1 All ER 756.

5   The cause of action against the builders accrues when physical damage occurs. Any claim in negligence against the local authority in respect of negligent inspection accrues later, when that damage poses a threat to health and safety: *Governors of the Peabody Donation Fund v Sir Lindsay Parkinson & Co Ltd* [1985] AC 210, [1984] 3 All ER 529, HL.

6   *Dove v Banham Patent Locks* [1983] 2 All ER 833, [1983] 1 WLR 1436.

7   *Forster v Outred & Co* [1982] 2 All ER 753, [1982] 1 WLR 86, CA; *Secretary of State for the Environment v Essex Goodman & Suggitt* [1986] 2 All ER 69, [1986] 1 WLR 1432.

8   *UBAF Ltd v European American Banking Corpn* [1984] QB 713, [1984] 2 All ER 226; *First National Commercial Bank plc v Humberts* [1995] 2 All ER 673, CA.

8a   [1997] 1 WLR 1627, HL.

8b   Ibid.

of negligence special provision is now made for all forms of latent damage with separate rules for personal injuries and other forms of damage.

(C)   SPECIAL RULES FOR PERSONAL INJURIES

The impetus for reform of the limitation rules concerning personal injuries came from cases relating to industrial disease. Where the plaintiff contracts some form of pneumoconiosis such as silicosis from inhaling dust, his cause of action in negligence arises even though he is unaware of the onset of the disease. In *Cartledge v E Jopling & Sons Ltd*[9] the House of Lords held that, at common law, time started to run as soon as the damage was suffered; in this case, therefore, time ran once material scarring of the lung tissue has occurred, even though X-ray examination would not have revealed it. The Limitation Act 1980[10] seeks to avoid the injustice that might otherwise result when a cause of action for personal injuries becomes time-barred before the plaintiff knows of it. The three-year limitation period begins to run either from the date of the accrual of the cause of action (ie the date of the damage) or from the date of the plaintiff's knowledge of that damage, whichever is the later. The limitation period ends only three years after the date of the plaintiff's knowledge of the cause of action if that date is after three years from the accrual of the cause of action. If the plaintiff dies before the expiration of the period, the period as respects the cause of action surviving for the benefit of the estate of the deceased by virtue of section 1 of the Law Reform (Miscellaneous Provisions) Act 1934 is three years from the date of death or the date of knowledge of the personal representative.[11]

The Act provides in section 14 a detailed definition of 'knowledge', the interpretation of which has given rise to complicated case law. When, in a personal injuries case, time runs from the date of a person's knowledge, the date is the date on which he first had knowledge of the following facts:[12]

1   that the injury in question was significant. Any injury is significant if the person whose date of knowledge is in question would reasonably have considered it sufficiently serious to justify his instituting proceedings for damages against a defendant who did not dispute liability and was able to satisfy a judgment.[13] It would appear that the particular plaintiff's intelligence should be considered,[14] but that his personal reasons for not suing are irrelevant;[15]

2   that the injury was attributable in whole or in part to the alleged wrongful act or omission.[16] This means that the plaintiff must know that the wrongful act was a cause in fact of his injury.[17] But it is generally not relevant that the plaintiff was unaware that, as a matter of law, the defendant's act was an actionable tort;[18]

---

9   [1963] AC 758, [1963] 1 All ER 341, HL.
10   Section 11.
11   Section 11(5), (6). For the corresponding application of these provisions to claims under the Fatal Accidents Act see ss 12(1) and 33.
12   Section 14(1). Note that there is an important distinction between 'knowledge' and 'belief': see *Nash v Eli Lilly & Co* [1993] 4 All ER 383, [1993] 1 WLR 782.
13   Section 14(2).
14   *McCafferty v Metropolitan Police District Receiver* [1977] 2 All ER 756 at 775, CA (per Geoffrey Lane LJ).
15   *Miller v London Electrical Manufacturing Co Ltd* [1976] 2 Lloyd's Rep 284, CA (not suing for dermatitis through fear of losing job); *Buck v English Electric Co Ltd* [1978] 1 All ER 271 (not suing for pneumoconiosis because he was receiving wages and did not wish to 'sponge').
16   See *Wilkinson v Ancliff (BLT) Ltd* [1986] 3 All ER 427, [1986] 1 WLR 1352. The plaintiff need not know the precise details of the defendant's acts or omissions to set time running, only the essence of the act or omission: *Nash v Eli Lilly & Co* [1993] 1 WLR 782.
17   *Pickles v National Coal Board* [1968] 2 All ER 598.
18   *Brooks v J and P Coates (UK) Ltd* [1984] 1 All ER 702; *Broadly v Guy Clapham Co* [1994] 4 All ER 439, CA; *Dobbie v Medway Health Authority* [1994] 4 All ER 450, CA.

3   the identity of the defendant;[19]
4   the identity of a third person (and any additional facts supporting the bringing of an action against the defendant) where that third person was guilty of the act or omission on which the plaintiff's case hangs. If, therefore, the plaintiff seeks to hold an employer vicariously liable, time does not run until he identifies the employee and ascertains whether he was acting in the course of his employment.

Section 14(1) expressly states that knowledge that any acts or omissions did, or did not, as a matter of law, involve negligence, nuisance or breach of duty is irrelevant.[20] In effect he is deemed to know the legal significance of facts.[1] Yet it is not the plaintiff's actual knowledge alone which is relevant. Section 14(3) makes the following provision for constructive knowledge.

> For the purposes of this section, a person's knowledge includes knowledge which he might reasonably have been expected to acquire:
> a   from facts observable or ascertainable by him; or
> b   from facts ascertainable by him with the help of medical or other appropriate expert advice which it is reasonable for him to seek; but a person shall not be fixed under this subsection with knowledge of a fact ascertainable only with the help of expert advice so long as he has taken all reasonable steps to obtain (and, where appropriate, act on) that advice.

If he consults the expert, he is not prejudiced if the expert fails to find, or inform him of, the ascertainable facts.[2] The subsection applies only to knowledge of a 'fact' – if the plaintiff delays suing because he has received erroneous legal advice, time will run against him if he has not issued a writ.[3] Similarly, the subsection is confined to knowledge and what ought to be known and it does not extend to reasonable belief or reasonable suspicion.[4]

Nevertheless, in exceptional cases, the victim of personal injuries who fails to start his action in due time may, with permission of the court, still be able to proceed. Thus the plaintiff who had knowledge of all the relevant facts but was unaware of his legal rights, or the plaintiff who has received duff legal advice, has one last chance to seek a remedy. By section 33(1) the court may still allow an action to proceed notwithstanding the expiry of the limitation periods. The court has a discretion to extend the statutory time limits if it considers it equitable to do so having regard to the degree to which the ordinary limitation rules prejudice the plaintiff and the degree to which any exercise of the power would prejudice the defendant. The court must have regard to all the circumstances, including:

a   the length of, and the reasons for, the delay on the part of the plaintiff;[5]
b   the effect of the delay on the cogency of the evidence in the case,
c   the conduct of the defendant after the cause of action arose, including his response to the plaintiff's request for information,
d   the duration of any disability of the plaintiff arising after the cause of action,

---

19   The plaintiff may have been knocked down by a hit-and-run driver, or the defendant's firm may be a member of a group of interlocking companies – see *Simpson v Norwest Holst Southern Ltd* [1980] 2 All ER 471, [1980] 1 WLR 968, CA.
20   That said, where P's action relies on D's omission, 'knowledge' cannot exist until P knows that something else could and should have been done: *Forbes v Wandsworth Health Authority* [1997] QB 402, [1996] 4 All ER 881.
1   See *Brooks v J & P Coates (UK) Ltd* [1984] 1 All ER 702.
2   *Marston v British Railways Board* [1976] ICR 124.
3   If the solicitor's advice is wrong on the facts (as distinct from the law), time does not start to run.
4   *Nash v Eli Lilly & Co* [1993] 4 All ER 383, [1993] 1 WLR 782.
5   *Thompson v Brown Construction (Ebbw Vale) Ltd* [1981] 2 All ER 296, HL.

e   the extent to which the plaintiff acted promptly and reasonably once he knew of the facts which afforded him a cause of action, and

f   the steps taken by the plaintiff to obtain medical, legal, or other expert advice and the nature of any such advice received.

A very wide discretion, and one not limited to the six named factors, is given to the court.[6] So, for example, the fact that the defendant is insured is a relevant consideration[7] as, too, is the fact that the case may involve putting the defendant to greater expense in defending the action than the action is actually worth.[8] There is, however, one restriction: where the plaintiff has commenced proceedings and then discontinued them, only in the most exceptional case will discretion be exercised in his favour.[9] And remember that the decision of the House of Lords in *Stubbings v Webb*[10] denied the benefit of any such discretion to the victim of a deliberate tort.

(D)   LATENT DAMAGE OTHER THAN PERSONAL INJURIES

The special provision made by section 11 of the Limitation Act to assist plaintiffs who lacked the necessary knowledge to start an action was restricted to actions for personal injuries. Yet the problems limitation periods pose for the victim of a latent defect can be just as acute in relation to damage to property. A series of Court of Appeal decisions sought to establish that the cause of action in such cases accrued only when the defect was discoverable.[11] But in *Pirelli General Cable Works Ltd v Oscar Faber and Partners*[12] the House of Lords overruled those decisions as inconsistent with *Cartledge v E Jopling & Sons Ltd*.[13] The facts in *Pirelli* highlight the problems of latent damage.

> In 1969, the plaintiff engaged the defendants to advise them in relation to building a new chimney. The defendants' design was negligently produced. Cracks occurred in the chimney and it had to be replaced. The plaintiffs first discovered the cracks in 1977 but they first occurred in 1970. The plaintiffs served their writ in 1978 contending that the (six-year) limitation period did not begin to run until 1977 when they could first reasonably have discovered the defect.

The House of Lords held that the cause of action accrued in 1970 when the damage first occurred so the claim was time-barred. Two further acute difficulties for plaintiffs emerged from the decision in *Pirelli*. Lord Fraser, in an obiter dictum,[14] suggested that where a defect was so gross that the building was 'doomed from the start',[15] time would begin to run even earlier: from the completion of the building. The result of such a doctrine that the worse the negligence the more favourable the limitation period would

---

6   *Firman v Ellis* [1978] QB 886, [1978] 2 All ER 851, CA. See also *Birkett v James* [1978] AC 297, [1977] 2 All ER 801, HL, and *Liff v Peasley* [1980] 1 All ER 623, CA; *Hartley v Birmingham City Council* [1992] 2 All ER 213, CA.

7   *Kelly v Bastible* (1996) 36 BMLR 51.

8   *Nash v Eli Lilly & Co* [1993] 4 All ER 383, [1993] 1 WLR 782, CA.

9   *Walkley v Precision Forgings Ltd* [1979] 2 All ER 548, HL; *Deerness v John R Keeble & Son (Brantham) Ltd* [1983] 2 Lloyd's Rep 260, HL.

10   [1993] AC 498 at 552, [1993] 1 All ER 322, HL. And see *Halford v Brookes* [1992] PIQR P175 though in substance the judgment must now be considered incorrect.

11   See *Sparham-Souter v Town and Country Developments (Essex) Ltd* [1976] QB 858, [1976] 2 All ER 65; *Dennis v Charnwood Borough Council* [1983] QB 409, [1982] 3 All ER 486.

12   [1983] 2 AC 1, [1983] 1 All ER 65, HL.

13   [1963] AC 758, [1963] 1 All ER 341; see above.

14   [1983] 2 AC 1 at 16, HL.

15   See *Dove v Banhams Patent Locks Ltd* [1983] 2 All ER 833, [1983] 1 WLR 1436; *Jones v Stroud District Council* [1988] 1 All ER 5, [1986] 1 WLR 1141.

be to the defendant did not find favour in later decisions.[16] The second difficulty arising from the case in relation to latent defects affected 'subsequent owners' of buildings. In *Pirelli* it was said that time did not start to run again in favour of the subsequent owner once he acquired the property.[17] But subsequent owners' problems were in fact more acute than simply being entitled only to the tag end of their predecessors' limitation period. Had they any claim at all in respect of damage to property to which, at the time damage occurred, they had no title? The essence of the claim in such a case is a claim for economic loss, for the diminished value of the property the subsequent owner has acquired. In general, the House of Lords' decision in *Murphy v Brentwood District Council*[18] has now ruled such claims to be inadmissible, yet their Lordships also managed to approve *Pirelli* as falling within the principle of *Hedley-Byrne v Heller*.[19] The ensuing result is continuing chaos.[20]

The Law Reform Committee reported on these several problems concerning latent damage to property in 1984.[1] Their proposals are largely embodied in the Latent Damage Act 1986 which applies not solely to latent damage to property but to all negligence actions other than claims in respect of personal injury or death. The Act first inserts new sections 14A and 14B into the Limitation Act 1980. The limitation period in actions to which sections 14A and 14B apply shall be either six years from the date on which the cause of action accrued or three years from the 'starting date' when the plaintiff had the necessary knowledge of the facts to bring an action. 'Knowledge' is defined in section 14A(6)-(8) in terms virtually identical to those used to define 'knowledge' in the original section 14 of the 1980 Act for the purpose of extending the three-year period to bring an action in respect of personal injuries.[2] Section 14B imposes a 'long stop' of 15 years from the date of the alleged negligence. Once 15 years have elapsed, no action may be brought, even though the plaintiff may not have discovered the relevant damage: there is no provision similar to section 33 of the 1980 Act for a judge to exercise his discretion to override this final limitation period in section 14B.[3]

The Latent Damage Act represents a worthy attempt at compromise between the rights of plaintiffs and defendants, but it still leaves some key questions unanswered. First, sections 14A and 14B apply to actions for negligence. Will they be applied, for example, to actions for nuisance or breach of statutory duty where the essence of the wrong complained of is also absence of reasonable care?[4] Secondly, no clear definition of damage is provided. Thus, as damage to buildings is often progressive, will the cause of action accrue when the first slight crack is judged to have occurred or, if at a later stage, when?

One matter that was once unclear has now been clarified by the Court of Appeal. The Latent Damage Act 1986 is applicable only to actions in tort.[5] But, notwithstanding its inapplicability to contractual duties of care, some contractual relationships may still be governed by this limitation period where concurrent duties are owed in both contract

16 See, eg, *Kettemann v Hansel Properties* [1987] AC 189, [1988] 1 All ER 38 where the House of Lords adopted a severely restrictive view of 'doomed from the start'. The doctrine, if it existed, did not embrace any latent defect bound at some stage to result in damage to the property: [1987] AC 189, [1988] 1 All ER 38, HL.
17 Supra, at 18.
18 [1991] 1 AC 398, [1990] 2 All ER 908, HL. See ch 12 ante.
19 Ibid, at 919 (per Lord Keith).
20 See McKendrick '*Pirelli* re-examined' (1991) 11 Legal Studies 326.
1   *Twenty-fourth Report; Latent Damage* Cmnd 9390.
2   *Spencer-Ward v Humberts* [1995] 06 EG 148, CA.
3   But see s 2 of the 1986 Act regarding fraud, concealment or mistake.
4   For a 'yes' answer, see James 'Statutory Liability for Negligence and the Latent Damage Act 1986' (1994) 45 NILQ 301.
5   *Iron Trades Mutual Insurance Co Ltd v JK Buckenham Ltd* [1990] 1 All ER 808; *Société Commerciale de Reassurance v ERAS (International) Ltd* [1992] 2 All ER 82n, CA.

and tort.[6] According to *Henderson v Merrett Syndicates Ltd*,[7] the plaintiff is entitled to rely on that limitation period which is most advantageous to him.

Section 3 of the 1986 Act addresses the rights of successive owners of property. It provides that where a cause of action has accrued to A while he has an interest in that property, 'then providing B acquires the property' ... after the date on which the original cause of action accrued,

> but before the material facts about the damage have become known to any person who, at the time when he first had knowledge of the facts, has any interest in the property; a fresh cause of action in respect of that negligence shall accrue to that other person on the date on which he acquires his interest in the property.

The limitation period as against the new owner is once again either six years from when his cause of action accrued (ie his acquisition of the property) or three years from when he acquired knowledge of the relevant facts (subject once again to the 15-year 'long stop' in section 14B).

Three further points must be noted about section 3. First, and most importantly, how can section 3 be reconciled with *Murphy v Brentwood District Council* which generally denies the existence of any duty of care in such cases?[8] Note that in *Murphy*, section 3 did not even get a passing mention from their Lordships! Secondly, although drafted with defective buildings in mind, it applies to all property including goods. Finally, the new cause of action for the subsequent property owner arises only where his predecessor did not have any actual or constructive knowledge of the relevant defect.[9]

(E) CONTINUING WRONGS

Where the act of the defendant is a continuing wrong, for example if he erects a building on the plaintiff's land, there will be a continuing trespass;[10] so long as it remains there, any cause of action will lie, which is based on the continuance of that wrong during the six years (or three years in the case of personal injuries) immediately preceding the action.[11]

(F) EFFECT OF DISABILITY OF THE PLAINTIFF

If, on the date when any right of action accrued, the person to whom it accrued was a minor or a person of unsound mind,[12] the action may be brought at any time before the

---

6 Note that many professional-client relationships would fall into this bracket.
7 [1995] 2 AC 145, [1994] 3 All ER 506, HL.
8 *Murphy* does not deny a duty of care where the defective property poses a threat of damage to other property, nor does it do so where the property damage is of the kind often referred to as 'complex structure' damage. These would appear to be the only two exceptions to the seeming redundancy of s 3 in this context.
9 In what circumstances (if any) could the subsequent owner sue the vendor who failed to disclose his knowledge of the relevant defects?
10 See ch 5, ante.
11 *Hardy v Ryle* (1829) 9 B & C 603; *Earl of Harrington v Derby Corpn* [1905] 1 Ch 205.
12 By s 38(3) 'a person is of unsound mind if he is a person who, by reason of mental disorder within the meaning of the Mental Health Act 1983 is incapable of managing and administering his property and affairs'. The court will not strike out an action by an infant plaintiff for negligence for mere inactivity on his part before his 21st birthday: *Tolley v Morris* [1979] 2 All ER 561, [1979] 1 WLR 592, HL.

expiration of six years (or three years in the case of personal injuries) from the date when the person ceased to be under that disability, or died, whichever event first occurred.[13]

Where the cause of action has once vested in a person who is free from disability, and the period has therefore began to run, should that person or some other person to whom the cause of action has passed subsequently become disabled, the period will not on that account be further extended.[14] When a right of action which has accrued to a person under disability vests, on the death of that person while still under a disability, in another person also under a disability, there, too, no further extension of time shall be allowed by reason of the disability of the second person.[15] Where a person, in whom a cause of action has vested, was, at the moment of vesting, under one disability, for example minority, and, at or before the cessation of that disability, becomes insane, time does not begin to run until he has 'ceased to be under a disability',[16] that is until the last of his disabilities has ended.

The fact that disability may persist for a very long time obviously works to the disadvantage of the defendant. But according to *Headford v Bristol and District Health Authority*[17] it was not an abuse of process to institute proceedings after a 28-year delay, even though the delay was apparently unjustified other than in terms of the Act's provision for extension of the limitation period.

(G) POSTPONEMENT OF LIMITATION PERIOD IN CASE OF FRAUD OR CONCEALMENT

Where the action is based upon the fraud of the defendant or his agent, or of any person through whom he claims[18] (or that person's agent), or where any fact relevant to the right of action is deliberately concealed by any such person, the period shall not begin to run until the plaintiff has, or with reasonable diligence could have, discovered the fraud or concealment.[19] It is not sufficient if the defendant has merely concealed facts that would strengthen the plaintiff's claim; they must be central to him framing such a claim in the first place.[20] On the other hand, once a cause of action has arisen, subsequent concealment of facts relevant to the plaintiff's action will postpone the running of the limitation period.[1]

A tort is 'based upon fraud' only where fraud is a necessary allegation in order to constitute the cause of action.[2] Presumably, deceit is the only tort based upon fraud in this sense. Deliberate commission of a breach of duty in circumstances in which it is

---

13 Sections 28(1), 28A (inserted by the Latent Damage Act 1986) and 38(1). For an illustration of the operation of these provisions see again *Stubbings v Webb* [1993] AC 498, [1993] 1 All ER 322, HL. And see *Tolley v Morris* [1979] 2 All ER 561, [1979] 1 WLR 592, HL.
14 Section 28(2). But in personal injury actions, the court may take account of this factor in deciding to exercise its s 33 discretion to extend the limitation period.
15 Section 28(3).
16 Section 28(1).
17 [1995] 6 Med LR 1, CA.
18 In *Eddis v Chichester Constable* [1969] 2 Ch 345, [1969] 2 All ER 912, CA, these words included the tenant for life where the plaintiffs were the trustees and owners of an heirloom fraudulently sold by the tenant for life.
19 Section 32(1).
20 *C v Mirror Group Newspapers Ltd* [1996] 4 All ER 511, [1997] 1 WLR 131.
1 *Sheldon v RHM Outhwaite (Underwriting Agencies) Ltd* [1996] AC 102, [1995] 2 All ER 562, HL.
2 *Beaman v ARTS Ltd* [1949] 1 KB 550, [1949] 1 All ER 465, CA (conversion not an action based on fraud).

unlikely to be discovered for some time amounts to deliberate concealment of the facts involved in that breach of duty.[3]

'Fraud' in the Act is to be interpreted very widely;[4] it appears, rather than to bear any technical meaning, to signify simply 'conscious wrongdoing'.[5]

SECTION 7.   DEATH

The Law Reform (Miscellaneous Provisions) Act 1934[6] provides that on the death of any person all causes of action subsisting against or vested in him shall survive against, or as the case may be, for the benefit of, his estate. But this does not apply to causes of action for defamation. If the plaintiff dies, the damages recoverable for the benefit of his estate shall not include exemplary damages.

The right of a person to claim under section 1A of the Fatal Accidents Act 1976 for bereavement[7] does not survive for the benefit of his estate.[8] No damages may be awarded for loss of income in respect of any period after the death of the injured person.[9] If the plaintiff dies after the expiry of the limitation period, the claim does not survive in cases of personal injury. However, it is open to his personal representatives to ask the court, under the discretionary provisions of section 33 of the Limitation Act 1980,[10] to waive the limitation period.

If the plaintiff died before the limitation period expired, a new limitation period begins to run under the Limitation Act 1980.[11] This new period is three years from either the date of death, or from the date of the personal representative's knowledge, whichever is the later.

---

3   Section 32(2). And see *Beaman v ARTS* (supra).
4   *Kitchen v Royal Air Force Association* [1958] 2 All ER 241, CA.
5   *Beaman v ARTS* (supra) at 572 (per Singleton LJ).
6   Section 1(1).
7   See ante.
8   Section 1(2)(a) of the 1934 Act.
9   Ibid.
10   Section 33(4), (5). And see ante.
11   Section 11(5).

Chapter 29

Parties

SECTION 1. THE CROWN

(A) VICARIOUS LIABILITY

By section 2(1) of the Crown Proceedings Act 1947:

> ... the Crown shall be subject to all those liabilities in tort to which, if it were a private person of full age and capacity, it would be subject in respect of torts committed by its servants or agents.

For the Crown to be vicariously liable, an employee must be directly or indirectly appointed by the Crown and paid wholly out of the Consolidated Fund or other specified national funds.[1] The Crown is not, therefore, vicariously liable for the torts of police officers,[2] or for the torts of borrowed servants.

The Act does not apply to the employees of those bodies which are not deemed to be agents of the Crown – in such cases the ordinary law affecting public bodies and public officers will apply. Many public bodies are therefore outside the Act. The former nationalised industries, for example, fell outside the ambit of the Act.[3] In order to determine this question, which is often thorny, the nature of the functions of the body in question and the extent to which it is under ministerial control, are especially relevant.[4]

(B) NON-VICARIOUS LIABILITY

Section 2(1)(b) and (c) make the Crown liable for any breach of those duties owed at common law to employees, agents or independent contractors by an employer, and for

---

1 Section 2(6); unless the tort complained of is infringement of copyright or any other tort within s 3 of the Act, or detinue or any other tort affecting property, for which a petition of right formerly lay (s 1).
2 For the liability of the chief constable to pay damages out of public funds to those harmed by a policeman's torts, see the Police Act 1964, s 48.
3 *Tamlin v Hannaford* [1950] 1 KB 18, [1949] 2 All ER 327, CA.
4 *Bank voor Handel en Scheepvaart NV v Administrator of Hungarian Property* [1954] AC 584, [1954] 1 All ER 969, HL.

any breach of the duties attaching at common law to the ownership, occupation, possession or control of property.

Section 2(1) does not seem sufficiently wide to take account of all the cases where an employer is liable otherwise than vicariously: it has been shown that employers are frequently answerable for acts of independent contractors, not because the independent contractor has committed a tort in the course of his work, but because a duty is imposed on the employer. Section 2 may not be wide enough to cover non-delegable duties of this sort.[5] The Crown is liable in tort to the same extent as private persons for breaches of statutory duty which have been imposed on it, provided that the duty is also imposed on persons other than the Crown and its officers.[6] If the duty is imposed, not on the Crown, but directly on its employees, and an employee commits a tort while performing or purporting to perform those statutory functions established by the Act, 'the liabilities of the Crown in respect of the tort shall be such as they would have been if those functions had been conferred or imposed solely by virtue of instructions lawfully given by the Crown'.[7] The Crown also has the same liability as other employers under the Employer's Liability (Defective Equipment) Act 1969.[8]

(C) EXCEPTIONS

(1) JUDICIAL ERRORS

Section 2(5) provides that the Crown shall not be liable 'in respect of anything done or omitted to be done by any person while discharging or purporting to discharge any responsibilities of a judicial nature vested in him, or any responsibilities which he has in connection with the execution of the judicial process'.

The first part of the subsection would be otiose if it merely provided that the Crown shall not be liable wherever the judge has the defence of 'judicial act'. It seems, therefore, that whatever doubts there may be about the liability of inferior courts for acts done in excess of jurisdiction which purport to be in discharge of the judicial function, the Crown is exempted from liability.[9] Presumably the first part of the subsection extends not only to that limited class of bodies not being courts, stricto sensu, to which the defence of 'judicial acts' applies, but also to other administrative tribunals.[10]

(2) ARMED FORCES

The Crown Proceedings (Armed Forces) Act 1987 repealed section 10 of the 1947 Act which prevented members of the armed forces suing the Crown in respect of injuries suffered in the course of their duties, caused by another member of the armed forces

---

5 See ante. Yet in *Egerton v Home Office* [1978] Crim LR 494 the court held that a duty was owed to a sexual offender in prison to keep a protective watch to guard against his being attacked by fellow prisoners.
6 Section 2(2). Section 6 of the Occupiers' Liability Act 1957 provides that that Act shall bind the Crown and that the common duty of care imposed by it shall apply as a statutory duty for the purpose of the Crown Proceedings Act 1947.
7 Section 2(3). Presumably, this rule also applies where the duty in question is not also imposed on persons other than employees of the Crown.
8 See ante.
9 *Welsh v Chief Constable of Merseyside Police* [1993] 1 All ER 692.
10 Is the Crown vicariously liable for a malicious prosecution by the Director of Public Prosecutions?

who was on duty. The Act applies only to causes of action arising after its passing,[11] but the 1987 Act did make provision for the Secretary of State to revive section 10 for 'the purpose of any warlike operations in any part of the world outside the United Kingdom'.

Beyond the statute, it was also established in *Mulcahy v Ministry of Defence*[12] that no (alternative) common law liability exists. There, the Court of Appeal held that a serviceman did not owe his fellow servicemen a duty of care in warlike conditions for it would not be fair, just and reasonable to impose such a duty.

(3)   CERTAIN STATUTES IMPOSING LIABILITY IN TORT

It is doubtful whether the Crown is bound by statutes imposing tortious liabilities unless the particular statute has clearly made the Crown liable. Most modern Acts making substantial changes in the law of torts have been made expressly applicable to the Crown: for example, the Law Reform (Contributory Negligence) Act 1945, the Congenital Disabilities (Civil Liberties) Act 1976, the Civil Liability (Contribution) Act 1978 and the Limitation Act 1980.[13] Statutes about which the doubt persists include the Defamation Acts of 1952 and 1996.

SECTION 2.   FOREIGN STATES

Foreign states cannot be sued in tort in the English courts except as provided in the State Immunity Act 1978.[14] Under that Act, the foreign state is no longer immune for (1) an act or omission in the UK,[15] causing death or personal injury or damage to or loss of property,[16] (2) obligations arising out of the ownership, possession or use of property[17] and (3) actions for purely financial loss arising from a commercial transaction.[18] In this last instance, however, according to *Playa Larga v I Congreso del Partido*,[19] an ostensibly commercial transaction that is, in truth, undertaken by a state acting in its governmental capacity is afforded immunity.

SECTION 3.   AMBASSADORS

The relevant law is contained in the Diplomatic Privileges Act 1964.[20] Ambassadors and their staffs and families are exempt from the jurisdiction of English courts so long

---

11 See Boyd [1989] PL 237. And note that the effect of s 10 had already been narrowed somewhat by judicial interpretation of that section: *Bell v Secretary of State for Defence* [1986] QB 322, [1985] 3 All ER 661; *Pearce v Secretary of State for Defence* [1988] AC 755, [1988] 2 All ER 348, HL.
12 [1996] QB 732, [1996] 2 All ER 758, CA.
13 Because the sea collision regulations did not bind the Crown, it was held not liable for negligence based on such a breach in *Thomas Stone (Shipping) Ltd v Admiralty, The Albion* [1952] 1 Lloyd's Rep 104 – an important Crown immunity.
14 Section 1.
15 For application, see *Al-Adsani v Kuwait* [1994] PIQR P 236, CA where the alleged acts of torture took place in Kuwait.
16 Section 5.
17 Section 6.
18 Section 3.
19 [1983] 1 AC 244, [1981] 2 All ER 1064, HL.
20 See Sch 1 thereto.

as they continue to exercise their diplomatic functions.[1] They are not immune from legal liability: they may waive their procedural privilege and submit to the jurisdiction. Further, once their diplomatic immunity has ended, actions may be brought against them in respect of causes of action which accrued during their employment.[2] Members of the administrative, technical and service staffs have no immunity for torts committed outside the course of their duties.

SECTION 4.   POSTAL AUTHORITIES

By the Post Office Act 1969, the Post Office is now a public authority which is not an agent of the Crown.[3] It is liable, subject to the financial limits and conditions prescribed by Post Office Regulations, for loss of, or damage to, inland registered postal packets.[4] Subject to that, neither the Post Office nor any of its employees, officers or sub-postmasters is liable for anything done or omitted to be done in relation to anything in the post[5] or for any omission to collect post.[6] Nobody engaged in the carriage of mail, or their employees, agents or sub-contractors is liable for loss or damage in relation to the post.[7] This means, technically, that there is immunity in relation to a postman who throws away cards sent at Christmas simply because he thinks his sack is too heavy.

SECTION 5.   HIGHWAY AUTHORITIES

Persons who suffer injuries caused by the defective state of a highway may have causes of action against highway authorities in negligence, in public nuisance, or for breach of statutory duty. Indeed, they will often have a choice of action.[8]

The liability of all highway authorities (including the Crown) for all these torts is regulated by the Highways Act 1980. The Act applies regardless of whether the plaintiff is suing in public nuisance, negligence or for breach of statutory duty. Section 58(1) provides that:

1   The immunity extends to such a reasonable period after an ambassador has presented his letters of recall as is necessary to enable him to wind up his official business and prepare for his return to his own country: *Musurus Bey v Gadban* [1894] 2 QB 352, CA.
2   Nor does the period of limitation begin to run until the privilege expires: *Musurus Bey v Gadban* [1894] 2 QB 352, CA.
3   Section 6(1) and (5).
4   Section 30. For an interpretation of the extent of liability see *Building and Civil Engineering Holidays Scheme Management Ltd v Post Office* [1966] 1 QB 247, [1965] 1 All ER 163, CA (construing s 9 of the Crown Proceedings Act 1947 – now repealed by, but substantially re-enacted in, the Post Office Act 1969).
5   The addressee of a letter, on the envelope of which the Post Office stamped 'Remember that Road Accidents are caused by People Like You', could not recover damage in libel when the Postmaster-General pleaded s 9 of the Crown Proceedings Act (which was similar to s 29 of the 1969 Act): *Boakes v Postmaster-General* (1962) Times, 27 October, CA.
6   Section 29(1) and (2). In *Harold Stephen & Co Ltd v Post Office* [1978] 1 All ER 939, CA, the court left open whether the Post Office was liable for failing to sort mail during a strike. In *American Express Co v British Airways Board* [1983] 1 All ER 557, [1983] 1 WLR 701, it was held that this section exempted the Post Office and its sub-contractors from liability for breach of bailment and for breach of Article 18 of the Warsaw Convention relating to liability for international carriage.
7   Section 29(3). Similar immunities afforded to British Telecom while in public ownership have now been repealed. Presumably if proposals to privatise the Post Office go through, its immunities will also be revoked.
8   *Simon v Islington Borough Council* [1943] KB 188, [1943] 1 All ER 41, CA.

in an action against a highway authority in respect of damage resulting from their failure to maintain a highway maintainable at the public expense, it is a defence (without prejudice to any other defence or the application of the law relating to contributory negligence) to prove that the authority had taken such care as in all the circumstances was reasonably required to secure that the part of the highway to which the action relates was not dangerous for traffic.

Following the pattern of the Occupiers' Liability Act 1957, the section proceeds to define some of the criteria which will be relevant in deciding whether the highway authority has discharged its burden of proving that it took reasonable care. These criteria, set out in section 58(2), are:

(a) the character of the highway, and the traffic which was reasonably to be expected to use it;

(b) the standard of maintenance appropriate for a highway of that character and used by such traffic;

(c) the state of repair in which a reasonable person would have expected to find the highway;

(d) whether the highway authority knew, or could reasonably have been expected to know, that the condition of the part of the highway to which the action relates was likely to cause danger to users of the highway;

(e) where the highway authority could not reasonably have been expected to repair that part of the highway before the cause of action arose, what warning notices of its condition had been displayed.

The Act has received judicial interpretation in a series of cases. The plaintiff must prove that the highway is dangerous; a trifling defect such as one flagstone being an inch higher than the next will not avail the pedestrian who trips.[9] The plaintiff must further prove that the danger was caused by failure to maintain: an occasional flooding or an icy patch in winter is not evidence of failure to maintain.[10] But failure to drain a trunk road that was flooded in consequence rendered the Department of Environment liable.[11] Once the plaintiff has established these points, the onus is on the defendant to prove that he did what was reasonably required.[12]

The section also provides that:

it is not relevant to prove that the highway authority had arranged for a competent person to carry out or supervise the maintenance of the part of the highway to which the action relates unless it is also proved that the authority had given him proper instructions with regard to the maintenance of the highway and that he had carried out the instructions.

Presumably the object is to make the highway authority liable whenever an independent contractor has negligently failed to maintain the highway. And despite some ambiguity in the language, the courts may be expected to construe it in that way. The intention of

---

9   *Meggs v Liverpool Corpn* [1968] 1 All ER 1137, CA; *Burnside v Emerson* [1968] 3 All ER 741, CA. A hole 12' x 6' x 3' deep was held dangerous in *Bird v Tower Hamlets London Borough Council* (1969) 67 LGR 682.

10 *Burnside v Emerson* (supra) at 743 (per Lord Denning MR).

11 *Tarrant v Rowlands* [1979] RTR 144. In *Bird v Pearce and Somerset County Council* (1979) 77 LGR 753, CA a local authority was held liable for a collision after it had obliterated white lines at a junction while resurfacing.

12 *Pridham v Hemel Hempstead Corpn* (1970) 69 LGR 523, CA (proof that it inspected the footpath of a minor residential road every three months and kept a complaints book excluded it from liability). And see *Griffiths v Liverpool Corpn* [1967] 1 QB 374, [1966] 2 All ER 1015, CA. The duty to maintain a highway imposed by s 41 of the Highways Act 1980 includes a duty to remove snow and ice from footpaths, but a plaintiff who slipped on an icy footpath would have to prove that the authority had failed to take reasonable remedial measures in the circumstances: *Haydon v Kent County Council* [1978] QB 343, [1978] 2 All ER 97, CA.

the Act is to safeguard users of the highway from personal injury. Economic loss occasioned to traders and others by disrepair of nearby roads is not recoverable in an action for breach of this statutory duty.[13]

SECTION 6.　CORPORATIONS

(A)　LIABILITY

Where the liability of an employer for the acts of his employees is in issue, there are normally four possible situations.

1　The act may be treated as the act of the employer himself so that no issue of vicarious liability arises.
2　The employer has authorised the employee to commit the tort.
3　The employee has committed the tort in the course of his employment.
4　The employee has committed the tort while acting outside the scope of his employment.[14]

The same four possibilities presumably apply where the employer is a corporation. In the House of Lords case of *Lennard's Carrying Co Ltd v Asiatic Petroleum Co Ltd*,[15] dealing with the defendant's plea that the 'fault' of a corporation was co-extensive with that of its employees, Viscount Haldane said of a corporation that:[16]

> [it] has no mind of its own any more than it has a body of its own; its active and directing will must consequently be sought in the person of somebody who for some purposes may be called an agent, but who is really the directing mind and will of the corporation ... That person may be under the direction of the shareholders in general meeting; that person may be the board of directors itself...

In order, then, to be the act of the company in this sense, the act must be of 'somebody who is not merely a servant or agent for whom the company is liable on the footing *respondeat superior*, but somebody for whom the company is liable because his action is the very action of the company itself'.[17] If somebody of such authority in the company acts tortiously on behalf of the company the company is liable, not by way of vicarious liability, but because the tortious act is that of the company itself.[18]

Poulton v London and South Western Rly Co[19] provides a clear example of the fourth case, an act outside the scope of employment.

> A stationmaster arrested the plaintiff for non-payment of the freight in respect of his horse. Because the defendant railway company, his employers, were empowered by statute to arrest passengers for non-payment of fares but for no other reasons, the court held that the

13　*Wentworth v Wiltshire County Council* [1993] 2 All ER 256, CA.
14　This is the only one of the four cases where the employer is not liable.
15　[1915] AC 705, HL.
16　[1915] AC 705 at 713, HL.
17　[1915] AC 705, HL. In *The Lady Gwendolen* [1965] P 294, [1965] 2 All ER 283, CA, the Guinness company were liable for their managerial failure to detect and stop the habitual practice of their ship's captain in going full steam ahead in fog through reliance on the fact that his ship was fitted with radar.
18　The director may himself be liable as bailee when goods are stored with his company and he assumes personal responsibility for their storage: *Fairline Shipping Corpn v Adamson* [1975] QB 180, [1974] 2 All ER 967. On other circumstances in which a company director may be personally liable for a company employee's tort see *C Evans & Sons Ltd v Spritebrand Ltd* [1985] 2 All ER 415, [1985] 1 WLR 317, CA.
19　(1867) LR 2 QB 534.

stationmaster was acting outside the scope of his employment, and that the defendants were therefore not liable.

Thus, in deciding what an employee is or is not impliedly authorised to do, one may be assisted by considering what his employers may lawfully do.

The law reports abound with the commonplace event of a limited company being held vicariously liable for torts committed by its employees in the course of their employment, especially claims arising out of road accidents and claims by its workmen in respect of the negligence of their fellow workmen.

Campbell v Paddington Corpn is a case in the second class: a corporation was held liable for the tortious act of its employees on the basis that it had authorised the commission of the tort.[20]

> In pursuance of a resolution of the council of the defendant corporation, its employees erected a stand on the highway so that members of the public could view a procession. This act was a public nuisance which the corporation, seemingly, had no authority to perform: the fact that the act was ultra vires did not prevent the corporation from being held liable in tort.

Lush J distinguished *Poulton v London and South Western Rly Co* (and, hence, the fourth case) as follows:[1]

> That case was only an illustration of the principle that where the wrongful act is done without the express authority of the corporation, an authority from the corporation to do it cannot be implied if the act is outside the statutory powers of the corporation. That principle has no application to a case where the corporation has resolved to do and has, in the only way in which it can do any act, actually done the thing which is unlawful and which causes the damage complained of.

This case – the only one on the point – seems to support the proposition that a corporation can be liable for a tortious act arising from an activity beyond the powers of the corporation. Though unique on the point, the case is perfectly in kilter with sections 35, 35A and 35B of the Companies Act 1985 which abolished the application of the ultra vires doctrine in connection with those dealings which take place between a company and third parties.

(B)   POWER TO SUE

Corporations can sue for any tort other than those of which, in the nature of things, they could not be victims – for example, assault.

SECTION 7.   TRADE UNIONS AND OTHER UNINCORPORATED BODIES

(A)   TRADE UNIONS

Trade unions are no longer generally immune from liability for their own torts. As far as liability in negligence, nuisance or other non-economic torts is in issue, if the requisite

---

20   [1911] 1 KB 869.
1   [1911] 1 KB 869 at 878.

elements of the tort are proved, the union is liable just as an individual would be.[2] Trade unions are further liable for acts of their members committing one of the various economic torts concerned with interference with economic and business interests other than in contemplation or furtherance of a trade dispute,[3] where the member's act has been authorised by a 'responsible person'[4] within the union. Financial limits related to the union's total membership restrict the amount of damages which may be awarded in such a case.[5] The remaining immunities afforded in respect of the commission of torts of interfering with contracts or business in the course of a trade dispute are made dependent on support for the action being approved in a ballot.[6]

As regards the capacity to sue, section 10 of TULRCA stipulates that trade unions are not to be treated as bodies corporate. Accordingly, it has been held that those unions which are not special register bodies – and few are – cannot sue for defamation.[7]

(B) OTHER UNINCORPORATED BODIES

Here we are concerned with those bodies which apparently exist and carry on their activities as separate units, but which are not incorporated: members' clubs, many students' unions and friendly societies are important examples.[8]

(1) LIABILITY AS DEFENDANTS

(a) Substantive
There are no special rules of the law of torts which determine whether a cause of action subsists against the members of an unincorporated association as such. If, according to ordinary principles, there is vicarious liability for the tort of an employee of the association, if someone has been ordered to commit an act constituting a tort, or if there is a breach of the duties of an employer to an employee, a cause of action will be established.

(b) Procedural
More difficult is the problem of who may be made a defendant when such a cause of action is made out. Four possible solutions must be examined.

1   The body cannot ordinarily be sued in its group name.[9] In a few cases, statutes setting up certain bodies have been interpreted as imposing on them a liability to be sued in their collective names – friendly societies are an example.[10]

2   There is no legal obstacle to joining all the members of the association as defendants in proceedings, but the practical inconveniences of doing this in the case of a large club with a possibly fluctuating membership are obvious.

---

2   Section 20 of the Trade Union and Labour Relations (Consolidation) Act 1992 (TULRCA).
3   On the narrow definition of trade dispute see s 244 of TULRCA.
4   Widely defined: see TULRCA, s 20.
5   TULRCA, s 23.
6   TULRCA, s 226.
7   *Electrical, Electronic Telecommunication and Plumbing Union v Times Newspapers Ltd* [1980] QB 585, [1980] 1 All ER 1097.
8   But note that friendly societies may be registered as incorporated friendly societies under the Friendly Societies Act 1992, s 93.
9   *London Association for Protection of Trade v Greenlands Ltd* [1916] 2 AC 15, HL.
10   Friendly Societies Act 1992; *London-Griffiths v Smith* [1950] 2 All ER 662, a fuller report on this point than [1951] 1 KB 295.

3   RSC Ord 15, r 12 does, however, provide that where numerous persons have the same interest in any proceedings, the proceedings may be begun[11] and continued by or against any one or more of them as representing all of them. It will often be impossible to make use of this rule in tort proceedings because not all the defendants will have the same common interest. Thus, in *Mercantile Marine Service Association v Toms* the facts were as follows.[12]

> The plaintiffs wished to make three officers of a guild for the protection of seamen representative defendants in a libel action. The Court of Appeal refused to allow this on the ground that not all the general body of members had the same interest in resisting the proceedings.

Obviously, the requirement that all the persons represented should have the same interest was not met, because not all members of the guild could have published, or authorised the publication of, the libel. Furthermore, there are, no doubt, many circumstances where a representative action may be held inappropriate because different defences are available to the various defendants represented.

4   Actions may sometimes be brought against officers of clubs. There is no procedural problem here, but it must be stressed that such actions will fail unless, according to the ordinary substantive principles of the law of torts, those officials can be shown to have committed a tort. So in *Robertson v Ridley*[13] it was held that members of the club committee were not liable to a member for injuries resulting from the unsafe condition of club premises simply because they were committee members. Nothing in the rules of the club expressly imposed such liability on them.[14] On the other hand, in *Owen v Northampton Borough Council*[15] it was held that once a committee member, or indeed any ordinary member of the club, carrying out a task for the common good – in this case, hiring a room at a sports centre – becomes aware of a risk of injury to others, he owes a duty of care to his fellow members.

(2)   CAPACITY AS PLAINTIFFS

The body cannot ordinarily sue in its own name, except, as in the case of friendly societies and trade unions, where an intention to permit this can be spelt out in a statute.

It will be recalled that RSC Ord 15, r 12 provides for representation orders being made for plaintiffs in the same circumstances as those laid down for defendants. This raises the question of the extent to which the English courts are prepared to follow practice in the US and allow class actions by representatives of very large numbers alleging the infringement of similar rights. *Prudential Assurance Co Ltd v Newman Industries Ltd*[16] shows that English courts are keeping such actions on a fairly tight rein. A representative action may be brought by a plaintiff suing on behalf of himself and all other members of a class, where each member has a separate cause of action in tort, provided that (i) the relief claimed could not have the effect of conferring a cause of action on a member who would not have had a separate cause of action, (ii) all the members shared the same interest, and (iii) the action benefited the class. The normal

11   *Prudential Assurance Co Ltd v Newman Industries Ltd* [1981] Ch 229, [1979] 3 All ER 507.
12   [1916] 2 KB 243, CA.
13   [1989] 2 All ER 474, [1989] 1 WLR 872, CA.
14   The authority to look to club rules for these purposes derives from the decision in *Prole v Allen* reported at (1950) 209 LT 183. It has been endorsed, more recently, in *Grice v Stourport Tennis, Hockey and Squash Club* [1997] CLY 3859, CA. Relying on the decision in *Grice*, Hooper J has since questioned the correctness (but not the ratio) of the decision in *Robertson* in *Melhuish v Clifford* (18 August 1998, unreported, QBD).
15   (1992) 156 LG Rev 23, CA.
16   [1981] Ch 229, [1979] 3 All ER 507.

relief is a declaration, and sometimes an injunction (which is obviously useful where there are numerous small claims of a similar kind). Damages would also appear to be available: although the court in the *Prudential* case went on to say that damages could not be awarded in representative tort actions,[17] it has since transpired that this statement goes to far. In *EMI Records Ltd v Riley*,[18] the court directed an inquiry into damages in a representative action for infringement of copyright, as well as granting an injunction. It was held that where the damage is to a property interest, in which the members of the body have a common interest, it is open to a court to award damages in a representative action.

SECTION 8.   PARTNERS

Partners may be jointly and severally liable to any persons not themselves partners[19] for torts committed by any one of them either while acting in the ordinary course of the business of the firm, or with the authority of co-partners.[20] In order to be so liable, the plaintiff must establish that he relied upon the individual partner's status *as a partner*.[1] In addition to this vicarious liability statutorily imposed on partners, each partner may have a primary duty in tort; for example the occupier's duty of care to visitors is owed by each partner in a firm which occupies premises.[2]

SECTION 9.   HUSBAND AND WIFE

The liability of one partner in a marriage for the torts of the other is to be decided on the same principles as those applying where the parties are not married. There is no presumption that one is responsible for the other.[3]

Section 1(1) of the Law Reform (Husband and Wife) Act 1962 provides that 'each of the parties to a marriage shall have the like right of action in tort against the other as if they were not married'. In most cases where spouses wish to sue each other, the spouse is a nominal defendant, and the real defendant is an insurance company. The most important consequence of the Act is that where one spouse is injured in a car accident through the tortious driving of the other spouse, the victim can collect from the other's motor vehicle insurers. If another negligent driver is involved, his insurers will be able to claim a contribution from the spouse's insurers on the basis of the principles to be discussed later in this chapter. Notwithstanding section 1(1), Parliament was also anxious to discourage actions founded on petty grievances between spouses. Section 1(2), therefore, allows the court to stay the action 'if it appears … that no substantial benefit would accrue to either party from the continuation of the proceedings'.[4] The

---

17 See also obiter dicta in *Markt & Co Ltd v Knight Steamship Co Ltd* [1910] 2 KB 1021.

18 [1981] 2 All ER 838, [1981] 1 WLR 923.

19 *Mair v Wood* 1948 SC 83 (M, one of five partners of a trawler, injured through negligence of another partner. Held that neither under the Partnership Act nor under any common law rule unaffected by the Act could the other three partners be vicariously liable for the negligence of one partner to a fellow partner).

20 Partnership Act 1890, ss 10 and 12; *Hamlyn v John Houston & Co* [1903] 1 KB 81, CA.

1   *Nationwide Building Society v Lewis* [1998] Ch 482, [1998] 3 All ER 143.

2   See *Meekins v Henson* [1964] 1 QB 472, [1962] 1 All ER 899.

3   Section 3 of the Law Reform (Married Women and Joint Tortfeasors) Act 1935. Husband and wife can be jointly liable in conspiracy: *Midland Bank Trust Co Ltd v Green (No 3)* [1982] Ch 529, [1981] 3 All ER 744, CA.

4   Note, too, the provision in s 1(2)(b) to allow property disputes to be dealt with under s 17 of the Married Women's Property Act 1882.

expression 'substantial benefit' may give the courts some trouble. For example, when deciding whether to exercise its discretionary power to stay, the court may have to balance its estimate of how much cash the plaintiff spouse is likely to collect in the form of damages against the chance of unhappiness or even disruption of the marriage resulting from the litigation. It may also inquire whether any damages awarded will be paid by the spouse's insurers. Furthermore, just what constitutes a trivial grievance? Should we, for instance, tolerate at the turn of the millennium any notion of a 'trivial battery' against a wife?

SECTION 10.   MENTALLY DISORDERED PERSONS

The problems here arise mainly from the incomplete analyses often made by the judges of the states of mind required in particular torts. The case most directly in point is *Morriss v Marsden*.[5]

> The defendant violently attacked the plaintiff, a complete stranger, while he was standing in the entrance hall of a hotel, and was sued for battery. The defence raised was insanity. The judge found that the defendant was not in a condition of automatism or trance at the time of the attack on the plaintiff, but that his mind directed the blows which he struck; he also found that at the material time, he was a certifiable lunatic who knew the nature and quality of his act but, because of his lunacy, did not know that what he was doing was wrong. He nevertheless held that the defence of insanity not to be applicable.

This case is therefore authority for the proposition that if a mentally disordered person has that state of mind which is required for liability in battery, then his insanity is no defence – all that is required in battery is that the defendant must intend to strike the blow at the plaintiff. The judge found that he did so intend, and it therefore followed that he was liable. At a more general level, the case decides that, in tort (as distinct from criminal law), a defendant who intentionally invades the plaintiff's protected interest will not be excused simply because he was unaware that the invasion was a wrongful act.

These rules are definite. In every case one has to ask: what state of mind did the particular tort require? Did the defendant have that state of mind? It follows that in all torts – including those of 'strict' liability – if the defendant's conduct is, because of his mental disorder, involuntary and purely automatic, he has a valid defence. Thus, in *Morriss v Marsden* Stable J said:[6]

> ... if a person in a condition of complete automatism inflicted grievous injury, that would not be actionable. In the same way, if a sleepwalker inadvertently, without intention or without carelessness, broke a valuable vase, that would not be actionable.

In short, one is never liable in torts requiring deliberate acts for one's involuntary conduct: if the defendant is so mentally disordered that his conduct is involuntary, then he has a sound defence. Furthermore, if the tort requires an improper purpose or malice, his insanity – although it does not render his act unintentional – nevertheless prevents him from consciously forming the requisite improper purpose. Accordingly, the insanity will afford him a defence.[7]

5   [1952] 1 All ER 925.
6   [1952] 1 All ER 925 at 927.
7   Obiter dicta in some old cases such as *Weaver v Ward* (1616) Hob 134, which might suggest that insanity is no defence in trespass, are easily explained: they were voiced at a time when the courts regarded trespass as a tort of strict liability, and merely inferred, therefore, that want of

If the defendant's insanity causes him to be under a delusion about the surrounding circumstances, then it seems that this will not afford him a defence provided that he did have that state of mind which the tort requires.[8]

SECTION II. MINORS

(A) LIABILITY

A person is a minor until he attains the age of 18 years.[9] Minority as such is not a defence:[10] but like all other defendants, a minor is not liable for a specific tort if it is shown that he lacked the required state of mind. Should a one-year-old child pick up a letter defamatory of X, written by his father, and throw it through the window, whereupon Y picks it up and reads it, X will have no cause of action for libel against the baby. On the other hand, a 15-year-old youth who pushed a man into a swimming pool, was held liable in negligence and trespass.[11]

(1) WHERE THE ACT OF THE MINOR IS ALSO A BREACH OF CONTRACT

With certain exceptions a minor is not liable for breach of contract.[12] Therefore, where the act of the minor is merely an improper performance of one of the acts contemplated by such a contract, it will not be open to the person aggrieved to sue him in tort so as to evade the contractual immunity. On the other hand, if the act complained of, though performed upon the occasion of a contract, is independent of it, the plaintiff may then sue in tort. Of course, this rule will be very difficult to apply in marginal cases, but its judicial recognition is beyond doubt. Thus, a minor who had possession of goods under a hire-purchase agreement, and who wrongfully disposed of them to a third party was liable to the true owner for the independent tort of detinue which he committed by wrongfully disposing of them.[13] The hirer of a mare, hired for riding only, is liable in tort for doing an act of a nature not contemplated by the contract (namely jumping the mare); but if he were merely to ride her too far, this would not be an act of a different nature and no action in tort would lie.[14] The fact that the contract was, in both cases, void against the minor did not prevent him from being liable in tort.

In this context, the question of suing a minor in tort arises most often where he has obtained goods or a loan of money under contract by misrepresenting his real age. The

---

intention through insanity would be no defence. Given the premise, the conclusion is sound, but now that trespass is held not to be a tort of strict liability (see ch 2 ante), they are irrelevant. And see Denning LJ (obiter) in *White v White* [1950] P 39 at 48, [1949] 2 All ER 339, CA, who would support the dicta in *Weaver v Ward*.

8   In *Buckley and Toronto Transportation Commission v Smith Transport Ltd* [1946] 4 DLR 721 (Ontario CA), the defendant driver had the delusion that his truck was under remote control from head office. This was a defence to negligence based on a road accident caused by his truck – not on the ground that delusion as such is a defence, but because by reason of the delusion 'he did not understand the duty which rested upon him to take care'.

9   Section 1(1) of the Family Law Reform Act 1969.

10   See the discussion with regard to negligence, ante.

11   *Williams v Humphrey* (1975) Times, 20 February; cf *Wilson v Pringle* [1987] QB 237, [1986] 2 All ER 440 (13-year-old schoolboy pulling bag off another).

12   See now Minors' Contracts Act 1987.

13   *Ballett v Mingay* [1943] KB 281, [1943] 1 All ER 143, CA.

14   *Burnard v Haggis* (1863) 14 CBNS 45; *Jennings v Rundall* (1799) 8 Term Rep 335. See also *Walley v Holt* (1876) 35 LT 631 and *Fawcett v Smethurst* (1914) 84 LJKB 473.

courts have decided that no action in deceit then lies, because that would be tantamount to allowing the enforcement of a void contract.[15]

(2) LIABILITY OF THE PARENT

Although a plaintiff may have no cause of action against the minor, he may sometimes be able to recover from its parent. The parent is liable only where he is accountable according to some other general principle of torts. He may be vicariously liable – for example if the minor is acting as her father's chauffeur and drives the car negligently. Similarly, the father will be liable if he instigates the son's commission of a tort, and he will be liable if he himself has been personally negligent.[16] Accordingly, a father is not liable merely because his son has thrown a stone through his neighbour's window. Unless the father ordered him to do so, or unless his negligent supervision is proved to have caused the act complained of, he will not be liable.

(B) CAPACITY TO SUE

Except that he must normally sue by his next friend, a minor is in the same position as any other plaintiff when suing in tort. A child may sue either parent, and may wish to do so where the parent has an insurance policy (usually a comprehensive household insurance) which covers the particular liability – for example if a loose tile from the family home is carelessly allowed to fall on the child while it is playing in the garden.[17] The Court of Appeal has warned against the danger of too readily imposing liability for the 'rough and tumble of family life'.[18] Their admonition may be in part motivated by a spate of litigation by children formerly in care against foster parents and local authorities. Do we risk diminishing children's rights? One other case that clearly does have that effect is *Stubbings v Webb*.[19] By imposing an absolute six year-limitation period for actions in trespass to the person, victims of child abuse are effectively denied a remedy for their suffering. The capacity of children to sue for injuries sustained before birth has been considered earlier.[20]

SECTION 12. BANKRUPTS

(A) LIABILITY

In respect of the liability arising from torts committed before bankruptcy, section 382 of the Insolvency Act 1986 provides that such liability is a bankruptcy debt and provable against the trustee in bankruptcy. In respect of torts subsequently committed, the bankrupt remains personally liable but may not, of course, be worth suing.

---

15 *R Leslie Ltd v Sheill* [1914] 3 KB 607 at 612, CA (per Lord Sumner MR).
16 *Donaldson v McNiven* [1952] 2 All ER 691, CA; *Newton v Edgerley* [1959] 3 All ER 337. The duty of school authorities is also to take the care which a reasonable parent would take: see, eg, *Ricketts v Erith Borough Council* [1943] 2 All ER 629 and *Rich v LCC* [1953] 2 All ER 376, [1953] 1 WLR 895, CA.
17 In *Ash v Lady Ash* (1696) Comb 357, a daughter sued her mother in false imprisonment and battery and succeeded, subject to a new trial, to fix damages. In a Scottish case, *Young v Rankin* 1934 SC 499, it was held that a child, who was injured by the negligent driving of his father, could sue his father.
18 *Surtees v Kingston-upon-Thames Borough Council* [1991] 2 FLR 559, CA.
19 [1993] AC 498, [1993] 1 All ER 322, HL.
20 See ch 12, ante.

(B)   CAPACITY TO SUE

Where the tort protects only a purely personal interest – for example, assault or slander[1] – the bankrupt retains the right to sue, and the claim does not pass to the trustee for the benefit of creditors. Where, however, the purpose of the tort is to preserve property – for example, the action for recovery of land – or where the damage is in the form of purely economic loss,[2] the cause of action passes to the trustee and any suit by the bankrupt personally may be met by the valid defence that the plaintiff is a bankrupt.

If there are two separate causes of action, one of which is personal – for example, in respect of loss of reputation – and the other of which is a tort to property – such as in respect of damage to business interests – the personal right remains with the bankrupt and the proprietary one vests in the trustee.[3] A split of this kind, between trustee and bankrupt, may only be made where there is more than one cause of action. If there is only a single cause of action where the main head of loss is related to a proprietary interest while the remaining head of loss is of a personal character, the cause of action passes to the trustee. Consider *Hodgson v Sidney* as an illustration.[4]

> The plaintiff claimed damages for both pecuniary loss and loss of reputation in consequence of the deceit of the defendant. The plaintiff had become bankrupt and the court held that the defendant had a valid defence to the suit by the bankrupt in respect of both heads of damage, because the main element of the tort was pecuniary loss, and the personal claim was merely a separate head of damage, not a separate cause of action remaining available to the bankrupt plaintiff.

The courts have made some surprising decisions in respect of actions for trespass to land. They have allowed a bankrupt to sue in trespass where he has maintained that the major part of the damage was not to his property but in connection with his personal enjoyment of the property.[5] The principle on which all these decisions have been based is summarised in the following dictum.[6]

> those rights of action are given in respect of the immediate and present violation of the possession of the bankrupt, independently of his rights of property, and are an extension of the protection given to his person, and the primary personal injury to the bankrupt is the principal and essential cause of action.

We submit that while the principle may be correct in relation to other torts, it is inappropriate to apply it in relation to trespass. Trespass is actionable per se[7] and personal injury is not essential in such an action. Accordingly the cause of action for trespass to land should be seen as principally (if not entirely) a proprietary one which ought to pass to the trustee.

---

1   *Re Wilson, ex p Vine* (1878) 8 Ch D 364, CA.
2   In *Ramsey v Hartley* [1977] 2 All ER 673, CA it was held that a cause of action for negligent misstatement passed to the trustee. See also *Weddell v JA Pearce & Major* [1988] Ch 26, [1987] 3 All ER 634.
3   *Wilson v United Counties Bank Ltd* [1920] AC 102 at 131, HL (per Lord Atkinson); cf *Re Kavanagh* (1950) 66 (Pt 1) TLR 65, CA (the fuller report).
4   (1866) LR 1 Exch 313, followed in *Wenlock v Moloney* (1967) 111 Sol Jo 437, CA: the bankrupt's conspiracy action was mainly for business and property damage, so that not even the consequential claim for injured feelings and loss of reputation could be pursued by him.
5   *Brewer v Dew* (1843) 11 M & W 625; *Rogers v Spence* (1844) 13 M & W 571; *Rose v Buckett* [1901] 2 KB 449, CA.
6   Per Cresswell J in *Beckham v Drake* (1849) 2 HL Cas 579 at 612.
7   *Bush v Smith* (1953) 162 Estates Gazette 430, CA.

SECTION 13.   ASSIGNEES

It is settled that a right to sue in tort is not in general assignable[8] because the law has an interest in preventing rights of action in tort from being a marketable commodity.[9] There are, however, several glosses on this rule.

1   There is an obiter dictum from the Court of Appeal that 'an assignment of a mere right of litigation is bad ... but an assignment of property is valid, even although that property may be incapable of being recovered without litigation'.[10] This rule, if substantiated,[11] would be a sensible acknowledgement of the fact that the function of the torts of action for the recovery of land and of wrongful interference with goods is often to settle title to property.[12]

2   A trustee in bankruptcy can assign any cause of action in tort vested in him to a third party or even to the bankrupt.[13]

3   The damages to be recovered in an action in tort, as distinct from the cause of action itself, can be assigned; that is, the plaintiff may transfer to another the right to any damages recovered in a pending action, but of course must continue to bring the action in his own name.[14]

4   Where a plaintiff's insurers have paid a claim made by him in respect of circumstances which afford him a cause of action in tort against another, and, in consideration of the settlement of that claim on the insurance policy, have taken an assignment of the right to sue in tort, the insurers may maintain that suit.[15] This wise concession to commercial convenience applies even if subsequent investigation shows that the insured did not have in fact a valid claim on his policy, provided that the settlement by the insurers of his claim was a bona fide transaction.[16]

SECTION 14.   CONVICTED PERSONS

Those convicted of crimes, whether or not they be in prison, have virtually the same tortious rights and liabilities as others.[17] The only difference is that in disciplining prisoners and segregating them in a way that would ordinarily constitute a battery, the prison authorities are exempt from liability.[18]

8   Eg, per Farwell LJ in *Defries v Milne* [1913] 1 Ch 98 at 109, CA.
9   See, eg, the comments of Hobhouse LJ in *Camdex International Ltd v Bank of Zambia* [1998] QB 22, CA. However, it has long been recognised that the assignee of a claim who has 'a genuine commercial interest in the enforcement of the claim of another' is entitled to enforce that claim so assigned to him: *Trendtex Trading Corpn v Crédit Suisse* [1982] AC 679 at 703, HL (per Lord Roskill). See further *Clerk and Lindsell* para 4.42.
10   Per Stirling LJ in *Dawson v Great Northern and City Rly Co* [1905] 1 KB 260 at 271, CA.
11   *HEL* vol vii 533–4 n 7, deduces the same rule from *Prosser v Edmonds* (1835) 1 Y & C Ex 481 and *Dickinson v Burrell* (1866) LR 1 Eq 337 but these cases also fail to establish the point authoritatively.
12   At the same time it is not thought likely that the exception would extend to injuries to property, where title is not in dispute: eg, damage to a ship. See *Trendtex Trading Corpn v Crédit Suisse* (supra).
13   *Ramsey v Hartley* [1977] 2 All ER 673, CA (where an action based on a negligent misstatement was validly assigned to the bankrupt, even though it was a term of the assignment that the bankrupt should retain only 65% of the net proceeds of the action); *Stein v Blake* [1995] 2 All ER 961. See also *Weddell v Pearce* (supra).
14   *Glegg v Bromley* [1912] 3 KB 474, CA.
15   *King v Victoria Insurance Co* [1896] AC 250, PC; *Compania Colombiana de Seguros v Pacific Steam Navigation Co* [1965] 1 QB 101, [1964] 1 All ER 216.
16   *King v Victoria Insurance Co* (supra).
17   Criminal Justice Act 1948, s 70.
18   *R v Deputy Governor of Parkhurst Prison, ex p Hague* [1991] 1 AC 58, [1991] 3 All ER 733, HL.

SECTION 15.   JOINT TORTS[19]

(A)   CATEGORIES

There are three broad categories of circumstances where one person may suffer damage as the result of torts committed by two or more defendants.

(1)   JOINT TORTFEASORS

In this category are the following.[20]

(a)   Employer and employee in those cases where the employer is vicariously liable for the tort of the employee.[1]

(b)   Where one person instigates another to commit a tort. Thus, a landlord who invited his lodger to help him detect an escape of gas on the premises by striking a match was a joint tortfeasor along with the lodger in respect of the damage caused by the ensuing explosion.[2] But a person who merely facilitated (rather than procured) a tort would not be a joint tortfeasor.[3]

(c)   Where there is a breach of a duty imposed jointly on two or more persons. Thus, two occupiers are joint tortfeasors if they are sued by a visitor for failure to take reasonable care in respect of the premises jointly occupied by them.

(d)   Where persons take 'concerted action to a common end'[4] and, in the course of executing that joint purpose, any one of them commits a tort, all of them are joint tortfeasors. The liability of partners for a tort committed by one of them in connection with the firm's business, and the liability of joint employers of an employee who commits a tort in the course of his employment, are two examples; *Brooke v Bool* furnishes another.[5] The landlord and his lodger were looking for an escape of gas, and an explosion occurred as a result of the careless exposure by the lodger of a naked light to the escaping gas. Besides holding that they were joint tortfeasors because the landlord had authorised the lodger to do the act, the court held that they were joint tortfeasors for the further reasons that[6] 'the enterprise in which he [the landlord] and M [the lodger] were engaged was the joint enterprise of both, and that the act which was the immediate cause of the explosion was their joint act done in pursuance of a concerted purpose'. Similarly,

---

19 See Williams *Joint Torts*.
20 Cf Scrutton LJ in *The Koursk* [1924] P 140 at 155, CA.
1   See ch 25, ante.
2   *Brooke v Bool* [1928] 2 KB 578, Div Ct; *Ash v Hutchinson & Co Ltd* [1936] Ch 489, [1936] 2 All ER 1496, CA.
3   *PLG Research Ltd v Ardon International Ltd* [1993] FSR 197.
4   Per Bankes LJ in *The Koursk* [1924] P 140 at 152, CA. Directors may be joint tortfeasors with a limited company where they directed or procured the tortious act, or informed the company for the express purpose of doing a wrongful act: *Rainham Chemical Works Ltd v Belvedere Fish Guano Co* [1921] 2 AC 465 at 476, HL (per Lord Buckmaster); or if, after formation, the company adopted a deliberate policy of wrongdoing: *Oertli A G v E J Bowman (London) Ltd* [1956] RPC 282 at 292.
5   [1928] 2 KB 578, Div Ct. Perhaps *Scarsbrook v Mason* [1961] 3 All ER 767 furnishes the most remarkable recent example. There it was held that where passengers and the driver of a car combine on equal terms for the enterprise of a specific journey by the car of another, each is jointly liable for the driver's negligence.
6   [1928] 2 KB 578, at 585 (per Salter J).

where D1 imprisoned P, and D2 threatened to strike P if he resisted, they were joint tortfeasors in respect of P's false imprisonment even though D2's act was also an assault.[7]

The Porter Committee summarised the position in defamation as follows:[8]

Where defamatory matter is contained in a book, periodical or newspaper, there is normally a series of publications each of which constitutes a separate tort. First, there is a publication by the author to the publisher for which the author is solely liable. Secondly, there is the publication by the author and publisher jointly to the printer, for which the author and publisher are jointly liable. Thirdly, there is the publication of the printed work to the trade and the public, for which the author, publisher and printer are jointly liable.

(2) SEVERAL CONCURRENT TORTFEASORS[9]

Several, or separate, or independent, tortfeasors are of two kinds; either those whose tortious acts combine to produce the same damage, or those whose acts cause different damage, to the same plaintiff. It is convenient to call the first group several concurrent tortfeasors, and they alone are being illustrated in the present subsection. This subsection is, then, concerned with acts which do not fit into any of the four sub-heads of joint torts already listed, but which result in the infliction of the same damage to the plaintiff. In *Drinkwater v Kimber*,[10] a passenger in a motor car was injured in a collision between that car and another. Morris LJ said that the two drivers, both of whom were negligent, 'were separate tortfeasors whose concurrent acts caused injury to the female plaintiff'. Another example of tortfeasors who were not joint, but several concurrent tortfeasors is supplied by *Thompson v LCC*.[11]

The plaintiff's house was damaged when its foundations subsided. This was caused by (i) negligent excavation by D1 and (ii) a water company, D2, negligently allowing water to escape from their main.

By way of final illustration, the facts in *The Koursk* were as follows.[12]

The Koursk, while sailing in convoy, negligently changed course so that it bore down on the *Clan Chisholm*, which was careless in failing to reverse its engines in order to avoid a collision. Immediately after the impact, the *Clan Chisholm* collided with the *Itria*. Having recovered damages against the *Clan Chisholm* for an amount less than the loss suffered (because of a special statutory provision), the *Itria* sued *The Koursk*. *The Koursk* and *Clan Chisholm* were held not to be joint tortfeasors, but only several tortfeasors causing the same damage.

The feature common to all these cases is that there was only one unit of damage which it was impossible to divide between the various tortfeasors.

---

7 *Boyce v Douglas* (1807) 1 Camp 60; see also the view of Bankes LJ at 149 in *The Koursk* (supra) that if A, B and C conspired to attack P, and A and B carried out the attack, the fact that A and B were sued in battery, and C was sued in conspiracy, would not prevent them from being joint tortfeasors.
8 Cmd 7536 at p 29. If the plaintiff must prove malice in order to defeat a plea of qualified privilege, only those defendants who are malicious are joint tortfeasors: *Gardiner v Moore* [1969] 1 QB 55, [1966] 1 All ER 365.
9 This terminology has been borrowed from Williams *Joint Torts*.
10 [1952] 2 QB 281 at 292, [1952] 1 All ER 701, CA. And see *Fitzgerald v Lane* [1989] AC 328, [1988] 2 All ER 961, HL.
11 [1899] 1 QB 840, CA; cf *Sadler v Great Western Rly Co* [1896] AC 450, HL.
12 [1924] P 140, CA.

(3)   SEVERAL TORTFEASORS CAUSING DIFFERENT DAMAGE

Where two or more persons not acting in concert cause different damage to the same plaintiff, they are treated differently in law from either joint or several concurrent tortfeasors. In the straightforward kind of case, the two defendants inflict quite separate harm on the plaintiff. For example, D1 gouges out P's eye, and D2 fractures his skull, whereupon D1 is answerable for the damage resulting from the loss of the eye and D2 for the damage attributable to the fracture of the skull. Similarly, suppose that a motorist carelessly knocked down a pedestrian who sustained multiple injuries to his leg, and a surgeon later amputated the wrong leg. Since the motorist would not be answerable for the further damage occasioned to the pedestrian by the surgeon's negligence, the motorist and the surgeon would be several tortfeasors who had caused different damage to the same plaintiff.

In other cases it is much more difficult to decide whether there was an indivisible unit of damage, or whether the harm may be treated as capable of apportionment among the several defendants. The courts appear to have taken a sensible attitude, namely to avoid, if possible, saddling any one defendant with responsibility for more harm than he has caused. They will, therefore, be very ready to declare harm to be divisible.[13] For example, in the common kinds of case of harm caused by the independent acts of various defendants, such as pollution of rivers, and nuisance by noise or smell, the courts will not hold each defendant liable for the entire damage; they will endeavour to ascertain the respective contributions to the harm made by each defendant, and, failing that, they will apportion the loss equally between them.[14] Flooding is a more difficult problem. If P's land is flooded for 30 days by the combined flood water of D1 and D2, and would have been flooded for 15 days by the flood water of either of them, each is liable for 15 days' loss of farming activity; if however the flooding does not hinder P's work, but actually destroys his crops in circumstances where the flood water of either D1 or D2 alone would not have destroyed the crops, both D1 and D2 will be liable for the entire loss – the harm being indivisible. When the act of the defendant impinges on existing circumstances – for example, where D1 and D2 are already discharging water into a stream and not causing a flood – and D3, knowing of D1 and D2's acts, discharges such a further amount as causes P's lands to be flooded, then D3 is answerable for the entire flood damage.

(B)   THE IMPORTANCE OF THE DISTINCTION BETWEEN JOINT TORTFEASORS, SEVERAL CONCURRENT TORTFEASORS AND OTHER TORTFEASORS

1   Concurrent tortfeasors, whether joint or several, are each answerable in full for the whole damage caused to the plaintiff. Other several tortfeasors are merely answerable for that damage which each has caused. It is therefore often of prime

---

13 In *Friends' Provident Life Office v Hillier Parker* [1997] QB 85, [1995] 4 All ER 260, CA, for example, the element of damage caused by D1 was restitutionary in nature while that caused by D2 was tortious in nature; the court nonetheless treated the loss as the 'same damage' for the purposes of the 1978 Act. See also *Birse Construction v Hastie Ltd* [1996] 1 WLR 675, CA.

14 *Bank View Mills Ltd v Nelson Corpn* [1942] 2 All ER 477, especially per Stable J at 483; reversed [1943] KB 337, [1943] 1 All ER 299, CA; *Pride of Derby and Derbyshire Angling Association Ltd v British Celanese Ltd* [1953] 1 All ER 179, CA. See also *Dingle v Associated Newspapers Ltd* [1961] 2 QB 162, [1961] 1 All ER 897 at 916, CA (per Devlin LJ). The point was not discussed in the House of Lords [1964] AC 371. Sometimes the cumulative effect of D1 and D2's actions is greater than the sum of their respective contributions – this does not deter the courts from making them liable proportionately to the amount of harm which each would have caused in any event.

importance to decide whether the defendants were acting in concert. Suppose that A and B are engaged on a hunting expedition and both of them simultaneously fire across a highway at game beyond the highway. If a shot injures a highway user, but it is not known which of A or B fired it, they are joint tortfeasors acting in concert, enabling the plaintiff to recover full damages from either.[15] If, however, they are several tortfeasors, they have not committed the same damage (for only one has caused damage), and the success of the action depends on proof of the commission of a tort by the one who is sued.[16] Questions of divisible harm do not arise where the defendants are joint tortfeasors for each joint tortfeasor is liable in full for all the harm sustained by the plaintiff.

2   Satisfaction[17] by any concurrent tortfeasor discharges the liability of all the others, whereas satisfaction by a several non-concurrent one does not.[18]

3   The courts are less willing to exercise their discretion under RSC Ord 16, r 4 to allow joinder of defendants where the defendants concerned are not concurrent tortfeasors.

4   As will be seen shortly, there is in general a right to contribution in the case of concurrent tortfeasors, but not in respect of other tortfeasors.

(C)   THE DISTINCTION BETWEEN JOINT TORTFEASORS AND SEVERAL CONCURRENT TORTFEASORS

The distinction between joint and several concurrent tortfeasors is of minor importance since the abolition by section 6(1) of the Law Reform (Married Woman and Tortfeasors) Act 1935[19] of the rule in *Brinsmead v Harrison*[20] that a judgment against one joint tortfeasor barred the action or the continuance of the action against the others.[1] One minor difference survives: a release under seal or a release by way of accord and satisfaction[2] (but not a mere covenant not to sue[3]) in respect of one joint tortfeasor discharges the others, but does not have this effect in the case of several concurrent tortfeasors.[4] The significance of this distinction is further limited by the fact that the courts are reluctant to construe an agreement between one joint tortfeasor and the plaintiff as an agreement to release by way of accord; they show a marked preference for construing such agreements, where possible, as mere covenants not to sue.[5]

15   *Arneil v Paterson* [1931] AC 560, [1931] All ER Rep 90, HL.
16   Cf *Cook v Lewis* [1952] 1 DLR 1.
17   See ch 28 ante.
18   And see *Bryanston Finance Ltd v de Vries* [1975] QB 703, [1975] 2 All ER 609, CA. For the effect of the plaintiff's accepting payment into court by one defendant on his right to sue others jointly liable, see *Townsend v Stone Toms and Partners* [1981] 2 All ER 690, CA.
19   Section 6(1) has been repealed, and in this respect substantially re-enacted in s 1 of the Civil Liability (Contribution) Act 1978.
20   (1872) LR 7 CP 547.
1   If P had an unsatisfied judgment against D1 and a retrial is ordered of his action against D2 the judgment against D1 does not prevent P from recovering judgment against D2: *Wah Tat Bank Ltd v Chan Cheng Kum* [1975] AC 507, [1975] 2 All ER 257, PC.
2   See ch 28 ante.
3   *Apley Estates Co Ltd v de Bernales* [1947] Ch 217, [1947] 1 All ER 213.
4   *Duck v Mayeu* [1892] 2 QB 511, CA; *Cutler v McPhail* [1962] 2 QB 292, [1962] 2 All ER 474; *Gardiner v Moore* [1969] 1 QB 55, [1966] 1 All ER 365.
5   See, eg, *Watts v Aldington* (1993) Times, 16 December. In similar vein, it has been held that 'the same damage' for the purpose of s 1(1) of the 1978 Act means 'the wrong causing injury and/or death' and does not mean either death or loss of dependency so that where an employer had already paid an employee damages for injuries attributable to exposure to asbestos 'in full and final settlement' his executors were not debarred from claiming for loss of dependency under the Fatal Accidents Act 1976: *Jameson v Central Electricity Generating Board* [1998] QB 323, CA. Cf *Birse Construction v Haiste Ltd* [1996] 1 WLR 675, CA.

The following two rules apply to both joint and several concurrent tortfeasors. A plaintiff who has obtained judgment against one wrongdoer for any damage is free to obtain judgment later against anyone else jointly liable for that damage,[6] and the damages in the later actions can exceed the award in the first. The plaintiff is not entitled to costs in any such later action, unless the court is of the opinion that there was reasonable ground for bringing that action.[7]

(D)   CONTRIBUTION

(1)   SCOPE

Section 1(1) of the Civil Liability (Contribution) Act 1978 enacts that 'any person liable in respect of any damage suffered by another person may recover contribution from any other person liable in respect of the same damage (whether jointly with him or otherwise)'. This section applies whatever the legal basis of liability, whether tort, breach of contract, breach of trust or otherwise.[8] If, therefore, a house owner had a cause of action in contract against her builder and one in tort against the architect who designed the house in respect of defective foundations, contribution could operate as between the two defendants. The same is true if one claim lies in restitution and the other in tort. In *Friends' Provident Life Office v Hillier Parker*,[9] for example, excessive charges levied upon the plaintiff by a developer gave rise to a restitutionary claim. However, the plaintiff preferred to sue only an alternative defendant who had negligently advised the plaintiff to pay those charges. The defendant sought a contribution from the developer and the Court of Appeal held that although one action was founded on restitution and the other on negligence, they both lay in respect of the 'same damage' (which was to be broadly construed).

(2)   WHO MAY CLAIM CONTRIBUTION

The 1978 Act reaffirms the general principle that a person who is liable is entitled to claim contribution.[10] Frequently a person agrees to make a payment in settlement or compromise of a claim against him. If he can show that, assuming that the factual basis of the claim against him could be established, he would have been liable, he may claim contribution for a bona fide payment.[11] If he has settled because he was doubtful about his liability in law, even though the facts were established, he would obtain contribution only if he could prove that he was legally answerable, however bona fide and reasonable his decision to settle the claim. If he were liable at the time he made, was ordered to make, or agreed to make the payment, he is still entitled to recover contribution, even though he has since ceased to be liable either because of the expiry of a limitation period, or otherwise.[12] The right to claim contribution passes on the defendant's death to his personal representatives, whether or not his liability had, before his death, been established or admitted.[13]

6   Civil Liability (Contribution) Act 1978, s 3.
7   Civil Liability (Contribution) Act 1978, s 4.
8   Civil Liability (Contribution) Act 1978, s 1(1). For resolution of the problems arising when the relevant breach of duty occurred prior to the coming into force of the 1978 Act, and damage was suffered subsequently, see *Lampitt v Poole Borough Council* [1991] 2 QB 545, [1990] 2 All ER 887, CA.
9   [1997] QB 85, [1995] 4 All ER 260, CA.
10 Civil Liability (Contribution) Act 1978, s 1(1).
11 Civil Liability (Contribution) Act 1978, s 1(4); *Arab Monetary Fund v Hashim (No 8)* (1993) Times, 17 June.
12 Civil Liability (Contribution) Act 1978, s 1(2).
13 *Ronex Properties Ltd v John Laing Construction Ltd* [1983] QB 398, [1982] 3 All ER 961, CA.

(3)   THOSE FROM WHOM CONTRIBUTION MAY BE CLAIMED

Contribution is recoverable from any one who is liable for the same damage,[14] and on the authority of *K v P*[15] it is clear that the defence of *ex turpi causa non oritur actio* may not be raised in order to defeat a claim for contribution.[16] If one party was originally liable, but then ceased to be liable since the time the damage occurred, he nonetheless remains liable to make a contribution.[17] Someone may have ceased to be liable because the plaintiff has waived his claim. The same is true, normally, where a settlement has been reached.[18] One exception to this latter rule, however, was created by the Court of Appeal in *Jameson v Central Electricity Generating Board*.[19]

> Jameson was exposed to asbestos at work due to the fault of his employer, X. He agreed a 'full and final settlement' with X. When Jameson died, his executors claimed for loss of dependency under the Fatal Accidents Act 1976 from the CEGB alleging similar negligence and breach of statutory duty. It was held that if the CEGB were found liable, they would be able to claim a contribution from X under the 1978 Act, notwithstanding X's settlement with Jameson. Their liabilities arose out of the same 'damage'.[20]

More commonly, the period of limitation for the plaintiff suing that defendant may have expired (the limitation period being two years after the right to contribution arose).[1] So long as contribution is sought before the expiry of the limitation period, however, he may still seek a contribution.[2]

(4)   AMOUNT OF CONTRIBUTION RECOVERABLE

By section 2(1) of the Civil Liability (Contribution) Act 1978:

> … in any proceedings for contribution under section 1 above the amount of the contribution recoverable from any person shall be such as may be found by the court to be just and equitable having regard to the extent of that person's responsibility for the damage in question.

Section 2(2) enacts that:

> The court shall have power in any such proceedings to exempt any person from liability to make contribution, or to direct that the contribution to be recovered from any person shall amount to a complete indemnity.

14   Civil Liability (Contribution) Act 1978, s 1(1).
15   [1993] Ch 140, [1993] 1 All ER 521.
16   On the other hand, those factors relevant to raising the defence are also factors of which the court may take note in fixing the level of contribution (which may be 0%).
17   Civil Liability (Contribution) Act 1978, s 1(3).
18   *Logan v Uttlesford District Council and Hammond* [1986] NLJ Rep 541, CA.
19   [1998] QB 323, [1997] 4 All ER 38, CA.
20   X argued that the damage in respect of which the CEGB were claiming was different – ie the loss of dependency. But as Auld J pointed out (ibid, at 17), damage for the purposes of the 1978 Act 'is the wrong causing injury and/or death; it does not mean death and it does not mean loss of dependency resulting from death'.
1   The relevant date is the date of judgment or, where the case has been settled out of court, the date of the agreement to pay: s 10(3), (4) of the Limitation Act 1980. The period may be extended where the person seeking contribution is under a disability or is the victim of fraud, concealment or mistake Limitation Act 1980, s 10(5).
2   Civil Liability (Contribution) Act 1978, s 1(3). The subsection has a proviso that he is not liable if, on the expiry of the period of limitation or prescription, the right on which the claim against him was based, was extinguished. But because most tort actions are not extinguished by limitation – conversion is the important exception – this proviso is unimportant here.

Neither causation nor culpability is the sole test to be applied in making the apportionment. It is not enough to discover merely who is guilty of moral blame, but, taking a commonsense view of the facts, the degree of 'responsibility' must be determined'[3] – both the blameworthiness and the extent to which the act is directly connected with the damage are material in making this apportionment.[4] This view that moral blame is not the only criterion is supported by the cases which have authorised apportionment between a defendant liable for negligence at common law and one who was not negligent but who was in breach of statutory duty.[5]

If there is a limit on the amount for which a defendant could be liable to the plaintiff, by reason of an agreement between the plaintiff and the defendant, or if the amount would have been reduced by reason of the Law Reform (Contributory Negligence) Act 1945,[6] then the maximum amount of contribution is that amount so limited or reduced.[7]

It will be noted that the statute contemplates tortfeasors being entitled to a complete indemnity in some circumstances. Where, for example, a person who knows that he is not entitled to sell goods authorises an auctioneer to sell them, and he immediately does, the auctioneer, having been held liable in conversion, is entitled to an indemnity from his principal.[8]

Most important is the relationship between master and servant. In *Lister v Romford Ice and Cold Storage Co Ltd*:[9]

> D, employed by P, took his father with him as mate. In backing his lorry he injured his father who, in an action against P, recovered damages in respect of D's negligent act. P brought an action against D claiming an indemnity in respect of the amount of the judgment and costs awarded against it.

The House of Lords held that P was entitled to recover from D for breach of D's contractual obligation of care to his employer.[10] It follows that an employer who has

3   *Weaver v Commercial Process Co Ltd* (1947) 63 TLR 466.
4   *Miraflores (owners) v George Livanos (owners)* [1967] 1 AC 826 at 845, HL (per Lord Pearce); *Brown v Thompson* [1968] 2 All ER 708 at 709, CA (per Winn LJ); *Cavanagh v London Passenger Transport Executive* (1956) Times, 23 October (per Devlin J).
5   Eg *Jerred v Roddam Dent & Son Ltd* [1948] 2 All ER 104; *Dooley v Cammell Laird & Co Ltd* [1951] 1 Lloyd's Rep 271.
6   Suppose that the plaintiff was injured by defective goods which he bought, but that he was also contributorily negligent. As contributory negligence is not a defence to actions for breach of contractual duties, which are strict (*Barclays Bank plc v Fairclough Building Ltd* [1995] QB 214, CA), the retailer will be liable in full to the plaintiff, but his claim for contribution against the negligent manufacturer will be reduced to the extent to which a claim by the plaintiff against the manufacturer would have been scaled down on account of the plaintiff's contributory negligence.
7   Civil Liability (Contribution) Act 1978, s 2(3). The reduction to represent the degree of the plaintiff's contributory negligence must be made before assessing the respective contributions of the tortfeasors: *Fitzgerald v Lane* [1989] AC 328, [1988] 2 All ER 961, HL.
8   *Adamson v Jarvis* (1827) 4 Bing 66. For an illustration of a statutory right of indemnity, see the Civil Aviation Act 1982, s 76(3).
9   [1957] AC 555, HL; distinguished in *Harvey v R G O'Dell Ltd* [1958] 2 QB 78 at 106, [1958] 1 All ER 657 at 666 (per McNair J): 'I find it difficult to see on what grounds of justice and reason I should hold that by making his motorcycle combination available for his employers' business on a particular occasion he should be held in law to have impliedly agreed to indemnify them if he committed a casual act of negligence'. And see *Vandyke v Fender* [1970] 2 QB 292 at 303, CA (per Lord Denning MR).
10 The Report of the Inter-Departmental Committee (1959) set up by the Ministry of Labour and National Service concluded that the decision raised no practical problem and that no legislative change was called for at present. Moreover, in *Morris v Ford Motor Co Ltd* [1973] QB 792, [1973] 2 All ER 1084, CA, it was held that the agreement in that case, being in an industrial setting so that subrogation against employees was unrealistic, contained an implied term excluding subrogation against them.

been made vicariously liable for the tort of his employee can claim an indemnity from the employee. It was clearly recognised before this decision that when the employer himself was also at fault he would not obtain a complete indemnity but must suffer a reduction in respect of his own fault.[11] But these cases were based on section 6 of the Law Reform (Married Women and Tortfeasors) Act 1935.[12] What remains to be decided is whether, and if so on what principles, a reduction can be made in a claim by the employer based on a breach by the employee of his contract of employment.[13]

---

11 Eg *Jones v Manchester Corpn* [1952] 2 QB 852, [1952] 2 All ER 125, CA. Where the master's liability is purely vicarious, involving no personal fault, the master will obtain a 100% contribution from the negligent servant under the Act of 1978, as in *Harvey v R G O'Dell Ltd* [1958] 2 QB 78, [1958] 1 All ER 657.
12 *Lister v Romford Ice and Cold Storage Co Ltd* [1957] AC 555, HL left open whether an indemnity under the Act could also have been given.
13 How far the Law Reform (Contributory Negligence) Act 1945 applies to a suit in contract is obviously pertinent. But see *Barclays Bank plc v Fairclough Building Ltd* [1995] QB 214, CA ruling out its applicability in relation to strict contractual duties.

Convention rights
(Human Rights Act 1998, Sch 1)

Section 1(3)

PART 1
THE CONVENTION

Rights and Freedoms

Article 2
Right to life

1 Everyone's right to life shall be protected by law. No one shall be deprived of his life intentionally save in the execution of a sentence of a court following his conviction of a crime for which this penalty is provided by law.

2 Deprivation of life shall not be regarded as inflicted in contravention of this Article when it results from the use of force which is no more than absolutely necessary:
  (a) in defence of any person from unlawful violence;
  (b) in order to effect a lawful arrest or to prevent the escape of a person lawfully detained;
  (c) in action lawfully taken for the purpose of quelling a riot or insurrection.

Article 3
Prohibition of torture

No one shall be subjected to torture or to inhuman or degrading treatment or punishment.

Article 4
Prohibition of slavery and forced labour

1 No one shall be held in slavery or servitude.

2   No one shall be required to perform forced or compulsory labour.

3   For the purpose of this Article the term 'forced or compulsory labour' shall not include:
  (a)   any work required to be done in the ordinary course of detention imposed according to the provisions of Article 5 of this Convention or during conditional release from such detention;
  (b)   any service of a military character or, in case of conscientious objectors in countries where they are recognised, service exacted instead of compulsory military service;
  (c)   any service exacted in case of an emergency or calamity threatening the life or well-being of the community;
  (d)   any work or service which forms part of normal civic obligations.

Article 5
Right to liberty and security

1   Everyone has the right to liberty and security of person. No one shall be deprived of his liberty save in the following cases and in accordance with a procedure prescribed by law:
  (a)   the lawful detention of a person after conviction by a competent court;
  (b)   the lawful arrest or detention of a person for non-compliance with the lawful order of a court or in order to secure the fulfilment of any obligation prescribed by law;
  (c)   the lawful arrest or detention of a person effected for the purpose of bringing him before the competent legal authority on reasonable suspicion of having committed an offence or when it is reasonably considered necessary to prevent his committing an offence or fleeing after having done so;
  (d)   the detention of a minor by lawful order for the purpose of educational supervision or his lawful detention for the purpose of bringing him before the competent legal authority;
  (e)   the lawful detention of persons for the prevention of the spreading of infectious diseases, of persons of unsound mind, alcoholics or drug addicts or vagrants;
  (f)   the lawful arrest or detention of a person to prevent his effecting an unauthorised entry into the country or of a person against whom action is being taken with a view to deportation or extradition.

2   Everyone who is arrested shall be informed promptly, in a language which he understands, of the reasons for his arrest and of any charge against him.

3   Everyone arrested or detained in accordance with the provisions of paragraph 1(c) of this Article shall be brought promptly before a judge or other officer authorised by law to exercise judicial power and shall be entitled to trial within a reasonable time or to release pending trial. Release may be conditioned by guarantees to appear for trial.

4   Everyone who is deprived of his liberty by arrest or detention shall be entitled to take proceedings by which the lawfulness of his detention shall be decided speedily by a court and his release ordered if the detention is not lawful.

5   Everyone who has been the victim of arrest or detention in contravention of the provisions of this Article shall have an enforceable right to compensation.

Article 6
Right to a fair trial

1 In the determination of his civil rights and obligations or of any criminal charge against him, everyone is entitled to a fair and public hearing within a reasonable time by an independent and impartial tribunal established by law. Judgment shall be pronounced publicly but the press and public may be excluded from all or part of the trial in the interest of morals, public order or national security in a democratic society, where the interests of juveniles or the protection of the private life of the parties so require, or to the extent strictly necessary in the opinion of the court in special circumstances where publicity would prejudice the interests of justice.

2 Everyone charged with a criminal offence shall be presumed innocent until proved guilty according to law.

3 Everyone charged with a criminal offence has the following minimum rights:
  (a) to be informed promptly, in a language which he understands and in detail, of the nature and cause of the accusation against him;
  (b) to have adequate time and facilities for the preparation of his defence;
  (c) to defend himself in person or through legal assistance of his own choosing or, if he has not sufficient means to pay for legal assistance, to be given it free when the interests of justice so require;
  (d) to examine or have examined witnesses against him and to obtain the attendance and examination of witnesses on his behalf under the same conditions as witnesses against him;
  (e) to have the free assistance of an interpreter if he cannot understand or speak the language used in court.

Article 7
No punishment without law

1 No one shall be held guilty of any criminal offence on account of any act or omission which did not constitute a criminal offence under national or international law at the time when it was committed. Nor shall a heavier penalty be imposed than the one that was applicable at the time the criminal offence was committed.

2 This Article shall not prejudice the trial and punishment of any person for any act or omission which, at the time when it was committed, was criminal according to the general principles of law recognised by civilised nations.

Article 8
Right to respect for private and family life

1 Everyone has the right to respect for his private and family life, his home and his correspondence.

2 There shall be no interference by a public authority with the exercise of this right except such as is in accordance with the law and is necessary in a democratic society in the interests of national security, public safety or the economic well-being of the country, for the prevention of disorder or crime, for the protection of health or morals, or for the protection of the rights and freedoms of others.

Article 9
Freedom of thought, conscience and religion

1   Everyone has the right to freedom of thought, conscience and religion; this right includes freedom to change his religion or belief and freedom, either alone or in community with others and in public or private, to manifest his religion or belief, in worship, teaching, practice and observance.

2   Freedom to manifest one's religion or beliefs shall be subject only to such limitations as are prescribed by law and are necessary in a democratic society in the interests of public safety, for the protection of public order, health or morals, or for the protection of the rights and freedoms of others.

Article 10
Freedom of expression

1   Everyone has the right to freedom of expression. This right shall include freedom to hold opinions and to receive and impart information and ideas without interference by public authority and regardless of frontiers. This Article shall not prevent States from requiring the licensing of broadcasting, television or cinema enterprises.

2   The exercise of these freedoms, since it carries with it duties and responsibilities, may be subject to such formalities, conditions, restrictions or penalties as are prescribed by law and are necessary in a democratic society, in the interests of national security, territorial integrity or public safety, for the prevention of disorder or crime, for the protection of health or morals, for the protection of the reputation or rights of others, for preventing the disclosure of information received in confidence, or for maintaining the authority and impartiality of the judiciary.

Article 11
Freedom of assembly and association

1   Everyone has the right to freedom of peaceful assembly and to freedom of association with others, including the right to form and to join trade unions for the protection of his interests.

2   No restrictions shall be placed on the exercise of these rights other than such as are prescribed by law and are necessary in a democratic society in the interests of national security or public safety, for the prevention of disorder or crime, for the protection of health or morals or for the protection of the rights and freedoms of others. This Article shall not prevent the imposition of lawful restrictions on the exercise of these rights by members of the armed forces, of the police or of the administration of the State.

Article 12
Right to marry

Men and women of marriageable age have the right to marry and to found a family, according to the national laws governing the exercise of this right.

Article 14
Prohibition of discrimination

The enjoyment of the rights and freedoms set forth in this Convention shall be secured without discrimination on any ground such as sex, race, colour, language, religion, political or other opinion, national or social origin, association with a national minority, property, birth or other status.

Article 16
Restrictions on political activity of aliens

Nothing in Articles 10, 11 and 14 shall be regarded as preventing the High Contracting Parties from imposing restrictions on the political activity of aliens.

Article 17
Prohibition of abuse of rights

Nothing in this Convention may be interpreted as implying for any State, group or person any right to engage in any activity or perform any act aimed at the destruction of any of the rights and freedoms set forth herein or at their limitation to a greater extent than is provided for in the Convention.

Article 18
Limitation on use of restrictions on rights

The restrictions permitted under this Convention to the said rights and freedoms shall not be applied for any purpose other than those for which they have been prescribed.

PART II
THE FIRST PROTOCOL

Article 1
Protection of property

Every natural or legal person is entitled to the peaceful enjoyment of his possessions. No one shall be deprived of his possessions except in the public interest and subject to the conditions provided for by law and by the general principles of international law.

The preceding provisions shall not, however, in any way impair the right of a State to enforce such laws as it deems necessary to control the use of property in accordance with the general interest or to secure the payment of taxes or other contributions or penalties.

Article 2
Right to education

No person shall be denied the right to education. In the exercise of any functions which it assumes in relation to education and to teaching, the State shall respect the right of parents to ensure such education and teaching in conformity with their own religious and philosophical convictions.

Article 3
Right to free elections

The High Contracting Parties undertake to hold free elections at reasonable intervals by secret ballot, under conditions which will ensure the free expression of the opinion of the people in the choice of the legislature.

Defamation Act 1996

(Sch 1, Parts 1 and 2)

SCHEDULE 1
QUALIFIED PRIVILEGE

PART 1
STATEMENTS HAVING QUALIFIED PRIVILEGE WITHOUT EXPLANATION OR CONTRADICTION

1   A fair and accurate report of proceedings in public of a legislature anywhere in the world.

2   A fair and accurate report of proceedings in public before a court anywhere in the world.

3   A fair and accurate report of proceedings in public of a person appointed to hold a public inquiry by a government or legislature anywhere in the world.

4   A fair and accurate report of proceedings in public anywhere in the world of an international organisation or an international conference.

5   A fair and accurate copy of or extract from any register or other document required by law to be open to public inspection.

6   A notice or advertisement published by or on the authority of a court, or of a judge or officer of a court, anywhere in the world.

7   A fair and accurate copy of or extract from matter published by or on the authority of a government or legislature anywhere in the world.

8   A fair and accurate copy of or extract from matter published anywhere in the world by an international organisation or an international conference.

PART II
STATEMENTS PRIVILEGED SUBJECT TO EXPLANATION OR CONTRADICTION

9 (1) A fair and accurate copy of or extract from a notice or other matter issued for the information of the public by or on behalf of—
- (a) a legislature in any member State or the European Parliament;
- (b) the government of any member State, or any authority performing governmental functions in any member State or part of a member State, or the European Commission;
- (c) an international organisation or international conference.

(2)   In this paragraph 'governmental functions' includes police functions.

10   A fair and accurate copy of or extract from a document made available by a court in any member State or the European Court of Justice (or any court attached to that court), or by a judge or officer of any such court.

11 (1)   A fair and accurate report of proceedings at any public meeting or sitting in the United Kingdom of—
- (a) a local authority or local authority committee;
- (b) a justice or justices of the peace acting otherwise than as a court exercising judicial authority;
- (c) a commission, tribunal, committee or person appointed for the purposes of any inquiry by any statutory provision, by Her Majesty or by a Minister of the Crown a member of the Scottish Executive or a Northern Ireland Department;
- (d) a person appointed by a local authority to hold a local inquiry in pursuance of any statutory provision;
- (e) any other tribunal, board, committee or body constituted by or under, and exercising functions under, any statutory provision.

(2)   In sub-paragraph (1)(a)—
'local authority' means—
- (a) in relation to England and Wales, a principal council within the meaning of the Local Government Act 1972, any body falling within any paragraph of section 100J(1) of that Act or an authority or body to which the Public Bodies (Admission to Meetings) Act 1960 applies,
- (b) in relation to Scotland, a council constituted under section 2 of the Local Government etc (Scotland) Act 1994 or an authority or body to which the Public Bodies (Admission to Meetings) Act 1960 applies,
- (c) in relation to Northern Ireland, any authority or body to which sections 23 to 27 of the Local Government Act (Northern Ireland) 1972 apply; and
'local authority committee' means any committee of a local authority or of local authorities, and includes—
- (a) any committee or sub-committee in relation to which sections 100A to 100D of the Local Government Act 1972 apply by virtue of section 100E of that Act (whether or not also by virtue of section 100J of that Act), and
- (b) any committee or sub-committee in relation to which sections 50A to 50D of the Local Government (Scotland) Act 1973 apply by virtue of section 50E of that Act.

(3)   A fair and accurate report of any corresponding proceedings in any of the Channel Islands or the Isle of Man or in another member State.

12   (1)   A fair and accurate report of proceedings at any public meeting held in a member State.

(2)   In this paragraph a 'public meeting' means a meeting bona fide and lawfully held for a lawful purpose and for the furtherance or discussion of a matter of public concern, whether admission to the meeting is general or restricted.

13   (1)   A fair and accurate report of proceedings at a general meeting of a UK public company.

(2)   A fair and accurate copy of or extract from any document circulated to members of a UK public company—
- (a) by or with the authority of the board of directors of the company,
- (b) by the auditors of the company, or
- (c) by any member of the company in pursuance of a right conferred by any statutory provision.

(3)   A fair and accurate copy of or extract from any document circulated to members of a UK public company which relates to the appointment, resignation, retirement or dismissal of directors of the company.

(4)   In this paragraph 'UK public company' means—
- (a) a public company within the meaning of section 1(3) of the Companies Act 1985 or Article 12(3) of the Companies (Northern Ireland) Order 1986, or
- (b) a body corporate incorporated by or registered under any other statutory provision, or by Royal Charter, or formed in pursuance of letters patent.

(5)   A fair and accurate report of proceedings at any corresponding meeting of, or copy of or extract from any corresponding document circulated to members of, a public company formed under the law of any of the Channel Islands or the Isle of Man or of another member State.

14   A fair and accurate report of any finding or decision of any of the following descriptions of association, formed in the United Kingdom or another member State, or of any committee or governing body of such an association—
- (a) an association formed for the purpose of promoting or encouraging the exercise of or interest in any art, science, religion or learning, and empowered by its constitution to exercise control over or adjudicate on matters of interest or concern to the association, or the actions or conduct of any person subject to such control or adjudication;
- (b) an association formed for the purpose of promoting or safeguarding the interests of any trade, business, industry or profession, or of the persons carrying on or engaged in any trade, business, industry or profession, and empowered by its constitution to exercise control over or adjudicate upon matters connected with that trade, business, industry or profession, or the actions or conduct of those persons;
- (c) an association formed for the purpose of promoting or safeguarding the interests of a game, sport or pastime to the playing or exercise of which members of the

public are invited or admitted, and empowered by its constitution to exercise control over or adjudicate upon persons connected with or taking part in the game, sport or pastime;

(d) an association formed for the purpose of promoting charitable objects or other objects beneficial to the community and empowered by its constitution to exercise control over or to adjudicate on matters of interest or concern to the association, or the actions or conduct of any person subject to such control or adjudication.

15 (1)   A fair and accurate report of, or copy of or extract from, any adjudication, report, statement or notice issued by a body, officer or other person designated for the purposes of this paragraph—

(a) for England and Wales or Northern Ireland, by order of the Lord Chancellor, and

(b) for Scotland, by order of the Secretary of State.

(2)   An order under this paragraph shall be made by statutory instrument which shall be subject to annulment in pursuance of a resolution of either House of Parliament.

Index

Abuse of process
tort of, 498

Accord and satisfaction
effect of, 568

Account
action for, 535

Act of State
defence, as, 104, 105

Agent
deceit by, 507
false representation by, 123, 124
privilege of, 472, 473
servant and independent contractor,
overlapping, 507
vehicle driven by, liability for, 508

Ambassadors
diplomatic privilege, 581, 582

Animals
dangerous–
liability for, 415
non-dangerous species of, 414
species of, 413, 414
dogs, liability for injury to livestock done
by, 416
duty of care, 413
straying livestock, liability for, 416
strict liability–
dangerous animals, damage by, 413-415
statutory regime, 413

Anton Piller order
effect of, 536

Armed forces
personal injuries actions, 580, 581
public service immunities, 192

Arrest
arrestable offences, 98
defence, powers as, 97
general, power of, 98
informing of grounds of, 100
manner of, 100, 101
police powers after, 101
policeman with warrant, by, 97

Arrest—*contd*
private citizens, by, 98, 100
reasonable cause, for, 99
statutory rules, 100
warrant, maliciously procuring, 493
warrant, without, 98

Assault
apprehension of contact, establishment
of, 35
defendant's conduct, character of, 35
meaning, 34
mere words as, 35
old and new cases, difficulty in
reconciling, 34
prevention of threat, effect of, 35
res judicata, 105
tort of, 30
trespass, overlap with, 27
unloaded pistol, brandishing, 35

Assignment
right to sue, of, 593

Bailment
at will, 47
conversion, action in, 47
dealing with goods in manner wholly
inconsistent with, 48
disregarding terms of, 72
loss or destruction of goods, 59, 60

Bankrupt
capacity to sue, 592
liability of, 591

Battery
act of defendant, character of, 33
consent of plaintiff, absence of, 32
contact, need for, 33
damages for, 34
defendant, state of mind of, 31
direct, act to be, 33
hostility, absence of, 31
meaning, 30
medical treatment, in context of, 27

Battery—*contd*
  person of another, defence of, 89, 90
  proof of injury or damage, no need for, 31
  res judicata, 105
  tort and crime, as, 31
  tort of, 30
Breach of confidence
  competing interests, 166
  confidentiality, obligation of, 164, 165
  contract, obligation arising in, 165
  personal information, protection of, 164,
      165
  privacy, protection of interest in, 165
  public interest, justification of disclosure
      in, 166
  remedies, 167
Breach of statutory duty
  action for–
      broad principle, 417, 418
      careless performance, for, 423
      local authorities, duties of, 418
      meaning, 417
      nature of, 423
      two-part test in, 419
  breach of regulation, deriving from, 422
  circumstances of harm, Parliament
      envisaging, 422, 423
  Crown, vicarious liability of, 523
  defective products, liability for, 347, 348
  defences–
      assumption of risk, 430, 431
      contributory negligence, 431, 432
      criminal and tortious liability, to, 430
      third party, act of, 432
  disrepair of highway, 421
  economic loss, recovery of, 421
  enforcement of obligation, 418
  industrial safety legislation, interpretation
      of, 420
  injury or loss of recognised type, showing,
      419
  land and goods, protection of interests in,
      421
  matters to be proved–
      breach of duty, 430
      burden on defendant, statute imposing,
          424
      causation, 430
      conduct of defendant, violation of
          statute by, 429
      damage, proof of, 429
      harm suffered within scope of general
          class of risks, 428
      obligation on defendant, 423, 424
      persons protected by statute, plaintiff
          as one of, 429
      plaintiff's interest, protection of–
          alternative statutory remedies, 426,
              427
          considerations, 425-428
          pre-existing common law, state of,
              425
          public and private rights, violation
              of, 427

Breach of statutory duty—*contd*
  negligence, confusion with, 423
  Parliamentary intent to confer right to
      compensation, identifying, 419-
      423
  performers' rights, protection of, 421
  precise terms, duty in, 422
  public authority, action against for failure
      to provide public services, 422
  reform, proposals for, 432
  vicarious liability for, 523
Careless misstatement
  economic loss resulting from, 216
  liability, test for, 216
  physical damage resulting from, 215
  re-examination of liability for, 216
  special relationships, 215-220
Causation
  all torts, relevant in, 264
  breach of statutory duty, proof for, 430
  burden of disproving, 268
  case and effect, establishing, 264, 265
  chain, breaking, 270
  common sense approach, 266
  concurrent causes, 273
  consecutive causes, 273, 274
  contributory negligence, 282-286
  defective products, injury caused by, 345,
      345
  establishment of, 171
  evidence of–
      burden of proof, 265, 266
      disease, injury being, 266
      loss or injury, occasioning, 265
      medical, 266-268
      'what if', question of, 269
  hypothetical action of third party, loss
      depending on, 267
  lost chance of complete recovery, of, 266,
      267
  materialisation of risk, responsibility in law
      for, 272
  multiple causes–
      concurrent, 273
      consecutive, 273, 274
      novus actus interveniens, 269-272
  negligence, cases arising in, 264
  novus actus interveniens–
      act of nature, intervening act as, 270
      alternative danger, plaintiff in position
          of, 269
      approach to, 269
      intervening act constituting, 269, 270
      plaintiff's own conduct as, 270, 271
      third party, act of, 270, 271
  product liability, in, 355, 356
  remoteness of damage, 272
  repetitive strain injury, of, 268
  risk of injury, increasing, 266, 267
  stages, analysis in, 264
  tort actionable per se, in, 264
Character merchandising
  passing off, 132

Civil liberties
development of, 4
Compensation
crimes, for, 42
Conspiracy
burden of proof, 147
combination, need for, 144, 145
damage, to inflict, 145
false and fraudulent representations,
    making, 146
illegal aim, with, 144
intent to injure plaintiff, proof of, 146
justification, scope of, 147
own interests, protection of, 146
purpose of defendants, 145-147
simple, 144-146
tort, forms of, 144
unlawful means, 144, 146
Contract
action for breach, contributory negligence
    invoked in, 290, 291
breach, inducing. *See* INDUCING BREACH OF
    CONTRACT
confidence, obligation of, 165
illegal transaction, arising from, 106
obligations defined by, no concurrent
    action in tort, 533
occupiers' liability in, 316
tort, concurrent action in–
    contributory negligence invoked in,
        290, 291
    negligence–
        common calling, exercise of, 196
        exclusion of, 196
        implied duty of care, 196
        remedy in tort, agreement to give
            up, 197
        restrictive rules, exclusion of, 197
        third party, duty sought to be
            established by, 198
        tort action, limits of, 197, 198
    obligations defined by contract, where,
        533
    professional duties, 246-248
    remedies, choice of, 533, 534
tort, juridical division between, 15, 16
Contribution
amount of, 599, 600
limit, agreement for, 600
persons claiming, 598
persons from whom claimed, 599
statutory provisions, scope of, 598
Contributory negligence
action for breach of contract, in, 290
assumption of risk, relationship with, 299,
    300
breach of statutory duty, defence to, 431,
    432
causation, 282-286
child, not imputed to, 289
collisions at sea, as to, 283
common law, at, 281
commonsense principles, 284
contributing factor, as, 282-286

Contributory negligence—*contd*
damage–
    cause of, 289, 290
    definition, 289
damages, apportionment of, 291, 292
deceit, no defence to, 122
duty of care after risk has materialised, 282
employee of plaintiff, of, 288
establishing, elements of, 281
examples of, 287
fact, as question of, 284
fault, definition of, 290
independent contractor, of, 288
injuries, contributing to, 289
last opportunity rule, 283, 285, 286
misrepresentation, as defence to, 125
negligence of plaintiff, and, 286-289
nuisance, as defence to, 386
occupiers' liability, as to, 313
plaintiff in position of danger, where, 287,
    288
product liability, as defence to, 354
reasonable behaviour of plaintiff, 288
reduction of damages for, 289
risk of danger, plaintiff deliberately
    encountering, 288
risk, nature of, 282
rule in *Rylands v Fletcher*, defence to claim
    under, 407, 408
seat belt, failure to wear, 292
severability of acts, 284
standard of care, 286, 287
statutory provisions–
    effect of, 281
    scope of, 289-291
strictly synchronous negligence, 284
Conversion
action for, 45
acts of, 54-60
co-owners, between, 60, 61
damages for–
    date of conversion, value at, 62-66
    detinue, previously available in, 64, 65
    full value, recovery of, 61
    market value, as, 62
    pecuniary loss, for, 64
    re-sale profit, 65, 66
    special, 64
    transfer of title on satisfaction of
        judgment, 65
    value of interest, limited to, 61
defendant, state of mind of, 53, 54
definition, 46
delivery, order for, 66
denial of title not being, 60
destruction or alteration of goods, 55
disposition with delivery, 57, 58
disposition without delivery, 57
dispossessing person of goods, 54, 55
goods subject to, 52
human body products, rights in, 52, 53
intentional conduct, need for, 53
limitation of actions, 67
loss or destruction of goods, 59, 60

Conversion—*contd*
misdelivery by carrier, 58
mistake, by, 54
plaintiff, interest of–
bailment, 47, 48
finder, of, 50, 51
jus tertii, 51
licensee, of, 49, 50
lien and pledge, 48, 49
possession or right to immediate
possession, 47
sale, on, 49
third party rights, 51
question in law as to, 45, 46
receiving as, 56
refusal to surrender goods on demand, 59
remedies, 66
residual acts amounting to, 60
subject matter of, 52
taking goods, 54, 55
use of goods, 55
voluntary act, absence of, 59
Convicted persons
rights of, 593
Corporations
power to sue, 585
vicarious liability of, 584, 585
Crime
use of force to prevent, 92
Criminal Injuries Compensation Scheme
compensation from, 562
Criminal law
tort law, overlap with, 16
Crown
armed forces, personal injuries actions by,
580, 581
judicial errors, not liable for, 580
non-vicarious liability, 579, 580
statutes imposing tortious liability, whether
bound by, 581
vicarious liability, 523, 579
Crown prerogative
acts under, 105

Damages. See also DEFAMATION, etc
aggravated, 527, 528
assignment of, 593
contemptuous, 526
exemplary–
application of rules on, 528, 529
object of, 528
punitive, being, 527, 528
range of torts for which available, 529
where granted, 529
fatal accidents. *See* FATAL ACCIDENTS
general and special distinguished, 526
injunction, in addition to, 535, 538
mitigation of damage, 530, 531
nominal, 525
parasitic, 527, 531
personal injuries, for. *See* PERSONAL INJURIES
restitution and tort, choice of action in,
535

Damages—*contd*
successive actions on same facts–
one tortious act causing damage on
different occasions, where, 533
policy as to, 531
successive acts, relating to, 532
two rights separately protected,
violation of, 531
two torts protecting same interest,
where, 532
tax on, 526
Death
cause of action, survival of, 553, 554, 578
damages incurred until time of, award of,
553, 554
defamation action not surviving, 438, 578
fatal accidents. *See* FATAL ACCIDENTS
Deceit
agent, by, 123, 124
contributory negligence no defence to, 122
damage, proof of, 122, 123
damages for, 122, 123
definition, 118
development of tort, 118
exemplary damages for, 123
extent of liability for, 274
false representation–
agent, by, 123, 124
change of circumstances, due to, 119
communication of, 120, 121
concealment of truth, 119
conduct being, 119
fraudulent, economic loss through
reliance on, 216
intention to deceive, 120, 121
intention, as to, 122
knowledge of falsity, 120
law, statements of, 122
motive for, 121
opinion, as to, 121
reliance on, 121, 122
use of, 118
written or spoken words, 119
misrepresentation–
contributory negligence as defence to,
125
entry into contract, inducing, 125
innocent, 126
statutory provisions, 125
principal, vicarious liability of, 123, 124,
507
Statute of Frauds, action under, 124, 125
Defamation
actions in–
damages, level of, 437
plaintiff's death, not surviving, 438,
578
wealthy persons, by, 436, 437
apology, effect of, 484
appeals, 437
background issues, 435-439
broadcasting and television, effect of, 10
class libels, 447, 448

Defamation—*contd*
commercial enterprises, action by, 442
constitutional significance, 438
damages for, 485-487
level of, 437, 485
death, action not surviving, 438, 578
defamatory statements–
abuse, words of, 440
commercial reputation of trading
corporation, defaming, 442
examples of, 441
innuendo, 443-445
interpretation, 443-446
judge and jury, roles of, 445, 446
knowledge of defendant, immateriality
of, 446, 447
living person, defaming, 442
opinion, words of, 441
reputation, injury to, 439-441
several meanings, capable of, 445
defences–
absolute privilege–
executive matters, 464-466
judicial proceedings–
reports of, 468
statements in, 466, 467
Parliamentary proceedings, 464
solicitor-client communications,
467, 468
amends, offer of, 463
assumption of risk, 457
consent, 457
fair comment–
burden of proof, 483, 484
definition, 479
honest, to be, 482, 483
malice, not to be actuated by, 482-
484
procedural complexities, 481
public interest, matters of, 479, 480
true facts, comment on, 480-482
innocent dissemination–
common law, 461
statutory provisions, 462
justification–
fact and opinion, statements of,
459
interpretation of defamatory
statement, 458, 459
malice, effect of, 460, 461
material statements, of, 459, 460
minor points of detail, inaccuracy
in, 459
press, freedom of, 460
qualified privilege–
common interest, instances of, 477
criminals, statements given to assist
in catching, 476
general principle, 473
instances of, 473-479
interest, statements to protect, 476,
477
joint publishers, 472, 473

Defamation—*contd*
defences—*contd*
qualified privilege—*contd*
legal, social or moral duty,
statements in pursuance of,
477-479
malice, relevance of, 469-473
misconduct of public officers,
statements concerning, 476
occasions of, 469
privileged reports, 474-476
publisher, interest of, 476
dishonesty, allegations of, 223, 224
extension of liability, 436
historical development, 435, 436
individual's interest and freedom of speech,
balancing, 438
injunction against, 487
injurious falsehood, and, 141
joint tortfeasors, 595
knowledge of defendant, immateriality of,
446, 447
legal aid not available for, 436
legislation, 436
libel–
actionable per se, 452
crime, as, 452
meaning, 450
repetition of, 456
slander distinguished–
criteria for, 450, 451
juridical differences, 452
limitation period, 569
malice–
burden of proof, 471
establishment of–
abuse of purpose of privilege, 470
extraneous matter, inclusion of, 471
persons outside scope of privilege,
unreasonable publication to,
471
truth of statement, defendant not
believing in, 469, 470
excess of privilege, 472
fair comment not to be actuated by,
482-484
joint publishers, problems of, 472, 473
judge and jury, roles of, 471
publication with, 469
malicious publication, 448-450
plaintiff, reference to, 447, 448
political import, 436
public authorities and governmental bodies,
no right of action by, 436
publication–
meaning, 449
omission, by, 450
proof of, 450
responsibility for, 449
third party, to, 450
remedies, 485-487
remoteness of damage, 455, 456
right to freedom of speech, and, 436, 438

Defamation—*contd*
slander–
actionable per se–
crime, implication of, 452, 453
disease, imputation of, 453, 454
office, profession, calling trade or
business, in respect of, 454
unchastity of woman, imputation
of, 454
damages for, 486
libel distinguished–
criteria for, 450, 451
juridical differences, 452
meaning, 450
special damage, 455, 456
proof of, 436
types of, 435
unintentional references, 448
witness immunity, 498, 499
Defective premises
inadequate foundations, 325
liability for–
builders and contractors, of–
duty of care, 327, 328
economic loss, for, 329-331
negligent construction, for, 328
omissions, 328
physical damage, for, 327, 328
property separate from building,
damage to, 330
state not fit for business, premises
in, 331
landlords, of, 332, 333
local authorities, of, 331, 332
non-occupiers, of, 325-333
occupier, of, 303. *See also* OCCUPIERS'
LIABILITY
physical injury, for, 303
professional advisers, of, 331
strict, 327
types of defendant, 303
work, for, 327
statutory duties in relation to, 326
statutory provisions, 325-327
work in relation to, strict liability for, 327
Defective products. *See also* PRODUCT
LIABILITY
breach of statutory duty, action for, 347,
348
common law stance, 337
consumer protection laws, 337
contract law, limitations of, 338, 339
loss of injury caused by, history of liability
for, 337
merchantability, 339
negligence, liability in–
burden of proof, 345, 346
causation, proving, 345, 345
continuing duty of care, 344
dangerous goods, for, 340
defendants, range of, 341, 342
design, container or labelling, defect in,
344, 346

Defective products—*contd*
negligence, liability in—*contd*
development of, 340
Donoghue v Stevenson, case of, 340,
341
economic loss, for, 344, 345
intermediate examination, no
possibility of, 343
manufacturer, of, 341
narrow rule, 341
neighbour principle, 340
principles of, 341
producers, of, 342
products, meaning, 342
proof of, 345-347
sale of goods, absence of, 343
thalidomide case, in, 347
ultimate consumer, to, 342
negligence, proof of, 338
potential remedies for, 338
privity of contract, rules of, 339
reform of law, calls for, 348
Sale of Goods Act, protection under, 337-
339
services, contract for, 339
statutory protection, 339
ultimate user, action by, 337
Defences
Act of State, 104, 105
arrest. *See* ARREST
breach of statutory duty, to. *See* BREACH OF
STATUTORY DUTY
consent–
act complained of, to, 84
burden of proof, 83
express, 83
forms of, 83
inferred, 83, 84
medical treatment, to, 85-88. *See also*
MEDICAL TREATMENT
contributory negligence, 88. *See also*
CONTRIBUTORY NEGLIGENCE
crime, prevention of, 92
defamation. *See* DEFAMATION
discipline. *See* DISCIPLINE
entry, search and seizure, powers of, 97,
101, 102
exclusion of liability, 300-302
executive acts, 104, 105
general, 11, 82
inevitable accident, 83
injurious falsehood, to, 141
intentional torts to person and property,
to, 82
judicial acts, 102, 103
malicious prosecution, to, 497
mistake, 82
necessity–
defence of property distinguished, 92
medical treatment, in context of, 87,
88, 93
private, 93
public, 94

Defences—*contd*
  necessity—*contd*
    rule in *Rylands v Fletcher*, claim under,
      410
    scope of, 93, 94
  nuisance, to. *See* NUISANCE
  Parliamentary proceedings, acts connected
    with, 104
  person of another, defence of, 89, 90
  plaintiff as wrongdoer, where–
    anti-social or disgraceful conduct, 107,
      108
    conceptual basis of, 106
    criminal act, injury arising from, 107
    entitlement to remedy, barring, 105
    ex turpi causa non oritur actio, source
      of maxim, 105, 106
    examples of, 107
    other defences, giving rise to, 108
    test for, 106
    uncertainty in applying, 105
  prerogative, 105
  product liability. *See* PRODUCT LIABILITY
  property, defence of–
    another, of, 92
    own, 90-92
  res judicata, 105
  Rylands v Fletcher, rule in. *See* RYLANDS V
    FLETCHER, RULE IN
  self-defence, 88, 89
  self-help remedies, 108
  statutory authority, 103, 104
  volenti non fit injuria. *See* VOLENTI NON FIT
    INJURIA
Detinue
  abolition, 59
  remedies, preservation of, 64, 65
  writ of, 45
Diplomatic privilege
  effect of, 581, 582
Discipline
  children, of–
    parents, by, 95
    schoolteachers, etc, by, 96
  defence to action, as, 95
  passengers in public transport, of, 97
  sanctions, 95
Dogs
  liability for injury to livestock done by,
    416
Duty of care
  animals, for. *See* ANIMALS
  boundaries, setting, 228
  breach, establishment of, 171
  contract, implied in, 246-248
  damage to property, to avoid, 212-214
  denial of, 173, 174
  Donoghue v Stevenson, principle in, 173
  duty-situations–
    analogous, 179
    Anns, rise and fall of, 174-179
    examples of, 173
    general, 172

Duty of care—*contd*
  duty-situations—*contd*
    necessary proximity giving rise to, 176
    new, incremental development of, 179
    novel, 177
    physical damage, carelessness causing,
      178
    two-stage test of, 174-176
  economic consequences of imposing, 193
  economic loss, to safeguard against, 215.
    See also ECONOMIC LOSS
  emergence of, 172
  employers' liability. *See* EMPLOYERS' LIABILITY
  existence and scope, identification of, 172,
    173
  foreseeability. *See* FORESEEABILITY
  harm, types of, 200
  Human Rights Act 1998, effect of
    implementation of, 230
  human rights, and, 228-230
  imposition of–
    fairness of, 210
    feasibility and enforceability of, 210
    insurance, implications for, 211
    moral questions involved, where, 211
  individual's rights, weight given to, 229
  neighbour principle–
    injury inflicted, parameters of, 199
    new situations, emergence of, 174
    restrictive interpretations of, 199
    statement of, 173
  new situations, emergence of, 174
  non-delegable, 510-513
  occupiers' liability. *See* OCCUPIERS' LIABILITY
  omissions, 182
  person to whom owed, 172
  personal injuries, to avoid, 199
  policy considerations excluding, 229
  policy grounds for existence of, 176
  professional, of, 246-248
  psychiatric harm, as to, 203-210. *See also*
    PSYCHIATRIC HARM
  public authorities, of. *See* PUBLIC AUTHORITIES
  public policy, limitation of liability for
    harm on basis of, 210-212
  rescuers, to, 202, 203
  situations imposing, 173
  standard of care. *See* STANDARD OF CARE
  strands to requirement of, 172
  third parties, as to damage by–
    absence of, 193
    adjoining property, cases involving,
      195, 196
    control by defendant, element of, 194
    positive duty, conditions for, 193,
      194
    special source of danger created, where,
      195
  tort and contract, in–
    common calling, exercise of, 196
    concurrent, 196
    exclusion of, 196
    implied duty, 196

Duty of care—*contd*
tort and contract, in—*contd*
remedy in tort, agreement to give up,
197
restrictive rules, exclusion of, 197
third party, duty sought to be
established by, 198
tort action, limits of, 197, 198
tort of negligence, establishment in, 171
unborn, to, 200-202
unforeseen plaintiff, to, 180, 181

Easement
nuisance, right to commit, 385
Economic interests, interference with.
See also ECONOMIC TORTS
careless, 116, 117
contract and tort, overlap of, 117
deliberately inflicted harm, 114
intentional harm, liability for, 113
negligent, 116, 117
right to protection of interests,
establishment of, 114
Economic loss
breach of statutory duty, recovery on, 421
builders and contractors, liability of, 329-
331
careless statements, caused by. *See* CARELESS
MISSTATEMENT; NEGLIGENT ADVICE
classification of loss as, 226, 227
defective floor, for, 225, 226
defective products, in relation to, 344, 345
economic torts. *See* ECONOMIC TORTS
foot and mouth disease, allowing cattle to
become infected by, 225
fraudulent statement, reliance on, 216
liability for, 175
principles governing, 223
limits of recovery for, 228
negligent interruption of services, caused
by, 225
never recoverable, where, 227
nuisance causing, 377, 376
physical damage, consequent on, 226
another person, to, 227, 228
predictability of, 226
property, damage to, 213, 214
proximity of parties, 226
pure, 215
relationship between parties, relevance of,
226
restrictive approach to, 215
rule in *Rylands v Fletcher*, claim under,
402
Economic torts
breach of contract, inducing, 115
Convention rights, lack of impact, 8
deceit. *See* DECEIT
economic regulation, and, 117
haphazard development of, 114
injurious falsehood. *See* INJURIOUS FALSEHOOD
intellectual property, protection of, 116
negligence, economic loss caused by, 117

Economic torts—*contd*
new issues in, 10
passing off. *See* PASSING OFF
scope of, 7
trade union immunities, 116, 162
unfair competition, 115, 116
unlawful acts, 115
unlawful interference with trade. *See*
UNLAWFUL INTERFERENCE WITH TRADE
Employee
employers' liability to. *See* EMPLOYERS'
LIABILITY
independent contractor distinguished. *See*
INDEPENDENT CONTRACTOR
Employers' liability
adequate premises and plant, for, 254
competent staff, provision of, 253
compulsory insurance, 251
contributory negligence by employee, 288
defective equipment, for, 253, 512
defences, 252
development of, 250
duty of care–
language of, 251
personal, non-delegable, 251-253
tripartite, 251
employee's family, to, 256
general, 250
negligence, for, 252
physically dangerous work environments,
responsibility for, 255
primary negligence, absence of, 251
proper system of working, provision of,
254-256
responsibilities, divisions of, 251
vicarious. *See* VICARIOUS LIABILITY
workmen, rights of, 256
Entry on premises
police powers of, 101, 102
Estate agent
negligent statement by, 508
European Community law
rights protected by, 9
Ex turpi causa non oritur actio
contribution, not defeating claim for, 599
effect of, 105-108
source of, 105, 106
Exclusion of liability
business liability, 300, 301
death or personal injury, for, 300, 301,
318
duty of care arising, where, 301, 302
statutory provisions, 300-302

False imprisonment
character of act, 38-41
conditions of detention, changes in, 39, 40
damages for, 42, 43
definition, 38
information leading to, giving, 42
initial act, wrongful nature of, 491
interest protected by, 5

False imprisonment—*contd*
justifiable, whether, 82
movement, restraint on, 39
omission, effect of, 40, 41
persons liable for, 41, 42
place of confinement, 39
plaintiff, knowledge of, 41
positive act of, 40
proof of damage, no need for, 42
remand beyond statutory limits as, 40
state of mind of defendant, 38
tort of, 30
voluntarily attending police station, 101
Fatal accidents
bereavement, claim for, 556, 557
damages, assessment of–
bereavement, for, 557
cohabitants, position of, 559
date of trial, to, 559
death and trial, taking account of
events between, 559
funeral expenses, 559
future earnings, for, 558, 559
parent, loss of, 560, 561
pecuniary loss, for, 557, 558
traditional method, 558
widow, payment to, 558
death as cause of action–
act complained of, nature of, 555, 556
contributory negligence, 555
executor or administrator, action by,
555
historical background, 554
interests protected, nature of, 556, 557
limitation period, 556, 557, 578
relatives, on behalf of, 555
wrongful act, neglect or default, caused
by, 555
dependant, claim by, 556, 557
issues arising, 553
statutory provisions, 554
Foreign states
immunity, 581
Foreseeability
extent of damage, of, 278
insufficiency of, 178
means by which harm caused, of, 276-278
precise mechanics of harm, of, 277
proof of, strong presumption of liability
on, 179
psychiatric harm, of, 206
public policy, limitation of liability for
harm on basis of, 210-212
rule in *Rylands v Fletcher*, claim under,
405, 406
shock, of, 275, 276
sole test of duty of care, as, 175
thin skull rule, 279
type of damage, of, 275, 276
unforeseen plaintiff, 180, 181
Wagon Mound principle, 275
Freedom of speech
right to, 436, 438

Goods
conversion. *See* CONVERSION
detinue, 45
interests not in possession, protection
of, 45
interference, protection against, 44
law of torts relating to, criticism of, 44
residual torts involving, 72
slander of, 136
trespass to. *See* TRESPASS TO GOODS
wrongful interference with–
remedies, 66
statutory provisions, 46
trespass to goods as, 71
Goodwill
injury to, 133, 134
passing off goods to cash in on, 131, 132
Harassment
meaning, 38
stalking, 37
tort of, 37
Health and safety
European provisions, 420
legislation, 420
Health service
non-delegable duties, 511, 512
Highway
disrepair as breach of statutory duty, 421
public nuisance. *See* PUBLIC NUISANCE
trespass on, 77
Highway authorities
liability of, 582-584
Human body products
property rights in, 52, 53
Human rights
Convention rights–
common law, remedy under, 6
domestic law, not established in, 5
interpretation of statutes consistently
with, 6
law of torts, recognition in, 5
meaning, 5
protection of, 5, 9
public authorities, enforceable against,
5
duty of care, and, 228-230
private individual, wrongdoer as, 6
Human Rights Act 1998
claims under, 5, 6
Convention rights, effecting, 5
intentional torts to the person, effect on,
30
law of torts, impact on, 4, 5
Husband and wife
actions between, 588, 589
liability of, 588

Independent contractor
agents, and, 507, 508
contributory negligence, 288
employee distinguished–
borrowed employees, 506

Independent contractor—*contd*
  employee distinguished—*contd*
    cases of, 505-507
    control, 504, 505
    criteria for, 504, 505
    hospital staff, 506
    importance of, 503, 504
  liability of employer for–
    authorising committing of tort, 509
    intentional or negligent conduct not
        required to be proved, 510
    negligence–
      non-delegable duties, 510-513
      personal, on part of employer, 510
  meaning, 503
  no liability of employer for–
    collateral negligence, 514
    duty imposed on employer, no breach
        of, 513
  nuisance, creation of, 382
  occupiers' liability for, 313, 314
Inducing breach of contract
  breach of obligation, proving, 150
  contracts, types of, 149
  damage, causing, 155
  damages for, 157
  defendant, state of mind of, 154, 155
  direct intervention, by, 152, 153
  direct persuasion or procurement, by, 152
  enticement of servant, 148
  extension of, 148
  forms of, 151
  inconsistent dealing, by, 154
  indirect procurement, by, 153
  inducement, 151
  injunction against, 157, 158
  interference, 151
  justification of, 155, 156
  knowledge of contract, need for, 151
  malice or ill-will, irrelevance of, 154
  other obligations, breach of, 149
  performance, preventing or hindering, 150
  remedies for, 157, 158
  secondary industrial action, by, 153
  secondary obligations, breach of, 149
  strike in breach of non-strike clause,
      inducing, 150
  tort of, 148
  types of breach, 149-151
Industrial injuries
  compensation for, 250, 563
Injunction. *See also* NUISANCE, etc
  Anton Piller order, 536
  balance of convenience, on, 537
  damages in addition to, 535, 538
  discretionary jurisdiction, 536, 537
  interlocutory, 536
  mandatory, 536
  Mareva, 536
  no tort established, where, 537, 538
  perpetual, 536
  prohibitory, 536
  remedy per se, as, 535

Injunction—*contd*
  right of property, protecting, 537, 538
Injurious falsehood
  ambit of, 137
  business reputation, protection of, 136
  damage, causing, 140, 141
  defamation, and, 141
  defences, 141
  definition, 136
  disparagement, 138
  economic damage, causing, 137
  false statement–
    pecuniary loss, causing, 140, 141
    proof of, 138
    publication, 139
  intellectual property, protection of, 137
  interests in land, protection of, 137
  interests protected, 136-138
  malice, element of, 139, 140
  slander of goods, as, 136
  trade libel, as, 137
  utility, extension of, 137
Insurance
  assignment of right to sue, 593
  employers' liability, 251
  expansion of scope of duty situations,
      implications of, 211
  loss distribution, 14
  personal injuries, compensation for, 563
  professional negligence, against, 246
Intellectual property
  breach of confidence. *See* BREACH OF
      CONFIDENCE
  definition, 163
  infringement, action for, 164
  interests, protection of, 8
  protection of, 116
  protection of, 163
  rights, grant and regulation of, 164
  statutory protection, 163
  threat of infringement proceedings, 138
Intimidation
  tort of, 158, 159

Judgment
  final, effects of, 567, 568
  res judicata, 568
  satisfaction, 567
Judicial acts
  liability in tort, negating, 102, 103

Land
  trespass to. *See* TRESPASS TO LAND
Latent damage
  limitation period, 574-576
Libel. See DEFAMATION
Lien
  goods, over, 48
Limitation period
  accrual of cause of action, 571
  continuing wrongs, for, 576
  conversion, action for, 67
  death of plaintiff after expiry of, 556, 578

Limitation period—*contd*
defamation, 569
disability of plaintiff, effect of, 576, 577
fraud or concealment, postponement in
case of, 577
latent damage, in case of, 574-576
need for, 569, 570
personal injuries action–
breach of duty, meaning, 570
extension for, 573
generally, 570
industrial diseases, 572
knowledge of injury, beginning to run
from, 572-574
special rules for, 572-574
product liability, 356, 569
statutory provisions, 569
trespass, action for, 570
Litigation
unjustifiable, protection from, 491
Livestock
dogs, liability for injury done by, 416
straying, liability for, 416
Local authority
defective premises, liability for, 331, 332

Malicious prosecution
conditions for, 492
defences, 497
defendant not believing in plaintiff's guilt,
evidence of, 495
guilt of plaintiff, person of ordinary
prudence not believing in, 495
improper purpose, evidence of, 496
malice, evidence of, 496
proceedings–
Crown Prosecution Service, by, 497
disciplinary, 493
institution of, involvement of
defendant, 492
nature of, 493
non-criminal, 493
termination in favour of plaintiff, 494
public interests, balance of, 492
purposes of procedural formalities,
concerned with, 491
reasonable and probable cause, absence of,
494-496
warrant of arrest, procuring, 493
Medical treatment
battery in context of, 27
consent to–
child, on behalf of, 86
implied, 85
informed, 249, 250
minor, by, 86
necessity, defence of, 87, 88, 93
person incapable of giving, position in
relation to, 86, 87
temporary incapacity, patient, under,
87
written, 85
counselling on, standard of care, 232

Medical treatment—*contd*
mental disorder, conduct towards persons
suffering from, 95
professional negligence. *See* PROFESSIONAL
NEGLIGENCE
Mentally disordered person
liability, relevance of state of mind, 589
medical treatment, 95
Minor
capacity to sue, 591
liability of–
breach of contract, act being, 590
state of mind, lacking, 590
meaning, 590
parent, liability of, 591
Misfeasance in public office
claims of, 499, 500
fabrication of evidence, 500
malicious refusal of bail, 500
public body, against, 499, 500
vicarious liability for, 500
witness immunity, 500
Misrepresentation
contributory negligence as defence to, 125
deceit. *See* DECEIT
entry into contract, inducing, 125
innocent, 126
passing off. *See* PASSING OFF
statutory provisions, 125

Negligence
animals, liability for. *See* ANIMALS
burden of proof, 257
categories–
expandable nature of, 175
limiting, 179, 180
category-based approach, return to, 176
causation. *See* CAUSATION
collateral, 514
defective products. *See* DEFECTIVE PRODUCTS
defences–
contributory negligence. *See*
CONTRIBUTORY NEGLIGENCE
exclusion of liability, 300-302
volenti non fit injuria. See VOLENTI NON FIT
INJURIA
duty of care. *See* DUTY OF CARE
economic loss, liability for, 175
Human Rights Act 1998, re-evaluation of
boundaries under, 200
professional. *See* PROFESSIONAL NEGLIGENCE
proof of–
law and fact, 256, 257
onus of, 257
procedure, background to, 256
res ipsa loquitur, 258-263. *See also* RES
IPSA LOQUITUR
public authorities, of. *See* PUBLIC AUTHORITIES
scope of, public interest limitation, 211,
212
separate tort, emergence as, 171
trespass, overlap with, 23-25

Negligent advice
duty of care–
auditors, of, 217, 218
extended principle, 220-224
special relationships, 217
surveyors, of, 219, 220
economic loss arising from, parameters of
liability for, 217
liability for–
assumption of responsibility, 220, 221
basis of, 220
disappointed beneficiaries, to, 221, 222
disclaimer of, 220
economic loss, redress for, 221-223
extended principle, 220-224
limits of, 218
person to whom owed, 221
reference, provision of, 223
placing faith in, situations of, 218, 219
professional negligence, 247
recovery for, criteria, 216, 217
special relationships, 217
Nervous shock. See PSYCHIATRIC HARM
Nuisance
action, persons bringing–
damage to chattels, persons suffering,
377, 376
economic loss, persons suffering, 377,
376
owners, 376
personal injuries, persons suffering,
377, 376
resident occupiers, 376
reversioners, 377
activities being, 358
acts of nature, 381
boundaries of, 360
creators of, 378-380
damages for, 387, 388
defences–
assumption of risk, 386
contributory negligence, 386
fire, accidental starting of, 386
plaintiff's conduct, 385, 386
prescription, 385
statutory authority, 384, 385
defendants–
creators, 378-380
landlords, 382, 383
occupiers, 380-382
definition, 357
environmental law, and, 359, 360
independent contractor, created by, 382
injunction against, 362, 388, 389
interests protected, 357
liability in–
strict or fault-based, being, 361
substantial interference, for, 362-368
unreasonableness, role of, 368-376
negligence, and–
elements eclipsed by, 359
relationship with, 360, 361

Nuisance—contd
outcome of conduct, reasonableness, 358,
359
personal injuries, no recovery for, 359
planning legislation, effect of, 360
previous occupier, acts of, 382
public and private, relationship between,
392, 393
public. See PUBLIC NUISANCE
remedies, 387-389
rule in *Rylands v Fletcher*, relationship
with, 361, 410-412
scope of, 357-359
substantial and unreasonable disturbance,
358
substantial interference with land–
abstraction of water, 372
amenity, 363
basis of liability, as, 362
character of neighbourhood, alteration
of, 366
damage, proof of, 362, 363
defendant's land, emanating from, 383
fault, 374
ill-conduct, 373
location of defendant's enterprise, 373
location of premises, relevance of, 365,
366
material damage, causing, 366-368
motive of defendant, 372, 373
nature of, 368
plaintiff, sensitivity of, 364, 365
preventing or avoiding, impracticability
of, 375
reasonable user, 371-376
seriousness of, 363, 364
servitudes, interference with, 368
type of user, 375
unreasonableness–
character of harm. 370, 371
duration of harm, 369
extent of harm, 370
issues to which relating, 368
reasonable user, 371-376
role of, 368-376
seriousness of, 369-371
type of user, 375
use interfered with, social value of,
371
use and enjoyment, with, 363-366
tenant, liability of, 383
trespasser, acts of, 380, 381

Occupiers' liability
activities on land, for, 322, 323
adjoining premises, to persons on, 324,
325
common law, at, 303, 322, 323
damage by animals, for, 413
movable structures, application of
principles to, 314, 315, 323
non-visitors, to–
age and capabilities of, 321

Occupiers' liability—*contd*
  non-visitors, to—*contd*
    awareness of danger, 320
    common law rules, replacement of, 320
    duty of care, test for existence and
        substance of, 321, 322
    likelihood of entry by, 320
    risk of injury, foreseeable, 320
    statutory provisions, 320-322
    warning, 321, 322
  occupier, meaning, 304
  persons outside premises, to, 323, 324
  statutory provisions, 303, 304
  visitors, to–
    activities not directly associated with
        occupation, 309
    children, 307, 311
    common duty of care–
      assumption of risk, 312, 313
      child, physical and mental powers
          of, 311
      chimney sweep, to, 311
      contributory negligence, 313
      exclusion of, 317, 318
      general principles, 309-312
      independent contractors, liability
          for, 313, 314
      particular profession, visitors of,
          311
      purposes for which invited, in
          relation to, 309, 310
      standard required, attaining, 310
      warning, giving, 312
      window cleaners, to, 311
    common law rules, use of, 309
    contract, in, 316
    damage to property of, 315
    exclusion of–
      common duty of care, modification
          of, 317, 318
      contract term, in form of, 318
      farmers and countryside owners, by,
          319
      notice, by, 318, 319
    fixed or movable structures, application
        of principles to, 314, 315
    implied invitation to, 307, 308
    independent contractors, liability for,
        313, 314
    invitees or licensees, irrelevance of
        distinction between, 305
    meaning, 305-308
    more than one occupier, in relation to,
        306
    occupier, meaning, 304
    public right of way, on, 306, 307
    right, persons entering as of, 308
    risks against which protected, 308,
        309
    scope of provisions, 305-309
    standard of care, 305
    trespassers, and, 306
  workmen on premises, to, 256

Omission
  acts distinguished, 182
  liability for, scope of, 200
  liability, not giving rise to, 182
  statutory power, failure to exercise, 188,
      189

Parliamentary proceedings
  acts connected with,, no liability for, 104
Partners
  liability of, 588
Passing off
  character merchandising, 132
  damage, proof of, 134
  damages for, 135
  defences, 134
  dishonest competitive practices, control
      of, 126
  elements of action, 127
  extent of, 126
  false advertising, 130, 131
  foundation of, 126
  goodwill–
    another's, cashing in on, 131, 132
    calculated to injure, 133, 134
  injunction against, 135
  misrepresentation–
    character merchandising, 132
    customers or ultimate customers, to,
        132, 133
    false advertising, 130, 131
    goodwill of another, cashing in on, 131,
        132
    imitating appearance of plaintiff's
        goods, 129
    inferior goods to that of plaintiff,
        selling to mislead purchaser,
        130
    marketing product as that of plaintiff,
        127
    plaintiff's name, using, 127
    plaintiff's trade mark, using, 129
    plaintiff's trade name, using, 128, 129
    trade, in course of, 132
  remedies, 135
  unfair trading, 135, 136
Perjury
  crime, as, 498, 499
Personal injuries
  compensation for–
    Criminal Injuries Compensation
        Scheme, 562
    debate on, 540
    fault system, 539, 540
    industrial injuries scheme, 563
    insurance, 563
    occupational pensions, 563
    occupational sick pay, 563
    Pearson Report, 563-565
    reform, 563-565
    social welfare approach, 564
    torts as system of loss distribution, 539
    trade unions, payments from, 563

Personal injuries—*contd*
Criminal Injuries Compensation Scheme, 562
damage or destruction of goods, claim for, 552
death. *See* DEATH; FATAL ACCIDENTS
disability payments, 562
limitation period–
breach of duty, meaning, 570
extension of, 573
generally, 570
industrial diseases, 572
knowledge of injury, beginning to run from, 572-574
special rules for, 572-574
living plaintiffs, damages for–
components of, 541, 542
interest on, 552
loss of amenities, for, 550
loss of earnings, for–
actuarial evidence, use of, 543
date of trial, up to, 542
early death, prospect of, 544
earning capacity, and, 544, 545
inflation, effects of, 543
Ogden Tables, 543
prospective, 542-544
non-pecuniary losses, for–
loss of amenities, 550
pain and suffering, 549, 550
provisional awards, 551, 552
quantum, assessing, 550, 551
once and for all lump sum, as, 540, 541
pain and suffering, for, 549, 550
pecuniary losses, for–
benefits received, deduction for, 548, 549
breakdown of marriage, associated with, 547
loss of earnings, 542-545
medical, nursing and hospital expenses, 545, 546
policy grounds, exclusion on, 547
special expenses, 546, 547
provisional damages, 551, 552
structured settlement, 541, 542
traditional approach to, 540, 541
meaning, 570
social security benefits, 561, 562
welfare state, role of, 561, 562
Physical harm
wilful act or statement causing–
disuse of tort, 37
examples of, 36
harassment, 37
injury, nature of, 37
intention, proof of, 36
nervous shock cases, 36
stalking, 37
tort, as, 36
Pledge
right conferred by, 48, 49

Postal authorities
liability of, 582
Privacy
infringement of, 438, 439
Product liability
blood and human tissues, exclusion of, 351
causation, 355, 356
construction and presentation defects, 353
defect, definition, 351-353
development risks defence, 338, 349, 354, 355
Directive–
construction of provisions in light of, 349
Consumer Protection Act regime, derivation of, 348, 39
requirements of, 338
drugs, side-effects of, 352
fault, proof of, 351
intermediate examination of product, 356
limitation of actions, 356, 569
plaintiffs, 349
producers, of, 342, 350
products, meaning, 342, 351
safety standards, judging, 353
statutory provisions, 338
strict liability–
benefits of regime, 355
defences–
contributory negligence, 354
development risks, 338, 349, 354, 355
general, 353, 354
improper or imprudent use, 354
no-fault liability, and, 351
persons on whom imposed, 350
Professional negligence
advice, as to, 247
background to, 246
breach of duty, 246-248
doctors, of–
action against, 249
difficulties faced by, 246
informed consent, problem of, 249, 250
duty of care, 246-248
errors of judgment, 249
implications of, 246
indemnity cover, 246
insurance against, 246
proper practice, evidence of, 248
reasonable professional, standard of, 248, 249
skill and competence, exercise of, 246, 248
standard of care, 246
third parties, duties to, 247, 248
tort and contract, concurrent duties in, 246-248
Property
damage to, duty to avoid, 212-214
defective premises. *See* DEFECTIVE PREMISES; OCCUPIERS' LIABILITY

Property—*contd*
economic loss to, 213
imminent danger, causing, 214
latent damage to, 574-576
Psychiatric harm
bystanders, liability to, 207, 208
categories of plaintiffs, 206
claim for damages, disorders giving rise to,
205
emergency services, to members of, 208,
209
examples of situations of, 209, 210
expansion of liability, halting, 209
foreseeability, approach relying on, 206
Hillsborough cases, 208
Human Rights Act 1998, effect of
implementation of, 230
liability for, 203-210
monetary value of, 203
other person's injuries, as reaction to,
204
post-traumatic stress disorder, 204
primary victim, liability of, 207
primary victims of negligence, victims as,
204, 205
proximity to events, establishment of,
206, 207
recovery of compensation for, 203, 204
reform of law, need for, 210
secondary victims, 205, 206
trauma of event or aftermath, resulting
from, 207
Public authorities
classification of persons as, 6
Convention rights enforceable against, 5
defamation, no right of action in, 436
discretionary powers, exercise of–
careless and unreasonable, 184
child care claims, 186
child protection, of, 185-188
common law duty, imposition of, 186
damage, likelihood of, 184
decision-making cases and
implementation cases
distinguished, 185
decisions outside statutory discretion,
186
education cases, 187
increase of cases on, 192
liability for, 185
negligent, 183, 184
policy and operational decisions, 184
duty of care, economic consequences of
imposing, 193
employees, vicarious liability for, 187
failure to provide public services, claim for
breach of statutory duty, 422
liability of–
compensation, ability to pay out, 183
discretionary powers, exercise of, 183-
188
general principle, lack of, 182, 183
public service immunities, 190-193

Public authorities—*contd*
liability of—*contd*
statutory power-
exercise of, 182
failure to exercise, 182, 188, 189
negligence claims against, complexities in,
183
public service immunities–
armed forces, of, 192
conferring, 192
criteria for, 192
development of, 190
fire brigade, of, 191, 192
Hillsborough cases, 191
just and reasonable test, 193
police, of, 190, 191
proximity and causation, analyses of,
192
statutory power, failure to exercise, 188,
189
Public nuisance
criminal offence, as, 357, 389
damages for, 394
defective premises, injuries caused by, 323,
324
highways, danger or obstruction on, 391,
382
injunction against, 393
nature of, 389
private nuisance, relationship with, 392,
393
relator action against, 389
remedies, 393, 394
special damage, civil action for, 390-392

Rape
trespass to the person, as, 27
Reference
bad, negligently giving, 267
liability for, 223, 224
qualified privilege, as example of, 224
Rehabilitation of offenders
spent convictions, 460, 461
Release
cause of action, of, 568
Remedies. *See also* NEGLIGENCE, etc
account, action for, 535
choice of, 566, 567
contract and tort, choice between, 533,
534
damages. *See* DAMAGES
injunctions. *See* INJUNCTION
restitution and tort, choice of action in–
election, 534, 535
measure of damages, 535
Remoteness of damage
causation, and, 272
defamation, in, 455, 456
extent of damage, 278
foreseeable type of harm, 275, 276
limitation of liability, 274
means by which harm caused, 276-278
Re Polemis, case of, 274, 275

Remoteness of damage—*contd*
thin skull rule, 279
trespass, in relation to, 24, 25
Wagon Mound principle, 275
Reputation
protection of, 9
Res ipsa loquitur
absence of explanation, 258, 259
effect of, 262, 263
harm being of kind not ordinarily
happening if proper care taken, 259
instrumentality causing within exclusive
control of plaintiff–
control, meaning, 260
two or more persons, control by, 261
onus, shifting, 263
prima facie evidence of negligence, as, 262
principle, as, 258
statement of, 258
Rescuers
duty to, 202, 203
emergency services, compensation to, 203
Human Rights Act 1998, effect of
implementation of, 230
psychiatric harm to, 208, 209
volenti non fit injuria not lying against,
299
Restitution
choice of action in, 534, 535
tort, juridical division between, 15, 16
Risk
voluntary assumption of. *See* VOLENTI NON FIT
INJURIA
Rylands v Fletcher, **rule in**
defences–
Act of God, 409, 410
consent of plaintiff, 407
contributory negligence, 407, 408
necessity, 410
statutory authority, 406
third party, act of, 408, 409
defendants to action, 398-401
economic loss, claim for, 402
escape, meaning, 404, 405
extension of liability, 396
foreseeability of harm, 405, 406
lessor of land, liability of, 400
negligence, relevance of, 408, 409
non-natural use of land–
application to, 402
definition, 396, 397, 403
essence of, 395
instances of, 403, 404
interpretation of, 403
munitions works, operation of, 397
nuisance, relationship with, 361, 396, 410-
412
occupier of land, recovery by, 401
original case, 395
personal injury, action by person suffering,
402
plaintiff in action, 401, 402
scope of, 395

Rylands v Fletcher, **rule in**—*contd*
strict liability tort, as, 395, 396
things within, 397, 398
vegetation, accumulation of, 399
water, artificial accumulation of, 399

Search and seizure
defence, powers as, 97
police powers of, 101, 102
reasonable cause, for, 99
Self-defence
defence of, 88, 89
Slander. *See* DEFAMATION
Social security
victims of personal accidents, benefits for,
561, 562
Standard of care
adults affected by disability or infirmity, in
relation to, 238
balance of rights and utility of activity,
taking account of, 232
children, in relation to, 237, 238
duty, relationship with, 235-237
general practice of community, 245
medical treatment, counselling on, 232
objective nature of, 237
occupiers' liability. *See* OCCUPIERS' LIABILITY
particular needs of plaintiff, relevance of,
242
plaintiff, circumstances of, 242
plaintiff, of, 286, 287
precedent, 235-237
principles of law–
act of defendant, utility of, 233, 234
balance of rights and utility of activity,
taking account of, 232
cost of avoiding harm, 234, 235
harm, likelihood of, 233
serious injury, risk of, 233
seriousness of risk, 233
professional negligence. *See* PROFESSIONAL
NEGLIGENCE
professional persons, skill of, 240, 241
reasonable anticipation, showing, 243, 244
reasonable person, of–
adults affected by disability or
infirmity, in relation to, 238
children, in relation to, 237, 238
facts and circumstance, knowledge of,
239, 240
hurly burly of life, allowance for, 243
hypothetical, 237
intelligence and knowledge of, 239, 240
legal standard, as, 231
memory and experience of, 239
objective nature of, 237
ordinary care and skill, using, 237
plaintiff, circumstances of, 242
reasonable anticipation, showing, 243,
244
skill of, 240, 241
third parties, foreseeable acts of, 244
skill, as to, 240, 241

Standard of care—*contd*
third parties, foreseeable acts of, 244
Statutory authority
compensation for acts under, 104
defence, as, 103, 104
nuisance, defence to, 384, 385
rule in *Rylands v Fletcher*, defence to claim
under, 406
Strict liability
animals, for. *See* ANIMALS
defective premises, for, 327
products, for. *See* PRODUCT LIABILITY
torts of, meaning, 336

Tort
contract and restitution, juridical division
between, 15, 16
crime, conduct constituting, 16
deterrent effect, 14
forms of action, 11, 12
interest, violation of, 4
malice or motive, relevance of, 11
meaning, 3
motive for, 491
non-material harms, judicial caution in
respect of, 13
other areas of law, and, 15, 16
other branches of law distinguished, 3
pleadings, 12
predictability of principles, need for, 180
situations held to be, 11
Tortfeasors
concurrent–
joint distinguished, 596-598
several, 595
contribution–
amount of, 599, 600
limit, agreement for, 600
persons claiming, 598
persons from whom claimed, 599
statutory provisions, scope of, 598
indemnity, 600, 601
joint–
defamation, in, 595
examples of, 594
several and others distinguished, 596-
598
several–
concurrent, 595
joint distinguished, 596-598
same damage, causing. 596
Torts, law of
administration of criminal law, aiding, 10
ancient history, having, 10
certainty and justice, conflict between, 12
changes, circumstances necessitating, 10
common issues, 10-12
compensation, providing for, 3, 4
Convention rights, recognition of, 5
economic analysis, 15
effectiveness, limits of, 13
function of, 3
fundamental human interests, protecting, 4

Torts, law of—*contd*
general defences, 11
Human Rights Act, effect of, 4, 5
interests protected by–
competing, 7
Convention rights, 9
economic relations, business and
trading, 7
Eurotorts, 9
intellectual property, 8
malicious abuse of judicial process, 9
negligent interference, 8
personal and proprietary, 7, 8
reputation, 9
laissez-faire, judicial acceptance of, 13
law of tort, or, 11
loss distribution, 13, 14
obligations imposed on members of society
to fellow members, as, 3
rights and wrongs, relationship of, 7
Trade union
immunities, 116, 162
liability of, 585, 586
Trespass
assault, overlap with, 27
boundaries set by, 27
careless conduct as, 24, 25
consent as defence, 83
discipline. *See* DISCIPLINE
goods, to. *See* TRESPASS TO GOODS
history of, 23
intention, and, 26
intentional invasion, as, 23, 25
justifiable, whether, 82
land, to. *See* TRESPASS TO LAND
limitation period, 570
medical treatment, in context of, 27
motive for, 26
negligence, overlap with, 23-25
negligent, 24
person of another, defence of, 89, 90
police behaviour as, 27
property, defence of–
another, of, 92
own, 90-92
relevance of, 27-29
remoteness of damage, and, 24, 25
security of person and property, deliberate
violation of, 23
self-defence, defence of, 88, 89
unintentional, 26
writ of, 12, 23
Trespass to goods
act of defendant, character of, 68, 69
action for, 44
actionable per se, whether, 68, 69
damages for, 71
direct interference, remedy for, 44
dispossession of plaintiff, need for, 68, 69
forms of, 68
indirect interference, 68
interest of plaintiff, 69-71
interests protected by, 67

Trespass to goods—*contd*
meaning, 67
question in law as to, 45, 46
state of mind of defendant, 69
wrongful interference, as, 71
Trespass to land
airspace, invasion of, 76
continuing, 74, 75
damages for, 80
defendant, state of mind of, 77 '
direct and consequential, 73, 74
exclusive possession, plaintiff having, 77,
78
highway, on, 77
interests protected by, 73
licence, withdrawal of, 75
meaning, 73
plaintiff, interest of, 77-79
reversioners, actions by, 81
subject matter of, 76
type of acts, 73-75
unlawful possession by plaintiff, effect of,
79
Trustee in bankruptcy
cause of action, assignment of, 593

Unborn persons
duty to, 200-202
mother, duty of, 201
wrongful life, action for, 201, 202
Unfair competition
torts of, 115
unlawful acts, 115
Unfair contract terms
business liability, in relation to, 300, 301
exclusion of liability, restricting, 300
statutory provisions, 300-302
Unincorporated body
liability of–
procedural, 586, 587
substantive, 586
plaintiffs, capacity as, 587, 588
Unlawful interference with trade
breach of contract, inducing. *See* INDUCING
BREACH OF CONTRACT
conspiracy. *See* CONSPIRACY
criminal acts, 160, 161
development of tort, 143
economic torts as species of, 143
ingredients of, 159, 160
intimidation, 158, 159
liability, rules for, 143
scope of, 158
unlawful conduct, 159-161
unlawful threats, 158, 159

Vicarious liability
breach of statutory duty, for, 523
corporations, of, 584, 585
Crown, of, 523, 579

Vicarious liability—*contd*
indemnity, employer claiming, 601
loss distribution, 14
misfeasance in public office, for, 500
tort of employee, for, 251, 503
commission by employee, 515
course of employment–
act in, 516
act unrelated to, 517
connection with work, 520
deliberate criminal conduct, 521-
523
detour by employee, 518
express prohibition of act, 518-
520
fraud, 522, 523
mode of doing work, 516
relevant factors, 516-523
time and space, authorised limits of,
517, 518
travel to and from work, 517
unauthorised mode of acting, 516
Volenti non fit injuria
breach of statutory duty, defence to, 430,
431
dangerous activities, participation in, 298
defamation, defence to, 457
defence, as, 292-294
defendant's negligent conduct, assumption
of risk of, 292
driver of vehicle, defence not used in
action by passenger against, 300
drunken drivers or pilots, in case of, 296-
298
employees, in suits by against employers,
294-296
employment context, in, 294
illustrations of, 294-298
judicial techniques, examples of, 293, 294
occupiers' liability, as to, 312, 313
sporting events, at, 293
summary of, 293
theoretical basis, debate on, 300
tortious act by defendant, presupposing,
294
voluntary act, assumption of risk by–
contributory negligence, relationship
with, 299, 300
economic pressures negativing, 298
employees, claims by, 298
rescuers, position of, 299

Waiver
liability in tort, extinguishing, 566, 567
Witness
immunity, 498-500
Wrongful life
claim for, 201, 202
public interest limitation on liability for,
211, 212